THE GLOBE GUIDE TO

Shakespeare

PEGASUS BOOKS
NEW YORK LONDON

Published in 2016 by
Pegasus Books LLC
80 Broad Street, 5th Floor
New York, NY 10004

in association with
Shakespeare's Globe

An earlier version of this book was published as
The Rough Guide to Shakespeare

The moral right of the author has been asserted

All quoted Shakespeare text is from the second edition of *William
Shakespeare: The Complete Works*, edited by Stanley Wells and Gary Taylor
(Oxford University Press, revised 2005) © Oxford University Press.

1 3 5 7 9 10 8 6 4 2

Typeset in Minion and TheSans
to a design by Henry Iles

A CIP catalogue record for this book is available from the British Library.
720 pages; includes index

ISBN 978-1-68177-260-8

Printed and bound in Great Britain by Bell and Bain Ltd, Glasgow
Distributed by W. W. Norton & Company, Inc.

MIX
Paper from
responsible sources
FSC
www.fsc.org   FSC® C007785

THE GLOBE GUIDE TO

Shakespeare

Andrew Dickson

With contributions by Joe Staines

First opened to the public in 1995, the reconstructed Globe in London now welcomes more than 350,000 ticket-buyers annually – the closest thing we have to Shakespeare's "wooden O", raised originally in 1599 (see p.589).

Contents

Part I ❖ **The plays**

Part II ❖ **The poems**

Part III ❖ **Contexts**

Othello is perhaps Shakespeare's most tightly focused and volatile tragedy – and also one of his most controversial, because of debates about how the "Moor" should be represented on stage. In this 2015 RSC production both Othello and the villainous Iago were played by actors of colour (Hugh Quarshie and Lucian Msamati respectively), which raised fascinating questions about the play's depiction of racism.

Key topics

How this book works

The Globe Guide to Shakespeare is designed to be easy to use. It divides into three sections: Plays, Poems and Contexts. Throughout the text you'll also find a series of small essays on key topics; see p.vii for a complete list.

Plays

Each of the 39 plays gets a chapter to itself, and, for ease of reference, chapters are arranged alphabetically. All conform to the same pattern, beginning with a short **introductory paragraph**, accompanied by a **synopsis**, a list of **major characters** and information about the play's approximate **date**, **sources** and **textual history**. This is followed by an **interpretative essay** – the heart of the chapter – that guides you through the play and introduces its crucial themes and ideas, as well as quoting sections from the text. The essay is followed by a

stage history, describing the play's life in the theatre from the earliest years to the present day, as globally inclusive as we can make it. At the end of the chapter are a series of reviews. First listed are **screen and audio adaptations**, highlighting the best and most interesting productions around and the format in which they are currently available.

The final section of each play chapter is devoted to **books**, with a recommendation of the best individual edition of the play in question, followed by selected works of literary criticism.

Poems

The Poems section follows almost exactly the same pattern as the plays, with individual chapters on *A Lover's Complaint*, *The Rape of Lucrece*, the Sonnets and *Venus and Adonis*. Each contains an

interpretative essay and **book recommendations**, with the obvious difference that there are no performance histories, and only a handful of audio or video versions are currently available.

Contexts

The final section of the book begins with a chapter outlining **Shakespeare's life**, focusing on the documented historical facts but also examining the many myths about him. It's followed by an account

of the **stages on which Shakespeare worked**, with specifics about the major acting companies and playhouses. Then comes an introduction to **Shakespeare's language**, describing the oral and written

Quotes and symbols

Quotations

Quotations from the plays and poems are found throughout *The Globe Guide to Shakespeare*. Each one is followed by a numerical reference identifying precisely where it's taken from. The plays are nearly always broken down into acts and scenes, and modern editors usually number the lines too. Following the standardized system, this book cites act numbers first, then the relevant scene number, and finally the line number – so "5.2.23–32" indicates that the quotation in question is taken from Act Five, scene two, and covers lines 23 to 32 ("SD" indicates that the text appears in a stage direction).

When referring to the poems, citations provide line numbers. The text used throughout is the second edition of *William Shakespeare: The Complete Works*, edited by Stanley Wells and Gary Taylor (Oxford University Press, revised 2005); other editions, including those recommended at the end of each chapter, will in all likelihood number things slightly differently. Text quoted from other writers is generally presented in modernized spelling.

In the review sections of each chapter, publishing information for **film and audio** versions appears as follows. Each is listed in date order, with cast and director details appearing first, followed by country and date of origin, then current distributor (in the order UK / US where the distributor is different in each territory):

Symbols

Coriolanus
R. Fiennes, V. Redgrave, B. Cox; Ralph Fiennes
(dir.) UK, 2011 > Lionsgate / Weinstein DVD

Macbeth
S. Dillane, F. Shaw, D. Conlan; Fiona Shaw (dir.)
UK, 1998 > Naxos ◉ / ⬇

DVD = DVD
CD = ◉
Download = ⬇

Book details

Book details follow a similar format throughout, listing author/editor, date of original publication, then current publisher (in the order UK / US where publishers are different). "UP" stands for "university press":

Arden Shakespeare (third series)
Peter Holland (ed.); 2013 > Bloomsbury

The Common Pursuit
F.R. Leavis; 1952 > Penguin / Yale UP [o/p]

Every effort has been made to indicate when books are currently out of print ("o/p"), but with online booksellers the distinction between titles that are available and those that aren't has become increasingly blurred. It's not impossible that a secondhand book ordered through a specialist retailer will be easier to find – and reach you faster – than something published only a few months ago. Ebook availability and format changes frequently, so it's well worth checking to see if books are available in digital form.

culture of Shakespeare and his contemporaries as well as the literary techniques they employed, including new words, rhetorical figures and blank verse. An outline of **Shakespeare's canon** – what he wrote and when – follows.

We have also included a chapter introducing Shakespeare's most significant **colleagues and rivals**: nine writers also at work in Elizabethan and Jacobean London. You'll find a detailed introduction to each, along with short descriptions of their best work. Following this, there is short chapter focusing on **Shakespeare for kids** – reviews of the best adaptations for young audiences.

The Globe Guide concludes with a list of **recommended books**, covering everything from music in Shakespeare to the works that he himself read. This is supplemented by a comprehensive roundup of the **best Shakespearian websites**, ranging from reference sources and DVD rental sites to blogs and discussion groups. Finally there's a **selective glossary**, defining some useful terminology common to this book and others in the area.

Introduction

There are many different Shakespeares. As the years pass, they multiply: theatre is an inquisitive and unpredictable medium, and Shakespeare, the world's most revived playwright, keeps mutating and evolving. Close to four centuries after his death, his plays continue to be seen by millions of people in thousands of locations across the globe. His words and phrases enrich the English language, rippling through casual, day-to-day speech and at the same time sustaining the very notion of "high" culture. His works have generated a major publishing industry and been translated into hundreds of different languages. His name has been pressed into the service of convictions and ideologies he could never have dreamed about, and he has become an icon in countries that didn't even exist when he was alive.

Just as there are many Shakespeares, there is no single way of explaining what makes his work so appealing. His plays and poems aren't just astonishing works of art, but gripping pieces of drama. They're remarkable social documents, but often touched with magic and fantasy. They're full of optimism and comedy about the human condition, yet also shot through with pain, anger and despair. And although they're of their historical moment, they touch something that feels universal. The completeness of Shakespeare's vision remains unmatched, whether he's writing about large-scale politics or the most intimate of love affairs. He is the most exciting, challenging and awe-inspiring writer in the language, and in many different languages too.

For all that, approaching Shakespeare can be a bewildering and intimidating experience. Partly this is because of his reputation as a cornerstone of the academic canon. It is also to do with sheer volume – an effect of the global Shakespeare industry, in which his name possesses significant cultural capital. At least twenty major editions of the *Complete Works* are currently in print, hundreds more academic articles and monographs pile up each year, and more films than ever take their cue from his work. Many of these interpretations offer something different, something new, and in all likelihood something worth pondering. Looking at things from contrasting angles is entirely Shakespearian; as critics long ago realized, no other playwright makes us think so hard about what it is like to experience life from radically different points of view. But you can't read or see everything: few people will wish to watch the more than fifty screen versions of *Hamlet*, examine all the competing theories about *King Lear*'s textual history or trudge their way through the countless critical studies devoted to Shakespeare's life and work.

Which is where this book comes in. In *The Globe Guide to Shakespeare* we've attempted to cut a path through the jungle, offering ways into each play and major poem: key critical studies, recommended editions, essential reference works. The opinions expressed aim to be balanced and accessible, giving a flavour of what's out

The World Shakespeare Festival in 2012 swept companies from countries all around the globe to British theatres – including the Globe. New Zealand's Ngakau Toa company kicked off festivities with a strutting, strident version of Troilus and Cressida that used many traditional Maori forms.

there while being carefully selective about what has been included. Above all, this isn't intended to be a textbook, and we hope it's fun to read: our ambition throughout has been to demystify Shakespeare, to show that there are interesting ways of thinking about his works without saturating them in academic jargon.

Also at this book's heart is a passionate belief in performance: the idea that Shakespeare's plays shouldn't be thought of as lifeless literary texts, but as living, breathing pieces of drama – three-dimensional works designed to be adapted and acted. We've included detailed and up to date stage histories for the plays, giving a flavour of hundreds of different productions around the world and over 400 years. You'll also find reviews of what we think are the most exciting film and TV adaptations on DVD and download, offering an opportunity to experience the plays in screen incarnations across more than a century of cinema – from the earliest silent treatments to big-budget modern movies. We've also made a point of including audio versions, partly because many of them boast such stellar casts, but also because Shakespeare's plays make for astonishing listening, somehow even more vivid when staging is left to the imagination. Even so, it's worth saying that the best place to get a taste of the action is where it always has been: inside a theatre. Nothing compares to the sensation of being in the same space as the actors, sharing in the unique and unrepeatable experience of live performance.

Yet there is more to Shakespeare than just the plays. As well as being a supremely talented dramatist, he is also one of the most absorbing poets in the English language. Shakespeare's Sonnets have long been admired for their subtlety and intellect, the way they enfold intimate confessions about love within dazzlingly intricate language. Less familiar – indeed sometimes overlooked entirely – are his narrative poems *Venus and Adonis*, *The Rape of Lucrece* and *A Lover's Complaint*: as varied a trio as you could imagine, and well worth getting to know. While acknowledging that some works will always be more popular than others, we've tried to be reasonably democratic, allotting a similar amount of space to plays and poems in the belief that all of them have something to offer, from the neglected early histories to the less popular late romances.

We have tried to make *The Globe Guide* of use to as many different people as possible. Theatregoers will hopefully find plot synopses helpful, and stage histories of interest when comparing how productions have varied across the years. Students will be able to find reference information, browse critical essays, research books and weblinks. Cinephiles can cut straight to the most rewarding and absorbing film adaptations. Parents and teachers can check out a handful of suggestions on the best adaptations for young audiences. Anyone needing a sense of the broader context can go straight to the chapters on Shakespeare's life, stages and language, or read up on his Elizabethan and Jacobean colleagues and rivals. Individual sections can be read straight through, or dipped into as and when.

Finally, it's worth remembering that no one owns Shakespeare: how you respond is entirely up to you. Although *The Globe Guide* is delighted to be published in assocation with Shakespeare's Globe, it is independently researched and written. And its aim isn't to tell you what you *should* think about Shakespeare and his writing; it's to encourage you to find out for yourself. This book is intended as a starting point.

Though often neglected, Shakespeare's late plays are experimental masterpieces, touched with fantasy as well as turbulent emotion. *The Winter's Tale* contains perhaps the most famous stage direction in the canon, "Exit, pursued by a bear" – the moment at which the traveller Antigonus is chased off stage by a wild animal. This is the scene as conjured by the English eighteenth-century artist Joseph Wright of Derby (engraved by S. Middiman); the question of how this was staged in Shakespeare's day is still hotly debated.

Q&As: The man and the myths

Was Shakespeare really Shakespeare?
Yes, he was. Some conspiracy theorists believe that Francis Bacon or the Earl of Oxford, among other candidates, wrote the plays, but all the evidence points the other way > p.566

Was Shakespeare gay?
For a variety of reasons it is almost impossible to say, although it is true that Shakespeare wrote over a hundred love poems that appear to be addressed to a man > p.539

Do we know what Shakespeare looked like?
Various portraits exist, but it is likely that none dates from his lifetime, and their accuracy is disputed > p.574

Is it true that Shakespeare abandoned his wife and family?
After marrying Anne Hathaway in 1582 and having three children with her, Shakespeare left Stratford to start work in London; it isn't known how often he returned home > p.562

Where did Shakespeare go to school?
The records have long since perished, but it is extremely likely that he attended the King's New School in Stratford > p.560

Did he speak any foreign languages?
Despite legends that he travelled in Europe as a young man, no records survive; he did, however, understand French and Italian as well as Latin and Greek > p.561

Was Shakespeare Catholic?
The evidence suggests that Shakespeare conformed to mainstream Protestant beliefs, though there is speculation that his father John remained a Catholic > p.564

Did Shakespeare die of syphilis?
Cause of death was not usually recorded in Renaissance England, so no one knows for sure what killed William Shakespeare > p.579

Numerous attempts to capture Shakespeare's likeness were made in the centuries after his death, and there are now memorials in numerous towns and cities worldwide, from Shakespeare Sarani (Street) in Kolkata to John Quincy Adams Ward's pensive statue in Central Park. Its foundation stone was laid in 1864, the 300th anniversary of the playwright's birth, but is highly unlikely to represent what he actually looked like (see p.574).

Did Shakespeare act in his own plays?

We know that he performed in at least two plays by his colleague Ben Jonson, and there is a long-standing tradition that he took roles in As You Like It and Hamlet ❯ p.570

Do any samples of Shakespeare's handwriting exist?

Yes: his signature survives on a number of documents and it is thought that he wrote part of a playtext now in the British Library ❯ p.190

How many plays did Shakespeare write?

Most scholars agree that Shakespeare was the main author of 39 surviving plays, but he may have contributed to several more, while others have been lost ❯ p.618

Do all his plays survive?

No: two are referred to in the records but have since disappeared ❯ p.242

This wide and vniuersall Thea

Presents more wofull Pagean

Wherein we play in.

Ia.   All the world's a stage,

And all the men and women, n

They haue their *Exits* and thei

And one man in his time playe

His Acts being seuen ages. At

Mewling and puking in

The plays

Made to his Mistresse eye-bro

Full of strange oaths, and bear

Ielous in honor, sodaine, and q

Seeking the bubble Reputatior

Euen in the Canons mouth : Ar

In faire round belly, with good

With eyes seuere, and beard of

Full of wise sawes, and moderne

And so he playes his part. The

Into the leane and slipper'd Par

With spectacles on nose, and p

His youthfull hose well sau'd, a

For his shrunke shanke, and his

Turning againe toward childish

And whistles in his sound. Las

That ends this strange euentful

Is second childishnesse, and me

All's Well That Ends Well

The central story woven by *All's Well* seems at first glance more socially optimistic than any other Shakespeare wrote: a poor physician's daughter finds her prince and succeeds in marrying him. But the uncomfortable truth exposed by this bittersweet play is that fairytale endings rarely mesh with real human needs. Helen, the play's questing heroine, needs only to convince her idol that she is worth wedding, but she ends up blackmailing him into it – a finale that the play's sardonic title renders profoundly disquieting. Some have wondered whether *All's Well* is an alternative title for the mysterious *Love's Labour's Won* (see p.240), but although Helen labours to win her love, the play's own ambiguous "end" is worlds away from those of earlier, brighter comedies. George Bernard Shaw compared the play to Ibsen's *A Doll's House* for the way that the "sovereign charm" of Helen is set against "a perfectly ordinary young man, whose unimaginative prejudices and selfish conventionality make him cut a very mean figure". Despite its considerable dramatic strength, *All's Well* and its small cast are not often given the chance to win over audiences; nevertheless, a handful of productions have demonstrated the special intensity and charm of this neglected play.

DATE > Though considered by some to be the lost *Love's Labour's Won* (see p.240), most scholars believe that *All's Well* dates from 1604–05, after *Othello* – making it the last "problem play".
SOURCES > Giovanni Boccaccio's *Decameron* (1353), a collection of tales told by a group of Florentines, passes on the basic story, though Shakespeare would have taken it from William Painter's translation *Palace of Pleasure* from 1566 (see p.5). He adds several characters.
TEXTS > Though only the Folio text (1623) survives, it is unusually messy and error-strewn, possibly set from the dramatist's working manuscripts.

Interpreting the play

Like *Twelfth Night* before it, *All's Well* – though ostensibly a comedy – begins in mourning. The stage is filled with characters clad in black; bereavement hangs in the air. The King of France is gravely ill and has commanded his young ward Bertram to attend him, while in the very first lines of the play Bertram's own departure is likened by his widowed mother, the Countess of Roussillon, to "burying a second husband" (1.1.1–2). Helen, too, is adjusting to the recent loss of her father – a man, moreover,

MAJOR CHARACTERS & SYNOPSIS

Countess of Roussillon, a widow
Bertram, Count of Roussillon, the Countess's son
Helen, a doctor's daughter and the Countess's servant
Lavatch, a clown in the Countess's service
Reynaldo, the Countess's steward
Paroles, a companion of Bertram
King of France
Lafeu, an old lord and friend of the Countess
First and **Second Lords Dumaine**, brothers
An **Interpreter**
Duke of Florence
Widow Capilet and **Diana**, her daughter
Mariana, a friend of the Widow

ACT 1 The King of France is dangerously ill and has summoned his ward Bertram (the son and heir of the late Count of Roussillon) to be with him during his last hours. As Bertram leaves his home in Roussillon, his mother the Countess notices that her gentlewoman Helen is upset, and realizes why – Helen secretly loves him. Giving Helen her blessing, the Countess encourages her to follow Bertram on the pretext of offering the medical skills that she has inherited from her father to the King.

ACT 2 The King agrees to Helen's treatment, promising that if she succeeds he will guarantee her any husband she wants. He rapidly improves under her care and summons all his lords so that she can make her choice. When she picks Bertram, however, he scornfully turns her down, refusing to touch a low-born doctor's daughter. Even though the King forces them to wed, Bertram decides to leave the marriage unconsummated and escape to the Italian wars with his disreputable companion Paroles.

ACT 3 The Countess's delight at news of the marriage sours when she receives a letter from Bertram declaring that he has fled. Helen announces that she has also received a letter in which Bertram states that he will agree to be her husband only if she removes the ancestral ring from his finger and bears his child – both, he boasts, impossible. Helen reflects that her only option is to disappear, and heads to Italy disguised as a pilgrim. She arrives to mixed news: Bertram has proved himself a brilliant soldier, but has been trying to seduce Diana, daughter of the Widow Capilet. Revealing her identity to Diana's mother, Helen suggests a bed-trick: Diana will agree to sleep with Bertram but be replaced at the last minute by Helen. Meanwhile, Paroles' boastfulness has irritated the other soldiers so much that the Dumaine brothers decide to humiliate him in public.

ACT 4 The two plots swing into action. Disguised as enemy soldiers, the Dumaines ambush Paroles and interrogate him. When he blithely slanders his comrades, they remove his blindfold and unmask themselves. In the meantime Diana has persuaded Bertram to swap his ring for one of her own (actually Helen's), on the agreement that he will visit her chamber at midnight. All goes to plan, and Helen – who has by now spread rumours of her own death – leaves for France with Widow Capilet and Diana, intending to tell the King everything. Believing Helen to be dead, however, Lafeu has negotiated with the Countess for Bertram to marry his own daughter.

ACT 5 Bertram returns to France and is pardoned by the King. When he offers an engagement ring for Lafeu's daughter, however, the King recognizes it as one he has given Helen and arrests Bertram on suspicion of having killed her. At that moment a letter arrives from Diana, revealing Bertram's promise to marry her on Helen's death; Diana and her mother appear, and produce his ring. Bertram admits to knowing them but denies offering to marry Diana, who he claims is a whore. Paroles does his best to confuse matters, but everything is resolved when the pregnant Helen makes her appearance. In a neat irony, Bertram has managed to fulfil his own contract without even knowing it. He has no choice but to accept Helen.

whose medical expertise is now sorely missed at court. The Countess reflects that if only he were here, the King's prognosis would be incalculably improved. Noting that Helen's father's "skill … would have made nature immortal", she plays wistfully with the reality of his loss:

> Would for the King's sake he were living. I think it would be the death
> of the King's disease.
>
> [1.1.20–22]

But once Bertram is gone, the subject of Helen's own "sorrows" proves more complicated than her companions think. "I think not on my father," she weeps. "My imagination / Carries no favour in't but Bertram's." Her description of him sounds strikingly like a remembrance:

> 'Twas pretty, though a plague,
> To see him every hour, to sit and draw
> His archèd brows, his hawking eye, his curls,
> In our heart's table—heart too capable
> Of every line and trick of his sweet favour.
> But now he's gone, and my idolatrous fancy
> Must sanctify his relics.
>
> [1.1.91–7]

KEY SOURCE > Boccaccio's *Decameron*

For both *All's Well That Ends Well* and *Cymbeline* Shakespeare drew upon a renowned collection of stories by the Italian humanist **Giovanni Boccaccio** (1313–75). Boccaccio's *Decameron* (1353) brings together a hundred popular tales, told over a period of ten days by ten people (hence the title, which means "ten days"). The occasion for their telling is the plague that ravaged Florence during 1348, which killed up to half the city's population. Boccaccio's aristocratic cast is safe, but only just: quarantined in a country retreat while the disease rages in the city, they are forced to recount stories to each other in order to pass the time and distract from the gruesome events outside. (Chaucer would borrow the tale-telling framework for his *Canterbury Tales*, begun a few decades later.)

Despite its grim setting, the *Decameron* is largely a collection of love stories, told in an atmosphere of insouciant flirtation between the female and male guests, and many of them stray into bawdy territory – Boccaccio's relaxed and enthusiastic view of sex often embarrassed later commentators. Indeed, the first English translation of the tales, William Painter's *Palace of Pleasure* (1566) was, despite its juicy title, a heavily expurgated version containing just sixteen of Boccaccio's politer stories (John Florio's complete English translation did not appear until 1620).

It was from Painter, not the original, that Shakespeare borrowed the stories of Gilette of Narbonne (who cures the King of France and marries Bertrand of Roussillon) and Bernabò of Genoa (tricked into believing that his wife has been unfaithful). Painter's version – which was among Shakespeare's favourite reading – also supplied source material for *Romeo and Juliet*, *The Merry Wives*, *Timon* and *Lucrece*.

Sounding somewhere between Hamlet and the anonymous maid in *A Lover's Complaint* (see p.519), Helen sighs that her heart is only too "capable of" (able to suck in) Bertram's beauty. His departure for the social whirl of the French court might as well be from life itself; she is left behind, an "idolatrous" disciple, to "sanctify his relics".

Doctor She

What happens next sounds as if it comes out of a fairy story. Under pressure, she confesses her love to Bertram's mother, but instead of being snobbishly appalled that one of her servants wants to marry her son, the Countess gives Helen her blessing and advises her to make a dash for Paris. Arriving at court, Helen gains access to the King and promises to use her father's wisdom on him. Though at first he is suspicious, when she offers to submit herself to death if her powers fail, he becomes convinced.

While his medical advisers have informed him that "labouring art" has little chance against the course of nature, Helen seems to promise something different, the kind of "immortal" power that the Countess claims was invested in her father. There is something undeniably magical about this "Doctor She", as the old retainer Lafeu remarks wonderingly to the King:

> I have seen a medicine
> That's able to breathe life into a stone,
> Quicken a rock, and make you dance canary
> With sprightly fire and motion ...

> [2.2.71–4]

But, while her royal master is healed, one man refuses to succumb to Helen's powers. When the King grants her "power to choose" a husband from among his lords as reward for her magic, Bertram obstinately refuses to take part:

> BERTRAM
> My wife, my liege? I shall beseech your highness,
> In such a business give me leave to use
> The help of mine own eyes.
> KING   Know'st thou not, Bertram,
> What she has done for me?
> BERTRAM   Yes, my good lord,
> But never hope to know why I should marry her.

> [2.3.107–11]

Bertram's disgusted explanation, that he will not debase his nobility by being forced to marry a "poor physician's daughter", is unappealing, and has earned him a consistently bad press; but, as ever, Shakespeare muddies the moral waters. His is also the honest response of a man being forced to play along with someone else's bizarre fairy tale. Though Helen has brought life to the King, in Bertram's eyes what faces him is a life sentence: marriage to a woman he does not love.

> *I cannot reconcile my heart to Bertram; a man noble without generosity,*
> *and young without truth; who marries Helen as a coward and leaves her as*
> *a profligate; when she is dead by his unkindness, sneaks home to a second*
> *marriage, is accused by a woman whom he has wronged, defends himself by*
> *falsehood, and is dismissed to happiness.*
>
> Samuel Johnson, commentary to *The Plays of William Shakespeare* (1765)

Bertram has little choice but to consent, though no sooner is the ceremony over than he announces his intention to escape France and head to the Tuscan wars. He leaves the marriage unconsummated, a state of affairs that he intends to preserve, vowing in a letter to the Countess that "I have wedded her, not bedded her, and sworn to make the 'not' eternal" (3.2.21–2). His callous pun ("not eternal" for "knot eternal") does not impress his mother, but his crowing message to his wife proves altogether more fateful. "When thou canst get the ring upon my finger, which shall never come off," he writes, "and show me a child begotten of thy body that I am father to, then call me husband" (3.2.57–9). Helen's quest to make those words ring true will exercise all her intelligence and ingenuity.

Whate'er the course

Wittily diverting Paroles's rude remarks about the idea of virginity back in Act One, Helen had asked him, coyly, "How might one do, sir, to lose it to her own liking?" (1.1.149). Her determination to do just that, to take responsibility for losing her own virginity and that of Bertram too (as seems likely, he is a virgin too) drives the second phase of the plot. Like Rosalind in *As You Like It*, she dons disguise in order to get what she wants, but unlike Rosalind remains a woman throughout – her cover, in a rather poignant gesture to her "sanctifying" of Bertram at the play's outset, being the cloak of a pilgrim.

But her stratagem requires that she wear that devout costume somewhat ironically. Once arrived in Italy, she rapidly finds that Bertram has been attempting to seduce the beautiful Diana – and though Diana has so far resisted his advances, she is clearly tempted to give in. Pointing out Bertram in the passing parade of soldiers, she sighs, "'Tis a most gallant fellow,"

> I would he loved his wife. If he were honester
> He were much goodlier.
>
> [3.5.79–81]

To which it might be replied that Bertram's problem is too much honesty, not too little – far from pretending to be in love with a wife forced upon him, he takes the first opportunity to flee the country and look elsewhere.

"Honest", a destructive and dangerous word in *Othello*, resonates loudly at this point in Shakespeare's career, and in *All's Well* it is put under unusual pressure. Helen, still in disguise, describes how Bertram's "poor lady" has a "reservèd honesty" (guarded chastity); the Widow speaks of Diana's "honestest defence" against Bertram's advances. But Helen's solution to the problem that afflicts them both will involve not honesty but calculated betrayal. Suggesting that Diana agree to sleep with Bertram (after demanding that he give her his precious ring), Helen advises a covert assignation with him – for which she, not Diana, will turn up. In the dark Bertram will be none the wiser, and before he knows it he will have consummated his marriage, given his wife a child and surrendered the ring. His scoffing challenge to Helen will have been met, point by point. "Let us essay our plot," Helen urges the Widow after paying her off,

> which if it speed
> Is wicked meaning in a lawful deed
> And lawful meaning in a wicked act,
> Where both not sin, and yet a sinful fact.

> [3.7.44–7]

As the Duke pronounces in *Measure for Measure*, "the doubleness of the benefit defends the deceit from reproof" (3.1.59–60); or as Helen (and the play's title) repeatedly expresses it, "All's well that ends well; still the fine's the crown. / Whate'er the course, the end is the renown" (4.4.35–6).

The paradoxes Helen describes – that a deed can be both "lawful" and "wicked", both "sinful" and virtuous, that something so morally questionable can yet "end well" – are brought into unpleasant proximity in the bed-trick. *All's Well* is the second and only other comedy in which Shakespeare uses the device, though numerous other plays, among them *Much Ado*, *Othello*, *The Winter's Tale* and *Cymbeline*, dwell on apparent sexual deceit by women. The difference here, of course, is that the deceit – though accomplished with what are for Helen the best of intentions – is fully real. Commonplace in the tales that were Shakespeare's sources for *Measure for Measure* and *All's Well*, on stage the bed-trick is an uneasy and unrealistic technique, a strange combination of intimacy and distance. It implies that sex – even love – is dizzyingly unspecific, so much so that Bertram will fail even to realize that he has slept with the wrong woman.

Some critics have defended the bed-trick with the line that (roughly speaking) Helen takes: that it aligns her "liking" with his, encourages Bertram back to the marital straight-and-narrow despite himself. But for most audiences it remains an immense stumbling block, the crowning problem in a play replete with them. It is so not least because Helen's own love for Bertram raises more questions than it answers. Is her unwavering devotion a sign of strength or weakness? Is she open-eyed about her husband's many flaws, or wilfully blind to them? Will her hoped-for triumph over Bertram alter Diana's suggestion that "'Tis a hard bondage to become the wife / Of a detesting lord" (3.5.64–5)?

The name and not the thing

Before any of these can be answered, though, *All's Well* swerves away from its main subject. It has a minor subplot, invented by Shakespeare, in which the "gallant militarist" Paroles (a bragging soldier straight out of Greek comedy) is shown to be as untrustworthy towards his apparent friends as we in the audience realize he is towards everyone else. In a storyline that echoes the ambush of Falstaff in *Henry IV Part One* (see p.114), his fellow soldiers concoct a ruse whereby, disguised as Russian troops, they will capture Paroles, blindfold him, and expose him as a lying coward.

All goes to plan: Paroles gives up all the military secrets he has sworn to keep without pausing for breath, and is equally forthright with his opinions on his fellow officers – much to their private displeasure. They then discover that he is carrying a letter addressed to Diana, warning her of Bertram's intentions. Still fooled, Paroles freely explains all:

> My meaning in't, I protest, was very honest in the behalf of the maid, for
> I knew the young Count to be a dangerous and lascivious boy, who is a
> whale to virginity, and devours up all the fry it finds.
>
> [4.3.223–6]

The irony is, naturally, that the inveterate liar Paroles is nothing other than "honest" here, as Bertram well – and furiously – knows. Though at first sight this scene seems to sit outside the main curve of the play, as the action develops it becomes apparent how closely it informs on the central plot. In this topsy-turvy world a professional con-artist can as easily tell the truth as a woman can guarantee her husband's virtue by arranging him an affair.

By this time, moreover, Bertram has proved himself false to his word, and abandoned Diana to return home – to which Helen compounds her own dishonesty by arranging for a priest to put out word that she herself has died. As Bertram returns to the French court, all seems resolved: his wife is apparently dead, he has forgiven by the King and he is on the point of marrying Lafeu's daughter. But then the King spots that the ring he is about to give his new bride is the same one that he gave Helen.

Abruptly, the plot accelerates. Suspecting foul play, the King is about to accuse Bertram of her murder when a note arrives from Diana, swiftly followed by Diana herself. The court becomes a kind of courtroom as the King tries to ascertain precisely what is going on. Rejecting Diana's paradoxical evidence, he commands her to be sent to be prison. But then her "bail" appears:

> KING   Is there no exorcist
>   Beguiles the truer office of mine eyes?
>   Is't real that I see?
> HELEN   No, my good lord,
>   'Tis but the shadow of a wife you see,
>   The name and not the thing.
>
> [5.3.307–10]

Helen's final miracle is to raise herself, as she raised the King, from the dead – but to do so she has had to divorce her "name" as wife from her real identity. Her next question, to Bertram, reunites them: "Will you be mine, now that you are doubly won?" He has little choice but to acquiesce, but it is striking – and somehow strikingly sad – that he does not even reply directly. "If she, my liege, can make me know this clearly," he tells the King, "I'll love her dearly, ever ever dearly" (5.3.316–8). The audience is left pondering the consequences of that "if". The play refuses to resolve it for us.

Stage history and adaptations

Beyond its likely date of 1604–05 – placing it as one of Shakespeare's first Jacobean plays – there is no evidence of *All's Well's* initial life on stage. Though there is nothing unusual about that, some have conjectured that it was as unpopular then as it has been until recent years. The first performance on record took place in 1741, put on by **Henry Giffard**, who advertised the play as "written by Shakespeare and not acted since his time". Giffard himself acted Bertram and his wife Helen, but a few weeks into the run the young **David Garrick** joined the company and the comedy was axed so that Garrick could concentrate on more "serious" Shakespeare.

This faltering start cast a shadow over many subsequent productions. The Drury Lane version of 1742 was cut short when **Peg Woffington**'s Helen fell ill and her King, **William Milward**, died (despite jokingly professing faith in Woffington's "Doctor She"). Even **Theophilus Cibber**'s Paroles – audiences were reputedly moved to laughter just by the sight of his face – failed to save it, so the company rapidly nicknamed *All's Well* "the unfortunate comedy" and it soon closed. A Covent Garden attempt in 1746, with **Henry Woodward** as Paroles to **Hannah Pritchard**'s Helen, fared no better, achieving just one performance before Woodward jumped ship. **Garrick**, meanwhile, decided that *All's Well's* only redeeming feature was Paroles (described by the actor and writer Thomas Davies as "inferior only to the great master of stage gaiety and mirth, Sir John Falstaff") and penned an adaptation, premiered in 1756, which focused almost exclusively on him. Though **Woodward** took the role and would continue doing so for the next twenty years, the prompter recorded that "the play went off dull". Even so, Garrick doggedly mounted a revival in 1762 and Covent Garden replied the same year with a more popular version starring Woodward and **Maria Macklin**.

Another adaptation, this time by **Frederick Pilon**, was mounted at the Haymarket in 1785 to a warm reception – perhaps because it cut the first three acts. Yet another was staged at Drury Lane in 1794 at the behest of **John Philip Kemble**. Instead of concentrating on Paroles, however, Kemble saw potential in sentimentalizing *All's Well*, with himself as Bertram to **Dorothy Jordan**'s hoydenish Helen. John Philip's brother **Charles** mounted another production in 1811, again with himself as Bertram and **Nanette Johnston** as Helen. Although some reviewers made positive noises about the play itself, by general consensus it disgraced Kemble's Covent Garden. An operatic version by the industrious **Frederick Reynolds** appeared in 1832 – enlivened with lyrics stolen from other Shakespeare plays – but had a mixed reception, as did **Samuel Phelps**'s version at Sadler's Wells two decades later. Despite Phelps's attempts to refine the behaviour of **Fanny Cooper**'s heroine, played alongside Phelps's own Paroles and **Frederic Robinson**'s Bertram, *All's Well* was savaged by the critics. The *Athenaeum* derided the "rude nature of the plot" and its "exceedingly gross" manners.

The Countess (Clare Higgins) and Helen (Michelle Terry) conspire: a scene from Marianne Elliott's 2009 production of *All's Well That Ends Well* at the National Theatre in London.

This was to be a familiar refrain during the Victorian era and *All's Well* received precious few stagings, on the basis that Helen's behaviour was self-evidently brazen and indecent. George Bernard Shaw's was a lone voice of support, but as late as 1928 he wrote that the public was unprepared for its unsettling, Ibsenesque qualities. By the time **Frank Benson** came to the play in 1916, only it and *Titus* had failed to be produced at the Stratford Memorial Theatre. But once again fate intervened – Benson had just been knighted, and applause whenever he appeared on stage all but swamped the play. The iconoclastic **William Poel** put on an "Elizabethan" production at Bayswater in 1920, but audiences were puzzled by his decision to cross-cast many of the parts and some were incensed by his overtly political reading, which cast Helen as a Suffragette figure, demanding love as others did the vote.

Robert Atkins emphasized the play's comedy rather than its problems in the first of his three productions in 1921, but his efforts were attacked for lacking depth and the *Observer* concluded that *All's Well* was "very nearly the worst play its distinguished author ever wrote". The Poel disciple **William Bridges-Adams** found more success in his Stratford version the following year, but though critics praised **Baliol Holloway**'s Paroles, **Maureen Shaw**'s Helen was considered "too beautiful to be taken seriously" (as the *Birmingham Post* puzzlingly put it). The decade's final performance in 1927 was more innovative, set in modern-day France by **Barry Jackson**'s Birmingham Rep and with a teenage **Laurence Olivier** as Paroles.

In 1953 **Tyrone Guthrie** launched at Stratford, Ontario what was probably the first production of *All's Well* on the North American continent since a fleeting Bostonian appearance in 1799. Edwardian in setting, it starred **Irene Worth** as Helen and **Alec Guinness** as the King, and became a watershed production, adeptly balanced between tragedy and comedy. Guthrie repeated his success at the English Stratford six years later, this time with **Zoe Caldwell** as Helen, **Edward de Souza** as Bertram and **Cyril Luckham** as Paroles. **Edith Evans** played the Countess, the first grande dame to take what Shaw called "the most beautiful old woman's part ever written". **Michael Benthall**'s Old Vic production of 1953 was attacked for whimsy (**Claire Bloom**'s Helen merely ornamental and **Benthall**'s Paroles stealing the show); and **Noël Willman**'s Stratford staging, with **Joyce Redman**'s Helen and **Keith Michell**'s Paroles, also received criticism for prettifying the play's difficulties with Louis XIV picturesque.

John Barton took the play's contrast between youth and age as the keynote of his 1967 RSC production, with **Estelle Kohler**'s schoolgirlish Helen and **Ian Richardson**'s sympathetic Bertram, and opted for a Caroline setting. Also historically conservative was **Jonathan Miller**'s stripped-down Elizabethan version at the Greenwich Theatre in 1975. Following **David Jones**'s Stratford, Ontario staging in 1977 – once more Louis XIV in design – the play's most sympathetic 1980s production was directed at the RSC by **Trevor Nunn** in 1982. As with Guthrie, Nunn's Edwardian setting and Chekhovian inflections made sense for reviewers, not least because it was clouded by premonitions of World War I. **Harriet Walter** appeared as Helen to the Bertrams of **Mike Gwilym** and **Philip Franks**, but most audiences were entranced by **Peggy Ashcroft**'s Countess, full of worldly wisdom and compassion.

The reawakening of interest in the play was evidenced by its appearance at Stratfords both Canadian and English in 2003: the Ontario version was directed by **Richard Monette**, with **Lucy Peacock** as Helen and **David Snelgrove**'s Bertram; while in **Gregory Doran**'s RSC production (firmly set in the seventeenth century) **Judi Dench** brilliantly conveyed the Countess's split emotions, torn between her affection for **Claudie Blakley**'s sympathetic Helen and her gradual realization that **Jamie Glover**'s narcissistic Bertram has feet of clay.

In recent years *All's Well* has become, if not exactly a favourite, then not the dusty museum piece it once was. In 2009, director **Marianne Elliott** boldly put it on the main Olivier stage at Britain's National Theatre in a high-concept, fairytale-style production. Not all the critics adored the show ("ugly and overemphatic", declared the *Independent*), but **Michelle Terry**'s downtrodden yet ardent Helen won praise. The London Globe, meanwhile, has offered the play twice: first in 2011, in a solid if somewhat conventional home-grown version directed by **John Dove**; then again the following year, with a fleet-footed – and surprisingly upbeat – Gujarati production by the Mumbai-based **Arpana** troupe, part of the World Shakespeare Festival. In 2013, the RSC gave the play yet another outing, with **Nancy Meckler** directing a sharply feminist reimagining in which it was clear that **Joanna Horton**'s Helen had a much more immediate connection with the Countess and Diana than she did with Alex Waldmann's petulant Bertram.

All's Well does not dominate Shakespearian filmographies. The Jonathan Miller-produced BBC/Time-Life version of 1980, directed by **Elijah Moshinsky**, was made for TV. More recently there have been several live theatre recordings, notably of Dove's Globe production.

SCREEN

All's Well That Ends Well
A. Down, I. Charleson, C. Johnson;
Elijah Moshinsky (dir.) UK, 1980 > BBC **DVD**

Does it say something about the BBC/Time-Life Shakespeare project that the plays it excels at are the problem comedies? As with Desmond Davis's 1979 *Measure*, this *All's Well* from the following year receives a gloomy, slightly stifling treatment that captures the play's essence well. David Myerscough-Jones's designs resemble the interiors of seventeenth-century Dutch painting (transforming studio-bound necessity into a kind of virtue), though there is little Vermeerian tranquillity here as Angela Down's steely and solid Helen attempts to ensnare Ian Charleson's peevish Bertram. Donald Sinden is hammy as the King, but on the whole this production is one of the most satisfactory in a famously uneven series.

All's Well That Ends Well
E. Piercy, S. Crane, J. Dee; John Dove (dir.)
UK, 2013 > Globe > Opus Arte **DVD**

There have been more imaginative versions of *All's Well*, but so far none committed to video. First seen in 2011 and filmed two years later in front of a live audience at Shakespeare's Globe in London, John Dove's production is squarely seventeenth-century in design, all rustling velvet and lace collars, and makes a solid case for the play as a predecessor of Jacobean masterpieces by Middleton and Fletcher: tragedy only narrowly averted. Ellie Piercy makes an earnest but worldy-wise Helen, nicely cast against Sam Crane's priggish but not unsympathetic Bertram, a toff too young to realize how much is at stake until it's nearly too late. James Garnon does nice work as a pouting Paroles, but, as so often, the Countess – a wonderfully youthful and un-grand Janie Dee – steals the show. Is the ending heart-stoppingly moving or too sugary by half? You decide.

AUDIO

All's Well That Ends Well
C. Bloom, J. Stride, F. Robson; H. Sackler (dir.)
UK, 1965 > HarperCollins (Caedmon)

Like others in the Caedmon series, this 1965 *All's Well* casts a nostalgic glow – a refugee from another Shakespearian age – but, in doing so, somehow gets to the heart of the play's poignant ambiguity. It is dominated by Claire Bloom's measured but wonderfully rich Helen and John Stride's callow but not entirely unsympathetic Bertram. Flora Robson (herself a Dame) is a suitably stately and august presence as the Countess, but Robert Stephens's somewhat over-saturated Paroles might try the patience of some.

EDITIONS

Oxford Shakespeare
Susan Snyder (ed.); 1993 > Oxford UP

In the preface to her edition, Snyder relates how she was fortunate to have first come across *All's Well* not as a dry text in a dusty classroom, but via Noël Willman's 1955 version at the RSC, and her book is illustrated with production shots that take up interpretative points she raises. All the more bizarre, then, that she includes a mere paragraph of performance history – a frustrating omission in what would otherwise be a near-flawless edition. (Russell Fraser's Cambridge edition, updated in 2003, has some useful detail.) That said, Snyder's intellectual savvy is considerable and the attention she pays to the uncomfortable roles played by Helen is adroit. The introduction concludes, neatly, with an in-depth examination of every single element in the play's problematic title.

SOME CRITICISM

The Unfortunate Comedy
J.G. Price; 1968 > Liverpool UP / Toronto UP [o/p]

Price's work has the distinction of being the first book devoted to *All's Well*, a comedy that has often struggled to make its voice heard (the title refers to the nickname attached to the play after an ill-fated 1742 production). Price's study breaks down into two main parts, looking at the play's often troubled stage history and contrasting that with its critical reception. He concludes with an impassioned "Defence" of the play, one of the most sympathetic pieces of criticism around.

Reading Shakespeare Historically
Lisa Jardine; 1996 > Routledge

Lisa Jardine sprang onto the academic scene with her 1983 *Still Harping On Daughters: Women and drama in the age of Shakespeare* and was a highly visible part of it until her death in 2015. *Reading Shakespeare Historically* adopts some of the feminist concerns of her earlier Shakespeare book but groups together eight separate essays that form an engaging commentary on the new historicist practice of reading literature through its engagement with social and cultural history. The piece that covers *All's Well*, "Cultural Confusion and Shakespeare's Learned Heroines", is Jardine at her best – insightful, sympathetic and astute.

Antony and Cleopatra

Dramatically adventurous, richly characterized, linguistically gorgeous, *Antony and Cleopatra* is one of the surging triumphs of Shakespeare's late career. It sits closer than anything else he wrote to the Romantic ideal of sublimity – something so magnificent it inspires reverence and awe – and received corresponding praise from Samuel Taylor Coleridge, who extolled its "fiery force" and "giant power", and suggested there are probably no other works by the playwright in which "he impresses the notion of angelic strength so much". In its depiction of the titanic conflict between Rome and Egypt, the play is one of Shakespeare's most ambitious political dramas, but in every way the grand passion of the two lovers lies at the heart of its action, and is ultimately the impetus behind its tragedy. For all its vastnesses the play is also disarmingly domestic in scale; with their middle-aged squabbles and tantrums Antony and his Egyptian Queen embody something touchingly human and fragile at the centre of global politics.

DATE > First recorded in May 1608, the play is likely to have been written a few years before: Christmas 1606–07 is possible.

SOURCES > Sir Thomas North's translation of Plutarch, *Lives of the Noble Grecians and Romans* (1579), is the main source – Shakespeare lifts some passages almost verbatim. Samuel Daniel's *Cleopatra* (1594) and Barnabe Barnes's *The Devil's Charter* (1607) were also influences as was, to a lesser extent, the Countess of Pembroke's tragic *Antonius* (1592).

TEXTS > Although the publisher Edward Blount registered the right to print *Antony and Cleopatra*, it seems he never actually did. The only surviving text is that in the 1623 First Folio; numerous quirks suggest that it was probably copied from Shakespeare's manuscript.

Interpreting the play

Sublime though it may be, *Antony and Cleopatra* is mighty hard to perform, and is always threatening to come apart at the seams. Despite a mere handful of main roles and no crowd scenes, there are around forty characters and some 220 entrances and exits. The stage empties over forty times (scenes are not marked in the only printed text), and as the action builds everything gets progressively faster. Yet, as recent Jacobean-style stagings have revealed, that is very much the point. In the fluid, rapid-fire theatre of Shakespeare's time the effect must have been dazzling: a constant parade of people across the space; cross-cutting, filmic scenes that no sooner begin than they come to an end. Here, more than in any other work by Shakespeare, there is a powerful sense of ancient history in all its pomp and lavish spectacle.

MAJOR CHARACTERS & SYNOPSIS

Mark Antony, a triumvir (one of three co-rulers) of Rome

Octavius Caesar, triumvir

Lepidus, triumvir

Cleopatra, Queen of Egypt and Antony's lover

Domitius Enobarbus, companion to Antony

Octavia, Caesar's sister (later Antony's wife)

Sextus Pompey (Pompeius), rebel against the triumvirs

Antony's followers: **Demetrius, Philo, Ventidius, Silius, Eros, Camidius, Scarus** and **Decretas**

Caesar's followers: **Maecenas, Agrippa, Taurus, Dolabella, Thidias, Gallus** and **Proculeius**

Pompey's followers: **Menecrates, Menas** and **Varrius**

Cleopatra's followers: **Charmian, Iras, Alexas**, the eunuch **Mardian, Diomed** and **Seleucus**

A **Soothsayer**

A **Clown**

ACT 1 Antony, Rome's finest general, idles away his days far from home. Seduced by the good life in Egypt – the feasting, the parties, and above all by Cleopatra, his lover and Egypt's queen – he is a shadow of the man he was. Such at least is the view of Caesar and his councillors, who are eager to have Antony back in Rome to deal with the threat of rebellion from Pompey, all to no avail. But when Antony hears of his wife Fulvia's death, he realizes that he can delay no longer. Cleopatra is dismayed that he is returning to Rome, and although she eventually agrees, cannot get him out of her mind. In the meantime, though, a soothsayer has predicted that the fortunes of the world's most glamorous couple are on the wane.

ACT 2 At Pompey's camp, the news that Caesar has assembled an army is not well received; worse, Antony has returned. Meanwhile, Rome's three rulers are locked in argument: Antony is criticized for Fulvia's erstwhile rebellion but denies undermining Caesar. Agrippa suggests that in order to strengthen their alliance and be reconciled, Antony should marry Caesar's sister Octavia. Both agree, but it isn't long before Antony longs to return to Egypt. News of Antony's conduct has already reached Cleopatra, however, and she is devastated. And although the threat of civil war is averted when Pompey agrees to cease his campaign, it becomes clear at the peace dinner that his intentions are far darker than anyone realizes.

ACT 3 Rome's campaign against the Parthians has been successful, but old wounds rapidly reopen as Antony, on the way to Athens with his new wife, criticizes Caesar's renewal of hostilities against Pompey. Octavia is sent to Rome to mediate, but it is soon reported that Antony has made his way back to Egypt without Octavia's knowledge, and that he has promised the eastern empire to Cleopatra. Caesar, fresh from his trouncing of Pompey, intends to fight. And Antony, accompanied by his lover, is showing dangerous lapses of judgement: spurning the advice of their military advisers, they prepare for an ill-fated sea assault. As predicted, they lose. Caesar rejects their peace terms, in which Antony is permitted to retire into private life with Cleopatra, and attempts to turn them against each other.

ACT 4 Having had his challenge of single combat derisively rejected by Caesar, Antony prepares for a decisive second battle. Though the omens are not good – his soldiers are convinced that Hercules has deserted them, and Enobarbus has defected – the first day's fighting goes well for Antony and he returns to Cleopatra in triumph. But catastrophe strikes the next day when the Egyptian ships suddenly surrender. Antony, watching from land, blames Cleopatra and threatens to murder them both. When Cleopatra responds by sending news of her own feigned suicide to Antony, he takes it seriously and attempts to kill himself. Fatally wounded, he is carried off to see her one last time.

ACT 5 When Antony dies Cleopatra sees death as the only option, but she is prevented from stabbing herself by Caesar's soldiers. When Dolabella reveals that Caesar intends her to be paraded through Rome, Cleopatra is appalled and resolves to die at once. Placing asps to her breast and arm, she predicts reunion with Antony in the afterlife. Caesar, discovering her body, arranges for the lovers to share a tomb.

In contrast to Shakespeare's earlier historical Roman play, *Julius Caesar, Antony and Cleopatra* wilfully refuses to be Roman in tone – even though it has good grounds to be considered a sequel, picking up political events as the post-Caesar triumvirate of Antony, Octavius and Lepidus explodes under the pressure of clashing personalities. Whereas the action of *Julius Caesar* moves most often through reasoned debate, via persuasion and counter-persuasion, *Antony and Cleopatra* delights in ornament, fancy, excess. Shakespeare has sometimes been accused of indulging his love of language in this late play: there may be some truth in the charge, but then this tragedy is all about showing off. Its most famous speech, Enobarbus's rapt description of Cleopatra's arrival in her barge – the entrance that puts Antony fatefully under her spell – appeals to the heart, not the head. "The barge she sat in," he declares, "like a burnished throne / Burned on the water."

> The poop was beaten gold;
> Purple the sails, and so perfumèd that
> The winds were love-sick with them. The oars were silver,
> Which to the tune of flutes kept stroke, and made
> The water which they beat to follow faster,
> As amorous of their strokes. For her own person,
> It beggared all description. She did lie
> In her pavilion—cloth of gold, of tissue—
> O'er-picturing that Venus where we see
> The fancy outwork nature. On each side her
> Stood pretty dimpled boys, like smiling Cupids,
> With divers-coloured fans whose wind did seem
> To glow the delicate cheeks which they did cool,
> And what they undid did.

[2.2.198–212]

In this almost impossibly sensual image, life simply comes to a halt: the oars and the waves beat time, but to little impression of movement, just as the "dimpled boys" fan the Queen's cheeks and yet make them glow, doing "what they undid". Nothing happens – beautifully.

For all *Antony and Cleopatra*'s bustle, it is often observed that in the wider play, too, not much goes on. Shakespeare streamlines the material in Plutarch's *Life* of Antony, compressing or deleting many events and dwelling instead on their personal and emotional implications. When the play begins, Antony has already fallen under Cleopatra's spell, and whatever happens we sense that he will be unable to stay away from "his Egyptian dish" (2.6.126) – as Enobarbus harshly describes her – for long. The on-off affair between the protagonists persists in its maddeningly unsettled state for nearly all the play. Much the same happens with the global events that *Antony and Cleopatra* ostensibly spans: the political match with Octavia, designed to hold Antony and her brother Octavius "in perpetual amity", breaks down almost as soon as it is agreed; while it is only too characteristic that the play's defining political turning point, the sea battle between the Egyptian forces and the Roman army of Octavius at Actium, ends in chaos.

Antony and Cleopatra can be read as the fall of a great general, betrayed in his dotage by a treacherous strumpet, or else it can be viewed as a celebration of transcendental love.

A.P. Riemer, "A Reading of Shakespeare's *Antony and Cleopatra*" (1968)

Pleasure now

The Romans themselves are quite sure that Antony, formerly their greatest captain, the towering example of Roman values, is now an ageing joke. Plutarch, Shakespeare's source, often comments on the morality (or otherwise) of his subjects, and in *Antony and Cleopatra* those juicy comments often find their way into the mouths of Antony's former colleagues. "He fishes, drinks, and wastes / The lamps of night in revel," Octavius acidly observes (1.4.4–5), and even earlier in the play Philo and Demetrius, supposedly Antony's followers, join him in condemnation. "This dotage of our General's / O'erflows the measure," Philo remarks:

> Those his goodly eyes,
> That o'er the files and musters of the war
> Have glowed like plated Mars, now bend, now turn
> The office and devotion of their view
> Upon a tawny front. His captain's heart
> Which in the scuffles of great fights hath burst
> The buckles on his breast, reneges all temper,
> And is become the bellows and the fan
> To cool a gipsy's lust.
>
> [1.1.1–10]

Sexually enslaved to Cleopatra, the titanic Antony has thrown himself on the scrapheap. While on campaign with his Roman men, Octavius laments, Antony would "deign [accept] the roughest berry on the rudest hedge …" (1.4.64); now he wastes his time in "lascivious wassails", the endless round of parties that constitute life at the Egyptian court.

Egypt is, of course, the key to Antony's decline and the storehouse for his "pleasure". For Jacobeans no less than Greek historians Egypt held a seductive, exotic appeal – a land of desert yet dominated by the mysterious, all-delivering Nile; the repository of wise yet alien ancient civilizations. In Shakespeare's play, Egypt is evoked by melting, fluid language, a direct challenge to the chiselled certainties of Rome. Attempting to rid himself of his Roman responsibilities near the opening of the play, Antony snarls, "Let Rome in Tiber melt, and the wide arch / Of the ranged empire fall" (1.1.35–6). And these words receive a resonant echo in Cleopatra's curse a few scenes later, when she is confronted with a recalcitrant messenger:

> Melt Egypt into Nile, and kindly creatures
> Turn all to serpents!
>
> [2.5.78–9]

Decadent, death-risking excess characterizes life in Egypt – the twelve wild boars slaughtered for a single breakfast, the "Alexandrian feast" and "Egyptian bacchanals" with which Antony and his followers entertain the Romans after his fateful marriage to Octavia.

Perhaps most importantly, Egypt, sensual and sexual, poses a subversive threat to the brute world of Roman masculinity. The only Roman woman in the play is Octavia herself, whose "holy, cold, and still conversation" (2.6.122–3) will, Enobarbus predicts, soon tire Antony. In rich contrast, Cleopatra is surrounded by swarms of hand-maidens and attendants, who, when Antony departs for Rome, amuse themselves by gossiping about sex. Even the eunuch Mardian, though "unseminared" (emasculated), indulges in the occasional risqué fantasy. "I can do nothing / But what indeed is honest to be done," he informs his mistress, his words thick with puns,

> Yet I have fierce affections, and think
> What Venus did with Mars.
>
> [1.5.15–18]

Little wonder that the militant Octavius, serving the Roman god of war in a more straightforward sense, insists coldly at Antony's Egyptian feast that, given the choice, he would "rather fast from all" for four days than become dangerously drunk in one. He has no desire to suffer Antony's – or indeed Mardian's – fate and become "not more manlike / Than Cleopatra" (1.4.5–6).

No more

In every sense the heartbeat of *Antony and Cleopatra* is the relationship – quixotic, captivating – between the lovers themselves. Like so much in the play, this too is gran-diosely unrealistic: more the stuff of poetry than real life. Often there is the sense that Cleopatra and Antony are talking themselves into a love affair, rather than genuinely inhabiting it:

CLEOPATRA
    If it be love indeed, tell me how much.
ANTONY
    There's beggary in the love that can be reckoned.
CLEOPATRA
    I'll set a bourn how far to be beloved.
ANTONY
    Then must thou needs find out new heaven, new earth.

> [1.1.14–17]

The lovers can conceive of no "bourn" (limit) to their love other than of what they themselves are capable. Cleopatra later accuses Antony of forgetting that "eternity was in our lips and eyes, / Bliss in our brow's bent; none our parts so poor / But was a race of heaven" (1.3.33–7).

Constance Collier was Herbert Beerbohm Tree's leading lady from 1901 to 1906. Cleopatra (to Tree's Antony) was one of her finest achievements.

Cleopatra herself, perhaps Shakespeare's greatest female role, seems eminently capable of constructing new worlds should she so desire. She makes a habit of dressing in "th'habiliments of the goddess Isis" (3.6.17), and in Enobarbus's rapt description appears almost immortal: "Age cannot wither her," he declares, "nor custom stale / Her infinite variety" (2.2.241–2). To many characters in the play she is also infinitely unknowable: on the one hand "great Egypt", "most sovereign creature", a "triumphant lady"; on the other, a "foul Egyptian", a "witch", a "cow in June". That shimmering variety is the key to her appeal – for audiences as well as Antony – but is also frequently a source of frustration. She fishes for his commitment even as she makes herself impossible to love. "See where he is, who's with him, what he does," she orders her servants as soon as Antony disappears from the room:

> If you find him sad,
> Say I am dancing; if in mirth, report
> That I am sudden sick.

[1.3.2–5]

The moment is comic, but also comically human. Cleopatra is capable of astounding changes of temper, and like the great actress she is ranges from comedy to tragedy in an instant. Struck by Shakespeare's portrayal, the seventeenth-century poet Margaret Cavendish exclaimed, "One would think that he had been Metamorphosed from a Man to a Woman," in order to create a character herself so consistently changeful.

The scene in which she discovers that Antony has betrayed her by marrying Octavia is a glorious set piece for Cleopatra and the actor who plays her: after receiving one of the play's many messengers ("twenty several" of hers alone pursue Antony to Rome), she is so frantic for news that she will not even permit him to speak. Responding to his guarantee that her lover is "well", she barks:

CLEOPATRA   But, sirrah, mark: we use
  To say the dead are well. Bring it to that,
  The gold I give thee will I melt and pour
  Down thy ill-uttering throat.
MESSENGER
  Good madam, hear me.
CLEOPATRA   Well go to, I will.
  But there's no goodness in thy face. If Antony
  Be free and healthful, so tart a favour
  To trumpet such good tidings! If not well,
  Thou shouldst come like a Fury crowned with snakes,
  Not like a formal man.
MESSENGER   Will't please you hear me?
CLEOPATRA
  I have a mind to strike thee ere thou speak'st.

[2.5.30–42]

Though the scene becomes still more broadly comic – particularly when she "hales him up and down" in a rage, as the stage directions have it – it is also coloured by a lingering pathos. As we watch Cleopatra fight her urge to hear Octavia's beauty described (albeit by a messenger now too terrified to tell her anything remotely unpalatable), it seems clear that she feels the loss of what she touchingly calls her "salad days" keenly.

In their solipsistic, self-magnifying obsession with themselves and each other, Antony and Cleopatra resemble Shakespeare's other headlining couple, Romeo and Juliet. But whereas the young lovers are torn apart by a strife that they cannot hold back, their middle-aged counterparts are fatefully implicated in the events that are their undoing. "These strong Egyptian fetters I must break, / Or lose myself in dotage," mutters Antony just two scenes into the play (1.2.109–10), but Shakespeare makes his task far more muddled, and by the play's end he is still floundering. As his commanders fear, Antony's military instincts have blunted, and against their advice he confronts Caesar at Actium by sea. After losing disastrously he dares Octavius to single combat, only for Octavius to scorn the challenge, and though the subsequent battle goes well for Cleopatra and her forces, their apparent betrayal is Antony's undoing. When news arrives that the Egyptian Queen has committed suicide, it is the end. Preparing for a valiant Roman suicide, Antony muses to Eros that

  Sometime we see a cloud that's dragonish,
  A vapour sometime like a bear or lion,
  A towered citadel, a pendent rock,
  With trees upon't that nod unto the world
  And mock our eyes with air.

[4.15.2–7]

"My good knave Eros," he continues, "now thy captain is / Even such a body." It isn't just Antony's reputation that has dissolved – he sees himself disappearing before his own eyes.

Let's pretend

The dusty documentary evidence of Shakespeare's time on earth – all those legal records, lists of land holdings, tax records – leaves many readers craving more in the way of human contact. Diary entries or the first drafts of *Othello* may be too much to hope for – but couldn't there at least be a letter in the great man's hand, or a record of the books he owned? A note to his wife, or at least his publisher? It's hard not to hope that someone might yet turn up the literary discover of all time, buried in an attic or at the bottom of a long-forgotten trunk.

That impulse goes some way towards explaining the many colourful myths surrounding Shakespeare, from the dramatist William Davenant's claim to be his love child to the theory – actually far more unlikely – that someone entirely different wrote the plays (see p.566). It also impels several lurid tales of Shakespearian fakery. The most famous case dates back to the last years of the eighteenth century, with the chance discovery of several documents featuring Shakespeare's signature by a teenager named **William Henry Ireland** (1777–1835). Ireland managed to persuade the experts of the documents' authenticity and his father, a prominent London bookdealer, printed them in 1796 as *Miscellaneous Papers and Legal Instruments under the Hand and Seal of William Shakespeare*. Among the treasure trove they ostensibly unearthed was correspondence between Shakespeare and the Earl of Southampton, a confession of Catholicism in Shakespeare's own writing, a note from Elizabeth I and – most tantalizingly – a love letter from Shakespeare to Anne Hathaway enclosed with a poem:

Is there inne heavenne aught more rare
Thanne thou sweete Nymphe of Avon fayre
Is there onne Earthe a Mann more trewe
Thanne Willy Shakspeare is to you

Of course the whole lot were fakes, forged by the young Ireland in homemade ink and littered with – as well as some distinctly dodgy spelling – glaring errors of fact. Even so, many were fooled, and, relishing the attention, Ireland "discovered" ever more astonishing things: manuscripts for *Hamlet* and *Lear*, several entirely new plays. One, colourfully entitled *Vortigern and Rowena*, was even scheduled for performance at Drury Lane in 1796. As it turned out, the decision to stage *Vortigern* proved Ireland's undoing. Following a brutal demolition of the Shakespeare papers by the great scholar and editor **Edmond Malone** two days before, a capacity audience was overcome by laughter, and the performance descended into chaos. It was obviously with some relief that Ireland, still only in his early twenties, admitted that he had made up the whole thing, though in a poignant footnote to the affair his own father refused to believe him.

Far more troubling is the case of **John Payne Collier** (1789–1883), a respected scholar who appeared in 1852 to have made an unbelievably lucky discovery: a copy of the 1632 Second Folio full of corrections by a member of Shakespeare's own company. Persuaded by several earlier documents he claimed to have found (some of which were indeed authentic), fellow academics rushed to believe Collier's story; indeed, many of the textual alterations he proposed seemed entirely reasonable. Even when a British Museum team spotted that the "seventeenth-century" handwriting was actually done in nineteenth-century watercolour, many refused to accept that Collier could have been responsible. The man himself kept quiet.

To this day some maintain that Collier's only sin was to be taken in by forgeries perpetrated by someone else, though it seems more likely that the mysterious handwriting he found (or wrote) was a desperate attempt to beat his rivals – an admittedly extreme version of the Victorian quest for the "perfect" text. And in one respect at least, Collier has had the last laugh: he was an early proponent of the long-disputed history play *Edward III*, which has recently been readmitted to the canon (see p.81).

In the event, somehow fittingly, Antony bungles his suicide – a suicide initiated by news that Cleopatra is dead. It is the play's bitter joke (and again testament to her "infinite variety") that she is nothing of the kind: Cleopatra put out the news in an attempt to defuse Antony's anger after battle. The truth arrives only once Antony has tried, and failed, to kill himself; and he is doomed to die a lingering death, trying to get her to listen even in his last moments. Although (unlike Romeo and Juliet) they are given a last chance to see each other, Antony and Cleopatra do so at the cost of conventional tragic dignity: Antony's last words are "no more" as his beloved begs, characteristically, "hast thou no care of me?" (4.16.62).

The play does not end with Antony, however, and in its drawn-out final scene, located throughout at Cleopatra's monument as the Romans close in, *Antony and Cleopatra* proves that it is after all a double tragedy. Some of Cleopatra's most passionate speeches about her lover occur once he is dead, and point to the fantasy that sustained their relationship. "I dreamt there was an Emperor Antony," she exclaims to Dolabella. "His legs bestrid the ocean; his reared arm / Crested the world ... Realms and islands were / As plates dropped from his pocket." The image is deliberately unreal, and when Cleopatra asks, "Think you there was, or might be, such a man / As this I dreamt of?", Dolabella's only reply is "Gentle madam, no" (5.2.81–93).

Aside from fantasy, however, the only other option for Cleopatra is the grim reality of life under Roman control – and control is not something she is prepared to relinquish. She will not live to be paraded through Rome like a "strumpet", jeered at by the multitude; she cannot bear the thought that "quick comedians" will put them on stage, that

> Antony
> Shall be brought drunken forth, and I shall see
> Some squeaking Cleopatra boy my greatness
> I'th' posture of a whore.
>
> [5.2.214–7]

The dramatic irony is powerful: on Shakespeare's stage Cleopatra was already being played by a "boy", possibly the same talented actor who created the roles of Lady Macbeth and Volumnia. But Cleopatra wants to star in her own tragedy, and as she puts on her queenly garments for the last time, expressing her "immortal longings" (5.2.276), she arranges her death like the great performer she is.

Stage history and adaptations

We don't know for certain at which theatre *Antony and Cleopatra* was first produced, though the indoor **Blackfriars** has been suggested – partly owing to the play's surprisingly intimate theatrics, which, unlike the other Roman dramas, require no crowd scenes. No records survive, however, and it's likely that even if the tragedy was written for an indoor space Shakespeare's company would have done it during the summer at the open-air Globe. The existence of two other Cleopatra dramas, **John Fletcher** and

"A most triumphant lady" ... Gregory Doran's 2006 RSC production brought Patrick Stewart back to the stage after many years in TV, but it was Harriet Walter's glittering, capricious heroine that captured the critics' hearts.

Philip Massinger's *False One* (1619–23) and **Thomas May's** *Cleopatra, Queen of Egypt* (1626) hint that his subject matter (if not necessarily his script) was still in vogue a few years after his death.

Although **John Dryden** claimed to "imitate" Shakespeare in his well-known neo-classical adaptation, *All for Love, or, The World Well Lost* (1678), in fact his version deviates more markedly from Shakespeare than any other Restoration reworking. Cleopatra's skimpy role barely compares and the focus is firmly on our hero's moral dilemmas as he struggles to balance various calls on his energies – one of whom, Caesar, even fails to make it on stage. In 1759, **David Garrick** boldly attempted a revival of something approaching Shakespeare's play at Drury Lane, but the text was cut and conflated in all but the final act, Garrick relying instead on ornate scenery and his own powers as Antony. That the former dwarfed the latter may account for the production's failure – a fellow actor griped that Garrick was "not sufficiently important and commanding".

Throughout the nineteenth century, the scenery just kept getting larger. Despite the anxieties of his leading lady, **Sarah Siddons**, that playing the "foul Egyptian" might injure her reputation, **John Philip Kemble** went ahead in 1813 with a version that set the tone for years to come. Designed for the vast new Theatre Royal at Covent Garden, it boasted a sea fight complete with galleys, and an elaborate funeral procession with a massed choir. Again, though, it was a flop, and critic William Hazlitt publicly attacked

Kemble's decision to retain some of Dryden's text. **William Charles Macready** revived Kemble in 1833 still more spectacularly, but ironically enough **Clarkson Stanfield's** magnificent painted scenery attracted the only positive reviews.

Shakespeare himself, now divested of Dryden, was judged the winner in **Samuel Phelps's** 1849 production at Sadler's Wells. The *Illustrated London News* thought its treatment of the Egyptian scenes "exceedingly *vraisemblable*", though Isabella Glyn as Cleopatra still looked extavagantly stately and Victorian. Perhaps it was only inevitable that archeological accuracy would predominate in **Frederick Chatterton's** 1873 Drury Lane staging, which advertised the fact that its costumes were modelled on the British Museum's Egyptian collection. Though Chatterton achieved sour enough notices, the critical horror that greeted **Lewis Wingfield's** unwieldy production at the Princess's Theatre in London seventeen years later was revealing: a soporific four and a half hours long, it was panned by *The Times* as an "Oriental pantomime". Even **Lillie Langtry**, the Prince of Wales's lover, failed to enliven proceedings as Cleopatra. Arrigo Boito's Italian translation of the play had three performances at the Lyric Theatre in 1893, starring the great Italian actress **Eleonora Duse**, but it was not one of her successes and was attacked by leading critic William Archer. Nor were things much better with **Herbert Beerbohm Tree's** 1906 production, described a "Magnificent Spectacle" by the *Daily Telegraph*, although it did boast the formidable beauty **Constance Collier** as Cleopatra.

It took **Harley Granville-Barker**, influenced by **William Poel**, to call a halt to Orientalist megalomania. Though neither man ever managed to put on *Antony and Cleopatra*, Granville-Barker's *Preface* on the play celebrated its "old fluidity" and argued for sensitive staging. **Robert Atkins** complied at the Old Vic in 1922, using cut-out scenery and a practically bare stage. In 1951 **Michael Benthall** staged a rather more opulent production at the St James's Theatre for the husband-and-wife team of **Laurence Olivier** and **Vivien Leigh**. But it was **Glen Byam Shaw's** somewhat cooler 1953 Stratford production that really defined the play for the mid-century. Supposedly cast against type, **Peggy Ashcroft** triumphed as a Cleopatra who was sharply intelligent rather than merely capricious while **Michael Redgrave** brought a poetic world-weariness to the role of Antony. **Trevor Nunn's** 1972 Stratford production marked something of a return to epic luxuriousness, but did so in order to underscore the play's exaggerated view of imperialism. **Richard Johnson** was a robust Antony and **Janet Suzman** a coolly calculating Cleopatra, although some commentators complained that she failed to achieve the requisite grandeur. For **Peter Brook** in 1978 (yet again at Stratford) **Glenda Jackson's** haughty Cleopatra battled with **Alan Howard** as a petulant and preening Antony, in a designer-chic setting that managed to be both minimalist and sensuous.

The debate about whether the leading couple live up to their roles has dominated responses to most modern productions. While **Tony Richardson** (1973) diverted the audience's attention with offbeat iconoclasm (a red-haired **Vanessa Redgrave** vamped it up in a white silk trouser suit), in 1987 **Peter Hall** played it straight at the National, casting a grizzled **Anthony Hopkins** against **Judi Dench's** earthy Queen. Both actors gave their all in what was regarded as a keynote staging, one in which the lovers had a tangible sexual chemistry. **Adrian Noble** also went for big names with **Helen**

Mirren and Michael Gambon in 1982, but with less success. Mirren – an ideal actress for the part – repeated the role at the National Theatre in 1998 but this time a sadly undercharged Alan Rickman as Antony meant that the production failed to take off. More subversive interpretations have included an all-male production directed by Giles Havergal at the Citizens' Theatre in Glasgow in 1972 and Michael Kahn's version of 1988, which cast the African American actor Franchelle Stewart Dorn as Cleopatra (much of her court was also black, in a studied statement about the play's interest in race).

The 1999 production at Shakespeare's Globe in London attempted an even more radical approach, presenting the play as a kind of comedy. In this all-male version, Mark Rylance played for laughs as Cleopatra but also brought out much of the character's wistfulness. Opposite him, in a Jacobean-style staging by Giles Block, were Paul Shelley as Antony and John McEnery as Enobarbus. Twenty-odd years after playing Enobarbus under Trevor Nunn – and by now more famous for Star Trek than for Shakespeare – Patrick Stewart returned to the RSC to play Antony in 2006. Gregory Doran's fluent direction won rave reviews, as did Harriet Walter's searchingly intelligent heroine. The following year, Belgian director Ivo van Hove and Toneelgroep Amsterdam debuted Roman Tragedies, an epic version of the three Roman plays updated for the era of 24-hour news and a constantly churning political spin cycle. Antony was played by actor Hans Kesting as a fixer nonetheless deeply scarred by the death of Caesar.

A more recent RSC production, this time in the hands of American playwright Tarell Alvin McCraney, caused controversy in 2013 for attempting to examine the play's colonial dimensions, featuring depictions of slavery and voodoo and using an "edited" script that reordered several scenes (Egypt was eighteenth-century Saint-Domingue, with the Romans frock coat-wearing French invaders). The critics were given no such qualms by Jonathan Munby's Jacobean-ish staging for the London Globe the following year, dominated by a heartfelt if not especially passionate relationship between Eve Best's highly strung Cleopatra and Clive Wood's battered, battle-scarred Antony.

Antony and Cleopatra proper has reached the screen several times. To date, the only full-scale, English-language movie version has been that undertaken by Charlton Heston in 1972, which features abundant alterations to Shakespeare's text in the best nineteenth-century tradition. Never released in the US, it was widely regarded (like Heston's Antony) as a noble failure. Trevor Nunn's more convincing TV adaptation two years later, like his later Macbeth and Othello, reworked his stage production and retained the services of Johnson and Suzman. Jonathan Miller's 1981 BBC/Time-Life production in Elizabethan costume, in which Jane Lapotaire's coquettish Cleopatra played against the down-to-earth ruggedness of Colin Blakely, was comparably intimate, though here the constraints seemed financial rather than artistic. More impressive in every sense is Kannaki, the free Malayalam-language adaptation (2002) by Jayaraaj, which relocates the action to a rural Indian community and wryly transforms the epic power struggles of Shakespeare's original into a series of village cockfights.

SCREEN

Antony and Cleopatra

C. Heston, H. Neil, J. Castle; Charlton Heston (dir.)
UK/Spain/Switzerland, 1972 ❯ Warner **DVD** ⬇

After acting Antony in Stuart Burge's *Julius Caesar* (see p.210), Heston became convinced that he was the man to take on the headline role in Shakespeare's grandest Roman play. Orson Welles declined to be involved, so Heston took the director's chair and put everything together himself, cutting and reordering most of the text along the way. It was a brave decision, and the film is certainly not as bad as its slimline budget might so easily have ensured, but is damaged (as in so many stage productions) by the limitations of the lead couple. Heston makes a valiant attempt not to sink into self-parody, but Hildegard Neil is simply not up to the job.

Antony and Cleopatra

R. Johnson, J. Suzman, C. Redgrave; John Scoffield (dir.) UK, 1974 ❯ Lions Gate **DVD**

One complaint about Trevor Nunn's 1972 staging of the play was that Janet Suzman failed to scale Cleopatra's monumental heights. On video you get a ringside seat as the leading couple slug it out, and it's true that neither is overly imposing – Suzman sometimes too skittish, Johnson's Burtonesque bluffery occasionally false. But deflation is among the play's obsessions, and what they bring to this production – captivating, chameleonic humanity – is of supreme value, and in the end almost unbearably sad. Elsewhere in the cast, Corin Redgrave's sub-zero Octavius has passed into legend (it's all in the lips), and even Patrick Stewart's gruff Enobarbus isn't as irritating as at first he seems. Despite it being a production filmed for TV (like Nunn's *Macbeth*; see p.266), Scoffield's camerawork is always inventive, suggestively employing an enforced studio-bound setting to recreate the play's overlapping and often mirage-like spaces. Among the best Shakespeare television has produced – which makes it doubly frustrating that at the time of writing the only copies available on DVD seem to be secondhand.

Kannaki

Lal, N. Das, Siddique; Jayaraaj (dir.)
India, 2002 ❯ Moser Baer **DVD**

Antony is an expert at cockfighting in a small Kerala village, Cleopatra a local beauty and folk healer: nothing is quite what you expect in this strange but beguiling adaptation by Malayalam director Jayaraaj, also responsible for *Kaliyattam* (1997), a fascinating version of *Othello* remade in the South Indian dance form *teyyam*. Taking its cue from the throwaway line that Caesar's "cocks do win the battle," Jayaraaj imagines what Shakespeare's play might look like set in a tightly knit rural Indian community every bit as stratified and status-obsessed as Rome and Egypt. It's a beautiful film, poetically shot in a sultry, water-logged environment that is a fine match for Cleopatra's Nile; and its tormenting conclusion throbs with emotion. The movie is only available from Indian-based sellers (with excerpts available online), but it's well worth making the effort.

AUDIO

Antony and Cleopatra

A. Quayle, P. Brown, P. Daneman
UK, 1965 ❯ HarperCollins (Caedmon) ⬇

Any *Antony and Cleopatra* is made, or unmade, by its lead couple, and despite an acting style that might strike some listeners as old-fashioned both Anthony Quayle and Pamela Brown are more than up to their shared task. Quayle presents a small-scale yet utterly persuasive Antony, convincingly irritated that he is going to seed, while Brown does her matriarchal best as Cleopatra, a grande dame permanently conscious of her audience – and who refuses to go gently. Other members of the cast are also first-rate, among them Jack Gwillim's oaky Enobarbus and Paul Daneman's curt Octavius. Ultimately, though, it's this recording's fast pace, which makes convincing sense of the play's boundless energy – not to mention its Egyptian revels – that makes it a top choice. Only its boxy sound, which sometimes makes the lovers seem as if they're quarrelling in a bedsit, lets it down.

EDITIONS

Oxford Shakespeare

Michael Neill (ed.); 1994 ❯ Oxford UP

Neill's edition is probably the most comprehensive currently available – particularly useful for this, one of Shakespeare's densest and richest works. His book-length introduction is suggestive and astute, and probes some interesting thematic links within the play. Neill also deals with performance history in some detail, and usefully includes relevant excerpts from Thomas North's translation of Plutarch, one of Shakespeare's main sources. One slightly idiosyncratic editorial decision, to spell "Anthony" with an "h", receives learned backup, and a notoriously messy text is cleaned up well. If you're in search of more recent criticism and stage history, David Bevington's updated New Cambridge edition (2005) also comes recommended.

SOME CRITICISM

The Common Liar
Janet Adelman; 1973 ❯ Yale UP [o/p]

The Common Liar modestly subtitles itself "an essay on *Antony and Cleopatra*", but at some 235 pages long that's something of an understatement. It's one of the best places to start: Adelman provides readable, sane and intelligent commentary to many of the play's main concerns, brought together under her overall argument that its compound uncertainties are a measure of its explorative nature. The book also contains appendices on Plutarch, Virgil, and also Cleopatra's ethnicity – the last a topic still infrequently discussed, but something deliberately provoked by the play.

Enter the Body
Carol Chillington Rutter; 2001 ❯ Routledge

Taking issue with critics like Stephen Orgel (see p.42) who have focused on the homoerotic frisson of Shakespeare's cross-dressing boy actors – yet another male-obsessed view of Shakespeare, she argues – Carol Rutter wants us instead to focus on the plays themselves, and their eloquence when it comes to bodies, especially female ones. Few roles are as fascinating or as self-aware in this regard as Cleopatra, and Rutter unpicks questions of representation with impressive precision, notably the centuries-long trend of playing the Egyptian queen as "white" when the text contains nearly as many references to blackness as does the script of *Othello*. Though it's not without its flaws – Rutter's near-exclusive concentration on British stage productions limits her conclusions unnecessarily – this is bracing stuff and powerfully argued.

As You Like It

Written during the same period as *Twelfth Night*, *As You Like It* has little of the obvious darkness of the other mature comedies. Perhaps that is because it spends so much time in the Elizabethan "green world" of the Ardenne forest, a rejuvenating environment that allows all the play's erotic entanglements to untie themselves with ease, preparing for a barnstorming finale in which no fewer than eight characters are paired off simultaneously. The play's take-it-or-leave-it title makes the conclusion seem all the more light-hearted, and perhaps excuses the playwright from the accusation, levelled by some, that its plot is paper-thin. It could be argued that the comedy's genius lies not in its happenings but in its characters, who include perhaps Shakespeare's most engaging heroine, Rosalind – one in a line of confident and sparklingly witty women who dominate the middle comedies. Though it is by no means frivolous, as Helen Gardner, one of *As You Like It*'s most attentive critics, writes, this is "the last play in the world to be solemn over".

DATE > *As You Like It* was entered in the Stationers' Register on August 4, 1600, alongside *Henry V*, *Much Ado* and Ben Jonson's *Every Man in His Humour*. It was presumably written either that year or just before.

SOURCES > Thomas Lodge's hugely popular *Rosalynde* (1590), a slender but eventful prose tale written while the author was en route to the West Indies, provided Shakespeare with the substance for *As You Like It*, though he refashions its plot and renames its characters.

TEXTS > Despite being entered in the Register, the play wasn't to reach print until the 1623 Folio, meaning that its entry there was probably a "staying order" – a device to prevent piracy or forestall censorship. The Folio text was perhaps typeset from a promptbook rather than Shakespeare's own papers.

Interpreting the play

Shakespeare's characters in *As You Like It* have it easy – at least compared to those in his main source, Thomas Lodge's Elizabethan classic *Rosalynde* (1590). Forsaking treachery at court for the wildness of the forest, Lodge's female characters have to confront outlaws, rape and even the threat of incest before they are permitted to reach the story's end; while his male hero, Rosader (Shakespeare's Orlando), faces up to the wrestling challenge knowing that all the previous combatants have died horribly in the attempt. Shakespeare's characters, by contrast, lead lives which can only be described as blessed. As numerous critics have observed, *As You Like It* is the only Shakespearian comedy in which death is kept at arm's length, Oliver's doomed attempts to get rid of Orlando being just that – doomed. It is not altogether surprising that the adjective

MAJOR CHARACTERS & SYNOPSIS

Duke Senior, deposed and living in banishment in the forest of Ardenne,

Rosalind, Duke Senior's daughter (later disguised as Ganymede)

Amiens and **Jaques**, Lords attending on Duke Senior

Duke Frederick, Duke Senior's brother, the usurper

Celia, Duke Frederick's daughter and Rosalind's companion (later disguised as "Aliena")

Le Beau, a courtier attending Duke Frederick

Charles, Duke Frederick's wrestler

Touchstone, a clown in Duke Frederick's service

Oliver, the eldest son of Sir Rowland de Bois

Jaques and **Orlando**, Oliver's younger brothers

Adam, an old servant of Sir Rowland

Denis, Oliver's servant

Corin, an old shepherd and his companion **Silvius**, a young shepherd in love with the shepherdess **Phoebe**

William, a countryman, in love with **Audrey**, a goatherd

Sir Oliver Martext, a country clergyman

Hymen, the god of marriage

ACT 1 Ever since Orlando's father's death, his brother Oliver has kept him in poverty and denied him an education. When the two argue, Oliver plots how he can be rid of him: hearing that Orlando intends to fight in the forthcoming wrestling competition, he orders Charles the wrestler to kill him. At court, Rosalind is dejectedly reflecting on her father's banishment by Duke Frederick when she and Celia are cheered by news of the wrestling match. Both are struck by the brave appearance of a young man taking part – Orlando – and his surprising defeat of Charles. The cousins congratulate him, but Orlando is so smitten by Rosalind that he cannot speak. Duke Frederick, however, is fearful his niece will betray him and banishes her, but Celia secretly arranges for them both to escape in disguise and join Duke Senior in the forest of Ardenne.

ACT 2 Rumour quickly spreads of the cousins' disappearance, and Duke Frederick recruits Oliver to join the search. Hearing that his brother intends to kill him, Orlando flees. In the forest, Duke Senior and his companions are about to eat when Orlando rushes in with Adam close behind, both faint with hunger. Realizing who Orlando is, the Duke tells of his respect for Orlando's father and invites both Orlando and Adam to dine.

ACT 3 Orlando is pining for love, leaving poems about Rosalind throughout the forest. When Rosalind appears with one such poem, Celia teasingly reveals who the author is; when he enters, Rosalind hits on a plan. Disguised as Ganymede, she interrogates Orlando about his love before prescribing a possible cure – to be administered by her. Later, the cousins come across Phoebe who falls immediately in love with Ganymede – despite being wooed by Silvius.

ACT 4 Rosalind/Ganymede has convinced Orlando to take a more realistic view of love, but complicates things still further by taking on the personality of Rosalind while still dressed as Ganymede, and persuading Celia/Aliena to "marry" them in a mock ceremony. Phoebe has meanwhile addressed a love letter to Ganymede, but Rosalind returns it scornfully. Oliver bursts in, clutching a bloodied cloth, and narrates how he has been saved from a lioness by Orlando's valour, and the two brothers have been reconciled. Rosalind/Ganymede faints.

ACT 5 Touchstone, meanwhile, has decided to marry Audrey, and bullies William, her current suitor into leaving her. For his part, Oliver has fallen for Celia/Aliena, and agrees to marry her in front of Duke Senior the next day, leaving his estate to Orlando. Rosalind – still in the guise of Ganymede – promises Orlando that she will make his beloved appear by magic, and they will be married too. She also guarantees success to Silvius if he turns up with Phoebe. The big day arrives: while everyone prepares, the disguised Rosalind and Celia slip out, before returning in their own clothes and accompanied by Hymen. Loose ends are tied and weddings finalized – Rosalind to Orlando, Celia to Oliver, Audrey to Touchstone and, lastly, Phoebe (who realizes she cannot marry Ganymede) to Silvius. All are leaving joyfully when news arrives that Frederick has become a hermit, leaving the kingdom in Duke Senior's rightful hands.

"fairytale" is often applied to the play. Though its "good" characters are depicted in rounded human complexity, evil has a distinctly two-dimensional presence, ultimately evaporating with ease.

That is not to say that all is well in the court of Duke Frederick (Duke Senior's usurping brother), in which we initially find ourselves. In another change to his source, Shakespeare creates a set of neat symmetries between the play's good and bad sides. Just as Duke Frederick has usurped Duke Senior, Orlando has been disinherited by his elder brother Oliver – a device that will recur in Shakespeare's final solo play, *The Tempest*. But Oliver's villainy – like that of Don John in *Much Ado* – is essentially motiveless, as he himself admits while plotting to have Orlando removed from the frame:

> I hope I shall see an end of him, for my soul—yet I know not why— hates nothing more than he. Yet he's gentle; never schooled, and yet learned; full of noble device; of all sorts enchantingly beloved; and, indeed, so much in the heart of the world, and especially of my own people, who best know him, that I am altogether misprized. But it shall not be so long.
>
> [1.1.154–61]

It won't be "long" because Oliver has prepared for Orlando to meet his end in a wrestling bout with his henchman Charles, a contest he is confident that the young hero can never win. It is precisely the kind of capricious cruelty that Frederick's court, which has banished Rosalind's father but not Rosalind herself, delights in – indeed, as Touchstone notes, the women will be encouraged to watch ("It is the first time that ever I heard breaking of ribs was sport for ladies," he tartly notes (1.2.128–9)). But Oliver's grudging litany of Orlando's heroic qualities alerts us to the fact that evil will not prevail. Playing the part of the wandering knight to perfection, Orlando wins the contest against all the odds and captures the greatest prize of all – Rosalind's affection.

Let the forest judge

But the malevolent world of court does not prove a propitious location for love, and both Rosalind and Orlando soon find themselves banished from its boundaries, catapulted into the forest of Ardenne (spelt "Arden" in the First Folio and many subsequent editions; see p.33). Ardenne provides the setting for the majority of the play's scenes, if not most of its plot; and in the forest, with the initial rush of actions completed, time slows down to a near standstill. Ardenne is, as its name seems to indicate, a cross between Arcadia and Eden, the rustic "Golden World" imagined by pagan poets and the biblical garden all in one. Yet it can also be a perplexing – even menacing – location, as the characters from court discover when they enter it for the first time. Orlando describes it as an "uncouth forest", "bleak", a "desert"; and even Rosalind's bright exclamation, "this is the forest of Ardenne", does not impress Touchstone, who acidly replies, "Ay, now am I in Ardenne; the more fool I. When I was at home I was in a better place" (2.4.14–16).

Duke Senior and his lords make what they can of the forest, but the mixed nature of life there is somehow epitomized in Amiens's song, performed as the company sits down to dinner in the wood:

> Blow, blow, thou winter wind,
> Thou art not so unkind
>   As man's ingratitude.
> Thy tooth is not so keen,
>   Because thou art not seen,
> Although thy breath be rude.
> Hey-ho, sing hey-ho, unto the green holly.
> Most friendship is feigning, most loving, mere folly.
> Then hey-ho, the holly;
> This life is most jolly.

[2.7.175–84]

It is "ingratitude" of sorts that has banished the Duke and his lords to Ardenne – proof that the court is a brittle world in which "most friendship is feigning". Yet the song, celebrating the rustic life, finds a kind of liberation in adversity, like the Duke who, as Amiens earlier says, "can translate the stubbornness of fortune / Into so quiet and sweet a style" (2.1.18–20). "Let the forest judge," Touchstone comments (3.2.119–20), and here it grants the Duke and his men respite from the world's troubles.

Not everyone is convinced by that transformation, however. The Duke's gloomy companion Jaques takes every opportunity to expound bad grace, for as he himself boasts, "I can suck melancholy out of a song as a weasel sucks eggs" (2.5.11–12). Despite the Duke's optimism about their condition, Jaques – with one of the most famous metaphors in literature – remains cynical:

DUKE SENIOR
    Thou seest we are not all alone unhappy.
    This wide and universal theatre
    Presents more woeful pageants than the scene
    Wherein we play in.
JAQUES   All the world's a stage,
    And all the men and women merely players.
    They have their exits and their entrances,
    And one man in his time plays many parts,
    His acts being seven ages.

[2.7.136–43]

The miserabilist "ages" that Jaques goes on to sketch – all the way from the "infant, / Mewling and puking in the nurse's arms" to the "second childishness and mere oblivion, / Sans teeth, sans eyes, sans taste, sans everything" – make rich capital from the human comedy, but his laughter is hollow.

Arden or Ardenne?

"Shakespeare, when he wrote this idyllic play," declared Edward Dowden in 1881, "was himself in Arden." Though Dowden meant these words metaphorically – the forest, he suggested, was a kind of rest-cure – the bond between Shakespeare and the real-life **forest of Arden**, which lay to the north of Stratford-upon-Avon, was strong. The poet's mother took her maiden name from the wood, and the farmhouse that Anne Hathaway inherited, her "Cottage", stood close to its boundary.

As well as providing the title for a respected edition of Shakespeare's works, tradition also holds that *As You Like It* is set – and has often been performed as if it were set – in the Warwickshire Arden, deep in the English countryside. Why, then, does this book call it "Ardenne"? The answer lies in Shakespeare's source, Lodge's *Rosalynde*, which locates the scene not in England, but France. Pointing towards the numerous French names in *As You Like It* and drawing attention to the great continental forest of the Ardennes, which now borders France, Belgium and Luxembourg, the editors of the Oxford complete works spell the word "Ardenne"; this guide, following that text, does likewise. In truth, Shakespeare's play – which features both palm trees and lionesses – seems to have a less geographically circumscribed (and more imaginatively exotic) location in mind than either.

His cynicism, furthermore, is decisively rejected by the play. The all-inclusive forest delivers the antidote to Jaques's maudlin satire, as Rosalind discovers when she finds Orlando's love poems pinned to the trees. She does so not as herself but in male camouflage, the unravelling of which takes up much of the rest of the play. Although she is forced to dress as a man in order to travel into the forest, Rosalind's initial panic about how to approach her lover in disguise ("Alas the day, what shall I do with my doublet and hose!" (3.2.214–5)) turns into a realization that in fact she can use it to advantage. Dressing as a man liberates her to explore the quality of her love – and her lover – as she would never be able to do as a woman.

Whereas the gender of Lodge's disguised Rosalynde is always clear (even to Rosader), Shakespeare's Rosalind takes full advantage of the sexual ambiguity of her costume. With breathtaking cheek, she even proposes to Orlando an outrageous scheme whereby she will stop him pining for love by imitating Rosalind herself. She explains, breezily, that she has already tried out the "cure" on another man:

He was to imagine me his love, his mistress; and I set him every day to woo me. At which time would I, being but a moonish youth, grieve, be effeminate, changeable, longing and liking, proud, fantastical, apish, shallow, inconstant, full of tears, full of smiles; for every passion something, and for no passion truly anything, as boys and women are for the most part cattle of this colour—would now like him, now loathe him; then entertain him, then forswear him; now weep for him, then spit at him, that I drave my suitor from his mad humour of love to a living humour of madness, which was to forswear the full stream of the world and to live in a nook merely monastic. And thus I cured him ...

[3.2.392–405]

"Moonish youth" ... Naomi Frederick was a plucky Rosalind at Shakespeare's Globe in 2009, but came touchingly adrift when she fell for Jack Laskey's Orlando. Thea Sharrock directed this Elizabethan-style production.

Though Celia will later claim, angrily, that "you have simply misused our sex in your love-prate" (4.1.191–2), Rosalind wittily disengages herself from the battle of the sexes by satirizing both sides. The infuriatingly changeable "mistress" she acts is the stuff of male stereotype, but Rosalind manages to blur the boundaries, concluding that "boys and women" are as bad as each other.

Paradoxical as it seems, disguise enables Rosalind to be entirely herself – quizzical, interrogative, scurrilous, irrepressible. It has often been thought that she outshines

Orlando, her supposed equal, entirely; indeed, the exchanges between them frequently have an air of pupil and teacher. Discussing the strategies by which Orlando might best woo his beloved, she decides that they will rehearse what to do if she refuses him:

ROSALIND   Well, in her person I say I will not have you.
ORLANDO   Then in my own person I die.
ROSALIND   No, faith; die by attorney. The poor world is almost six thousand
        years old, and in all this time there was not any man died in his own per-
        son, videlicet, in a love-cause. Troilus had his brains dashed out with a
        Grecian club, yet he did what he could to die before, and he is one of the
        patterns of love. Leander, he would have lived many a fair year though
        Hero had turned nun if it had not been for a hot midsummer night, for,
        good youth, he went but forth to wash him in the Hellespont and, being
        taken with the cramp, was drowned, and the foolish chroniclers of that
        age found it was Hero of Sestos. But these are all lies. Men have died
        from time to time, and worms have eaten them, but not for love.
                                                [4.1.86–101]

Rosalind calls cheerily upon the great lovers of antiquity to illustrate her point – Troilus and Cressida, whose tragic love affair was caught across the battle lines of Troy (dramatized by Shakespeare a few years later); and Hero and Leander, separated when Leander drowned while swimming the Hellespont to see his lover. Despite the flippancy of her tone, there is good sense in what she says: it is all very well for men to moon over their mistresses, but there is more to life than star-crossed love. Rosalind sees exactly what Jaques sees, but is not deterred by the prospect.

Fathom deep

But Rosalind is not impregnable. She confides in Celia that, for all her sardonic words on the subject, she is already sunk "fathom deep" in love, so outright that she "cannot be out of the sight of Orlando" (4.1.195, 206). Her emotions towards him are frequently close to the surface: she has already been reduced to the point of tears by his apparent inability to turn up on time, and it isn't long before she comes close to giving the game away by swooning, in a dangerously unmanly fashion, at the news that he has been hurt by a lioness.

Some sage critics have discovered as a great geographical fault in Shakespeare that he introduces the tropical lion and serpent into Arden, which it appears they have ascertained to lie in some temperate zone. I wish them joy of their sagacity. Monsters more wonderful are to be found in that forest; for never yet, since water ran and tall tree bloomed, were there gathered together such a company as those who compose the dramatis personae of As You Like It.

William Maginn, writing in *Bentley's Miscellany* (1837)

About clowning

Like any nervous amateur director, Hamlet does not trust the professionals to get it right. "And let those your clowns," he anxiously advises the players, "speak no more than is set down for them" (3.2.38–9). The fear that a company's fools (as they were also known) might run amok and swamp what the Prince soberly calls the "necessary question of the play" must have been an occupational hazard for Jacobethan playwrights, though Shakespeare characteristically makes his comedians work for their laughs in esoteric and unusual places – as the "antic" Hamlet, wisecracking in Ophelia's grave, knows full well.

Professional fools were for a long time the real stars of the stage, and were instrumental in making sixteenth-century secular theatre the rowdy and irreverent thing it became. The most famous clown of the generation immediately before Shakespeare was **Richard Tarlton** (d.1588), so idolized that the Queen's Men, set up by royal command in 1583 to tour the nation, was built around him; and so funny that Elizabeth reputedly ordered him to stay away because he made her laugh too much.

Tarlton's talents extended far beyond comedy: he was an adept dancer and fencer, and his "wondrous" witticisms spawned a minor publishing industry; but most importantly he never failed to steal the show, whichever part he took (the root, perhaps, of Hamlet's anxiety).

Tarlton's close rival was the more refined **Robert Wilson**, though in Shakespeare's own company **William Kempe** (d.1603) would later challenge both by dint of physical athleticism: he once danced a jig all the way from London to Norwich, a feat that lasted nine days. Kempe's replacement, **Robert Armin** (c. 1568–1615), took a more thoughtful approach to his work, and published a book about his experiences in the profession, entitled *Fool upon Fool*. He also inspired most of Shakespeare's great clowning roles, including those of Touchstone in *As You Like It* and Feste in *Twelfth Night*.

And in Shakespeare's plays clowns – rather like the satirical comics who are their closest modern equivalents – also have serious jobs to perform. *Twelfth Night's* Olivia comments that "there is no slander in an allowed fool" (1.5.89–90), and as Enid Welsford's classic 1935 study of the subject reveals, throughout the middle ages and into the Renaissance fools were a social as well as theatrical reality. Many were employed in courts and wealthy households not only to provide entertainment, but were also "allowed" to speak about whatever they wanted – the idea being that someone outside normal social conventions could say what flattering advisers dare not. The "**Feast of Fools**", a carnivalesque festival in which life became topsy-turvy during the twelve nights of Christmas immortalized in Shakespeare's play, lasted well into the seventeenth century on the European continent; and none other than the humanist Desiderius Erasmus expounded the necessity of foolery in his satirical *Moriae Encomium* ("Praise of Folly") from 1511.

Touchstone's very name alludes to a truth-revealing trait Erasmus would condone, while Feste's skittish experiments with language frequently undercut the wider events of the play and ridicule its characters even more than they ridicule themselves. But by the time Shakespeare reaches the emotional wilds of *King Lear*, the jokes have become caustically bitter. "I am better than thou art, now," Lear's nameless Fool tells his master. "I am a fool; thou art nothing" (1.4.175–6). In the late tragedy *Antony and Cleopatra*, the final, cruel joke of the play – after Antony has botched his suicide – is that Cleopatra's attempts to satisfy her "immortal longings" are entrusted to a rustic clown, who delivers the fatal asps with the solemn assurance that "those that do die of it do seldom or never recover" (5.2.242–3).

By this stage in *As You Like It*, falling in love has become infectious. Following Oliver's lightning conversion to the side of good (inspired by Orlando's nobility in saving him from the lioness), he rapidly proposes to Celia – a match some critics have found hard to defend, but which is nonetheless a guarantee that his redemption is authentic. And love becomes so rife in Ardenne that even Touchstone longs to leave the incurably single life of a Shakespearian fool and develops a crush on Audrey. The unlikely pairing of the professional man of words and the tongue-tied goatherd somehow exemplifies not just the range of love accommodated in the play, but its power to draw even the most unusual couples together. Touchstone's reasons for marrying at least have the merit of being honest, as he tells Jaques:

> As the ox hath his bow, sir, the horse his curb, and the falcon her bells, so
> man hath his desires; and as pigeons bill, so wedlock would be nibbling.
>
> [3.3.72–4]

A rather different perspective on love is offered by the shepherd Silvius, who first enters the play in the company of his "true labourer" colleague Corin. Given that Silvius sounds like he's never been near a sheep in his life, it is difficult at first to imagine what they have to talk about – until, that is, Silvius begins a lament about the cruelty of his mistress, Phoebe, which continues unabated for the rest of the play. In a comedy in which falling in love seems implausibly easy, the relationship between Silvius and Phoebe will prove the most tortured of the lot – not least because Phoebe, spurning Silvius, then falls for Rosalind/Ganymede. This is a neat twist on the theory of scornful mistresses outlined by Rosalind earlier in the play, but nonetheless creates the only barrier to love that *As You Like It* presents.

Fittingly, Rosalind herself, having created the problem, resolves it. Gathering everyone together – promising to Orlando that she will produce Rosalind as if by magic and guaranteeing to Phoebe that "I will marry you if ever I marry woman" (5.2.107–8) – she orchestrates what proves to be a flurry of weddings officiated over by no less a presence than that of the god of marriage, Hymen. Yet Rosalind is not permitted to end the play, just as its characters know they cannot remain in Ardenne for ever. Addressing the lovers, Hymen insists, "'Tis I must make conclusion / Of these most strange events":

> Whiles a wedlock hymn we sing,
> Feed yourself with questioning,
> That reason wonder may diminish
> How thus we met, and these things finish.
>
> [5.4.135–8]

However our "wonder" diminishes, it will not disappear entirely. *As You Like It* deliberately teases its audience with the highest marriage count of any Shakespearian comedy, yet asks us to believe in each and every one.

Stage history and adaptations

There is no hard evidence that *As You Like It* was acted during Shakespeare's lifetime, but the eighteenth-century editor George Steevens reported that the playwright played Old Adam and it may have been performed during Christmas 1603 for James I at **Gillingham House** in Kent. Though **Thomas Killigrew** won the rights to the play after the Restoration, no production ensued and it was an adaptation – **Charles Johnson's** *Love in a Forest* (1723) – that introduced *As You Like It* to the eighteenth century. Johnson's version bore little resemblance to the original, extraneous characters being cut and chunks from other Shakespeare plays inserted instead, and his most surprising innovation was to marry off **Colley Cibber's** Jaques to the play's Celia. It flopped.

The way lay open for **Charles Macklin**, who restored the original play at Drury Lane in 1740 and, spotting an opportunity left open by his colleague David Garrick (who preferred the tragedies), launched a fashion for Shakespearian comedy. Macklin was blessed in **Kitty Clive's** Celia and the orotund **James Quin's** Jaques, but above all in **Hannah Pritchard's** superlative Rosalind, bursting with "genuine, sprightly, unaffected Nature", as one witness put it. Pritchard's success encouraged others to follow, and Rosalind became a favourite of such long-standing luminaries as **Peg Woffington** (who acted her from 1741 to 1757, when she collapsed mid-performance); **Ann Barry** (1766–78); and **Dorothy Jordan** (1787–1817). Even **Sarah Siddons**, better known for her Lady Macbeth, had a go in 1785 – albeit to limited success.

The fashion for breeches roles ensured *As You Like It's* near-continual success into the nineteenth century. **William Charles Macready's** production (Drury Lane, 1842) had Macready himself as Jaques and, initially, **Ada Nesbitt** as Rosalind. But the young **Helen Faucit** soon took over and made a career of Rosalind, the radiance and honesty of her performances winning hearts along the way – among them Ellen Terry's, who spoke admiringly of her "deep and true emotion" in the role. To her great regret Terry herself never got to play Rosalind; when the work was staged at the Lyceum in 1890 it was the Irish-American **Ada Rehan** who took the role, which subsequently became something of a calling card. **Madge Kendal**, who played opposite her husband **W.H. Kendal's** Orlando, was another outstanding Rosalind of the 1870s and 80s. But by the time Faucit retired in 1879, the Victorian taste for hyper-realistic staging had become endemic. That year, performances at Stratford featured a freshly culled deer from Charlecote in Warwickshire – a descendant of the flock reputedly poached by Shakespeare – and a turnip from Anne Hathaway's garden. (The stuffed deer appeared regularly until 1919, though presumably the same is not true of the turnip.) In a similar vein was **Oscar Asche's** production at His Majesty's Theatre in London in 1907, in which **Lily Brayton's** blithe Rosalind and Asche's Jaques roamed around a forest created from two thousand ferns, stacks of bamboo and leaves left over from the previous autumn.

Nigel Playfair turned his back on this over-literal approach with his lively and controversial Stratford production in 1919, distinguished by **Claude Lovat Fraser's** "futurist" sets. Esme Church directed a Gainsborough-inspired production at the Old Vic in 1936 with **Edith Evans** as Rosalind and **Michael Redgrave** as Orlando. Though Evans was twenty years older than Redgrave, their partnership convinced the critics – perhaps because they were having an affair at the time.

Mad about the boy: Adrian Lester's Rosalind (centre) flirts with Patrick Toomey's Orlando while Tom Hollander's Celia looks on. Declan Donnellan's much-revived, all-male Cheek by Jowl production (1992 onwards) had great fun experimenting with the play's homoerotic tensions.

Redgrave's daughter, **Vanessa**, launched the play's most famous postwar production under **Michael Elliott**'s direction at the RSC in 1961. Her gamine Rosalind, often barefoot and sporting a cute cap, received lustrous reviews and added a tangible sparkle to the forest scenes, which became the imaginative focus for Elliott's production. Redgrave was supported by **Ian Bannen** as a serious-minded Orlando and **Max Adrian** as a sardonic, fur-coated Jaques. The homoerotic undertow hinted at by Redgrave was more stridently voiced by **Clifford Williams** in 1967 at the Old Vic, with an all-male cast (including **Ronald Pickup**'s Rosalind, **Charles Kay**'s Celia and **Jeremy Brett** as Orlando) acting what some saw as an *As You Like It* way ahead of its time in its exploration of gender and identity – others as camp, drag-act Shakespeare. **Buzz Goodbody**'s RSC rendering of 1973, with **Eileen Atkins** as a denim-clad Rosalind, advertised the play's feminism, but struggled to communicate its grace.

1977 saw three wildly different major versions, indicating not just the comedy's appeal but its kaleidoscopic opportunities. **Trevor Nunn**'s outlandish version at the RSC nearly drowned out its cast – among them **Kate Nelligan**'s Rosalind and **Peter McEnery**'s Orlando – with Purcellian opera, but after complaints the musical content was scaled back. No such compromises for **Peter Stein** at the Schaubühne in Berlin, who treated his audiences to extravagant and highly stylized *Regietheater* (director's theatre), making them troop from Frederick's stern court to a magical forest in a nearby film studio for the Ardenne scenes. **Robin Phillips**'s staging at

Stratford, Ontario gazed back decorously at the eighteenth century, with **Maggie Smith** as a well-bred and fine-boned Rosalind.

More recent stagings, especially British ones, have attempted to find a visual language that suggests the forest as a world outside of the world. In **Adrian Noble's** RSC version (1985) the designer Bob Crowley presented Ardenne as a landscape swathed in white silk sheeting in which the powerful double act of **Juliet Stevenson** as Rosalind and **Fiona Shaw** as Celia could come to self-knowledge – not least about their role within patriarchal society. **Declan Donnellan's** all-male production for his own Cheek by Jowl company had little time for such seriousness (or budget for such designs) when they toured the play six years later. Their performance space was a simple canvas box, their interpretation joyously irreverent – envisioning an affair between **Adrian Lester's** Rosalind and **Tom Hollander's** Celia yet preventing **Patrick Toomey's** straight Orlando from kissing Ganymede. In a riotous and noisy finale even Hymen and Jaques got together.

Lucy Bailey's Globe production of 1998 likewise used little by way of sets, but the point this time was historical – the Elizabethan staging attracted attention to Shakespeare's sly (mis)use of theatrical conventions. **Gregory Thompson** also used staging in enterprising ways at the RSC in 2003: **Nina Sosanya's** Rosalind found herself in a forest made of people rather than trees (the cast also pretended to be sheep when required). **Samuel West's** Sheffield Crucible production of 2007 imagined the play in self-consciously theatrical terms, with a single balloon doubling as sun and moon, and a forest in which hats sprouted from the ground. As Rosalind, **Eve Best** provided, according to the *Times* critic, "all the symptoms of a sparkling wit with a gnawing need inside".

The play has attracted the welcome attention of leading female British directors in recent years. **Thea Sharrock's** 2009 production at the Globe in London was full of mischief and mayhem, all the better for taking the comedy seriously, and had a joyously intelligent Rosalind in **Naomi Frederick**. **Blanche McIntyre's** 2015 version at the same venue was less skittish, built around **Michelle Terry's** older, more restrained Rosalind. At the RSC, **Maria Arberg's** "joyous, big-hearted" 2014 production (*Independent*) won comparisons with Donnellan's Cheek by Jowl version years before – and considerable praise for its music, by folk superstar **Laura Marling**. Stranger and more intriguing than any of these was a free reimagining by controversial Catalan director **Calixto Bieto** called *Forests*, part of the 2012 World Shakespeare Festival. Acted by a cast of six beneath a blasted tree like something out of *Waiting for Godot*, it offered a doomy, death-haunted evocation of Shakespeare's pastoral universe.

With its pastoral perspectives and ambling pace, *As You Like It* has provided as many problems as possibilities for film-makers. **Paul Czinner's** movie of 1936 (starring **Elisabeth Bergner** as Rosalind and **Laurence Olivier** as Orlando) blended fairytale whimsy with a script from which some of the most exciting moments were excised. **Basil Coleman's** BBC/Time-Life version of 1978 was hamstrung by its heritage location shoots but boasted a fine cast, including **Helen Mirren** as a feisty Rosalind and **Richard Pasco** as a particularly acidic Jaques. In 1992 **Christine Edzard** relocated Ardenne to the London Docklands, an imaginative leap which worked more effectively than **Kenneth Branagh's** decision to set his 2007 *As You Like It* in nineteenth-century Japan.

SCREEN

As You Like It

E. Bergner, L. Olivier, L. Quartermaine; Paul Czinner (dir.) UK, 1936 > AG Plate / Alpha **DVD** 🔻

Olivier in front of the camera, Jack Cardiff (Powell and Pressburger's legendary head of photography) behind it, David Lean editing, William Walton providing the music – quite a bunch, which makes their combined efforts all the more disappointing. The fault unfortunately lies with a husband-and-wife team of director (Paul Czinner) and star (Elizabeth Bergner), recent exiles from Nazi Germany who settled on a Shakespearian talkie – Britain's first – as a follow-up to their historical epic *Catherine the Great*. It isn't Bergner's fault that she struggles with English, though she makes no obvious attempt to sound Rosalind's depths despite plentiful fluttering eyelashes. Czinner, meanwhile, offers fussy direction and a production so whimsically designed that you rather wish Monty Python would blunder in en route to the Holy Grail. Even the young Larry – glummer than you'd expect, all doe eyes and cowlick – seems bland. A silk purse somehow made into a sow's ear.

As You Like It

E. Croft, A. Tiernan, C. Bannerman; Christine Edzard (dir.) UK, 1992 > Squirrel / Canal Plus **DVD** 🔻

Ardenne? London's Docklands. Love poems on trees? Graffiti on walls. A magical lion? A half-seen mugger. Such are the transformations wrought by Christine Edzard in this deliberately edgy *As You Like It*, which sees Emma Croft's Rosalind slip into baggy jeans and hooded tops instead of doublet and hose. Despite the film's commercial failure, its political point is potent. The fractured worlds of Frederick's court and the forest transplant well to the London of the early 1990s (locations are a City bank foyer and a cardboard city somewhere in Rotherhithe), itself locked into ever-widening divisions between rich and poor. But the production is scuttled by a host of problems: Andrew Tiernan is abysmal as both Oliver and Orlando (a doubling which robs the play of much-needed electricity); the wrestling scene is a wimpish cop-out; and the finale is played between bursts of credits.

As You Like It

R. Garai, D. Oleweyo, K. Kline; Kenneth Branagh (dir.) US/UK, 2007 > Lionsgate / HBO **DVD** 🔻

Branagh's productions can seem like the Marks & Spencer of screened Shakespeare: reassuringly expensive, nicely produced but ineffably middle-aged. This *As You Like It*, although mellow enough, is no different. Goodness only knows what possessed Branagh to set the action in Japan with an Anglo-American cast (we're offered some flim-flam about nineteenth-century merchant adventurers), a cultural translation that feels significantly thinner than skin-deep, especially when everything else is so doughtily English. Tim Harvey's interiors are pretty enough, but the forest scenes are so toffee-coated it's a wonder Disney rabbits haven't taken up residence. And while it was nice to see fresh faces – David Oyelowo as Orlando, Romola Garai as Rosalind and Adrian Lester as Oliver all make attractive screen presences – it was surely time for Branagh to put some old pals out to pasture.

As You Like It

N. Frederick, J. Laskey, L. Rogers; Thea Sharrock (dir.) UK, 2009 > Globe / Opus Arte **DVD** 🔻

Recorded live at the Globe in summer 2009, Thea Sharrock's fast, funny Elizabethan-style production has fizz aplenty, and the vocal prescence (and laughter) of the groundlings only helps. This is very much a double act, dominated by Naomi Frederick's wonderfully ardent Rosalind and Laura Rogers's effervescent Celia – Frederick only too keen to tear off her farthingale and slip into a leather jerkin, Rogers driven to a foot-stamping tantrum at being forced to drag her skirts through the mud. Not everyone in the cast is quite so strong – Dominic Rowan as Touchstone is more wooden than the oak boards he lumbers around on – but Jack Laskey's boyish Orlando is unable to keep a smile off his lips, and Tim McMullan offers a masterclass in sardonic sourpussery as Jaques. An irresistibly pleasurable performance, not least because everyone on stage looks like they're having a blast.

AUDIO

As You Like It

H. Bonham-Carter, N. Little, D. Morrissey; Kate Rowland (dir.) UK, 2000 > BBC ◉ 🔻

Helena Bonham-Carter is – at least on audio – a pretty much perfect Rosalind: fleet-footed and girlish, gloriously witty and possessed of a touching humanity. Kate Rowland's direction sets her very much at the centre of this version with the result that some of the rest of the cast are forced into the shade (Natasha Little, in particular, could do with more vigour as Celia). On the whole, however, this is a well-rounded and, more importantly, often very funny production. James Fleet's worldly wise Touchstone is the icing on the cake.

EDITIONS

New Cambridge Shakespeare
Michael Hattaway; rev. 2009 > Cambridge UP

Hattaway's edition is superlative, taking account of the pastoral motifs Shakespeare employs (perhaps one of the play's more difficult aspects for modern readers) and giving plentiful background on them. Hattaway's introduction also spends time discussing the politics of

As You Like It, both the politics of land – Elizabethans experienced a series of bad harvests and property scandals during the 1590s, events dimly reflected by the play – and those of gender and sexuality. Despite this serious matter, though, Hattaway is a lively critic and never loses sight of the comedy's playful dramatic texture, or indeed its multiple meanings on stage, both backed up by an excellent stage history (recently updated in a revision of the book). Lodge's *Rosalynde* is printed in excerpts at the back, and a short appendix provides some detail on the songs.

SOME CRITICISM

Essays, Mainly Shakespearean
Anne Barton; 1994 > Cambridge UP

Born in the US but based for most of her career at Cambridge, Anne Barton was one of the most distinguished Shakespearian critics of her generation. From her hugely successful *Shakespeare and the Idea of the Play* (1962; see p.312) to her involvement with the Riverside Shakespeare, she contributed a vast amount to critical understanding of Renaissance drama, and this book collects some of her best articles, originally published in far-flung places. *As You Like It* is a frequent presence in Barton's thinking, and here it features mainly in two essays written three decades apart: one on "Shakespeare's sense of an ending" (1972), the other on "Parks and Ardens" (1992), the latter of which contains many useful nuggets on Shakespearian forests and the social realities behind them. Her essays on the late plays are also particularly acute.

Impersonations
Stephen Orgel; 1996 > Cambridge UP

Impersonations: The performance of desire in Shakespeare's England takes its cue from recent interest in the idea of gender in the Renaissance – a debate sparked by French theorist Michel Foucault, who famously argued that sexuality as we understand it today is a modern invention, things being both more fluid and less dogmatic four centuries ago. They were certainly that in the transvestite theatre of Shakespeare and his contemporaries, and Orgel argues not only that the English theatre was the odd one out (other countries accepted actresses), but that for native audiences to insist on seeing boys playing female roles involved a complex kind of social doublethink. The significance for *As You Like It* and *Twelfth Night* is obvious enough, and both plays flit in and out of Orgel's book, but *Impersonations* also touches on Dekker's *Roaring Girl*, Marlowe's *Edward II*, Jonson's masques and even the penchant of James I's wife for masculine headgear.

The Comedy of Errors

T he madcap tale related by *The Comedy of Errors* is difficult to credit. Featuring two sets of identical twin brothers with the same name, separated while still young but who all end up in the same location by chance, the plot can seem wilfully confusing. Yet that is very much the point: Shakespeare borrows the story of long-lost twins who are continually mistaken for each other from the Roman playwright Plautus, and surpasses it in complexity, creating an intricately constructed masterpiece full of youthful brio (he might well have been in his late twenties when he wrote it). *The Comedy of Errors* was performed at a London law college in 1594, and perhaps intended to flatter that well-educated audience, but there is also a more poignant side to the play, one that connects this apprentice work to Shakespeare's last writing for the theatre. Its concern with anxiety and madness probes the brittle nature of human identity, while its heartstopping finale looks forward to the magical reunions of the late romances.

DATE > A play sounding very much like *The Comedy of Errors* was performed at the law college of Gray's Inn on December 28, 1594. Internal evidence suggests, though, that it might have been written earlier – perhaps as early as 1591.

SOURCES > The play's main source is *Menaechmi* by the Roman playwright Plautus (c.250–184 BC).

Shakespeare expands this with material from Plautus's *Amphitruo* and the framing narrative derives from Gower's *Confessio Amantis* (1390s), the main source for *Pericles*. George Gascoigne's play *Supposes* (acted 1566) has a number of similarities to Shakespeare's play.

TEXTS > The Folio text of 1623, possibly printed from Shakespeare's papers, is the only one.

Interpreting the play

"However can you stage such a conglomeration of improbabilities?" exclaimed an exasperated reviewer after seeing Clifford Williams's 1962 production at the Royal Shakespeare Company. On paper as much as on stage, those "improbabilities" loom large: a father and two sets of twins somehow end up in the same place, are consistently mistaken for one another (but never meet their own doubles), then are eventually reunited. Though it has been on stage for over four centuries, and is one of the most translated texts in the canon, many directors have preferred to tinker with or adapt *The Comedy of Errors* rather than offering the script as Shakespeare wrote it.

At some level there seems to be a deep discontent with the play itself, a reluctance to trust it on its own terms – or at least to believe that people will ever really take to it. The eighteenth-century editor George Steevens declared that "in this play we find more intricacy of plot than distinction of character", while Coleridge held that it

MAJOR CHARACTERS & SYNOPSIS

Duke of Ephesus

Egeon, an old merchant from Syracuse

Antipholus of Ephesus and **Antipholus of Syracuse**, Egeon's twin sons

Dromio of Ephesus and **Dromio of Syracuse**, twin servants of the two Antipholuses

Adriana, Antipholus of Ephesus's wife

Luciana, Adriana's sister

Nell, Adriana's kitchen-maid

Angelo, a goldsmith; and **Balthasar**, a merchant

A **Courtesan**

Doctor Pinch, a schoolmaster and exorcist

A **Merchant** from Ephesus, Antipholus of Syracuse's friend

A **second Merchant**, Angelo's creditor

Emilia, an abbess from Ephesus

ACT 1 Ephesus and Syracuse are at war and Egeon (a native of Syracuse) faces the death penalty for having entered Ephesus illegally. Interrogated by the Duke, Egeon reveals that he is on a quest: he and his wife Emilia had identical twin sons (both called Antipholus), but the family was split up for years following a shipwreck, he and the younger Antipholus plus one of the Dromio twins being separated from Emilia and the other two twins. Years later, Antipholus of Syracuse (Antipholus S) went looking for his brother, but never returned – and now Egeon has arrived in Ephesus in search of them both. Touched by Egeon's story, the Duke delays his execution. Coincidentally, Antipholus S has also landed in Ephesus with his servant Dromio. Left alone, Antipholus S bumps into the other Dromio (who of course lives there), and is mistaken for his twin, Antipholus of Ephesus (Antipholus E) – setting up the chain of transposed identities that dominates the rest of the play.

ACT 2 Incensed that her husband has not arrived for dinner, Adriana hears from Dromio E that his master (the wrong one, naturally) is behaving oddly. They set off to find him and meet Antipholus S, who is understandably perplexed by her insistence that he should come home and eat.

ACT 3 Meanwhile, Antipholus E has been with his friends Angelo and Balthasar. Realizing he

is running late, he invites them home – only to discover that his wife is already dining and they are locked out. They head off elsewhere, Antipholus E promising to have his revenge by giving the gold chain intended for his wife to a courtesan instead. The house, meanwhile, is in uproar: Luciana (Adriana's sister) cannot understand why Antipholus S pretends not to know his wife, and is horrified when he tries to woo her instead. For his part, Dromio S is appalled to find that he is engaged to a kitchen wench, and leaves to find a ship so that he and his master can escape.

ACT 4 Antipholus E accuses Angelo of not delivering the gold chain as promised – which Angelo (having given it to Antipholus S by mistake) denies, and instead arrests Antipholus E for non-payment. Dromio S rushes in, having procured a ship, but his master is bewildered by the offer and demands money for bail instead. Dromio S is sent to fetch cash from Adriana, and meets Antipholus S on the way back; astonished to find his master at liberty, Dromio S gives him the bail money anyway. The pleasant surprise quickly sours, however, when the Courtesan appears and demands the chain from around Antipholus S's neck. Certain that she is a witch, Antipholus S and Dromio S escape. Antipholus E, meanwhile, is still under arrest and his friends are convinced he has gone mad. Fetching an exorcist, they send him home captive – but are terrified when the other twins suddenly appear, having apparently escaped.

ACT 5 Confronted by a crowd of people attempting to arrest them, Antipholus and Dromio S make a dash for a nearby priory. Demanding her husband back from the Abbess, Adriana is persuading the Duke – who has arrived with Egeon – to intervene when Antipholus and Dromio E appear, having actually escaped. The Duke is struggling to make sense of it all when the Abbess enters with Antipholus and Dromio S. After protracted confusion, the Abbess recognizes Egeon as her long-lost husband and the twins' identities are revealed. The day's events are unscrambled, Antipholus S proposes to Luciana and Egeon is reprieved.

was "in exactest consonance with the philosophical principles and character of farce" (despite the fact that this is the only play of Shakespeare's with the word "comedy" in its title). At just 1800 lines, it is by some distance the shortest work Shakespeare wrote. Perhaps it is inevitable that it has often been written off as froth.

The thing I cannot get

Yet *The Comedy of Errors* is much deeper than it seems. Largely influenced by the Roman dramatist Plautus, whose witty, unsentimental and brittle comedies had a lasting impact on drama in Renaissance England, *Errors* represents an abrupt change of gear from the harsh world of plays like the *Henry VI* cycle and *Titus Andronicus*. Plautus's reputation was largely based on his skill for intricate plotting and diverting devices. *Menaechmi*, upon which *Errors* is based, is a virtuosic example: it concerns a merchant who has twin sons, Menaechmus and Sosicles. When Menaechmus is stolen as a young child, Sosicles is renamed "Menaechmus" in memory of his absent twin, before growing up and resolving to find his brother. Sosicles/Menaechmus eventually arrives in the right place, Epidaurus, but creates understandable confusion there – first the real Menaechmus's mistress, then his wife and father-in-law, mistake him for the man they know and chaos ensues until the twins are eventually reunited and all is resolved.

Shakespeare follows the same basic plot, while heightening the tale's implausibility by creating a matching pair of servants for his Antipholus twins (all four, apparently, born on the same night and in the same place). But where Plautus concentrates solely on the wild misunderstandings that drive his plot, Shakespeare's characters are fleshed-out people. Antipholus of Syracuse enters the play tormented by grief, convinced that he will never find his long-lost brother. "He that commends me to mine own content," he begins,

The Japanese Mansaku Company's Kyogen-influenced *Errors*, performed at the London Globe in summer 2001, came up with a novel way of representing the play's visual perplexities: the twins wore indistinguishable masks. Mansai Nomura (left) and Yuki Takeyama (right) played energetic Dromios.

Commends me to the thing I cannot get.
I to the world am like a drop of water
That in the ocean seeks another drop,
Who, falling there to find his fellow forth,
Unseen, inquisitive, confounds himself.
So I, to find a mother and a brother,
In quest of them, unhappy, lose myself.

[1.2.33–40]

Like another melancholy Shakespearian twin, Viola in *Twelfth Night*, Antipholus feels deeply the pain of separation. While later in the play Antipholus will indeed "lose himself" more thoroughly than even he realizes, here the tone is tragic, not comic.

Sadness often threatens to encroach upon the central narrative: what Egeon movingly describes as "this unjust divorce of us" (1.1.104), the shipwreck that splits apart his family, forces Egeon, like his Syracusan son, to be a wanderer:

My youngest boy, and yet my eldest care,
At eighteen years became inquisitive
After his brother, and importuned me
That his attendant—so his cause was like,
Reft of his brother, but retained in his name—
Might bear him company in the quest of him;
Whom whilst I laboured of a love to see,
I hazarded the loss of whom I loved.

[1.1.124–31]

"Love" and "hazard" are forced together: love of family condemns Egeon – and Antipholus, and Dromio – to the life of a nomad.

Indeed, Egeon's very existence seems a counterbalance to the comic giddiness of the rest of the play. While in Plautus the twins' father is barely mentioned, Shakespeare drew upon the tale of Apollonius of Tyre, another much-wronged hero forced into a quest for his family – and the main source for *Pericles* – to create the figure of a father ready to risk all for his sons. Egeon is in fact prepared to risk death: after entering Ephesus illegally, he is arrested and told to await execution. The play hinges on the fact that he has been given only a few hours to live; if there is to be a happy ending, it must be secured within that time (there are more references to "time" in *Errors* than in any other Shakespeare play).

Strange to me

This sense that the play needs to accomplish an apparently impossible task against the clock is both serious and seriously amusing, and in a similar fashion many of the play's funniest moments flirt with genuine danger. Initially Antipholus of Syracuse can't believe his luck – Ephesus is a bemusing paradise where everyone seems not just to know him, but to treat him like an old friend. "There's not a man I meet but doth salute me," he exclaims,

And everyone doth call me by my name.
Some tender money to me, some invite me,
Some other give me thanks for kindnesses ...

[4.3.1–5]

So when a local merchant marches up, presents him with an expensive gold chain and refuses to accept any money, Antipholus grabs the opportunity. The chain is of course intended for his twin, and before long Antipholus of Ephesus will be in prison for refusing to pay for it (on the entirely reasonable grounds that he has yet to receive the goods). The joke very quickly turns sour, and when Antipholus sends his servant to collect money for his bail, things really start to unravel. Dromio hands it to Antipholus of Ephesus by mistake – another gift he feels he can't refuse – and for a while it looks as if his twin will never be released.

Shakespeare adeptly balances the fates of his Antipholus twins, ensuring that as one rises, the other falls. The comedy is at its keenest when the identities of the pair are closest to collapsing into one another, the central "error" of the comedy. Yet, again, there are real emotions at stake. One of the play's subplots concerns Antipholus of Syracuse's marriage to Adriana, which is apparently on the rocks even before his twin – and all the confusion he brings – arrives in Ephesus. When her husband fails to arrive for dinner, Adriana is quick to round on her "unkind mate" (2.1.38), and the problems only intensify when Antipholus of Syracuse falls for Adriana's sister, Luciana:

She that doth call me husband, even my soul
Doth for a wife abhor. But her fair sister,
Possessed with such a gentle sovereign grace,
Of such enchanting presence and discourse,
Hath almost made me traitor to myself.

[3.2.162–8]

Antipholus of Syracuse's attempts to woo Luciana are farcically counterpointed by Dromio's anxious attempts to escape the clutches of the kitchen wench who is betrothed to his twin, but the point is the same. Love is not everything it seems – and can be as shallow as a mere matter of appearances.

Nor are the Antipoluses the only victims. Hearing that Antipholus has been attempting to seduce her sister, Adriana is justifiably appalled (she would be even more appalled to discover that her real husband, locked out by his wife, has been spending time with a prostitute), and confronts him in a passion:

The main action takes place in a time gone crazy, twisted, looped, turning in on itself, not so much the medium of existence as a manifestation of its perplexities, even, at times, of its horror.

Gamini Salgado, "'Time's Deformed Hand': Sequence, Consequence, and Inconsequence in *The Comedy of Errors*" (1972)

How comes it now, my husband, O how comes it
That thou art then estrangèd from thyself?—
Thy 'self' I call it, being strange to me
That, undividable, incorporate,
Am better than thy dear self's better part.
Ah, do not tear away thyself from me;
For know, my love, as easy mayst thou fall
A drop of water in the breaking gulf,
And take unmingled thence that drop again
Without addition or diminishing,
As take from me thyself, and not me too.

[2.2.122–32]

Echoing Antipholus's water imagery, she tries in vain to understand what has happened to their marriage. Shakespeare gives her words further resonance (one that his earliest audiences would certainly have picked up on) by having her echo Saint Paul's Letter to the Ephesians – aptly enough given the play's geographical setting. The moment may in one sense be funny, but it is also painfully touching: while Antipholus of Syracuse is beginning to doubt his sanity, the woman who thinks she is his wife is trying to persuade herself that he still loves her.

As in *The Taming of the Shrew*, the sometimes tortured relationships between women and men come under scrutiny and – unlike many Elizabethan plays that have fun with similar issues – *The Comedy of Errors* gives women a strong and independent voice. In contrast to her sister, Luciana has a more hard-bitten view of the realities of marriage. "If you did wed my sister for her wealth," she begs Antipholus of Syracuse,

Then for her wealth's sake use her with more kindness;
Or if you like elsewhere, do it by stealth:
Muffle your false love with some show of blindness.
Let not my sister read it in your eye.

[3.2.5–9]

From the outside, of course, Antipholus's insistence that he loves Luciana rather than his wife looks like a man doing his utmost to have an affair; the joke is that this supposedly illicit romance is in fact one of the truest relationships in the play.

Much, much different

Money and the problems it buys are a recurrent feature in *Errors*, as is the topic of madness (the connection between the two is made much more extensively in *Timon of Athens*). "Lapland sorcerers inhabit here," mutters Antipholus of Syracuse to himself (4.3.11), but in the event it will be his twin who ends up in the madhouse. Desperately trying to straighten everything out, the imprisoned Antipholus of Ephesus is enraged to discover that Dromio has apparently mislaid the money for his bail. Everyone

responds, however, by assuming that it is Antipholus that is mad, and he is bound
and submitted to the ministrations of the unappealingly named Doctor Pinch. The
Doctor's considered verdict – frighteningly reasonable in the circumstances – is
that "both man and master is possessed … I know it by their pale and deadly looks"
(4.4.93–4), and he begins an exorcism:

PINCH
    I charge thee, Satan, housed within this man,
    To yield possession to my holy prayers,
    And to thy state of darkness hie thee straight:
    I conjure thee by all the saints in heaven.
ANTIPHOLUS OF EPHESUS
    Peace, doting wizard, peace! I am not mad.
ADRIANA
    O that thou wert not, poor distressèd soul.

                                [4.4.55–60]

Antipholus is caught in the same unenviable catch-22 as Malvolio in *Twelfth Night*.
Unable to prove that they are in their wits and that everyone else is behaving irration-
ally, both characters begin to fret that they are going crazy – because if everyone else
thinks you're mad, you might as well be. Adriana's bewildered observation that her
husband is "much, much different from the man he was" (5.1.46) is true enough, but
at this point it looks as if no one will ever find out why.

Fortunately, however, *The Comedy of Errors* allows itself to resolve these complicated human muddles – not least the muddle of Egeon, waiting patiently all this time
for his death sentence to be carried out. But Shakespeare is reluctant to relinquish the
suspense. When Antipholus of Syracuse is spotted on the loose, everyone assumes that
his twin has broken free, and after he and Dromio of Syracuse take refuge in a nearby
priory, a crowd gathers impatiently outside and demands their release. The Abbess
refuses, and it is left to the Duke to sort everything out. With him is Egeon, who
immediately recognizes Antipholus and Dromio. The last joke of the play (though
again a poignant one) is that he too gets it wrong:

EGEON
    Why look you strange on me? You know me well.
ANTIPHOLUS OF EPHESUS
    I never saw you in my life till now.
EGEON
    O, grief hath changed me since you saw me last,
    And careful hours with time's deformèd hand
    Have written strange defeatures in my face.
    But tell me yet, dost thou not know my voice?
ANTIPHOLUS OF EPHESUS
    Neither.

                                [5.1.296–302]

Egeon once more gets his sons muddled up, and it is not until Antipholus and Dromio of Syracuse stumble onstage that the truth begins to dawn. Even as the twins are reunited, the play keeps its most astonishing revelation for last: the Abbess is none other than their mother. Though the "errors" are finally over, the comedy keeps a solemn promise.

Stage history and adaptations

From the records of the law college **Gray's Inn** in London, we know that a play resembling *The Comedy of Errors* was performed on the night of December 28, 1594 as part of the Christmas festivities. Another gala performance took place a decade later to the day: the accounts of **James I's court** record "The play of Errors" by "Shaxberd", raising the intriguing possibility that some legally trained audience members may have seen both performances. The script was also a success on the public stage, at least judging by the fact that **Middleton** and **Dekker's** *Honest Whore* (1604) cheerfully steals its locking-out scene.

Nonetheless, it was not revived at the Restoration and its eighteenth-century stage history is dominated by a range of adaptations under a variety of madcap titles. The first was the farcical *Every Body Mistaken* (1716), but this was quickly challenged by the anonymous *See If You Like It, or 'Tis All a Mistake* (1734), which interspersed Shakespeare with Plautus and was acted for the next seventy-odd years. **Thomas Hull** got in on the act in 1762 with *The Twins, or The Comedy of Errors*, which aspired to limited seriousness and would be acted with a few tweaks by **John Philip Kemble** in 1808. Kemble played Egeon with his younger brother **Charles** as Antipholus of Ephesus. One **W. Woods** had himself adapted it under the title of *The Twins, or Which is Which?* back in 1780, and the two *Twins* competed over stage time for a number of years.

Samuel Phelps was more textually dutiful at Sadler's Wells in 1855, and his production was a triumph. Equally successful was the uncut tercentenary performance mounted in 1864 at the Princess's Theatre. This had siblings **Charles** and **Henry Webb** as near-identical Dromios, while **George Vining** and **J. Nelson** played their masters. The play reached the Stratford Memorial Theatre in a production by **Edward Compton** in 1888, but the Elizabethan revivalist **William Poel** gained full marks for authenticity six years later: his version of *Errors* was staged at Gray's Inn in 1894 – in the same venue as the first recorded performance, precisely 300 years on.

The play was put on several times over the ensuing decades: **Frank Benson** directed and played Antipholus of Syracuse in 1905, while **Ben Greet** presented **Sybil Thorndike** as Adriana in 1915. But the play's fortunes were most drastically revived by **Theodor Komisarjevsky** in 1938, whose Stratford production indulged in joyous topsy-turvydom: its set was a huddle of colourful houses dominated by a huge clock which took on a life of its own at several key moments, while costuming ranged freely across the centuries. Though Komisarjevsky's liberties incensed some (one critic pronounced that "the one thing it is determined not to be is Shakespeare's play"), on the whole the production was well received. That same year, on the other side of the

Atlantic, the musical theatre powerhouse of musician **Richard Rogers** and lyricist **Lorenz Hart** opened *The Boys from Syracuse*, the first Broadway musical to be based on a Shakespeare source and often revived since.

More authentic than either of these versions was the *Errors* directed at Stratford-upon-Avon by **Clifford Williams** in 1962, one of the play's most successful twentieth-century incarnations. Where Komisarjevsky had conjured carnival, Williams offered pathos: the cast was praised for picking out the disquieting elements of the play and included **Ian Richardson** as Antipholus of Ephesus and **Alec McCowen** as his twin; **Ian Hewitson** and **Barry MacGregor** as the two Dromios; and **Diana Rigg**'s Adriana opposite **Pauline Letts**'s Emilia (Letts had played Luciana with Komisarjevsky a quarter-century earlier). The next major UK production was undertaken by **Trevor Nunn** at Stratford in 1976. Nunn imagined Ephesus as a Mediterranean tourist trap, complete with what one critic called a "lively crowd of tarts, slinky pimps, priests, policemen". An outstanding cast included **Judi Dench**'s pouting Adriana and **Francesca Annis**'s earnest, bespectacled Luciana, as well as **Richard Griffiths**, **Michael Williams** and **Roger Rees**, but many felt that Nunn's decision to enliven the play with musical numbers was gratuitous.

RSC productions over the last thirty years have illuminated various sides to the play. **Adrian Noble**'s (1983) was a hotchpotch of different comic styles and (some felt) too gimmicky by half; he suspended a large cradle above the stage, serving both as balcony and interior, but it had an alarming tendency to break down mid-performance, leaving **Zoë Wanamaker** (Adriana) and **Jane Booker** (Luciana) stranded in mid-air. **Ian Judge**'s gag-filled version of 1990 was largely felt to be a failure: his decision to double the twins with one actor for each, thus obliterating the pathos of their reunion, attracted particular criticism. Subtler was **Tim Supple**'s staging six years later, which used the intimate space of The Other Place to provide a fresh and surprisingly dark view of the play; a youthful cast included **Sarah C. Cameron**, **Eric Mallet**, **Simon Coates** and **Maeve Larkin**. Back in the RSC's main house in 2000, **Lynne Parker** put on an energetic and zany production with gimmicks aplenty: an onstage chase at the end of Act Four co-opted a few spare actors, in costume, from the *1 Henry IV* then playing at the Swan.

Equally funny was the Mansaku Company's *Kyogen of Errors*, rewritten by **Yasunari Takahashi**, which played at Shakespeare's Globe on Bankside in 2001. This translated English comedy into Japanese Kyogen, and invited audiences to chant *Ya-ya-koshi-ya* ("How complicated!") at pivotal moments. Drawing on her work with experimental theatre troupe Shared Experience, **Nancy Meckler**'s 2005 RSC version delved into the world of Dickensian London, bustling with pickpockets and spivs on the make. The *Telegraph*'s Charles Spencer suggested that Meckler "pays the play the compliment of taking it seriously".

The RSC intelligently made *The Comedy of Errors* part of a "shipwreck trilogy" during the World Shakespeare Festival in 2012, pairing it with *The Tempest* and *Twelfth Night*, and brought out (in **Amir Nizar Zuabi**'s production) its bleak and nightmarish qualities, notoriously featuring a scene of waterboarding. Similar themes surfaced in the Globe's contribution to the same festival, offered in Dari Persian by the **Rah-e-Sabz** troupe from Afghanistan; notionally set in contemporary Kabul, it made much of the emotional schisms and torments that dominate the action. Less powerful was the English-language Globe version by **Blanche McIntyre's** approximately Elizabethan version in 2014, which despite some strong performances was distinguished largely by some frantic slapstick (including at one point an octopus deployed as a weapon).

Given the rich potential it offers for visual trickery, it's perhaps surprising that *Errors* has yet to reach the silver screen in anything like its original form, though in **India** (where adaptations were numerous from the late nineteenth century onwards), successful movie remakes include the Bengali *Bhranti Bilas* (1963) and the Hindi-language *Do Dooni Char* ("Two Twos are Four", 1968), as well as **Gulzar's** much-loved *Angoor* (1982). English-language audiences have had to settle for the film version of *The Boys from Syracuse* (1940), the **Bette Midler–Lily Tomlin** comedy vehicle *Big Business*, loosely based on the play (1988), and two TV versions, both BBC – one an operetta starring **Joan Plowright** (1954), and the BBC/Time-Life Shakespeare, with **Michael Kitchen** playing both Antipholuses and **Roger Daltrey** the Dromios.

SCREEN

The Comedy of Errors

R. Rees, J. Dench, F. Annis; Philip Casson (dir.) UK, 1978 > Network **DVD**

As his excursions into musical theatre attest, Trevor Nunn has never been averse to making his actors sing and dance as well as act. His RSC *Errors*, which debuted in 1976 and was filmed for TV two years later, is tricked out with plenty of tunes and choreography, not to mention various comic high-jinks absent from Shakespeare's script. A great idea, but badly realized: Nunn's fine cast looks ill at ease, and after a few minutes Guy Woolfenden's jaunty intro music will have you scurrying for fast-forward. A shame, as the production is otherwise funny and adroit, picturing Ephesus as a kind of Costa del Sol overrun with holidaymakers and ruled by a banana-republic dictator, and into which Judi Dench, Roger Rees and Francesca Annis inject sympathetic performances. It's certainly a lot better than the woebegone BBC version.

Angoor

S. Kumar, D. Verma, M. Chatterjee; Gulzar (dir.) India, 1982 > Video Palace **DVD**

Given this comedy's lowly status in the west, it might be disconcerting to discover that *Errors* – albeit heavily adapted – has been wildly popular in India, first translated by Mumbai-based playwrights in the 1860s and frequently remade since. *Angoor*, by the renowned Bollywood lyricist-director Gulzar, is squarely in this tradition, a re-re-make of earlier cinematic versions, but is unusually faithful to its source – if not quite line-by-line then at least scene-by-scene. Legendary leading man Sanjeev Kumar plays the Ashoks/Antipholuses with

panicked pathos (he looks perennially on the point of tears) and is ably assisted by the pleasingly lumpen Deven Verma as the Bahadurs/Dromios. Classic Hindi comedy, this isn't sophisticated film-making – the cinematography is wobbly and the wildly noisy musical score should come with a health warning – but it's done with huge heart. See if you can spot the cunning intertextual reference to *Twelfth Night* buried in the final scene. The DVD is an Indian import but it's also worth trying YouTube.

The Comedy of Errors

J. Tucker, R. Katz, C. Entwisle; Paul Hunter (dir.) UK, 2009 > Digital Theatre 🔊

A mere 84 minutes long, this cut-down version of *Errors* was created by the barnstorming Told By an Idiot Troupe and the RSC education team for people who might be expected to respond well to the madcap humour of this zaniest of plays: kids under the age of 11. Despite the intended audience – the production was filmed live in a school hall – there's plenty here for everyone to enjoy. Paul Hunter encourages his actors to play things fast and loose, and looks to have drawn design inspiration from a dressing-up box – Egeon emerges from a broken fridge standing in for a prison, and there's liberal use of the silliest wigs you're ever likely to see in an RSC production. Yet it's wittily and imaginatively done, and the cast is excellent: James Tucker and Richard Katz are finely matched as the puzzled Antipholi, Christine Entwisle brings broken-down pathos to the role of Adriana and there's a star turn from Jonjo O'Neill as a sweetly long-suffering Dromio of Syracuse. Noisy, cheerful and boisterously charming, the show is what productions of this comedy so often aren't – genuinely funny.

The Comedy of Errors
A. Haq, G. Tanha, P. Mushtahel; Corinne Jaber (dir.)
UK, 2012 > Globe 📥

One of the surprise successes of the 2012 World Shakespeare Festival, held to coincide with the London Olympic Games, was this contribution from Team Afghanistan. Despite being a scratch company who had only ever performed one Shakespeare play before – and though they were forced to rehearse in Bangalore after their rehearsal space in Kabul was suicide-bombed – Rah-e-Sabz offered an interpretation of the play that was by turns painful and painfully funny, captured here in this live Globe recording. Despite a cavalcade of crowd-pleasing sight gags and more comic disguises than an episode of *Monty Python* (pleasurably emphasized by the vocal presence of the audience), the company underscore Shakespeare's obsession with exile and separation, insanity and isolation; when this family is finally reunited, your heart will be in your throat. The use of scene synopses instead of detailed subtitles is the only real frustration – unless you're lucky enough to speak Dari Persian, it might be best to watch with a text to hand.

AUDIO

The Comedy of Errors
D. Tennant, B. Coyle, N. Cusack; Clive Brill (dir.) UK, 1998 > Arkangel ◎ 📥

Managing the comic and tragic elements of *The Comedy of Errors* is something most productions find difficult to do, but this Arkangel version generally succeeds, delivering a moving opening scene built around Trevor Peacock's Egeon and plenty of fleet wit afterwards. This Ephesus is dominated by Irish voices – a welcome novelty, especially for Dromios usually played in bad Cockney – among whom are siblings Niamh and Sorcha Cusack (Adriana and Luciana respectively). Both David Tennant (Antipholus of Syracuse) and Brendan Coyle (Antipholus of Ephesus) are excellent, and fortunately they don't sound too similar. The only problem is the continuously cartoonish sound effects, which strive too hard for laughs.

EDITIONS

Oxford Shakespeare
Charles Whitworth (ed.); 2002 > Oxford UP

Charles Whitworth's newish Oxford edition just beats R.A. Foakes's classic Arden 2 equivalent (1962). Both print a version of Plautus's *Menaechmi* as an appendix (it's worth dipping into Plautus just to see how much more interesting Shakespeare makes his interpretation of the story), but Whitworth offers the translation by William Warner (1595) which appeared at about the same time that *Errors* was first performed. Whitworth is also in a position to comment on the critical and theatrical re-evaluation the play has experienced in the last few decades, and his account usefully interleaves the play's life on page and stage.

SOME CRITICISM

Shakespeare and the Traditions of Comedy
Leo Salingar; 1974 > Cambridge UP

One of the best general introductions, pleasingly returned to print, Salingar's study helps to elucidate what the word and concept of "comedy" might have meant to Shakespeare and his dramatic colleagues – and of course to audiences too. *Shakespeare and the Traditions of Comedy* ranges fleet-footedly across history (medieval stage romances, classical comedy), geography (Italian *commedia dell'arte* versus English comedy) and themes ("trickster" figures, trial scenes and the role of the Wheel of Fortune) to present a view of its subject that is both nuanced and – more importantly – not as po-faced as some other studies. Alexander Leggatt's excellent *Cambridge Companion to Shakespearean Comedy* (2002) offers some more recent perspectives.

The Comedy of Errors: Critical Essays
Robert S. Miola (ed.); 1997 > Routledge

As the author of *Shakespeare and Classical Comedy* (1994), Robert Miola is well placed to offer opinions on *Errors*, Shakespeare's Plautine experiment. This reader is terrific: you'll find an in-depth account of the play's critical history, particularly detailed on its use of sources; some twenty articles on productions spanning 398 years; and many of the most influential essays on the play – among them G.R. Elliott on "weirdness" and Harold Brooks on its themes and structure. The only puzzle is that Gamini Salgado's superlative piece on time in the play (*Shakespeare Survey*, 1972) isn't among them.

Coriolanus

S hakespeare's muscular final tragedy, *Coriolanus* is also his purest expression of a tragic form, Greek in origin, in which a hero meets a sudden and brutal reversal of fate. While researching his earlier Roman tragedies *Julius Caesar* and *Antony and Cleopatra* in Plutarch's histories, the playwright's eye was caught by the glittering but ultimately catastrophic career of Caius Martius Coriolanus, a Roman general whose brilliance on the battlefield was matched only by his failings as a popular politician. The story is a fable however you look at it, but it points in different directions: in one reading, Coriolanus is a hero deserted by a fickle populace; in another, he is a villain whose arrogance threatens dictatorship. Shakespeare makes room for both those positions and more besides, drawing on the politics of his own day to press home urgent and thorny questions about how democracy should operate. During its performance history *Coriolanus* has been interpreted as everything from fascist propaganda for Hitler's Third Reich to a communist tract enshrining the power of the people. As the soldier Aufidius, watching Coriolanus's star plummet, balefully notes: "our virtues / Lie in th'interpretation of the time" (4.7.49–50).

DATE > Uncertain, though the language of *Coriolanus* puts it close to *Antony and Cleopatra*, *Pericles* and *Timon of Athens* in 1608–09. Allusions within the play to historical events, notably the Midlands food riots and "great frost" of 1607–08, seem to support this. As such it is the last of the tragedies, and perhaps the first of Shakespeare's plays intended for indoor performance at the Blackfriars theatre.

SOURCES > As with the other Roman plays, North's 1595 edition of Plutarch's *Lives* is the central source, and, as in the case of *Antony and Cleopatra*, some passages are lifted almost verbatim.

TEXTS > The 1623 Folio provides the sole authoritative text, probably set from a transcript of Shakespeare's foul papers.

Interpreting the play

Rome, the most powerful empire the world has ever known, stalks Shakespeare's career. Four of his plays and one of his poems have Roman settings, and a Roman army even sneaks into the early Britain of *Cymbeline*. The Empire crops up in the most surprising places. Henry V's triumphant return from Agincourt becomes, in the Chorus's words, the arrival of a "conqu'ring Caesar". For his part, Macbeth scorns to "play the Roman fool" and die on his sword as he realizes Macduff's army is upon him. Even Falstaff manages to name-check the most famous Roman victory of all: "He saw me and yielded," Sir John boasts as he bags a rebel prisoner in *Henry IV Part II*, "that I may justly say, with the hook-nosed fellow of Rome, 'I came, saw and overcame.' "

MAJOR CHARACTERS & SYNOPSIS

Caius Martius, later known as **Coriolanus**, a patrician (aristocrat) of Rome
Menenius Agrippa, another patrician
Titus Lartius and **Cominius**, generals and patricians
Volumnia, Coriolanus's mother
Virgilia, Coriolanus's wife
Young Martius, Coriolanus's son
Valeria, a lady from Rome
Sicinius Velutus and **Junius Brutus**, tribunes (representatives) of the Roman people
Roman Citizens and **Soldiers**
Tullus Aufidius, a Volscian general
Volscian Lords, **Citizens** and **Soldiers**
Adrian, a Volscian
Nicanor, a Roman

ACT 1 Struck by famine, Rome is starving and its citizens are in revolt. A mob, on its way to lynch the city's most hated patrician, Caius Martius, is halted in the streets by Menenius, a fellow patrician. Making the most of his fair-dealing reputation, Menenius holds the crowd back, but reckons without Martius's own appearance and his announcement that the mob should be hanged. But Rome has worries other than famine: Aufidius's Volscian army is marching on the city, and Martius is soon appointed to join Cominius's retaliatory force. As the city waits for news of the battle, Volumnia boasts to Virgilia of her son's military prowess and notes with satisfaction that her young grandson, also called Martius, is taking after his father. At the battlefront, meanwhile, the wounded Martius performs with astonishing bravery, reversing a Roman retreat and masterminding the occupation of Corioles. Once Roman victory is confirmed, Cominius confers the honorific "Coriolanus" on his brilliant deputy. Aufidius, defeated and humiliated, contemplates revenge.

ACT 2 At the Senate, the tribunes are dissecting Martius's personal flaws when Virgilia announces his victorious return. Coriolanus enters the city to an enormous welcome, horrifying Brutus and Sicinius with the thought that he

will be promoted. Their fears are confirmed when the Senate make him a consul. Coriolanus himself remains aloof, but is eventually encouraged to address the commoners directly and beg for their votes – a process he finds as distasteful as it is democratic. And, though he eventually gets their support, the tribunes soon convince the citizens to reconsider.

ACT 3 Coriolanus is about to be made a consul when the tribunes gleefully inform him that his popularity has evaporated. Incensed, he declares that the people don't deserve him, at which point the tribunes attempt to arrest him. They fail, but Coriolanus is forced to appear in the marketplace and answer the people's objections. Despite Volumnia's entreaties to stay calm, he loses his temper once more, railing at both citizens and tribunes alike. This time he is banished permanently.

ACT 4 Although the tribunes make no secret of their joy at Coriolanus's departure, it isn't long before rumour spreads that the Volscians will take advantage of his absence and launch another attack on Rome. For his part, Coriolanus heads directly for enemy headquarters at Antium and offers his services to Aufidius, who gratefully accepts. As their army heads for Rome, Aufidius's agenda becomes apparent: as soon as Coriolanus outlasts his usefulness, Aufidius will destroy him.

ACT 5 Rome, meanwhile, is desperate to win back its saviour, and first Cominius, then Menenius, attempt to persuade him to return. Both fail, but Virgilia, Volumnia, Valeria and Young Martius make a final plea, to which Coriolanus at last relents, fully aware of the danger this puts him in. While Rome celebrates the news, Aufidius accuses Coriolanus of treachery and the Volscians demand his head. The end has come. Coriolanus is first stabbed to death, then trampled by the Volscian crowd. Aufidius, weeping at what he has done, orders him to be buried with full military honours.

Coriolanus, almost certainly Shakespeare's final tragedy, takes us inside Rome itself. What we find there is grim. Where *Antony and Cleopatra* counterpoises an oppressive Rome with the wide, luxurious, exotic expanses of Egypt, in this play we are trapped inside the city as the Volscian enemy circles outside. There has been famine, and the people are out on the streets, inflamed by rumours that the city leaders have been (as the politician Menenius delicately puts it) "cupboarding the viand", hoarding food while everyone else starves. Despite Menenius's desperate attempts to make peace, insisting that the patricians have "most charitable care" for the people, the citizens are scandalized:

> FIRST CITIZEN   Care for us? True, indeed! They ne'er cared for us yet: suffer us to famish, and their storehouses crammed with grain; make edicts for usury to support usurers; repeal daily any unwholesome act established against the rich; and provide more piercing statutes daily to chain up and restrain the poor. If the wars eat us not up, they will; and there's all the love they bear us.
>
> [1.1.77–84]

These complaints about the abuse of political power have an eerily modern ring, but few among today's audiences (in the industrialized west at least) know what it is really like to "famish". The same could not be said of Shakespeare's first spectators. At the time *Coriolanus* was premiered, times had been hard in England, especially in the playwright's home county of Warwickshire. The so-called "Midlands Riots" during the early summer of 1607 had been touched off by a cycle of bad harvests and rampant inflation in food prices, exacerbated by illegal enclosure of common land. Peasants protested, but were brutally suppressed by local gentry – events whose repercussions were witnessed by Shakespeare, who seems to have spent some of 1608 in Stratford attending to his mother's funeral. As a local landowner himself, it has been argued that the playwright must automatically have sided against the rioters. But *Coriolanus* makes that hard to believe. Trying to disperse the starving crowd (Shakespeare conflates his sources' two riots into one for dramatic impact), Menenius insists that there is simply no point in complaining. "For your wants, / Your suffering in this dearth," he begins,

> you may as well
> Strike at the heaven with your staves as lift them
> Against the Roman state, whose course will on
> The way it takes, cracking ten thousand curbs
> Of more strong link asunder than can ever
> Appear in your impediment.
>
> [1.1.64–70]

Protest is useless; the state simply rolls on regardless. Though Menenius's words have sometimes been taken to imply that *Coriolanus* is a politically conservative play, what seems striking here is the way in which the crowd, desperately hungry, is being fobbed off with mere words – words guaranteeing that, far from being at the heart of Roman democracy, they have no say in how the city is run.

Mᴿ KEAN,

AS CORIOLANUS.

Engraved by Thomson from an original drawing by Wageman

Published 1820, by Simpkin & Marshall, Stationers Cᵗ & Chapple, Pall Mall.

Edmund Kean's Caius Martius was – like nearly every role he played – quixotic and full of fire, but the show was still a failure: the production ran at Drury Lane for just four nights in January 1820 before being forced to close. Nonetheless, it was commemorated in this engraving, taken from Thomas Charles Wageman's original drawing.

The common file

Menenius's clumsy attempts to calm the crowd are upset by the sudden arrival of Caius Martius, the man whose downfall they are really after. His view of the plebs, though hardly palatable, is at least honest. "What would you have, you curs?", he demands,

> He that trusts to you,
> Where he should find you lions finds you hares,
> Where foxes, geese. You are no surer, no,
> Than is the coal of fire upon the ice,
> Or hailstone in the sun. Your virtue is
> To make him worthy whose offence subdues him,
> And curse that justice did it. Who deserves greatness
> Deserves your hate, and your affections are
> A sick man's appetite, who desires most that
> Which would increase his evil. He that depends
> Upon your favours swims with fins of lead,
> And hews down oaks with rushes.

[1.1.168–79]

This splenetic, almost frantic language colours what is an otherwise linguistically austere play. The view of Shakespeare's main source, an English translation of Plutarch's

KEY SOURCE > Plutarch's *Lives*

Directly after polishing off the chronicle-based English histories, Shakespeare turned towards the ancient past. His major source for the Roman plays (plus a good few others) was the collection of *Parallel Lives* by Greek historian L. Mestrius Plutarchus (c. 50–120 AD), known by the Anglicized name of **Plutarch** well before his biographical works reached English – which they did in 1579 in a big-boned translation, *The Lives of the Noble Grecians and Romans*, by diplomat **Sir Thomas North** (1523–c. 1601). Not that things are quite as straightforward as that: North was working from a French version by his near contemporary, scholar and bishop **Jacques Amyot** (1513–93), so the text that reached Shakespeare was at some distance from Plutarch's original.

Even so, North's *Lives* are one of Shakespeare's most fertile sources: in places, particularly in *Coriolanus* and *Antony and Cleopatra*, he quotes them almost directly. It's not hard to see why. Instead of writing broad-brush political history, Plutarch com-piled compelling biographies of the most powerful men in the ancient world – the 23 that have survived include giants like **Alexander the Great**, **Theseus** and **Romulus** as well as **Coriolanus**, **Julius Caesar** and **Mark Antony**. As Amyot's celebrated preface to his readers explains, "an history is the very treasury of man's life, whereby the notable doings and sayings of men, and the wonderful adventures and strange cases ... are preserved from the death of forgetfulness". What that meant in practice was history that did its utmost to make great men live again, and which exposes their vices along with their virtues. Thus it's from the gossipy (and frequently scandalized) Plutarch that we learn some juicy historical titbits: that Antony was once so drunk that he vomited over a council table; that Coriolanus "never left his mother's house" despite taking a wife; and that Caesar was first wooed by Cleopatra when she wrapped herself up in a mattress and had the bundle smuggled into his bedroom.

Life of Coriolanus, that Caius Martius was "choleric and impatient" here seems a dangerous understatement. Irascible and disdainful, Martius detests the crowd, but (in his terms at least) that makes him deserving of "greatness". The Romantic critic William Hazlitt fought against a lifetime's passionately held liberalism to admit that in *Coriolanus* "the language of poetry naturally falls in with the language of power", and indeed there is something almost hypnotic in Martius's unstoppable raging against the mob. Among Shakespeare's heroes, he is the only one able to transform insatiable contempt into something that seems almost positive.

Plutarch describes how "valiantness was honoured in Rome above all other virtues", and in Martius's person we see where that philosophy really leads. Combining lofty aristocracy and effortless machismo with near-suicidal valour on the battlefield, Martius acquires his familiar title while performing a particularly spectacular piece of derring-do outside the city of Corioles – hence "Coriolanus". Reborn in the fire and smoke of battle, he "cannot in the world", the smooth-tongued politician Cominius suggests, "be singly counterpoised". In war, Cominius continues, Coriolanus has no equal:

> His sword, death's stamp,
> Where it did mark, it took. From face to foot
> He was a thing of blood, whose every motion
> Was timed with dying cries. Alone he entered
> The mortal gate of th'city, which he, painted
> With shunless destiny, aidless came off,
> And with a sudden reinforcement struck
> Corioles like a planet.
>
> [2.2.107–14]

Coriolanus is a machine "timed with dying cries"; nourished by battle, he is prepared to go on for ever as if he were "a perpetual spoil", not even pausing to catch his breath.

The admiring portrait Cominius draws is, of course, horrendous: this unstoppable, blood-soaked warrior is not a man, but a ravening beast. "There is no more mercy in him than there is milk in the male tiger," (5.4.28–9) says Menenius. Still more shocking is the attitude of his mother, the fearsome Volumnia. As the women of Rome wait nervously for news of the battle at Corioles, Virgilia plaintively hopes that her husband has not been injured. It is all Volumnia can do to hold back her disdain: blood "more becomes a man," she scornfully replies, "than gilt his trophy."

> The breasts of Hecuba
> When she did suckle Hector looked not lovelier
> Than Hector's forehead when it spit forth blood
> At Grecian sword, contemning.
>
> [1.3.41–5]

The warrior who becomes on the battlefield "a thing of blood" is eerily predicted in these grim words. Volumnia and her son are a kind of nightmare perversion of

Roman values: the city's fetish for military prowess approves Coriolanus's brutality in war just as it encourages the kind of sadistic outlook voiced by his mother. A few moments later Volumnia describes approvingly how Coriolanus's little son shows every sign of following after his father – by tormenting a butterfly, then ripping it apart with his teeth.

O' me alone

Coriolanus depicts, again and again, the madness of life in Rome. Though the people have genuine complaints with the way they are ruled, they allow themselves to be bought off with words (Shakespeare deliberately muddies his source, which explains that as a result of the grain riots the people won political representation). And although Roman ideas about "valiantness" seem comprehensible enough, in Coriolanus and his mother they reach an apex of inhumanity. And though the crowd detests the man who calls them "curs", they find themselves persuaded that he deserves to wield power over them.

At the urging of politicians eager to capitalize on his military victories, Coriolanus agrees to stand for the Senate – the ironic catch being that, in order to be elected by the people, he must first beg for their "voices" (votes). A curious tussle ensues: though the commoners can decide whether to elect him or not, most seem to believe that it would be embarrassing to show "ingratitude" to a man who has done so much for their city. Admitting that they are prepared to vote for him on condition that he shows them his battle scars, they reveal that they too are entangled in the ideology worshipped by Volumnia and Coriolanus.

Coriolanus himself is not even sure he can bring himself to go that far. The irony that he has become the very man he despises, the man who must "depend" on the crowd's "favours" as he stands begging votes, is not lost on the hero. "Better it is to die, better to starve," he bitterly exclaims, "than crave the hire which first we do deserve" (2.3.113–7). Longing for the solitary simplicities of the battlefield, Coriolanus simply cannot understand the complexities of democracy.

Even so, he very nearly gets into office – until, that is, the tribunes Sicinius and Brutus succeed in convincing the crowd to turn against him and have him declared a traitor. Like Plutarch, they make much of his supposed "pride", but Shakespeare makes that view seem too simplistic. Coriolanus's reluctance to hear his "nothings monstered" by Cominius after Corioles demonstrates his personal humility; his refusal to wear the gown of humility exhibits his moral probity; and his determination to avoid flattering the citizens and showing his scars underlines his loathing of hypocrisy. Yet somehow Coriolanus manages to transform these virtues into fatal flaws, undone by his inability to swerve from his own view of the world. Under attack from the Volscians, he is unflappable; under fire from his own people, he is unredeemable. Though he is

The whole dramatic moral of Coriolanus is, that those who have little shall have less, and that those who have much shall take all that others have left.

William Hazlitt, writing in *The Examiner*, December 15, 1816 accused of treachery and banished from the city, he decides he must banish Rome, not the other way around:

> You common cry of curs, whose breath I hate
> As reek o'th' rotten fens, whose loves I prize
> As the dead carcasses of unburied men
> That do corrupt my air: I banish you.

[3.3.124–7]

With those three magisterial words Coriolanus throws himself into the wilderness. Aristotle famously observed that a man who cannot live in the *polis* is either a beast or a god, and we know enough about Martius to sense that the "city of kites and crows" (4.5.42) outside Rome's walls is where he and the play have always been heading. The soldier who cried "O' me alone!" (1.7.76) at the gates of Corioles has, perhaps, nowhere else to go; and though he is not alone for long – he joins with his enemy Aufidius in order to get hold of his army – Coriolanus's terrible vengeance on Rome is a brooding solitary obsession.

As his and Aufidius's forces encamp outside Rome, ready to lay waste to it, the tribunes send out envoys desperately persuading Coriolanus to spare the city. But Coriolanus remains unmoved. "He does sit in gold," Cominius stammers, "his eye / Red as 'twould burn Rome" (5.1.63–4), and the only way the city's elders can see to save themselves is to send out the women closest to Coriolanus: Volumnia, Virgilia and Valeria, accompanied by Young Martius. Despite Coriolanus's insistence that they should not try "t'allay / My rages and revenges with your colder reasons" (5.3.85–6), over the course of an extraordinarily long and moving scene of pleading – in every way the climax of the play – he is eventually persuaded to back down. Though earlier he attempted to claim that he stood isolated, "As if a man were author of himself / And knew no other kin" (5.3.36–7), the hero is forced to recognize that his family cannot so easily be disowned. Yet his acceptance, painfully won, is also dark with foreboding. "O mother, mother!" he cries, holding her hand in an isolated symbol of empathy,

> What have you done? Behold, the heavens do ope,
> The gods look down, and this unnatural scene
> They laugh at. O my mother, mother, O!
> You have won a happy victory to Rome;
> But for your son, believe it, O believe it,
> Most dangerously you have with him prevailed,
> If not most mortal to him.

[5.3.183–90]

"But let it come," he concludes, and with that he knows that his fate is sealed. Though he gives in to Volumnia's pleas, her earlier lesson that "Thy valiantness was mine, thou suck'dst it from me" (3.2.128) proves more enduring.

By this time we know Aufidius jealously believes that Coriolanus is, as his own servants snigger, "the greater soldier" (4.5.170), and is plotting his rival's downfall.

"A thing of blood": years before filming the role, Ralph Fiennes made a violent and short-tempered Coriolanus on stage in London in 2000.

Characteristically, though, Coriolanus beats him to it. Angrily denying that the tears of his family – what Aufidius sneeringly calls "certain drops of salt" (5.6.95) – have weakened his resolve, Coriolanus angrily turns upon the Volscians once more. Aufidius's taunt that he is nothing but a "boy of tears" proves the end. "Cut me to pieces, Volsces," Coriolanus cries, commanding even his own death:

> Stain all your edges on me. 'Boy'! False hound,
> If you have writ your annals true, 'tis there
> That, like an eagle in a dove-cote, I
> Fluttered your Volscians in Corioles.
> Alone I did it.

[5.6.112–6]

The crowd, clutching knives, surges forward. In the crush of people, Coriolanus is "alone" one last time.

Stage history and adaptations

Coriolanus might well have been the first Shakespeare play to be performed at his brand-new winter venue, the indoor **Blackfriars** playhouse. Intriguingly for a play so concerned with the will of the people, this means that it would have been viewed by a far more exclusive audience than at the Southwark amphitheatres, though if it was a hit (there are no records) it's likely that it would have transferred to the Globe during the summer months. Either way, early productions of this conspicuously noisy play would have been filled with music, and it is almost certain that **Richard Burbage**, the troupe's leading tragedian, took the role of Martius. Given that Burbage was about 40 at the time, scholars are divided as to who played Volumnia, a boy or an older man.

The next we hear is of **Nahum Tate**'s Restoration rewrite, entitled *The Ingratitude of a Commonwealth*, premiered in 1681. The country was then embroiled in anti-Catholic witch-hunts centring on Charles II, and Tate's piece (as its title reveals) was an unapologetic piece of royalist propaganda: in the dedication the author confessed that "I chose rather to set the *Parallel* nearer to sight, then to throw it off at futher Distance". This was the first expressly topical remake, but it would hardly be the last. **John Dennis**'s version, *The Invader of His Country* – a patriotic (and anti-Catholic) manifesto – reached the stage in 1719. Less contentious were the Lincoln's Inn Fields performances the previous year, possibly with **James Quin** in the title role (plus some comic parts not in the original). Quin might also have acted in another adaptation, *Coriolanus: or The Roman Matron*, which amalgamated sections of an original play by **James Thomson** with Shakespeare's at the behest of **Thomas Sheridan** (father of playwright Richard). Debuting in Dublin with Sheridan as Coriolanus and **Peg Woffington** as his mother in 1747, this version successfully transferred to Covent Garden.

Following a failed production by **David Garrick** a few years later, the play might have sunk without trace were it not for the efforts of **John Philip Kemble**, who detected in Coriolanus a fine match for his patrician, declamatory demeanour, and from 1789 until 1817 it was his signature role. Assisted by two-inch lifts in his sandals, Kemble presented a brooding, grave Martius alongside his celebrated sister **Sarah Siddons** as Volumnia – the only problem arriving with the unrest following the French Revolution, which forced a temporary suspension of performances. The firebrand **Edmund Kean** failed to break Kemble's spell in 1820, lacking his stature (or his heels), and **William Charles Macready**, too, was criticized for lack of gravitas. **Samuel Phelps** gained plaudits at Sadler's Wells thirty years later, but mainly for the quality of his scenery.

In the fiercely republican United States, meanwhile, actors breathed fresh life into the role. **Edwin Forrest**, perhaps America's first true home-grown star, played Martius as a frontier hero in the 1860s (one commentator said he was "not so much patrician by status as by mind"), and **Tommaso Salvini** also toured in 1885 as an impetuous Coriolanus, performing in Italian while the rest of the cast spoke English.

Less interested in novelty was **Frank Benson**, the first man to bring *Coriolanus* to Stratford-upon-Avon: his own boyish interpretation remained unchanged between 1893 and 1919, though the same could hardly be said for British politics. A nod to the fearsome power of the mob was included in 1910, however, when they were instructed to lynch the Tribunes at the end of Act Four. By that time **Henry Irving**'s ill-fated staging had come and gone (Irving, 63 at the time, was too frail for the fight scenes), and the Victorian taste for grandiloquent Roman staging was on the wane. **William Bridges-Adams** had a particularly fierce crowd in 1933, but, revisiting the play in 1939, did his best to play down the uncomfortable parallels between *Coriolanus* and events on the continent, with a studiously Elizabethan production.

Companies elsewhere in Europe had no such luxury, as **Hans Rothe** discovered when his modernist translations of the plays (among them *Coriolanus*) were banned by Goebbels, and the writer forced into exile in 1934 – whereupon the play became a primer for the Nazis, depicting the "true hero and *Führer*, Coriolanus, who desires to lead the misguided *Volk* to restoration" (as one loyalist put it). That Shakespeare's work could, however, equally be put to anti-fascist ends became clear in England in 1935, where a production at Manchester's **Royal Exchange** became an anti-Mussolini allegory complete with shiny uniforms and a Sicinius resembling Lenin. **Laurence Olivier** also had *Il Duce* in mind under **Lewis Casson** at the Old Vic in 1938, his first attempt on the role. Nearly two decades later, his death scene for **Peter Hall**'s famous Stratford version of 1959 deliberately aped the dictator's gruesome end, suspended from a meathook by cheering crowds. Olivier's spoilt Coriolanus, clearly in thrall to **Edith Evans**'s Volumnia, set the tone for many later English stagings (most obviously **Tyrone Guthrie**'s at the Nottingham Playhouse in 1963, which played up the homo-erotic frisson between **John Neville**'s Martius and the Aufidius of **Ian McKellen**). **Alan Howard**'s narcissistic, macho and black-leather-clad Martius, directed by **Terry Hands** at Stratford in 1977, was the zenith – for some, the nadir – of this view of the play.

In mainland Europe, contemporary politics was very much on the mind of **Bertolt Brecht**, whose Marxist variation, *Coriolan*, foregrounded class struggle and the role of the proletariat; though it remained unfinished at his death, it was premiered by the Berliner Ensemble in 1964. Employing theories already put into practice in **Giorgio Strehler**'s celebrated production in Milan in 1957, Brecht insisted that the play should be read as a tragedy not of the individual, but of the "individual's indispensability". **Anthony Hopkins**'s Coriolanus at London's National Theatre (1971) benefited not just from Brecht's ideas, but the direction of two of his collaborators, Manfred Wekwerth and Joachim Tenschert. **John Osborne**'s *A Place Calling Itself Rome*, though it appeared the same year, folded *Coriolanus* into the drab realities of 1970s Britain in a decidedly right-wing take on the play.

Since then, *Coriolanus*'s political relevance has never been more in fashion, not least in Eastern Europe, where it had a lively life on stage in the communist era, often staged as a coded commentary on real-life events. In Britain, **Peter Hall**, returning to the play in 1984 at the National (with a strutting **Ian McKellen** opposite **Irene Worth**'s matronly Volumnia), seized the opportunity to satirize post-Falklands England with an intriguing blend of medieval costuming and Thatcherite power suits; while **William Gaskill**'s 1991 production for the Folger Shakespeare Company, in the wake of the Gulf War, had a Desert Storm-ish Coriolanus face down groups of Palestinian-like Volscians. **Tim Supple**'s 1992 production for **Kenneth Branagh**'s Renaissance Theatre Company at Chichester boasted not merely Branagh's supremely sneering Martius and **Judi Dench**'s haughty Volumnia ("a domestic tyrant with the heart and stomach of a lion", commented one reviewer) but a mob of fifty extras to swell Shakespeare's crowd scenes.

And though stylish postmodern interpretations have had their say – notably at the behest of **Stephen Berkoff**, who has staged *Coriolanus* three times, in 1988 with **Christopher Walken** in the lead – many directors have continued to confront the play's politics head-on. For **David Thacker** at the RSC's Swan Theatre in 1994 that meant draping a sketch of Delacroix's painting *Liberty Guiding the People* across the back of the stage (**Toby Stephens**, his Coriolanus, was just 24). For **David Farr** at the same venue in 2002 it involved recreating the distant territory of samurai Japan, where the pre-eminence of the warrior class remained unquestioned, with **Greg Hicks** as a testy Martius. A few years earlier, in 2000, **Ralph Fiennes** played the role for **Jonathan Kent** at a disused film studio in north London, offering an interpretation suggesting that the hero was (in the words of the *Guardian*) "a lonely dragon whose only real relationship is with his martial mother".

Recent productions have again returned to the question of scale. Belgian director **Ivo van Hove** made *Coriolanus* part of the epic, six-hour *Roman Tragedies*, which opened in Amsterdam in 2007. The show offered Roman history as multimedia political spectacle, in an attempt to explore "how politicians make good decisions, how they make mistakes, why they make mistakes", as Van Hove put it. In 2012 directors **Mike Pearson** and **Mike Brookes** mounted an epic staging in a disused aircraft hangar in the Glamorgan countryside for the newly established **National Theatre Wales**, blending Shakespeare's text with Brecht's adaptation and inviting the audience to track the action on foot. More suffocating and intimate was **Josie Rourke**'s Donmar version the following year, which referenced the Occupy protest movement and reimagined the play as a modern-dress chamber piece with **Tom Hiddleston** as a surprisingly soulful, sorrowful hero.

Coriolanus has made little impact on screen. To date, the only major film version is **Ralph Fiennes**'s Balkanized version of 2011, with Fiennes himself in the lead alongside **Vanessa Redgrave** and **Jessica Chastain**. Other than that, just the BBC's complete Shakespeare series (directed by **Elijah Moshinsky** with the pairing of **Alan Howard** and **Irene Worth** as Martius and mother) and a small clutch of live recordings have made it into production.

SCREEN

Coriolanus
A. Howard, I. Worth, J. Ackland; Elijah Moshinsky (dir.) UK, 1984 > BBC **DVD**

Alan Howard was a famous Coriolanus at Stratford in 1977, and so it was little surprise that he was invited to reprise the role a few years later for the BBC. Elijah Moshinsky's production is more conservative in both tone and style than Terry Hands's at the RSC, however, and while Howard undeniably has plenty of vocal power this version makes him look mannered and struggles to support him effectively. Moshinsky's impressionistic screenwork – particularly in the battle scenes – might have looked effective on film, but on TV too often fails to have any real impact. Yet Irene Worth's Volumnia, another veteran of the Stratford production, brings a surprising warmth to her role and Joss Ackland's fruity Menenius is also worth watching out for. Ultimately, however, this version simply fails to catch fire.

Coriolanus
R. Fiennes, V. Redgrave, B. Cox; Ralph Fiennes (dir.) UK, 2011 > Lionsgate / Weinstein **DVD** 🔵

For his directorial debut, Ralph Fiennes chose a role he'd already attempted once, nearly a decade before. It's a fine fit – Fiennes does few things better than snarling, caustic contempt; and his shifting of the play's territory from ancient Rome to a contemporary-ish Balkans splintering into chaos makes smart sense for an audience reared on *The Hurt Locker* and video game *Call of Duty*, both of which the film somewhat resembles. The cast, too, is fine, with Gerard Butler as a glowering Aufidius, Brian Cox as a meaty Menenius and Vanessa Redgrave as a plausibly deranged Volumnia (with ace screenwriter John Logan editing and tightening the script). Despite the goriness of the setting – rarely has the hero been so literally a "thing of blood" – the movie feels oddly anaemic, though, easier to admire than get inside, particularly once the pace starts to flag in the second half. Intelligent without ever being fully gripping.

AUDIO

Coriolanus
P. Jesson, M. Yates, E. Hooper; Clive Brill (dir.) UK, 1998 > Arkangel ◉ ⬇

Any Coriolanus needs a magnetic lead star, and in Paul Jesson's grizzled and wonderfully scornful hero Arkangel certainly has that. It also has a fine Volumnia (the splendid Marjorie Yates), a fittingly patrician Menenius (Ewan Hooper), vigorously characterized crowd scenes and some very gruesome battle noises. This recording likewise contains good performances from an unusually steely Virgilia (Sarah Woodward) and Martin Marquez's testy Aufidius (though his "northern" accent betrays a few cracks), and the scene in which Jesson's Coriolanus melts for the first and last time – there is no more moving silence in the canon than the moment when he gives in, and it's well done here – is impressively affecting. What more could you want? (Possibly not the slightly bizarre brass band music which punctuates the action.)

EDITIONS

Arden Shakespeare
Peter Holland (ed.); 2013 > Bloomsbury

Arden Shakespeare editions keep getting fatter – good news for readers, if bad news for our wrists. This latest leviathan (503 pages), edited by Peter Holland, is one of the finest of the new bunch. Holland begins, unusually, with the story of *Coriolanus* in the 1930s and uses contrasting interpretations of the play that surfaced during that strange, tense period (militaristic,

poetic, anti-fascist) to draw out many different shades of interpretation over the play's broader history. His expertise is in performance history, so there's generous coverage of its life on stage (with a helpful table of key performances in appendix), and the text is rendered cleanly.

SOME CRITICISM

Disowning Knowledge
Stanley Cavell; rev. 2003 > Cambridge UP

Disowning Knowledge in Six Plays of Shakespeare has classic status – and indeed has been updated with a new essay on *Macbeth*, taking the count up to seven. This book takes as its premise the notion that the philosophical scepticism manifest in the philosophy of the French thinker René Descartes receives some of its most intriguing exposition in Shakespeare. This leads Cavell into a brilliant development of what he terms the "sceptical problematic", touching *Hamlet*, *Lear*, *Othello* and *The Winter's Tale*. In *Coriolanus* Cavell argues that scepticism about politics is integral to the play, and that its multiple images of feeding and starvation present a Rome suffering from a "famine of words". Cavell can be a hard critic to live with – he is a philosopher by trade – and he makes few concessions to readerly comfort, but *Disowning Knowledge* is very much worth the effort.

Suffocating Mothers
Janet Adelman; 1992 > Routledge

Janet Adelman's criticism is consistently engaging and challenging, rarely more so than in *Suffocating Mothers: Fantasies of maternal origin in Shakespeare's plays, "Hamlet" to "The Tempest"*. As her title implies, Adelman is deeply committed to psychoanalytic readings of these plays, stimulated by her observation that in his last dramatic works Shakespeare creates a series of powerful (and, yes, suffocating) mothers, figures who have been all but absent since his early work. *Coriolanus* is very much the seedbed for Adelman's thesis, and in fact her brilliant piece on the hero's troubled masculine identity – one constructed in famously close symbiosis with his mother – dates all the way back to 1975, nearly twenty years before the book finally made it into print.

Cymbeline

No one is quite sure why *Cymbeline*, one of Shakespeare's final comedies, was included in the list of "Tragedies" in the First Folio, but if this was a mistake it was fortuitous. Everyone who has written about – or seen – the play notices its haunting, bittersweet qualities, perhaps more truly tragicomic than anything else Shakespeare wrote. And though its historical background is esoteric and its plot famously labyrinthine – the playwright drew upon a hotchpotch of sources, something that irritated Samuel Johnson among others – in the right hands *Cymbeline* can be intensely moving as well as theatrically persuasive. The flurry of breathtaking revelations that brings this late comedy to an end reflects the Jacobean vogue for intricate plotting (the play was put together in 1610 or 1611), but also demonstrates Shakespeare using the improvisatory qualities of his art more freely and brilliantly than ever before.

DATE > The play was seen by Simon Forman (an astrologer who witnessed early performances of several of Shakespeare's works), and it was certainly on the stage before September 1611. It was probably finished by autumn 1610 – shortly before *The Tempest*.

SOURCES > The play's historical substance, concerning Cunobelinus (Cymbeline), derives from Holinshed's *Chronicles*, the major source for his English history plays; other details of *Cymbeline*'s notably knotty plot derive from Boccaccio's *Decameron* (1353) and the anonymous play *The Rare Triumphs of Love and Fortune* (1589).

TEXTS > The Folio of 1623 provides the sole authoritative text. It describes the heroine as "Imogen", but this is probably a misprint; the Oxford *Complete Works* (which this book follows) prefers "Innogen".

Interpreting the play

A terse entry in Holinshed's *Chronicles* describing the reign of "Kymbeline" seems to have caught Shakespeare's attention. At first glance it is difficult to see why: Cunobelinus (Cymbeline) was an obscure British king who ruled over much of southern England at around the time Augustus Caesar was putting the finishing touches to his Pax Romana. As Holinshed tells it, the most remarkable event to happen during Cunobelinus's reign was entirely unconnected to it: the birth of Christ.

But then Shakespeare's play, though historical, is very little about history. Pushing the tussles between the British and the Romans largely to one side, at least until the final act, the playwright places in the spotlight a very human story: the trials and tribulations of the heroine Innogen (or Imogen, as she is spelt in the First Folio and elsewhere) and her new husband Posthumus Leonatus. In this patchwork of a play, the

MAJOR CHARACTERS & SYNOPSIS

Cymbeline, King of Britain
Princess Innogen, Cymbeline's daughter (later disguised as **Fidele**)
Posthumus Leonatus, Innogen's husband, a poor gentleman
Queen, Cymbeline's second wife and Innogen's stepmother
Lord Cloten, the Queen's son by a former husband, Innogen's suitor
Pisanio, Posthumus's servant
Cornelius, a doctor
Helen, a lady attending Innogen
Two **Lords** attending Cloten
Belarius, a banished British lord (going under the name of **Morgan**)
Guiderius (known as **Polydore**) and **Arviragus** (**Cadwal**), Cymbeline's sons, stolen by Belarius
Filario, Posthumus's host in Rome
Giacomo, an Italian friend of Posthumus
Posthumus's other friends: a **Frenchman,** a **Dutchman** and a **Spaniard**
Caius Lucius, a Roman ambassador, later general of the Roman army
Various Romans: **Senators**, **Tribunes** and a **Captain**
Philharmonus, a soothsayer
Apparitions: **Jupiter**, King of the gods; **Sicilius Leonatus**, Posthumus's father; Posthumus's **Mother**; Posthumus's two **Brothers**

ACT 1 By marrying Posthumus, Innogen has dismayed her father and angered her stepmother, who wanted her son, the doltish Cloten, to marry her. Posthumus is banished and heads for Rome, after exchanging tokens and vows of fidelity with Innogen. Abroad, Posthumus and his friends debate the relative chastity of their countrywomen, and Giacomo wagers Posthumus that he can seduce his wife. Arriving in Britain, Giacomo finds his attempts resisted by Innogen. The Queen, meanwhile, has obtained what she thinks is poison from the doctor, which she presents as a gift to Pisanio, persuading him it is a life-restoring medicine.

ACT 2 Determined to win his bet, Giacomo asks Innogen to safeguard a large trunk, which he hides in, emerging as she sleeps and stealing her bracelet. Returning to Rome, he presents it to Posthumus as proof that she has slept with him.

ACT 3 In Britain, Cymbeline has refused to pay the annual tribute to Rome; the Roman ambassador Lucius responds by declaring war. Meanwhile, Pisanio has received a letter from his master telling him to kill Innogen, but informs her instead. Horrified, she begs him to go through with it, but he persuades her to disguise herself as a man and travel to Rome with Lucius. In the Welsh countryside, Belarius is out with his two sons (actually Cymbeline's sons, stolen in infancy to avenge Belarius's banishment) when a hungry Innogen/Fidele appears. At court, her absence has been noticed, and Cloten decides to hunt her down.

ACT 4 While out hunting, Belarius and his "sons" meet Cloten and kill him after he challenges them. Innogen, feeling unwell, takes the Queen's "medicine" given her by Pisanio, and falls into a death-like slumber. Assuming she is dead, Belarius's "sons" place her alongside Cloten's headless corpse. She awakens to what she thinks is her husband's body (Cloten is wearing Posthumus's clothes), and despairingly concludes that she has been betrayed. In the meantime, the Romans have invaded. Lucius comes across the mourning Innogen and takes her into his service.

ACT 5 Persuaded that Innogen is dead, Posthumus repents and joins the British side; disguised as a peasant, he saves Giacomo (who fails to recognize him). Belarius and his "sons" rescue Cymbeline and reverse a British defeat. But Posthumus wishes to die, and dresses as a Roman before being captured. In prison, he has a vision of his dead family, and of the god Jupiter, who leaves a mysterious message. With the British victorious, Belarius and others are rewarded by the King. After news arrives that the Queen is dead and her evil exposed, Lucius, Innogen/Fidele, Giacomo and Posthumus are brought in as prisoners. Seeing Giacomo, Innogen asks about his ring and he reveals that he cheated Posthumus out of it. Pisanio then recognizes Innogen, before Belarius reveals his own identity and those of Cymbeline's sons. Embracing them, Cymbeline decides to resume the payment of Roman tribute as Jupiter's words, prophesying peace, are decoded.

story has more twists and turns than anyone in the audience could reasonably expect. After Posthumus becomes convinced that Innogen has been unfaithful to him, she runs away in disguise to the forests of Wales, where she undergoes a bizarre series of mishaps: first falling into a death-like slumber when she drinks a magic potion by mistake, then waking to discover a headless corpse wearing her husband's clothes. While in the country, she has been taken in by kindly hunters, who are in fact – though none of them yet knows it – her own brothers, stolen years earlier by a disgruntled courtier and raised in ignorance of their royal blood. The truth eventually outs when all (Posthumus included) are drawn back to Cymbeline's court. Shakespeare contrives a jaw-dropping finale in which a captivating sequence of revelations and reunions are plucked, hair-breadth, from disaster.

I'th' eye

Not for nothing has the play frequently been compared to fairy tales such as *Snow-White* and *Goldilocks*, and indeed Cymbeline's cackling Queen (she has no other name) has more than a whiff of Wicked Stepmother about her. Angling for her moronic son Cloten to seize her stepdaughter from the "poor but worthy" Leonatus, she tries to persuade Innogen that "you shall not find me, daughter, / After the slander of most stepmothers, / Evil-eyed" (1.1.71–3). But Innogen, the doctor Cornelius and the audience know that to be false. "I do not like her," Cornelius mutters just out of earshot,

> She doth think she has
> Strange ling'ring poisons. I do know her spirit,
> And will not trust one of her malice with
> A drug of such damned nature.
>
> [1.5.33–6]

With "poisonous compounds" the Queen intends to murder Innogen and her husband's servant Pisanio, but she is (for the moment) foiled: the "drugs" Cornelius supplies merely tranquillize, not kill. This cheerful resistance to evil seems built into the plot: though the King is furious that his daughter has flouted his wishes by marrying below her station, he has done little to prevent it. Likewise, Cloten is presented as too dim-witted to offer much of a threat. Cymbeline's stepson is simply "Too bad for bad report" (1.1.17), so hopeless as barely to be worth the effort of describing.

But these hard outlines between characters – the wicked queen and her idiot son, the virtuous daughter, the constant husband – begin to blur as soon as Posthumus is banished from Cymbeline's court. His departure does something to the play's optics, hinting that things will change and shift beyond all recognition. First to be deceived is Posthumus himself. No sooner has he arrived in Italy than his supposed friend Giacomo is goading him into betting on his "unparagoned" and absent wife's fidelity, a segment of the plot that takes its cue from Boccaccio's courtly compendium of tales, the *Decameron* (see p.5). Bragging that "strange fowl light upon neighbouring ponds" (1.4.87), Giacomo successfully persuades Posthumus that he will be able to seduce

In 1786 the publisher John Boydell planned an edition of Shakespeare to be illustrated by the leading artists of the day. This engraving, after a painting by Richard Westall, shows a scene from Act Three of *Cymbeline* – Innogen outside the cave of Belarius.

Innogen. Posthumus's sealing of the bargain strays into the kind of misogyny only too familiar from *The Winter's Tale*. "Only thus far you shall answer," he addresses his rival:

> If you make your voyage upon her and give me directly to understand
> you have prevailed, I am no further your enemy; she is not worth our
> debate.
>
> [1.4.154–7]

Fortunately, though, Innogen proves herself less easily misled than her husband – at least initially. When Giacomo arrives in Britain, attempting to sway Innogen with brazen flattery, his attempts fall on stony ground. Then he tries a nastier trick, hinting that Posthumus himself has been unfaithful to her. "Are men mad?" he wonders, apparently commenting on their inability to value beauty (and by extension Posthumus's insanity in abandoning his wife):

> It cannot be i'th' eye—for apes and monkeys,
> 'Twixt two such shes, would chatter this way and
> Contemn with mows the other; nor i'th' judgement,
> For idiots in this case of favour would
> Be wisely definite; nor i'th' appetite—
> Sluttery, to such neat excellence opposed,
> Should make desire vomit emptiness,
> Not so allured to feed.
>
> [1.6.40–7]

Giacomo is coldly calculating here, trying to perplex Innogen while also intimating that she has been betrayed. In this cruel trick language itself becomes twisted almost beyond recognition, with the thrust of Giacomo's words (that the "eye" of the absent Posthumus prefers the beauty of "shes" other than his own wife, even though "apes and monkeys" or "idiots" would make the right choice) all but disappearing behind sinister insinuation.

In the event, however, Innogen proves more resistant than Giacomo had hoped, so he switches tack once again, claiming merely to be testing whether her "affiance / Were deeply rooted" (1.6.164–5). Immediately persuaded, Innogen then makes the mistake of falling for the Italian's final ploy: agreeing to keep in her chamber a large trunk, supposedly containing a "present for the Emperor" but in fact harbouring Giacomo himself. As soon as she is asleep, he creeps out – the first of the play's many daring moments of visual staging. Reaching for her bracelet (a token from Posthumus), he exclaims gleefully that the happily married couple are both undone. "'Tis mine," he whispers,

> and this will witness outwardly,
> As strongly as the conscience does within,
> To th' madding of her lord. On her left breast
> A mole, cinque-spotted, like the crimson drops
> I'th' bottom of a cowslip. Here's a voucher

Stronger than ever law could make. This secret
Will force him think I have picked the lock and ta'en
The treasure of her honour.

[2.2.35–42]

This too-innocent visible evidence – not just the bracelet but the marks on Innogen's own body, voyeuristically noted down – will condemn her to Posthumus. It is difficult

KEY SOURCE > Spenser's *The Faerie Queene*

Although not many of Shakespeare's works make direct reference to **Edmund Spenser**, the playwright was undoubtedly influenced by the poetry of one of his most famous contemporaries – particularly Spenser's nationalistic verse epic *The Faerie Queene*.

Born in London around 1552, making him just over a decade older than Shakespeare, Spenser came from a similar background. His father was probably a cloth-maker, although Edmund liked to claim a connection with the aristocratic Spencers of Althorp (the same family from which Princess Diana was descended). After studying at Merchant Taylor's, one of the newly founded grammar schools (see p.561), Spenser went on to Cambridge, where he formed a close friendship with Gabriel Harvey, a fellow of Pembroke Hall and the young writer's earliest collaborator.

While still at university Spenser developed a reputation as a poet, before securing posts in various high-powered households, culminating in a friendship with the poet **Sir Philip Sidney** and a job serving Lord Grey of Wilton, Elizabeth I's representative in Ireland, who was tasked with subjugating the country to English rule and importing settlers. Spenser travelled out in 1580 and witnessed the implementation of Wilton's scorched-earth policies, which ranged from large-scale military intervention to ethnic cleansing – policies applauded in Spenser's *A View of the Present State of Ireland* (1596), a calculatedly brutal piece of political analysis arguing that the only way to defeat the Irish was to obliterate their language and culture. After nearly twenty years living at Kilcolman Castle in County Cork, a rebellion by Irish chieftains forced Spenser and his family to flee in 1598, and he returned to England a broken man. He died a year later.

Alongside his job as a colonial bureaucrat, Spenser maintained a busy career as a poet, composing complaints (see p.523) and several groups of pastoral poems, including *The Shepheardes Calender* (1579). But in every sense his life work was *The Faerie Queene*, a monumental, medieval-style epic centred on the adventures of a group of knights serving at an idealized version of Queen Elizabeth's court. Spenser completed only six of his projected twelve books, and despite its elaborate celebration of the monarch the poem never won its author the status (or the salary) he craved. Nonetheless *The Faerie Queene* stands as one of the greatest literary achievements of the Elizabethan era, as poetically inspired as it is often wilfully eccentric.

Spenser's influence on Shakespeare is difficult to pin down – at once elusive and pervasive. A few plays, notably *Much Ado*, *King Lear* and *Cymbeline*, draw plot details or character sketches from *The Faerie Queene*. *A Lover's Complaint* uses a poetic mode perfected by Spenser, and some of the Sonnets (notably 106) make clear reference to his work. And it is difficult not to feel that *As You Like It*, by some stretch Shakespeare's most pastoral and chivalric play, comes into sharper focus when filtered through the world view of this particular eminent Elizabethan, whose questing knights and elaborate verse style it playfully echoes.

not to think, as Shakespeare himself must have thought, back to the early poem *The Rape of Lucrece* and another guiltless heroine who is undone when a man forces himself into her private chamber.

Mortal joy

Posthumus's inability to trust his feelings rather than his eyes proves Innogen's downfall. It also introduces another strand of deceit in a play that braids them tightly together. Inventing for her a sequence of "faults" ("For even to vice," he rages, women "are not constant" (2.5.29–30)), he writes to her claiming his undying love while simultaneously arranging for his servant Pisanio to murder her in cold blood. But unlike his master, Pisanio is unable to lie – he is the closest the play has to a hero – and reveals the truth to Innogen. Hit hard, she responds in pain. "Come, fellow, be thou honest," she cries,

> Do thy master's bidding. When thou seest him,
> A little witness my obedience. Look,
> I draw the sword myself. Take it, and hit
> The innocent mansion of my love, my heart.
>
> [3.4.64–8]

Innogen's urgent wish for death does not prevail (Pisanio finds that he cannot go through with the suicide), and tragedy is for the moment averted, but Innogen opts to undergo a metaphorical death instead – "forgetting" her womanly identity and exchanging her clothes, like many a Shakespearian heroine before her, for those of a young man, in order to flee to Wales. The touching pseudonym she chooses, "Fidele", means "the faithful one".

Yet death proves difficult to charm away, and before long makes its presence more insistent. After reaching Wales, Innogen comes across, then is adopted by, a group of men living wild in the forest yet – like Duke Senior and his companions in *As You Like It* – who possess all the dignity of gentlemen. The two youths, Guiderius and Arviragus, bristle with what are described as "sparks of nature" (3.3.79), but neither is aware of their royal identity. This deception also entangles Innogen – herself in disguise, she has no idea that they are her brothers – and the confusion only intensifies when, feeling unwell, she takes the draught that Pisanio had been given by her evil stepmother earlier in the play. In a nightmarish echo of her previous slumber, she immediately falls into a death-like sleep, and Guiderius and Arviragus are left to conclude, sorrowfully, that their new-found companion has died. They address her silent body with one of Shakespeare's simplest but most moving lyrics. "Fear no more the heat o'th' sun," Guiderius sings,

> Nor the furious winter's rages.
> Thou thy worldly task hast done,
>   Home art gone and ta'en thy wages.
> Golden lads and girls all must,
> As chimney-sweepers, come to dust.
>
> [4.2.259–64]

In Act V of Cymbeline there is a Vision, a Masque, and a Prophecy, which interrupt the Fable without the least necessity, and unmeasurably lengthen this act. I think it plainly foisted in afterwards for mere show, and apparently not of Shakespeare.

Alexander Pope, *Works of William Shakespeare* (1725)

Yet of course Innogen/Fidele still has much of her "worldly task" to do, and the deathly stillness that her brothers invoke is yet, fortunately, far in the distance.

Though she turns out to be alive, Innogen – with a distant husband still convinced that she has betrayed him – has not been granted peace of mind, still less come "home". The sight that greets her when she awakes, that of a blood-spattered, headless trunk wearing her husband's clothes, could barely be more horrible, and makes a ghastly mockery of her desire to be reunited with him. "But soft, no bedfellow!", she starts, lifting the funeral garlands laid by Guiderius and Arviragus from her body,

> These flowers are like the pleasures of the world,
> This bloody man the care on't. I hope I dream,
> For so I thought I was a cavekeeper,
> And cook to honest creatures. But 'tis not so.
> 'Twas but a bolt of nothing, shot of nothing,
> Which the brain makes of fumes. Our very eyes
> Are sometimes like our judgements, blind. Good faith,
> I tremble still with fear; but if there be
> Yet left in heaven as small a drop of pity
> As a wren's eye, feared gods, a part of it!
> The dream's here still. Even when I wake it is
> Without me as within me; not imagined, felt.

> [4.2.297–309]

Touching the body, Innogen "feels" what she fears: that it is Posthumus lying next to her. Shakespeare condenses an almost untenable mixture of emotions into one theatrical moment. Cloten had dressed in Posthumus's clothes in order to rape her, but, challenging Guiderius to a fight, met an aptly ignoble end. Now Innogen "dreams" (and she will believe it until the play's final few minutes) that the body next to her is her husband's. Stroking his leg, his hand, then grotesquely smearing herself with his blood, she is fooled – like Posthumus himself before her – by the evidence of her "very eyes", a mistaking that has been made all the more likely in performance by using the same actor to play both Posthumus and Cloten. Observing all this, Shakespeare's audiences may well feel – the piercing intensity of this instant makes the cliché seem worthwhile – that they don't know whether to laugh or cry.

As so often in these late romances, however, recognition is allowed to work itself out, albeit via more jackknifing of the plot. Having been discovered by Roman soldiers led by Lucius, Innogen invents a story that the body is her master's, "a very valiant Briton" (4.2.371), and begs to be taken into Roman service. Posthumus, meanwhile, has discovered Giacomo's treachery and announced his intention to be killed in battle. "I'll die / For thee, O Innogen," he swears, in an unknowing echo of her earlier suicide attempt,

> even for whom my life
> Is every breath a death; and, thus unknown,
> Pitied nor hated, to the face of peril
> Myself I'll dedicate.

[5.1.25–9]

In an apt image of *Cymbeline* itself, that "peril" brings Posthumus close to death but also, ultimately, to happiness. Captured by the British forces, he falls asleep in prison, and with breathtaking bravura Shakespeare dramatizes the vision that appears in his hero's sleep. As "solemn music" plays, the stage directions instruct:

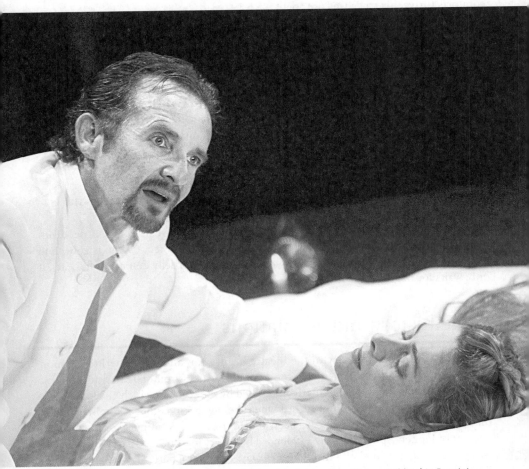

"'Tis mine ..." Giacomo (Anton Lesser) bends over the sleeping Innogen (Emma Fielding) in Dominic Cooke's 2003 RSC production.

Enter, as in an apparition, Sicilius Leonatus (father to Posthumus, an old man), attired like a warrior, leading in his hand an ancient matron, his wife, and mother to Posthumus, with music before them. Then, after other music, follows the two young Leonati, brothers to Posthumus, with wounds as they died in the wars. They circle Posthumus round as he lies sleeping

[5.5.123 SD]

These instructions – taken word for word from the Folio text – have given directors free rein to come up with some impressive theatrics, and from *Cymbeline*'s first days in the theatre the apparition will most likely have been spectacular. As Posthumus slumbers on, it becomes even more so: after his dead family complete their round of song, they call on the god Jupiter to reverse Posthumus's "miseries". And when Jupiter himself appears, he announces that "Your low-laid son our godhead will uplift. / His comforts thrive, his trials well are spent" (5.5.197–8).

Jupiter's words indicate that *Cymbeline* will end in joy rather than pain. Even so, it nearly fails to get there. Posthumus is on the point of being executed by the Britons when news arrives that he is to be freed and taken to Cymbeline's court instead. Innogen, meanwhile, is still in disguise; when she also arrives at court, it seems that the lovers will be reunited at last. But the grief-stricken Posthumus, thinking that Fidele scorns his sorrow, lashes out – and it is only when Pisanio exclaims, "O my lord Posthumus, / You ne'er killed Innogen till now" that anyone realizes what is going on. "Does the world go round?" exclaims Innogen's father, dumbstruck:

If this be so, the gods do mean to strike me
To death with mortal joy.

[5.6.232–5]

Fortunately the gods intend no such thing and, as *Cymbeline* comes to a close, death works finally in the service of good. The wicked Queen has died, Cloten is gone, and as Innogen comes round in her father's arms (a reunion cruelly denied King Lear), it only waits for her brothers to be revealed.

Stage history and adaptations

Records of *Cymbeline*'s history in the theatre begin soon after it was written. Simon Forman, doctor and astrologer, saw the play performed around 1610 and noted it down in his diary. He was particularly impressed by the scene in which Giacomo leaps out of the trunk, though did not record where he saw it – possibly at the **Blackfriars** theatre, where Shakespeare will have been able to use stage machinery for the magical descent of Jupiter. Aptly for a play influenced by Stuart masque (see p.629), *Cymbeline* was performed at **Whitehall** on New Year's Day, 1634, for Charles I, who approved of it despite its portrayal of a scheming, manipulative Queen – a charge often levelled at his wife, who pointedly didn't attend.

Cymbeline appears to have disappeared from the stage until 1682, when it surfaced in an adaptation by **Thomas D'Urfey** entitled *The Injured Princess, or The Fatal Wager*. To suit the taste of the age, D'Urfey made Innogen a purely passive victim while Posthumus kills the rakish Giacomo in revenge. Another adaptation by **William Hawkins** arrived in 1759, recast in neoclassical fashion, but Shakespeare's text had reappeared on stage back in 1746 and with **David Garrick** came once more into favour. After playing Posthumus first in 1761, Garrick came to specialize in the role, and his successor **John Philip Kemble** acted it from 1785 onwards. Kemble's Innogen was his formidable sister **Sarah Siddons**, marking a trend which would come to dominate the next era: the age of headlining heroines.

The American actress **Nancy Hallam** had scored great success as Innogen as early as the 1770s (her talent was captured in an impressive painting by Charles Willson Peele), but from 1837 the British **Helen Faucit** came to epitomize the role during the thirty-odd years she played it. Faucit's characterization was placid and virtuous (she was described by a Victorian commentator as "the purest and most womanly of Shakespeare's women ... who includes among her virtues aptitude for cookery") – too much so for some. **Adelaide Neilson**, who played Innogen in 1872, presented a more headstrong interpretation when she toured the role in the United States. By the time that the great **Ellen Terry** came to play the part in 1896, aged nearly 50, she had resolved to present a less angelic and more womanly heroine – a decision influenced by George Bernard Shaw, who corresponded with her throughout rehearsals. Nevertheless, according to Harley Granville-Barker, when Terry spoke, her voice "seemed to fill the Lyceum Theatre with dancing sunbeams". Her Giacomo was **Henry Irving**, the latest in a line of actors from **William Charles Macready** onwards to have seen star potential in the play's antihero rather than in Posthumus. Courtesy of the British Raj, *Cymbeline* became popular in India during the late nineteenth century, first translated into Bengali in 1868 and adapted in over twelve separate versions in subsequent decades. An all-male Marathi version called *Tara* was seen in **Vadodara** in 1880 by a visiting British academic, who suggested – with palpable surprise – that the staging "would have astonished Mr [Henry] Irving", particularly the performance of the "exquisitely girlish" boy playing Innogen.

Back in the UK, *Cymbeline* waned in popularity during the latter half of the nineteenth century and it would not be put on in a major British production until 1923, at **Barry Jackson**'s Birmingham Rep. Like his *Hamlet* two years later, this scandalized audiences by opting for modern dress, though **Cedric Hardwicke**'s Giacomo was universally loved by the critics. Innovation continued in 1937, with **Ben Iden Payne**'s Stratford production, which boasted sets based on Jacobean masques and gained good reviews. But it would be another two decades before *Cymbeline* appeared again in Shakespeare's birthplace, this time at the behest of the young **Peter Hall**, who teamed up with Italian painter **Lila de Nobili** to present a visually spectacular production in 1957 (and one that used an uncut text). Hall's Innogen was **Peggy Ashcroft**, both experienced in the role – she had played it at the Old Vic 25 years earlier – and then at the peak of her career.

Another Stratford production appeared in 1962 but its director, **William Gaskill**, eschewed Hall's fairytale setting for a set clothed entirely in white in which **Vanessa**

Redgrave played a typically impetuous Innogen. A similarly pared-down staging dominated **Jean Gascon**'s production eight years later at Stratford, Ontario.

Other directions have proved less successful: **John Barton**'s attempt to politicize *Cymbeline* at the RSC in 1974, drawing on British angst about the oil crisis and the EEC, flopped (Barton also attempted to readjust the play by introducing a narrator and cutting around a thousand lines). **Robin Phillips**'s decision to go for a 1940s-style staging at Stratford, Ontario in 1986 won points for novelty; while **Bill Alexander**'s production two years later gained from the intimacy of the RSC's The Other Place and had, in **Harriet Walter**, an Innogen of startling emotional immediacy. In fact 1988 proved something of a turning point for *Cymbeline*'s fortunes, with Alexander's production at Stratford running concurrently with a similarly small-scale version at the National Theatre, directed by **Peter Hall**. Hall's production, over thirty years since his first attempt on the play, focused on the tension between **Geraldine James**'s strong-willed Innogen and **Peter Woodward**'s powerful Giacomo. Although Hall opted to put his cast in Jacobean costume, the Cottesloe stage was dominated by a stylized zodiac from which Jupiter descended in full glory.

More recent versions have likewise stressed *Cymbeline*'s eclecticism. **JoAnne Akalaitis**'s production at New York's Newman Theatre in 1989 was inspired by surrealism, while closer to the present day **Bartlett Sher**'s 2001 staging, once more at The Other Place in Stratford, freely blended cowboys and samurai warriors. The 1997 RSC production, directed by **Adrian Noble** in an Oriental-ish setting, faced hostility for his decision to use a narrator to make sense of the plot, but his cast – which included **Damian Lewis**'s Posthumus, **Joanne Pearce**'s Innogen and **Edward Petherbridge**'s King – received praise. The Bankside Globe's fluid production from summer 2001, starkly staged in white by **Mike Alfreds**, attempted to find coherence in a play all too often criticized for lacking it and employed a cast of just six, among them **Mark Rylance**'s impressive Posthumus/Cloten/Cornelius. Another British production, directed at the RSC by **Dominic Cooke**, was acclaimed as one of the high points of the 2003 season: **Emma Fielding**'s Innogen, **Daniel Evans**'s Posthumus and **Anton Lesser**'s Giacomo shared plaudits for an emotionally rich account of the play. **Declan Donnellan**'s pared-down Cheek by Jowl troupe toured *Cymbeline* through Europe and the US for six months in 2007, winning ecstatic notices en route. **Jodie McNee**'s Innogen was praised for her freshness, while a touch of intriguing grotesquery was added by casting **Tom Hiddleston** as both Posthumus and Cloten.

The play still counts as a rarity on British stages, and is only marginally more popular on American ones. The RSC dutifully staged it as part of their 2006–07 Complete Works festival in a "freely adapted" version by Cornish troupe **Kneehigh**, which came under heavy fire for what the *Guardian* called its "coarsely reductive" rendering of the text. During the World Shakespeare Festival in 2012, the **South Sudan Theatre Company** brought a rollicking translation in Juba Arabic to the London Globe, which offered intriguing parallels between their fledgling nation's struggles with decades of conflict and the warring Britain of Shakespeare's play. Later that same year, the **American Shakespeare Center** in Staunton, Virgina, offered a fast-paced, loosely original-practices production at their replica Blackfriars Playhouse – a rare opportunity to see the play in a space resembling that in which it was originally performed.

In 2014 *Cymbeline* at last made it on to a movie lot, in a grittily contemporary collaboration between Michael Almereyda and Ethan Hawke, fourteen years after their successful *Hamlet*. Various TV versions also exist. The one generally regarded as the best, and a high-quality addition to the BBC/Time-Life series, was screened in 1982 under **Elijah Moshinsky's** direction; **Helen Mirren** and **Michael Pennington** played the lovers.

SCREEN

Cymbeline
H. Mirren, M. Pennington, R. Johnson; Elijah Moshinsky (dir.) UK, 1982 ❯ BBC `DVD`

Making sense of *Cymbeline*'s many locations – never mind its plot – is a hard task, and probably the most difficult thing for any TV version to bring off. In interior scenes the BBC does well to capture the play's sometimes claustrophobic atmosphere (particularly so at the elaborately Jacobean court of Cymbeline), and the moments at which it excels are also intimate in scale: Helen Mirren's quiet and touching Innogen reaches a moving climax in her awakening scene, grotesquely smearing Cloten's blood on her face. Other moments are less successful: the appearance of Michael Hordern's Jupiter to Michael Pennington's earnest Posthumus makes little attempt to astound, while the play's conclusion struggles to keep up the intensity – despite Richard Johnson's excellent Cymbeline.

Cymbeline
M. Jovovich, E. Hawke, E. Harris; Michael Almereyda (dir.) US, 2014 ❯ Koch / Lionsgate `DVD` 🔊

Perhaps it's fitting that the most eclectic play in the canon should receive one of the weirdest movie treatments in recent history, but even so – Michael Almereyda and Ethan Hawke's return to Shakespeare after their imaginative version of *Hamlet* (see p.000) is a strange and ungovernable beast. Cymbeline (a brooding Ed Harris) is a New York drugs kingpin, Innogen (a pre-*Fifty Shades* Dakota Johnson) his eye-rolling indie-kid daughter. Rome is the name of the local police force, and Posthumus (a hipster-ish Penn Badgley) ... well, Posthumus has a curious obsession with communicating via woodblock prints, for reasons left unclear. None of it is terrible, exactly – and in setting the rural scenes in a surprisingly frontier-like bit of upstate it finds a nicely American twang – but it feels like no one's heart is quite in it. Almereyda's direction is unusually slack, and the dangling plot threads (where is Posthumus being banished to *exactly*?) will leave you more confused than ever. Hawke does his best as an insinuating and ratlike Giacomo, but generally speaking this film is gruesome in the wrong ways.

AUDIO

Cymbeline
S. Thompson, B. Porter, J. Shepherd; Clive Brill (dir.) UK, 1998 ❯ Arkangel ◉ 🔊

One of the distinguishing features of this *Cymbeline* is that the cast speak wonderfully clearly – entirely necessary when the verse is as knotty as this. Sophie Thompson's steely Innogen especially shines, and although Ben Porter's Posthumus is slightly underpowered the scenes between them are effectively done. Stephen Mangan adds welcome comic detail as an impressively doltish Cloten, and Suzanne Bertish is delightful as his cackling mother. The final scene is (perhaps inevitably) baffling, however, and the "solemn music" of the play's masque – along with Jupiter's descent – has the unintended effect of provoking giggles rather than wonder.

EDITIONS

New Cambridge Shakespeare
Martin Butler (ed.); 2005 ❯ Cambridge UP

Confronting Dr Johnson's notorious charge that *Cymbeline*'s best bits were "obtained at the expense of much incongruity", Martin Butler delicately suggests that, rather, they "differ from those anticipated by readers trained to admire singularity of effect" – a tactful rebuke that typifies his lucid and insightful introduction. This edition is especially good on the folktale origins to the play, and has interesting things to say on Innogen's place within the context of Jacobean gender politics, awkwardly poised between demands for chaste wifeliness and fantasies about female physical sexuality. The notes do an excellent job with the play's complex syntax, and Butler's treatment of the stage history covers a great deal of ground.

SOME CRITICISM

Prefaces to Shakespeare
Harley Granville-Barker; 2 vols, 1946–47 >
B.T. Batsford / Princeton UP [o/p]

Granville-Barker's *Prefaces* to various Shakespeare plays were assembled over a 25-year period and distil a lifetime's thinking and theatrical practice. Heavily influenced by William Poel (see p.588), Granville-Barker was perhaps England's most inspirational pre-war director, responsible for a succession of revolutionary productions that changed the face of British theatre and redefined approaches to Shakespeare. The *Prefaces* began life as introductions to a multi-volume edition of the plays that subsequently foundered, and as a consequence they were published independently. They are all terrific pieces, sometimes eccentric but never dull, and despite their dated scholarly views they have an unerring habit of illuminating what the plays are really like to experience and stage. *Cymbeline* benefits from Granville-Barker's practical wisdom (particularly his advice on speaking the verse), but so do all the other plays he covers: *Hamlet, Lear, The Merchant, Antony and Cleopatra* (volume 1) and *Othello, Coriolanus, Romeo and Juliet, Julius Caesar* and *Love's Labour's Lost* (volume 2). The essays are also available in individual volumes, published by Nick Hern Books.

Shakespeare's Romances: Contemporary Critical Essays
Alison Thorne (ed.); 2002 > Palgrave Macmillan

A good snapshot of recentish approaches to the late plays is included in Alison Thorne's anthology, which brings together scattered pieces published in the 1990s and 2000s from a variety of scholars. Kiernan Ryan offers a thoughtful, Marxist-influenced analysis of what the concept of "romance" might have meant to Shakespeare (even if, as he points out, it's a word the poet never himself used), after which the plays get two essays apiece. Ruth Nevo offers an absorbing post-Freudian account of King Cymbeline's unresolved feelings for his daughter, while Jodi Mikalachki probes the historical context of the play's interest in emerging British nationalism. Jyotsna Singh on the race and gender conflicts in postcolonial versions of *The Tempest* is also very much worth consulting.

Edward III

Excluded by Shakespeare's colleagues from the 1623 First Folio, *Edward III* has led a shadowy life for the past four centuries, regarded with suspicion by scholars and rarely – in fact almost never – performed. It's only in the past couple of decades that editors have accepted that Shakespeare had anything to do with the play, and even now most believe that he wrote only a handful of scenes. Even so, *Edward III* rewards attention. Likely to have been written in the early 1590s, it forms an intriguing addendum to the cycle of history dramas the young playwright was developing at the time, employing the no-frills dramatic style of *Henry VI Part I* to narrate the story of Richard II's father and grandfather as they attempt to capture France. Seen simply in its own terms, the tragedy also stands up to scrutiny. Its portrait of a king whose moral flaws are only too obvious raises troubling questions about the ethics of power, while its interest in the relationship between father and son touches one of Shakespeare's most resonant themes. And by counterpointing a series of illustrious English victories with graphic depictions of war's brutality – nearly all of it visited on the long-suffering French – the play clearly prepares the ground for *Henry V*.

DATE > Published in 1596 but definitely in existence a year earlier, *Edward III* was written in 1592–93, perhaps during one of the periods when London theatres were closed by plague.

SOURCES > An early Tudor translation of the fourteenth-century *Chroniques* by French historian Jean Froissart is the play's main source, though other details derive from Holinshed's *Chronicles*. The anonymous *Famous Victories of Henry V* (c. 1580s), also a key source for Shakespeare's *Henry V*, may have provided a cue, as might documentary reports of the Spanish Armada in 1588.

TEXTS > The first quarto (Q1), printed in 1596 and republished in a corrected version three years later (Q2), is the only surviving text. *Edward III* did not feature in the 1623 First Folio – taken by some to mean that Shakespeare had no involvement with it (see p.84).

Interpreting the play

Early on in *Richard II*, John of Gaunt, Richard's elderly uncle, decides that it falls to him to confront the King about his failings as a ruler. As Richard and his entourage sweep in, Gaunt launches into a scathing denunciation of everything that his nephew stands for. "Thou liest in reputation sick," he warns. "A thousand flatterers sit within thy crown, / Whose compass is no bigger than thy head." He goes on:

> O, had thy grandsire with a prophet's eye
> Seen how his son's son should destroy his sons,

MAJOR CHARACTERS & SYNOPSIS

THE ENGLISH AND THEIR ALLIES

King Edward III of England
Queen Philippa, Edward's wife
Edward, Prince of Wales, their eldest son
(historically known as the "Black Prince")
Earl of Salisbury and his wife, the **Countess of Salisbury**
Earl of Warwick, the Countess of Salisbury's father
Sir William de Montague, Salisbury's nephew
Other nobles: **Earl of Derby**, **Lord Audley**, **Lord Percy**
John Copland, an esquire (later knighted)
Lodowick, King Edward's secretary
Robert, Count of Artois and Earl of Richmond
Jean, Count of Montfort (later **Duc de Bretagne**)
Gobin de Grâce, a French prisoner

THE FRENCH AND THEIR ALLIES

King Jean II of France
Prince Charles, Jean's eldest son, the dauphin
Prince Philippe, Jean's youngest son
Duke of Lorraine
Villiers, a Norman lord and envoy
Six Poor Men and six wealthy **Citizens,** all from Calais, and a **Woman** with **two children**
King of Bohemia
Polish Captain
King David II of Scotland
Sir William Douglas

This synopsis retains traditional act divisions, but follows the scene numbering of the Oxford Complete Works

SCENES 1–2 At the English court King Edward is discussing, with the renegade French Count of Artois, his claim to the French throne. When Lorraine enters with a message from the French King demanding fealty, Edward refuses and war looms. In the north, meanwhile, Roxborough castle is under siege from Scottish forces, and the Countess of Salisbury, whose husband is in France, is a virtual prisoner. News of the imminent arrival of the English prompts the Scots to flee. When Edward arrives, the grateful Countess invites the King to stay. Aroused by her beauty, he accepts.

SCENES 3–4 The next morning, as Edward is composing a love letter to the Countess, she

enters. When the King declares his love, she reminds him they are both married. Unabashed, he tricks her father into acting as his go-between. The arrival of his son pricks Edward's conscience, but he is only brought to his senses when the Countess strikes a grim bargain with him.

SCENES 5–8 The English defeat the French at sea. On land, the Black Prince is also victorious, pardoning the French soldiers who surrender but killing those who do not. After withdrawing his army to Crécy, King John meets with Edward and tries to buy him off. Edward demands the crown but John refuses to resign it and battle recommences. Amid the confusion, word arrives that the Prince is surrounded, but Edward declines to send help, trusting his son to prove himself. The Prince enters in triumph and is knighted by his father. Having won the day, Edward sets out to besiege Calais while the Prince pursues King John.

SCENES 9–17 Salisbury offers the captured Villiers his freedom in exchange for safe passage to Calais. Outside Calais, Edward plans to starve the city into surrender. When six of its poorest citizens are expelled, he shows them mercy, but when the city falls, Edward demands obeisance from six rich merchants. Meanwhile, John and his son Charles discuss a strange prophecy which they believe is favourable. In danger again, the Black Prince spurns offers of mercy and, when the French army begins to panic at strange portents, seizes the advantage. Captured by the French, Salisbury is to be executed until Charles argues for his release. Triumphant, and with King John as his prisoner, the Black Prince prepares to join his father.

SCENE 18 Edward is on the point of entering Calais and executing its inhabitants when six merchants plead for mercy. The King agrees to spare the city but is about to kill the merchants when his wife intercedes for them. Salisbury then arrives and informs the King that the Black Prince has been killed at Crécy, but as Edward prepares to be revenged, a herald brings news that the Prince is alive and has captured King John and his son. With the arrival of the Prince and his prisoners, the victory is complete.

From forth thy reach he would have laid thy shame,
Deposing thee before thou wert possessed,
Which art possessed now to depose thyself.

[2.1.96–108]

Of all the insults that Gaunt can sling, it is the reference to Richard's "grandsire", King Edward III, that is most calculated to wound. Edward was feted by late medieval and Tudor historians as the greatest of warriors, one of the most successful English monarchs ever to have lived. He seized the throne from his mother and her lover in 1337, the same year that he launched a campaign for the French throne, and battled doggedly to establish English power there, winning stunning victories and doing much to restore the country's confidence following the calamitous reign of Edward II (with whom Richard II was often compared). The chronicler Jean Froissart, whose works were translated into English early in the sixteenth century, met Edward and claimed that "his like had not been seen since the days of King Arthur". Shakespeare's Richard is only too aware of this and cannot abide his uncle's allusion. A few moments later he turns on Gaunt, condemning him as a "lunatic, lean-witted fool" for daring to lecture him on "great Edward" (2.1.116–22).

Soon begun

Many scholars now agree that a few years before turning his mind to *Richard II*, Shakespeare somehow got involved in writing a collaborative play on Edward III himself, travelling back past the exhausting, messy Wars of the Roses and narrating the exploits of England's greatest warrior king. No one is quite sure how the project developed, still less who Shakespeare's collaborators were (see p.84), but what seems clear is that the dramatic style perfected by other history plays of the period – fast-paced, boisterous, rousing and often very funny – obviously influences *Edward III* itself, which compresses the major events of Edward's fifty-year reign into just eighteen action-packed scenes. The action rapidly covers the origins of the Hundred Years' War and touches on England's ongoing strife with Scotland, whistles through the great military victories at Sluys and Crécy, and ends in another triumph at Poitiers. By the play's end the French are left cowering in defeat, while Edward's son, the so-called "Black Prince" (Richard II's father), has decisively won his spurs.

The play opens at the English court in scenes that unmistakably foreshadow Shakespeare's *Henry V*. Edward is debating his claim to rule over France when the Duke of Lorraine arrives as an ambassador from the enemy, demanding that Edward renounce his territorial ambitions. "Repair to France within these forty days," Lorraine loftily instructs, to which the English king offers a characteristically gung-ho response. "See how occasion laughs me in the face," he chuckles:

No sooner minded to prepare for France,
But straight I am invited—nay, with threats,
Upon a penalty, enjoined to come!

[Sc. 1, 67–70]

Edward III – playwriting by committee?

Not even the most evangelical scholars claim that Shakespeare alone was responsible for a drama that is more unevenly written than any of his canonical works. Most accept that he is behind a maximum of three or four scenes, and was perhaps called in as a specialist to provide certain dramatic effects while other writers handled other sections and laid out the plot.

Because Renaissance theatre companies, not playwrights, generally retained control over what happened to a text (the concept of intellectual property was still emerging), freelancers were often paid to adapt, revise or otherwise tinker with someone else's script, as in the film or TV industries today. We assume that Shakespeare worked in this way several times in his career, and indeed polishing and revising old scripts is perhaps how he got started as a writer. That he continued to do so even after becoming established is attested by the collaborative play **Sir Thomas More**, whose troublesome genesis illustrates how convoluted such projects could be. The play, which survives as a manuscript in the British Library, was authored mainly by Anthony Munday and Henry Chettle in the early 1590s, but hit problems with the censor and was left untouched for more than a decade. It appears to have been taken up again in the early 1600s, with Shakespeare and two other writers employed to make additions – Shakespeare contributed just 164 lines – but appears nonetheless never to have made it on stage. It is remarkable chiefly for being the only surviving sample of Shakespeare's handwriting on a playscript (see p.190).

Edward III, too, might well have offered Shakespeare an opportunity to flex his poetic muscles while other writers handled more humdrum parts of the action. Aided by so-called **stylometric analysis** (which compares features such as spelling and word usage with other texts to help ascertain authorship), scholars think that Shakespeare most likely composed scenes 2 and 3, those in which Edward attempts to seduce the Countess of Warwick – a less violent replay of *Lucrece*, which he was in the middle of writing at this time – and perhaps also scenes 12 and 13, where the speculative battlefield philosophy offered by the Black Prince seems to foreshadow *Hamlet*. The texture of the writing is noticeably different at these points, richer and more lyrical, as befits someone in the midst of planning *Richard II* (?1595), likewise a history drama full of surprising poetic touches.

Yet, assuming Shakespeare did write parts of *Edward III*, editors have yet to settle on who his collaborators were. **George Peele**, who may have worked with Shakespeare on *Titus Andronicus*, is supposed by some to have been involved, while for others **Thomas Kyd**, author of *The Spanish Tragedy*, is a more likely candidate. The mystery remains.

The joke is a good one, and delivered with the bullish energy that characterizes the play's first scene and a half. Events happen at a similarly cracking pace: Edward and Lorraine are soon at each other's throats, swords drawn, and hostilities are officially declared. "Our gage is thrown, and war is soon begun," Edward aptly remarks (Sc.1, 119). And no sooner has news arrived of problems on the Scottish front than Edward seizes control, ordering his army to be mobilized in defence of Roxborough Castle and promising to lead them to victory in person.

Almost as soon as it begins, though, the play's attention swerves away from military matters. With the Scots fleeing as the English approach, the focus turns to Edward himself. Resident at the castle is the beautiful Countess of Salisbury, whose husband is away fighting in France and whose gratitude at being rescued affects Edward in ways that will become fateful. As he sets eyes on the Countess, it is clearly love at first sight:

KING EDWARD
    This is the Countess, Warwick, is it not?
EARL OF WARWICK
    Even she, my liege, whose beauty tyrants' fear—
    As a May blossom with pernicious winds—
    Hath sullied, withered, overcast and done.
KING EDWARD
    Hath she been fairer, Warwick, than she is?
EARL OF WARWICK
    My gracious King, fair is she not at all
    If that her self were by to stain herself
    As I have seen her when she was her self.

[Sc. 2, 94–101]

The abrupt change of gear apparent in Warwick's reply – which plays dazzling games with the word "herself" to imply that captivity has taken its toll on his daughter's beauty – has been taken by scholars to indicate that a different hand, presumably Shakespeare's, wrote this section of the play. To an extent it doesn't matter: whoever wrote these lines clearly intended to make their audience listen in a new way, and perhaps more attentively, than before.

What follows next is indeed riveting, for it shows a disturbing and unexpected side to the hero. Immediately smitten, the King abandons all thoughts of military action and instead lays siege to the Countess, despite the fact that she has a husband and he a wife. Following the approach adopted by many a Shakespearian lover, he employs an underling, Lodowick, to help him compose love letters in her praise. "Forget not to set down how passionate, / How heart-sick and how full of languishment / Her beauty makes me," Edward sighs to Lodowick, who pretends not to get the point:

LODOWICK   Write I to a woman?
KING EDWARD
    What beauty else could triumph over me,
    Or who but women to our love-lays greet?
    What think'st thou I did bid thee praise? A horse?

[Sc. 2, 259–64]

Again the joke is nicely timed, but Lodowick's reluctance to play along illuminates a seamier aspect to Edward's actions, which are of course shamelessly corrupt as well as politically suspect. For her part the Countess is equally adamant, though her polite refusals to submit have little effect, so much so that Edward soon forces the horror-struck Warwick to pimp his own daughter and convince her to go to bed with him.

In every way *Edward III*'s most complete recent production, Anthony Clark's 2003 version for the RSC hinged on a power struggle between David Rintoul's King (seated) and Jamie Glover's Black Prince (left).

The episodes between the King and the Countess have proved popular on stage – and have sometimes been performed in isolation from the rest of the play – but for all their dramatic appeal these are far from light-hearted wooing scenes. Ground down, the Countess finds no option but to offer an unappealing bargain: she will relent only on the condition that he murder both their partners first. Astonishingly, he agrees:

KING EDWARD
>   Thy beauty makes them guilty of their death,
>   And gives in evidence that they shall die—
>   Upon which verdict I, their judge, condemn them.

COUNTESS OF SALISBURY
>   O, perjured beauty! More corrupted judge!
>   When to the great star-chamber o'er our heads
>   The universal sessions calls to 'count
>   This packing evil, we both shall tremble for it.

[Sc. 3, 157–63]

If Shakespeare did write these scenes, he was probably also in the midst of working on *Lucrece*, which tells the story of a Roman woman raped by a friend of her husband, and perhaps had recently finished *Richard III*, in which another English king has his way with a recently widowed woman. Furthermore, Warwick's description of how "lilies that fester smell far worse than weeds" (Sc. 2, 619) is an apt description of Edward's fall from grace, but is also a line used in Shakespeare's Sonnet 94, a meditation on power and its moral obligations.

Fortunately, however, in *Edward III* tragedy is averted when the King – not before time – staggers to his senses at the sight of the Countess kneeling before him and is overwhelmed by guilt. "Even by that power I swear, that gives me now / The power to be ashamèd of myself," he cries:

> I never mean to part my lips again
> In any words that tends to such a suit.
> Arise, true English lady, whom our isle
> May better boast of than ever Roman might
> Of her, whose ransacked treasury hath tasked
> The vain endeavour of so many pens.
>
> [Sc. 3, 186–93]

If Shakespeare wasn't responsible for these scenes, the reference to "so many pens" scribbling away about the Romans' Lucrece suggests that someone at least knew his work. If he was, these lines sound rather like an advert for his own poem.

Like victories

Somewhat ironically, as soon as Edward III regains control of himself and his passions, uttering a few perfunctory commands towards his officers with respect to the French, he disappears from view. The next scenes of the play switch to the French side and cover the sea battle between the two nations off Sluys in the present-day Netherlands, a battle in which the French navy was almost totally destroyed. Given the near impossibility of staging naval conflict on the scenery-free Elizabethan stage, the dramatists concentrate instead on the political machinations during the build-up to war, then the immediate aftermath. The play's eyewitness reports, which rely heavily on those of contemporary chroniclers, are particularly striking, bringing to life action that could never be compassed on stage. A French mariner reports the outcome of the battle in lurid terms:

> Purple the sea whose channel filled as fast
> With streaming gore that from the maimèd fell,
> As did her gushing moisture break into
> The cranny cleftures of the through-shot planks.
> Here flew a head dissevered from the trunk;
> There mangled arms and legs were tossed aloft,
> As when a whirlwind takes the summer dust
> And scatters it in middle of the air.
>
> [Sc. 4, 161–8]

As an account of a medieval sea battle – some 20,000 sailors were killed at Sluys – this is remarkably chilling, not least because it isn't clear to which side, English or French, all those heads, arms and legs lost in the chaos actually belong. And in the following scene we hear not from the victorious English, but from ordinary French refugees as they flee in terror. "'Tis good to fear the worst," says one panicked man (Sc. 5, 29), movingly described in the stage directions as "without baggage". In fact *Edward III*, like Shakespeare's *Henry V*, spends a striking amount of time focusing not on the spoils of war, but on its immense costs. As the two armies count their dead, the French King appears in front of Edward and the Black Prince offering to buy them off, accusing the conquering forces of little more than theft. "Yet in respect thy thirst is all for gold," he spits,

> Thy labour rather to be feared than loved,
> To satisfy thy lust, in either part,
> Here am I come and with me have I brought
> Exceeding store of treasure, pearl and coin.
> Leave, therefore, now to persecute the weak,
> And armèd ent'ring conflict with the armed,
> Let it be seen, 'mongst other petty thefts,
> How thou canst win this pillage manfully.

[Sc. 6, 62–70]

Although the English naturally deny the charge, the dramatic effect is unexpected, rendering them not as brave conquerors but as greedy, lustful tyrants. The parallel with Edward's assault on the unarmed Countess is underlined a few moments later when the French King accuses his opposite number of being "a belly-god, / A tender and lascivious wantonness, / That th'other day was almost dead for love," drawing a clear line between Edward's would-be extramarital affair and his martial ambitions (Sc. 6, 154–6). Edward is obviously stung, declaring to his officers immediately afterwards that they must either "clear us of that scandalous crime, / Or be entombèd in our innocence," which – somewhat unappealingly – sounds rather like an offer to make everyone else pay for his misdeeds (169–70).

The lingering memory of Edward's behaviour colours, too, the ensuing battle scene at Crécy, which is carefully set up as young Prince Edward's opportunity to redeem his – and by implication his father's – reputation. It isn't long before the French are on the run, but news filters through to the English that the Black Prince is in trouble, "beset / With turning Frenchmen" (Sc. 8, 13–14) and urgently in need of aid. But King Edward steadfastly refuses to send any assistance, insisting instead that the Prince prove his honour alone. "The Prince, my lord, the Prince!" exclaims the Earl of Derby. "He's close compassed with a world of odds." But Edward's reply is chillingly offhand:

> Then will he win a world of honour too
> If he by valour can redeem him thence.
> If not, what remedy? We have more sons
> Than one to comfort our declining age.

[Sc. 8, 19–24]

Though it is perfectly possible to play Edward's words as those of a worried father unwilling to admit his anxiety, the script makes this hard. And when the Prince does in the end appear safely, his father returns to the worry about his own reputation that has been nagging him all along. "Now, Jean of France," he says grimly as he congratulates his son, "I hope / Thou know'st King Edward for no wantonness, / No love-sick cockney" (Sc. 8, 99–102).

If anything, *Edward III*'s concluding phase seems to ingrain the divide between father and child still more deeply. As the play readies itself for the final contest between the French and the English, the Prince is dispatched to Poitiers to lead his troops into battle, while King Edward takes on the job of besieging Calais. In uniting these two events – in reality they occurred a decade apart – the playwrights clearly want their audience to pay attention to the contrasting approaches of these two soldiers, young and old, and in ways that are not entirely flattering to the monarch. While Prince Edward is off in the midst of war, fighting the French all but single-handedly, his father elects to play politics with the citizens of a starving town. Yet again, the suffering of civilians is put centre stage, as six poor Frenchmen, tenderly described as "patterns of despair and woe" by one of the English commanders (Sc. 10, 12), appear in order to beg mercy – a request which Edward initially affects to refuse. "We are your enemies," he taunts them:

> in such a case
> We can no less but put ye to the sword,
> Since, when we proffered truce, it was refused.
>
> [Sc. 10, 24–6]

And even though Edward changes his mind just moments later, offering to feed the famished citizens as well as pay them off, it is made clear that the gesture is entirely pragmatic. "The lion scorns to touch the yielding prey," the King loftily declares as they creep off. "And Edward's sword must fresh itself in such / As wilful stubbornness hath made perverse" (Sc. 10, 33–5).

The fact is, of course, that Edward's sword remains firmly in his scabbard, even as his son is facing mortal danger at Poitiers. The Earl of Salisbury's description, delivered to the waiting King and his frantically worried wife, depicts the Prince in heroic terms as he stands alone on the battlefield:

> And in the midst, like to a slender point
> Within the compass of the hòrizon,
> As 'twere a rising bubble in the sea,
> A hazel wand amidst a wood of pines,
> Or as a bear fast-chained upon a stake,
> Stood famous Edward, still expecting when
> Those dogs of France would fasten on his flesh.
>
> [Sc. 18, 140–6]

At this moment it looks very much as if the Prince will not succeed in beating the odds, leaving his mother wishing for death and his father to stand impotently by.

Fortunately for England, it is not to be: only a few moments later the Prince makes what will be his last and most decisive surprise entrance, returning in triumph as if from the dead, and – in a gesture that recalls a famous scene in Marlowe's *Tamburlaine* – with prisoners in tow. His final speech, almost the play's last, makes it clear where power now lies. "The bloody scars I bear / The weary nights that I have watched in field," young Edward declares,

> The dangerous conflicts I have often had,
> The fearful menaces that were proffered me,
> The heat and cold, and what else might displease,
> I wish were now redoubled twentyfold,
> So that hereafter ages, when they read
> The painful traffic of my tender youth,
> Might thereby be inflame with such resolve
> As not the territories of France alone,
> But likewise Spain, Turkey and what countries else
> That justly would provoke fair England's ire,
> Might at thy presence tremble and retire.
>
> [Sc. 18, 224–36]

Edward's rabble-rousing address brings the action firmly up to date, playing knowingly with the notion of historical theatre to assert his strength down the ages. Yet there is an irony here too: as Shakespeare's audience knew full well, only twenty years later the Prince would be dead – a year before his father – and the ten-year-old Richard II would be installed on the throne, with all the catastrophes that resulted. It is an irony to which the playwright would often return.

Stage history and adaptations

Dogged by doubts about its authorship, *Edward III* has enjoyed none of the success of more unambiguously Shakespearian history plays, and the number of professional performances remains nearly non-existent. That said, apparently the play was popular when first aired, at least according to the title-page of the 1595 first edition, which proclaimed that it had been "sundry times played about the city of London". It's not known by whom, but some have guessed that **Lord Pembroke's Men**, who might have employed the young Shakespeare (the company also performed *Titus Andronicus* and a version of *3 Henry VI*), kept it in their repertoire. If so, it wouldn't have been theirs for long: following the intermittent but gruelling bouts of plague that closed theatres in the early 1590s, the company split and its playbooks were dispersed. Given that *Edward III*'s casting is relatively light, it's possible that it survived the break-up and was smuggled into the repertoire of a small touring company. Tantalizing evidence suggests that a play of that name was performed in **Poland** in 1591 by a troupe of English actors, but whether this was an early version of *Edward III* or a separate script no one is sure.

After this, the play seems to have disappeared entirely from the stage for nearly three centuries. The great revivalist **William Poel** (see p.588) dusted it off at London's Little Theatre in 1911, but was too cautious to put on the full work, instead presenting merely the sections he thought to be Shakespeare's – essentially the wooing scenes of Act Two – under the title *The King and the Countess*. Co-directing with him was **Gertrude Kingston**, while **Arthur Wontner** and **Helen Haye** took the main roles. Although the press focused their attention on the other parts of the programme, the *Sketch* reviewer remarked that "the supposed Shakespearian extract certainly seemed like Shakespeare".

Another half-century passed before record of another production, this time a radio version for the BBC Third Programme in 1963, featuring **Stephen Murray** and **Googie Withers** as the King and Countess, with **Raymond Raikes** directing. This version was trimmed heavily for broadcast, and prefaced on-air with the remarks of the eighteenth-century editor Edward Capell, who suggested that "it must be confessed that its being Shakespeare's is conjecture only". Twenty years later, producers **R. Thad Taylor** and **Jay Uhley** put on an amateur version of the play at the Globe Playhouse in Los Angeles in summer 1986 as part of their Shakespeare "apocrypha" project, bracketing *Edward III* with texts including *The Two Noble Kinsmen* and *Sir Thomas More* as well as less likely candidates including *Edmund Ironside* and *A Yorkshire Tragedy*. It was directed by **Dick Dotterer**, with **Martitia Palmer** as the Countess and **Edward Dloughy** as Edward.

Far more attention was paid to Theatr Clwyd's performance in 1987, directed by **Toby Robertson**, the first professional staging of the full text for nearly 400 years – albeit one flagged up as the work of an "anonymous" playwright rather than Shakespeare himself. **Ian McCulloch** played a strident Edward to **Annabel Leventon**'s virtuous if somewhat stern Countess, with **Colin Hurley** appearing as a lively, swaggering Prince. The set was dominated by a timber scaffold tower that doubled as a siege engine, while soldiers in the cast wore menacing black costumes that reminded at least one reviewer of the Droogs from Stanley Kubrick's movie of *A Clockwork Orange*. Others were struck by the play's similarity to *Henry V*, but didn't find the comparison flattering: according to the *Sunday Times*, "if it is by Shakespeare he was quite right to keep quiet about it", although the *Financial Times* grudgingly admitted that this was "the work of an accomplished craftsman at the very least". The *Independent*'s critic was won over, however, remarking that "Toby Robertson has done us a big favour by rescuing it from the Shakespeare apocrypha".

For all that, the play would not be produced on another professional British stage for another 15 years. Several small-scale North American performances appeared in the interim, including a version by the **Council of Doom Theatre Company** at Minneapolis in 1998; an outdoors, modern-dress staging directed by **David Frydrychowski** for Ohio's Cleveland Shakespeare Festival in 1999 (again using the subtitle "The King and Countess"); and a staged reading directed by **Rosemary Dunsmore** and attached to an academic conference held in Toronto in 2000. A year later, the **Pacific Repertory Theatre** in Carmel, California, staged what is claimed to be the first professional American performance of the play.

But in every sense the largest recent staging of *Edward III* has appeared courtesy of the RSC, who presented it – somewhat cheekily – as "a 'new' play by Shakespeare" in 2002, initially at Stratford and then in London's West End as part of a season of Jacobethan rarities. Alongside impressive, stark designs by **Patrick Connellan**, director **Anthony Clark** (a last-minute stand-in after Edward Hall stormed out of rehearsals) offered a crisp and militaristic reading, initially focused on **David Rintoul's** forceful, somewhat chilly Edward but soon dominated by **Jamie Glover's** public-school Prince. Much was made of the French plight, especially that of **Michael Thomas's** sombre King Jean, echoing **Caroline Faber's** trials as a poised Countess.

Critics generally liked the production but were less enthusiastic about the writing. "If the play is all by Shakespeare," wrote Charles Spencer in the *Telegraph*, "it is Shakespeare in hack rather than inspirational mode," while the *Evening Standard's* Nicholas de Jongh acidly remarked that the script offered merely "a dullish canter around the fields of war, with the English always maintaining their top-dog status". Paul Taylor in the *Independent* concluded "this is not a piece that audiences are ever going to warm to, nor the repertoire likely to clasp to its bosom". Prophetic words, given that the company has left *Edward III* unperformed since, and left it out of their 2006–07 Complete Works festival as well as their keynote cycle of Shakespeare histories in 2007–08. Likewise, the Globe eschewed the play in their otherwise complete celebration of global Shakespeare in 2012.

No recent film or TV adaptations have been made, although the Internet Movie Database records an American silent version of *The Death of King Edward III* from 1911, directed by **J. Stuart Blackton** and starring **Charles Kent** as the King; it's not clear whether, or to what extent, it derives from Shakespeare, although Blackton did make several other Shakespeare-inspired silent films.

EDITIONS

New Cambridge Shakespeare
Giorgio Melchiori (ed.); 1998 > Cambridge UP

Cambridge took a brave decision to publish a solo edition of *Edward III*, only the second time in 120 years that the play had been allowed into the consecrated ground of a mainstream Shakespeare series, and this edition remains the best. Melchiori, a long-term champion of the work, is a scrupulous editor and includes plenty of background detail. He deals with authorship questions but doesn't get bogged down in them, and has much to offer on the play's contents and context. Particularly helpful is his appendix on the play's chronicle sources.

SOME CRITICISM

Shakespeare's Kings
John Julius Norwich; 1999 > Penguin

Sensibly remaining aloof from the question of the play's authorship (characteristically remarking that "we cannot get involved here"), Norwich's excellent study briskly tells the tale of Edward III and the monarchs who succeeded him in a novelistic but nonetheless detailed way. The book deftly weaves together Shakespeare's sources with current historiography, piecing together an image of what really happened when, but never forgets that its primary job is to inform an understanding of the plays themselves. An excellent read for anyone wanting to know more about English history as well as anyone wanting to know more about Shakespeare.

Hamlet

The longest of Shakespeare's plays, *Hamlet* is arguably also his very greatest: a pinnacle of Renaissance culture and a forerunner of modernity. Yet hiving it off from the rest of Shakespeare's works is to do it a disservice: this is a sublime work of intellect and art, the most speculative piece of writing Shakespeare ever produced, but it is also the most brilliant – and brilliantly self-aware – of plays. So lengthy in its most extended version that it is near impossible to perform uncut, *Hamlet* presents such challenges to performers that it's been thought that Shakespeare was writing simply to please himself. Even if that were so, this product of the most fruitful and inventive period of his career is a theatrical masterpiece, a thrilling drama of revenge and politics that has never been off the stage since it was written. Authored on the cusp of the seventeenth century, the play transposes a story of brutal Norse revenge into a sophisticated Renaissance setting. But it is perhaps in the character of the hero, the most compelling, beguiling and unknowable of Shakespeare's creations, that the play comes most alive. As the Romantic critic William Hazlitt commented, "it is we who are Hamlet". Over the four centuries he has been in existence, audiences and readers have never relinquished their fascination with the Prince.

DATE > It's hard to be precise. The play was registered to be printed in July 1602, but on internal evidence probably postdates *Julius Caesar* (1599); one version was on the stage by 1600.

SOURCES > Numerous. An earlier play of the same name (dubbed the "ur-*Hamlet*" by critics) was apparently a key source, but has since disappeared. Another might be the sixteenth-century French writer François de Belleforest's version of the Norse tale of Amleth – which appears in Saxo Grammaticus's *Historiae Danicae* (c. 1200) – but it's not clear whether Shakespeare had access to this version or not.

TEXTS > One version of the play (Q1) was printed in 1603, but seems to have been assembled from memory – most likely by an actor playing bit parts (see p.100). Another (Q2) appeared in 1604, longer and more authoritative. Yet another version (F1) is included in the 1623 Folio, possibly revised by Shakespeare.

Interpreting the play

Perhaps fittingly for a man whose words echo through western culture, Hamlet's roots reach back to the cradle of the middle ages. Scholars have been able to trace his story to twelfth-century Scandinavia and a history of the Danish people by a writer known as Saxo Grammaticus. Though even earlier sources have been unearthed, Saxo's Norse saga is the first to treat Prince Amleth, as he is called, as a hero – albeit one distinctly less urbane than his Shakespearian descendant ("Amleth" means "the stupid one").

MAJOR CHARACTERS & SYNOPSIS

Prince Hamlet of Denmark, son of King Hamlet and Gertrude

Horatio, a student friend of Hamlet

Ghost of King Hamlet

King Claudius of Denmark, King Hamlet's brother

Gertrude, King Hamlet's widow and Claudius's wife

Polonius, a lord

Laertes, Polonius's son

Ophelia, Polonius's daughter

Reynaldo, Polonius's servant

Rosencrantz and **Guildenstern**, old friends of Prince Hamlet

Valtemand, **Cornelius** and **Osric**, courtiers

Francisco, **Barnardo** and **Marcellus**, soldiers

Two **Clowns**, a gravedigger and his companion

Fortinbras, Prince of Norway

ACT 1 At Elsinore castle in Denmark, the ghost of the recently deceased King is confronted by soldiers. At court, Hamlet – in mourning for his father's sudden death – expresses his disgust that Gertrude, his widowed mother, has married his uncle Claudius. Alerted by his friend Horatio, Hamlet meets his father's ghost, who tells of his murder by Claudius and demands revenge. Meanwhile, Laertes, who is leaving to study in France, warns his sister Ophelia not to trust the Prince, who has apparently tried to woo her; their father Polonius agrees.

ACT 2 Hamlet decides to feign madness in order to investigate his father's death, and the whole court is thrown into confusion – Ophelia is stunned, Polonius thinks it is because Ophelia has rejected him, and the King and Queen hire Rosencrantz and Guildenstern to spy on him. When the news arrives that a company of actors is about to arrive at Elsinore, Hamlet sees an opportunity. He will get them to perform a play that he jokingly names "The Mousetrap", one scene of which closely resembles his father's murder, and, with Horatio, will observe Claudius's reaction.

ACT 3 Listening in on a meeting between Hamlet and Ophelia – at which Hamlet seems utterly unhinged – Claudius plots to send him to England. The court gathers to watch the players, and at the moment where the murder is re-enacted Claudius starts up in shock and the play is abandoned; Horatio and Hamlet agree that he must be guilty. On the way to speak with Gertrude, Hamlet sees Claudius praying for forgiveness, and is about to kill him but changes his mind. He angrily accuses Gertrude of unfaithfulness, and when he hears Polonius hiding behind the screen in her room, stabs him to death.

ACT 4 Realizing the danger he is in, Claudius sends Hamlet away to England with Rosencrantz and Guildenstern, secretly arranging for him to be killed on arrival. Ophelia has meanwhile been driven mad by her father's death, while Laertes has rushed back from Paris. When news arrives that Hamlet has escaped his companions and is returning to Denmark, Claudius promises to help Laertes kill the Prince. Laertes's anger only intensifies when it transpires that Ophelia has drowned herself.

ACT 5 On his way back to court, Hamlet meets two gravediggers preparing for Ophelia's burial. When the funeral procession arrives, Hamlet initially hides before suddenly revealing himself, to Laertes's fury. Claudius announces that the two should duel, but (unbeknown to Hamlet) arranges for the tip of Laertes's sword to be poisoned. He also prepares a backup plan by poisoning Hamlet's wine. The duel begins: Laertes wounds Hamlet, but they exchange swords and Laertes is also cut. Events spiral out of control as it becomes apparent that Gertrude has unwittingly drunk from Hamlet's cup and has been poisoned. The dying Laertes blames Claudius and reveals what their plan had been, and Hamlet finally stabs his uncle before himself collapsing. The grisly scene closes as the invading army of Fortinbras, a Norwegian prince who has arrived to restore rightful rule to Denmark, enters. He arranges for Hamlet to have a full military funeral.

The tale Saxo tells could hardly be described as sophisticated: Prince Amleth's father, Horwendil, is publicly killed by his jealous brother, the evocatively named Feng, who then marries his erstwhile wife Gerutha. The child Amleth craves revenge, but is too young to act, so decides that the only way he has any chance is to pretend to lose his wits, thus convincing Feng that he offers no threat. After a succession of close shaves and plot convolutions, Amleth makes it through to adulthood and puts into practice his long-held desire – with the added twist that he succeeds in running Feng through with the King's own sword. This is politics as the Norse sagas understand the term: brutal, violent, and with power and revenge side by side.

Shakespeare might have come into contact with this tale in any number of ways, but one of the most fascinating possibilities is that the playwright had a personal connection with the windswept castle of Kronborg, near Elsinore (or Helsingør) in Denmark, where he opts to set his play. A troupe of English actors – among them several of Shakespeare's closest colleagues – played Kronborg on tour in the 1580s, and it's more than possible that Shakespeare's interest in writing about Denmark began from hearing stories about his companions' experiences there. At any rate it's unlikely that he read the story of Amleth in the twelfth-century original: his Hamlet is rather more a Renaissance man.

A version of Saxo's saga was translated by the sixteenth-century poet François de Belleforest, but even if Shakespeare didn't have access to this version (or enough French to read it), by the early 1590s a play about Hamlet was being performed by the playwright's own company. Though the text has not survived, critics are confident that a drama they call the "ur-*Hamlet*" (the German *ur* meaning "original") was one of a number of gory revenge tragedies of the period, among them Thomas Kyd's *Spanish Tragedy* and Shakespeare's own *Titus Andronicus*. The reputation of its illustrious ancestor notwithstanding, the ur-*Hamlet* itself (possibly Kyd's handiwork) was not well reviewed by contemporaries. The writer Thomas Lodge had nothing but scorn for it in 1596, describing a play in which a white-bearded ghost – sounding like nothing so much as an "oyster-wife" on the streets of London – screeched, "Hamlet, revenge". For one of the most famous works in world literature, it is not the most impressive of origins.

Remember me

Even so, it's perhaps fitting that *Hamlet*, a story at least four centuries old by the time Shakespeare came to it, constantly finds itself shuttling between different versions of the past. For all that most people forget the fact, the play in fact has two Hamlets, not one: father and son. Amid the pomp of the Danish court, fresh from celebrating the marriage of Claudius and Gertrude, the "inky-cloaked" figure of young Hamlet makes a striking contrast. Scorning the advice of his uncle, who proclaims that mourning for the old King Hamlet must be balanced with "remembrance of ourselves" (1.2.7), the Prince, in the first of his many soliloquies in the play, is tormented by thoughts of suicide:

> O that this too too solid flesh would melt,
> Thaw, and resolve itself into a dew,

Or that the Everlasting had not fixed
His canon 'gainst self-slaughter! O God, O God,
How weary, stale, flat, and unprofitable
Seem to me all the uses of this world!

[1.2.129–43]

Like Antonio's in *The Merchant of Venice*, Hamlet's melancholy is a kind of *Weltschmerz* ("world-weariness"), but unlike Antonio he goes on to diagnose its cause. Recalling

"Good mother ..." Following Freud, the agonized relationship between Hamlet and Gertrude has been a major source of interest for many armchair psychologists. Here the American actor John Barrymore cosies up to Constance Collier (in real life, only four years older than him).

with horror his father's death and what his mother later, candidly, calls her "o'er-hasty marriage", Hamlet struggles to unscramble his emotions and sense of self. His tone is distracted, broken, but as his thoughts develop it becomes clear that he is grappling with memory itself ("But two months dead—nay, not so much, not two", he exclaims, as if struggling to pin down the event).

He is trapped by the prison of his body, the "too too solid flesh", and his anguished question to himself a few lines later, "Heaven and earth, / Must I remember?", reveals his urgent but painful struggle to hang on to what remains – especially as everyone else in Elsinore, it seems, has forgotten. Claudius chides his new son that his grief is "unmanly", urging him to forget that his father ever existed, to "think of us / As of a father" (1.2.107–8). Gertrude, who has herself demonstrated her capability to move with the times, argues: "all that lives must die, / Passing through nature to eternity" (1.2.72–3). Even Horatio, Hamlet sourly jokes, has visited the court not to pay respects to the old King, but to see the wedding that quickly followed.

Hamlet's savagely disconsolate voice is all the more remarkable because it fore-shadows what we already know – that the past is in fact very much alive. T.S. Eliot peevishly complained that Hamlet's emotion is "in *excess* of the facts as they appear", but part of the wonder of *Hamlet* is the way in which the facts themselves are in glorious excess. The play's unforgettable opening scene, the eerie appearance of the old King's ghost on the battlements at Elsinore, reanimates – in a frighteningly literal sense – something dead and buried:

HAMLET
   My father—methinks I see my father.
HORATIO
   O where, my lord?
HAMLET   In my mind's eye, Horatio.
HORATIO
   I saw him once. A was a goodly king.
HAMLET
   A was a man. Take him for all in all,
   I shall not look upon his like again.
HORATIO
   My lord, I think I saw him yesternight.

                                                    [1.2.183–8]

Even over the offhand intimacy of the conversation between Hamlet and his close com-panion – an intimacy Shakespeare or his scribe renders by using "a" instead of "he", a subtle shading that has long since passed out of the language – the Ghost casts its chill.

Hamlet's encounter with the Ghost, when it occurs, forces the Prince to keep on remembering. Echoing the Ghost's urgent promptings to "Remember me", his son responds, "Remember thee?",

   Ay, thou poor ghost, while memory holds a seat
   In this distracted globe. Remember thee?

Yea, from the table of my memory
I'll wipe away all trivial fond records,
All saws of books, all forms, all pressures past,
That youth and observation copied there,
And thy commandment all alone shall live
Within the book and volume of my brain
Unmixed with baser matter.

[1.5.95–104]

Intoning again the Ghost's words, Hamlet then incants them once more (repetition is a verbal tic of the play, one reason among many for its sprawling size), picturing his memory being erased and rewritten by them. "Remembering" is all.

Unfortunately, though, this is where the problems begin. Though Hamlet presents his mind as if it were a commonplace book (Shakespeare, along with many Elizabethan schoolchildren, will have assembled one as a way of developing his memory), the point about scrapbooks is that they can't be erased or rewritten. Despite swearing that "from this time forth, / My thoughts be bloody, or be nothing worth!" (words that are cut from the Folio text), Hamlet's brain cannot stop thinking of other things. Though the Ghost casts him in the role of revenger (a role played so well by his long-distant ancestor Amleth), it is a part Hamlet knows he will have great difficulty performing:

The time is out of joint. O cursèd spite
That ever I was born to set it right!

[1.5.189–90]

Try as he might, Shakespeare's most self-consciously complex character cannot reduce himself to the simplifications required by the role. In startling contrast to Laertes, the play's other key revenger, who coldly vows to "cut [Hamlet's] throat i'th' church" if necessary to avenge his father Polonius, Hamlet has the greatest of trouble negotiating his scruples. First pausing to see if the Ghost's word is accurate, Hamlet then fluffs the opportunity to kill Claudius at his prayers, not wishing to send his father's murderer to heaven. By the time he does achieve his revenge – not at his own initiative, it might be added – events will have spiralled out of control.

Even in its unmanageable length – a length that often sees it trimmed in performance – *Hamlet* is dominated by postponement and hesitancy. As critics since the mid-eighteenth century have commented in their droves, the issue of Hamlet's own delay is perhaps the biggest question of all, not least because its hero spends a good deal of his precious time ruminating on just what it is to act. Furiously protesting that, despite being "prompted to my revenge by heaven and hell," he "must, like a whore, unpack my heart with words" (2.2.586–8), Hamlet continues to debate the issue almost non-stop – and with over 1500 lines, almost half as much again as Richard III, the Danish Prince is the most voluble character in Shakespeare. Some of those "words" are the most renowned not just in the canon but in the language:

To be, or not to be; that is the question:
Whether 'tis nobler in the mind to suffer
The slings and arrows of outrageous fortune,
Or to take arms against a sea of troubles,
And, by opposing, end them. To die, to sleep—
No more, and by a sleep to say we end
The heartache and the thousand natural shocks
That flesh is heir to—'tis a consummation
Devoutly to be wished. To die, to sleep.
To sleep, perchance to dream. Ay, there's the rub,
For in that sleep of death what dreams may come
When we have shuffled off this mortal coil
Must give us pause. There's the respect
That makes calamity of so long life,
For who would bear the whips and scorns of time,
Th'oppressor's wrong, the proud man's contumely,
The pangs of disprized love, the law's delay,
The insolence of office, and the spurns
That patient merit of th'unworthy takes,
When he himself might with his quietus make
With a bare bodkin? Who would these fardels bear,
To grunt and sweat under a weary life,
But that the dread of something after death,
The undiscovered country from whose bourn
No traveller returns, puzzles the will,
And makes us rather bear those ills we have
Than fly to others that we known not of?
Thus conscience does make cowards of us all,
And thus the native hue of resolution
Is sicklied o'er with the pale cast of thought,
And enterprises of great pith and moment
With this regard their currents turn awry,
And lose the name of action.

[3.1.58–90]

Though Hamlet's thoughts are dizzyingly on the wing, they circle around the idea of stasis. What begins as a rational enquiry into the state of being – "To be, or not to be" – transmutes into a speculative meditation on the ways in which humans are persuaded out of "action". Suicide is on the hero's mind, but even this "resolution" (escapist though he argues it is) stumbles and "turn[s] awry", undone by conscience. Despite his determination to answer the "question", a statement that makes him sound like a schoolboy dutifully arguing the point, Hamlet's thinking is spasmodic, broken – a new kind of dramatic style for Shakespeare, and arguably an entirely new dramatic language. One of Shakespeare's greatest German advocates, August Wilhelm Schlegel, regarded the play as a *Gedankentrauerspiel*, a "tragedy of thought", and this speech

Remember me!

The Argentinian writer **Jorge Luis Borges** once wrote a haunting short story entitled "Shakespeare's Memory" (1983), in which the protagonist, a German scholar by the name of Hermann Sörgel, is offered the chance to possess his idol's memory by a man who claims to have access to it. Sörgel jumps at the chance, a mysterious mental transfer occurs – and the academic suddenly becomes aware that he can remember shady, unsettling things belonging to a life other than his own. But the gift ultimately proves a curse: Shakespeare's memory begins to dominate its victim until Sörgel begins to lose his own mind. Reaching for the telephone book, he dials numbers at random until finally someone agrees to try the experiment for themselves.

Borges' eerie tale suggests that Shakespeare haunts all of us who have come into contact with him. *Hamlet* is perhaps the most haunting play of all, and in a ghostly kind of way it has always been so. The first printed version of the text to hit the market (1603) was a so-called "**memorial reconstruction**" of the play sold to the printers by an actor who claimed to know the script, almost certainly without the permission of Shakespeare's company. This "pirated" text has become known as the **bad quarto**, mainly because whichever parts the nameless actor took (the best guess so far is Marcellus, Valtemand and Lucellus) he had trouble remembering anything else. He is reasonably accurate in some places – presumably when he was on stage and able to listen properly – but elsewhere forgets massive swaths of the script. In his version, Hamlet's soliloquy, probably the most well-remembered Shakespearian speech of all, gets completely garbled. This is how it comes out (original spelling and all):

To be, or not to be, I there's the point,
To Die, to sleepe, is that all? I all:
No, to sleepe, to dreame, I mary there it goes,
For in that dreame of deathe, when we
* awake,*
And borne before an euerlasting Iudge,
From whence no passenger euer retur'nd,
The vndiscouered country, at whose sight
The happy smile, and the accursed damn'd.

Unsurprisingly, Shakespeare or his company scrambled to set the record straight: a "newly imprinted and enlarged" version of the play appeared in print the following year.

A more successful attempt to remember *Hamlet* was pioneered nearly two centuries later by the eighteenth-century language expert **Joshua Steele**, whose life work was a study called *An Essay Towards Establishing the Melody and Measure of Speech* (1775), which attempted to set down in writing, with the aid of musical notation, how people actually spoke. Steele attended **David Garrick**'s performances of *Hamlet*, and his records of what must have been an astonishing occasion appear actually in the book – in which Garrick's every intonation, pitch and shade of voice is meticulously transcribed for posterity. If you can work out Steele's notation, you can even reproduce the great man's delivery for yourself.

demonstrates just how in one sense that might be true. Even in its prodigious length and complexity, Hamlet's most famous soliloquy exhibits the way in which thoughts – inspired, unique thoughts – can get in the way.

It is a fact not often observed that this famous soliloquy contains not a single "I" or "me", and its relationship to Hamlet's own situation is complex. Even so, Shakespeare makes us see the tangible as well as philosophical difficulties of the Prince's position. Hamlet is never entirely sure that what the Ghost says is actually true (unlike the audience, who is allowed to witness Claudius's desperate penitence at his prayers), and his options concerning what to do with the knowledge are also sorely limited. The court at Elsinore, ruled by a usurping murderer, is hardly likely to provide any kind of justice, and Hamlet has little choice but to embark on what the Elizabethan politician and sage Francis Bacon called the "wild justice" of revenge, a course prompted by a Ghost who could also (as Shakespeare's audiences would be well aware) be a demon sent from Hell. That course is wild indeed: in his early political dramas especially Shakespeare shows that the ethic of revenge tears societies apart. In the *King Henry VI* plays it is revenge that finally rips England to pieces during the Wars of the Roses; in Shakespeare's first Roman tragedy *Titus Andronicus*, revenge transforms the city of Rome into a "wilderness of tigers" where violence consumes the world of the play. Knowledge of the political and ethical problems with revenge haunts Hamlet as much as his father's ghost, or indeed his own sense of self.

Even so, as we might guess given that he spends so long riddling with it, "action" is a word Hamlet understands differently from nearly everyone else in the play. As is abundantly obvious on stage, Claudius, not his nephew, is the great doer of *Hamlet*: it is he who kills the King, marries the wife, incessantly agitates behind the scenes for the hero's removal from the plot. Hamlet's deeds are, by contrast, second-hand: he stabs Polonius after mistaking his identity, and sentences his companions Rosencrantz and Guildenstern to death by rewriting Claudius's commission to England. Even the Prince's death is scripted for him in advance by his uncle, who arranges a duel with Laertes in which the swords and Hamlet's wine are both "envenomed" with poison. Hamlet's two great "acts" in the tragedy – his "antic disposition" of madness and the play he puts on to test his uncle's conscience – are revealing, for they interpret "acting" as theatrical display rather than purposeful achievement.

Hamlet is continually searching for his role, and Shakespeare develops the theme by filling the play with characters who echo or reflect aspects of the hero. The Prince's way with "words" is comically counterpointed by the excruciating verbal excursions of the royal adviser Polonius, whose reluctance to be "brief" (2.2.93) becomes one of *Hamlet*'s verbal tics. (Ironically, Polonius's inability to keep his mouth shut, hidden in Gertrude's bedchamber, will be his downfall.) Also servants at the slippery world of court are Rosencrantz and Guildenstern, two men who appear on stage only in each other's company and are sometimes even mistaken for one another. As well as being Hamlet's "dear friends", their situation somewhat mirrors that of the Prince, the difference being that they are entirely happy to do what they are told – a model of dutiful service Hamlet wishes to emulate yet is also right to despise. Hamlet's closest companion Horatio is another of the Prince's doubles, stoic and stalwart, as brief in words as his friend is verbally expansive. Unlike Hamlet, Horatio seems innately attuned to the savage politics of Elsinore (politics as dangerous as those in the Norse saga which is the play's ultimate source). "You will lose this wager, my lord," he tells Hamlet as news of the duel arrives (5.2.155), and his instinct is fatally accurate.

> *In Hamlet the problems the audience thinks about and the intellectual action of thinking about them are very similar. Hamlet is the tragedy of an audience that cannot make up its mind.*
>
> Stephen Booth, "On the value of *Hamlet*" (1969)

But Hamlet's closest living doppelgänger is the Norwegian prince Fortinbras, whose father (also named Fortinbras) lost in battle to the old King Hamlet – an indignity the young Fortinbras is eager to revenge. Though the character is offstage for nearly all the play, Shakespeare never allows Fortinbras to leave our minds, dropping in rumours about his conquest in Poland, his marching through Denmark, his gung-ho bravery in battle. Hamlet himself is only too aware of the difference between the man he calls a "delicate and tender prince" (a character assessment that has rather more Hamlet than Fortinbras in it) and himself, a "rogue and peasant slave" (2.2.552). In the last moments of the play, it is Fortinbras to whom Hamlet gives his "dying voice" as the next King of Denmark, a prince far more warlike – and far more like old Hamlet – than the rightful candidate, young Hamlet himself.

To what base uses

Though Schlegel may have been right in one respect, *Hamlet* is not merely an intellectual tragedy. It is not even a tragedy of the hero alone; as the play develops, tragedies begin to cluster. Hamlet's musings on the "thousand natural shocks / That flesh is heir to" are interrupted by the arrival of Ophelia, the "Nymph" whose relationship with the hero is as fraught as his relationship with himself. Fevered speculation has attempted to unravel just what lies between them, but the play itself gives little away. Polonius is only too ready to attribute Hamlet's distracted behaviour to frustrated love (particularly after both he and Laertes advise Ophelia to steer clear of him), and it seems that the Prince has indeed sent her love letters, but beyond this there lies little but uncertainty. It does not help that the only time we see the couple alone together, Hamlet's supposedly feigned madness (yet another huge question in the play) is beginning to look rather more real. When Ophelia announces that she has "remembrances" from him to return, Hamlet denies even this much, retorting, "No, no, I never gave you aught" (3.1.95–8). What follows is one of the most perplexing episodes in the tragedy, and certainly one of the most distressing to watch:

HAMLET I did love you once.
OPHELIA Indeed, my lord, you made me believe so.
HAMLET You should not have believed me, for virtue cannot so inoculate
    our old stock but we shall relish of it. I loved you not.
OPHELIA I was the more deceived.
HAMLET Get thee to a nunnery. Why wouldst thou be a breeder of sinners?

[3.1.117–24]

At first claiming that he loved Ophelia, then in the next breath denying it, Hamlet's words are almost wilfully obscure. He may mean that because "virtue" can do nothing to "inoculate" humanity ("our old stock") from its essential sinfulness, his "love" was not authentic; but in practice his language is even more broken and splintered than before. Typically, the Prince has transformed the situation into something beyond itself, arguing that humanity is so tainted by sin that love itself is delusive. That does not soften the savagery of his words, though, nor the cruelty of his insistence, repeated five times in this scene, that Ophelia should "get … to a nunnery" (also Jacobethan slang for a brothel) rather than feel as she does.

When Hamlet confronts his mother a few scenes later, his thoughts return to the themes of "breeding" and sinfulness. As Freudian critics have noted, Hamlet's projection onto Ophelia of intemperate lust (the kind that breeds "sinners") seems suspiciously close to his feelings about Gertrude. When he accuses his mother of "compulsive ardour", it seems clear that his feelings about the incurable sinfulness of humanity are magnified by his belief that in marrying her husband's murderer Gertrude has performed a kind of nightmarish adultery:

HAMLET   Nay, but to live
    In the rank sweat of an enseamèd bed
    Stewed in corruption, honeying and making love
    Over the nasty sty—
QUEEN GERTRUDE   O, speak to me no more!
    Those words like daggers enter in mine ears.
    No more, sweet Hamlet.

                                            [3.4.81–6]

Though we don't have to diagnose Hamlet as suffering from a full-scale Oedipal complex (a famous theory initiated by Ernest Jones in his slim 1949 book *Hamlet and Oedipus*), it is interesting to note the connections that complicate his relationships with the play's two female characters, not least the nightmarish links he constructs between sexuality, sin and death. The brute irony is that Hamlet's spiralling obsession with sins of the body is played out while there is a real corpse to be dealt with – that of Polonius, whom he has just stabbed (suddenly and sinfully) behind a wall-hanging.

It is fitting, perhaps, that sooner or later Hamlet will take his thoughts to the grave itself – a literal as well as symbolic destination for the play. Escaping from the clutches of Rosencrantz and Guildenstern by a hair's-breadth scheme involving pirates on the high seas, Hamlet returns to Denmark and finds himself, with Horatio, in a churchyard. There he finally comes across a man who has the expertise to answer his inquisitiveness about death: a gravedigger. Their debate about the human condition, with reference to the conditions humans find themselves in, becomes a kind of grim comic repartee (aptly, for the gravedigger is a "Clown" in the text):

HAMLET How long will a man lie i'th' earth ere he rot?
FIRST CLOWN I'faith, if a be not rotten before a die—as we have many
        pocky corpses nowadays, that will scarce hold the laying in—a will last
        you some eight year or nine year. A tanner will last you nine year.
HAMLET Why he more than another?
FIRST CLOWN Why, sir, his hide is so tanned with his trade that a will keep
        out water a great while …

                                            [5.1.159–66]

> *The poet places [Hamlet] in the most stimulating circumstances that a human being can be placed in. He is the heir-apparent of a throne: his father dies suspiciously; his mother excluded her son from his throne by marrying his uncle. This is not enough; but the Ghost of the murdered father is introduced to assure the son that he was put to death by his own brother. What is the effect upon the son? – instant action and pursuit of revenge? No: endless reasoning and hesitating ...*
>
> Samuel Taylor Coleridge, *Table-Talk* (1812)

Neoclassical critics – famously Voltaire – objected to this scene because it debased Hamlet's tragedy, but what is striking here is that the Prince's bleakly comic routine echoes with delicious vulgarity some of the biggest ideas in the play. "To what base uses we may return, Horatio!" Hamlet exclaims (5.1.198) – when it comes down to it, we end up in the grave. Even "a king may go a progress through the guts of a beggar" (4.3.30–1) after he rots and is eaten by worms.

The laughter, dark though it is, is short-lived: the grave at which Hamlet and Horatio are conversing has been dug for Ophelia, driven mad by her own father's death (a painfully real echo of Hamlet's feigned insanity, itself caused by bereavement) and who has drowned herself. With this news, the tone of the play begins to narrow: death is no longer a subject for speculative enquiry, but a savage reality. Though Polonius's own end was messy and squalid – Hamlet lunges behind the arras for a "rat", unceremoniously lugging the body offstage afterwards – here we sense that even the fate of "intruding fools" like him (or clowns like Hamlet's long-dead jester Yorick) has a terrible tragic dimension.

Death is of course where Hamlet (and *Hamlet*) conclude, but despite his insistent desire to escape the prison of his flesh, the hero does not in the end go gently. Having put up Laertes to challenge the Prince to a duel, Claudius does his utmost to ensure that Hamlet is finally dispatched – Laertes's swordsmanship, a "treacherous" weapon, poisoned wine. Yet Hamlet, newly aware that "the readiness is all" (5.2.168), fails to be compliant. He fights back. Having hung so long in irresolution, *Hamlet* becomes a full revenge tragedy only in its concluding – its dying – moments. But the play never loses its interest in the chaotic, unpredictable nature of death. Laertes is wounded by his own sword, Gertrude drinks the poison intended for her son, Claudius is stabbed only when Hamlet realizes that he himself has been mortally wounded. Shakespeare's pacing of this final scene is astonishing, something only really comprehensible in performance: from Osric's announcement of the duel to the moment where Gertrude collapses occupies nearly two hundred lines, perhaps ten minutes on stage; yet it is only another fifty lines before Laertes, Claudius and finally Hamlet are finished. Quite suddenly, the revenge is complete, the revenger is dying, and everything is very nearly over.

Though the hero is, characteristically, thinking of his audience as he readies himself for his terminal interruption, the certainty that "the rest is silence" (5.2.310), he is also aware that events have come full circle. The play ends, as it began, with the death of a Hamlet. "You that look pale and tremble at this chance," he addresses spectators both on and off stage,

That are but mutes or audience to this act,
Had I but time—as this fell sergeant Death
Is strict in his arrest—O, I could tell you—
But let it be.

[5.2.286–90]

Yet the play will not quite let Hamlet be: just after he begins his overdue journey to the "undiscovered country from whose bourn / No traveller returns" (3.1.81–2), the stage is filled with "warlike noise", drums and trumpets, as the Norwegian army of Fortinbras swarms on. Hamlet's corpse is lifted and carried off, destined for what the new King of Denmark announces will be a soldier's funeral. It is the final misunderstanding, tragic and bittersweet, and the hero is no longer around to protest.

Stage history and adaptations

Hamlet is almost unique among Shakespeare's works in never having been off the stage, as far as we can make out, since it was written. Here there is barely space to render even the outlines of that history.

While there are no surviving records of its first years at the Globe (it perhaps debuted there around 1600), there is little doubt that then – as now – the play seized the imagination of audiences. **Richard Burbage** created the Prince's role, and the "bad" 1603 quarto presumably appeared in response to popular demand for a text, its title-page claiming that early performances occurred in **Oxford**, **Cambridge** and the **city of London**. It was also played at court with **Joseph Taylor**, Burbage's successor, in 1619 and 1637, and travelled widely, notably in the German and Baltic states, courtesy of travelling English actors. There is even a story that *Hamlet* reached **Sierra Leone**, where the crew of an East India Company ship called the *Dragon* acted it alongside *Richard II* in September 1607, repeating their performance off what is now Yemen the following March. If true, this would be the first known appearnce of a Shakespeare play on the African continent, but the evidence has – mysteriously and unfortunately – disappeared.

Taylor continued acting *Hamlet* up to the closure of the theatres in 1642, after which time the gravedigging scene was smuggled into a skit entitled *The Gravediggers*, performed by **Robert Cox's** company. Once Charles II returned from exile in 1660, *Hamlet* swiftly followed, with the young **Thomas Betterton** appearing in the lead the following year (he would act it for another five decades, last playing the Prince in 1709 at the age of 74). Betterton's stamina would be challenged, but never equalled, by the self-anointed king of the eighteenth-century stage, **David Garrick** (1742–76), who developed a painstakingly fleshed-out interpretation (according to one witness, he "preserve[d] every gradation and transition of the passions"). Garrick's decisiveness in the role, played to **Susannah Cibber's** Ophelia, was assisted by cutting the Prince's more irresolute speeches and eventually most of Act Five – and he employed a special hydraulic wig to make his hair stand on end at the sight of the Ghost. **John Henderson** took over from Garrick in 1777, and imitated his master's style with some success.

Both sad and sweetly funny, quizzical yet slyly alert, Mark Rylance's Hamlet at Shakespeare's Globe in 2000 was his second attempt on the role – and perhaps his finest.

Hamlet, albeit heavily cut, was Shakespeare's most popular play during the eighteenth century, and under **John Philip Kemble** it continued its pre-eminence into the nineteenth. Despite his stately style Kemble communicated the gnawing melancholy at the Prince's heart, though was too cool for some – especially when compared with his sister **Sarah Siddons**, who attempted the role herself. The same criticism could never be levelled at **Edmund Kean**, who acted Hamlet from 1814 in a portrayal that outlined all the character's "turbulent delineations of passion" (*The Stage*) and, doing so, scandalized audiences used to the more classical acting of Kemble. A decade later **William Charles Macready** attempted to combine the best elements of Kean's and Kemble's styles, but only after Kean's untimely death in 1833 did he become the leading Hamlet of his generation. Kean's son **Charles** acted the play from 1838 onwards to a succession of Ophelias including **Eliza Smith** and his wife **Ellen Tree**.

By this time *Hamlet* had become an intercontinental phenomenon. A performance by **Charles Kemble**'s company at the Paris Odéon in 1827 caused a sensation, not least because **Harriet Smithson** as Ophelia mesmerized Romantic artists like Delacroix and Berlioz (so much so in the latter's case that he married her). In America it was popular early on and became especially so on the frontier circuit, when travelling companies toured it around the expanding United States in the 1830s, 40s and 50s. **Edwin Booth**, who was encouraged to take up the play by his British actor father **Junius Brutus**, cut his teeth touring in California and later became synonymous with the role in New York from the 1860s. During the following decades several London-based managers would tour in the US. One was **Henry Irving**, who acted Hamlet in a sprawling 1878 Lyceum performance that offered a Victorian version of Hamlet's conundrum – torn between duty to his father and love for **Ellen Terry**'s sensitive Ophelia. The great Italian **Tommaso Salvini**, famous for his titanic Othello, also toured as Hamlet in the 1870s, winning plaudits even though few critics could understand what he was saying (he insisted in acting in Italian). Still more unusual was **Sarah Bernhardt**'s Parisian Prince (1899), who offered a "boyish" interpretation despite being 54 (and, of course, a girl).

Though *Hamlet*'s days as a star vehicle were by no means over, the late nineteenth century witnessed a growing desire to produce the play as it might have been known by Shakespeare. The great revivalist **William Poel** began his adventures with "Elizabethan" staging in 1881 with a first quarto *Hamlet*, and masterminded three subsequent versions. Elsewhere, the playtext came under scrutiny, initially with **Johnston Forbes-Robertson**'s celebrated Lyceum version from 1897, which restored the Fortinbras subplot for the first time in two hundred years; and then with **Frank Benson**'s "full text" productions at Stratford from the turn of the century, which lasted a breathtaking six hours. Even more ambitious was an extraordinary production at the Moscow Arts Theatre which opened in January 1912. Designed and directed by the visionary theatrical innovator **Edward Gordon Craig** (who had played the title role in London fifteen years earlier), the production attempted to create a new idiom for Shakespeare – a kind of epic symbolism that would convey the essence of the play without any distracting naturalistic details.

Craig's influence can be seen in the boldly simplified designs that **Robert Edmond Jones** made for a celebrated New York production in 1925. This starred **John Barrymore**, who discarded poetic introspection in favour of a more assertive and physically dynamic portrayal of the Prince ("the realest Hamlet we have known", claimed the *Herald*). In the same year **Barry Jackson**'s Birmingham Rep mounted an infamous modern-dress production – the "plus-fours" *Hamlet* – that infuriated as many as it impressed. Throughout the 1930s and 40s *Hamlet* was played by an astonishing sequence of British stars based at London's Old Vic. **Ernest Milton**, **Laurence Olivier**, **Maurice Evans** and **Michael Redgrave** were all acclaimed Princes, though the most famous of them all was **John Gielgud**, who first played Hamlet in 1930 – aged just 26 – and acted him in four subsequent versions. Though Gielgud attempted to find something new in the character each time – all the way from the early "angry young man" to a hero for whom, as one critic put it, "wickedness is no surprise" – his noble demeanour and impressive verse-speaking were consistently singled out for praise. During World War II the play was drafted into the war effort: a pared-down wartime *G.I. Hamlet* was put on to rally American troops by **Maurice Evans**, who had played the role at the Old Vic and later took it to Broadway.

Since then, *Hamlet* has continued to be performed more often than any other play by Shakespeare, and perhaps any other play: London has sometimes seen more than three performances running concurrently, and any attempt to describe more than a handful would be impossible here.

In 1953 **Richard Burton**'s swashbuckling performance at the Old Vic was wildly successful (with eighteen curtain calls on the first night); while the same theatre four years later saw **John Neville** in a more poetic reading, complete with Ruritanian costumes and a touching Ophelia from a very young Judi Dench. But for many, it was **Paul Scofield**'s measured, unhistrionic Hamlet – at Stratford in 1948 and for **Peter Brook** in 1955 – that most truly penetrated the character's multifaceted complexity, and best defined the role for his generation.

Ten years later, **David Warner**'s disaffected and nihilistic student Prince captured the mood of the post-nuclear age – leading one esteemed critic to comment that "even the oldest of us feel that we are seeing the play for the first time". And in **Peter Hall**'s Stratford production, the cast provided further surprises, **Tony Church**'s politico Polonius and **Glenda Jackson**'s feisty Ophelia among them. At London's Roundhouse in 1969 **Tony Richardson**'s production, dominated by **Nicol Williamson**'s savage Prince, divided the critics, not least because of the laid-back Ophelia of **Marianne Faithfull** – better known as a pop singer. **Buzz Goodbody**'s 1975 production performed at The Other Place (a corrugated iron shed down the road from the RSC's main house), was notable for its powerful immediacy and **Ben Kingsley**'s unheroic prince. Five years later, at London's Royal Court theatre, **Jonathan Pryce**'s Hamlet created a sensation, in a claustrophobic production by **Richard Eyre**, by speaking his father's lines as if physically possessed by the ghost. At the RSC, in the same year, **Michael Pennington** bucked the trend by playing Hamlet as a sensitive and intelligent aristocrat, who balked at the murder of his uncle (**Derek Godfrey**). **John Barton**'s production, aided by **Ralph Koltai**'s stark and minimal set, firmly laid the emphasis on the Prince's struggle between an emotional and an intellectual response to his situation.

Ron Daniels's RSC production of 1989 was hailed as one of that decade's best, with **Mark Rylance**'s vulnerable, little-boy Prince enthusiastically received. In 2000, by now artistic director of Shakespeare's Globe in London, Rylance made another attempt on the role in a Jacobean-style production directed by **Giles Block** – and was even finer the second time round, according to many. The *Guardian*'s Michael Billington declared him "one of nature's Hamlets: alert, humorous and capable of combining whimsical dottiness with a troubled inner life".

Kenneth Branagh's various performances, most successfully under **Adrian Noble** in 1992, demonstrated that Hamlet could be physical, too, and even something of a film star. This was even truer of **Ralph Fiennes**, who played the Prince for **Jonathan Kent** at the Almeida Theatre in 1995 as an over-sensitive and confused toff. Controversy attended **Matthew Warchus**'s RSC version of 1997, with **Alex Jennings** as a sardonic Prince, because of the director's decision to cut over a thousand lines of text in order to streamline the play and emphasize its familial aspects. A bold piece of casting saw a rather plump **Simon Russell Beale** project a probing intelligence and palpable disgust in an otherwise lacklustre National Theatre production in 2000. Other directors have identified political undercurrents: **Steven Pimlott**'s 2001 version, again at the RSC, stressed the brutalist aspects of Claudius's regime and had **Sam West** as a youthful but edgy Prince. *Hamlet*'s first internationally successful production of the twenty-first century was directed by one of the biggest directorial names of the twentieth, **Peter Brook**, whose adaptation, *The Tragedy of Hamlet* (2001), explored the metaphysical conundrums of the play. **Adrian Lester** played a philosophical, introspective hero.

At the Old Vic in 2004, **Trevor Nunn** emphasized the gulf between the generations, casting the scarecrow-like **Ben Whishaw**, fresh from drama school, as a nervy student prince alongside **Samantha Whittaker**'s teenagey Ophelia. Contemporary events touched the Cape Town-based Baxter Theatre Company's production in 2006, which nearly didn't reach the Stratford Complete Works festival after one of the company was shot dead a week before opening. In 2007, New York's avant-garde **Wooster Group** debuted a *Hamlet* that delved even further into the past – a restaging of **Richard Burton**'s 1964 Broadway version, originally captured with the then-futuristic "Electronovision" film technology and beamed to 1,000 cinemas. With characteristic slyness, the Woosters presented a tragedy suspended somewhere between digital remix, ghoulish seance and post-mortem, with live actors channelling Burton's performance, projected onto a huge screen upstage.

In the years since, the play has remained as popular as ever on British and American stages, with big-name actors queueing up to play the Dane – notably **David Tennant** (2008), **Jude Law** (2009), **Rory Kinnear** (2010), **Michael Sheen** (2011) and **Benedict Cumberbatch** (2015). Kinnear's version, directed at the National Theatre by **Nicholas Hytner**, was one of the most thoughtful reinterpretations, a detailed examination of a surveillance society gone mad. Cumberbatch's, despite selling out in mere minutes and being subject to intense pre-publicity in the press and social media, attracted a mixed critical reception: the hero was praised for what the *Independent*'s reviewer described as his "racing, ironic intellect", but there was common consent that he was trapped inside what the *Guardian* called an "intellectual ragbag of a production" by **Lyndsey Turner**, too stylized and stylish to cohere.

More intriguingly, female actors have returned to explore the role too, including **Maxine Peake** at Manchester's Royal Exchange in 2014, who offered – according to the *Observer* – a "stripling Prince, almost pre-sexual, who glides without swagger and without girlishness". In 2014, the London **Globe** launched an ambitious (and mildly lunatic) project to tour a stripped-down *Hamlet* to every country in the world; visas and war zones allowing, the aim is for it to be complete by April 2016, the 400th anniversary of Shakespeare's death.

Of *Hamlet*'s varied life in translation, all the way from Afrikaans (1945) to Zulu (1954), little of detail can be said in this space, save perhaps its special popularity in Russia (where "Hamletism", a word that appears in the 1840s, became a familiar malady among a certain brand of intellectual). Performed as early as 1837 in Moscow by **Pavel Mochalov**, the play was given an innovative production at the Moscow Arts Theatre in 1912 (see p.107), and more recently **Yuri Lyubimov**'s 1971 production, starring **Vladimir Vysotsky**, gained much attention outside its home country.

Germany has also provided a congenial environment for the Danish Prince. Cut-down and part-translated versions of the text were toured through northern Europe by English actors as early as the opening years of the seventeenth century, and certainly by 1626. The play became massively popular in **Friedrich Ludwig Schröder**'s eighteenth-century performances, inspiring a whole generation of *Sturm und Drang* writers, among them Goethe, whose *Wilhelm Meister's Apprenticeship* of 1795–96 is heavily in its shadow. Promoted to the status of a German classic after **August Wilhelm Schlegel** completed his translation in 1798, *Hamlet* remained popular through the nineteenth century – the poet Ferdinand Freiligrath proclaimed in 1844 that "*Deutschland ist Hamlet!*" – and into the twentieth.

Perhaps surprisingly, it remained so during the Nazi period, when a production starring the blonde-wigged **Gustaf Gründgens** ran for over 200 performances in Berlin from 1936 – acclaimed by one critic (somewhat strangely) as a "Hamlet who knows precisely what he wants". Forty years later, the play found a quite different edge courtesy of playwright **Heiner Müller**, whose savagely distilled *Hamletmachine*, completed in 1977 and premiered in Brussels the following year, protested against the lack of intellectual freedom on offer in the GDR. In 2008, a radically rearranged production by wild-child director **Thomas Ostermeier** and actor **Lars Eidinger** – whose Prince resembled a spoiled, overweight toddler romping across a vast field of black earth – opened in Berlin to a mixture of acclaim and mild horror; it has since toured the world, achieving over 200 performances.

People have wanted to film *Hamlet* from the first days of cinema. Although a French short appeared in 1900, the films of **Johnston Forbes-Robertson** (1913) and **Sven Gade** (1920) – the latter starring the great **Asta Nielsen** in an intriguing cross-gender experiment – are perhaps the most celebrated silent versions. The first ever talkie *Hamlet* to be made anywhere in the world was in Hindi, adapted and directed in 1935 by the renowned actor **Sohrab Modi** under the melodramatic title *Khoon-ka-Khoon* ("Blood for Blood"). Itself based on Parsi plays from the late nineteenth century, Modi's movie is now lost, but photographs and its script have informed later Indian films, including **Kishore Sahu's** of 1954 and *Haider*, the latest Shakespeare adaptation by Bollywood auteur **Vishal Bhardwaj** (2014).

In the west **Laurence Olivier's** movie of 1948 has dominated the canon, though **Grigori Kozintsev's** 1964 film, with **Innokenti Smoktunovsky** in the lead, is a masterpiece on a par with his *King Lear*. The 1960s saw the filmed stage versions of **Philip Savile** (1964) and **Tony Richardson** (1969), starring **Christopher Plummer** and **Nicol Williamson** respectively. More recently, the play has attracted major studios – notably via **Franco Zeffirelli**, who in 1990 cast Hollywood star **Mel Gibson** as a vigorous and heroic (if mother-obsessed) Prince; and **Kenneth Branagh**, who offered a response to Zeffirelli's swingeingly cut version by releasing a full-text version with himself in the lead. **Michael Almereyda's** 2000 film relocated the play to modern-day New York and starred **Ethan Hawke** as the Prince.

TV versions include **Richard Chamberlain's** Byronic Hamlet in 1970 (with **Michael Redgrave** as Polonius, **Richard Johnson** as Claudius, and Gielgud's Ghost); and **Rodney Bennett's** lengthy BBC/Time-Life version from 1980, with **Derek Jacobi** as a watchful yet capricious Hamlet to **Patrick Stewart's** domineering Claudius and **Eric Porter's** bustling Polonius. **Joseph Papp's** New York Shakespeare Festival version of the play, with **Kevin Kline** in the lead, was recorded for PBS in 1990 and is now available on DVD, as is the RSC version of **David Tennant's** Hamlet, directed by **Gregory Doran**.

SCREEN

Hamlet

L. Olivier, J. Simmons, P. Cushing; Laurence Olivier (dir.) UK, 1948 > ITV / Criterion DVD ⬤

"Mr Olivier does not speak poetry badly," opined one critic of his 1937 debut as Hamlet. "He does not speak it at all." His verbal eccentricities won't trouble you here (in fact they're rather terrific), but then Olivier gets to do a lot more than just use his voice. *Hamlet*, his second Shakespeare film, is probably the most daring and brilliant of the lot, done out in high-contrast monochrome with obvious debts to German Expressionism and *film noir*. Equally insistent is Olivier's obsession with Hamlet's Oedipal conundrum, which led him to cast Eileen Herlie as Gertrude (she was in fact thirteen years his junior), though in all other respects his glacial and imperious interpretation of the role is finely balanced. Even if some have criticized the visuals as fussy – the vertiginous camerawork, exploring the murky recesses of the Prince's imagination, invites strong reactions – the film is bolstered by its sure-footed dramatic pacing, some excellent supporting performances and William Walton's atmospheric music.

Hamlet (Gamlet)

I. Smoktunovsky, A. Vertinskaya, M. Nazavanov; Grigori Kozintsev (dir.) USSR, 1964 > Ruscico / Facets DVD

At times Kozintsev's *Hamlet* seems to echo Olivier's, but it is richer in insight and more cinematically mature. Whereas Olivier employs the meandering staircases of Elsinore to represent Hamlet's quest for identity, Kozintsev presents a castle of massy walls and airless spaces: never has the "prison" of Denmark seemed so inescapable as when the drawbridge thunders down during his opening sequence. This subtext must have had a horribly personal resonance for Innokenti Smoktunovsky, a war hero sent to the Gulag by Stalin, and he delivers an inspired performance as a Prince trapped as much by his position (most memorably when he wanders through crowds of courtiers, soliloquies raging in voice-over) as by the cry for revenge. Also ensnared is Anastasia Vertinskaya's girlish Ophelia, almost literally a wind-up toy for her baleful father (Yuri Tolubeyev) and his thickset boss (Mikhail Nazavanov), though via cuts in the text Elsa Radzina's Gertrude becomes a bystander, her death mere misadventure. It's the film's political dimension that makes it most thrilling: this Prince is a genuine threat to stability, and the arrival of Fortinbras heralds a political dawn so defining it's been seen as Kozintsev's nod to Khrushchev. Shostakovich's propulsive music is an organic part of the drama, though some may feel that it's too intrusive.

Hamlet

N. Williamson, M. Faithfull, A. Hopkins; Tony Richardson (dir.) UK, 1969 > UCA / SPE DVD

Whereas other filmed *Hamlet*s use grandiloquent architecture to enlarge their scope, Tony Richardson's doomy interpretation offers nary a glimpse of its location (the action was shot inside the Roundhouse in north London, a disused Victorian trainshed rediscovered as a cult arts venue). Instead the camera works in remorseless close-up and via long, fluid takes. Based on Richardson's hugely successful stage production, the effect is both highly theatrical and persuasively filmic, painting a portrait of Hamlet's inner torments amid crowded tableaux of fast-moving events. Nicol Williamson's balding, bearded hero suggests self-disgust rather than self-pity, spitting and snarling the verse at top speed throughout, while Anthony Hopkins brings a fast-thinking pragmatism to Claudius. Look out for Marianne Faithfull's throaty rendition of Ophelia's mad songs and a spry double cameo by Roger Livesey as Player King and Gravedigger.

Hamlet

K. Branagh, K. Winslet, D. Jacobi; Kenneth Branagh (dir.) UK, 1996 > Warner DVD ⬤

An oft-repeated fact about *Hamlet* is that, from its first days at the Globe, a full performance will have been impossible. Enter Kenneth Branagh, a fat chequebook and an uncut quarto text. His attempt to see if multiplex audiences will run out of patience – or popcorn – by the time Hamlet flings his rapier into Claudius (just past the 3hr 45min mark) is magnificently brave, but Branagh just doesn't trust the script. He interpolates fussy silent episodes presumably designed to aid comprehension, but which just add to the hair-tearing excess of it all: any director who wastes Judi Dench and John Gielgud on a wordless sequence has more contacts than sense. They are not the only ill-served luminaries: Branagh's capacious cast ranges from the underused (Simon Russell Beale, Ray Fearon), the undercooked (Winslet, Julie Christie, Billy Crystal, Richard Briers) to the downright bizarre (Ken Dodd, Gérard Depardieu). Branagh's own performance is mixed, not to say limited by his habit of welling up each time he approaches an emotional crux. Centred around Blenheim Palace, the sets are great, but Branagh's bid for Viscontian grandeur too often resembles low-grade Hollywood.

Hamlet

E. Hawke, J. Stiles, K. MacLachlan; Michael Almereyda (dir.) US, 2000 > Arthaus / Miramax DVD ⬤

For all the millennial modernity – it's set in a New York of "Denmark Corp", swish limousines and designer apartments – the director presents a drama whose previous incarnations are as inescapable as Sam Shepard's glowering Ghost. Hamlet can't verbalize his emotions without replaying them on his Handicam, and instead of hiring players to tug at his uncle's conscience he montages *The Mousetrap: A Film/Video*. All very wry, but such gimmickry only encourages the film to topple into parody. Despite the semiotic seductions, playing "To be, or not to be" in Blockbuster Video was surely a mistake, and the movie's air-con setting maroons rather than liberates the play. Hawke plays the heir presumptive as a wised-up student rebel who wears his pinstripes with a Peruvian woolly hat and an air of bad grace, while Julia Stiles scowls efficiently as Ophelia (she hasn't opportunity to do much else; the couple's emotional entanglements are drastically ironed out). This *Hamlet* does well to capture the portmanteau layering of the play, but ultimately fails to convince.

The Banquet
Daniel Wu, Zhang Ziyi, You Ge; Feng Xiaogang (dir.) China, 2006 > Metrodome DVD 🔊

No need to wait for the fencing scene at the end: in this Chinese adaptation you're barely ten minutes in before the first hand-to-hand combat, and courtesy of ace fight director Wo-Ping Yuen (best known in the west for *Crouching Tiger, Hidden Dragon*), elaborately choreographed martial arts scenes pop up more frequently than the inky-cloaked imperial guard of You Ge's scowling and usurping Emperor Li. Combined with motifs drawn from Ibsen's *Ghosts*, the plot of Shakespeare's play is thinned out to a not-so-subtle Oedipal romance between Daniel Wu's androgynous Prince and Zhang Ziyi's kung-fu kicking Gertrude/Empress. But it's none the worse for that, and Xun Zhou is a touching Ophelia/Qing Nu who looks to be made from porcelain and could shatter at any moment. There's gore aplenty, but the visuals – heavily influenced by Kurosawa's *Ran* (see p.237) – are lavish and undeniably spectacular; and in a final plot twist Feng's movie makes the bold suggestion that the real tragedy here is Gertrude's. Released in the US under the fittingly over-the-top title *Legend of the Black Scorpion*.

Hamlet
D. Tennant, P. Stewart, P. Downie; Gregory Doran (dir.) UK, 2009 > BBC/RSC/Illuminations DVD 🔊

A major hit for the RSC when it opened in 2008, David Tennant's Dane – the *Doctor Who* star was in every sense the main attraction – was filmed for TV the following year. Though the adaptation sometimes seems unsure whether it's trying to be a piece of theatre or a television special (the snow-filled Fortinbras scenes look awkwardly studio-bound), it is unfussy and intelligently done, with minimal camerawork and a fluid, dramatic pace. The setting is Ruritanian but not invasively so, and it's a top-notch cast: Patrick Stewart is sly and sharp as Claudius,

Penny Downie torn between emotions as Gertrude, and Oliver Ford Davies makes a Polonius far more sympathetic than usual. Tennant's Prince is towards the emotive end of the scale (he's often choking back the tears) but in the mad scenes is brilliantly loopy, rapier-sharp and genuinely funny. Only a shame they didn't record it live: a Hamlet this good at scoring laughs deserves an audience.

Haider
S. Kapoor, Tabu, K. Kharbanda; Vishal Bhardwaj (dir.) India, 2014 > Reliance DVD 🔊

India seems to have an obsession with the Danish Prince: the world's first talkie version of *Hamlet* was released in Mumbai in 1935, and there have been multiple reincarnations since – notably Kishore Sahu's 1954 Hindi-Urdu adaptation, notionally a tribute to Olivier but done with irresistible Bollywood panache. Vishal Bhardwaj's *Haider*, the director's third Shakespeare movie, is perhaps his glossiest and most accomplished, eminently appealing in its own right as well as by Shakespearian lights. Bhardwaj astutely relocates the action to disputed Kashmir during its terrorist-rife recent history, and Shahid Kapoor's eponymous Muslim hero is driven into the arms of militants after his father is "disappeared" by the Indian authorities (a ghostly touch that keeps him somewhere between dead and alive). The pace is thriller-ish, the script taut; only the conclusion – a gory shoot-em-up in the winter snow that makes the OK Corral look like a pleasant day out – risks overdoing it. Bhardwaj's final plot twist is too tantalizing to give away, but suffice it to say that Tabu's seductive but sympathetic Ghazala/Gertrude gives up everything for her son, and finally her life.

AUDIO

Hamlet
A. Lesser, E. de Souza, E. Fielding; Neville Jason (dir.) UK, 1997 > Naxos ◎ 🔊

Choosing an audio *Hamlet* is an invidious task, and a long one – this version stretches across four CDs, a total of three-and-a-half hours' listening. Nevertheless Naxos provides the best long-term audio experience, in part because production values are higher here than with some of the competition: the Ghost scenes are actually pretty unnerving, while the music involves real instruments rather than synthesized electronics. All this is incidental compared to the actors, most especially Anton Lesser, who makes a vigorous, mature Hamlet, never afraid to experiment with both voice and verse (he played the role on stage for Jonathan Miller in 1982). Emma Fielding's Ophelia is attractively ungirlish, and Susan Engel gives her all as Gertrude. Edward de Souza's Claudius is not as oily as he might be, though Peter Jeffery is nicely over-fussy as Polonius, as much a victim of events as the Prince himself.

Hamlet

J. Gielgud, B. Kroeger, D. McGuire; John Gielgud (dir.) USA, 1951 > Pearl ◉

Taking the dying Hamlet at his word when he begs Horatio to "absent [himself] from felicity awhile" and "tell" the Prince's story, this recording has John Merivale's earnest Horatio acting as narrator – a necessity given that this cut-down version axes a large portion of the script (it lasts just 74 minutes) and edits scenes like a film, creating short bursts of dialogue and punctuating highlights with music. One effect is to throw even more limelight on John Gielgud's Hamlet, a Prince not yet corroded by bitterness: despite his introspection, anger lies close to the surface and he seizes upon revenge with real impetuosity. While there is a sense that Gielgud is often singing rather than speaking the lines, this is a captivating reading. Barry Kroeger's surprisingly reasonable Claudius forms a nice duo with Pamela Brown's wonderfully mumsy Gertrude, as do Dorothy McGuire's wide-eyed Ophelia and George Howe's spry Polonius.

EDITIONS

Arden Shakespeare (second series)

Harold Jenkins; 1982 > Bloomsbury [o/p]

The final Arden 2 edition to appear, Jenkins's 1982 *Hamlet*, painstakingly assembled over many years, embodies the best of a certain brand of Shakespeare editing, and that series in particular: capacious notes, serious treatment of sources, date and so on, a muscular critical introduction unembarrassed about making bold statements about the play. But it's the "Longer Notes", about a quarter of this very bulky book, that make this edition really worth using. This is the place to go if you want to find out all about the sources informing Ophelia's insanity (twelve pages), the role of miniature paintings on the Elizabethan stage (three pages) or what on earth a "handsaw" is doing in the play (one page). But Jenkins has no space for *Hamlet*'s performance history and takes a traditionalist view of the text – that the second quarto is the one to follow. Although the book is now out-of-print, it's easy to pick up a secondhand copy for next to nothing.

Arden Shakespeare (third series)

Ann Thompson & Neil Taylor; 2006 > Bloomsbury

Lauded by some for its relativistic approach to *Hamlet*'s many scripts, derided by others as textual correctness gone mad, Thompson and Taylor's edition – the Arden successor to Jenkins – has divided critics. It embodies a sort of DIY editing, suggesting value in every incarnation of a text but refusing to rule between them – in this case three texts, with an edition of the full second quarto script filling one fat volume and separately edited versions of Q1 and F1 the other. This approach will inevitably interest only specialists, but what makes this Arden 3 particularly worth consulting are the on-page notes, offering a rare sense of the play in the theatre, and the stage histories, which are more complete than anything available elsewhere.

SOME CRITICISM

Shakespearean Tragedy

A.C. Bradley; 1904 > Penguin

It was estimated in 2000 that criticism on *Hamlet* exceeded the entire literary output of several European nations. Whether or not this is true, *Shakespearean Tragedy*, written around the same time, has proved more magisterially influential than the entire lot. Bradley enshrined the centrality of what's still known as the "big four" – *Othello*, *Macbeth*, *Lear* and, of course, *Hamlet* – and focused on moments he saw as of climactic significance. His view of the plays is correspondingly narrow in focus: he has little time for the plays' language, treats Shakespeare most often like a novelist, and his late-Victorian morality sometimes proves burdensome. But the readability of Bradley's analysis (though that is a term he scorned), as well as its resilient interest in humanity, wins through. You won't agree with everything he says, but you will be convinced once again that Shakespeare is the *only* writer worth attending to. An interesting postmodern response to Bradley is Ewan Fernie's monograph *Shame in Shakespeare* (2002), which argues suggestively that this very emotion – enshrined in Hamlet's question "O shame, where is thy blush?" – is the grounding idea of the play, as with the other major tragedies.

Murder Most Foul

David Bevington; 2011 > Oxford UP

Beginning with the bold premise that "the history of *Hamlet* can be seen as a kind of paradigm for the cultural history of the English-speaking world", Bevington's sprightly survey races through the centuries in an attempt to find out what the Prince of Denmark has meant to many ages – from the hectic and turbulent environment of late-Elizabethan London to the postmodern cinematic worlds of Branagh and Almereyda (with a useful bit of prehistory thrown in). Bevington is an alert critic, especially sensitive to how questions of staging can illuminate the play's substance, and offers a bravura section on how Shakespeare used the resources of the Globe theatre to the maximum. The only pity is that he restricts himself largely to English-speaking countries: there's not much here on Hamlet's global influence, whether it's Germany during the *Sturm und Drang* or the numerous Indian remakes of the drama. If you're interested in zooming in for the close-up, Martin Dodsworth's *Hamlet Closely Observed* (1985), which burrows into the text in absorbing detail, is well worth a look.

Henry IV Part I

I f *Richard II* is a play about behind-the-scenes power-broking, and *King John* unsparingly analyses the cynicism of politics, then both *Henry IV* plays examine how fragile a king's authority can be. Just glancing at the list of characters in *Henry IV Part I* reveals how much this drama is concerned with rebellion: the King's party is just five men strong; opposing them are more than twice that number. The canny and wordly-wise Bolingbroke of *Richard II*, who manoeuvred himself onto the throne with almost imperceptible fluency, is beginning to look fatally undermined, and England's future hangs once more in the balance. Despite its weighty subject matter, however, a thick comic vein runs through the play, and Shakespeare is liberated rather than constrained by his historical materials. *1 Henry IV* spends as much of its time in Eastcheap pubs as in the corridors of power, and of course it introduces one of Shakespeare's most famous double acts: that of Prince Hal, the glamorous but profligate heir to the throne, and his unlikely alter ego Sir John Falstaff – the "fat knight" who has proved one of the playwright's most enduring creations.

DATE > In print by 1598, *1 Henry IV* was most likely first performed in the summer of 1596 (soon after *Richard II*, its chronological predecessor).

SOURCES > As with his other histories, Shakespeare put Holinshed's *Chronicles* (1587 edition) and possibly Halle's *Union* (1548) to good use. It seems likely that he also read Samuel Daniel's verse *Civil Wars* (1595), chronicles by John Stow and the anonymous play *The Famous Victories of Henry V* (c. 1580s).

TEXTS > Both highly topical and immediately popular, the play was published in 1598 (a few fragments survive of what is called Q0) and reprinted seven more times (Q1–7) by 1632. A version was printed in the First Folio of 1623.

Interpreting the play

The grand theme of Shakespeare's "second tetralogy", the group of four plays stretching from *Richard II* to *Henry V*, is the so-called "Tudor Myth" (see p.154), which held that the deposition of Richard II by Bolingbroke fatally weakened the English throne and directly instigated the Wars of the Roses – a conflict brought to a close only by the accession of Henry Tudor in 1485. In *1 Henry IV* those abstract arguments, extensively worked over by the Elizabethan historiographers who constituted Shakespeare's source material, acquire a sombre human dimension. Raphael Holinshed's 1587 *Chronicles* make it clear that Henry's "unquiet" rule was caused by his usurpation: "his regiment [reign]", the historian explains, confronted "the hatred of his people, the heart grudgings of his courtiers, and the peremptory practices of both together".

MAJOR CHARACTERS & SYNOPSIS

King Henry IV (sometimes known as Bolingbroke)

Prince Harry, Prince of Wales, Henry IV's eldest son and heir (known as Hal)

Lord John of Lancaster, a younger son of Henry IV

Earl of Westmorland and **Sir Walter Blunt**, supporters of the King

REBELS AGAINST THE KING

Henry Percy, Earl of Northumberland, leader of the rebels

Thomas Percy, Earl of Worcester, Northumberland's younger brother

Sir Henry (Harry) Percy, Northumberland's son and heir (known as Hotspur)

Lord Edmund Mortimer, Earl of March, Hotspur's brother-in-law

Owain Glyndŵr, Welsh lord, Lady Mortimer's father

Archibald, Earl of Douglas, a Scottish lord

Sir Richard Vernon, an English knight

Richard le Scrope, Archbishop of York

Sir Michael, a member of the Archbishop's household

Lady Percy, Hotspur's wife and Mortimer's sister (known as Kate)

Lady Mortimer, Glyndŵr's daughter and Mortimer's wife

OTHER CHARACTERS

Sir John Falstaff, one of Hal's companions (called "Oldcastle" in the early printed texts)

Falstaff's followers: **Edward (Ned) Poins**, **Bardolph** and **Peto**

Mistress Quickly, hostess of an Eastcheap tavern

Francis, a barman, and a **Vintner** (tavern-keeper)

[ACTION CONTINUED FROM RICHARD II]

ACT 1 Henry Bolingbroke, new to the throne, is already battling his first rebellion. Mortimer has been taken prisoner by the Welsh rebel Glyndŵr, though the King's forces have succeeded in the north, where Hotspur has defeated the Scots. In contrast, Henry's wastrel son, Prince Hal, is boozing with cronies rather than fighting for his father. At an Eastcheap tavern Hal conspires with Poins to play a practical joke on their friend Falstaff – who has turned to highway robbery to pay his bills – by robbing him in disguise. Hotspur,

meanwhile, has withdrawn support until the King pays Mortimer's ransom. When he refuses – denouncing Mortimer as a traitor – Hotspur is enraged and plots rebellion against him.

ACT 2 After Falstaff and his crew rob a group of travellers, Hal and Poins ambush their friends and steal their booty. They are already in Eastcheap by the time Falstaff returns, and pretend to believe his account of the attack before exposing the truth. Falstaff is recovering from the embarrassment when Hotspur's rebellion is announced. Recalled to court and convinced that the King will take the opportunity to condemn his behaviour, Hal briefly plays out the scene of his father's wrath with his companions before they are forced to hide from the sheriff and his men, who are on Falstaff's trail.

ACT 3 King Henry is unimpressed with his son's antics, but is won round by Hal's promise to prove himself and fight. In Wales, the rebellion gathers pace: Mortimer has joined forces with Glyndŵr, Hotspur and Worcester, and war is certain. On his way to battle, Hal calls on the tavern and per-suades Falstaff to join him.

ACT 4 Rumours of Hal's unexpected appearance reach the rebels, who have been hit by sudden bad news about Northumberland (seriously ill) and Glyndŵr's army (badly under-prepared). Challenged by the King, they squabble among themselves. Falstaff, meanwhile, is doing his bit for the royal cause by accepting bribes to dismiss good soldiers.

ACT 5 Distrusting the King's offer of clemency, Worcester is convinced that the rebels must fight. Battle at Shrewsbury commences. Although Henry has arranged for several soldiers to impersonate him in order to confuse the enemy, Douglas discovers the real King and is about to kill him when Hal bursts in and saves his father. Hotspur appears and the two fight, Hal finally killing his rival. He then notices Falstaff's body lying close by, and laments the death of his old friend – at which point Falstaff gets up. The battle is won, Worcester and Vernon are sentenced to death, and King Henry prepares to rout the remaining rebels.

But in Shakespeare's masterful *Part I*, the King's tragedy – which will eventually grow into the tragedy of England, as we already know from the *Henry VI* plays – is less than half the story. The playwright shunts the conflict into another generation, and what results is a kind of competitive comedy between King Henry's wastrel son Hal, Prince of Wales, and his dashing rival Hotspur, son of the King's main foe, Northumberland. Historically spurious though it is (the real-life Henry Percy was over twenty years older than Henry), this dynamic story of two young bloods competing for supremacy dominates the action of the play, offsetting the political narrative and often threatening to eclipse it altogether.

So blest a son

At first it seems as if there will not be much in the way of competition: while Hotspur is where any young noble should be, on the battlefield, Hal whiles away his time in inns and taverns – a source of some discomfort to the Prince, who wittily, but perhaps nervously, satirizes his rival as a man "that kills some six or seven dozen of Scots at a breakfast, washes his hands, and says to his wife, 'Fie upon this quiet life! I want work'" (2.5.103–6). Hal's father is altogether less sanguine about the contrast between the two, unable to think about much else. Henry expresses his "envy" that "my lord Northumberland / Should be the father to so blest a son—"

> A son who is the theme of honour's tongue,
> Amongst a grove the very straightest plant,
> Who is sweet Fortune's minion and her pride—
> Whilst I by looking on the praise of him
> See riot and dishonour stain the brow
> Of my young Harry. O, that it could be proved
> That some night-tripping fairy had exchanged
> In cradle clothes our children where they lay,
> And called mine Percy, his Plantagenet!
>
> [1.1.78–88]

Far from fearing that Hal is not his own child, the King actively wishes he were someone else's. Though his frustration is hemmed in by irony – this disregard for the niceties of inheritance is one reason why he is on the throne – it is also agonizingly real: a father's grief that his son simply will not be as he should.

Not that Hotspur's relationship with his own father is any more productive. While Northumberland is a wily politician (wily enough not to turn up at Shrewsbury when it becomes apparent that the rebels have no chance), his son is the polar opposite. Hotspur's brilliance and chutzpah make him a natural in battle – and a fiery figure on stage – but leave him utterly stranded in the messier world of interpersonal politics. Committed to knightly integrity and a strict moral code, he cannot stand "this ingrate and cankered Bolingbroke", "this vile politician", the "king of smiles" who has (in his view) glad-handed himself to the English throne. While Richard II's usurpation is a matter of minor political regret for King Henry –

a miscalculation, perhaps – Hotspur vows to "empty all these veins, / And shed my dear blood drop by drop in the dust" in order to avenge it. "By heaven," he exclaims imperiously to his father,

> methinks it were an easy leap
> To pluck bright honour from the pale-faced moon,
> Or dive into the bottom of the deep,
> Where fathom-line could never touch the ground,
> And pluck up drownèd honour by the locks,
> So he that doth redeem her thence might wear,
> Without corrival, all her dignities.

[1.3.199–205]

In the canon of angry young Shakespearien men, only Coriolanus comes close – and the parallel does not bode well. As Worcester wearily notes, Hotspur is addicted to his imagination: "he apprehends a world of figures here, / Not the form of what he should attend" (1.3.207–8). Brilliant though his wit is – and we see it deployed to brilliant effect as he vies with the other rebels for supremacy – it will be one reason for his downfall.

A tun of man

From snatched hints in Holinshed about the "great resort of people" who hung around the Prince, encouraging him to waste time in "such recreations, exercises and sports as he fancied", in the *Henry IV* plays Shakespeare builds an evolving cast of low-life comic characters who are as varied in personality as they are consistent in their determination to shirk, drink and steal – traits that only endear them to the "mad wag" Prince. There's Poins, Hal's close companion and his co-conspirator in the plot to fool Falstaff by robbing him in disguise at Gads Hill. There's Russell (later renamed Bardolph; see box overpage), with his grotesque nose, "all bubuncles and knobs and flames o' fire" (*Henry V*, 3.6.103–4); and Harvey/Peto, cowardly but ultimately honest. There's Francis, well-meaning but dim. There's also Mistress Quickly, a pub hostess with a gift for unwitting double entendres. In later plays Shakespeare adds to their number with Pistol, a braggart soldier who sounds as if he's just stepped out of the pages of Marlowe; and his nemesis Nim, whose favourite – and almost only – word is "humour" (an Elizabethan joke lost on us).

But the leader of this motley group is Shakespeare's largest comic creation in every sense, Sir John Falstaff (or Oldcastle, as he was originally called; see box overpage), who first appears in *1 Henry IV* and irresistibly dominates both play and stage. Even the subject of his size is a major concern of *1 Henry IV* and a rich seam of the play's linguistic texture: he is "fat-witted", "fat guts", "fat rogue", "woolsack", "huge hill of flesh", "as fat as butter". Until relatively recently he was unquestionably Shakespeare's most popular character; in fact there are so many references to him that *The Shakespeare Allusion-Book* (1909) treats him not as a character but as a work in his own right. The critic A.C. Bradley, writing that same year, merely echoed audiences across the centuries when he

Zounds!

Shakespeare's gaffes are few but famous; one came close to endangering his career. In the first versions of *1 Henry IV* Sir John Falstaff is nowhere to be seen: his place is taken by "**Sir John Oldcastle**". All well and good, except that Shakespeare had made the mistake of naming one of his finest comic creations, the "whoreson round man" of the second tetralogy, after an unimpeachably zealous Protestant martyr. Oldcastle's descendants – one of whom was Elizabeth I's influential Lord Chamberlain – were none too impressed, and the playwright was forced not only to rechristen him, along with Russell (Bardolph) and Harvey (Peto), but to insert a grovelling retraction in the epilogue to *2 Henry IV* insisting that "Oldcastle died a martyr, and this is not the man" (Epilogue, 30).

Shakespeare was usually more careful, for Elizabeth I's government kept a wary eye on members of the theatrical profession. In 1581 the Queen made **Edmund Tilney**, her Master of the Revels, responsible for approving all plays that were publicly produced, and as Tilney's interventions to tone down the collaborative *Sir Thomas More* (c. 1595) demonstrate, he took his role seriously – as did his successor **George Buck**, in the job during the last years of Shakespeare's career. By that stage things had got even harder for the players. With the passing of the notorious "**Act to Restrain the Abuses of Players**" in 1606, a sop to Puritan parliamentary leaders and popular campaigners, they were banned from acting anything that took the Lord's name in vain. An energetic tradition of stage swearing celebrated by Shakespeare's deliciously rude *Henry IV*s was over at a stroke. Those plays and others, among them *King John*, were henceforth purged of irreligious language (outlawed words included "zounds", short for "God's wounds", "'S'blood"/"Christ's blood" and many others).

The Act initiated a (dis)honourable tradition of cleaning up Shakespeare to suit the supposed sensitivities of his audiences. In this curious pantheon the name of the Reverend **Thomas Bowdler** looms large. Bowdler's *Family Shakespeare* (1818), assembled in collaboration with his sisters (who in fact did most of the work), deleted anything that "cannot with propriety be read aloud in a family", though their swingeing cuts to *Othello* rendered the play so nonsensical that they recommended it be hidden from children just in case they realized. Other plays suffered nearly as much, with the result that the verb "to Bowdlerize" was current in the language just a few decades later.

For some, the idea that Britain's national poet could have penned anything remotely off-colour has simply been too much. The cornerstone of **Joseph C. Hart**'s argument in his splendidly eccentric *The Romance of Yachting* (1848), that Shakespeare did not author the plays, is ingeniously simple: no one man could have written all the filth they contain. Having been "purchased or obtained surreptitiously", Hart thundered, "they were first spiced with obscenity, blackguardism and impurities, before they were produced." Nor are those days entirely past. The prize for misplaced prudery must surely go to the film censors employed by the State of Massachusetts exactly a century later, who insisted that references to "The rank sweat of an adulterous bed" be cut from Olivier's version of *Hamlet* before it could safely be screened.

proclaimed that "no one in the play understands Falstaff fully, any more than Hamlet was understood by the persons around him. They are both men of genius."

Falstaff comes from a long literary pedigree of vast wenchers, eaters and drinkers, but it is his subversive resistance to the historical patterns of the *Henry IV* plays that make him so attractive. Like the Bastard Falconbridge in *King John*, he considers himself outside the main action. While the rest of the King's army readies itself for battle at Shrewsbury, for instance, Falstaff is openly unimpressed. "What is honour?" he enquires,

> A word. What is in that word 'honour'? What is that 'honour'? Air. A trim reckoning! Who hath it? He that died o' Wednesday. Doth he feel it? No. Doth he hear it? No. 'Tis insensible then? Yea, to the dead. But will it not live with the living? No. Why? Detraction will not suffer it. Therefore I'll none of it. Honour is a mere scutcheon.
>
> [5.1.133–40]

Falstaff concludes that "honour", so much a central issue for Hotspur (and ultimately for Hal too), is "a mere scutcheon" (a cheap heraldic emblem). That Falstaff has little taste for bravery is clear enough following the episode at Gads Hill in the first half of the play, where the disguised Hal and Poins rob their companions in order to see what ludicrous stories of derring-do Falstaff will invent – invention is very much his forte – after the event.

Falstaff is, in an obvious sense, a surrogate father for Hal (indeed, the one character who actually calls him "Hal"), albeit one with whom his relationship is as fraught as the real thing. The relationship between the two is gloriously complicated, and Hal frequently takes the opportunity to test its limits. He stage-manages a role-play at Eastcheap in which Falstaff impersonates King Henry grilling Hal about his antics, but they soon exchange roles and Falstaff is left to defend himself. In response to Hal's accusations about "that villainous, abominable misleader of youth … that old white-bearded Satan," Sir John is moved to respond:

> That he is old, the more the pity … If to be old and merry be a sin, then many an old host that I know is damned. If to be fat be to be hated, then Pharaoh's lean kine are to be loved. No, my good lord, banish Harvey, banish Russell, banish Poins, but for sweet Jack Oldcastle, kind Jack Oldcastle, true Jack Oldcastle, valiant Jack Oldcastle, and therefore the more valiant being, as he is, old Jack Oldcastle … Banish plump Jack, and banish all the world.
>
> HAL I do; I will.
>
> [2.5.472–86]

The tone of Hal's response is famously inscrutable – it can be played as a light-hearted joke just as easily as an open threat (and is perhaps both at once). But it is difficult to watch this moment without thinking of Hal's statement only two scenes into the play that he has every intention of disposing of his "loose behaviour". Imitating Richard II's

---

No play of Shakespeare's is better than Henry IV … History as a dramatic form ripens here to a point past which no further growth is possible.

Mark Van Doren, *Shakespeare* (1939)

---

beloved solar imagery, he proclaims "Yet herein will I imitate the sun, / Who doth permit the base contagious clouds / To smother up his beauty from the world,"

> That when he please again to be himself,
> Being wanted he may be more wondered at
> By breaking through the foul and ugly mists
> Of vapours that did seem to strangle him ...
> And like bright metal on a sullen ground,
> My reformation, glitt'ring oe'r my fault,
> Shall show more goodly and attract more eyes
> Than that which hath no foil to set it off.
> I'll so offend to make offence a skill,
> Redeeming time when men least think I will.
>
> [1.2.194–214]

We glimpse here a Prince who is not making excuses for his wayward existence, but calculating and weighing its advantage with the kingly life to come. His language is impersonal – his companions are "base contagious clouds", the "sullen ground" – but there is no mistaking its thrust. Hal hints that his "reformation", when it arrives, will be a show-stealing change from what has come before.

The finale of *1 Henry IV*, then, has all the ingredients for a blockbuster finish: a military showdown between the royal forces and the rebels; the long-awaited combat between Hal and Hotspur; most importantly, perhaps, the moment where we get to see what will happen between father and son – whether Hal will continue as Henry's "near'st and dearest enemy" (3.3.123) or prove himself his father's heir. Masterfully plotted throughout, the play keeps its audience hanging on to the very end. It is not until the rebels begin to falter, lacking Northumberland's support, that it becomes clear that the King will prevail, and that father and son will indeed be reunited. The outcome of the combat between Hal and Hotspur is somewhat simpler, however. Meeting in battle, Hal crisply warns Hotspur that he can no longer tolerate rivalry. "Think not, Percy, / To share with me in glory any more," he announces,

> Two stars keep not their motion in one sphere,
> Nor can one England brook a double reign
> Of Harry Percy and the Prince of Wales.
>
> [5.4.62–6]

Slaying his double, stepping out of his shadow, Hal defines himself.

But the play has one more surprise in store. Near Hotspur's corpse, Hal sees Falstaff lying on the ground, and is struck by emotion:

> What, old acquaintance! Could not all this flesh
> Keep in a little life? Poor Jack, farewell.
> I could have spared a better man.
>
> [5.4.101–3]

Hal wants his address to Falstaff's corpse to be a defining moment, his attempt at "reformation". The only problem is that reality isn't compliant with Hal's neat ending – Falstaff is only pretending to be dead in order to steer clear of trouble, and his typically obstreperous resurrection from the battlefield, a jokey taste of the reawakening scenes Shakespeare employs in his late romances, refuses to finish things off. One thing is clear: there is going to have to be a sequel.

Stage history and adaptations

Bursting with actorly and comic detail, both parts of *Henry IV* have long been favourites on stage, and it's been estimated that *Part I* was Shakespeare's most successful play in his lifetime. **Richard Burbage** seems to have created the role of Hal, and **John Heminges** (future co-editor of the First Folio) Falstaff. Both will presumably have played before the Flemish Ambassador in 1600, and again at court in 1612 to mark the marriage of James I's daughter Elizabeth (*Part I* is called "The Hotspur" in the records), though by then Burbage will have made a rather elderly prince. Other command performances seem to have occurred in 1625 and 1638, and an adaptation of both plays was prepared for performance at the country house of antiquarian **Sir Edward Dering**, *Part I* taking the lion's share.

The runaway fame of Sir John Falstaff – there are over a hundred mentions of him in surviving seventeenth-century documents – makes subsequent references to the plays difficult to untangle. *The First Part of Sir John Falstaff* (1635) is most likely *Part I*, but the dramas described as *Sir John Falstaff* in 1635 and *Oldcastle* in 1638 could be any of Shakespeare's Falstaff plays. Sir John's celebrity even protected him from the theatrical ban imposed by Cromwell's government – a skit entitled *The Bouncing Knight, or, The Robbers Robbed* did the rounds in the 1650s. After the Restoration, the *Henry IV* plays were acted by **Thomas Killigrew**'s company with **William Cartwright** as Falstaff, who was much admired by Pepys. Actor-manager **Thomas Betterton** began as Hotspur in 1682 (playing the role with "fierce and flashing fire", according to one observer), but by the end of the century had migrated to the fat knight.

Betterton's move proved prophetic, for in the eighteenth century *Part I*'s story becomes a roll call of career Falstaffs: first the austere **James Quin**, who gave the knight lofty dignity from 1718 (and who inspired **William Kenrick**'s 1760 spin-off *Falstaff's Wedding*); then actors including **James Love** (from 1761), **Francis Gentleman** (1770) and **John Henderson** (1777). **David Garrick** steered well clear, but did play Hotspur. **John Philip Kemble** also tried Hotspur, leaving Falstaff to his brothers **Stephen**, then **Charles** – although Stephen's talents were limited, he had the advantage of requiring no padding. The most famous Hotspur of the age, however, was **William Charles Macready**, who first acted him in 1815 and continued for the next thirty years.

As evidenced by an adaptation by **Charles Short** called *The Life and Humours of Falstaff* (1826), Sir John's heyday lasted well into the nineteenth century, and he landed on new and remote shores. The first recorded Shakespearian production in Australia was a version of *Henry IV*, performed in 1800, and *Part I* was also among the first Shakespeare plays to be staged in sub-Saharan Africa, in English, at the African Theatre

Richard Burton brought not only youthful intensity but palpable menace to the part of Prince Hal at Stratford in 1951. Critic Kenneth Tynan remarked that "Burton is first and last an animal actor, with an animal's accidental grace and unsentimental passions."

in Cape Town in 1801. The American **James Henry Hackett** acted Falstaff with considerable success in both New York and London's Covent Garden – to the horror of some English critics, unused to the notion of an American doing Shakespeare – and his rival **Samuel Phelps** kept Sir John's flame alive at Sadler's Wells for over two decades, famously acting him in a tercentenary *Part I* at Drury Lane in 1864. By this stage grand "historical" productions were all the rage, meaning that *Part I*, lacking in opportunities for pageantry (unlike *Part II*), was less frequently mounted – though **Herbert Beerbohm Tree** did introduce an impressive Battle of Shrewsbury into his version of 1896. After staging it at Stratford a few years later, **Frank Benson** did away with *Part I* altogether in his ground-breaking cycle of histories, replacing it with Marlowe's *Edward II* instead.

Part I would not always fare so badly. The English histories were surprisingly popular in Germany from the 1850s onwards, and **Max Reinhardt** put on both plays in a fine production at the Berlin Deutsches Theatre in 1912, with **Wilhelm Diegelmann** as Falstaff to **Alessandro Moissi**'s Hal. **Barry Jackson** went one better nine years later at the Birmingham Rep, presenting both parts on Shakespeare's 357th birthday – *Part I* in the afternoon, *Part II* in the evening. A similar arrangement, directed by **William Bridges-Adams**, marked the opening of the new Memorial Theatre at Stratford in 1932. Seven years later **Orson Welles** presented an adaptation called *Five Kings* in Boston: the *Henry IV*s and *Henry V* became a single play, with excerpts from Holinshed filling the gaps, but it was a flop.

Immediately after World War II, **John Burrell** directed starry productions of both plays at the Old Vic, with **Laurence Olivier** as a memorable Hotspur (complete with stammer), **Sybil Thorndike** as Mistress Quickly and **Ralph Richardson** as a particularly nuanced and sensitive Sir John. **Anthony Quayle**'s cast at Stratford in 1951 was equally impressive, with **Michael Redgrave** as Hotspur, Quayle himself as a gentlemanly Falstaff and **Richard Burton** as a hard-boiled Hal. Quayle placed much emphasis on the divisive relationship between Sir John and his protégé, as did **Douglas Seale** at the Old Vic in 1955, but in the later production **Robert Hardy**'s Hal revealed a soft spot for **Paul Rogers**'s Falstaff that only political events hardened.

Since **Clifford Williams**'s epochal staging of the *Henry IV*s as part of the Barton–Hall *Wars of the Roses* cycle in 1964, with **Roy Dotrice** as Hotspur, **Hugh Griffith** as a roguish Falstaff and **Ian Holm** as Hal, the tendency has been for both histories to be played as part of the Henriad cycle, and sometimes of both cycles. The RSC has hosted nearly all: first under **Terry Hands** (1975), who directed a cynical second tetralogy, focused on **Alan Howard**'s graceless prince, that divided audiences – some admiring its imaginative unity, others viewing it as too monochrome (especially with *1 Henry IV*, which was played darkly, Hands's staging making Howard dominant over **Brewster Mason**'s Falstaff throughout). Opposite in conception was **Trevor Nunn**'s Barbican version seven years later, relying on the rich resources of **Joss Ackland** as Sir John (see p.135).

Adrian Noble's response in 1991, with a two-play *Henry IV* that opened his reign as director of the RSC, was to emphasize *1 Henry IV*'s vivid spectacle, culminating in an impressively staged Battle of Shrewsbury. Not that this production lacked human detail: **Michael Maloney**'s Hal had plenty of restless energy, **Owen Teale**'s Hotspur was roundly portrayed and **Robert Stephens** was impressive as Falstaff, described by the *Observer* as "a bleak Government health warning on the effects of sack". Also at the RSC, 2000 saw a grand two-tetralogy staging of the histories entitled *This England*, which boasted uncut texts and ran for nearly 24 hours in all. **Michael Attenborough** offered a sombre realization of the *Henry IV*s, with a cast including **David Troughton**'s earnest King Henry and **William Houston** as his wayward son; **Desmond Barrit** made a memorable first appearance as an irrepressible Falstaff, clambering through a trap-door to puncture the power-broking atmosphere.

Nicholas Hytner's 2005 National Theatre production was eagerly awaited, not least for the prospect of **Michael Gambon**'s Falstaff, but in the end his shambling interpretation of a needy Sir John failed to project sufficiently into the Olivier theatre's large expanse. Another RSC complete cycle was mounted in 2007–08, this time directed by **Michael Boyd**. **David Warner** brought to Falstaff a gimlet-eyed menace few had expected, though was criticized for failing to develop much of a relationship with **Geoffrey Streatfield**'s puppyish Hal. The company again staged the two *Henry IV* plays, this time in isolation, in new productions in 2014, with **Antony Sher** donning the fattest fatsuit in the company's wardrobe to play Falstaff. It was **Trevor White**'s Hotspur, however, who seized the attention of many critics – a "blonde hothead who is impatient to the point of derangement", in the words of the *Independent*.

Not all royal Shakespeare cycles have appeared courtesy of the Royal Shakespeare Company. **Michael Bogdanov**'s politically confrontational English Shakespeare Company histories toured the UK as *The Wars of the Roses* from 1986, while a more esoteric approach was tried by the Italian **Collettivo di Parma**, who presented hypnotic postmodern versions of their *Enrico IV* at London's Riverside Studios in 1983. Equally radical was the staging of *Part I* by **Ariane Mnouchkine** and her Paris-based Théâtre du Soleil the following year. Over in New York a decade later, a one-evening abridged version of both parts of *Henry IV* debuted at the Lincoln Center in late 2003. It boasted an impressive cast – **Ethan Hawke**'s Hal to **Kevin Kline**'s Falstaff – and received considerable acclaim.

In 2010, the *Henry IV* plays made a long-overdue appearance at the rebuilt Globe in London, in a measured, medieval-style production directed by **Dominic Dromgoole**. Central in every sense was **Roger Allam**'s sardonic Falstaff, acclaimed by the *Telegraph* for his "ripe, roguish charisma" (**Jamie Parker**'s cool, public-school Hal, meanwhile, was compared by the same critic to British prime minister David Cameron). Two years later, the plays were staged as part of the theatre's contribution to the World Shakespeare Festival; *Part I* was offered by Mexico's **Compañia Nacional de Teatro** in a production that, despite its strolling-player-style costumes, brought to mind the ugly power struggles that have dogged recent Mexican politics. One of the most fascinating recent British versions – the *Henry IVs* have never been especially popular in America since the days of James Henry Hackett– was staged in 2014 by director **Phyllida Lloyd** at the Donmar in London, an informal follow-up to her all-female *Julius Caesar* two years earlier (see p.209). Again set in a women's prison, it cut the plays down to sharp, two-hour versions and featured **Harriet Walter** as an agonized King, **Ashley McGuire** as a Cockneyfied Falstaff and **Clare Dunn**'s hot-blooded Hal.

The most artistically memorable film version of the *Henry IV* plays remains **Orson Welles**'s *Chimes at Midnight* (1966), but variations on the play surface in **Gus Van Sant**'s *My Own Private Idaho* (1991), in which **William Richert**'s Falstaffian Bob joins **Keanu Reeves**'s rent boy Scott/Hal on the road as they traverse the Pacific Northwest. None other than **Sean Connery** played Hotspur to **Robert Hardy**'s Hal in a 1960 BBC adaptation of *Part I*, part of the fifteen-part *Age of Kings* series, while the BBC/Time-Life Shakespeare version was directed by **David Giles** (1979). The BBC returned to the play in 2012 with *The Hollow Crown*, a lushly produced costume drama that put the first part of the cycle, *Richard II* to *Henry V*, on TV screens: in *Part I*, **Tom Hiddleston** took Hal to **Jeremy Irons**'s Henry, with **Simon Russell Beale** as Falstaff and **Richard Eyre** directing.

SCREEN

Chimes at Midnight

O. Welles, K. Baxter, J. Gielgud; Orson Welles (dir.)
Spain/Switzerland, 1966 > Mr Bongo `DVD` 🔊

Compared to his *Macbeth* (1948) and *Othello* (1952), *Chimes at Midnight* is the most straightforward work of Orson Welles's three Shakespeare adaptations and also one of his greatest films. Half the wonder lies in the patchworking of material from both *Henry IV*s and the supple pacing. While incipient tragedy is never distant (Hal's "yet herein will I imitate the sun" speech is played with Welles's mountainous Falstaff within anxious earshot), Welles still manages to make the Battle of Shrewsbury — filmed in stomach-churning proximity — a truly impressive first climax, despite limitations of budget. Norman Rodway's fiery Hotspur is both genuinely funny and terribly sad, a verdict that perhaps stands for *Chimes* as a whole, which ditches even more of the historical narrative than Shakespeare in order to concentrate on the personal relationships Welles sees at its centre. Even better, the film has recently been restored and is available on HD Blu-ray.

Henry IV Part I

R. Allam, J. Parker, O. Cotton; Dominic Dromgoole (dir.) UK, 2010 > Shakespeare's Globe 🔊

Roger Allam's turn as Falstaff was a recent highlight at the Globe — the fat-suited, red-nosed Allam waddled away with a Olivier award — and is well caught in this live recording. The political and court scenes are efficiently done, but this version of *Part I* is in every way happiest down the pub, never better than when Allam's sardonic, Havana-voiced Sir John is sparking off Jamie Parker's Estuary-accented Hal. If some of the japery is forced — the Gads Hill scene is like something out of *Blackadder* — the performances have an appealing warmth, particularly that of Sam Crane as an anxious and likeable Hotspur. But it's hard to take your eyes off Allam. His speech railing against "honour" is a masterclass in how to use the space: without the tiniest hint of bombast, he seems to make 1,400 people both laugh and hold their breath.

The Hollow Crown

S. Beale, T. Hiddleston, J. Irons; Richard Eyre (dir.) UK, 2012 > BBC `DVD` 🔊

After a slightly wobbly start with Rupert Goold's stylish but uneven *Richard II* (see p.372), the *Hollow Crown* series finds its rhythm courtesy of old hand Richard Eyre, who both adapts and directs this highly watchable *Henry IV Part I*. Starkly divided between the blood-and-butchery world of Eastcheap and the icy chill of the court, it has fine performances from a rasping, choleric Jeremy Irons

as King Henry and Simon Russell Beale as a badger-like Falstaff, rather more watchful and fretful than you might expect. Apart from some over-soupy music, almost this film's only flaw — perhaps Shakespeare's too — is that it's hard to believe Tom Hiddleston's chilly and efficient Hal will play the wastrel for a moment longer than necessary. But then perhaps it's not even Hal's play: one of the fascinations of this version is the light it throws on Hotspur, played with sparking wit and energy by Joe Armstrong alongside his real-life father Alun as Northumberland and Michelle Dockery's fiery Lady Percy. When Hal and Hotspur finish their single combat at a snow-blighted Shrewsbury, you can't help feeling that the best man lost.

AUDIO

Henry IV Part I

J. Glover, J. Glover, T. West; Gordon House (dir.) UK, 2000 > BBC ⊙ 🔊

Casting a real-life father and son as King Henry and Hal is attention-grabbing, but with performances like these it is much more than that. Glovers both senior and junior seem truly to inhabit the roles — Jamie does a good line in slightly unsettling levity, while Julian's King is politically efficient but emotionally troubled. Timothy West is persuasively grizzled as Falstaff, and while this performance may be more reflective than some would like (one occasionally wishes for more fireworks), it makes for excellent listening. Jonathan Keeble brings a north-country edge to his surprisingly sober Hotspur.

EDITIONS

Oxford Shakespeare

David Bevington (ed.); 1987 > Oxford UP

Though now one of the older Oxford editions, Bevington's terrific edition of *1 Henry IV* is still highly recommended. It offers a no-holds-barred critical introduction to the play and lashings of detail on its textual background, which Bevington takes from the 1598 quarto, one of the neatest texts published during its author's lifetime as well as one of his most popular. Bevington looks hard at the literary and popular models feeding Shakespeare's Falstaff, and touches on events that occur in *Part II* but are hinted at from early on in the first play — notably Sir John's rejection. Bevington elects to retain the names of Falstaff, Bardolph and Peto as they are usually known (see p.118), arguing continuity. Historical phrases in the text are keyed to passages from Halle and Holinshed at the back. More recent stage history is available in David Scott Kastan's Arden 3 edition (2002).

SOME CRITICISM

Oxford Lectures on Poetry
A.C. Bradley; 1909 > HardPress / Atlantic

After his *Shakespearean Tragedy* (see p.113), Bradley's other great work is this collection of lectures delivered while Professor of Poetry at Oxford. The volume indulges his Romantic tastes (with articles on Wordsworth, Shelley and "The Sublime") but heads inexorably towards Bradley's great love, Shakespeare – and one of his greatest loves of all, Falstaff. In this classic essay Bradley's thesis is simple: "In Falstaff", he declares, the poet "created so extraordinary a being, and fixed him so firmly on his intellectual throne, that when he sought to dethrone him he could not." This sense that Shakespeare simply cannot kill off someone so touched by genius has remained influential, and even Bradley's suggestion that poet and Falstaff are locked into a kind of battle to the death is persuasive.

Sodometries
Jonathan Goldberg; 1992 > Fordham UP

Forget Falstaff – what about Hal? Now a classic of queer theory, *Sodometries* looks at different presentations of male homosexuality in Renaissance texts, among them Spenser and Shakespeare. In the *Henry IV* plays, Goldberg investigates just why we (and the characters in the *Henry IV* plays) seem to find the youthful Prince so attractive, and uncovers some interesting detail about how the play presents his sexuality. Goldberg has interesting as well as provocative things to say about sex in this period – as about sex in the late twentieth century – and has another particularly excellent chapter on Shakespeare's rival Christopher Marlowe.

Henry IV Part II

G iven that they have so much in common, it is a surprise to realize how different the two *Henry IV* plays in fact are. Whereas *Part I* is dominated by youth – by two charismatic young men locked in rivalry – its follow-up is both older and gloomier. Though the historical record for the decade compressed into *Part II* is packed with incident, that is not true for the play itself, which witnesses just one abortive battle and a lingering royal death. Shakespeare allows the action to become dominated by response to events already past, and soured by reminiscence and regret. With Hotspur dead, young characters recede into the distance, and the cast becomes populated by people who are starting to seem past their best. Repetition, too, is a major concern as we watch King Henry face yet more rebellion and Hal, having promised his father (and us) a "reformation", pointedly reverting to his bad old ways. And although its humour is often as fresh as ever, the play produces a final twist that still has the capacity to shock. It is no accident that *2 Henry IV* has been called Shakespeare's first tragicomedy.

DATE > Though presumably *Part II* was written soon after *1 Henry IV*, another "Falstaff" play – *The Merry Wives of Windsor* – may have come between the pair. A composition date of between late 1597 and early 1598 is generally accepted.

SOURCES > *2 Henry IV* uses the same set of sources as its predecessor (see p.114).

Other details may derive from a source itself employed by John Stow, *The Governor* (1531) by the Tudor courtier Thomas Elyot, and another work, John Eliot's *Ortho-epia Gallica* (1593).

TEXTS > In contrast to *1 Henry IV*, only one quarto printing (Q1, 1600) is recorded before the play appeared in the 1623 First Folio. Some passages appear in the Folio text alone.

Interpreting the play

Many have wondered how exactly the two *Henry IV*s fit together: did the playwright plan a two-part structure, or was he spurred by the success of *Part I* to pen a follow-up? The so-called "structural problem" of *Henry IV* – whether it is one play or two – still vexes scholars, but perhaps that is because it is really both. Dramatically speaking, what really matters is that *2 Henry IV* is dominated by fallout from events that have already happened, particularly events that have occurred in *Part I*. Though Shakespeare gives no suggestion that time has elapsed between the two parts – quite the opposite, in fact – there is an unmistakable sense that things have changed.

Part II turns the fact that it is a sequel into a morbid theatrical preoccupation. With Hotspur dead, it becomes starkly apparent that the play's central political argument – Henry Bolingbroke's usurpation of Richard II's throne – is a quarrel between old men.

MAJOR CHARACTERS & SYNOPSIS

King Henry IV of England
Prince Henry (known as Hal), later crowned **King Henry V**
Hal's brothers: **Prince John of Lancaster**; Humphrey, **Duke of Gloucester**; Thomas, **Duke of Clarence**
The King's supporters: **Earls of Warwick, Surrey** and **Westmoreland**; **Harcourt**; **Gower**; **Sir John Blunt**

REBELS AGAINST THE KING

Earl of Northumberland and his wife, **Lady Northumberland**
Kate, Lady Percy, Hotspur's widow
Travers, Northumberland's servant; and **Morton**, a messenger
Rebellious nobles: **Archbishop of York**; **Lord Bardolph**; **Mowbray**; **Lord Hastings**; **Sir John Coleville**

OTHER CHARACTERS

Sir John Falstaff, one of Hal's companions
Falstaff's followers: **Edward (Ned) Poins, Bardolph, Pistol** and **Peto**; and his **Page**
Mistress Quickly, hostess of an Eastcheap tavern
Doll Tearsheet, a prostitute
Shallow and his companion **Silence**, elderly country justices
Davy, Shallow's servant
Soldiers recruited by Falstaff: **Mouldy, Shadow, Wart, Feeble** and **Bullcalf**
Rumour, the Presenter

[ACTION CONTINUED FROM HENRY IV PART I]

ACT 1 Northumberland is frantic for news of the rebellion. Initial reports seem good, but the truth soon arrives – the rebels are defeated and his son Hotspur is dead. Northumberland is devastated, but Morton and Lord Bardolph assure him that the fight is not over: the Archbishop of York and others are mustering their forces, and the King's position is not as secure as it seems. Falstaff, meanwhile, is being harangued by the Lord Chief Justice for his influence on Hal, the heir to the throne. Unperturbed by the accusations against him, Falstaff asks for financial support – to no avail.

ACT 2 Mistress Quickly attempts to have Falstaff arrested for fraud, but he manages to talk his way out of it by renewing his promise to marry her, even persuading her to pawn her silver to raise cash. Hal, meanwhile, worries about his father's illness, but is diverted from state business when Falstaff sends a letter slandering Poins. Poins denies the allegations, and the pair resolve to spy on Falstaff and find out what he is up to. They sneak into the Eastcheap tavern and overhear Falstaff complaining about the Prince while canoodling with Doll Tearsheet. When confronted, Sir John attempts to convince them he has Hal's best interests at heart. The Prince is interrupted by a summons to court.

ACT 3 The pressures of leadership are taking their toll on King Henry. Unable to sleep, he reflects ruefully with Warwick and Surrey on his betrayal by the very nobles who helped him to power. Falstaff, visiting Warwickshire to recruit soldiers for the royal army, is on the make – taking bribes to turn down good men.

ACT 4 York, Mowbray and Hastings, commanding the rebel forces in Gaultres Forest, are unimpressed by Northumberland's flight to Scotland. When they outline their grievances to Hal's brother, Prince John, he promises redress – but as soon as they agree, arrests them for treason. Falstaff, surprisingly, has also succeeded in capturing some enemy troops. The King, meanwhile, is in such poor health that news of his victory causes him to collapse. Arriving at court, Hal assumes his father has died and sadly takes up the crown. The awakening King angrily thinks he covets the throne for himself, but Hal convinces him otherwise and the two are reconciled. The old King dies, hoping that his son's reign will be more peaceful than his own.

ACT 5 As reports spread that Hal has inherited the throne, courtiers question his abilities. Falstaff certainly believes that his friend has no intention of reforming, and rushes to London to be by his side – also hoping to release Mistress Quickly and Doll Tearsheet from prison. But a shock awaits them: the new King Henry renounces his previous life, pointedly refusing to recognize Falstaff and his companions. Henry V promises to be every inch a king and is rumoured to be planning a campaign against the French.

The visibly wilting Northumberland is almost a different character from the proactive politician of *Part I*, and the news of his son's demise destabilizes him further. Though he attempts to make light of his sickness, casting away his crutches and claiming that "these news, / Having been well, that would have made me sick, / Being sick, have in some measure made me well" (1.1.137–9), it is clear that he is no longer really in control. Struggling to assert his youthful strength, he finds he cannot; in "robbing" Hotspur of his youth (*1 Henry IV*, 5.4.76), Hal has all but finished off his rival's father.

The revolution of the times

King Henry is even more obviously on borrowed time; his demise is the long-deferred event on which both plays hang. In *Part I*, Henry was careworn, weighed down by the double yoke of the crown and his machinations in order to hang on to it; in *Part II*, he is ailing physically, plagued by illness and insomnia. When we first see him (over a third of the way into the play), he makes a more pitiful figure even than Northumberland. Bitterly asking, "How many thousand of my poorest subjects / Are at this hour asleep?", he continues,

> O sleep, O gentle sleep,
> Nature's soft nurse, how have I frighted thee,
> That thou no more wilt weigh my eyelids down
> And steep my senses in forgetfulness? ...
> Wilt thou upon the high and giddy mast
> Seal up the ship-boy's eyes, and rock his brains
> In cradle of the rude imperious surge,
> And in the visitation of the winds,
> Who take the ruffian billows by the top,
> Curling their monstrous heads, and hanging them
> With deafening clamour in the slippery clouds,
> That, with the hurly, death itself awakes?
> Canst thou, O partial sleep, give thy repose
> To the wet sea-boy in an hour so rude,
> And in the calmest and most stillest night,
> With all appliances and means to boot,
> Deny it to a king? Then happy low, lie down.
> Uneasy lies the head that wears a crown.

[3.1.4–31]

Henry longs for "forgetfulness", craves the amnesia of sleep – perhaps even the sleep of death. Shakespeare makes the most of hints in Holinshed's *Chronicles* that the King found himself unable to "compose or settle himself to sleep for fear of strangling" after an assassination attempt in 1401, but he gives them a broader motive, and introduces a heavy note of irony. It is Henry's very kingliness, an office he had no right to expect, that corrodes his well-being; even a "ship-boy", whose life is constantly in danger on the high seas, leads a happier existence than his monarch.

Regret is very much on Henry's mind, as he explains to his supporters Warwick and Surrey, as are the harsh mechanics of time:

> O God, that one might read the book of fate,
> And see the revolution of the times
> Make mountains level, and the continent,
> Weary of solid firmness, melt itself
> Into the sea; and other times to see
> The beachy girdle of the ocean
> Too wide for Neptune's hips; how chance's mocks
> And changes fill the cup of alteration
> With divers liquors! 'Tis not ten years gone
> Since Richard and Northumberland, great friends,
> Did feast together; and in two year after
> Were they at wars …

[3.1.44–55]

Time brings change, and change lays waste to man. Though the span of years in Henry's mind is only small, it dilates into a geological frame, placed alongside the collapse of mountains and the melting of the earth. As in Shakespeare's Sonnets – a portion of which were probably complete by the time he wrote *2 Henry IV* – "this bloody tyrant", "devouring time", dwarfs mere humanity; man's "stay" on this earth is but "inconstant" (as Sonnets 15, 16 and 19 put it). As Warwick rejoins, "such things become the hatch and brood of time" (3.1.81); time will bring all human actions – both bad and good – to light.

The kingdom at large is, Henry frets, poisoned with "rank diseases" and has "danger near the heart of it" (3.1.37–9); and so too are many of its inhabitants (at least as the play sees it). Into *2 Henry IV* Shakespeare introduces two new characters, Justices Shallow and Silence of Warwickshire, the playwright's home county. In many ways irrelevant to the plot, this pair of old men nevertheless embody what much of the play is about. While Henry's memory is a burden to him, Shallow and Silence are only too pleased to launch into reminiscence. As they discuss Falstaff, "this Sir John … that comes hither anon about soldiers", their thoughts turn at once to that other country, the distant past:

SHALLOW The same Sir John, the very same. I see him breaking Scoggin's head at the court gate when a was a crack, not thus high. And the very same day did I fight with one Samson Stockfish, a fruiterer, behind Gray's Inn. Jesu, Jesu, the mad days that I have spent! And to see how many of my old acquaintance are dead.

SILENCE We shall all follow, cousin.

SHALLOW Certain, 'tis certain; very sure, very sure. Death, as the Psalmist saith, is certain to all; all shall die.

[3.2.26–36]

It seems probable that 2 Henry IV was written some three years before Troilus, some six before Measure for Measure, yet here Shakespeare anticipates the objectivity of manner, fused with a suggestion of deep and personal concern, which is characteristic of these two later plays.

Clifford Leech, "The Unity of 2 Henry IV" (1953)

Meandering though their conversation is – further hobbled by Shallow's habit of repeating everything – the subject of their thoughts is definite enough. Death haunts them at least as much as it haunts the King, for they are closer to it than most. The "mad days", like the youthful combats between Hal and Hotspur they echo, are well and truly over.

Even the subject of Shallow and Silence's musings, Falstaff, is feeling twinges of mortality. If his sheer bulk is an obsessive topic of conversation in *Part I*, in its sequel it is that same body's steady breakdown. Falstaff enters the play enquiring what the doctor thinks of his "water" (urine), and learning (in his brand-new Page's words) that "the water itself was a good healthy water, but, for the party that owed it, he might have more diseases than he knew for" (1.2.3–5). The comedy is obvious, but it sounds a serious theme. Whereas in *1 Henry IV* Falstaff is gleefully happy to twist the time of day to his own ends – never mind his time of life – in *Part II* even he is striving, and failing, to stave away thoughts of death. "I am old, I am old," he frets to his mistress in Eastcheap, Doll Tearsheet, "Thou'lt forget me when I am gone" (2.4.273–80). When she wonders "when wilt thou leave fighting o'days, and foining o'nights, and begin to patch up thine old body for heaven?", Falstaff is terrified. "Peace, good Doll," he urges, "do not speak like a death's-head, do not bid me remember mine end" (2.4.233–7).

Tears and heavy sorrows

But the one major death that does occur in *Part II* proves more complicated than these repeated dramatic premonitions might suggest. Hal is spending less time than before in Eastcheap – his main visit is spent with Poins, setting up Falstaff for yet another comedown – and is being drawn more and more to the court. Everyone knows why. Following the news that Prince John has managed to capture the ringleaders of the rebellion, the King is seized not by joy, but sickness, and rapidly worsens to the point where his closest advisers fear for his life. Finding his father slumbering in the royal bedchamber, Hal assumes the worst – that Henry is dead. "By his gates of breath / There lies a downy feather which stirs not," the Prince exclaims,

> My gracious lord, my father!—
> This sleep is sound indeed. This is a sleep
> That from this golden rigol hath divorced
> So many English kings.—Thy due from me
> Is tears and heavy sorrows of the blood,
> Which nature, love, and filial tenderness
> Shall, O dear father, pay thee plenteously.

My due from thee is this imperial crown,
Which, as immediate from thy place and blood,
Derives itself to me.
    He puts the crown on his head
        Lo where it sits,
Which God shall guard; and put the world's whole strength
Into one giant arm, it shall not force
This lineal honour from me. This from thee
Will I to mine leave, as 'tis left to me.

                                       [4.3.162–78]

This moment is the climax of the play and fraught with all sorts of meanings – a teasing metatheatrical moment for an actor feigning deathlike sleep on stage, it is also an ironic reconstruction of the deposition scene in *Richard II*, in which the very same crown was handed from Richard to Henry Bolingbroke. As he plays the part for himself, it's striking that Hal is every bit as calculating as his father had been; though invoking "God" as he takes up the precious object in his hands, his words are undeniably legalistic in tone. His part of the bargain is "tears and heavy sorrows of the blood"; his father's is far more tangible, "this imperial crown".

But Hal's spontaneous self-coronation is premature. The King is still alive – just – and when he wakes he is furious, until Hal persuades him of his honest intentions. As the two are finally reconciled, Henry turns once more to the past:

           God knows, my son,
By what bypaths and indirect crook'd ways
I met this crown; and I myself know well
How troublesome it sat upon my head.
To thee it descend with better quiet,
Better opinion, better confirmation;
For all the soil of the achievement goes
With me into the earth …

                                       [4.3.312–9]

"For all my reign," he goes on, "hath been but as a scene / Acting that argument." The pageant – and Shakespeare's play – will only be halted with his demise.

Just before Henry dies, he comments, "and now my death / Changes the mood" (4.3.327–8), but if we expect a comic conclusion like that in *Part I* we are to be disappointed. Falstaff's own fate, obliquely hinted at throughout the *Henry IV* plays, hastens closer. Prepared by debunkings galore and Hal's chilly words on the matter, the audience knows that it is only a matter of time before Falstaff is rejected – a conclusion even rehearsed in Falstaff's apparent "death" at Shrewsbury. Yet, as news breaks that old King Henry is dead, Falstaff and his followers are seemingly the last people in the theatre to realize which way the wind is blowing. Grabbing the first horses he finds, Sir John is sure that "the young King is sick for me". But when he reaches out from the crowd that throngs the new King Henry, the gesture is tragic:

SIR JOHN God save thee, my sweet boy!

KING HARRY

My Lord Chief Justice, speak to that vain man.

LORD CHIEF JUSTICE *(to Sir John)*

Have you your wits? Know you what 'tis you speak?

SIR JOHN

My king, my Jove, I speak to thee, my heart!

KING HARRY

I know thee not, old man. Fall to thy prayers.

How ill white hairs becomes a fool and jester!

I have long dreamt of such a kind of man.

So surfeit-swelled, so old, and so profane;

But being awake, I do despise my dream.

(5.4.43–51)

"Presume not that I am the thing I was," Henry continues, "I have turned away my former self." His reformation is over almost before it has begun, even if some critics (notably the great A.C. Bradley) have questioned whether one of Shakespeare's finest comic creations can be disposed of so easily. Yet when Falstaff attempts to make light of the situation, arguing to Shallow that "this that you heard was but a colour [pretext]", the effect is heart-rending. Shallow's response, that it is "a colour I fear that you will die in" (5.3.85), is typically morbid, but in this instance unusually prescient.

Having wasted time with Falstaff, and watched his father serve it, Hal now attempts to redeem his misspent hours. His education as a prince, one of the major strands in the *Henry IV* plays, has been achieved, but Shakespeare does not hide from us its personal cost, nor does he cosset us by insisting that the perfect prince has to be a perfect man. Questions concerning the sacrifices of kingship are at the forefront of *2 Henry IV*; in the next play in the cycle, *Henry V*, they will loom even larger.

Stage history and adaptations

The performance history of *2 Henry IV* largely shadows that of *Part I* (see p.121), but judging by the popularity of printed versions the first, more straightforwardly funny play seems to have been performed more during Shakespeare's lifetime. Even so, both parts were acted at **court** in celebration of the 1612 marriage between James I's daughter Elizabeth and a German prince (*Part II* appears as "Sir John Falstaff" in the paperwork). The bulky **John Lowin**, the King's Men's longest-serving actor, probably took over the role from Heminges (see p.121), and was certainly playing it by the 1620s. The papers of the antiquarian **Sir Edward Dering** contain an conflation of both parts made around the same time, presumably for performance by an amateur company at his estate at Surrenden in Kent.

Aside from various references to plays and adaptations starring Falstaff (see p.121), the first specific mentions of *Part II* occur at the behest of **Thomas Betterton**, who

Roger Allam was a fine Falstaff at Shakespeare's Globe in 2010, well-upholstered but not in the least bit cuddly. Here he holds forth in Eastcheap, with an unimpressed-looking Bardolph (Paul Rider) and Mistress Quickly (Barbara Marten) as his audience.

revived it with the other Falstaff plays during the 1690s. It appeared as a separate piece in 1720 at Drury Lane, with **Colley Cibber** as Shallow and his son **Theophilus** a swaggering Pistol. Despite his initial reluctance to stage either *Henry IV* at Covent Garden, **David Garrick** relented and played King Henry from 1758 onwards – staging Hal's coronation with plenty of pomp, not to mention period costume (a recent innovation). A few years later a pastiche entitled *Falstaff's Wedding* by **William Kenrick** appeared, which developed an entire plot from loose ends in *Part II*.

A Falstaff-centred adaptation of *Part II* by **John Philip Kemble** took the boards in 1804, continuing a steady trend towards ever grander spectacle that reached new heights in **William Charles Macready**'s production of 1821 with **Charles Kemble** as Hal. This featured no fewer than four additional coronation scenes, catering for the coronation fever that attended the crowning of George IV that year (George responded by lavishing free tickets for Covent Garden on his subjects). After touring to New York, Macready presented a spiced-up *Part II* at Drury Lane in 1834 complete with musical interludes. Following his triumph as a richly comic Falstaff in *Part I* (he delighted audiences by being unable to sit down without assistance),

Samuel Phelps turned his talents to both King Henry and Shallow in versions of *Part II* that appeared at Sadler's Wells from 1853.

Frank Benson had a preference for *Part II* in the productions he put on at Stratford from 1894 (*Part I* disappeared entirely in 1906) and played Falstaff himself before **Louis Calvert** took over the role, while his wife **Constance** acted Doll Tearsheet. As **Max Reinhardt**'s versions of both plays wowed audiences in Berlin in 1912, **Barry Jackson** was preparing his own stagings at the pioneering Birmingham Rep in which full-text *Henry IVs* were performed on the same day. **Ben Greet** revived *Part II* at the Old Vic in 1917, following with its predecessor three years later, and **William Bridges-Adams** celebrated the opening of the new main house at Stratford in 1932 with productions of both – **Dorothy Massingham**'s haunting Doll garnered praise, though the rest of the cast was described as "tired out" after an exhausting rehearsal schedule.

After the cessation of hostilities in 1945 **John Burrell** opened twin Old Vic productions of the *Henry IVs* with an impressive cast, many of whom had cut their teeth with the same company before the war. **Ralph Richardson**'s Falstaff was regarded as one of the finest ever – "not a *comic* performance", in Kenneth Tynan's words – and after his extraordinary Hotspur **Laurence Olivier** excelled as Shallow, described by Tynan as "a paltering scarecrow of a man" yet bursting with generosity. At Stratford, in the Festival of Britain season of 1951, **Michael Redgrave** directed *Part II* after playing Hotspur in *Part I*; **Anthony Quayle** remained as a superlative Falstaff, and **Richard Burton** a commanding Hal who really showed his mettle in the second play. Four years later **Douglas Seale**'s Old Vic production headlined the young **Robert Hardy** as Hal and **Paul Rogers** as Falstaff, but also with **John Neville**'s Pistol and **Rachel Roberts**'s Mistress Quickly.

Seale's vision of the histories as a single unit would influence subsequent directors, most famously **Peter Hall** and **John Barton**, who produced the *Wars of the Roses* cycle in 1964, one of the defining postwar adaptations. *2 Henry IV* was subcontracted to director **Clifford Williams**, with **Hugh Griffiths** as a moving Falstaff adrift in the turbulent politics that surrounded him – politics in which **Ian Holm**'s watchful Hal was entirely comfortable. Since then the play has nearly always been produced in company with *Part I*, frequently in large cycles put on by the RSC. **Terry Hands**'s sober version of 1975, presenting the second tetralogy, centred on **Alan Howard**'s sourly calculating prince (according to one observer, the oats he sowed "were never very wild"), who consistently suborned **Brewster Mason**'s patient and dignified Falstaff until the inevitable betrayal – a rejection scene in which Henry appeared, statue-like, clad in gold from top to toe. In thought-provoking contrast **Trevor Nunn**'s staging from 1982 made both parts of *Henry IV* Falstaff's via the talents of **Joss Ackland**, who delivered an interpretation of the role that plumbed its tragic depths alongside its comedy. Nunn's Hal, **Gerard Murphy**, was a bland dropout ("less hell-raiser than housemaid", said one reviewer), although **Patrick Stewart**'s politically astute King generated positive notices.

Adrian Noble's RSC production in 1991 was applauded by critics for its subtle touches of staging, many of which connected both parts of *Henry IV*; **Michael Maloney** played Hal to **Julian Glover**'s Henry with **David Bradley**'s fussy Shallow attracting particular attention. **Michael Attenborough**'s version of the *Henry IV*s, part of the RSC's history extravaganza *This England* in 2000 handled the different styles of the two plays more impressively even than Noble – **Desmond Barrit**'s previously energetic Falstaff was visibly ailing in *Part II*, a hostage to affairs beyond his control, while the manic double act of **Benjamin Whitrow** and **Peter Copley** as Shallow and Silence captured the bizarre futility of rural escape.

Michael Bogdanov's English Shakespeare Company production, which opened in 1986, saw **John Woodvine**'s Falstaff – "sly as a fox and warm as a coal-fire", according to Michael Billington – play against **Jenny Quayle**'s Doll. In 2003, New York audiences were treated to a one-evening version of *Henry IV*; its glittering cast – **Ethan Hawke**'s Hal to **Kevin Kline**'s Falstaff – was met by equally glowing reviews. The play was given historical point in **Michael Boyd**'s epic staging of the histories at the RSC in 2007–08 (directed here by **Richard Twyman**), which buried its idiosyncrasies beneath the march of history – most clearly when **Jonathan Slinger**'s long-dead Richard II clambered out of his coffin at the opening. The simmering enmity between **David Warner**'s Falstaff and **Geoffrey Streatfield**'s Hal broke out into open warfare over **Alexia Healey**'s Doll.

In the RSC's 2014 version of the two *Henry IV*s, staged by artistic director **Gregory Doran** as informal sequels to his *Richard II* the previous year, **Antony Sher** offered an energetically predatory Falstaff who found himself outplayed in *Part II*, a genuine victim of circumstance (and **Alex Hassell**'s quietly scheming Hal). While the Globe's version a few years earlier, directed by **Dominic Dromgoole**, contained few overt surprises, it nonetheless boasted a fine Falstaff in **Roger Allam**, who visibly crumpled in the rejection scene, blindsided by an entirely unforeseen turn of events. In the theatre's 2012 follow-up, part of the World Shakespeare Festival, an all-Latino Henriad was completed by **Elkafka Espacio Teatral** from Buenos Aires, whose postmodern staging (hi-vis jackets, punkish prostitutes) struggled in the open-air Globe, but was distinguished by a meaty Falstaff from **Horacio Peña**. Two years later, having successfully reimagined *Julius Caesar* for an all-female cast (see p.209), director Phyllida Lloyd turned her attention to the *Henry IV* plays at the Donmar. *Part II* was cut to the quick – Shallow and Silence the most obvious casualties – and some felt Lloyd's steely interpretation underplayed the plays' wistfulness, but her cast was widely praised. **Harriet Walter** was superb as a guilt-ridden King Henry, but **Ashley McGuire**'s Falstaff stole the show: "a one-person vindication of the all-female enterprise," in the words of the *Observer*.

The most original cinema adaptation of both *Henry IV*s remains **Orson Welles**'s *Chimes at Midnight*, which uses more *Part II* text than *Part I*, and which in turn inspired **Gus Van Sant**'s *My Own Private Idaho* (see p.124). The BBC/Time-Life version, directed like *Part I* by **David Giles**, was aired in 1979; **Anthony Quayle**'s return as Falstaff after playing him nearly thirty years before was perhaps the production's most noteworthy aspect. In addition to its Brechtian TV epic *An Age of Kings* (1960), the BBC included the play in its 2012 series *The Hollow Crown*, with a similarly blue-blooded cast as featured in *Part I*, all under the expert direction of **Richard Eyre**.

SCREEN

Chimes at Midnight
O. Welles, K. Baxter, J. Gielgud; Orson Welles (dir.)
Spain/Switzerland, 1966 > Mr Bongo DVD

Even in the midst of 1 Henry IV's comic highlights Orson Welles always seems to be thinking of Part II – Falstaff's glum observation to Shallow that "we have heard the chimes at midnight" forms part of its opening sequence – and in truth the second play's darkness is closer to his conception of what they are both about. Here the central intimacy between Welles's Falstaff and Keith Baxter's shady Hal is always doomed, and often it seems that only Falstaff's incessant guzzling of sack insulates him from the chilly winds of reality. In Chimes that chill is memorably embodied in Gielgud's icily precise King Henry and even Jeanne Moreau's passionate Doll (a terrific cameo) proves entirely unable to protect her man. But Welles's skill is such that the film's conclusion – a typically deft insertion from Henry V – still feels like an appalling shock, while even Henry's own death is unexpectedly moving. At long last restored, the film is also available on HD Blu-ray.

Henry IV Part II
R. Allam, J. Parker, O. Cotton; Dominic Dromgoole (dir.) UK, 2010 > Shakespeare's Globe

Stolidly Elizabethan, Dominic Dromgoole's production, designed by Jonathan Fensom and recorded live in front of the Globe audience, has blokeish bravura and features a disconcerting density of leather boots and jerkins. Though there have undeniably been more surprising versions, it canters through the play respectably enough, slowing to a pleasing potter when Shallow and Silence appear. As with Part I (see p.125), the main draw is Roger Allam's Falstaff, a star turn in every sense. If anything, Allam suits the darker tones of Part II even better, offering a Sir John who even at his most wildly extravagant always seems aware of how rapidly his world is shrinking. His relationship with Jade Williams's Doll Tearsheet is genuinely affecting, funny and sweetly sad; and if you don't have a lump in your throat during the rejection scene you're made of even stonier stuff than Jamie Parker's chameleonic but cold-blooded Hal.

The Hollow Crown
S.R. Beale, T. Hiddleston, J. Irons; Richard Eyre (dir.)
UK, 2012 > BBC DVD

After the youthful high spirits of Part I, Richard Eyre's BBC adaptation steers a firm course into the choppier waters of 2 Henry IV, equally purposeful in its pacing but shadowier and more muted in tone. The divisions between the court and the Boar are less stark than before, and everyone seems to be suffering from the same lingering ennui, which eventually claims Jeremy Irons's tottering King. The main plot is efficiently delivered, but this version is at its best in its most intimate moments – notably the lingering bed scene between Simon Russell Beale's rueful Falstaff and a dignified, fierce Doll Tearsheet (Maxine Peake), which comes painfully close to outright tragedy. The only thing that doesn't come off, curiously, is Falstaff's summary dismissal: it seems all too likely that Tom Hiddleston's posh-boy Hal will do exactly this, and a silent tableau of the Eastcheap crew being carted off to jail is a poor stand-in for genuine emotion. Infinitely more moving is the Shallow–Silence scene; lit by failing firelight, Beale's Falstaff hears the "chimes at midnight" for what he knows will be the final time, and there is nothing but terror in his eyes.

AUDIO

Henry IV Part II
J. Glover, J. Glover, T. West; Gordon House (dir.) UK, 1999 > BBC

Continuity is the order of the day with the BBC's Henry IVs: a near-identical cast features, and in the director's chair once again is Gordon House. In truth the slightly cool style of this production suits Part II better, and the scenes between Prunella Scale's earthy Mistress Quickly, Timothy West's dark-toned Falstaff and Lucy Briers's Doll have a particular poignancy. Jamie Glover makes a particularly earnest Hal, a man on a mission who is genuinely conscious that time is pressing, while his father Julian Glover seems completely destroyed by King Henry's countless woes. As Shallow and Silence, Richard Briers and Timothy Bateson bring some welcome comedy to the proceedings.

EDITIONS

New Cambridge Shakespeare
Giorgio Melchiori; rev. 2007 > Cambridge UP

The perils facing any Shakespearian editor are great, greater still when you consider that one of the most banal pieces of text in this play (Bardolph's "Who keeps the gate there, ho!" at 1.1.1) was footnoted in such preposterous detail in the 1923 Arden edition that those notes were once included in an anthology of comic writing. Fortunately, Giorgio Melchiori makes no such mistakes, presenting a brisk critical introduction to 2 Henry IV that deals sensibly with all its major concerns. Much of his time is taken up with stage history, assisted by C. Walter Hodges's masterly pen-and-ink impressions of Elizabethan performance. Melchiori's text is taken from the 1600 quarto, but includes various passages unique to the Folio edition. Various sources, including a segment of The Famous Victories of Henry V, are included in an appendix.

SOME CRITICISM

Henry IV Parts One and Two
Nigel Wood; 1995 > Open UP [o/p]

Renaissance critics concentrating on hard-core literary theory can be gnomic to the point of impenetrability. *Henry IV Parts One and Two: Theory in Practice* does occasionally veer towards mystification, but it does at least set out to show that readings informed by literary theory can be tied to specific texts and work convincingly – and without implying that Shakespeare had the works of Derrida and Bakhtin alongside his Halle and Holinshed. Four essays feature, each introduced by an explanatory editorial piece and followed by a dialogue between Nigel Wood and the contributor. Peter Womack's piece suggesting ways in which the *Henry IV* plays are a kind of Brechtian "epic theatre" and make audiences aware of their problematic design, is perhaps the best of the bunch; but Donald MacDonald's article on the relationship between Bakhtin and the carnival sides of Shakespeare is also persuasive.

Memory in Shakespeare's Histories
Jonathan Baldo; 2012 > Routledge

Peter Saccio's *Shakespeare's Kings* (rev. 2000) remains an excellent introduction to the historical background, but if you're interested in taking a different approach – how the plays themselves remember as well as forget the past – Baldo's recent study is well worth investigating. Focusing largely on the second tetralogy, Baldo is subtle on the accretions of history in these dramas, as a Tudor playwright attempted to bring medieval England back to life, and also has plenty to say on how "memory" itself was changing in the face of new print technology and the growth of a market economy. This approach to *2 Henry IV* is especially acute, set as it is in a world where everyone seems to remember both too much and too little, and moves on smoothly to an examination of Welsh, Irish and Scottish contexts in the tetralogy as a whole – an island history Shakespeare's audiences would remember only too keenly.

Henry V

With its depiction of a miraculous English triumph at Agincourt under a glamorous, youthful king, *Henry V* is often thought of as Shakespeare's most overtly patriotic play. Rousing, flag-waving productions have made it into a symbol – even a cliché – of England and English resoluteness. Stirring snippets have passed into the language; politicians regularly cite it as their favourite play; even the history books still seem in thrall to Shakespeare's boyish King. By the same token, *Henry V* has sometimes been treated with wariness by writers and directors embarrassed by its supposedly nationalistic message. Director Michael Bogdanov transformed it into a crudely jingoistic pantomime in the 1980s, and in 2003 audiences at the National Theatre in London witnessed a production by Nick Hytner which drew parallels between conflict in fifteenth-century France and twenty-first-century Iraq. But there are more complex meanings to Shakespeare's drama than its critics sometimes allow. *Henry V* does not shy away from the savage realities of war, and though it celebrates military glory and heroism, those who ignore its complicating counter-currents are blind to much of what the play is about. Like all great works of art – and unlike propaganda – the play contains the potential to be understood in radically and creatively different ways.

DATE > Perhaps the easiest play of all to date because of a reference it makes to the Earl of Essex's campaign in Ireland, *Henry V* was almost certainly first acted in the summer of 1599.

SOURCES > As with Shakespeare's other histories, the combination of Holinshed's *Chronicles* (1587) and Halle's *Union* (1548) provides the basic narrative. These were bulked out by *The Famous Victories of Henry V* (c. 1580s), Samuel Daniel's poem *The Civil Wars* (1595), and John Stow's *Chronicles* (1580) and *Annals* (1592).

TEXTS > While the Folio text (F1, 1623) was printed from Shakespeare's own papers, the play had already circulated in a "bad" quarto version published in 1600 (Q1) and reprinted twice more.

Interpreting the play

Henry V is eager to put the past to rest. An old king is dead, his youthful son is on the throne and the internecine wrangling of the two *Henry IV* plays promises at last to recede. Shunning the insidious figure of Rumour, who acts as the presenter to *Part II*, Shakespeare's Chorus (who introduces the story at the beginning of each Act) in *Henry V* has an altogether braver message. "O for a muse of fire, that would ascend / The brightest heaven of invention," he cries at the very opening of the play:

MAJOR CHARACTERS & SYNOPSIS

Chorus, introducing the action

THE ENGLISH

King Henry V of England (known as Harry)
Dukes of Gloucester and **Clarence**, Henry's brothers
Duke of Exeter, Henry's uncle
Duke of York
Earls of Salisbury, Westmorland and **Warwick**
Archbishop of Canterbury
Bishop of Ely
Traitors to King Henry: **Richard, Earl of Cambridge**; **Henry, Lord Scrope of Masham**; **Sir Thomas Grey**
Falstaff's former companions **Pistol, Nim** and **Bardolph**; a **Boy**, formerly in Falstaff's service
Hostess, formerly **Mistress Quickly**, Pistol's wife
Captains Gower, Fluellen, Macmorris and **Jamy**, serving in Henry's army
Sir Thomas Erpingham
John Bates, Alexander Court and **Michael Williams**, English soldiers

THE FRENCH

King Charles VI of France
Queen Isabel, Charles's wife
Louis the Dauphin, their son and heir
Princess Catherine, their daughter
Alice, a lady attending Catherine
French noblemen: **Constable of France; Dukes of Bourbon, Orléans, Berri** and **Normandy; Lord Rambures** and **Lord Grandpré**
Montjoy, the French herald
Governor of Harfleur and **Ambassadors** to the English court

[ACTION CONTINUED FROM 2 HENRY IV]

ACT 1 The relationship between England and France has sunk to new depths. King Henry's religious advisers are convincing him to claim the French throne, and the Dauphin has sent a barrel of tennis balls to the English king, mocking his youth and his reputation as a wastrel. Stung by the insult, Henry decides to invade.

ACT 2 As the country prepares for war, Bardolph, Nim and Pistol plan to enlist, but end up brawling. They are interrupted by a summons to Falstaff who, broken by Henry's rejection, dies soon after their visit. Embarking at Southampton,

the King narrowly avoids an assassination attempt organized by Scrope, Cambridge and Grey, who are arrested for treason. Meanwhile, France's leaders are divided: King Charles is nervous about the English threat, while the Dauphin refuses to take it seriously.

ACT 3 Fighting rages outside Harfleur, where Henry exhorts his forces to drive through the town walls. Bardolph is keen to advance, but his companions have to be driven on by Fluellen, who then argues with his fellow captains. They are interrupted by Henry's address to the Governor of Harfleur, warning of atrocities if the town resists. The Governor surrenders – a triumph for Henry, whose forces are flagging. At the French court, where Princess Catherine is secretly learning English, King Charles is so shocked by events that he commits a huge army to engage the invaders. Back among the English, Bardolph is to be executed for stealing. King Henry tells the French herald that though his army is weak he will not avoid an encounter with the French.

ACT 4 The night before battle, Henry visits his demoralized troops in disguise. One soldier, Williams, is challenged by the King for doubting their mission. In the morning, the English (outnumbered five to one) are glumly saying farewell to each other when Henry raises them with an inspiring speech. They head for what seems certain death at Agincourt, but the battle unexpectedly turns their way. As the French are regrouping, Henry orders all enemy prisoners to be killed, just as news arrives that the French have murdered the boys guarding the English camp. Henry's victory finally assured, it is confirmed that French casualties are 10,000 to just 25 English. The King goes in search of Williams, and reveals his true identity before forgiving him.

ACT 5 At a peace conference in France, the two sides negotiate terms – one of which is a marriage between Henry and Catherine. Henry privately woos her and she relents, at which peace is concluded and their wedding agreed. All seems resolved, but the Chorus warns that it won't remain so – the reign of Henry's son (Henry VI) will bring only sorrow for England.

A kingdom for a stage, princes to act,
And monarchs to behold the swelling scene.
Then should the warlike Harry, like himself,
Assume the port of Mars, and at his heels,
Leashed in like hounds, should famine, sword, and fire
Crouch for employment.

[PROLOGUE, 1–8]

"Can this cock-pit hold / The vasty fields of France?" he continues, his voice charged with the strong vowel sounds that were the powerhouse of the Elizabethan stage, "Or may we cram / Within this wooden O the very casques / That did affright the air at Agincourt?" Though it's possible that *Henry V* premiered at the Curtain, a temporary home for the Lord Chamberlain's Men, it seems more likely that it was the new Bankside Globe – which had room for some three thousand spectators – that first played host to these stirring words. Their meaning is plain: this is to be the moment when history becomes History.

Warlike Harry

Our first introductions to the new King leave us in no doubt that the wild days of his youth is past. When the Archbishop of Canterbury and Bishop of Ely get together to discuss the possibility of a war in France, they are full of praise for a King they consider "full of grace and fair regard", as Canterbury exclaims:

The breath no sooner left his father's body
But that his wildness, mortified in him,
Seemed to die too. Yea, at that very moment
Consideration like an angel came
And whipped th'offending Adam out of him,
Leaving his body as a paradise
T'envelop and contain celestial spirits.

[1.1.26–32]

The reformation is complete – and in explicitly religious terms, with an "angel" purifying the King from his earthly dross. One of Shakespeare's sources, Edward Halle's chronicle, emphasizes that Henry was a monarch "whose life was immaculate and his living without spot ... the mirror of Christendom and the glory of his country". This connection between godliness and Englishness might make us think of Gaunt's description of the "blessèd plot" in *Richard II*, but in *Henry V* God's support for the English cause is never in doubt. "O God, thy arm was here," Henry exclaims after his victory at Agincourt and the revelation that the English losses are miraculously (and unhistorically) slight. "Take it God, / For it is none but thine" (4.8.106–12).

Henry is equipped with the lion's share of words in the play (his is Shakespeare's largest role to date), and his skills as an orator have passed into legend. "Once more unto the breach, dear friends, once more," he urges his compatriots outside the walls of Harfleur:

Dedicated to the Allied forces who liberated Europe, Laurence Olivier's wartime *Henry V* (1944) closely identified the struggle against Nazism with the English triumph at Agincourt – and won an honorary Oscar for its director, producer and star.

Or close the wall up with our English dead.
In peace there's nothing so becomes a man
As modest stillness and humility,
But when the blast of war blows in our ears,
Then imitate the action of the tiger,
Stiffen the sinews, conjure up the blood,
Disguise fair nature with hard-favoured rage …
                             … And you, good yeomen,
Whose limbs were made in England, show us here
The mettle of your pasture; let us swear
That you are worth your breeding—which I doubt not,
For there is none of you so mean and base
That hath not noble lustre in your eyes.
I see you stand like greyhounds in the slips,
Straining upon the start. The game's afoot.
Follow your spirit, and upon this charge
Cry, 'God for Harry! England and Saint George!'

[3.1.1–34]

The appeal of Henry's speech, one of the most famous in the Shakespearian canon – and which actually occupies a whole scene – is undeniable, and it has frequently been included in literary anthologies for soldiers heading to war (not just in Britain). But the King's rhetoric, though thrilling, is intrinsically euphemistic: war is a "game", the English soldiers "greyhounds", not killers. Even class divisions are erased: the King addresses his subjects as "friends"; the "mean and base" are made "noble" fighting side by side with their countrymen. Henry's equalizing spirit will appear again at Agincourt, where he urges his troops, calling them "We few, we happy few, we band of brothers" (4.3.60).

Meeting stiffer resistance, however, the King offers a less appealing analysis of battle. Faced with the intractable citizens of Harfleur – who have the effrontery to resist the occupying English army – Henry's tone darkens as he threatens the townspeople with the consequences of their actions. "Take pity of your town and of your people," he coldly suggests,

> Whiles yet my soldiers are in my command,
> Whiles yet the cool and temperate wind of grace
> O'erblows the filthy and contagious clouds
> Of heady murder, spoil, and villainy.
> If not—why, in a moment look to see
> The blind and bloody soldier with foul hand
> Defile the locks of your shrill-shrieking daughters;
> Your fathers taken by the silver beards,
> And their most reverend heads dashed to the walls;
> Your naked infants spitted upon pikes,
> Whiles the mad mothers with their howls confused
> Do break the clouds, as did the wives of Jewry
> At Herod's bloody-hunting slaughtermen.
>
> [3.3.110–24]

A threat it may be – and, as it proves, effective enough to prevent its implementation – but there is no disguising the calculated violence in Henry's words, nor the fact that it foreshadows one of *Henry V*'s most obscene actions, the execution by both sides of their prisoners. Though the King will later insist that God's "arm" was at Agincourt, here his own soldiers are compared to King Herod's "bloody-hunting slaughtermen", the biblical soldiers whose grim task it was to hunt down the infant Jesus. In little more than the space of two scenes, we are confronted with the extreme realities of war – its pity along with its glory.

Some of the King's soldiers, many of them conscripts, are openly cynical about their commander-in-chief's gung-ho spirit. Though the Chorus is eager to describe the restorative effect of Henry's incognito night-time visit to his troops (eagerly promising "a little touch of Harry in the night"), in the event the King's common touch all but deserts him when he encounters a group of English squaddies while disguised as an officer. One, Williams, is not impressed by Henry's unctuous assertion that "methinks I could not die anywhere so contented as in the King's company, his cause being just and his quarrel honourable". Williams angrily retorts:

But if the cause be not good, the King himself hath a heavy reckoning to make, when all those legs and arms and heads chopped off in a battle shall join together at the latter day, and cry all, 'We died at such a place'— some swearing, some crying for a surgeon, some upon their wives left poor behind them, some upon the debts they owe, some upon their children rawly left. I am afeard there are few die well that die in a battle, for how can they charitably dispose of anything, when blood is their argument? Now, if these men do not die well, it will be a black matter for the King that led them to it ...

[4.1.133–44]

Williams's fears are forceful ones: not to be allowed to "die well", and to put one's earthly and spiritual affairs in order, is a heavy price for serving an earthly king. His nightmarish vision of the "latter day" (the Day of Judgement), awash with truncated body parts, provides a strong pacifistic argument. But his chief worry is about the justness of this particular conflict – and it is a question Henry evades, preferring to argue merely that "the King is not bound to answer the particular endings of his soldiers" (4.1.154–5). Though the religious justification for Henry's war in France is carefully laid out in the first few scenes of the play, there are jarring notes – among them the fact that the church is backing it in order to divert attention from a royal inquiry into their coffers. Williams's concerns aired, audiences in the know may well think back to the dying King's advice to his son in *Henry V*'s predecessor, "to busy giddy minds / With foreign quarrels" (*2 Henry IV*, 4.3.342–3). Crusade or smokescreen?

Entertain conjecture

At least Williams's courage is not under question; that is not true for all the King's troops. The men the Chorus rather hopefully calls "culled and choice-drawn cavaliers" (3.0.24) include some of Henry's erstwhile Eastcheap pals, Bardolph, Nim and Pistol – none of whom is distinguished by their bravery. Though Bardolph is briefly fired up by the King's speech at Harfleur, echoing, "On, on, on, on, on! To the breach, to the breach!" (3.2.1–2), his exhortation to his comrades falls on stony ground. The Boy provides the most astute analysis of all:

Would I were in an alehouse in London. I would give all my fame for a pot of ale, and safety.

[3.2.12–3]

Shakespeare can scarcely have intended that the force of preconception should, hundreds of years after his death, still be preventing the careful, the learned, and the sympathetic from seeing what he so definitely put down. The play is ironic.

Gerald Gould, "A New Reading of *Henry V*" (1919)

Cowering in their foxhole – a parodic version of *esprit de corps* – until they are chased out by Captain Fluellen (a Welshman), they represent an England which is rather less patriotic in practice than it might like to believe.

The story of the Eastcheap soldiers, sordid and unhappy as it is, is a powerful undercurrent to the view of events presented by the Chorus and Henry himself. The kind of vivacious and rumbustious comedy they offer in the *Henry IV* plays is all but silenced in *Henry V*, something first noticed by Samuel Johnson, who commented ruefully that "the comic personages are now dismissed". Before long Bardolph manages to get himself executed for robbing a church (his death underwritten by the King himself), while Pistol leaves the play as a solitary figure, having heard that "my Nell is dead ... of a malady of France" (5.1.77–8), a euphemism for venereal disease which ironically underscores the nature of his own position. King Henry may have adapted winningly to his changed circumstances, but other characters do not have that luxury.

And if the "mad wag" Hal disappeared into the grave alongside his father's corpse, the gaping absence of another father figure – one whose body is a good deal larger – dominates *Henry V*. Falstaff dies during the play, but he does so without once coming on stage. *2 Henry IV*'s Epilogue promised that "If you be not too much cloyed with fat meat, our humble author will continue the story with Sir John in it," going on, "where, for anything I know, Falstaff shall die of a sweat—unless already a be killed with your hard opinions" (Epilogue, 24–8). Given Falstaff's instantaneous celebrity on the Elizabethan stage, that last comment must have seemed like a jovial quip, no more, to its first hearers. But Shakespeare turns the joke back on his audiences. Falstaff's sordid rejection by his erstwhile companion in the dying moments of *Part II* turns out, against all expectation, to have been his swansong. There is little doubt as to what lies behind his death. As Mistress Quickly tearfully relates, "The King has killed his heart" (2.1.84).

All Elizabethan comedies end with marriage, and *Henry V*, though a history play, is no exception. But the alliance between Henry and Catherine of Valois, frequently acted as a light-hearted coda to the English victory at Agincourt, is not without its problems – or affected by some of the other questions of the play. As the English and French diplomats meet in order to thrash out how to guarantee what Burgundy calls "gentle peace" for France, Henry insists that they must "buy that peace"; part of his ransom ("our capital demand") is the French princess. But she will not be bought – at first reacting with what seems like disgust to the praise he heaps on her head, then recoiling from his brute swagger as the conquerer of her land. "Is it possible dat I sould love de *ennemi* of France?" she enquires, to which Henry's answer is blunt:

> KING HARRY No, it is not possible that you should love the enemy of
> France, Kate. But in loving me, you should love the friend of France, for
> I love France so well that I will not part with a village of it, I will have it
> all mine; and Kate, when France is mine, and I am yours, then yours is
> France, and you are mine.
> CATHERINE I cannot tell vat is dat.
>
> [5.2.169–77]

Catherine's baffled incomprehension, though Shakespeare makes it linguistic, might echo our own. Henry's casual intermingling of the language of love with that of military conquest could be a gruff soldier's attempt to speak well – he claims it is – but from a King as linguistically versatile as Henry that seems to ring false. It is perhaps no accident that his choice of words echoes Richard II's resignation speech ("Your own is yours, and I am yours, and all" (3.3.195)), nor even that it foreshadows the marriage proposal offered to Isabella by the Duke in *Measure for Measure*. Henry's status as the owner of France is above all what concerns him here; he is intent on implementing his particular version of *droit du seigneur*.

Given that this scene is so delicately balanced between comedy and something darker, it offers a thought-provoking conclusion to a drama that continually asks its audiences to consider what kind of play it really is. The Chorus's invitation to "entertain conjecture" (4.0.1) reminds us of Shakespeare's stagecraft, but also asks us to think very hard about what we've just seen. Henry may exclaim at Agincourt that those not present "shall think themselves accursed that they were not here" (4.3.65) – but, Shakespeare asks, do we feel the same way?

Stage history and adaptations

Henry V has enjoyed a rich life on stage, though not in mainland Europe, where it is the only one of Shakespeare's histories to have been virtually ignored. Although it may have premiered in 1599 at the newly erected **Globe** (probably with **Richard Burbage** in the lead), there is little to suggest that the play was popular initially, and the next recorded performance took place in 1605 at James I's **court**. Nor was it revived after the restoration of James's grandson, Charles II, though a spin-off was staged by **Thomas Betterton** in 1664.

Shakespeare's play had to wait until 1738, when it returned to the London stage. It became particularly popular whenever war with France beckoned (as later in the century it often did), one of its most famous appearances being **David Garrick**'s in 1747, the same year as the catastrophic English loss at Lauffeld. **William Smith** appeared frequently as Henry during the 1750s and 60s, but **John Philip Kemble**'s adaptation of 1789 became the standard acting version for many years. **William Charles Macready** acted a restored version exactly half a century later, but still cut it so as not to distract from **Clarkson Stanfield**'s impressive dioramas. These paled beside **William Telbin**'s extravagant designs for **Charles Kean**'s 1859 production, which called for no fewer than two hundred extras. Kean inserted a triumphal entry for Henry after Act Four in which the King was showered in gold by a cavalcade of angels, with his wife **Ellen** appearing as the choric "Clio", the muse of history.

Charles Calvert's Manchester version of 1879 was the most popular of Victorian revivals; and actor-manager **George Rignold** also won success in the 1870s, touring Henry to acclaim as far afield as New York and Sydney. **Lewis Waller**'s 1900 staging typified this heroic, patriotic view of the play: from the moment Waller's Henry bounded on stage, he "radiated power" (according to one observer) and won as many female admirers as critical plaudits. In the same mould were **Frank Benson**'s Stratford

KEY SOURCE > Holinshed's *Chronicles*

All of Shakespeare's English history plays – and several others including *Macbeth* and *Cymbeline* – are indebted to one key source, the sprawling *Chronicles of England, Scotland and Ireland*, first printed in 1577. The work's general editor was **Raphael Holinshed**, who began his career as a translator but soon found himself in charge of a unique historical enterprise, an attempt to catalogue the history and topography of "Great Britain" – a term that first appears under Henry VIII, who annexed Wales and had himself declared King of Ireland. Declaring their intention to have "an especial eye unto the truth of things", Holinshed and his team mined many sources to bring to an Elizabethan readership a lively and patriotic account of their nation, starting from its semi-legendary beginnings and providing plenty of engaging detail along the way. The book was hugely successful, and in fact outlived Holinshed himself; he died around 1580 and it was left to his co-authors, among whom were **Edmund Campion**, **William Harrison**, **Richard Hooker**, **Richard Stanyhurst** and **John Stow**, to bring the *Chronicles* up to date. Doing so was politically risky – the second edition covered events as recent as ten years before – and the new edition they published in 1587 came under fire from the censors, who demanded large-scale changes before the book could be distributed. These alterations survive in some extant copies, which have pages curiously misnumbered or lines simply missed out.

Shakespeare repeatedly turned to this 1587 edition, and he also drew directly upon one of Holinshed's key sources, **Edward Halle**'s Tudor-friendly and hyper-moralistic *Union of the Two Noble and Illustrious Families of Lancaster and York* (1548). The only puzzle is how a youthful and probably impoverished playwright could have afforded to buy such expensive tomes in the first place (his earliest history play to use them, probably *2 Henry VI*, dates from 1590–91). One theory is that he simply borrowed them from his friend and fellow Stratfordian, the printer **Richard Field**, but if that is so then the loan might have been more long-standing than either party was expecting – Shakespeare's last play to use Holinshed, *Henry VIII*, dates from over twenty years later.

productions, which toured from 1897 to 1916 with Benson in the lead. His sheer energy – which included pole-vaulting onto the walls at Harfleur – wowed many, but Max Beerbohm sardonically described this as a "university cricket" *Henry V*, in which "speech after speech was sent spinning across the boundary".

Others attempted to subvert expectations, most obviously **Tyrone Guthrie**'s Old Vic staging of 1937, in which **Laurence Olivier** tried a bombast-free Henry in a version pushing an overtly pacifistic message (somewhat ironic, given his later film version). Neither of the productions mounted in 1951, Festival of Britain year, were quite so challenging, but they did locate hitherto hidden qualities in the play. **Glen Byam Shaw**'s emotionally rich Old Vic version had **Alec Clunes** in the lead; while over at Stratford **Richard Burton**'s wily, calculating King (directed by **Anthony Quayle**) demonstrated that there could be a good deal more to Henry than boyish pluck.

Quayle's production placed *Henry V* in the context of its companion plays, a path also trod by **John Barton** and **Peter Hall**, who in 1964, four centuries after Shakespeare's birth, put on a version as part of their two-tetralogy cycle, entitled *The Wars of the Roses*. Following series policy, *Henry V* was cynical about war and focused on the careworn figure of **Ian Holm**'s Henry. Though winning approval in some quarters, others felt (with critic Robert Speaight) that it was too tendentious, and "every moment of every play had been squeezed for the last ounce of meaning it contained". Other 1960s directors went for altogether simpler messages. That same year an overtly anti-war translation ironically entitled *Held Henry* ("Hero Henry") appeared in Bremen, directed by **Peter Zadek**. Four years later, **Michael Kahn** went for outright controversy at Stratford, Connecticut, with an anti-Vietnam *Henry V* in which the King's pre-Agincourt speech was surmounted by a message reading "The Machine Creates The Believable Lie".

Terry Hands's RSC productions of 1975 (once more as part of a Henriad cycle) attempted to roughen the play's gloss with Brechtian Alienation-effects – notably a decision to act sections of the play in "rehearsal" clothes – but were nevertheless dominated by **Alan Howard**'s commanding hero. **Kenneth Branagh**'s King was similarly dominant in **Adrian Noble**'s Stratford version of 1984, and despite the production's brutality it apparently persuaded Charles and Diana to name their second son Harry. The first British production properly to confront the results of the 1982 Falklands campaign – interpreted by some as Thatcher's Agincourt – was that toured by **Michael Bogdanov**'s English Shakespeare Company from 1986, with **Michael Pennington** as Henry. The anti-war message was displayed at some cost to subtlety: the English were portrayed as football hooligans, memorably unfurling a banner proclaiming "FUCK THE FROGS" to the strains of Parry's "Jerusalem".

Productions since have concentrated instead on *Henry V*'s human cost. **Matthew Warchus**'s RSC version of 1994 led **Iain Glen**'s godly monarch to a poppy-saturated finale, while his Stratford successor **Ron Daniels** (1997) created a set which reminded many of the Vietnam Veterans' Memorial in Washington DC. **Edward Hall**'s 2000 production, part of the RSC's *This England* jamboree, was closer to the spirit of Bogdanov – it interpolated songs by the left-wing activist Billy Bragg – but many felt short-changed by **William Houston**'s low-key King. Few made the same criticism of **Mark Rylance**'s subtly characterized monarch at the London Globe in 1997, but the rest of the production (directed by **Richard Olivier**, son of Laurence and famous for preaching *Henry V*'s leadership lessons to businesspeople) offered an unabashedly triumphalist reading of the play, rewarded with crowd cheers when the French prisoners were executed.

In 2003, **Barrie Rutter**'s Northern Broadsides company toured a typically pared-down version that ignored overall politics in favour of an emotional message. Altogether different was **Nicholas Hytner**'s debut as artistic director of the National Theatre, which drew pointed parallels between the play's "foreign quarrels" and British involvement in the invasion of Iraq; **Adrian Lester**'s on-message Henry exchanged his tailored suit for combat fatigues for the TV cameras. **Michael Boyd**'s brisk retelling four years later, as part of the 2007–08 RSC histories marathon, presented Agincourt as a kind of medieval Verdun, albeit one where the French played camp poseurs. **Geoffrey Streatfield** held on to the schoolboyish enthusiasm of his Hal as King, though his victory was celebrated on a dais formed from the coffins of dead soldiers.

Recent productions of *Henry V* have touched – yet again – on questions of nationhood and national identity. In 2012, the Bankside Globe staged the play as part of its season celebrating the World Shakespeare Festival. After six weeks of productions in a blizzard of languages, **Dominic Dromgoole**'s heart-of-oak production, with **Jamie Parker** as a keenly self-aware King, became (perhaps too overtly) a repossession of the space by an English-speaking cast. In 2013, **Jude Law**'s appearance in the role as part of **Michael Grandage**'s West End season was notable mainly for its starry casting, as well as being the first commercial revival of the play in Britain since the 1930s. Far more intellectually interesting was the London Unicorn theatre's version the same year, adapted for young audiences by **Ignace Cornelissen** and directed by **Ellen McDougall**, which relocated Agincourt to a sandpit and made the battle for France into a Brechtian playground squabble – "*Regietheater* [director's theatre] for children", according to one online commentator. **Gregory Doran**'s account at the RSC in 2015 was more traditional in design, albeit offered on a bare stage populated by holograms, but it was nonetheless acclaimed by the *Evening Standard* as "a Harry for our times": **Alex Hassell** offered a King more than capable of doing the military tough stuff, but nonetheless soulful as required.

In addition to the two celebrated movies of *Henry V* by arch-popularizers **Olivier** (1944) and **Branagh** (1989), the play has had various outings on the small screen. The BBC/Time-Life production of 1979 was directed by **David Giles**, with **David Gwillim** as Henry, and it also formed the culmination of the BBC's *The Hollow Crown* cycle, filmed in 2012, with **Tom Hiddleston** claiming his just dues in a production directed by **Thea Sharrock**.

SCREEN

Henry V
L. Olivier, R. Asherson, L. Banks; Laurence Olivier (dir.) UK, 1944 > ITV / Criterion DVD

Dedicated to the fighting men who liberated Europe at the close of World War II, Olivier's *Henry V* was regarded by the British authorities as such a boost for morale that schoolchildren were escorted to special mass screenings on its release. Seventy-odd years later, it is indeed the pep-talk patriotism that hits first; then bewilderment that a movie which caricatures the French so grotesquely can have been made when they were allies. Olivier, as ever, works with broad brushstrokes. Though the film is often visually disappointing – the colour garish, the sets winsome (especially the French court's cartoonish battlements) – William Walton's score is arguably his finest and Agincourt, the film's sole location shoot, is breathtakingly done (albeit with help from Eisenstein, whose battle scenes in *Alexander Nevsky* Olivier quotes repeatedly). The acting is uneven, too, and while Olivier is often impressive he can also be irritatingly mannered. But *Henry V*'s intriguing conceit – the main action is framed by a quaintly realized Elizabethan production – is more imaginative and successful than the film's detractors make out. Also available on high-definition Blu-ray.

Henry V
K. Branagh, E. Thompson, D. Jacobi; Kenneth Branagh (dir.) UK, 1989 > Icon / MGM DVD

When Branagh's version of *Henry V* premiered it was touted as the darker, messier rival to Olivier; the one that was prepared to tell war like it is. While there's some truth in that – Branagh restores the second Harfleur speech and emphasizes the ghoulish execution of Bardolph, both cut by Olivier – it's interesting to note that Shakespeare still demands atrocities (such as the massacre of French prisoners) that even latter-day film-makers can't stomach. And although Branagh's own Henry is more intimately sketched that Olivier's, it is far from antiheroic: appropriating the language of Hollywood, Branagh makes him a troubled Eighties action hero, *Die Hard* rather than *Dam Busters*. *Henry V* was targeted as a mass-market movie, and it succeeds in that role, Oscars and all. Though there are some errors of judgement – the silent insert of Robbie Coltrane's sweaty death as Falstaff and Derek Jacobi's hammy Chorus are just two – strong performances from Paul Scofield (the French King) and Ian Holm (Fluellen) save the day.

The Hollow Crown
T. Hiddleston, P. Joseph, A. Lesser; Thea Sharrock (dir.) UK, 2012 > BBC 📀 ➕

Though it's the climax to the Henriad, *Henry V* can feel like a let-down when you've watched the full sweep of plays, Shakespeare exchanging the cavalcade of comic characters he created in *Henry IV* for a suite of bland politicians. Despite a typically excellent cast, Thea Sharrock's *Hollow Crown* version doesn't entirely escape that trap, a workmanlike adaptation that is honest to the play (it restores controversies such as the massacre of the prisoners and Henry's threats of rape at Harfleur) but somehow slightly dull. Nonetheless, there's some very good acting on display. Tom Hiddleston, thin-faced and earnest, has grown into the role and offers a decisive but troubled monarch – a warrior king haunted by the inevitable costs of war – and the wooing scene with Mélanie Thierry's blushing Catherine is poised between romance and something much more bleak. Sharrock's decision to frame the action with scenes from Henry's funeral (he would be dead aged just 35) is a worthwhile reminder that history is always on the march.

AUDIO

Henry V
J. Glover, S. Todd, B. Cox; Clive Brill (dir.) UK, 1998 > Arkangel ◉ ➕

Same names, different label – a logical way to follow up the excellent BBC *Henry IV*s is this Arkangel version with Jamie Glover making the transfer from Hal to Henry. This he does adeptly, with an urgent and serious-minded performance that makes a good case for Henry's heroism. Not that this version shies away from the less appealing sides to the play: war is somehow acutely disturbing in audio, and Clive Brill's direction (admirably taut on the whole) captures well the tense hours pre-Agincourt and the nerves of the English soldiers. Brian Cox puts in a powerful cameo as the Chorus, a role ideally suited to this medium.

EDITIONS

Arden Shakespeare (third series)
T.W. Craik (ed.); 1995 > Bloomsbury

Gary Taylor's 1982 Oxford edition, one of the first in that series and indeed one of its best, is well worth taking a look at. But despite the Oxford's strengths, Craik's Arden version has just that bit more to offer and is able to discuss two major recent milestones in the play's performance history, Michael Bogdanov's 1986 ESC production and Kenneth Branagh's film three years later. Craik's introduction is organized along traditional Arden lines, with sections on Date, Sources, Texts, Criticism and so forth, but is easily navigable and he includes a facsimile of Q1 at the back along with some useful maps. The text itself is helpfully glossed with liberal quotations from Holinshed and *The Famous Victories*.

SOME CRITICISM

Shakespeare and the Problem of Meaning
Norman Rabkin; 1981 > Chicago UP

This slender volume unites several of Rabkin's essays from a variety of sources. It's held together by its conviction that exploring what Shakespeare *means* can be a process as complicated – and illuminating – as reading or seeing the plays themselves; and also that they will wriggle free from whatever we attempt to make them mean. At the heart of this collection is Rabkin's famous piece on *Henry V*, in which he compares the play to one of those two-dimensional optical illusions that seems like a duck one moment and a rabbit the next – and which cannot be both at the same time, however much you want it to. Also included are essays on *The Merchant of Venice* and the romances.

Shakespeare Left and Right
Ivo Kamps (ed.); 1991 > Routledge

Few plays have found themselves more caught up in political ideology (or ideologies) than *Henry V*, and in Kamps's confrontational collection the play finds itself under cross-examination several times – notably from Harry Berger (on the Henriad), David Scott Kastan (in an essay exploring new historicist approaches to the histories) and Chris Fitter (who puts Branagh's film under the microscope and exposes "an establishment cover-up"). *Shakespeare Left and Right* is varied in quality, but the contributors' urgent arguments, from all angles of the political debate, will not leave you on the sidelines. Recently republished in the "Routledge Revivals" series.

Henry VI Part I

Historically speaking, *Henry VI Part I* kicks off what is sometimes called the "first tetralogy" – the sequence of four plays covering the turbulent period in English history through the life and death of Henry VI, his usurpation by Edward IV and the murderous succession of Edward's brother, Richard of Gloucester, as Richard III. If it is the earliest play of the four, *Part I* is Shakespeare's first attempt to wrestle with the Wars of the Roses – still uncomfortably recent history when he was writing. But the play is not some abstract treatise, nor a Tudor propaganda piece: it is a vivid and powerful drama about high-stakes international politics, albeit one whose potential has been exploited all too rarely on the modern stage. Dominated by the impressive and terrifying character of Joan la Pucelle (better known as Joan of Arc), one of Shakespeare's first great female roles, it offers plenty of spectacle and excitement – not least in its vivid battle scenes and onstage fights.

DATE > *1 Henry VI* was a roaring success from 1592 onwards – although a prequel to the two other *Henry VI* plays, it could have been written after them. Thomas Nashe has been suggested as one of at least two other likely collaborators with Shakespeare.

SOURCES > Raphael Holinshed's 1587 *Chronicles of England, Scotland and Ireland* and Edward Halle's *Union of the Two Noble and Illustrious Families of Lancaster and York* (1548) provide the story's backbone. Some scenes also derive from Robert Fabyan's *New Chronicle of England and France* (1516).

TEXTS > The 1623 Folio provides the only authoritative text – unlike the other *Henry VI* plays, which were published in quarto.

Interpreting the play

The closing lines of *Henry V* offer an eloquent and moving description of what will follow the miraculous English victory at Agincourt. The omens are not good, the Chorus suggests:

> Thus far with rough and all-unable pen
>   Our bending author hath pursued the story,
> In little room confining mighty men,
>   Mangling by starts the full course of their glory.
> Small time, but in that small most greatly lived
>   This star of England. Fortune made his sword,
> By which the world's best garden he achieved,
>   And of it left his son imperial lord.
> Henry the Sixth, in infant bands crowned king

MAJOR CHARACTERS & SYNOPSIS

THE ENGLISH

King Henry VI of England and France
Duke of Gloucester, Henry's uncle and Protector
Bishop of Winchester, Henry's great-uncle, later
Cardinal
Richard Plantagenet (later **Duke of York**)
Edmund Mortimer, Plantagenet's uncle
Duke of Bedford, Henry's uncle and Regent of
France
Duke of Exeter, King Henry's great-uncle
Duke of Somerset, Exeter's nephew
Earls of Warwick, Salisbury and Suffolk
Lord Talbot (later **Earl of Shrewsbury**) and **John
Talbot**, his son
Various English dignitaries, including **Sir William
Glasdale**, **Sir Thomas Gargrave**, **Sir John
Fastolf** and **Sir William Lucy**

THE FRENCH

Charles, Dauphin of France
René, **Duke of Anjou** (later **King of Naples**)
Margaret, René's daughter
Duke of Alençon
Bastard of Orléans, the Duke of Orléans's
illegitimate son
Duke of Burgundy, King Henry's uncle
Countess of Auvergne
Joan la Pucelle, a peasant (also known as Joan
of Arc)

ACT 1 Henry V, England's greatest king, is dead.
The funeral is interrupted by news that his hard-
won legacy – the conquest of France – is under
threat: in fact, territory has already been lost to
the French. The English nobles squabble among
themselves in the absence of the young King,
Henry VI; Gloucester and Winchester in particular
jostle for political advantage and their hatred
spills over into brawling between their followers.
Meanwhile, in the battle for Orléans, the French
are beaten back. The peasant Joan la Pucelle
arrives, however, and presents herself as France's
saviour; when she beats the Dauphin in single
combat, it seems she is gifted with superhuman
powers. Under her direction the French fire on
English positions, Salisbury is mortally wounded
and Talbot is disarmed. Orléans is once more in
French hands.

ACT 2 The battle turns once again as the English
assault Orléans and drive out the French. Back in
England, political infighting reaches new levels
as rivals Richard Plantagenet and Somerset face
each other in the Temple garden, plucking red
and white roses to mark their opposing loyalties.
The Wars of the Roses – the battle between the
houses of York and Lancaster – have symbolically
begun, and when Plantagenet visits his uncle, the
dying Edmund Mortimer, the Wars' argument
is rehearsed: Plantagenet's claim to the English
throne rests on the fact that Richard II (York) was
deposed by Henry IV (Lancaster). The hold of the
present king, Henry VI (Lancaster), is weak.

ACT 3 The King struggles to smooth relations
between Gloucester and Winchester. Attempting
to calm the York–Lancaster quarrel, he makes
Plantagenet Duke of York – so alienating his
kinsman Somerset. Henry heads to France to
be crowned, but finds more strife between supporters of York and Lancaster. Joan continues her
devilish machinations: she leads the French in
disguise to take Rouen and persuades the Duke of
Burgundy (Henry's uncle) to switch sides.

ACT 4 Henry's coronation is interrupted by
news of Burgundy's treason, and his problems
deepen when he attempts to mediate in another
quarrel between York and Lancaster supporters,
unwittingly favouring the Lancastrians. It seems
barely surprising that the battle for Bordeaux
goes spectacularly wrong: Talbot's forces are left
stranded and the two English commanders, York
and Somerset, blame each other.

ACT 5 As part of a peace deal with France, Henry
agrees to marry the Earl of Armagnac's daughter,
but Suffolk has other plans – he woos the beautiful Margaret of Anjou for the King, plotting to
keep her as his own mistress. Paris rebels against
the Dauphin and Joan, and Joan is captured by
York, later being condemned to death. The play
closes as Henry accepts Margaret in the face of
bitter opposition from his nobles: her dowry is
non-existent and England must give up more
French territory as part of the bargain. More strife
seems inevitable.

> Of France and England, did this king succeed,
> Whose state so many had the managing
> That they lost France and made his England bleed,
> Which oft our stage hath shown—and, for their sake,
> In your fair minds this acceptance take.
>
> [*Henry V*, Epilogue 1–14]

The lines are not simply a reminder about what will come next historically, once the cast have taken off their costumes: they also look back, to the outset of the "bending author's" career. In the early 1590s, nearly a decade earlier – a long time for the industrious Shakespeare – he began a series of history plays that were unlike anything the London stage had yet seen. Their subject was a different Henry, Henry V's son, and the civil strife and broils that filled his unhappy life and tore England apart as never before. Shakespeare's colleague and possible collaborator Thomas Nashe wrote admiringly of *Henry VI Part I* and its effect on "ten thousand spectators at least (at several times)", and the series did much to cement Shakespeare's reputation as the most exciting young dramatist in London.

No one had written English history plays on this scale before. Although Christopher Marlowe's *Tamburlaine* (1587–90) began a fashion for writing multi-decker drama, Shakespeare's *Henry VI* sequence in its final form is the only professional three-part play from this period. That said, many critics think that *1 Henry VI* was in fact the last of the trilogy to be penned, capitalizing on the success Shakespeare had already experienced with *The First Part of the Contention of the Two Famous Houses of York and Lancaster* (now known as *2 Henry VI*) and *The True Tragedy of Richard Duke of York and the Good King Henry the Sixth* (*3 Henry VI*). If this is true, the young playwright's decision to write a prequel dramatizing the origins of the York–Lancaster conflict was logical enough.

John Heminges and Henry Condell, actor-editors of the 1623 First Folio, placed the (numbered) *Henry VI* plays in historical order, directly inviting readers to interpret them as a "real" sequence – a kind of national epic whose interior cohesion reinforces its continuity with the Elizabethan present. Taking that view, some nineteenth-century critics compared it to Aeschylus's *Oresteia* trilogy or Wagner's *Ring* cycle; others have linked it to the medieval mystery plays; still others have made comparisons with TV period drama. It's worth observing that one of Nashe's reasons for picking out *1 Henry VI* is to demonstrate that it had an improving purpose: to make the past live again for the edification of its audiences.

Civil broils

But if *1 Henry VI* is a history lesson, what does it teach? Following the doyen of mid-twentieth-century historical criticism, E.M.W. Tillyard, who declared in 1944 that "throughout the *Henry VIs* and *Richard III* Shakespeare links the present happenings with the past", many commentators have argued that the plays argue for what Tillyard christened the "Tudor myth" (see box overpage). This depicts Henry VI's reign as a period of horror-filled instability: the King loses his grip on power, in

Mything the point

Taken together, eight of Shakespeare's ten history plays – *Richard II*, the two *Henry IVs*, *Henry V*, the three *Henry VIs* and *Richard III* – tell an unbroken tale of English monarchy from the deposition of Richard II to the deposition of Richard III. The man responsible for the latter was **Henry Tudor**, whose triumph at the Battle of Bosworth in 1485 inaugurated the Tudor dynasty, which proclaimed to heal the wounds inflicted by the Wars of the Roses and bring peace and prosperity to an England wracked by civil conflict. As Shakespeare's Henry declares in words that close *Richard III*: "Now civil wounds are stopped; peace lives again. / That she may long live here, God say 'Amen'." (5.8.40–1).

Ironically enough, for critics of Shakespeare's histories, this soothing speech has been tantamount to a declaration of war. One of the opening salvoes was fired by **E.M.W. Tillyard**, whose 1943 study *The Elizabethan World Picture* developed the view that "ordinary" Elizabethans believed solidly what their masters told them to: in the strength of church, state and monarchy. Developing these ideas in *Shakespeare's History Plays* (1944), Tillyard stated that Shakespeare went along with all this; furthermore, his history plays consistently promote what he called the "**Tudor myth**" – the idea peddled by Tudor historiographers such as Polydore Vergil (c. 1470–c. 1555), Edward Halle (c. 1498–1547) and Raphael Holinshed (d. c. 1582), that Henry VII's accession was divinely ordained, and

that his granddaughter Elizabeth's reign was, as Tillyard puts it, the "acknowledged outcome" of God's providence. In using Halle and Holinshed, Tillyard's Shakespeare is reassuringly conservative, at his "most individual when most orthodox and of his age".

Subsequent critics would come to radically different conclusions about the lesson(s) the histories offer. The Polish critic **Jan Kott**'s *Shakespeare Our Contemporary* (1964) famously recast the myth as a "Grand Mechanism", a "great staircase on which there treads a constant procession of kings", all of them functions of the same depersonalized system. As opponents have eagerly noted, though, while Kott stressed faceless chaos rather than Tillyardian order, this simply replaces one overriding structure with another. **A.P. Rossiter** suggested that the histories are ambivalent and evasive about the morals of kingship, while **Norman Rabkin**'s *Shakespeare and the Common Understanding* (1967) posited that they were dominated by "illogicality, irregularity, complexity, contrariety, complementarity, polyphony, doubleness, ambivalence, even *discoherence*". This taste for transgressive ambiguity has naturally found favour among latter-day writers unwilling to accept Shakespeare as an establishment lackey – though, intriguingly, so-called **new historicist** critics have most often stressed the state-friendly "ideology" of the plays so enthusiastically that they all but accuse him of precisely that.

the process throwing true-bred English heroes like Talbot to the wolves and bringing England to the brink of chaos. In this view, the histories present a stark message: war is bad, peace good. But in recent years Tillyard's position has come under fire from more rebellious critics, who insist that Shakespeare is not complicit with the Tudor regime, but a critic of it. And far from criticizing events such as Talbot's death, Shakespeare is dramatically dependent on them. Both viewpoints have their strengths: on one level, it might be said that the playwright takes an "official" line, and presents arguments that worthily call for peace and civility; on another, his task is complicated by the fact that strife is the life-blood of drama. Though grimly unpleasant in real life, war can be terrific fun on stage.

This latter view receives strong backing in *1 Henry VI*, which vividly animates the two conflicts which dominate its action – war in France and internecine strife at home. There is little doubt that this is one of Shakespeare's most action-packed dramas, for all that it is infrequently revived. Over twenty fights take place, many of which occur hand-to-hand on stage. Often – as with Joan la Pucelle's breathtaking defeat of the French Dauphin – those combats provide its most stunning effects. And, as recent critics have pointed out, late sixteenth-century audiences (a large proportion of them young men) would hardly have put up with the dull and stylized choreography some present-day directors call "fighting". Real weapons would have been used – and swordsmanship was something in which such audiences took a near-professional interest. Given that the play was probably first performed at the Rose, whose shallow stage will have added a frisson of real danger to fight scenes, it is difficult to avoid the conclusion that *1 Henry VI* was written to show off its writer's ability to create explosive, dangerous drama. It's likely that a significant percentage of Nashe's "ten thousand spectators" were there for the battle scenes, not the tears.

1 Henry VI specializes in depicting grand set-piece occasions that are violently disrupted. Nowhere is this more apparent than with the funeral of Henry V at its very opening. England's lords are grouped around the coffin to pay their last respects when an argument suddenly flares up:

WINCHESTER
> He was a king blest of the King of Kings.
> Unto the French, the dreadful judgement day
> So dreadful will not be as was his sight.
> The battles of the Lord of Hosts he fought.
> The Church's prayers made him so prosperous.

GLOUCESTER
> The Church? Where is it? Had not churchmen prayed,
> His thread of life had not so soon decayed.

> [1.1.28–34]

What is so brilliantly dramatic here is the way in which Shakespeare transforms innocent eulogy into naked aggression. *1 Henry VI's* lords are full-time politicians: even the funeral of their erstwhile monarch turns into an opportunity for point-scoring. Bedford attempts to make peace:

> Cease, cease these jars, and rest your minds in peace.
> Let's to the altar. Heralds, wait on us.
> Instead of gold, we'll offer up our arms—
> Since arms avail not, now that Henry's dead.
> Posterity, await for wretched years,
> When, at their mothers' moistened eyes, babes shall suck,
> Our isle be made a marish of salt tears,
> And none but women left to wail the dead.
> Henry the Fifth, thy ghost I invocate:

Prosper this realm; keep it from civil broils;
Combat with adverse planets in the heavens.
A far more glorious star thy soul will make
Than Julius Caesar or bright—
    Enter a Messenger

[1.1.44–56]

Bedford's attempt to conjure Henry V's "ghost" is abruptly broken off, and his attempt to restore calm is, aptly, left incomplete. In a neat linkage, the messenger interrupting him brings news that the conquest of France, the dead King's greatest success, is under threat. The twin themes, international and domestic war, are sounded simultaneously. Henry's funeral rites are forgotten, and the play's depiction of political fragmentation gets underway – before long, in fact, the servants of Gloucester and Winchester will be brawling openly on stage. Something curiously similar happens in the two other ceremonies that dominate *1 Henry VI*'s action: the new King's coronation is interrupted by news that Burgundy has defected, then by warring supporters of York and Somerset; and the proposed marriage of Henry to the Earl of Armagnac's daughter doesn't even get past the planning stage because Henry changes his mind for factional reasons.

One of the play's most impressive scenes in this vein occurs at the very centre of its action, soon after the English armies have been shown fighting to uproot the French from Orléans. Back in London, the Lancaster and York factions are vying for place at court when they meet in the garden of the Temple Church. Richard Plantagenet (York) believes that Somerset (Lancaster) has wronged him and, as in France, violence is very much on everyone's minds:

RICHARD PLANTAGENET
    The truth appears so naked on my side
    That any purblind eye may find it out.
SOMERSET
    And on my side it is so well apparelled,
    So clear, so shining, and so evident,
    That it will glimmer through a blind man's eye.
RICHARD PLANTAGENET
    Since you are tongue-tied and so loath to speak,
    In dumb significants proclaim your thoughts.
    Let him that is a true-born gentlemen
    And stands upon the honour of his birth,
    If he suppose that I have pleaded truth,
    From off this briar pluck a white rose with me.
        He plucks a white rose

[2.4.20–30]

Somerset responds by defiantly choosing a red rose, and with that gesture, the Wars of the Roses (a nineteenth-century name for a conflict first described by the Tudor historians Shakespeare was reading) are under way.

So fair a dame

But competition between men is just one of *1 Henry VI*'s many enmeshed conflicts. It is also a play in which war crosses gender boundaries. Talbot, "the terror of the French", a man whose very name strikes fear into the enemy, faces his biggest challenge in outwitting the Countess of Auvergne, a seductress who attempts to ensnare him with her feminine wiles. In a similar way, the entire *Henry VI* sequence comes to rest on Henry's biggest blunder: marrying Margaret of Anjou, possibly one of Shakespeare's most satisfyingly evil female roles, a character whom the Duke of York will memorably describe as a "tiger's heart wrapped in a woman's hide" (*3 Henry VI*, 1.4.138) but who appears in this first play as "so fair a dame" that the Earl of Suffolk cannot resist her charms.

Then, of course, there is the "holy maid" Joan la Pucelle, a character who has been described by one critic as "a composite portrait of the ways women are dangerous to men" – a character who uproots not just gender conventions but those of religion, society and politics. Once she has defeated the Dauphin in single combat, it barely seems surprising that she can face down the entire English army; nor that she employs witchcraft in order to do so. While this last element might seem to introduce a note of wilful fantasy into Shakespeare's history, in fact the historical Jeanne d'Arc was accused by the English of being "a disciple and limb of the Fiend … that used false enchantment and sorcery". Joan herself sees her mission as something simpler, to rescue France from English destruction, and Shakespeare gives her plenty of verbal as well as magical power with which to do so. "Look on thy country, look on fertile France," she begs the Duke of Burgundy, who has gone over to the English side:

> And see the cities and the towns defaced
> By wasting ruin of the cruel foe.
> As looks the mother on her lowly babe
> When death doth close his tender-dying eyes,
> See, see the pining malady of France,
> Behold the wounds, the most unnatural wounds,
> Which thou thyself hast given her woeful breast.

> [3.7.44–51]

Burgundy is soon won over and persuaded to rejoin the French: "either she hath bewitched me with her words," he exclaims, "or nature makes me suddenly relent" (3.7.58–9). Indeed, all three female characters in *1 Henry VI* seek control over men and attempt to suborn them to their ends (which are, needless to say, wicked through and through) – a fact which has led some to caricature the young Shakespeare as a woman-hater, others to claim that this play's stereotypes strike an early blow for feminism by satirizing male anxieties.

The subsurface, "mythic" war waged in this play is a war against women, identified with sexuality: it is a war against the outlaw feminine principle.

Marilyn French, *Shakespeare's Division of Experience* (1982)

One of the most striking aspects of Shakespeare's early histories is their powerful female roles. Here Joan (Beatriz Romilly) finally submits to David Harley's guard near the end of *Henry VI Part I* at the Globe in 2013 – but she doesn't give in without a fight.

Whatever the truth, the male world the play depicts is in serious trouble. For *1 Henry VI*'s male characters – in particular Henry VI himself – things are becoming unstuck: haunted by the triumphs of their fathers' generation, they are struggling to prove themselves worthy heirs. Though the King is older in the play than his historical counterpart (who was just nine months old at his father Henry V's death), he is still depicted as dangerously young, both naive and ineffectual. His first words in the play, which attempt to quell the growing argument between Gloucester and Winchester, sound as if his only knowledge of conflict is what he has read in school textbooks:

> O what a scandal it is to our crown
> That two such noble peers as ye should jar!
> Believe me, lords, my tender years can tell
> Civil dissension is a viperous worm
> That gnaws the bowels of the commonwealth.

[3.1.70–4]

Accurate though his words unquestionably are, they are a sign – if any were needed – that Henry VI will fail to hold his father's "commonwealth" together. That very failing will rapidly lead to the deaths of another father and child, Talbot and his son, who perish due to the high-level feud between Somerset and York. Their twinned death is in that sense symbolic: it represents the fracturing of a world in which male certainties are being rendered impotent. It is a framing irony in the *Henry VI* plays that the Wars of the Roses are to do with bloodlines, inheritance, family; and yet they remorselessly tear families apart, separate father from son.

Stage history and adaptations

The early public life of *1 Henry VI* is recorded in unusually precise detail by **Thomas Nashe's** impressionistic description of it in 1592; in the role of Talbot was possibly **Edward Alleyn**. That the play was a staggering success is confirmed by the owner-manager of the Rose theatre, **Philip Henslowe**, who noted receipts totalling over £33 for this, a "new" play – far outstripping other hits of the season such as Kyd's *The Spanish Tragedy* and Marlowe's *The Jew of Malta*. Even so, this initial triumph is the first we hear until 1738, when *1 Henry VI* was acted by request at **Covent Garden**, apparently in a performance that featured numerous dance episodes.

Thereafter, as with the other *Henry VI* plays, adaptations provided the only opportunities for airing. The celebrated **Edmund Kean** revived it in December 1817 as part of **J.H. Merivale's** five-act *Richard Duke of York; or the Contention of York and Lancaster*, which also stirred gobbets of Chapman and Webster into the brew. Kean shone as Richard, one commentator declaring him (somewhat lukewarmly) "in many scenes, unusually great". Another one-evening adaptation was undertaken by **Charles Kemble**, John Philip Kemble's little brother, later in the century, but that clearly proved a dead end – no performance is recorded. Slightly more success seems to have occurred on the continent; the play was acted in Germany and a particularly notable performance took place in Vienna in 1873. Back in England, **G. Osmond Tearle** put on *1 Henry VI* in 1889 with himself as Talbot, **Erskine Lewis** as Henry and **Ellen Cranston** as Margaret.

In 1906 **Frank Benson** decided to present all three *Henry VI*s on different evenings. With *3 Henry VI* billed as the "revival play" (none too successfully, at least judging from the takings), Benson cut props down to a minimum and did away with scene changes entirely. Though the intention was to revive the practice of fluid staging, one reviewer's eye was still caught by the atmosphere of the production: "everything … blended with perfect harmony to give the prevailing sentiment of mournful grandeur due precision".

Robert Atkins built a thrust stage jutting out from the London Old Vic's proscenium for his 1923 adaptation, but was textually less radical than Benson – he opted once more to compress three plays into one *Henry VI*. But the ground was laid for several influential English productions, the first of which transferred from Birmingham Rep to Atkins's former haunt, the Old Vic, under the aegis of **Barry Jackson**. Jackson's 1953 version, directed by **Douglas Seale**, was praised for its "clean thrusting style" and featured **Jack May** as King Henry and **Rosalind Boxall** as his wife, in a Gothicky set designed by **Finlay James**. More radical still was an amateur production in 1959, which used an uncut text and presented Joan as sympathetically as possible.

Back in the professional theatre, **Peter Hall** and **John Barton**'s RSC cycle, *The Wars of the Roses* (1963), engineered two plays – *Henry VI* and *Edward IV* – out of Shakespeare's three (with *Richard III* making *Roses* a trilogy) for reasons partly artistic, partly financial. The text was not only cut in numerous places, but, in the best eighteenth-century traditions, Hall and Barton added new material – some selected from the chronicles, some written by themselves. (Barton coolly remarked later that he "wouldn't dream of trying to write bits into *Lear*".) John Bury designed an austere metallic set that reinforced the harshness and brutality of the play's world. The result was a huge critical and popular success, with **David Warner**'s Henry, **Peggy Ashcroft**'s lisping Margaret and **Janet Suzman**'s Joan attracting particular enthusiasm. **Terry Hands** played down comparisons with Barton and Hall when he directed the cycle fourteen years later at the Swan, again for the RSC, but could not help but be influenced by their approach. In many ways this production was every bit as epic – the set was dominated by an imposing iron bridge – but attempted to be more searching in terms of characterization. **Alan Howard**, who played nearly all Hands's kings in the cycle, offered a Henry simply uninterested in politics, while **Helen Mirren** smouldered as Margaret.

Political relevance was back on the agenda for **Michael Bogdanov**'s ESC versions of 1987, once more cut and spliced as part of a two-tetralogy touring series entitled, yet again, *The Wars of the Roses*. *Part I* came out relatively well, being in the main preserved: **Mary Rutherford**'s Joan made a serene martyr, her death provocatively got up as a South African-style execution with a burning tyre placed around her neck. At the RSC, meanwhile, **Adrian Noble** presented *The Plantagenets* (1988), a two-play adaptation more theatrically conventional than Bogdanov's and certainly more grandiose, which was distinguished by **Ralph Fiennes**'s excellent King. In 2000 the RSC once more put on a cycle of Shakespeare's histories, but unlike previous adaptations the texts remained uncut; the *Henry VIs* were directed by **Michael Boyd** at the small-scale Swan theatre with **David Oyelowo** as Henry (the first black actor to play an RSC monarch). **Edward Hall** presented a two-part version of the *Henry VIs* radically different from that of his father, which toured the UK in 2001–02 under the kitschy title of *Rose Rage*. Hall's youthful, all-male company stressed the plays' heedless violence by setting them in a slaughterhouse. Typically, *Part I* was the one to suffer, made to share one evening with a compressed *Part II* and deprived of nearly all its interest.

The play had better luck at the RSC in 2007–08 when it appeared during **Michael Boyd**'s retread as part of a two-tetralogy cycle. Boyd's brisk direction gave *Part I* plenty of no-nonsense vigour, pitting a hearty squad of English against **Katy Stephens**'s zealous Joan and **John Mackay**'s fey, blonde-ringleted Dauphin. And it took on fresh life as part of a novel experiment by Shakespeare's Globe in London in summer 2013, a project to perform the plays on the battlefields where they are set (not, alas, in France). Sections of *Part I* appeared as a tight, two-hour-long script called *Harry the Sixth*, directed by **Nick Bagnall**.

Influential non-English versions have included **Giorgio Strehler**'s 1965 adaptation, *Il Gioco dei Potente*, influenced by both Barton–Hall and Strindberg; **Peter Palisch**'s stark *Krieg der Rosen* (1967); and **Denis Llorca's** 1978 French adaptation, entitled *Kings, ou les adieux à Shakespeare*, which attempted to approach the plays from the "enemy" perspective. The play was also part of the World Shakespeare Festival in 2012, with troupes from the recently war-torn Balkans each taking part of the *Henry VI* trilogy at the London Globe. **Nikita Milivojević** and National Theatre Belgrade offered a Serbian version that looked disconcertingly English, with leather jerkins and an Arthurian-style round table; instead of plucking roses, the warring barons smeared their faces with red and white paint. In 2014, a starkly modern, through-written adaptation by the Rennes-born director **Thomas Jolly** debuted at the Avignon arts festival; *Libération* acclaimed the show as "legendary", though it mainly seemed impressed by the eighteen-hour duration ("veterans" were awarded a jacket pin).

On screen, the Hall-Barton *Roses* cycle made a powerful impact when adapted for TV in 1965, but otherwise the *Henry VI* plays have not proved popular with film-makers: only two versions currently exist, both courtesy of the BBC. One was made in 1960 as part of the sprawling *An Age of Kings* series, the other as part of the complete BBC Shakespeare project. The latter, directed by **Jane Howell**, concentrated on the plays' childish, game-like elements and gained mixed reviews. More warmly received were the tapings of **Bogdanov's** ESC productions, which were recorded live, pre-serving something of the excitement and vitality of the original performances. At the time of writing, a cut-down version of the play is being filmed – as a two-part *Henriad* – as a follow-up to the BBC's 2012 *The Hollow Crown*. **Dominic Cooke** directs, while the cast includes **Sophie Okenedo** (Margaret), **Hugh Bonneville** (Humphrey) and **Tom Sturridge** (Henry VI). Release is expected in April 2016.

SCREEN

An Age of Kings
T. Scully, J. May, E. Atkins; Michael Hayes (dir.) UK, 1960 > BBC/Illuminations **DVD**

Decades before the BBC made *The Hollow Crown*, there came *The Age of Kings* – a mould-breaking series that was not merely the first attempt to put the entire cycle of histories on screen in hour-long instalments, but one of the first times it had been performed in its entirety in the UK. Filmed in black and white, which comes across as rather hazy on DVD (despite the best efforts of the Illuminations production company), the programmes look their age, but boast a youthful and energetic cast, and at their best are more than a match for glossier subsequent versions. *Henry VI Part I* gets a raw deal, cut to a single episode by adapter Eric Crozier and little more than a prequel to the civil broils that follow, but is cleanly done, with a seething Robert Lang as Winchester and Terry Scully's fluting King Henry. Commanding in every sense is the young Eileen Atkins as a crop-haired Joan la Pucelle – boldly sexual and defiantly ballsy, hers is a performance that makes you think Shakespeare found the original for later cross-dressing heroines in the mists of French history.

King Henry VI: House of Lancaster
P. Brennen, B. Stanton, C. Farrell; Michael Bogdanov (dir.) UK, 1990 > Vision **DVD** [o/p]

Though it might seem unflattering to call Bogdanov's *Wars of the Roses* production-line Shakespeare, in turnaround time this seems apt enough: the plays were filmed on consecutive nights at the Grand Theatre in Swansea and the "live" results released on video. Though this didn't allow the luxury of retakes or fine-tuning (witness the occasionally crude editing), the interpretations are slick and have dated surprisingly well (despite the odd dodgy moustache). All of *1 Henry VI* and part of *2 Henry VI* are here combined with some success: the action is fast-paced and performances are excellent if undemonstrative – Richard Jarvis, who returns in the title role of *Richard III*, is a strongly characterized exception, sparkling in cameo as the Dauphin. Paul Brennen's earnest Henry looks as if it's his first day at school throughout, and only Brenda Blethyn's spaced-out Joan seems a disappointment. Despite a rumoured official release, the recordings are – frustratingly – only available on bootleg DVD and in online clips.

AUDIO

Henry VI Part I
D. Tennant, N. Rodway, J. Bowe; Clive Brill (dir.) UK, 1998 > Arkangel ◉ ⬇

There's plenty of excitement in the military scenes of this *1 Henry VI*, even if some of it seems excessively shouty (the sound effects, reminiscent of World War I, are equally noisy). Plenty of excitement elsewhere, too: little surprise that David Tennant's kindly Henry has trouble reining nobles as hot-headed as these, while Amanda Root's Joan crackles with righteous aggression. The play's comic energy is somewhat sacrificed to this approach, but with rounded performances from the likes of Norman Rodway, as an earnest Gloucester, and Nigel Cooke, urbane and sly as Suffolk, it's difficult to complain.

EDITIONS

Arden Shakespeare (third series)
Edward Burns (ed.); 2000 > Bloomsbury

Unlike the New Cambridge general editors, who gave Michael Hattaway the job of editing all three *Henry VI*s, Arden has decided to separate the task out – laudably regarding them as individual artistic entities. Edward Burns's *1 Henry VI* offers an excellent way into this still undervalued play, and presents a closely argued case for multi-authorship. Whether you're convinced by this or not, Burns's introduction will certainly provide food for thought. His cursory treatment of stage history is the only irritation.

SOME CRITICISM

Shakespeare's History Plays
E.M.W. Tillyard; 1944 > Penguin / Athlone [o/p]

Tillyard's study has cast a long shadow over the critical history of the *Henry VI* plays, not least because it became cheaply available to a generation of students after being issued in paperback in 1962. In it Tillyard honed theories from his earlier *The Elizabethan World Picture* (1943), which set out his notion of the "great chain of being", beginning with God's place at the centre of the universe and moving outward and downwards through kings and princes to common people and even lower forms of life. This static image of commonplace assumptions to which all Elizabethans had access is notable chiefly for its emphasis on order and degree, a fearlessly orthodox interpretation. This book has been doggedly attacked from the 1960s onwards, but it remains a key text in the history of Shakespearian criticism.

Shakespeare: The Histories
Graham Holderness; 2000 > Macmillan

If you're looking to do battle with E.M.W. Tillyard, look no further. Graham Holderness has published extensively on the history plays, and nearly everything Tillyard takes for granted – that they were written sequentially, that they even count as "chronicles" – is disposed of neatly in the first few pages, with Holderness arguing forcefully that the genre is both more complex and stranger than a mere recitation of past events (it's revealing that his first text is, of all things, *Hamlet*). Holderness sometimes pushes his postmodern, materialist argument too far – it is quite likely that the Tudors' view of the Wars of the Roses was more straightforward than he allows – but this study abounds in spiky detail and will make you think deeply about what history and its presentation on stage really mean.

Henry VI Part II

enry VI Part II begins, appropriately enough, in the thick of things. As events in France fade into the background, the English court begins to fragment more dramatically than ever before – Gloucester's enemies finish him off, the King is pushed onto the defensive and York exposes his own ambition for the crown. But in *2 Henry VI* Shakespeare expands the scene beyond dynastic wrangling: he steps back from the main narrative at several key moments, showing that history means more than baronial families quarrelling over bloodlines. One of its most celebrated episodes concerns Jack Cade's Kentish rebellion, which comes close to destabilizing the country (and the play) in ways that even England's leaders find impossible to control. In what might have been the first drama in the *Henry VI* sequence to be written, Shakespeare also dwells on some of the stranger aspects of the past: the plot includes a man whose blindness is apparently cured by a miracle, a colourful tale borrowed from John Foxe's anti-Catholic collection, the *Book of Martyrs* (1563).

DATE > If the play was the first of the *Henry VI* sequence to be penned (a currently fashionable view), it most likely dates from 1590–91.

SOURCES > Halle's *Union* and Holinshed's *Chronicles*, as with the other two plays, provide the substance of *2 Henry VI*. Eleanor's penance may derive from an Elizabethan biographical collection, *The Mirror for Magistrates*, while the

miracle scene probably comes from John Foxe's *Book of Martyrs* (1583).

TEXTS > A quarto version (Q1) entitled *The First Part of the Contention* was printed in 1594, to be followed by others in 1600 (Q2) and 1619 (Q3), though all these texts were perhaps reconstructed from memory. The 1623 Folio version was almost certainly printed from Shakespeare's papers.

Interpreting the play

In *2 Henry VI*, Shakespeare takes up the political narrative from King Henry's marriage to Margaret of Anjou, through the Duke of Gloucester's fall and Cade's rebellion, to the Duke of York's long-intended bid for the crown and the clash between his forces and those of the King at St Albans. In contrast to *1 Henry VI*, the focus is shifted decisively from the clash of nations to disputes on the home front: problems in France continue to dog Henry's regime, but they are pushed almost completely off stage. Even the sudden announcement at court that England has lost all its domains in France, the moment where Henry's international star is at its lowest, is remarkably underplayed:

MAJOR CHARACTERS & SYNOPSIS

LANCASTRIANS
King Henry VI of England and France
Queen Margaret, Henry's wife
William de la Pole, **Marquis** (later **Duke**) **of Suffolk**, the Queen's lover
Duke Humphrey of Gloucester, the King's uncle and Protector
Duchess of Gloucester, Duke Humphrey's wife
Cardinal Beaufort, Bishop of Winchester, Henry's great-uncle
Dukes of Buckingham and **Somerset**
Old **Lord Clifford** and **Young Clifford**, his son

YORKISTS
Richard Plantagenet, Duke of York
York's sons: **Edward**, Earl of March and **Richard**, Earl of Salisbury
Earl of Warwick, Salisbury's son

OTHER CHARACTERS
The combatants: **Thomas Horner** and **Peter Thump**, Horner's man
The conjurors: the witch **Margery Jordan**, the conjuror **Roger Bolingbroke** and **Asnath**, a spirit
Simon Simpcox, supposedly cured by a "miracle", and his **Wife**
The rebels: the Kentishman **Jack Cade** (secretly supported by the Duke of York and pretending to be John Mortimer) and his supporters
Opponents of the rebels: **Clerk of Chatham**; **Sir Humphrey Stafford** and his **Brother**; **Lords Saye** and **Scales**
Alexander Iden, from Kent, who kills Cade

[**ACTION CONTINUED FROM HENRY VI PART I**]

ACT 1 The English court is in uproar. King Henry is to marry Margaret of Anjou, even though she has no dowry and the English must renounce French land in the deal. Gloucester, the King's Protector, is appalled, and his enemies Winchester and Buckingham demand his removal. York wants the crown for himself, but bides his time. Gloucester's wife is equally ambitious for the throne and is tricked by her enemies at court into consulting witches; York and Buckingham are lying in wait at the séance and arrest her. Political unrest has also reached the commoners, and a small group petitions Queen Margaret and her lover Suffolk for help – to their scorn. Back in council, the bickering continues: Gloucester denies

accusations of corruption while King Henry struggles to control the deepening row between York, Somerset and their supporters.

***

ACT 2 Out hawking with the King, Gloucester and Winchester continue to argue when they are interrupted by a man who claims his blindness has been cured by a miracle. Henry naively believes him, and, though Gloucester exposes the hoax, news soon arrives of the Duchess of Gloucester's arrest; Gloucester resigns the protectorship in disgrace, and his wife is banished.

***

ACT 3 Gloucester's opponents close in on him. The Queen denounces him in parliament and he is blamed for the loss of the remaining French territories. Arresting his uncle, Henry announces that Gloucester will be tried fairly, but Margaret plots with York and Suffolk to have him killed. York secretly begins his campaign for the crown, revealing that he has convinced a commoner, Jack Cade, to impersonate John Mortimer (York's dead ancestor) and incite rebellion against the Lancastrian rule of Henry. News of Gloucester's sudden death reaches Henry, who accuses Suffolk of murder and has him exiled. Winchester dies, driven mad by guilt.

***

ACT 4 Suffolk is murdered at sea by the ship's captain and crew in revenge for Gloucester's death and because of his affair with the Queen. In Kent, Cade's rebellion is beginning: his supporters kill Sir Humphrey Stafford and his brother, who intervene on the King's side. Cade's rioters attack London before executing Lord Say and his son-in-law, but the rebellion falters when Old Clifford and Buckingham offer to pardon those who will support Henry V's son. Cade flees, a broken man, and is killed by Iden. Meanwhile it is reported that York's army is marching towards the King.

***

ACT 5 York and his sons challenge Henry, and their armies fight at St Albans. York kills Old Clifford (whose son vows revenge) and Richard kills Somerset, before Margaret and Henry admit defeat and escape for London. They are pursued by the Yorkists, determined to seize the crown itself.

KING HENRY   What news from France?
SOMERSET
   That all your interest in those territories
   Is utterly bereft you—all is lost.
KING HENRY
   Cold news, Lord Somerset; but God's will be done.
YORK *(aside)*
   Cold news for me, for I had hope of France,
   As firmly as I hope for fertile England.

[3.1.83–8]

While Henry is content to take the loss of France as part of some divine plan (something, therefore, he is powerless to resist), the Duke of York's response is wholly selfish: his thoughts focus on how it impinges on his designs on the crown. This moment is crucial not merely because it demonstrates how irrelevant the struggle for France has become, but because it illuminates the extent to which the English court has torn itself apart. While *1 Henry VI* depicts nobles so terrified of losing in war that, in Bedford's words, news of it will make the old King Henry "burst his lead and rise from death" (*1 Henry VI*, 1.1.64), in the sequel France is little more than an excuse for political infighting.

In this play dynamic, opportunistic figures such as Richard of York (and of course his son, Richard of Gloucester, later Richard III) leave others standing by the wayside. While Henry fiddles and his lords bicker, York is after power. He speaks one of the play's few soliloquies after his colleagues unwittingly dispatch him to Ireland:

   My brain, more busy than the labouring spider,
   Weaves tedious snares to trap mine enemies.
   Well, nobles, well: 'tis politicly done
   To send me packing with an host of men.
   I fear me you but warm the starvèd snake,
   Who, cherished in your breasts, will sting your hearts.
   'Twas men I lacked, and you will give them me.
   I take it kindly. Yet be well assured
   You put sharp weapons in a madman's hands.

[3.1.339–47]

His language is blunt rather than artful (Shakespeare will give his son, Richard of Gloucester, sharper oratory), but York, toying with the meaning of "politic", knows full well what he is after.

Hope of harmony

This kind of brute political philosophy is utterly at odds with that espoused by the King. His celebrated address to the arguing nobles in Act Two has been widely commented upon:

The winds grow high; so do your stomachs, lords.
How irksome is this music to my heart!
When such strings jar, what hope of harmony?

[2.1.58–60]

Henry speaks in terms which would have been familiar to his audience – that musical and political discord function alike and are equally unnatural. But Henry's fine words, unlike York's, get him nowhere: they are simply a commentary on events of which Henry is no longer in control – and an analogy which is beginning to look rather hopeless. While an Elizabethan audience (parts of it at least) might well have agreed with Henry's well-meaning sentiments, the action of the play is already leaving him behind.

Whereas we now know the play as *Henry VI Part II*, when published in 1594 the King's name was conspicuously absent from the title-page, which described "The First Part of the Contention betwixt the two famous Houses of York and Lancaster, with the death of the good Duke Humphrey: And the banishment and death of the Duke of Suffolk, and the Tragical end of the proud Cardinal of Winchester, with the notable Rebellion of Jack Cade: And the Duke of York's first claim unto the Crown". Almost everyone is present, in fact, apart from Henry: it is the people surrounding him – Gloucester, Suffolk, Winchester, Cade, York – who get top billing. This is symptomatic of the King's creeping irrelevance, an irrelevance he actually seems to invite. As the battle at St Albans begins to turn against the Lancastrian forces, Queen Margaret simply cannot believe that her husband can be so comprehensively inactive:

KING HENRY
 Can we outrun the heavens? Good Margaret, stay.
QUEEN MARGARET
 What are you made of? You'll nor fight nor fly.
 Now it is manhood, wisdom and defence,
 To give the enemy way, and to secure us
 By what we can, which can no more but fly.

[5.4.2–6]

Henry will "nor fight nor fly"; Margaret can describe him only by what he will not do. Where the sources presented the reign of King Henry as a byword for weak governance, in this play Shakespeare develops a character whose inability to do anything – even run away from his enemies – makes his existence as a dramatic entity somewhat questionable.

Henry's piety might seem to form the moral centre of a conspicuously amoral play, but what events emphasize is that morals are out of fashion in these "dangerous" days. Henry has been described as a medieval character adrift in a Renaissance play: his appeals to divine providence have the ring of sincerity, but they advertise his dislocation from the real business of life. Nowhere is this truer than in the so-called "mock miracle" scene, when the royal party is visited by a man falsely claiming to have been cured of blindness at the shrine of St Alban. While Henry – ever the believer – takes

The English Shakespeare Company brought Shakespeare's histories to audiences across the land during the late 1980s. In its two-play remake of the *Henry VI*s, Paul Brennen was a bright but fatally naive Henry, while June Watson's steely Margaret reminded many of the then prime minister, Margaret Thatcher.

Simpcox at his word, Gloucester plays the sceptic, fooling him into revealing that the miracle is manufactured. Shakespeare bases this incident not on Halle or Holinshed, his main sources, but on Foxe's *Acts and Monuments*, a virulently anti-Catholic tract and history of Protestant martyrdom better known as the *Book of Martyrs*, which by the time of Elizabeth's reign had become the most significant Protestant work after the Bible. In Foxe's rendering, the tale is simply a demonstration of Duke Humphrey's wisdom – and of course a swipe at miracle-touting Catholics. Shakespeare, however, makes it more than that. The King's Christian credulousness seems not just naive, but desperately outdated; Gloucester's empirical rationalism carries the day. Ominously, this is Henry's first embarrassment at St Albans. His second, in battle with the Yorkists, will endanger his very throne.

Henry is not alone in being out of step with the times. The Duchess of Gloucester attempts to employ witchcraft to control events (like Joan la Pucelle in *1 Henry VI*), but this simply leads her into a trap laid by her enemies. Medieval chivalry, too, does not escape Shakespeare's hard-edged satire. During an argument between the armourer Horner and his man Peter in which Horner accuses Peter of treason, the two men are ordered to fight it out in feudal style, but the knightly trial-by-combat turns into brutal farce when Horner turns up drunk and Peter bludgeons him to death. Even the ancient rule of law, upheld by Gloucester, is up for grabs, as the plotters against him realize when conspiring how best to dispose of him:

> That he should die is worthy policy;
> But yet we want a colour for his death.
> 'Tis meet he be condemned by course of law.
>
> [3.1.235–7]

"Colour" could translate as "pretext" or "pretence" – a word Shakespeare frequently uses in this dissembling sense (adding a further irony to Gloucester's exposing of Simpcox, which rests on the "blind" man's uncanny ability to spot colours). Equally shifty are words such as "worthy", "policy" and "meet" – which, in Winchester's lexicon, are all about playing the game to best advantage.

Wild Moriscos

Another inset into the story of the Wars of the Roses throws a different light on its dynastic squabbles. At the beginning of Act Three, York reveals that he has recruited the talents of a dynamic Kentish troublemaker, Jack Cade, and persuaded him to rebel against the King. This uprising comes to occupy most of Act Four, and in it Shakespeare focuses for the first time in his career (but certainly not the last) on politics at the grassroots. It would be hard to describe Shakespeare's portrait of the crowd as sympathetic: his commoners are dim-witted, destructive and fickle, galvanized into revolt by Cade's promises of easy takings but easily dispersed when threatened. This perspective matches that of Shakespeare's sources, Halle and Holinshed, both of whom are critical of the revolt – Holinshed in particular describes Cade as a "villainous rebel" leading an army composed of "idle and vagrant persons".

For all that, though, Shakespeare deliberately complicates matters. Cade is one of the most attractive characters in the play, and he promises revolution:

> Be brave, then, for your captain is brave and vows reformation. There shall be in England seven halfpenny loaves sold for a penny, the three-hooped pot shall have ten hoops, and I will make it felony to drink small beer. All the realm shall be in common, and in Cheapside shall my palfrey go to grass ... [T]here shall be no money. All shall eat and drink on my score, and I will apparel them all in one livery that they may agree like brothers, and worship me their lord.
>
> [4.2.66–77]

In this alluring jumble of philosophies, communist utopianism, theocracy and decent beer somehow combine. Small wonder, perhaps, that Cade is described by York as a "wild Morisco" (morris dancer), and indeed some theatre historians have suggested that Shakespeare's colleague William Kempe, the most famous clown of his day, might have taken the part. Whether this is accurate or not, Cade exhibits an anarchic, carnivalesque power. And ironically he might well have gathered popular support among Shakespeare's audiences: his fantasies of low prices exploit anxieties about inflation (a pressing problem in the last years of Elizabeth's reign), and one critic has argued that Shakespeare drew on a reservoir of rebellion-friendly popular debate in constructing this section of the play. In a history otherwise so concerned with the suffocating intricacies of dynastic politics, Cade's own perspective on life can seem like a breath of fresh air.

Attractive though those alternatives might seem at first, as the rebels gather in strength events take a turn for the worse. As soon as they learn that the captured Clerk of Chatham can "write and read and cast account", Cade puts his manifesto to work:

> CADE Dost thou use to write thy name? Or hast thou a mark to thyself like an honest plain-dealing man?
> CLERK Sir, I thank God I have been so well brought up that I can write my name.
> ALL CADE'S FOLLOWERS He hath confessed—away with him! He's a villain and a traitor.
> CADE Away with him, I say, hang him with his pen and inkhorn about his neck.
>
> [4.2.101–9]

> *In Margaret we have a foreshadowing of Lady Macbeth finely contrasted with the meek and holy Henry, whose gentle lowliness of spirit is brought out with a prominence and beauty a good deal beyond what history alone would have suggested to the Poet ...*
>
> G.C. Verplanck, *The Illustrated Shakespeare* (1844–47)

In depicting this savage attack on literacy, Shakespeare drew not just on the account of Cade's rebellion in Halle and Holinshed, but turned back several chapters to the Peasants' Revolt of Wat Tyler – which was notably more brutal than its latter-day equivalent. Shakespeare is obviously keen to make his audiences think hard about precisely what this kind of unregulated rule can really mean.

Perhaps this suggests the role played by the Jack Cade scenes within the wider action of the play. While the rebellion comes from a different world from the feud between the Lancastrians and Yorkists, in fact the two are closely linked: the revolt is nourished by popular support, but initiated by a shady aristocratic backer. And, just as the scenes at court present a world in which Henry's inertia is outclassed by York's breathtaking dynamism, the rebellion offers an image of power at its most fluid – and its most dangerous. Both York and Cade are arresting figures when compared to the fatally weak King, but the kind of violence and brutality they represent offers a grim premonition of the future.

Stage history and adaptations

Unlike with the other two *Henry VI* plays, there is no direct evidence of early performance of *Part II* – though this is hardly uncommon. The only information we do possess derives from the 1594 quarto, whose unusually detailed stage directions appear to reflect the play as it might have been staged at the **Rose** playhouse. Some editors have speculated that the play must also have toured when the city theatres were closed because of plague, though there is no documentary proof. In any case, it's a reasonable bet that *Part II*, like its companions, was popular when first performed.

The next we hear is via **Thomas Crowne**, who in 1681 created an expanded version of Acts One to Three of *Part II*, literalistically – if misleadingly – entitled *Henry the Sixth, the First Part, With the Murder of Humphrey Duke of Gloucester*. Crowne, an ardent royalist and anti-Catholic, cut the Cade rebellion and moved it to his sequel, *The Misery of Civil War* (see p.180), while also making the Cardinal of Winchester into a full-blown papist villain. **Ambrose Philips** attempted something similar in his 1723 *Humfrey Duke of Gloucester*, performed at Drury Lane, but also jettisoned most of Shakespeare's text – only around thirty lines of the original survive. The wisdom of this decision was thrown into question by the quality of Philips's own poetry, which was limp-wristed enough to earn its author the nickname "Namby-Pamby". **Theophilus Cibber**, son of the more renowned Colley, turned his own hand to the plays a few months later, this time retaining a good deal more text. His *Henry VI* combined the first few Acts of *Part III* with the last of *Part II*, and dwelt on the pathos-filled death of York's son Rutland (see p.176).

In December 1817, **Edmund Kean** played the titular hero in **J.H. Merivale's** five-act, star-vehicle *Richard Duke of York; or the Contention of York and Lancaster*, the script for which was *Part II* bulked out with a few scenes from *Part I*. In Shakespeare's tercentenary year, 1864, the Surrey Theatre put on a "restoration" of *2 Henry VI* with **James Anderson** as both York and Cade. Though the English histories have never been widely popular in mainland Europe, there are records of some stagings in Germany and Austria during the nineteenth century. Back in England, **G. Osmond Tearle** put *1 Henry VI* on in 1889 with himself as Talbot, **Erskine Lewis** as Henry and **Ellen Cranston** as Margaret.

In 1906 **Frank Benson** presented all three *Henry VI* plays on successive evenings (he had first acted them at the Shakespeare Memorial Theatre five years earlier), trimming back on props and doing away with scene changes entirely. This fluid staging was well received, even if the *Athenaeum* objected that for Benson's death scene as the Cardinal, the set was "strewn unaccountably with sheaves of straw, which distracted from his tragic intensity".

Despite a specially erected thrust stage at the Old Vic, **Robert Atkins** reverted to eighteenth-century type by compressing three plays into one *Henry VI*. But the ground was laid for several influential English productions, the first of which transferred from Birmingham Rep to Atkins's former haunt, the Old Vic, under the aegis of **Barry Jackson**. Jackson's 1951 version (*Part II* was the first to be revived, with the others following in successive years), directed by **Douglas Seale**, featured **Jack May** as King Henry and **Rosalind Boxall** as Margaret. In 1957, the three plays were made into two evenings' entertainment, with **Barbara Jefford** replacing Boxall (Jackson described Margaret as "one of the greatest feminine roles in the whole gallery"). The play was also performed in the United States several times, first in 1935 at the Pasadena Community Playhouse in California.

Peter Hall and **John Barton**'s ground-breaking RSC cycle from 1963, *The Wars of the Roses*, made Shakespeare's three *Henry VI* plays into two, *Henry VI* and *Edward IV*, freely cutting – and even inventing – text before adding them to *Richard III*. The productions struck a chord with critics and audiences alike, not least for their parallels with contemporary realpolitik. They were also terrifically cast, with **David Warner** presenting Henry as a kind of "Holy Fool" and **Peggy Ashcroft** letting rip with a chillingly fierce depiction of Margaret. This version established the *Henry VI* plays in the modern theatre and they returned to the RSC (in less mangled form) under **Terry Hands** in 1977, with **Alan Howard**'s thoughtfully characterized King particularly praised.

Thatcherite politics proved the driving force behind **Michael Bogdanov**'s English Shakespeare Company touring version from 1987, which inserted *Part II* into a series entitled (again) *The Wars of the Roses*. **June Watson**'s handbag-touting Queen Margaret reminded many audiences of a real-life politician of the same name, although **Michael Pennington** came close to stealing the show as a punkish, Union flag-wearing Cade. **Adrian Noble**'s RSC company attempted no such contemporary parallels a year later with their carefully historicized *Plantagenets* adaptation, which (like Barton and Hall before) compressed the three *Henry VI*s into two. Though some felt an opportunity had been missed, **Ralph Fiennes**'s Henry and **David Waller**'s Duke Humphrey gained glowing reviews, and **Anton Lesser**'s dynamic Richard of Gloucester was widely acclaimed.

In 2000, the *Henry VI*s popped up once again at the Royal Shakespeare Company, this time under **Michael Boyd** at the intimate Swan Theatre. Though Boyd used uncut texts, his decision to introduce a spurious fiend-like character who mysteriously appeared as characters died was somewhat less authentic. The same criticism could be levelled at **Edward Hall**'s two-evening version from 2001, entitled *Rose Rage*. Hall used a text adapted in collaboration with **Roger Warren**, and *Part II* did well, with the Cade scenes (played by a lively **Tony Bell**) making a great impression. Cade, this time played by **John Mackay**, once again formed the antic focus of **Michael Boyd**'s return to the play in 2007–08, which gave its medieval riot scenes an extra whiff of danger by dressing up one of Cade's victims as a member of the audience. **Katy Stephens** excelled as a wide-eyed but spine-chilling Margaret, opposite **Geoffrey Streatfield**'s genteel Suffolk. Even more realistic – at least in some senses – was the touring version taken by **Nick Bagnall** and a troupe from the London Globe around English battle sites over the summer of 2013. *2 Henry VI*, adapted and pruned into a piece called *The Houses of York and Lancaster*, was staged in – among other places – the cathedral grounds at St Albans, near the real-life location for Act Five.

Non-English versions featuring *Part II* have included **Giorgio Strehler**'s 1965 adaptation, *Il Gioco dei Potente*; **Peter Palisch**'s stark *Krieg der Rosen* (1967), which put its characters on Jan Kott's "treadmill of power"; and **Denis Llorca**'s 1978 French adaptation, entitled *Kings, ou les adieux à Shakespeare*. More recently, the cycle proved its popularity with French audiences at the 2014 Avignon festival, where an eighteen-hour version of all three plays was directed by **Thomas Jolly**. According to an excitable *Le Monde*, the epic, which ran from 10 a.m. and finished at 4 a.m. next day, was "wonderful, stunning, hypnotic … [the festival's] Himalayas". Back in Britain, *Part II* was staged by the **National Theatre of Albania** in their own language during the World Shakespeare Festival. For the *Guardian*'s reviewer, **Bujar Asqueriu**'s Rambo-like Jack Cade stood out, but the representation of his rioting followers was less successful: "the full gamut of disabled stereotypes".

On screen, the Barton–Hall *Roses* cycle (adapted for TV in 1965 by Peter Hall and Robin Midgely) is, sadly, the stuff of specialist archives, though the BBC's 1960 *An Age of Kings*, in which the play fills two episodes, has recently been re-released. So far, the only purpose-built production of the *Henry VI* plays to be finished is in the BBC Shakespeare series. Directed by **Jane Howell**, it is decidedly patchy. The filming of **Bogdanov**'s ESC productions are more impressive and preserve much of the vigour of the original performances. At the time of writing, **Dominic Cooke**'s two-part *Henriad*, part of the ongoing BBC *Hollow Crown* series – with **Tom Sturridge** as Henry VI and **Sophie Okenedo** as Margaret – was in post-production, due for release in April 2016.

SCREEN

An Age of Kings

T. Scully, J. May, M. Morris; Michael Hayes (dir.) UK, 1960 > BBC/Illuminations **DVD**

Adapter Eric Crozier and producer Michael Hayes afforded *2 Henry VI* a pair of episodes, "The Fall of the Protector" and "The Rabble from Kent", cleanly dividing the action between machinations at court and those among Cade's restive rebels. Even if Shakespeare's interplay of contrasting scenes is lost, the action rattles along, aided – as in other parts of the series – by some stand-out performances. Terry Scully is rather one-note as a milquetoast King, but Mary Morris's sharp-eyed Margaret is terrific fun to watch and Jack May is appealingly adamantine as York. The sets (what you can see of them) appear to be made of egg boxes and the battling nobles sometimes stray into the holler-to-hit-the-back-wall acting style sent up by Jonathan Miller in *Beyond the Fringe* ("O saucy Worcester, dost thou lie so still ..."), yet it's a genuine political thriller, and way ahead of its time.

King Henry VI: House of Lancaster

P. Brennen, B. Stanton, C. Farrell; Michael Bogdanov (dir.) UK, 1990 > Vision **DVD** [o/p]

Preserved for posterity in front of a live audience at Swansea, Michael Bogdanov's successful *Wars of the Roses* series remains a good way into the *Henry VI* plays (even if it's currently only available on bootleg DVD and via online clips). This touring production keeps everything pretty basic but crafts virtue from necessity:

it's unpretentious stuff, convincingly delivered, and at least the verse drowns out some of the tiniest music you're likely to hear this side of a shopping mall. The first segment of *2 Henry VI* is grafted onto its predecessor to make *House of Lancaster*; particularly noteworthy are the double act of Siôn Probert's drawling public-school Somerset and Barry Stanton's blunt York.

King Henry VI: House of York

P. Brennen, A. Jarvis, B. Stanton; Michael Bogdanov (dir.) UK, 1990 > Vision **DVD** [o/p]

House of York has all the attractions and minor flaws of its predecessor: punchy, no-nonsense acting in front of a live audience and some appealing production touches. *2 Henry VI* loses some of its coherence in Bogdanov's adaptation, but the Cade scenes are famously lively – Michael Pennington, Bogdanov's co-director, plays the rebel as a punkish yob wearing a Union flag singlet – while Andrew Jarvis's Richard of Gloucester is already dominating the action.

AUDIO

Henry VI Part II

D. Tennant, K. Hunter, N. Rodway; Clive Brill (dir.) UK, 1998 > Arkangel ◉ ☁

Arkangel's second instalment in the *Henry VI* cycle retains many of the personnel from *Part I*, and the recording is every bit as well made. In the opening scenes there's a nagging sense that Kelly Hunter isn't putting her all into Margaret, but as the production develops she adds more fire to the role and produces a fearsome interpretation, but also a persuasively human one – not a sadistic battleaxe, but a woman driven to extreme ends. The scrum of lords at court (and their machinations to get the head of Norman Rodway's forbearing Duke Humphrey) is properly oppressive, with Steve Hodson's Winchester adding grizzled menace. And as the play nears its end Clive Merrison's forthright York and David Troughton's wry Richard of Gloucester, both men of business, already sound like leaders of England.

EDITIONS

Arden Shakespeare (third series)

Ronald Knowles (ed.); 1999 > Bloomsbury

Though it predates Edward Burns's Arden *1 Henry VI* (see p.162) by a year, Ronald Knowles's surprisingly fat version of *2 Henry VI* is even more complete –

among its six appendices are a page-by-page facsimile of the first quarto and a chart suggesting doubling for all parts. His coverage of the play's chequered critical history is similarly detailed, distinguished by its even-handedness and its focus on the carnivalesque elements of the play.

SOME CRITICISM

Shakespeare and the Popular Voice

Annabel Patterson; 1989 > Blackwell

Patterson has no time for those who would deify the "Bard", or even (as the nineteenth century was fond of doing) promote him socially: for her he is a glover's son, actor and theatrical shareholder, man of business – and, most importantly, someone whose work often finds itself speaking in the "popular voice". Her larger project, of locating Shakespeare's "social assumptions" and his attitude to "the ordinary working people inside and outside his plays" might strike some as foolhardy, but for the fresh light this sheds on the political postures of his drama it seems worth it. *2 Henry VI* is an obvious text on which to focus – even though the "ordinary" people in it are conspicuously not working – and Patterson clarifies the contemporary significance of Cade's revolt by drawing attention to some Elizabethan experiences of rebellion.

Shakespeare's History Plays

Ton Hoenselaars (ed.); 2004 > Cambridge UP

Not by any stretch of the imagination to be confused with Tillyard's study of the same name (see p.162), this essay collection sees Dutch scholar Ton Hoenselaars assemble a cohort of international contributors to demonstrate the remarkable life of Shakespeare's history plays in mainland Europe and far beyond. The story begins close to home, with essays on Irishness by Andrew Murphy and Welshness by Lisa Hopkins, and extends quickly to an eye-opening French account of *Henry V* by Jean-Michel Déprats, before ranging across performance and interpretative history in countries including Japan, Spain, Italy and Bulgaria. The first tetralogy plays a surprisingly large role, with James N. Lohelin describing Bertolt Brecht's pivotal influence on its twentieth-century rehabilitation and Manfred Draudt offering fascinating detail on history cycles at Vienna's Burgtheater, where the plays entered the repertoire far earlier than they did in Britain. A valuable corrective to the assumption that Shakespeare's English histories have nothing to say to anyone who isn't English.

Henry VI Part III

I f ever a play provided evidence of what the Polish critic Jan Kott called the "constant procession of kings" in Shakespeare's histories, it is *Henry VI Part III*. The action, which follows Queen Margaret's fleeting triumph at Wakefield to the Lancastrians' last stand at Tewkesbury and Henry's subsequent murder, sees no fewer than three characters claiming the throne – with one more, Richard of Gloucester, poised to make his bid as the curtain falls. But *Part III* is also Shakespeare's clearest exposition yet of the horrors of civil war. For the conservative critic M.M. Reese, it presented "a dreadful example of what happened when God's kindly watchfulness was turned to wrath by the crimes, ambition and misgovernment of men"; for more recent commentators it radically undermines all of those assumptions. The play was originally known as *The True Tragedy of Richard, Duke of York*, and York's gruesome end forms one of its most traumatic images – after being captured by Margaret's forces, the Duke is mockingly crowned with a paper coronet and taunted with the murder of his own son, before being stabbed to death by Margaret herself. As that scene hints, *3 Henry VI*, which draws extensively on the revenge dramas then popular on the Elizabethan stage, is one of Shakespeare's most violent plays, and perhaps the darkest history of all.

DATE > On the theory that the play was written after *Part II*, probably 1591; it was definitely complete by 1592.

SOURCES > As with the two other *Henry VI* plays, Shakespeare used Edward Halle's *Union* (1548) and Raphael Holinshed's 1587 *Chronicles* to provide the narrative basis of *3 Henry VI*. Thomas More's *History of King Richard III*

(c. 1513) influences some scenes, as does work by Kyd and Marlowe.

TEXTS > An octavo edition (O), possibly reconstructed from memory, was published in 1595 and was followed by various printings (Q2, 1600; Q3, 1619) based on the same text. The Folio version (1623) is thought to derive from Shakespeare's manuscript.

Interpreting the play

3 Henry VI has sometimes struggled to win friends. After his cagey approval of the other two parts, the British critic E.M.W. Tillyard thought *Part III* was uneven at best, postulating that Shakespeare was "either tired or bored" with his material and remarking that "there are indeed splendid things in it, but they are rather islands sticking out of a sea of mediocrity than hills arising from the valleys or undulations of an organic landscape". Shakespeare's younger contemporary, Ben Jonson, expressed contempt for the *Henry VIs* more generally when he sneered in the Prologue to *Every Man In His Humour* (1601) about plays that "with three rusty swords, / And help of

MAJOR CHARACTERS & SYNOPSIS

LANCASTRIANS

King Henry VI of England and France
Queen Margaret, Henry's wife
Prince Edward, Henry and Margaret's son
Dukes of Somerset, **Exeter** and **Northumberland**
Earl of Westmorland
Lords Clifford and **Stafford**
Somerville
Henry, Earl of Richmond (later **Henry VII**)

YORKISTS

Richard Plantagenet, Duke of York
York's sons: **Edward, Earl of March** (later
 Edward IV), **George** (later **Duke of Clarence**)
 and **Richard** (later **Duke of Gloucester**),
 Earl of Rutland
York's uncles: **Sir John** and **Sir Hugh Mortimer**
Lady Gray, a widow (later Edward's wife)
Earl Rivers, Lady Gray's brother
Rutland's Tutor
Other Yorkists: **Earl of Pembroke**, **Duke of
 Norfolk**, **Sir John Montgomery** and
 Sir William Stanley

THE NEVILLES

Earl of Warwick, first a Yorkist, then a Lancastrian
Marquis of Montague, Warwick's brother, a
 Yorkist
Earl of Oxford, Warwick and Montague's brother-
 in-law, a Lancastrian
Lord Hastings, Warwick and Montague's brother-
 in-law, a Yorkist

THE FRENCH

King Louis of France
Lady Bona, Louis' sister-in-law

[ACTION CONTINUED FROM HENRY VI PART II]

ACT 1 After their success at the Battle of St
Albans, the Yorkists force King Henry to compromise: he will remain in power, but after his
death Richard, Duke of York, will inherit the
throne. Queen Margaret is outraged that her son,
Prince Edward, has been disinherited and prepares to fight. In the meantime, York has decided
to break his oath and seize the crown. His forces
meet Margaret's at Wakefield, where his young
son, Rutland, is killed and he himself is captured
and murdered by Clifford and the Queen.

ACT 2 Despite his father's death, Edward
Plantagenet is proclaimed king. In the royal camp
Henry knights his own son, but declines to fight.
When Edward appears and repeats his claim to
the throne, Margaret and her supporters reject it
and the armies fight at Towton. Henry ponders on
the country's suffering but is interrupted by news
that Margaret's army has lost. Clifford is killed,
and Edward heads to London to be crowned.

ACT 3 Edward (now King Edward IV) desires the
widow Lady Gray and blackmails her into
marriage. Once alone, Richard Plantagenet (now
Duke of Gloucester) reveals that he wants the
crown for himself. Henry, meanwhile, has been
captured and sent to the Tower. Margaret appeals
for help from King Louis of France, only to find
that Warwick is trying to arrange a marriage
between King Edward and Louis's sister, Lady
Bona. When he discovers that Edward has already
married Lady Gray, Warwick angrily switches his
allegiance to Margaret and King Henry.

ACT 4 In England unrest continues as Richard
and George Plantagenet criticize their brother's
choice of wife. George (now Duke of Clarence)
deserts for Warwick's camp; the two men capture
Edward and remove his crown, only for Richard
to free him once more. Henry is in turn released
from the Tower by Warwick and George, whom
he appoints protectors, but shortly after is recap-
tured by the Yorkists. Edward is back in control.

ACT 5 Warwick's forces meet the Yorkists at
Coventry, but the Lancastrians are dealt a series
of heavy blows: George rejoins his brother
Edward, Warwick's brother Montague is killed,
and Warwick himself dies from his wounds. The
victorious Edward sets off to face Margaret, who
is struggling to rally her troops at Tewkesbury.
Margaret and her son Prince Edward are soon
in Yorkist hands, and despite his mother's pleas
the young Prince is murdered. In the commotion,
Richard slips away to the Tower and enters Henry's
cell. The deposed King predicts that the evil
omens at Richard's birth foretell more bloodshed;
Richard responds by stabbing him and declaring
that nothing will keep him from the throne.

> *In Henry VI the sacrificial idea, which makes catastrophe a consequence of sin, is sharply challenged by the "machiavellian" idea that makes it a consequence of weakness.*
>
> Philip Brockbank, "The frame of disorder – *Henry VI*" (1961)

some few foot-and-half-foot words, / Fight over York and Lancaster's long jars: / And in the tiring-house bring wounds to scars". The playwright and poet Robert Greene, older than both Shakespeare and Jonson, addressed part of his 1592 pamphlet, *Greene's Groatsworth of Wit, bought with a million of Repentance*, supposedly composed on his deathbed, to his colleagues in the theatre. He warned them to watch out for one man in particular:

> There is an upstart crow, beautified with our feathers, that with his *tiger's heart wrapped in a player's hide* supposes he is as well able to bombast out a blank verse as the best of you; and, being an absolute *Johannes Factotum* [Jack-of-all-trades], is in his own conceit the only Shake-scene in a country.

This bitter denunciation contrasts Greene's own poverty and struggle for fickle success with that of a mystery dramatist whose identity is obscured, none too subtly, behind an allusion to "the only Shake-scene". It also contains a good deal of snobbery: what seems to incense Greene most is the fact that he and his colleagues – university "scholars" to a man – are being upstaged by a mere "upstart crow" who has stolen their "feathers". That this can only refer to Shakespeare is confirmed by Greene's twisting of a line from *3 Henry VI*, "O tiger's heart wrapped in a woman's hide!" (1.4.138), into a professional insult. What is less frequently commented upon is that Greene steals the line from Shakespeare's Duke of York, who is himself railing against Queen Margaret just before his execution – so Greene, similarly near death, actually offers a kind of backhanded compliment to the power of Shakespeare's verse. He had clearly been listening attentively: none of Shakespeare's plays was yet in print.

Heavy times

Greene's comments are the first contemporaneous mention of a man called Shakespeare writing plays, and at the very least they confirm that by the early 1590s he was making waves as a dramatist. In some ways, the fact that Greene picked out a fragment from a grand set-piece speech is fitting: this play demonstrates Shakespeare exploring the possibilities of rhetoric more widely than ever before. Quoted more fully, York's speech shows the character (perhaps the playwright himself) straining at the limits of invention to express hatred for the Queen who has murdered Rutland, his youngest son:

> O tiger's heart wrapped in a woman's hide!
> How couldst thou drain the life-blood of the child
> To bid the father wipe his eyes withal,

And yet be seen to bear a woman's face?
Women are soft, mild, pitiful, and flexible—
Thou stern, obdurate, flinty, rough, remorseless.
Bidd'st thou me rage? Why, now thou hast thy wish.
Would'st have me weep? Why, now thou hast thy will.
For raging wind blows up incessant showers,
And when the rage allays the rain begins.

[1.4.138–47]

York rushes through a kind of mental thesaurus, searching for insults to fling towards Margaret. The speech is also remarkable in its dramatic self-consciousness: York draws attention to his own actions, his raging, his weeping, in terms that make him sound like an actor drawing attention to the skill of his own spectacle.

If the dying York is attempting to make sense of inhuman actions, some critics have suggested that the play represents the final stage in Shakespeare's representation of moral anarchy. The action of *Henry VI Part III* is spread over four tremendous battles – at Wakefield, Towton, Barnet and Tewkesbury. In real life some 50,000 men fought at Towton, and over half were killed, more than in any conflict on British soil before or since. Unable to call upon anything like that number of extras, Shakespeare crystallizes the slaughter into one poignant scene. A man enters lugging a body which he hopes to rob, but, removing the helmet, he makes a grim realization. "Who's this?" he cries,

O God! It is my father's face
Whom in this conflict I, unawares, have killed.
O, heavy times, begetting such events!

[2.5.61–3]

As if this irony were not enough, from the other side of the stage another man enters, this time a father carrying the body of his son. Shakespeare seems to have taken the cue for this entire scene from a chance remark by one of his chronicle sources, Edward Halle, who states that "this conflict was in manner unnatural, for in it the son fought against the father, the brother against the brother, the nephew against the uncle, and the tenant against his lord, which slaughter did sore and much weaken the puissance [power] of this realm".

Shakespeare deepens the irony still further by centring the scene on the presence of Henry VI himself, the very man whose inability to hold things together is responsible for the chaos that surrounds him. The King enters longing for an existence away from regal cares ("O God! Methinks it were a happy life / To be no better than a homely swain" (2.5.21–2)), but the folly of this fantasy is exposed when he witnesses the dead sons and fathers. He cries out:

Woe above woe! Grief more than common grief!
O that my death would stay these ruthful deeds!
O, pity, pity, gentle heaven, pity!

The red rose and the white are on his face,
The fatal colours of our striving houses …

[2.5.94–7]

The savage beauty of this description shows Shakespeare using the formal resources of the Elizabethan stage – ritualized scenes, powerful laments – to intensify his audience's sense of the characters' suffering. Where the other *Henry VI* plays allow Shakespeare to show off his skill in reportage, here he uses highly patterned devices to depict the breakdown of moral order.

Revenge sufficient

It's been said, too, that the play brings into serious question exactly what we think of as "moral order". In a further development of the father-son theme that occupies Shakespeare first in *1 Henry VI* and then in that scene at Towton, one of *Part III*'s dominant figures is the revenger Young Clifford. Clifford's father is killed by York in *Part II* and the son swears to avenge his death. Moments before killing the young Rutland, he boasts that he will stop at nothing:

Had I thy brethren here, their lives and thine
Were not revenge sufficient for me.
No—if I digged up thy forefathers' graves,
And hung their rotten coffins up in chains,
It could not slake mine ire nor ease my heart.
The sight of any of the house of York
Is as a fury to torment my soul.
And till I root out their accursèd line,
And leave not one alive, I live in hell.

[1.3.26–34]

Clifford's love for his father and wish to see justice done is here twisted into unjust vengeance; it is gruesomely apt that he declares his intention to root up York's entire family in order to avenge the murder of one of his own.

The cycle of gory retaliation is ingrained in the play's fabric: York is killed for his crimes; Clifford (one of the architects of York's death) is tormented by Warwick, Edward and Richard as he lies dying; even the mighty Warwick gets his comeuppance. It scarcely seems surprising that among Shakespeare's plays *3 Henry VI* is second only to *Titus Andronicus* in the number of times it uses words with the root "venge": both plays dwell on unstoppable cycles of violence. Where in *Part II* the seductive dangers of power are fully on display, *Part III* depicts the moral repercussions – that war is not simply a matter of personal loss or individual action, but corrodes the foundations of society itself.

And where in *Part II* Gloucester's enemies were eager to hide their Machiavellian actions behind the "colour" of legality, few of *Part III*'s characters have such scruples. Nearly all the central players go back on their word at some point in the action, setting

"O tiger's heart wrapped in a woman's hide ..." Peggy Ashcroft's Margaret taunts Donald Sinden as the Duke of York at the climax of the RSC's *Wars of the Roses* sequence in 1963 – a landmark production that restored the early history plays to a central place in the canon.

up another kind of cycle – this time of untrustworthiness. Edward breaks his compact with Warwick over the marriage to Lady Bona, Warwick responds by changing sides to fight for the Lancastrians, George follows by switching to Henry's cause (and then back again in the latter stages of the play). But the play's most important oath occurs at the climax of the very first scene, when Henry brokers a deal with York enabling him to hold onto the throne:

> KING HENRY   I here entail
>   The crown to thee and to thine heirs for ever,
>   Conditionally, that here thou take thine oath
>   To cease this civil war, and whilst I live
>   To honour me as thy king and thy sovereign,
>   And nor by treason nor hostility
>   To seek to put me down and reign thyself.
> YORK
>   This oath I willingly take and will perform.

[1.1.195–202]

Though York later claims to mean what he says – in sharp contrast to his sons, who do their best to persuade him that the oath is "vain and frivolous" – it isn't long before he resolves to turn once more against Henry. But, as it turns out, he needn't have bothered: news arrives that Margaret has broken Henry's side of the oath for him. While Samuel Johnson was keen to draw "moral instruction" from this tale – pointing to the irony that, if only York had waited, he would have kept his hands clean – it might be said that the lesson is, if anything, conspicuously amoral: this turn of events demonstrates that oaths have no value whatsoever. It is a chilling new world order. York's son, Richard of Gloucester, who flatly states that "But for a kingdom any oath may be broken. / I would break a thousand oaths to reign one year" (1.2.16–17), is its persuasive spokesman.

Indeed, if anyone can prosper in the ethical vacuum around him, it is Richard. It is perhaps not too extreme to say that the horrors of the play give birth to a character who is as morally twisted as (he boasts) he is physically distorted. Pondering on his "indigested and deformèd shape", Gloucester rejoices in his demonic capabilities:

> Then, since the heavens have shaped my body so,
> Let hell make crooked my mind to answer it.
> I had no father, I am like no father;
> I have no brother, I am like no brother;
> And this word, 'love', which greybeards call divine,
> Be resident in men like one another
> And not in me—I am myself alone.

[5.6.78–84]

Richard is isolating himself from the conflicts around him – the wars fought by two great families – by claiming to be author of himself. In an ominous new twist, he is prepared to murder not merely his enemies but his own kin to seize it. Power for its own sake is the attraction.

If there is a continuity to the *Henry VI* plays, perhaps it's that they demonstrate an unremitting breakdown of values: *Part I* begins as a patriotic adventure but ends with its nobles ranged against one another; *Part II* depicts the fragmentation of society, with different sections of English society in conflict; *Part III* shows a country in break-down as fathers murder their own sons and sons their fathers. But Richard is prepared to turn against not merely his own country, nor even his political enemies, but his own family – and it is his bloody path to power which occupies *Richard III*, the next and final play in the historical sequence.

Stage history and adaptations

Like its brethren, the stage history of *3 Henry VI* is a tale of initial success followed by a struggle (dogged by doubts about authorship) to be performed in anything approaching its early form. Though there is no other sixteenth-century record of it on the stage, **Robert Greene**'s coded reference to the play in 1592 (see p.176) doesn't merely catalogue the author's resentment at a younger rival, but confirms that *Part III* was popular when initially acted (apparently by the **Earl of Pembroke**'s men, if the title-page of the first quarto is accurate).

Then all goes quiet until 1681, when **Thomas Crowne** put on the first of many adaptations. *The Misery of Civil War*, based on *3 Henry VI*, was a Restoration reworking whose title baldly states its main concerns. Evidently not anxious about labouring the point, Crowne added Cade's rebellion from *Part II* to underscore the horrors of civil conflict, and employed painted scenery depicting grisly scenes of soldiers on the rampage. In a more domestic touch, Crowne also provided King Edward with a mistress (killed in battle, in delightfully cod-Shakespearian fashion, while disguised as a boy). The play's political resonances were clearly too strong for others – in 1700, **Colley Cibber** was refused permission to stage the murder of Henry VI in his version of *Richard III*, lest it stir Jacobite sympathies for the exiled King James II. Cibber's son **Theophilus** was more fortunate 23 years later, his version grafting Acts One to Three of *Part III* onto the final act of *Part II* in what was regarded as a successful adaptation.

In the early nineteenth century, **J.H.** Merivale's *Richard Duke of York; or the Contention of York and Lancaster* (1817) compressed all three parts into an evening's entertainment and utilized the electrifying talent of **Edmund Kean**, who had made his name as Richard III, in the central role. Another one-evening adaptation was apparently undertaken by **Charles Kemble** later in the century, but seems not to have made it onto the boards. Following **James Anderson**'s lead – Anderson celebrated 1864, the year of Shakespeare's tercentenary, by staging an unexpanded *2 Henry VI* – in 1906 **Frank Benson** bravely put on all three plays. In this, the first time that *3 Henry VI* had been performed in its entirety since the 1590s, Benson attempted to restore some sense of the Elizabethan theatre – though his efforts were not to everyone's liking, one critic cavilling that "there was an unnecessary amount of fighting, never very effective on the stage". Shouldering the role of Richard of Gloucester himself, following one performance Benson even spoke to the audience as soon as the applause had died down, expounding his own (patriotic) views about the cycle. In the end, though, *Part III* brought in the smallest houses of the week.

After **Robert Atkins**'s 1923 production of *Henry VI* (which, like Merivale's a century before, squeezed three plays into one), several twentieth-century performances have restored the reputation of Shakespeare's earliest histories. The first was undertaken in 1951 by **Barry Jackson**, who had seen Benson fifty years before. He made the most of the tiny space offered by the Birmingham Repertory Theatre and built a strong, cohesive company in which doubling was used to great effect.

Peter Hall and **John Barton** did things differently in their RSC cycle, *The Wars of the Roses* (1963), which consisted of three plays (*Henry VI*, *Edward IV* and *Richard III*), the first two derived from Shakespeare's work plus other material. As with Peter Brook's infamous *King Lear* of the previous year, the radical politics and bleak world-view of Jan Kott's *Shakespeare Our Contemporary* held sway, and the set was dominated by an intimidatingly massive conference table. **David Warner** played Henry as a boyish martyr, **Peggy Ashcroft** made an impressive Margaret (terrifyingly intense in her murder of York) and a young **Ian Holm** appeared as Gloucester. More politically cautious was the widely praised production mounted in 1977 by **Terry Hands** at the Swan in Stratford, in which the director used near-uncut texts and focused on characterization rather than ostentatious thematic gestures. A seasoned **Alan Howard** played the King to **Helen Mirren**'s Margaret – despite her conspicuous success in the role, Mirren still claimed to suffer physical nausea every time York's death scene was performed.

Political relevance was back on the agenda for **Michael Bogdanov**'s ESC versions of 1987, once more cut and spliced as part of a two-tetralogy series entitled, yet again, *The Wars of the Roses*. In this slimline touring production, Thatcherite power politics wrestled with yob culture in an ultimately cynical reading. At the RSC, meanwhile, **Adrian Noble** presented *The Plantagenets* (1988), a two-play adaptation whose imaginative designs (by **Bob Crowley**) and intellectual breadth were enthusiastically received; **Ralph Fiennes** played the King to **Anton Lesser**'s (sometimes literally) satanic Richard Gloucester. In 2000 the RSC once more put on a cycle of Shakespeare's histories entitled *This England*, this time with uncut texts; the *Henry VIs* were directed by **Michael Boyd** at the small-scale Swan theatre. The following year, **Edward Hall** presented a two-part version of the *Henry VIs* drastically different from that of his father, which toured the UK in 2001–02 under the kitschy title of *Rose Rage*. Hall's youthful, all-male company Propeller offered a vigorous interpretation of the plays set in a slaughterhouse, in which cartoonish violence, butcher's off-cuts and Victorian hymns formed an unlikely melange. Boyd used a full version of *Part III* as part of his epic RSC histories project of 2007–08, subtitling it "the Chaos" and making it an orgy of premeditated slaughter. Even **Katy Stephens**'s Margaret was appalled by events, which also engulfed **Chuk Iwuji**'s fragile monarch, gifting the fidgety, sniggering Richard of **Jonathan Slinger** a straightforward path to the throne.

Continuing a long and successful tradition of touring the *Henry VIs* to the England they represent, the Globe's cut-down productions, taken to battlefield sites including Towton by director **Nick Bagnall** in summer 2013, were acclaimed as vivid and energetic. The *Guardian*'s eye was caught by the scene in which **Graham Butler**'s innocent Henry sat on an upturned pail (rather than a molehill) to deliver his famous soliloquy, while the *Telegraph*'s critic confessed that it was a "pole-axing thing" to see Shakespeare's plays performed on tranquil farmland that had once been a blood-soaked killing field.

At the Globe itself the year before, a Balkan Henriad, part of the World Shakespeare Festival, was brought to a close by the **National Theatre of Bitola** from Macedonia, directed by the American **John Blondell**. This energetic, forceful production put the *Guardian* in mind of Propeller's earlier version, but **Petar Gorko**'s unusual decision to play King Henry as an overweening tyrant struck many as brilliantly original. Other notable non-English versions have included **Giorgio Strehler**'s 1965 adaptation, *Il Gioco dei Potente*, influenced by both Barton–Hall and Strindberg; **Peter Palisch**'s stark *Krieg der Rosen* (1967); and **Denis Llorca**'s 1978 French adaptation, entitled *Kings, ou les adieux à Shakespeare*, which attempted to approach the plays from the "enemy" perspective. In 2014, a modernized, through-written adaptation by the French director **Thomas Jolly** debuted in Avignon, eighteen hours long and with a cast of twenty-one – "without doubt the biggest spectacle of the festival", according to *Le Monde*.

With the exception of the BBC's heavily edited 1960 *An Age of Kings* series, the only production currently on release is one directed by **Jane Howell** for BBC and Time-Life in 1983. Howell's interpretation, which imagined the plays as a public-school brawl, gained mixed reviews, delighting some but appalling others. More warmly received were the tapings of Bogdanov's ESC productions, recorded live. The

BBC's latest version – with the *Henry VI* cut down to two parts – is currently in post-production, part of the second *Hollow Crown* series directed by **Dominic Cooke**. The second instalment, which will centre on *Part III*, is keenly anticipated because it offers the prospect of TV and movie star **Benedict Cumberbatch** as Gloucester, alongside **Geoffrey Streatfeild** as Edward IV and **Tom Sturridge**'s King Henry. Release is scheduled for 2016.

SCREEN

An Age of Kings

T. Scully, P. Daneman, M. Morris; Michael Hayes (dir.) UK, 1960 › BBC/Illuminations 🆅🅳🆅

Crisp and concise, the BBC's *Age of Kings* series rounds off the first Henriad in brisk style, offering *Part III* in two hour-long sections entitled "The Morning's War" and "The Sun in Splendour". As in previous instalments, the acting is muscular and some of the plays' subtler shadings are lost (murky 1960s black and white doesn't help), but the pace more than makes up for it; no sooner is Terry Scully's weary-looking Henry unkinged than he's kinged again, and it's a mere matter of minutes between Jack May's virile York planting himself on the throne and kneeling for execution in front of Mary Morris's harridan-like Margaret. A young Julian Glover is nicely self-satisfied as Edward IV, but it's his brother Gloucester – a crackling performance by Paul Daneman, more tormented than you expect – who catches the eye. His murder of King Henry at the play's end has the grim aspect of a psychopath finally snaring his victim.

King Henry VI: House of York

P. Brennen, A. Jarvis, B. Stanton; Michael Bogdanov (dir.) UK, 1990 › Vision 🆅🅳🆅 [o/p]

Adapting the *Henry VI*s into a two-part play emphasizes Richard Gloucester's hold on the plot, and with Andrew Jarvis in the role, Bogdanov has a star worthy of the attention: his gleeful, toothy and bald-pated Richard is frankly irresistible (and someone the live audience obviously appreciates). Also impressive is June Watson's Queen Margaret, who bears an uncanny resemblance to Margaret Thatcher. Some of the ESC's theatrical techniques – khaki battle scenes contrasted with black-tie cocktail parties – now seem like clichés and don't always capture *3 Henry VI*'s subtler resonances, but they get near its combination of warring brutality and power politics. And Bogdanov's is very much a sequence: Jarvis utters the famous first lines of *Richard III* as the lights come down. Frustratingly, the episodes only appear to be available as online clips or on bootleg DVDs.

AUDIO

Henry VI Part III

D. Tennant, K. Hunter, J. Bowe; Clive Brill (dir.) UK, 1998 › Arkangel ◉ 🔊

3 Henry VI sees Shakespeare exploring the language of brutality more fully than ever before, and on audio there's little to insulate against it: the scene in which Jamie Glover's fierce Clifford murders the boy Rutland (a very convincing Jay Barrimore) is in some ways more horrible to listen to than see, but it is just one of a series of vicious moments in this disturbingly violent play. Much of that violence is captured in Clive Brill's excellent Arkangel trilogy, and like its predecessors *3 Henry VI* has an excellent cast with some genuinely terrific performances (Kelly Hunter's Margaret comes into her own here, while David Troughton's strongly characterized Richard of Gloucester is as restlessly energetic as ever).

EDITIONS

Arden Shakespeare (third series)

John D. Cox & Eric Rasmussen (eds); 2001 › Bloomsbury

John D. Cox has a reputation as a card-carrying new historicist – his *Shakespeare and the Dramaturgy of Power* (1989) is a classic of the movement – but this collaborative edition is gratifyingly unbiased in its appraisal of the play's critical history. Although Michael Hattaway's Cambridge version offers strong competition, Arden is more complete, full of vivid historical information – a photo of the mangled skull of a soldier from Towton, one of 24,000 dead, is a salient reminder that the Wars of the Roses weren't mere play-acting. If your curiosity is pricked by the play's contorted textual history, note that the 1595 octavo *True Tragedy* is reproduced in facsimile as an appendix.

SOME CRITICISM

Shakespeare's English Histories and their Afterlives
Peter Holland (ed.); 2010 > Cambridge UP

As the history plays have become more widely studied, so they have appeared more often in theatres – and vice versa. A mutually supportive relationship lies behind this excellent and pleasingly heterogeneous collection, Issue 63 of the well-respected *Shakespeare Survey* journal, which was compiled in the aftermath of a major RSC staging of the two tetralogies in 2007–08. There is plenty on performance history here, and much more besides: thoughtful pieces by Christy Desmet on "Shakespeare the Historian", Jean-Christophe Mayer on the relationship between differing chronicle accounts, and a particularly good essay by Anna Kamaralli on the sometimes questionable ways in which female characters in the histories have been portrayed on stage, from Joan of Arc to Queen Margaret.

Shakespeare and the Staging of English History
Janette Dillon; 2012 > Oxford UP

This volume, part of the Oxford Shakespeare Topics series, is slim but provides a hugely useful introduction to what the "history play" might have meant to Shakespeare, and explores how he both worked within and infinitely expanded the form. Dillon is insightful on the ceremonial structures that underpin the early histories in particular, and acutely aware of how they worked in the cramped confines of the Elizabethan theatre – her division of their action into "horizontal" and "vertical" axes not only helps you picture how their first audiences might have read their stage pictures, but underlines their interest in symbolic symmetry. Coverage of *3 Henry VI* is offered alongside the rest of the two tetralogies, and also touches suggestively on *King John* and *Henry VIII*.

Henry VIII

Written with John Fletcher, *Henry VIII* (or *All Is True*) is one of Shakespeare's most ostentatiously spectacular works – Coleridge called it a "show play". But it was also responsible for burning down his playhouse. During a performance on June 29, 1613, material from a cannon fired in Act One ignited the Globe's roof; within hours the theatre was in ashes. This event foreshadowed an even larger loss: Shakespeare's retirement to Stratford following *The Two Noble Kinsmen*, his final collaboration with Fletcher. *Henry VIII* itself, however, gives little hint of imminent departure, slotting tightly into the mould of the early history plays. Picking up events a generation after the close of *Richard III*, it redeploys the kind of court chicanery and high-level politics familiar from the *Henry VI* cycle, albeit with a more jaundiced eye than ever before. But, like *Antony and Cleopatra*, it also deals with the personal suffering that results from political events – touchingly displayed in the humiliating treatment of Katherine of Aragon, stripped of her position as King Henry's first wife. The fact that her successor, Anne Boleyn (the mother of Queen Elizabeth I), was executed three years later makes *Henry VIII*'s reflections on the ever-turning wheel of fortune seem utterly prescient.

DATE > According to evidence describing the Globe fire on June 29, 1613 (see above), *Henry VIII* – or *All Is True*, as it was probably first known – was a new play when the incident occurred, perhaps finished by Shakespeare and Fletcher earlier that year.

SOURCES > As with the other history plays, the *Chronicles* by Raphael Holinshed and others (1587) and Edward Halle's *Union of the Two Noble and Illustrious Houses of Lancaster and York* (1548) provide *Henry VIII*'s main sources. Other details derive from John Foxe's anti-Catholic *Book of Martyrs* (1563) and Samuel Rowley's play *When You See Me, You Know Me* (1603), as well as George Cavendish's 1592 *Life* of Wolsey.

TEXTS > Only one text, that in the 1623 First Folio, survives. It was probably typeset from a scribe's copy of the play.

Interpreting the play

One reason the Globe burnt down so quickly – so it seems – was that its audience was too engrossed to notice. While their eyes were "more attentive to the show," wrote the diplomat Sir Henry Wotton to his nephew, the flames "kindled inwardly, and ran round like a train, consuming within less than an hour the whole house to the very grounds". The authors may thus have had cause to rue the success of *Henry VIII*, only on its third or fourth performance at the time: if some of the spectators had allowed their attention to wander, the theatre might have been saved. The very fact that a cannon was being fired to welcome King Henry, not as the more usual

MAJOR CHARACTERS & SYNOPSIS

Prologue and **Epilogue**
King Henry VIII of England
Katherine of Aragon, Henry's wife, later his divorcée
Anne Boleyn, Katherine's maid of honour and Henry's second wife
Cardinal Wolsey
Thomas Cranmer, later Archbishop of Canterbury and his colleague the **Bishop of Lincoln**
Stephen Gardiner, Henry's new secretary, later Bishop of Winchester
Cardinal Campeius, ambassador of the Pope
Lord Caputius, ambassador of Emperor Charles V
Thomas Cromwell, Henry's adviser
Duke of Buckingham
Lord Abergavenny and the **Earl of Surrey,** Buckingham's sons-in-law
Nobles, gentlemen and officials at the English court: **Dukes of Norfolk** and **Suffolk, Lord Sands, Sir Thomas Lovell, Sir Anthony Denny, Sir Henry Guildford, Sir Nicholas Vaux,** the **Lord Chamberlain** and the **Lord Chancellor**
Three Gentlemen at the court
Buckingham's **Surveyor**
Griffith, Katherine's usher
Patience, Katherine's waiting woman
Old Lady, Anne Boleyn's companion
Doctor Butts, Henry's physician

ACT 1 The English court is abuzz with news from the Field of Cloth of Gold, a spectacular peace conference between England and France. But the influence wielded by Cardinal Wolsey (who is Lord Chancellor and the mastermind of the event) is the source of much jealousy among certain lords. Sneering at his ambition and low birth, Buckingham, Abergavenny and Norfolk grumble that the peace deal with the French is already falling apart. But Wolsey is one step ahead of his enemies, and Buckingham is arrested. The Cardinal seems unstoppable: though news of his damaging taxes reaches the King, no sooner are they repealed than Wolsey craftily puts out word that it is he who has called for the changes. Though suspicions remain high, the

King has other matters on his mind: namely the beautiful Anne Boleyn, his wife's maid of honour, whom he dances with and kisses at the Cardinal's palace.

ACT 2 As Buckingham heads to his execution, rumours begin to circulate that Henry intends to divorce his wife Katherine at Wolsey's behest, and in fact that Cardinal Campeius has travelled from Rome especially to arrange matters. Meanwhile, Anne Boleyn confides her qualms about queenship to the Old Lady. At the divorce court being held in Blackfriars Katherine puts up strong resistance, however, and refuses to be intimidated by Cardinal Wolsey and his henchmen.

ACT 3 The case stalls until Katherine decides to relent following a visit from Wolsey and Campeius. But a further hold-up occurs when deceitful letters sent by Wolsey to the Pope are revealed to the King. With his career in ruins, Wolsey is replaced as Chancellor by Sir Thomas More.

ACT 4 The coronation of Anne has taken place with great ceremony, but her triumph cruelly coincides with Katherine's decline. Lying sick at Kimbolton, Katherine has a vision of angels and celestial spirits before receiving a visit from Lord Caputius. She dies after commending her daughter to the King's care.

ACT 5 The new Queen is soon pregnant, but the news only antagonizes the King's secretary Gardiner, who vows to attack her and Cranmer, Henry's virtuous Archbishop of Canterbury (and latest confidant). But the King is not to be outplayed: when Gardiner and his cronies turn against Cranmer in council, Henry's support is steadfast. Amid scenes of wild public rejoicing, Anne's newborn daughter Elizabeth – the future queen – is christened. Cranmer predicts that her reign, and that of her successor, will be blessed.

shorthand for a battle scene, speaks volumes. *Henry VIII* was intended to astound its first audiences.

Even in a four-hundred-year-old playscript, *Henry VIII* still packs a strong visual punch. Many of the play's pivotal moments are attended by grand theatrical set pieces, all described with unusually detailed stage directions. The first big moment, Wolsey's banquet in Act One – the first scene that hints that the King, dancing with Anne Boleyn, will stray from his marriage – requires several tables on stage, copious guests and plenty of music (considerable resources for a playhouse like the Globe). In Act Two, the aftermath of the Duke of Buckingham's trial is designed to seize our attention with his ignominious entrance, flanked as he is by "halberdiers" (armed soldiers) and a throng of noblemen and commoners.

But these pale compared to the visual splendours later in that same Act when Queen Katherine herself is tried. As scene four begins, both "trumpets" and "cornetts" sound as the court proceeds majestically into session, led by a train of twenty-four named personnel, ranging from functionaries, such as "two vergers with silver wands" and "two gentlemen bearing two great silver pillars", all the way up to a gang of some five bishops – not to mention the estranged King and Queen themselves, each attended by numerous flunkies (2.4.0. SD). As is attested by the extravagant 1520 peace conference between England and France known as the Field of Cloth of Gold (with which the play begins), Henry VIII's real-life court was acutely conscious of the political value of majestic ceremonial trappings. *Henry VIII* does its utmost to reproduce them. Following that court scene, three other spectacular events map out the course of the rest of the play: Anne's coronation, represented by an extensive "royal train"; Queen Katherine's dream vision, featuring "six personages in white robes" who dance around her to the accompaniment of music; and finally the christening of the young Princess Elizabeth (Anne Boleyn's daughter and the future Queen) that brings the play to its conclusion.

The very persons

The play itself urges audiences to take this kind of realism seriously. From Wotton's letter describing the fire, we gather that "The Life of King Henry the Eight", as it was printed in the 1623 First Folio, was more usually known by a jaunty alternative title, *All Is True*. There was a brief Jacobean fad for colloquial, playful titles – Samuel Rowley's play *When You See Me, You Know Me* (revived in 1613) was also about Henry VIII, while Thomas Heywood's *If You Know Not Me, You Know Nobody* (1605) appears to have been a source for Shakespeare and Fletcher. Shakespeare's own taste for tongue-in-cheek names appears in the comedies as *Much Ado About Nothing* and *What You Will*, the latter better known as *Twelfth Night*. But "All Is True" is more outrageously daring than any of these: it suggests not merely that "all" will be "true" in the end, but insists that what the playwrights are putting on stage really did happen. As the Prologue puts it:

> To rank our chosen truth with such a show
> As fool and fight is, beside forfeiting
> Our own brains, and the opinion that we bring
> To make that only true we now intend,

Will leave us never an understanding friend.
Therefore, for goodness' sake, and as you are known
The first and happiest hearers of the town,
Be sad as we would make ye. Think ye see
The very persons of our noble story
As they were living; think you see them great,
And followed with the general throng and sweat
Of thousand friends; then, in a moment, see
How soon this mightiness meets misery.

[PROLOGUE, 17–30]

This is no knockabout farce, no "fool and fight" show, but a drama to feed the mind. Furthermore, it is drama intended to be indistinguishable from the "truth" of real life: unlike *Henry V*'s Chorus, who urges spectators to "piece out our imperfections with your thoughts" (Prologue, 23), there is no apology here for the limitations of the Globe. And there would have been an even more heightened sense of "truth" at the King's Men's new venue, the Blackfriars, where the play may have transferred after the fire. Located in an upmarket area north of the river, this recently refurbished indoor theatre occupied the site of an old Dominican monastery and contained the very hall in which Queen Katherine's divorce case was tried, eighty-odd years earlier. When the trial occurs on stage in Act Two, it must have been difficult to avoid a sense that events were being played out on stage as they had once been for real.

Even if the play's early audiences were ignorant of the location of Katherine's downfall, the dizzying sense that history was intimately entwined with the present must have been inescapable if they paused to "think" about the monastery itself, whose change of use was instigated by Henry VIII's most wide-reaching political act: the split with the Catholic hierarchy, the foundation of the Church of England and the dissolution of religious houses. Indeed, the fact that *Henry VIII* hinges on the momentous events of the English Reformation – a schism instigated by Henry's wish to divorce Katherine despite being refused by the Pope – has been taken by many to argue that Fletcher and Shakespeare's play is Protestant propaganda dressed up as history. After all, it climaxes with the birth of Princess Elizabeth, a Protestant monarch who will preside over a country in which "God shall be truly known", as Archbishop Cranmer puts it in the play's closing minutes (5.4.36). Writing a full decade after that same Elizabeth's death, the playwrights were freed from the Queen's injunction not to perform plays touching "either matters of religion or of the governance of the estate of the common weal", and took the opportunity to retell some of the events of her father's reign, events that were only just beyond living memory for some of their spectators.

> *In architectural elevation there may not be anything very imposing in Henry VIII. It is no towering edifice, based and buttressed, one substructure resting upon another. But everything is meshed, consequential, and more subtly interrelated than one may suspect at first.*
>
> Kristian Smidt, *Unconformities in Shakespeare's History Plays* (1982)

In one sense the play's overall trajectory does seem to confirm a Protestant message: it also pivots on the downfall of Cardinal Wolsey, the lord chancellor historically sacked by Henry as soon as it became clear that he would be unable to broker the King's "great matter" and arrange a divorce. During his time as chief royal adviser, many were appalled at Wolsey's influence over Henry: all-powerful, vainglorious and with a larger household even than the royal one (the magnificent royal palace at Hampton Court was in fact originally his), the Cardinal was seen to embody everything that was wrong with England. By the time that Wolsey had outlasted his usefulness, Protestant commentators rejoiced that he would be rejected alongside the devilish Roman Church he represented. The play itself makes the reason for Wolsey's downfall more specific, and more ironic. Wolsey's bitter enemy Suffolk gleefully narrates the ins and outs:

Henry VIII, as illustrated in Nicholas Rowe's 1709 edition of Shakespeare. Despite its "modern-dress" setting (the gossiping courtiers sport periwigs and breeches), both Henry and Wolsey appear in Tudor garb.

> The Cardinal's letters to the Pope miscarried,
> And came to th'eye o'th' King, wherein was read
> How that the Cardinal did entreat his holiness
> To stay the judgement o'th' divorce, for if
> It did take place, 'I do', quoth he, 'perceive
> My king is tangled in affection to
> A creature of the Queen's, Lady Anne Boleyn'.
>
> [3.2.30–6]

With these words Wolsey signs what will eventually prove his death sentence as well as his ejection from office. The complicating factor is of course that, at least in this instance, he has done absolutely nothing wrong: in fact the Cardinal has simply told the truth. The difficulty is that this truth is rather too sensitive to bear – it makes the King's actions seem somewhat grubbier than he would prefer.

Many hands

Given that Shakespeare is often regarded as the greatest writer in the English language, it can be a substantial disappointment to discover that we possess practically no examples of the great man's hand – no manuscripts, no printed books with his jottings. All that remain are six scratchy but authenticated signatures on various legal documents (the infamous will was written out by a professional scribe, the client simply signing in the appropriate places).

That isn't quite the end of the story, however. Many believe that at least some of the handwriting in a unique surviving copy of a text entitled "**The Booke of Sir Thomas Moore**" (c. 1603), preserved in the British Library, is Shakespeare's. This manuscript is a playtext (in this instance "book" equals "promptbook") based on the life of the eponymous politician, writer and Catholic martyr – executed on the orders of Henry VIII – but it seems never to have been acted or published. One reason for that might have been the involvement of Elizabeth I's Master of the Revels, Sir Edmund Tilney, who apparently rejected the play and refused to allow it to be performed. Perhaps in response to this censorship, various rewritings and additions seem to have been made to the text – and some of those changes are in handwriting subsequently (and somewhat unromantically) described as "**Hand D**". Since the nineteenth century scholars have argued that this hand is Shakespeare's

and excerpts from the text are included in many *Complete Works* and have even been performed on stage.

If Hand D *is* Shakespeare's – watertight identification is difficult – it prompts fascinating questions about his involvement in collaborative playwriting. The hands of dramatists **Anthony Munday, Henry Chettle, Thomas Dekker** and possibly **Thomas Heywood** also feature in the More manuscript, indicating that in this instance at least the work was shared. Heywood later claimed to have had "a entire hand or at least a main finger" in over two hundred plays, and in recent years theatre historians have argued that writing plays in collaboration was the rule for Elizabethan dramatists rather than the exception. *Sir Thomas More* also provides tantalizing hints about Shakespeare's creative process: the insertions ascribed to Hand D have plenty of false starts and crossings-out, suggesting that the playwright's patterns of work were both messy and fairly rapid. And the fact that these insertions include a powerful speech by More addressed to the citizens of London, in which he successfully quells a riot against foreigners, also implies that Shakespeare had become well known among his contemporaries for producing emotive work – and work that showed an affinity with what the text calls "wretched strangers", the minority victims of mob violence.

For more on the story behind *Sir Thomas More*, along with Shakespeare's involvement in collaborative projects, see p.84.

By this stage everyone knows that Henry has tired of Katherine and fallen for Anne Boleyn (after dancing with her in Wolsey's house, ironically enough). Even so, Henry is hasty to claim that he desires a divorce not because his eye has been caught by another woman, but because Katherine has been unable to give him a male heir. It is a curse that has resulted, the King claims, because the match between them is actually void: Katherine was initially married to his older brother Arthur, but Arthur died soon afterwards. Rather than England break the political alliance with Spain, she was handed to Henry instead. "Hence I took a thought," Henry explains to the papal legate Campeius,

This was a judgement on me that my kingdom,
Well worthy the best heir o'th' world, should not
Be gladded in't by me.

[2.4.190–3]

If Campeius is unimpressed by these arguments (as Henry suspects he is), it is a cynicism only encouraged by the play. The King has often been portrayed as the play's out-and-out hero, a Protestant monarch who finally banishes the arch-tempter Wolsey (as a previous King Henry banished Falstaff) and takes control of England for himself. Yet that exemplary image is hardly to be found in *Henry VIII*. Whereas in real life Henry wed Anne Boleyn some four years after the rift with Katherine, in the play the marriage follows with scrambled haste. Likewise, for all the King's bluster about his "wounded conscience", his courtiers have little doubt as to the reality:

LORD CHAMBERLAIN
    It seems the marriage with his brother's wife
    Has crept too near his conscience.
    SUFFOLK   No, his conscience
    Has crept too near another lady.

[2.2.16–18]

The rib-nudging tone of the exchange – and its unfussy language, somewhat characteristic of the play – speaks volumes. And though Henry publicly undertakes to stay with his wife if the cardinals prove the marriage "lawful", Katherine sadly reveals that he has long since banished her from his bed.

A glist'ring grief

If Henry isn't a spotless hero, neither is Wolsey an out-and-out villain. Eager though *Henry VIII* might seem to offer a tale of regal redemption – the kind of tale that Shakespeare's earlier romances had created a taste for – its commitment to historical "truth" among the web of Tudor politics (even the unpalatable truth about Henry's sexual interests) opens up plenty of other options. The play began with a grim demonstration of the Cardinal's malevolence: the downfall of the Duke of Buckingham, whose error is to criticize too openly Wolsey's dominance, and who pays the price soon afterwards. But as we watch Wolsey's snarling enemies turn on the former lord chancellor himself, Buckingham's earlier words on the fickleness of power seem more acute than ever. Heading to his execution, Buckingham grimly warns anyone within earshot that the court is a dangerous place to eke out a career. "You that hear me," he calls,

This from a dying man may receive as certain—
Where you are liberal of your loves and counsels,
Be sure you be not loose; for those that you make friends
And give your hearts to, when they once perceive
The least rub in your fortunes, fall away

> Like water from ye, never found again
> But where they mean to sink ye.

[2.1.125–32]

It is the kind of counsel given weight by the speaker's proximity to death: like John of Gaunt in *Richard II*, who insists that "the tongues of dying men / Enforce attention" (2.1.5–6), Buckingham hopes that his stark message will be taken for truth. Power is slippery, he warns: anyone can suffer a fall, and friends inevitably become enemies, "fall[ing] away / Like water" (a vivid and surprising poetic image) before they turn against you. In the treacherous world of the sixteenth-century court – *Henry VIII* is the only one of Shakespeare's histories to be set in the Renaissance – the only person you can trust to be true is yourself.

In time Wolsey too has good reason to rue these realities (his fine speech acknowledging his weaknesses has been much anthologized), and the insistent parallels between Buckingham and Wolsey's respective fates – both tell the truth, both are undone by omnipresent enemies – overcome the differences between them. The play begins to look less like the straightforward story it seems at first, and more like a satire on the ever-rumbling treadmill of power.

But like *King John*, another play that looks unsparingly at the messy business of politics, the next downfall depicted in *Henry VIII* presents a properly tragic aspect: the suffering of the blameless Queen Katherine, who forms another and more pitiful embodiment of truth – the kind of truth hinted at by Buckingham, the commitment to absolute constancy. Initially the play sets her up (ahistorically) as a kind of heroine, ranged against Wolsey in a fight for the people. In the play's second scene we see her kneeling in front of Henry and exclaiming that his subjects are "in great grievance" because of what she earnestly calls "exactions" – ruinously high taxes set by Wolsey in defiance of his royal master (1.2.20–6). As soon as the matter comes to light, Henry rescinds them and the royal couple are confirmed in their strength.

But Katherine's next involvement with power politics will not be so successful: after the banquet at Wolsey's, rumours begin to circulate of the King's eagerness to seek a divorce, and when we next see the Queen it is at her trial. Kneeling once more to her husband, she movingly describes what it is like to be outmanoeuvred politically (in a speech probably written by Shakespeare, who might have contributed around half of the play, around two scenes per act). "Heaven witness / I have been to you a true and humble wife," she addresses Henry,

> At all times to your will conformable,
> Ever in fear to kindle your dislike,
> Yea, subject to your countenance, glad or sorry
> As I saw it inclined. When was the hour
> I ever contradicted your desire,
> Or made it not mine too? Or which of your friends
> Have I not strove to love, although I knew
> He were mine enemy?

[2.4.20–9]

These are questions for which Henry cannot provide answers – he will not even speak until much later in the scene – and in fact Katherine's "enemies" are already gaining the upper hand. The Queen eloquently attempts to clear her name of any taint of suspicion, but she had little idea until now that being "true" could harm her. "Have I lived thus long," she cries, "a wife, a true one?"

> A woman, I dare say, without vainglory,
> Never yet branded with suspicion?
> Have I with all my full affections
> Still met the King, loved him next heav'n, obeyed him,
> Been out of fondness superstitious to him,
> Almost forgot my prayers to content him?

[3.1.124–31]

"Truth loves open dealing," she earlier warned the scheming Wolsey (3.1.39), and as she finds herself gambled out of her throne, truth has never seemed more isolated among the chicanery at court. Before the play is out Katherine will be dead – but not before experiencing a miraculous vision in which "spirits of peace" crown her with garlands in a symbol of divine innocence.

Katherine's prominently unlovely fate makes it difficult to accept the role of her successor as Queen, Anne Boleyn, who is crowned even before Katherine's death. The play leaves Anne's motives and experience largely in shadow, and although it ends with yet another spectacular occasion celebrating the birth of Elizabeth (a daughter Henry is desperate to avoid in his eagerness for a male heir), the Queen's silent presence at the ceremony of thanksgiving seems almost foreboding. Though everyone else present looks towards the future, to the "thousand thousand blessings" of Elizabeth's reign as Queen (5.4.19), from the perspectives enabled by the play it is hard to avoid the sense that before that comes to pass Anne herself will be accused of adultery and beheaded, Henry will have remarried another four times and England will have been plunged into roiling religious turmoil.

Anne's own words on the subject much earlier in the play, though they dissolve amid the pomp and ceremony of the closing scene, seem uncannily accurate. Discussing the sorry state of Katherine with her companion the Old Lady, Anne's opinion is strongly – truthfully – held. "Verily, I swear," she declares,

> 'tis better to be lowly born
> And range with humble livers in content
> Than to be perked up in a glist'ring grief
> And wear a golden sorrow.

[2.3.19–22]

"Our content / Is our best having," the Old Lady agrees; wanting any more is incalculably dangerous. That message is one of the truest things *Henry VIII*, or *All Is True*, contains.

Stage history and adaptations

Though the **Globe** fire of June 1613 proved devastating, a rebuilt theatre was up and running within the year and performances of *All Is True* no doubt continued at the indoor **Blackfriars**, probably with the corpulent **John Lowin** as Henry. Another performance was commissioned in 1628 by the widely reviled **Duke of Buckingham**, apparently as a device to increase his popularity (he pointedly left the performance after his namesake's unjust execution), but satirists wondered why he failed to spot the play's more obvious message – the downfall of a hugely unpopular courtier.

This is all we know until the 1660s, when *Henry VIII* (as it became known in this period) was put on by **William Davenant** at Lincoln's Inn Fields. Sponsored by the newly restored Charles II, Davenant emphasized the play's propagandistic purposes, employing impressive Tudor pageantry and employing the talents of **Thomas Betterton**'s noble Henry and **John Verbrugger**'s Wolsey. Pepys was one of many satisfied customers – he saw it twice, thinking it "better than I ever expected". **John Banks** mounted a strongly Protestant adaptation entitled *Virtue Betrayed, or Ann Bullen* in 1682, **Barton Booth** playing Henry in both this and Shakespeare's play (itself much curtailed).

Brushes with literal royalty continued in the next century. *Henry VIII* was played at **court** in front of George I in 1717 (the Hanoverian monarch's English being limited, the jokes had to be explained), and then a decade later to coincide with George II's coronation. **Colley Cibber** was responsible for the latter, the royal connections paying off handsomely in 1728 when George announced he would attend a performance: people responded by breaking into Drury Lane in order to procure seats with a good view not of the stage but the King. Cibber's productions starred **Peg Woffington** and **Hannah Pritchard** from the 1740s, and **James Quin** also played redoubtable Henrys. Coronation fever in 1761 again inspired stagings of *Henry VIII*, this time in a showdown between **David Garrick** at Drury Lane and **John Rich** at Covent Garden (Garrick's performances were accused of being shabby by comparison). Near the century's end the play would receive new life in the hands of **John Philip Kemble** – or, more accurately, his sister **Sarah Siddons**. Renowned as a tragic actress, Siddons was recommended to play Queen Katherine by none other than Dr Johnson, and the results were apparently spectacular: one actor reputedly refused to go on stage with her, so searing was her performance; and audiences commonly refused to applaud, out of respect, until her body had left the stage.

But it was the historical realism of Kemble's production that would influence directors throughout the nineteenth century, perhaps *Henry VIII*'s most popular period. **William Charles Macready** and **Samuel Phelps** put on competing performances at their respective houses, but in 1848 came together at **Drury Lane** to perform (yet again) in front of royalty, this time Queen Victoria and her consort Albert. Their Katherine was the charismatic American actor **Charlotte Cushman**, who later toured the role in the States (building upon the success of **Charles** and **Fanny Kemble**, who had taken the play to New York in 1834) and even, in 1859, played Wolsey. By that time **Charles Kean**'s 1855 performance in London was infamous, if only because of its vast scale and cutting-edge technology. Pioneering the use of spotlighting and

Henry Irving as Cardinal Wolsey dominated the 1892 production of *Henry VIII* at London's Lyceum Theatre. His performance won high praise for what the *Saturday Review* called "the soul struggle which rends the heart and intellect of the great statesman".

so-called "raking flats" (backcloths set at an angle to give the impression of distance), Kean's version employed a cavalcade of angels to represent Katherine's vision and built up to a "Grand Moving Panorama" of Tudor London scrupulously copied from a 1543 drawing. Unsurprisingly, the text was severely cut – Kean reasoning that there simply wasn't space for everything.

This production would seem restrained compared to those mounted by **Henry Irving** in 1892 and **Herbert Beerbohm Tree** in 1910, both of which broke extravagant new ground. Though Irving called upon the services of **Ellen Terry** (Katherine) and **William Terriss** (Henry) and played Wolsey himself, he cut most of the final two acts and surrounded them with lavish "historical" scenery. Tree did much the same, constructing monumental fan-vaulted sets and filling the stage with extras in the belief that the period required "great sumptuousness". But his obsession with detail rebounded when he toured to the US in 1916, shipping over some 375 costumes and 135 items of furniture in the process: having little else to comment on (half the play was cut), critics simply accused it of looking scruffy.

The Victorian and Edwardian taste for "authenticity" was passing, and ripe for satire – which is precisely what happened at the Cambridge Festival Theatre under **Terence Gray** in 1931. Instead of Holbein, Gray took inspiration from the topsy-turvy worlds of Lewis Carroll, creating weirdly modernist designs that ended up dominating the action, culminating in a baptism scene in which a cardboard infant Elizabeth I was shown to have a sixty-year-old face before being tossed blithely to the audience. **Tyrone Guthrie**'s *Henry VIII* at the Old Vic two years later was much more traditional and had in **Charles Laughton** the epitome of the "bluff King Hal" approach to the role. Guthrie's 1949 staging at Stratford won him even warmer reviews. Using a full text, he filled the stage not with vast sets but bustle and colour, and also emphasized the play's comedy. **Diana Wynard**'s Katherine and **Anthony Quayle**'s Henry were well received, and the production was subsequently revived in the coronation year of 1953.

Since then this still-unpopular play has appeared only infrequently, most often at the behest of the state-subsidized Royal Shakespeare Company. By general consent the most satisfying postwar production was staged in 1970 by **Trevor Nunn**, who largely ignored *Henry VIII*'s politics in favour of its psychological drama, with **Donald Sinden**'s tormented Henry and **Peggy Ashcroft**'s fine Katherine much praised (Ashcroft, for one, seems to have taken her role every bit as seriously as Siddons did). **Howard Davies** put on an aggressively radical production in 1983, again at the RSC, which underscored the play's power politics with all manner of Brechtian conceits, including a coronation scene which was "rehearsed" on stage. **Ian Judge**'s insipid Chichester Festival production of 1991 was coolly received, but **Gregory Doran**'s efforts at the RSC's Swan Theatre in 1996 received positive notices for bringing the play's pageantry into harmony with its political and personal realism. **Paul Jesson**'s Henry and **Jane Lapotaire**'s conspicuously Spanish Katherine were both sensitively performed; in a pointed reference to the play's original title and its contemporary resonances, "All Is True" was emblazoned across the back of the stage.

Perhaps nervous about *Henry VIII*'s inflammatory reputation, the team at the rebuilt Globe on Bankside didn't stage the play there until 2010, in a faithful if slightly pedestrian version by **Mark Rosenblatt**. Two years later – having successfully failed to set the place alight – it returned as part of the World Shakespeare Festival, with the Madrid-based **Rakatá** company performing a sprightly and refreshingly non-Tudor version in Castilian Spanish.

Sections of **Beerbohm Tree**'s 1910 production were captured on silent film – making *Henry VIII* one of the first Shakespeares to make it onto celluloid – but nothing survives. To date, the BBC/Time-Life production of 1979 is the only other screen version; it was directed by **Kevin Billington**.

SCREEN

Henry VIII
J. Stride, C. Bloom, T. West; Kevin Billington (dir.) UK, 1979 ❯ BBC **DVD**

Billington's decision to shoot *Henry VIII* on location might seem like a much-needed liberation, or it could be seen as the inevitable conclusion of a nineteenth-century aesthetic (epitomized by Irving and Tree) of staging the plays in as historically "realistic" a manner as possible. But although the great Tudor rooms it lives in are undeniably more impressive than anything cobbled together by the props department, the play's subversive ironies are perhaps stifled as a result. The cast are mixed: John Stride's Henry is attractive but lacks depth while Timothy West plays Wolsey efficiently yet with a touch of perfunctoriness. Claire Bloom produces a moving performance as the betrayed Katherine, however.

Henry VIII
D. Rowan, I. McNeice, J. Cummins; Mark Rosenblatt (dir.) UK, 2010 ❯ Shakespeare's Globe **DVD**

Though *Henry VIII* was often treated as costume drama in the nineteenth century, there is more to this Tudor-style Globe production than codpieces and fur capes (though there are indeed plenty of those, and some well-populated processions besides). It's striking how much of a drama of words this is, with Ian MacNeice's plumptiously jowled Wolsey and Kate Duchêne's emphatic Katharine going toe to toe in a battle for political survival while fixers and placemen look on. Mark Rosenblatt's stagecraft is somewhat stand-and-deliver and Dominic Rowan seems slightly underpowered as the King, though it's nice to see Henry VIII played with less harrumphing hey-nonny-nonny than is usual. Whether you interpret the appearance of the child Elizabeth I in the extravagantly choreographed final scene as satire or entirely straight-laced will say much about your attitude to politics – and the play.

AUDIO

King Henry VIII
P. Jesson, J. Lapotaire, T. West; Clive Brill (dir.) UK, 1998 ❯ Arkangel ◉ ⬇

This Arkangel *Henry VIII* potters along pleasantly enough, though it's slightly lacking in vividness – but perhaps that's inevitable for a play so inescapably visual. Paul Jesson's Henry is ill-advisedly bluff at times (the banqueting scene is annoying in this respect), but Jane Lapotaire's Katherine is appropriately dignified, as in her stage performance for Doran and the RSC a few years earlier, and the other parts are thoughtfully cast: Anton Lesser makes a rounded Duke of Northumberland and Timothy West gets the opportunity to reprise the role of Wolsey, this time with greater conviction. *Henry VIII*'s gossipy character, too, comes across well: intimate recording (particularly of the two gentlemen who repeatedly murmur about the ins and outs at court) takes you to the very centre of the action.

EDITIONS

Arden Shakespeare (third series)
Gordon McMullan (ed.); 2000 ❯ Bloomsbury

R.A. Foakes's Arden edition of *Henry VIII* (1957) was the first to take the play – and its place in the Shakespearian canon – seriously, and his third-series successor Gordon McMullan does a fine job of bringing things more up to date. As with other Arden 3s (notably the *Henry VI* editions, published around the same time), McMullan's text is chunky, bulked out by no fewer than seven appendices, among them a handy historical chronology and a doubling chart rationalizing the play's extensive *dramatis personae*. At the other end of the book, McMullan's sizeable introduction makes spirited – though sometimes tendentious – reading, exploring various spins on the play's concern with "truth", and he makes a neatly argued case for co-authorship between Shakespeare and Fletcher.

SOME CRITICISM

King John and Henry VIII: Critical essays
Frances A. Shirley; 1988 > Routledge

King John and *Henry VIII* have little obvious in common other than their relative isolation in the Shakespearian canon (neither forms part of a historical sequence), but this essay collection covering both plays makes it invaluable. Slightly over half the book is devoted to *All Is True*, and there are some excellent pieces here – theatre reviews of early productions alongside conventional academic essays. Among the latter, Lee Bliss's piece on Fortune in the play (1975) and an excerpt from Kristian Smidt's *Unconformities in Shakespeare's History Plays* (1982) are particularly perceptive on the play's thematic patterns.

Shakespeare and Early Modern Political Thought
David Armitage, Conal Condren and Andrew Fitzmaurice (eds); 2009 > Cambridge UP

The word "politics" appears nowhere in Shakespeare's oeuvre, but – as his English history and Roman plays eloquently reveal – the concept was rarely distant from his mind, and persisted until very nearly the end of his career. This collection, drawn from papers delivered at a 2006 conference, has an admirably wide range, aiming to place Shakespeare's work in the tumultous debates about political matters that occurred in the Renaissance. Only one essay, Jennifer Richards's "Shakespeare and the Politics of Co-Authorship", confronts *Henry VIII* head-on (Richards is perceptive on the differences between Fletcher and his co-author's approach to their subject matter), but its concerns – the slipperiness of power, the difficulties of governing justly – flicker through the book. Conal Condren on political theory in *Measure for Measure* and Stephen Greenblatt on the ethics of political authority are particularly engaging.

Julius Caesar

Though in many ways a drama of ideas, *Julius Caesar* is probably Shakespeare's tautest study of political intrigue. It is also one of his leanest plays: nearly half the size of *Hamlet*, with the action compressed into just sixteen high-voltage scenes. Though it shows that Shakespeare had learnt from the experience of his recently completed English histories, the tragedy also marks a turning point for the playwright, the first of his scripts to employ the Greek historian Plutarch's richly characterized *Lives of the Noble Grecians and Romans*. The measured, cool style of the play – in which even private conversations take on the tone of public oration – can seem monochrome at first glance. But the closer one looks, the stranger and more intriguing *Julius Caesar* gets, not least in its thrilling self-consciousness about performance and rhetoric – fittingly enough, for it was one of the first plays to be acted at the new Globe. And as a drama whose ostensible protagonist dies early in Act Three, it probes not only the ancient debate of whether Caesar is a tyrant or the greatest of men, and thus whether his assassination is defensible or disastrous, but questions whether anyone's actions can be called heroic amid the cross-currents and rip tides of history.

DATE > The play was seen at the Globe by a Swiss tourist in autumn 1599, and other evidence suggests that it was written that year for the opening season of the new theatre.

SOURCES > For *Julius Caesar* Shakespeare turned for the first time to a book that would dominate his subsequent career – Thomas North's translation of Plutarch, *Lives of the*

Noble Grecians and Romans (1579). In addition to freely plundering North, he may well have been influenced by the anonymous drama, *The Tragedy of Caesar and Pompey* (1595).

TEXTS > *Julius Caesar* was treated well in the 1623 Folio, where it was first printed – the text is unusually free of errors.

Interpreting the play

Understood as a unit, the so-called "Henriad" – *Richard II*, the *Henry IV*s and *Henry V* – explores, along with much else, the big questions of government. Is it better for a monarch to be rightful (like Richard II) or effective (like Henry IV)? Can there be such a thing as a perfect ruler? The play that Shakespeare wrote almost immediately afterwards turns to those imperatives once again, but with a stark difference. Using for the first time Sir Thomas North's English translation of Plutarch's *Lives*, Shakespeare was free to explore more fundamental questions of kingship and legitimacy. *Julius Caesar*, set in classical Rome at the moment it became the most important and powerful city in the world, asks whether we need monarchs at all.

MAJOR CHARACTERS & SYNOPSIS

Julius Caesar (later a **Ghost**)
Calpurnia, Caesar's wife
The conspirators against Caesar: **Marcus Brutus**,
   Caius Cassius, Casca, Trebonius, Decius Brutus,
   Metellus Cimber, Cinna and **Caius Ligarius**
Portia, Brutus's wife
Lucius, Brutus's servant
The triumvirs (three co-rulers) after Caesar's
   death: **Mark Antony, Octavius Caesar** (Julius
   Caesar's great-nephew) and **Lepidus**
Tribunes of the people: **Flavius** and **Murellus**
Senators: **Cicero, Publius** and **Popillius Laena**
Cinna, a poet
A **Soothsayer**
Artemidorus, a Doctor of Rhetoric
Pindarus, Cassius's servant
Titinius, an officer in Cassius's army
Officers and soldiers in Brutus's army: **Lucillius,**
   Messala, Varrus, Claudio, Young Cato, Strato,
   Volumnius, Flavius, Dardanius and **Clitus**
Another **Poet**
Plebeians: a **Cobbler**, a **Carpenter** and others

ACT 1 Julius Caesar has triumphed over Pompey in the civil wars, and Rome celebrates with him – to the annoyance of the tribunes Flavius and Murellus. Caesar prepares to address the people, ignoring the warnings of the Soothsayer. While Caesar speaks offstage, Cassius and Brutus discuss his rising power and popularity. Casca relates to Cassius and Brutus how, during his speech, Caesar was offered the crown but felt obliged to turn it down. That night, panic spreads as fearful portents appear. Cassius interprets the signs as omens against Caesar, and encourages Brutus to join a conspiracy against him.

ACT 2 Brutus privately resolves that Caesar's ambition means he must die. Joined by Cassius and other conspirators, he agrees to kill Caesar, but Brutus vetoes the suggestion that Antony should also be killed. Portia has noticed that her husband is troubled but reluctant to explain why. Caesar is also nervous about the portents, and when a sacrifice goes wrong Calpurnia begs him not to leave home, revealing that she has dreamed of his death. Caesar initially agrees, but changes his mind when Decius (a conspirator) tells Caesar how the Senate wish to make him king. Other conspirators, and Antony, arrive to escort him to the Capitol. Artemidorus, meanwhile, plans to warn Caesar by giving him a letter as he walks by.

ACT 3 At the Capitol, Caesar rejects Artemidorus's letter but instead listens to a petition requesting that the banishment of Metellus's brother be repealed. When he refuses, the conspirators stab him to death. Antony arrives at the scene and mourns Caesar's death but promises to delay judgement until the murderers have explained themselves at Caesar's funeral, at which Antony intends to speak. At the funeral all goes well for the conspirators when the popular Brutus speaks, but Antony's address to the crowd wins them round. Convinced of their treason, the crowd begins to bay for the conspirators' blood, but they have already fled. In the ensuing riot, citizens murder a poet called Cinna, mistaking him for a conspirator of the same name.

ACT 4 Antony, Octavius Caesar and Lepidus have assumed the leadership of Rome. Meanwhile Brutus and Cassius combine their forces at Sardis, but the two men quarrel when Brutus accuses Cassius of accepting bribes. Though momentarily reconciled (just as news arrives that Portia has killed herself), they clash again over tactics. Receiving information that Antony and Octavius's army is heading towards Philippi, Cassius wants to remain where they are, while Brutus is for marching to meet them. Brutus's decision prevails, but left alone he is disturbed by the ghost of Caesar, who tells him that they will meet again at Philippi.

ACT 5 As news reaches Antony and Octavius that the enemy is approaching, the two leaders quarrel. As battle commences, Brutus attacks Octavius's troops but Cassius, believing that his own forces are surrounded, commits suicide with the help of his servant Pindarus. Titinius arrives from Brutus with news of imminent victory but when he sees Cassius's body he too kills himself. Brutus and Young Cato resolve to fight on, but Cato is killed and Brutus realizes that the cause is lost. Brutus begs his colleagues to kill him and finally dies by falling on Strato's sword. When the victorious Antony and Octavius find his corpse, they swear to bury him with honour.

It begins as the story of a man whose ambition, military success and unparalleled popular support put him within reach – quite literally – of the Roman crown. Yet Caesar's career climaxes not in coronation but assassination: he is brutally cut down by a coalition who cite the defence of Rome's republican ethic as justification. Some Renaissance thinkers agreed, arguing that Caesar was a dangerous tyrant; for others, he was a blameless hero. Dante put Brutus and Cassius, ringleaders of the conspiracy, in the lowest circle of Hell in his *Inferno*, while the English historian John Stow, arguing that Caesar was "the most ambitious and greatest traitor that ever was to the Roman state", presumably thought that Caesar should take their place.

There's the question

Julius Caesar throws its audiences immediately into these turbulent debates. Rome is in ferment: crowds are out on the streets, "rejoicing" at Caesar's defeat of his rival (and former co-ruler) Pompey by declaring a holiday. But the tribunes Flavius and Murellus are aghast at their fickleness. Murellus cries out:

> Wherefore rejoice? What conquest brings he home?
> What tributaries follow him to Rome
> To grace in captive bonds his chariot wheels?
> You blocks, you stones, you worse than senseless things!
> O, you hard hearts, you cruel men of Rome,
> Knew you not Pompey?
>
> [1.1.32–7]

Caesar, Murellus notes, has done nothing to deserve Rome's rejoicing; its citizens are "worse than senseless" to think he has. Recalling the days when Caesar returned from conquest in some far-flung corner of the empire with "tributaries" (captives) in tow, Murellus insists that this domestic political victory is not a Roman triumph: it is a tragedy.

The man himself makes an appearance in the next scene, but the atmosphere surrounding him remains tense and uneasy. As Caesar enters, thronged by citizens, a Soothsayer is pushed out from the crowd, warning sinisterly that Caesar should "beware the ides of March" (1.2.25, the "ides" being the midpoint of the month and the next day in the play). Despite the heavy dramatic irony, however – we know only too well the risk Caesar is in – the Soothsayer is not given the opportunity to elaborate and Caesar moves on. As the crowd passes by, another pair of men are left on stage, and again they have little good to say about Caesar. The fluctuating relationship between Brutus and Cassius will become crucial to the play, but here it's enough to notice how brilliantly Shakespeare manages to conjure up the different currents of emotion in Rome. As the two men earnestly talk, their conversation is punctuated by cries from the crowd nearby, shouts of adulation as "new honours", Brutus comments, are "heaped on Caesar" (1.2.135). And though their business is private, it has everything to do with what is going on outside, as Cassius rancorously explains:

Why, man, he doth bestride the narrow world
Like a Colossus, and we petty men
Walk under his huge legs, and peep about
To find ourselves dishonourable graves.
Men at sometime were masters of their fates.
The fault, dear Brutus, is not in our stars,
But in ourselves, that we are underlings.
Brutus and Caesar: what should be in that 'Caesar'?
Why should that name be sounded more than yours?
Write them together: yours is as fair a name.
Sound them: it doth become the mouth as well.
Weigh them: it is as heavy. Conjure with 'em:
'Brutus' will start a spirit as soon as 'Caesar'.
Now in the names of all the gods at once,
Upon what meat doth this our Caesar feed
That he is grown so great?

[1.2.136–51]

Cassius's caustic analysis of the mystique of power refuses to admit that Caesar is anything other than a man, but it does so by grotesquely magnifying him – he is a "Colossus" that looms over Rome, a city whose "wide walls … encompa[ss] but one man" (1.2.156). The nightmare he conjures is of complete tyranny: a leviathan Caesar whose shadow eclipses the figures of men who are in every way his equal.

Julius Caesar is Shakespeare's most subtle analysis of the power of oratory, and Cassius's words form the first big speech of the play. They work on us as much as on the stoic Brutus, making us hear the word "Caesar" – the most frequently uttered name in the drama – in new and unsettling ways. It is much to the point, likewise, that Cassius's words to Brutus are allowed to eclipse the political crux going on in the wings, which sees Caesar being offered the crown by an increasingly enthusiastic people. Shakespeare allows us to hear about this scene only through the words of Casca, who narrates that Caesar collapsed in front of the crowd (historically, he probably suffered from epilepsy) – an event which seems, if anything, to have increased their leader's popular standing. "Three or four wenches where I stood cried 'Alas, good soul!' and forgave him with all their hearts," Casca waspishly observes:

But there's no heed to be taken of them: if Caesar had stabbed their mothers they would have done no less.

[1.2.273–5]

Caesar's collapse is made to seem like a strategy to win favour, and for all we know it is.

Caesar's actions, in fact, remain mostly in shadow. He is on stage for just three scenes, and it is no accident that Shakespeare emphasizes the human failings of this world-conqueror – his indecision, his physical frailty (the playwright even makes him, ahistorically, deaf in one ear). Persuaded to join the conspirators against him, Brutus seems only too aware that the arguments for assassinating this man also leave plenty of unanswered questions. Even so, "it must be by his death," he resolves,

> And for my part
> I know no personal cause to spurn at him,
> But for the general. He would be crowned.
> How that might change his nature, there's the question ...
> Th'abuse of greatness is when it disjoins
> Remorse from power. And to speak truth of Caesar,
> I have not known when his affections swayed
> More than his reason. But 'tis a common proof
> That lowliness is young ambition's ladder,
> Whereto the climber-upward turns his face;
> But when he once attains the upmost round,
> He then unto the ladder turns his back,
> Looks in the clouds, scorning the base degrees
> By which he did ascend. So Caesar may.
>
> [2.1.10–27]

"May" is very much the operative word in this masterfully ambiguous speech; the question of how Caesar would really behave as king is one the play is never permitted to answer. Likewise Brutus, for all his show of logic, starts from a presumption that Caesar's "death" is necessary. His words are a remarkable example of someone preventing themselves being argued out of a case.

Lend me your ears

So is Caesar a "Colossus" who threatens to swallow up Rome, or a sick man who struggles to get through a public meeting without collapsing? Are the citizens right to hail him as their leader, or does he represent a danger to their city? In short: will his death be defensible assassination (what Brutus calls "the even virtue of our enterprise" (2.1.132)) or cold-blooded murder? One answer is that Caesar is all of these things and more: he is the great paradox at the centre of the play. Another answer is that Shakespeare doesn't let us make up our minds – or rather, doesn't permit us to hold to just one view. Meanwhile, the conspirators have forced events to a head. Surrounding Caesar in the Senate while he hears Metellus's plea to reverse the banishment of his brother, they suddenly surge forward and unsheath their knives.

But when Caesar is dead the conspirators, too, cannot make up their minds. Against Cassius's instincts, Brutus decides that, lest their course "seem too bloody", Antony should not be killed along with his master:

> For Antony is but a limb of Caesar.
> Let's be sacrificers, but not butchers, Caius.
>
> [2.1.165–6]

Brutus demonstrates that he has little capacity for dealing with the reality of what he is about to unleash; that reality includes a wound-riddled body and a live Antony who has every intention of doing something about it. As soon as the assassins are out of earshot, Antony exclaims movingly to the corpse, "O pardon me, thou bleeding piece of earth, / That I am meek and gentle with these butchers," (3.1.257–8), as if turning Brutus's feeble words back on him. In the long term, he prophesies, "Domestic fury and fierce civil strife / Shall cumber all the parts of Italy" (3.1.266–7). In the shorter term, he does everything possible to ensure that the conspirators' triumph turns rapidly into disaster.

The contest between those views becomes the centrepiece and climax of the play. Brutus announces his intention to "appeas[e] / The multitude" almost as soon as Caesar is dead, and sets to work convincing the restless crowd of his good intentions. "Romans, countrymen, and lovers," he begins,

> Hear me for my cause, and be silent that you may hear. Believe me for mine honour, and have respect to mine honour, that you may believe. Censure me in your wisdom, and awake your senses, that you may the better judge.
>
> [3.2.13–17]

So he continues, arguing calmly by stages that his hands are bloody not because "I loved Caesar less, but that I loved Rome more" (3.1.21–2). The strategy works: as Brutus prepares to leave, the people are behind him, promising to "give him a statue with his ancestors".

But it does not last. In another well-meaning yet deadly mistake – again against Cassius's better judgement – Brutus allows Antony to speak to the crowd. The results are both infamous and, for the conspirators, fatal. "Friends, Romans, countrymen, lend me your ears," Antony begins, reusing Brutus's words in an attempt to reclaim the crowd. Then he begins to work them:

> I come to bury Caesar, not to praise him.
> The evil that men do lives after them;
> The good is oft interrèd with their bones.
> So let it be with Caesar. The noble Brutus
> Hath told you Caesar was ambitious.
> If it were so, it were a grievous fault,
> And grievously hath Caesar answered it.
> Here, under leave of Brutus and the rest—
> For Brutus is an honourable man,
> So are they all, all honourable men—
> Come I to speak in Caesar's funeral.
> He was my friend, faithful and just to me.
> But Brutus says he was ambitious,
> And Brutus is an honourable man …
>
> [3.2.74–88]

How too could Brutus say he finds no personal cause, i.e. none in Caesar's past conduct as a man? Had he not passed the Rubicon? Entered Rome as a conqueror? Placed his Gauls in the Senate? Shakespeare (it may be said) has not brought these things forward. True! and this is the just ground of my perplexity. What character does Shakespeare mean his Brutus to be?

Samuel Taylor Coleridge, *Marginalia on "Julius Caesar"* (1818)

And so it goes on, each clanging "honourable" another nail in their collective coffin. In this extraordinary speech Antony employs many rhetorical techniques – the most insistent being one that Shakespeare would have learnt at school whereby as phrases are repeated they grow in intensity, the words gradually shifting from apparent straightforwardness to biting sarcasm. The persuasive rhythms of Antony's speech aptly recreate what Plutarch called Antony's "study of eloquence". He conforms entirely to the brief agreed with the conspirators, but depth-charges their whole operation.

The crowd, ever-fickle, immediately revolt. The terrible dangers unleashed by his words are underlined when a poet whose name happens to be Cinna is torn apart by citizens under the impression that he is one of the conspirators, and soon Rome slides as predicted into a bitter civil war. But Shakespeare focuses tightly on the personal consequences of these political actions. Brutus is at the centre of them all – so much so that he, not Caesar, has sometimes been taken as the play's real tragic hero. Persuaded into action by dire warnings of tyranny, he is alone among the conspirators in his belief that he is fighting for "peace, freedom and liberty", and his inability to keep the crowd on his side begins to seem symptomatic. As he and Cassius take sides against the combined forces of Antony, Lepidus and Caesar's great-nephew Octavius, quarrels with Cassius over strategy take centre stage.

As they all prepare for war, Brutus is tormented by a vision of Caesar's ghost, arrived to remind him that "thou shalt see me at Philippi" (4.2.335). And after Cassius's senseless death (in a tragic mistake he becomes convinced that Brutus's camp has been overrun by the enemy), Brutus is left to fight a final, futile battle, one that ends in his suicide. Coming across his corpse, Antony is generous but even-handed. "This was the noblest Roman of them all," he says:

> All the conspirators save only he
> Did that they did in envy of great Caesar;
> He only in a general honest thought
> And common good to all made one of them.
> His life was gentle, and the elements
> So mixed in him that Nature might stand up
> And say to all the world 'This was a man.'
>
> [5.5.67–74]

But if this is so, Antony's audiences might feel prompted to ask, what does this say about the state of the world? If it is politicians like Antony who end up on top, the ethics of your cause don't come into it; presentation is everything. As Cassius said, standing over the newly slain Caesar's body,

> How many ages hence
> Shall in this lofty scene be acted over
> In states unborn and accents yet unknown!

[3.1.112–4]

In this boldly metatheatrical gesture, the actor playing Cassius, and the audience in front of him, together know what Brutus and the others do not. The play will keep being performed – but its message will seem different every single time.

Stage history and adaptations

In the diary of one Thomas Platter, a Swiss tourist visiting Elizabethan England, we have a description of a very early performance of *Julius Caesar*. Platter records that in September 1599 he and some friends crossed the Thames to the new **Globe** and "saw the tragedy of the first Emperor Julius Caesar, very pleasingly performed ... at the end of the play they danced together admirably and exceedingly gracefully, according to their custom". The play may have been on the stage for a few months by then, and it remained popular into the next century: "Caesars Tragedye" was performed for the court at **Whitehall** in 1612, and again at **St James's Palace** in 1637 – an irony, perhaps, given that Charles I had proclaimed several years earlier that he would rule without parliament, an act that saw him accused of Caesar-like tyranny.

Julius Caesar resurfaced after the Restoration and reopening of the theatres, when it was allotted to **Thomas Killigrew** and the King's Company. But its emphasis had changed: Caesar's role was reduced to that of petty tyrant, while Brutus – especially in the hands of **Thomas Betterton** – became the stoic, philosophical hero of the piece. Betterton acted him until 1708, often in the company of **Colley Cibber**'s Cassius and **Edward Kynaston**'s Antony. After Betterton's retirement, **Barton Booth** took up the role, followed in 1728 by **James Quin**. All three acted in a version of the play prepared by **John Dryden** and **William Davenant**, which made Brutus into a genuine tragic hero by cutting any lines that distracted from his moral probity, and had him commit suicide by his own hand. The play was further simplified by transforming the mob into a comic turn, but even so it's probably no coincidence that Shakespeare's tale of tyrannicide received no London productions after George III began suffering mental illness amid demands that he be removed from power.

On the other side of the Atlantic, however, *Julius Caesar* became something of a rallying cry for the restive colonies. A 1770 production in **Philadelphia** advertized it as depicting "The noble struggles for Liberty by that renowned patriot Marcus Brutus", launching an enthusiasm for the play in the post-Independence US that culminated in the enormously popular nineteenth-century productions by **E.L Davenport**, **Edwin Booth**, and a number of others. In 1864 Booth gave a single performance of the play in New York as a fundraiser for a Shakespeare statue in Central Park, playing Brutus

"1 Min. until Julius Caesar's death ..." Glossily modern and conducted at a furious pace, Ivo van Hove's Dutch-language *Roman Tragedies*, which first went on stage in 2007, updated *Julius Caesar* for the world of rolling political news and ever-moving social media.

opposite the Cassius of his older brother **Junius Brutus Booth Jr**. Ironically, the part of Antony was played by their younger brother, **John Wilkes Booth**, who five months later lived out what he saw as the play's libertarian ideals by assassinating Abraham Lincoln. (It is a further irony that both murderer and victim were enthusiastic Shakespearians: Lincoln was known to carry a copy of the complete works around the White House, while Booth later quoted Brutus's "Alas, / Caesar must bleed for it" in a letter sent to the papers.)

Back in London, **John Philip Kemble** brought the "noble drama", as the *Times* called it, out of retirement in 1812, near the end of his career. His own Brutus was acclaimed, as was his brother **Charles**'s Cassius, but the production's main attraction was its scale, enhanced by seventy-odd extras. The German playwright and dramaturg Ludwig Tieck – who would later put his name to Germany's most successful Shakespeare translation – sneered that Kemble's stylized stagecraft was merely "clever ballet", but the die was cast. Immense, unwieldly productions soon became the norm. **William Charles Macready** and **Samuel Phelps** staged the play at Covent Garden and Sadler's Wells respectively throughout the 1830s, 40s and 50s, acting together in 1838 (Macready's Brutus to Phelps's Cassius). The **Duke of Saxe-Meinigen**'s company brought a German version to London in 1881, resplendent in historically researched costumes, but with a new emphasis on ensemble work rather than star performances. **Herbert Beerbohm Tree**'s staging at Her Majesty's Theatre from 1898 was the apogee of the Victorian tradition: Tree pruned the text to three acts, each foregrounding his own Antony; recruited a cast of hundreds; and invested heavily in gargantuan Roman sets from **Lawrence Alma-Tadema**, a painter who specialized in luxurious classical subject matter. **Charles Fulton**'s powerful Caesar played to **Lewis Waller**'s Brutus, and the production remained in the repertoire for the next fifteen years.

Though Tree's staging was grander than anything previously seen, it also sounded the death knell of Victorian theatrics, and subsequent performances tried hard to relocate the play's authentic essence. **William Bridges-Adams** used an uncut text and "Elizabethan" stagecraft in his Stratford production of 1919, but it was the rediscovery of the play's political resonance in the tense days of the 1930s that would prove more influential. The young **Orson Welles** opened his Mercury Theatre in New York in 1937 with an adaptation of *Julius Caesar* subtitled "Death of a Dictator", set in Mussolini's Italy. It saw Welles's own Brutus squaring up to the decidedly *Il Duce*-like Caesar of **Joseph Holland**; the *Washington Post* thought that "the touch of genius is upon it". **Henry Cass**'s Old Vic version, back in London, employed similar techniques in 1939 on the eve of World War II, but to less critical success.

Postwar productions have rarely been that overt, but the play's echoes of recent history have hardly been ignored. The version co-directed at Stratford in 1950 by **Anthony Quayle** and **Michael Langham** was relatively conservative, relying on the enviable quality of its cast, which included **John Gielgud**'s Cassius, **Harry Andrews**'s Brutus and **Alan Badel**'s Octavius. **Glen Byam Shaw**'s version at the same venue seven years later was bolder in focusing on the struggles of its all-too-human titular hero, played by **Cyril Luckham** with **Alec Clunes** as Brutus and **Geoffrey Keen**'s Cassius. **John Barton** once more found fascistic overtones at the RSC in 1968, but **Brewster Mason**'s Caesar made many reviewers think of de Gaulle rather than Mussolini or Hitler. **Trevor Nunn**'s Stratford production of 1972, as part of a sequence of Roman plays, was quite literally built around **Mark Dignam**'s Caesar – or rather a vast statue of him that remained insistently on stage long after its model's death. The past was similarly inescapable under **John Schlesinger** at the National Theatre in 1977, with **Brian Cox**'s truculent Brutus tormented at Philippi by a ghost represented by face masks peering out from the set. Not everyone was won over, however: the *Guardian*'s Michael Billington suggested that the conspiracy against **John Gielgud**'s mellifluous Caesar seemed merely like "a gratuitous attempt to kill off the best verse-speaker on the English stage".

David Thacker's staging at the RSC's The Other Place in 1993 invited audiences to compare its actions to events then occurring in Bosnia, while a year earlier **Peter Stein**'s acclaimed version with the Berlin Schaubühne company filled the stage with a yobbish crowd that threatened to overrun the theatre itself; Stein transported the entire lot to a former aircraft hanger near Edinburgh airport for the 2003 festival. The libertarian message of *Julius Caesar* has made it particularly resonant in apartheid South Africa: a multilingual adaptation by the South African **Yael Farber**, *SeZaR*, toured in 2002, notable for featuring part of a Setswana version by **Solomon Plaatje**, the first ever full version of the text to be translated into any African language.

Several notable productions have appeared since. **David Farr** toured a smart, modern-dress RSC version in 2004 in which **Christopher Saul**'s polo-necked Caesar reminded some of a minor TV celebrity. Fame was also a theme in **Deborah Warner**'s epic Barbican staging two years later, which, like the Stein production, boasted a convincingly large and vociferous crowd. **Ralph Fiennes** as Mark Antony was a self-consciously starry cheerleader for **John Shrapnel**'s business-suited Caesar. Elsewere in the cast, **Simon Russell Beale** made Cassius into a twitchy, anxious operator, opposite **Anton Lesser**'s notably impatient Brutus. **Ivo van Hove**'s *Roman Tragedies*, which first appeared at Toneelgroep Amsterdam in 2007, was not dissimilar, if framed on an even larger scale. A six-hour epic that ran together versions of *Coriolanus*, *Julius Caesar* and *Antony and Cleopatra*, it was set in an urgently contemporary world of Twitter, rolling news and media management, and invited the audience to sit on stage or drift in and out of the performance space as they pleased.

Recent British productions have been, despite various reinventions, less radical. **Gregory Doran**'s 2012 version, an RSC contribution to the World Shakespeare Festival, set the play in a nameless African country and featured an all-black cast, playing up the sub-Saharan dimensions of Shakespeare's "African" play. More intriguing was **Phyllida Lloyd**'s version for the Donmar later the same year: set in a female penitentiary, it offered *Julius Caesar* as a play-within-a-play, with inmates acting out the script as a prison entertainment. The concept was perhaps less striking than the cast, which featured **Harriet Walter** as a thin-faced, edgy Brutus, **Jenny Jules** as an ardent Cassius and **Frances Barber** as a properly magisterial Caesar. **Dominic Dromgoole**'s 2014 version at Shakespeare's Globe brought out the bustle and clamour of the Roman streets – groundlings shouldered their way through hooting commoners celebrating the feast of Lupercalia – but lacked dramatic punch (though it was at least a chance to see the play in togas, these days a rarity).

Although *Julius Caesar* was once one of the most popular scripts in the American canon, its appeal has waned. The most recent Broadway version, a lumbering vehicle for movie star **Denzel Washington**, dates from 2005, although the play remains a regular on the US festival circuit, notably at **Colorado** (2007), **Oregon** (2011, with a female Ceasar), Virginia's **American Shakespeare Center** and the **Chicago Shakespeare Theatre** (both 2013).

On screen, the play has experienced several reworkings, led by the big-budget versions of **Joseph L. Mankiewicz** (1953) and **Stuart Burge** (1970). Both had impressive casts, but Mankiewicz's is usually thought the finer achievement. The BBC/Time-Life version (1978) was directed by **Herbert Wise**, starring **Charles Gray** as Caesar, **Richard Pasco** as Brutus and **David Collings** as Cassius. More recently, the RSC's 2012 version has been filmed for TV and DVD release.

SCREEN

Julius Caesar

M. Brando, J. Gielgud, J. Mason; Joseph L. Mankiewicz (dir.) US, 1953 > Warner DVD 📥

Mankiewicz's *Caesar* has gone down in Hollywood legend as the film that got everything right – impressive cast, impressive staging, impressive filming – but watching it a half-century later it's difficult not to feel, well, a bit stupefied. The exception, of course, is Brando, who gives an electrifying performance as Mark Antony, particularly compelling in his rendition of the funeral oration. But John Gielgud seems miscast as a rather pallid Cassius while James Mason is fatally underpowered as Brutus. The pacing is leaden, and ultimately the whole production is rather too cool, dominated by monumental Roman sets and bleakly monochrome visuals (Roland Barthes, in a famous essay, noted how every character in the film, from principals to extras, sported a fringe as a sign of their Roman-ness). After Brando does his stuff outside the Senate it's just too tempting to switch off. If you do, you won't miss a great deal: Mankiewicz's Battle of Philippi strays too deep into Cowboy-and-Injun territory to be taken entirely seriously.

Julius Caesar

J. Gielgud, C. Heston, R. Johnson; Stuart Burge (dir.) UK, 1970 > Olive DVD

Widely known as a stage and TV director in the UK, Stuart Burge never shone on film, despite some big projects – Olivier's hotly contentious *Othello* (see p.346) being one. The other is his 1970 *Julius Caesar*, his second foray into the play (his first, from 1959, is all but forgotten now). Though it holds little by way of surprise and tends towards the over-literal – Cassius's bitter "what should be in that 'Caesar'?" speech is conducted in front of a wall helpfully covered with graffiti – it is ably done and has some quality touches. These chiefly stem from casting, Burge's great strength: Richard Johnson grumbles effectively as Cassius, Heston makes a nobly shaggy Antony, a glacial Gielgud is more at home as Caesar than as Cassius, and Jason Robards quietly falls apart as Brutus. Aficionados of classic TV spy drama will have a ball: Robert Vaughn (Casca) and Diana Rigg (Portia) share screen time. Also available on HD Blu-ray.

Julius Caesar

J. Kissoon, P. Joseph, C. Nri; Gregory Doran (dir.) UK, 2012 > RSC DVD

Struck by what he saw as the parallels between Julius Caesar and contemporary Africa, RSC director Gregory Doran decided to set the play in a nameless sub-Saharan state and employ a cast of black British actors for his contribution to the World Shakespeare Festival in 2012. Even discounting the dubious concept (there's more to the politics of a continent than gory assassination and witch-doctor-style soothsaying), this TV version is a strange hybrid – sometimes shot in the theatre, elsewhere on low-budget locations (Caesar appears to meet his end on a shopping centre escalator). No wonder so many of the actors, obliged to put on "African" accents of varying quality, look ill at ease. Yet in the end the cast save it: Jeffery Kissoon is superb as Caesar, by turns tetchy and oleaginous, and Paterson Joseph's fatally naive Brutus is an excellent foil for Cyril Nri's jumpy Cassius. Ray Fearon all but steals the show as Antony – nobly oratorical and coldly manipulative as it suits him.

AUDIO

Julius Caesar

M. Feast, J. Bowe, A. Lester; Clive Brill (dir.) UK, 1998 > Arkangel ◉ 📥

In common with many of the Arkangel series, the pace of this *Julius Caesar* feels rapid, even if it's actually a full ten minutes longer than the BBC version (see below). There are other differences, too, and some excellent solo performances make this recording an interesting contrast. Adrian Lester's Antony is perhaps the star of the piece, delivering a convincing mix of political self-interest and genuinely righteous anger that seems as effective in private as in the tumult of the Forum, though Estelle Kohler's urgent and womanly Portia makes you wish that the play gave them an opportunity to meet. Cassius, however, seems to lack energy (Geoffrey Whitehead makes him an embittered civil servant rather than the lean and hungry man we might expect), and Brutus himself, a slightly plodding John Bowe, rarely hints at his character's interior conflict.

Julius Caesar

G. Murphy, N. Farrell, J. Firth; Eoin O'Callaghan (dir.) UK, 1999 > BBC ◉ 📥

This BBC offering is perhaps a little too cool and relaxed to be genuinely gripping, but it contains some excellent moments: among them the scene of the assassination itself, which leaves you in no doubt of the conspirators' personal enmity towards Caesar. The bustle of the play's many public scenes comes across well – this Rome is convincingly busy – and Nicholas Farrell's measured Brutus particularly shines, as does Gerard Murphy's irascible Caesar, although Colin McFarlane's Cassius may not be edgy enough for some, and Jonathan Firth's youthful Antony is perhaps too lightweight for this role. The 1920s setting advertized in the booklet doesn't really make a great deal of aural impact, too, and portentous music often distracts from the tension that the play conjures perfectly well on its own.

EDITIONS

Arden Shakespeare (third series)
David Daniell (ed.); 1998 > Bloomsbury

Daniell is undeterred by *Julius Caesar*'s school-play image and keen to play up its strengths, which he takes to rest in Shakespeare's dispassionate eagerness not to "endorse anyone", still less come down on one side of the play's incessant debates. While this view of the tragedy can leave it looking somewhat diffuse – an impression not aided by Daniell's sometimes gnomic prose style – it does have the merit of leaving readers to make up their own minds. There is plentiful detail on the historical background to Shakespeare's drama, and extended excerpts from Plutarch's *Lives* are included at the back. The text itself is cleanly and helpfully presented. Marvin Spevack's Cambridge edition (revised 2003) has more recent stage history, and is particularly strong on this republican play's long and fascinating history in America.

SOME CRITICISM

Shakespeare: The Roman plays
Derek Traversi; 1963 > Stanford UP [o/p]

Long a standard work on the "standard", Plutarch-based Roman plays (*Julius Caesar, Antony and Cleopatra* and *Coriolanus*) Traversi's book remains a useful and humane companion, seeing in Shakespeare's continued engagement with Roman materials the development of his mature tragic art. Traversi's work on *Julius Caesar* in particular is excellent, escorting readers through the play and paying close attention to the text while never losing sight of its larger complicating themes. Some might find it hard to agree with Traversi that Shakespeare's tragedies are almost exclusively about their heroes, but the force of his arguments is still difficult to resist.

Roman Shakespeare
Coppélia Kahn; 1997 > Routledge

This is part of the Routledge "Feminist Readings of Shakespeare" series, and so no prizes for guessing where Kahn's interest lies. Nevertheless its extended exploration of Shakespeare's Roman work – all the way from *Lucrece* and *Titus* to *Cymbeline*, via more familiar stopping points *Julius Caesar, Antony and Cleopatra* and *Coriolanus* – shows that this book is interested in asking bigger questions. Kahn's reading of *Julius Caesar* looks carefully at the paradoxes within the play's presentation of Rome; what emerges is a closely nuanced reading of masculinity and the idea of the state (in England as much as Italy). Kahn also has some interesting thoughts on Portia's "voluntary wound", inflicted to prove her scorn for womanish weakness.

King John

King John is the chronicle play that got away. Set in an earlier medieval period than the two cycles of *Henry* plays, it is even less well known than that other isolated historical drama, *Henry VIII*. Despite a vivid life on stage during the nineteenth century – mainly because of its potential for pomp and pageantry – it escaped the theatrical revival of interest in the English histories during the twentieth century, and until recently has rarely figured in scholarly debates about Shakespeare's political writing. Part of the reason might be its tone: even more so than in the earlier plays, *King John* depicts politics as cynical, hard-edged and ultimately corrosive. The plot ranges across the defining events of John's reign – though it leaves out the most famous of them all, Magna Carta – but continually takes risks with its material, representing the chaotic and messy workings of reality in unsparing (and frequently unflattering) detail. Though located furthest from the present day, from a twenty-first-century perspective *King John* seems one of Shakespeare's most modern works, as well as his boldest experiment in making living drama out of the distant past.

DATE > No records of early performances survive, but stylistic evidence indicates 1595–97, close to *Richard III*, *The Merchant of Venice* and *1 Henry IV*.

SOURCES > An anonymous play, *The Troublesome Reign of King John* (printed 1591), is strikingly close in certain respects to Shakespeare's – the relationship between the two is still disputed. Holinshed's 1587 *Chronicles* is the main printed source.

TEXTS > *King John* was first printed in the 1623 Folio in a text purged of profanities, suggesting that it was prepared after a clampdown by the authorities (see p.118).

Interpreting the play

Though much is made of *King John*'s isolation from the rest of Shakespeare's "histories", it is the links between them, not the differences, that are striking. The *Henry VI* plays, written a few years before in the early 1590s, are much concerned with the problems of a monarch who is unable to hold together the fragile coalition that sustains him in power, and who is eventually ejected from the throne. *Richard II* (1594–95), though dating from later in Shakespeare's career, returns to the root of those problems, dramatizing the terrible conundrum of a rightful but inept king removed from his throne by a man who is the polar opposite – effective and convincing, but undeniably illegitimate. As the *Henry IV* plays are worked out, we see the corrosive effects of past indiscretions: Henry is first weighed down by worry and constant rebellion, then ultimately killed by it. For its part, *Henry V* asks us to look at a king who is both glamorous and morally beyond reproach – and then square that image with his response to the squalid realities of war.

MAJOR CHARACTERS & SYNOPSIS

King John of England, brother of the deceased Richard I

Queen Eleanor, their mother

Prince Henry, John's son (later **King Henry III** of England)

Lady Blanche of Spain, John's niece, later married to Louis the Dauphin

Hubert, a follower of King John

Rebellious English nobles: **Earls of Essex, Salisbury, Pembroke** and **Lord Bigot**

Lady Falconbridge

Philip Falconbridge, also known as the **Bastard**, her illegitimate son by King Richard I

Robert Falconbridge, her legitimate son

James Gurney, her servant

King Philip of France

Louis the Dauphin of France, Philip's son

Arthur, later **Duke of Brittaine**, King John's young nephew (the son of his elder brother Geoffrey)

Lady Constance, Arthur's mother

Duke of Austria

Châtillon, ambassador from France to England

Count Melun

Citizen of Angers

Cardinal Pandolf, a legate from the Pope

Peter Pomfret, a prophet

ACT 1 At the English court Châtillon challenges King John's right to the English crown and declares France's support for the claim of his nephew Arthur. The two nations face war. John then hears a dispute between the two Falconbridge brothers. Robert, the younger, accuses Philip, the elder, of being the bastard son of Richard I and claims his inheritance. Presented with a choice – accept bastardy and become Sir Richard Plantagenet, or keep the land – Philip ("the Bastard") chooses the former and swears allegiance to Queen Eleanor. Lady Falconbridge arrives to defend her name but eventually admits the truth.

ACT 2 The two armies confront each other at Angers. The French claim the city for Arthur; King John demands it as his. A citizen, acting as spokesman, vows loyalty to the King of England, but insists that the battle will determine who that is. The armies fight and both claim victory but still the city denies them entry. Infuriated, the enemy kings are about to join forces against Angers when the citizen suggests a solution: the warring sides

will be united by a marriage between the Dauphin Louis and Lady Blanche (John's niece). The parties agree and, in addition, John gives the city to Arthur. All are happy except Constance, who is horrified that the French have abandoned her son's cause.

ACT 3 After the wedding, Constance berates King Philip and the Duke of Austria for their weakness but is interrupted by the arrival of Cardinal Pandolf, the papal legate. The Cardinal tells John that he must accept the Pope's candidate for Archbishop of Canterbury. John refuses and is excommunicated by Pandolf, who then threatens the same for King Philip unless he turns against John. Philip reluctantly agrees and prepares to fight once more. In the ensuing battle the Duke of Austria is killed and Arthur is captured. King John then commissions Hubert to murder Arthur. Meanwhile in the French camp, Cardinal Pandolf exhorts the Dauphin to continue the fight against John and claim the English throne for himself.

ACT 4 Back in England, Hubert visits the cell where Arthur is held, but cannot bring himself to kill him. At court, the support of Salisbury, Pembroke and Bigot – already weakened by John's decision to be crowned a second time – is further damaged by news of Arthur's apparent death. The situation worsens as John hears of the arrival of a huge French army, and that both Eleanor and Constance are dead. Rumours circulate, stirred up by Peter of Pomfret, of John's imminent downfall. In alarm, he blames Arthur's death on Hubert, who reveals that the boy is still alive. Neither knows, however, that Arthur has been killed in a fall when escaping from captivity. When his body is discovered by Salisbury, Pembroke and Bigot, they assume it is murder and join the Dauphin's army.

ACT 5 John accedes to the Pope's wish, but Pandolf fails to call off the Dauphin. As war breaks out, news arrives that the French reinforcements have been shipwrecked. Suffering from fever, John cannot celebrate but is forced to take refuge in Swineshead Abbey. The English receive a further boost when Salisbury, Pembroke and Bigot leave the French, but the situation collapses with the news that John has been poisoned and half the English army drowned at the Wash. John dies just as peace is being negotiated.

These themes also surface in *King John*, probably written soon after *Richard II* but before its sequels. Like that of Bolingbroke, Richard II's usurper, King John's claim to the English throne is disputed – in this case because he inherited the crown from his brother, Richard I (known as *Coeur de Lion*, "Lion-heart") rather than giving it to Arthur, son of their brother Geoffrey. This dilemma, and the political machinations that surround it, launch the action. Only seven lines in, the French ambassador Châtillon presents the case that will dominate the rest of the play:

CHÂTILLON
    Philip of France, in right and true behalf
    Of thy deceasèd brother Geoffrey's son,
    Arthur Plantagenet, lays most lawful claim
    To this fair island and the territories,
    To Ireland, Poitou, Anjou, Touraine, Maine;
    Desiring thee to lay aside the sword
    Which sways usurpingly these several titles,
    And put the same into young Arthur's hand,
    Thy nephew and right royal sovereign.
KING JOHN
    What follows if we disallow of this?
CHÂTILLON
    The proud control of fierce and bloody war,
    To enforce these rights so forcibly withheld—
KING JOHN
    Here have we war for war, and blood for blood,
    Controlment for controlment: so answer France.

[1.1.7–20]

The language of legitimacy rings out clearly: Philip's cause is "right" and "true"; Arthur's claim is "lawful" and, again, "right". But John is uninterested in words. His curt question demands outcomes. What translates is simple: "war for war", "blood for blood", "controlment [restraint] for controlment". That's politics.

This question receives a new colouring just moments later, with the entry of the Falconbridge brothers. They, too, are engaged in a battle over rights, this time over which sibling is their father's rightful heir – Robert accusing Philip of being illegitimate, and therefore not entitled to his land. The man claimed as Philip's real father is Richard I, who is supposed to have had an affair with Lady Falconbridge while her husband was away. For the King this question is close to home in more ways than one. His opinion that "your brother is legitimate" is not unconnected to his own determination to hang onto the English throne:

    My mother's son did get your father's heir;
    Your father's heir must have your father's land.

[1.1.128–9]

This fudge will seem even more suspicious in the next meeting with the French, when Eleanor accuses Arthur of being a "bastard", and therefore unable to claim the crown. In the wider perspective, the quarrel between the brothers Falconbridge over their father's "fair five hundred pound" of inheritance points up the argument over who should be king of England for what it is: a tussle over property.

The story of the Bastard Falconbridge (as he becomes known) could not be more crucial to the play. He has been called Shakespeare's first real hero, for he demonstrates that it doesn't much matter whether you're legitimate or not – it is what you make of it that counts. Given the opportunity to choose between his two identities, he decides to spurn his father's inheritance, admit illegitimacy and become Sir Richard Plantagenet. In so doing he represents a spirit of opportunism that animates the play – a forerunner, perhaps, of Shakespeare's more famous illegitimate son, Edmund in *King Lear*. Reflecting on "new-made honour", the Bastard rejoices in his recent promotion into a higher social class. "This is a worshipful society," he neatly observes:

> And fits the mounting spirit like myself;
> For he is but a bastard to the time
> That doth not smack of observation …

[1.1.205–8]

Flexing the meaning of his identity, the Bastard claims that, for "the time", he is utterly legitimate. So is anyone with "observation", or the ability to watch for changing opportunities and make the most of them. Often stepping out of the action and speaking directly to the audience, the Bastard acts as a chorus to the play, commenting on – and often smirking at – events as they scroll past. If we're complicit with anyone in *King John*, it's him.

Mad world, mad kings

The opportunistic principles the Bastard embodies reach a climax in Act Two at Angers, in which the French and English armies attempt to face each other down. Both need to win the town in order to claim victory, but, with an interest in self-preservation entirely characteristic of the play, Angers' citizens decline to declare their colours until they know who will win. Though one of those citizens admits that "we are the King of England's subjects", that King's appeals go unheard:

KING JOHN
> Acknowledge then the King, and let me in.

CITIZEN
> That can we not; but he that proves the king,
> To him will we prove loyal; till that time
> Have we rammed up our gates against the world.

[2.1.267–72]

Falconbridge (Lewis Waller, left) squares up to a French lord (Norman McKinnell) in Beerbohm Tree's grandiose London production of 1899.

Their demand for "proof" remains. Yet proof is not swift in arriving: the battle fought between the English and the French ends inconclusively, and, when the citizens again defer judgement, both kings decide to join forces – and, as John bluntly puts it, "lay this Angers even with the ground" (2.1.399). The irony of this situation is staggering: instead of coming together in the interests of their people, the two rulers unite to obliterate them. This is a novel spin on John's desire to match his enemy "war for war" and "blood for blood".

Aptly, the town is only saved through a still more staggering political ploy, a speedily concluded marriage between Dauphin Louis and Lady Blanche. As John resigns areas of France as part of the deal, it isn't hard to agree with the Bastard that it is all a pointless charade:

> Mad world, mad kings, mad composition!
> John, to stop Arthur's title in the whole,
> Hath willingly departed with a part;
> And France, whose armour conscience buckled on,
> Whom zeal and charity brought to the field
> As God's own soldier, rounded in the ear
> With that same purpose-changer, that sly devil,
> That broker that still breaks the pate of faith,
> That daily break-vow, he that wins of all,
> Of kings, of beggars, old men, young men, maids—
> Who having no external thing to lose
> But the word 'maid', cheats the poor maid of that—
> That smooth-faced gentleman, tickling commodity;
> Commodity, the bias of the world …

> [2.1.562–75]

John's impassioned defence of his realm, France's religious fervour; all are undone by "commodity" (self-interest). Given the Bastard's wisecracking speech, it will be little surprise to learn that, just a few scenes later, the brief peace is over. Cardinal Pandolf – having excommunicated John – puts pressure on King Louis to reconsider his self-interest, and turn against the "cursed" John instead.

Many acts in *King John* are cynical, some are brazenly so. One of its most unappealing events is the plot concocted by King John to rid himself of his nephew Arthur, who has been captured from the French. The tone of their exchange, one of the most remarkable in the play, is as spine-tinglingly sinister as anything in *Richard III*. "Good Hubert, Hubert, Hubert, throw thine eye / On yon young boy," John coos,

> I'll tell thee what, my friend,
> He is a very serpent in my way,
> And wheresoe'er this foot of mine doth tread,
> He lies before me. Dost thou understand me?
> Thou art his keeper.

HUBERT   And I'll keep him so
That he shall not offend your majesty.
KING JOHN
    Death.
HUBERT   My lord.
KING JOHN   A grave.
HUBERT   He shall not live.
KING JOHN   Enough.

[3.3.59–66]

Strung across one line of verse, Hubert's and the King's thoughts are all of a piece: curt, evasive, euphemistic. John concentrates on Arthur's eventual destination, not the act of killing him; Hubert puts it all safely in the negative. Everything is read between the lines. The aim, of course, is deniability, and indeed as it turns out the King will attempt to refute that he ever ordered Arthur's death – which, strictly speaking, is accurate enough.

Arthur will be saved, however, and for a while it looks as if the play will redeem itself from cynicism. Moved by the boy's eloquent appeals to his "heart", Hubert undergoes a miraculous conversion from henchman to saviour and spares him. Wrongly persuaded that Arthur has been murdered, King John undergoes a transformation that is no less striking: he tries to blame Hubert for persuading *him* into "bloody villainy" and frets that the boy's death will blot his copybook at the "last account", the Day of Judgement (4.2.217). But his sorrow is as nothing compared to that of Arthur's mother Constance, likewise convinced since his capture that her young son is dead. Her words are heartbreaking in their simplicity. "Grief fills the room up of my absent child," she cries,

> Lies in his bed, walks up and down with me,
> Puts on his pretty looks, repeats his words,
> Remembers me of all his gracious parts,
> Stuffs out his vacant garments with his form ...

[3.4.93–7]

Constance lives up to her name, providing – as do other female figures in the history plays – a strong ethical centre in a world otherwise amoral. Shakespeare's only son Hamnet was buried in August 1596, around the same time that *King John* was premiered, and it is tempting to read into these plain but moving words the feelings of a man who knew her kind of "grief" only too well.

But the play itself makes little further attempt to spare our feelings. Though Arthur has survived the King's plotting, it is only to face death a few scenes later, jumping from a wall while disguised as a ship-boy. This is just the kind of senseless event that *King John* frequently delivers – a chaos reflecting what the Bastard describes as the "tug and scramble" of the world (4.3.147). For all that, though, as territorial intrigues and political chicanery continue, our eyes are caught by the fate of the King. Already ill by the time he engages one last time with the French in Act Five, John travels to the monastery at Swineshead for relief, but – in a bizarre final twist – is poisoned there by a monk. As he lies on his deathbed, the monarch's mind wanders around the consequences of his actions. "Ay marry, now my soul hath elbow-room," he says, talking in riddles,

> It would not out at windows nor at doors.
> There is so hot a summer in my bosom
> That all my bowels crumble up to dust;
> I am a scribbled form, drawn with a pen
> Upon a parchment, and against this fire
> Do I shrink up.
>
> [5.7.28–34]

There is a macabre irony in John's words: just as he attempted to have Arthur eliminated by means of a note passed to Hubert, so his very body has become a "scribbled form" shrinking into the fires of Hell.

Although the King is meted out a form of just deserts – in the manner of the moralized history books that Shakespeare often used – the play nevertheless teases its audience right up to the end. No sooner is King John dead and Prince Henry on the throne than news arrives, in another sudden reversal, of a French offer of peace. All of a sudden, the play is over. Allowed the final word, the Bastard Falconbridge makes of these events what he can, but his attempt to end things on a rousing patriotic note cannot but sound a little hollow. Reflecting that "England never did, nor never shall, / Lie at the proud foot of a conqueror," he attempts to turn a lucky escape into a national triumph:

> Now these her princes are come home again,
> Come the three corners of the world in arms
> And we shall shock them. Naught shall make us rue
> If England to itself do rest but true.
>
> [5.7.112–8]

Do we allow ourselves to believe that this is *King John's* ultimate message? The question is as open-ended as the play itself.

Stage history and adaptations

We know practically nothing about *King John's* first years in the theatre. It might have been written after an anonymous play entitled *The Troublesome Reign of King John* which was published in 1591 but performed by **Queen Elizabeth**'s own company several years earlier. Shakespeare's version didn't reach print until the 1623 First Folio and there is no indication of when – or even whether – it was acted. It is possible to guess, however, that the boy role of Arthur would have been a gift for a young actor, and the part of Constance (also acted by a man in Shakespeare's all-male company) would have provided opportunities for virtuoso performing.

Although the script was allotted to **Thomas Killigrew's** company after the Restoration, there is no other record of *King John* until 1737. In that year it was performed under the aegis of **John Rich** in London, possibly with the support of the Shakespeare Ladies' Club – a mysterious organization, led by the **Countess of Shaftesbury,** dedicated to reviving the plays. Also in 1737 the celebrated dramatist **Colley Cibber** prepared a revised adaptation entitled *Papal Tyranny in the Reign of King John,* which (as its title baldly states) was strongly anti-Catholic. Because of political sensitivities Colley's version stayed off the stage, however, and would not appear until 1745, the same year that **David Garrick** began performing an abbreviated version of Shakespeare's text at Drury Lane. As usual, Garrick transformed the play into a star vehicle for himself as John (the scene in which he received the news of Arthur's death particularly impressed spectators), and for the next few years *King John* became an integral part of the London scene.

It would become popular again in the era of **John Philip Kemble,** who first acted the play at the request of George III in 1783 and played it intermittently thereafter. Kemble made a fittingly villainous King, but as ever his sister **Sarah Siddons** won hearts as Constance – her "eagle-like power" in the role was particularly admired. Kemble's son **Charles,** who had played the Bastard Falconbridge under his father, took on *King John* in 1823 and toured it to America two decades later in a production, designed by the antiquarian **J.R. Planché,** which broke new ground for the historical accuracy of its staging (the US tour carted around no fewer than 170 costumes and 150 actors). **William Charles Macready's** 1842 version was again led by pictorial design, this time by **William Telbin,** but Macready's thoughtfully presented King John also attracted comment. Later in the 1840s, **Samuel Phelps's** productions at Sadler's Wells gained some success, while **Charles Kean's** 1852 staging was another lavishly detailed extravaganza.

King John escaped the notice of most other producers and it was left to **Herbert Beerbohm Tree** to mount a large-scale revival in 1899. Large it certainly was: Tree introduced silent tableaux representing battle in Act Five and, unimpeded by Shakespeare's script, the signing of Magna Carta (one historical episode the playwright leaves well out of his play). The *Athenaeum* commended this approach, commenting that "a play such as *King John* is to be regarded as a vehicle for stage pageant". In the end Tree's version ran for 114 performances.

In the twentieth century, the play's popularity began to dwindle. **Frank Benson** put it on at Stratford several times before World War I, but it never rivalled his larger productions, and at the same venue **William Bridges-Adams** produced it in 1925 but met with failure. Nevertheless, during this era **Sybil Thorndike's** monumental Constance became well known in a variety of productions, as did **Ralph Richardson's** gung-ho Bastard under **Harcourt Williams** in 1931. **Paul Scofield** played the Bastard at Birmingham Rep under **Peter Brook** in a well received staging from 1945, while at Stratford three years later **Robert Helpmann's** sinister John was supported by a sternly resolute **Anthony Quayle** as the Bastard. At the Old Vic in 1953, **George Devine** was lucky in having as his Bastard the swashbuckling **Richard Burton,** and although there were some problems with the production – audiences tended to laugh in the wrong places – the *Times* commented that it was "unusually satisfying".

The problem is less history's meaninglessness than its excessive meaningfulness: the plot promises more coherence than it delivers. The apparent trajectory of events repeatedly proves illusory; seemingly decisive moments turn out to be mere episodes in the open-ended, ironic, unpredictable movement of history.

Walter Cohen on *King John*, in *The Norton Shakespeare* (1997)

Apart from a politically cynical German translation by **Friedrich Dürrenmatt**, which opened at Basle in 1968, and a celebrated production in 1964 by Northampton Repertory Players, in which **Pauline Letts** was a remarkably moving Constance, *King John* had little opportunity to be seen anywhere but the state-subsidized Royal Shakespeare Company in the later twentieth century. **Buzz Goodbody**'s low-tech 1970 production cut swaths of the text and introduced a Brechtian slant, but undeniably the decade's most tendentious reading was provided by **John Barton**'s company four seasons later. As in his *Cymbeline* of the same year (see p.78), Barton stressed the play's political resonance and erased much of the script in what was described as "a parable for our times", but was again slated by the critics – one of whom was sufficiently angered to write a full-scale academic article about the fiasco.

A 1980 production by the **Weimar National Theatre** received warmer reviews (its unsparing view of war was particularly commended), as did **Deborah Warner**'s RSC production eight years later. Warner received plaudits for not shying away from the play's multiple shifts of tone, with her English and French sides brawling in front of Angers before the niceties of diplomacy took hold. **Nicholas Woodeson**'s short-statured King John brought out the comedy of his role, as did **David Morrissey** as the Bastard. *King John* surfaced once more ten years later at the rebuilt Globe theatre, but for one night only: in summer 1998 **Patrick Tucker**'s Original Shakespeare Company performed it after just a day's rehearsal in an attempt to reconstruct Elizabethan theatre conditions.

2001 saw no fewer than two major productions in the UK. **Barrie Rutter**'s Yorkshire-based Northern Broadsides company came first with a touring production whose clarity and verve impressed the critics; Rutter himself starred as a wily Cardinal Pandolf, while **Marie Louise O'Donnell** made a plangent Constance. Soon afterwards **Gregory Doran**'s RSC production opened in Stratford to considerable acclaim: **Guy Henry**'s flippant John was well received, as was **Jo Stone-Fewing**'s Bastard. The *Guardian* described Doran's interpretation as like "a series of playground games played for high stakes". **Josie Rourke** gave *King John* another airing in 2006 as part of the RSC's Complete Works festival, with **Tamsin Greig** and **Joseph Millson** alternating Constance and the Bastard with Beatrice and Benedick in a parallel production of *Much Ado*. The production was given a defiantly ironic spin, with religious music and formal pageantry undercut by the march of events. Restaging the play in Stratford in 2014, **Maria Aberg** opted for a modern-dress take, defiantly feminist, with cross-gender casting (notably **Pippa Nixon** as an impish Bastard and **Paola Dionisotti** as Pandolf) deployed to memorable effect. Not everyone was impressed – too many party balloons, one critic thought – but it made a powerful case for the script's contemporaneity.

Despite Shakespeare's inconvenient reluctance to show the signing of Magna Carta, the 800th anniversary of the document's sealing in 2015 gave *King John* some much-needed publicity, notably in a full Globe production directed by **James Dacre**, which opened in the atmospheric setting of a Northamptonshire church before transferring to London. Though medieval pageantry was far from absent, the staging was acclaimed for its subtly contemporary resonances: "More than any of Shakespeare's political plays, this one records the genesis of the modern state and a modern dynamic in which everything is up for grabs," declared the *Telegraph*.

Although the chances of *King John* being produced as a movie remain slim, scenes from **Beerbohm Tree**'s staging are, in fact, the earliest surviving Shakespeare on film, dating all the way back to 1899. Closer to the present day, it has seen little interest: **Donald Wolfit** played John for TV in 1952 but the most recent production is the BBC/Time-Life version from 1984, directed by **David Giles** and starring **Leonard Rossiter** (John) and **Claire Bloom** (Constance).

SCREEN

King John
L. Rossiter, C. Bloom, J. Thaw; David Giles (dir.) UK, 1984 > BBC DVD

Leonard Rossiter was probably best known as a TV sitcom actor, but in fact he had an extensive stage career – he was a notable Richard III in 1980 – and makes a robustly characterized and precisely spoken King John. Also worth mentioning is Claire Bloom's touching Constance, while the Hubert of John Thaw, another distinguished TV actor, is appropriately gritty. Unfortunately the production itself has few attractions: its staging is unconvincing – a two-dimensional Angers is perhaps intended to resemble Olivier's *Henry V* but simply looks cheap – while the pacing isn't smart enough to retain much interest. George Costigan's Bastard is good, but the part seems almost pointless without the presence of an audience.

AUDIO

King John
M. Feast, E. Atkins, M. Maloney; Clive Brill (dir.) UK, 1998 > Arkangel ◉ ⬇

Balancing *King John*'s warring sides – caustic political satire versus startling depictions of personal suffering – is hard, arguably impossible. Here Clive Brill tries to have it both ways, ramping up the camp and the comedy (most of all in Michael Maloney's crazed and somewhat overplayed Bastard), but also giving his cast plenty of emotional space. Eileen Atkins is unbearably tender as Constance, mother rather than matriarch, and in a quiet performance Michael Feast illuminates King John's progress from cynicism to devouring and

pathetic paranoia. Things sound slightly imbalanced as a result (sudden switches of mood, emphasized by Brill's rapid editing, can startle), but as a view of the play it's persuasive, and the cast clearly believe wholeheartedly in what they're doing. A welcome addition to the series.

EDITIONS

Oxford Shakespeare
A.R. Braunmuller (ed.); 1989 > Oxford UP

Braunmuller's Oxford *King John* is as easy to recommend as his more recent Cambridge *Macbeth* – both present strong and involving arguments about the plays' meanings couched in wider critical debates but not coerced by them. This is especially welcome in the case of *King John*, which until recently had few defenders and languished in the obscurer corners of the canon. Braunmuller's handling of a sometimes tricky text is well done, and he makes a good case that it was revised before printing in the Folio. A reasonably detailed stage history covers the play's mixed fortunes in the theatre up to the 1980s, but more up to date detail will doubtless be supplied by John Tobin and Jesser Lander's Arden 3 edition, scheduled to publish in 2016.

SOME CRITICISM

Shakespearean Meanings
Sigurd Burckhardt; 1968 > Princeton UP [o/p]

A collection of essays on various Shakespearian topics left very nearly finished at its author's death, *Shakespearean Meanings* starts from two bold assertions: that Shakespeare should be *read* (the italics are Burckhardt's) rather than performed; and that we can uncover what

"Acknowledge then the king …" Jo Stone-Fewings made a decisive ruler in James Dacre's touring Globe production of 2015, which began in Northampton before making a royal progress to the Temple Church in London.

he intended his plays to *mean* (ditto). There is much to disagree with in this, to be sure, but in the instance of *King John* Burckhardt does a persuasive job – perhaps because in this play, he argues, Shakespeare shows himself becoming restless with the kind of "Elizabethan World Picture" described by E.M.W. Tillyard (see p.154) and permits himself to send it up.

King John: New Perspectives

Deborah Curren-Aquino (ed.); 1989 > Delaware UP [o/p]

In our cynical age, scholarly interest in *King John* has blossomed, and as the editor of this collection comments,

"Shakespeare creates in *King John* a play provocatively charged with the urgency, anguish and relevance of 'now'". Several of the pieces collected here take up that sense of latter-day political anxiety – most clearly Virginia M. Vaughan's argumentative reading of the history as "A Study in Subversion and Containment" and Larry S. Champion's suggestion that it simply defies "artistic form". Also highly recommended is Phyllis Rackin's article on the play's eloquent but trapped women. Refreshingly for an academic collection, *King John: New Perspectives* suggestthat the theatre holds the key to many of the play's most interesting problems, and several essays probe its life in performance. Another anthology, Frances Shirley's essay collection (1988), is reviewed on p.198.

King Lear

This harrowing tale of an irascible father driven mad by the cruelty of his children asks more searching questions of its audiences than commentators can answer. A.C. Bradley thought *Lear* to be "Shakespeare's greatest achievement"; William Hazlitt declared it "the best of all Shakespeare's plays"; G. Wilson Knight was so in awe that he spoke of "the *Lear* universe". But many have also found the brutality and sheer imaginative immensity of this rawest of tragedies too much to handle – Tolstoy called it "unnatural"; Charles Lamb complained that it "cannot be acted"; Bradley went on to qualify his praise by saying that "it seems to me *not* his best play". This overwhelming bleakness helps explain why Shakespeare's script disappeared from the stage for nearly two centuries, being replaced by a sentimental rewrite by Restoration dramatist Nahum Tate, who somehow contrived a happy ending from the brutal wreckage of the original. Even so, four centuries after it was first written, the tragedy seems more in tune with the pessimism and emptiness of the modern era than any other Shakespeare text. The Polish critic Jan Kott radically compared it to Beckett and Ionesco's theatre of the absurd, commenting that in *Lear* "the abyss, into which one can jump, is everywhere".

DATE > Probably written in 1605, although *Lear*'s first recorded performance took place on December 26, 1606, at the court of King James I.
SOURCES > Shakespeare's most obvious source was an anonymous play performed by the Queen's company, *The Chronicle History of King Leir and His Three Daughters* (published in 1605, perhaps because of Shakespeare's play). The Duke of Gloucester subplot is taken from Philip Sidney's *Arcadia* and some of Poor Tom's language derives from a viciously anti-Catholic pamphlet (1603) by Anglican cleric Samuel Harsnett. Michel de Montaigne's *Essays* also seem to have been fresh in Shakespeare's mind at this point.
TEXTS > Two distinct versions of the play exist (see p.228). The first was printed in quarto in 1608 and seems to represent an early version; the 1623 First Folio includes a different text, possibly revised by Shakespeare after performance.

Interpreting the play

Looked at one way, *King Lear* is all about politics. It begins with a ruler's casual resignation from power, and ends in catastrophe when rival factions tear his country apart. There's reason to think that Shakespeare's earliest spectators would have seen at once the relevance of this fable – particularly on December 26, 1606, when the audience for this new play included King James I, a ruler who had brought Scotland and England into uneasy political union for the first time. Read as a warning to princes, *King Lear*'s message is stark: power is yours, it says, but so are the gravest of responsibilities.

MAJOR CHARACTERS & SYNOPSIS

King Lear of Britain
Goneril, Lear's eldest daughter
Duke of Albany, Goneril's husband
Regan, Lear's second daughter
Duke of Cornwall, Regan's husband
Cordelia, Lear's youngest daughter
Duke of Burgundy, Cordelia's first suitor
King of France, Cordelia's second suitor
Earl of Kent, a follower of Lear (later disguised as
    "Caius", a servant of the King)
Earl of Gloucester
Edgar, Gloucester's legitimate son, and his eldest
    (later disguised as "Poor Tom")
Edmund, Gloucester's illegitimate younger son
Old Man, a tenant of Gloucester
Curan, a courtier
Fool in Lear's service
Oswald, Goneril's steward

ACT 1 King Lear wants to divide his kingdom among his three daughters, according to whoever loves him most. Goneril and Regan speak sycophantically and are rewarded, but his youngest and favourite daughter, Cordelia, refuses to flatter him. Angered by her response, Lear gives her share to her sisters – with whom he now intends to spend his time. Despite Cordelia's loss of favour, the King of France agrees to marry her, but when Kent defends her, Lear banishes him. Meanwhile, Gloucester's illegitimate son Edmund is planning to frame his brother Edgar and steal his land; he shows Gloucester a forged letter revealing Edgar's plans to kill him. At Goneril's castle Lear and his retinue are accused of being too rowdy, so he departs in a rage for Regan's palace, along with the Fool and a disguised Kent.

ACT 2 Edmund tells Edgar of their father's anger and persuades him to flee, whereupon Edgar resolves to disguise himself as a beggar. Meanwhile Kent has attacked Goneril's steward Oswald and is put in the stocks by Regan and Cornwall; Lear and the Fool discover him there and demand to know why he has been punished, and although Regan and Cornwall release him they demand the King dismisses his retinue. When Goneril arrives and also refuses her father access, Lear leaves in a fury, bitterly vowing to contend with the wilderness instead.

ACT 3 Lear appears with his Fool, raging against the storm and his daughters' cruelty. Kent arrives and tries to persuade them to shelter in a nearby hovel, where the Fool finds Edgar, disguised and feigning madness. Lear, now genuinely mad, takes pity on him. Gloucester – though forbidden to do so – seeks out Lear and offers to house him. Meanwhile Edmund has informed Cornwall of his father's contact with France. Gloucester is captured and his eyes gouged out, but a servant who defends him fatally wounds Cornwall.

ACT 4 Edgar finds his blinded father who – ignorant of Edgar's identity – asks to be taken to Dover to commit suicide. Edmund, Goneril and Oswald enter, discussing Albany's inaction; Goneril gives Edmund a love token; Albany appears and accuses Goneril of cruelty towards her father. Meanwhile Cordelia, heading a French army, has landed in Britain. Goneril's and Regan's armies separately prepare for battle. Near Dover, Gloucester attempts to throw himself off a cliff but Edgar arranges it so his father is on level ground; Edgar pretends to be a stranger and convinces him that he has jumped and survived. When Oswald appears, with a message from Goneril to Edmund, Edgar kills him. At the French camp Cordelia and Kent are reunited and Lear is carried in, asleep; he awakes and recognizes Cordelia.

ACT 5 Regan, also in love with Edmund, demands to know whether he has feelings for Goneril but he denies everything. As Goneril and Albany plan war with France, the disguised Edgar hands Albany Goneril's love letter and demands to fight Edmund in single combat after the battle. The British forces rout the French, and Lear and Cordelia are captured and imprisoned. Albany having read Goneril's letter accuses Edmund of treason, and Edgar, disguised as a mysterious knight, fights his brother, only revealing his identity (and that Gloucester has died) after Edmund is mortally wounded. Just as news arrives that Goneril has poisoned Regan and killed herself over Edmund, Edmund confesses that Lear and Cordelia are to be executed on his orders. Albany orders their immediate release, but the message arrives too late. Lear enters, carrying Cordelia's body, and dies, demented by grief.

King Lear, with Stonehenge in the background, bewails the death of Cordelia. An engraving after the painting by James Barry (1786).

People's lives, the lives of what the play calls the "poor naked wretches" who make up the commonwealth, matter (3.4.28). It is only by being driven mad that King Lear realizes that truth, but one of the play's many tragedies is that by then it is too late: his kingdom has already gone.

King Lear pushes the political and the personal into painful conjunction, and it addresses not just politicians but ordinary mortals too: it shows that it matters who has power, and that problems afflicting a country's rulers can have terrifying consequences. Shakespeare makes the story of what happens "when majesty falls to folly", as the Earl of Kent bluntly puts it (1.1.148), the epicentre of his tragedy. It famously opens with the King's declaration that it is only by displaying "love" towards him (a love that has to find its way into polished words) that his daughters can be rewarded with a share in the kingdom he is so recklessly breaking up. "Tell me, my daughters", the King begins,

> Since now we will divest us both of rule,
> Interest of territory, cares of state—
> Which of you shall we say doth love us most,
> That we our largest bounty may extend
> Where nature doth with merit challenge?

> [1.1.48–53]

Lear's first mistake is to divide his realm; his second is to mix "love" with politics, and to misinterpret speeches describing love for the real thing. Two of his daughters, the devious Goneril and Regan, effortlessly perform as required, declaring their commitment "beyond what can be valued", as Goneril sycophantically puts it (1.1.57). But Lear's third child, Cordelia, is not prepared to flatter her father, and her treatment is severe. Her inheritance is cut off and she is left no dowry to attract a husband.

The 40-year-old Shakespeare, by this stage a veteran of at least thirty major plays, probably found the skeletal story of *Lear* in a text he'd encountered in his early career. He seems to have had links with an Elizabethan company who were performing a play called *The Chronicle History of King Leir and His Three Daughters* in the early 1590s, when he was most likely training as an actor. This old play is different from the new one in countless ways – Shakespeare prunes some of its plot and makes innumerable changes – but it contains the story of a father and his daughters and the breakdown of the relationship between them, ingredients that the playwright would use to construct one of the most disturbing and shocking tragedies ever written.

The bond cracked

For it isn't only politics that makes *King Lear* a masterwork: it is the horrifying story of a man driven to madness that gives this tragedy its unique intensity. The King is often reminded that he is too old, that as Regan callously puts it, "Nature in you stands on the very verge / Of his confine" (2.2.320–1), and as the play develops Lear begins to fret that he will topple over into madness. Though at first it is simply his political actions that are described as "mad" (Kent forces the point in the very first scene), it becomes clear that the threat to the King's sanity is quite real.

Shakespeare makes madness in multiple forms one of the biggest concerns of the play. At first it is rooted in Lear's terrible anger, which foreshadows his mental collapse. Lear's famous rant against the storm, delivered as Goneril and Regan make it clear that they are no longer prepared to house the ageing King and his rowdy knights, brings his bitter wrath to a head. Declaring his intention to "abjure all roofs" and confront "the enmity o'th' air" (2.2.381–3) rather than stay with such heartless children, Lear rages at the cosmic forces in one of the play's most memorable images. "Blow, winds, and crack your cheeks!" he cries,

> Rage, blow
> You cataracts and hurricanoes, spout
> Till you have drenched our steeples, drowned the cocks!
> You sulph'rous and thought-executing fires,
> Vaunt-couriers of oak-cleaving thunderbolts,
> Singe my white head; and thou all-shaking thunder,
> Strike flat the thick rotundity o'th' world,
> Crack nature's moulds, all germens spill at once
> That makes ungrateful man.

> [3.2.1–9]

Lear or Lears?

As if the existential pain of the script weren't enough, for students of *King Lear* there's a further headache: the texts. "Texts" plural, because there are in fact three separate versions of the play. One is known as the **first quarto** (Q1), for the simple reason that it is the earliest edition of *Lear* to have been printed (it appeared in 1608) and is in the small-format "quarto" size (see p.620). A slightly different **second quarto**, Q2 for short, was published eleven years later in 1619; and the 1623 First Folio (F1) also includes a text of "The Tragedie of King Lear" quite different from either of its predecessors.

For a long time it was assumed that all three derived from a lost authorial manuscript, and editors from the eighteenth century onwards cobbled them together as best they could. But it's now thought that the Q texts correspond to an early version of the play, with F1 representing a **revision** made a few years later. The Folio loses around three hundred lines and adds another hundred, and because it is dramatically punchier it's been argued that these changes were made post-performance. Linguistic evidence suggests that Shakespeare made the additions and it is possible that he was behind the cuts too – so what these two sets of texts seem to offer is a precious insight into the ways he wrote and rewrote for the theatre.

Around half of Shakespeare's plays exist in multiple texts – *Hamlet* has three, while the problems reconciling *Othello*'s two versions are notorious – but because of the extreme divergences in *Lear* many have been tempted to treat the Folio and quarto versions separately, arguing that they should be considered, and performed, as distinct entities.

The Oxford Shakespeare caused a storm in 1988 by doing just that, calling the quarto text **The History of King Lear** and the Folio the **Tragedy**. *The Norton Shakespeare* prints these side by side, making the differences obvious, though it also (confusingly) offers a conflated edition "so that readers can encounter the tragedy in the form that it assumed in most editions from the eighteenth century until very recently".

For the purposes of this book, the *King Lear* cited is the Folio *Tragedy* as it appears in *The Oxford Shakespeare*.

Lear makes the storm raging around him into a symbol of his suffering, but though addressing these elemental forces he is not in control of them, and the destruction they wreak will in the end seem directed against him alone.

The storm scene is Shakespeare's invention, as is Lear's companion on the heath, his faithful but in some ways equally mad Fool. Lear's Fool (he has no other name) is, like his equivalents in *Twelfth Night* and *All's Well*, a wry commentator on events, "licensed" by his position – as many Fools were in the households of real-life nobles – to ridicule those in authority and say things that others could not. In *King Lear* the humour is bleak, and the wisecracks of Lear's Fool, bizarre as they are, never stray far from the subject of his master's own folly. "Canst tell how an oyster makes his shell?" the Fool enquires, mock-innocently:

LEAR No.

FOOL Nor I neither; but I can tell why a snail has a house.

LEAR Why?

FOOL Why, to put 's head in, not to give it away to his daughters and leave
    his horns without a case.

[1.5.26–32]

"If thou wert my fool," the Fool continues, "I'd have thee beaten for being old before thy time." (1.5.40). This bitter little punchline echoes Regan's conclusion early on that for all her father's advancing years, "he hath ever but slenderly known himself" (1.2.292–3), but the Fool's counsel is ignored by the King, who seems perpetually unable to hear those who have most concern for his welfare.

Lear's progress to self-knowledge is halting, and before he gains any further insight he will become, through madness, an utterly different person. His distress – like ours, watching it – is intense. And he is far from the only character to suffer during the course of the play: in *King Lear* terrible pain touches nearly everyone. Lear's experience is shadowed by that of one of his courtiers, the Duke of Gloucester, who falls prey to a plot by his illegitimate son Edmund to disinherit his brother Edgar, who as Gloucester's lawful offspring stands to inherit his father's land. The parallels with Lear and his children are obvious, and when the machiavellian Edmund manages to convince Gloucester that it is Edgar who has turned against *him*, Gloucester frets that the world itself is coming to pieces. Reflecting on the King's own behaviour, Gloucester anxiously exclaims, "These late eclipses in the sun and moon portend no good to us":

> Love cools, friendship falls off, brothers divide; in cities, mutinies; in countries, discord; in palaces, treason; and the bond cracked 'twixt son and father. This villain of mine comes under the prediction: there's son against father. The King falls from bias of nature: there's father against child. We have seen the best of our time.
>
> [1.2.101–10]

Gloucester correctly sees that if families are wrenched apart, the state itself will follow, and he notes that what he delicately calls the King's "bias of nature" (his temperament, though we might think of his developing insanity) has the capacity to destroy everything in its path. Yet Gloucester fails to understand how his own "bias" towards Edgar has been overcome by Edmund, who resembles *Othello*'s Iago (and of course Shakespeare's sometime Duke of Gloucester, Richard III) in his ability to convince others of his goodness while plotting to ensnare them all. And in this play Gloucester will be made to suffer terribly for his error: when Edmund informs on his father, revealing that he has been in contact with the forces of Cordelia and the King of France, plotting to invade Britain and recapture it, Gloucester is captured by Goneril, Regan and Cornwall and as punishment his eyes are gouged out. He pays for his metaphorical blindness in the most grotesquely literal of ways. In this his plight resembles that of his son Edgar, who is forced on to the run and decides that

> *There are no longer kings and subjects, fathers and children, husbands and wives. There are only huge Renaissance monsters, devouring one another like beasts of prey ... All that remains at the end of this gigantic pantomime is the earth – empty and bleeding.*
>
> Jan Kott, *Shakespeare Our Contemporary* (1964)

New and improved

With the death of Oliver Cromwell in 1658 and the subsequent collapse of his son's government, the path opened for King Charles II to return from French exile and take up the English throne. Among the many changes initiated by his **Restoration**, those in the theatre were both immediate and profound: before 1660 was out Charles had rescinded the ban on drama brought in by parliament eighteen years earlier. London could once again become the hub of a thriving entertainment industry.

But the theatres desperately needed material. While playwrights busily set about writing new scripts, managers plundered the pre-Civil War repertoire for ideas. Among their finds were the plays of Shakespeare. When King Charles licensed two play-wrights, **William Davenant** and **Thomas Killigrew**, to recruit theatrical companies in August 1660, they split Shakespeare's work – along with Ben Jonson's and Beaumont and Fletcher's – between them. The well-connected Davenant (who liked to claim that he was Shakespeare's love child) got the slightly better deal – among his haul were *The Tempest, Lear* and *Hamlet* – though for his part Killigrew gained the much-loved English histories and *Othello*.

Shakespeare would have found the Restoration theatres bewildering, however. As part of the new licensing arrangements King Charles announced that professional actresses were to be allowed, while the new indoor theatres built by Davenant and Killigrew boasted cutting-edge design, including proscenium arches and "flats" for three-dimensional sets. If Shakespeare's plays were to survive, they too needed drastic surgery – and at the hands of Restoration rewriters, they got it. Davenant was himself involved with an adaptation

of *The Tempest* in collaboration with the youthful **John Dryden**, which debuted in 1667 and saw astounding success. In addition to pruning Shakespeare's knottier language (felt to be a constant problem), they took advantage of the presence of female actors by inserting another set of lovers to keep Ferdinand and Miranda company. Dryden's solo work *All For Love* (1677) was a freer version of *Antony and Cleopatra* and retained practically none of the original script, but it too catered for the neoclassical tastes of Dryden's audiences, setting the action after the Battle of Actium and transforming the play into the story of Antony's tragic failure to pull himself together.

Both these versions pale, though, alongside **Nahum Tate**'s reworking of *King Lear*. His 1681 adaptation removes the Fool entirely and cuts Gloucester's suicide attempt, but saves its most swingeing alterations for the very end. In Tate's own words, "the tale conclude[s] in a success to the innocent distressed persons": King Lear is allowed to live out his last years in peace, while Cordelia survives in order to marry Edgar in the joyful closing moments. While Tate has rarely been forgiven for this perceived abomination ("Tatefication" became a dirty word in the Victorian era), his younger colleague **Colley Cibber** has largely escaped vitriol: lines from his version of *Richard III* (1700) even made it into Laurence Olivier's infamous 1955 film (see p.385).

Texts of these wayward gems are available not only in Sandra Clark's handy anthology *Shakespeare Made Fit: Restoration adaptations of Shakespeare* (1997) but the more wide-ranging *Adaptations of Shakespeare: A critical anthology of plays* (2000), edited by Daniel Fischlin and Mark Fortier.

his only chance of survival is to disguise himself as an insane beggar, a refugee from the "Bedlam" madhouse. The irony of his disguise becomes starkly obvious when the pretend madman meets Lear, the real one, on the heath. *King Lear* has a way of turning the most lurid of nightmares into reality.

Joy and grief

This sense that the most horrific things imaginable are being acted out for real dominates the experience of seeing or reading *King Lear*, but as ever Shakespeare retains the ability to surprise his audiences. One of the tragedy's most poignant but eeriest moments occurs in the final third of the play, when Gloucester decides that, now blind, his only option is to commit suicide. Encountering a man calling himself "Poor Tom" (in fact his disguised son Edgar), he asks to be led to a cliff at Dover so that he can throw himself off. And instead of revealing himself, Edgar agrees to show him the way: it is as if the play will not let them be reconciled so easily, and so the two undergo a bizarre charade in which Edgar persuades his father that they have arrived at Dover, then tells him to jump. As Edgar well knows, they are nowhere near a cliff, and Gloucester ends up throwing himself merely onto the ground. But this is not the end of Edgar's game: now pretending to be a passer-by, he attempts to convince his father that he has in fact fallen, and has only survived by the unlikeliest of miracles. "Hadst thou been aught but gossamer, feathers, air," he tells the incredulous Gloucester,

> So many fathom down precipitating
> Thou'dst shivered like an egg. But thou dost breathe,
> Hast heavy substance, bleed'st not, speak'st, art sound.
> Ten masts a-length make not the altitude
> Which thou has perpendicularly fell.
> Thy life's a miracle.
>
> [4.5.49–55]

Yet the "miracle" is entirely of Edgar's doing, and it is also cruelly absurd, an unreal pre-echo of the mystical transformations and revelations that close Shakespeare's final plays, and – some have thought – the playwright's mocking exposé of the triviality of his craft. "Why I do trifle thus with his despair / Is done to cure it," Edgar says (4.5.32–3), but it is not clear that performing this ritual has done anything of the kind, still less granted Gloucester any measure of happiness. Later on Edgar finally reveals himself, and father and son are reconciled, but it is tragically fitting that the joy of reunion – the joy of discovering love – ends tragically. "I asked his blessing," Edgar tells Albany long after the event,

> and from first to last
> Told him our pilgrimage; but his flawed heart—
> Alas, too weak the conflict to support—
> 'Twixt two extremes of passion, joy and grief,
> Burst smilingly.
>
> [5.3.187–91]

It is not true to say that *King Lear* is loveless or cold, as some critics have insisted: the problem it perhaps explores is how difficult it can be to communicate that love. Lear mistakes Cordelia's love for arrogance; Kent has to pretend he is someone else in order to convince his lord of his faithfulness; Gloucester's misplaced love ends in

> *I was many years ago so shocked by Cordelia's death, that I know not whether I ever endured to read again the last scenes of the play till I undertook to revise them as editor.*
>
> Samuel Johnson, commentary to *The Plays of William Shakespeare* (1765)

his physical torture; and both Goneril and Regan fall for Edmund, a doomed passion that he chillingly betrays. Even so, when Cordelia and France's army finally arrives in Britain, it seems as if further tragedy might somehow be averted. Lear is found and taken in, and – in contrast to the fractured meetings between Edgar and Gloucester – father and daughter are movingly reunited. Kneeling in front of Lear, Cordelia prays, "O look upon me, sir,"

> And hold your hands in benediction o'er me.
> You must not kneel.
> LEAR   Pray do not mock.
> I am a very foolish, fond old man,
> Fourscore and upward,
> Not an hour more nor less; and to deal plainly,
> I fear I am not in my perfect mind.
> Methinks I should know you, and know this man;
> Yet I am doubtful, for I am mainly ignorant
> What place this is; and all the skill I have
> Remembers not these garments; nor I know not
> Where I did lodge last night.
>
> [4.6.50–61]

Though still suffering from his ordeal on the heath, Lear does eventually recognize Cordelia and for the moment his insanity dissolves. Touching her weeping eyes and finding them "wet", he is brought into physical contact with his child – a moment echoed in *The Winter's Tale*, when it is touch that alerts Leontes to his wife's survival – as well as with his own plight. It might be said that just as his experiences on the heath teach him what it is to suffer, in this reconciliation the King learns for the first time what it is to love.

The moment is so precious that it is difficult not to interpret it as a sign of Lear's redemption, but if that is true Shakespeare does not grant him any lasting peace. The long-awaited battle between the French army and those of Edmund and the two sisters is both rapid (it is placed almost entirely offstage) and brutal: the invading forces are crushed, and Cordelia is captured with her father. At this point Shakespeare's audiences – at least those who knew the old *King Leir* and were expecting a happy ending – would feel they were on familar ground. After Edmund is fatally wounded by Edgar in single combat, it looks as though the play will right itself at the last moment: overtaken by a last-minute conversion to good, the dying Edmund reveals that his "writ / Is on the life of Lear and on Cordelia" (5.3.220–1) and a messenger is sent to save them before it is too late. The question of whether it *is* too late is one that Shakespeare refuses at first to answer, and the suspense is perhaps more horrific than anything else in the play. Clutching Cordelia's apparently lifeless body as he limps on stage, Lear at first thinks she is dead – but grief soon gives way to desperate hope:

> Howl, howl, howl, howl! O, you are men of stones.
> Had I your tongues and eyes, I'd use them so
> That heaven's vault should crack. She's gone for ever …
> She's dead as earth. Lend me a looking-glass.
> If that her breath will mist or stain the stone,
> Why, then she lives.
>
> [5.3.232–8]

"Is this the promised end?" Kent asks (5.3.238), and we are surely intended to share his bewilderment. Holding a "looking-glass" to the mouth of the living, breathing actor playing Cordelia can only intensify the confusion, and despite Lear's initial certainty ("She's dead as earth") a few seconds later he becomes convinced that she is still breathing. When it becomes apparent that this hope is mere fantasy, the shock of her loss, strung out until the final moment, is almost unspeakable. Lear puts it into plain monosyllables, among the last words he has:

> No, no, no life?
> Why should a dog, a horse, a rat have life,
> And thou no breath at all?
>
> [5.3.281–3]

"Never, never, never, never, never," he concludes, an empty jangle that says both everything and nothing. Nothing makes sense, and it's with that terrifying thought that King Lear dies – and *King Lear* ends.

Stage history and adaptations

The play's early life is mysterious. It was successful enough to be played in front of James I at court, probably with **Richard Burbage** in the lead role and **Robert Armin** as the Fool (that performance, in December 1606, is the first on record), but only one other seventeenth-century reference to the script being acted survives. Perhaps this was why Shakespeare was encouraged to tinker with it (see p.228); at any rate, the existence of an anonymous **ballad** called "A Lamentable Song of the Death of King Lear and his Three Daughters" indicates that the story was well-known enough to be a popular song.

Then came **Nahum Tate**'s 1681 adaptation with the great **Thomas Betterton** as Lear, which introduced a happy ending (see p.230) and was still performed in preference to Shakespeare until the 1830s. **David Garrick** – who first played Lear in 1742 at the age of 25 and continued until retirement 34 years later – progressively restored

Shakespeare's text (while still clinging to Tate's ending), and did much to turn the role into a star vehicle: apparently his final performance reduced even the actresses playing Goneril and Regan to tears. Nevertheless, forty or so years later, the tragedy disappeared from the stage altogether: during the illness of what Shelley memorably called "an old, mad, blind, despised, and dying King" (George III), it was out of the question even to think of putting on *Lear*.

After much hesitation, **William Charles Macready** took the plunge and used a shortened version of Shakespeare's play – and its ending – in 1838, which eventually proved a success. But nineteenth-century audiences proved hard to win over, despite heavy cuts to the text and spectacular, pictorially elaborate staging. **Ernesto Rossi** and **Tommaso Salvini** toured Europe in the 1870s and 80s, both performing in their native Italian, but Henry James, writing in 1883, couldn't imagine "a drama that accommodates itself less to the stage". **Henry Irving**'s 1892 production, which boasted elaborate sets with Druidical and Viking costuming, was a flop.

Only with **William Poel**, and his turn-of-the-century attempts to revive fluid "Elizabethan" staging, did *Lear* regain lost ground. Since then, the play has become a core part of the repertoire and once again a test of the expressive potential of designers as well as actors. **Theodor Komisarjevsky** led the way in 1936 with an expressionistic staging that used lighting for most of its effects, although in **Randle Ayrton** he had an old-fashioned, declamatory actor as the King. One of Poel's actors, **Harley Granville-Barker**, directed an outstanding version at the Old Vic in 1940, with **John Gielgud** in the central role, which stressed what he saw as the play's mythic, fairytale dimension. Four years later the maverick actor-manager **Donald Wolfit** triumphed in his own production at London's Scala Theatre, giving a performance that brought out both the grandeur and the frailty of Lear's character. James Agate in the *Sunday Times* said that Wolfit "opened abysses at our feet", but the fact that the actor continued to tour the same production for years to come rather took the shine off its reputation.

At the New Theatre in 1946 the 39-year-old **Laurence Olivier** directed and played the title role; his performance, if not the production, is widely regarded as one of his greatest achievements. Critics were particularly struck by Olivier's power and vocal brilliance: Harold Hobson felt that "the cries and the lamentations ... that are torn out of his breast are like the crash of thunder and the stab of lightning. They are not the whimpering of a weak old man: they are the groaning and the weeping of the universe."

Gielgud's second attempt at the role, at Stratford in 1950, was distinguished in particular by the tenderness of his scenes with **Peggy Ashcroft**'s Cordelia; while his third, for **George Devine** five years later, became infamous for the bold abstract designs of sculptor **Isamu Noguchi**, which ultimately overwhelmed the play. At Stratford in 1959 **Charles Laughton** was thought to be stronger on pathos than rage: indeed, some found his performance in the play's post-storm scenes almost unbearably moving.

But it was **Peter Brook**'s influential 1962 RSC production, with **Paul Scofield** as the King, that marked a real sea change. Brook pitched *Lear* in bleak postwar terms, with bare staging and minimal costuming – all much influenced by the critic Jan Kott, whose comparisons of the play with Samuel Beckett's *Endgame* had caused a stir. The approach would become one of the defining motifs of twentieth-century

"The two crowns of the egg ..." Belarus Free Theatre offered Lear as a savage folk tale at the Globe in 2012, with Aleh Sidorchik as a bleakly funny King struggling to keep his dignity in the face of insurmountable odds.

performance, as directors attempted to represent the alienation and cynicism of a nuclear and post-nuclear age. **Adrian Noble** also reached for his Beckett in a bleakly comic RSC production from 1982, dominated by **Antony Sher**'s energetic Fool, but with Sher's death (killed by **Michael Gambon**'s Lear in Act Three) the comedy leached out of the play and it became solely tragic.

For all that, more recent productions – of which there are too many to attempt to list here – have avoided obvious approaches to the play. **Peter Zadek**'s 1974 version in the German city of Bochum caused controversy by pitching *Lear* in circus tents and depicting the King sexually assaulting Cordelia. Equally experimental was a version directed by **J.A. Seazer** at the Tokyo Globe in 1991, which interpolated mime scenes to draw out underlying themes. The previous year had seen two major British productions running concurrently: those by **Deborah Warner** at London's National Theatre and **Nicholas Hytner** at the RSC. Critics found themselves divided: some preferred Hytner's sheer theatricality, embodied in **John Wood**'s craggy Lear; others went for Warner's inventiveness, which saw **Brian Cox**'s King enter on a wheelchair sporting a celebratory red nose.

Another year in which British productions competed, 1997, again saw contrasting approaches: **Peter Hall**'s Old Vic staging opted for carefully researched Jacobean dress, but in **Alan Howard** had a vocally mannered and unsympathetic Lear; at the National Theatre **Richard Eyre** found something more timeless in the play, with **Ian Holm** presenting an often child-like King who was nevertheless capable of bouts of terrifying, uncontrollable anger. Rather more radical was a production by **Helena Kaut-Howson** at the Leicester Haymarket; the versatile **Kathryn Hunter** took the title role, and everything was presented as a literal nightmare – the play opening and closing in a run-down nursing home.

At the other end of the imaginative scale was **Jonathan Miller**'s 2002 production at Stratford, Ontario (revived in New York in 2004), which offered a claustrophobic seventeenth-century setting instead of cosmic open spaces, emphasizing *Lear*'s brutal comedy and Hobbesian pessimism. In the lead was **Christopher Plummer**, who produced what some described as the best performance of his lengthy career (the *New York Times* commenting that his was a finely shaded "portrait for the ages, drawn in self-consuming fire"), though **Barry MacGregor**'s music-hall cockney Fool and **Claire Jullien**'s somewhat priggish Cordelia (clearly her father's daughter) were also singled out for praise.

At the RSC in 2007, **Ian McKellen** and **Trevor Nunn** were united for a grandiose staging, paired with *The Seagull,* whose Ruritanian opulence made some think of grand opera, others of *Phantom of the Opera*. McKellen's tottering Lear was notably human in scale, befuddled and self-conscious about the loss of his powers. Not many were impressed by **Kevin Kline**'s attempt at the role later that year at New York's Public Theater, which brought a barrage of dismal press. "I have sat through worse productions," the *New York Times*'s Ben Brantley wrote, "but never have I seen one that left me so utterly unmoved."

King Lear has been more fortunate in its recent British interpreters. **David Calder** won praise in 2008 at Shakespeare's Globe in London, in a Jacobean-style staging directed by **Dominic Dromgoole** – Calder displayed "a humanity, vulnerability and spiritual beauty in the role that is as moving as any I have seen," according to the *Telegraph*'s critic. In 2010 **Michael Grandage** mounted it in a fast, fluent production at London's studio-sized Donmar – consort music rather than epic Romantic symphony. **Derek Jacobi** was a King prim with authority who subsided quietly under the pressures of circumstance, memorably whispering "Blow, winds!" rather than yelling them to the gods. Two years later, Jonathan Pryce appeared as Lear in a production by **Michael Attenborough** at the similarly small-scale Almeida that emphasized a father's abusive relationship with his daughters: "a family, rather than cosmic, tragedy," according to the *Guardian*.

Much larger than either was **Sam Mendes**'s long-awaited version with **Simon Russell Beale** in 2014, staged in the National Theatre's largest auditorium, the Olivier. Beale's bull-necked, bearded Lear was wrathful and powerfully deliberate, yet touchingly fragile once his mental storms had subsided (the recognition scene with **Olivia Vinall** was almost unbearably moving); but Mendes's production, cluttered with supernumeraries, felt unwieldy, and many felt that the decision to show Lear beating his Fool to death with an iron bar was a brutality too far.

Utterly different – refreshingly so – was the pared-down version staged at Shakespeare's Globe in 2012 by the **Belarus Free Theatre** as part of the World Shakespeare Festival, which took the play back to its roots as a savage, ironic folk tale. Dominated by **Aleh Sidorchik**'s lupine Lear, it presented the script as a battle between the generations in which Ancient Britain (or perhaps present-day Belarus) was being thrown to the wolves. Even earthier was the radical reimagining by Dutch auteur **Johan Simons** that opened at Munich's Kammerspiele in 2014: set in what looked like a half-demolished circus (an echo, perhaps, of Zadek at Bochum forty years earlier), it featured a cast of live pigs, who were free to trundle across the stage whenever they wished.

The story of *Lear* on film begins with a 1909 silent version directed by **William Ranous**, and continues through **Grigori Kozintsev**'s 1970 Russian adaptation, translated by Boris Pasternak; **Peter Brook**'s of the following year (derived from his stage production); and **Akira Kurosawa**'s epic *Ran* (a 1985 feudal interpretation in Japanese). The 1980s saw two TV productions, both a little underwhelming. **Jonathan Miller**, who had directed a fine *Lear* with **Michael Hordern** at the Nottingham Playhouse in 1969, filmed a version for the BBC in 1982, again with Hordern as the King and **Frank Middlemass** as an elderly Fool; unfortunately Miller's decision to film his excellent cast almost exclusively in close-up dissipated much of the plays' tension. The next year, Granada wheeled on **Laurence Olivier**, by now far too frail for the role, in a rather earnest and literal production directed by **Michael Elliott**. Much more worthwhile are the filmed versions of two recent stage versions: **Richard Eyre**'s intense National Theatre production, filmed in 1998, and **Trevor Nunn**'s rather more opulent RSC staging, which was released on DVD in late 2008.

SCREEN

King Lear (Korol Lir)

Y. Yarvet, O. Dal, E. Radzin; Grigori Kozintsev (dir.)
USSR, 1970 ➤ Mr Bongo / Facets 𝗗𝗩𝗗

At about the same time Peter Brook was struggling to keep warm in Jutland (see below), across in Estonia Grigori Kozintsev was putting the finishing touches to his Russian film of *Lear*. The two versions have similarities (among them bleak locations and morose black and white texture), but it's the differences that make Kozintsev's version stand out, and a more rewarding cinematic experience. While Brook concentrates unremittingly on the central characters, Kozintsev's opening sequence, which tracks a crowd of peasants limping up to Lear's castle, reveals that this tragedy will shake an entire population. This socialist interpretation is further stressed by the Fool, who remains until the very end – when he is kicked out of the way by one of the King's retinue. At its centre is the Estonian Yuri Yarvet (Kozintsev cast him even though he couldn't speak a word of Russian), whose small frame and imploring eyes make his Lear childish rather than regal; where Scofield is stony, Yarvet is pathetic, conveying perhaps a more

rounded impression of the role. And if you're bilingual you get the best of both worlds: Pasternak's masterly Russian spoken, Shakespeare's text in subtitles.

King Lear

P. Scofield, J. McGowran, I. Worth; Peter Brook (dir.)
UK, 1971 ➤ UCA 𝗗𝗩𝗗

Brook writes approvingly in his book *The Empty Space* (1968) of the cinema's "mobility" versus the static qualities of theatre, and it's tempting to regard his film of *Lear*, released three years later – though distilled from his 1962 Stratford production – as the director's conclusive view of the play. It's a bleak vision: the film's grim, Beckettian no-man's-land (actually Jutland) is permanently snowbound; no human love, it seems, will melt the permafrost. On stage, Scofield's Lear was widely acclaimed as among the finest of its time; on celluloid, it's his face, etched with inexpressible pain and bewilderment, that does all the work – and is sometimes too painful to watch. In fact the whole film presents challenges to its audience: it contains not a note of music; is sufficiently uninterested in narrative flow that on-screen plot summaries become a necessity; and Brook's meandering camera alienates and unsettles – particularly in the "mad" scenes, when the choppy jump-cuts make it feel like you're watching unedited film. This isn't a reading which reflects the complex multifariousness of the play (it cuts Edmund's dying speech, along with much else), but for sheer force it remains unequalled.

Ran

T. Nakadai, A. Tereo, J. Nezu; Akira Kurosawa (dir.) Japan, 1985 ❯ Studio Canal / Lionsgate `DVD` 📥

Akira Kurosawa's second homage to Shakespeare builds on the techniques of his 1957 *Throne of Blood* (see p.265) – translating the story of *Lear* to feudal Japan and freely adapting its contents. The Gloucester subplot is gone, and Hidetora (Lear) has sons, not daughters (Mieko Harada provides the obligatory demonic woman as Lady Kaede, wife of one of the sons). This interpretation, which alternates stretches of remarkable tranquillity with scenes of luridly colourful violence, won't be for everyone – but it is thought-provoking viewing. Inflected by Kurosawa's pessimism about global politics, the entire film seems poised on the brink of the civil "chaos" its title describes. Also available on high-definition Blu-ray.

King Lear

I. Holm, M. Bryant, B. Flynn; Richard Eyre (dir.) UK, 1998 ❯ Metrodome `DVD`

Distilled from Eyre's National Theatre production of 1997, this *Lear* presents all the virtues of a finely honed, well-rounded theatrical production without aspiring to cinematic grandeur. It begins in confined spaces, Bob Crowley's geometric interiors gradually fading away beneath the pelting rain of the heath then onto the miasmatic, eerie setting of Dover and beyond. Holm's Lear is small in stature but every inch the martinet, given to sclerotic spurts of rage at the merest whim. Yet this is very much an ensemble project: there's barely a weak performance here, from Timothy West's doomy Gloucester to Paul Rhys's wide-eyed Edgar, plus Michael Bryant's sourly tubercular Fool and a pair of impressively un-Cruella-like sisters from Barbara Flynn and Amanda Redman. Eyre's sensitivity to nuance keeps the script very much alive, and even though some moments feel a tad rushed, this version's only lasting fault is that it offers little sense of the cosmic abyss into which everyone is plunged.

AUDIO

King Lear

C. Redgrave, J. Waddell, D. Troughton; Cherry Cookson (dir.) UK, 2001 ❯ BBC ◉ 📥

Getting Lear right – even getting just some of him right – is an awesome undertaking, one often compared to mountaineering without the security of ropes. Corin Redgrave does formidably well, rapidly ascending

from cosy indulgence and childish whimsy to howling irascibility: his is a truly astonishing performance. Though the rest of the cast have their work cut out attempting to compete, they manage impressively: also deserving of mention are David Troughton's gruff Kent and Justine Waddell's earnest Cordelia, while William Houston's gleefully mocking Edmund makes an excellent foil to Robert Glenister's quiet and affecting Edgar. Geraldine James is perhaps not haughty enough as Goneril (Kika Markham's part-kittenish, part-wolvish Regan leads the way), though Paul Copley does his utmost to make the Fool's role work convincingly on audio – and very nearly succeeds. A few touches of music aside (and the obligatory rumbles of canned thunder), the soundscape is restrained but atmospheric – some of it was recorded in a chapel – making the whole production a remarkably intense experience.

King Lear

P. Scofield, A. McCowen, K. Branagh; John Tydeman (dir.) UK, 2002 ❯ Naxos ◉ 📥

Of Paul Scofield's many Shakespearian roles, his Lear under Peter Brook has passed most firmly into legend, an early summit in a sixty-year career on stage and among the century's finest. His return to the role on audio forty years later (at 80, he was at last the right textual age) is more measured than earlier incarnations, and takes time to warm up: this Lear is solid granite to Redgrave's seething lava. If Scofield's collapse into despair is surprisingly quiet, his puzzled insanity feels disconcertingly real – though the creaking sound effects that recreate the storm all but ruin his carefully shaded performance. Still, this production is directed by one of the most experienced names in radio drama and the cast is to die for. Decades after they appeared on stage in the play, Alec McCowen rejoins Scofield as a twinkling Gloucester (his successor as the Fool, Kenneth Branagh, displays an under-exploited gift for this kind of comedy); Harriet Walter is a nervy Goneril to Toby Stephens's urbanely malevolent Edmund, and David Burke is deep-hearted Kent. The text follows Jay Halio's Folio-based edition (see below).

EDITIONS

New Cambridge Shakespeare

Jay L. Halio (ed.); 1992 ❯ Cambridge UP

Halio's edition (one of the fattest in the New Cambridge series) is based on the 1623 Folio version of *King Lear* (see p.228), and it's an impressive way into this version of Shakespeare's text. If sometimes a little prolix, Italio's introduction is a model of its kind, and provides an exhaustive survey of the play's thematic concerns and its various spin-offs, paying welcome attention to its life on screen as well as in the theatre. Halio also includes an extensive analysis of *Lear*'s textual history, defending his choice of text with vigour but providing plenty of detail on the issues at stake, including parallel passages drawn from both quarto and Folio. The notes will be erudite and detailed enough for even the most enquiring of readers, and the editor also presents some sensible suggestions for further reading. A terrific achievement.

King Lear: A Parallel Text Edition
René Weis (ed.); rev. 2010 > Routledge

If you're interested in the variant texts of *Lear* – and there is much that's genuinely fascinating – René Weis's ingenious edition, recently revised, presents Folio and quarto side by side, allowing you to see just what the differences and similarities are. His notes are hugely helpful, and the introduction takes readers through the suggestive if sometimes technical opportunities offered by a two-text *Lear*. A new preface argues suggestively that the ways in which the texts connect reveals a great deal about the ways in which the playwright's company (rather than the author himself) reshaped the play for later performances. Stanley Wells's Oxford edition (2001), based solely on the quarto version, is also well worth looking up.

SOME CRITICISM

The Wheel of Fire
G. Wilson Knight; rev. 1949 > Routledge

This collection of Shakespearian essays, two of which focus on *King Lear*, is as readable and as thought-provoking in its fourth edition as when it first appeared in 1930. The first piece looks at the play's grotesque comedy, while the second focuses on what the author memorably christens "the *Lear* Universe", its larger-than-life philosophical scope and deployment of apparently cosmic forces (Knight insists that "mankind's relation to the universe is [the play's] theme"). Though critical fashions may have moved on, Knight's eloquent analysis of the contradictions at the heart of *Lear* is a persuasive example of the image-based and thematic readings he pioneered. The play seems large enough for this brand of interpretation, which has the further advantage of appearing less fatalistic (or indeed less black and white) than some other approaches. If you're eager to test Knight's larger claims against more sceptical recent approaches, *Shakespeare Survey 55*, edited by Peter Holland, contains valuable essays on *Lear* and its afterlife.

Shakespearean Negotiations
Stephen Greenblatt; 1988 > Oxford UP

Authored by the founding member of the new historicist movement, this book is idiosyncratic, dense and sometimes downright bizarre. But it's also a virtuosic display, and Greenblatt's essay on *Lear*, "Shakespeare and the Exorcists", showcases the insights that can result from approaching it via contemporaneous, non-"literary" documents – in this case a Catholic-bashing pamphlet that was a key source. Though the entire new historicist movement have come under fire for their sometimes eccentric approaches to texts (Greenblatt freely admits that he is most interested in "what can only be glimpsed, as it were, in the margins"), it's bracing stuff. The book also contains provocative accounts of several other plays, including *Twelfth Night*, the *Henry IV*s and *Henry V*, and *The Tempest*.

Love's Labour's Lost

L
ove's Labour's Lost has sometimes been compared to the "curious-
knotted garden" that the Spanish braggart Don Armado rhapsodizes
about early in the play: a winding comic maze, filled with interesting
corners and diverting patterns but not a great deal else. Though a drama
of love, it has been said to lack the romantic intensity of *Romeo and Juliet*,
while its plot (which seems to be the playwright's own invention) has been
criticized for its whimsically farcical qualities, one reason it disappeared from
the stage for the best part of two centuries. But the play can also be one of
Shakespeare's most fleet-footed and funniest, and it is above all a transitional
work – a comedy which dares to end in near tragedy, a conclusion that keeps
both critics and audiences guessing. The first of what have been called the
"lyrical" dramas, followed by *A Midsummer Night's Dream* and *Richard II*,
Love's Labour's Lost showcases the pleasures of delighting in language, but
also the dangers. The social worlds of the play collide with sometimes prickly
hostility, and beneath the extravagant verbal sparring enjoyed by everyone
there lies a vein of painful pathos.

DATE > Most likely 1594 or 1595, around the same time as *A Midsummer Night's Dream*, *Romeo and Juliet* and *Richard II*.

SOURCES > No direct sources survive, though given that the real-life Henri of Navarre (1553–1610) had two lords named Biron and Longueville, it has been conjectured that the play derives from a lost account of them. Other possible analogues include Pierre de la Primaudaye's *L'Académie Française* (1577) and Robert Wilson's play *The Cobbler's Prophecy* (c. 1594), and there are clear debts to the Italian *commedia dell'arte* tradition.

TEXTS > Two: the quarto of 1598 (Q) – actually impossible to act owing to its confusing speech-prefixes, probably the result of foul-ups by the author – and the 1623 Folio (F1).

Interpreting the play

Love's Labour's Lost relishes games – games with words, games of acting, games of
love. It opens in apparent seriousness, with a resolution by the King of Navarre and
his three lords to devote themselves to stern and stringent pursuits. In the name of
what Dumaine proudly calls "philosophy" (1.1.32), they will study, fast, be celibate
and sleep for three hours a night, for a whole three years. The joke, of course, is that
they haven't the remotest chance of achieving it. Biron, the most cynical of the lords
as well as by far the wittiest, is reading the agreement among them aloud when he
realizes there are problems:

MAJOR CHARACTERS & SYNOPSIS

King Ferdinand of Navarre
Biron, **Longueville** and **Dumaine**, lords attending
  the King
Princess of France
Rosaline, **Catherine** and **Maria**, ladies attending
  the Princess
Boyet, a French lord attending the Princess
Don Adriano de Armado, a braggart from Spain
Mote, Don Armado's page
Mercadé, a French messenger
Costard, a clown
Jaquenetta, a dairymaid
Sir Nathaniel, a curate
Holofernes, a schoolmaster
Anthony Dull, a constable

ACT 1 King Ferdinand has proclaimed a new
moral order. Persuading his lords to sign an
agreement renouncing women and dedicating
themselves to three years of study, he hopes
to turn the court into the academic envy of the
world. But aristocrats aren't alone in feeling
the effects: the countryman Costard is brought
before the King and punished for attempting
to woo Jaquenetta. The insufferably pompous
Don Armado, who has informed against
Costard, reveals why – he covets Jaquenetta
for himself.

ACT 2 But the King's plan hits an unexpected
obstacle. The Princess of France has arrived
in Navarre with three ladies, announcing that
her father will repay an outstanding loan – but
Ferdinand disputes the figures, claiming he is
owed more. While the legalities are clarified,
Ferdinand is forced to accommodate the party
(much to the secret delight of his lords). Each
clandestinely asks for details about their female
guests: Longueville likes Maria, Dumaine fancies
Catherine, while Biron is keen on Rosaline. Even
King Ferdinand seems to have a crush on the
Princess.

ACT 3 Don Armado makes a move for
Jaquenetta by employing Costard to send her an
impassioned love letter. Thinking along the same
lines, Biron recruits Costard to deliver his own
letter to Rosaline.

ACT 4 Finding the ladies out hunting, Costard
produces Don Armado's letter by mistake.
Without realizing his error, Costard then delivers
the other letter to Jaquenetta and they ask the
pretentious schoolmaster Holofernes to read it
out. Biron, meanwhile, has overheard the King
composing love poems in private, and they both
hear Longueville doing the same. Dumaine
then walks by, trying out his own poetry, at
which point Longueville emerges from hiding
and accuses him of breaking their agreement.
The King follows, criticizing them both, but
Biron waits until last and accuses all three of
hypocrisy. Unluckily for him, though, Jaquenetta
and Costard arrive, brandishing his own letter to
Rosaline. The four men agree to forget their pact
and set about wooing the ladies in earnest.

ACT 5 Don Armado greets Holofernes,
Nathaniel and Dull with news that he has been
commanded by the King to provide an entertainment for the Princess. The four suitors, meanwhile, disguise themselves in order to win their
ladies; having been forewarned, the ladies mask
up and pose as each other in order to embarrass
their visitors. When the lords reappear, this time
as themselves, the ladies pretend not to have
recognized them, but Biron realizes that they
have been duped. Renouncing all stratagems,
the lords promise to woo honestly from now
on and everyone settles down to watch the
entertainment performed in their honour.
Don Armado and the others boldly attempt to
present a pageant of the nine most famous
people in history (the "Nine Worthies"), but
the result is predictably risible, Don Armado's
own self-important impersonation of Hector
coming unstuck when Costard announces that
Jaquenetta is pregnant by the Spaniard. Don
Armado and Costard are scuffling when Mercadé
suddenly arrives with a message that the
Princess's father has died. Despite entreaties to
stay and agree to marriage, the Princess resolves
to return home and mourn for her father.
However, she announces that she will reconsider
the King's proposal one year on – subject to his
good behaviour. The other ladies make the same
demand of their respective suitors.

'Item: if any man be seen to talk with a woman within the term of three years, he shall endure such public shame as the rest of the court can possibly devise.'

This article, my liege, yourself must break;
   For well you know here comes in embassy
The French king's daughter with yourself to speak—
   A maid of grace and complete majesty—
About surrender-up of Aquitaine
   To her decrepit, sick and berid father.
Therefore this article is made in vain …

[1.1.128–37]

Lost en route

Quite apart from the debates concerning Shakespeare's real identity, other questions about his work nag editors and students – not least how many works he actually wrote (see p.618). There is another problem, too: some texts have apparently disappeared for good.

The oldest mystery concerns **Love's Labour's Won**, a play mentioned by Elizabethan writer Francis Meres in a gushing list of Shakespeare's early works. No play by that name survives, and some have argued that the title is merely an alternative for a canonical work such as *Much Ado About Nothing* or *All's Well That Ends Well*. But that hasn't dampened speculation. Not so long ago the eminent Shakespearian Cedric Watts attempted to conjure up a plot – commenting gleefully that "to do so is a temptation that it seems sinful to resist" – and the fictional discovery of a missing manuscript even formed the basis for a 1948 detective story by high-class thriller writer Edmund Crispin. Real life has proved almost as exciting (at least for scholars): five years after Crispin's novel was published, a bookseller's inventory from 1603 was unearthed, recording a work named "loves labours won" and thus implying that a separate play really did exist. If this is indeed the case, the puzzlingly sombre ending of *Love's Labour's Lost* – where marriage between the main characters is left hanging in the air in a most un-Shakespearian fashion – might make more sense. Perhaps the playwright decided on a multi-part comedy to rival his experiments with the histories of *Henry VI*.

Questions also hang over a play from the other end of Shakespeare's career. In 1613 the King's Men performed at court a drama the records call "Cardenno" or "Cardenna", but the work (attributed to Shakespeare and John Fletcher) doesn't surface again in the records until 1653, well after the closure of the theatres under Oliver Cromwell, and appears never to have made it into print. **Cardenio**, as it's now known, was apparently based on Cervantes's *Don Quixote*, and if it was new when the King's Men performed it, it was probably Fletcher and Shakespeare's first collaboration. Heminges and Condell failed to feature it in the First Folio (but probably not on the grounds of co-authorship; they included *Henry VIII*), and it passed into obscurity. Notwithstanding, a spin-off entitled *Double Falsehood; or, The Distressed Lovers*, "Written Originally by w. shakespeare", appeared courtesy of playwright **Lewis Theobald** in 1728 and was performed successfully at Drury Lane. But the original script – Theobald claimed to have access to three separate copies – has long since vanished, perhaps in one of the numerous fires that plagued candlelit eighteenth-century theatres.

And with that, in one sense, much of the plot is over. From the speed with which their compact breaks down, it is easy to guess that it won't be long before the King and his lords have fallen further; in fact fallen head over heels for the French Princess and her three ladies. The King is "shamed" by his own ridiculous edict, and with the entry of the women the real game of the play – the game of love – can begin.

For all that it seems inevitable, the process by which the lords come to the realization that love has ensnared them occupies over half the action. It approaches its comic climax near the end of Act Four in a gloriously witty scene in which the lords are forced to admit that, far from keeping to their vow of chastity, each and every one intends to dispose with it. The entire plot hinges on this event, and yet what might be the tensest moment in the comedy is also its most tongue-in-cheek, a simultaneously daring and silly piece of stagecraft. Safely hidden up a tree, Biron overhears first the King, then Longueville, then Dumaine, all rehearsing love poems. At its most complicated, there are no fewer than three lords hidden from view (invisible to each other but visible to Biron) while the unfortunate Dumaine reads out a halting "sonnet" for his lover. Intricately constructed though it is, the scene is patently ridiculous. As Biron gleefully exclaims, "All hid, all hid—an old infant play."

> Like a demigod here sit I in the sky,
> And wretched fools' secrets heedfully o'er-eye.
>
> [4.3.75–7]

As the scene builds up, so it unravels: Longueville appears, accusing Dumaine of hypocrisy; the King steps in, rounding on them both; and finally Biron descends from his hiding place, reproaching them all and exclaiming with breathtaking self-righteousness that "I that am honest, I that hold it sin / To break the vow I am engagèd in" (4.3.175–6). Except, of course, that he has broken the vow, too, as everyone realizes when Jaquenetta and the clownish Costard burst in with Biron's own missive to the "celestial" Rosaline.

The scene never becomes too serious: the lords' progress towards self-awareness is constructed through a series of comic blunders – first believing that they are alone in love, then that they can hide it from the others, then that they have exposed someone else. Though they are transformed, they are transformed into the same thing. As Biron declares:

> Sweet lords, sweet lovers!—O, let us embrace.
>   As true we are as flesh and blood can be.
> The sea will ebb and flow, heaven show his face.
>   Young blood doth not obey an old decree.
> We cannot cross the cause why we were born,
> Therefore of all hands must we be forsworn.
>
> [4.3.212–7]

The chiming rhymes and jaunty pulse of Biron's speech confirm that all's well that ends well: everyone is in love (as we, the audience, knew they were all along), and there's no more to say.

"Discourse peremptory ..." Christopher Godwin brought a nicely fustian fussiness to the part of the schoolmaster Holofernes in Dominic Dromgoole's Globe production of 2007.

Obscene and most preposterous

There is in fact plenty more to say, for *Love's Labour's Lost* is also one of Shakespeare's most talkative plays. According to one count, it uses more "new" words (words the playwright hadn't used before) than any other work. Critic Frank Kermode noted that, just as its characters adore wordplay and fast-talking quibbles, so over sixty per cent of the comedy's lines are rhymed, a figure unrivalled by any other Shakespearian play. But what those figures don't indicate is that in *Love's Labour's Lost* language is often wildly out of control. While the King and his lords are in the process of repenting their hasty words, also resident in Navarre are two characters, the schoolmaster Holofernes and his curate sidekick Nathaniel, who provide an extreme example of what it is like to have too much language. Their speech is peppered with obscure literary allusions and classical tags, while mere conversation provides the opportunity for rhetorical one-upmanship and grammatical point-scoring. The Princess's killing of a deer while out hunting furnishes the schoolmaster with an excuse to put his linguistic virtuosity to the test. Promising to "something affect the letter" (use alliteration in the manner of old-fashioned verse), he launches into an "extemporal epitaph" celebrating the occasion:

> The preyful Princess pierced and pricked a pretty pleasing pricket.
>   Some say a sore, but not a sore till now made sore with shooting.
> The dogs did yell; put 'l' to 'sore', then 'sorel' jumps from thicket—
>   Or pricket sore, or else sorel. The people fall a-hooting.
> If sore be sore, then 'l' to 'sore' makes fifty sores—O sore 'l'!
> Of one sore I an hundred make by adding one more 'l'.

[4.2.56–62]

It's tempting to think that this speech has lost something in historical translation, but in fact Elizabethan audiences would probably have been as puzzled by it as we are. This monstrous exercise, rather like Holofernes himself, is amusing but socially dysfunctional: it fails to make language useful. Congratulated by Nathaniel on his "rare talent", Holofernes, flattered, replies: "This is a gift that I have, simple, simple—a foolish extravagant spirit, full of forms, figures, shapes, objects, ideas, apprehensions, motions, revolutions ..." (4.2.66–8). The more he cycles through synonyms, the less he seems to mean.

Where Holofernes and Nathaniel are content to impress each other, yet another resident at court, the Spaniard Don Armado, has grander ambitions – to cement a friendship with the people he aspires to regard as equals, King Ferdinand and his intimates. The problem is that Don Armado's addiction to what he calls the "sweet smoke of rhetoric" (3.1.61) illustrates some of the social dangers of saying the wrong things. Blissfully unaware that even his page, Mote, sneers at him, he writes to the King, informing on Costard's illegal liaison with Jaquenetta. He aims to impress: addressing the King somewhat implausibly as "Great deputy, the welkin's vicegerent and sole dominator of Navarre, my soul's earth's god, and body's fostering patron", he continues in awkwardly grandiose style:

> So it is, besieged with sable-coloured melancholy, I did commend the black-oppressing humour to the most wholesome physic of thy health-giving air, and, as I am a gentleman, betook myself to walk. The time when? About the sixth hour, when beasts most graze, birds best peck, and men sit down to that nourishment which is called supper. So much for the time when. Now for the ground which—which, I mean, I walked upon. It is yclept thy park. Then for the place where—where, I mean, I did encounter that obscene and most preposterous event that draweth from my snow-white pen the ebon-coloured ink which here thou viewest, beholdest, surveyest, or seest ...
>
> [1.1.216–39]

Searching desperately for a courtly tone, Armado gets it stunningly wrong. Rather like his performance as Hector in the pageant of the Nine Worthies near the end of the play – which ends in even greater fiasco than the artisans' play in *A Midsummer Night's Dream* – Armado's incapacity to judge how he appears, and how he speaks, renders him an ignominious figure of fun. A similar fate meets Holofernes, whose own impersonation of Judas Maccabeus is destroyed by heckling, and who wretchedly exclaims that his treatment is "not generous, nor gentle, nor humble" (5.2.622). In moments such as these, it is possible to see Shakespeare hinting at what will become increasingly apparent in his later comedies: that words really can bruise.

Well mocked

For, while the characters in *Love's Labour's Lost* are frequently playing games with one another, the stakes are sometimes perilously high. While the King and his lords

> *The disruptions perpetrated by the characters eventuate in the destruction of the romantic form, the form which is ideally the literary celebration of the wedding of individuals, sexes, and classes. The King's last-minute plea for the Princess's hand has already been disgraced by death.*
>
> Louis A. Montrose, "'Sport by sport o'erthrown': *Love's Labour's Lost* and the politics of play" (1977).

indulge in ivory-tower fantasies, the Princess and her three ladies, in the critic Anne Barton's words, "come from a world outside the confines of Navarre that is colder and more realistic than the playground of the park". They arrive on financial business, sent to repay an outstanding loan from the French court, and from the first they refuse to indulge the niceties of politesse – or insist on seeing through it. Meeting the party outside the court, the King nobly declares them "welcome to the court of Navarre". But the Princess does not hide her disapproval that they are to be left camping outside. "'Fair, I give you back again,'" she indignantly exclaims,

> and welcome I have not yet. The roof of this court is too high to be yours,
> and welcome to the wide fields too base to be mine.

[2.1.91–4]

Her skill at deflation is even sharper in the scene where the lords decide to dress up as "frozen Muscovites" in order to represent their enslavement to love. Tipped off beforehand and with Boyet as go-between, Rosaline and her companions set to work on wilfully misinterpreting their suitors' claim to have "measured many miles" in pursuit:

BOYET
    If to come hither you have measured miles,
    And many miles, the Princess bids you tell
    How many inches doth fill up one mile.
BIRON
    Tell her we measure them by weary steps ...

ROSALINE   How many weary steps
    Of many weary miles you have o'ergone
    Are numbered in the travel of one mile?
BIRON
    We number nothing that we spend for you.
    Our duty is so rich, so infinite,
    That we may do it still without account.

[5.2.190–9]

Biron survives what Boyet later calls "the tongues of mocking wenches", but only just – and, anyway, the game is already lost. The disguised ladies have baffled their suitors, and when Biron later realizes that they have all been duped, the Princess has succeeded in doing what she declared at the outset:

To make theirs ours and ours none but our own.
So shall we stay, mocking intended game,
And they well mocked depart away with shame.

[5.2.153–5]

It's for these kind of reasons that *Love's Labour's Lost* has sometimes been interpreted as a reply to the male-supremacist attitudes prevalent in *The Taming of the Shrew*. But the play is about more than the battle of the sexes: it is ultimately cynical about the ability of any of its characters to transcend reality. Far from concluding as Biron and the others expect it will, *Love's Labour's Lost*, as its title suggests, ends unhappily. Just as the comedy is at its sharpest, news arrives that the Princess's father has died, the "scene begins to cloud" (5.2.714) and the ladies refuse – for the moment – to wed their suitors. Biron is sent by Rosaline to use his wit on the "speechless sick", and similar trials are constructed for his colleagues. The lords will need to do more than say they are in love if their lovers are to believe them. As Biron ruefully comments, "Our wooing doth not end like an old play":

> Jack hath not Jill. These ladies' courtesy
> Might well have made our sport a comedy.
> KING
> Come, sir, it wants a twelvemonth an' a day,
> And then 'twill end.
> BIRON   That's too long for a play.

[5.2.860–4]

"Too long" indeed – the playing has come to an end. Some have interpreted this dark ending as a forcible growing-up; others have read into it Shakespeare's unhappiness with comic form itself; still others have suggested that he is preparing for a now-lost sequel (see p.242). Whatever the truth, *Love's Labour's Lost* gives its audiences plenty of serious things to think about.

Stage history and adaptations

Though the 1598 **first quarto** loudly proclaims that *Love's Labour's Lost* was "presented before her Highness [Elizabeth I] this last Christmas" (presumably the winter of 1596–97, though possibly a year earlier), it was also popular on the public stage – as the publication of a poem by one Robert Tofte, in which the poet describes taking his girlfriend to see the play, testifies. The year 1598 also saw the publication of **Francis Meres**'s *Palladis Tamia*, a pioneering work of literary criticism that set out to compare "our English poets, with the Greek, Latin and Italian poets" and spoke glowingly of twelve of Shakespeare's plays, among them *Love's Labour's Lost*.

At any rate, the play stayed very much in repertoire. It was performed for James I's wife, Anne, at the **Earl of Southampton**'s house during the extended festivities over Christmas 1604–05. (Though Shakespeare's colleague Richard Burbage apparently recommended the comedy for its "wit and mirth", he hadn't much choice – the Queen had already seen every new play they were offering.) We also know that *Love's Labour's Lost* was played at the **Blackfriars**, the permanent winter home of Shakespeare's company from about 1609 onwards, but what we don't know is how they performed the extended final act – which appears to be longer than candles of the time could cope with without guttering and filling the theatre with smoke.

It wasn't lighting issues, though, that kept *Love's Labour's Lost* off the stage for nearly two hundred years. Regarded as the least revivable play in the canon, it was the only one of Shakespeare's dramas not to be performed in the eighteenth century. An anonymous adaptation entitled *The Students* (1762) seems never to have been acted, and even the dogged **David Garrick** failed to get the "musical" version he commissioned in 1771 onto the boards – suggesting that other producers shared **John Dryden**'s view that *Love's Labour's Lost*, *The Winter's Tale* and *Measure for Measure* were "either grounded on impossibilities, or at least, so meanly written, that the Comedy neither caus'd your mirth, nor the serious part your concernment".

In fact, *Love's Labour's Lost* had to wait until 1839 and the redoubtable **Elizabeth Vestris**, one of the great actress-managers of the period, to see the inside of a theatre again. Her production was lavish, with gorgeous costumes by **J.R. Planché**, but on the opening night at Covent Garden the audience was more concerned by the high ticket prices and came close to rioting. The next staging came in 1857 under the industrious **Samuel Phelps** in an Arcadian setting which won some plaudits, but the play failed to catch on and was infrequently acted for the rest of the century (though it reached the US in 1874, in a Broadway production by **Augustin Daly**, favourably received by the *New York Times* as "an unquestionable success"). It was performed at the birthday celebrations in Stratford-upon-Avon in 1885 – apparently its sheer obscurity singled it out for attention – but soon afterwards **George Bernard Shaw** wondered whether it was "worth viewing at this time of day".

Despite **Harley Granville-Barker**'s assumption that *Love's Labour's Lost* was an apprentice piece, his influential *Preface* (1927) to the play claimed that all a successful production needed was "style in the acting". At the Westminster Theatre five years later, his advice was heeded by **Tyrone Guthrie,** who employed eighteenth-century costumes and staging, and even persuaded the arch-sceptic editor John Dover Wilson to change his mind. Guthrie directed the play again in 1936, this time at the Old Vic with a strong cast (but rather threadbare set) that included **Alec Clunes** as Biron and **Michael Redgrave** as the King of Navarre.

But it was the next major production of *Love's Labour's Lost* that proved to be a watershed: it was the 1946 Stratford debut of the 21-year-old *wunderkind* **Peter Brook**, who – like Guthrie – raided the early eighteenth century, this time in imitation of the wistful Rococo paintings of Jean-Antoine Watteau. Brook presented the play elegiacally, with **Paul Scofield** as a mournful, Don Quixote-like Armado. **Hugh Hunt** put it on just three years later, with **Redgrave** as Biron and **Diana Churchill** as Rosaline (this time in Elizabethan costume), and also saw success. **Laurence Olivier** staged the play at the National Theatre in 1969, but offered it in starker terms – unlike Brook, who gradually dimmed the lights towards the end, Olivier's Mercadé appeared suddenly, "as if from nowhere".

Since then, *Love's Labour's Lost* has become a solid favourite, being mounted four times in major British productions during the 1970s and frequently in the US. **David Jones's** production at the RSC was well received in 1973, with **Estelle Kohler** as Rosaline opposite **Ian Richardson**'s show-stealing Biron. **John Barton**, again at Stratford, told his actors to "think Chekhov" five years later, exploring the painful side of love. Barton attempted to be deliberately anti-romantic, with **Richard Griffiths** a distinctly podgy King opposite **Carmen Du Sautoy**'s spectacles-wearing Princess; **Michael Pennington** played Biron to **Jane Lapotaire**'s Rosaline. Over in Stratford, Ontario, in the same year **Robin Phillips** further underscored the play's sense of doom by setting it in 1914 to the rumbling of distant guns. **Trevor Nunn** deployed a similar strategy with his 2003 National Theatre version in London, which emphasized the play's icier elements by opening it with a tableau of the Western Front to which **Joseph Fiennes**'s consummately sarcastic Biron and **Kate Fleetwood**'s mischievous Rosaline were destined to be sent.

Dominic Dromgoole's 2007 Globe production bucked this elegiac, modernizing trend with an Elizabethan setting and an emphatically broad comedic approach, in which **Trystan Gravelle**'s Welsh-accented Biron and **Gemma Arteton**'s elegant Rosaline were a sparky double act. At Stratford a year later, **David Tennant** played a Scottish Biron with the same energy and charm that he had brought to Hamlet in the same season. His engaging performance was let down by what some critics felt was **Gregory Doran**'s fussy Elizabethan-style production. **Peter Hall**'s approach, in the same year, was much more respectful – some thought *too* respectful – of the play's textual subtleties. Austerely staged at the Rose Theatre at Kingston upon Thames (a modern theatre based on the dimensions of the Elizabethan Rose), it featured **Finbar Lynch** as a sombre but intelligently spoken Biron and **Peter Bowles** haughtily absurd as Don Armado – but the comedic honours went to **William Chubb** as a pompous yet sympathetic Holofernes.

Despite the play's challenge to translators, *Love's Labour's* has experienced a healthy life in non-Anglophone countries, often appearing in surprisingly political guises, especially in the Soviet Union – a 1987 production in Prague using a translation by **Martin Hilsky** made pointed use of the theatre's "iron" or fire curtain, which threatened to descend and cut off the action at any time, interpreted as sardonic commentary on the USSR. Even more fraught was the production mounted inside the ruined Babur Garden in Kabul, Afghanistan, by the French director **Corinne Jaber** in 2005; the Lords' decision to renounce women had a powerful resonance given the presence of the Taliban, and Jaber's mixed local cast faced death threats for performing alongside each other, the women bravely not wearing traditional burqas.

Exploring the play's linguistic experimentalism, Shakespeare's Globe commissioned the Deaf-led theatre company **Deafinitely** to adapt the play into British Sign Language for its contribution to the World Shakespeare Festival in 2012, thought to be the first time ever that the play has been translated into BSL. In **Paula Garfield**'s production, the cast used the Globe space with winning physicality and verve, with **Charly Arrowsmith** an antic and scene-stealing Rosaline. In 2014, the RSC mounted their own experiment, coupling *Love's Labour's Lost* with *Much Ado About Nothing* (here subtitled *Love's Labour's Won*). In **Christopher Luscombe**'s paired productions, the setting became an elegant English country house, with *Love's Labour's* ending during World War I and *Much Ado* picking up immediately after the end of hostilities – "shades of *Downton Abbey*," according to one critic – with a musical score that made knowing reference to Noël Coward and Gilbert and Sullivan.

In North America, meanwhile, the play remains perhaps surprisingly popular: a musical adaptation by **Alex Timbers** with songs by **Michael Friedman** debuted at New York's Shakespeare in the Park in 2013, albeit to lukewarm reviews, while **John Caird**'s Poussin-influenced revival was enthusiastically received at the Stratford, Ontario festival of 2015: "so much love in it," declared the Toronto *Star*, "that nothing is lost".

There have been no fewer than five silent films from 1912 onwards, but **Kenneth Branagh**'s 1999 version has been the only English-language movie to make the modern big screen; though wanly reviewed, its intriguing decision to present Shakespearian conceits through the prism of golden-age musicals had the benefit of novelty. In 2014, Argentinian writer-director **Matias Pineiro** released *The Princess of France*, a loose Spanish-language adaptation-cum-tribute to *Love's Labour's Lost* set in contemporary Buenos Aires. Despite the relocation, critics were unimpressed: "flimsy and thin, like clever scribblings in the margin of a book," according to the *New York Times*. **Elijah Moshinsky** directed the BBC TV Shakespeare version in a Regency-style staging in 1984, but this production (despite **Maureen Lipman**'s dignified Princess) was generally considered one of the weakest in the series.

SCREEN

Love's Labour's Lost
K. Branagh, A. Silverstone, N. Lane; Kenneth Branagh (dir.) UK, 1999 > Fox / Miramax **DVD** ⬇

Easy-going it may be, but this version of *Love's Labour's Lost* is not without charm. In homage to the heyday of Hollywood musicals, Branagh sets the action in a kind of soundstagey Oxbridge (wittily designed by Tim Harvey) and at crucial moments has his cast spin on their heels and croon American songbook standards by Porter, Kern, Gershwin and company instead of launching into sonnets and masques. This cleverly translates the play's own stylization into something cinematically more approachable, even if most of its linguistic crossfire ends up on the cutting-room floor (and it has to be said that Branagh's own singing voice, along with others in his cast, wouldn't have made it past Irving Berlin). In the end, though, you can't help thinking that it would all look so much better with the colour turned down.

Love's Labour's Lost
E. Bennett, M. Terry, S. Alexander; Christopher Luscombe (dir.) UK, 2015 > RSC / Opus Arte **DVD**

Offered as a two-disc set with something called "Love's Labour's Won" (known to the rest of us as *Much Ado*),

Christopher Luscombe's live 2014 RSC production cleverly offers a diptych in which World War II forms the central panel. *Love's Labour's Lost*, set in something resembling an all-male 1930s college, goes heavy on the tennis whites, but is none the worse for that, and it's a useful solution to the colliding worlds of the play. The action is sensitively staged, centred on Edward Bennett's plummy Biron and Michelle Terry's gimlet-eyed Rosaline, who have plenty of world-weary chemistry and are very much a study for Beatrice and Benedick. Courtesy of John Hodgkinson, even the Don Armado scenes aren't overdone, and the conclusion, set against the gathering clouds of war, offers a genuine chill.

AUDIO

Love's Labour's Lost
A. Jennings, E. Fielding, S. Bond; Clive Brill (dir.) UK, 1998 > Arkangel ◉ ⬇

Perhaps it's only in audio that you can get the true measure of the wordiest play in the canon, but *Love's Labour's Lost* needs careful handling: done too slowly it fails to take flight, too fast and it becomes a blur of wordplay. Generally speaking this production gets the mix just right, and it's helped along the way by a genuinely terrific cast, one that must make Clive Brill the envy of many a stage director: Alex Jennings as a homely

Biron, Samantha Bond's delightfully pointed Princess and Emma Fielding's sprightly Rosaline are just some of the highlights. Alan Howard rather hams it up as Don Armado, but it's the kind of role in which you can get away with it.

EDITIONS

New Cambridge
William C. Carroll (ed.); 2009 > Cambridge UP

Despite strong competition from Henry Woudhuysen's Arden 3 (1998), William C. Carroll's more recent edition is the one to use. Carroll is one of the foremost authorities on the play, author of the pioneering study *The Great Feast of Language* (see below), and offers a thoughtful yet no-nonsense account of its many different aspects, from its interest in homoerotic tension to its fascination with showy stagecraft. A complex first quarto text is spruced up well, and Carroll's performance history is the most up to date currently available, impressively including Corinne Jaber's remarkable 2005 production in Kabul (see p.249).

SOME CRITICISM

The Great Feast of Language
William C. Carroll; 1976 > Princeton UP

Even a few moments spent watching or reading *Love's Labour's Lost* makes it clear that Mote is only too accurate to remark on "the great feast of language" in the play (a feast from which Holofernes and company have merely "stolen the scraps"). There is so much to say on the subject that the reader might seem at risk of being swamped, but Carroll's approach is clear, presenting various different aspects of the play's language – linguistic style, theatrical devices, self-conscious "poetry" – before moving on to link these with its larger themes. *The Great Feast of Language* is a welcome rehabilitation of a comedy which has often been (as Carroll puts it) "the darling of the Shakespearean lunatic fringe", and it is one of the first examples of the language-based analyses that have done so much to revive interest in Shakespeare's comedies. Keir Elam's *Shakespeare's Universe of Discourse* (1984) goes even further, taking the comedies and testing them against linguistic theory.

Shakespeare's Comedies
Emma Smith (ed.); 2004 > Blackwell

Smith's reader, one of Blackwell's valuable guides to criticism, is hugely useful on the concept of Shakespearian comedy as a whole and on *Love's Labour's Lost* (which plays so teasingly with the form) in particular. Particularly valuable are a classic feminist account of the play from Katherine Eisaman Maus (1991), a perceptive examination of the homoerotic tensions in the comedies by Valerie Traub (1992) and Russ McDonald on Shakespeare's linguistic games (2001). Smith's account of varied critical trends from the 1590s to the present is expertly done, and Lisa Hopkins's essay on "Marriage as Comic Closure" is a timely reminder that *Love's Labour's* is not the only play to subvert the expectation that wedding bells invariably produce happy endings.

Macbeth

Macbeth, Shakespeare's shortest and darkest tragedy, has never lost its ability to shock. "The Scottish play", as it is still nervously known in the theatre, is attached by long-standing tradition to all manner of unlucky occurrences – quite apart from those dictated by the script, which are unlucky enough. It was more than likely written to honour King James VI of Scotland, who took the English throne in 1603, and whose distant ancestor Banquo appears as the most honourable of Macbeth's victims. But the tragedy itself refuses to be cast in black and white: whereas *Othello* distils its evil into the tempter Iago, in *Macbeth* the hero steadily, inexorably becomes the villain. So it is, too, with the merciless Lady Macbeth, who despite being in many ways the most fearsome character of all (far more so, in fact, than her husband) ends up a victim of the play, her sanity shattered by the brutal march of events. Though many fine productions have responded sensitively to the otherworldly, eerie aspects of this unique tragedy, *Macbeth* never forgets that the demons we conjure ourselves are the ones we should fear.

DATE > From internal evidence – notably a cryptic reference to the trial of the Gunpowder Plot conspirators – *Macbeth* was probably first performed in 1606, around the time that *Antony and Cleopatra* was written.

SOURCES > Raphael Holinshed's massive *Chronicles* (revised 1587) provided Shakespeare with the story of Macbeth and Duncan, as well as other material. George Buchanan's *Rerum* *Scoticarum Historia* (1582) possibly offered further leads, and Matthew Gwynne's Latin pageant *Tres Sibyllae* (performed for James I in 1605) has been linked to *Macbeth*.

TEXTS > Only the Folio version (1623) survives. This was probably derived from a playhouse script, thought to be an adaptation by Shakespeare's younger colleague Thomas Middleton.

Interpreting the play

Macbeth is, quite literally, a murky play. The great critic A.C. Bradley put on paper what is obvious to audiences from its very first moments. "Darkness, we may even say blackness, broods over this tragedy," he wrote. "It is remarkable that almost all the scenes which at once recur to memory take place either at night or in some dark spot." Those dark corners – Macbeth's vision of the dagger, Duncan's murder, Banquo's murder, Lady Macbeth's tormented sleepwalking – guide us rapidly through the action of the play, from the Macbeths' craving for power and the savage murders they per-form to secure it to the erosion into dusty nothingness of everything they hold dear.

But one major component is missing from Bradley's scheme, and it is far more memorable to audiences:

MAJOR CHARACTERS & SYNOPSIS

King Duncan of Scotland
Malcom, Duncan's elder son
Donalbain, Duncan's younger son
A **Captain** in Duncan's army
Macbeth, Thane of Glamis
Lady Macbeth, Macbeth's wife
Porter at Macbeth's castle
Seyton, servant of Macbeth
Banquo, a thane, and his son Fleance
Macduff, Thane of Fife
Lady Macduff, Macduff's wife
Lennox, **Ross**, **Angus**, **Caithness** and **Menteith**, thanes
Siward, Earl of Northumberland, and his son **Young Siward**
Hecate, Queen of the Witches
Six **Sisters/Witches**

ACT 1 War divides Scotland as the rebellious Macdonald fights against King Duncan. But Duncan has the resolute Thane of Glamis, Macbeth, on his side and the battle goes their way. Returning from the war, Macbeth and his fellow general Banquo suddenly encounter three witch-like Sisters, who prophesy that Macbeth will be rewarded and one day become king, while his companion's ancestors will prosper. As the witches vanish, a party from Duncan arrives, announcing that – as predicted – Macbeth is now Thane of Cawdor. Reeling from the news, Macbeth writes to his wife, who resolves that her husband needs to be helped on his way to power. So when news arrives that King Duncan intends to stay at their castle overnight, she persuades the reluctant Macbeth that their only option is to murder him.

ACT 2 As Macbeth steals towards Duncan's chamber, his resolve weakens as he comes across Banquo and then is troubled by strange hallucinations. Nonetheless, as Lady Macbeth waits and Duncan's drugged guards sleep, Macbeth kills the King. Shortly afterwards Macduff arrives at the palace and discovers Duncan's corpse. Feigning horror, Macbeth murders the guards, who Lady Macbeth has attempted to frame by smearing

them with blood. Fearing for their own lives, Donalbain and Malcom flee – thus arousing suspicion of their involvement. Macbeth is now king: the Sisters' prophecy has come true.

ACT 3 Although Banquo harbours doubts about his friend's role in events, he agrees to celebrate the coronation at a banquet. But Macbeth wants Banquo dead, and arranges for assassins to murder him and his son Fleance. The attempt is botched, however, and Fleance escapes. That night at the banquet, Macbeth alarms his guests when he sees what he thinks is Banquo's ghost. The dinner breaks up in disarray. Lennox and another lord discuss their misgivings about Macbeth and how Macduff is trying to raise an army against him.

ACT 4 Macbeth visits the Sisters, desperate for information about his future. He is warned about Macduff but also told that "none of woman born / Shall harm Macbeth". Hearing that Macduff has escaped to England, Macbeth orders the deaths of his wife and children. In England, meanwhile, Malcom falsely describes himself to Macduff as dissolute and unfit to be King; when Macduff recoils, Malcom knows him to be loyal to Scotland. The two men are discussing the campaign against Macbeth when news arrives that Macduff's entire family has been slaughtered.

ACT 5 Back in Scotland, Lady Macbeth has been sleepwalking and raving about the various murders. By this time Malcom's forces are marching on the King's castle, Dunsinane, carrying branches to disguise their approach. Macbeth – convinced that the Sisters have predicted his invincibility – refuses to acknowledge the threat until he hears that Lady Macbeth is dead and that Birnam Wood is moving towards them. He fights on, eventually coming face to face with Macduff, whom he learns was delivered by Caesarian section. Macduff succeeds in killing him and presents his head to Malcom, hailing him as the new King of Scotland.

FIRST WITCH
> When shall we three meet again?
> In thunder, lightning, or in rain?

SECOND WITCH
> When the hurly-burly's done,
> When the battle's lost and won.

THIRD WITCH
> That will be ere the set of sun.

FIRST WITCH
> Where the place?

SECOND WITCH   Upon the heath.

THIRD WITCH
> There to meet with Macbeth.

FIRST WITCH
> I come, Grimalkin.

SECOND WITCH
> Paddock calls.

THIRD WITCH   Anon.

ALL
> Fair is foul, and foul is fair,
> Hover through the fog and filthy air.

[1.1.1–11]

Though centuries of theatrical familiarity and an increasingly secularized culture have done a fine job of stripping the "Weird" or "Weyard" Sisters of their capacity to inspire terror ("weird" in this instance retaining its medieval meaning of someone who has prophetic skills), Shakespeare's audiences, brought up on lurid tales about the potency of witchcraft, and who might have witnessed first-hand the persecution of women believed to be witches, would not have been nearly so relaxed. Though it is unclear whether this brief scene, the very first in the play, takes place at night, it deserves to appear in any list of *Macbeth*'s eeriest moments. If played convincingly, the Sisters unleash something genuinely terrifying into the play, bridging the gap between the world that we know and comprehend, and the wild, chaotic space beyond it. The Sisters "look not like th'inhabitants o'th' earth," Banquo exclaims, "and yet are on't" (1.3.39–40).

The message the Weird Sisters deliver to Macbeth, that he will be "king hereafter", confirms that they live up to their name – as he himself realizes once their first prediction, that he will be made Thane of Cawdor, comes true. "This supernatural soliciting," he murmurs, "cannot be ill, cannot be good."

> [T]hough in Macbeth the strife of mind is greater than in his wife, the tiger spirit not so awake, and his feelings caught chiefly by contagion from her,—yet, as both were finally involved in the guilt of murder, the murderous mind of necessity is finally to be presumed in both.
>
> Thomas De Quincey, "On the Knocking at the Gate in *Macbeth*" (1823)

> If ill,
> Why hath it given me earnest of success
> Commencing in a truth? I am Thane of Cawdor.
> If good, why do I yield up to that suggestion
> Whose horrid image doth unfix my hair
> And make my seated heart knock at my ribs
> Against the use of nature?
>
> [1.3.129–36]

One man who took witches sufficiently seriously to publish a book about them was the monarch for whom *Macbeth* was almost certainly written: James I. Many scholars believe that Shakespeare's Scottish play was composed to honour the Edinburgh-born king who had recently taken control of the English throne, uniting the two nations for the first time and also extending his patronage to Shakespeare's company, which became the King's Men. Shakespeare repaid his and his colleagues' debt in fine style, returning to the main source for his English histories, the sprawling *Chronicles* (1587) published by Raphael Holinshed and others, and drawing out from the "History of Scotland" the tale of the eleventh-century thane Banquo, believed to be the ultimate ancestor of all Scottish monarchs, James included.

Yet of course Shakespeare decided not to write a story directly about Banquo, but about the erstwhile colleague and companion who became his murderer – the infinitely more fascinating figure of Macbeth. As well as being more dramatically engaging, Holinshed's account contained the suggestive hint that Macbeth relied on supernatural advice to govern Scotland, something that in *Macbeth* becomes a defining theme. Partly this must have been to catch King James's interest in such matters, but in so doing Shakespeare also creates a dramatic world in which witchcraft and humankind become dangerously – and tragically – entangled. In a strange kind of way (and the play is nothing if not strange), the Sisters are intended to be "the heroines of the piece", as critic Terry Eagleton puts it.

Unsex me here

It would be interesting to know what James – or his contemporaries – made of another rogue female who dominates *Macbeth*: the hero's wife. Building, again, on stray hints in Holinshed (that Lady Macbeth was "very ambitious"), Shakespeare conjures a character who, despite the many things about her that remain enigmatic (not least her first name, which is never mentioned, even by her doting husband) has exercised a powerful influence over the imagination of audiences and critics alike. Shakespeare had already created malevolent women who wrestle with demons (Joan la Pucelle in *Henry VI Part I* is the clearest example), but Lady Macbeth outstrips them effortlessly, being both theatrically powerful and ruthlessly chilling. Receiving the news that Duncan is to stay that night at their castle, she calls upon "you spirits / That tend on mortal thoughts" to

> unsex me here,
> And fill me from the crown to the toe top-full

Of direst cruelty. Make thick my blood,
Stop up th'access and passage to remorse,
That no compunctious visitings of nature
Shake my fell purpose, nor keep peace between
Th'effect and it. Come to my woman's breasts,
And take my milk for gall, you murd'ring ministers ...

[1.5.39–47]

Lady Macbeth seems to make her very femaleness paradoxical and dangerous, "stopping up" her sensitivity to "remorse" as if it were menstrual blood; giving out "gall" from her "woman's breasts" as well as taking it in. To the cultural stereotype that a woman's rightful place is to rear and care for children, she has a brutal answer. "I have given suck," she declares,

and know
How tender 'tis to love the babe that milks me.
I would, while it was smiling in my face,
Have plucked my nipple from his boneless gums
And dashed the brains out, had I so sworn
As you have done to this.

[1.7.54–9]

By "this" she means the murder of King Duncan, and Lady Macbeth stops at nothing in driving her husband on – at first taunting his manliness ("Was the hope drunk /

David Garrick as Macbeth and Hannah Pritchard as Lady Macbeth, roles they played regularly between 1748 and 1768. As Johann Zoffany's depiction indicates, it was customary to perform Shakespeare in contemporary dress in the eighteenth century.

Wherein you dressed yourself?" she scoffs), then claiming that she would "dash the brains out" of their own child had she promised to do so. Though the question of whether the Macbeths actually have children – they are not mentioned elsewhere – remains a puzzling lacuna in the play (a lacuna male critics have spent a great deal of energy attempting to fill), what is important here is that Lady Macbeth's ghastly words make her sound still more like the Sisters: both mother and murderer, good and evil, fair and foul.

The word of promise

The play would be meaningless, however, if witchcraft had sole sway: it would be over before it began. The Sisters may ordain, but they do not perform the many "horrid deed[s]" Macbeth and his wife take upon themselves on their bloody path to the throne. Yet they do make the hero's grip on events seem disturbingly slippery. Though almost impossible to observe in performance (events move too fast), what is striking when reading *Macbeth* is that the idea of killing Duncan, the play's all-important point of no return, seems to originate from nowhere. The Sisters insinuate that Macbeth will be King of Scotland, but not how he should go about achieving it. Even Lady Macbeth, after hearing of their prophecies, skirts coyly around the subject, noting that though her absent husband is "not without ambition", he is "too full o'th' milk of human kindness / To catch the nearest way" (1.5.16–18) – "the nearest way" meaning, of course, murdering their ruler (and guest) in cold blood. Though the milk she has eradicated from herself apparently lingers in her husband, ironically it is she who can't quite bring herself to spell out what murder might mean.

Macbeth, by contrast, does his utmost to confront the philosophical complexity of his situation. Though initially comforting himself with the thought that "if chance will have me king, why chance may crown me / Without my stir" (1.3.142–3), it soon becomes apparent that things require considerably more than that. By the time that Duncan has entered the castle and a feast prepared in his honour, Macbeth is already imagining in a kind of jumpy doublethink past the murder to what lies beyond:

> If it were done when 'tis done, then 'twere well
> It were done quickly. If th'assassination
> Could trammel up the consequence, and catch
> With his surcease success: that but this blow
> Might be the be-all and the end-all, here,
> But here upon this bank and shoal of time,
> We'd jump the life to come.

[1.7.1–7]

The extraordinarily choppy texture of these lines, and their tongue-tripping quality for actors, show Macbeth trying to think through what seems unthinkable. His language is thick with euphemisms – "assassination" is a chilly coinage for "murder" (this is its first appearance in the English language); "his surcease" means "Duncan's death" – and Macbeth seems to be arguing, or at least hoping, that this one killing will

The Scottish Play

Perhaps inevitably for a tragedy that lends witchcraft such a major role (let alone one that takes place almost entirely at night), *Macbeth* has long been associated with malign theatrical forces. Legend has it that its curse began during an early run when a boy actor named **Hal Berridge** died of pleurisy while playing Lady Macbeth. Although the story is probably apocryphal – most likely an invention of Victorian wit Max Beerbohm – his ghost has proved difficult to exorcize: scholars have discovered a child christened "Henry Berredge" in July 1593, making him just the right age for the part.

Even if Beerbohm was making all this up, he might have been seeking to explain an already established tradition. Some attribute it to the fact that *Macbeth*, a sure-fire hit, was used as a standby when less successful productions foundered. Others date it to the great Irish actor **Charles Macklin**, whose ground-breaking 1772 production, which imposed "authentic" Scottish costume and made the Weird Sisters spooky rather than comic, ended up provoking a riot after supporters of his rival, Garrick, stormed the stage. Although he soldiered through to the end, Macklin was sacked soon afterwards. An even worse riot occurred in May 1849 when the English tragedian, **William Charles Macready**, attempted to appear as Macbeth at the Astor Place Opera House. Opposing him were the supporters of his former friend, but by now arch-rival, the American **Edwin Forrest**. Whipped up by rabble-rousing nationalists, an estimated 20,000 people hit the streets and, as the play began, hurled paving stones and other debris at the theatre. Eventually the National Guard were called in, and in the ensuing chaos some thirty people were shot dead.

In the twentieth century the curse has gained further high-profile victims. An early casualty was the Russian pioneer of "method" acting, **Konstantin Stanislavsky**: when his Macbeth suffered a memory lapse during the dress rehearsal, the prompter failed to deliver his cue – and was found dead in his box, a grim omen that closed the show. Likewise, **Laurence Olivier**'s 1937 staging at the Old Vic was beset by a catalogue of woes including sets that didn't fit, a director who had to be replaced after a car crash, and Olivier himself narrowly escaping being crushed by a stage weight. When Lilian Baylis, the Old Vic's redoubtable founder, died during final preparations, it seemed that the curse had truly taken hold.

Peter Hall, staging the play at Stratford thirty years later with Paul Scofield and Vivien Merchant, urged his actors to ignore the superstition – and was rewarded with a vicious case of shingles. The show had to be postponed, and when it finally reached the stage, was judged a failure despite its impressive cast. But these disasters pale in comparison to **Oldham Rep**'s revival of *Macbeth* in 1947. A few nights into the run, the climactic fight between Antony Oakley's Macduff and Harold Norman's Macbeth seemed to audiences to be more realistic than usual, and as the curtain fell it became obvious why – Norman had been stabbed in the chest. He died soon afterwards.

Theatre is a notoriously superstitious profession, and while nothing more sinister than low lighting and a higher than usual density of sharp objects may account for the play's ill luck, many actors are unwilling to take on the curse. Except when performing it, they never refer to *Macbeth* by name in a theatre or quote from the text (acceptable euphemisms include "The Scottish Play"). If these rules are broken, the offender must leave the building, turn around three times, then spit or swear. But the curse surfaces in the oddest of places, as the ever-industrious actor-manager **Donald Wolfit** discovered to his cost during a touring version of *Macbeth* in the 1940s. Disgruntled about his low wages, a young actor playing a Messenger decided to make a few last-minute adjustments to the script in order to register his feelings. So instead of announcing Lady Macbeth's sudden death to Wolfit's expectant King, he coolly walked on stage and declared: "My lord, the Queen is much better ... and is even now at dinner." It may have been the only time in his lengthy and voluble career that Wolfit was lost for words.

be the last, that it will be the "be-all and the end-all". He imagines cause and effect being "trammelled" (bundled up) together into one instant, feverishly plotting far beyond the immediate moment ("this bank and shoal of time") into "the life to come". The critic William Empson commented on this speech that "the meanings cannot be remembered all at once, however often you read it. It remains the incantation of a murderer, dishevelled and fumbling among the powers of darkness."

Despite Macbeth's best hopes, however, Duncan's murder isn't by any means the "be-all and the end-all"; it is only the beginning. "Blood will have blood" (3.5.121)," as the hero remarks later on, and the lurid vision of a dagger stained with "gouts of blood" that led him to Duncan's chamber proves an apt symbol of what Macduff calls the "bloody-sceptred" tyrant who wrests control of Scotland. Just after the deed is done, Macbeth gazes at his blood-stained hands, imagining them polluting the visible world:

> Will all great Neptune's ocean wash this blood
> Clean from my hand? No, this my hand will rather
> The multitudinous seas incarnadine,
> Making the green one red.

> [2.2.58–61]

Macbeth's terror is more than the fear that their crime will be discovered: it is that he has unleashed forces that will ultimately tear him apart. The vision of the oceans stained crimson by Duncan's assassination is too gruesomely extravagant to be true, but when Macbeth's coronation supper is interrupted by the "gory" ghost of the recently murdered Banquo (the Macbeths' second major victim), it seems that anything is possible. "The time has been / That, when the brains were out, the man would die, /And there an end," Macbeth cries out, to his wife's horror, "But now they rise again …" (3.4.77–9).

Baffled and panicked by Banquo's ghost, Macbeth heads once again to the Sisters. What he finds there, instead of the appealing certainties of before, is a series of dark riddles. Though the Sisters say that "none of woman born / Shall harm Macbeth" (4.1.96–7), Macduff is somehow still a threat; though Macbeth has nothing to fear until "Great Birnam Wood to high Dunsinane Hill … come against him", the last vision he sees depicts a sequence of Banquo's descendants stretching out as far as Doomsday. From these mixed assurances, equivocal as anything in the play, Macbeth constructs a kind of comfort – after all, if you can't conceive of a forest rising up against you, what have you to be scared of? What is a talisman protecting you against anyone "of woman born" if not a guarantee of immortality? What the Sisters offer Macbeth is the certainty that his mind is the only limit: he only need imagine it for it to be true.

But Macbeth's brain is, as he anxiously reflects to his wife, "full of scorpions" (3.2.37), and, like her – as the Doctor later comments to a serving woman – he has known what he should not. Although he isn't the first casualty of this knowledge (Lady Macbeth, discovered sleepwalking and guiltily washing her hands of Duncan's blood, is that), the sudden announcement that his wife is dead

– presumably suicide, though the play leaves the verdict open – initiates a speech in which Macbeth pictures himself gazing into the abyss. "She should have died hereafter," he mutters,

> There would have been a time for such a word.
> Tomorrow, and tomorrow, and tomorrow
> Creeps in this petty pace from day to day
> To the last syllable of recorded time,
> And all our yesterdays have lighted fools
> The way to dusty death.

> [5.5.16–22]

Life is, he concludes, "a tale / Told by an idiot, full of sound and fury, / Signifying nothing" (5.5.25–7). Endlessly repetitive, it is also ultimately futile, a stuttering sequence of tomorrows.

As the tragedy hurtles towards its conclusion, the sequence of horrors Macbeth has performed and provoked – Duncan's murder, Banquo's death, the slaughter of Macduff's wife and children – turn decisively against him. In a bizarre spin on the perversion of nature for which he is responsible, Birnam Wood does indeed rise up against Macbeth, in the form of Malcom's and Macduff's soldiers carrying branches in the hope of confusing enemy scouts. But *Macbeth* reserves its biggest twist for last. Confident of immortality, Macbeth vows to fight until "from my bones the flesh be hacked" (5.3.33), slaying Young Siward and facing Macduff undaunted. When the pair finally meet in combat, Macbeth taunts, "Thou losest labour … I bear a charmèd life" (5.10.8–12). But Macduff's reply stops him dead:

> Despair thy charm,
> And let the angel whom thou still hast served
> Tell thee Macduff was from his mother's womb
> Untimely ripped.

> [5.10.8–16]

Macduff boasts that he was delivered via Caesarean section – a dangerous last-ditch operation in seventeenth-century England, let alone feudal Scotland, and one that invariably resulted in the death of the mother. The revelation is fittingly unreal (another word that appears for the very first time in the play), and in it Macbeth recognizes a bitter irony. "Accursed be the tongue that tells me so," he gasps,

> For it hath cowed my better part of man;
> And be these juggling fiends no more believed,
> That palter with us in a double sense,
> That keep the word of promise to our ear
> And break it to our hope.

> [5.11.17–22]

Suicide is either a protest or an admission of guilt. Macbeth does not feel guilty, and there is nothing for him to protest about. All he can do before he dies is to drag with him into nothingness as many living beings as possible.

Jan Kott, *Shakespeare Our Contemporary* (1964)

By his "better part" Macbeth means his courage; we know as well as he that anything good has long since drained away. The circumstances of Macduff's birth have sentenced Macbeth to death; the Sisters' "promise" proves worthless. And like so much else in the play, Macbeth realizes that his "hope", too, signifies absolutely nothing.

Stage history and adaptations

It's likely that *Macbeth* was popular when it reached the **Globe** in around 1606, probably with **Richard Burbage** as Macbeth and **Robert Armin** as the Porter. The astrologer Simon Forman saw it there four years later and, like many subsequent theatregoers, was impressed by the "3 women fairies or nymphs" and Lady Macbeth's sleepwalking scene. **Thomas Middleton** (possible collaborator on *Timon*) overhauled the play a few years later, adding Hecate and some dance scenes for the Sisters. But the most famous seventeenth-century adaptation was **William Davenant's** (1664), which beefed up the Macduffs' roles while underscoring Macbeth's similarities to the hated Cromwell and adding some spectacular flying witches (achievable with Restoration stage technology). **Thomas Betterton** and his wife **Mary** acted, to triumphant receptions: Pepys saw them no fewer than eight times, and one night his own wife walked out rather than suffer Betterton's understudy.

James Quin succeeded Betterton from 1717, but in 1744 was eclipsed by **David Garrick**, who announced that his performances alongside **Hannah Pritchard** would be "as written by Shakespeare" (not wholly true, but the text was more authentic than anything seen since the 1660s). The next great Macbeth, **Charles Macklin**, didn't dare challenge Garrick's signature role until his seventies, and outdid him only sartorially – with "authentic" Highland costume. Later in the 1770s **John Philip Kemble** turned his attention to the play, and, despite his own impressive performance in the lead, had the mixed fortune to be acting alongside his remarkable sister, **Sarah Siddons**, perhaps the greatest of all Lady Macbeths. Pre-empting Stanislavskian techniques by over a century, Siddons observed sleepwalkers in order to get inside the role, and was acclaimed for a "womanly" interpretation that nonetheless led her to seem almost "above nature", as the critic William Hazlitt breathlessly exclaimed.

Macbeth also became popular in Germany in this era, with **Friedrich von Schiller's** adaptation of 1800 and **Ferdinand Fleck's** celebrated acting leading the way. **Edmund Kean** was perhaps Fleck's English equivalent, and he guided the play into the Romantic era, but compared to his sensational Richard III, his Macbeth hit the heights only in bursts. **William Charles Macready**, who played him constantly from 1821 to 1848, was more successful and Macbeth soon became one of his most celebrated roles, with critics singling out the terrifying way he recoiled at the sight of Banquo's ghost. By 1847, when **Samuel Phelps** put on *Macbeth* at Sadler's Wells, the fashion for extravagant staging had begun to take over. Phelps's productions indicated witchcraft by spreading green gauze across the front of the stage, but as ever **Charles Kean**'s vast sets and massive reserves of extras stole a march on his rivals, in this instance when his ultra-"Scottish" *Macbeth* debuted in 1853.

The American **Charlotte Cushman**, famed for her Romeo (see p.394), was Macready's leading lady for a time, and during the latter end of the nineteenth century the play became more than ever Lady Macbeth's drama. The remarkable Italian actress **Adelaide Ristori** toured an adaptation by **Giulio Carcano** (later used as the basis for **Giuseppe Verdi**'s celebrated opera) in the 1850s, yet the most celebrated Lady Macbeth of the era was probably **Ellen Terry** – though several critics felt she wasn't sharp-edged enough for the role. First seen in **Henry Irving**'s Lyceum production of 1888, Terry was unforgettable in an incandescent red wig and a dress covered with glittering beetle-cases, and outshone not merely Irving's Macbeth but also his gargantuan Pre-Raphaelite sets. Not all Macbeths would be so easily outdone. The towering Italian **Tommaso Salvini** toured the play during the 1870s and 80s, and the virtuosic Austrian actor **Friedrich Mitterwurzer**, who acted it from 1877 onwards, did his utmost to upstage everything else (even Banquo's ghost, which he attacked in a frenzy).

Herbert Beerbohm Tree's staging, though it premiered in 1911, was virtually the last gasp for overblown Victorian *Macbeths*. Within twenty years **Barry Jackson**'s Birmingham Rep had staged a modern-dress version, and by 1933 the avant-garde **Theodor Komisarjevsky** was directing it at Stratford as an Expressionist nightmare, with an aluminium set dominated by a large staircase. Even more radical was the version mounted in Harlem, New York by the 21-year-old **Orson Welles** three years later: known as the "voodoo" *Macbeth*, it was set in nineteenth-century Haiti and had an all-black, mainly amateur, cast. **Donald Wolfit** provided a momentary throwback to Victorian times with his blood-and-thunder touring production, which began life in 1937. Employing such devices as a change of wig for the hero (red in the first half, white in the second), it was loved by the public but the critics were merciless, James Agate describing it as a "ranting, raving, Saturday night melodrama". **Margaret Webster**'s production at New York's National Theatre in 1941 was conventional but rather less corny, and it boasted two outstanding performances – from **Maurice Evans** as Macbeth and **Judith Anderson** as Lady Macbeth.

Macbeth's difficulty – or curse – is such that most critics list just a handful of defining postwar productions. **Paul Rogers** earned rave reviews at the Old Vic in 1954, but it is **Glen Byam Shaw**'s production at Stratford in 1955 that remains the touchstone, partly because of its glamorous leading couple, **Laurence Olivier** and **Vivien Leigh**. Despite his idiosyncratic way with the verse, Olivier received almost unanimous praise ("he radiates a kind of brooding sinister energy," wrote one critic, "a dazzling darkness"), perhaps because he took the unusual step of building in intensity towards the end of the play; and even Leigh, long dismissed as a pretty face and not much else, won plaudits. By contrast, the reviewers savaged **William Gaskill**'s modish Royal Court production eleven years later, not least because **Alec Guinness** as Macbeth was too

Lady Macbeth (Judi Dench) tries to persuade her husband (Ian McKellen) to return the daggers to the scene of Duncan's murder – exactly the same moment as depicted in the Zoffany painting on p.256.

low-key and **Simone Signoret** as Lady Macbeth largely unintelligible, but also because with its pared-down sets it refused to glamorize the play.

That reluctance to approach *Macbeth* as a heroic work also characterized what has been for many its most powerful late-twentieth-century incarnation, that directed at the RSC by **Trevor Nunn** from 1976 onwards. Audiences at Stratford's intimate The Other Place (and later in London) were exposed to an interpretation that magnified the play's unnerving darkness. With the production design restricted originally by a budget of just £250, all the action took place within a small chalk circle – which Macbeth traversed anticlockwise, a demonic device – and gave unusual prominence to the Sisters. Yet it was also psychologically gripping, notably in the compelling relationship between **Ian McKellen**'s twitchy but magnetic Macbeth and **Judi Dench**'s powerhouse of a wife.

Few modern productions have been blessed with such effusive reviews. One was **Gregory Doran**'s 1999 RSC version, set in a nameless but clearly contemporary militaristic state, with **Antony Sher** as a bluff soldier and **Harriet Walter** as his wild-eyed spouse (later filmed for TV). Another was **Rupert Goold**'s 2007 staging, which opened at the Chichester festival before transferring successfully to the West End. Set in a bleak 1940s hospital ward, it offered comparisons between medieval Scotland and Stalinist Russia, with **Patrick Stewart**'s blunt officer-turned-psychopath and **Kate Fleetwood**'s steely accomplice. The *Evening Standard* gushed that it was "the *Macbeth* of a lifetime". Back at the RSC in 2011, the play became – bravely, given its cursed reputation – the first production to be seen inside the remodelled Royal Shakespeare Theatre. **Michael Boyd**'s blood-soaked production was acclaimed for its chilling unreality, with **Jonathan Slinger** playing a peroxide-blonde soldier only too keen to turn into a serial killer, and **Aislin McGuckin** equally creepy as his wife.

Shakespeare's Globe in London has played host to two recent stagings: one a modern-dress version by the Polish company **Kochanowski**, part of the World Shakespeare Festival in 2012; and a Jacobean-style staging directed by **Eve Best** the following year, which was warmly if not over-enthusiastically received. Somewhat stronger was the reaction to **Rob Ashford**'s hyper-realistic version for the Manchester International Festival in 2013, which transformed a deconsecrated church into a bloody, muddy medieval battlefield, with **Kenneth Branagh** statuesque and forthright as the hero.

Macbeth has never been as much of a star vehicle as *Hamlet*, but big-name castings have begun to make their presence felt in recent years, particularly in Britain and America (notably **Ethan Hawke** in a dismally received version at New York's Lincoln Center in 2013 and **James McAvoy** in a rather better West End one in 2014). Undeniably the play's most egocentric recent reinterpretation featured Scottish actor **Alan Cumming** in an absorbing one-man adaptation directed by **John Tiffany** first in Glasgow, then in New York. Nervily patrolling a set that resembled a psychiatric hospital, Cumming offered a literally schizophrenic approach to the play, acting out every major role as if reliving the psychological trauma of its events.

The play has also had a number of innovative non-English reworkings – particularly in places where its political or philosophical content has acquired resonance. a production by **Xu Xiaozhong** made many think of the tyrannical Mao Ze Dong when it appeared in Beijing in 1980, and elsewhere on the globe *Macbeth* has been grafted successfully onto folk drama, notably in India, with **Utpal Dutt**'s various Bengali versions, one of which was staged during the Indian Emergency in 1975, **B.V. Karanth**'s *Barnam Vana* (1979) from the southwestern state of Karnataka, and **Lokendra Arambam**'s well-regarded *Stage of Blood*, which premiered in 1997 at Imphal in the northeast of the subcontinent. The UK has seen a number of touring foreign-language productions, notably **Yukio Ninagawa**'s picturesque but powerful Japanese version, which arrived in 1985; and **Welcome Msomi**'s popular Zulu reworking *uMabatha*, which has toured the world and appeared most recently at the London Globe in 2000.

Though regarded as theatrically troublesome, *Macbeth* has received considerable attention on screen, most clearly with big-budget movies such as those by **Akira Kurosawa** (1957) and **Roman Polanski** (1971); but also with smaller projects developed from stage productions – notably **Orson Welles's** typically distinctive 1948 film; Hall of Fame's 1960 TV version with **Maurice Evans** and **Judith Anderson**; and **Trevor Nunn**'s TV adaptation (1978). It has also occasioned several spin-offs, among them gangster movies by **Ken Hughes** (*Joe Macbeth* from 1955) and **William Reilly** (*Men of Respect*, 1991). Another gangsterized adaptation was **Geoffrey Wright**'s 2007 version, which set the action in a blinged-up Melbourne underworld; the Sisters were naughty schoolgirls, while **Sam Worthington**'s Macbeth sported designer threads. The 1982 BBC/Time-Life production was directed by **Jack Gold**, starring **Nicol Williamson** and **Jane Lapotaire**. In 2003 Indian director **Vishal Bhardwaj** imaginatively relocated the play to Mumbai in a *Godfather*-inspired version called *Maqbool*.

More recently, in 2015, a British-produced movie, directed by Australian **Justin Kurzel** and starring **Michael Fassbender** and **Marion Cotillard**, received considerable acclaim; the *Telegraph* delivered the somewhat breathless verdict that it "unseams the famous Shakespearian tragedy open from the nave to the chops, letting its insides spill out across the rock underfoot".

SCREEN

Throne of Blood (Kumonosu-Jo)
T. Mifune, I. Yamada, M. Chiaki; Akira Kurosawa (dir.) Japan, 1957 ➤ BFI / Criterion **DVD** ⬇

Akira Kurosawa had long aspired to transplant Shakespeare's own retelling of distant Scottish history to the screen, but, hearing that Orson Welles planned likewise, delayed doing so. Yet *Throne of Blood* (*Kumonosu-Jo*, "The Castle of the Spider's Web", in Japanese) is in an entirely different league from most films of Shakespeare. Set amid a painstakingly realized warrior aristocracy of medieval Japan, it retains practically none of Shakespeare's language, thins out his characters (though the lead couple are powerfully played by the ever-fierce Toshiro Mifune and a chilling Isuzu Amada) and removes several key components of his plot. But what *Throne of Blood* lacks in linguistic texture it recreates through vibrant visual poetry and an impressive command of atmosphere, all marshalled by typically expert editing. Kurosawa has

an innate grasp of what makes inspirational film, even if that means ignoring Shakespeare – so Tsusuki/Duncan's murder is handled wordlessly, while Washizu/Macbeth dies not in single combat but under a storm of arrows in a truly astonishing final sequence. Quintessential auteur cinema, and the most perfect Shakespearian movie in existence.

Macbeth
J. Finch, F. Annis, J. Stride; Roman Polanski (dir.) UK, 1971 ➤ Sony **DVD** ⬇

Immediately notorious because it was part-funded by Playboy mogul Hugh Hefner, this violent *Macbeth* also attracted scandal because it seemed to draw on the director's own personal experiences – notably the brutal murder of his wife by followers of Charles Manson's cult. Behind the headlines, though, there lies a fine movie, co-scripted with drama critic Kenneth Tynan and filmed with thoroughgoing realism in a moody medieval Scotland (actually Wales). Polanski's emphasis is heavily on the lead couple, Jon Finch and the gamine Francesca Annis – both young, sexy and credible, if somewhat raw. Things fall apart, however, when it comes to audio: Polanski redubbed a large percentage of the film, and the results are mixed – partly because soliloquies are frequently done in voice-over, partly because it is clearly difficult to muster with's-end terror in a sound booth. Two nuggets of trivia: contrary to popular rumour, Hefner did not insist that Annis's sleepwalking scene should be done in the nude (that was Polanski's idea); and fans of British low-end TV might enjoy spotting a youthful – and jowly – Keith Chegwin vamping it up as Fleance.

Macbeth
I. McKellen, J. Dench, J. Woodvine; Philip Casson (dir.) UK, 1978 **>** Fremantle / A&E **DVD**

Trevor Nunn's innovative 1976 RSC production stressed the play's suffocating claustrophobia by locking the action within a small circle, emphasizing its demonic qualities and deploying Ian McKellen's histrionic powers in the title role to devastating effect. Collaborating with Philip Casson in this reworking for Thames TV, Nunn determined to "photograph the text", nothing more, attempting to preserve what McKellen has called the "intimate horror" of the whole experience. In many ways video is the ideal medium for what is sometimes regarded as the finest of all TV Shakespeare adaptations, and it features particularly impressive performances from Judi Dench (Lady Macbeth) – her unearthly scream near the end of the play will have you cowering into the cushions – and John Woodvine as a granitic Banquo. McKellen himself occasionally risks overdoing it, but in a scenario this terrifying who could blame him?

Maqbool
I. Khan, Tabu, P. Kapoor; Vishal Bhardwaj (dir.) India, 2003 **>** Eagle **DVD**

Director Vishal Bhardwaj might have decided to make this version of Macbeth almost by accident (he was lacking a plot for a gangster movie until he came across his nephew's copy of Tales from Shakespeare), but it made his name in India, and reminded the outside world of the subcontinent's rich seam of Shakespeare, both on screen and stage. As well as being Bhardwaj's earliest adaptation, Maqbool is in some ways his best – a white-knuckle gangster thriller with the hero (Irrfan Khan) plotting to take over a Muslim crime gang in Mumbai run by a Godfather-like don (Pankaj Kapoor). The Weird Sisters are, brilliantly, cast as corrupt cops obsessed with astrology, and in a fine Bollywood plot twist the Lady M character (Tabu) is Maqbool's mistress, not his wife. The star, though, is Mumbai – oozing mist, skulduggery and murk, it is the stuff of delirious subtropical nightmares. The film is only available as an Indian import, but it's reasonably straightforward to find.

Macbeth
M. Fassbender, M. Cotillard, P. Considine; Justin Kurzel (dir.) UK, 2015 **>** StudioCanal **DVD**

With something like ten major movies now in existence – not counting TV versions and adaptations – Macbeth now rivals Hamlet for the title of most-filmed play in the canon. The latest pretender to the Scottish throne is Justin Kurzel's UK/French co-production, which premiered to wild acclaim at the 2015 Cannes festival. It certainly looks the part, shot in a malevolent and moody Scotland (this time some of it really is Scotland) soaked in blood and mud, and whose very skies glower with thunderous vindictiveness. The cast is fine, too, centreing on intimate performances from the ethereal Marion Cotillard and a brutish Michael Fassbender, whose descent into the role of psychopath is – refreshingly – far more rapid than his wife's. Despite its good points, though, the film doesn't quite ring true, stagily paced and full of art-directed slo-mo that's a bit too Game of Thrones for comfort. There's plenty of fury and a great deal of sound (the battlefield effects are retch-worthy), but this version doesn't signify nearly as much as it should.

AUDIO

Macbeth
S. Dillane, F. Shaw, D. Conlan; Fiona Shaw (dir.) UK, 1998 **>** Naxos ◉ ⬇

Your ears prick up at the very opening of this Macbeth: over Stephen Warbeck's eerie music Fiona Shaw places the sound of shallow and anxious breathing – even before the Sisters begin their incantation. Shaw's taste for aural theatricality permeates this version: the spaces it creates are hallucinatory rather than sound-effects realistic, an adventurous strategy that works surprisingly well. Excellent performances, too, notably Shaw's own (unhistrionic, but all the better for it) Lady Macbeth alongside Stephen Dillane's soft-spoken hero, and there's a terrific cameo from Bill Paterson as the Porter. Some might feel this production could be swifter, but it does at least emphasize Macbeth's reflective qualities.

Macbeth
A. Guinness, P. Brown, A. Cruikshank UK, 1953 **>** Pearl ◉ ⬇

Alec Guinness's one major shot at the role of Macbeth, at the Royal Court in 1966, was largely rubbished and he never attempted it again. That makes this 1953 recording his definitive version, and despite its dated air – most evident in some rather excitable sound effects – it has its attractions. Guinness himself sounds quiet and even weary in the role ("If it were done when 'tis done …" has the air, rather brilliantly, of a middle-ranking civil servant planning a memo), and his attempts at tyrannical command ring increasingly false as the play progresses. Opposite him is Pamela Brown's caustic Lady Macbeth, never more alive than when scolding her low-performing husband yet able to raise hairs with the merest of whispers. Andrew Cruikshank is an aristocratic and resonant Banquo, more of a genuine power broker than Macbeth will ever be, and the auld-world partnership of Macduff (Robin Bailey) and Malcom (Anthony Service) signal that Scotland will be more firmly ruled from now on.

EDITIONS

New Cambridge Shakespeare
A.R. Braunmuller (ed.); 1997 > Cambridge UP

Braunmuller's admirably full edition is an excellent choice, full of fresh angles on a play so critically worked over that editors sometimes struggle for new things to say. Thus here you'll find an engraving illustrating precisely what the Captain means when he describes Macbeth hacking into an enemy "from the nave to th' chaps"; plentiful information on the eerie context of Shakespeare's Weird Sisters; and historical detail on contemporary practice regarding the nursing of children. Nor does Braunmuller avoid the play's core issues: his thoughts are subtle and intelligently argued, drawing a useful distinction between "*Macbeth* in the mind" and "*Macbeth* in performance", the latter providing a detailed stage history. There is an intriguing appendix on "casting Macbeth", a perennial problem for directors and actors alike. Sandra Clark and Pamela Mason's Arden 3 edition (2015) is also recommended, particuarly welcome for its focus on the play's female characters, notably Lady M and the witches.

SOME CRITICISM

The Well Wrought Urn
Cleanth Brooks; 1947 > Harvest [o/p]

This methodical, calm but brilliant account of *Macbeth*'s unsettling poetic qualities might seem a perverse recommendation were it not that many of the play's finest poetic moments seem in performance to be gone in a flash, such is the breakneck pace of its plot. Brooks was one of the shapers of the so-called "New Criticism" movement that appeared in the US during the 1940s and his essay on *Macbeth* is a classic, launching itself from the incandescent (if near-indecipherable) speech in which the hero compares the "pity" released at Duncan's death to "a naked new-born babe" (1.7.21) and hitching it to the submerged symbols that run throughout the play's language. Brooks refuses to give up on its difficulties, and what emerges is a reading of the play's imagery that will transform your understanding of Shakespeare's writing – even if it leaves your theatrical awareness none the wiser.

Supernatural Environments in Shakespeare's England
Kristen Poole; 2011 > Cambridge UP

Tantalizingly subtitled "spaces of demonism, divinity and drama", Kristen Poole's absorbing study examines the often hazy boundaries between changing Christian beliefs, cultic practices and folk superstition in Renaissance Europe. The field has thrown up some fascinating research in recent years, and this work ranges ambitiously from the spells and enchantings in Marlowe's *Doctor Faustus* through a number of Shakespeare's dramas, including *Hamlet*, *Othello* and *The Tempest*. The Scottish play, seemingly written for a King who not only believed in witchcraft but published a book on it, is a key text, and Poole places the Weird Sisters in a suggestive context that includes Calvin and Hooker, and illuminates *Macbeth*'s eerily elastic sense of time, which seems to dissolve the difference between the Protestant present and Doomsday in an instant. It's demanding stuff, but eloquently argued.

Measure for Measure

Though technically it is set in Vienna, *Measure for Measure*, Shakespeare's unsettling comedy of sex in the city, reflects more closely than anything else the playwright wrote the Jacobean London he knew. Saturated with moral decline – something that all but killed its chances in the Victorian theatre – it moves between courtroom, prison, nunnery and brothel as the old tale of a corrupt judge who propositions the sister of a defendant is worked through to a newly troubling conclusion. Coleridge thought it "the most painful – say rather the only painful" play of Shakespeare's, and it is most often known as the first of his "problem comedies", a group of plays whose hard-edged and cynical tone often seems to preclude fantasies of lasting happiness. Yet this fable of justice, morality and power, perhaps intended for performance in front of King James I, is by no means clinical. The rich and scabrous humour of the play's Viennese flesh-pots has an energy that frequently threatens to overwhelm the main business of the plot, while the moral ambiguity of nearly every character on stage (impossible to ignore in performance) makes it difficult to track the course of *Measure for Measure* on a straightforward ethical spectrum.

DATE > Played at court on December 26, 1604, *Measure for Measure* was probably written up to a year before. That performance, coupled with its thematic interest in Puritanism, law and governance, suggests that it draws topical parallels with the rule of James I, who came to the throne the previous year.

SOURCES > The play's chief sources are Giraldi Cinthio's Italian novella *Hecatommithi* (1565) and an English play along similar lines,

George Whetstone's *Promos and Cassandra* (1578). Other elements derive from dramas by Shakespeare's contemporaries – Middleton's *The Phoenix*, Marston's *The Malcontent* and Jonson's *Sejanus*.

TEXTS > The Folio of 1623 provides the sole authoritative text, probably set from a promptbook; it possibly bears the fingerprints of Thomas Middleton (see p.637), who may have been involved in adapting it.

Interpreting the play

Hearing of a play named *Measure for Measure*, Shakespeare's contemporaries would in all likelihood have thought of one thing: God. More specifically, they would have thought of the biblical injunction, contained in Matthew's gospel, about how a good Christian should behave towards others. "Judge not, that ye be not judged," Christ advises his followers during the Sermon on the Mount,

> With what judgement ye judge, ye shall be judged: And with what measure ye mete, it shall be measured to you again. Seest thou a mote in thy brother's eye, but perceivest not the beam that is in thine own eye? Or, how

MAJOR CHARACTERS & SYNOPSIS

Duke Vincentio of Vienna
Angelo, the Duke's deputy
Escalus, an old councillor
Claudio, a young gentleman
Juliet, Claudio's betrothed
Isabella, Claudio's sister, a novice in a nunnery
Lucio, a "fantastic" (extravagant young man)
Froth, another gentleman
Mistress Overdone, a brothel-keeper
Pompey, Mistress Overdone's servant
Elbow, a constable
Abhorson, an executioner
Barnadine, a condemned prisoner
Mariana, Angelo's ex-fiancée
Friar Peter
Francesca, a nun
Varrius, a lord and friend of the Duke
A **Provost**, a Justice and others

ACT 1 Vienna is lawless and morally corrupt. Its ruler, the Duke, has decided to leave the city in the care of his puritanical deputy, Angelo, in the hope that he will reintroduce order while the Duke is away. But the Duke has an ulterior motive: instead of leaving town, he plans to disguise himself as a friar in order to observe Angelo's actions. Angelo immediately announces that brothels are to be pulled down and the city's laws to be strictly applied. At one such brothel Pompey and Mistress Overdone are worriedly discussing the proclamation when they are interrupted by Claudio, who has been arrested for getting Juliet, his betrothed, pregnant. Under the new regime Claudio faces execution, and in desperation sends Lucio to find his sister Isabella (who has just entered a nunnery) so that she can plead with Angelo on his behalf.

ACT 2 The practical problems of the clampdown are exposed when the doltish constable Elbow attempts to have Pompey and Froth tried for corrupting his wife. Isabella is then brought before Angelo to plead for her brother. The deputy is initially unmoved by her arguments, but gradually becomes touched by her virtue and courage. But he is also attracted to her, and when they meet again declares that he will save her brother's

life on one condition – that she sleeps with him. She is horrified and threatens to tell everyone, but realizes that she will not be believed. At the prison, meanwhile, the Duke reappears in disguise and lectures a penitent Juliet on her sinfulness.

ACT 3 The Duke (still in disguise) visits Claudio, and prepares him to meet death. Isabella arrives at the prison, and reluctantly tells her brother about Angelo's proposition. When he begs her to consent and save his life, she is outraged. The Duke has overheard their conversation, however, and intervenes to suggest a solution: Isabella must trick Angelo into sleeping with his ex-fiancée, Mariana, in the belief that she is actually Isabella.

ACT 4 The bed-trick works, but the Duke discovers that Angelo has failed to keep his side of the bargain: Claudio still faces execution. Invoking the Duke's authority, he persuades the Provost that another prisoner – also under sentence of death – should be executed early, and that his head be sent to Angelo as proof of Claudio's death. He hides this from Isabella, however, who believes her brother is dead. The Duke then sends word to Escalus and Angelo that he is ready to return to Vienna.

ACT 5 At the city gates, the Duke (no longer disguised) meets Escalus and Angelo. Isabella is brought before him – unaware that he and the friar are the same – and denounces Angelo for his corruption. The Duke demands evidence and Mariana enters, claiming that she and Angelo are betrothed and have consummated their marriage. The confusion deepens as the Duke re-enters in disguise and backs up her story. But when he is accidentally unmasked, Angelo realizes that the truth is out and begs to be executed. Mariana then pleads for him and, as Claudio is revealed to be alive, Angelo is pardoned on condition he marries Mariana. The play closes with a final twist, however: the Duke asks Isabella whether she will marry *him* ...

sayest thou to thy brother: Suffer me, I will pluck out a mote out of thine eye: and behold, a beam is in thine own eye? Thou hypocrite, first cast out the beam out of thine own eye: and then shalt thou see clearly, to pluck out the mote out of thy brother's eye.

[MATTHEW 7:1–5]

Christ's famous words insist that we should think before judging others; before presuming to criticize another person (noticing the "mote" or speck in their eye) we should be careful not to be blinded by our failings (the "beam" or block in our own).

Nor does the playwright avoid the confrontational aspects of the parallel: while Jesus warns against the perils of passing judgement because we ourselves are fallible, *Measure for Measure* dramatizes an Italian tale about a corrupt official who falls into precisely that trap. In Giraldi Cinthio's *Hecatommithi*, a collection of stories that also provided the inspiration for *Othello*, Shakespeare found the story of a strict judge named Juriste who falls in love with Epitia, the younger sister of a man Juriste has condemned for rape, when she comes to plead for his life. Under pressure from her brother, the young woman relents to the judge's demands, but no sooner has he taken her to bed than he orders that the brother be beheaded anyway. Epitia finds out and demands justice from the city's ruler, but is informed that Juriste's punishment is to be married to none other than her. In a plot twist that might strike us as surprising, she realizes that she has subsequently fallen in love with him. Everything ends happily.

Shakespeare makes the story both richer in texture and even more replete with problems. His Isabella is not merely virtuous, she is a nun; her brother Claudio is guilty not of rape, but has merely slept with his betrothed. And Shakespeare makes a major role for the shadowy figure of Vienna's Duke, who leaves his deputy Angelo ruling in his absence and yet stays in the city disguised as a friar, safeguarding the comic resolution of a play which frequently threatens to be anything but. The Duke's motivation for involving himself in the lives of his subjects may be mysterious, but it does divert the play from outright tragedy. And yet the conclusion of Shakespeare's *Measure for Measure* is for most audiences its most surprising and perplexing aspect: having saved Isabella and her brother from the depredations of Angelo, Duke Vincentio decides that he wants the nun for himself.

Most biting laws

The first words of *Measure for Measure* are "Of government", and the action of the play might be interpreted as a form of sociological experiment. Its aim is to see how the people of Vienna can be governed – whether, in fact, they *can* be governed. The initial evidence is not promising. Having ruled Vienna leniently, Duke Vincentio has

Almost all that is here worthy of Shakespeare at any time is worthy of Shakespeare at his highest: and of this every touch, every line, every incident, every syllable, belongs to pure and simple tragedy.

A.C. Swinburne on *Measure for Measure*, in *A Study of Shakespeare* (1879)

decided to try a stricter approach, but instead of implementing the crackdown himself he leaves his puritanical deputy Angelo (a man "whose blood / Is very snow-broth", according to the libertine Lucio (1.4.56–7)) in charge. As the Duke explains to Friar Peter, the city needs harsh measures, and fast:

> We have strict statutes and most biting laws,
> The needful bits and curbs to headstrong weeds,
> Which for this fourteen years we have let slip;
> Even like an o'ergrown lion in a cave
> That goes not out to prey. Now, as fond fathers,
> Having bound up the threat'ning twigs of birch
> Only to stick it in their children's sight
> For terror, not to use, in time the rod
> More mocked becomes than feared: so our decrees,
> Dead to infliction, to themselves are dead;
> And Liberty plucks Justice by the nose,
> The baby beats the nurse, and quite athwart
> Goes all decorum.

> [1.3.19–31]

Just as the Duke has been struggling (and failing) to maintain his power for all those years in office, here it his language that runs riot. He manages to say "headstrong weeds" rather than "headstrong steeds", so making nonsense of his own figure of speech, and the jumble of metaphors he calls on to describe the way in which "decorum" has been thwarted sounds every bit as chaotic as the city he describes. Though he does his best to speak like a Puritan zealot, the Duke is clearly finding his way into the role.

At least Vincentio, fleeing the city, is no longer having to deal with the real business of government. His deputy Angelo is confronted in the first scene of Act Two with the gravest threat yet to the new regime – people themselves. Despite his insistence to Escalus that "we must not make a scarecrow of the law" (2.1.1), Angelo has reckoned without officials like Constable Elbow, who manages to transform the task of making the law look ridiculous into a full-time occupation. Elbow has arrested the pimp Pompey on the basis that Pompey has done something to Elbow's wife (quite what Pompey has done Elbow never gets round to explaining), and the comic routine between the two – Elbow's malapropisms, Pompey's rambling answers – lasts the rest of the scene. Angelo survives only a few minutes before storming off, leaving Escalus to deal with the mess. Though the scene is funny, it soon hits some of the bigger questions investigated by the play. When Escalus demands, "What do you think of the trade [prostitution], Pompey? Is it a lawful trade?", Pompey's reply is disarmingly simple:

POMPEY If the law would allow it, sir.
ESCALUS But the law will not allow it, Pompey; nor it shall not be allowed
    in Vienna.

POMPEY Does your worship mean to geld and spay all the youth of the city?
ESCALUS No, Pompey.
POMPEY Truly, sir, in my poor opinion they will to't then.

[2.1.215–23]

In other words, until such time as there is no call for sex (because Escalus and his colleagues would "geld and spay", or sterilize, the city's young people), illicit sexual activity will thrive. The comedy here is double-edged: though Pompey's interpretation of "lawful" wouldn't stand up in court, it suggests the futility of banning something which, however morally repugnant, is a constant of human nature – Pompey's "trade" is, after all, the oldest trade there is. And though these issues vex lawmakers today as much as ever, they would have had a special resonance for Jacobean audiences visiting a theatre located in Southwark, part of the so-called "liberties" outside city jurisdiction. Prostitution thrived just outside the Globe's doors, and the playwright's Vienna is pointedly similar to the London he knew so intimately.

Early audiences would also have had sympathy with another victim of Angelo's new moral order, Claudio. He has been arrested for sleeping with his fiancée, Juliet, before they are officially married – technically fornication, but a common offence in early modern England, and one that Shakespeare knew only too well (when he married Anne Hathaway in 1582, she was several months pregnant). To make matters more complicated, Claudio claims that "upon a true contract, / I got possession of Julietta's bed" (1.2.133–4), in effect that they are engaged – in this era often interpreted as serious a commitment as marriage itself. And yet he faces the death penalty.

Isabella's predicament is different, but it is no less ethically problematic. Dragged from the convent in which she is about to become a nun, Isabella has the unenviable task of pleading for a brother whose "vice" (as she admits to Angelo) she "abhors". Unlike Portia in *The Merchant of Venice*, Isabella – on the point of cutting herself off from male company for good – has no masculine disguise behind which to hide. Quite the contrary: it is her womanliness that Claudio is relying upon ("in her youth," he remarks, "There is a prone and speechless dialect / Such as move men" (1.2.170–2)). Those persuasive gifts are undeniable: arguing in front of Angelo that "it is excellent / To have a giant's strength, but it is tyrannous / To use it like a giant," she draws upon the full rhetoric of Christianity to argue her position:

Merciful heaven,
Thou rather with thy sharp and sulphurous bolt
Split'st the unwedgeable and gnarlèd oak
Than the soft myrtle. But man, proud man,
Dressed in a little brief authority,
Most ignorant of what he's most assured,
His glassy essence, like an angry ape
Plays such fantastic tricks before high heaven
As makes the angels weep, who, with our spleens,
Would all themselves laugh mortal.

[2.2.117–26]

Though Isabella's impassioned words are not easy to untangle (she pictures apish, "proud man" laughing at sins that make angels "weep", but also those angels laughing themselves to death at our weakness), their argument – that "merciful heaven" should be reflected here on earth – is impossible to misunderstand.

Th'offence pardons itself

But Isabella's speech has a disconcerting effect on its auditor. Angelo is smitten, and – stunned by these new feelings – soon offers the grim bargain we have been expecting all along. This is the lurching crux on which *Measure for Measure* will turn – whether Isabella will sleep with him in order to save her brother, or hold onto her convictions and allow Claudio to die. Her response, which is to decide that "more than our brother is our chastity" (2.4.185) has attracted violent disagreement: she has been attacked as a "vixen" and "self-absorbed" (by male critics, perhaps unsurprisingly); but also defended as "saintly", utterly committed to ideals few of us have the courage to face. For his part Claudio initially thinks – or claims to think – that she must save herself, but soon changes his mind. "Death is a fearful thing," he reminds a horrified Isabella:

ISABELLA And shamèd life a hateful.
CLAUDIO
    Ay, but to die, and go we know not where;
    To lie in cold obstruction, and to rot;
    This sensible warm motion to become
    A kneaded clod, and the dilated spirit
    To bathe in fiery floods, or to reside
    In thrilling region of thick-ribbèd ice;
    To be imprisoned in the viewless winds,
    And blown with restless violence round about
    The pendent world; or to be worse than worst
    Of those that lawless and incertain thought
    Imagine howling—'tis too horrible!

                                      [3.1.116–28]

Though he is hardly a Hamlet, Claudio takes up the Prince's musings on "the undiscovered country" and argues, mapping it out in fearful detail, that it must be more horrific than anything life can offer. Though nearer to it than most, he articulates the main problem repeatedly posed by the play: whether it is preferable to allow life, in all its flawed corruption; or cut it off.

In *Measure for Measure* we are forced to see every point of view, and to ask every question. Claudio has sinned, but should he die? Is it right that his sister should submit to Angelo in order to save him? Can the end (saving a life) ever justify the means (rape)? Can "measure" answer for "measure"? Following its title, the play places these incommensurable issues side by side and demands that they be resolved.

Its proposed solution is, if anything, yet more fraught. Disguised as a friar, the Duke has observed Isabella's predicament. Revealing that Angelo has all this time

From left to right: the Duke (David Troughton), the Provost (Angus Wright) and Escalus (Mike Grady) discuss the imminent execution of Angelo. A Complicite/National Theatre co-production, 2004.

been "affianced" to another woman (an uncomfortable echo of Claudio's situation), Vincentio improvises a plan that will solve everything at a stroke: Mariana will sleep with Angelo in Isabella's place. The so-called "bed-trick" is Shakespeare's addition to the story, as theatrically appealing as it is morally suspect. "Th'offence pardons itself," as the Duke breezily observes later in the play (5.1.533), though we in the audience might wonder if things are entirely as simple as that.

Though deceit and disguise are familiar enough devices in Shakespearian comedy, the Duke's actions as *Measure for Measure* heads towards its denouement put comic ideals under almost impossible strain. As in *All's Well*, the climax is extended over a breathtakingly tense final scene. Here Vincentio virtuosically shuttles between his multiple personae, staging a grand return to Vienna as the Duke while also maintaining his friar's disguise. First Isabella arrives, unaware that Claudio has been spared and hysterically demanding "justice, justice, justice, justice" (5.1.25); then Mariana appears, claiming to have slept with Angelo as strongly as Isabella claims that he raped her. The mystery deepens:

DUKE What, are you married?
MARIANA No, my lord.
DUKE Are you a maid?
MARIANA No, my lord.

274

DUKE A widow then?

MARIANA Neither, my lord.

DUKE Why, you are nothing then; neither maid, widow, nor wife!

[5.1.170–7]

The Duke puts himself in a position where only he can solve the conundrums Mariana speaks of, and, after further delay, he does so, theatrically emerging from disguise to the disbelief of everyone present.

The punishments and rewards he produces, however dazzling, leave many of the play's characters stunned into silence. Angelo is married to Mariana, but promptly sentenced to death – until, that is, Claudio is produced, apparently back from the dead. For his impertinence to the Duke, Lucio is initially threatened with the hangman's noose, then told to marry a prostitute whom he has made pregnant instead. Though it is impossible to take it entirely seriously, the ferocity of Lucio's response to his apparently lucky escape nevertheless hangs in the air:

Marrying a punk, my lord, is pressing to death, whipping, and hanging.

[5.1.521–2]

And the Duke's insistence that his comedy must end in marriages goes even further. "Dear Isabel," he calls,

I have a motion much imports your good,
Whereto, if you'll a willing ear incline,
What's mine is yours, and what is yours is mine.

[5.1.533–6]

Isabella is given no opportunity to respond. Unlike Shakespeare's earlier comedies, here marriage does not grow organically from the plot or its characters: it is brought down with all the suddenness of an axe. As *Measure for Measure* ends, Shakespeare makes it seem as if happiness has never seemed further away.

Stage history and adaptations

A play recorded as "Mesur for Mesur" by one "Shaxberd" was acted at **court** in front of James I on December 26, 1604 – the first performance we know of, probably with **Richard Burbage**, the company's star actor, as the Duke. In 1621, **Thomas Middleton**, possibly a collaborator on *Timon of Athens*, adapted *Measure*; in his version the city comedy aspects of the plot are beefed up to suit late Jacobean taste.

Shakespeare might well have approved, but it's difficult to imagine that he would have felt the same for **William Davenant**'s *The Law Against Lovers*, staged in 1662. This excised most of the play's underworld characters and replaced them with Beatrice and Benedick from *Much Ado*, while Angelo became a Cromwellian Puritan. Another adaptation, this time premiered in 1700 by **Charles Gildon**, sounds, if anything, even odder: breezily entitled *Measure for Measure, or Beauty the Best Advocate*, it interspersed stretches of Shakespeare with Purcell's *Dido and Aeneas*. Gildon's Angelo and Mariana are already married, presumably to give the bed-trick a sheen of respectability.

Neither Davenant nor Gildon's versions enjoyed popularity, and it wasn't long before Shakespeare's play returned. During the eighteenth century and into the next, the star roles of Isabella and the Duke became much-prized vehicles for leading actors: **James Quin** first played Vincentio in 1720, and was joined by **Susannah Cibber**'s Isabella in 1731; **John Henderson** and **Mary Yates** stepped into their shoes in the 1770s and 80s. But it was the pairing of **John Philip Kemble** and his sister **Sarah Siddons** from 1794 onwards that defined this phase in the play's history. Kemble's version of *Measure* was typically conservative, with sexual and subversive overtones airbrushed out, emphasis being placed instead on Siddons's Isabella and her brother's patrician Duke. Siddons dominated the role so effectively that she was still playing it in 1812 at the age of 57, creaking joints notwithstanding.

Doubts about *Measure*'s morals had become widespread by the first decades of the nineteenth century, and it was produced with declining frequency. New York audiences were first given the chance to see it in 1818, but versions in London fared badly. Though **Samuel Phelps** at Sadler's Wells employed a text from which all indecorous language had been rooted out ("not an offensive phrase left", applauded the *Athenaeum*), it failed to take off and the play languished in the doldrums during the rest of the Victorian era.

Its fortunes were to change, however. **William Poel** chose *Measure* as the first play on which to attempt his experiments in historicist staging, and his production of 1893 was hailed as revolutionary. Though Poel constructed an "Elizabethan" stage for the play, his interpretative ideas were less radical: the text was still heavily cut and the *Leamington Courier* felt able to proclaim that it was a "great purifying influence" when Poel brought it to Stratford in 1908 (admittedly to resistance from the local vicar). Poel's disciple **William Bridges-Adams** risked an uncut text at the same venue in 1923, leading the *Birmingham Post* to suggest that, if Shakespeare were still alive, he would certainly be censored. **Tyrone Guthrie**'s fine Old Vic production ten years later was notable for the sinister Angelo of **Charles Laughton** ("a lustful black bat" was how the *Daily Telegraph* described him), but it still failed to attract audiences – despite supportive letters by T.S. Eliot and John Gielgud.

Gielgud's enthusiasm for the play proved prescient: he was to play Angelo in a Stratford production of 1950 mounted by the young **Peter Brook** (one of several Shakespearian comedies Brook rescued from relative obscurity), in what turned out to be *Measure*'s defining postwar staging. A foreboding fixed set looming throughout, Brook caught the play's darkness and, bravely, its comedy (many thought of Bruegel, but to the director it was "Dostoevskian"). But he still pushed a conformist line: the script was skewed to flatter **Harry Andrews**'s benevolent Duke, and **Barbara Jefford** brought to Isabella all the innocence of her 19 years – though in the final scene she was instructed to pause for as long as she thought the audience could stand before deciding to plead for Angelo's life. Kenneth Tynan thought this production "a perfect marriage of shrill imagination and sober experience".

This advocacy – along with a burgeoning interest in the play's audacious blend of repression, power and sexuality – saw *Measure* more popular postwar than ever before.

Bertolt Brecht's Berliner Ensemble acted their version in 1952, and two years later James Mason, who had played Claudio in Guthrie's Old Vic production, played Angelo for the same director at Stratford, Ontario. But in British theatre the play's equivocal view of politics was stressed most persuasively by John Barton at Stratford in 1970, with Sebastian Shaw playing a capricious Duke to Ian Richardson's icy Angelo. Barton also made the comedy's conclusion truly problematic – following the Duke's marriage offer, Estelle Kohler's Isabella simply turned to the audience in despair. Keith Hack's expressionistic, Brechtian staging at the same venue four years later proved notorious, not least because in the closing scene the Duke was flown in on a bar labelled "Deus ex machina".

Charles Marowitz penned a typically fierce adaptation in 1975 at the Open Space, which restored much of Cinthio's narrative yet added new material to create a satire on power – most jarringly when Isabella (Ciaran Madden) was denied justice by the Duke. Since then two different kinds of *Measure* have predominated in English-language productions. The first was launched in 1974 by Jonathan Miller, who set the play in a pre-Nazi Austria steadily overtaken by fascism – an approach echoed by Nicholas Hytner at the RSC in 1988 and Michael Boyd with the same company a decade later. The other tendency has been to portray another kind of Vienna, that inhabited by Sigmund Freud. Robin Phillips tried this at Stratford, Ontario in 1975, but for many critics Trevor Nunn's 1991 version at the studio-scale The Other Place has been the most revealing attempt to date to view the play through its intimate psychology: David Haig's fussy, nervous Angelo became coldly brutal when confronted by Claire Skinner's schoolgirlish Isabella.

Other directors have brought out the contemporary relevance of the play, notably Declan Donnellan in his 1994 Cheek by Jowl production, which witnessed Isabella becoming an increasingly isolated figure in a world of slippery moral relativism. Donnellan would return to the text in 2015 with a company of Russian actors, in a translated, cut-down version that drew illuminating parallels between the moral clampdowns of Jacobean London and those in Vladimir Putin's Russia – not dissimilar to Moscow's Vakhtangov company, who brought a modernized version to Shakespeare's Globe in 2012 (the latter production raised eyebrows for casting one actor, Sergey Epishev, as both Angelo and the Duke).

In 2004, Simon McBurney emphasized the symbiotic relationship between the world of politics and the world of the brothel, dovetailing their respective scenes in a fast and fluid Complicite production at the National Theatre. TV monitors were employed both for the surveillance of political prisoners (dressed in Guantánamo Bay orange) and for the projection of pornography. The Duke's moral ambiguity – powerfully conveyed by David Troughton – culminated in the chilling image of him coaxing a stunned Isabella (Naomi Frederick) towards a double bed that had suddenly been illuminated at the back of the stage.

In Bath in 2006, Peter Hall brought out the script's puritanical power play, swathing it in dour Jacobean costume with Richard Dormer as a frosty Angelo and Andrea Riseborough a girlish Isabella. By contrast, Michael Attenborough's staging at the Almeida in London in 2010 was modern-dress and icily exact, dominated by Rory Kinnear's arrestingly original Angelo ("like some bearded, geeky, think-tank wonk," according to the *Independent*). The following year, Roxana Silbert's version for the

RSC foregrounded the tribulations of **Jodie McNee's** bluestocking heroine, adrift in a sordid S&M world of black leather, whips and chains.

After such severe interpretations, **Dominic Dromgoole's** 2015 production, one of his last as artistic director of Shakespeare's Globe, came as a surprise for emphasizing *Measure for Measure's* antic, zany comedy; according to the *Observer*, "though it might seem madness to think of a jolly production of one of Shakespeare's most troubling plays, Dromgoole's staging comes near." Another 2015 London production, directed by **Joe Hill-Gibbins** at the Young Vic with **Romola Garai** in the lead, raised eyebrows for its use of inflatable sex dolls and video footage of Claudio and Julietta in bed – but, thought the *Guardian*, "[it] gets closer to the heart of Shakespeare's strange fable than many more orthodox versions".

Despite its recent popularity, there is no full film version of *Measure for Measure*. Only one TV version exists, part of the BBC/Time-Life complete Shakespeare and widely regarded as one of the best in that series. It was directed by **Desmond Davis**, with **Tim Pigott-Smith**, **Kenneth Colley** and **Kate Nelligan** as Angelo, the Duke and Isabella respectively, and aired in 1979.

SCREEN

Measure for Measure
K. Colley, K. Nelligan, T. Pigott-Smith; Desmond Davis (dir.) UK, 1979 ❯ BBC `DVD`

The BBC/Time-Life Shakespeare series was always a bit hit-and-miss, and has not worn the years well: this seventeenth-century *Measure* is as close as the project has to a jewel in the crown. The budgetary and creative restrictions that torpedoed others in the series – flimsy sets, tawdry costuming, woeful picture quality – here become a kind of virtue, with gloomy interior spaces and a down-at-heel feel adding to the play's subterranean atmosphere (an atmosphere only occasionally punctured by over-zealous sound effects). The cast, too, is excellent: Kate Nelligan's Isabella is full of righteous (but sympathetic) virtue; Kenneth Colley's Duke can twinkle when he wants, but has plentiful reserves of shadiness; Tim Pigott-Smith's Angelo has unsettling menace; John McEnery's pompous Lucio has it coming to him. The only real flaws surface in the underworld scenes – difficult enough on stage, never mind in a studio. How do they handle the end? Well, that would be telling …

AUDIO

Measure for Measure
R. Allam, S.R. Beale, S. Gonet; Clive Brill (dir.) UK, 1998 ❯ Arkangel ◉ ☁

The contrasting worlds of *Measure for Measure* – its schizoid splits between the room of state, the brothel, the jail and the confessional – are convincingly conveyed in this production. It is all too clear that decisions made at the clipped and somewhat sterile court (memorably embodied in Roger Allam's nicely anxious Duke and Christopher Benjamin's sober Escalus) have little hope of restraining life elsewhere in the city (as becomes clear in the wild exchange between Desmond Barritt's irrepressibly Welsh Pompey and Simon Russell Beale's fatefully precise Angelo). Beale is perfectly cast, capable of evoking sympathy yet deploying an undertow of megalomania that makes his resignation to "our evils" both inevitable and shocking. As Isabella, Stella Gonet communicates well the character's unwitting sexuality as well as her fierce rage when cornered, and the intense scenes between her and Angelo are in many ways the highlight of this recording.

EDITIONS

New Cambridge Shakespeare
Brian Gibbons (ed.); 1991 ❯ Cambridge UP

There is no shying away from the challenges of *Measure for Measure*, and the play seems to bring out the best in editors. J.W. Lever's scrupulous and engaging Arden 2 edition (1965) was one of the best in that series, and is still well worth consulting. But Brian Gibbons's version for New Cambridge is even better, aided by a stage history that takes into account the late twentieth-century revival of interest in the play and provides a decent amount of space on the critical dogfights it has spawned. Gibbons's notes are also exemplary, and his treatment of a quirky text, while more invasive than some would prefer, is subtle and intelligent.

SOME CRITICISM

Speechless Dialect
Philip C. McGuire; 1985 > California UP [o/p]

Isabella's notorious wordlessness at the end of *Measure for Measure*, as McGuire shows, is just one of many Shakespearian "open silences" whose meaning is as debatable – and significant – as any of the words in the script. McGuire focuses closely on performance history and text to develop a study into the "silences that Shakespeare's words impose upon characters who remain alive". His results suggest the complex and suggestive possibilities offered by plays as rich as *Twelfth Night, The Tempest, Lear* – and, of course, *Measure for Measure*.

Theory in Practice: Measure for Measure
Nigel Wood (ed.); 1996 > Open UP [o/p]

Measure for Measure provokes passionately different responses, and a number of them are marshalled into this excellent collection, part of the "Theory in Practice" series. It offers four contrasting points of view – Peter Corbin on the play's performance history, Amanda Piesse on gender and new historicism, Nicholas Radel on the play's challenges to feminist critics and Richard Wilson on the long shadow of Michel Foucault (particularly suggestive here, given Shakespeare's interest in power, surveillance and imprisonment). Touching usefully on other interpretations, editor Nigel Wood points out that the play is only a problem if we expect it to be a cohesive experience; one of the great powers of drama is that it is usually anything but. This could be read in conjunction/argument with a more traditionalist approach, such as that offered by G. Wilson Knight in *The Wheel of Fire* (see p.239).

The Merchant of Venice

V iewed one way, *The Merchant of Venice* looks like anti-Semitic propaganda: a Christian merchant becomes indebted to a rapacious Jewish moneylender, Shylock, who seizes on the merchant's bankruptcy to demand repayment in the grisly form of a pound of the debtor's flesh. Viewed another way, the play's most tragic character is Shylock himself: a man abused by the Christians of Venice, robbed and deserted by his own daughter, and finally humiliated by being forced to abandon his own religion and convert to Christianity. Both sides of the story are there in this brilliant and troubling play, and it's easy to feel that they're irreconcilable; what Keats called Shakespeare's "negative capability" – his capacity for making audiences see things from multiple angles – here makes for disturbing viewing. Shylock may be descended from the devilish Jewish villains that were a staple of Christian storytelling, but Shakespeare makes it impossible to view him as straightforward evil; while the Christians of the play, for all their apparent civility, are racist, fixated by money and in the end brutally vicious. Yet *The Merchant*, which contains so much hatred, is also a comedy of love, and it's in this – in the collision between the two folk stories that were Shakespeare's sources – that the play throws up its most searching questions, in particular the involvement of the wealthy heroine Portia in the grubby battle for money and life at the centre of the plot. It is impossible to sit on the fence when watching *The Merchant*, and the issues it raises about religious intolerance and conflict seem more pressing now than ever.

DATE > Certainly in existence by July 1598, the *Merchant* was possibly being acted 1596–97.
SOURCES > Barabas, the antihero of Marlowe's *The Jew of Malta* (c. 1589), looms large, but a more specific source is Giovanni Fiorentino's fourteenth-century tale collection *Il Pecorone* ("The Dunce"). Myriad other analogues include an anonymous play, *The Jew* (c. 1578), though the major plot elements – the flesh-bond and the story of the three caskets – may derive from folk roots.
TEXTS > The play's most important text is its first quarto printing, Q1 (1600), probably set from a scribal copy of Shakespeare's manuscript; both the second quarto (Q2, dated 1600 but in fact 1619) and the First Folio versions are based upon it.

Interpreting the play

Given its deliberately flat title, the plot of *The Merchant of Venice* can seem strange, even bizarre. It meshes two powerful folk stories – the story of the creditor who

MAJOR CHARACTERS & SYNOPSIS

Antonio, a merchant from Venice
Bassanio, Antonio's friend, suitor to Portia
Lorenzo, a friend of Antonio and Bassanio, in love
with Jessica
Graziano, another friend
Saliero and **Soliano**, acquaintances
Leonardo, Bassanio's servant
Shylock, a Jewish moneylender
Jessica, Shylock's daughter
Tubal, another Jewish moneylender
Lancelot, Shylock's clownish servant, later
Bassanio's
Gobbo, Lancelot's father
Portia, an heiress from Belmont (later disguised
as "Balthasar", a lawyer)
Nerissa, Portia's gentlewoman (later disguised as
Balthasar's clerk)
Balthasar and **Stephano**, Portia's servants
Princes of Morocco and **Aragon**, Portia's
suitors
Duke of Venice

ACT 1 Bassanio badly needs a favour from his
close friend Antonio – money in order to woo
the wealthy heiress Portia. Though Antonio's
capital is tied up overseas, he gladly agrees to
let Bassanio borrow the money in his name.
Bassanio arranges a loan with the moneylender
Shylock, who spots an opportunity to be
revenged on his old foe Antonio – jokingly
suggesting a contract stipulating that if the
money is not repaid on time, Shylock can have
a pound of Antonio's flesh. Confident that his
cash flow will improve, Antonio consents. In
Belmont, meanwhile, Portia reviews her father's
will, which insists that she must marry the suitor
who correctly chooses among three caskets
of gold, silver and lead. Unfortunately, the
candidates so far – excepting Bassanio – do not
look promising.

ACT 2 Lancelot informs his old father that he
has decided to leave Shylock's service and the pair
ask Bassanio if Lancelot can serve him instead.
Shylock's daughter, Jessica, is also planning to
desert her father, in order to elope with Lorenzo, a
Christian. Back in Belmont, the Prince of Morocco
agrees to take part in the contest for Portia's
hand but loses when he opens the gold casket.

The Prince of Aragon, who chooses the silver one,
fares no better.

ACT 3 Shylock is incensed by his daughter's
flight and the fact that she has stolen money
from him, but is cheered by news that one of
Antonio's merchant ships has sunk, and he looks
likely to go bankrupt. In Belmont, Portia tries to
dissuade Bassanio from choosing a casket, in
order to prolong his company. Undeterred, he
chooses the leaden casket, and is rewarded with
a message granting him Portia's hand. Inspired,
Graziano announces that he and Nerissa (Portia's
gentlewoman) also wish to marry. But the two
couples' joy is soured by news that Antonio's
business has indeed collapsed and Shylock is after
his flesh. While Bassanio rushes back to Venice
with the money, Portia has another plan: she and
Nerissa will follow him undercover and see how
they can help.

ACT 4 Though Bassanio has arrived back in
Venice and offers to repay Antonio's debt twice
over, Shylock demands nothing less than his
legal rights. The Duke is stalling for time when
a young lawyer, "Balthasar" (Portia in disguise),
arrives with Nerissa (also disguised) acting as her
clerk. When their appeals to Shylock's mercy fail,
Antonio's fate seems sealed and Shylock prepares
to make the fatal incision. Suddenly, however,
Balthasar/Portia stops him, stating that although
he is entitled to a pound of flesh he may shed not
a drop of blood. Stunned by this brilliant legal
technicality, Shylock agrees to take the money
after all. But the judgement is not over: she also
informs him that, as an alien attempting to take
the life of a Venetian, he faces the death penalty.
Though Shylock is immediately pardoned by the
Duke, he is forced to give up half his wealth and
convert to Christianity.

ACT 5 Returning in triumph to Belmont,
the men are met by their wives, who are not
impressed to learn that Bassanio and Graziano
have given away their wedding rings to the
"lawyers" who defeated Shylock. Portia and
Nerissa make them squirm for as long as possible
– before, brandishing the rings, they gleefully
relate their coup.

> *For the Venetians, money is a medium of exchange representing not the goods and services of academic economists, but the passions of love and hate.*
>
> Alexander Leggatt, *Shakespeare's Comedy of Love* (1974)

attempts to secure a pound of flesh instead of repayment; the tale of the lover who wins his lady through a riddle game and three caskets – and works them out in painstaking detail. Though hardly the only comedy of Shakespeare's to use folk motifs, critics have frequently been struck by *The Merchant*'s fantastical, even improbable, qualities: the director Harley Granville-Barker infamously declared it a "fairy tale", adding that "there is no more reality in Shylock's bond and the Lord of Belmont's will than in *Jack and the Beanstalk*".

This is not to say that the play shirks the everyday messiness of human psychology; in fact the opposite. At its centre is Antonio, the merchant of the title, who begins the action with famous words dwelling on the shortcomings of rational explanation. "In sooth," he complains to his acquaintances Saliero and Soliano, "I know not why I am so sad,"

> It wearies me, you say it wearies you,
> But how I caught it, found it, or came by it,
> What stuff 'tis made of, whereof it is born,
> I am to learn;
> And such a want-wit sadness makes of me
> That I have much ado to know myself.

> [1.1.1–7]

Antonio is not on speaking terms with his "sadness", and though many critics have tried to explain it, the answer eludes them too. Noting that Antonio travels through the play as an outsider – never more clearly than in the last scene, where he is a solitary figure surrounded by couples – some have suggested that he is a kind of scapegoat in the play, the "tainted wether of the flock" (4.1.113), as he puts it, who will inevitably suffer for his friends' sake. Less complicatedly, perhaps, his melancholy has been called a kind of *Weltschmertz* ("world-weariness"), and in a play where happiness is as much a commodity as anything else he is not the only sufferer.

And now worth nothing

It is revealing of Shakespeare's Venice that Antonio's companions do not hesitate to speculate what they think is the matter. "Your mind is tossing on the ocean," Saliero suggests, among the "argosies" (merchant ships) Antonio's trade relies on. "Should I go to church," Saliero continues,

> And see the holy edifice of stone
> And not bethink me straight of dangerous rocks
> Which, touching but my gentle vessel's side,

Would scatter all her spices on the stream,
Enrobe the roaring waters with my silks,
And, in a word, but even now worth this,
And now worth nothing?

[1.1.29–36]

The thought of religion does not inspire religious thoughts in Saliero – or at least only makes him think on Mammon. Though capital is all, its perilous instability is part of the bargain: worth "this" one moment, "nothing" the next. And though Antonio rejects Saliero's diagnosis, the merchant is not about to deny the significance of money.

Historically famous as a centre of European commerce, Venice in Shakespeare's play oozes conspicuous consumption: its citizens organize masques, music and revels, and splash a great deal of cash – as the moneylender Shylock realizes, quite literally to his cost, when his daughter Jessica splurges in "one night fourscore ducats" after running off with Lorenzo and much of her father's wealth. This leads, of course, into the play's central issue, which dwells heavily on borrowing and debt. The young blade Bassanio's own taste for the high life has left him in dire financial straits, as he explains to Antonio early on:

'Tis not unknown to you, Antonio,
How much I have disabled mine estate
By something showing a more swelling port
Than my faint means would grant continuance,
Nor do I now make moan to be abridged
From such a noble rate; but my chief care
Is to come fairly off from the great debts
Wherein my time, something too prodigal,
Hath left me gaged.

[1.1.122–30]

Though Bassanio expresses his indebtedness somewhat coyly, it is clear that in Venice money talks. His solution is to get more of it, by launching an expedition to woo the "richly left" heiress Portia, which he hopes will secure his long-term economic future.

There are shades here of Petruccio in the *Shrew*, but the tone is more serious, not least because money actually delineates the friendship between the two men. "To you, Antonio, / I owe the most in money and in love," Bassanio insists, and Antonio urges him in turn not to doubt their relationship:

You know me well, and herein spend but time
To wind about my love with circumstance;
And out of doubt you do me now more wrong
In making question of my uttermost
Than if you had made waste of all I have.

[1.1.153–7]

Backed by Antonio's coffers (or rather a debt made to refill them), Bassanio travels from Venice to Belmont in order to woo Portia and, in the climax of the plot's first phase, takes part in the bizarre game laid out in her father's will: selecting from three caskets by working out the riddles inscribed on them. Portia's first suitor, the Prince of Morocco, chooses the golden casket and loses out; as does the Prince of Aragon, who opts for the silver. It is left to Bassanio – inevitably – to choose the leaden casket (paradoxically the most valuable, as Bassanio realizes) and with it win Portia's hand. Lest we should ignore this commodification of the play's heroine, Shakespeare makes Portia herself sketch its terms. Taking Bassanio's hand, she explains, "myself and what is mine to you and yours / Is now converted,"

> But now I was the lord
> Of this fair mansion, master of my servants,
> Queen o'er myself; and even now, but now,
> This house, these servants, and this same myself
> Are yours, my lord's.
>
> [3.2.66–71]

This verbal balance sheet is, as she describes it a few lines earlier, the "full sum of me", and the lot is now in her lover's possession.

The means whereby I live

The first and most comic phase of the play is over. But, as we already know, it has always been underpinned by more unsettling forces. "When I told you / My state was nothing," Bassanio tells Portia soon after their marriage is agreed,

> I should then have told you
> That I was worse than nothing, for indeed
> I have engaged myself to a dear friend,
> Engaged my friend to his mere enemy,
> To feed my means.
>
> [3.2.256–61]

Antonio's "mere enemy", as Bassanio calls him, is Shylock, the moneylender who stands as close to the centre of the play as his real-life counterparts were integral to the Elizabethan economy. Usurers were hated as a matter of course, but in Shakespeare's Venice that loathing takes on a specific racial colouring. The Jewish Shylock is never permitted to forget the fact of his religion. Most often the Venetians simply call him "the Jew" and, for those content to borrow from him while simultaneously despising his religion and people, he may as well have no other identity (in Shakespeare's source, an Italian tale entitled *Il Pecorone*, he is not even given a name).

Shylock himself continually asserts his exclusion from those who make no attempt to hide their hatred for him. Angered and grief-stricken by his daughter's elopement, he savagely turns on the Venetians Saliero and Soliano when they jokingly assert that he has nothing against Antonio. "He hath disgraced me, and hindered me half a million," Shylock cries,

> laughed at my losses, mocked at my gains, scorned my nation, thwarted my bargains, cooled my friends, heated mine enemies, and what's his reason?—I am a Jew. Hath not a Jew eyes? Hath not a Jew hands, organs, dimensions, senses, affections, passions; fed with the same food, hurt with the same weapons, subject to the same diseases, healed by the same means, warmed and cooled by the same winter and summer as a Christian is? If you prick us do we not bleed? If you tickle us do we not laugh? If you poison us do we not die? And if you wrong us do we not revenge?
>
> [3.1.50–62]

We have no reason to doubt a word, for even when taking his money Antonio made no secret of his distaste for Shylock, his willingness to "spit" on the usurer (1.3.129).

It's hard to know how Shylock's impassioned speech would have been heard by Shakespeare's first audiences. Some Jews did live in Elizabethan London, working mostly as merchants, and sixteenth-century Venice was notorious for its Ghetto, into which all of the city's large Jewish community was demeaningly crammed. On the English stage, meanwhile, Jews were unremittingly caricatured as villains, and Marlowe's *The Jew of Malta* (c. 1589) – a play that Shakespeare certainly knew – has an antihero called Barabas who, however striking, snugly fits the archetype of a Jew who is both miserly and gleefully murderous.

Shakespeare's Shylock is not nearly as crude as that, though, and the play makes it difficult to demonize him – one reason among many why *The Merchant* has had such a varied and rich stage history, witnessing performances in which the Jew has been played as anything from out-and-out villain to nobly tragic hero. Though the play does not make him seem attractive, Shakespeare is careful to imply (like Marlowe before him) that the mercenary Christians are not much more appealing: and they, unlike the Jew, have the luxury of appearing otherwise. And for all that Shylock and his co-religionists seem integral to the economy of Venice and its reputation for tolerance, the city's Christian community never permits the moneylender to forget that he exists there only on sufferance – the moneylender is socially as well as legally alien in Venice. More than that, in this play he is quite literally alone: his servant and daughter both desert him during its course, and his wife, the fleetingly mentioned "Leah", is long in her grave. It is not too much to say that Shylock's loneliness – an isolation confirmed and strengthened by jarring religious and cultural differences from those around him – is the ground for his tragedy.

But it is also the ground for his gruesome revenge. When news arrives that Antonio's ships have miscarried, the merchant is plunged into bankruptcy and events take a sickening twist. Determined not to squander his opportunity for "revenge", Shylock demands that his "merry jest" with Antonio must stand. Refusing to be bought off, the moneylender insists that he is owed a pound of the merchant's flesh, nothing less. While this grisly detail usually strikes modern viewers as savage and bewildering, for Elizabethan audiences living in a period of heavy inflation and soaring debt (Shakespeare's own father fell into heavy arrears in the 1570s), Antonio's looming sacrifice must have seemed a vivid metaphor for those real-life debtors who were sent by bloodsucking creditors to notorious London jails such as Newgate and Ludgate. And the insistent sacrificial metaphors of Shakespeare's play begin to seem frighteningly real as Shylock's demand reaches fever pitch. Hamstrung by Venice's need for Jewish investment, the Duke cannot persuade Shylock to provide a "gentle [gentile] answer", as he ill-advisedly warns the usurer (4.1.33). The Jew's insistence for "a weight of carrion flesh" (4.1.40) looks unstoppable.

Henry Irving's 1879 performance of Shylock was notable for its haunting intensity and the high degree of sympathy he brought to the character.

Shylock's mistake, however, is to rely on the legal literalness of his claim. As the final strand of his plot, Shakespeare introduces a device familiar from his early play *The Two Gentlemen of Verona*, and which dominates his great middle-period comedies – the disguised heroine. Despite giving Bassanio all the money he needs, Portia itches to be involved in the plan to free Antonio, and as soon as Bassanio is gone she arranges, with Nerissa, to dress up as lawyers, and sends word to Venice that they are legal experts. They enter the court just as Shylock is sharpening his knife. Portia's pleas for (Christian) mercy falling on deaf ears, the tension mounts inexorably. It is Portia who breaks it. "A pound of that same merchant's flesh is thine," she tells Shylock, examining the bond while the flummoxed Venetians sit by, but then reveals that the contract has a legalistic sting in the tail:

> There is something else.
> This bond doth give thee here no jot of blood.
> The words expressly are 'a pound of flesh'.
> Take then thy bond. Take thou thy pound of flesh.

But in the cutting it, if thou dost shed
One drop of Christian blood, thy lands and goods
Are by the laws of Venice confiscate
Unto the state of Venice.

[4.1.299–309]

With that, Shylock's case falls apart. A technicality it may be, but – at least in this court – it is enough to free Antonio. Portia's triumph is a victory for women (and it is capped by a ruse in which she and Nerissa humiliate their new husbands by persuading them to relinquish their wedding rings), and ostensibly for humanity too.

But Shylock sees little of the latter, and this strand of the comedy – the play is officially that – ends bitterly. Initially taunted by his eagerness to take the money and run, Shylock finds that he has been snared in a catch-22. Another law unearthed by Portia states that if an "alien … seek the life of any citizen", his goods and money have every right to be confiscated (4.1.346–8). For all that his comeuppance is inevitable, Shylock is keenly aware of the singular nature of his treatment. "Nay, take my life and all, pardon not that," he desperately exclaims,

You take my house when you do take the prop
That doth sustain my house; you take my life
When you do take the means whereby I live.

[4.1.371–4]

Shylock's words, those of a man unable to see much beyond money, may not redeem him – but in the Venice of the play his obsession with the things of this world is hardly unique. In any case the Christians hardly seem to care. Though notionally "pardoned", Shylock is stripped of half his income before being forcibly and humiliatingly converted to Christianity. *The Merchant* ends, like other comedies, with its community brought together. But rarely does Shakespeare make us so sensitive to the cost.

Stage history and adaptations

Practically all our knowledge about the early performance history of the *Merchant* arrives from its only text, the 1600 quarto, which states that "it hath been divers times acted by the Lord Chamberlain his Servants", presumably at the **Theatre** in Shoreditch, the company's main home until 1597. The question of personnel is likewise uncertain: some have proposed that Shakespeare's lead comedian, **William Kempe**, took the part of Shylock; others that it was created by the tragedian **Richard Burbage**. Knowing the answer might help us understand how Shakespeare conceived the role – but perhaps it is better that we don't.

An early performance took place in front of James I at **court** on Shrove Tuesday, 1605, and was repeated two days later. *The Merchant*'s celebrity in the Jacobean theatre is also suggested by various plays containing Jewish characters – among them *The Travels of the Three English Brothers* (1607) by **John Day**, **William Rowley** and

George Wilkins. Nonetheless, we have no records of any other seventeenth-century performance of Shakespeare's text: although it passed into the hands of **Thomas Killigrew** and the King's Company in 1669, it was apparently never acted.

Just into the eighteenth century, the Tory politician **George Granville** remedied this deficiency by putting the script under the Marlovian title of *The Jew of Venice* and putting it on at Lincoln's Inn Fields in London. Reworking the play for the neo-classical taste of his day, Granville deleted much of Shakespeare's text and replaced it with his own (introducing, according to critic John Gross, "a note of wearisome vulgarity"). He also thinned out Shylock's role to that of a conventional villain, played by a well-known comedian, **Thomas Doggett**. Though never hugely popular, *The Jew of Venice* held the stage until 1741, when **Charles Macklin** put on a triumphant revival of Shakespeare's own text at Drury Lane. Macklin's portrayal of Shylock was a revelation: in place of the conventional comic characterization, he presented a fully rounded figure – touched by pathos as well as embittered and malevolent. It became one of the most successful productions of the period and made Macklin's career – he was still acting Shylock at 89 and stopped only when his memory failed completely.

Though the *Merchant* reached North America in 1752 – courtesy of **Lewis Hallam** and his English company, who staged it at Williamsburg, Virginia in 1752, seemingly the first ever professional staging of Shakespeare in the US – most eighteenth-century performances occurred back in England. It was produced a number of times by **David Garrick** (with whom the great **Sarah Siddons** debuted as Portia in 1775), **George Colman**, **George Frederick Cooke** and **John Philip Kemble**, but audiences had to wait until 1814 and **Edmund Kean** for an interpretation of the central role as ground-breaking as Macklin's – Shylock as hero. Though the auditorium at Drury Lane was three-quarters empty, Kean's tragic portrayal was to propel him into superstardom (he celebrated by buying a stallion and naming it "Shylock"). As importantly, it resonated with Romantic critics headed by William Hazlitt – who, borrowing from *Lear*, reverently described Kean's Jew as a man "more sinned against than sinning". G.H. Lewes later wrote that it was impossible to watch him "without being strangely shaken by the terror, and the pathos, and the passion of a stormy spirit uttering itself in tones of irresistible power".

William Charles Macready acted the play from 1823 onwards, but was never entirely comfortable in the role of Shylock. **Charles Kean** (Edmund's surviving son) followed him at the Princess's Theatre in 1858 but distracted attention from the actors by evoking all the fun of the *Carnevale*, complete with colourful crowds, gondolas and "real" canals. In the US, meanwhile, the *Merchant* had flourished, not least among companies who toured the frontiers of the burgeoning nation. One of the most successful Shylocks of the century was **Edwin Booth**, the first American talent to make a name for himself in Europe. His performance at New York's Winter Garden in 1867 was enthusiastically acclaimed, but turned its back on Kean's sympathetic interpretation – in Booth's view, Shylock was obsessed by money and malice, and the text was cut to emphasize those qualities.

The African American **Ira Aldridge** (see p.337) added the Jew to his extensive list of roles in the 1850s, but the most influential exponent of a sympathetic Shylock in the late nineteenth century was **Henry Irving**, who based his 1879 characterization on a

"Moorish Jew" he had seen while travelling. Acting opposite **Ellen Terry**'s Portia at the Lyceum in the conviction that Shylock was "the type of a persecuted race; almost the only gentleman in the play, and the most ill-used", Irving didn't stint on pathos, even to the point of adding an emotive wordless scene in which the Jew returned home to discover Jessica fled. Though Henry James thought Irving "rigid and frigid", most agreed with F.J. Furnivall, who declared in a fan letter that "one longs Shakespeare could be here to see you".

Irving's designs – like his dramatic approach – were elevated and spectacular, but they invited a backlash. The first stirrings were masterminded by **William Poel** (see p.588), whose "authentic" reinterpretation included his own villainous Shylock in an 1898 production. The year 1932 saw conservative and radical forces meet at Stratford-upon-Avon. **Frank Benson**'s company played a well-worn *Merchant* in his farewell outing, while in a portent of things to come **Theodor Komisarjevsky** put on his brand-new version later in the summer. As in his later *Comedy of Errors* (see p.50), the

Jonathan Pryce brought a hunted quality to the role of Shylock in Jonathan Munby's Renaissance-Venetian production at the Globe in 2015, making it clear that revenge was the refuge of a man driven to extremes.

director's vision was eclectic: his higgledy-piggledy Venice was populated with mimed *commedia dell'arte* episodes and clowning galore. The subtext, though, was satirical: his Christians were dissolute wastrels, while **Randle Ayrton**'s Shylock was a "twisting, comic devil". Given what was then happening in Germany, though, Komisarjevsky's critique now looks naive – as **Max Reinhardt**, a Jewish director who had regularly staged the *Merchant* since 1905, discovered when he left Germany for the US in 1938, having turned down an offer of "honorary Aryanship". One of Reinhardt's colleagues, **Werner Krauss**, would later act in Nazi-sponsored productions of the play, Shakespeare being exempted from Hitler's ban on foreign writers. Krauss's interpretation of Shylock reached its anti-Semitic height in a notoriously rabble-rousing production staged by **Lothar Muthel** at Vienna's Burgtheater in 1943.

Though the horrors of Hitler's "Final Solution" became widely apparent in the last months of World War II, it took some time for the implications to filter down to British productions of the *Merchant*. Following **Donald Wolfit**'s success in the role, Shylock was acted as a stage villain well into the 1950s, and even **Michael Redgrave**'s sensitive performance at Stratford in 1953 was notable mainly for its brooding intensity and rage. It was only in 1960, in **Michael Langham**'s Stratford version with the young **Peter O'Toole**'s heroic Shylock, that some kind of response was formulated. Perhaps the most searching postwar production in England was **Jonathan Miller**'s, at the National in 1970. **Laurence Olivier** played Shylock as a Jew trying hard – too hard – to assimilate in a Venice of the 1880s, Miller's aim being to demonstrate that economic forces lay at the root of anti-Semitism. His cast – **Joan Plowright**'s Portia and **Jeremy Brett**'s Bassanio among them – suggested the *froideur* and emptiness at the heart of the play.

Successive productions in both the UK and US have dealt with its ethnicity in different ways, but all have paid close heed. **John Barton**'s 1978 version at The Other Place cast **Patrick Stewart**'s Shylock as a mean-spirited miser, but above all a bad Jew; directing it again in 1981, Barton used the Jewish **David Suchet**, who kept his character's religion at the centre of his interpretation but faced corresponding anxieties from reviewers. Much the same difficulties faced **Antony Sher** (again of Jewish heritage) when he essayed the role at the RSC in 1987 under **Bill Alexander**'s direction: Sher adopted a Turkish accent and was equipped with flowing Oriental robes. This self-consciously "foreign" Shylock faced outright hostility from the play's Christians, as he did in **Barry Edelstein**'s 1995 production in New York; **Ron Liebman** donned yarmulke and beard in a visual statement of Shylock's Jewishness.

A few years earlier **Peter Hall** directed **Dustin Hoffman** in London, once again portraying the Christians as unapologetic racists. **Peter Zadek**'s 1995 production, originating in Germany but later touring internationally, stressed the capitalist problems at the root of the play – even bringing Shylock to Belmont to advise on the casket wager. By contrast, the Holocaust was never very distant from **Trevor Nunn**'s 1999 National Theatre production, with **Henry Goodman** playing Shylock in a setting reminiscent of 1930s Berlin. Goodman spoke Yiddish to his daughter in what the *Times* acclaimed as "the best *Merchant* for many years". Also excellent was **Barrie Rutter**'s searching production with Northern Broadsides in 2004, which had at its centre Rutter's sympathetic Shylock in a reading that brought out the clash of personalities at the play's centre.

Although the play has remained popular in the UK, it has been less so in the US, its subject matter perhaps too much for many producers to stomach. Nonetheless, **Rupert Goold**'s Royal Shakespeare Company version of 2011, set in a contemporary American casino, boldly exchanged Venice for Las Vegas and ducats for dollars. Many critics were suspicious, but it brought home how money was at the root of the play's evils, with **Patrick Stewart** playing a miserly Shylock and even **Susannah Fielding**'s brightly optimistic Southern-belle Portia reduced to a breakdown by the end. **Polly Findlay**'s 2015 staging at the same venue was also highly conceptual but only lukewarmly received ("reduces some strong actors to mechanical playthings," according to one critic), and suffered from comparison with the concurrent production by **Jonathan Munby** at Shakespeare's Globe in London, in which **Jonathan Pryce** offerd a dignified and anguished Shylock in a carefully realized sixteenth-century Venice. The closing tableau, in which the audience observed his forced conversion to Christianity, was almost unbearably moving.

Merchant has been hugely popular globally since the mid-nineteenth century, notably in places where the Jewish population has traditionally been small – implying that a Judaeo-Christian framework is not the only way of understanding the play. Adapted in the 1860s as a Bengali drama called *Bhanumati Cittavilasa* by the writer **Hara Chandra Ghosh**, it was the first Shakespearian text to be remade in an Indian language, and sparked a run of localized versions that continued into the 1910s, many of them written for the popular theatres of Mumbai. More surprisingly, the play has also been hugely popular in **China**, both the first Shakespearian play ever to be translated into Mandarin (in a version adapted from the Lambs' *Tales from Shakespeare*) and the first drama to reach the stage, a version staged in 1913 called *Rou quan* ("Bond of Flesh"). The play has often been revived since, perhaps because its near-Marxist interest in high finance was attractive to China's communist leaders (*Merchant* has long been a set text in Chinese schools).

Things have understandably been very different in Israel, where the play's concern with the Jewish faith has been an abiding focus. The play was first performed in 1932 under the great German director **Leopold Jessner**, with **Aharon Meskin** in the lead. **Tyrone Guthrie** was the next to direct in 1959, a generation later and well after the formation of the State of Israel – as well as after the Holocaust. He felt free to experiment, introducing modern dress but bringing back Meskin to play Shylock, this time as a capitalist financier. The production had other problems, however, and did badly – as did **Yossi Yzraeli**'s version in 1972, which risked a deeply unsympathetic Shylock, the comedian **Avner Hyskiahu**, and paid the price at the box-office. Another Israeli production of *The Merchant*, this time directed by **Yossi Alfi** in a translation by **Avraham Oz**, failed even to make the stage of the Bet-Lessin Theatre, pulled because of financing difficulties. A Hebrew-language production by the Israeli company **Habima** toured to London in 2012 as part of the World Shakespeare Festival, but was almost as controversial: the performance was picketed to protest the fact that the company had previously performed in the Occupied Territories. Nonetheless **Jacob Cohen** made a powerful and mournful Shylock, visibly worn down by events.

At least seven *Merchant*s were filmed in the silent era alone, a number of them in India. These include a 1916 version starring the renowned **Matheson Lang** as Shylock opposite his wife **Nellie Hutin Britton** as Portia; the Indian *Dil Farosh* ("The Seller of

Hearts", 1927), based on an earlier script by **Syed Mehdi Hasan Ahsan**; and a German production of 1923 with **Werner Krauss**. Since then, non-English productions have dominated the big screen: a Hindi version (*Zaalin Sandagar*) in 1941, a French-Italian co-production with **Michel Simon** as Shylock in 1953 and a Maori-language adaptation directed by **Don Selwyn** in 2002 with a largely Maori cast. Hollywood has only produced one version to date, directed by **Michael Radford**, and starring **Al Pacino** as Shylock (2004), who also took the role to Broadway in 2010. Various well-regarded TV productions (in addition to the adaptation of Jonathan Miller's 1970 *Merchant*) include the BBC/Time-Life version directed by **Jack Gold**, with **Warren Mitchell** as Shylock.

SCREEN

The Merchant of Venice

L. Olivier, A. Nicholls, J. Plowright; John Sichel (dir.)
UK, 1973 ❯ Network / 01 Distribution DVD 🔊

Produced by Jonathan Miller and based on his celebrated 1970 production for the National Theatre, this *Merchant* is certainly slick. Set in 1880s Venice, the staging brings to mind the damasked interiors of Freud's Vienna as well as mid-century London – all gloomy tapestries and thin-lipped *politesse*. The problem is that the sheer physical horror of the play feels worlds away: the flesh-bond is just too incredible to believe, and Anthony Nicholls's Antonio barely has to remove his frock coat before Plowright's immaculate Portia steps in. But then Antonio isn't the emotional centre here: it's Olivier's Shylock, cast as tragic hero in true Irving style (the "I hate him for he is a Christian" speech is cut, for instance). His is a big performance, perhaps a bit too big, though it's persuasively finessed and doesn't duck controversy – some critics thought Olivier was impersonating the Rothschilds, others Trollope's Augustus Melmotte, still others Hitler. Though partial, Miller's is a consummately intelligent reading of the play, and there isn't a weak performance to be found.

The Merchant of Venice

H. Goodman, A. Hanson, D. Crotty; Trevor Nunn (dir.) UK, 2000 ❯ Metrodome / Image DVD

Henry Goodman's searing, masterful performance was reason enough to record Trevor Nunn's award-winning 1999 National Theatre production. His mild-mannered Shylock seems benign at first, but clearly possesses a groundswell of torment he does not fully understand – he flinches even as he draws the knife, as if unable to comprehend quite what prompts his ghastly revenge. But Shylock's decision to turn his back on "mercy" here sunders him from his religion (and in a brilliant touch his kinsman Tubal stalks out of the court in disgust), a moment of critical importance and one echoed in a tremendously moving finale, which sees Gabrielle Jordan's anguished Jessica break tearfully into Yiddish song as she is handed her father's wealth. The production, set in a Venice artfully reminiscent of interwar Berlin, bristles with attentive detail, and rarely have the play's intimate psychological shadings seemed so freshly real. Every character travels into uncomfortable and irredeemable emotional territory – not least David Bamber's careworn and pallid Antonio, Alexander Hanson's thoughtful Bassanio and a highly strung (and utterly brilliant) Portia from Derbhle Crotty.

The Merchant of Venice

A. Pacino, J. Irons, J. Fiennes; Michael Radford (dir.)
Italy/US, 2004 ❯ MGM / Sony DVD 🔊

Michael Radford's polished *Merchant* certainly looks the part. The cinematography is done in burnished, Giorgionesque tones, the Venetian backdrop oozes authenticity – but as drama this struggles to rise above the level of historically accurate window-dressing. The pacing is languorous going on lethargic, there's precious little tension, while the acting is merely tolerable. Joseph Fiennes seems superficial as Bassanio, Lynn Collins offers a breathily posh and mildly prim Portia, while Jeremy Irons's openly gay Antonio appears to be struggling with indigestion rather than caustic inner torment. Only Al Pacino's turn as a hulking, watchful and intensely sympathetic Shylock rescues this picture from Merchant Ivory-level ordinariness: without a hint of barnstorming, he makes the trial scene a study in wounded self-destruction.

AUDIO

The Merchant of Venice

W. Mitchell, M. Jarvis, S. West; Peter Kavanagh (dir.)
UK, 2000 ❯ BBC ◉ 🔊

A twinkling-eyed Warren Mitchell squints out from the cover of this BBC *Merchant*, and given that Mitchell's most famous role was that of the comical bigot Alf Garnett in the 1960s sitcom *Till Death Us Do Part*, some listeners might approach this recording with trepidation.

This cackling cockney Shylock does surprise after Olivier's assimilative tones (see above), but he has both history and ethnicity on his side: the East End was for many years the centre of London's Jewish community (Mitchell himself grew up there) and his interpretation sparkles with life. It also marks him off aurally from the drawling world of Sam West's Bassanio and Martin Jarvis's Antonio, a class distinction that lies at the heart of this version. Juliet Aubrey's Portia is excellent, but after her humiliation of Shylock amid jeering and spitting Christian crowds it's difficult to think there is much harmony in the play's conclusion.

EDITIONS

New Cambridge Shakespeare
M.M. Mahood (ed.); rev. 2003 > Cambridge UP

Though the core of Mahood's edition of the *Merchant* dates back to 1987, it has been revamped with new information on recent critical and theatrical debates. These bring up to date what was already an excellent title: Mahood's introduction explores a variety of intellectual approaches but never loses sight of what "experiencing the play" in the theatre is like. While some might quibble with her assertion that "first and foremost *The Merchant of Venice* is a romantic play", she makes a persuasive case and Charles Edelman's contributions, taking into account recent books by James Shapiro and others, finesse it.

SOME CRITICISM

Shakespeare's Comedy of Love
Alexander Leggatt; 1974 > Routledge / Methuen

Alexander Leggatt is the editor of *The Cambridge Companion to Shakespearean Comedy* and author of much else besides, but his most celebrated book is probably his early *Shakespeare's Comedy of Love*. It

remains one of the most sympathetic, suggestive and humane studies of Shakespearian comedy around, consistently alive to the wistful and even tragic qualities present in these plays, yet celebrating their diverse and inventive explorations of comic romantic love. His essay on *The Merchant* is superlative, demonstrating how love (and not just romantic heterosexual love) seems here as much a part of the commercial environment as anything else, a thematic link that yokes together its two contrasting plots; Leggatt's final conviction that the play shows "a larger world than it can finally bring into harmony" seems as fine a description of the play as it's possible to conceive. Alongside *The Merchant*, the book also contains chapters on each of the major comedies: *Dream, Much Ado, The Merry Wives, As You Like It* and *Twelfth Night*. Hard copy is print-on-demand, but it's also available in ebook format.

Shylock
John Gross; 1992 > Touchstone

When *The Merchant* was first printed in 1600, its title-page drew attention to the "extreme cruelty of Shylock the Jew towards the said merchant", and the moneylender has, understandably enough, rarely been absent from discussion about the play. Literary and theatre critic John Gross refuses to close off debate, instead providing information along with further questions: why is Shylock forcibly baptized when Church policy went against it? How does the legal substance of the play stand up? Why "Shylock", even? The book is really a cultural history of attitudes to Jewishness brought into focus by versions of Shakespeare's play, and its range – extending from medieval Jewry to T.S. Eliot's Bleistein – is impressive. Attending to the complexity of his task in our post-Holocaust world, Gross senses a "permanent chill in the air" in *The Merchant*. Also well worth looking at in this context is James Shapiro's *Shakespeare and the Jews* (1996).

The Merry Wives of Windsor

T he only full play of Shakespeare's to be located in the England he knew, *The Merry Wives of Windsor* takes rich delight in its social and geographical setting, eschewing the verbal artfulness of earlier comedies for an earthy, prosy texture. In this subtly crafted and often genuinely funny play, Shakespeare removes Sir John Falstaff and several of his followers from the world of *Henry IV* and transplants them to the alien territory of Elizabethan Windsor – perhaps in order to keep a pact with the audience, who were promised at the end of *Part II* that the playwright would "continue the story with Sir John in it". Further background for its genesis is provided by the (possibly apocryphal) theory that it was performed in front of Queen Elizabeth in 1597 in order to celebrate the knightly Order of the Garter. Whatever the exact reasons behind its creation, though, its generic affinities are easily defined. The story of two wives who gain the upper hand over their husbands and the interloping Falstaff borrows elements from the folk-tale tradition, and the play is a sharp and pointed social comedy, one in which the good people of Windsor – in particular the "wives" – emerge gloriously triumphant.

DATE > It seems likely that an entertainment performed in front of Elizabeth I in April 1597 was *The Merry Wives of Windsor*, or at least part of it. The play was probably finished by 1598 (when the cycle of history plays starring Falstaff was completed).

SOURCES > This spin-off from the *Henry IV–V* cycle has no direct sources, and is the only play of Shakespeare's to be wholly set in England – a fact that has encouraged critics to detect any number of Elizabethan in-jokes.

TEXTS > A quarto version, perhaps reconstructed from an actor's memory of the play, appeared in 1602 (Q1), and was popular enough to be reprinted in 1619 (Q2). A more authoritative text was included in the 1623 Folio, but it was cleansed of "profanities" in response to new legislation (see p.118).

Interpreting the play

Written only a year or two after *The Merchant of Venice*, another play with markedly middle-class credentials, *The Merry Wives* is set among the provincial milieu of Windsor – then, as now, a well-to-do satellite of London – and portrays a bustling, vivid tapestry of small-town life. In contrast to so-called "city comedy" (a hard-bitten, satirical genre pioneered by younger colleagues like Thomas Dekker, John Marston and Thomas Middleton), *The Merry Wives* might best be described as suburban in

MAJOR CHARACTERS & SYNOPSIS

TOWNSPEOPLE OF WINDSOR

Margaret Page (the first "wife")
George Page, Margaret Page's husband
Anne Page, their daughter
William Page, their son, a schoolboy
Alice Ford (the second "wife")
Frank Ford, Alice Ford's husband (later disguised as "Brooke")
John and **Robert**, the Fords' servants
Sir Hugh Evans, a Welsh parson
Doctor Caius, a French physician
Mistress Quickly, Dr Caius's housekeeper and Anne Page's confidante
John Rugby, Dr Caius's servant

AT THE GARTER INN

Sir John Falstaff, lodging at the Garter Inn
Bardolph, **Pistol** and **Nim**, Falstaff's followers
Robin, Falstaff's page
The **Host** of the Garter
Robert Shallow, a justice of the peace
Master Abraham Slender, Shallow's nephew
Peter Simple, Slender's servant
Master Fenton, a young gentleman

ACT 1 Justice Shallow is complaining to Sir Hugh Evans about the presence in Windsor of the unruly Sir John Falstaff, who has been poaching his deer. Also present is the doltish Slender, who hopes to marry the Pages' daughter Anne. When Falstaff appears, Shallow denounces him, but trouble is averted, and all dine together at Page's house. Back at the Garter Inn, Falstaff, convinced that Mistress Ford and Mistress Page fancy him, intends to seduce them both and get hold of their husbands' money. Pistol and Nim, however, reveal all to Ford and Page. At Dr Caius's house, meanwhile, Simple has arrived with a letter from Evans to Mistress Quickly enlisting her support in Slender's cause. When Caius unexpectedly returns, he is incensed (he also hopes to win Anne's hand) and challenges Evans to a duel. Finally, another suitor, Fenton, turns up seeking Mistress Quickly's advice.

ACT 2 Mistresses Page and Ford have been sent identical love letters by Falstaff. The two plot revenge: they will pretend to play along but bankrupt Falstaff in the process. Ford – aware of Falstaff's scheme and consumed with jealousy –

decides to disguise himself as Brooke, an invented suitor of Mistress Ford who wishes Falstaff to seduce her on his behalf. Falstaff willingly agrees.

ACT 3 The duel between Caius and Evans fails to occur when the Host of the Garter sends them to different places; reconciled, the two men agree to be revenged on him instead. In the meantime, Ford grows more jealous, unaware that the wives plan to humiliate Falstaff by hiding him in a laundry basket (on the pretext of Ford's sudden arrival) and dumping him in the Thames. When Ford does indeed arrive home, expecting to find Sir John, this is precisely what happens. Recovering at the Garter, Falstaff is persuaded by Mistress Quickly that the whole thing was a mistake and that Mistress Ford wants another meeting. Unfortunately, Ford (as Brooke) finds out about it. Meanwhile Fenton has been competing for Anne's hand, and though she is tempted by his offer, her father still favours Slender.

ACT 4 At Ford's house, Falstaff's seduction of Mistress Ford is stalled again by the arrival of Mistress Page, warning that an angry Ford is on the prowl. The two women disguise Falstaff as an old woman before Ford enters; again, he is baffled to have missed his wife's supposed lover. But Mistress Ford reveals the truth, and the two reconciled couples plot Falstaff's humiliation – to occur that night in Windsor Park. On top of this, Page has secretly arranged for Anne to elope with Slender, while his wife (not knowing her husband's plan) plots the same, but with Caius.

ACT 5 At midnight, Falstaff waits in the Park disguised, as instructed, as Herne the Hunter – an ancient woodland spirit. Just as Mistresses Ford and Page arrive, the forest is filled with noise. To Falstaff's disbelief, a group of fairies appear (local children shepherded by Evans and Anne Page). Falstaff panics, but they drag him from his hiding place and condemn his sinfulness. At a signal they are replaced by the Pages and Fords, and Falstaff realizes that it has all been a hoax. Just as the entire party is about to leave for Windsor, however, Slender runs in, followed by Caius. Anne has evaded everyone and marries Fenton instead.

tone. Among its population are a parson, a doctor and an innkeeper – not to forget the "wives" of the title and the network of servants who surround and support them. Unusually for a Shakespearian comedy, the play also depicts family life in some detail; it even includes a scene set in a schoolroom (via Mistress Quickly's impromptu involvement, even young William Page's Latin lesson becomes a convincing comic routine). No direct sources for the play appear to exist: it seems that Shakespeare assembled it from venerable English folk-tale traditions, as certain threads – the jealous husband, the game of suitors – imply.

All this, however, is to ignore the man who, in an early printed text, shares top billing with the "wives": Sir John Falstaff. The roguish "fat knight", who first took a bow in *1 Henry IV*, seems to have been so popular that Shakespeare decided to write a spin-off featuring the comic characters from the history plays. Unruly, fractious and funny, Falstaff and his cronies always threaten to overwhelm (and undermine) the epic kingly narrative played out in the histories. Though caught up in its events, they are gleefully resistant to their historical role, preferring – if at all possible – to while away their lives in Eastcheap taverns, surrounded by cheap booze and women of questionable repute. And *The Merry Wives*, in which they get a play all to themselves, is barely grazed by the courtly and military world of *Henry IV* and *Henry V*.

That said, this comedy has an open-ended relationship with its predecessors. The action must presumably take place before Falstaff's broken-hearted death in *Henry V*, but Shakespeare has no intention of making the linkages neat. Mistress Quickly, for instance, behaves exactly like her namesake in the *Henry IV* plays but seems not even to know Falstaff, still less be desperate to marry him (as she is in *Part II*). Forcibly relocating his historical cast to the provinces, Shakespeare gives us characters who are – and are not – the same as those we know.

Ashore at Windsor

We are not the only ones striving to make sense of Falstaff's presence: the good folk of Windsor – or at least some of them – are having trouble with the unexpected (and unwelcome) new arrivals. As the play gets underway, Justice Shallow is heatedly threatening legal action against Falstaff for poaching Shallow's deer and attacking his men. "If he were twenty Sir John Falstaffs, he shall not abuse Robert Shallow, Esquire" (1.1.2–11), Shallow fumes, his rage fuelled by the unpalatable fact that, as a knight, Falstaff actually outranks him socially. But "abuse" is precisely what he gets, as becomes clear when Falstaff eventually appears:

SIR JOHN Now, Master Shallow, you'll complain of me to the King?
SHALLOW Knight, you have beaten my men, killed my deer, and broke open
    my lodge.
SIR JOHN But not kissed your keeper's daughter?
SHALLOW Tut, a pin. This shall be answered.
SIR JOHN I will answer it straight: I have done all this. That is now answered.
[1.1.102–9]

> *The first act of the Merry Wives alone contains more life and reality than all German literature.*
>
> Friedrich Engels, writing to Karl Marx (1868)

Punning on "answer" ("legal redress"/"reply"), one of Shakespeare's most verbally dextrous characters demonstrates that he is more than a match for rural folk of this stripe. It has long been suspected that in allowing Falstaff to run rings around Shallow and Slender, with all their petty snobberies, the playwright is poking fun at minor gentry around Stratford – one hoary tale is that Shakespeare spent his youth poaching deer, just like Falstaff – but we don't need to know that to enjoy the put-down. The age-old tension between city and country is integral to this scene – and the play.

As with many of his real-life knightly counterparts, Falstaff's claims to social superiority are offset by his need for hard cash, and Windsor, he thinks, offers a solution. It isn't long before he hits on a sure-fire moneymaking scheme that involves seducing both Mistresses Page and Ford and thereby gaining access to their husbands' wealth. Concocting a plan to woo them via letter, he boasts to Nim and Pistol that it will be an easy job to bend Mistress Ford to his will. "I spy entertainment in her," he smirks,

> She discourses, she carves, she gives the leer of invitation. I can construe the action of her familiar style; and the hardest voice of her behaviour, to be Englished rightly, is 'I am Sir John Falstaff's'.
> PISTOL   He hath studied her well, and translated her will: out of honesty, into English.
>
> [1.3.39–45]

Having an affair is as simple as a cheerful exchange of words – the kind of relaxed attitude to infidelity (and the kind of plot for making a fast buck) that dominates contemporary city comedy.

But Windsor is not the city. Though the town is content to let its visitor poach deer, poaching housewives is assuredly off-limits, as Mistress Ford insists, scandalized, when she reads her love letter from the "greasy knight":

> What tempest, I trow, threw this whale, with so many tuns of oil in his belly, ashore at Windsor? … Did you ever hear the like?
>
> [2.1.61–6]

"Perceive how I might be knighted," she exclaims, turning what Falstaff presumes is his key attraction smartly back on him. When it transpires that the letters are duplicates, Mistress Page is even more shocked, and the pair immediately agree to be "revenged" on Falstaff by any means that "may not sully the chariness of our honesty", as Mistress Ford puts it (2.1.94–5).

The rest of the main plot tracks the progress of that richly deserved comeuppance, but Shakespeare introduces a twist. Master Ford is obsessed with the idea that his wife is being unfaithful with Falstaff behind his back, and the playwright, naturally, brings them together. Driven on by reports that Sir John has his eye on her, Ford goes to the unlikely lengths of disguising himself as one "Master Brooke" and paying Falstaff to attempt to seduce her. Once Falstaff assures him that it will be an easy task to lure Mistress Ford away, her husband thinks he has all the evidence against his wife he needs. "Who says this is improvident jealousy?" he seethes:

> My wife hath sent to him, the hour is fixed, the match is made. Would any man have thought this? See the hell of having a false woman! My bed shall be abused, my coffers ransacked, my reputation gnawn at … I will rather trust a Fleming with my butter, Parson Hugh the Welshman with my cheese, an Irishman with my aqua-vitae bottle, or a thief to walk my ambling gelding, than my wife with herself.
>
> [2.2.280–95]

The misogynistic little-Englander Ford regards his "woman" as a commodity, like so much home-churned butter or cheese. The extent to which his rage is directed at characters such as Sir Hugh Evans, the Welsh parson, marks his distance from a community that has taken outsiders such as Evans and the French Dr Caius to its heart (for all that the play itself gives them what appear to be "funny" foreign accents). And although Ford's speech is comic because we have the confidence that his wife's good sense will win through, it hints at jealousy's destructive force. While on one level he is undeniably the "poor cuckoldly knave" that Falstaff later describes, what appears comic in *The Merry Wives* will have altogether darker ramifications in *Othello* and, later still, *The Winter's Tale*.

Sinful fantasy

Fortunately Mistresses Page and Ford never allow affairs to become that serious: they are as well equipped to deal with Ford's jealousy as they are to neutralize Sir John. The process of the two men's re-education, via a mounting sequence of comic emasculations, takes up the rest of the play. While allowing Ford's ludicrous suspicions to build, they first engineer a scene in which both men are shown up to be the fools they really are.

After scheduling a romantic tête-à-tête between Mistress Ford and Falstaff, both wives arrange for Master Ford to make a surprise entrance, forcing Falstaff to hide in a conveniently placed wash basket – which is then emptied into the nearby Thames (exposing him to household drudgery first-hand, as it were, as well as administering a well-deserved soaking). Satisfyingly, all goes to plan: Ford is duped, Falstaff dumped and neither are any the wiser. But this is just the start of his sufferings, as Falstaff discovers to his dismay when he reschedules a meeting with Mistresses Ford and Page. Hearing that Ford is threatening to burst in once again, his wife has an inspirational idea – to disguise Falstaff as her maid's aunt and smuggle him out. Unfortunately for Sir John, Ford loathes Mother Prat, the "fat woman of Brentford", with a passion unique even for him. "I'll prat her!" he exclaims and lunges, howling:

> Out of my door, you witch, you rag, you baggage, you polecat, you runnion! Out, out! I'll conjure you, I'll fortune-tell you! ... Hang her, witch!
>
> [4.2.170–8]

Though the comedy is broad, it is not without depth. There is a gratifying aptness in seeing Ford's misogyny addressing itself to one of Shakespeare's most resolutely masculine characters; the pleasure is compounded by the irony that this is the only time in all of Shakespeare's plays that a man appears on stage dressed as a woman (an irony not without force, given the transvestite theatre in which he operated). Ford's own response to the situation is unwittingly to ridicule himself. "Come hither, Mistress Ford!" he yells,

> Mistress Ford, the honest woman, the modest wife, the virtuous creature, that hath the jealous fool to her husband. I suspect without cause, mistress, do I?
> MISTRESS FORD God be my witness you do, if you suspect me in any dishonesty.
>
> [4.2.117–22]

Following this incident, the wives decide that Ford has suffered enough and let him into their big secret.

But Falstaff's final disgrace is yet to come. After the robust comedy of his earlier treatment, his final humiliation, in which he is persuaded into Windsor Great Park in the dead of night and attacked by malicious fairies (in fact local children), can seem strange. It makes rather more sense, as critics have emphasized, when understood in relation to the folk-tale ancestry of *The Merry Wives*. Drawing attention to the ancient rituals that underpin the final scene, the scholar Jeanne Addison Roberts suggests that the townspeople of Windsor treat Falstaff as a scapegoat who must be slaughtered because his sexual aggression threatens the community of the play. The fairies' chant, which intones, "Fie on sinful fantasy! / Fie on lust and luxury!" (5.5.92–3) draws this out. It's also worth observing that Shakespeare's comedies frequently end by isolating single characters as everyone else is paired off around them: in *As You Like It* it's Jaques, in *Twelfth Night* it's Malvolio, in *Much Ado* it's Don John. If the comic community of *The Merry Wives* is to heal its wounds, Shakespeare suggests, Falstaff needs not just to be thrown out but to be utterly humiliated, crowned with horns like a cuckolded husband. If the wives are to prove themselves "merry, and yet honest too" (4.2.95), the duper needs to be duped.

Thus the play's finale concerns more than Falstaff: it is about the wives' reassertion of control over their community. But in the dying moments of the comedy they, too, are taught a lesson. While the rest of the plot has been working satisfyingly away, the Pages' daughter Anne has been pursued by a variety of suitors. The dimwit Slender has ambitions, and despite his inability to string together a cogent sentence is secretly supported by Anne's father. Mistress Page, meanwhile, has her hopes pinned on Dr Caius, the town's irascible and near-nonsensical French physician. But Anne has other dreams, and in making them reality she outwits both parents. While everyone else is busy fooling Falstaff in the wood, Anne manages to get herself married to young Fenton instead. As Fenton tells it, the climax of *The Merry Wives* is nothing less than a victory for love. "Hear the truth of it," he addresses his new parents-in-law:

> You would have married her, most shamefully,
> Where there was no proportion held in love.
> The truth is, she and I, long since contracted,
> Are now so sure that nothing can dissolve us.
> Th'offence is holy that she hath committed,
> And this deceit loses the name of craft,
> Of disobedience, or unduteous title,
> Since therein she doth evitate and shun
> A thousand irreligious cursèd hours
> Which forced marriage would have brought upon her.

> [5.5.212–23]

The wider movement of the play suggests that we – and the people of Windsor – should take Fenton's grave words seriously. It is a lesson Master Ford, recently reconciled with his own wife, would do well to observe.

Stage history and adaptations

Until recently it was believed that *The Merry Wives* was written specifically for Queen Elizabeth I (there is an apocryphal tale that she commanded Shakespeare to write a play showing Falstaff "in love"), or perhaps for a 1597 feast celebrating the **Order of the Garter**, but in the absence of hard evidence it's thought that the comedy was intended for public performance from early on and it seems it did well. Among its first casts seem to have been **Richard Burbage** (Ford), **Robert Armin** (Evans) and **John Heminges** (Falstaff). "A Play of the Merry Wives of Windsor" was played at **court** in 1604; and another performance is recorded in 1638 at Inigo Jones's Cockpit-at-Court Theatre, this time with the portly **John Lowin** as Falstaff.

It was one of the first Shakespeare plays to be resurrected following the Restoration, initially at the Vere Street Theatre (where Pepys saw it on several occasions, liking it less each time), and though **John Dennis** launched an adaptation he entitled *The Comical Gallant: or The Amours of Sir John Falstaff* in 1702, claiming that "all those men of extraordinary parts, who were the Ornament of that Court … were in love with the Beauties of this Comedy", it failed to dislodge the original from the repertoire of **Thomas Killigrew**'s King's Company. **Thomas Betterton** performed *The Merry Wives* at court in 1705, with **Anne Bracegirdle** and **Ann Barry** playing the leads; and it appeared at **John Rich**'s Lincoln's Inn Fields fifteen years later, with **James Quin** as Falstaff. Though novelist Tobias Smollett likened Quin's declamatory style to "heaving ballast into the hold of a ship", Quin continued to play the part successfully until his

Gossiping beneath twin beehive hairdryers, Mistress Page (Janet Dale) and Mistress Ford (Lindsey Duncan) plot Falstaff's humiliation in Bill Alexander's "new Elizabethan" *Merry Wives* at the RSC (1985).

retirement in 1751. Nearer the century's end **Charles Kemble** was another famous Falstaff, and his brother **John Philip** first staged it at Covent Garden in 1803.

The period also saw one of the few non-native successes for the play – a Russian adaptation attributed to none other than **Catherine the Great** but most probably worked on in collaboration with other writers, which debuted in 1786. In addition to frequent English performances during the eighteenth and nineteenth centuries (some thirty or so at major venues), during this era *The Merry Wives* also reached the continental operatic stage in versions set by **Antonio Salieri** (1799), **Otto Nicolai** (1849) and, most famously, **Giuseppe Verdi**, whose much-loved *Falstaff* premiered in 1893. The best that England could come up with, meanwhile, was an "operatized" adaptation by **Frederick Reynolds** from 1824, incorporating lyrics from other Shakespearian plays and with **Eliza Vestris** starring (and singing) as Mistress Page. Vestris took Reynolds's version to Covent Garden with her in 1839, this time with a cast including **Louisa**

Nisbett as Mistress Ford and **George Bartley**'s Falstaff, and it was also performed at the Haymarket under **Benjamin West** five years later.

Bartley transported the role to the Princess's Theatre in London when **Charles Kean** put on the original play in 1851, where Kean acted Ford with his wife **Ellen Tree** as his onstage spouse. **John Hollingshed**'s 1874 production at the Gaiety Theatre was notable not merely for the experienced actor-manager **Samuel Phelps** in the role of Falstaff, but incidental music by **Arthur Sullivan**. Close to the century's end, **Herbert Beerbohm Tree** would mount several versions of *The Merry Wives*: the first, in 1889, was also his first Shakespeare (it starred his wife, **Helen Maud**, as Anne Page), while the second was a lavish and painstakingly historicized spectacle mounted in 1902 to celebrate the coronation of Edward VII. Alongside **Madge Kendal**'s and **Ellen Terry**'s middle-aged Wives, Tree was widely acclaimed as "the finest Falstaff of them all".

The Merry Wives continued to be acted every few years, though after Tree's grand fifteenth-century treatment, it wasn't wholly surprising that **Oscar Asche**'s production of 1911 at the Garrick Theatre, featuring spare and snowbound sets, was not well received. (His subsequent Haymarket staging in 1929, boasting modern dress and a motorcycle upon which Anne Page rode pillion, did better.) Outrage once again greeted **Theodor Komisarjevsky**'s colourfully Viennese production of 1935, though traditionalist sympathies would be assuaged by **Donald Wolfit**'s patriotic wartime performances at the Strand Theatre in 1940 and 1942.

As with other less popular plays, *The Merry Wives* has found the Stratford Memorial Theatre (and its state-subsidized successor, the Royal Shakespeare Company) its most eager postwar advocates. Numerous productions have appeared at their behest, beginning with **Glen Byam Shaw**'s 1955 version – in which **Anthony Quayle** injected a dose of melancholy into Sir John – and continuing with **Terry Hands**'s staging of 1968, with **Brewster Mason** as Falstaff, **Brenda Bruce** and **Elizabeth Spriggs** tackling the role of the Wives, and **Ian Richardson**'s coldly cynical Ford.

Hands revived the play seven years later with a similar cast (the sole novelty being **Barbara Leigh-Hunt**'s Mistress Ford), this time as part of a cycle of the *Henry IV–V* plays. Though **Trevor Nunn** and **John Caird**'s RSC version of 1979, with **John Woodvine** as Falstaff and **Ben Kingsley**'s Ford, was well received, by common consent the most memorable RSC late twentieth-century production was put on by **Bill Alexander** in 1985. Set in 1950s suburbia, this saw **Janet Dale** and **Lindsey Duncan**'s Wives plotting under adjacent hairdryers how to ensnare **Peter Jeffrey**'s raffish Falstaff, and featured memorable design touches including a Herne's Oak cut down by the Ministry of Works and replaced by an "Ancient Monument" sign.

Rachel Kavanaugh's 2002–03 touring version, again for the RSC, opted to retread this route with **Richard Cordery**'s gentle-giant knight lording it over a postwar, demobbed Windsor. Again at the RSC, **Gregory Doran** directed a musical version during panto season in 2006 as part of the Complete Works festival. **Judi Dench** (Mistress Quickly) and **Simon Callow** (Falstaff) led an all-star cast, with **Ranjit Bolt**'s book set to music by **Paul Englishby**, but critics were not won over. "This is a soufflé," Michael Billington noted grimly in the *Guardian*, "that takes a long time to rise." More enthusiastically received was the Renaissance-style 2010 production at Shakespeare's Globe in London, directed by **Christopher Luscombe**, which eschewed the play's textual trickery in favour of broad physical humour, notably in **Christopher Benjamin**'s roué-ish Falstaff (like a "helium-filled satyr," according to the *New York Times*).

Although *Merry Wives* has never been nearly as popular outside the UK as other comedies, there have been isolated stagings, particularly on the American festival circuit, notably at the **American Players Theatre** in Wisconsin and Florida's **Orlando Shakespeare Theatre**, both in 2015. In 2012 it was translated into Swahili by a scratch company starring Kenyan comedian **Mrisho Mpoto** as Falstaff, who brought a joyous and slapstick-heavy production to the the Globe as part of the World Shakespeare Festival.

SCREEN

The Merry Wives of Windsor
J. Davis, P. Scales, R. Griffiths; David Hugh Jones (dir.) UK, 1982 > BBC DVD

Comedy is something the BBC Shakespeare project always struggled with, straitjacketed by an Elizabethan-style quest for "authenticity" that left directors little option but to emphasize the verbal wit of the plays (notoriously difficult on screen) over any other kind of humour. That restriction all but sinks David Hugh Jones's Elizabethan *Merry Wives* in comic terms – the cast simply cannot make the laughs work – though the social dynamics that drive the play do come through. The Wives are nicely counterpointed as petit bourgeois (Judy Davis's Mistress Page) and nouveau riche (Prunella Scales), while Ben Kingsley attempts a properly paranoiac Ford. But Richard Griffiths makes little apparent effort as Falstaff, robbing the play of much of its interest, and in general Jones's straight-faced interpretation is neither persuasively serious nor honestly funny. It almost goes without saying that the staging (plenty of Tudor beams and cardboard trees, complete with a sealed-down model of Windsor for distance shots) does not do this production any favours.

The Merry Wives of Windsor
C. Benjamin, S. Evans, S. Woodward; Christopher Luscombe (dir.) UK, 2010 > Shakespeare's Globe DVD

Shakespeare's most resolutely Elizabethan play deserves to be seen in an original-practices production, and Luscombe's, filmed in front of a live Globe audience, does the trick. The ruffs are the size of serving plates, the music squawks away nicely, and there is clinking of tankards aplenty. Despite some drifts into Merrie England territory, the cast is well balanced, with Sarah Woodward and Serena Evans's hoity-toity Mistresses running rings around Christopher Benjamin's well-upholstered Falstaff (who resembles a cross between Father Christmas and late-period Ralph Richardson). The comedy doesn't always come off – the Welsh/French scenes are unavoidably trying – but seeing the purple-stockinged Falstaff being stuffed into a linen basket the size of a small family car just about makes up for it. Even the flat grey skies glimpsed above the roof of the theatre seem appropriately English, and the climatic forest scene has a pleasingly folksy twang.

AUDIO

The Merry Wives of Windsor
J. Redman, J. Jago, A. Quayle UK, 1966 > HarperCollins (Caedmon) ⬇

Despite some suspicions that this 1966 *Merry Wives* might prove insufferably old-fashioned, its cast is enviable and in many ways its character-led approach makes the play seem freshly minted. Quayle was one of the century's most famous Falstaffs and his performance here is absolutely magisterial, though he has plenty of competition: Ronnie Stevens is poignantly wonderful as Slender, Hazel Hughes is ideal as Mistress Quickly and even Dr Caius comes alive in the hands of Micheál MacLiammóir. Almost the best thing about this recording is that everyone sounds as if they're doing it for fun.

EDITIONS

Arden Shakespeare (third series)
Giorgio Melchiori (ed.); 1999 > Bloomsbury

Melchiori's edition of the companion play *2 Henry IV* for the New Cambridge Shakespeare comes highly recommended, and his version of *The Merry Wives* is every bit as good. Although often treated as a mere spin-off, the comedy is not without its critical difficulties – among them the matter of its date and provenance. Melchiori takes a controversial line, arguing that the Garter entertainment presented in front of Elizabeth I could not possibly have been the play, and is thus free to date it after *2 Henry IV*. On less vexed topics Melchiori is informative and argumentative, arguing that the play is Falstaff's as much as the Wives'. The main text is helpfully glossed, and a facsimile of the 1602 first quarto is included in appendix.

SOME CRITICISM

Shakespeare's English Comedy
Jeanne Addison Roberts; 1979 > Nebraska UP
[o/p]

Roberts's interest in the "Englishness" of *The Merry Wives* relates mainly to its use of native folk and ritual motifs – such as those used to humiliate male adulterers – going back many hundreds of years, analogues (or, in her term, "contexts") she employs to construct a persuasive defence of its dramatic techniques as well as its place in the Shakespearian canon. As well as providing a thorough symbolic analysis of the play – one that has a good deal to recommend it – Roberts also offers information on textual history and critical reception.

The Metamorphoses of Shakespearean Comedy
William Carroll; 1985 > Princeton UP

Carroll's engaging exploration of metamorphosis and its place within Shakespearian comedy from the *Shrew* to the romances finds a natural midpoint in *The Merry Wives*, in which both Falstaff and Ford find their worlds turned upside down by the play: Falstaff (until now, Carroll remarks, "like Frankenstein's monster ... still on the loose") is conquered, Ford apparently reformed. While covering some of the same ground as Roberts, Carroll suggests that the play's final trick may be on its audiences, and perhaps that we too are meant to be chastened by its conclusion – a conclusion leading inexorably towards Falstaff's death in *Henry V*.

A Midsummer Night's Dream

One of the most enduringly popular of Shakespeare's comedies and the playwright's first mature masterpiece, *A Midsummer Night's Dream* is probably the most widely acted play in the canon. Curiously, that's been a mixed blessing: mined by Victorian producers for its spectacular potential and indelibly associated with hosts of fluttering fairies, *Dream* has only recently been acknowledged as the dangerous, high-wire piece of theatre it really is. Though Shakespeare's cast of sprites could come from any number of Elizabethan masques – there's a long-standing theory that he drew upon boyhood recollections of royal festivities held in Warwickshire – in this play his fairies influence, and subvert, mortal life and love with mischievous and often unsettling power. Indeed, audiences and critics have often thought that the emotional tussles between Oberon, Puck and Titania are the most dramatic of all, nearly eclipsing those of Shakespeare's Athenian lovers as they wander in the forest at night-time. But perhaps it's the collisions between the play's varied social worlds that most surprise and enchant. Plenty of unexpected transformations and translations occur; and in the pseudo-tragedy that brings things to a halt, performed for the Athenians by a troupe of local artisans, Shakespeare even sends up the business of theatre itself.

DATE > Probably 1595–96, towards the end of a group of plays including *Love's Labour's Lost*, *Richard II*, *Romeo and Juliet* and *The Merchant of Venice*.

SOURCES > Shakespeare amplifies Chaucer's "Knight's Tale" (c. 1388), which provides the wedding narrative, with classical sources including Ovid's *Metamorphoses* in Arthur Golding's 1567 translation and Apuleius's *The Golden Ass* (trans. 1566). Myriad other sources have also been detected – more than in any other play.

TEXTS > A quarto version (Q1) typeset from the dramatist's papers appeared in 1600, and was reprinted in 1619 (Q2). The Folio edition (1623) suggests that Shakespeare tinkered with Act Five.

Interpreting the play

One of the reasons that *A Midsummer Night's Dream* is so popular is that it offers so much to so many. It is a comedy of love and lovers in the lyrical vein of *Love's Labour's Lost*. It is festive, too: framed by a wedding which is to be celebrated, as Theseus promises his bride, "with pomp, with triumph, and with revelling" (1.1.19), it also has close resonances with the ancient festival of midsummer, traditionally a celebration

MAJOR CHARACTERS & SYNOPSIS

Theseus, Duke of Athens
Hippolyta, Queen of the Amazons, engaged to Theseus
Philostrate, Theseus's master of revels
Egeus, an Athenian gentleman, Hermia's father
Hermia, Egeus's daughter, in love with Lysander
Lysander, loved by Hermia
Demetrius, also in love with Hermia (with Egeus's support)
Helena, in love with Demetrius
Oberon, King of the Fairies
Titania, Queen of the Fairies
Robin Goodfellow (known as **Puck**), Oberon's fairy attendant
Fairies, among them **Peaseblossom**, **Cobweb**, **Mote** and **Mustardseed**
The artisans: **Peter Quince,** a carpenter (acts **Prologue** in the play *Pyramus and Thisbe*); **Nick Bottom**, a weaver (**Pyramus**); **Francis Flute**, a bellows-mender (**Thisbe**); **Tom Snout**, a tinker (**Wall**); **Robin Starveling**, a tailor (**Moonshine**); **Snug**, a joiner (**Lion**)

ACT 1 At the Athenian court, preparations are underway for the marriage of Theseus and Hippolyta. The royal couple is discussing arrangements when an angry Egeus storms in: his rebellious daughter Hermia refuses to marry Demetrius as arranged, but instead prefers Lysander. Although Demetrius formerly courted Helena (who still loves him), Theseus decrees that Hermia should obey her father, and announces that she has until the day of his own marriage (in four days' time) to decide. Left alone, Hermia and Lysander resolve to elope, and arrange to meet in the forest. But they reveal as much to Helena – who reflects that alerting Demetrius might be the way to win him back. Elsewhere, a group of workers led by Peter Quince are making their own plans: they hope to perform their play, *Pyramus and Thisbe*, at the royal wedding celebrations.

ACT 2 In the woods, Oberon and Titania bicker over a boy in Titania's service, whom Oberon wants as an attendant. When Titania refuses, Oberon plots revenge, sending Puck to find him a magic flower, the juice of which (when dropped on the eyelids of a sleeping person) makes them fall in love with whatever they see first. Oberon applies

it to Titania's eyes. By this time, Demetrius and Helena have entered the forest on Hermia and Lysander's trail, and Oberon orders Puck to bewitch Demetrius, too, hoping that he will fall for Helena. But Puck gets the wrong man, applying the juice of the flower to Lysander's eyes by mistake. When he is woken by Helena, Lysander immediately falls in love with her and abandons Hermia.

ACT 3 When Puck sees the artisans rehearsing their play, he mischievously changes Bottom's head to that of a donkey, causing his companions to flee in horror. Slumbering nearby, Titania awakes and, as intended, immediately falls for the puzzled (but flattered) Bottom and leads him to her bower. Puck gleefully relates this to Oberon, but when Lysander and Demetrius appear, it becomes apparent that something has gone appallingly wrong. Attempting to resolve the situation, Puck applies the juice to Demetrius's eyes, but when he falls in love with Helena too, she merely concludes that it is all a cruel joke. Matters worsen when the women turn on each other, just as the men are deciding to duel. All eventually fall asleep, exhausted, and Puck sets about fixing affairs.

ACT 4 Oberon takes pity on Titania and decides to undo the spell. She is appalled to find Bottom in her arms, but when Oberon removes Bottom's ass-head, the fairy couple is reconciled. Meanwhile, Theseus and Hippolyta are out hunting with Egeus in the forest, when they discover the sleeping lovers. Waking them, Theseus overrules Egeus and commands that Hermia should marry Lysander and Demetrius Helena.

ACT 5 Following the weddings of all three couples, Theseus demands entertainment, which the artisans provide – to the court's mounting bemusement. The plot concerns Pyramus and Thisbe, divided lovers, who arrange to meet and communicate through a chink in a wall. Later, Thisbe sees a lion and flees, dropping her mantle, which Pyramus picks up, woefully concluding that his lover has been eaten. He kills himself just before Thisbe reappears, finds the dead Pyramus, and does likewise. The court struggles to hold back its laughter as Theseus orders everyone to bed.

of fertility and fecundity. It is a play that dwells extensively in the Elizabethan "fairy land", which interacts – and collides – with the human world of the play to an extent unparalleled in any other drama of the period. And it is a comedy in the more modern sense of that word. In his rendering of the entertainment mounted earnestly but mis-guidedly by Bottom and his pals, Shakespeare doesn't just poke fun at the labours of the poet Arthur Golding (from whose translation of Ovid's *Metamorphoses* the tale of Pyramus and Thisbe derives), but produces effects so richly comic that audiences still laugh out loud, four centuries on.

Perhaps it is Shakespeare's skill in synthesizing and shaping all these materials – the play has more sources than any other in the canon – that is most impressive. Though drawing his three groups of characters – the lovers, the fairies and the artisans – from utterly different walks of life, their experiences and fates are bound up in surprising and illuminating ways. For some critics, this a demonstration of Shakespeare's funda-mental optimism about the human condition, if only that when it comes down to it we're all as ridiculous as each other.

O strange!

One common thread is Shakespeare's interest in the ways in which people change – or, rather, the tension between the ways in which they change and yet remain the same. In part this is a continuing dialogue with Shakespeare's sources, in particular Ovid, whose *Metamorphoses* ("Transformations") provide patterns of transformation that dominate the play. Most obvious is the case of the pugnacious weaver Nick Bottom, who, like Ovid's Midas, is given an ass's head by the mischievous spirit Puck. This unfortunate gestation occurs while the "hempen homespuns", as Puck calls them, are rehearsing a play for Theseus's wedding in the forest. Bottom is about to make his grand entrance as the hero Pyramus, unaware of his asinine makeover, when chaos ensues:

> BOTTOM *(as Pyramus)*
>   If I were fair, Thisbe, I were only thine.
> QUINCE O monstrous! O strange! We are haunted. Pray, masters; fly, masters:
>   help!
>
> [3.1.99–100]

The artisans dash for cover, terrified by an apparition that is half-man, half-beast. As we might guess given its distinguished literary pedigree, this transformation is more than an excuse to use a comic prop – though eager directors have often equipped the transmogrified Bottom with a mechanical head, complete with rolling eyes and wag-ging ears. On one level, Bottom's new appearance literalizes what the audience have known all along: that he is an ass (indeed, his name points to another meaning of the word). On another, the joke is that he simply doesn't realize that he is any different – much as, the rest of the time, he is unable to connect his own elevated view of himself with what others inevitably think. He simply cannot understand why his colleagues address him in fear:

SNOUT O Bottom, thou art changed. What do I see on thee?
BOTTOM What do you see? You see an ass-head of your own, do you?
QUINCE Bless thee, Bottom, bless thee. Thou art translated.
BOTTOM I see their knavery. This to make an ass of me, to fright me, if they
could …

[3.1.110–5]

Bottom, though it would pain him to realize it, is already an "ass". Despite the terror expressed by the other artisans and the apparent seriousness of the transformation, Bottom more or less stays as he is. He may develop a bemused taste for "good dry oats" and "great desire to a bottle of hay" (4.1.31–2), but the overriding comedy of the situation cushions it. When Bottom comes round, he is not distressed, but impressed by his "rare vision … past the wit of man to say what dream it was" (4.1.202–3).

We might feel more disturbed, however, by other ambiguous alterations in the play. The Athenian lovers are forced to confront bewildering changes as they traverse the wild, sometimes frightening, territory of the moonlit forest. They end up there partly by accident: after Hermia's father threatens her with death for refusing to marry Demetrius, she elopes with Lysander, but Demetrius and Helena quickly pursue, and all four lovers find themselves in the wood. Once there, they find it near impossible to leave: the fairy king Oberon (a father figure often doubled successfully with Theseus) attempts to resolve the love triangle by casting a spell on Demetrius, but his messenger Puck blunders and anoints the slumbering Lysander with a "love juice" distilled from a magical flower of the forest by mistake. Lysander awakes, falls promptly in love with Helena, and everything immediately begins to go wrong. Though the wood offers liberation from the stifling oppressiveness at court, here it complicates rather than resolves the lovers' experience.

This initial confusion sets up a chain of other transpositions, and the lovers turn against each other with alarming rapidity. The effect is terrifying for those who have to deal with it – which is to say, not those who are actually transformed (Lysander and Demetrius remain oblivious), but those around them. The issues at stake are anxiously expressed by Hermia as she struggles to deal with the fact that Lysander has apparently changed from her devoted lover to a man who claims to "hate" her and adore Helena instead:

Hate me—wherefore? O me, what news, my love?
Am I not Hermia? Are not you Lysander?
I am as fair now as I was erewhile.

[3.2.273–5]

Hermia cannot believe that Lysander looks the same, yet behaves so differently – and demands whether she, too, has visibly changed. (Lysander, though drugged, has already introduced the issue to Helena, crying: "Who will not change a raven for a dove?" (2.2.120)).

Nor are they the only ones caught up in the confusion. Demetrius, recently anointed by Puck in order to straighten things out, has just announced that he once again loves

Helena (as apparently he did before the play began). But instead of accepting him gladly, she switches her position, believing – rather like Bottom – that her erstwhile friends are "bent / To set against me for your merriment" (3.2.146). The irony of this turnaround is sharp: just a few scenes before, she had lamented that she was not as "fair" as Hermia, and that all would be well if only they could switch identities:

KEY SOURCE > Ovid's *Metamorphoses*

"Ovidius Naso," sniffs Holofernes in *Love's Labour's Lost*, "was the man." That this supreme compliment issues from a pompous windbag of a schoolteacher is a sly joke – Ovid was by some distance Shakespeare's favourite classical poet, perhaps even his favourite author in any language.

Publius Ovidius Naso was born in 43 BC at Sulmo (Sulmona), among the Apennines, and was educated in Rome. After making a few half-hearted stabs at a government career, he devoted himself to a life of poetry. He enjoyed conspicuous success until 8 AD, when he was suddenly banished by Augustus Caesar for reasons apparently connected with his licentious *Ars Amatoria* ("Art of Love"), which fell foul of the emperor's severe moral taste. Settling unhappily in Tomis, on the bleak western shores of the Black Sea, he set about recording his despair in works such as *Tristia* (9 AD) and *Epistulae ex Ponto* (13 AD), and died a few years later. Ovid's work was highly esteemed by medieval readers – **Chaucer** and **Gower** among them – and his fame continued into the Renaissance, where his works became a backbone of the humanist curriculum. Shakespeare will almost certainly have discovered Ovid at school, and been required to rehearse his Latin by memorizing sections of the poetry – thus initiating an intense dialogue with the Roman author that continued throughout his working life.

The critic Jonathan Bate points out that Shakespeare was at his most Ovidian at both ends of his career: his early narrative poems "demand to be read side by side with the narratives upon which they improvise", while *The Winter's Tale* and *The Tempest* both betray strong links with the *Metamorphoses* ("Transformations"), a compendium of myths and tales that Ovid

himself transformed into an epic poem prior to his banishment. Something like ninety per cent of Shakespeare's allusions to classical mythology refer to narratives contained in this volume: the tale told in *Venus and Adonis* uses Book 10, where it appears amid a sequence of stories relating frustrated love; and *Titus Andronicus* turns to Book 7's rape of Philomel and her subsequent transformation into a nightingale – so knowingly, in fact, that the play's Lavinia, herself raped and tongueless in a queasy echo of Ovid, brings the *Metamorphoses* on stage in order to relate her plight. With other plays (in particular *Cymbeline, The Merchant of Venice* and *Twelfth Night*) the playwright's debt is more muted, but in *A Midsummer Night's Dream* Shakespeare allowed himself an extended riff on the possibilities – and impossibilities – of Ovidian transformation.

Characteristically, Shakespeare points up differences as much as similarities. Bottom's fate resembles Midas's in *Metamorphoses* Book 11 (after failing to praise Apollo's musical abilities highly enough, Midas is given ass's ears), but the fact that the weaver has to appear "translated" in the flesh and on stage – usually with an obviously fake head – only highlights the fragile realities of theatrical illusion. Likewise, when Shakespeare introduces the tragic tale of Pyramus and Thisbe from Book 4 to the play, he plays it entirely for laughs – and even sends up the sometimes lumbering translation of *Metamorphoses* by **Arthur Golding** (1564). While Francis Meres was right to declare in 1598 that "the sweet witty soul of Ovid lives in mellifluous and honey-tongued Shakespeare", Shakespeare was not above debunking his classical predecessor once in a while – as Holofernes's eulogy testifies.

Demetrius loves your fair—O happy fair!
Your eyes are lodestars, and your tongue's sweet air
More tuneable than lark to shepherd's ear
When wheat is green, when hawthorn buds appear.
Sickness is catching. O, were favour so!
Your words I catch, fair Hermia; ere I go,
My ear should catch your voice, my eye your eye,
My tongue should catch your tongue's sweet melody.
Were the world mine, Demetrius being bated,
The rest I'd give to be to you translated.

[1.1.181–91]

Yet, being "translated", as the whole situation has been translated, Helena finds that she cannot adjust – something hinted at, too, by the straitened and forced texture of her language, all the more obvious in a play that is otherwise so linguistically rich and imaginative.

This unnerving sense of familiarity and alienation is climactically expressed in the mock fight between Demetrius and Lysander in Act Three, orchestrated throughout by the magic of Puck. Their rivalry goes back to the play's opening – except that Helena, not Hermia, is now being fought over. Like the farcical combat between Sir Andrew Aguecheek and the disguised Viola in *Twelfth Night*, this battle is all in the mind; but, as *Dream* repeatedly demonstrates, the deluded mind can be a terrifying place to be. Yet again, the situation is neither one thing nor the other. Though both men are being led "so astray / As one come not within another's way" (3.3.359–60), their aggression is desperate – and desperately personal. Having boasted of the ease with which he shifts shape, "Sometime a horse I'll be, sometime a hound, / A hog, a headless bear, sometime a fire" (3.1.103–4), Puck is the perfect symbol of what Demetrius and Lysander are both fighting and fighting over. As the critic Terry Eagleton puts it, he is the "delusive space", both everything and nothing, that represents their whole experience in the forest.

But with the mind

One of Shakespeare's most teasing suggestions is that love itself may be at fault. While Demetrius and Lysander charge around the forest, all too neatly symbolizing what Helena calls "winged Cupid painted blind", the fairy queen Titania is experiencing her own variation on the theme. At Oberon's behest she too has been drugged, and sweetly calls her love to "sit thee down upon this flow'ry bed,"

While I thy amiable cheeks do coy,
And stick musk-roses in thy sleek smooth head,
And kiss thy fair large ears, my gentle joy.

[4.1.1–4]

The object of her deluded affection is Bottom. She is not convinced that he is an ass, merely that those facets of him that are ass-like are suddenly attractive: love makes

> *What matters in the end is not whether characters "really" love each other or not – since anyone after all can love anyone else – but whether their illusions interlock.*
>
> Terry Eagleton, *William Shakespeare* (1986)

her an ass by making her fall in love with one. These instances upend Helena's early assertion that "Things base and vile, holding no quantity, / Love can transpose to form and dignity" and unflatteringly gloss her belief that "Love looks not with the eyes but with the mind" (1.1.232–4). In *A Midsummer Night's Dream* love does indeed transpose, but rarely does it dignify. As the Polish critic Jan Kott phrases it, in this play "the world is mad and love is mad": something Titania will realize only when she recovers and finds that she has been sleeping with a donkey (not entirely innocently, the play hints, characteristically tongue in cheek).

Another approach to love is put forward by the Mechanicals, whose performance of their drama *Pyramus and Thisbe* at the long-deferred royal marriage celebrations strives for literary seriousness (it is based on the omnipresent *Metamorphoses*) but, "very tragical mirth", unwittingly sends up all the conventions of its genre. Still more, it plays motifs which until now have been serious – lovers meeting by moonlight, the threat of death – as comedy, allowing them to be purged in laughter and revelling. Bottom's turn as the heroic Pyramus is supremely funny in its own terms, but opens out beyond them:

> O grim-looked night, O night with hue so black,
>   O night which ever art when day is not;
> O night, O night, alack, alack, alack …

> [5.1.168–71]

Taken seriously – which of course they are not meant to be – Pyramus's words echo those spoken by Helena ("O weary night, O long and tedious night" (3.3.19)) just a few scenes ago: the entertainment is not as distant from real life as the lovers like to imagine (and, notably, it is surprisingly close to the denouement of *Romeo and Juliet*, perhaps written concurrently with *Dream*). Burlesque though it is, *Pyramus and Thisbe* sends up the kind of melodramatic behaviour we have already seen acted out for real.

There is perhaps a rich joke here. Despite being more or less incidental to the plot (Bottom is, characteristically, the exception), the artisans are not only the most realistic characters in *Dream* – they are beautifully observed, certainly when compared to the interchangeable lovers – but provide a wryly accurate commentary on its main action. Though the aristocrats find themselves chortling at the homespun play offered in their honour, that is only because they fail to see how prescient and humane it is. Shakespeare encourages us to think otherwise. Far from being "nothing, nothing in the world" (as Egeus snootily describes it), it might be said that the artisans' play, in Hippolyta's apt expression, like *Dream* itself, "grows to something of great constancy; / But howsoever, strange and admirable" (5.1.26–7).

At the Old Vic in 1937 Vivien Leigh proved both a beautiful and a beguiling Titania in Tyrone Guthrie's Victorian-style production.

Stage history and adaptations

We know nothing concrete about the earliest years of *Dream*; the first recorded performance took place on New Year's Day at **Hampton Court** in 1604, in front of James I (scholars presume that the "play of Robin good-fellow" in the records was Shakespeare's), but the play was probably a decade old by then. Its transgressive power is attested to by another seventeenth-century staging, which took place around 1631 at **Buckdale** in Huntingdonshire: it broke the Sabbath and the actor playing Bottom ended up in the stocks for twelve hours – still wearing his ass's head. Restoration audiences were unimpressed by the play's magical qualities, however: Pepys saw a performance in 1662 and, though he noted some "handsome women", described it as "the most insipid ridiculous play that ever I saw". A year before it had been truncated into a playlet entitled *The Merry Conceited Humours of Bottom the Weaver*.

This focus on the Athenian workers continued in the eighteenth century with versions including **Richard Leveridge**'s *Comic Masque of Pyramus and Thisbe* (1716) and **John Frederick Lampe**'s *Pyramus and Thisbe – a Mock-opera* (1745). By then, another way of dealing with this troublesome drama had appeared: the musical adaptation. **Henry Purcell**'s *Fairy Queen*, commissioned by **Thomas Betterton** and first performed in 1692, was the first and best. This kept the spoken play (heavily reworked) and inserted separate musical masques at the end of each act. Another musical attempt was masterminded by **David Garrick**, whose *Fairies* (1755) inserted songs with music by **John Smith** (Handel's pupil), cut three-quarters of the text and eliminated the Mechanicals. Garrick was uncharacteristically coy about the finished result – Horace Walpole described the libretto as "forty times more nonsensical than the worst translation of any Italian opera-books" – and left a revised version in the hands of **George Colman**, whose initial performance in November 1763 was so catastrophic that he rewrote it in three days as a two-act afterpiece entitled *A Fairy Tale*. This unhappy story didn't deter the last of the large-scale musical adapters, **Frederick Reynolds**. As with Reynolds's *Comedy of Errors* three years later, the production was antiquarian in style and spectacular in scope, retaining some of Garrick's lyrics but utilizing new music. Popular though it was, it nearly put critic William Hazlitt off theatre for life.

Shakespeare's play, meanwhile, hadn't seen the stage for nearly two centuries by the time **Elizabeth Vestris** followed up the success of her *Love's Labour's Lost* of the previous year (see p.248) by resurrecting *Dream* with something like its original text. She played Oberon herself, with **J.R. Planché**'s Athenian designs featuring a spectacular entrance for Puck, who ascended on a giant mushroom. While in Germany **Ludwig Tieck** was directing ground-breaking "authentic" stagings in Schlegel's translation, launching a lost-lasting German affection for the play (**Mendelssohn**'s sparkling incidental music was written for a Tieck production at Potsdam in 1843), in England directors were seeing fairies: **Charles Kean**'s 1856 production had no fewer than ninety tutu'd sprites on stage for the finale, while Oberon and Puck were both played by actresses (the latter was the 8-year-old **Ellen Terry**). Still more spectacular were **Augustin Daly**'s Broadway production of 1888, which employed an onstage pleasure-barge and scrolling dioramic scenery; **Frank Benson**'s version the following year, which was particularly commended for its "mirth-provoking ass's head" and employed the services of 24 dancing girls; and **Herbert Beerbohm Tree**'s 1900 staging, which the *Athenaeum* described as having reached "the limits of the conceivable". That reviewer clearly reckoned without **Max Reinhardt**, whose Berlin productions (1905 onwards) represented the apotheosis of grandiose staging – his stage productions employed real trees, while his 1935 film used an estimated 600,000 yards of cellophane.

But a revolt was underway. In 1914 **Harley Granville-Barker** mounted a futuristic production which used just two sets, an uncut text and folk song instead of Mendelssohn. No corps de ballet here: in the words of one spectator, **Norman Wilkinson**'s menacing adult fairies "look[ed] like Cambodian idols and posture like Nijinsky". Reviewers were hostile, and when Wilkinson designed *Dream* again – for **William Bridges-Adams** in 1932 – he was noticeably less radical. Bridges-Adams had directed the play at Stratford as early as 1920, and there too had deliberately avoided controversy: his Puck was female, his fairies children, and the *Observer* commended it for being "not freakish, or futurist, or rebellious". The 1937 productions of **Tyrone Guthrie** also stuck resolutely with tradition: taking his inspiration from the world of Pollock's Toy Theatres and Victorian children's books, Guthrie created a magical fairy land of muslin-clad fairies (choreographed by **Ninette de Valois**) and offered the glamorous partnership of **Robert Helpmann** as Oberon and **Vivien Leigh** as Titania, although most critics singled out **Ralph Richardson**'s endearing, Cockneyfied Bottom. **George Devine**, directing in 1954, aimed to avoid such "conventional prettinesses" and achieved something like the shock value of Granville-Barker, with fairies who were harsh and birdlike. Again, though, reviewers were unhappy – as they were with **Peter Hall**'s 1959 production at Stratford, which aimed for novelty by playing the lovers unsympathetically as stroppy, oversexed teenagers, and the fairies as near-feral.

Among the vast number of postwar productions on both sides of the Atlantic, perhaps the most revelatory was, typically, the most controversial: **Peter Brook**'s at Stratford in 1970. Designed by **Sally Jacobs**, this set the action in a three-sided white box hung with trapezes; Brook claimed that it celebrated "the theme of theatre", but many detected a darker undertow. **Alan Howard** and **Sara Kestelman** doubled Theseus and Hippolyta with Oberon and Titania, suggesting the tense continuities between the couples; and the nature of Titania's relationship with **David Waller**'s Bottom was obviously far from innocent. Though audiences loved it, some critics felt that Brook's sexualized interpretation was too dogmatic.

Much the same accusation dogged the Canadian **Robert Lepage**'s visually spectacular production at the National Theatre in 1992: his set was dominated by a large muddy pond around and into which the fairies and lovers periodically slithered. Puck was played by the Francophone contortionist **Angela Laurier** and **Timothy Spall** appeared as a truculent Bottom. The Halifax-based Northern Broadsides under actor-director **Barrie Rutter** took a similar, though more well received, route: their touring version of 1994 erased discrimination towards the Mechanicals (who are usually given "regional" accents in British productions) because the entire cast spoke in Yorkshire accents.

The play's magical transformations have encouraged directors to attempt their own rich and strange translations. **Karin Beier**'s German production of 1995 employed fourteen actors from nine countries, all speaking their own languages in what one critic described as "a UN meeting without simultaneous translation". Linguistics were

The World Shakespeare Festival of 2012 brought together hundreds of theatre-makers in a celebration of the global reach of the world's most translated and staged playwright. This athletic, audacious production of *Dream* by Korea's Yohangza Theatre Company was one of many highlights.

again the key for **Tim Supple**, who opened a boisterous, boldly sexual version in Chennai in 2006 before touring it abroad. This featured eight different Indian tongues (including English), and a cast of jugglers, acrobats and musicians from across the subcontinent. Indian critics were largely unimpressed (it was pointed out that almost no one could understand all of the text), but reviewers in the UK and America lapped it up. More broadly successful was the **Yohangza** company's carnivalesque, colourful and breathtakingly choreographed Korean-language version, which first appeared at Shakespeare's Globe in London in 2010 and was reprised two years later for the World Shakespeare Festival, the same year as Russian director **Dmitry Krymov**'s puppet-filled mash-up of *Dream* and *As You Like It*.

Numerous productions have appeared in recent years around the world. Notable in Europe and America have been experimental company **Filter**'s stripped-down and jazzed-up version (2012); a starry revival in London's West End with comedian **David Walliams** as Bottom and **Sheridan Smith** as Titania (2013); **Julie Taymor**'s otherworldly and lushly conceptual Broadway production ("eye-popping", according to the *New York Times*, also 2013); and **Michael Thalheimer**'s bleak reimagining at Munich's Residenztheater in 2014, which overturned long-standing German theatre tradition by turning *Dream* into an expressionistic, Jan Kott-influenced nightmare.

The play has proved irresistible to directors on film as well as stage. **J. Stuart Blackton** and **Charles Kent**'s silent film (1909) uses an open-air setting, while **Max Reinhardt** and **William Dieterle**'s talkie of 1935 visited all the places his stage version couldn't quite reach – owls, deer and unicorns included. Reinhardt's desired cast of Greta Garbo as Titania and Charlie Chaplin as Bottom unfortunately didn't come off, but the final line-up did include **James Cagney** as Bottom, **Olivia de Havilland** as Hermia and **Mickey Rooney** as Puck. Another fine cast was assembled by Peter Hall for the 1968 film (based on his RSC production): **Helen Mirren, Ian Holm, Diana Rigg, Ian Richardson** and a near-naked **Judi Dench** all frolicked gamely in a muddy Warwickshire wood. **Adrian Noble**'s 1996 version was likewise based on his RSC production, while **Michael Hoffman**'s Hollywood rendering tried to replicate the appeal of Branagh's *Much Ado* (see p.329). Eight TV productions have been made in all, plus a cinematic recording of Taymor's 2013 staging: the BBC/Time-Life version of 1981 was directed by **Elijah Moshinsky** and produced by **Jonathan Miller**; and a CGI-heavy version adapted by *Doctor Who* writer **Russell T. Davies** is set to screen on the BBC in 2016.

SCREEN

A Midsummer Night's Dream
W.V. Ranous, M. Costello, J. Swayne Gordon;
J. Stuart Blackthorn & Charles Kent (dirs) USA, 1909
> On Silent Shakespeare (BFI) DVD

One of the pre-eminent American silent film houses, Vitagraph specialized in what are nowadays called art-house productions. Shot in a gorgeous sun-dappled setting, this ten-minute *Dream* (1909) is charming: the stylized perambulations of the lovers make excellent sense, while Gladys Hulette's girlish Puck effortlessly zips in and out of the frame, aided by the magic of cinema (one adventurous shot has her putting "a girdle round about the earth" suspended over a giant rotating globe). Vitagraph's decision to replace Oberon with a female character called "Penelope" is mystifying, but William V. Ranous's strongly characterized Bottom more than makes up for it. Even Laura Rossi's music – which elsewhere may have you reaching for the mute button – doesn't cast too much of a pall. This *Silent Shakespeare* video from the BFI also features versions of *Lear, The Tempest* (see p.425), *Twelfth Night* (see p.478), *The Merchant of Venice* and *Richard III* (see p.385).

A Midsummer Night's Dream
V. Jory, A. Louise, J. Cagney; Max Reinhardt &
William Dieterle (dirs) US, 1935 **>** Warner DVD

John Gielgud claimed that watching it was akin to having surgery – but then he was never the most generous of critics. In fact this adaptation, adapted from Reinhardt's live Hollywood Bowl production, sustained with oodles of Warner Bros cash and illuminated with all the stars that

the studio could fling at it, is far better than its reputation implies. Yes, those are phalanxes of child fairies tripping through the sky; yes, that is a gnome orchestra sawing away in the forest; and, yes, that was a unicorn you glimpsed wandering past. But, fed by the astonishing fecundity of Reinhardt's imagination, none of this feels like mere prettification. The costumes are majestic, Korngold's reworking of Mendelssohn is a triumph of concision and Hal Mohr's high-contrast cinematography turns the play into an epic battle between light and dark. Olivia de Havilland sparkles as a quick-witted Hermia, Cagney puts in a forthright turn as Bottom and the young Mickey Rooney offers an unforgettable and faintly unnerving Puck, full of Mowgli-like whoops and cries. There's genuinely nothing like it.

A Midsummer Night's Dream
I. Richardson, J. Dench, P. Rogers; Peter Hall (dir.)
UK, 1968 **>** MGM DVD

This Peter Hall / RSC version feels like a riposte to Reinhardt's classic *Dream* (see above). Instead of cavernous studio sound stages, we have a muddy and damp Warwickshire. Where that was bursting with opulent fantasy, this is dowdily realistic. And where Reinhardt sought to make film-making into high art, Hall's own low-budget, modern-dress adaptation sometimes feels like a home movie. But it's impossible not to fall for it. Crafting virtue out of necessity, Hall plays the lovers mainly for comic effect – all four look as if they'd rather be sauntering up the King's Road – while finding real interest in the relationship between Ian Richardson's marvellously chilly Oberon and Judi Dench's husky Titania. The rest of the cast, all expert verse-speakers, are impeccable (Ian Holm's froglike Puck and Diana Rigg's self-pitying Helena deserve special mention), while the gala performance of *Pyramus and Thisbe*, though funny, has all the curious solemnity of a school play. Plus there can be few sights in cinema like that of the semi-naked Dench cuddling up to Paul Rogers's awestruck Bottom. The DVD is only available as a US import, but is reasonably easy to get hold of.

A Midsummer Night's Dream
A. Jennings, L. Duncan, D. Barrit; Adrian Noble (dir.) UK, 1996 > Cinema Club / Miramax `DVD`

Capturing the theatrics of *Dream* on celluloid has proved an elusive art, arguably never really achieved. Noble's adaptation of his RSC production at least confronts the play's anti-filmic qualities head-on: it is obviously filmed in a studio, with lots of good old-fashioned stage magic (trapdoors, cradles aloft, invisible wires) jazzed up by the occasional sprinkle of digital effects. As a filmed play it is excellent, with assured ensemble performances (Desmond Barrit's large-framed Bottom and Barry Lynch's Puck/Philostrate are particularly good) and an attractively quirky jumble of visual styles. As a movie it is rather less so, hobbled by Noble's bizarre introduction of a crisply pyjama'd young boy as a kind of wordless spectator, through whose wondering eyes we are presumably supposed to encounter events (combined with Howard Blake's chocolate-box score, he's redolent of nothing so much as *The Snowman*). Perhaps too much *Poppins* or *Potter* to be seriously convincing.

A Midsummer Night's Dream
R. Everett, M. Pfeiffer, K. Kline; Michael Hoffman (dir.) USA, 1999 > Fox `DVD`

The film's full title, *William Shakespeare's A Midsummer Night's Dream*, makes you wonder if it's possible to sue for defamation four hundred years on. Someone clearly told Michael Hoffman (perhaps it was Kenneth Branagh) that filming Shakespeare was a doddle: select quaint Tuscan backdrop – don't forget a smattering of picturesque rural poor, bless their worn-out socks – assemble starry cast, cut in a few seconds of Mendelssohn. It's tempting to say that the result is vacuous, but that seems unnecessarily hostile towards vacuums. The best that can probably be said is that Kevin Kline brings some pathos to a hen-pecked Bottom, while Calista Flockhart does little more than pout. Both Anna Friel (Hermia) and Michelle Pfeiffer (Titania) flounder in attempting to keep their heads above water, and the ever self-sacrificing Rupert Everett (Oberon) does a fine job of making everything else look more charismatic (buildings included). Come back, Ken – all is forgiven.

AUDIO

A Midsummer Night's Dream
W. Mitchell, M. Maloney, S. Woodward; Neville Jason (dir.) UK, 1997 > Naxos ◉

Interspersing Purcell's glorious music for *The Fairy Queen* makes it very hard for a director to go wrong, and fortunately the rest of this *Dream* lives up to the soundtrack. The scenes between the lovers overcome what can sometimes seem like perfunctoriness in less well cast productions (those between Emily Raymond's Helena and Jamie Glover's Demetrius are impressive), and in the fairy world too this performance very nearly retains its magic: only some slightly cheap sound effects and Michael Maloney's slightly overblown Oberon endanger things. The Mechanicals are alike impressive, though the Bottom played by Warren Mitchell (also a fine Shylock; see p.292) dominates – as perhaps he should.

EDITIONS

Oxford Shakespeare
Peter Holland (ed.); 1994 > Oxford UP

Holland's edition has many attractions. One is his extensive discussion (surprisingly uncommon) of the meanings of "dream" to Renaissance thinkers and writers, drawing on a long inheritance of dream-science extending all the way back to classical writers such as Artemidorus of Daldis and Macrobius. The rest of the introduction is divided among the different groups of characters, neatly reconstructing its competing social strata, and the editor provides sensible and sane commentary on many of the play's major themes (perhaps too sensible for some – Holland has no truck with radical theories about the play's interest in sexuality). Shakespeare's revisions to Act Five – some speeches are apparently reworked – are printed as an appendix. Those in search of more recent stage history could try the updated edition of R.A. Foakes's somewhat thinner New Cambridge text (2003), but even this is not especially up to date.

SOME CRITICISM

Something of Great Constancy
David Young; 1966 > Yale UP [o/p]

Young begins his study of *A Midsummer Night's Dream* with a disarming declaration: "a work of criticism that exceeds its subject in length", he notes, "is rightly regarded with suspicion." No such worries here, though: Young's account seems so in tune with the play's spirit that it would be churlish to complain about its size. And in fact *Something of Great Constancy* is slender and feels even smaller, made up of a set of brief points on pertinent themes (folklore, the idea of transformation, the play's imagery, the use of "art") that together illuminate the tapestry of influences that make up the play. Young never condescends to the reader, nor – best of all – to the play itself, seeming somehow to preserve its atmosphere of mystery and magic. A broader examination of its debt to ancient customs and folk rites is on offer in C.L. Barber's classic study, *Shakespeare's Festive Comedy* (revised 2011; see p.660).

Shakespeare and Comedy
Peter Holland (ed.); 2003 > Cambridge UP

Published as part of the invaluable *Shakespeare Survey* series (a journal that is helpfully organized by theme as well as time), this collection brings together some fine recent writing on the topic of Shakespearian comedy, a subject that was undervalued for many years but is now blossoming. The *Dream* looms large, as well it might, and there are some fine pieces here, including Patricia Parker on love potions, Alan Sinfield on the play's queer intertexualities and A.B. Taylor on the play's *other* playwright, Peter Quince. Particularly treasurable is Michael Dobson's essay on adaptations of the Pyramus and Thisbe episode, from seventeenth-century versions right up to the Beatles' spoof for TV in 1964. The broader topic of comedy is well covered, with excellent contributions from Stephen Orgel and Dympna Callaghan among others, as well as an illuminating in-conversation-with director Declan Donnellan, whose Cheek by Jowl troupe have infused many Elizabethan comedies with joyous new life.

Much Ado About Nothing

S et in the Sicilian town of Messina, *Much Ado About Nothing* fizzes with holiday spirit. Its rich humour was singled out early on by Elizabethan writer Francis Meres, who included it in a 1598 list of plays demonstrating that Shakespeare was "most excellent" in comedy, and the play is every bit as fascinated by verbal wit as an earlier work mentioned by Meres, *Love's Labour's Lost*. The lead couple in that comedy, Biron and Rosaline, may well have inspired Shakespeare to create the feisty Beatrice and Benedick, whose battle to out-talk each other dominates *Much Ado* – at least until they are tricked into falling in tongue-tied love, raising suspicions that their verbal jousting was repressed flirtation all along. Technically, however, their romance forms the subplot, grafted on to an Italian tale concerning another pair of lovers (in *Much Ado* named Hero and Claudio) who fall prey to a sinister scheme to drive them apart. In connecting the two stories of deception, Shakespeare forces both sets of lovers to rethink their understandings of love and each other; and for everyone on stage painful loss precedes resolution. Genuine tragedy clouds the scene for an uncomfortable amount of time, and (ironically enough) the device by which comedy is restored puts the sunny atmosphere of the play under the greatest strain of all.

DATE > Between mid-1598 and early 1599 – flanked by *2 Henry IV* and *Henry V*.

SOURCES > Ariosto's *Orlando Furioso* (1516) is a possible source for the Hero–Claudio plot, possibly filtered through Matteo Bandello's *La Prima Parte de le Novelle* (though the tale occurs in multiple versions). The Beatrice–Benedick story is most likely Shakespeare's own, as is the clownish Watch.

TEXTS > The 1600 quarto *Much Ado* was set from Shakespeare's working papers; some of the speech prefixes mistakenly use actors' names rather than characters. This text was reprinted in the 1623 Folio with a few amendments.

Interpreting the play

Shakespeare's penchant for throwaway titles is often commented on, and in his middle period, around the turn of the sixteenth century, he seems to have been especially fond of choosing names with a kind of cheeky, take-it-or-leave-it quality. *As You Like It* and *What You Will* (the latter better known as *Twelfth Night*) tease their audiences not to take things too seriously; while later comedies such as *Measure for Measure* and *All's Well That Ends Well* dare spectators to take *their* titles – and the contortions of their plots – at face value.

MAJOR CHARACTERS & SYNOPSIS

Don Pedro, Prince of Aragon
Benedick, a young lord from Padua
Claudio, Benedick's companion, a young lord from Florence
Balthasar, a singer attending Don Pedro
Don John, Don Pedro's illegitimate brother
Borachio and **Conrad**, followers of Don John
Leonato, governor of Messina
Hero, Leonato's daughter
Beatrice, Leonato's niece, an orphan
Antonio, Leonato's brother, an old man
Margaret and **Ursula**, Hero's attendants
Friar Francis
Dogberry, a parish constable in charge of the Watchmen
Verges, Dogberry's partner, a lower-ranking constable
A **Sexton** (church officer)

ACT 1 Accompanied by his daughter Hero and niece Beatrice, Leonato, governor of Messina, awaits the return of Don Pedro, fresh from victory over his disaffected brother Don John. Don Pedro arrives along with Claudio and Benedick, the latter an acquaintance of Beatrice – with whom he has a relationship of mutual mockery. When, after Leonato's party has left, Claudio reveals that he is in love with Hero, Don Pedro offers to help win her by impersonating Claudio at a masked ball that evening. When the plan reaches Leonato, he advises Hero to accept. Casting a shadow over events, however, is Don John – still determined to create mischief.

ACT 2 At the ball, Don Pedro successfully woos Hero for Claudio, but the latter is persuaded by Don John that he has actually done so for himself. After Don Pedro convinces Claudio of the truth and marriage is agreed, he outlines a further plan: the sparring Beatrice and Benedick will be tricked into falling in love. To this end, Don Pedro arranges for Benedick to overhear a staged conversation in which he and Leonato discuss Beatrice's supposed love for him. Benedick is taken in and resolves to respond. Elsewhere, Don John continues to scheme: his man Borachio will court Margaret (Hero's gentlewoman), who will disguise herself as Hero, thus suggesting to Claudio Hero's infidelity.

ACT 3 Don Pedro's plan continues to work when Beatrice overhears Hero and Ursula describing Benedick's secret passion for her. At this point Don John arrives and announces that Hero has been unfaithful. Claudio and Don Pedro refuse to believe him, but Don John claims to have evidence: that night they will see her with another man. Sure enough, when they spy on Margaret and Borachio, Claudio is convinced that the woman is Hero. By a freak chance, though, the dim-witted Watch (newly recruited by Dogberry and Verges) catch Borachio bragging about his success to Conrad soon afterwards, and arrest them both. They inform Leonato, but he is preoccupied with the impending marriage.

ACT 4 As the wedding ceremony begins, Claudio savagely denounces Hero, backed up by Don Pedro and Don John. Hero faints, thus convincing her father of her guilt. Friar Francis stands by her, however, and advises that her death be announced while she hides away till her innocence can be proven. Benedick tells Beatrice that he does not believe the accusations; when he then admits that he loves her, she reciprocates but urges him to kill Claudio. The Watch, meanwhile, have taken their prisoners to the Sexton, who realizes that Hero has been framed.

ACT 5 Leonato and Antonio confront Claudio and Don Pedro and accuse them of killing Hero, but they refuse to be drawn, and are surprised when Benedick enters and challenges Claudio to a duel. They are even more shocked when Dogberry and Verges reveal the truth about Don John's plan. Appalled, Don Pedro and Claudio beg Leonato's forgiveness, and he instructs them to write an epitaph that will clear his daughter's name, and tells Claudio he must marry Antonio's daughter. Claudio agrees. Benedick, meanwhile, has been struggling to write Beatrice love poems. Next morning, as Claudio is about to marry Antonio's daughter, she lifts her veil and reveals herself to be Hero. Beatrice and Benedick realize they have been tricked, but when his poems and her love letters are revealed, bow to the inevitable and admit their love. All are reconciled – with the exception of the captured Don John, whose punishment is postponed until another day.

Much Ado About Nothing sits squarely in the middle of this period, and its title plays multiple games with readers and audiences alike. On one level the phrase seems to deny that there's anything worth getting fussed about: there may well be "much ado" as the lovers sort themselves out, but things will be all right in the end. The well-known song sung by Balthasar to Benedick midway through the play picks up on just this sentiment. "Sigh no more, ladies, sigh no more," he croons,

> Men were deceivers ever,
> One foot in sea, and one on shore,
>   To one thing constant never.
> Then sigh not so, but let them go,
>   And be you blithe and bonny,
> Converting all your sounds of woe
>   Into hey nonny, nonny.
>
> [2.3.61–8]

Whatever happens, the song insists – bitterness, betrayal – you have to keep on singing, converting "sounds of woe" into nonsense like the old refrain "hey nonny, nonny". "These are very crotchets [trivialities] that he speaks," says Don Pedro to Balthasar just beforehand, reaching for a musical pun. "Note notes, forsooth, and nothing!" (2.3.55–6).

Shakespeare's audiences would also have heard a bawdier joke in the play's title. "Nothing" was risqué Elizabethan slang, usually referring to the female sex organs, but in practice pretty much all-purpose. In this light the play's concern with love and sex seems a little more cynical (where does all that "ado" get you?), but the playfulness remains. Yet another possible meaning of "nothing" can be obtained by removing the "h", as Elizabethan pronunciation often did. The comedy and tragedy of the play rest alike on observation and overhearing, whether it's Benedick and Beatrice listening in to reports of the other's frenzied love or Claudio being persuaded that Hero has been unfaithful to him. All of us, Shakespeare implies, are sometimes inclined to "note" things that are in fact "nothing".

Talk themselves mad

The play is as witty as its title. Most of *Much Ado*'s impressive verbal fireworks appear courtesy of Beatrice and Benedick, Shakespeare's infamously talkative couple (and his sole addition to a story sourced from several Renaissance romances). Though in some ways they resemble the *Shrew*'s Katherine and Petruccio, who likewise spend much of their time together fighting, Beatrice and Benedick prefer to wage what Leonato calls their "merry war" with words alone. But what words they are. Though Don Pedro and his gentlemanly retinue have only just arrived in Messina, it is not long before Beatrice and Benedick renew their acquaintance. They do so, as ever, by being – verbally speaking – at one another's throats:

BEATRICE I wonder that you will still be talking, Signor Benedick. Nobody
 marks you.

BENEDICK What, my dear Lady Disdain! Are you yet living?

BEATRICE Is it possible disdain should die while she hath such meet food to feed it as Signor Benedick? Courtesy itself must convert to disdain if you come in her presence.

BENEDICK Then is courtesy a turncoat. But it is certain I am loved of all ladies, only you excepted. And I would I could find in my heart that I had not a hard heart, for truly I love none.

BEATRICE A dear happiness to women. They would else have been troubled with a pernicious suitor. I thank God and my cold blood I am of your humour for that. I had rather hear my dog bark at a crow than a man swear he loves me.

BENEDICK God keep your ladyship still in that mind. So some gentleman or other shall escape a predestinate scratched face.

BEATRICE Scratching could not make it worse an 'twere such a face as yours were.

BENEDICK Well you are a rare parrot-teacher.

BEATRICE A bird of my tongue is better than a beast of yours.

BENEDICK I would my horse had the speed of your tongue …

[1.1.110–35]

And so it continues. Beatrice and Benedick often sound as if they could go on for ever, thrusting and parrying, each trying to dispatch the other with yet more spectacular linguistic flourishes. Even the masked ball, set up once Don Pedro and his lords arrive in town and providing a suggestive opportunity for the lovers to woo in disguise, gives Beatrice the chance to insult her counterpart. Encountering the masked Benedick, she announces that the very same man is "the Prince's jester, a very dull fool" (2.1.127).

Despite Leonato's warning to his niece that "thou wilt never get thee a husband if thou be so shrewd of thy tongue" (2.1.16–17), Beatrice has already met her match – in every sense of the word. Or at least that is what the other characters think, plotting to bring them together by a stratagem somewhat more complicated than a masked ball. Don Pedro first stage-manages a meeting with Claudio and Leonato in which they are to discuss – within earshot of Benedick – the news that Beatrice has been pining for him all this time. Immediately convinced, Benedick decides that "this can be no trick", and resolves at once to be "horribly in love with her" (2.3.209, 223) in response. Beatrice is "limed" soon afterwards – this time by Ursula and Hero, who pretend to have discovered that Benedick is "wast[ing] inwardly" for *her*:

BEATRICE (*coming forward*)
    What fire is in mine ears? Can this be true?
        Stand I condemned for pride and scorn so much?
    Contempt, farewell; and maiden pride, adieu.
        No glory lives behind the back of such.
    And Benedick, love on. I will requite thee,
        Taming my wild heart to thy loving hand.

[3.1.107–12]

Beatrice is so taken in that she promises to "tame" herself – the *Shrew*'s Katherine makes no such concessions – and even forsakes her usual prose to launch into an abbreviated sonnet saying as much.

Lest such immediate conversions ring false, Shakespeare is careful to hint that Beatrice's apparent antagonism towards Benedick stems from a long-past affair which has never healed. And he creates a good deal of comedy from their creaking attempts to go through the motions once again. Despite his ear for language, Benedick is soon forced to admit, frustratedly, that he is having the greatest of trouble compressing his feelings into "rhyme":

Beatrice was the Shakespearian role closest to Ellen Terry's own lively personality, and one she excelled in. Her Benedick at the Lyceum Theatre was Henry Irving, whom she described as "too deliberate, though polished and thoughtful".

> I have tried. I can find out no rhyme for 'lady' but 'baby', an innocent rhyme; for 'scorn' 'horn', a hard rhyme; for 'school' 'fool', a babbling rhyme. Very ominous endings. No, I was not born under a rhyming planet …
>
> [5.2.35–9]

As Benedick "suffer[s] love" for Beatrice (5.2.60), his wit is brought low – to a recycling of nonsensical vowel sounds. Contrary to Leonato's amused insistence that "if they were but a week married they would talk themselves mad" (2.1.330–1), in fact the effort of wooing has them both tied up in verbal knots. And when Beatrice and Benedick do eventually find out that they have been duped, it is the evidence of their "halting" letters and poems to each other that persuades them to go through with the marriage.

The wonder of her infamy

Before the lovers can get to the altar, however, more malign deceptive forces make their presence felt in Messina. Don Pedro's bastard brother Don John is for reasons only known to himself determined to force apart the play's other new couple, Claudio and Hero. Arranging for his henchman Borachio to woo Hero's gentlewoman Margaret, Don John escorts Claudio and Don Pedro to a dark spot from where they can see Borachio conversing with her. Persuaded that the woman they see is Hero, Claudio immediately swears (as Borachio tells it) to "meet her as he was appointed next morning at the temple, and there, before the whole congregation, shame her with what he saw" (3.3.152–5). Instead of formalizing the marriage in front of the whole of Messinan society, Claudio will turn the ceremony into one of ritual humiliation.

And as soon as Leonato gives her away, Claudio does just that. "Give not this rotten orange to your friend," he cries:

> She's but the sign and semblance of her honour.
> Behold how like a maid she blushes here!
> O, what authority and show of truth
> Can cunning sin cover itself withal!
> Comes not that blood as modest evidence
> To witness simple virtue? Would you not swear,
> All you that see her, that she were a maid,
> By these exterior shows? But she is none.
> She knows the heat of a luxurious bed.
> Her blush is guiltiness, not modesty.

[4.1.32–42]

In his obsession with female hypocrisy Claudio echoes Master Ford, but in *Merry Wives* no one doubts for a moment that Ford's jealousy exists solely in his mind. Here even Leonato, Hero's good-natured father, is immediately convinced of her guilt, crying, "O she is fallen / Into a pit of ink, that the wide sea / Hath drops too few to wash her clean again" (4.1.140–2).

This is the very bleakest moment in the play, and it should be noted that the only evidence behind Claudio's wild accusations is that, as Don Pedro explains, she talked "with a ruffian at her chamber window" – an act they witnessed at night and with only Borachio's word to confirm it. This bond of trust between men, which is able to erase at a stroke an entire heterosexual relationship, seems to confirm what some commentators have claimed, that Messina is a less tolerant society than might at first appear. In this respect it points forward to the anguished world of *Troilus and Cressida*, whose heroine becomes guilty (if guilty is the word) of what Hero is not when she is observed flirting with a rival wooer. In both plays, it is women who bear the brunt of restrictive social codes that delineated behaviour between the sexes in the Renaissance, and in presenting Hero's suffering so powerfully *Much Ado* pointedly suggests that it doesn't much matter whether a woman deserves "dishonour" or not: it's what society thinks

---

It is here [in the church scene] that the social abnormality of aristocratic society in Messina is exposed once and for all for what it is – a shallow and perverse application of a standard of behaviour that is both automatic and uncharitable.

Walter N. King, "Much Ado About Something" (1964)

that counts. When Hero is condemned by not merely her suitor and his comrades but her own father, a rigid culture of shame and honour turns in full force against her, a catastrophe caused by the flimsiest of fabrications.

It is the ferocity of this culture that most appals in *Much Ado*: stung by Hero's stunned inability to reply (she has in fact fainted), Leonato is terrifyingly quick to believe his daughter's accusers rather than Hero herself, and so frantic with rage that he several times threatens to "tear her" with his own bare hands. Shakespeare does indeed make Hero die as a result of her shame, but fortunately not as literally as Leonato demands – the resourceful Friar suggests that Hero should fake her own decease, arguing that "the supposition of the lady's death / Will quench the wonder of her infamy" (4.1.240–1), in effect that everyone (especially Claudio) will be so overcome by grief that they will forget all about the scandal. It is a desperate measure, but Hero's plight is extreme – so extreme, it seems, that social reputation outweighs life itself. It is left to Beatrice to voice the corollary, that Claudio too should not escape the consequences of his actions. She demands from an unsuspecting Benedick a real sign of love:

BEATRICE I love you with so much of my heart that none is left to protest.
BENEDICK Come, bid me do anything for thee.
BEATRICE Kill Claudio.

[4.1.287–90]

The comic world of *Much Ado* seems a long way away at this emotion-filled crux, not least because, having been pushed finally to fall in love, it now seems possible that circumstances will drive Benedick and Beatrice apart.

Fortunately, however, the play does not allow that to happen. Claudio and Don Pedro are not the only characters to have been eavesdropping. The conversation between Borachio and Conrad, in which Borachio boasted about his "villainy", has been overheard by members of Messina's comically useless Watch, led by constable Dogberry and his sidekick Verges. By rights the Watch should be too hopeless to achieve anything at all, but somehow a couple of its members succeed in arresting Borachio and Conrad, thereby setting in motion events that will expose Don John's malicious hoax. The well-meaning Verges attempts to inform Leonato about their recent coup, but Dogberry – doing his level best to impress – wants to have the governor all to himself. Urging Verges to stop waffling, he takes it upon himself to criticize his companion's way with words:

VERGES Yes, I thank God, I am as honest as any man living that is an old man and no honester than I.
DOGBERRY Comparisons are odorous. Palabras, neighbour Verges.
LEONATO Neighbours, you are tedious.
DOGBERRY It pleases your worship to say so, but we are the poor Duke's officers. But truly, for mine own part, if I were as tedious as a king I could find in my heart to bestow it all on your worship.

[3.5.13–21]

Enumerating Dogberry's linguistic limitations has proved an engaging pastime for editors, but it is the spontaneous felicity of his errors that stands out – the Duke is "poor" indeed to have such "tedious" officials (clearly Dogberry interprets the word as a compliment) on his side.

Dogberry makes an unlikely fairy godmother, but he possesses all the means for a happy ending. *Much Ado*'s final scene is characterized by relief as various truths are outed, but the conclusion is not facile. Persuaded that Hero was innocent after all, the guilt-stricken Claudio agrees to Leonato's offer to marry his niece instead. Even Leonato's assurance that she is "almost the copy of my child that's dead" (5.1.281) does not prepare Claudio for her unveiling at the ceremony:

CLAUDIO
    Another Hero!
HERO   Nothing certainer.
    One Hero died defiled, but I do live,
    And surely as I live, I am a maid.

                                [5.3.62–4]

"She died, my lord, but whiles her slander lived," echoes Leonato, pointing to the kind of mythic rebirth that will so inspire Shakespeare in his last plays. For the moment, though, the comic community of Messina is allowed to heal its wounds and gather once more (as the script puts it) in a "Dance".

Stage history and adaptations

The title-page of the 1600 quarto claims that *Much Ado* was "sundry times publicly acted" by the **Chamberlain's Men**. The text also helpfully includes some speech prefixes telling us who took various roles – among them **William Kempe**'s Dogberry and **Richard Cowley**'s Verges. Subesequent references to the comedy indicate its steady popularity, and it was one of fourteen plays provided by **John Heminges** and the King's Men (as they became known) at **court** for the festivities celebrating the marriage of James I's daughter in 1613. It appears in the records as "Benedicte and Betteris", suggesting that even early on its lead couple had become dominant; for his part, Charles I renamed it "Benedik and Betrice" in the royal copy of the 1632 Second Folio.

William Davenant took on the play following the Restoration, and promptly squeezed it into his 1662 *The Law Against Lovers*, a version of *Measure for Measure* that stole the Beatrice–Benedick subplot and much else (see p.275). But it flopped, and the unadapted *Much Ado* bounced back in 1721 at the behest of theatre manager **John Rich**. Though elements of the comedy found their way into other reworkings (among them **Charles Johnson**'s 1723 *Love in a Forest* and **James Miller**'s 1737 *The Universal Passion*), the play itself prospered during the eighteenth century, most impressively under **David Garrick** at Drury Lane from 1748. Garrick's Benedick was one of the few comic parts in which he excelled, and he played it over a hundred times to a roll call of lively Beatrices including **Hannah Pritchard**, **Elizabeth Pope** and **Frances Abbington**. Abbington herself continued with the role for twenty years after Garrick's retirement, and **Sarah Siddons,** **Elizabeth Farren** and **Dorothy Jordan** also tried their hands before the century's end.

Siddons's younger brother **Charles Kemble** challenged Garrick's longevity, performing *Much Ado* from 1803 with actresses including **Anne Brunton,** his daughter **Fanny** and **Louisa Nisbett.** By the time of his farewell appearance in 1836, his leading lady was the 19-year-old **Helen Faucit** and there was a 42-year age gap between the two. Faucit did more than any other to convert Beatrice from fire-breathing vixen into rounded human being; a review from 1846 describes the "rare beauty" of her performances. **Henry Irving**'s co-star **Ellen Terry** took the role in 1882, a few years after Faucit's retirement, and produced a Beatrice who was "buoyant, winsome, merry, enchanting" (in Bram Stoker's words). Though she outclassed Irving's Benedick, their Lyceum production notched up nearly 250 performances and toured to the US. It was no less famous for its lavish sets, designed by **William Telbin**: Hero's denunciation took place in an exquisite Italianate church with columns thirty feet high.

Herbert Beerbohm Tree's 1905 version, equally grand, was the end of an era: an Ellen Terry revival two years earlier, designed by her son **Edward Gordon Craig,** featured stripped-down sets, and in 1904 **William Poel** put on an "Elizabethan" production boasting period music. Even so, through the first decades of the twentieth century *Much Ado* became once again a star vehicle, chiefly at the Old Vic. **Sybil Thorndike** and **Edith Evans** both played Beatrice pre- and interwar, joined by the Benedicks of **Lewis Casson** and **Baliol Holloway. John Gielgud** acted opposite **Dorothy Green** in 1930, and returned to the play at Stratford in 1949 in what became its first successful postwar production. Gielgud initially directed **Anthony Quayle**'s Benedick and **Diana Wynard**'s Beatrice, but during three subsequent revivals took the lead himself, first with **Peggy Ashcroft,** then **Margaret Leighton.**

Much Ado has remained one of Shakespeare's most revived comedies, as the bewildering variety of its subsequent stagings suggests. Within a few years it would appear in guises ranging from Tex-Mex (Stratford, Connecticut in 1957) to Regency-Risorgimento (at Stratford, UK in 1958 under **Douglas Seale** with **Michael Redgrave** and **Googie Withers**). **Michael Langham**'s RSC incarnation of 1961 also returned to Regency England, but **Geraldine McEwan**'s Beatrice was apparently "a modern young woman" nonetheless. **Franco Zeffirelli**'s National Theatre version (1965) and another RSC version by **Trevor Nunn** (1968) both attempted to historicize the play: Zeffirelli in a typically operatic nineteenth-century Sicily; Nunn in one of the few Elizabethan settings to have made it into performance. Both had up-and-coming stars (**Maggie Smith** with **Robert Stephens** and **Janet Suzman** with **Alan Howard** respectively), in contrast to one of the most famous twentieth-century UK productions, **John Barton**'s RSC version of 1976, which struck an autumnal tone with a mature **Donald Sinden** and **Judi Dench.** Barton set the play in colonial nineteenth-century India, focusing on the officers' mess posturing of Don Pedro and his men and undercutting the low comedy by making the Watch (somewhat dubiously) into a "native" force.

Among more recent versions, a handful have succeeded in bringing innovation to *Much Ado* without trampling on its sensibilities. **Terry Hands**'s 1982 RSC production, starring **Sinead Cusack** and **Derek Jacobi,** was dominated by **Ralph Koltai**'s mirrored sets, representing the play's shifting representations of truth and falsehood.

Catherine Tate and David Tennant brought comic fizz to Beatrice and Benedick in Josie Rourke's 2011 *Much Ado* in London's West End, set in an off-duty garrison town where almost anything went.

Judi Dench directed **Kenneth Branagh**'s Renaissance Theatre Company in 1988 (in another Regency setting) with Branagh's Benedick well matched by **Samantha Bond**'s feisty Beatrice. **Declan Donnellan**'s irreverent Cheek by Jowl company took it on in 1993 in a downbeat production that emphasized the characters' mutual shabbiness, while the following year **Mark Rylance** and **Janet McTeer** proved a particularly effective pairing in **Matthew Warchus**'s lively West End production – he slightly diffident with a soft Ulster accent, she tall and domineering.

Marianne Elliot's RSC version in 2006 set TV star **Tamsin Greig** opposite **Joseph Millson** in a rum-soaked, pre-Castro Cuba; despite some deftly choreographed salsa, an onstage Vespa succeeded in stealing the show. More surprising was **Nicholas Hytner**'s uncluttered, unfussy version at the National Theatre the following year, which cast **Simon Russell Beale** and **Zoë Wanamaker** as a Beatrice and Benedick rapidly running out of time (the actors were 46 and 58 respectively). Wistfulness and regret were never far away for this awkward, sometimes odd couple; "instead of discovering love," suggested Susannah Clapp in the *Observer*, "they are recovering it".

TV stars **David Tennant** and **Catherine Tate** shared the honours in a production by **Josie Rourke**, wittily updated to 1980s Gibraltar, that opened in London's West End in 2011; a more cautious, Renaissance-style production starring **Eve Best** and **Charles Edwards**, directed by **Jeremy Herrin** opened a few days earlier at Shakespeare's Globe. The Royal Shakespeare Company's Indian-style reimagining in 2012, directed by **Iqbal Khan**, was altogether more globalized. Taking issue with the RSC's 1976 version, which featured white actors "browning up", it featured a British-Asian cast led by **Meera Syal** and **Paul Bhattacharjee**, and was set in an emphatically postcolonial Delhi. Another kind of repossession was offered back at the Globe the same year, with the Paris-based **Compagnie Hypermobile** offering a *Much Ado* full of froth and *jeux d'esprit*.

Outside the UK the comedy has continued to be widely performed, with myriad productions in English-speaking territories such as North America and Australia (where it debuted in Melbourne, courtesy of American actor **Edwin Booth**, in 1843). Foreign-language versions range all the way from **Stanislavsky**'s Russian performances in 1893 to **Jiang Weiguo**'s adaptation, which debuted in China in 1986 and soldered *Much Ado* onto the Huangmeixi folk tradition. Remarkably, a Chinese production translated by **Zhu Shenghao** was almost the last Shakespeare play to go on stage in 1961, before the Cultural Revolution (when Shakespeare was banned), and the very first to reappear after it, in 1979. Cast, staging and Renaissance-style costumes were identical, with **Jiao Huang** and **Zhu Xijuan** playing Benedick and Beatrice as if nothing had happened in the intervening 18 years.

As well as **Kenneth Branagh**'s film of 1993, *Much Ado* has appeared in various screen incarnations. **Franco Zeffirelli**'s production was adapted for TV in 1969, and the BBC/Time-Life Shakespeare has seen not one version but two: **Donald McWhinnie**'s of 1978 (with **Michael York**, **Penelope Keith** and **Ian Richardson**), originally designed to open the series; and **Stuart Burge**'s replacement from six years later, with **Robert Lindsay** and **Cherie Lunghi** in the leads. In 2013, American director **Joss Whedon** – perhaps best known for *Buffy the Vampire Slayer* and Pixar's *Toy Story* – unveiled a surprise adaptation of the play, set in California and boldly filmed in black and white.

SCREEN

Much Ado About Nothing
K. Branagh, E. Thompson, D. Washington; Kenneth Branagh (dir.) UK, 1993 > MGM DVD ⬇

Perhaps the most-watched Shakespeare movie of the last 25 years, this Tuscan *Much Ado* persuaded Hollywood producers that having the Bard as co-screenwriter didn't necessarily entail commercial suicide. The Branagh formula has since become both familiar and imitated – Hollywood stars alongside British talent, period settings, plenty of warm-hearted sentiment – but back then it was a novelty. And now? Well, it still looks fresh (if you discount the 1990s perma-tans) and contains some pleasing moments. Branagh's Benedick is as spry – and intermittently fatuous – as ever, but it's Thompson's womanly Beatrice who is scripted to win our sympathy, and that she does with a performance that Helen Faucit and Ellen Terry (so one guesses) would be proud of.

Much Ado About Nothing
D. Tennant, C. Tate, A. James; Josie Rourke (dir.) UK, 2011 > Digital Theatre ⬇

British actor David Tennant cut his teeth in comic roles at the RSC, and his quicksilver wit and deft timing make him a mercurial and somewhat sardonic Benedick, albeit somewhat more world-weary than his audio version a decade before (see below). He's well-matched here by Catherine Tate, who is just as skilled at raising laughs and yet allows a quiet sadness to break through. Recorded in front of a live audience, Josie Rourke's production transfers well to video, even if the stage revolve becomes mildly dizzying after a while. It's set in a holidaying Gibraltar stuffed with off-duty servicemen in dress whites and girls in clothes the colour of cocktail umbrellas, a garrison town of wild stag dos and hen parties where a woman's reputation can be shredded in an instant. The tragedy that threatens to swamp Tate and Tennant is never far away.

Much Ado About Nothing
A. Acker, A. Denisof, R. Diamond; Joss Whedon (dir.) US, 2012 > Kaleidoscope DVD ⬇

Better known for *Buffy the Vampire Slayer* than the Bard, Joss Whedon filmed this good-natured, contemporary version of *Much Ado* during an enforced two-week holiday after finishing *The Avengers* – and used his own Santa Monica mansion as its setting. It's a delight, and the home-made feel (Whedon even wrote some of the music) extends to the cast, largely pals and *Buffy* alumni, none of them marquee names. Whedon's decision to film in black and white was partly for simplicity's sake, but also adds a nice touch of screwball comedy, particularly in the pairing of Alexis Denisof's lugubrious, downbeat Benedick with Amy Acker's highly strung and funny-sad Beatrice – not quite Grant and Hepburn, perhaps, but an excellent double act nonetheless. Much of the play's bleakness is evaded, which makes for a slightly cloying conclusion (hard to believe that Jillian Morgese's Hero would forgive Fran Kranz's expensively educated frat-boy Claudio so immediately), but Whedon's touch is so light that it seems entirely forgivable. Also available in HD Blu-ray format.

AUDIO

Much Ado About Nothing
D. Tennant, S. Spiro, D. Swift; Sally Avens (dir.) UK, 2001 > BBC ◉ ☁

On tape as much as on stage, it's the casting of Beatrice and Benedick that decides whether *Much Ado* sinks or swims. This version emphatically does the latter, with some gloriously fast-paced scenes between David Tennant's cynical, Scottish Benedick and Samantha Spiro's wry Beatrice (the gulling scenes come across surprisingly well with some adept sound balance). Elsewhere among the cast Chiwetel Ejiofor brings a sombre sympathy to Claudio – a character who might not seem to deserve it – and David Haig's Dogberry, thankfully, avoids overdoing things, a trap other actors do not always resist. Sally Avens does not avoid tinkering with the text, however, and there are some transpositions and excisions.

EDITIONS

Arden Shakespeare
Claire McEachern (ed.); 2005 > Bloomsbury

A.R. Humphreys's 1981 Arden 2 edition, much reprinted, was a favourite for many years – not least because Humphreys seems so in tune with *Much Ado*'s spirit – but its successor, edited by Claire McEachern, is the more obvious and contemporary choice. McEachern is refreshingly alert to the social pressures that threaten the play's community, particularly the women that populate it, and points out that one of those pressures is the community itself: there is a welcome amount of detail on the folk narratives of cuckolding and shame that underpin the

Claudio–Hero story. But the editor is also aware of the play's mischievous fun, and provides a clear text with helpful glosses. The slightly skimpy critical history is the only obvious flaw. An update with expanded stage history is scheduled for early 2016.

SOME CRITICISM

Shakespeare's Comedies of Play
J. Dennis Huston; 1981 > Columbia UP [o/p]

Though initially concerned with the earliest comedies, *Shakespeare's Comedies of Play* revels in the honing of Shakespeare's dramatic powers. Huston interprets "play" in a rich variety of ways, arguing that, in *Much Ado*, "playing" – in the sense of social performance – becomes more serious than ever before. Huston's overall thesis, that Shakespeare's work radically changes between the earlier comedies and plays such as *Much Ado*, sometimes feels strained, but he is an observant and interesting reader of these works, constantly illuminating new connections between them. And while noting *Much Ado*'s unsettling qualities, Huston maintains that Dogberry is its saving grace, "unaccountably tied to the spirits of goodness".

Shakespeare's Comedies
Kiernan Ryan; 2009 > Macmillan

Although Kiernan Ryan came to prominence as part of the new historicist and cultural materialist movements in the 1980s, his writing has always been enjoyably various, Conrad and Ian McEwan alongside Thomas Nashe. *Shakespeare's Comedies* is a surprisingly old-fashioned study that focuses on ten plays, *The Comedy of Errors* to *Twelfth Night*, offering readable and lively accounts that try to escape from theory-heavy interpretation and return us to a close engagement with the texts. Some might find all this a bit well-meaning and soft-edged – though it's hard to disagree with his assertion that some critics are "more interested in maps, make-up or medicine than in the power of plays" – but Ryan's approach to *Much Ado* is subtle, focusing on deception and public reputation as the play's grounding themes, and does not duck its troubling aspects (including plentiful hints in the script that Beatrice and Benedick might not live happily ever after).

Othello

A lthough it may not have the cosmic or philosophical resonance of *Hamlet* or *Lear*, the playwright's second great tragedy, *Othello*, is often felt to be his most gripping play. The story of a soldier propelled into murderous fury by his wife's apparent unfaithfulness first appears in a sensationalist Italian novella, but Shakespeare transforms this small-scale, somewhat squalid drama into a maelstrom of turbulent emotion. *Othello* is, unavoidably, also about race: its hero is a black man in a society governed by whites, and from its first days on the stage audiences have been forced to confront the complex issues it presents. Othello is a hero, not a devil – Shakespeare's contemporaries would have assumed the reverse – and ends as an isolated and tragic figure. The calculating killer of an innocent white girl, he might easily have been the lurid villain of racist stereotype, but instead, crucially, he becomes another victim. For we in the audience see what Othello does not: the demonic nature of the play's real villain, the white Venetian Iago, who, unbeknown to everyone on stage, directs every moment of the action. It is impossible not to respond strongly to *Othello*, and passionate reactions also dominate its history in the theatre: there are numerous stories of audience members fainting or screaming – or even begging the cast not to go through with the tormenting final scenes. The tragedy of *Othello* draws us in like no other, and for that reason it is one of Shakespeare's very greatest achievements.

DATE > Possibly as early as 1601–02; perhaps as late as 1603–04 – any reckoning rests on a number of resemblances to *Hamlet*. At any rate, *Othello* was composed during the period when Shakespeare wrote his major tragedies.

SOURCES > Shakespeare's greatest debt is to a novella from Giraldi Cinthio's *Hecatommithi* (1565), which he read in either the original Italian or a French version by G. Chappuys

(1583). Facts about the Turkish invasion may come courtesy of Richard Knolles's *History of the Turks* (1603), while the *History and Description of Africa* by Leo Africanus (1600) is another possible source.

TEXTS > Famously problematic. A quarto printing (Q1) was published in 1622, just a year before the First Folio text, but is different in many details (and 160 lines shorter).

Interpreting the play

Elizabethan and Jacobean plays featuring black characters were a rarity; ones in which they took centre-stage were unheard of. In England there was a long tradition of blacking up in order to represent evil or exotic characters for the medieval mystery and morality cycles, and in courtly entertainment acting "black" became briefly fashionable – as in Ben Jonson's *Masque of Blackness* from 1605, during which white

MAJOR CHARACTERS & SYNOPSIS

Othello, a black soldier, the "Moor" of Venice
Desdemona, Othello's new wife
Michael Cassio, Othello's lieutenant
Bianca, a courtesan in love with Cassio
Iago, Othello's ensign (a low-ranking officer)
Emilia, Iago's wife
Brabanzio, Desdemona's father, a Venetian
   senator
Graziano, Brabanzio's brother
Lodovico, a relation of Brabanzio
Roderigo, a Venetian gentleman in love with
   Desdemona
The **Duke of Venice**
Montano, Governor of Cyprus
Senators of Venice
A **Clown** in Othello's employment

ACT 1 Roderigo and Iago are on their way
to inform Brabanzio that his daughter has
eloped with Othello – the black commander of
Venice's military forces. Roderigo is in love with
Desdemona, while Iago claims to be angry at
being passed over for promotion by Othello in
favour of Cassio. Brabanzio is appalled by the
news of his daughter's marriage and sets off
with his kinsmen to confront Othello. But the
Duke of Venice has already summoned his senators and advisers to discuss the sighting of a
hostile Turkish fleet advancing towards Cyprus, a
Venetian colony. Othello arrives and is ordered to
defend Cyprus, while Brabanzio's wild claim that
his daughter has been bewitched is dismissed
when Desdemona enters and confirms her love,
after which the couple immediately leave for
Cyprus. But their problems are only beginning:
Iago, who has the general's absolute trust, is plotting Othello's downfall.

ACT 2 Though battered by storms, the Venetians
arrive safely in Cyprus to news that the Turkish
fleet has dispersed. Roderigo is also in Cyprus, and
Iago is quick to exploit his jealousy. Persuading
him that Desdemona is now in love with Cassio,
he encourages him to pick a fight with Cassio
later that evening. To make this more likely, Iago
gets Cassio drunk and in the ensuing brawl Cassio
strikes a fellow officer. Dragged from his bed,
Othello demands an explanation, which Iago gives
in such a way that – without directly blaming

him – Cassio is dismissed. Iago then advises Cassio
to win back Othello's favour via Desdemona's
influence; but his own secret plan is to convince
Othello that Cassio is having an affair with her.

ACT 3 When Desdemona intercedes on Cassio's
behalf, Iago suggests to Othello that she does
so out of more than mere friendship. Othello
is resistant at first, but as Iago gradually works
on him, the idea of her adultery comes to seem
more and more feasible. When Desdemona
reappears, she tries to soothe her husband's
obvious disquiet by binding his head with her
handkerchief. Iago's wife Emilia later finds the
handkerchief on the floor and gives it to Iago,
who seizes the opportunity to play on Othello's
suspicion. Told by Iago that Desdemona has
given it to Cassio as a love token, Othello
demands it back from his wife – who, innocently,
tries to turn the subject back to Cassio. By now
convinced of her infidelity, Othello decides on
revenge.

ACT 4 Iago continues to fuel Othello's jealousy,
to the point where he collapses in a fit. When
he recovers, Iago arranges for him to overhear
a meeting with Cassio, during which Othello
becomes even more certain that Desdemona
is unfaithful. He resolves to kill her, while Iago
undertakes to murder Cassio. When a deputation
arrives from Venice recalling Othello, he publicly
abuses Desdemona (to everyone's horror) and
later, in private, accuses her of being a whore.

ACT 5 At Iago's bidding, Roderigo attacks
Cassio but only wounds him, and in the confusion that follows Iago stabs Roderigo to death.
Othello, meanwhile, is about to kill the sleeping
Desdemona when she awakens; despite her
anguished denials, he smothers her in their
own bed. Discovering them both, Emilia insists
on her mistress's innocence, and when Othello
mentions the handkerchief the extent of Iago's
villainy is finally revealed. Iago has arrived in
the meantime, but when Othello attacks him,
he escapes after killing Emilia. Returning under
arrest, he refuses to give any reason for his
actions. Othello finally realizes the truth and,
after asking Cassio's forgiveness, stabs himself.

> *In the first half of the play the main conflict is merely incubating; then it bursts
> into life, and goes storming, without intermission or change of direction, to its
> close.*
>
> A.C. Bradley, *Shakespearean Tragedy* (1904)

female courtiers disported themselves as "blackamoors". Yet in real life, even with
the expansion of colonial trade involving far-flung corners of the globe, there were
few black people resident in England itself during Shakespeare's lifetime. The globe-
revealing public theatres were one of the few means by which the public, at least in
London, experienced such worlds first-hand.

Shakespeare himself had introduced a "Moor", Aaron, into the Roman environment
of *Titus Andronicus*, and another, the Prince of Morocco, makes an appearance in
The Merchant of Venice, itself a play hugely concerned with the idea of an ethnic outsider living in the metropolis. Neither character makes much of a positive precedent:
Morocco is a pompous bore, while Aaron is a fearsome yet thinly sketched villain, as
close as the young playwright gets to evil incarnate, – both characterizations doing
little to challenge commonplace Elizabethan assumptions about the moral or intellectual qualities of men who were black, let alone lurid fears about miscegenation (both
men are involved with white women). Yet in *Othello* everything changes. A black man
is the tragic hero, the noble "Moor of Venice" for whom the play is named; it is a white
Italian, Iago, who is the villain.

That apparent contradiction must have struck *Othello*'s first audiences hard, and
indeed the Duke of Venice admits to feeling it too, hearing that Desdemona, daughter of
one of his senators, has married a black soldier. "Noble signor," he addresses her father,

> If virtue no delighted beauty lack,
> Your son-in-law is far more fair than black.
>
> [1.3.289–90]

The division between outward appearance and inner reality will prove a crucial – and
increasingly malignant – idea in *Othello*, but for the moment it seems that at least
some Venetians recognize that a man who happens to be black need not be a savage.

This realization is hard-won. In opening scenes of unparalleled bitterness and
brutality, we have watched as Iago and Roderigo – Othello's ensign, and his rival for
Desdemona's hand – do their utmost to slander his name. Before the first scene is
out, and before he even appears on stage, "the Moor" (as Iago sneeringly calls him)
is described as a "thick-lips", a "Barbary [Arab] horse", "lascivious". Iago puts it in
the basest terms he can think of. "'Swounds, sir, you're robbed," he taunts her father
Brabanzio,

> Your heart is burst, you have lost half your soul.
> Even now, now, very now, an old black ram
> Is tupping your white ewe.
>
> [1.1.86–9]

Shakespeare's "Moors"

At least three "Moors" appear in Shakespeare's plays: Aaron in *Titus Andronicus*, the Prince of Morocco in *The Merchant of Venice*, and of course the most famous of all, Othello, the "Moor of Venice" (though a fourth, a nameless Moorish girl made pregnant by Lancelot Gobbo in *The Merchant*, also surfaces briefly). The word "**Moor**" has its roots in ancient Mauretania in North Africa, approximately modern-day Algeria and Morocco, but shifted northwest during the eighth century when people of mixed Arab and Berber descent, called *Moro*, conquered Spain and made it part of the Islamic empire.

However, Shakespeare's use of the term, like that of many of his contemporaries – indeed, people much later – is vague at best, and in *Othello* still causes confusion. On the one hand Iago describes the hero as a "Barbarian" (hinting that he is from Barbary in North Africa, perhaps having lighter skin); on the other, Othello calls himself "black", and Roderigo tauntingly refers to him as

"the thick-lips", implying that he is perhaps from sub-Saharan Africa. But Roderigo and Iago's crude racist insults don't exactly make for trustworthy evidence – and the debate would have had little practical value for Shakespeare, still less the white actor blacking up for the part (see p.282). "Moor", "Blackamoor" and "Muslim" were often interchangeable in this period (all three thought to portray an exotic, godless and brutish people), and even if the playwright's sensitivity to his hero's ethnicity were more sophisticated than his countrymen's, this play reminds us that apparently reliable facts about appearance are often anything but. Othello himself relates some more crucial reasons why he feels like an alien: his age, military background and social status all make him an awkward guest in Venice, and Jacobethan audiences would have been quick to observe the strangeness of his marriage to a young society girl. In *Othello*, of all plays, we have to do more than look skin deep.

What we are soon to see described (in Othello's rapt words) as a love "too much of joy" (2.1.198), a love upon which the play will hinge, is here reduced to brute animal lust – and crude racist stereotype.

Over the four centuries *Othello* has been upon the stage, actors and audiences have likewise struggled with the idea that Othello could be both black and the hero of the piece – one commentator, writing in the southern United States only a few years after slavery was abolished, declared that, in her view, "Shakespeare was too correct a delineator of human nature to have coloured Othello *black* … Othello *was* a *white* man." Such colour-blindness (in the worst sense of that phrase) was hardly at a premium. Though there were occasional exceptions, notably the nineteenth-century African American star Ira Aldridge, in Britain and the US Othellos were played by white actors in make-up right up to the 1980s, and in some countries, notably Germany, still are. Critics have fussed over the hero's precise ethnicity, as if by being proved not to be a "veritable negro" (as Samuel Taylor Coleridge argued), he could more easily be understood.

The surprising thing is, those shocking first few scenes aside, *Othello* is not a play that explores racism in any real detail – *The Merchant*, also set in the racial melting pot of Venice, is far more analytical in that respect. As Othello himself testifies, he is employed as a general by the Venetian state and has every reason to expect his position to be respected. And in a sense, it is: though Brabanzio is inflamed by racist slander, his real irritation is that his daughter has flouted his wishes; likewise, Roderigo's grudge against Othello is simply that Desdemona prefers her new, more exciting, suitor to a drab Venetian.

Enmesh them all

Othello has, it seems, not the slightest clue that there is anything at work against him. All that changes when the action relocates to the far-flung island of Cyprus. Posted there in order to confront the encroaching Turkish army, the party of Venetians – Othello, his wife and Cassio, plus soldiers – arrives to the welcome news that the Turkish fleet has been broken up by the storm. But though the military threat has evaporated, Iago has not. Trapped as he is in this suffocating outpost, his plot to devastate the fragile colony and Othello, the man at its centre, develops and builds strength uninterrupted.

We might wonder why Iago is so desperate to destroy Othello, but the play has no real answer – or rather, presents too many to believe. Coleridge famously commented on Iago's "motive-hunting of motiveless malignity", and though more literal-minded commentators have taken up the scattered clues Iago tosses to the audience (which include everything from professional envy to the belief that Othello has, in Iago's grim expression, "leapt into my seat" by sleeping with his wife), Coleridge comes close to defining the sense of absolute evil Iago represents. There is a terrifying void at the centre of his character, an apparently psychopathic urge to destroy a genuinely good man while posing as his best friend. In one of his most chilling soliloquies, Iago even plays tricks with the one thing that is certain about him – his wickedness. "And what's he then that says I play the villain?" he taunts,

When this advice is free I give, and honest …?

[3.1.327–8]

Dispensing "advice" to all and sundry under the cover of plain-speaking honesty, Iago's devilishness, as he goes on to boast, lies in his ability to produce "heavenly shows" while all the time plotting the "blackest sins" imaginable – a triumphant duplicity that will see Othello calling his ensign "honest Iago" until practically the last moment of the play.

Iago sets to work by telling tales – more specifically a single story, that Desdemona has been unfaithful with Cassio, whom she innocently likes and admires:

So will I turn her virtue into pitch,
And out of her own goodness make the net
That shall enmesh them all.

[2.3.351–3]

Relying on Desdemona's open-heartedness and Othello's absolute trust, Iago deftly turns each and every "virtue" into a flaw, and each character into their own most destructive enemy. In this sense he rewrites *Othello* itself, which begins like a comedy, with a marriage achieved against all odds by a rebellious daughter (like, say, *The Merry*

Wives or *Dream*), followed by a storm that presents deliverance, not evil – and yet which turns into monstrous tragedy, one that, as Iago boasts, does indeed trap everyone.

Shakespeare gives Iago nearly a third of the lines in the play, many more than Othello, and while actors have often seen him as the natural leading role, he has also been intrepreted almost as a surrogate playwright. His control of the plot and his willingness to improvise is a work of malign genius. On their first night in Cyprus, Iago arranges for Cassio to get drunk and start a fight with Roderigo (who has accompanied Iago, goaded on by Iago's promise that it's only a matter of time before Desdemona is his). As Iago well knows, that night is also the wedding night, and Othello is so irritated at being disturbed that he strips Cassio of his post on the spot. Cassio is mortified and desperate to recover his "reputation", so Iago persuades him that the quickest way to the general's heart is to appeal to his wife. With all this in place, Iago begins to work Othello. When the two men are alone, Iago innocently asks, "Did Michael Cassio, when you wooed my lady, / Know of your love?"

OTHELLO
    He did, from first to last. Why dost thou ask?
IAGO
    But for a satisfaction of my thought,
      No further harm.
OTHELLO   Why of thy thought, Iago?
IAGO
    I did not think he had been acquainted with her.
OTHELLO
    O yes, and went between us very oft.
IAGO Indeed?
OTHELLO
    Indeed? Ay, indeed. Discern'st thou aught in that?
    Is he not honest?
IAGO Honest, my lord?
OTHELLO Honest? Ay, honest.
IAGO
    My lord, for aught I know.
OTHELLO   What dost thou think?
IAGO Think, my lord?
OTHELLO
    'Think, my lord?' By heaven, thou echo'st me
    As if there were some monster in thy thought
    Too hideous to be shown! Thou dost mean something.

                            [3.3.96–112]

While what Iago wants Othello to think he "means" is already becoming clear, the plain truth, that the whole thing is a monstrous fiction, will not be exposed until it is far too late. Iago uses his control over language to run rings around his master – hinting and insinuating, never stating. Deniability is a key component of Iago's

A veritable negro

Coleridge's notorious assertion that "it would be something monstrous to conceive this beautiful Venetian girl falling in love with a veritable negro" speaks of the anxieties nineteenth-century audiences felt about the subject of *Othello* and race. On the one hand, Othello was black (though Coleridge tried hard to prove he wasn't); on the other, he was the hero – and some had trouble reconciling the two. The striking thing about Coleridge's nervousness is its newness: the few surviving seventeenth-century references to the play simply admire the power of the role, and even in the eighteenth century *Othello* seems to have been understood as a play about jealousy rather than race.

It's interesting to counterpoint this with its performance history. When *Othello* first appeared around 1604, there would have been no question of a black man taking the lead – few were resident in London and were unknown as performers on the public stage. Shakespeare's theatre was well practised at illusion: just as boys played girls, white actors played black roles in *Titus Andronicus*, *The Merchant of Venice* and *Othello*. The same remained true into the nineteenth century and nearly to the end of the twentieth.

Jonathan Miller, who cast the white Bob Hoskins in the role for the BBC in 1981 to some controversy, argued that the play was not really about ethnicity. But the first great black Othello, the nineteenth-century actor **Ira Aldridge**, felt differently: *Othello* became a symbol of his struggle to win over audiences unwilling to see a "negro" act Shakespeare. Having found little success in the United States but some in Britain, Aldridge embarked on a wide-ranging European tour in the 1850s, winning ecstatic praise wherever he went. As the anti-slavery movement was gathering pace, a Russian liberal,

K. Zvantsev, wrote fervently that Aldridge's Othello voiced "the far-off groans of his own people, oppressed by unbelievable slavery, and more than that – the groans of the whole of suffering mankind". Not until **Paul Robeson**'s performances in the 1930s and 40s would *Othello* again have such passionate resonance with the politics of racial oppression.

In recent decades, with theatre directors eager to escape the grim legacy of minstrel shows and the like, it has become impossible to cast anyone other than an actor of colour in the role of Othello. At least in the English-speaking world: in Germany, curiously, there have been several productions in which white actors black up, albeit to some controversy; and in opera it is still commonplace for singers to black up for the title role in Verdi's *Otello*.

A bold 1997 experiment by Jude Kelly at the Washington Shakespeare Theater – a so-called **"photonegative" production** – attempted to re-evaluate the racial dynamics of the play, but many felt that by employing Patrick Stewart's white Othello amid an otherwise African American cast, Kelly had made things even harder for black actors trying to secure lead roles. Something of the same anger makes itself felt in the novelist **Ben Okri**'s account of watching Ben Kingsley play a Moorish Othello at the RSC in 1985. For all that Kingsley is himself of mixed heritage, Okri remarks in *A Way of Being Free* (1997) on feeling like "the only black person in the audience" and insists that the play is unavoidably about colour: "any black man who has gone out with a white woman", he argues, "knows that there are a lot of Iagos around". Even in 2015, when the RSC cast the British-Tanzanian actor **Lucian Msamati** as Iago, "colour-blind" casting is perhaps impossible for a play like *Othello*.

subterfuge, as is his technique of ensuring that Othello is left to construct his own nightmare, breed his own "monsters".

It works, horribly. Soon afterwards, Othello is raging at Iago, unable to make sense of what he suspects:

> I think my wife be honest, and think she is not.
> I think that thou art just, and think thou art not.
> I'll have some proof. My name, that was as fresh
> As Dian's visage, is now begrimed and black
> As mine own face. If there be cords, or knives,
> Poison, or fire, or suffocating streams,
> I'll not endure it.

> [3.3.388–95]

Othello's emotions will not be assuaged, and over the next scenes of the play his doubts about Desdemona's faithfulness (and Cassio's "honesty") will harden into certainty. Iago, typically, is the first to mention the word "jealousy", warning his master with apparent concern that "it is the green-eyed monster which doth mock / The meat it feeds on" (3.3.170–1). For his part Othello is already becoming convinced that his "name" is destroyed and that murderous violence is inevitable.

Confirmations strong

Othello persuades himself that he is acting rationally by demanding "some proof", but again he reckons without Iago's skill – or the workings of chance. As Iago had planned, Othello's is "a jealousy so strong / That judgement cannot cure" (2.1.300–1), and he will be convinced by the flimsiest of grounds. That "proof", almost farcically, is a handkerchief, "spotted with strawberries", that Desdemona happens to drop. Seized on by Emilia, who hands it to her husband, the handkerchief makes its way to Cassio's chamber and thereby becomes the sum total of the physical evidence proving Desdemona's guilt. As Iago jubilantly remarks, "trifles light as air /Are to the jealous confirmations strong / As proofs of holy writ" (3.3.326–7).

The eighteenth-century dramatist Thomas Rymer famously belittled *Othello* as a "bloody Farce", irreverently suggesting that it should be called "the *Tragedy of the Handkerchief*", and though few have felt brave enough to defend him, Rymer puts his finger on the sheer horror of what the play presents: a husband persuaded into murderous jealousy by mere rumour, a wife sent to her death by a "little napkin" – even if, as Othello later claims, the handkerchief was woven for his mother and has "magic in the web of it" (3.4.69). But perhaps that is the point: even the tiniest or apparently most insignificant details are put under huge pressure, and when they fail to take the weight, the avalanche is spectacular. Desdemona's well-meaning eagerness to help Cassio rebounds terribly against her; Emilia's desperate efforts to earn her husband's love makes her an unwitting accessory to his plot.

The play's greatest perversity, though, is built into its very structure. *Othello* is the site of one of Shakespeare's most virtuosic theatrical coups, the so-called "double time-scheme". Othello and Desdemona have, on one level of the play, almost implausibly little time together: their new marriage is threatened by her father's wild intervention, then by the news that Othello must be sent to Cyprus. Later, their wedding night is disturbed by Cassio's brawl (leading some critics to infer that the match remains unconsummated), then by the witless group of musicians he pays to play outside their window in a misguided attempt to curry favour. It has been calculated from internal references that, once in Cyprus, the action of the play occupies no more than 33 hours – just under a day and a half. On stage, however, *Othello* feels much longer, apparently lengthened by Shakespeare's scattered gestures to more extended time periods. The effect is of a play at once too long and too short: long enough for Othello and Desdemona's marriage to feel convincing, yet short enough for it to be insecure; short enough for Iago's plot to remain secret, yet long enough for it to work its way to completion. Though he is ignorant of it, Othello himself picks up on this impossible, torturing tension. "What sense had I of her stol'n hours of lust?" he cries,

> I saw't not, thought it not; it harmed not me ...
> He that is robbed, not wanting what is stol'n,
> Let him not know't and he's not robbed at all.
>
> [3.3.343–8]

Those "stol'n hours" are, of course, an impossibility; there is simply no time in the action of the play (even if there were reason) for Desdemona to be unfaithful. Shakespeare steals time from us too, just as Iago steals from Othello his mind.

Nor does Shakespeare give us space to draw breath. Just a few minutes after beginning to suspect Desdemona, Othello is racked by doubt; another few minutes after that, he is swearing "capable and wide revenge" (3.3.462), convinced by the evidence and resolved not to go back. After the handkerchief makes its appearance and Cassio is framed, the effect on the hero is devastating. "Lie with her? Lie on her?" Othello cries,

> We say 'lie on her' when they belie her. Lie with her? 'Swounds, that's
> fulsome! Handkerchief—confessions—handkerchief. To confess and be
> hanged for his labour. First to be hanged and then to confess! I tremble
> at it. Nature would not invest herself in such shadowing passion without
> some instruction. It is not words that shakes me thus. Pish! Noses, ears,
> and lips! Is't possible? Confess? Handkerchief? O devil!
>
> *He falls down in a trance*
>
> [4.1.33–42]

Though Othello will rapidly recover from this fit, the mental turmoil it represents will stay with him until his death.

But first the blameless Desdemona must die. Although Iago plants the idea of her infidelity in Othello's mind, the notion of killing her in revenge is all her husband's. "O, blood, blood, blood!" he rages just moments before his wife appears, as innocent of the knowledge as she is in character. She assumes that state business has distracted Othello, made him unwell, but her ministrations do nothing but infuriate him. The terrible cycle of jealousy does its work. After a horrific public shaming during which Othello hits Desdemona in front of guests from Venice, the lovers have a tearful final argument. Othello taunts her with his own certainties, refuses to listen to her denials. "What, not a whore?" he yells,

DESDEMONA   No, as I shall be saved.
OTHELLO Is't possible?
DESDEMONA O heaven forgive us!
OTHELLO I cry you mercy then.
   I took you for that cunning whore of Venice
   That married with Othello.

[4.2.89–94]

There is something infinitely moving about Othello's lingering torment, but of course he is not its main victim. Instructing Desdemona to prepare for bed, he readies himself for an execution in cold blood. Even so, the testimony of her sleeping body almost persuades him not to go through with it. "It is the cause, it is the cause," he murmurs, stepping silently into her bedroom,

Let me not name it to you, you chaste stars.
It is the cause. Yet I'll not shed her blood,
Nor scar that whiter skin of hers than snow,
And smooth as monumental alabaster.
Yet she must die, else she'll betray more men.

[5.2.1–6]

He will not "scar" her alabaster skin, but he will kill her before the scene is out. This is perhaps the most chilling of Iago's many malicious victories: as well as robbing Othello of his sanity, he makes him into the villain imagined by racist fantasy – a black murderer stealing into a white girl's bedchamber. Worse still, Othello seems aware of the fact, drawing attention to her "whiter" complexion rather than his "foul", "filthy" murder. Emilia informs Othello what many early seventeenth-century audiences will have suspected all along: "O, the more angel she, and you the blacker devil!" (5.2.140).

The play is very nearly over – but not quite. Though it is too late for Desdemona (and indeed for Othello), in the dying moments the truth does out. Following Emilia's furious testimony – like her namesake in *The Winter's Tale* she is a fierce guardian of the truth – the real story emerges. "O thou dull Moor," Emilia cries, "that handkerchief thou speak'st of / I found by fortune and did give my husband..." (5.2.232–3). Realizing that his fictions are collapsing, Iago makes a last attempt to rewrite the conclusion and lunges brutally at his wife, mortally wounding her.

Othello, meanwhile, begins the slow and tragic journey to realization. He, too, is desperate to be understood. "When you shall these unlucky deeds relate," he tells the assembled throng, as it gathers around the corpses on stage,

> Speak of me as I am. Nothing extenuate,
> Nor set down aught in malice. Then must you speak
> Of one that loved not wisely but too well,
> Of one not easily jealous but, being wrought,
> Perplexed in the extreme; of one whose hand,
> Like the base Indian, threw a pearl away
> Richer than all his tribe …
>
> [5.2.350–7]

For Iago, however, the storytelling has come to an end. "Demand me nothing," he says. "What you know, you know." (5.2.309–10). There will be no other answers.

Stage history and adaptations

The first performance of *Othello* on record is at James I's **court** on November 1, 1604, almost certainly with **Richard Burbage** in the lead (after his death he was applauded for his "grieved Moor"). Opposite him as Iago was possibly **John Lowin**, better known for his Falstaff. Fifteen or so years later Burbage's heir **Ellyaert Swanston** took on Othello and **Joseph Taylor** Iago. Another early staging was recorded at **Oxford** in 1610, where the performance apparently moved spectators to tears, and the play was being performed in London right up to the Civil Wars.

It soon returned, almost unique among Shakespeare's output in not being rewritten for the Restoration stage, and Desdemona was one of the first roles to be taken by a professional actress, possibly **Margaret Hughes** or **Anne Marshall**, in a production for Thomas Killigrew's King's Company in 1660. A decade later **Michael Mohun** was a celebrated Iago and the play was possibly performed at Dublin's Smock Alley Theatre later in the 1670s, but from 1682 *Othello* became indelibly associated with **Thomas Betterton**'s magisterial Moor, much commended for his "Rage and Jealousy" in the role. Those words came from **Colley Cibber**, who played a smirking Iago to **Barton Booth**'s heroic and noble Othello from 1710 to 1727. Booth's reputation was so great that **James Quin** struggled when he attempted the role in 1720 (again to Cibber's Iago), and when **Charles Macklin** turned to the play in 1734 he opted for Iago instead, producing one of the subtlest interpretations of the century. **David Garrick**, too, would be defeated by the Moor, playing the role just three times before giving it up in 1747 in favour of Iago. Alongside him was **Spranger Barry**'s electrifying Othello – so passionate that female audience members are reported to have shrieked whenever he came on stage.

Barry's Desdemona was the excellent **Susannah Cibber**, and a generation later it was **Sarah Siddons** who transformed Desdemona into a central role, acting her alongside the stately Othello of her brother, **John Philip Kemble**, from 1785. Soon afterwards the play became known in French via **Jean-François Ducis**'s translation. Parisian audiences were said to be so stunned by the play that Ducis had to scribble an emergency happy ending in case they rioted.

The mercurial **Edmund Kean** seized upon the possibilities offered by Othello in 1814, opting for lighter make-up than usual and emphasizing the facial expressions and the emotional extremes that became his hallmark. Kean downplayed the first two acts of the play, but came into his own during Othello's breakdown, producing, according to Hazlitt, "the finest piece of acting in the world". In his first season, Kean played the role of Iago – equally successfully – on alternate nights, before establishing the precedent of hiring rival tragedians to play Iago with the aim of destroying their reputations in the process. **Junius Brutus Booth** was humiliated in this way in 1817, the Kemble disciple **Charles Mayne Young** fared slightly better in 1822, but by the time Kean took on **William Charles Macready** in 1832 he was a broken man. A year later, during his final performance, he collapsed into the arms of his son **Charles Kean,** who was playing Iago, and died two months later.

By this time the brawny **Edwin Forrest** had become well known in the US, and played the role for the next half-century. But in every way the nineteenth century's most important Othello was the African American **Ira Aldridge**, who was forced to leave the US in order to make his career. Aldridge's European tour in the 1850s turned him into a folk hero, but in Britain and the States audiences were often openly racist (see p.337). His pan-European success would be replicated a few decades later by the Italians **Tommaso Salvini** and **Ernesto Rossi**, both playing impressive Othellos in their native language; Salvini won praise for being "supremely, paralyzingly real" in the role.

English actors failed to match the grandeur of these foreign stars, and during the late Victorian era *Othello* became more than ever Iago's play. **Henry Irving** attempted the Moor in 1876, but even his leading lady **Ellen Terry** (herself an impressive Desdemona) admitted that watching him was "painful" in the worst sense, and when they revived it in 1881 Irving took Iago to **Edwin Booth**'s Othello. By the end of the decade **Giuseppe Verdi**'s grand opera had become known in England and Shakespeare's play, more domestic in its compass, suffered as a result. Different approaches were required: **Baliol Holloway** took the risk of performing an egotistical Othello in 1922, while in 1929 **H.K. Ayliff**'s Birmingham Rep gave the play modern dress. The most famous Othello of the era was **Paul Robeson**, who closely associated the role, like Aldridge before him, with the struggle against racist oppression and played it a number of times. He first did so in 1930, opposite a young **Peggy Ashcroft** as Desdemona at London's Savoy Theatre (audiences were audibly shocked when the lovers kissed, and would have been even more horrified to discover that the couple were having a real-life affair). Robeson returned to the role in 1943 in a production directed by **Margaret Webster**; and finally at Stratford in 1959 with **Sam Wanamaker** as Iago and **Mary Ure** as Desdemona. Though Robeson was sometimes accused of lacking depth, he brought to the part (according to one witness) a "tranquil dignity and a melancholy infinitely sad".

By contrast, **Ralph Richardson**'s Othello under **Tyrone Guthrie** at the Old Vic in 1938 was underpowered, and the show was stolen by **Laurence Olivier**, who played Iago as a repressed homosexual. **Donald Wolfit** took the role in his many touring productions during the 1940s, while over in the States **Orson Welles** acted in the 1951 production that he would eventually make into a film. By this time black actors had become more familiar in the role: **Earle Hyman** played Othello in the 1950s, but it was **James Earl Jones**'s resonant 1964 New York Shakespeare Festival performance that became most celebrated (Jones repeated the role on Broadway in 1982, but this time

The climactic moment from Paul Robeson's 1943 Broadway production of *Othello*, the murder of Desdemona (here played by Uta Hagen). Robeson, a prominent activist, identified closely with the role of Othello and played it several times as part of his tireless campaign to see performers from all backgrounds accepted in mainstream performances – Shakespeare included.

Christopher Plummer's Iago got the rave reviews). The quatercentenary year of 1964 was also the year of **John Dexter**'s National Theatre production, which had **Laurence Olivier** attempt an antiheroic Othello in deference to the critic F.R. Leavis, who had criticized the character's self-absorption. Olivier's efforts to act against type (and to be as "black" as possible) torpedoed an otherwise finely judged production, marked by **Maggie Smith**'s reserved Desdemona and **Frank Finlay**'s icy Iago.

Charles Marowitz's *An Othello* (1972) made both hero and villain black and ditched much of Shakespeare's language, while in Hamburg four years later **Peter Zadek** caused controversy by making his Othello wear a King Kong costume in an attempt to shock audiences out of their complacency. **John Barton**'s 1971 RSC version was perhaps more influential, set in a nineteenth-century colonial outpost; **Brewster Mason**'s stolid Othello played second fiddle to **Emrys James**'s energetic Iago. The last two white Othellos in major British productions, **Donald Sinden** (RSC, 1979) and **Paul Scofield** (National, 1980), both opted for light brown make-up rather than trying to convince audiences that they were actually of a different ethnicity.

In South Africa, for reasons that are grimly obvious, *Othello* has a long and often disreputable history. It was one of the first Shakespeare plays to be performed in the British Cape Colony, with a "gentleman and three ladies" from the **Theatre Royal, Liverpool** arriving in 1818 to offer it alongside a cast of local European amateurs. Revivals became reasonably frequent during the nineteenth century, sometimes in adapted form, as in an 1836 performance of a Dutch play baldly called *Othello, of de Jaloersche Zwart* ("Othello, or the Jealous Black"), but more often done straight, as evidenced by the version by touring British actor **Gustavus V. Brooke**, who visited Cape Town in 1854. During the apartheid regime the play was still sometimes staged – with white men blacking up – but also helped challenge the status quo. In 1971 the British playwright **Donald Howarth** created an adaptation pointedly called *Othello Slegs Blankes* ("Othello Whites Only") in which the hero was written out of the script entirely; one critic wrote that it helped "lay bare the absurdities that so many of us accept as commonplace". In 1983 **Joko Scott** became the first black South African to play Othello, in a production by **Phyllis Klotz**; and was followed by **John Kani** at Johannesburg's Market Theatre in a staging by **Janet Suzman**. Performed just two years after the repeal of the so-called "Immorality" laws, which outlawed sexual relationships between people of different races, it became an international symbol of the struggle.

Back in Britain, **Terry Hands**'s 1985 production at the RSC stressed the dangerous affinities between the Othello of **Ben Kingsley**, of mixed Indian and Jewish heritage, and **David Suchet**'s Iago, but it was Suchet's decision to play Iago as obviously gay that proved most influential. **Ian McKellen** hinted something similar in **Trevor Nunn**'s 1987 production – with **Willard White** a statuesque and commanding Othello to **Imogen Stubbs**'s girlish Desdemona – as did **Simon Russell Beale** under **Sam Mendes** at the Old Vic in 1998. While Nunn once more drew on the nineteenth century for his production, Mendes opted to set *Othello* in the 1930s, drawing out the play's militarism with Russell Beale's bully-boy villain dominating **David Harewood**'s youthful hero – an approach emulated at **Michael Attenborough**'s RSC in 1999, with **Ray Fearon**'s Othello in thrall to **Richard McCabe**'s bluff Iago. Conceivably the boldest attempt to redefine *Othello* in the late twentieth century, however, was the Washington Shakespeare Theatre production by **Jude Kelly**, which staged a "photonegative" version of the play in 1997: **Patrick Stewart** played a white Othello surrounded by blacks, among them **Patrice Johnson**'s moving Desdemona and the hefty Iago of **Ron Canada**. Many critics were unconvinced, though, arguing that Kelly's approach created more problems than it solved.

In 2004 **Declan Donnellan**'s touring production for Cheek by Jowl had a gentle, almost boyish hero from **Nonso Anozie**, bewildered by **Jonny Philips**'s brilliant, cooing Iago. Over at the RSC the same year **Antony Sher** took the role opposite **Sello Maake ka-Ncube**'s Othello. **Gregory Doran**'s production was much-hyped for its South African connections – the stars grew up on the different sides of apartheid – but it was its near-operatic intensity that most captured reviewers, embodied in Sher's defiantly energetic villain as much as ka-Ncube's histrionic downfall. At London's Donmar in 2007, in a Jacobean-style production directed by **Michael Grandage**, the stars of the evening were **Chiwetel Ejiofor**'s distinguished, generous Othello and **Kelly Reilly** as a fragile Desdemona, **Ewan McGregor**'s Iago winning merely pallid reviews. The same year also saw **Wilson Milam** stage a similarly historicized version at Shakespeare's Globe, with a dignified Othello from **Eamonn Walker** and a snarling **Tim McInnery** as Iago. Altogether different from either was the updated hip-hop version brought by American group the **Q Brothers** to the World Shakespeare Festival in 2012, which featured everything from nods to the Beastie Boys to descriptions of "boning" and "shagging".

Othello remains as popular as ever in the US, where it is a standby of the festival and non-profit circuit, though it has not been staged on Broadway since the 1980s. Strikingly, given the play's history, **Nicholas Hytner**'s 2013 sleekly contemporary production at London's National Theatre seemed almost post-racial, with **Adrian Lester** offering a modern-day soldier who just happened to be black; opposite him as a blunt Iago was **Rory Kinnear**. Even more fascinating – and echoing Marowitz 40 years before – was **Iqbal Khan**'s 2015 Stratford version, which cast the British-Ghanaian **Hugh Quarshie** alongside **Lucian Msamati**, who is of Tanzanian heritage. As well as being the first RSC staging to feature an Iago of colour, the production was also noteworthy because Quarshie had decades earlier declared that "of all the parts in the canon, perhaps Othello is the one which should most definitely not be played by a black actor."

Until the TV adaptation of Nunn's 1990 production, no footage existed of a black actor playing Othello in a mainstream version. A 1922 silent film by **Dmitri Buchowetzki** (with **Emil Jannings** as Othello and **Werner Krauss** as Iago) and **Sergei Yutkevich**'s 1955 Russian version aside, the dominant English-language productions are those by **Orson Welles** (1952), **Stuart Burge** (a 1965 rendering of the Dexter–Olivier staging), **Oliver Parker** (1995), with **Laurence Fishburne** as Othello, and **Tim Blake Nelson**'s 2001 American high-school adaptation, *O*. For the BBC, **Jonathan Miller** initially tried to secure James Earl Jones as Othello, but in the end cast **Anthony Hopkins** opposite **Bob Hoskins**'s Iago (1981). Two fascinating cinematic versions hail from India, **Jayaraaj**'s *Kaliyattam* (1997), a Malayalam-language version that blends Shakespeare's plot with the highly ritualized theyyam performance tradition; and **Vishal Bhardwaj**'s predominantly Hindi *Omkara* (2006), in which the caste tensions of the contemporary subcontinent throw those of the drama into stark relief.

SCREEN

Othello

O. Welles, S. Cloutier, M. MacLiammóir; Orson Welles (dir.) Morocco/Italy, 1952/1993
> Upfront / Image **DVD**

Like pretty much everything Orson Welles did, his reconstructed and restored *Othello* has divided audiences. Some have junked it as eccentric bilge, others consider it a masterpiece in the best traditions of *film noir*. Whichever camp you find yourself drawn into, when you consider the terrible labours of production, it's a wonder anything got made at all: with funding practically non-existent, shooting took, on and off, four years – two weeks for every minute of film. Though there is much that will offend purists (not least the savage cuts, which shrink the action to a hurtling 87 minutes and render the immaculately paced onset of jealousy all but nonsensical), it's the shards of brilliance that remain lodged in the memory: Welles's sturdy Othello, sunlit at first but trapped in cloying shadow as he descends into madness; Micheál MacLiammóir's febrile Iago; superbly inventive flashes of cinematography and stage business. While it may not comply with the letter of Shakespeare's play, this *Othello* is a loving tribute to its spirit.

Othello

L. Olivier, M. Smith, F. Finlay; Stuart Burge (dir.) UK, 1965 **>** British / Warner **DVD**

Anyone expecting a noble, Robeson-like Moor will be shocked by Laurence Olivier's portrayal in this filmed version of the 1964 National Theatre production. Olivier presents a vividly unsympathetic Othello, an arrogant fraud only tolerated in Venice because of his usefulness to the state. This is interesting and radical stuff, much indebted to Leavis (see p.348), but Olivier, characteristically, goes too far. Quite apart from his colour, which makes Othello look as if he's been dipped in antique wood-stain, Olivier's efforts "to be black" (in his words) by lowering his voice, altering his gait and attempting a Jamaican accent will strike most audiences as outright offensive. In striving for "blackness" as a mark of "otherness", this interpretation veers too close to racist caricature – and is often too embarrassingly comic – for its many insights to be taken seriously. Almost as importantly, it doesn't allow Othello's character to go anywhere: what Shakespeare scores as a series of infinitesimal psychological fractures become variations on a theme. Frank Finlay's smirking, NCO Iago barely has to lift a finger to return his master to savagery.

Othello

J. Kani, J. Weinberg, R. Haines; Janet Suzman (dir.) South Africa, 1987 **>** ArtHaus **DVD**

Staged at Johannesburg's Market Theatre during the grim last years of apartheid, Janet Suzman's *Othello* had history on its side, and made a name for itself internationally for being the first major staging of the play with a black South African, John Kani, in the lead. This TV recording doesn't have quite the punch-you-in-the-guts intensity audiences reported in the theatre, but it is still a remarkable achievement, a record of an epoch-making production as well as a compelling piece of drama. Kani is more timid than you might expect as the hero, almost boyish and clearly adrift in the polite Venetian society inhabited by Joanna Weinberg's well-bred Desdemona and Neil McCarthy's smooth-jowled Cassio. But in every sense the focus is Richard Haines's bullish, bullying Iago, effortlessly in command until almost the last. As he rages bitterly against the "Moor", it's impossible to forget that in South Africa just a few years before it would have been impossible for Othello and Desdemona to be seen together in public, still less get married.

Othello

W. White, I. Stubbs, I. McKellen; T. Nunn (dir.) UK, 1990 **>** Metrodome **DVD**

Qualities that marked out Nunn's 1978 filming of *Macbeth* – pared-down setting, taut atmosphere, excellent casting – are very much in evidence here, in what remains probably *Othello*'s best translation to video. Shakespeare's domestic tragedy feels naturally at home on the small screen, and particularly so when Nunn's claustrophobic sets and dour nineteenth-century staging, originally designed for the RSC's tiny The Other Place, begin to do their work. Willard White, better known as an opera singer, has the stature and the voice to make a superb Othello, and Imogen Stubbs brings an appealingly fragile quality to Desdemona. Zoë Wanamaker's Emilia, too, deserves praise for her blend of strength and neediness. But in Nunn's hands the play belongs throughout to Ian McKellen's restless Iago, as impressively flexible as the play needs him to be yet always teetering on the brink of sanity.

Othello

L. Fishburne, I. Jacobs, K. Branagh; Oliver Parker (dir.) UK, 1995 **>** Warner **DVD** **🔊**

A film starring Kenneth Branagh in which he isn't the director? True enough, though you could get through watching this picture without realizing it: some of the old crew are here (Tim Harvey's lush designs are unmistakable) and Oliver Parker's debut film is solidly in the style of Hollywood Shakespeare *à la* Branagh. Its gorgeously shot Italian settings will be an antidote to too many studio-bound versions, though in most other respects this film simply fails to come alive. Laurence Fishburne's Moor did not deserve the critical mauling it received upon release, but despite Fishburne's impressive screen presence he sorely lacks depth and often seems rudderless in the verse. That might be Parker's fault: everyone attempts to keep the dialogue naturalistically low-key, and with the play's melodrama pumped up (most famously for fantasy sequences in which Othello imagines Desdemona's infidelity) the results are oddly imbalanced. Branagh himself looks uneasy playing his first Shakespearian villain, and with about half the script gone (including Iago's crucial final lines), this *Othello* is more lightweight than it needed to be.

Omkara

Ajay Devgn, K. Kapoor, S.A. Khan; Vishal Bhardwaj (dir.) India, 2006 > Shemaroo DVD

Vishal Bhardwaj's follow-up to his sleeper hit *Maqbool* (see p.266) is an altogether larger and brassier affair, lavishly shot in the lawless terrain of Uttar Pradesh with Ajay Devgan's Omkara/Othello the scowling leader of a gang whose job is to terrorize the local area on behalf of a corrupt politician. He's mixed-race; Dolly/Desdemona (Kareena Kapoor) is fair-skinned, which in caste-sensitive India lends their romance a genuinely illicit thrill. There's dancing and songs aplenty, but by mainstream Bollywood standards it's restrained as well as sensitively acted, and in Saif Ali Khan's snarling villain it has an Iago who's up there with the best of them.

AUDIO

Othello

P. Robeson, J. Ferrer, U. Hagen; Godard Lieberson (dir.) USA, 1944 > Pearl ◉

Paul Robeson's life was intimately bound up with *Othello*: the role itself became a crucial part of his struggle for civil rights, and gave him a much-valued opportunity to extend his acting skills beyond the stereotyping confines of Hollywood. For that reason alone this 1944 recording is unique testament to a man who has still perhaps to receive his full due. Unfortunately it doesn't hold many other attractions: José Ferrer's unruffled Iago barely breaks into a trot, Alexander Scourby sounds insipid as both Cassio and Brabanzio and while the script is quite heavily trimmed this taping somehow lacks any real tension. The goods are delivered, however, by the lead couple (who were having an affair at the time): Uta Hagen is

passionate and persuasive as Desdemona, and opposite her Robeson is calmly adamantine. While he doesn't find the fire in the role you might expect, the detailed modulation of his astonishing voice offers its own rich insights – particularly as the play develops and Othello disappears into the depths of his inner soul (the final scene is extraordinarily intense). In addition, three of Robeson's song recordings close disc two of this set.

Othello

H. Quarshie, A. Lesser, E. Fielding; David Timson (dir.) UK, 2000 > Naxos ◉ ☁

Despite Hugh Quarshie's very public doubts about *Othello*, long before battling his demons and appearing on stage at the RSC in 2015 he took the role in this audio version. He presents a different take on hero to Fearon (see below): older, cooler, oakier in vocal tone, somewhat more thoughtful, yet alert to the quiet humour of the role; his breakdown is like watching a building subside, but brick by brick. Anton Lesser as Iago might struggle to persuade that he's a career soldier, but nevertheless his is a versatile high-wire performance, one that might almost convince you (as Othello is convinced) of Iago's bluff but hard-edged honesty. Emma Fielding makes a mature and searching Desdemona, resigning herself to the wreckage of her marriage (like that of Patience Tomlinson's wry Emilia) with clear but saddened sight. Supporting parts are also well filled: John McAndrew whines delightfully as Roderigo, and Peter Yapp is surprisingly sympathetic as Brabanzio. Not as searing an experience as the BBC version, but this is a considered and well-rounded production.

Othello

R. Fearon, J. Frain, A. Hille; Jeremy Mortimer (dir.) UK, 2001 > BBC ◉ ☁

A few years before recording this, Ray Fearon provided a memorable Othello at the RSC. On audio he is less vocally resonant than some (Hugh Quarshie, above, offers strong competition) but nevertheless manages to deliver an interpretation that is both intelligent and terrifyingly sad – particularly in the scenes with James Frain's bullying Iago, which are so intimately recorded that Frain merely has to whisper to tighten the screws on his master's sanity. Fearon's hero is young and virile, but comes to pieces with almost startling ease: listening to the bleached-out monotone of his voice in the latter stages of the play you sense that his revenge will be terrible and unstoppable – that of a man who has confronted his devils and will not return. Anastasia Hille's rather quiet Desdemona is sensitively done and Lindsey Coulson pulls out all the stops as Emilia.

EDITIONS

Oxford Shakespeare
Michael Neill; 2006 > Oxford UP

If *Hamlet* was the play of choice for angst-ridden Romantics, and *Lear* the only text that made sense to a shattered postwar world, then *Othello* is the work that speaks most readily to our postcolonial, postracial society – so at least claims editor Michael Neill. Neill is an eloquent advocate for *Othello*'s merits as well as an astute guide to its challenges, notably on the issue of ethnicity, an issue that he manages with extraordinary subtlety and tact. The handling of a famously bothersome text – Neill favours the Folio – is all but flawless, and the editorial matter is as richly revealing on the play's life in performance as it is on matters such as military history and music. A fine first choice.

SOME CRITICISM

The Common Pursuit
F. R. Leavis; 1952 > Faber

Fearless as well as ferocious, F.R. Leavis trampled on many toes during the course of a distinguished and provocative academic career. One of the leading lights of the so-called "Cambridge" school, Leavis set up his own journal, *Scrutiny*, to publish his views and those resembling it, and many of the essays in *The Common Pursuit* appeared there first. Though they cover plenty of non-Elizabethan ground (Milton, Gerard Manley Hopkins, Johnson, Henry James), Shakespeare was always integral to Leavis's literary pantheon and three pieces confront him directly. The essay on *Othello* is the most famous, not least for the fact that it relegates the hero to a subtitle: "Diabolic Intellect and the Noble Hero: or the Sentimentalist's Othello" describes the dignified Moor of legend but insists that he figures nowhere in the play. Instead Othello has "a habit of approving self-dramatization", is fatally "self-centred" while also lacking in "self-knowledge", and, in short, has it coming to him. Plenty to disagree with, but that's the point: if Leavis doesn't make you livid there's little point in reading him.

The Masks of Othello
Marvin Rosenberg; 1961 > Delaware UP [o/p]

First published in the early 1960s and reprinted by Delaware, Marvin Rosenberg's terrific work has helped generations of readers get inside *Othello*. Like later examples in his "Masks" series – notably *Lear* (1972), *Macbeth* (1978) and his immense *Hamlet* (1992) – *The Masks of Othello* goes straight to the heart of the play's appeal, tracking what Rosenberg's subtitle calls "the search for identity of Othello, Iago and Desdemona by three centuries of actors and critics". Examining how some of the greatest practitioners in history have approached the play provides rich rewards for a tragedy with such power to woo audiences, and this study is as enlightening about *Othello*'s deep themes as it is about its extensive life on stage. Leavis would pour scorn on Rosenberg's conclusions about Othello's essential "nobility" (built on the theories of A.C. Bradley and many after him), but Rosenberg is with the majority.

Pericles

P*ericles* embodies a new mode of work for Shakespeare – away from the grand run of tragedies capped by *Antony and Cleopatra* and *Coriolanus*, and towards the world of romance. The playwright's source was the medieval poet John Gower, who actually appears on stage to relate the story of the Tyrean hero, his numerous adventures and his hardships, all experiences comparable to those of wanderers in classical epic such as Odysseus and Aeneas. *Pericles* itself, excluded from the all-important First Folio, has had an equally hard time of it, still rarely performed. No one is quite sure why Heminges and Condell decided not to include the play, but their reasoning probably had little to do with its literary or theatrical merit, for even in the text we possess, which appears to be corrupt or otherwise unpolished (some think it was co-written with the minor dramatist George Wilkins), it contains moments of outstanding beauty. As those who have been fortunate enough to have seen it in the theatre can testify, *Pericles* delivers a finale which is among Shakespeare's most intensely moving.

DATE > *Pericles* was seen by the Venetian ambassador probably in 1608, and was most likely written the previous year – the earliest of the "romances".

SOURCES > The Greek story of Apollonius (Pericles) of Tyre was widely known, but John Gower's version in *Confessio Amantis* (1390s) is the central source – the poet even stars as the play's narrator. Laurence Twine's novella *The Pattern of Painful Adventures* (1576) also furnished some details.

TEXTS > *Pericles*'s sole text was printed in 1609 in an unauthorized edition, perhaps reconstructed from memory. Because it was not included in the 1623 Folio, it has been argued that *Pericles* is a collaboration with the poet George Wilkins, whose novella, *The Painful Adventures of Pericles Prince of Tyre* (1608), recalls the play. Some modern editions divide the play into scenes, but not acts.

Interpreting the play

Pericles never allows us to forget that it is a story – an ancient tale worked up anew. The first person on stage, and a recurrent presence thereafter, is Gower, medieval poet and author of the *Confessio Amantis* ("The Lover's Confession"), Shakespeare's main source. "To sing a song that old was sung / From ashes ancient Gower is come," he begins,

> Assuming man's infirmities
> To glad your ear and please your eyes.
> It hath been sung at festivals,

MAJOR CHARACTERS & SYNOPSIS

Gower, the narrator
Pericles, Prince of Tyre
Marina, Pericles' daughter
Helicanus and **Aeschines**, counsellors of Tyre
King Antiochus of Antioch
Antiochus's Daughter
Thaliart, a villain
King Simonides of Pentapolis
Thaisa, Simonides's daughter
Cleon, governor of Tarsus
Dionyza, Cleon's wife
Leonine, a villain
Lychorida, Thaisa's nurse
Cerimon, a physician from Ephesus
Philemon, Cerimon's servant
Lysimachus, governor of Mytilene
Various brothel characters, including a **Bawd**, a
  Pander and **Boult**, the Pander's servant
Diana, goddess of chastity

*This synopsis retains traditional act divisions,
but follows the scene numbering of the Oxford
Complete Works*

SCENES 1–4 Gower relates an old story: how
King Antiochus has had an incestuous affair with
his daughter, and tries to keep her for himself by
setting her many suitors an impossible riddle.
When each one fails to solve it, he sentences
them to death. Antiochus enters with Pericles,
who intends to woo the princess, and sets him
the riddle; when Pericles astutely works out the
correct answer, Antiochus secretly orders him to
be murdered. But before Thaliart can poison the
Prince, Pericles arranges with Helicanus to escape
to Tarsus. Thaliart arrives in Tyre, but misses
Pericles, who has meanwhile arrived in Tarsus and
delivered its citizens from famine by bringing corn.

SCENES 5–9 As news arrives about Thaliart's
plot, Pericles leaves once more but is shipwrecked
in a storm. He is washed up on the shore near
Pentapolis, and is looked after by a group of kindly
fishermen. When they drag his armour from the
sea, Pericles decides to travel incognito to the court
of King Simonides and take part in the tournament
there, which is intended to test the prowess of his
daughter's suitors. The mysterious knight wins the
jousting, and also the princess's heart, but refuses

to divulge his identity. Back in Tyre, Pericles' own
knights complain about his absence and try to persuade Helicanus to take the crown in his place – but
Helicanus nobly refuses. In Pentapolis, Simonides
tests Pericles' feelings for his daughter by showing
him a forged love letter to Thaisa; after hearing
Pericles' protestations of virtue, the King grants
the couple permission to marry. Their wedding is
described by Gower with the aid of a dumb show.

SCENES 10–14 Pericles and his pregnant bride
sail for Tyre, but during a terrible storm Thaisa
seemingly dies in childbirth and the superstitious
sailors insist that her body be thrown overboard.
Horrified and grief-stricken, Pericles complies but
resolves to transport their newborn daughter,
Marina, to Tarsus, where her upbringing will be
entrusted to the governor Cleon and his wife
Dionyza. Thaisa's coffin, meanwhile, has washed
ashore at Ephesus, where the physician Cerimon
manages to revive her from a deathlike sleep.
Unable to remember the birth, Thaisa is taken to
join the temple of Diana.

SCENES 15–19 Gower narrates Marina's
development into a beautiful young woman,
and how Dionyza grows jealous of her charge,
arranging to have the girl murdered by Leonine.
Before Leonine can succeed, however, Marina is
kidnapped by pirates and sold into prostitution at
Mytilene. There she stoutly refuses to co-operate
with customers – to the Bawd's despair – and
when the governor Lysimachus appears, she
persuades him to help. Pericles has meanwhile
returned to Tarsus and is told that Marina has
died in his absence; he sadly vows to spend the
rest of his life in mourning.

SCENES 20 - 23 Pericles' ship arrives at
Mytilene, and – not knowing of their relationship – Lysimachus sends Marina to sing to the
grief-stricken Prince and ease his sorrow. Pericles
does not recognize his daughter immediately, but
after a heart-stopping pause they are reunited.
Moments later, the goddess Diana appears to
Pericles in a vision and persuades him to go to
Ephesus, where he discovers Thaisa. All are joyfully brought back together, and Lysimachus is
betrothed to Marina.

On ember-eves and holy-ales,
And lords and ladies in their lives
Have read it for restoratives.

[Sc. 1, 1–8]

Unlike the Chorus of *Henry V*, who apologizes for the theatre itself, "this unworthy scaffold", Gower, like all the best storytellers, begs forgiveness for his tale by simultaneously advertising its pedigree. That apology goes for *Pericles* as a whole, the first of Shakespeare's so-called "romances", which draws attention to its artifice while simultaneously celebrating the fact. Rejuvenating the long-dead Gower from his grave – which was just around the corner from the Globe in what is now Southwark Cathedral – and putting him on stage is the first of the miracles the play will perform.

Not that this impressed Ben Jonson, the first of *Pericles*'s many critics, who sullenly dismissed it as a "mouldy tale ... and stale / As the shrieve's crusts, and nasty as his fish- / Scraps". Though editors and scholars have agreed – many conjecture that the play is co-written and the text damaged or not quite finalized – it is hard not to think that this misses the point. *Pericles* has that "once upon a time" quality: it is *meant* to seem magically and wonderfully antique.

Unknown travels

Gower's expedition through the centuries is merely the first of many journeys in *Pericles*, which moves restlessly from place to place, "bourn to bourn, region to region", as Gower puts it (Sc. 18, 4). Though Shakespeare himself had no use for the word "romance", like many of his contemporaries, *Pericles* is his fullest expression of romance motifs, themes that ultimately have their root in ancient epics such as Homer's *Odyssey* but became formalized during the early medieval era and flowered for at least another three centuries. Integral to romance tales is the idea of the quest – the task that the hero (there are few romance heroines) must perform, and the adventures he encounters along the way. *Pericles* has all the right ingredients. The hero is compelled to take up what seems like an endless journey across the eastern Mediterranean, a story of love and loss, seemingly impossible feats, and multiple tragedies averted only by the most magical of realizations. The first of Pericles's many quests is to win the hand of King Antiochus's beautiful daughter, but he is compelled to flee when he discovers a dark secret at the heart of the Syrian court. This sets up a chain of expeditions that takes in such exotic centres of the ancient world as Ephesus, Tarsus and Myteline. Like Odysseus in Homer's epic – and indeed like Egeon and Antipholus of Syracuse in *The Comedy of Errors*, which also uses Gower as a source (see p.43) – he becomes nomadic, almost rootless.

The restlessness that lies at the heart of *Pericles*'s source material has often attracted comment. What Laurence Twine, the sixteenth-century author of *The Pattern of Painful Adventures* (1576), which Shakespeare also seems to have used, billed the "delectable variety ... chances and changes" of his story has been less well received nearer the present day. The critic G. Wilson Knight, though one of *Pericles*'s champions, famously described its plot as "merely a succession of happenings linked by

Yukio Ninagawa's production of *Pericles*, which visited the UK in 2003, was a stunning visual experience. Masaaki Uchino played the long-suffering hero, seen here about to be reunited with his wife Thaisa.

sea-journeys", while editor J.C. Maxwell catalogued what he saw as the "fantastic and often irrational narrative". But it is one of the play's most telling themes that in the face of powerful natural forces humans have little opportunity to control their own fates. Even ending other people's lives can prove a problem, as Thaliart (the assassin hired by Antiochus to murder Pericles) finds to his cost when he arrives at Tyre in hot pursuit, only to discover that the King has "betook himself to unknown travels" (Sc. 3, 35), and is already en route elsewhere.

The dangers that the play's characters face are starkly presented by the all-encompassing role of the sea in *Pericles*. Even more so than *The Tempest* (written perhaps two years later), the play is obsessed with the risks of travelling by water. Two terrible storms occur in the course of the action: in the first Pericles is shipwrecked and all his possessions drowned; in the second he loses his wife to the flood. Though in one sense these tempests enable the plot to develop and turn in unexpected directions – *Twelfth Night*, too, relies on the shipwreck that separates the heroine Viola from her brother – in *Pericles* the sea often features as a malevolent dramatic force: a fearful barrier rather than a liberating medium. By heading to Tarsus, Helicanus worries that his friend Pericles "puts himself unto the ship-man's toil, / With whom each minute threatens life or death" (Sc. 3, 24–5), and indeed the frustrated assassin Thaliart contents himself that the King has done his job for him by taking ship, grimly noting that "he scaped the land to perish on the seas" (Sc. 3, 29). Though these dark forebodings will not prove quite accurate – Pericles will not die during this first storm – other troubles soon strike.

For although Pericles will survive the second tempest, too, it is at appalling cost. When his new wife, Thaisa, appears to have died in childbirth, the sailors insist her body must be dumped overboard; the "venomous" ocean will not be satisfied until it has swallowed her corpse. Pericles's moving farewell speech to his wife carries the play to its first climax, and in it he attempts to negotiate with the vast forces that surround them both. "A terrible childbed hast thou had, my dear," he says,

> No light, no fire. Th'unfriendly elements
> Forgot thee utterly, nor have I time
> To give thee hallowed to thy grave, but straight
> Must cast thee, scarcely coffined, in the ooze,
> Where, for a monument upon thy bones
> And aye-remaining lamps, the belching whale
> And humming water must o'erwhelm thy corpse,
> Lying with simple shells.
>
> [Sc. 11, 55–63]

Passionately simple and movingly homely in tone, Pericles's obsequy attempts to find a human, personal space in the "great vast" for his dead wife. Though the play's language is not always this fine, here it calls down themes that resonate with the great tragedies. And yet Pericles does not, like Lear, rant against the elements. As he later admits, "Should I rage and roar / As doth the sea she lies in, yet the end / Must be as 'tis" (Sc. 13, 9–12).

This great sea of joys

Into the sea, Thaisa's immense grave, go Pericles's hopes: this is the play's bleakest moment. Yet the "ooze" – both the end of life and its source, a word that becomes densely suggestive in Shakespeare's late plays – will not swallow her body forever, and in fact it will deliver her. Lord Cerimon, the virtuous doctor, speaks of "the disturbances / That nature works, and of her cures" (Sc. 12, 34–5), describing the inherent balance that lies at the heart of creation. Sure enough, in the scene that follows, Thaisa's casket arrives out of the "turbulent and stormy night", presenting Cerimon with the opportunity to revive its living but unconscious cargo; a miraculous reawakening that proves the first of several. Calling for "still and woeful music", Cerimon observes how, as it works, Thaisa "'gins to blow / Into life's flow'r again" (Sc. 12, 92–3) – both a breathtakingly theatrical moment and a figurative rebirth for the Queen, herself just free from the pangs of childbed. When she

> As [Pericles] elaborates, feature by feature, on the similarity he senses, the remembered past merges with the perceived actuality, until the images of the wife who "was" and that of the daughter who "might have been" dissolve ... into the girl before him.
>
> Inga-Stina Ewbank, "'My name is Marina': the language of recognition" (1980)

exclaims breathlessly, "Where am I? Where's my lord? What world is this?" (Sc. 12, 104) it is as if she begins to relearn what it is to live.

Thaisa's escape from the storm's clutches echoes that of her husband after the first tempest just a few scenes before. "Cast up" (vomited) by the "drunken" sea after his shipwreck (and with all his possessions drowned), Pericles is on the verge of collapse when he comes across a group of fishermen by the shore:

PERICLES
What I have been, I have forgot to know,
But what I am, want teaches me to think on:
A man thronged up with cold; my veins are chill,
And have no more of life than may suffice
To give my tongue that heat to crave your help,
Which if you shall refuse, when I am dead,
For that I am a man, pray see me burièd.
He falls down

MASTER Die, quotha? Now, gods forbid't an I have a gown here! Come, put it on, keep thee warm. Now, afore me, a handsome fellow! Come, thou shalt go home, and we'll have flesh for holidays, fish for fasting-days, and moreoe'r puddings and flapjacks, and thou shalt be welcome.

[Sc. 5, 112–24]

Again, humanity intervenes. Though this scene has none of the magical splendour of Thaisa's reawakening, the fishermen's homespun generosity is powerful enough. A stranger and a survivor, Pericles is warmly welcomed into their society. And as if in response to their kindness, the "rough seas" that provide their livelihood suddenly disgorge the King's armour – giving Pericles the opportunity to prove his heroic worth at King Simonides's court and ultimately win Thaisa's hand in marriage.

Perhaps the most expressive example of the sea's changefulness appears on the dreadful night of Thaisa's loss – indeed, is the reason for her apparent death. Marina, "born in a tempest" and named after the ocean that carries away her mother, is less rooted even than her father, as she exclaims mournfully:

The world to me is but a ceaseless storm,
Whirring me from my friends.

[Sc. 15, 71–2]

After being forced to flee from the court of Cleon and the wicked Dionyza (recalling her father), and suffering "death" (shades of her mother), Marina is kidnapped by pirates and ends up in a brothel. Cast once again to the mercy of fate, she is nevertheless able to talk her way out through sheer strength of personality: sending her would-be clients away with prayers on their lips and charity in their hearts, she is so chaste, her baffled pimp exclaims, that she would "undo the whole of generation" if she could (Sc. 19, 13).

Marina's radiant virtue saves her from the depredations of "lewdly inclined" clients, but it also prepares for the play's emotional highpoint. Brought unknowingly to meet

Tragical-comical-historical-pastoral

It's obvious enough that Shakespeare's plays defy easy categorization, and commentators these days often fight shy of affixing labels. The playwright's colleagues Heminges and Condell had few such anxieties, however, cheerfully dividing the 36 works included in the First Folio into **"Comedies, Histories, and Tragedies"**, as the title infamously puts it. Occasionally their decisions have raised eyebrows. *Cymbeline*, although it ends happily for the major characters, appears among the tragedies, while some of the Folio's "histories", among them *3 Henry VI* and *Richard II*, were originally published as "tragedies".

That said, sixteenth-century audiences would know what to expect with a **comedy**: laughter, yes, and probably stock characters, but also varieties of satire – the world gone mad or held up to ridicule. Renaissance theorists and their classical forebears did come up with more complex definitions based on Roman dramatists such as Plautus and Terence, yet although Shakespeare learned extensively from classical precedents he crafted an idiosyncratic comic world. His comedies use witty wordplay, ingenious plotting and have satiric elements (often via clowns; see p.400), but they almost invariably deliver some kind of social resolution, usually sealed by marriage between his protagonists – a device that hints at festive modes of renewal and reconciliation.

Critics have often compared Shakes-pearian **tragedy** to the work of the revered Greek tragedians Aeschylus, Sophocles and Euripides. **Aristotle**'s fragmentary musings on the genre in his *Poetics* received much attention after they were redis-covered in the sixteenth century, but again Shakespeare's own tragedies don't draw directly on Greek traditions and often operate quite differently, not least in their penchant for inserting comedy where neo-classical writers, following Aristotle, felt it vulgar. The definition of the Elizabethan translator **John Florio** is Aristotelian but workmanlike: he wrote in 1598 that "a tragedy or mournful play" was "a lofty kind of poetry and representing personages of great state and matters of much trouble, a great broil or stir: it beginneth prosperously and endeth unfortunately or sometimes doubtfully, and is contrary to comedy". Closer to home is the observation that, in many of Shakespeare's plays – to reverse the famous aphorism – tragedy equals comedy plus time.

Though a majority of the plays could convincingly be called "tragicomic" (a term of abuse until his colleague John Fletcher attempted to write a tragicomedy), another genre is used by critics: that of the **romance**. This has the least claim to authenticity, and was seemingly first used to describe Shakespeare's work by the nineteenth-century scholar Edward Dowden, who attempted to isolate what was unique about the final group of plays (often just called the "last comedies"). In them, Dowden suggested, "the dissonances are resolved into harmony; the spirit of the plays is one of large benignity; they tell of the blessedness of the forgiveness of injuries; they show how the broken bonds between heart and heart may be repaired and reunited; each play closes with a victory of love". But Shakespeare never used the word "romance", and his contemporaries would have found it hard to comprehend what modern critics mean by it. Whether we even accept Dowden's sentimental opinions is another – and much larger – critical question.

Pericles – who thinks that his daughter, like his wife, is dead and buried – she thinks at first that Pericles is too catatonic in grief to be saved. But the fractured, sea-borne story of Marina's life ("If I should tell / My history," she exclaims, "it would seem like lies" (Sc. 21, 106–7)) begins to work at his curiosity until the truth about her parentage steadily –

and incredibly – becomes clear. Beginning to realize that she is his child (a fantasy too improbable to be true), Pericles cries out, "Give me a gash, put me to present pain,"

> Lest this great sea of joys rushing upon me
> O'erbear the shores of my mortality
> And drown me with their sweetness!

[Sc. 21, 179–82]

"Thou that begett'st him that did thee beget," he continues, a wonderstruck father addressing the daughter who has given him life once more. The sea has delivered more than pain and death: it has metamorphosed into the bringer of "joy". It seems only fitting that the goddess Diana should descend from the heavens to crown the event, as Shakespeare (perhaps assisted by a newly installed winch at the Blackfriars playhouse, a likely early venue) makes her do just moments later.

Once daughter and father are together once more, all that remains for the story to have worked itself through is for Thaisa, too, to be recovered. Shakespeare does not try his audience's patience: in the very next scene Pericles announces that he will give thanks to Diana when one of her attendant nuns suddenly swoons; she is none other than Thaisa. The recognition this time is immediate, but no less astonishing. "O, let me look upon him," Thaisa begs,

> If he be none of mine, my sanctity
> Will to my sense bend no licentious ear,
> But curb it, spite of seeing. O, my lord,
> Are you not Pericles? Like him you spake,
> Like him you are. Did you not name a tempest,
> A birth and death?

[Sc. 22, 48–54]

As with Marina, it is the story that tells all: the tempest, birth and death that are the lineaments of Pericles's tale reunite him with his family. In the first of these romance plays, Shakespeare steers a way through tragedy – the storms, the long-lost child, the death – and finds something new and miraculous at his journey's end.

Stage history and adaptations

Amid the shifting sands of theatrical taste, *Pericles*'s fate seems especially harsh. Seemingly a huge hit in the first years of its life (one of its author's biggest), it sank into almost total obscurity during the late seventeenth century, disappearing from the stage in its original form for over two hundred years. Even now, shadowed by doubts about its authenticity, it is one of the most rarely revived of Shakespeare's dramas.

The runaway success of **printed editions** suggests the play's early popularity – the 1609 quarto was reprinted five times, despite being error-strewn – and it was performed at James I's **court** that same year (though not in front of the King, whose wife had recently died and who therefore had good reason to stay away). A poem published in 1646 describes *Pericles* as one of Shakespeare's finest achievements, and that seems to have been the view of Restoration actors and managers too. The young **Thomas Betterton**, then a trainee bookseller, performed it at the Cockpit playhouse in London in 1659, making the play one of the earliest to appear after the reopening of the theatres under Charles II.

But after the carving up of Shakespeare's repertoire between impresarios William Davenant and Thomas Killigrew, *Pericles* disappeared from favour for the best part of a century. In 1738, the playwright **George Lillo** put together an adaptation he dubbed *Marina*, which debuted at Covent Garden. Lillo cut the first two acts of Shakespeare's romance in order to focus on Pericles's daughter and added a moralizing prologue apologizing for the original's "rude wild scenes" (which, naturally, he had done his utmost to smooth over).

It was over a hundred years before *Pericles* proper appeared again. The great **Samuel Phelps**, once described as "a diligent labourer in the vineyard of old plays", revived it at Sadler's Wells in 1854 in a lavish production – and gained little but condescension from the *Times*, who noted "the paucity of the dramatic interest". Soon afterwards the husband-and-wife team **Sarah** and **James Stark**, both Americans who trained in Britain, introduced the play to California, one of the very few times it was staged in America (or anywhere else) in the nineteenth century. It was not until 1900 that the play would be seen again back in Britain, courtesy of **Frank Benson** at Stratford. Benson wrote to a friend that in veteran actor **John Coleman**'s acting version there was "nothing objectionable" (the brothel scene was cut, along with much else), and it achieved some acclaim, one reviewer declaring that "the production of such a work filled me with wonder". *Pericles* was staged only twice more before World War I, both times in Germany.

Robert Atkins put on a production during 1921 at London's Old Vic that was noted for its simplicity, directness and use of an uncut text. Just before World War II, **Robert Eddison** appeared as Pericles at London's Regent's Park Theatre, and after hostilities ceased, his success was matched by **Paul Scofield** and **Daphne Slater**, who appeared at Stratford in 1947 in a heavily edited version. Another Stratfordian leading couple, **Richard Johnson** (Pericles) and **Geraldine McEwan** (Marina), wowed audiences in a spectacular staging directed by **Glen Byam Shaw** in 1958, particularly noted for its fairytale magic and moving recognition scene.

Terry Hands revived the play at Stratford-upon-Avon in 1969 in a production that emphasized the hero's place in the action by putting a vast copy of Leonardo's famous Vitruvian Man on the front curtains, but savagely cut the script. By contrast, **Ron Daniels**, directing at the studio-size Other Place a decade later, retained some of the so-called "Wilkins" text and drew attention instead to the role of **Julie Peasgood**'s impassioned Marina. The English Stratford has not been the play's only champion: its Canadian cousin presented an enthusiastically received production (1973) directed by **Jean Gascon** and starring **Nicholas Pennell** and **Pamela Brook**, the same year that **Toby Robertson**'s Prospect company presented a carnivalesque reading of the play at the Edinburgh Festival.

For all that, however, *Pericles* remains one of Shakespeare's least revived plays. **Declan Donnellan**'s Cheek by Jowl staged a touring production in 1984 that was a model of narrative clarity using the simplest of means, but many remained unconvinced, and the play was excluded from Peter Hall's survey of the romances at the National Theatre in 1987. At the Ontario Shakespeare Festival the previous year it had appeared in an acclaimed production by **Richard Ouzounian** starring **Geraint Wyn Davies** as Pericles and **Goldie Semple** as Thaisa. **David Thacker**'s RSC version of 1989 attracted notice for casting **Helen Blatch** in the male part of Cerimon as well as its experimental approach to the text, and the production's refreshingly low-tech staging also gained plaudits. The same could not be said for **Adrian Noble**'s RSC production of 2002, which involved plenty of high-wire theatrics – not least a breathtaking descent from the lighting rig by Diana. **Ray Fearon**'s Pericles was noble yet searching and **Kananu Kirimi** shone as Marina, though Noble's self-consciously "Oriental" staging gained mixed reviews.

In contrast, excitement greeted the arrival of **Yukio Ninagawa**'s Japanese company at London's National Theatre in 2003. Ninagawa's approach tended towards the symbolic, seeing in *Pericles* a "restorative" message (as Gower puts it) for refugees across the world – the action was framed by a crowd of dispossessed people shambling across the stage to the sound of gunfire and helicopters. Brilliantly executed stage effects, among them human puppet shows, created a fairytale world, but it was the strength of the cast – notably **Masaaki Uchino**'s forceful Pericles and a delicate **Yuko Tanaka** as Thaisa and Marina – that made this production a landmark. **Kathryn Hunter**'s radical, modern-dress reimagining for Shakespeare's Globe in 2005 featured a troupe of aerialists and divided the central role between **Robert Luckay** and **Corin Redgrave** to underscore the remorseless passage of time. Another interesting interpretative turn was taken as part of the RSC's Complete Works festival in 2006 by **Dominic Cooke**, who cross-cast *Pericles* with *The Winter's Tale* to draw out the plays' thematic links. In Cooke's promenade production, which perambulated from Greek taverns to Soho pole-dancing clubs, **Lucian Msamati** offered a stoical hero, with **Ony Uhihara** a sweet, gentle Marina.

The play is increasingly popular in North America, where it has recently been revived in lavishly stylized productions at the Chicago Shakespeare Theatre (**David Bell**, 2014) and Oregon Shakespeare Festival (**Joseph Haj**, 2015), and director **Scott Wentworth**, staging it at Stratford, Ontario in 2115, won plaudits for taking it to an entirely new place: the Victorian world of Charles Dickens. Arguably more authentic – at least in the Mediterranean sense – was the Greek-language production staged by the **National Theatre of Greece** at the Globe in 2012, but it won lukewarm reviews for relying too heavily on physical comedy.

Pericles seems to have little chance of gracing the silver screen in the imminent future, even recorded live in a theatre, and the only TV production in existence is that for the BBC/Time-Life series (1983), directed by **David Hugh Jones** and featuring **Mike Gwilym**'s Pericles opposite **Juliet Stevenson**'s Thaisa.

SCREEN

Pericles

M. Gwilym, J. Stevenson, E. Petherbridge; David Hugh Jones (dir.) UK, 1984 > BBC DVD

The great selling point of the BBC Shakespeare series was that it would explore the further reaches of the canon as well as the better known plays. Unfortunately, with this timid, unadventurous *Pericles* their heart doesn't seem to have been in it. Given Pericles's incessant travels, lack of access to any kind of exotic location is a shortcoming (the studio-bound fishermen scene, complete with added-in coastal background, is poor, while the shipwreck scene is little better), and the whole thing feels more than slightly lukewarm. Mike Gwilym's callow Pericles struggles to impress, although the women surrounding him are better: Juliet Stevenson is poignant as Thaisa while Amanda Redman's clear-eyed Marina is strong – if somehow a bit spooky.

AUDIO

Pericles

N. Terry, S. Gonet, J. Cox; Clive Brill (dir.) UK, 1998 > Arkangel ◉ ☁

This 1999 *Pericles* was one of the last projects John Gielgud ever did, and his august tones – a throwback to a lost age of Shakespearian verse-speaking – make him ideal in all sorts of ways as Gower. In fact on audio all of *Pericles* comes across very strongly, more strongly than critics of its verse style would have you believe, and it often has a wonderfully colourful tang. Nigel Terry speaks particularly well, presenting a rounded interpretation of the hero, and Stella Gonet's womanly Thaisa is also fine. Julie Cox sounds youthful as Marina but produces extensive reserves of inner strength – especially during some vigorously realized brothel scenes. It may be one of the very few spoken-word versions available, but this Arkangel recording is genuinely compelling.

EDITIONS

Arden Shakespeare (third series)

Suzanne Gossett (ed.); 2004 > Bloomsbury

Calmly credited to "William Shakespeare and George Wilkins", Gossett's edition feels refreshingly free of the kind of wild-eyed fervour that touches some other scholarly accounts of *Pericles*. The play isn't perfect, Gossett readily admits (and you wouldn't want to hang around Shakespeare's collaborator, the decidedly unsavoury Wilkins), but in a decent production – such as Yukio Ninagawa's 2003 staging, described warmly in her introduction – it has plenty to offer. This edition covers all the usual ground with style, provides an elegant argument for co-authorship and suggests plenty of ways into the imaginative fabric of the play.

SOME CRITICISM

The Crown of Life

G. Wilson Knight; 1947 > Routledge

The book that put *Pericles* on the critical map, *The Crown of Life* is subtitled "essays in interpretation of Shakespeare's final plays" and is every bit as lapidary as its quasi-biblical title suggests. "Interpretation" in the grandest sense of the word is what concerns Knight, who remains splendidly aloof from debates about authorship, preferring instead to probe the play's artistic merits – what he terms its "organic" qualities, the sense that (despite the textual problems) everything is imaginatively coherent. Unabashedly Christianized though his philosophical framework is (Pericles's discovery of sin at Antioch is seen as an Adam-like Fall), Knight avoids the sentimentality that afflicts many later studies of the romances and is refreshingly upfront about the play's attractions – and limitations.

Pericles: Critical Essays

David Skeele (ed.); 2000 > Routledge

As ever with plays that risk falling off the critical radar, Routledge's Garland collections of essays prove invaluable. David Skeele's imaginative cull of criticism reveals how far understanding of *Pericles* has come over the years, all the way from Jonson's peeved declaration that it was "mouldy" to Janet Adelman's suggestion that it forms the mother-obsessed heart of the final plays. And his selection of theatre pieces ranges from eyewitness accounts of Samuel Phelps in 1854 to analysis of the play's intriguing popularity in Japan. This is easily the best place to start, and might also be supplemented with Kiernan Ryan's similarly excellent anthology, *Shakespeare: The Last Plays* (1999), reviewed on p.516.

Richard II

F or his fifth foray into English history, Shakespeare dug up the roots of the feud whose consequences are played out in the three parts of his early *Henry VIs*: the deposition of Richard II by his cousin Henry Bolingbroke in 1399. That event ignited a slow-burning conflict, the Wars of the Roses, that destabilized British politics for the next ninety-odd years and fragmented England's ruling class. In *Richard II* these fissures lie mostly hidden, though the play's central quandary – how a country can be ruled by a rightful but weak monarch – must have engaged Elizabethan audiences, well aware that their own Queen was sometimes compared to Richard. The play is experimental among Shakespeare's histories: it contains not a word of prose, and its rich verbal texture closely resembles comedies such as *Love's Labour's Lost*. At the centre of this operatic drama stands King Richard himself, whose preternatural skill with words is matched by his limitations as a ruler, a polar opposite to his efficient but chilly replacement. Obsessed with the performance of his own life, Richard – and his downfall – make for compelling theatre.

DATE > Probably 1594–95. *Richard II* has stylistic similarities to the "lyrical" comedies, including *Love's Labour's Lost, Romeo and Juliet* and *A Midsummer Night's Dream*.

SOURCES > Shakespeare worked closely with Holinshed's *Chronicles* (1587), and also used Edward Halle's *Union* (1548). Samuel Daniel's epic *Civil Wars* (1595) is a key source, as is the anonymous play *Woodstock* (c. 1592). Marlowe's *Edward II* also had an influence.

TEXTS > The quarto (Q1) of 1597 sold well, and was reprinted twice. Q4 (1608) restores several politically sensitive sections cut from Q1, and was itself reprinted as Q5 in 1615. The 1623 Folio text is based mainly on Q3, but includes Richard's abdication scene.

Interpreting the play

In real life, the reign of Richard II was marred by popular revolt and bitter aristocratic feuding, and he was ejected from the English throne not once but twice. To succeeding generations, his flaws as a leader attracted widespread condemnation, and by the nineteenth century his rule had become a byword for incompetence and cronyism. The Elizabethans appear to have thought likewise: no fewer than three plays concerning the king appeared on the London stage during the dramatist's career, not including his own, and all were unforgiving – dwelling on Richard's culpability for the murder of his uncle, the Duke of Gloucester, and satirizing his notorious weakness for flatterers.

Behind this thriving trade in portrayals of a long-dead monarch was the example of his very much alive (though somewhat elderly) successor, Elizabeth I, who was herself accused of being misled by her favourites, and about the matter of whose succession –

MAJOR CHARACTERS & SYNOPSIS

King Richard II of England
Queen Isabel, Richard's wife
John of Gaunt, Duke of Lancaster, Richard's uncle
Harry Bolingbroke, Duke of Hereford, Gaunt's son (later **King Henry IV**)
Duchess of Gloucester, widow of the murdered Duke (Gaunt's and York's brother)
Duke of York, Richard's uncle, and his wife, the **Duchess of York**
Duke of Aumerle, the Yorks' son
Thomas Mowbray, Duke of Norfolk
Green, **Bushy** and **Bagot**, intimates of King Richard
Percy, Earl of Northumberland
Harry Percy, Northumberland's son
Lord Ross
Lord Willoughby
Earl of Salisbury
Bishop of Carlisle
Sir Stephen Scrope
Other nobles, including **Lord Berkeley**, **Lord Fitzwalter**, the **Duke of Surrey**, the **Abbot of Westminster** and **Sir Piers Exton**
A **Groom** from King Richard's stable

ACT 1 The old Duke of Gloucester has been murdered and the English court is riven by faction. On one side Harry Bolingbroke accuses his enemy Mowbray of the murder, but Mowbray denies the charge. The pair are eager to prove themselves in combat, and King Richard eventually consents. But when the day of the duel arrives, Richard suddenly changes his mind, deciding to banish the two troublesome lords instead – Bolingbroke for ten years, Mowbray permanently. This does little to enhance Richard's popularity, nor does it dampen suspicions (held by the widowed Duchess of Gloucester and John of Gaunt) that the King himself is implicated in Gloucester's violent death. Back at court, Richard and his favourites carp about Bolingbroke's departure from England and his ballooning popular support when news arrives of a rebellion in Ireland.

ACT 2 Joined by York, the dying Gaunt bemoans the state of the country, which is struggling under Richard's unpopular rule – a point that Gaunt makes to the King personally. Richard is unmoved, however, and as soon as Gaunt expires makes a point of seizing his estates. Rumour has it that Bolingbroke is gathering forces to return home, and, sure enough, as soon as Richard departs for Ireland he lands at Ravenspurgh. Richard's supporters panic, while York (made regent in Richard's absence) finds his loyalties divided, and when Bolingbroke and his army reach Berkeley Castle he reluctantly allows them to enter.

ACT 3 Returning in emergency from Ireland, Richard faces a terrible situation: his army has dispersed, three of his closest friends have been executed by Bolingbroke, and York has defected. In despair he travels to meet his enemies at Flint Castle. Despite Bolingbroke's protestations that he has no wish to seize the throne, Richard admits he is powerless. A coup begins to seem inevitable when the Queen overhears her gardeners discussing Bolingbroke's intentions towards the throne.

ACT 4 As Bolingbroke attempts to search for the truth behind Gloucester's murder in Parliament, Richard's abdication is announced. Carlisle warns that civil war will break out if Bolingbroke becomes king, but Northumberland has him arrested. When Richard arrives to abdicate in public, he succeeds in upstaging his successor with a histrionic and self-pitying performance in which he refuses to acknowledge the legitimacy of his deposition. Carlisle, Westminster and Aumerle are persuaded by his cause and vow to fight back.

ACT 5 York and his wife are discussing Bolingbroke's enormous popular support when they discover that none other than their son Aumerle is guilty of plotting against Bolingbroke. York rushes to plead with the new King that his son should be punished, but Aumerle escapes with a pardon. Richard is less lucky. Believing that Henry has ordered the ex-king to be murdered, Exton heads to Pomfret Castle, where Richard is imprisoned, and stabs him to death. Hearing the news, King Henry vows to go on a penitential pilgrimage.

given her childlessness – there was continued anxiety throughout the 1590s. Elizabeth herself recognized the resemblance only too well, remarking acidly to the antiquarian William Lambarde a few years before her death that "I am Richard II, know ye not that?", and observing that a "tragedy" of the King had been "played forty times in open streets and houses".

Whether Shakespeare's play was the "tragedy" to which Elizabeth alluded we will never know. But elsewhere the part it took in her life seems more definite. On the eve of the Earl of Essex's rebellion against the Queen in 1601, his supporters paid the Lord Chamberlain's Men to revive a play about "the deposing and killing of Richard II", possibly Shakespeare's. Though the performance at the Globe went ahead as arranged on February 7, Essex's attempted coup foundered the following day and he was captured, then beheaded, before the end of the month.

This realm

The parallels between *Richard II* and Elizabeth's reign were sensitive enough for the scene depicting the King's abdication to be blue-pencilled by the censors (or cut by Shakespeare before they got to it), and it was only restored in a text published long after the Queen's death. The resonances are distinctly unflattering. Much is made of Richard's political mismanagement and unpopularity: the Earl of Northumberland accuses him of financial largesse and being "basely led / By flatterers"; Ross laments the "grievous taxes" he has imposed; Willoughby grumbles how "daily new exactions are devised" (2.1.242–250). Nahum Tate, whose adaptation of the play briefly graced the Restoration stage, observed that Shakespeare's Richard was "painted in the worst Colours of History".

Furthermore, England itself – as critic E.M.W. Tillyard suggests, the ever-present "hero" of Shakespeare's histories – seems to be in mortal danger. Close to death at the start of Act Two, Gaunt gives impassioned voice to his nephew's fickle betrayal of "this royal throne of kings, this sceptred isle,"

> This earth of majesty, this seat of Mars,
> This other Eden, demi-paradise,
> This fortress built by nature for herself
> Against infection and the hand of war,
> This happy breed of men, this little world,
> This precious stone set in the silver sea,
> Which serves it in the office of a wall,
> Or as the moat defensive to a house
> Against the envy of less happier lands;
> This blessèd plot, this earth, this realm, this England ...

[2.1.40–50]

Though this speech is often (too often) quoted as a patriotic celebration of England and Englishness – it was anthologized as one of "the Choicest Flowers of our English Poets" as early as 1600 – its dramatic purpose is altogether different. Gaunt underlines everything that England should be under Richard's command but conspicuously isn't. The nation is, Gaunt objects, "leased out ... Like to a tenement or a pelting farm", "bound in with shame" (2.1.59–63); the King is its "landlord", not its ruler. And Richard's betrayal of England is compounded by a personal betrayal. Just moments after Gaunt's death, the King coolly announces that he will seize his "plate, coin, revenues, and movables" in order to fund the Irish wars – in effect disinheriting Gaunt's banished son, Bolingbroke, and setting in train events that will culminate in Richard's own deposition.

Up to this point in the play, the case against Richard seems watertight – particularly because Bolingbroke, his opponent and eventual successor, is presented in terms starkly antithetical to those of the King. Banished by Richard, ostensibly for challenging Mowbray (but more likely because Richard seems anxious about his mounting power), his cousin's response to the news is calm rather than histrionic. Although Bolingbroke expresses pain at bidding England farewell, he undertakes to carry consoling thoughts of its "sweet soil" with him:

> Whe'er I wander, boast of this I can:
> Though banished, yet a trueborn Englishman.
>
> [1.3.271–2]

Bolingbroke astutely plays the patriotic card, a successful strategy underscored just a scene later by reports of his mounting popular support – and Richard's rancorous jealousy at it. Though Bolingbroke is never that outspoken, the play begins to present him as England's saviour, a "trueborn" liberator who will combat the (French-born) King. As Northumberland puts it, it is Bolingbroke who will "shake off our slavish yoke",

> Redeem from broking pawn the blemished crown,
> Wipe off the dust that hides our sceptre's gilt,
> And make high majesty look like itself ...
>
> [2.1.293–7]

Yet Bolingbroke's own views on the progress of his career rarely receive a public airing. His main attraction – that he is utterly different from his rival for the throne – is also his most enigmatic quality. Shakespeare never permits him to speak in soliloquy, and his motives remain consistently in shadow. Even so, his opportunism is undeniable: as soon as Richard is out of the country, Bolingbroke stages a surprise reappearance with several thousand men. The question of precisely what he will do is left open: the return from banishment takes place off stage, and it is left to Bolingbroke's ally Northumberland to insist that "the noble Duke hath sworn his coming is / But for his own" (2.3.147–8), in effect that he has come to reclaim the property illegally seized from his father. Nearly everyone else suspects that he is after the throne itself, however, and when the King disappears to Ireland during the crucial centre of the play, the balance of power suddenly shifts. York, left in control of England, cannot resist the invading army; Richard's favourites, "the caterpillars of the commonwealth" (2.3.165) fall into Bolingbroke's hands and are summarily dispatched; the King's Welsh troops melt away.

But the closer Bolingbroke gets to power, the more opaque his words seem. Warned by York to "Take not … further than you should, / Lest you mistake the heavens are over our heads", Bolingbroke's reply is elegant doublespeak:

> I know it, uncle, and oppose not myself
> Against their will.

[3.3.18–19]

If the "will" of the heavens reads two ways, then so can Bolingbroke's intentions towards the King when they meet again at Flint Castle after Richard's hurried (and disastrous) return from Ireland. Richard cries, "Up, cousin, up," urging his cousin not to kneel in front of him:

> Your heart is up, I know,
> Thus high at least, although your knee be low.
> BOLINGBROKE
> My gracious lord, I come but for my own.
> KING RICHARD
> Your own is yours, and I am yours, and all.

[3.3.192–5]

Kinged again

It seems astonishing that an entire kingdom can be resigned in words of such painstaking ambiguity (it may be that Shakespeare didn't dare risk anything more politically overt), but a reaction against this seemingly unstoppable procession of events is not long in arriving. Moments after Bolingbroke accepts Richard's resignation, the Bishop of Carlisle retorts, "Marry, God forbid!"

> Worst in this royal presence may I speak,
> Yet best beseeming me to speak the truth.
> Would God that any in this noble presence
> Were enough noble to be upright judge
> Of noble Richard.

[4.1.104–10]

Carlisle identifies the central conundrum of *Richard II*: how can mere subjects condemn their monarch? Landing in Wales, Richard insisted that "Not all the water in the rough rude sea / Can wash the balm from an anointed king" (3.2.50–1), and his assertion, articulating the so-called "divine right" of monarchy, was a commonplace of Tudor political theory. But it was not uncontested, and Shakespeare makes it plain just how vulnerable a king can be. The irony of Richard's metaphor proves sharp: Bolingbroke (whose name, spelt "Bullingbrooke" in early texts, could mean "boiling brook") will find it all too easy to wash away the King's political foundations.

Unusually self-conscious in its use of language, *Richard II* is filled with poetic images identifying both protagonists with the elements. Richard begins the play as a "sun-king of fire" opposed to Bolingbroke's flood, but as the action progresses the two steadily change place. On his way to surrender, Richard casts himself as "glist'ring Phaethon" (Apollo's doomed son, who stole his father's sun-chariot and drove it too close to the earth), but before long he imagines his body as "a mockery king of snow, / Standing before the sun of Bolingbroke" (4.1.250–1). The balancing point occurs when Richard is called upon to hand over his crown "in common view". He pictures it as "like a deep well / That owes two buckets filling one another,"

> The emptier ever dancing in the air,
> The other down, unseen, and full of water.
> That bucket down and full of tears am I,
> Drinking my griefs whilst you mount up on high.
>
> [4.1.174–9]

Rewriting Bolingbroke's coronation into his own "unkinging", Richard takes charge of the event. But the speech also marks a decisive shift in the tone and focus of the play. Once Bolingbroke actually takes the crown (Richard wittily insists he "seize" it), the focus moves decisively away from him. Bereft of political power, meanwhile, Shakespeare makes Richard free to express himself on stage. His *coup de théâtre* in front of his enemy occurs when he requests a "mirror" to "show me what a face I have". Looking into it, he exclaims, "No deeper wrinkles yet?"

> Hath sorrow struck
> So many blows upon this face of mine
> And made no deeper wounds? O flatt'ring glass,
> Like to my followers in prosperity,
> Though dost beguile me!
>
> [4.1.268–71]

Richard's examination of his reflection – which reaches a peak when he dashes the mirror to pieces – is a persuasive gesture, and like all solo performances it reverberates powerfully in the theatre.

The question of how to perceive Richard is one that Shakespeare makes remarkably hard. Critics have been divided (Coleridge dismissed Richard's "constant flow of emotions from a total incapability of controlling them … a waste of that energy which should have been reserved for action"), but few have questioned that as the play goes on Shakespeare displaces our sympathy for Richard's victims and redirects it instead to Richard himself. Doing so, his play becomes less a history and more what its first printed title promises, "The Tragedy of King Richard the Second", with Richard the hero at its centre.

Though to some extent the form of *Richard II*'s title is conventional, in Aristotle's use of the term, Richard really is a tragic hero: a man who (like Sophocles's Oedipus or Ajax) blunders and is culpable, and who suffers terribly for his mistakes. Richard's

"O flatt'ring glass" ... Alternating roles on different nights, Richard (Richard Pasco) and Bolingbroke (Ian Richardson) played mirror images of each other in John Barton's heavily conceptual 1973 production.

awareness of his own experience is more solipsistic, but no less solemn: he repeatedly compares himself to Jesus and his enemies to Judas, exclaiming during the climactic deposition scene that "[Christ] in twelve / Found truth in all but one; I, in twelve thousand, none" (4.1.161–2), tragically aware of the gulf between them – a gulf all the more obvious because of Richard's supposedly godly role. Like Gaunt, who declares (for all his criticisms of his nephew's reign) that "God's is the quarrel" (1.2.37) and that humans should not intervene, Richard appears genuinely to believe that – sanctioned by the King of Heaven – he has quasi-divine powers. Newly arrived on the coast of Wales after returning from Ireland, Richard gives short shrift to Aumerle's warning that Bolingbroke threatens the realm. "Discomfortable cousin," Richard cries,

> know'st thou not
> That when the searching eye of heaven is hid
> Behind the globe, that lights the lower world,
> Then thieves and robbers range abroad unseen
> In murders and in outrage bloody here;
> But when from under this terrestrial ball
> He fires the proud tops of the eastern pines,
> And darts his light through every guilty hole,
> Then murders, treasons, and detested sins,
> The cloak of night being plucked from off their backs,
> Stand bare and naked, trembling at themselves?
>
> [3.2.32–42]

Richard talks here of the "eye of heaven": a metaphor for the sun (one of his favourite self-images, as we have seen), but also a literal representation of God – the ferocious Old Testament God who will scourge "thieves and robbers" like Bolingbroke and bring their sins to light. Yet, like much else, Richard's sense of divinity changes through the play: in his last minutes alive he will recall the New Testament teaching of Christ, which insists that Heaven will house those who are powerless and impoverished – the "seely [simple-minded] beggars" rather than the great monarchs (5.5.25). Richard's new awareness of a consoling God adds an unexpected pathos to his deposition, a fate that God himself has apparently done little to prevent.

As soon as Bolingbroke takes power it is clear that Richard's liberty is at an end – and indeed it won't be long before he is dead, murdered by Exton (who believes, perhaps rightly, that Bolingbroke set him on). Sent under guard to Pomfret Castle after an emotional farewell from his wife, Richard is left to contemplate his shattered being. Alone on stage once more, he eloquently ruminates, "Thus play I in one person many people, / And none contented."

> Sometimes am I king;
> Then treason makes me wish myself a beggar,
> And so I am. Then crushing penury
> Persuades me I was better when a king.
> Then am I kinged again, and by and by

Think that I am unkinged by Bolingbroke,
And straight am nothing. But whate'er I be,
Nor I, nor any man that but man is,
With nothing shall be pleased till he be eased
With being nothing.

[5.5.31–41]

Richard has sometimes been called an actor rather than a monarch, but if so he is unable to relinquish his key role, or perhaps is doing his utmost to escape. "Any man that but man is" – anyone alive – needs to realize that "nothing" is where we come from, and it is to nothingness that we return. Richard's flawed journey to this difficult self-knowledge anticipates, however partially, that of King Lear.

Richard makes a finer victim than he does a king, arranging the tragic spectacle of himself with impressive aplomb. His last long speech is in some ways his most candid, but it is also the most rhetorically gorgeous of many in this strange and beautiful play. "I wasted time, and now doth time waste me," he reflects,

For now hath time made me his numb'ring clock.
My thoughts are minutes, and with sighs they jar
Their watches on unto mine eyes, the outward watch
Whereto my finger, like a dial's point,
Is pointing still in cleansing them from tears.
Now, sir, the sounds that tell what hour it is
Are clamorous groans that strike upon my heart,
Which is the bell. So sighs, and tears, and groans
Show minutes, hours, and times. But my time
Runs posting on in Bolingbroke's proud joy,
While I stand fooling here, his jack of the clock.

[5.5.49–60]

Having earlier compared himself to Christ, Richard's image here is rueful. Haunted by the absurdity of his position, the only self-image he can find is that of a "fool".

Stage history and adaptations

Richard II has long been one of Shakespeare's most frequently revived dramas, almost his only English history play to achieve a defining stage tradition, ironically enough, outside of "this sceptred isle". It was popular initially, possibly at the **Theatre** in Shoreditch, and also thrived in print, with six editions appearing before its author's death. It may have been performed at the residence of **Sir Edward Hoby** in 1595, and was perhaps the "play of King Henry the Fourth, and of the killing of Richard the Second" put on by Shakespeare's company and paid for by the **Earl of Essex's** supporters in 1601, just as he rebelled against Elizabeth I. In addition to being played in London and perhaps on tour, *Richard II* has been rumoured to have reached the coast of West Africa in 1607, when it was performed alongside *Hamlet* on board a ship belonging to the East India Company, but many historians doubt the theory.

Though the Restoration dramatist **Nahum Tate** did his best to disown historical parallels between King Charles II and his ancestor – insisting in his preface that "why a History of those Times should be suppressed as a Libel upon Ours, is past my Understanding" – the authorities banned it as soon as it appeared on stage in 1680, Tate's newly blameless Richard notwithstanding. This was the first of several adaptations, among them **Lewis Theobald**'s (1719) and **Francis Gentleman**'s (1755), designed to answer contemporary disquiet with *Richard II*'s orotund dramatic style and subject matter. Although **John Rich** staged an unadapted version at Covent Garden in 1738, it would be the eighteenth century's last.

The way lay clear for the Romantics to rediscover the play's soloistic potential, which in **Edmund Kean**'s hands they did. Kean's 1815 text – a version by company member **Richard Wroughton** – emphasized the King at the cost of almost everything else, offering Richard as a courageous figure; an interpretation that Hazlitt took issue with ("Mr Kean made it a character of *passion*, that is of feeling combined with energy; whereas it is a character of *pathos*, that is to say of feeling combined with weakness"). Where Edmund went for naked emotion, his son **Charles**, a lesser actor, kept the box-office of his Princess's Theatre busy with scenography, debuting, in 1857, the most lavish production of the play anyone had seen. Though again the plight of Kean's own King was underscored, audiences flooded in to see the triumphal procession of Bolingbroke with the defeated Richard – an event only described in Shakespeare's play, but which in Kean's vision became "one of the most gorgeous and effective scenes that we have ever witnessed on stage" (*The Illustrated London News*). By then *Richard II* had made its way the US, with productions mounted by **Junius Brutus Booth** in the 1830s and 40s, then by his American-born son **Edwin** later in the century. But after Edwin was shot at by a member of the audience in Chicago in 1879, he refused to play it again and the play's popularity declined.

Back in England, **Frank Benson**'s Stratford productions with himself as a sympathetic but weak-minded Richard, kept old traditions alive from 1896 onwards, but soon afterwards the revolutionary **William Poel** staged an "authentic" version in London with the young **Harley Granville-Barker** as the King (it still lasted a reported four hours). By the time **Herbert Beerbohm Tree** mounted his spectacular version in 1903, boasting real horses, fashions were changing. In **Harcourt Williams**'s 1929 Old Vic version, with **John Gielgud** in the lead, the play's actorly potential became apparent, and **George Hayes** and **Maurice Evans** later excelled in the role. The year 1937 saw two defining productions: **Margaret Webster**'s on Broadway, with Evans's Richard (the first *Richard II* to be seen in America since Booth); and **Gielgud**'s own Queen's Theatre production in London. Gielgud relished the poetry of the role, and was well supported by an enviable cast that included **Michael Redgrave** as Bolingbroke and **Peggy Ashcroft** as the Queen.

At Stratford in 1951 **Anthony Quayle** directed a production most notable for **Redgrave**'s insistence on playing Richard as "an out-and-out pussy queer" (as Laurence Olivier indecorously put it). **Paul Scofield**'s Richard, directed by Gielgud at the Lyric in Hammersmith the following year, on the other hand, possessed a chilly

Fiona Shaw brought a captivating stillness and fragility to the part of Richard in Deborah Warner's 1995 production at the National Theatre in London; she is one of only a handful of female actors who have played the role.

hauteur that made him seem fatally detached from what was happening. The concept that Richard might be gay was reinforced in **Richard Cotterell**'s 1969 Prospect Theatre production, which played Shakespeare's tragedy in parallel with Marlowe's *Edward II*. **Ian McKellen** acted both monarchs with show-stopping theatricality, while **Timothy West** was contrastingly gruff as Bolingbroke and Mortimer. By then **John Barton** and **Peter Hall**'s "Henriad" cycles of 1964 had come and gone – **David Warner** playing an overtly Christian Richard to **Eric Porter**'s Bolingbroke – but Barton would return in 1973 with an RSC *Richard* that shocked as many audiences as it delighted. In a production that became a byword for director's theatre, Barton had **Ian Richardson** and **Richard Pasco** alternate as Richard and Bolingbroke on successive nights to underline the ritualized similarities between them, and also featured escalators representing their relative positions on the treadmill of power – there was even a snowman literalizing Richard's "mockery king of snow".

Subsequent RSC Richards have included **Alan Howard** (1980), **Jeremy Irons** (1986) and a youthful **Sam West** (2000), while away from Stratford *Richard II* has appeared in some strikingly different incarnations. In 1981 **Ariane Mnouchkine** stressed the play's ritualistic aspect in a Kabuki- and Noh-influenced production at the Théâtre du Soleil in Paris. At the National Theatre in 1995 **Deborah Warner** daringly cast **Fiona Shaw** as a de-sexualized King, literally cocooned in his medieval world, in stark contrast to **David Threlfall**'s pragmatic, modern Bolingbroke. Compared to these two, the painstaking "original practices" theatre seen at Shakespeare's Globe in summer 2003 seemed positively conservative. What was unusual was **Mark Rylance**'s interpretation, which found a surprising degree of comedy in Richard's capriciousness and, as with Fiona Shaw, emphasized the character's childishness. A complete contrast was offered by **Trevor Nunn**'s 2005 modern-dress production at the Old Vic, which foregrounded the play's power politics. **Kevin Spacey** excelled as an arrogant Richard prone to fits of real anger, who spectacularly broke down at being bested by the ruthless efficiency of **Ben Miles**'s Bolingbroke.

In 2006, the Berliner Ensemble visited Britain with a more stylized modern take on the play. On a stage that filled up with the mud and debris of civil strife as the play progressed, a white-faced and white-suited Richard (**Michael Maertens**) was overwhelmed by events. **Claus Peymann**'s vivid production deftly balanced a stark absurdism with an almost vaudevillian humour. By contrast, **Jonathan Slinger**, who bookended **Michael Boyd**'s RSC histories marathon by playing both Richards II and III in 2007–08, mustered a surprising degree of menace, alternating between infantile whimsy and middle-aged choler (and also managing a passing resemblance to Elizabeth I). Apart from a stunning piece of stagecraft when Richard was parted from **Hannah Barrie**'s Queen Isabel beneath a cascade of white sand, the production was restrained, given over to **Clive Wood**'s middle-manager Bolingbroke. The same could not be said for Michael Grandage's 2011 revival at the Donmar in London, which despite its small scale was dominated by a petulant, choleric **Eddie Redmayne**, almost literally a boy. Grandiose in a different way was the operatic, medievalized production directed by **Gregory Doran** at the RSC in 2013, in which **David Tennant**'s vaguely Christ-like Richard sported hair extensions and was given to wafting dolefully across the stage in a white gown, effortlessly outmanouevred by **Nigel Lindsay**'s coolly menacing Bolingbroke.

Shakespeare's Globe, meanwhile, has staged two strikingly different productions. In 2012 the **Ashtar Theatre** from Ramallah brought a richly poetic Arabic version to the theatre as part of the World Shakespeare Festival that nonetheless made pointed reference to the real-life events of the Arab Spring. In **Simon Godwin**'s traditionalist 2015 staging, dominated by a capricious **Charles Edwards**, the play reverted to being Richard's tragedy, the action preceded by a silent tableau of his coronation at the age of ten.

The BBC has a near monopoly on screenings of *Richard II* – initially with its 1960 *Age of Kings* television extravaganza; then with a Prospect-based version from 1970 featuring **Ian McKellen** and **Timothy West**; and most recently tapings of Warner's 1995 staging. The 1978 Time-Life production was directed by **David Giles** and starred **Derek Jacobi, Jon Finch** and **John Gielgud,** and the Corporation returned to the play once again in 2012 for the *Hollow Crown* histories cycle, with **Ben Whishaw** going head to head with **Rory Kinnear** in a realistic but somewhat ritualized medieval production by **Rupert Goold**.

SCREEN

Richard II

D. Jacobi, J. Finch, J. Gielgud; David Giles (dir.) UK, 1978 > BBC **DVD**

It's about as dramatically radical as an episode of *The Archers*, but this version of *Richard II* brings out many of the play's essential qualities. It is primarily an actors' vehicle, strongly differentiated between Jacobi's arrogant, camp, often histrionic – but finely spoken – King and Jon Finch's guarded Bolingbroke; while Gielgud, who made the play his own in the 1930s, delivers a fine "This England" speech as a convincingly emaciated Gaunt. The studio setting is if anything a boon, adding to the sense of rigidity and stylization, and Giles's camerawork is effective and unobtrusive – even if his decision to have Richard gossip with his favourites in what looks suspiciously like a Turkish bath could hardly be described as a subtle commentary on his sexuality. Not a masterpiece, but very watchable nevertheless.

The Hollow Crown

B. Whishaw, R. Kinnear, P. Stewart; Rupert Goold (dir.) UK, 2012 > BBC **DVD** 🔊

One of the biggest challenges of filming *Richard II* is the play's poetic, almost sensual formality: how to make it come alive in a medium where pictures, not words, do all the talking? Charged with this first instalment of the BBC histories, director Rupert Goold lingers on HD shots of shimmering silk canopies and sun-dappled medieval stone, attempting to find a visual poetry to match the

script (St David's Cathedral and Pembroke Castle stand in for Whitehall and Pomfret). But it's a tricky balance, and the whiff of the medieval miniseries somehow clings to the enterprise, particularly as everyone on screen looks so improbably well scrubbed. What saves it is the cast, which has a breadth and depth few Shakespeare adaptations can match (when you can afford to cast the wonderful David Bradley as a gardener you know you're on to a good thing). Central is Ben Whishaw, who plays Richard as a waxen-faced, helium-voiced martyr, almost extraterrestrial in his strangeness but no less sympathetic for it. Though Rory Kinnear's thuggish, balding Bolingbroke takes a little while to warm up, he is a fine match, and when the two clash during the deposition scene it's like seeing chess grandmasters playing to the death. You want to watch on, and find out what happens next.

AUDIO

Richard II

S. West, J. Ackland, D. Lewis; Jeremy Mortimer (dir.) UK, 2000 > BBC ◉ 🔊

Sam West's devil-may-care Richard II gained plaudits at Stratford in 2000, and so it's good that he had an opportunity to record it for the BBC just beforehand. On audio he is every bit as impressive, making the character less effete and tougher than is customary, while injecting a touching humanity into the play's closing scenes. Damian Lewis brings hauteur and impetuosity aplenty to Bolingbroke (a welcome change from more inscrutable interpretations), and Joss Ackland is finely grained as Gaunt. Jeremy Mortimer's decision to have Richard's nobles playing billiards isn't going to shock anyone these days – why does modern-dress have to be visual, after all? – but his reordering of the play's opening scenes might raise eyebrows. Even so, this is creatively directed and utterly absorbing.

EDITIONS

Arden Shakespeare (third edition)
Charles Forker (ed.); 2002 > Bloomsbury

Arden 3 editions keep on getting fatter, and Charles Forker's *Richard II* is one of the fattest – nearly six hundred pages all told. What you get for your money is impressive: 170-odd pages of critical introduction, extensive "longer notes" presenting mini-essays on various phrases in the text, an extensive textual analysis along with various other appendices, and detailed footnotes quoting liberally from Halle and Holinshed. Some may feel that Forker's eagerness to cover every possibility produces more heat than light, but his treatment of the text is admirably clear – passages unique to the Folio version are enclosed by superscript "F"s.

SOME CRITICISM

Shakespeare and the Idea of the Play
Anne Righter; 1962 > Chatto / Vintage [o/p]

Anne Righter's slimline and very readable *Shakespeare and the Idea of the Play* (published before she married director John Barton) is justifiably a classic. Righter's broad thesis is that Shakespeare's peculiar self-consciousness about the business of the theatre is both an inheritance and a break from his medieval and early Tudor precursors, one

that produces a quite different approach to the drama of power. According to Righter, plays such as *Richard II* weave dramatic awarenesses so tightly into the fabric of the action that, as she puts it, "the image of the actor pursues Richard relentlessly" on his path to infamy. The book covers nearly all the plays in varying amounts of detail as well as providing plenty of background on older dramatic traditions, making it a fine introduction not just to Shakespeare's work but to the theatre that provided him with employment and inspiration.

Shakespeare's Histories and Counter-Histories
Dermot Cavanagh, Stuart Hampton-Reeves and Stephen Longstaffe (eds); 2006 > Manchester UP

In recent years historians have placed more and more emphasis on the fissures that lay beneath the surface of the Elizabethan world, and literary scholars too have tried to grapple with how Shakespeare's representations of history were a sometimes cracked mirror for his own times. *Richard II* is a compelling text in this regard – the deposition scene was apparently too sensitive to be printed while Elizabeth I was alive – and several essays in this collection probe its darker purpose, notably the teasing relationship between the play's Queen Isabel and controversies over Mary, Queen of Scots (a suggestive piece by Alison Findlay) and its echoes of the anonymous drama *Woodstock* and other representations of the Peasants' Revolt (Stephen Longstaffe). John Joughin's "*Richard II* and the performance of grief" is a tour de force, moving adeptly from medieval theories about "the King's two bodies" (his physical and sacramental roles) to a wryly sceptical account of new historicist approaches to the past.

Richard III

Shakespeare's first great villain and his lengthiest early role, Richard III has long been a gift for actors. All the greats have played him, and each has made the irresistibly evil king their own. To many, it's Richard's breathtaking theatricality that makes him what he is: the smiling murderer, the seductive humpback, the man who engages with the audience outside the action yet nevertheless controls it until almost the last moment. In some ways Richard is a stock villain, a fusion of the medieval "Vice" character and the Elizabethan "Machiavel" of Marlowe and others, but he is above all a chillingly convincing one – so much so that Shakespeare's Crookback creation has been accused of obliterating the real King Richard in the historical record. Stepping out from the carnage of the *Henry VI* plays and the devastation wrought by the Wars of the Roses, he embodies a new and brutal age of politics, one on which the laws of society (even God) seem to have no purchase. And even though we know that Richard's oppressive and violent reign will come to an end, and that the play will culminate in England's deliverance, *Richard III*'s lively stage history testifies that it's more difficult to lay Richard's ghost to rest than his Tudor chroniclers can ever have suspected.

DATE > Presumably written once *1 Henry VI* was finished, *Richard III* is likely to have been completed 1592–93 (the same period as *Titus*), perhaps for the newly formed Lord Pembroke's Men.

SOURCES > As with the *Henry VI* plays, two Tudor historical accounts – Holinshed's *Chronicles* (1587) and Halle's *Union* (1548) – provide the basic matter and many of its colourful details. Both sources reprint Thomas More's unflattering *History* of Richard (c. 1513), and Senecan tragedy must also have been in Shakespeare's mind.

TEXTS > Notoriously complicated. A quarto edition (Q1, 1597) was reprinted seven times, but it's likely to be a later version of the play than the 1623 Folio one – possibly revised for touring.

Interpreting the play

As *Richard III* opens, some of its audience could be forgiven for feeling a sense of déjà-vu. The brilliant, twisted Richard of Gloucester is alone, centre-stage – acting like a malevolent chorus on the action even though it is yet to begin, and even though it will involve him too. It isn't long before his warm praise of King Edward's victory over the Lancastrians, "Now is the winter of our discontent / Made glorious summer by this son of York", dissipates and he shifts to a much darker and more revealing key:

MAJOR CHARACTERS & SYNOPSIS

Richard, Duke of Gloucester (later **King Richard III**)

Richard's brothers: **King Edward IV** and **George, Duke of Clarence**

Duchess of York, their mother

Queen Elizabeth, Edward IV's wife

Anthony Woodville, Lord Rivers, Queen Elizabeth's brother

The two young princes: **Edward, Prince of Wales** and **Richard, Duke of York**, sons of King Edward and Queen Elizabeth

Marquis of Dorset and **Lord Gray**, Queen Elizabeth's sons by her previous marriage

Lady Anne (later **Anne, Duchess of Gloucester**), widow of Henry VI's son, Edward

Queen Margaret, Henry VI's widow

William, Lord Hastings, the Lord Chamberlain

Lord Stanley, Earl of Derby, Hastings's friend

Henry, Earl of Richmond (later **King Henry VII**)

Richmond's followers: **Earl of Oxford, Sir James Blunt, Sir Walter Herbert**

Richard of Gloucester's followers: **Duke of Buckingham, Duke of Norfolk, Sir Richard Ratcliffe, Sir William Catesby, Sir James Tyrrel**

Cardinal Bourchier, Archbishop of Canterbury

Archbishop of York

Lord Mayor of London

Sir Robert Brackenbury, Lieutenant of the Tower

Ghosts of King Henry VI, Prince Edward, Clarence, Lady Anne, Buckingham and Hastings

[ACTION CONTINUED FROM HENRY VI PART III]

ACT 1 Edward Plantagenet is now King, but already his brother Richard is plotting against him. Having turned Edward against Clarence, Richard now proceeds to woo Lady Anne, widow of the Lancastrian Prince Edward: despite having a hand in her husband's murder, he manages to seduce her over the coffin of her father-in-law. With the King now ill, Queen Elizabeth fears that Richard will seize the throne if he dies. Richard and Elizabeth are arguing when Queen Margaret arrives, denouncing her Plantagenet usurpers. In the Tower, Clarence's nightmares turn to reality when two murderers in Richard's pay appear.

ACT 2 Having ordered Clarence's execution to be revoked, Edward is recovering when Richard coolly announces that he has been killed after all.

Everyone is appalled and King Edward dies shortly afterwards. When Richard and Buckingham imprison Lords Rivers and Gray, Queen Elizabeth's family, she decides to seek sanctuary with her youngest son, the Duke of York.

ACT 3 As Prince Edward arrives in London, Buckingham persuades the Archbishop of Canterbury to remove the Duke of York from sanctuary. Richard then conveys both princes to the Tower. Attempting to build support, Richard sends Catesby to sound out Hastings and promises Buckingham high office when he becomes King. Hastings refuses to support Richard, and after arriving in London (to plan Prince Edward's coronation), he is summarily executed on Richard's orders. Buckingham and Richard then convince the Mayor of London that Hastings was a traitor and suggest Edward IV and his heirs are illegitimate. In front of the Mayor, Richard feigns devoutness and seems reluctant to accept the throne when Buckingham insists it is his by right.

ACT 4 At his coronation Richard suggests to Buckingham that the two Princes should die. When Buckingham hesitates, Richard turns on him and gets Tyrrell to arrange the deed. Richard also plans the murder of his wife so that he can marry his niece Elizabeth. Buckingham reminds Richard of his promise of high office, but Richard stalls and Buckingham flees. Queen Elizabeth and the Duchess of York meet with Queen Margaret and bewail the loss of their loved ones. Richard enters and is cursed by his mother; he then asks Queen Elizabeth for help in wooing her daughter and she pretends to agree. As news arrives of Richmond's invasion, Richard's grip on power begins to falter.

ACT 5 Buckingham is captured by Richard's allies and is executed. Meanwhile, Richard, marching to meet Richmond, pitches camp at Bosworth. The night before battle, he is visited by the ghosts of those he killed en route to power. Richard's forces are defeated when Stanley switches to Richmond (his son-in-law). Richmond kills King Richard in single combat and Stanley presents him with the crown. Richmond promises to restore peace and unite the Houses of York and Lancaster by marrying Elizabeth, Edward IV's daughter.

> I that am rudely stamped and want love's majesty
> To strut before a wanton ambling nymph,
> I that am curtailed of this fair proportion,
> Cheated of feature by dissembling nature,
> Deformed, unfinished, sent before my time
> Into this breathing world scarce half made up—
> And that so lamely and unfashionable
> That dogs bark at me as I halt by them—
> Why, I in this weak piping time of peace
> Have no delight to pass away the time,
> Unless to spy my shadow in the sun
> And descant on mine own deformity.
> And therefore since I cannot prove a lover
> To entertain these fair well-spoken days,
> I am determinèd to prove a villain ...

[1.1.14–30]

All this might seem familiar to audiences who have witnessed *3 Henry VI* and heard Richard declaring, in strikingly similar terms, that "love foreswore me in my mother's womb" and resolving that

> since this earth affords no joy to me
> But to command, to check, to o'erbear such
> As are of better person than myself,
> I'll make my heaven to dream upon the crown ...

[3 HENRY VI, 3.2.165–8]

Gloucester's repeated statement of ambition is more than a link between *Richard III* and its "Henriad" predecessors – it is the keynote of Richard's own personality.

Not surprisingly, critics have seized on these lines. Led by Freud, who famously saw in Richard the archetype of a personality bruised by childhood experience and bent on revenge, commentators have worried away at the connection between Richard's deformity and his lust for power – "to o'erbear such / As are of better person than myself". The French critic René Girard suggests that "Richard's deformed body is a mirror for the self-confessed ugliness of his soul", making a strikingly similar point to that proposed several centuries earlier by Francis Bacon, who argued in his essay "Of Deformity" that "all deformed persons are extreme bold ... [I]t stirreth in them industry ... to watch and observe the weakness in others that they may have somewhat to repay".

Anxious about drawing too easy a link between Richard Gloucester's disability and his propensity for evil, recent writers have been disturbed by what this seems to imply, and much psychological effort has gone into diagnosing what really drives him. Is it hatred of his mother? Envy of his brothers? Anything at all? What such critics have been reluctant to notice is that Richard himself makes the link. In fact, his own account of himself ("cheated of feature", "deformed, unfinished", "scarce half made up") produces such a monstrous reflection that it cannot help but be an exaggeration. Richard is, as he says, "descanting" on his own deformity – playing with it, spinning it out, drawing us in.

Change shapes with Proteus

In another speech from *3 Henry VI* so closely identified with Gloucester that, from Cibber onwards (see p.381), it has often found its way into versions of *Richard III*, the Duke trumpets his skill as an actor, turning his unusually mutable identity to his own advantage:

> Why, I can smile, and murder whiles I smile,
> And cry 'Content!' to that which grieves my heart,
> And wet my cheeks with artificial tears,
> And frame my face to all occasions ...
> I can add colours to the chameleon,
> Change shapes with Proteus for advantages,
> And set the murderous Machiavel to school.
> Can I do this, and cannot get a crown?
> Tut, were it farther off, I'll pluck it down.
>
> [*3 HENRY VI*, 3.4.183–95]

Shakespeare stresses Richard's theatricality so much that even as we gasp at his deeds, we are astonished by his control over events. The strength of that power is revealed by the fact that other people think him honesty incarnate: Clarence attempts to persuade his very murderers that Gloucester "loves me"; Hastings is dispatched just moments after declaring confidently that "by his face straight shall you know his heart". Only to himself (and, importantly, to the audience) does Richard admit that he is backed by "the plain devil and dissembling looks" (1.2.224). It has long been recognized that Richard is a great role which was almost certainly designed for Shakespeare's most celebrated star, Richard Burbage, who would go on to play Hamlet, Othello, Malvolio and Lear. It's surely no accident that Burbage was himself described as a "Protean" talent: both Richards fit that billing.

Richard's success on the stage is also due to his descent from a long pedigree of Vice characters in medieval "Morality" plays, whose task it is to persuade good characters to stray from the path of righteousness; it is a pedigree Richard himself revels in. But equally important is Richard's relationship to one of Shakespeare's main sources, Thomas More's *History of King Richard III*, which was influential enough to be partly reprinted by both Tudor chroniclers, Holinshed and Halle, in their own histories of

---

That this play has scenes noble in themselves and very well contrived to strike in the exhibition, cannot be denied. But some parts are trifling, others shocking, and some improbable.

Samuel Johnson, commentary to *The Plays of William Shakespeare* (1765)

Appearing in a gender-bending, all-female production at Shakespeare's Globe in 2003, Kathryn Hunter radiated menace and impish glee as Shakespeare's Crookback.

the period. In More's text, "ill-featured", "crook-backed" Richard is "close and secret, a deep dissembler, lowly of countenance, arrogant of heart, outwardly companionable where he inwardly hated, not letting to kiss whom he thought to kill". But where More, Halle and Holinshed produce (and reproduce) an image of Richard which is nothing but evil – for reasons that have much to do with their Tudor affiliations – Shakespeare, ever-alert, realizes something crucial about this twisted genius: a man that good at being bad must be fascinating to watch.

Some tormenting dream

Richard's skill at remaking himself transforms political events just as rapidly. His wooing of Lady Anne over her father-in-law's coffin is a sublime example of theatrical daring – almost a literalization of the argument put forward by the real-life Machiavelli in his book *Il Principe* ("The Prince"), that "fortune [*fortuna*] is a woman, and if you want to control her, it is necessary to treat her roughly". We watch as Richard's power over words remakes Anne's terms of abuse – again, dwelling on his physical deformity – into flirtatious banter, reworking a situation in which he cannot win into one that he has no chance of losing:

LADY ANNE
    Never hung poison on a fouler toad.
    Out of my sight! Thou dost infect mine eyes.

RICHARD GLOUCESTER
    Thine eyes, sweet lady, have infected mine.
LADY ANNE
    Would they were basilisks to strike thee dead.
RICHARD GLOUCESTER
    I would they were, that I might die at once,
    For now they kill me with a living death.

[1.2.147–52]

When Lady Anne enters the play, it is as the mourner of her husband and her father-in-law, one of the female voices of lamentation and remembrance that dominate *Richard III*. But in persuading Anne to be his wife, Richard rewrites her role. Instead of defusing the situation, he redirects its power by casting her as scornful mistress, himself as wounded lover. His creative potential even redefines the ring he instructs her to wear: "Look how my ring encompasseth thy finger; / Even so thy breast encloseth my poor heart" (1.2.191–2). Despite Richard's malign persuasiveness, Anne's capitulation, gruesome as it is, has infinite capacity to shock – as of course Shakespeare intended. It is as if Richard's willpower – and here his will is sexual too – simply overcomes all opposition, no matter how righteous and strong. Only with Queen Elizabeth's double-crossing of Richard later in the plot will events (and the women that surround him) produce any kind of effective revenge.

    Richard's dealings with another woman in the play – Margaret of Anjou, who makes a spectral but powerful appearance (particularly spectral because she is historically dead at the time the action takes place) – have comparable transformative electricity. Like Anne, she bitterly denounces the usurping Plantagenets before cursing Richard himself:

> No sleep close up that deadly eye of thine,
> Unless it be with some tormenting dream
> Afrights thee with hell of ugly devils.
> Thou elvish-marked, abortive, rooting hog,
> Thou that wast sealed in thy nativity
> The slave of nature and the son of hell,
> Thou slander of thy heavy mother's womb,
> Thou loathèd issue of thy father's loins,
> Thou rag of honour, thou detested—

[1.3.222–30]

But Richard does not give her the opportunity to finish. He breaks in by shouting out "Margaret", turning the curse back on the curser. It is a moment of élan and wit, but a revealingly ironic one too. While Margaret's call for vengeance on the Plantagenets ("God I pray him, / That none of you may live his natural age" (1.3.209–211)), certainly bears fruit, it is Richard's agency that brings it all about.

    Some critics have pointed to Margaret's threat of "some tormenting dream" and noted that *Richard III* is the play of Shakespeare's in which the word "dream" occurs most often. Many characters express the sense that, as events take new and agitating turns, their whole experience is being turned into a waking nightmare. Nowhere is this truer than with Clarence, who is sent to the Tower because of King Edward's "prophecies and dreams" (in fact Richard's prompting) and whose description of the eerie nightmare he suffers occurs just moments before his execution. Bemoaning his "miserable night, / So full of fearful dreams", he describes how he dreamt he was voyaging away from imprisonment with his brother:

> As we paced along
> Upon the giddy footing of the hatches,
> Methought that Gloucester stumbled, and in falling
> Struck me—that sought to stay him—overboard
> Into the tumbling billows of the main.
> O Lord! Methought what pain it was to drown,
> What dreadful noise of waters in my ears,
> What sights of ugly death within my eyes.
> Methoughts I saw a thousand fearful wrecks,
> Ten thousand men that fishes gnawed upon,
> Wedges of gold, great ouches, heaps of pearl,
> Inestimable stones, unvalued jewels,
> All scattered in the bottom of the sea.
>
> [1.4.16–28]

Clarence's words come from any number of sources, but the Tudor commonplace that drowned riches represent worldly vanity is perhaps strongest here – and yet "simple, plain" Clarence has no vanity, just naive faith in Richard. He doesn't deserve a dream like this, and yet it plots the outline of his downfall and that of Richard's route to the throne. In a similar (if less appalling) way to the scene involving Lady Anne, it is as if the play makes him complicit in his own fate.

Ultimately, though, Richard loses control over what he himself has set in motion: almost as soon as he gains the crown, that long-held obsession, things start to unravel – and, during Act Four, do so with frightening rapidity. Richard's process of decline reaches its nadir the night before battle at Bosworth as, with eerie inevitability, Margaret's curse comes true. Richard's victims, quite literally, come back to haunt him: the ghosts of the young princes, King Henry, Clarence, Rivers, Gray, Vaughan, Hastings, Anne and Buckingham troop through Richard's sleeping mind, sending him into chaotic confusion:

> O coward conscience, how dost thou afflict me?
> The lights turn blue. It is now dead midnight.
> Cold fearful drops stand upon my trembling flesh.
> What do I fear? Myself? There's none else by.
> Richard loves Richard; that is, I am I.
> Is there a murderer here? No. Yes, I am.
> Then fly! What, from myself? Great reason. Why?
> Lest I revenge. Myself upon myself?

Alack, I love myself. Wherefore? For any good
That I myself have done unto myself?
O no, alas, I rather hate myself
For hateful deeds committed by myself.
I am a villain. Yet I lie: I am not.

[5.5.132–45]

"Richard loves Richard … I am I", the self-possessed mantra of isolation, first voiced at the end of *3 Henry VI* (see p.180), has left him friendless, just as his effortless skill at changing shape leaves him uncertain about what he is. As Richard's psychology spills out once more on stage, these ghosts become both imaginary and real, a blurred distinction that mirrors the final breakdown in his mind. Not in full control for the first time in the play, Richard simply collapses. The consummate actor has created a world so fluid and changeable that he himself cannot survive it. Far from being able to master Fortune, he is ultimately her victim.

Stage history and adaptations

Richard III is unusual among Shakespeare's oeuvre in having been almost continually on the stage in one form or another ever since it was written. The first quarto of 1597 describes it as having been "lately acted" by the **Lord Chamberlain's Men**, and it survived the transition to the indoor Blackfriars theatre in 1609. The play was a star vehicle from its inception: **Richard Burbage**, the greatest actor in the company, created the part of Richard; and it was taken by **Ellyaerdt Swanston** in the next generation King's Men. It remained in the repertoire, and was performed at **court** before Charles I and his French wife, Henrietta Maria – both of whom had an abiding interest in theatre – in 1633. Nor did it disappear after the reopening of the theatres in 1660: several performances are recorded (one, in 1690, had **Samuel Sandford**, an expert in playing villains, in the lead role), though it was apparently not popular, despite productions which played up Richard's apparent resemblance to Oliver Cromwell.

In 1700, the enterprising actor-dramatist **Colley Cibber** published an adaptation that would become one of the most popular plays on the stage for the next two centuries in both Britain and North America. Cibber cut over three-quarters of Shakespeare's text, added a thousand lines and deleted Margaret and Clarence entirely. This version made the career of **David Garrick**, who debuted in the title role in 1741 and acted it continually thereafter. Garrick was naturalistic but mercurial in the lead – Fanny Burney caught a performance in 1772 and declared him "sublimely horrible" – but his crown would be challenged by a new generation of stars, most notably **George Frederick Cooke**, who stressed the character's sarcasm at the expense of his nobility, and **Edmund Kean**, whose Drury Lane debut as Richard in 1814 caused a sensation. The diminutive Kean conveyed a vitality and a casual menace which mesmerized his audience; the battle scenes in particular were singled out by critics as a thrilling depiction of a disintegrating and desperate personality who yet retained a core of kingliness.

Cibber's adaptation was an early and riotous success in the American colonies. It was staged in 1750–51 in a version by **Walter Murray** and **Thomas Kean** (no relation to Edmund), who made it a hit in a makeshift theatre in New York, before touring the show to Maryland and Virginia; then again by the English actor-manager **Robert Upton** the following year; and reappeared frequently afterwards, being regarded as a reliable standby by both American actors and visiting British stars. **George Frederick Cooke** and **Edmund Kean** both brought their Richards to the East Coast in the early nineteenth century, but although Kean was lionized by an adoring press during his first tour in 1820 ("the most complete actor … that ever appeared on our boards," according to the *New York Post*), his second, in 1825, caused a riot in Boston after Kean was perceived to have insulted the audience. An early American star, the strapping "native tragedian" **Edwin Forrest**, excelled as a forceful Richard in the 1840s, as did the British-born **Junius Brutus Booth**. Booth's son **Edwin** made his debut in the play and acted its leading role intermittently from the 1850s to the 1870s. Cibber's adaptation was also wildly popular in touring versions that traversed the expanding United States – perhaps the most popular Shakespearian drama (albeit adapted) of the nineteenth century.

Back in Britain, Shakespeare's own stock was on the rise. **William Charles Macready**, whose 1819 debut in the part was a daring challenge to Kean's supremacy, restored the original text two years later, as did **Samuel Phelps** at Sadler's Wells in 1845, but the script was still doctored to throw more limelight onto the lead role (Phelps played Richard to **Mary Amelia Warner**'s Margaret). The situation was more enlightened in Germany, where full translations of Shakespeare's play had been performed for years. **Bogumil Dawison** excelled as Richard at the Dresden Court Theatre in the 1850s (and might well have been witnessed by the young Henrik Ibsen).

In an otherwise conventional Broadway production of 1920, **John Barrymore** brought a dynamic physicality to Richard, his performance partly inspired by the movements of the tarantula spider. Over in Berlin the same year **Leopold Jessner** mounted an Expressionist staging, in which the set was dominated by a huge flight of stairs. Jessner's reading would provide the inspiration for another innovative Berlin production, that by **Jürgen Fehling** in 1937, which bravely made links to totalitarianism (**Bertolt Brecht**'s 1941 *The Resistible Rise of Arturo Ui*, loosely based on *Richard III*, cloaked the parallel beneath references to American gangsterism). The notion of parodying Hitler himself had occurred to **Donald Wolfit** in wartime England, as it had **Laurence Olivier**, whose startling personification of the hunchback – complete with false nose and wheedling, sanctimonious voice – was first aired at the New Theatre in 1944. Touring widely, then preserved in his 1955 film, Olivier's Richard was highly idiosyncratic, but also in the pedigree of Cibber and Garrick: the consummate actor playing the consummate actor.

Successors attempted to escape from Olivier's shadow. In 1953 **Alec Guinness** played Richard with a light touch at the brand-new theatre in Stratford, Ontario; **Marius Goring** opted for subtle insanity in **Glen Byam Shaw**'s pared-down version at Stratford in 1953; while eight years later, also at Stratford, **Christopher Plummer** presented a weary and neurotic Richard. But the most successful break with the past was masterminded by directors **John Barton** and **Peter Hall**, whose politicized *Wars of the Roses* of 1963 melded the *Henry VI* plays with *Richard III*. **Ian Holm**'s insinuating Richard had the energy of a coiled spring but in the greater scheme of things was

"Mr Kean as Richard the Third". A popular print ("penny plain, tuppence coloured") produced by William West reflects the huge popularity of the greatest English actor of the early nineteenth century. Of Kean's enactment of Richard's death, the critic of the *Examiner* wrote: "we never felt stronger emotion, more overpowering sensations, than those kindled by the novel sublimity of the catastrophe".

just another monarch on the treadmill of power; and it was **Peggy Ashcroft**'s tragic Margaret who dominated.

John Hirsch drew upon Brecht's theatre of alienation at Stratford, Ontario in 1967, while at the Nottingham Playhouse in 1971 **Leonard Rossiter** (a brilliant Arturo Ui the year before) invested the role with his own unique brand of twitchy grotesquerie – often to highly comic effect. A heavily stylized Georgian-language production toured by **Robert Sturua** in 1980 was heavily Brechtian in its satire on power politics, but infused with carnivalesque spirit. Perhaps the most widely admired English portrayal of Richard of the 1980s was that by **Antony Sher** in **Bill Alexander**'s RSC production of 1984. Sher offered a charismatic "bottled spider", scuttling with crutches in a highly physical but intelligent performance; in a reversal of tradition, he faltered as the play went on. In contrast, **Ian McKellen**, in **Richard Eyre**'s 1930s vision at the National Theatre (1990), was a stylish and powerful man of action – every inch the fascist tyrant – who met his end with valour.

Also in 1990, **Andrew Jarvis** played a pinstriped, power-crazed and impeccably Thatcherite monarch in **Michael Bodganov**'s ESC *Wars of the Roses*. **Simon Russell Beale** made a heavyweight, toad-like but slightly camp Richard in **Sam Mendes**'s RSC version of 1992, while **David Troughton** emphasized the hero's comedy, but also his vulnerability, at Stratford three years later. In **Michael Grandage**'s 2002 production at the Crucible Theatre in Sheffield, **Kenneth Branagh** was described by the *Times Literary Supplement* as a "villain for the era of smile politics". A novel twist (not without historical precedent) appeared the following summer at Shakespeare's Globe in London, with **Barry Kyle**'s all-female troupe taking on the play: **Kathryn Hunter** excelled as a mischievous monarch who revelled in acting up for the groundlings. Also surprising was **Mark Rylance**'s turn as Gloucester, which opened at the Globe in 2012 before touring to New York; Rylance was quiet and whimsically sad in the role, visibly crushed by the march of events – a proto-Macbeth rather than a snarling Iago.

Jonathan Slinger's Richard at the RSC in 2007–08, part of **Michael Boyd**'s massive two-tetralogy cycle, stole the show as well as the crown, offering a psychopathic portrait of Gloucester – a man whose grin resembled that of the space-hopper he offered to the Princes and whose gait, as Michael Billington observed in the *Guardian*, "resembles one of those children's toys that resiliently refuse to fall over".

Richard III's attraction for leading actors remains undimmed. *Hobbit* star **Martin Freeman** played it in London's West End in 2014, but a bigger production – in every sense – was that by **Kevin Spacey**, who opened a production by **Sam Mendes** at the Old Vic in 2011 before touring worldwide. This was an epic interpretation, but nonetheless dominated by Spacey's Richard, who with his oversized military uniform and aviator shades brought to mind Middle East dictators too numerous to mention (the portrayal later influenced Spacey's turn in the Netflix political thriller *House of Cards*, itself based on the British TV version starring Shakespearian actor Ian Richardson). The play has also found some success in the politically repressive conditions of China, notably by **Lin Zhaohua**, whose avant-garde 2001 production made the hero resemble former Chinese leader Jiang Zemin. Visiting the London Globe as part of the World Shakespeare Festival in 2012, the **National Theatre of China** were more cautious, burying any political parallels beneath stylized and ritualistic acting (in a complication that Shakespeare would perhaps have appreciated, their costumes had become stuck in a shipping container en route, though they were able to perform as intended on a return visit in 2015).

Richard III has been finely caught on celluloid: in addition to the two stage-inspired films of Olivier (1955) and McKellen (1995), the earliest surviving American feature film is a version of the play starring **Frederick B. Warde** in 1912. Another silent movie was made by **J. Stuart Blackton** (1908), and **Frank Benson**'s Stratford version is preserved in a 1911 film. **Al Pacino** remixed the play in his 1996 *Looking for Richard*, framing his own powerful performance in the title role with a documentary in which he pounded the streets of New York searching for the play's essence. *Richard III* has also made fine TV: a segment was broadcast by the BBC in 1937 – one of the earliest ever transmissions of Shakespeare – and **Jane Howell**'s BBC production of 1982 was well received. It is intended to form the climax of the BBC's second *Hollow Crown* series in 2016, with **Benedict Cumberbatch** as a keenly anticipated Gloucester.

SCREEN

Richard III

F. Benson, M. Carrington, M. Johnston; Frank Benson (dir.) UK, 1911 ❯ on Silent Shakespeare (BFI) `DVD`

The British Film Institute's terrific *Silent Shakespeare* compilation includes early versions of seven plays – among them *Dream* (see p.316), *Twelfth Night* (see p.478) and *The Tempest* (see p.425). Most were adapted specially for the silent screen, but Frank Benson's 23-minute *Richard III* is a condensation of his infamous Stratford production; less engaging cinematically but historically priceless. What makes this film of more than antiquarian interest, though, is Benson himself: he reveals more with one malicious gesture than many lesser actors manage with an entire script – gleefully snatching up an apple after sending Hastings to his doom, momentarily unsteady on his feet as combat with Richmond looms. It's worth keeping this film silent, however – Laura Rossi's music isn't great.

Richard III

F.B. Warde, V. Stuart, R. Gemp; André Calmettes & James Kean (dirs) USA, 1912 ❯ Kino `DVD`

When the American Film Institute announced in 1996 that they had located the earliest surviving feature in the United States canon in a basement in Oregon, the reaction was disbelief. But it was true: a former movie projectionist had hung on to the nitrate reels and kept them in near-perfect condition. Even more astonishingly for Shakespearians, the movie – with the charismatic English-born Frederick B. Warde in the lead – is a silent version of *Richard III*, a living link to the barnstorming American Richards of the nineteenth century. Restored and set to a lush score by Ennio Morricone, the movie is an impressive experience: 55 minutes long, shot in upstate New York with a cast of 1,500 extras, its production values make Benson's version (above) resemble am-dram. But in every sense the most watchable thing on screen is Warde, a forgotten hero of the US stage who struts and stamps his way through the story with breathtaking chutzpah and aplomb.

Richard III

L. Olivier, J. Gielgud, R. Richardson; Laurence Olivier (dir.) UK, 1955 ❯ Network / Criterion `DVD` 🔊

This *Richard III* encapsulates what many people probably dread about Shakespeare on film: affected acting, kitschy sets, bad wigs. Indeed, Olivier's crookback King was so successfully parodied by Peter Sellers that it's sometimes hard to take this movie entirely at face value. For all that, it is one of *the* Shakespeare classics, perhaps best appreciated as an eighteenth-century star vehicle

(complete with Cibber and Garrick interpolations) which has somehow survived into the Technicolor age. Olivier is mesmeric in the lead – both repellent and fatally irresistible – and declaims the verse with a panache that would simply be impossible nowadays. He flirts with the camera, guiding the viewer through the play with malevolent glee and often shot in close-up as the grim tableau of his deeds unfolds behind him. When the central performance is this strong, it's even possible to understand how Claire Bloom's quiescent Anne feels she has no options left. Unmissable, particularly in the Blu-ray version, which includes lots of extra features.

Richard III

I. McKellen, N. Hawthorne, J. Carter; Richard Loncraine (dir.) UK, 1995 ❯ Pathé / MGM `DVD`

Made a full forty years after Olivier's version, Ian McKellen and Richard Loncraine's film steers a very different course to its illustrious predecessor. No medieval trimmings here: the setting is upper-crust 1930s England (with *arriviste* elements courtesy of Americans Annette Bening and Robert Downey, Jr), enlivened by a Cole Porter-ish soundtrack and intelligently shot in megalomaniacal locations including Brighton Pavilion, and London's St Pancras Station and Shell-Mex House. Though hardly the first actor to sense fascistic overtones in Richard's character (Donald Wolfit and indeed Olivier, both performing in wartime England, made a similar imaginative leap), McKellen makes a persuasive dictator and conveys a carefully judged balance between suaveness and menace. He is quieter than Olivier, but every bit as fine – full of sardonic humour and gleeful glances to camera. Yet visual style and postmodern wit smother most of the play's brute nastiness, which makes it feel curiously shallow at times. It will make you smirk rather than quake.

Looking for Richard

A. Pacino, K. Spacey, W. Rider; Al Pacino (dir.) USA, 1996 ❯ Fox `DVD` 🔊

"Ya know Shakespeare?" Pacino bawls amiably to a surprised six-year-old on a Manhattan sidewalk. "We're peddling Shakespeare on the streets." That's probably the best description of this strange but personable documentary, which chronicles Pacino's efforts to get on speaking terms with *Richard III*. The project occupied three years and saw Al and pals criss-cross not only New York but the Atlantic too – paying homage at Stratford and London, getting the low-down from a couple of academics, and chin-wagging with Famous English Thesps. Everything is woven around preparations for an abbreviated film version of the play starring Pacino as a mafioso-style Richard, a smirking Kevin Spacey as Buckingham and Penelope Allen's awesome Queen Elizabeth. If this sounds like a jumble it's intentionally so, and while *Looking for Richard* has its dire moments, it is redeemed by its insights into the mysteries of rehearsal, its frankness about American inhibitions concerning the Bard, and its genuine eagerness about Shakespeare's many wonders.

AUDIO

King Richard III
K. Branagh, M. Maloney, S. Gonet; David Timson (dir.) UK, 2001 ➤ Naxos ◉ ☁

Perhaps it's fitting to recommend an audio version starring the actor-director who's done more to manhandle Shakespeare into the popular cultural mainstream than anyone since Olivier – Kenneth Branagh. In fact, Branagh's CV has little to do with it: a year before he performed the role on stage, he puts in a genuinely involving performance, sometimes surprisingly moving, and his distinctive voice is here disconcertingly varied – so much so that you'll be hard-pressed to recognize him in the infamous opening soliloquy. No less impressive are Geraldine McEwan's commanding and well-spoken Margaret and Celia Imrie's sharply authoritative Elizabeth. Only Michael Maloney's slightly hysterical Clarence fails to evoke any sympathy. Under David Timson's direction the pace never slackens and – a rarity in audio Shakespeare – the music works well.

EDITIONS

Oxford Shakespeare
John Jowett (ed.); 2000 ➤ Oxford UP

As Associate General Editor of the Oxford *Complete Works*, John Jowett has an excellent track record in the bibliographical nitty-gritty of Shakespearian scholarship, and his edition of *Richard III* is typically scrupulous. Jowett's control text is the 1597 quarto, an unusual choice but selected on the basis that it represents something close to the play as first performed. With Folio additions listed in an appendix, the result is an unusually complete picture of the script and its various forms (including plenty on Cibber's adaptation). These are further complemented by detailed appendices, among them excerpts from More's *History* – otherwise surprisingly

tricky to get hold of – and an index of directors and actors. More recent stage history and critical trends are picked up in James R. Siemon's equally full Arden 3 edition (2009).

SOME CRITICISM

Angel with Horns
A.P. Rossiter (ed. Graham Storey); 1961 ➤ Longman [o/p]

In this wide-ranging collection of fifteen lectures delivered at Cambridge University by Rossiter and published after his death, the "Angel" of the book's title is the gloriously paradoxical Richard III, the brutal tyrant who is also irresistibly alluring. The opening essay was one of the first studies of the play to challenge critical orthodoxy and propose what theatregoers have known all along – that Richard is a great deal more exciting than anyone else who surrounds him. In doing so, it offers a reading of the play that sits quite happily with its customary role as a star vehicle, though which perhaps undervalues its wider political arguments – critics such as Jan Kott, who famously proclaimed that Richard "has no face", find fault with this character-based brand of interpretation. Despite these shortcomings, Rossiter's charm and offhand brilliance are likely to win you over.

Engendering a Nation
Jean E. Howard & Phyllis Rackin; 1997 ➤ Routledge

Subtitled "A feminist account of Shakespeare's English histories", Howard and Rackin's study, completed twenty or so years after feminist analysis of Shakespeare first took hold, does exactly what it says on the tin – and is none the worse for that. Their examination of the role of women in the first tetralogy under the heading "Weak kings, warrior women, and the assault on dynastic authority" is bracing and instructive. This approach works particularly well for *Richard III*, and throws useful light on women characters manipulated and victimized (and all too often obscured) by their celebrity king. A valuable counterbalance and corrective to Rossiter and much male-centred criticism.

Romeo and Juliet

I t is perhaps the most timeless Shakespearian image of all: the star-crossed lovers, united by passion yet doomed to separation. But *Romeo and Juliet* is all about time, and the fact that the lovers are given so little of it lends their love affair a volatile and turbulent intensity. Shakespeare's Juliet and Romeo fall in love on the instant, are married almost immediately, and are allowed just one precious night together before their feuding families drive them apart. They are not permitted to grow old, in other words, and *Romeo and Juliet* describes better than perhaps any other Shakespearian work what it feels like to be young. Indeed, it draws its power from violent conflict: between youth and age, life and death, fate and free will. Some have felt this makes it too schematic – the work of a man still learning his craft. Yet *Romeo and Juliet* is also a bold theatrical experiment, one that Shakespeare would never quite repeat. It begins in a world of bantering comedy and teenage rebellion, but when danger and death intervene, full-blooded tragedy consumes the action. The play at once portrays the power of romantic ideals and their fragility in the face of crushing social forces. The lovers may attempt to transcend their fractured world, but they are in the end unable to escape it.

DATE > Given its stylistic similarities to *Love's Labour's Lost* and *A Midsummer Night's Dream*, probably 1595 or 1596.

SOURCES > Arthur Brooke's poem *The Tragical History of Romeus and Juliet* (1562) is the play's largest source (*The Two Gentlemen of Verona* also uses it), though the basic tale exists in many versions – one of which, William Painter's *Palace of Pleasure* (1566–67), Shakespeare may have consulted.

TEXTS > Trading on *Romeo*'s apparent popularity, an unlicensed text (Q1) was printed in 1597, though its precise relationship with Shakespeare's version is disputed. Q2 appeared two years later, loudly advertised as "newly corrected, augmented, and amended", and was reprinted in 1609 (Q3), c. 1622 (Q4) and 1637 (Q5). The 1623 Folio version is based on the third, 1609 printing.

Interpreting the play

It is testament to the power of what is frequently billed as the greatest love story ever that, every year, thousands of love-struck correspondents write to "Juliet" in Verona asking for her blessing; so many, in fact, that there is a volunteer organization dedicated to replying on her behalf. That appeal to universality is part of *Romeo and Juliet*'s attraction. The couple are overwhelmingly in love yet fatally divided; conjoined in what Juliet achingly calls "my true-love passion" (2.1.146) yet separated by destiny. Their relationship, it's been said, taps into some mythic vein, an example

MAJOR CHARACTERS & SYNOPSIS

THE MONTAGUES

Romeo, a young man from Verona
Montague, Romeo's father, head of the household
Lady Montague, Montague's wife
Benvolio, Romeo's cousin and friend
Abraham, Montague's servant
Balthasar, Romeo's servant

THE CAPULETS

Juliet, a young lady from Verona
Capulet, Juliet's father, head of the household
Lady Capulet, Capulet's wife
Tybalt, Juliet's cousin
Juliet's **Nurse**
Peter, **Samson** and **Gregory**, the Capulets' servants

OTHERS

Escalus, Prince of Verona
Mercutio, a young nobleman related to the Prince, Romeo's friend
Count Paris, a young nobleman related to the Prince
Paris's Page
Friars Laurence and **John**, Franciscan monks
An **Apothecary**
Chorus, introducing the action

ACT 1 Verona is riven by a feud between the Capulets and the Montagues, powerful local families. Even a minor skirmish between servants rapidly escalates into a full-scale riot, halted only by the arrival of the Prince. After order is restored, Montague asks Benvolio to find out why his son Romeo is so melancholy; when Romeo reveals that he's in love with a woman who has sworn never to marry, Benvolio suggests he finds another lover. The Capulets, meanwhile, have agreed to let Paris, the Prince's kinsman, woo their daughter Juliet, and invite him to a feast to be held that night. Learning of the feast from a servant, Benvolio persuades Romeo that the two of them should attend. Despite Romeo's misgivings that it will end badly, they put on masks and – joining up with their friend Mercutio – succeed in getting in. Romeo catches sight of Juliet while dancing, and is immediately captivated. Though recognized by Tybalt, Romeo succeeds in speaking to her and they exchange kisses before Juliet is called away.

ACT 2 Romeo is hiding in Capulet's orchard when Juliet appears on her balcony; the two exchange loving words and agree to marry as soon as possible. The next morning, Romeo rushes to Friar Laurence, who undertakes to marry them in the hope of ending the feud. After meeting up with Mercutio and Benvolio (who are relieved to find him in good humour), Romeo arranges with the Nurse for Juliet to join him at Friar Laurence's cell that afternoon.

ACT 3 Benvolio and Mercutio are walking through the streets when they are approached by an aggrieved Tybalt, who is looking to challenge Romeo. Arriving from his marriage, Romeo fails to placate Tybalt, who then fights with Mercutio, fatally wounding him. Enraged by the death of his friend, Romeo fights and kills Tybalt. When the Prince hears of the murder, he banishes Romeo. The news reaches Juliet, but the Nurse and Friar Laurence arrange for the lovers to spend the night together before Romeo flees to Mantua. No sooner is Romeo gone, though, than Capulet insists that Juliet must marry Paris.

ACT 4 Friar Laurence outlines a solution to the desperate Juliet: she will agree to marry Paris, but on the evening of the wedding take a drug which will put her into a death-like sleep. When she is laid in the family tomb, Romeo will be waiting there and the two can elope. Juliet takes the potion as planned, and Friar Laurence takes charge of the funeral arrangements.

ACT 5 But the message explaining the plan never reaches Romeo, and the first he hears is that Juliet is dead. Grief-stricken, he rushes to Verona to Juliet's tomb. Paris is lying in wait and the two fight – Paris is killed and Romeo enters the tomb. There he finds the unconscious Juliet, kisses her one last time and takes poison. As Juliet begins to awaken, Friar Laurence arrives, but is frightened away by the appearance of the Watch. Seeing Romeo's body, Juliet resolves on suicide and stabs herself. As the Capulets and Montagues arrive, the Prince reflects that the lovers' deaths are punishment for the feud, and the two families finally resolve to be reconciled.

of the kind of "separation romance" that animates ancient tales such as those of Hero and Leander, Troilus and Cressida, Tristan and Isolde. Richard Wagner, whose opera on the last couple magnifies the myth to earth-shattering proportions, called it *Liebstod* ("love-death"), and *Romeo and Juliet* has frequently been interpreted in similarly totalizing terms.

Shakespeare, like countless writers before him, found inspiration in separation: that's why the balcony scene, with its gorgeous speeches between the divided lovers, works so powerfully – and perhaps why it has become the play's most potent image. Nor does *Romeo and Juliet* discourage its audiences from thinking of it as a kind of myth. As the play prepares to close, the Prince instructs the assembled citizens of Verona to "have more talk of these sad things":

> Some shall be pardoned, and some punishèd;
> For never was a story of more woe
> Than this of Juliet and her Romeo.

> [5.3.306–9]

"Never was a story of more woe" transforms the couple into something beyond themselves, like the "statue[s] in pure gold" that Capulet and Montague undertake to raise in their memory. They and their story have become examples, models, precedents – and for Shakespeare, who based his play on several retellings of this old story, perhaps they already were.

In a name

All of which makes it surprising that Shakespeare's main source interprets the tale in a starkly contrasting light. *The Tragical History of Romeus and Juliet* was published in 1562 by Arthur Brooke, poet, translator and soldier (he drowned the following year while travelling to fight abroad), and his 3,000-line poem provided Shakespeare with the most accessible narrative version. Like the play's Prince, Brooke is eager to impose a strict way of interpreting the story he is to tell, as his note "To the Reader" attests:

> And to this end (good Reader) is this tragical matter written, to describe unto thee a couple of unfortunate lovers, thralling themselves to unhonest desire, neglecting the authority and advice of parents and friends, conferring their principal counsels with drunken gossips, and superstitious friars (the naturally fit instruments of unchastity) attempting all adventures of peril, for the attaining of their wished lust … abusing the honourable name of lawful marriage, to cloak the shame of stolen contracts, finally, by all means of unhonest life, hasting to most unhappy death.

Brooke intends to make an example of the lovers, but in the darker sense of that phrase. Far from being caught up in fateful events far beyond their control – still less being tragic victims whose only sin, as Othello says of himself, is to love "not wisely but too well" – the damning fault of the lovers is their selfishness. They reject the sensible advice of "parents and friends", allow themselves to be overtaken by "unhonest desire" – and get their just deserts. Brooke pits the lovers against the rest of the city, but they are decisively on the wrong side.

Reading Brooke, Shakespeare evidently noted that the same story could be told differently. Instead of providing a cautionary tale addressed to young lovers, warning them to buckle under or face the penalties, he demonstrates in graphic terms where the "will" of senior Capulets and Montagues has actually landed Verona. His Chorus sketches out the terms:

> Two households, both alike in dignity
>> In fair Verona, where we lay our scene,
> From ancient grudge break to new mutiny
>> Where civil blood makes civil hands unclean.

[PROLOGUE, 1–4]

In those remorseless puns on the word "civil", the Chorus prepares the ground for the "new mutiny" that immediately and brutally follows, the argument between servants from the two opposing houses which rapidly spirals into a full-blown brawl. Aggression is total in Verona: the city's streets are war zones. At pains to emphasize this, Shakespeare has the play open with Capulet servants Samson and Gregory, clearly spoiling for a fight:

GREGORY The quarrel is between our masters and us their men.
SAMSON 'Tis all one. I will show myself a tyrant: when I have fought with the men I will be civil with the maids—I will cut off their heads.
GREGORY The heads of the maids?
SAMSON Ay, the heads of the maids, or their maidenheads, take it in what sense thou wilt.

[1.1.18–25]

Even though both are Capulets, the instinct to vie is inveterate – and in striving to out-brag each other, Gregory and Samson further twist that word "civil" into still darker realms, those of sexual violence. Raping and killing Montague women is just another way to get one over on the enemy.

Some commentators have taken this harshly masculine world as the keynote of the play. Men are the driving force behind the violence – and engaging in violence, as Samson and Gregory idly reveal, becomes synonymous with proving masculinity. Confronted with Benvolio's protestation that he is simply trying to "keep the peace", Tybalt angrily declares that "I hate the word / As I hate hell, all Montagues, and thee" (1.1.65–8). This is not civil society in any sense of that word: it is a world in which the masculine "name" swamps everything else. Juliet astutely realizes this in her much-quoted lines on the balcony:

> O Romeo, Romeo, wherefore art thou Romeo?

> Deny thy father and refuse thy name,
> Or if thou wilt not, be but sworn my love,
> And I'll no longer be a Capulet.

[2.1.75–8]

Calling upon Romeo to refuse his "name" will force him to "deny" his father and the legacy of his family. Protesting that "'Tis but thy name that is my enemy", Juliet attempts to separate the name from the object – or, rather, to restore the name to some true sense of what it really is. "What's in a name?", she questions,

> That which we call a rose
> By any other word would smell as sweet.
> So Romeo would, were he not Romeo called,
> Retain that dear perfection which he owes
> Without that title. Romeo, doff thy name,
> And for thy name—which is no part of thee—
> Take all myself.

[2.1.85–91]

Juliet offers to replace Romeo's name with her own body, but the irony this speech introduces is not just that Romeo and Juliet will not eventually be able to transcend their surnames (at least not in life), but that Romeo's first name – which means "a roamer, a wanderer" – points towards his banishment and their ultimate separation. The irony is compounded as soon as Romeo is banished, when he begs Friar Laurence, "tell me, friar, tell me, / In what vile part of this anatomy / Doth my name lodge?" so that he can "sack / The hateful mansion" (3.3.104–7). This realization that his name has become a death sentence is one of the play's sharpest. There is a further irony, too, in the site of the lovers' death: they end up in the Capulet family tomb, along with all the feud's previous victims.

My love as deep

As the great twentieth-century actor and director Harley Granville-Barker commented in his perceptive *Preface* to the play, "this is a tragedy of youth, as youth sees it", and some have argued that *Romeo and Juliet*, with all its turmoil and extremes, is about nothing less than the process of adolescence. Romeo enters the play every inch the moody teen, mooning distractedly over the previous object of his affection, Rosaline. Significantly, Rosaline herself never appears – she doesn't need to, for Romeo is clearly in love with love itself, and his passion evaporates as soon as her Capulet kinswoman, Juliet, arrives on the scene.

Juliet is similarly on the cusp of maturity: though her father initially considers her "yet a stranger in the world" (her fourteenth birthday is two weeks away at the play's opening), at the lovers' breathless initial meeting she is more than able to hold her own, calmly parrying Romeo's flirtatious words – and in fact Shakespeare makes their first exchange into a fourteen-line love sonnet, as if urging Juliet that, despite her

Johnston Forbes-Robertson as Romeo and Mrs Patrick Campbell as Juliet in the 1895 production of the play at London's Lyceum theatre, which ran for 79 performances. Though admired for her Pre-Raphaelite beauty, Mrs Campbell's Juliet divided critics; George Bernard Shaw called it "an immature performance at all the exceptional points".

youth, she has not a moment to lose. The fact that the lovers speak a poem almost without realizing it also acts as a kind of miraculous confirmation that their destinies are fatefully tied to each other, yet in its very intensity it also hints that, like poetic lovers before and since, they are doomed to separation.

Again, speed dominates: just a handful of lines after encountering each other, the lovers exchange their very first kiss. In just five scenes' time, they will be married; Mercutio and Tybalt will be dead a few scenes later; and in that brief period this comedy of romantic love will have become a full-blown tragedy. But though the couple's time together is agonizingly short, Shakespeare refuses to make it one-dimensional. Juliet, if anything, matures faster than Romeo. In the balcony scene, as he vows to love her "by yonder blessèd moon", she urges him: "O swear not by the moon, th' inconstant moon … Do not swear at all", fearing that "if thou swear'st / Thou may prove false". For her, their love lies not in immediate vows, but is organic, ever-growing:

My bounty is as boundless as the sea,
My love as deep. The more I give to thee
The more I have, for both are infinite.

[2.1.175–7]

But of course the sea is controlled by the moon, and Romeo and Juliet's love, while it will not become shallower, will eventually be betrayed. The lovers often attempt to alter the fabric of the universe, to push on time when apart but arrest it when together. Yearning for her wedding night, Juliet cries, "Gallop apace, you fiery-footed steeds, / Towards Phoebus's lodging" to the heavens,

Such a waggoner
As Phaëton would whip you to the west
And bring in cloudy night immediately.
Spread thy close curtain, love-performing night,
That runaways' eyes may wink, and Romeo
Leap to these arms untalked of and unseen.

[3.2.1–7]

Juliet here is trying to manipulate the passage of time, just as she is attempting to uproot convention by calling for night instead of day (a theme that much concerns the lovers); furthermore, her sexual language displays her as a woman – so much so that many nineteenth-century actresses refused to perform this speech altogether, regarding Juliet's description of "love-performing night", and, later, "amorous rites" unfitting for a girl not yet fourteen. In yet another irony, Juliet's wish is partly granted – time does fly – but so urgently that the lovers' rush to death rapidly becomes unstoppable.

Given the fact that the lovers don't escape their fate – and given the ways in which we're constantly reminded that they won't – some have even wondered whether *Romeo and Juliet* counts as tragedy. If they are predestined by "some consequence yet hanging in the stars" (1.4.107), if Friar Laurence is right that "these violent delights have violent ends" (2.5.9), do they ever reach tragic greatness? Or are they, as Capulet sadly notes, "Poor sacrifices to our enmity" – blameless, "star-crossed" victims? Perhaps the answer is that, in this early tragedy, Shakespeare wants to have it both ways. He constantly reminds the audience of the hastening inevitability of betrayal, while presenting us with the couple's growing maturity and the deepening of their love. Romeo and Juliet try to seize control of their story, but ultimately they cannot – and in that juxtaposition lies the tragedy.

Stage history and adaptations

It seems probable that *Romeo and Juliet* was put on initially at the **Theatre** in Shoreditch, then perhaps at the nearby **Curtain** after Shakespeare's company moved there temporarily in 1597, but all we can really be sure of is that its use of contrastive theatrical spaces (especially the gallery "aloft" and the curtained-in area behind the main stage) will have used the resources of both theatres to the full. It's likely that **Richard Burbage** took the part of Romeo and **Master Richard Goffe** Juliet. It even achieved international popularity, adaptations being performed early in the seventeenth century by Anglo-German companies touring northern Europe.

The next we know is of a version prepared by **William Davenant** (who liked to boast that he was Shakespeare's love child, but was most likely his godson). This appeared in 1662 at Lincoln's Inn Fields, and was witnessed by Pepys – who couldn't decide which he detested more, the play or the actors. The latter were **Mary Sanderson** as Juliet, one of the first women to appear on the English public stage, her future husband **Thomas Betterton** as Mercutio, and **Henry Harris** as Romeo. Just over fifteen years later, **Thomas Otway** decided to rejig Shakespeare's play and set it in ancient Rome; the finished work, *The History and Fall of Caius Marius*, was premiered in 1679 with Betterton in the title role. Underscoring the drama's political dimensions, it was a timely arrival given the crisis over Charles II's succession then gripping the nation.

The next significant production, that undertaken by **Theophilus Cibber** in 1744, claimed to be the real *Romeo and Juliet*, but retained Otway's revised ending – in which Juliet awakes before Romeo's death and the lovers are allowed a frenzied parting dialogue. Its success was muted, however, and it took the theatrical genius of **David Garrick**, who mounted a revival at Drury Lane four years later, to make the play into a sure-fire hit – which it certainly was, being performed some 329 times before 1776, even more than Garrick's *Hamlet*. It was not without competition, however: Garrick's original Romeo, **Spranger Barry**, jumped ship to Covent Garden in 1750 and forced Garrick to act the role himself, igniting a showdown between the two productions that lasted eight years. While Barry was considered better in the love scenes, Garrick's forte was tragedy – so, when both versions were performed on the same night, many theatregoers simply swapped venues halfway through. The era also saw a succession of fine Juliets grace the stage: **Susannah Cibber, Anne Bellamy, Isabella Nossiter** and **Hannah Pritchard**.

While the big names of the early nineteenth century – **John Philip Kemble, Edmund Kean** and **William Charles Macready** – all played Romeo in Garrick's version, it was commonly felt that the part lacked virility. Ironically, the actor responsible for changing that was the iconoclastic American **Charlotte Cushman**, who caused a sensation when she played Romeo to her sister's Juliet at the Haymarket in 1845. The critics were unanimous in their praise: the *Athenaeum* declared it "one of the most extraordinary pieces of acting, perhaps, ever exhibited by a woman", while the *Times* gushed that "Miss Cushman's Romeo is a creative, a living, breathing, animated, ardent, human being" – and, furthermore, not at all bad with a sword. The great Italian actress **Eleonora Duse** had one of her earliest successes in 1872, when, at the age of 14 (the "correct" age for the role), she played Juliet in the vast amphitheatre at Verona. Trailing rose petals whenever she met Romeo, and smothering his corpse with them, an idea she dreamt up just before the first performance, her complete identification with the character created a sensation.

The chief fixation of late nineteenth-century performers – pictorial realism, the grander the better – touched *Romeo* relatively late on, most magnificently in **Henry Irving**'s monumental production of 1882. Irving played Romeo to **Ellen Terry**'s

> *Romeo is Hamlet in love. There is the same rich exuberance of passion and sentiment in the one, that there is of thought and sentiment in the other. Both are absent and self-involved, both live out of themselves in a world of imagination.*
>
> William Hazlitt, *Characters from Shakespeare's Plays* (1817)

Juliet (she would act the Nurse at the other end of her career, in 1919), but it was his double set for the final scene that really made audiences gasp: after slaying Paris in the churchyard, Romeo descended a set of steps and, following a miraculous scene-change, reappeared in an eerie Gothic crypt. In 1895 **Johnston Forbes-Robertson** took over the management of the Lyceum, and scored a notable success with a dreamily romantic account of the play, starring himself as Romeo and **Mrs Patrick Campbell** as Juliet.

Into the new century, **William Poel**'s pioneering attempts at quasi-Elizabethan staging were well received, but even so his 1905 performance of *Romeo and Juliet* came to a halt after just four performances. It was **John Gielgud**'s sprightly production at the New Theatre (1935) that defined the play for a new era. Selecting an Italian Renaissance setting and costumes that emphasized the division between old and young, Gielgud alternated the roles of Romeo and Mercutio with **Laurence Olivier**. As with the Garrick–Barry contest, the two actors were acclaimed for the differences they brought to the lead role. Olivier later commented (with the hint of a sneer) that Gielgud was "all spirituality, all beauty, all abstract things; and myself ... all earth, blood, humanity". **Peggy Ashcroft** played Juliet, while **Edith Evans**'s Nurse was memorably described as "earthy as a potato, as slow as a cart horse and as cunning as a badger".

Peter Brook staged a markedly unsentimental *Romeo* at Stratford in 1947 with the youthful **Laurence Payne** and **Daphne Slater** taking the leads. On a virtually bare stage, Brook emphasized the play's violence and contrasted the lovers' youthful idealism with suffocating Veronese society; the mood was further darkened by **Paul Scofield**'s intense Mercutio, and the fact that the closing reconciliation between the Capulets and Montagues was cut. **Franco Zeffirelli**, directing at the Old Vic in 1960, administered an injection of zeitgeist – commissioning a set that looked like a real Italian street, cutting about a third of the lines and encouraging his actors to speak naturalistically. **Judi Dench** (and later **Joanna Dunham**) played Juliet to **John Stride**'s teenagey Romeo, while **Alec McCowen**'s Mercutio was applauded as an "angry young man".

Since these ground-breaking productions *Romeo and Juliet* has become a massive big-hitter, revived over 450 times internationally in the seventy years following World War II. That it continues to offer real possibilities for contrast is indicated by productions at the RSC over recent decades. In 1973, **Terry Hands** foregrounded the play's masculine violence, with **Bernard Lloyd**'s misogynistic Mercutio dismembering a life-size doll on stage. Three years later, **Trevor Nunn** and **Barry Kyle**'s production had a similarly dangerous feel, with **Ian McKellen**'s Romeo more neurotically than erotically charged. A decade later, in 1986, **Michael Bodganov** interpreted the play as a capitalist tragedy (though ironically his production was nicknamed "Alfa-Romeo and Juliet" for its sharp Italian tailoring); while, in 2008, **Neil Bartlett** added a touch of *The Godfather* to his jazzy and highly choreographed version with **Anneika Rose** and

Adapted for young audiences by the British National Theatre's Ben Power, this 2013 Romeo and Juliet, with Tendayi Jembere and Natalie Drew as the star-crossed lovers, brought out the energy and charm of Shakespeare's most youthful play.

Daniel Dawson. Something similar could be said about the almost countless recent stagings of the play in North America, which have ranged from **Laird Williamson's** Gold Rush-era version for the Oregon Shakespeare Festival in 2012 to an "original-practices" Elizabethan production by **Tim Carroll** at Stratford, Ontario (2013) and the James Dean-style New York revival, which featured **Orlando Bloom** and **Condola Rashad** alongside a vintage Triumph motorcycle (also 2013, the first on Broadway since John Neville and Claire Bloom in 1956).

Back in Britain, **Tim Supple's** version at the National Theatre in 2000 was widely attacked for its poor verse-speaking and muddled direction, while **Michael Boyd's** 2001 staging at the RSC was criticized for a set described by the *Daily Mail* as looking like "an underground car-park", while its leading lady, **Alexandra Gilbreath**, came under fire for being too old for the part. Much more positively received was **Rupert Goold's** charged, contemporary 2010 staging, again the RSC, which featured **Mariah Gale** and **Sam Troughton** and was acclaimed by the *Guardian* as the most exciting revival since Zeffirelli in 1960. At Shakespeare's Globe in London, **Dominic Dromgoole's** Elizabethan-style version of 2009, with **Adetomiwa Edun** and **Ellie Kendrick**, was full of youthful verve but struggled to maintain intensity. The same year **Ben Power** went in the opposite direction, with a touching adaptation called *A Tender Thing* that debuted at the RSC; it imagined Juliet and Romeo in old age, with the text shuffled and reset accordingly. Four years later, Power returned to the play yet again, this time at the National Theatre, in a version specially adapted for young audiences, full of colour and verve.

Perhaps the most adventurous reimaginings of *Romeo and Juliet* have appeared in locations where conflict has been dangerously real – from **Otomar Krejča** and **Josef Svoboda's** acclaimed Prague production, which caught the disaffection of Cold War

Czech youth (1964), to the Romany company **Pralipe** (Brotherhood), forced into exile from their native Macedonia, who set the play in Bosnia with a Muslim Juliet and a Christian Romeo (1994). In 2015 the play was performed by **Syrian refugees** on the rooftop of a makeshift hospital in Amman, Jordan, with Romeo only able to communicate with Juliet via Skype.

At least 61 film versions of *Romeo* have been counted over the century or so following the appearance of the earliest, directed by **Clement Maurice** (1900). The 1936 film directed by **George Cukor** is probably the least loved of the major versions, stymied by the casting of **Leslie Howard** (aged 44) and **Norma Shearer** (aged 36). John Gielgud claimed that "for unspeakable vulgarity, appalling hammery, and utter silliness, I have seen nothing worse," but even so it was remade in a famous Indian version from 1947 featuring *Mother India* star **Nargis** and **D.K. Sapru**, now unfortunately lost.

Renato Castellani's neo-realist version of 1954 won plaudits, but was soon eclipsed by **Franco Zeffirelli**'s 1968 movie, chock-full of youthful sex appeal and Italianate passion. Zeffirelli's hold on the youth market has been challenged by **Baz Luhrmann**, whose 1996 *Romeo + Juliet* made the play comprehensible (and appealing) to the MTV generation. Rejoicing in a different kind of anachronism, **John Madden**'s *Shakespeare in Love* (1998), written by **Marc Norman** and **Tom Stoppard**, played *Romeo and Juliet* autobiographically, with **Joseph Fiennes**'s Bard bidding for the manicured hand of **Gwyneth Paltrow**, his aristocratic, boy-actor-impersonating inamorata. *Downton Abbey*'s **Julian Fellowes** was the moving force behind **Carlo Carlei**'s naturalistic and lushly shot 2013 version, with the teenage **Hailee Steinfeld** and **Douglas Booth**, but the film was almost universally panned, not least for Fellowes's own cod-Shakespearian verse, added to the text at numerous points.

SCREEN

Romeo and Juliet

L. Whiting, O. Hussey, J. McEnery; Franco Zeffirelli
(dir.) Italy/UK, 1968 › Paramount DVD 🔽

Zeffirelli's film took his 1960 stage production to its logical extreme: much of the text is eradicated, the quest for realism takes him to the Tuscan hill town of Pienza, and the story is angled from the lovers' perspective as they battle against their tedious, overbearing parents. All this is risky, given the limited resources of the teenage leads, Olivia Hussey and Leonard Whiting, and the fact that Zeffirelli's cuts render their roles atoms away from two-dimensional. Any hint at Juliet's emotional maturity is airbrushed out, and for all the sultry passion ostensibly on display, the film feels oddly chaste. Hussey's balcony speech delivered as if to a favourite puppy. John McEnery's emotionally tormented Mercutio is much more successful, as is Michael York's pouting Tybalt. In some ways the scenes without the lovers are the ones that work: Zeffirelli distils the "mad blood" of the play with typical verve, his cat-calling young men purring with aggression and machismo.

Romeo + Juliet

L. DiCaprio, C. Danes, H. Perrineau; Baz Luhrmann
(dir.) USA, 1996 › Fox DVD 🔽

"Shakespeare has never been this sexy", screamed *Rolling Stone*, and after watching Zeffirelli you can see where they're coming from. But that does a disservice both to Shakespeare and to Luhrmann, whose adaptation is sharper than the shoutlines would have you believe. It centres on the fictional Verona Beach, a half-futuristic US city suspended somewhere between Miami and Mexico – violent, trashy and brash. The feud is fought out at gas stations and policed by helicopters, while the lovers meet to the strains of Des'Ree at the Capulets' gated mansion and woo each other in a swimming pool. Though the visuals are pure Luhrmann – channel-surfing, freeze-framing, jump-cutting – the real surprise is how well this suits Shakespeare's own restive depiction of a society at war with itself. *Romeo + Juliet* is consistently smart without being earnest: Elizabethan wit effortlessly becomes punchy street-speak, while the film's in-your-face Catholicism brilliantly animates an aspect of the play many have thought irretrievable. Neither DiCaprio nor

Danes were ever going to win Oscars, but that doesn't matter: Luhrmann does all the work for them, crafting an intense – and tense – denouement that actually, amazingly, has the power to shock.

Shakespeare in Love
J. Fiennes, G. Paltrow, G. Rush; John Madden (dir.)
UK, 1998 > UCA / Lionsgate DVD

Purists, look away – there's as much authenticity in this freewheeling spin on Shakespearian comedy as in many more straightforward movie adaptations. There are references to everything from *Two Gentlemen of Verona* to *Doctor Faustus* and *Twelfth Night* (learned ones at that), but *Romeo and Juliet* is the grounding narrative in this story of frustrated passion between Joseph Fiennes's brooding, blocked playwright and Gwyneth Paltrow's cross-dressing female aristo. The genius is in Tom Stoppard's script, smartened and polished from ignoble origins into a gem sparkling with wit, yet what makes the movie truly winning is its unashamed love for Shakespeare's work. Even if the idea of romcom with ruffs makes you wince, you'll leave with a smile on your face.

AUDIO

Romeo and Juliet
D. Henshall, S. Dahl, S. York; Peter Kavanagh (dir.)
UK, 1999 > BBC

Douglas Henshall and Sophie Dahl are the excellent leads, albeit ones who might struggle to convince you that they are in their teens. No matter: Henshall is persuasive as Romeo while Dahl brings an appealing innocence to the role of Juliet. Elsewhere Kavanagh's production is more mixed: its modern-day Veronese setting sounds a bit props department (roaring Vespas and Italian cursing) and other cast members are not so strong – Milo O'Shea's Friar Laurence is breathless and Freddie Jones's Capulet is almost too plummy for words. At least the lovers don't sound as if they're unblocking a sink when kissing (as they do in the rival Naxos version).

EDITIONS

Arden Shakespeare (third edition)
René Weis (ed.); 2012 > Bloomsbury

René Weis's Arden 3 edition is a fine work, and a fat one: weighing in at a shade under 450 pages, it is the fullest currently available. Some of this bulk is down to Weis's decision to print the first quarto in facsimile after his main edited text, in recognition that it is perhaps not as "bad" as scholars once believed; nonetheless this edition is still based on the Q2 version, originally published as "newly corrected, augmented and extended" and perhaps

never seen on stage. Even if you're not interested in the bibliographical nitty-gritty there's a huge amount here: subtle writing on the play's poetry and style, good detail on sources, and an admirably extended section on Romeo and Juliet's long and fruitful stage history, particularly its life in film. Engaging and enthusiastic, Weis even claims to solve one of the play's oldest mysteries – the Christian name of Juliet's Nurse.

SOME CRITICISM

Shakespeare's Mercutio
Joseph A. Porter; 1988 > North Carolina UP [o/p]

Though the play's title might not admit it, there's much more to *Romeo and Juliet* than the fresh-faced lovers. Among its more intriguing residents is Mercutio, one of Shakespeare's most astonishing characters yet whose untimely death at the hands of Tybalt shifts him decisively out of the action (Dryden thought that Shakespeare was forced to kill Mercutio lest he take over the play). Joseph Porter's study takes an extended look at Romeo's incendiary companion across theatrical and critical history, beginning with the merest of hints in Brooke's *Romeus* and underpinning this with an insightful exposition of Mercutio's most important facet – his name, derived from the god Mercury. Porter also has some intriguing thoughts on Marlowe, suggesting that in Mercutio Shakespeare might even have been celebrating the work of his recently dead rival.

Young Hamlet
Barbara Everett; 1989 > Oxford UP [o/p]

Young Hamlet: Essays on Shakespeare's Tragedies is in two parts, its first section a group of lectures delivered at University College London in 1988 on Bradley's "big four" (*Hamlet*, *Othello*, *Lear* and *Macbeth*), its second bringing together older pieces from a variety of sources. All are informed by Everett's wit and wisdom, as well as her commitment to what is sometimes thought to be a dying art – the skill of intensely close reading. As the book's title indicates, *Hamlet* is the centrifugal force here, but Everett's early article "*Romeo and Juliet*: The Nurse's Story", which looks carefully at Juliet's Nurse and what less intelligent critics have dismissed as her wasteful prattle, is exemplary and involving, suggesting that she (like Mercutio) is utterly central to the human story of the play. Everett can be cryptic at times – her most resonant statements often have an air of mystery about them – but her ability to pick up tiny details and work them into rich patterns is invaluable. Though Everett's work isn't included, other essay-length pieces on the play can be found in John F. Andrews's excellent Routledge anthology, *Romeo and Juliet: Critical Essays* (1993).

The Taming of the Shrew

I t is difficult not to feel that *The Taming of the Shrew* is a problem in need of solving. It depicts an unruly and strong-willed woman forced into marriage, then "tamed" into obedience by her new husband, who employs violent means to get his way. While some commentators have simply written off the *Shrew* as a delinquent farce, since the rise of feminist criticism it has attracted growing attention – albeit much of it unsympathetic. Opinion still remains sharply divided: one leading theatre critic has described the play as "totally offensive ... barbaric and disgusting"; elsewhere, it has been held up as an Elizabethan celebration of wifely triumph. On stage, where solemn rules rarely function, Shakespeare's most deliberately outrageous drama can be all of those things at once – and more. A didactic and savage folk tale becomes something infinitely richer, and the relationship between Katherine (the play's spirited "shrew") and her gold-digging suitor Petruccio suggests that love can blossom from the most unlikely of ingredients. Above all, perhaps, this is a play about playing: itself an experiment in dramatic form (the main action is a play-within-a-play), in performance it can be one of the most challenging and surprising of all Shakespeare's works.

DATE > Although it is undeniably one of Shakespeare's earliest comedies, theories about the play's precise date are complicated by its textual history (see below). It was probably written in 1590 or slightly later, close to *The Two Gentlemen of Verona*.

SOURCES > The main story probably derives from folk tale or ballad. The subplot appears in George Gascoigne's drama *Supposes* (1566), while some parallels recall the anonymous play *A Knack to Know a Knave* (1592).

TEXTS > Two versions exist: one printed in anonymous quarto in 1594 as *The Taming of a Shrew*, the other in the 1623 Folio as *The Taming of the Shrew*. Their relationship remains puzzling, though most scholars believe *A Shrew* is not directly Shakespeare's work.

Interpreting the play

Tales about "taming" women whom society deems to be unruly have a long and gruesome history. The misogynistic archetype of the shrewish woman crops up repeatedly in oral storytelling, and tales about taming apparently difficult wives were a staple of the early-modern world – as indeed they had been for centuries. One broadside ballad from 1635 even has the same name as Shakespeare's play, though

MAJOR CHARACTERS & SYNOPSIS

THE INDUCTION

Christopher Sly, a drunken tinker
Hostess of an alehouse
A **Lord**
Bartholomew, the Lord's page
Players acting the play-within-the-play

THE PLAY-WITHIN-THE-PLAY

Katherine (Kate) Minola of Padua, the "shrew"
Bianca, Katherine's younger sister
Baptista, Katherine's father
Petruccio, a gentleman from Verona, Katherine's
suitor (later her husband)
Grumio and **Curtis**, Petruccio's servants
Gremio, a rich old man from Padua, Bianca's suitor
Hortensio, another suitor for Bianca (later
disguised as "Licio")
Lucentio, a gentleman from Pisa (later disguised
as "Cambio", a teacher)
Tranio and **Biondello**, Lucentio's servants
Vincentio, Lucentio's father
A **Merchant** from Mantua (later disguised as
"Vincentio")

INDUCTION Christopher Sly, a drunken tinker,
is thrown out of an alehouse and falls asleep. He
is discovered by a Lord, who gets his servants to
play an elaborate trick on him. Taking him to their
master's house, they convince Sly that he has
been insane for the last fifteen years and is actually a Lord. After much ado he eventually believes
them, and settles down to watch the players
perform an Italian play, in which ...

ACT 1 Hortensio and Gremio both seek the
hand of the lovely Bianca, the younger daughter
of Baptista. Unfortunately Baptista has vowed
that she cannot marry until her sister, the
shrewish Katherine, has done so. All this is
overheard by Lucentio, newly arrived in Padua,
who – having seen Bianca – falls for her himself.
Knowing that Baptista is seeking tutors for
his daughters, Lucentio concocts a plan – he
will gain access to her by disguising himself
as a schoolteacher while his servant Tranio
impersonates him. Petruccio has also arrived in
town; hearing from Hortensio about Katherine's
substantial dowry, (and undeterred by her
reputation), he resolves to win her – much to the
relief of Bianca's numerous suitors.

ACT 2 Katherine is bullying Bianca into revealing
which suitor she prefers when the men arrive.
Petruccio offers himself as a suitor for Katherine,
and presents Hortensio (disguised as Licio) as a
music master for the two sisters. Gremio responds
by introducing Lucentio (disguised as Cambio)
as a teacher, while Tranio (disguised as Lucentio)
presents himself as a third suitor for Bianca.
Hortensio/Licio immediately suffers at Katherine's
hands, but Petruccio defiantly gives as good as he
gets in their first meeting. Meanwhile, Gremio
and Tranio (still disguised as Lucentio) attempt to
win Baptista's consent by boasting of their riches.

ACT 3 Bianca is already under siege from
Hortensio and Lucentio, both of whom covertly
reveal their identities in an attempt to win
her. Petruccio turns up late for his wedding to
Katherine, shocking Baptista by his bizarre and
unkempt dress. After the ceremony, Petruccio
insists that he and his wife cannot attend the
wedding dinner but must leave straightaway.

ACT 4 After an awful journey, during which
Katherine falls off her horse and is covered in
mud, the newlyweds arrive at Petruccio's house.
Petruccio denies his wife food and prevents her
from going to sleep, intending to tame her by
making her life miserable. Bianca, meanwhile,
has chosen Lucentio – to the feigned disgust of
Tranio and the disappointment of Hortensio (who
marries a widow instead). However, Lucentio still
lacks funds, so Tranio is forced to trick a passing
Merchant into imitating Vincentio, Lucentio's
father, in front of Baptista. All goes well, and
Lucentio and Bianca rush off to marry. Petruccio
continues to break Katherine's will, forbidding her
to contradict anything he says.

ACT 5 When the real Vincentio turns up at
Lucentio's lodgings, he is amazed to meet the
impostor Merchant; and when Tranio emerges
in Lucentio's clothes, Vincentio fears the worst.
He is about to be arrested when Lucentio (and
wife) appear; begging forgiveness, he reveals
everything. All are reconciled, but Petruccio has
one final test in store for Katherine: at a banquet
that evening he wagers Lucentio and Hortensio
that his wife is more obedient than theirs.

its subtitle "The only way to make a Bad WIFE Good: At least, To keep her quiet" suggests that its function is less to entertain than to advise. Another, entitled "A Merry Jest of a Shrewd and Curst Wife Lapped in Morel's Skin for Her Good Behaviour", is different again – it relates the tale of a defiant wife whose husband makes her behave by beating her violently, then wrapping her in the skin of a dead horse.

Though the "shrew" of Shakespeare's title, Katherine, is described by Hortensio as "intolerable curst, / And shrewd and froward so beyond all measure" (1.2.88–9), she is not made to suffer anything quite so violent as her counterparts in ballads and broadside tales. But in telling the story of Katherine's taming by Petruccio, a man who freely admits that he wants to marry her simply for her money, Shakespeare deploys motifs his audiences would be easily and deeply familiar with. Some of them would probably approve of the hero's actions, which include forcing her into marriage, then denying her food and sleep. Newly arrived in Padua, Petruccio's servant Grumio promises that if Katherine attempts to resist, his master will not be sparing. "An she stand him but a little," he chortles,

> he will throw a figure in her face and so disfigure her with it that she shall
> have no more eyes to see withal than a cat.
>
> [1.2.111–4]

While the subplot of *The Taming of the Shrew*, the wooing of Bianca by several disguised suitors, has an unimpeachably literary source – ultimately from Ariosto's *I Suppositi* via George Gascoigne's witty comedy *Supposes* – the main "taming" story comes straight out of low culture, and it has the brutality to prove it.

Right supremacy

It's tempting to dismiss the play as a simple-minded farce – not as physically fierce as ballads such as the "Merry Jest", but every bit as emotionally violent. Those who do dismiss it point to scenes such as the one in which Petruccio's servants nervously describe the fearful behaviour of their master towards his new wife. Petruccio, says his man Curtis, is at that moment

> In her chamber,
> Making a sermon of continency to her,
> And rails, and swears, and rates, that she, poor soul,
> Knows not which way to stand, to look, to speak,
> And sits as one new risen from a dream.
>
> [4.1.168–72]

There is a bitter kind of irony here: Petruccio rails on "continency" (restraint or self-control) while he himself indulges in unrestrained aggression.

Petruccio's harsh words follow hard upon Katherine's very public humiliation at her wedding, where Petruccio offends everyone by turning up late, wearing hideously inappropriate clothing and boasting that his new wife is his to order around as he wishes. Nor is Katherine's re-education complete at this. Confronted by her habit of talking back and refusing to stay quiet, Petruccio decides to repossess nothing less than her language. Over the course of several scenes he forces her to follow his every verbal whim. Near the end of the play, he takes advantage of the daytime to impose a bizarre demonstration, exclaiming, "how bright and goodly shines the moon!":

PETRUCCIO
I say it is the moon.
KATHERINE
I know it is the moon.
PETRUCCIO
Nay then you lie, it is the blessèd sun.
KATHERINE
Then God be blessed, it is the blessèd sun,
But sun it is not when you say it is not,
And the moon changes even as your mind.
What you will have it named, even that it is,
And so it shall still be for Katherine.

[4.5.16–23]

By imposing this doublethink, Petruccio bends to his will not just his wife, but the physical universe they share. It's little surprise to note that, when describing his relationship to his wife in this phase of the play, Petruccio reaches most often for the language of hawking – Katherine is, he claims, a "falcon" trained to respond to "her keeper's call" (4.1.180), and he is even prepared to literalize the metaphor by starving her into obedience. Katherine is simply not permitted to contradict the view of the world he demands – and it's interesting to note in passing that his diminutive nickname for her, "Kate" (she herself sticks resolutely to "Katherine"), is one many critics of the play unthinkingly use.

Katherine's trials climax in the closing scene of the play, when Petruccio, Lucentio and Hortensio set up a wager to see which of their wives is the most compliant. Both Hortensio's newly found Widow and Lucentio's Bianca fail to appear when called, but the apparently reformed Katherine dutifully turns up on cue, wins her husband the bet and so confirms what he calls his "aweful rule and right supremacy" (5.2.114). And Katherine goes still further, lecturing the other two wives on the obedience a true wife should display. Describing "a woman moved [angered]" as "like a fountain troubled, / Muddy, ill-seeming, thick, bereft of beauty," she piously continues,

Thy husband is thy lord, thy life, thy keeper,
Thy head, thy sovereign, one that cares for thee,
And for thy maintenance commits his body
To painful labour both by sea and land,
To watch the night in storms, the day in cold,
Whilst thou liest warm at home, secure and safe,
And craves no other tribute at thy hands

Lily Brayton was a formidable Katherine at the start of the twentieth century, playing the role opposite her husband Oscar Asche.

But love, fair looks, and true obedience,
Too little payment for so great a debt.

[5.2.147–59]

Whether she is actually pious, still less sincere, is a moot point, and some actresses have deliberately played up the irony of this speech – perhaps noting that Lucentio, exclaiming in the very last line of the play that "'Tis a wonder ... she will be tamed

403

> *Depending on how we take her tone, Kate is seriously tamed, is ironic at*
> *Petruchio's expense, has learned comradeship and harmonious co-existence, or*
> *will remain a shrew till her death.*
>
> Lisa Jardine, *Still Harping On Daughters* (1983)

so" (5.2.194), apparently finds her conversion difficult to credit. Other actors and directors have seen the darker side of Katherine's "taming", having her mumble this final speech like a victim of torture, her spirit visibly crushed. After all, she has been told to call the "sun" the "moon", and then on a whim the "sun" again; she has been forced to accept a rigidly hierarchical view of marriage – one in which it is only natural that a woman obey her husband. It is genuinely difficult, nearly impossible, to come to a firm view on this issue: as a glance at its stage history testifies, the *Shrew* can be played in countless different – and entirely contradictory – ways, perhaps more so than any other Shakespeare play.

And less agonizing possibilities certainly exist, all of them tenable. Some have seen Katherine's journey away from shrewishness as a good thing: a humanizing process that reflects her sincere love for Petruccio, and perhaps too his love for her – a genuine relationship shared by two damaged and difficult people. Others prefer to interpret Shakespeare's indulgence in extremes as a kind of knowing nod-and-wink to audiences (or readers) who know better – *Shrew* as satire. Others go even further, arguing that what Katherine actually declares in this infamous speech is more radical than we might suspect. As she goes on, they point out, her words become more intriguing:

> Such duty as the subject owes the prince,
> Even such a woman oweth to her husband,
> And when she is forward, peevish, sullen, sour,
> And not obedient to his honest will,
> What is she but a foul contending rebel,
> And graceless traitor to her loving lord?
>
> [5.2.159–65]

It is not too much to say that there is an implicit contract in action here: the wife is bound to obey, but her husband must be "loving" and "honest" too; Katherine may be publicly toeing the line, but she does so in her own terms – and it's notable that of the other couples competing in this final scene, only Katherine and Petruccio seem, albeit roughly, to have got the measure of each other. As some critics have commented, what Katherine actually declares to the other wives is on a par with arguments put forward by sixteenth-century Protestant reformers, who held that marriage should be a union of like-minded belief, not domestic tyranny. An early response to the play, John Fletcher's seventeenth-century sequel *The Woman's Prize*, makes something of the same point: the newly widowed Petruccio decides to marry again but is put through a sequence of trials by his new wife – all in the name of making him reject male supremacy and learn the importance of marital harmony.

Dreamed till now

But perhaps there is a danger of becoming too serious about this. The *Shrew* is a comedy – notionally at least – and many of its most troublesome moments for readers (particularly twenty-first-century readers) come across in performance as rather more tongue-in-cheek. In the event, most of the violence presented by Shakespeare's play is rhetorical – a battle of wit and spirit which, though it is hard-fought, is often very funny. Responding to Katherine's incessant put-downs at their first ever meeting, Petruccio chuckles, "Come, come, you wasp, i'faith you are too angry":

KATHERINE   If I be waspish, best beware my sting.
PETRUCCIO   My remedy is then to pluck it out.
KATHERINE   Ay, if the fool could find it where it lies.
PETRUCCIO   Who knows not where the wasp does wear his sting? In his tail.
KATHERINE   In his tongue.
PETRUCCIO   Whose tongue?
KATHERINE   Yours, if you talk of tales, and so farewell.
PETRUCCIO   What, with my tongue in your tail?

[2.1.209–16]

Beneath the sharp-edged banter a flirtatious current seems to ripple, and though Petruccio here succeeds in silencing Katherine with an obscene pun (she goes on to slap him, infuriated), he will by no means have the last word. Shakespeare hints that sexual attraction can blossom from this kind of banter, and indeed in later comedies including *As You Like It* and *Much Ado* (whose own Beatrice and Benedick owe much to Katherine and Petruccio) it forms a witty component of the wooing process, enabling characters to sound each other out without risking their feelings. Katherine, though she later chooses to conform, can more than hold her own; and in that way she is not that different from a Rosalind or a Beatrice.

One of the things that makes it difficult to take the story of Katherine's reformation entirely at face value, however, is that she doesn't actually exist – and nor do any of the characters in the so-called "taming" story. Though few productions acknowledge the fact, the main subject of the *Shrew* (indeed, the subject of its title and what most people mean when they talk about the play) is actually a play-within-a-play. Its characters are presented as fictions, acted by hired players in front of a beggar called Christopher Sly. At the farcical opening of the action, Sly crashes in halfway through a fight with the hostess of an inn, and collapses drunkenly on stage. While he sleeps, a nameless Lord happens by and decides to play a bizarre trick on the slumbering beggar – arranging for Sly to wake up and be persuaded that he is wealthy beyond his wildest dreams. The Lord's servants are primed by their master to fool Sly, and when he awakens everything goes to plan. Astonished to hear that he is not a beggar after all, but a great lord, Sly is thrown into bewildered confusion. "Am I a lord?" he cries,

Or do I dream? Or have I dreamed till now?
I do not sleep. I see, I hear, I speak.
I smell sweet savours, and I feel soft things.

Upon my life, I am a lord indeed,
And not a tinker, nor Christopher Sly.

[INDUCTION, 2.67–72]

Shakespeare is fond of experimenting with ever-receding dramatic perspectives: *Love's Labour's Lost* ends with a farcical pageant of the "Nine Worthies", while its successor among the lyrical comedies, *A Midsummer Night's Dream*, closes with the play put on by the hard-handed artisans. Still later, *Hamlet* binds its own play-within-the-play tightly within the main plot when its princely protagonist makes his father-in-law confess to murder by having a reconstruction of the deed performed in front of him. But the *Shrew* is the only drama of Shakespeare's in which he allows the interior action to become dominant, in which the story of Katherine and Bianca and their suitors takes over.

It takes over so completely, in fact, that once Sly settles down to watch it – and, after nodding off in boredom, wishes anxiously that "would 'twere done" (1.1.252) – he disappears from the text. This really is baffling: a competing version of the play, the anonymous quarto published in 1594 as *The Taming of a Shrew*, finishes with a conclusion in which Sly is risen from his drunken slumbers to exclaim that "thou has waked me out of the best dream / That ever I had in my life" – an ending that at least matches up with the beginning. But the Folio *Shrew*, apparently Shakespeare's text, has nothing of the kind. There are any number of reasons why this might be so, ranging all the way from typesetting cock-up to difficulties with staging – even a conscious artistic decision. The Oxford single-volume edition tidies things up by printing "Additional passages" from *A Shrew*, but Shakespeare's play as it stands is reluctant to conform in this way.

The effect is intriguingly open-ended, and in the end it makes *The Taming of the Shrew* even harder to pin down. Even if Sly's disappearance from the text is a simple error, the very fact that the taming plot is presented as a fit entertainment for a bewildered drunkard makes it hard to take in the soberest of terms. And while *A Shrew* ends with Sly declaring that he has learnt his lesson, that "I know now how to tame a shrew", Shakespeare's play conspicuously avoids making any such easy judgement. Near the end of the action, Petruccio admits that his approach might not in fact be the most effective. "This is a way to kill a wife with kindness," he muses,

And thus I'll curb her headstrong humour.
He that knows better how to tame a shrew,
Now let him speak.

[4.1.195–7]

Trusting to his actors and the dramatic moment, Shakespeare dares his audiences to make up their own minds.

Stage history and adaptations

The Taming of the Shrew has been widely performed, in one form or another, until relatively recently – when anxieties about its message have made many directors think twice. Although we know little about the play's early stage history, it appears to have remained in repertoire for at least two decades, and translations-cum-adaptations of the script seem to have been toured by English actors across northern Europe. But doubts about the ending seem to have existed even then: **John Fletcher** (Shakespeare's collaborator on *Henry VIII* and *The Two Noble Kinsmen*) wrote a sequel entitled *The Woman's Prize, or The Tamer Tamed* (see p.637), which gives the recently widowed Petruccio a new wife, Maria, who proves to be more of a handful than Katherine ever was. In its attempt to prove that husbands "should not reign as Tyrants o'er their wives", it even has Maria revenging herself by persuading Petruccio that he is dying of the plague. Shakespeare's play and this were performed within a few days of each other at court in 1633.

Fletcher's eagerness to tamper would prove prophetic. In 1667 it was seized on by **John Lacy**, who cut the last act and played Grumio himself – or, rather, "Sauney", Lacy's name for the character. This offshoot was published in 1698 as *Sauney the Scot: or, The Taming of the Shrew*. Though it was still being performed thirty years later, en route it had been challenged by three other pretenders. In 1716, two farces entitled *The Cobbler of Preston* appeared, one by **Charles Johnson**, the other by **Christopher Bullock** – both were loose adaptations emphasizing Sly. These were followed in 1735 by **James Worldale**'s *A Cure for a Scold*, a two-act "ballad-farce" that again revised the ending and erased most of Shakespeare's text. But the most influential spin-off would be one of **David Garrick**'s successful Shakespeare redactions, *Catharine and Petruchio*, which was first aired in 1754. Despite claiming that not "one drop" of Shakespeare was lost, Garrick in fact cut plenty – including Sly and the subplot – and removed much of the play's moral ambiguity. Garrick also initiated a venerable tradition by issuing himself as Petruchio with a whip (the prop would remain obligatory well into the twentieth century). **Hannah Pritchard** played Catharine in the debut production before **Henry Woodward** revived it a few years later with himself in the lead; **Kitty Clive** later took over from Mrs Pritchard. That great theatrical dynasty, the Kembles, kept Garrick's version in the family as well as on the stage: **Sarah Siddons** played Catharine to her brother, **John Philip Kemble**, as Petruchio in 1788, who was still playing the role opposite his wife in 1810. Both **Henry Irving** (playing Petruchio to **Ellen Terry**'s Catharine in 1867) and **Herbert Beerbohm Tree** (1867) used Garrick. *Catharine and Petruchio* was also a success in America: it was premiered in Philadelphia in 1766, and was frequently revived through the nineteenth century, being particularly popular with husband-and-wife troupes who toured the frontiers of the burgeoning nation.

But all was not lost for Shakespeare. In 1844, **J.R. Planché** mounted a production of the uncut *Taming of the Shrew* in the "Elizabethan manner", with just two sets and simple placards announcing locations. Clearly impressed by Planché's resurrection, **Samuel Phelps** played Sly in his own production at Sadler's Wells in 1856, but was less happy with the final act, which he edited heavily. The American **Augustin Daly** also made cuts in his 1887 version of Shakespeare's play, but with conspicuously more success than Phelps: it ran for over 120 nights, **Ada Rehan** being especially acclaimed for a Katherine who was, in Rehan's own words, "high-strung and nervous, though at the same time strong and thoroughly healthy".

Petruccio (Jasper Britton) and Katherine (Alexandra Gilbreath) often saw the funny side of the *Shrew* in Gregory Doran's energetic RSC production (2003).

One of the first twentieth-century productions to create a real impact was that mounted by husband-and-wife team **Oscar Asche** and **Lily Brayton** at the Adelphi Theatre, London in 1904 and again at the Aldwych in 1908. Asche's approach was direct and irreverent: "we played it as a jolly farce and it always went with a scream" was his own rather dubious description. From then on, the *Shrew* entered one of its most popular periods, being performed at Stratford-upon-Avon every year for nearly a decade – in the view of one 1930s reviewer, in reaction to the militant activities of "vote-hungry viragoes" at the time. But it took the mischievous modern-dress production by **Barry Jackson** in 1928 – complete with a Ford car, fashionable tailoring and press photographers – to remind audiences of the play's up-to-the-minute resonances. Jackson's version had the young **Laurence Olivier** supporting, though **Ralph Richardson** stole the show as a cheeky cockney Tranio.

Katherine was a popular apprentice part throughout the twentieth century: she was played by **Sybil Thorndike** (1927), **Edith Evans** (1937), **Siân Phillips** (1960), **Vanessa Redgrave** (1961), **Janet Suzman** (1967) and **Joan Plowright** (1972). It was also **John Barton**'s first production at the RSC in 1960, with **Peter O'Toole** as Petruccio and **Peggy Ashcroft** as Katherine – who relented gracefully, prompting Kenneth Tynan to declare that her performance "almost prompts one to regret the triumph of the suffragette movement". **Clifford Williams**'s version of 1973 also played it safe by dissolving any hint of gender struggle and concentrating on the play's farcical qualities. **Michael Bodganov**'s RSC staging of five years later made an apposite contrast: its first audiences were terrified by what appeared to be a football hooligan breaking into the auditorium, only for him to turn into **Jonathan Pryce**'s Sly (and later his controlling Petruccio). Viewing the play as a "male wish-fulfilment dream of revenge upon women", Bogdanov had **Paola Dionisotti**'s Katherine utter her final sermon in unreal, ironic tones – to the discomfort of many critics. Both **Barry Kyle**'s exuberant 1982 production (with **Sinéad Cusack** and **Alun Armstrong**) and **Jonathan Miller**'s chillier version of 1987 (with **Fiona Shaw**) created less divided reactions. By common consent, though, one of the most interesting productions of the last thirty years was that directed by **Di Trevis** for the RSC regional tour in 1985, which underlined connections between the subjection of women and that of the *Shrew*'s players in a shabby Victorian setting.

Phyllida Lloyd's Globe staging from 2003 gained points for novelty as well as ensemble acting with an all-female company headed by **Janet McTeer** as Petruccio (a wonderful caricature of swaggering machismo) and **Kathryn Hunter** as Katherine. Also offering fresh insights was **Gregory Doran** at the RSC a few months later, who smartly set the *Shrew* alongside Fletcher's *The Tamer Tamed* (see p.637) with the same cast. The thought-provoking conclusion of Shakespeare's play was, as **Alexandra Gilbreath**'s Katherine and **Jasper Britton**'s Petruccio reminded us, not quite the end. Less enjoyable was **Edward Hall**'s all-male Propeller version at the Old Vic in 2007, which reintroduced the Christopher Sly scenes, but played the main action as a coarse, brutal romp, embodied by **Simon Scardifield**'s sullen, hairy-chested Kate and **Tony Bell**'s toddlerish Tranio.

Toby Frow's version at Shakespeare's Globe in 2010 began (like Bogdanov at the RSC decades before) with Sly bursting drunkenly from the audience and clambering up on to the stage; after that point it became distinctly more dignified, with the same actor, **Simon Paisley Day**, offering a surprisingly debonair Petruccio to **Samantha Spiro**'s flashing-eyed Katherine. Revived two years later as part of the World Shakespeare Festival by the Pakistani troupe **Theatre Wallay**, the comedy (translated into Urdu by a three-woman team) became somewhat more ironic, with Katherine as unquestioned heroine and the play's men depicted as callow adventurers. Across in North America, *Shrew*'s popularity has diminished owing to anxieties about its gender politics, but is still sometimes revived. It got a rockabilly remake at the **Oregon Shakespeare Festival** in 2013, and festivals in Utah and Stratford, Ontario both unveiled new stagings in 2015. **Chris Abraham** at Stratford aimed to make the audience complicit in the goings-on on stage; Utah's was more straightforward, a Renaissance-style production that emphasized the play's broad comedy.

The *Shrew* has also inspired a number of spin-offs – some political, many less so. In India it was adapted a number of times in the nineteenth century, notably in a Gujarati version from 1852 staged in **Surat** whose title translates literally as "A Bad European Woman Brought to Her Senses". It was also popular in China, where it was one of the first stories to be translated into Mandarin early in the twentieth century, and where it has been staged a number of times – including a touring version from the **Shanghai Dramatic Arts Centre** in 2010, which despite its 1930s setting was every bit as chastening as the Elizabethan original. Back in Europe, **Charles Marowitz**'s savage adaptation of 1973, *The Shrew*, depicted **Thelma Holt**'s Katherine being cruelly bru- talized and culminated in her anal rape.

Less contentiously, the play has also inspired numerous composers: at least six musical versions exist, the most famous of which is probably **Hermann Goetz**'s opera of 1874. Better known is **Cole Porter**'s enduringly popular musical, *Kiss Me Kate* (1948), which sets its action around a staging of Shakespeare's play. But it is in the cinema that the *Shrew* has been best-served: at least eight films have been made in countries as far afield as Italy, Denmark and India. **D.W. Griffith**'s 1908 silent version (shot in just two days) is now too fragile to be shown, and **Sam Taylor**'s adaptation of 1929, with **Mary Pickford** and **Douglas Fairbanks** – the first Shakespeare "talkie" – is rarely screened. More familiar is the film by **Franco Zeffirelli**, starring a couple renowned for offstage fireworks on a par with the script – **Richard Burton** and **Elizabeth Taylor**. The play's most recent cinematic incarnation is perhaps the most unexpected: the teen-movie spin-off *10 Things I Hate About You* (1999), which translates elements of the play to a high school in present-day Seattle. On TV, the BBC production (1980) was directed by **Jonathan Miller**, who took the unusual step of casting comedian **John Cleese** as Petruccio opposite **Sarah Badel**'s Katherine.

SCREEN

The Taming of the Shrew

E. Taylor, R. Burton, M. York; Franco Zeffirelli (dir.)
USA/Italy, 1966 > Sony DVD

A mere pit stop for the Burton–Taylor bandwagon it may be, but Zeffirelli's carnivalesque *Shrew* offers many of the attractions – and flaws – of his *Romeo and Juliet*. Large chunks of the text are nowhere to be seen (our playwright gets a minor writing credit), and all the limelight illuminates the lead couple – cast for their off-screen shenanigans as much as their on-screen talent. That said, Taylor brings some depth to Katherine and Burton could do Petruccio in his sleep (the drink presumably helps). Theirs are big, physical performances, matching Zeffirelli's operatic style: the screen is cluttered and the comedy, little of it Shakespeare's, is broadly done. While this makes for amenable cinema, the film's view of women leaves a bitter taste in the mouth: Katherine's metamorphosis from fierce-eyed vixen to placid wifey is uncomfortably managed, and her simpering sister (Natasha Pyne) is hardly an admirable role model.

10 Things I Hate About You

J. Stiles, H. Ledger, L. Oleynik; Gil Junger (dir.) USA, 1999 > Touchstone DVD

Spin-off, schminoff. *10 Things I Hate About You* stands as an interesting alternative to Taylor and Burton. In Karen McCullah Lutz and Kirsten Smith's script, the narrative of the play – troublesome woman brought into line, social norms reinforced – becomes its modern analogue, the teen romance movie. The tomboyish Kat (Julia Stiles) hates men because she's had bad experiences, while oddball newcomer Patrick Verona (Heath Ledger) is happy to be bribed into dating her. There's no attempt to keep the text, but cute Shakespearian references are smuggled in nonetheless. One girl is so smitten with the Bard that she has his picture in her locker; the "10 things" of the title concerns a homework exercise to rewrite Sonnet 141 ("In faith, I do not love thee with mine eyes") in modern language. Kat's rendition of her poem proves the film's emotional climax, but, unsurprisingly, there's no attempt to replicate a sermon on obedience: that would be so, like, not cool. Not as satisfying as Luhrmann's *Romeo + Juliet*, but fun nonetheless.

The Taming of the Shrew

S. Spiro, S.P. Day, S. MacRae; Toby Frow (dir.) UK, 2012 > Shakespeare's Globe DVD

After the ruffs and farthingales more usually associated with the Globe, the first minutes of this video come as a surprise: a drunken yob clad in the England football strip ranting in the yard, lager can in hand. Still more surprising when he clambers on stage past the hey-nonny-nonnying musicians and urinates on a pillar. It is, of course, a set-up: the players get started and the yob (Simon Paisley Day) transforms from Christopher Sly to a roustabout Petruccio. Toby Frow's production, filmed in front of a live audience, and after this prologue straightforwardly Elizabethan, isn't always this subtle, but it's full of zany energy, even if the comedy is often so broad it's hard to take anything seriously. Samantha Spiro roars and rasps as a spitfire Katherine but perhaps misses the character's inner sadness, and her relationship with Day remains more or less on one note. When the pair do fall in love, it's hard to see exactly why – other than the script demanding it.

AUDIO

The Taming of the Shrew
G. McSorley, R. Mitchell, J. Ford; Melanie Harris (dir.)
UK, 2000 > BBC ◉ ☁

Few stage producers opt to retain the Christopher Sly scenes, so it's not entirely surprising to see the same policy in this BBC version – though it is a little disappointing, as they are certainly easier to get around without the problems of visual staging. Melanie Harris's decision was swayed by her determination to "get more immediately to the heart of the play", though, and this she undeniably does. Ruth Mitchell as Katherine brings plenty of energetic unruliness to the role without making her unsympathetic. Gerard McSorley could perhaps do with a touch more brio as Petruccio, but his Irish burr has plenty of appeal and the scenes between the couple are nicely done. Perhaps this production's best recommendation is that it refuses to moralize: despite the callowness of the men's bar-room barracking, Katherine speaks her famous speech with fervour and leaves them in stunned silence – a victory of sorts.

EDITIONS

Arden Shakespeare (third edition)
Barbara Hodgdon; 2010 > Bloomsbury

Barbara Hodgdon has written about the *Shrew* for decades, and her extended engagement with a play that many critics still avoid pays off in this thoughtful and detailed edition. She deals with the Sly epilogue upfront – wittily describing it as "ripped, one might say, from the Warwickshire police report" – and moves briskly on to the broad context of "taming" narratives that were a staple of folk literature, lingering on their violent aspects but also pointing out that Shakespeare's play doesn't quite share them (though it's a shame she doesn't tackle the contradictory character of Katherine more directly). Performance history fills an impressive

sixty pages, and *The Taming of a Shrew* is printed in full facsimile at the back.

SOME CRITICISM

Clamorous Voices
Carol Rutter; 1985 > Routledge [o/p]

Clamorous Voices corrals five British actresses (Sinéad Cusack, Paola Dionisotti, Fiona Shaw, Juliet Stevenson, Harriet Walter), who among them played nearly all Shakespeare's heroines in landmark RSC productions dating from the mid-1970s onwards. The format is that of a round-table discussion – for the *Shrew* the speakers are Dionisotti, Shaw and Cusack – held together by comments from theatre historian Carol Rutter. While the views of the panel sometimes stray into luvviedom, their contrasting thoughts on the *Shrew* in particular (often sharpened by their own feminism and conflict with male directors) bespeak not just the problems the play presents but the different solutions they found. As theatrical history this book is enlightening enough, but *Clamorous Voices* offers a great deal more: the kind of close reading and interpretive sanity on offer here should make academics green with envy.

Shakespeare and the Nature of Women
Juliet Dusinberre; rev. 2003 > Macmillan

Sometimes described as the first major feminist work on Shakespeare, Dusinberre's study (originally published in 1975) makes a revolutionary claim for its subject – as feminist *avant la lettre*. Her reading of the *Shrew* makes much of Shakespeare's rejection of convention and sees him siding with radical elements in Elizabethan society, particularly Puritan marriage reformers, in their bid to equalize the balance between the sexes. This progressive approach is not without its problems – her claim that Katherine's sermon is actually a libertarian document seems hard to sustain – but it's sympathetic and engaging.

The Tempest

I f *The Tempest* is one of Shakespeare's most cherished works, it can also seem his most abstruse, even unfathomable. It recounts the story of an exiled Italian ruler who inflicts revenge upon his usurpers by calling up a magical "tempest" that shipwrecks them on his island; a story apparently of the playwright's own devising, and which has tempted any number of competing analyses. Some have seen the plot as an allegory of divine learning, as the mage Prospero uses his celestial powers to conquer evil and restore the forces of good. Others have been engaged by *The Tempest*'s dissident colonial themes, its depiction of an island colonized by white Europeans who enslave its indigenous inhabitants. Still others interpret it as the veteran playwright's bewitching swansong, Prospero "drowning" his book at the play's end just as Shakespeare turned his back on the stage and entered retirement soon afterwards. Though that last theory is sentimental – no one knows for sure when Shakespeare retired, and there would be three more co-written plays to come – it is true that *The Tempest* dwells more than any other work upon the vivid transformations wrought by dramatic poetry and spectacle, and some of its most astonishing moments harness Prospero's magic to the illusions conjured in the theatre. Though all the author's plays are dazzling in their way, *The Tempest* holds a special charge for audiences and readers alike.

DATE > The first recorded performance of *The Tempest*, quite probably the last play that Shakespeare wrote on his own, was at court in November 1611. It's likely to have been written earlier that year, or possibly late in 1610 – around the same time as *The Winter's Tale*.

SOURCES > *The Tempest*'s plot seems to be original – uniquely among Shakespeare's plays – but may have been inspired by reports of an actual shipwreck in 1610 (see below). It quotes Michel de Montaigne's essay "Of the Cannibals" (translated by John Florio in 1605), and the influence of Virgil's *Aeneid* and Ovid's *Metamorphoses* has also been identified.

TEXTS > The 1623 Folio version provides the only authoritative text, and contains unusually detailed stage directions – suggesting that the person who typeset it might have seen the play performed.

Interpreting the play

In 1607, four years into James I's reign, the Virginia Company, dedicated to investing in the recently colonized Americas, founded a settlement they called "Jamestown" in his honour. Two years later, the Company attempted its boldest venture yet, the settlement of no fewer than four hundred colonists, shipped across the Atlantic during the summer of 1609. Disaster struck: caught in a hurricane, the fleet was broken up, one

MAJOR CHARACTERS & SYNOPSIS

Prospero, the deposed Duke of Milan, living in banishment on an island
Miranda, Prospero's daughter
Antonio, Prospero's brother, the usurping Duke of Milan
Alonso, King of Naples
Sebastian, Alonso's brother
Ferdinand, Alonso's son
Gonzalo, an honest old counsellor from Naples
Adrian and **Francisco**, lords
Ariel, a spirit attending on Prospero
Caliban, a wild "savage" enslaved by Prospero
Trinculo, Alonso's jester
Stephano, Alonso's drunken butler
Master of a ship and his **sailors**

ACT 1 Antonio, Alonso and his son Ferdinand are travelling by sea when their boat is caught in a terrible storm. Shipwrecked, they and their party are cast ashore on a strange and apparently deserted island – wholly unaware that the tempest has been caused by the magic of Prospero, their former duke and now the island's ruler. Responding to questions from his daughter Miranda, Prospero relates how they arrived on the island twelve years earlier: as Duke of Milan he had handed some duties to his brother Antonio who, gaining a taste for power, usurped Prospero with the aid of Alonso, King of Naples. Cast adrift in a boat, Prospero and the young Miranda eventually landed on the island, where they took as servants the spirit Ariel and the savage Caliban – whose island it originally was. When Ariel reveals to Prospero that his enemies are exactly where he wants them, the magician initiates the next stage of his plan. Enticing Ferdinand to them by magic, he encourages him and Miranda to fall in love, while pretending to disapprove.

ACT 2 Alonso and his companions are searching for Ferdinand. Ariel, who remains invisible, sends everyone to sleep except Antonio and Sebastian, Alonso's brother. These two then plot to murder Alonso and the courtier Gonzago, but before they manage it Ariel wakes the others. On another part of the island, Trinculo comes across Caliban, to their mutual shock; when the drunken Stefano arrives, Caliban thinks he must be a god and offers to serve him in the hope of escaping Prospero's control.

ACT 3 Prospero has enslaved Ferdinand and made him carry logs, but the young man does so willingly in order to serve his beloved Miranda. Watched secretly by Prospero, the two pledge to marry each other. Caliban tells Trinculo and Stephano that he is Prospero's slave; he proposes that they murder the magician, and that Stephano marry Miranda and rule in Prospero's stead. When the voice of Ariel interrupts, Caliban and Stephano think that it is Trinculo speaking, and the two men argue. Alonso and his party have given up hope of finding Ferdinand when, to the sound of strange music, spirits materialize in front of them and produce a banquet. Before they can eat, Ariel appears, and makes the banquet vanish before condemning Alonso, Antonio and Sebastian for their part in deposing Prospero.

ACT 4 Prospero admits that the tasks he set Ferdinand were to test his love for Miranda, and he now blesses their marriage with a masque performed by spirits. Suddenly remembering Caliban's plot against his life, Prospero angrily halts the performance and calls Ariel to him. Ariel tells how he has beguiled the would-be murderers into losing their bearings; when they finally arrive at Prospero's cell, Stephano and Trinculo are distracted by Prospero's regal robes before all three are chased away by spirits disguised as hunting dogs.

ACT 5 Ariel reports how the spirits of Alonso and the other Neapolitans have been broken, and Prospero instructs him to release them. Ariel leads the group in by magic, and to their amazement Prospero appears and reveals who he is. Prospero then produces Ferdinand and Miranda, and all are reunited and reconciled. Ariel is guaranteed freedom, Caliban is forgiven and Prospero renounces his magical arts and declares that he will return to Naples as Duke once again.

of the ships was sunk and another, the *Sea Venture*, driven onto the rocky coast of the Bermudas. Soon afterwards news began to filter back to Britain that the *Sea Venture's* human cargo had lived to tell the tale, and in September 1610 a sensational real-life story by one of the survivors, William Strachey, began circulating among London's chattering classes.

Strachey's "True Reportory of the Wreck" breathlessly describes how the passengers and crew encountered a miraculous and exotic island, its seas bursting with fish, its skies filled with strange but luscious birds, its forests teeming with massive wild boars. Unlike their unlucky and ill-prepared compatriots in Jamestown itself (who had been all but wiped out the previous winter by starvation and disease), the Bermudan colonists stayed for nine relatively tranquil months. Two of their members voted to stay behind when the rest set sail for Virginia, and became the uninhabited islands' first permanent settlers.

On November 1, 1611 – just over a year after the "Reportory" reached England – a partial reconstruction of some of those events was performed in front of the same King who had chartered the Virginia Company four years earlier. That play was *The Tempest*. Scholars agree that Shakespeare probably read Strachey's account and others that drew upon the chaotic experiences of the fledgling American colonies, and his subject matter had never been more topical. In what has been called Shakespeare's "American play", a group of Milanese voyagers are shipwrecked by a storm every bit as wild as that experienced by Strachey on the other side of the world. Washed ashore on a mysterious and apparently uninhabited island, they begin to confront the idea that they, too, are colonists – and might be stuck there for the rest of their lives. "Had I plantation of this isle, my lord," begins the counsellor Gonzalo,

> All things in common nature should produce
> Without sweat or endeavour. Treason, felony,
> Sword, pike, knife, gun, or need of any engine,
> Would I not have; but nature should bring forth
> Of its own kind all foison, all abundance,
> To feed my innocent people.

> [2.1.165–70]

Gonzalo's fantasy echoes those of many seventeenth-century Europeans, eager to read about the apparently infinite liberties promised by the New World. Though Shakespeare's reliance on colonial literature for *The Tempest* is difficult to pin down, his dramatization of colonial desires – the utopian wish to return to an older, simpler life, unfettered by the advances of civilization and nourished by all-giving Nature – shows just how seductive those dreams can be.

This thing of darkness

But Gonzalo and his aristocratic companions do not, in fact, have the place to themselves. Elsewhere on the island, two other survivors from the wreck, the jester Trinculo and the drunken butler Stefano, are making their own groping – and alcohol-hazed –

"Mercy on us! We split, we split!" The opening scene of *The Tempest* as depicted by engraver Elisha Kirkall for Nicholas Rowe's 1709 edition of Shakespeare, with Ariel hovering over the main-mast and Prospero directing the action from his island.

Rough magic

So powerful that it keeps the cast of *The Tempest* utterly in thrall – so powerful, in fact, that it dominates the experience of watching the play – Prospero's "so potent art" (5.1.50), his skill at magic, has long been a source of fascination. In placing a magician at the centre of his drama, Shakespeare wasn't doing anything particularly unusual: medieval and early Tudor plays often employed sorcerer-like figures, mostly evil, but these were succeeded in the Elizabethan era by more complex creations. Marlowe's **Doctor Faustus** (c. 1588), in which a scientist conjures up the devil and agrees to trade his soul for divine knowledge, is now the most famous, but other examples include Robert Greene's comedy **Friar Bacon and Friar Bungay** (c. 1594), which retells the life of medieval philosopher Roger Bacon with lashings of lurid necromancy, and Ben Jonson's **The Alchemist**, a satirical tale concerning a con man who uses "magic" to make a fast buck, which was performed by Shakespeare's company the year before *The Tempest*.

All these plays warn of the dangers of meddling in magic: its potential for evil, its power to pervert. Shakespeare often presents witchcraft in this light, notably in *1 Henry VI* and *Macbeth*. Not quite so in *The Tempest*, however, where Prospero's "Art" (the Folio script capitalizes it throughout) has often been seen as a benign force, perhaps like the "secret art" of the physician Cerimon in *Pericles*, which awakens the heroine Thaisa from a deathlike slumber. Both have been interpreted as so-called "white magic", which in the Renaissance became linked to Neoplatonic thought – a philosophical movement that sought to transcend earthly things and touch the divine, and which found in the rediscovered texts of Plato and his followers a model for mystical and spiritual intellectual exploration. German Neoplatonist **Cornelius Agrippa** (1486–1535) authored a survey entitled *De Occulta Philosophia* ("Of Occult Philosophy") that defended magic as being on the side of the angels. Later in the sixteenth century, the English mage **John Dee** (1527–1608) expounded what sounds strikingly like Prospero's "secret studies", describing how the contemplative mind should "deal speculatively in his own Art, and by good means mount above the clouds and stars". Dee first gained a reputation for sorcery at Cambridge, where his ultra-realistic stage effects for a performance of Arisophanes's *Peace* scandalized audiences, and later became astrologer to Queen Elizabeth. As well as being credited with the victory over the Armada in 1588 (he is supposed to have cursed the Spanish fleet), the most famous occultist of his age has also been interpreted as Shakespeare's original for Prospero.

But where Dee protested to hostile commentators that these powers were used – like Cerimon's – simply to cure, Prospero's motives are more complex. Though he claims that his "prosperous" government of the island is better than that of the "damned witch" Sycorax, the previous ruler, Prospero nevertheless keeps her son Caliban enslaved, torturing him with delusions, cramps and biting aches – symptoms that have been compared to **ergotism**, a form of rye-grain poisoning caused by fungus and commonplace in early modern Europe. Like Sycorax, too, Prospero forces Ariel to serve him, despite the spirit's repeated appeals for liberty. And the main role for Prospero's magic in *The Tempest* is to enact revenge on his usurping brother Antonio, first raising the storm that seems to wreck his ship, then pursuing him across the island with a series of hallucinatory visions. As interest in the play's colonial dimensions has grown, Prospero and his magic have come to seem exploitative as well as violent, and his hunger for absolute power on the island has been compared to that of the Stuart monarchs (James I dabbled in witchcraft and had a taste for Prospero-like masques). And if the ideal ruler should become expert in natural sciences, as philosopher **Francis Bacon** argued, Prospero is at best an ambiguous role-model: neglecting his Milanese dukedom for contemplative study, he was banished and left to lord it over a scantly populated island.

Perhaps that is why Prospero ultimately renounces his "Art", "drowning" his book and breaking his magical staff before returning to Milan – a decision that has puzzled those who have tried to present him as a Neoplatonist philosopher renouncing earthly cares. At the play's end Prospero heads not into retreat, but back to the daily grind – another reason why we should beware of reading *The Tempest* as Shakespeare's retirement note. The metatheatrical "revels" of this great and experimental play may be ended, "melted into air, into thin air" (4.1.148–50), but for playwright as much as for Prospero there was still a great deal of work to be done.

explorations of their new environment. Trinculo is first on the scene, and espies what he initially assumes to be a "fish", then "an islander that hath lately suffered by a thunderbolt" (2.2.35–6). After a fair amount of comic ado (in which Trinculo clambers in under the islander's coat, making Stefano believe that he is looking at a creature with "four legs"), the two Italians recognize each other and confront the "scurvy monster", who kisses Stefano's foot and promises to serve them both. "I prithee," the monster cries, "let me bring thee where crabs grow,"

> And I with my long nails will dig thee pig-nuts,
> Show thee a jay's nest, and instruct thee how
> To snare the nimble marmoset. I'll bring thee
> To clust'ring filberts, and sometimes I'll get thee
> Young seamews from the rock.
>
> [2.2.166–71]

This is Caliban, a "savage and deformed slave" (as the First Folio's dramatis personae expresses it) whose very name – a near-anagram of "cannibal" – identifies him as something far outside most Europeans' experience. The riches he offers, too, are wild and exotic, the dramatic equivalent of those that William Strachey described on Bermuda. But whereas Strachey and his companions had to unlock the island's assets for themselves, Caliban promises to do it all.

The scene is obviously meant to resemble those enacted in real life by colonists who found that the world they thought of as "new" in fact belonged to other people, with all the horrendous consequences that invited (not least the smallpox virus, introduced by European colonists, whose devastating effects on indigenous communities on the East Coast of America were recorded by English settlers). But Shakespeare's replay is satirical: here the wannabe colonists are from the dregs of society, their offerings alcoholic, their ambitions simply to get what they can out of Caliban (perhaps by shipping him to England and showing him off for money, as Trinculo speculates). The tragic farce of the encounter is captured by Trinculo: "A most ridiculous monster," he sniggers, "to make a wonder of a poor drunkard" (2.2.164–5).

Shakespeare was well acquainted with writing that expressed discomfort about the colonial enterprises of Europeans (he culled Gonzalo's dreamy speech about "plantation" from an essay by the French sage Michel de Montaigne, in which

Montaigne argues that the native inhabitants of what is now Brazil are not "savage" or "barbarous"), and pushes the parallel further in the all-powerful figure of Prospero, the mysterious magician who seized control of the island after being deposed from office in Milan. Encamped there with his young daughter Miranda, Prospero rules the place with an iron grip, enslaving and torturing Caliban and forcing the spirit Ariel to do his bidding. Caliban feels the pain of imprisonment bitterly, particularly as what was once a place of wonder is now a place of pain:

> The isle is full of noises,
> Sounds, and sweet airs, that give delight and hurt not.
> Sometimes a thousand twangling instruments
> Will hum about mine ears, and sometime voices
> That if I then had waked after long sleep
> Will make me sleep again; and then in dreaming
> The clouds methought would open and show riches
> Ready to drop upon me, that when I waked
> I cried to dream again.

[3.2.138–46]

In this heartbreaking and unexpectedly beautiful speech, "dreaming" becomes a kind of solace. Caliban is a collection of contradictions, far more complex than the innocent "noble savage" imagined by neoclassical philosophers such as Voltaire and Rousseau – he is cheerfully unrepentant about his attempt to rape Miranda, for instance – but coming into contact with "civilization" has only made things worse for him, even as it attempted to mould him to its needs. "You taught me language," he snarls at Prospero, "and my profit on't / Is I know how to curse" (1.2.365–6). Perhaps it is no surprise that Caliban, the character in *The Tempest* who most often steals the show, has sometimes been taken as its tragic hero.

No mortal business

But the play is not in Caliban's hands, and his one attempt to control its outcome – his plot, with the ineffective aid of Stefano and Trinculo, to topple Prospero and win the island back for himself – is doomed to failure. Prospero exerts absolute control, able through his "potent art" to summon up everything from a tempest to a pack of snarling dogs in order to baffle and torment the shipwrecked royal party. Though the comedy is, famously, the only one of Shakespeare's to fit the so-called "unities" of neoclassical drama (the law, supposedly derived from Aristotle, that a play should occupy real-time and a single location), Prospero's story began twelve years earlier, and a world away. As he tells Miranda:

> I, thus neglecting worldly ends, all dedicated
> To closeness and the bettering of my mind
> With that which but by being so retired
> O'er-priced all popular rate, in my false brother

Awaked an evil nature; and my trust,
Like a good parent, did beget of him
A falsehood, in its contrary as great
As my trust was, which had indeed no limit,
A confidence sans bound.

[1.2.89–97]

KEY SOURCE > Montaigne

It seems odd to describe works that no one is certain Shakespeare ever read as a "key source", but the writings of French sage **Michel de Montaigne** (1533–92) reach deep inside the thought-world of the mature plays – so much so that even if Shakespeare never actually encountered them, they would still illuminate much of his work.

Montaigne was born a generation before Shakespeare, a French aristocrat who, after practising law, dabbled genteelly in politics, initially at court, then later as the mayor of Bordeaux. Suffering increasingly from depression in his late 30s, he retired to his luxuriously appointed estate near the Dordogne, whose library he decorated with maxims from the great classical thinkers, and turned to writing. He called the texts he produced *essais*, used to signify a medium-sized piece of prose on a particular topic. In the various volumes of *Essais* published from 1580 onwards, and revised obsessively until his death, Montaigne ambled through a bewildering array of areas: from the nature of fear to the realities of earthly fame; from suggestions on the education of schoolchildren to speculation about why humans wear clothes; from ideas about Virgil to theories on modern-day cannibals. The essay form was effectively imitated in England by Shakespeare's great contemporary **Francis Bacon**, who published his first collection of English essays in 1597, and whose brother Anthony was a friend of Montaigne.

Translated more literally, as "experiment", or "trial", however, the word *essai* hints at the really startling thing about Montaigne's big project: his unsparing attempt to assess his own personality through prose. Montaigne's chief subject is himself, whether it's striving to order his thoughts on religion ("On prayer"), wondering at the power of his senses ("On smells"), or mentioning that he doesn't care much for salad, but rather likes melons ("On experience"). The essay "On the power of the imagination" is typically untypical: it begins in the elevated world of philosophy but moves swiftly, via several earthy stories, to ponder why penises are such erratic organs – Montaigne also confessing, with characteristic candour, that his own is not much to write home about. As the author put it in an introductory note to the first book of the *Essais*, translated into English by **John Florio** in 1603, "I desire therein to be delineated in mine own genuine, simple and ordinary fashion, without contention, art or study; for it is myself I portray."

This talent for erudite, questioning self-exposure makes many people think of Hamlet, the Shakespearian character that Montaigne most obviously resembles. But unless Shakespeare knew French well, or had access to an unpublished version of Florio's translation, the influence is difficult to trace – as it is in *King Lear*, whose sense of a universe larger than its gods might be borrowed from Montaigne's long essay on the subject, "An apology for Raymond Sebonde", but could just as easily be the playwright's own. In the end only two specific debts to Montaigne have so far been located, both in *The Tempest* (see p.412).

A more interesting way to understand Shakespeare's relationship to Montaigne, perhaps, is to think of them as fellow Renaissance travellers – men who put their formidable learning and curiosity about the human condition into practice not as politicians, diplomats or clergymen, but as writers.

"Rapt" in secret studies in Milan, Prospero fails to realize that his position there is under threat. This "evil" transformation in Antonio begins what Prospero calls his "sea sorrow": his romance-like ejection from power and flight to the island with the infant Miranda. But Prospero's magic enables him to set up his own poetic justices: Antonio and his retinue have fallen into his lap, and the fearsome sea storm he raises brings them once again under his control. In this sense, *The Tempest* is a story of revenge: Prospero shipwrecks his brother on the island in order to get his own back (quite literally, given that he succeeds in regaining the Milanese throne).

It is also a story that uses the full resources of Shakespeare's dramatic skill, to such an extent that Prospero has frequently been interpreted as a kind of stand-in for the poet himself, the magician's art and the playwright's merging into one. The similarities are arresting. The tempest that begins the play – and which gives it its name – would have been strikingly presented in its first performances at the candlelit Blackfriars theatre. *The Tempest's* unusually elaborate stage directions call first of all for "a tempestuous noise of thunder and lightning" (created either by offstage fireworks or perhaps cannon-balls rolled around a drum), and the fierceness of the storm, and the peril the ship is in, is emphasized by the "Mariners" who appear on stage soaked to the skin. All is hyper-realistic. And yet the whole thing, as we soon find out, is doubly make-believe – it is Prospero's play-within-a-play, and, as he comforts Miranda, for all the shipwrecking horror, "there's no harm done" (1.1.15). Though the sailors' clothes have been stained by salt water, the courtiers arrive on shore magically dry; "on their sustaining garments not a blemish," Ariel eagerly explains, "but fresher than before" (1.2.218–20). Gonzalo is quite right to urge Alonso to be "merry"; "You have cause," he says, "so have we all, of joy,"

> for our escape
> Is much beyond our loss. Our hint of woe
> Is common; every day some sailor's wife,
> The masters of some merchant, and the merchant,
> Have just our theme of woe. But for the miracle,
> I mean our preservation, few in millions
> Can speak like us.

> [2.1.1–8]

Amid the grinding, daily "woe" of life on the sea, their survival does seem extraordinary; it is still more so because Prospero plays the same tricks on the baffled Milanese as Shakespeare does on his audiences. They are spared, even as they are hoodwinked, by the miracles of theatre.

For, though Prospero brings the party to his island to achieve some kind of revenge – which he exacts by taunting them with spirits, culminating in Ariel's appearance as a scourging harpy to make them "mad" (3.3.58) – his treatment of them is ultimately beneficent. His cruellest trick is to make Alonso think that his son Ferdinand has perished in the shipwreck. Yet far from Sebastian's morbid certainty that Ferdinand cannot be "undrowned", undrowned is precisely what he is: a fact that Prospero reveals in the most impressive sleight of hand in the play, the sudden appearance of Miranda and Ferdinand innocently playing chess while the visitors to the island stand goggle-eyed at the front.

Despite his initial fierceness at Ferdinand's interest in Miranda, Prospero in fact encourages the young couple to fall in love, a redemption which, enshrined in their marriage, reaches out to involve nearly everyone in the play. It is the kind of strange metamorphosis captured in Ariel's haunting song "Full fathom five":

> Full fathom five thy father lies.
>   Of his bones are coral made;
> Those are pearls that were his eyes;
>   Nothing of him that doth fade
> But doth suffer a sea-change
> Into something rich and strange.

[1.2.399–404]

The words remind a puzzled Ferdinand of his "drowned father", little knowing that their reunion will be as "rich and strange" as the lyrics predict. "Full fathom five" is a song about transformation, about finding new life where none seemed possible. It is, as Ferdinand says, "no mortal business" (1.2.409).

With the lovers married and all reconciled, Prospero swears to "abjure" his "rough magic" and travel back to Milan – a promise of retirement that has been seen to foreshadow Shakespeare's own. But the transformations Prospero talks of are not unmingled in their happiness. "Be cheerful, sir," he tells Ferdinand after the magical masque celebrating the wedding, "our revels now are ended."

>   These our actors,
>   As I foretold you, were all spirits, and
>   Are melted into air, into thin air;
>   And like the baseless fabric of this vision,
>   The cloud-capped towers, the gorgeous palaces,
>   The solemn temples, the great globe itself,
>   Yea, all which it inherit, shall dissolve;
>   And, like this insubstantial pageant faded,
>   Leave not a rack behind.

[4.1.147–56]

"We are such stuff / As dreams are made on," he continues, "and our little life / Is rounded with a sleep" (4.1.156–8). If this is Shakespeare announcing retirement, even looking towards death – and another three plays, though co-written, lay in front of

In Caliban it is that Shakespeare has risen, I think, to the very height of creative power, and, by making what is absolutely unnatural thoroughly natural and consistent, has accomplished the impossible.

Horace Howard Furness, in the New Variorum *Tempest* (1892)

him – the tone is not indulgent. Leaving the magic of the stage, the "great globe itself", will be a painful and irrecoverable loss.

Stage history and adaptations

It's possible that *The Tempest* was specially written for the **Blackfriars theatre**, where Shakespeare's company began performing in 1609, but it was likely that it was also performed at the Globe during the summer months. In any case the only surviving text, that of the 1623 Folio, has unusually detailed stage directions and requires a great deal of music. It was also acted several times at **court**: once for James I in 1611, again during the celebrations for his daughter's wedding in 1613.

However spectacular those early performances, however, they would be trumped after the Restoration with the appearance of **William Davenant** and **John Dryden**'s adaptation *The Tempest, or the Enchanted Island* (1667), which featured impressive stage machinery but less than a third of the original text. Davenant introduced several new characters – among them "Hippolito", an innocent male counterpart to Miranda – and emphasized the piece's comedy (to the delight of Pepys, who saw it several times). Capitalizing on its runaway popularity, **Thomas Shadwell** mounted an "operatic" version of the same in 1674, with music mostly by **Matthew Locke**, which was so successful that remnants were still being performed in the nineteenth century.

Making the most of *The Tempest*'s popularity, **David Garrick** launched another operatic version in 1756, though he returned to Shakespeare's text the following year, albeit with cuts, and acted it frequently afterwards. **Thomas Sheridan** kept Garrick's text when he took over Drury Lane, but **John Philip Kemble** reinstated some of Davenant's changes in his productions of 1789, 1806 and 1815. During this period Prospero was presented as unwaveringly noble, at first by **Robert Bensley**, then the "majestic" Kemble himself, but even so **John Emery** was allowed to present a sympathetic, near-tragic Caliban.

The most influential production of the nineteenth century would prove to be **William Charles Macready**'s at Covent Garden in 1838, which finally restored most of Shakespeare's script (if not his opening scene, replaced by a "grand panoramic spectacle" depicting the shipwreck); **George Bennett**'s heart-rending Caliban appeared alongside the radiant Miranda of **Helen Faucit** and **Priscilla Horton**'s jaunty Ariel. **Samuel Phelps**'s productions at Sadler's Wells from the 1840s were also praised, the *Times* observing that they offered "the best combination of Shakespeare and scenery", but for sheer ostentation it would be hard to outdo **Charles Kean**'s 1857 staging at the Princess's Theatre. This opened with a storm scene so magnificent that the visiting Hans Christian Andersen was overawed (at least until his host Charles Dickens explained how it worked), and Kean's own "mysterious" Prospero was widely praised.

But in the high Victorian era *The Tempest* became more than ever Caliban's play. **Frank Benson** took on the part during his numerous touring productions in the last decades of the century and later at Stratford, basing an athletic interpretation on chimpanzees he had observed at the zoo and making a habit of appearing on stage with a real fish in his mouth. Also pursuing the theory that Caliban was a Darwinian

Declan Donnellan's 2011 fast-moving Cheek by Jowl production, with a Russian cast, pointed up *The Tempest*'s freshness and experimentalism – memorably concluding in a masque scene that resembled a Soviet peasant opera.

"missing link" was **Herbert Beerbohm Tree**, whose portrayal from 1904 became famous – not least because he expanded it to make the character more appealing, closing the play with a newly "civilized" Caliban waving farewell to the Milanese ships.

By this time **William Poel**'s radical productions with his Elizabethan Stage Society had come and gone, and innovation was all the rage. **Ben Greet**'s performances at the Old Vic from 1915 lasted just two hours and starred **Sybil Thorndike** as Ferdinand; while **John Drinkwater**'s Birmingham Rep production from the same year was designed by **Barry Jackson** and featured **E. Stewart Vinden** as Ariel, the first man in the role for some two centuries. **William Bridges-Adams**, a Poel disciple, put on a 1919 *Tempest* designed to look as it might have done in 1613, and staged it again at Stratford in 1934 with **Neil Porter** as Prospero. Going against a hoary stage tradition that the island's ruler was nothing if not kindly, Porter dared to present him as both irascible and distinctly unpleasant.

The most influential Prospero of the era – perhaps of the century – was **John Gielgud**, who first acted him under **Harcourt Williams** at the Old Vic in 1930 to **Ralph Richardson**'s Caliban. Gielgud, then just 26, dispensed with the flowing robes and beard of yore and instead created a man "rich in … melancholy", according to one witness. In **Peter Brook**'s 1957 production Prospero became an essentially noble figure, returning in triumph to his dukedom in the play's closing moments; whereas for **Peter Hall**, at the National in 1974, Gielgud's interpretation had hardened into brusque aloofness – a reading partly inspired by the Elizabethan magician and natural scientist John Dee (see p.416). **Michael Benthall**'s celebrated 1951 Stratford staging, by contrast, went the other way – initially featuring **Michael Redgrave**'s forceful Prospero, later replacing him with the more approachable **Ralph Richardson** (not to mention a conventionally female Ariel, **Margaret Leighton**, for **Alan Badel**).

If there is a single thread that connected postwar *Tempests*, it was a fresh concern with the play's colonial politics. Unsurprisingly, much of the impetus behind this re-evaluation has come from North America, where Shakespeare's "American play" was performed in New York as early as 1854 by **William Burton**. In 1945 **Canada Lee** was the first black actor to play Caliban, in a New York production directed by **Margaret Webster**, while **Nagel Jackson**'s 1970 staging in Washington had both Ariel and Caliban played by black actors (**Darryl Croxton** and **Henry Baker** respectively) in order to draw parallels with America's slave history. Over in the UK, **Jonathan Miller** directed a fiercely anti-colonialist production at the Mermaid Theatre in London, also in 1970, inflected by the director's reading of Octave Mannoni's *Prospero and Caliban*, a study of the French colonization of Madagascar. Even more illuminating was the Martinique-born **Aimé Césaire**'s rewriting, *Une Tempête* (1969), which posited Caliban as a revolutionary hero. Earnest approaches such as these were intriguingly mirrored in 1990 by **Peter Brook** with a touring multiracial troupe, among whose number were **David Bennent**'s boyish Caliban and **Sotugui Kouyate**'s benevolent Prospero. Nine years earlier, **Giorgio Strehler**'s Milanese version stunned audiences with its theatrical virtuosity – much, one suspects, as Shakespeare would have wanted.

Plurality of approach as well as of casting has, naturally enough, characterized more recent productions of this much-revived play. In just one year, 1988, British audiences were treated to **Peter Hall**'s second NT production, with **Michael Bryant**'s grizzled Prospero; **Declan Donnellan**'s typically playful Cheek by Jowl version; a modern-dress production from **Nicholas Hytner** at the RSC, focused on **John Wood**'s all-too-human Prospero; and a Noh-influenced Japanese version directed by **Yukio Ninagawa**. Ariel finally got his moment under **Sam Mendes** at the RSC in 1993, with **Simon Russell Beale**'s haughty sprite allowed to spit at his master (**Alec McCowen**) after being granted freedom. In **Jude Kelly**'s 1999 West Yorkshire Playhouse production, **Ian McKellen**'s Prospero, wearing a plastic raincoat and a battered hat, attracted comment and some condemnation for his unrepentant grumpiness. In an even more radical approach to the play's interpersonal relationships, the London Globe saw **Vanessa Redgrave** play Prospero in 2000, directed by **Lenka Udovicki** – though, like McKellen, Redgrave gave a pointedly gruff performance.

Derek Jacobi had his turn at imitating Gielgud at the Sheffield Crucible under **Michael Grandage** in 2002 in an actor-led production that nevertheless conjured plenty of theatrical magic, most striking when the ship's billowing sailcloth was sucked into Prospero's book. Although dramatically very different, **Tim Carroll**'s Elizabethan production at the Globe in 2005 also indulged author-hero fantasies by casting outgoing artistic director **Mark Rylance** both as Prospero and his usurping brother,; the magician plotted the action on a chessboard before casting away the pieces in disgust. By contrast, **Rupert Goold**'s eclectic production at the RSC the following year embedded the play in Arctic ice, with **Patrick Stewart**'s cabin-feverish hero lording it over **Mariah Gale**'s brutalized Miranda. Even doomier was **David Farr**'s staging at the same venue in 2012, dominated by **Jonathan Slinger**'s rasping and choleric Prospero.

Altogether more liquid than Goold's production was **Declan Donnellan**'s return to the play with a Russian cast in 2011 (it featured sea-bound video projections and gallons of real water sloshed around the stage), but it was again centred on the torments of **Anya Khalilulina**'s child-of-nature Miranda, visibly horrified by having to part from **Alexander Feklistov**'s tearful Caliban. Bangladesh's **Dhaka Theatre**, staging *The Tempest* in Bangla at the Globe as part of the World Shakespeare Festival, offered carnival and colour in the manner of the traditional *panchali* form, but also subtly emphasized the play's colonial dynamics by presenting **Chandan Chowdhury**'s Caliban and **Rubol Lodi**'s Prospero as cut from the same cloth. By contrast, the version done at the same venue by **Jeremy Herrin** the following year was – despite its Jacobean-ish costumes – an unrepentantly old-fashioned star vehicle, centred on **Roger Allam**'s fatherly magus. Something similar was true at New York's Shakespeare in the Park in summer 2015, with Public Theatre veteran **Sam Waterston** offering a beneficent, somewhat cuddly island ruler in a style long out of fashion.

On screen, *The Tempest* has inspired numerous tributes, many of them somewhat esoteric. The earliest, a filming of the shipwreck from **Herbert Beerbohm Tree**'s touring production, appeared in 1905; while other film adaptations range from the relatively faithful (**Derek Jarman**'s 1979 *Tempest*) to the ostentatious (**Peter Greenaway**'s *Prospero's Books*, 1991) and the wonderfully bizarre (the sci-fi *Forbidden Planet*, directed by **Fred McLeod Wilcox** and released in 1956). The 1979 BBC/Time-Life production was directed by **John Gorrie** and saw **Michael Hordern**'s Prospero opposite **Warren Clarke**'s Caliban. In 2010 **Julie Taymor** followed her well-regarded *Titus* (see p.45) with a version of *The Tempest*, featuring grande dame **Helen Mirren** as a character intriguingly called Prospera.

SCREEN

The Tempest
Percy Stow (dir.) UK, 1908 ❯ on Silent Shakespeare (BFI) DVD ⬇

Though not quite twelve minutes long, this silent *Tempest* from 1908 feels like a veritable odyssey, packing the play's highlights and its backstory into a succession of swift-flowing scenes. Details of the cast have long since disappeared, and although its members share equal screen-time the elfin little girl playing Ariel and an exaggeratedly hirsute Caliban (shown munching on roots, Timon-style) especially catch the eye. It's a charming version, made all the more appealing by its deft mixture of set-based footage and adventurous location shots (Ariel dances around a sun-dappled wood, Ferdinand literally clambers out of the sea), cinematography that comes together in one impressive split-screen shot in which Prospero is shown conjuring a real storm – with waves, pyrotechnics and a flock of real doves for good measure. It's available on the BFI's excellent *Silent*

Shakespeare anthology along with intriguing versions of *Twelfth Night* (see p.478), *Richard III* (see p.385) and *Dream* (see p.316).

Forbidden Planet
W. Pidgeon, A. Francis, L. Nielsen; Fred McLeod Wilcox (dir.) USA, 1956 ❯ Warner DVD ⬇

Esoteric plotting, an improbable love story and sometimes impenetrable dialogue? That's just the original. But this cult re-rendering of Shakespeare's final solo riff has many of those features too, translating Prospero's potent art into twenty-third-century sci-fi wizardry. We're beamed down to the green-skied planet of Altair-4, where a scientific colony has long since lost contact with Earth. A military team headed by Commander John J. Adams (Leslie Nielsen) heads into space to locate the problem, and ends up encountering the mysterious Dr Morbius (Walter Pidgeon) and his daughter Altaria (Anne Francis) – not to mention their dutiful servant, Robby the Robot. The film's borrowings from *The Tempest* pretty much halt there, though in its influential special effects

Forbidden Planet has surprisingly intimate affinities with the theatrical innovations of the play. What keeps it earthbound, unfortunately, is the script, which largely hobbles the cast (a pre-*Naked Gun* Nielsen rarely has a smirk off his lips). And in its lurching final twist, the film ditches any connections with Shakespeare and invests rather too much in 1950s American paranoia. Entertaining nonetheless.

The Tempest
H. Williams, T. Wilcox, K. Johnson; Derek Jarman (dir.) UK, 1979 > Second Sight / Viacom DVD ⬇

The Tempest may well be the most conspicuously unified play in the canon – all its action takes place in one location during the space of one day – but watching this idiosyncratic adaptation you'd hardly guess. Jarman hacks and rearranges the text, reflowing its narrative into a series of brief and disjunctive scenes, while the "island" is a series of firelit interiors in which rockinghorses, baroque furniture and straw liberally mingle. Though in a strange kind of way this emphasizes the play's bespoke originality, the film's successes are fragmentary – a series of vignettes rather than a satisfying composition. The mix of different performing styles adds to the oddness: poet Heathcote Williams' youngish but gruff Prospero seems strangely disengaged, but Toyah Wilcox's Miranda fizzes with quizzical energy, while the blind performance artist Jack Birkett very nearly steals the show as Caliban. Jarman reserves his greatest coup for a wonderfully camp finale, which succeeds in trumping even Shakespeare's magical masques with the help of elderly jazz diva Elisabeth Welch and a chorus of wheeling sailors. Also available in HD Blu-ray format.

Prospero's Books
J. Gielgud, I. Pasco, M. Rylance; Peter Greenaway (dir.) UK, 1991 > Allied Artists DVD

Prospero's Books takes Shakespeare's mage quite literally at his word. Greenaway's central conceit is familiar enough, equating the Bard and Prospero, but his way of broaching it is characteristically esoteric. The "books" of the title are those that tempted Shakespeare's rightful Duke away from the day job, and Greenaway imagines them to cover the panoply of Renaissance knowledge – from cosmology to pornography. These volumes structure the film, producing a series of meditations on aspects of *The Tempest* rather than a fully fleshed-out narrative. It's as much a paean to John Gielgud as anything else, and until the very end his spry but sober Prospero speaks all the play's lines as well as solemnly inscribing them in the last book of all, *The Tempest* itself. With most of the cast able to communicate only through body language, this often feels like a piece of performance art, and alongside Gielgud and a very young Mark Rylance its other star is

dancer Michael Clark's stunning Caliban. As an idea the film is attractive, but *Prospero's Books* ultimately feels hollow: not quite as smart as it thinks it is.

The Tempest
H. Mirren, B. Whishaw, R. Brand; Julie Taymor (dir.) USA, 2010 > Disney / Touchstone DVD ⬇

After scoring a surprise hit with her startling *Titus* (see p.451), Julie Taymor's return to Shakespeare seems at first glance to be cut from similarly eclectic cloth: Prospero is "Prospera", played by Helen Mirren; British comedian-cum-rabble-rouser Russell Brand plays the jester; and the action is relocated to Hawaii. On closer inspection, though, this *Tempest* is unexpectedly traditional, certainly compared to almost every other cinematic version. Nearly all the play is here, from shipwreck to final reconciliation, and a well-regarded Anglo-American cast puts in fine work, led by Mirren, more clear-eyed and thoughtful than the testy old tyrants who have become the norm. Making Prospero a mother rather than a father doesn't otherwise achieve a tremendous amount, and in some ways the best performance on offer is Ben Whishaw's waif-like Ariel, who despite being digitally manipulated to within an inch of his life is full of sharp and sceptical curiosity. In truth, the gee-whizz CGI seems somewhat wasted – shots of storming seas and the volcanic Hawaiian landscape do more than enough, and the Elizabethan-steampunk costumes by designer Sandy Powell are gorgeous. A note of advice: if you download the film you're spared the cringeworthy sight of Brand dressed as Shakespeare, being interviewed by Taymor, on the DVD/Blu-ray extras.

AUDIO

The Tempest
P. Madoc, N. Wadia, C. Rhys; David Hunter (dir.) UK, 2001 > BBC ◉ ⬇

Listening to recordings of *The Tempest* can be an odd experience: on audio the isle "full of noises" has a unique power to charm – and also a unique habit of going awry at the hands of over-enthusastic sound engineers. This version sits firmly in the first category (despite some odd silvery tinklings around Nina Wadia's giggly Ariel), and makes for excellent listening. Philip Madoc's rumbling Prospero has a voice to die for, as do many of this predominantly Welsh cast, who impart a rugged sonority to Shakespeare's late verse (particularly Joshua Richards's Caliban). The audio mix lends real intimacy to this production, although interpretatively it's hardly radical: Madoc stresses the inscrutable but benign aspects of the character, Wadia's Ariel is eager to please and the play's feel-good conclusion has reconciliation aplenty.

The Tempest
I. McKellen, S. Handy, E. Fox; John Tydeman (dir.)
UK, 2005 > Naxos ◉ ☁

A burst of thunder, and we're in – on the groaning deck of a soon-to-be-sunk ship, creaking and groaning amid the waves. The sound of this Naxos *Tempest* is realistic and vibrant, and magic is most often signalled by Renaissance music rather than gee-whiz sound effects (though there is some nifty digital fading accompanying Scott Handy's cooing Ariel). Pulling the levers is Ian McKellen's Prospero, though it's the quiet subtleties of his performance that impress most. Some might wish for a more dynamic approach to the miraculous poetry of the part – McKellen's growling "our revels now are ended" is almost thrown away – but it's effectively done, and suits this restrained and pensive production. Emilia Fox sounds a little prim as Miranda, though Benedict Cumberbatch makes a winningly earnest Ferdinand; and the colonial dimensions of the play are registered here by the dignified Caliban of Ben Onwukwe.

EDITIONS

Oxford Shakespeare
Stephen Orgel (ed.); 1987 > Oxford UP

Stephen Orgel's edition isn't the newest on offer (David Lindley's New Cambridge was updated in 2013 and is also recommended), but it is one of the best. Orgel is a distinguished writer and critic, particularly expert on the lavish seventeenth-century royal entertainments known as masques (many of his essays on these and other topics are collected in *The Authentic Shakespeare*, published in 2002). Given that *The Tempest*'s virtuosic staging contains elements of masque, Orgel is well placed to offer insights into its theatrical practice, but he is equally informative on a range of topics, ranging from the play's involvement with the New World to its use of history. No fewer than six appendices – one devoted to Montaigne – add formidable range to this edition.

SOME CRITICISM

Shakespeare's Caliban
**Alden T. Vaughan & Virginia Mason Vaughan; 1993
> Cambridge UP**

In the days when *The Tempest* was widely understood as a serene retirement note from Shakespeare, critics still found time to investigate the play's most puzzling and troubling component – Caliban. *Shakespeare's Caliban: A cultural history* joins (and describes) a long tradition of engagement with the "savage and deformed slave" of the Folio's job description. It was assembled in partnership by the Vaughans, literary critics both, who also edit the fine Arden 3 edition of the play (2003). Their work is predictably engaging, following Caliban's tracks from the historical contexts that most likely spawned him to recent concerns with the play's colonial ramifications. It also looks at his history on stage and screen as well as in visual art. In that sense *Shakespeare's Caliban* is partly a history of changing cultural taste, but the Vaughans' wider observation – that Caliban has been "endlessly transformed yet always recognizable" – underlines the extent to which his mutating shape reveals as much about us as about Shakespeare's play.

The Tempest and its Travels
Peter Hulme & William Sherman (eds.); 2000 >
Reaktion / Pennsylvania UP

It doesn't have much truck with traditionalist approaches to *The Tempest*, but in every other way this collection goes in for plurality: it includes poems and excerpts from theatrical reworkings of the play along with a welcome focus on visual art (there's a fine piece by David Dabydeen on Hogarth's well-known painting of Act One, scene two, showing Prospero, Miranda and Caliban). Many of the essays here touch on colonial and post-colonial topics located in the New World (somewhat de rigueur these days), but others go off in more unusual, if less exotic, directions – among them Robin Kirkpatrick's terrific article on the Italian background to the play and Donna Hamilton's piece on English versions of that great travelling epic, Virgil's *Aeneid*. An illuminating anthology. David Bevington and Peter Holland's collection *The Tempest: Shakespeare in Performance* (2008) also features excellent material about the play's life on stage.

Timon of Athens

T he fable of the big-spending man who uses, then loses, all his wealth – and with it his wits, then everything he owns – is probably as old as money itself, but Shakespeare's variation on the theme ranks as one of his most neglected works. Clearly indebted to the morality plays of medieval England, with all their stern warnings about the dangers of avarice, *Timon of Athens* also has certain affinities with Marlowe's *Doctor Faustus* in its portrayal of an (anti)hero who risks it all for supreme glory – in Faustus's case by trading his soul for knowledge of the divine, in Timon's by losing his vast Athenian fortune via a lifestyle of sensationally hedonistic proportions. Other contexts for *Timon* could be offered: some have suggested that the play is a philosophical debate between epicurianism and cynicism; others have seen in its bitter, hard-bitten tone shades of *King Lear*, which may have been written soon beforehand (Coleridge suggested it was "a *Lear* of domestic life"). But where *Faustus* and *Lear* are tragic masterpieces, *Timon of Athens* is less certain in tone, and more puzzling. Possibly co-written, the play's place in the canon is still earnestly debated, and despite its relative popularity in China – a legacy of communism – audiences in the west have had little opportunity to decide for themselves: it remains one of Shakespeare's least popular works, still infrequently revived.

DATE ➤ Conjectural: some critics argue for a date prior to *King Lear* (c. 1605); others put *Timon* close to *Antony and Cleopatra* and *Coriolanus* (1606–08); still others regard it as one of Shakespeare's very last plays – if it is, indeed, fully by him. Thomas Middleton, among others, has been suggested as a collaborator.

SOURCES ➤ As with the Roman plays, Plutarch's *Lives* in Thomas North's 1579 translation is a key source – enough to feature word-for-word in places. An anonymous play, *Timon* (c. 1602), seems to have had some influence, as does William Painter's collection of tales, *The Palace of Pleasure* (1566), the basis for numerous other works by Shakespeare.

TEXTS ➤ *Timon* first appeared in print in the 1623 Folio (F1) – seemingly in the place where *Troilus and Cressida* was originally meant to go.

Interpreting the play

The sixteenth-century essayist and philosopher Michel de Montaigne, observing that "what we hate we take to heart", chose Timon of Athens as an example of the kind of man who becomes so possessed by hatred of the world that he flees it. Timon's predicament – in Shakespeare's play he is driven to madness by his own insane generosity and the stinginess of his friends – has a tragic ring, but there is also something bitterly comic about his story. Forced into poverty, Timon digs for roots but, to his rage, unearths gold coins; abandoning the city, he becomes a hermit who has to deal

MAJOR CHARACTERS & SYNOPSIS

Lord Timon of Athens
Lords and Senators of Athens
Timon's false friends: **Lucius, Lucullus, Sempronius** and **Ventidius**
Alcibiades, an Athenian soldier
Apemantus, an ill-tempered philosopher
Servants of Timon's various creditors
Flavius, Timon's steward (head servant)
Timon's other servants: **Flaminius, Lucilius** and **Servilius**
Phrynia and **Timandra**, prostitutes with Alcibiades
Thieves
A **Poet**, a **Painter**, a **Jeweller** and a **Merchant**, all in Timon's pay
An **Old Athenian**
A **Fool**

ACT 1 Timon's immense wealth – and, more importantly, his generosity – are talked of throughout Athens, and artists and tradesmen queue up to gain his favour. Though the Poet has written a fable warning his patron that Fortune is fickle, Timon accepts his work, and that of all the others, without blinking, pausing only to pay his friend Ventidius's bail and to give his servant Lucilius some money so that he can marry his wealthy sweetheart. Timon has even invited the churlish philosopher Apemantus to a great banquet for his fawning friends. Apemantus hurls insults at the assembled guests and is particularly incensed when Timon insists on giving expensive gifts to all and sundry. But all is not as it seems. The fact that Timon is heavily in debt is known to one man alone – his steward Flavius.

ACT 2 Timon's creditors are getting restless and send their servants to request that he pay his debts. Flavius is attempting to stall them when Timon appears and demands to know what is going on. Flavius informs him that he has squandered his estate by his extravagance and that there is nothing left to pay off even half of what he owes. But Timon is undaunted, confident that his friends will help him out.

ACT 3 One by one Timon's so-called friends refuse to assist him, all citing the feeblest of excuses. As the servants of Timon's creditors pursue their claims, Timon enters enraged, but instead of paying them invites their masters to dinner one last time. His guests assemble (thinking that Timon's good fortune is restored), but when the meal is served it turns out to be nothing but warm water, which Timon throws at them as he rails against their falsity. Meanwhile the soldier Alcibiades has been banished from Athens for pleading for one of his men, who is under sentence of death for manslaughter. Alcibiades storms out, swearing to have his revenge on the city.

ACT 4 Though his servants stay loyal to him, Timon is now insane with anger; he curses the city and its inhabitants, and departs to live in the woods. While digging for roots in the forest, he discovers gold, but still remains implacable in his hatred – even when Alcibiades appears with two whores and offers to help him. Timon gives gold to Alcibiades for his campaign against Athens, and also to the whores, encouraging them to spread disease among the citizens. Timon is also visited by Apemantus, who insists that his misanthropy is just another kind of pride. Only the visit of Flavius touches his humanity, but Timon dismisses even him.

ACT 5 The Poet and Painter head to the forest in the hope of payment, but Timon drives them away. By this time Alcibiades and his forces are threatening Athens itself, and two Senators, accompanied by Flavius, hasten to Timon in the hope that he can help. But Timon, dreaming only of death, is unmoved, and proclaims that he could not care less if the city is destroyed. As Alcibiades enters Athens, the senators plead with him to spare the innocent, and he agrees to punish only his enemies and those of Timon. As the gates of the city are opened to him, news arrives that Timon has died, leaving an epitaph that curses his enemies and exhorts all others to pass by and ignore the gravestone in front of them.

with an unending stream of greedy visitors. Indeed, Montaigne describes Timon while discussing another philosophical paradox – whether one should weep over mankind's tragic situation; or, better still, simply laugh at the futility of it all.

Timon of Athens treads a similarly wild territory to *King Lear*, a play to which it has often been compared (and with which it is often dated) ever since Samuel Taylor Coleridge suggested that it was a kind of "after vibration" to that great tragedy. Both have heroes who descend into insanity in response to the unkindness of others, yet are themselves tragically culpable; both, too, expose the painful fact that, when madness arrives, there is nothing noble whatsoever about it. With its own hero who is unable to adjust to his place in society, *Coriolanus* resembles *Timon* too; but perhaps its closest Shakespearian cousin is the playwright's earliest tragedy, *Titus Andronicus*, which counterpoises comic and tragic themes with similarly unsettling effect. Where Titus's sufferings are so unbearably intense that he bursts out laughing, exclaiming that "I have not another tear to shed", Timon's bitter misanthropy expresses itself in brilliantly scabrous insults against anyone – or anything – who has the misfortune to get in his way. Watching the play, it is difficult to know whether to laugh, cry or rant with him.

Like *Titus*, *Timon*'s status in the canon is still often questioned. Dr Johnson, noting "perplexed, obscure, and probably corrupt" stretches of text, was among the first to query whether it was in fact unfinished, though he approved of its moral value (a quality he felt all too deficient in Shakespeare). By doing so he unleashed two large questions that still dominate critical discussion about the play: if *Timon* is finished; and whether it was co-written, perhaps with the young and brilliant Thomas Middleton. As Karl Klein, a recent editor, goes to some lengths to demonstrate, even with the aid of computerized statistical analysis it is almost impossible to prove that Shakespeare did *not* write significant sections of the play – so the question, for many, remains open. Though for many years critics assumed that the playwright suffered some kind of nervous breakdown during this phase of his career (Shakespeare-as-Timon, it might be said), as *Timon* has been more widely read – if not necessarily more frequently performed – it has been appreciated as a work of powerful drama in its own right.

Without price

Not that the play itself has unmixed thoughts about the status of art. *Timon* begins with a Poet, Painter and various other craftsmen and salesmen, all gathering to pay their respects to the "worthy lord" Timon – and of course to advertise their work in the hope of selling it to him. The importance of patrons like Timon was a fact of life for jobbing playwrights and poets (Shakespeare himself had dedicated two poems, *Venus and Adonis* and *The Rape of Lucrece*, to the Earl of Southampton), but nowhere else in Shakespeare's drama is the paradoxical place of art in the fiscal economy so openly explored. Commending the Painter's piece as "admirable", insisting that "it tutors nature", the Poet explains that his own work will do something similar. It warns Timon to beware of the "great flood of visitors" who cluster around him in the hope of material reward. Should Fortune decide to look the other way, the Poet insists, those crawling admirers will be the first to desert Timon:

When Fortune in her shift and change of mood
Spurns down her late belovèd, all his dependants,
Which laboured after him to the mountain's top
Even on their knees and hands, let him fall down,
Not one accompanying his declining foot.

[1.1.85–9]

Timon's fall, when it does come, will be horribly lonely: his fawning "dependants" will not hesitate to make themselves scarce as soon as trouble arises.

But the Poet's stark warning is not by any means without bias. For one thing, Timon accepts the poem without even reading it, warmly inviting the author to dinner without a second thought. For another, as Apemantus sourly jibes, the Poet is as bad as the rest – poetry, like painting or jewellery, is a flattering art, and the Poet writes in order to earn a living. Furthermore, as the Jeweller observes of the costly gem he presents to Timon,

My lord, 'tis rated
As those which sell would give; but you well know
Things of like value differing in the owners
Are prizèd by their masters.

[1.1.172–5]

Which is to say that everything is relative: value has no value when money is involved. What something is worth depends entirely on what someone else is prepared to pay for it. That goes for poetry too; and Timon is prepared, as with everything else, to pay the highest of prices. One question that the play poses is whether a Jeweller and a Poet can be thought of as the same type of salesman: one selling precious stones, the other pleasing words.

Another problem in *Timon* – in fact Timon's own problem – is that, contrary to the Jeweller's assertion, the hero doesn't "well know" the value of possessions at all. Or rather, his apparently boundless munificence blurs the meanings of value so grossly that it becomes impossible to know the real worth of anything, as gifts of astronomical price exchange hands between his intimates as liberally as if they were free. The word "priceless" does not appear in this play (Shakespeare seems to have invented it, but used it just once, in *The Rape of Lucrece*) but the concept of something that is worth everything and yet nothing hovers over it continually.

At the lavish banquet thrown for his friends at the end of Act One, Timon receives extravagant gifts from his acquaintances – "Four milk-white horses trapped in silver" from Lucius, "two brace of greyhounds" from Lucullus – but no sooner are they delivered than Timon demands that other, costlier, presents be returned to them in compensation. As he declares to Ventidius, "there's none / Can truly say he gives if he receives" (1.2.9–10). In this way the workings of gift exchange become as debased as those of the financial economy: Timon's friends give him things not out of "free love" (as Lucius obsequiously declares) but because they hope they will get something even more valuable in return. A concept familiar to cultures around the globe, for *Timon*'s

"A pretty mocking of the life": a debonair Timon (David Suchet) clutches the fruits of his patronage in Trevor Nunn's 1991 production at the Young Vic.

first audiences this competitive gift-giving may also have played on contemporary anxieties about inflation, a major worry in the debt-prone first years of James I's reign. It may have hit closer to home, too, given that James – who had taken Shakespeare's own company under his wing a few years before *Timon* was written – was accused of reckless spending on himself and his favourites at court, and sold off aristocratic titles to swell his thinning coffers.

As with James, there is a touch of fantasy to Timon's unstoppable largesse, and he is as free with his promises as he is with his possessions. "Methinks I could deal kingdoms to my friends, / And ne'er be weary," (1.2.220–1), he exclaims – and his friends no doubt hope that he will. But his faithful steward Flavius, watching helplessly as his lord dispenses jewels to his dinner guests, knows that Timon's spectacular behaviour is a spectacle. "What will this come to?" he asks,

> He commands us to provide and give great gifts,
> And all out of an empty coffer;
> Nor will he know his purse, or yield me this:

To show him what a beggar his heart is,
Being of no power to make his wishes good.
His promises fly so beyond his state
That what he speaks is all in debt, he owes
For every word.

[1.2.191–9]

"He is so kind," Flavius continues, "he now pays interest for it." Behind the appearance of infinite wealth lurks the spectre of poverty: despite acting as if nothing has a price tag (if you need to know, after all, you can't afford it), Timon is himself without worth, his very "words" indebted to his creditors.

The yellow slave

Despite Flavius's worries, when those creditors begin circling the steward is forced to tell all. Apprising his master about the state of his balance sheet – to Timon's disbelief – Flavius sets in train events that will fill the rest of the play. To his credit, Timon springs into action with impressive resolve, at first demanding that his land be sold (Flavius reveals it has already gone) and then suggesting that his "friends" will of course help him out. But Timon's judgement of character is even less finely attuned than his awareness of his accounts: one by one, over three extraordinary scenes, those friends decline to assist a man who has given them so much. Lucullus has the cheek to claim that Timon had it coming to him, and offers a far tinier amount than Timon had requested; Lucius is free with his promises but, when pushed, pleads poverty; and Sempronius affects to be offended that Timon did not come to him first – and then refuses altogether.

In a seemingly fateful echo of the events of *Titus Andronicus*, Timon decides to get his revenge by inviting them all to dinner. But his approach will be less grisly than his Roman counterpart Titus, who infamously bakes a pie from the sons of his guest of honour. Timon decides to give his former friends food for thought instead: serving them with bowls full of stones and warm water, he shouts, "Uncover, dogs, and lap":

May you a better feast never behold,
You knot of mouth-friends. Smoke and lukewarm water
Is your perfection. This is Timon's last,
Who, stuck and spangled with your flattery,
Washes it off, and sprinkles in your faces
Your reeking villainy.

[3.7.87–92]

It is fitting that events come to a head at dinner, given that at the play's previous feast – one sufficiently opulent to boast a chorus of dancing girls and a boy dressed as Cupid – the play's resident cynic, Apemantus, had exclaimed: "O you gods, what a number of men eats Timon, and he sees 'em not! It grieves me to see so many dip their meat in one man's blood" (1.2.38–40).

As Timon's situation worsens, images of cannibalism begin to echo through the play. Though the bloody events of *Titus* are not repeated, the script continually harks back to that earlier tragedy – and of course to another tragedy narrowly averted, that of Antonio in *The Merchant of Venice*, who nearly loses a pound of his flesh to a creditor bent on revenge. Timon offers his own creditors nothing less than his body in repayment:

TIMON
　Knock me down with 'em, cleave me to the girdle.
LUCIUS'S SERVANT Alas, my lord.
TIMON Cut my heart in sums.
TITUS'S SERVANT Mine fifty talents.
TIMON
　Tell out my blood.
LUCIUS'S SERVANT　　Five thousand crowns, my lord.
TIMON
　Five thousand drops pays that.

                                                                [3.4.88–93]

If comparisons with Antonio seem obvious, for some critics Timon's betrayal by his so-called "friends" is nothing less than an analogue to Christ's betrayal by Judas, especially so given that images of them drinking his blood and eating his body seem to tally with the flesh-and-blood substance of the Christian Eucharist, which itself replays Christ's final supper with his disciples. Other commentators, however, find it difficult to squeeze that much nobility out of the situation – particularly given that Timon's tragic mistake is, strictly speaking, his reluctance to look at his bank statements.

That is not quite how Timon sees it. In his view it is not his own behaviour that is at fault, but money itself – a conclusion that is reinforced by a bitter irony, for when he attempts to dig the ground for roots he somehow turns up gold. Counting it out in his hands, he addresses the "yellow slave" wonderingly:

O, thou sweet king-killer, and dear divorce
'Twixt natural son and sire; thou bright defiler
Of Hymen's purest bed; thou valiant Mars;
Thou ever young, fresh, loved, and delicate wooer,
Whose blush doth thaw the consecrated snow
That lies on Dian's lap; thou visible god,
That sold'rest close impossibilities
And mak'st them kiss, that speak'st with every tongue
To every purpose; O thou touch of hearts:
Think thy slave man rebels, and by thy virtue
Set them into confounding odds, that beasts
May have the world in empire.

                                                                [4.3.384–95]

> *The act of giving is for Timon its own aesthetic thrill; a man who will bestow anything on anybody is as superbly indifferent to particular persons and use values as the most mean-spirited miser ... His munificence is thus rather like money itself, perturbing all particular values in its restless expansiveness.*
>
> Terry Eagleton, *William Shakespeare* (1986)

Karl Marx cited Timon's words in notes for his early *Political Economy and Philosophy* (1844), describing the way in which money acts as "the universal whore ... the alienation of human capacity" in early capitalist societies, but it is tempting to say that in doing so he missed (or chose to ignore) Shakespeare's larger suggestion. Timon diagnoses money as the root of his woes – the alienating effect of money, which perverts good things into evil – when in fact it is his alienation from himself and others that initiates his downfall. Even in pouring scorn on the "sweet king-killer", in fact, Timon is unable to get away from its glistening allure. Blaming money for everything, like giving vast quantities of it away, has no meaning: the no-holds-barred totality of both acts strips them of any significance. As Apemantus declares to Timon on a trip to the forest, "the middle of humanity thou never knewest, but the extremity of both ends" (4.3.302–3).

In fact Timon's attack on money seems to express a kind of terrible poverty of spirit. While Lear's ravings, full of guilt and self-loathing, have a kind of savage grandeur, Timon's are passionate only in their absolute hatred of absolutely everything apart from himself. Handing gold to a group of thieves who come across his den in the forest, he promises to "example you with thievery", but his philosophy is limited in its scope:

> The sun's a thief, and with his great attraction
> Robs the vast sea. The moon's an arrant thief,
> And her pale fire she snatches from the sun.
> The sea's a thief, whose liquid surge resolves
> The moon into salt tears. The earth's a thief,
> That feeds and breeds by a composture stol'n
> From gen'ral excrement.

[4.3.437–44]

We can all understand Timon's feelings, but his problem is that he doesn't learn or change. Longing for death, he fails to repent or acknowledge his mistakes. All that is left is a curse, as his self-written epitaph records: "Here lies a wretched corpse," it begins,

> 'Of wretched soul bereft.
> Seek not my name. A plague consume
> You wicked caitiffs left!
> Here lie I, Timon, who alive
> All living men did hate.
> Pass by and curse thy fill, but pass
> And stay not here thy gait.'

[5.5.71–8]

Laid out like a morality play it may be, but in the end *Timon of Athens* denies there is anything to learn.

Stage history and adaptations

From a twenty-first-century perspective it seems apt that, in theatrical terms at least, *Timon of Athens* disappeared as soon as it was written. There is no evidence that the play was performed in Shakespeare's lifetime – fodder for critics who argue that it was unfinished or somehow suppressed for political reasons. But *As You Like It*, *All's Well*, *Antony and Cleopatra* and others are in a similar position, so it is difficult to draw firm conclusions, just as it's difficult to say whether **Thomas Middleton** was involved in writing it, as some believe, or not.

In any event, the first performance on record is that of an adaptation, **Thomas Shadwell's** *The History of Timon of Athens, the Man-Hater*, which first appeared in 1678 and lasted for the next half-century. Shadwell adjusted the dramatis personae as well as adding a love story, catering for the new fashion for actresses by giving Timon two mistresses. **Thomas Betterton** took the lead with his wife **Mary** as the faithful Evandra, while **Henry Purcell** put together the music. This adaptation was among the most popular of its time, but when in 1771 **David Garrick** wanted to put on the play at Drury Lane with **Spranger Barry** in the lead, he commissioned **Richard Cumberland** to come up with a more modern version, which further moralized Shakespeare's play. This saw twelve performances, but by this stage *Timon* was on the way out: another adaptation from 1786, this time by **Thomas Hull**, achieved only one performance before being pulled. One great might-have-been of the period is a translation by **Catherine the Great** of Russia, left unfinished at her death in 1796.

George Lamb put together a text somewhat resembling Shakespeare's for performance at Drury Lane in 1816, but it was his lead, the mercurial and charismatic **Edmund Kean**, who stole the show: with a script skewed to flatter Timon's better parts, Kean was described by one witness (with a newly fashionable adjective) as "electrical", but he gave a mere seven performances of the play. **Samuel Phelps** put on *Timon* in a more Shakespearian text at Sadler's Wells in 1851, and achieved a surprise hit – he staged it again five years later, this time with an impressive panorama of Athens dominating the set. Even so, this would be the last London production of the century, and *Timon* would not be staged again in Britain until **Frank Benson's** three-act redaction at Stratford in 1892. Benson continued the time-honoured tradition of playing Timon nobly, but the play was not one of his triumphs.

Several stagings were put on in the interwar period, but all of them struggled to find audiences. **Robert Atkins** at the Old Vic (1922) and **William Bridges-Adams** (1928) in Stratford attempted to find new angles, while in 1935, directing for London's Westminster Theatre, **Nugent Monck** simply decided to cut those parts of the text he assumed not to be by Shakespeare. Monck also inserted a ballet scene and employed the young **Benjamin Britten** to follow in Purcell's footsteps and write the music. All these versions would be thrown into relief, however, by **Willard Stoker's** boldly imaginative Birmingham Rep production of 1947, which emphasized the connections with a war-weary city by setting the play in a bomb-damaged Athens and making Timon's cave a crater.

Postwar productions offered contrasting presentation of Timon himself – all the way from **Tyrone Guthrie's** harshly satirical Old Vic version (1952), which painted the hero in an unflattering light, to **Paul Scofield's** sensitive interpretation for **John Schlesinger** at the RSC in 1965. As with Peter Brook's *Lear* a few years previously (see p.234), Schlesinger drew out the Beckettian images in Shakespeare's text, representing a society eating itself alive in corruption. Brook himself directed *Timon* in 1973 at the Bouffes-du-Nord complex, employing a French translation by **Jean-Claude Carrière** for his Parisian audience. Notable for its cheerful breaking of theatrical taboos (not least that of the stage's imaginary "fourth wall"), Brook's was a Marxist-inflected production that has been described as the play's finest twentieth-century incarnation. **Richard Pasco** sensed a defining humanity in Timon when he played him for **Ron Daniels** at Stratford's The Other Place ten years later, but many critics were unimpressed by the Japanese setting of Daniels's production.

Oddly, perhaps, for a play that seems so in touch with latter-day cynicism about conspicuous consumption, productions of *Timon* have remained few and far between. It has had some success in Germany: **Frank Patrick Steckel's** 1990 adaptation, heavily influenced by Brecht, attracted international attention, and the play has also been staged in Neuss (2004) and Munich (2014). There have also been a small number of stagings in North America, notably at Stratford, Ontario in 2004, in a contemporary production directed by **Stephen Oumette** with **Peter Donaldson** as an agonized hero; and at the Blackfriars Playhouse in **Staunton, Virginia** in 2014, a rare opportunity to see the play inside a space resembling one it may well have been written for.

To date only a handful of British productions have made it past the drawing board. **Trevor Nunn's** version at the Young Vic in 1991 looked askance at a newly post-Thatcherite London – money-obsessed and bitterly divided between rich and poor – but attracted criticism for being over-literal, although **David Suchet's** impressively characterized Timon was applauded by many. **Gregory Doran's** 1999 RSC version was perhaps a more rounded achievement, emphasizing *Timon's* links with the homosocial world of James I's court as well as its contemporary resonances; **Michael Pennington** was widely praised for his performance in the title role, as was **Duke Ellington's** musical score, originally composed for **Michael Langham's** 1963 production at Stratford, Ontario.

The English Stratford witnessed another powerful production in 2006–07, as part of the RSC Complete Works festival. **Adrian Jackson** and Cardboard Citizens troupe offered a politically inquisitive, site-specific version of the play, cutting the text and interleaving it with film and scripted testimony from homeless people and refugees. No fewer than three actors played Timon – **Simeon Moore, Agron Biba** and **Mahdad Majdian** – as he descended into madness. **Lucy Bailey** was also radical in her approach in her Globe production of 2008. Inspired by Hitchcock's film *The Birds*, she and designer **William Dudley** placed a net over the top of the theatre from which the actors descended on the defenceless Timon (**Simon Paisley Day**) like so many vultures attacking their prey. Four years later, in 2012, *Timon* received a long-overdue debut at Britain's National Theatre. Drawing attention to the lingering effects of the credit crunch, **Nicholas Hytner** set the action beneath gleaming skyscrapers and towers, with Timon's cave a rubbish-strewn underpass. **Simon Russell Beale** offered a consummately intelligent reading of the hero – oleaginously at ease in the corridors of power, frantic and pathetic out on the streets. Many critics were stunned by the play's power, though not many noticed that the script had been spliced with sections of *Coriolanus*.

Despite live cinema broadcasts of Hytner's production, *Timon* has not seen any success on the silver screen. The only English-language video version to make it into production has been the BBC's, directed by **Jonathan Miller** and with **Jonathan Pryce** in the lead.

SCREEN

Timon of Athens
J. Pryce, J. Welsh, N. Rodway; Jonathan Miller (dir.)
UK, 1981 > BBC DVD

The rarely produced *Timon* is one of those plays the BBC Shakespeare was designed to showcase to posterity, but its making proved unhappy: Michael Bogdanov was initially hired to direct, but his insistence on doing it in modern dress (an option ruled out by series policy) resulted in his ignominious exit. Miller took over the project, and despite those early troubles what emerges is persuasive, especially in the first half of the action – where Timon's spendthrift house is a forest of wealthy ruffs and conspicuous quaffing reminiscent of Dutch militia paintings. There are problems after this, however: Jonathan Pryce plays Timon as sympathetic and wronged throughout, and correspondingly struggles to present the crazed dementia the play demands. Miller's conclusion attempts tragedy, but *Timon* itself is reluctant to go that far.

AUDIO

Timon of Athens
A. Howard, N. Rodway, D. Lewis; Clive Brill (dir.) UK, 1998 > Arkangel ◉ ☁

It's a great shame that Alan Howard never got to play Timon on stage – the full-throttle reading he produces for this audio version makes you wish you had a chance to see him do the part. In contrast to Pryce, this Timon is petulant and misdirected from the off, and while Howard gives little hint of insecurity or eagerness to please, it's a strategy that delivers impressive results in the crazed latter stages of the play. In early scenes Norman Rodway's abrasive and embittered Apemantus forms an unlikely duet with John McAndrew's youthful and anxious steward Flavius in attempting to put on the brakes, but Howard's descent into madness is too much a juggernaut for that. The rest of the cast is mixed – those in supporting roles (and there are a fair few) sound a bit

uninspired and there is some over-enthusiastic chortling in the crowd scenes. That said, the giddy pace of Timon's court forms a vivid contrast with the wilderness outside Athens, and Damian Lewis is commanding and impressive as Alcibiades.

EDITIONS

Oxford Shakespeare
John Jowett (ed.); 2004 > Oxford UP

John Jowett's impressive edition continues the series policy of editorial radicalism, boldly crediting the script to "William Shakespeare and Thomas Middleton". The presentation of the text is meticulously done, but before getting to the script itself you're offered over 120 pages of introductory material. This might seem excessive, but Jowett uses thematic headings – "Misanthropy", "Giving and Sacrifice", "Debt" and so on – to break the flow, so the whole thing feels like a series of insightful and interlinked mini-essays. There's plenty to think about here, not least Jowett's verdict on the involvement of Middleton, based on textual analysis that purports to identify the playwrights' separate linguistic fingerprints. Not that you have to delve into bibliography to connect with the play: Jowett's introduction moves smoothly from critical questions on *Timon* to a decent stage history (which could usefully be extended by Anthony B. Dawson and Gretchen E. Minton's Arden 3 edition, published in 2008). The appendices include a list of Shakespeare's major source materials.

SOME CRITICISM

The Structure of Complex Words
William Empson; 1951 > Penguin / Michigan UP
[o/p]

One of the most brilliantly independent critics in the history of English studies, William Empson remained as cheerfully iconoclastic at the end of his career as at its outset, when he switched from studying maths at

Cambridge to focus on literature. Though the concept behind *Complex Words* is less esoteric than elsewhere (other studies include *Seven Types of Ambiguity* and *Some Versions of Pastoral*), Empson's rich insights do require navigation through tables and equations – his way of notating the relationships between certain words. Algebra-phobes would do best to skip to the tiny but terrific cadenzas on keywords in works from Pope, Milton, Wordsworth and many others. As Empson notes in *Seven Types*, "it is impossible to avoid Shakespeare in these matters", and words such as "honest" in *Othello* and "sense" in *Measure for Measure* bring into focus extended lines of enquiry. But it's the discursive nature of his approach that proves the most fun: his quizzical analysis of the strange permutations experienced by the word "dog" in *Timon* sees the author at his best. Also worth looking at is Empson's *Essays on Shakespeare* (1986), which collects his late work with some earlier pieces.

Timon of Athens
Rolf Soellner; 1979 > Ohio State UP [o/p]

Soellner's *Timon* is one of the only book-length surveys of the play (it is bulked out with various appendices, including a stage history by Gary Jay Williams, useful enough but obviously not up to date) – an interesting contrast with Empson's nine brilliant pages. Subtitling his study "Shakespeare's pessimistic tragedy", Soellner lays his cards decisively on the table, arguing that *Timon* deserves full tragic status and taking issue with those – like Wilson Knight in *The Wheel of Fire* (see p.239) – who defend the play solely by reading it in providential terms. Soellner persuasively insists that, instead of succumbing to such idealizations, we should understand the play as a study in pessimism and materialism. Though it's worth keeping your mind open as you read, Soellner's detail on the philosophical background to the play is engaging and instructive.

Titus Andronicus

B y some distance Shakespeare's most wilfully grisly play, for most of its history *Titus* has been written off as a sensationalistic excursion into the kind of blood-spattered drama that thrived on the 1590s stage – a chamber of horrors more extreme than any other. Commenting on the fact that several of its characters end up baked in a pie, the eighteenth-century editor George Steevens gaily proclaimed that in this play "*justice* and *cookery* go hand in hand", while his twentieth-century equivalent, John Dover Wilson, simply thought the whole thing "a huge joke". But in recent years critics have begun to take *Titus* more seriously: its exposition of the themes of tragic madness and cyclical revenge have been seen to foreshadow the grander achievements of *King Lear* and *Hamlet*; interest in the classical origins of this most fiercely well-read of tragedies has uncovered its inventiveness with source detail; and powerful productions by Peter Brook (1956), Deborah Warner (1988) and Lucy Bailey (2006), among others, have demonstrated that *Titus* has much to offer open-minded – and strong-stomached – audiences.

DATE > *Titus Andronicus* was an instant success when it hit the stage in January 1594, and was probably written shortly before, perhaps in collaboration with the dramatist George Peele.
SOURCES > The play has no direct sources, yet classical motifs predominate: a copy of Ovid's *Metamorphoses* actually appears on stage, and the story of Lucrece (employed in *The Rape of Lucrece*) is another analogue. The success of

Thomas Kyd's *The Spanish Tragedy* (1592) and other Elizabethan blockbusters indicates that blood-and-guts Senecan tragedy was all the rage in the 1590s.
TEXTS > A quarto (Q1) was printed in 1594, and went through two more editions – 1600 (Q2) and 1611 (Q3). The Folio version (1623) is based on the last.

Interpreting the play

The bad reviews are impossible to ignore. T.S. Eliot declared *Titus* "one of the stupidest and most uninspired plays ever written", complaining of "a wantonness, an irrelevance about the crimes". Much the same thing was said four hundred years earlier by one Jacques Petit, a French tutor who witnessed a private performance and was sufficiently unimpressed by it to record that "the spectacle had more value than the theme". Edward Ravenscroft, whose own version of *Titus* replaced Shakespeare's on the Restoration stage, was equally ungracious about his source, condemning it as "a most incorrect and undigested piece … rather a heap of Rubbish than a Structure". Editors have been, if anything, more damning: J.C. Maxwell wrote in 1953 that "*Titus* is neither a play with a complicated staging nor one which will ever be widely read";

MAJOR CHARACTERS & SYNOPSIS

THE ROMANS

Saturninus, eldest son of the late Emperor of Rome, later Emperor himself
Bassianus, Saturninus's younger brother
Titus Andronicus, a Roman general
Marcus Andronicus, Titus's brother, a tribune of the Roman people
Lucius, **Quintus**, **Martius** and **Mutius**, sons of Titus
Lavinia, Titus's only daughter
Young Lucius, Lucius's son
Publius, Marcus's son
Sempronius, **Caius** and **Valentine**, relations of the Andronici
Aemilius, a Roman

THE GOTHS

Tamora, Queen of the Goths (later Saturninus's wife)
Alarbus, **Demetrius** and **Chiron**, Tamora's sons
Aaron, a Moor in Tamora's service and her lover

ACT 1 The Emperor of Rome is dead and his sons, Saturninus and Bassianus, vie for the succession. A third candidate, the soldier Titus Andronicus, recently home from fighting the Goths, is the people's choice. As war reparation, he sacrifices the son of Tamora, Queen of the Goths, despite his mother's pleas. Titus then obediently rejects the crown in favour of Saturninus, who offers to marry Titus's daughter Lavinia. But Lavinia is already betrothed to Bassianus, and the two escape. Titus is outraged, and kills his son Mutius when he attempts to defend them. Saturninus denounces the Andronici family and decides to marry Tamora instead. Tamora appears to reconcile the quarrelling parties, but plots with Saturninus to wipe out the Andronici.

ACT 2 Tamora's sons, Chiron and Demetrius, are arguing over Lavinia when Aaron suggests that they take her by force. Titus, meanwhile, has gone hunting with Saturninus, during which Tamora (now Empress) slips away to find Aaron. Discovered by Bassianus and Lavinia, Tamora gets her two sons to murder Bassianus, after which they drag off Lavinia. Aaron then lures two of

Titus's sons, Quintus and Martius, into the pit where Bassianus's body has been dumped, further implicating them with a letter (fabricated by Aaron), and Saturninus orders their execution. In another part of the forest, Lavinia, who has been raped and had her hands and tongue cut off, is discovered by her uncle Marcus.

ACT 3 Titus vainly pleads for Quintus and Martius, and another son, Lucius, is banished for trying to rescue them. Marcus then enters with the mutilated Lavinia, and Titus and Lucius are filled with horror. Aaron interrupts with a message: the Emperor will release Quintus and Martius on condition that either Titus, Lucius or Marcus cut off one of their hands. Titus agrees, but his sacrifice is for nothing – his hand is returned with the heads of his two sons. Later that evening, when Marcus kills a fly, the crazed Titus denounces it as murder.

ACT 4 Lavinia identifies her attackers by pointing to the tale of Philomel in Ovid's *Metamorphoses* and inscribing their names in the sand. Titus responds by sending a mysterious gift to Chiron and Demetrius. Aaron alone realizes that Titus means revenge, but he is distracted by the arrival of a nurse with his newborn baby by Tamora, which she wants killed because of its dark skin. Aaron prevents the baby's murder but kills the nurse to stop her talking. At the palace, Saturninus is alarmed to hear that Lucius is marching on Rome at the head of a Goth army.

ACT 5 Assuming Titus has gone mad, Tamora, Chiron and Demetrius appear at his house dressed as Revenge, Rape and Murder. Realizing who they are, Titus agrees to summon Lucius to dine with the Emperor and Empress. But after Tamora leaves, Titus unleashes a gruesome plan. First he kills Chiron and Demetrius and bakes them in a pie, which he offers to Tamora and Saturninus. He then kills Lavinia, reveals the ingredients of the dinner, and stabs Tamora. Titus is immediately killed by Saturninus, who is himself killed by Lucius. Lucius becomes Emperor.

a few years earlier, John Dover Wilson thought it "like some broken-down cart, laden with bleeding corpses from the Elizabethan scaffold". As the critic Stanley Wells wryly remarks, "Shakespeare's earliest tragedy was a great success in its own time and has been regarded as a terrible mistake almost ever since."

On the face of it, the criticisms are easy enough to understand. One character is raped, then grotesquely mutilated to keep her quiet. The action culminates in a cannibalistic banquet, itself capped by a killing spree. It requires some of the most ghoulish props in the canon (one notorious stage direction instructs, "Enter a Messenger with two heads and a hand"). And *Titus* still manages to push the boundaries of taboo. Following their rape of Lavinia, Chiron and Demetrius first cut out her tongue, then amputate her hands. If that weren't enough, they then torment her (and the audience) with appalling wisecracks:

CHIRON
Go home, call for sweet water, wash thy hands.
DEMETRIUS
She hath no tongue to call, nor hands to wash …

[2.4.6–7]

The gouging-out of Gloucester's eyes in *King Lear* barely compares – that is perplexing and brutal, this is a craziness way beyond. So it is, too, when Titus finds out that cutting off his hand in order to save his imprisoned sons' lives has been pointless (they are already dead). He responds not with tears, but with laughter:

MARCUS
Why dost thou laugh? It fits not with this hour.
TITUS
Why, I have not another tear to shed.

[3.1.264–5]

It fits not

"It fits not" could stand as an epigraph for *Titus Andronicus*; it specializes in squeezing distressing events into beautiful patterns. Shakespeare uses classical sources throughout his career, but in *Titus* (if the play is solely by him; some think it is a collaboration with the minor dramatist George Peele) he often breaks them down, forces them into gruesome and unexpected new settings. To many critics, the most glaring disjunction occurs when Marcus catches sight of his mutilated, speechless niece. Instead of going to Lavinia's aid – instead, indeed, of being struck dumb by horror – he addresses her in bizarrely stylized rhetoric:

Why dost not speak to me?
Alas, a crimson river of warm blood,
Like to a bubbling fountain stirred with wind,
Doth rise and fall between thy rosèd lips,

Coming and going with thy honey breath.
Be sure, some Tereus hath deflowered thee
And, lest thou shouldst detect him, cut thy tongue ...
Fair Philomel, why she but lost her tongue
And in a tedious sampler sewed her mind.
But, lovely niece, that mean is cut from thee.
A craftier Tereus, cousin, hast thou met,
And he hath cut those pretty fingers off
That could have better sewed than Philomel.

[2.4.21–43]

It is one of the most difficult points in the play. Marcus's first reaction is not to deal with the primacy of Lavinia's (horribly real) injuries, but to reach for a classical precedent, that of Philomel's rape by Tereus in Book 7 of Ovid's *Metamorphoses*. Furthermore, the way in which Marcus aestheticizes her anguish – comparing her bleeding mouth to a "bubbling fountain", her amputated limbs to "sweet ornaments" – is deliberately confrontational. Marcus's lengthy speech does more than make us gaze in horror at the spectacle: it forces us to consider a terrible gulf between florid words and theatrical reality, made even more striking here by the play's otherwise clear and direct language.

Yet Marcus is quite right: Lavinia's suffering is in conscious imitation of Philomel's, as becomes still clearer when Lavinia is attempting to explain what has happened by the most efficient means possible – by finding a copy of the *Metamorphoses* and pointing to the relevant passage. Titus alone realizes what she is trying to communicate:

Lavinia, wert *thou* thus surprised, sweet girl,
Ravished and wronged as Philomela was,
Forced in the ruthless, vast, and gloomy woods?
See, see. Ay, such a place there is where we did hunt—
O, had we never, never hunted there!—
Patterned by that the poet here describes,
By nature made for murders and for rapes.

[4.1.51–7]

Ovid provides Shakespeare's "pattern", even the woods play out their preordained role. Lavinia, it might be said, is sacrificed to her source. Even her death at her father's own hands is modelled on the classical hero Virginius, who slew his own "enforced, stained, and deflowered daughter" to spare her shame – "a reason mighty, strong, effectual," as Titus grimly exclaims:

A pattern, precedent, and lively warrant
For me, most wretched, to perform the like.

[5.3.42–4]

It is not enough that Titus kills his daughter like a character in Livy; he provides reasons for his action like an obedient Renaissance schoolboy. Lavinia is hardly the

O, vengeance!

The tragedy of revenge is probably as old as drama itself. The Greek tragedian Aeschylus produced in around 458 BC what remains Western theatre's most ancient dramatic cycle: the *Oresteia*. This sequence of three plays tells the story of the hero Orestes, who is set on a murderous path to revenge when his mother Clytemnestra kills his father Agamemnon (itself an act of vengeance for Agamemnon's sacrifice of their daughter Iphigenia, Orestes's sister). Driven by fierce hatred and a command from Apollo, Orestes hunts down Clytemnestra and brutally butchers her – whereupon Furies rise up and pursue him. They are called off only after the intervention of Athena, goddess of justice and patroness of Athens.

This is both the problem and the – literally – fatal attraction of revenge: the cycle of violence is potentially inexhaustible. The attraction for dramatists is obvious, and in the work of the Roman playwright **Seneca** (d. 65 AD), much influenced by the Greeks, the genre became gorier than ever. Seneca's most famous revenge tragedy is *Thyestes*, which sees the eponymous hero seducing his brother Atreus's wife and stealing his kingdom. Atreus gets his own back in the grisliest way imaginable, by tricking Thyestes into eating a banquet prepared from the flesh of his own sons.

Elizabethan writers knew their Seneca, and in the first years of Shakespeare's career revenge tragedy was all the rage. The bestselling play of the 1590s was *The Spanish Tragedy*, written by trained legal clerk **Thomas Kyd** (see p.623). Watched over by a character actually named "Revenge", the *Tragedy* tells the lurid tale of a Spanish official named Hieronimo whose son is killed in cold blood. Though crazed by grief, Hieronimo manages to uncover the identities of the two murderers by putting on a play in which he himself stars, before killing them. Standing over their bodies, he declares that the revenge cycle has come full circle (before biting out his tongue rather than explain his actions):

> My guiltless son was by Lorenzo slain,
> And by Lorenzo and that Balthazar
> Am I at last revenged thoroughly,
> Upon whose souls may heavens be yet revenged,
> With greater far than these afflictions.
> Methinks since I grew inward with revenge,
> I cannot look with scorn enough on death.
>
> [4.4.191–9]

The end of Kyd's own life was nearly as sensationalistic as his play: after being imprisoned following the arrest of Christopher Marlowe in 1592, Kyd denounced his former roommate to the authorities and himself died soon afterwards, broken by his experiences in jail.

Shakespeare's Titus is closely modelled on Kyd's Hieronimo. Though there is no obvious source for *Titus Andronicus*, revenge might be said to co-write its plot: Titus executes Tamora's sons; she and Aaron arrange for Bassianus to be murdered and Lavinia raped; and Titus retaliates by capturing Chiron and Demetrius and cooking them in a pie. This gruesome finale glances back to *Thyestes*, but it also prepares the way for Shakespeare's later experiments with revenge motifs, which find their way into many of his works. Shakespeare's most famous revenge tragedy is of course *Hamlet*, but here it is the hero's difficulties acting as a revenger that dominate the tragedy. Although he puts on a play, just like Hieronimo, Hamlet misses his opportunity to kill Claudius in its aftermath. And by the time that he brings himself to act, Hamlet's own death – itself an act of revenge for the murder of Polonius – has already been arranged for him.

only abused woman to appear at Shakespeare's behest – *The Rape of Lucrece*, using many of the same sources, also dates from this period – but it is interesting to note how bookishly he treats her.

Critics have noted other classical parallels at work in *Titus*. In this, perhaps his earliest tragedy, Shakespeare adopts the motifs of revenge drama, then doing the rounds on the Elizabethan stage. Like Kyd's *The Spanish Tragedy*, a lurid and popular example of the genre, this play contains a cycle of revenge which involves three protagonists, Tamora, Aaron and Titus – all done along the lines of the Roman tragedian Seneca, whose own retellings of revenge exerted a powerful influence on Renaissance drama. Again, though, Shakespeare doesn't go for subtle remodelling. As with Lavinia's much-stressed parallels with Philomel, Tamora attempts to trap Titus not by acting out her revenge, but by actually *acting* Revenge, thinking him mad enough to believe her. Disguised in her "strange and sad habiliment", she announces: "I am Revenge,"

> sent from th'infernal kingdom
> To ease the gnawing vulture of thy mind
> By working wreakful vengeance on thy foes.
> Come down, and welcome me to this world's light.
> Confer with me of murder and of death.
> There's not a hollow cave or lurking-place,
> No vast obscurity or misty vale
> Where bloody murder or detested rape
> Can couch for fear, but I will find them out,
> And in their ears tell them my dreadful name …
>
> [5.2.30–39]

She has read the script, it seems, as has her paramour Aaron, who in one of his most cartoonishly villainous moments threatens "murders, rapes, and massacres, / Acts of black night, abominable deeds" (5.1.64–5).

A wilderness of tigers

But *Titus* does more than thumb through classical texts; it points forward to Shakespeare's greatest dramatic achievements. Titus is the most developed character in the play, and his journey as a father forms its emotional centre. His mourning farewell to his sons is moving (not least because of its pre-echoes of the extraordinary song from *Cymbeline*, "Fear no more the heat o'th' sun"):

> In peace and honour rest you here, my sons;
> Rome's readiest champions, repose you here in rest,
> Secure from worldly chances and mishaps.
> Here lurks no treason, here no envy swells,
> Here grow no damnèd drugs, here are no storms,
> No noise, but silence and eternal sleep.
>
> [1.1.150–5]

> [Titus Andronicus] shows a pitilessness, a sharp predilection for the ugly, a titanic quarrel with the gods, such as we find in the first works of the greatest poets.
>
> Heinrich Heine, *Shakespeare's Girls and Women* (1838)

But there is more than emotion at stake here. In Shakespeare's first dramatic exposition of the self-sacrificing severity of Rome, it is Titus's early mistake not to realize that, as he puts it later, the city has become a "wilderness of tigers" and "affords no prey / But me and mine" (3.1.53–5). Titus's faltering awareness of the importance of his family is strongly counterpointed in the play by the behaviour of his sons – one of whom, Mutius, he hacks to death after the young man defends his friend Bassianus. Solidarity is also embodied in the figure of Marcus, who stands alongside Titus throughout his sufferings and is one of the few survivors left on stage at the play's end, movingly promising his fellow Romans that they will come together once more as a people and a family, knitting "this scattered corn into one mutual sheaf" (5.3.69–70). It doesn't say a great deal for Titus that even the villainous Aaron is a more loving, if no less bloody, father to his newborn child: seizing the boy from (then stabbing) the Empress's Nurse, he refuses to let him be killed – something insisted on by Tamora, who will not tolerate the "treacherous hue" of the baby's black skin.

Notably, when Titus uses the word "love" first, it is to describe his service to his ruler. His journey towards a fuller understanding of the concept foreshadows that of Lear. Both are driven to the point of madness; both suffer for their lack of emotional understanding. As Titus struggles to comprehend the "reason for these miseries" (he can see none), his horrified empathy with his daughter gives way to powerful liquid imagery in one of the play's most impressive soliloquies:

> When heaven doth weep, doth not the earth o'erflow?
> If the winds rage, doth not the sea wax mad,
> Threat'ning the welkin with his big-swoll'n face?
> And wilt thou have a reason for this coil?
> I am the sea. Hark how her sighs doth blow.
> She is the weeping welkin, I the earth.
> Then must my sea be movèd with her sighs,
> Then must my earth with her continual tears
> Become a deluge overflowed and drowned,
> Forwhy my bowels cannot hide her woes,
> But like a drunkard must I vomit them.
>
> [3.1.220–30]

In this emotive speech – a sign of Shakespeare's growing dramatic skill – Titus describes himself conjoined not only with his daughter ("She is the weeping welkin [heavens], I the earth"), but with the distant memory of his sons, themselves insulated from "storms" like these.

But this speech propels Titus into the only expression of love the play allows him – to "vomit" revenge. In one sense, his tragedy is also the play's grimmest joke: his father's love is ridiculous in its futility. Titus cuts off his hand to save his surviving sons, but to no avail; love for his daughter eventually forces him to kill her. In this company, it is ironic but "fitting" that his sincerest expression of familial love concerns a fly killed by Marcus:

> How if that fly had a father, brother?
> How would he hang his slender gilded wings
> And buzz lamenting dirges in the air!
> Poor harmless fly,
> That with his pretty buzzing melody
> Came here to make us merry—and thou hast killed him!
>
> [3.2.60–5]

Just as the play's bizarre use of classicism makes its audiences think again, so this tender lament for a dead insect is counterpointed with the fact that its human characters are often treated like meat (literally so, given that two of them are baked in a pie). Even Lucius's closing promise, as he stands over the "poor remainder of Andronici", to "knit again … These broken limbs into one body" (5.3.69–71), is a kind of bitter joke. Far from being moronic, it might be said that *Titus* ranges across the extremes of human emotion – all the way from black humour to genuine sorrow and back again. Titus laughs because he has "not another tear to shed"; if we find some elements of the play difficult to understand, it is because it explores so much.

Stage history and adaptations

The first mention of the performance history of *Titus Andronicus* appears courtesy of **Philip Henslowe**, the owner of the Rose playhouse, who noted in his book of accounts that the play was "new" (probably completely new, rather than revived) in January 1594, and that it had done well at the box-office. **Richard Burbage**, who had already played Titus's model Hieronimo in *The Spanish Tragedy* and would later play Hamlet and Lear, presumably created the lead role. But what would probably have been a successful and long run for *Titus*, such as the *Henry VI* plays enjoyed, was cut short by an outbreak of plague at the end of the month, when the theatres were shut down. The play was rushed into print in February, in all likelihood to avert a financial crisis for the players. It was revived later in the year when Shakespeare's company toured outside the city, transferred to the Blackfriars – when the "fly scene" (3.2) was perhaps added – and was popular up to and beyond the closure of the theatres in 1642. (**Ben Jonson** was sufficiently jealous of its success that he inserted a barbed reference to it in *Bartholomew Fair*.)

Titus was also performed privately at the house of **Sir John Harington** in Rutland in 1596, though from the comments of his tutor Jacques Petit (see p.440), it appears to have been less suited to that exclusive audience. Its early life is further illustrated by the existence of a pen-and-ink drawing, supposedly by the draughtsman **Henry Peacham**; though it conflates several different episodes from the play, it reveals that Elizabethan actors made little effort to costume in "Roman" attire. Early on, *Titus* was also popular outside England: it was translated into German by **Frederick Menius** as *Eine Sehr Klägliche Tragaedia von Tito Andronico* and printed in 1620. A work by the Dutch dramatist **Jan Vos** as *Aren en Titus*, published first in 1641 then in no fewer than 28 editions by 1726, is more than likely an adaptation of Shakespeare's play.

Following the Restoration reopening of the theatres, Shakespeare's version continued to be acted but was shunted off the boards in 1678 by **Edward Ravenscroft's** adaptation, *Titus Andronicus; or, The Rape of Lavinia.* This gave Aaron a beefed-up role and had his young child killed by Tamora in yet another revenging twist, but was in other respects remarkably faithful to the original – particularly when compared with other Restoration remakes (see p.230). It was revived frequently, with the famously declamatory **James Quin**, an actor who insisted on performing only tragic parts, playing Aaron in the 1720s.

Equally enthusiastic about Aaron's potential was the African American actor **Ira Aldridge**, who commissioned in the 1850s what would turn out to be the only nineteenth-century British revival of *Titus*. Basing his interpretation on his other celebrated Shakespearian role, Othello, Aldridge made Aaron an essentially noble character whose relationship with Tamora was consciously legitimized. Aldridge's adapter, **C.A. Somerset**, was careful to omit anything that might offend squeamish audiences – including Lavinia's rape and mutilation – resulting in "a play not only presentable but actually attractive", as one reviewer put it. Another American, the actor-playwright **N.H. Bannister**, had introduced the play to Philadelphian audiences back in 1839. Though Bannister claimed that "the language of the Immortal Bard" was retained, he took pains to assure audiences that his text cut "every expression … calculated to offend the ear".

Difficulties of decorum also confronted **Robert Atkins** at the Old Vic in 1923, but he bravely dusted off Shakespeare's complete text nonetheless – the first time it had seen the stage for nearly 250 years. Though some theatregoers fainted, one commentator thought the production "thoroughly enjoyable in spite of the horrors". In contrast, the Japanese writer **Shoyo Tsubouchi** seems, if anything, to have revelled in the play's horrors when he translated *Titus* in 1926, comparing it to the notorious brutalities of Kabuki theatre.

The play's potential was most radically realized by **Peter Brook** at Stratford-upon-Avon in 1955, where abstract stylization was employed to dignify its subject: **Vivien Leigh's** glamorous Lavinia entered following her rape with ribbons, not blood, trailing from mouth and hands (Brook was accused of "squeamishness" by Evelyn Waugh), and some seven hundred lines were cut overall. The visual impression was similarly emblematic: Brook's enormous set was lit in visceral colours which advanced unremittingly towards a blood-red finale. **Anthony Quayle** played Aaron to **Maxine Audley's** hyper-exotic Tamora, but it was **Laurence Olivier's** haggardly lyrical Titus which most impressed the reviewers: Kenneth Tynan described how "a hundred campaigns have tanned his heart to leather, and from the cracking of that heart there issues a terrible music … the noise made in its last extremity by the cornered human soul". It was all

Memorably gruesome, Lucy Bailey's 2006 Globe production caused mass faintings when it was revived in summer 2014. Here Titus (William Houston) prepares his grisly banquet from the carcasses of Chiron and Demetrius, as Flora Spencer-Longhurst's mutilated Lavinia looks on.

the more remarkable an achievement given that Leigh and Olivier were splitting up at the time – she was reported to have taken advantage of her costume and whispered insults to her soon-to-be-ex-husband while they were actually performing.

In postwar German-speaking countries, attuned to theatrical experimentation, the play has been intermittently revived, and featured in notable adaptations by Swiss dramatist **Friedrich Dürrenmatt** (1970, revealingly subtitled "a comedy after Shakespeare"), and East German playwright **Heiner Müller**, whose *Titus, Fall of Rome*, written in 1984 in the shadow of the CIA-led coup in Chile, drew pointed parallels with colonial wars overseas.

In the English-speaking world, however, *Titus* has remained on the margins: along with *Timon of Athens*, it has featured on the RSC's secret list of productions guaranteed to make a loss – perhaps the only reason why **John Barton**'s bizarre double-bill of *Titus* and *The Two Gentlemen of Verona* (1981) actually made it past the drawing-board. But **Deborah Warner**, who directed the play at Stratford's Swan Theatre in 1987, demonstrated that the play could be trusted in its own terms. Where Brook stressed abstraction, Warner went for grim violence: **Sonia Ritter**'s bruised, groaning

Lavinia had the stumps of her arms covered with clay to stem their bleeding and **Brian Cox**'s Titus cut off his own hand on stage with a cheese wire – though Warner carefully avoided the use of fake blood until the deaths of Chiron and Demetrius in order to maximize the shock. The text remained intact, Warner deliberately courting the audience's laughter by Cox's chef's-hatted hero, who whistled an infamous tune from *Snow White* while preparing his grisly banquet.

Surprises lay in store for the cast of **Gregory Doran**'s 1994 production, which was rehearsed in Britain but featured a South African cast and toured to Johannesburg in the aftermath of the historic elections, the first in which black South Africans were able to vote. Aaron was applauded for his defiance by a predominantly black audience, but **Antony Sher**'s white-supremacist Titus came in for criticism, as did the play's comedy, which some thought played up to racial stereotypes. The play's next British staging, directed by **Bill Alexander** at the RSC in 2003, garnered praise for its unflinching representation of violence – even if most headlines were generated by the RSC's decision to team up with the National Blood Service, who parked a donation van outside the doors. **David Bradley** played a sardonic, cadaverous hero to **Eve Myles**'s forceful Lavinia (the rest of the cast, so it was claimed, kept a night-by-night "swoon count" of audience members fainting in shock).

As if in contrast, a more recent staging at the same venue, performed as part of the RSC's Complete Works festival in 2006, could barely have been more aestheticized. This was the work of legendary Japanese director **Yukio Ninagawa** and his Tokyo-based company, who together offered "a stark, glacial tone poem" – in the words of the *New York Times* – set in an abstractly feudal Japan. **Kotaro Yoshida** played a stiff samurai whose hand was never far from his sword, while **Hitomi Manaka**'s Lavinia did nothing so unsightly as bleed following her attack, but instead wreathed herself in skeins of red wool – shades of **Peter Brook**'s version of the same scene a half-century earlier.

Another production that also opened in 2006 was an altogether quicker and dirtier affair, directed by **Lucy Bailey** under a claustrophobic black canopy at Shakespeare's Globe. **Douglas Hodge** played Titus as a grizzled old soldier who transformed into a chuckling TV chef, with **Geraldine Alexander** as a bitchy, witchy Tamora. Although the *Independent* acclaimed it as the Globe's best yet, Benedict Nightingale in the *Times* argued that the mood was "more gleeful Grand Guignol than genuine, heart-stopping terror". When the show was revived in 2014 with **William Houston** and **Indira Varma**, the theatre experienced an unprecedented run of faintings among the groundlings, up to ten per performance. In contrast, some German theatregoers simply stormed out of a Berliner Ensemble adaptation by **Botho Strauss** entitled *Die Schändung* (Violation) in 2006, denouncing it as "Nazi theatre".

The habit among directors of either presenting the play as a piece of carefully ritualized violence or an excuse for Tarantino-like excess continues, at least in the UK. **Tang Shu-wing**'s Cantonese-language production, which visited the Globe in 2012 for the World Shakespeare Festival, was subtly acted but perhaps over-cautious in its minimalism; **Lai Yuk-ching** as Lavinia was given merely a polite spattering of stage blood and tasteful red gloves after the rape scene. **Michael Fentiman**'s RSC revival in 2013, in contrast, made some critics think of terrorist attacks in Syria and Iraq, others of outrages closer to home. It featured **Stephen Boxer** as a caustic hero and **Katy Stephens** as a sexily self-aware Tamora.

On screen, as inside theatres, *Titus* has not featured largely. Two screen versions have been made, both directed by women. **Jane Howell** directed the BBC TV version of 1985, with **Trevor Peacock** in the lead, in a warmly received production which attempted to position the action from the viewpoint of the play's sole innocent, Young Lucius. **Julie Taymor** attempted a similar strategy in her Hollywood version of 1999, which starred **Anthony Hopkins** as Titus and **Jessica Lange** as Tamora, but with far zanier results; her film enthused some critics but merely confused others.

SCREEN

Titus
A. Hopkins, A. Cumming, J. Lange; Julie Taymor (dir.) USA, 1999 ➤ Disney / Fox DVD

You have to admire Julie Taymor's courage: fresh from transferring Disney's cuddly *The Lion King* to the Broadway stage, she decided to do her first movie – basing it on Shakespeare's grisliest play. And, though the studios wouldn't touch it, she got it made. Whether you admire her film might be a different matter: the play's precarious balance between crazed brutality and crazed comedy is tilted decisively in favour of the latter, and Taymor's decision to go for high camp could be regarded as an easy way out of its moral ambiguities. But the cast redeem their director's excessive eclecticism: Anthony Hopkins is superbly cast as Titus, putting in a persuasively grizzled performance somewhat in the mould of Olivier, which illustrates well his character's naivety about matters political (even if it's difficult not to think of the inimitable Dr Lecter as the play approaches its flesh-munching climax). Alan Cumming, the campest of the lot, is also excellent as a ravingly extreme Saturninus, and Laura Taylor's poignant Lavinia is very finely done.

AUDIO

Titus Andronicus
D. Troughton, H. Walter, P. Joseph; Clive Brill (dir.) UK, 1998 ➤ Arkangel ◉ ☁

So how *do* you stage this most visually violent play on audio? If this Arkangel version is anything to go by, with plenty of sickening sound effects. But to concentrate on these would be entirely unfair, for this is a very well-cast and serious-minded version. Troughton sounds perhaps surprisingly young in the lead, but that's all to the good: his mad scenes have a touching tenderness about them that tougher actors might miss; while Harriet Walter, too, proves that there is plenty more to Tamora than wicked witch. Paterson Joseph is good as Aaron, but perhaps misses that last ounce of dangerous sarcasm. The rape

of Lavinia (Emma Gregory) is traumatically presented – her noisy weeping is a bitter counterpoint to the scenes afterwards – and in fact the whole middle section of the play makes for raw and uncomfortable listening. This is the way it should be, of course, but you are warned: *Titus* is upsetting, somehow especially so without the visuals.

EDITIONS

Arden Shakespeare (third series)
Jonathan Bate (ed.); 1995 ➤ Bloomsbury

As the Renaissance man behind *Shakespeare and Ovid* (1993), a tour-de-force analysis of Shakespeare's transformation of classical forms, Jonathan Bate proves an excellent guide to *Titus Andronicus*, perhaps the most perverse yet classically influenced play in the canon. A troublesome text receives sympathetic and scrupulous treatment, and Bate helpfully reprints some of its "patterns and precedents" – the material Shakespeare plundered to assemble his earliest tragedy. What emerges from this stout defence of *Titus*'s virtues is, in the editor's words, a drama which is a "complex and self-conscious improvisation upon classical sources". What it doesn't spend much time on, however, is the notion that the play is co-written – a topic on which Bate has shifted his ground, suggesting that George Peele may have been involved after all. Those in search of more recent stage history should note Alan Hughes's New Cambridge edition was updated in 2006.

SOME CRITICISM

Shakespeare and Classical Tragedy
Robert S. Miola; 1992 ➤ Oxford UP

Like Jonathan Bate, Robert Miola has written extensively on Renaissance reworkings of classical material. This slim study traces what T.S. Eliot called, rather too elegantly, "the penetration of Senecan sensibility" into the work of Shakespeare and his colleagues. Despite Eliot's loathing of the play, *Titus Andronicus* is an obvious calling point, and Miola's chapter on it is especially interesting both as a defence of *Titus* and of Seneca himself – perhaps the most maligned tragedian of all. Moving between the twin poles of "Heavy Seneca" (serious responses) to "Light Seneca" (comic and tragicomic retellings), the book also covers *Hamlet*, *Richard III*, *Macbeth*, *King Lear* and *A Midsummer Night's Dream*.

Titus Andronicus: Critical Essays
Philip C. Kolin (ed.); 1995 > Routledge

It has been the fate of *Titus Andronicus* to be sat awkwardly at the fringes: interesting things have been said about the play, but all too often in out-of-the-way crannies of Shakespearian scholarship. This makes Philip Kolin's labours in bringing together a substantial (518-page) slab of criticism on the play especially worthwhile. The essays here are cast into two sections, "*Titus* and the critics" and "*Titus* on stage", prefaced by Kolin's own detailed analysis of the critical legacy. They vary in quality, but there are some real gems – Heather James on cultural disintegration in the play, Robert Miola (see above) on "Rome and the Family" and David Bevington's analysis of stagecraft.

Troilus and Cressida

O nce memorably described as "the work of a man whose soul is poisoned with filth", *Troilus and Cressida* has scandalized critics over the four centuries or so since it was first produced. Audiences have had less opportunity: a cleaned-up version by Dryden notwithstanding, it was regarded as unperformable until the very end of the nineteenth century, and only in modern times has this most cynical and nihilistic of plays found a welcoming environment. Written as Shakespeare approached his forties, *Troilus and Cressida* is the earliest of his so-called "problem plays", and it nearly didn't make the First Folio owing to copyright issues, in the event being squeezed in between the Comedies and the Tragedies. And if ever there were a play that made those generic labels difficult to affix, it's *Troilus and Cressida*. Neither a history, comedy nor full-scale tragedy, despite having elements of all three, this story of a futile love affair trapped in the middle of an apparently endless conflict is also a scathing satire on the glory and chivalry of the Trojan War, which in this play often seems to be little more than a front for lust, vanity and misogyny. As Thersites, the play's most cynical character, sums it up: "Lechery, lechery; still, wars and lechery: nothing else holds fashion."

DATE > Though certainly penned after 1598, *Troilus and Cressida* resists more accurate dating: on the basis of internal style, 1601–02 seems most likely.

SOURCES > Chaucer's poem, *Troilus and Criseyde* (1385–87), is the most direct source – Shakespeare possibly recalled it from memory – but numerous others influence the play: Robert Henryson's fifteenth-century *Testament of Cresseid*, Chapman's *Homer* (1598), William Caxton's *Recuyell of the Histories of Troy* (1475).

TEXT > Perplexingly, two slightly variant quarto texts – Qa and Qb – were published in 1609 (see p.461). Despite copyright snags, it was squeezed into the 1623 Folio in a version perhaps based on a revised quarto text, including a Prologue not otherwise present.

Interpreting the play

The story of the Trojan War, canonized in the *Iliad*, the great Greek epic credited to Homer and written down some time in the eighth century BC, is one of the defining legends of western literature. Poem and poet alike were regarded with supreme reverence by the ancient Greeks, and the tale of Troy, along with the flamboyant manner of its telling, filtered down to Virgil, who took it as the basis for his founding Roman epic, the *Aeneid*, composed some eight hundred years later. It was another millennium and a half before the works of Homer made it into English, via the poet George Chapman – a masterly translation that took him eighteen years to complete.

MAJOR CHARACTERS & SYNOPSIS

Prologue, dressed as an armed man

THE TROJANS

Priam, King of Troy

Priam's sons: **Hector**, **Deiphobus**, **Helenus** (a
  priest), **Paris**, **Troilus** and **Margareton** (a bastard)

Cassandra, Priam's daughter, a prophetess

Andromache, Hector's wife

Aeneas and **Antenor**, Trojan commanders

Pandarus, a lord

Cressida, Pandarus's niece

Calchas, Cressida's father (who has defected to
  the Greeks)

Alexander, Cressida's servant

THE GREEKS

Agamemnon, commander-in-chief of the Greeks

Menelaus, Agamemnon's brother

Helen, Menelaus's wife (now living with Paris)

Greek commanders: **Nestor**, **Ulysses**, **Achilles**,
  Diomedes, **Ajax**

Patroclus, Achilles's companion

Thersites, an ill-tempered wit

A **Servant** attending on Diomedes

ACT 1 Seven years on, the Trojan War is locked
in stalemate. Inside Troy itself, however, Troilus
is more concerned with wooing Cressida via
her uncle Pandarus. Although Cressida affects
disdain, she is already in love with him. In the
Greeks' camp, meanwhile, Agamemnon bemoans
the war's lack of progress. Ulysses blames a
breakdown in control, intimating that their finest
warrior, Achilles, is undermining Agamemnon's
authority. When the Trojan warrior Aeneas arrives
with a message from Hector challenging any
Greek warrior to single combat (a challenge clearly
meant for Achilles), Ulysses and Nestor resolve to
humble Achilles by choosing the doltish Ajax.

ACT 2 Ajax is questioning Thersites about what
is going on, but is answered by insults. Achilles
arrives (with his friend Patroclus) and tells Ajax
of Hector's challenge, about which Achilles feigns
indifference. Back inside Troy, King Priam and his
sons are angrily debating whether they should
return Helen to the Greeks and end the war.
Hector argues that she is not worth fighting for,
but Troilus defends her, at which point Cassandra
bursts in raving and predicting the destruction

of Troy unless Helen is given up. Paris justifies his
original abduction of her, and the brothers are
temporarily reconciled – the war goes on.

ACT 3 Pandarus has finally arranged a meeting
between Troilus and Cressida, but fails to make
himself scarce. Initially nervous, the couple make
a vow of mutual constancy before retiring to the
bedroom – unaware that Cressida's father, the
defector Calchas, has arranged for his daughter
to be ransomed for the Trojan prisoner Antenor.
As Ajax prepares for the fight, the other Greek
commanders cold-shoulder Achilles and Ulysses
explains to him that his reputation is in decline.

ACT 4 Aeneas breaks the news to Troilus:
Diomedes has arrived with Antenor, who is to be
exchanged for Cressida. With little time left, the
couple tearfully exchange love tokens, and Troilus
begs Cressida to remain faithful. In the Greek
camp, meanwhile, preparations for the combat
have been finalized; Cressida and Diomedes arrive,
closely followed by Hector, Aeneas and Troilus.
Ajax and Hector begin to fight, but Hector calls
a halt on the grounds that the two are cousins.
Hector is then welcomed by the Greeks as an
honourable foe, but the mood is soured when the
piqued Achilles rashly challenges him to combat.

ACT 5 During the feasting on the eve of battle,
Ulysses takes Troilus to Calchas's tent to find
Cressida. As they approach, they witness Cressida
flirting with Diomedes and giving him one of
Troilus's love tokens. Troilus is soon beside himself
with rage and vows to kill Diomedes. Back inside
Troy, Hector arms himself for the fight – despite
his wife and sister's attempts to dissuade him.
Troilus also prepares for battle, tearing up an
unread letter sent by Cressida. As battle com-
mences, personal vendettas take precedence:
Troilus fights both Diomedes and Ajax, and
Achilles demands vengeance when his beloved
Patroclus is killed. Though beaten back by Hector,
Achilles sneaks up on him with a group of soldiers
and has him brutally murdered, even though he
is unarmed. As news reaches the Greeks, they
become convinced that victory will be theirs.
Troilus mourns the loss of Hector and plans
revenge; when Pandarus appears, he curses him.

By the early seventeenth century, when Shakespeare was in his late thirties, rework-ings of the Troy story had begun to stack up. In addition to Chapman's *Homer*, the first chunk of which was published in 1598, there had been several plays on the subject and a number of poems – all of which makes it hard to pin down precisely what the playwright drew upon when writing *Troilus and Cressida*. His title points to one major source, Chaucer's *Troilus and Criseyde* (1385–87), an elegant and poignant version of a fragment from the tale also related by Boccaccio, but it seems likely that Shakespeare also knew the very first book printed in English, William Caxton's *Recuyell* [Anthology] *of the Historyes of Troye* (1471–76), as well as John Lydgate's *Troy Book* (1412–21). These last provided him with a narrative which simply doesn't appear in Homer – the tale of the lovers Troilus and Cressida, whose tragic separation over the battle lines at Troy provides an eloquent inset to the nine-year war for the city.

All the argument

In Shakespeare's hands that story is not, as we might expect, all that noble. Troilus enters the play almost literally incapacitated by love, unable to fight or even sleep, he tells his go-between Pandarus:

> I tell thee I am mad
> In Cressid's love; thou answer'st 'She is fair',
> Pourest in the open ulcer of my heart
> Her eyes, her hair, her cheek, her gait, her voice;
> Handlest in thy discourse, O, that her hand,
> In whose comparison all whites are ink
> Writing their own reproach, to whose soft seizure
> The cygnet's down is harsh, and spirit of sense
> Hard as the palm of ploughman. This thou tell'st me—
> As true thou tell'st me—when I say I love her.
> But saying thus, instead of oil and balm
> Thou lay'st in every gash that love hath given me
> The knife that made it.
>
> [1.1.51–63]

Love is abject, painful: in the first of the play's many gruesome images of disease, Troilus describes how his heart is made such an "open ulcer" by love that even Pandarus's description of Cressida's beauty (especially her white hands, softer than the "cygnet's down") is a "knife" that wounds him. In Troilus's eyes there is nothing liber-ating, still less pleasurable, about passion: it is illness and injury, aptly enough given that the cause for which the Greeks and Trojans have fought so long is the retrieval of Helen, wife of the Spartan king, who has been abducted by the Trojan prince Paris.

Pandarus's advice is merely to "tarry", and as the play develops it becomes apparent why Troilus is being left to wait – Cressida's conviction that only by waiting do men learn the value of what they are after. "Women are angels, wooing," she observes,

Things won are done. Joy's soul lies in the doing.
That she beloved knows naught that knows not this:
Men prize the thing ungained more than it is.

[1.2.282–5]

Perhaps she is right: surrounded by men (Shakespeare never puts her on stage with the play's few other female characters), Cressida is keenly aware that she must retain her value in the sexual marketplace. Those same men, having "gained" Helen and thus triggered the Trojan War, are now debating whether the Queen is "worth what she doth cost", as Hector sourly puts it (2.2.50). Cressida's position is impossibly fragile.

If there is one thing in this play that the Greeks and Trojans have in common, iron-ically enough, it is disgust both for Helen and the war they are compelled to fight in her name. Though Troilus joins Paris in defending Helen's beauty and reputation, it is no accident that he describes her as a commodity, twisting Marlowe's famous lines from *Doctor Faustus* to emphasize the "price" of the woman who has "launched above a thousand ships / And turned crowned kings to merchants (2.2.81–2). The Greek Diomedes, discussing the same subject with his enemy Paris later in the play, is not convinced by Troilus's sense of Helen's value: "She's bitter to her country," he declares:

For every false drop in her bawdy veins
A Grecian's life hath sunk; for every scruple
Of her contaminated carrion weight
A Trojan hath been slain. Since she could speak
She hath not given so many good words breath
As, for her, Greeks and Trojans suffered death.

[4.1.70–6]

In Diomedes's unstinting analysis it is Helen's body, "contaminated" by the frank sexuality that has led her to desert her husband, that is the root of their trouble. The sardonic Thersites boils down still further what he thinks the war is really about: "All the argument is a whore and a cuckold," he remarks (2.3.71).

Thersites's point would perhaps have little force (he is, as he admits to Hector, "a rascal, a scurvy railing knave, a very filthy rogue" (5.4.26–7)) were it not for the fact that when we do get to see Paris and Helen together a scene later, as Pandarus tries to prepare the ground for Troilus and Cressida, it becomes only too obvious that there is nothing even faintly ennobling in their relationship. While Helen acts the skittish schoolgirl, petulantly demanding attention – and Pandarus is ordered to sing a grimly obscene song to amuse the court – Paris muses, to the best of his shallow abilities, on some insights into love. Troilus "eats nothing but doves, love," he nudgingly informs Helen,

and that breeds hot blood, and hot blood begets hot thoughts, and hot thoughts beget hot deeds, and hot deeds is love.

[3.1.124–6]

> *Troilus and Cressida has no story, or is as near to having none as a Renaissance play can be.*
>
> Barbara Everett, *Young Hamlet* (1989)

Every bit as obsessed with the body as Diomedes (or other of the play's male characters), Paris regards love and lust as entirely interchangeable. Perhaps Thersites is right: in *Troilus and Cressida* there is little to show for so much sacrifice. Blood – the blood of war as much as what Hector calls the "distempered blood" of passion (2.2.168) – is much of what the play is about.

Paris is not the only one of Shakespeare's characters to prove a disappointment – the play's subplot rests upon a tawdry attempt to undermine Achilles, the Greeks' greatest warrior but so insufferably arrogant that his compatriots Ulysses and Nestor agree to teach him a lesson. When the Trojan Hector sends a challenge to the Greeks to single combat, they deliberately exclude him from the competition and support the "blockish" Ajax instead, hoping to rile Achilles in the process. When the day for the combat arrives, Ajax and Hector begin fighting, only to stop when Hector realizes they are cousins. As a lull in the fighting beckons, the two sides seem momentarily to come to an understanding – until Achilles manages to puncture the bonhomie by turning up and challenging Hector to fight. In the bitter final battle of the play, Achilles even arranges to have his enemy murdered in cold blood. So much for chivalry.

No sooner got

The fraught issues that crowd the relationship between Paris and Helen – and which also touch Hector's macho scorn for his wife Andromache – do not bode well for the play's pivotal love affair. On hold for what seems like an eternity, by the time Troilus and Cressida finally manage to meet, over halfway into the play, the tension between them is cruelly painful. Waiting (yet again) for Cressida to arrive at their assignation, Troilus cannot stop thinking about death, comparing himself to "a strange soul upon the Stygian banks / Staying for waftage" (3.2.8–9). When Cressida does appear, the couple seem unable to find the right things to say, let alone understand what the other is thinking. Troilus exclaims, "You have bereft me of all words, lady," and the confusion between them does not dissipate:

> CRESSIDA Will you walk in, my lord?
> TROILUS O Cressida, how often have I wished me thus.
> CRESSIDA Wished, my lord? The gods grant—O, my lord!
> TROILUS What should they grant? What makes this pretty abruption? What too-curious dreg espies my sweet lady in the fountain of our love?
> CRESSIDA More dregs than water, if my fears have eyes.
>
> [3.2.53–65]

Cressida's first words can – and have – been interpreted in a bewildering multiplicity of ways, and acted in just as many. Her "will you walk in?" sounds disturbingly like a prostitute calling to her client, but it could just as easily be a plea to escape from the omnipresent Pandarus, who, as ever, is doing his utmost to ruin the occasion by hanging around and making leering wisecracks (the word "pander", meaning "pimp", is rooted in his name).

Shakespeare leaves it open, much as he leaves Cressida's character open to diametrically opposed interpretations. She has been characterized (usually by male critics) as a sex-hungry vixen; as an emblem of female independence in a misogynistic world; and as someone who is herself betrayed by actions over which she has no control. Though Cressida seems at first clear-eyed about the difficulties surrounding their relationship – far more so than Troilus, who is content to trot out clichés about the "fountain of our love" – just a few lines later she is struggling to explain why she played hard to get for so long:

> But though I loved you well, I wooed you not—
> And yet, good faith, I wished myself a man,
> Or that we women had men's privilege
> Of speaking first. Sweet, bid me hold my tongue,
> For in this rapture I shall surely speak
> The thing I shall repent.

[3.2.123–8]

Cressida's fear that her words will betray her provides a haunting pre-echo of the play's conclusion, further intensified by the vows that the lovers take almost immediately afterwards. While Troilus swears, awkwardly, that he will be "as true as truth's simplicity, / And simpler than the infancy of truth", Cressida rushes to seal her side of the bargain:

> If I be false, or swerve a hair from truth,
> When time is old and hath forgot itself,
> When water drops have worn the stones of Troy
> And blind oblivion swallowed cities up,
> And mighty states characterless are grated
> To dusty nothing, yet let memory
> From false to false among false maids in love
> Upbraid my falsehood. When they've said, 'as false
> As air, as water, wind or salty earth,
> As fox to lamb, or wolf to heifer's calf,
> Pard to the hind, or stepdame to her son',
> Yea, let them say, to stick the heart of falsehood,
> 'As false as Cressid'.

[3.2.180–92]

People did say "as true as Troilus" in the Renaissance, just as they did "as false as Cressida"; the lovers confront the historical aftershocks of their actions without realizing it. The dramatic irony here is so extreme as to be bitterly absurd. While Chaucer's

Criseyde frets that her behaviour towards Troilus will "shende" (ruin) not only her reputation but that of women everywhere, Shakespeare's Cressida blindly ensnares herself without even knowing it. Far from being a perfect relationship cruelly broken off by fate in the manner of *Romeo and Juliet*, in this play it seems stillborn from the first moment.

The morning after the lovers spend their one and only night together, news arrives that Cressida's traitorous father and the Greeks want to swap her – a literal exchange in a play full of metaphorical ones – for the Trojan prisoner Antenor. She must leave at once for the Greek camp, and their affair will be, as Pandarus exclaims in an

KEY SOURCE > Chaucer

When the man who brought the printing press to England, William Caxton, decided to publish a book of home-grown poetry, he needed a title that would sell. He turned immediately to **Geoffrey Chaucer**'s *Canterbury Tales*, arguably the greatest work of its kind ever written. Caxton's edition, which appeared around 1476, nearly 80 years after the poet's death, ensured that Chaucer remained on the bookshelves of the reading public not merely in his own period but well into the Renaissance, where he was frequently acclaimed as the father of English poetry.

Born into a well-to-do London family around 1340, Chaucer had an aristocratic childhood, serving in the household of Elizabeth de Burgh, wife of one of King Edward III's sons. He fought in France, was personally protected by the King, and later entered the royal household, where he grew close to John of Gaunt; when Gaunt's wife died in 1369, Chaucer paid tribute to her in *The Booke of the Duchesse*, a sophisticated early work that shows off his command of French verse style. A few years later Chaucer was awarded a lucrative government post as a customs official, and travelled in Europe on the King's service. All this time he was writing: *The Parliament of Fowls*, a dream-vision debating love; *The House of Fame*, a meditation on famous figures through the ages; and his great tragic love story, *Troilus and Criseyde*, a rhyme-royal work in five books set in the midst of the Trojan War. Other poems followed, notably *The Legend of Good Women*, a striking attempt to right the gender bias of his previous works and uncover the lives of famous historical women. But in every sense Chaucer's major work was *The Canterbury Tales*, the composition of which probably began soon after he relocated to Kent in the mid-1380s and lasted to his death in 1400. Originally planned as a vast series of 120 tales ostensibly told by pilgrims on the road from London to Canterbury, Chaucer in fact completed only 24 before being forced to call a halt. Even so, the work is one of a kind, a piece of panoptic social observation as well as a comic masterpiece touched with wry sympathy.

Like many Elizabethans, Shakespeare read Chaucer in the 1532 edition by **William Thynne**, and returned to the book repeatedly. *Troilus and Criseyde*, probably Chaucer's most famous poem in the Renaissance, was the major source for *Troilus and Cressida*, offering Shakespeare not only a basic plot but many intriguing details (though his portrait of Cressida, less generous than Chaucer's, is clearly influenced by later retellings of the story). Another popular work, the courtly "Knight's Tale" of Palamon and Arcite, told by Chaucer's "worthy" Knight as the first story in the Canterbury sequence, was used by Shakespeare to supply some backstory to *A Midsummer Night's Dream* and forms the basis of *The Two Noble Kinsmen*, written two decades later in collaboration with John Fletcher. Their debt is such that the poet is openly praised in the play's prologue, described as "Chaucer, of all admired".

These two major borrowings aside, Chaucer must rank as one of Shakespeare's favourite English writers, and fleeting references to *The Legend of Good Women* (which tells the story of Pyramus and Thisbe as well as that of Lucrece), *The Booke of the Duchesse* and other Canterbury stories abound.

uncomfortable echo of Cressida's words about wooing, "no sooner got but lost" (4.3.1). The Trojan leadership's eager consent to the deal – Antenor is militarily useful – is a compound betrayal, but Troilus, ever the loyalist, greets the news with a stiff upper lip. Yet his response to Cressida's apparent flirtation with Diomedes, which comes (though he does not know it) just after a welcome by the Greek generals in which she is required to kiss each in turn while they banter about her attractiveness, is less restrained. Watching in hiding as she surrenders to Diomedes the love token he gave her just a few scenes earlier, Troilus cannot believe what he sees:

> This, she? No, this is Diomed's Cressida.
> If beauty have a soul, this is not she.
> If souls guide vows, if vows be sanctimonies,
> If sanctimony be the gods' delight,
> If there be a rule in unity itself,
> This is not she.

> [5.2.140–5]

"This is and is not Cressid," he continues, battling to overlay his fantasized vision of her with the new reality. Far from believing that he and she are indissoluble, he is agonized by the fact that Cressida might have a life separate from his thoughts of her. As Troilus is coming to realize, there is in fact no "rule in unity itself".

Except that this lack of unity is not by any means new, as Cressida herself explained to him at their first, anxious meeting:

> I have a kind of self resides with you—
> But an unkind self, that itself will leave
> To be another's fool.

> [3.2.144–6]

Though her words are simple (a rarity in a play noted for its difficult, knotty language), Cressida's thoughts are densely intricate. She means – if she entirely knows what she means – that while part of her "resides", and wants to reside, with Troilus, she also despises herself for becoming "another's fool". That sense of internal dislocation goes some way to explaining why she acts as she does, and in so doing why she lives up to the reputation for which she had become notorious by the time Shakespeare's play reached the stage. Cressida's betrayal of Troilus is also a betrayal of herself – but then so was her getting together with Troilus in the first place.

Once Troilus is jilted – if he truly is (Cressida writes him a letter, but he dismisses it out of hand and we are not permitted to hear its contents) – the play brings to an end its cycle of betrayals. Despite Andromache's misgivings, and Cassandra's lurid premonitions of disaster, Hector is determined to fight and heads out to battle. Though he soon faces his arch-enemy Achilles, their first fight is inconclusive and they separate. But when news arrives that Patroclus, Achilles's favourite (and perhaps lover), has been killed, Achilles orders, then carries out, Hector's death – unarmed and in cold blood. This epic betrayal, so immense that it touches even *Hamlet*'s players, who act Hecuba's lament over Hector's corpse in front of the Prince, effectively ends the action of the play, which closes with Troilus's bitter insistence that "no space of earth shall sunder our two hates" (5.10.28).

But Troilus is not permitted to have the last word. In the earliest text of the play it is the bawd Pandarus who closes the action, ruminating on the betrayal of his own reputation. After being struck by Troilus for his behaviour, he complains:

> O world, world, world!—thus is the poor agent despised. O traitors and bawds, how earnestly are you set a work, and how ill requited! Why should our endeavour be so desired and the performance so loathed?
>
> [ADDITIONAL PASSAGE B]

Pandarus's final words are as grim as ever, and they provide a troubling ending to the play. The impression the audience is left with is hardly one of epic tragedy – the kind of tragedy enshrined in Hector's death – but nor are Pandarus's jokes about "endeavour" and "performance" easy to laugh at, given the horrendous separation endured by the lovers. *Troilus and Cressida* ends, like its position in the First Folio, stuck uncomfortably somewhere in the middle.

Stage history and adaptations

Mystery hangs over the early years of *Troilus and Cressida*, mainly because it was published in quarto in 1609 with two contradictory sets of front matter – one claiming that the play had never been "stal'd with the stage", the other insisting that it had been performed at the Globe by the King's Men, Shakespeare's regular troupe. The latter seems more likely, but for many years scholars believed (some still do) that the play was written for performance among learned spectators at an **Inns of Court** (law school), as with *The Comedy of Errors* and *Twelfth Night*.

The play's life in the following century is not much clearer: it possibly resurfaced at Dublin's Smock Alley Theatre in the 1670s, then was heavily adapted by **John Dryden** in 1679. Like his other rewritings, his approach in *Troilus and Cressida; Or, Truth Found Too Late* was drastic. Expressing his determination to save the play's "many excellent thoughts" from a "heap of rubbish", Dryden rewrote it almost entirely, transforming Cressida into a virtuous victim who only pretends to fall in love with Diomedes before conveniently committing suicide. In the first cast were **Thomas Betterton**'s Troilus alongside the Andromache of his wife **Mary**.

Aside from infrequent revivals of Dryden up to the 1730s, *Troilus and Cressida* genuinely disappeared from the stage until the very end of the nineteenth century – a fate not suffered even by *Timon of Athens* or *Pericles*. Translations of Shakespeare's text appeared in Germany and elsewhere in Europe (Berlin saw productions in 1899 and 1904, Munich one in 1898), but audiences in the UK had to wait until 1907 and **Charles Fry**'s London staging. In the event most critics were baffled by what they saw, though in **William Poel**'s Elizabethan production five years later they were won over, not least by a milliner turned actress called **Edith Evans**, then making her debut. By

Cressida (Lucy Briggs-Owen) and Troilus (Alex Waldmann) prepare to share a bittersweet first kiss, watched over by the ever-present Pandarus (David Collings). This 2008 Cheek by Jowl production emphasized the lovers' frailty in the face of implacable social forces.

this time, **Frank Benson** had put on all Shakespeare's plays up at Stratford with the exception of *Titus Andronicus* and *Troilus*, though Poel eagerly accepted the invitation to remedy half the deficit by touring *Troilus* there in 1913.

It was no accident that interest in so world-weary (and war-weary) a play as *Troilus* began to boom after the horrors of World War I. **Robert Atkins**'s Old Vic production from 1923 failed, mounted as the last in his series of plays put on to celebrate the tricentary of the First Folio, but **Ben Iden Payne** encountered more success with an Elizabethan staging at Stratford in 1936. Probably the play's defining production in this era was **Michael Macowan**'s at the Westminster Theatre in 1938, just a year before war was declared once again. Macowan put *Troilus* in a smart-set 1930s context, immortalized by **Max Adrian**'s dissolute, bow-tied Pandarus.

Anthony Quayle's 1948 Stratford production captured some of the exhaustion of postwar Britain, though **Glen Byam Shaw**'s 1954 successor was more openly cynical about conflict, starring Quayle as a fussy and wearisome Pandarus. The growing enthusiasm for the play is attested by **William Walton**'s opera from the following year, and in 1955 Shakespeare's text would receive infamous exposition in **Tyrone Guthrie**'s Old Vic production. This knowingly set the action just prior to World War I in decadent Edwardian society; the Trojan warriors were described as "callow specimens of a privileged caste".

The 1960s proved to be the play's busiest decade yet. The connection began early at Stratford, with **Peter Hall** and **John Barton**'s infamous "sand box" *Troilus* of 1960, focused on the sensual allure of **Dorothy Tutin**'s Cressida. **Peter O'Toole**'s acidic Thersites also gained glowing reviews, however, as did Max Adrian's return as Pandarus, and the political resonance of the production was underscored when the cast members scrawled "Ban The Horse!" in the sand at the height of the CND anti-nuclear rallies. Political campaigning was the hallmark of many 60s and 70s productions, particularly in the United States during the Civil Rights conflict and then the Vietnam years, and gender politics were also explored in **Joseph Papp**'s 1965 production in New York, which offered a pro-feminist Cressida who was a victim of unchecked male aggression. That approach would have its most influential recent incarnation in **Juliet Stevenson**'s fragile yet eloquent heroine at the RSC for **Howard Davies** in 1985. Stevenson was acclaimed for bringing to the role qualities many had thought absent – much like **Corinna Harfouch**'s Cressida with the Berliner Ensemble the following year, who repeatedly stressed her fragile position within a patriarchal community. By way of contrast, further productions by John Barton in 1968 and 1976 stressed the play's male sexualities; **Alan Howard**'s Achilles and **Richard Jones Barry**'s Patroclus were shown as openly gay in 1968.

Other directors have often seized on the play's ambiguous tone. Glasgow's Citizens' Theatre under **Philip Prowse** staged an all-male *Troilus* played for dangerous and somewhat crazed comedy, an approach mirrored by **Sam Mendes** at the RSC (1990), which was dominated by **Simon Russell Beale**'s acerbic Thersites. **Ralph Fiennes**'s nervy Troilus and **Amanda Root**'s emotive Cressida conducted their courtship with Thersites's insults ringing in the audience's ears. Mendes's approach was effectively postmodern (his Trojan War referenced many different eras), as was that by **Mark Wing-Davey** at the Public Theater in New York five years later, which spliced excerpts from CNN over Ulysses's famous speech on "degree". **Ian Judge**'s 1996 version, back at the RSC, was too tricksy for many critics, but its concern with **Victoria Hamilton**'s Cressida was one of its strongest features. The 1999 National Theatre production by **Trevor Nunn** steered a different course, instead sketching *Troilus* as an intimate and painful psychological study. **Sophie Okonedo**'s Cressida won plaudits for her depth of character, and the *Guardian* claimed that the whole thing was "a breakthrough".

German director **Peter Stein** brought an English-language version to the Edinburgh Festival in 2006, with **Annabel Scholey** and **Henry Pettigrew** in the lead. The production was sleek, dominated by a vast moveable wall at the back of the set and with the stage often packed with preening, bare-chested soldiers, but seemed curiously uncertain of its overall trajectory. More recently, **Declan Donnellan** and **Nick Ormerod**'s Cheek by Jowl company toured *Troilus* around Europe in 2008 in a conspicuously more stripped-down version. This saw the play primarily as a drama of ideas; among thought-provoking details were **Lucy Briggs-Owen**'s youthful Cressida, whose ebullient sexuality sometimes ran away with her, and **Richard Cant**'s Scouse, cross-dressed Thersites, played as a cleaning lady – one part Marlene Dietrich to two parts Lily Savage. In a striking image of the play's loneliness, the generals paused their barrack-room bravado to waltz with each other like teenagers at a school dance. Little of the same originality was present the following year in **Matthew Dunster**'s Globe production, which was dutiful but failed to spark into life, with the exception of **Matthew Kelly**'s oleaginous Thersites.

Troilus and Cressida has continued to see intermittent success in Germany (it was performed in a production by **Viet Schubert** at the replica Globe in Neuss in 2011), and has occasionally been staged in North America, too, notably at Stratford, Ontario in 2003 in a classically designed yet sexually vigorous production by **Richard Monette**; and at the Blackfriars Playhouse in Staunton, Virginia in 2013, where **Jim Warren**'s quickfire staging won plaudits for its stripped-down simplicity. Two productions seen in the UK during the 2012 World Shakespeare Festival illustrate the play's challenges as well as its potential for reinterpretation. At the Globe, New Zealand's **Ngakau Toa** company, performing in classical Maori, offered an epic version dominated by strutting warriors and preening aggression that made the love affair between **Kimo Houltham** and **Awhina Rose Henare Ashby** seem doomed before it even began. Radically different – and, to many, radically irritating – was the co-production between New York's avant-garde Wooster Group and the RSC, directed by **Elizabeth LeCompte** and **Mark Ravenhill**, which opened later that summer. The Americans were Trojans-cum-Native-Americans, the Brits played Greeks, and a great deal seemed to have got lost in transtlantic translation.

Troilus and Cressida has yet to appear on the big screen, though several TV adaptations have been made. Only **Jonathan Miller**'s BBC/Time-Life version from 1981, with **Anton Lesser**'s Troilus opposite **Suzanne Burden**'s Cressida, is still readily available.

SCREEN

Troilus and Cressida
A. Lesser, S. Burden, C. Gray; Jonathan Miller (dir.)
UK, 1981 > BBC **DVD**

Jonathan Miller's decision to get involved with the BBC Shakespeare halfway through turned around its artistic fortunes, and some of its finest achievements appeared under his stewardship. This *Troilus and Cressida* is perhaps not among them, but its rather serious-minded reading of the play nevertheless has virtues – and it is the only one available. Staging is Elizabethan, but less busily so than elsewhere in the series and Miller cleverly contrasts the Renaissance world of Troy and the grim muddle of the Greek camp. Suzanne Burden's Cressida is coolly measured, only hinting at the troubled passions beneath but registering her character's genuine lack of power; and opposite her Anton Lesser is painfully earnest as Troilus. Charles Gray is a bit too hammy as Pandarus, although Thersites receives a lively if somewhat bizarre performance at the hands of blind performance artist Jack Birkett (aka "The Incredible Orlando"), who also stars in Derek Jarman's *Tempest* (see p.426).

AUDIO

Troilus and Cressida
I. Pepperell, J. Ford, D. Troughton; Clive Brill (dir.)
UK, 1998 > Arkangel ◉ ⬇

There's plenty to like in this Arkangel *Troilus and Cressida*, if you discount the unpleasant events of the play. Despite the large size of the cast, there are many excellent performances: particularly worthy of note are David Troughton's superlatively sarcastic Thersites; a swaggering Achilles from Julian Wadham; an excellent Pandarus in Norman Rodway; and Gerard Murphy's dyspeptic and sanctimonious Ulysses. But if the play is to be anything more than bitter satire it needs a convincing couple in the lead, and Ian Pepperell and Julia Ford rise to the challenge. Ford makes it clear that Cressida's slightly shallow cynicism is a tactic forced by male locker-room posturing, and Pepperell's urgent but ultimately naive Troilus is effortlessly outmanoeuvred by almost everyone else – most notoriously Duncan Bell's suave Diomedes. These carefully considered touches are assisted by Clive Brill's clear and unsentimental production.

EDITIONS

Arden Shakespeare (third series)
David Bevington (ed.); rev. 2015 > Bloomsbury

Troilus is fortunate in having two excellent editions: this and Anthony Bawson's clean and no-nonsense New Cambridge (2003). Arden is pushed into pole position by virtue of having been updated and considerably extended (to 514 pages, which for one of the most neglected plays in the canon is impressive). Bevington is a sharp and thoughtful critic, and worries away at the play's many quiddities and paradoxes – its historical context, its sources, its complicated texts, its mysterious early performance history (perhaps limited by the script's political sensitivity, Bevington argues). Occasionally there is more heat than light, but no one could accuse the editor of not trying. The performance history, which now reaches up to 2013, is particularly welcome, and factors in recent critical studies too.

SOME CRITICISM

Shakespeare and the Common Understanding
Norman Rabkin; 1967 > Chicago UP [o/p]

While not exclusively concerned with *Troilus and Cressida*, the broad point of Norman Rabkin's masterful study – that it is the buried complexities within Shakespeare's work, not their surface appeal, that guarantees them resonance among our "common understanding" – means that he seems particularly sympathetic to the warts-and-all (or perhaps pox-and-all) world of this play. And although Rabkin covers nearly all Shakespeare's works in the course of this study, his half-chapter on *Troilus*'s contradictory views on worth and value is especially engaging. We have no need to apologize for this play, Rabkin argues, nor find a form of special pleading: its moral ambivalence and complex metaphysics are marks of a genius.

The Swan at the Well
E. Talbot Donaldson; 1985 > Yale UP [o/p]

Shakespeare used Chaucer quite sparingly but the medieval poet does crop up in intriguing places – as is witnessed by Feste's impersonation of a cleric called "Sir Thopas" in *Twelfth Night* (the name comes from one of the *Canterbury Tales*, although the play otherwise has little connection with Chaucer). E. Talbot Donaldson deals with more obvious connections, concentrating on *A Midsummer Night's Dream*, *The Two Noble Kinsmen* and *Troilus and Cressida* alongside various analogues. The strongest part of this slightly patchy book deals with the last of these: *Troilus and Criseyde* underpins every aspect of Shakespeare's play, and Donaldson's expert exposing of Chaucerian motifs demonstrates just how intimate the dialogue between the two masterpieces is.

Twelfth Night

L yrical, emotional and bittersweet, *Twelfth Night* has long been regarded as perhaps Shakespeare's most perfect comedy. Written soon after *Hamlet* and *As You Like It*, its mood is delicately poised: while its title promises carnival misrule, what the play delivers is grave and searching as well as riotously funny. It also stands at the very centre of Shakespeare's dramatic career, looking back on the twinned chaos of *The Comedy of Errors* and the boisterous laughs of Falstaff as well as anticipating the miraculous resolutions of *Cymbeline* and *The Winter's Tale*. As so often in Shakespearian comedy, here romantic love is both plague and cure – at the climax of the action nearly everyone on stage is in love with the wrong partner, and untangling the mess takes formidable and mischievous dramatic skill. The insanity of desire is a major theme in *Twelfth Night*, and so is its potential to humiliate, never more so than in the subplot of a household servant who is gulled into falling for his employer, a story the playwright does not allow to end happily. The play's alternative title, *What You Will*, teases its audiences with comic implausibilities alongside searching insights into human nature.

DATE > Performed at London's Middle Temple, a law college, on February 2, 1602, *Twelfth Night* was probably written the preceding year, soon after *Hamlet*. Numerous allusions tie it to this date, though an independent record of an unnamed entertainment performed before Elizabeth I on Twelfth Night 1601 is unlikely to be this one.

SOURCES > *Menaechmi*, by the Roman comedian Plautus, ultimately provides the twins story (it's also the main source for *The Comedy of Errors*), while the love interest derives from a titillating sixteenth-century Italian play called *Gl'Ingannati* ("The Deceived"), which Shakespeare could have read in a number of English and Italian versions.

TEXTS > The play was first printed in the 1623 Folio (F1) in an unusually trouble-free text, probably set from a scribe's copy.

Interpreting the play

Like Shakespearian comedies before and after, *Twelfth Night* begins in bleakness. There has been a shipwreck – one of Shakespeare's ever-malevolent tempests – with just a handful of survivors. The lady Viola, her sea journey cruelly interrupted, finds herself in a strange and possibly hostile land. Apart from the captain and sailors who accompany him (none of them reappears in the play), she is alone. She is also bereaved:

MAJOR CHARACTERS & SYNOPSIS

Orsino, Duke of Illyria
Valentine and **Curio**, Orsino's servants
Viola, a shipwrecked lady (later disguised as "Cesario")
Sebastian, her twin brother
A **Sea Captain**
Antonio, another sea captain
Olivia, a countess
Maria, Olivia's servant
Sir Toby Belch, Olivia's uncle
Sir Andrew Aguecheek, Sir Toby's companion
Malvolio, Olivia's steward
Fabian, Olivia's servant
Feste, Olivia's clown
A **Priest**

ACT 1 The Illyrian court is at a standstill – Duke Orsino is in love. But the object of his affections, Olivia, is in mourning for her brother and remains aloof. Orsino is not the only one in pursuit of Olivia: her uncle Sir Toby Belch has persuaded his friend, the rich but dim-witted Sir Andrew Aguecheek, to present himself as a suitor. Meanwhile on the coast of Illyria, two survivors of a shipwreck, Viola and the Sea Captain, are discussing what to do. Convinced that her twin brother Sebastian has drowned, Viola decides to disguise herself as a young man, Cesario, and serve at Orsino's court. She rapidly becomes a favourite of the Duke, who employs her as a go-between in his courtship of Olivia. The plan goes awry, however, when Olivia finds herself more charmed by the messenger than the message.

ACT 2 Sebastian has survived – rescued by Antonio – although he, too, thinks his twin is dead and resolves to head for the court of Orsino. Meanwhile Viola/Cesario has fallen in love with Orsino. Over at Olivia's house, Sir Toby and Sir Andrew are carousing with Feste, despite a warning from Maria, Olivia's maid. The revelry comes to an abrupt end, however, when Malvolio, Olivia's steward, storms in, complaining about the noise and threatening to throw them out. As soon as he leaves, the assembled company plans its revenge. Maria devises a scheme whereby, with the help of forged love letters, Malvolio will think that Olivia is in love with him. The plan

works: Malvolio discovers the anonymous letters and, assuming they are addressed to him, begins to fantasize about life as Olivia's husband.

ACT 3 Olivia confesses her love to Cesario/Viola but Viola tells her that it cannot be returned. Noting Cesario's apparent success with Olivia, the frustrated Sir Andrew is persuaded by Toby to challenge him to a duel. But Olivia now has another suitor: Malvolio, who hopes to win her by following the bizarre instructions supplied by the letters. Olivia, however, believes him to be mad and asks Sir Toby to keep an eye on him. The duellists are about to begin their fight when they are interrupted by Antonio, who has arranged to meet Sebastian. Mistaking Cesario/Viola for Sebastian, Antonio cannot understand when his friend fails to recognize him.

ACT 4 Sebastian is talking with Feste, who believes him to be Cesario, when he is attacked by Sir Andrew – who is under the same impression. Sebastian retaliates and Sir Toby joins in, before Olivia arrives and puts a halt to the fighting. Making the same mistake, and by now completely smitten, Olivia proposes to Sebastian that they marry; though bewildered, Sebastian falls in love on the instant and accepts. Things go from bad to worse for Malvolio – by now locked up for his own safety – when the fool Feste is persuaded by Maria and Sir Toby to imitate a priest and exorcize Malvolio's "demons".

ACT 5 Confusion mounts when discussion between Cesario/Viola and Orsino is interrupted by Olivia. As the Duke attempts to win his lady one last time, she triumphantly announces that she's already married to Cesario, who promptly denies it. Olivia then summons the priest, who seems to confirm the news, when Sir Andrew and Sir Toby limp in followed by Sebastian, who admits to having fought them both. After a few moments of astonishment, the twins joyfully recognize each other, Sebastian is reunited with Olivia (and Antonio), and Orsino proposes to Viola. All that remains is for the release of Malvolio who, when told of the trick that has been played on him, stomps off – vowing revenge on everyone present.

VIOLA
>What country, friends, is this?

CAPTAIN   This is Illyria, lady.

VIOLA
>And what should I do in Illyria?
>My brother, he is in Elysium.

[1.2.1–3]

Like the brothers Antipholus in *The Comedy of Errors*, Viola and her brother – his name is Sebastian – are identical twins, and from this impossible fact Shakespeare spins one of his most moving comedies. Though she cannot know it yet, Viola's similarity to the sibling she believes is drowned is something that will deliver her from sadness and ultimately reunite them both. Opting to "conceal" herself by dressing as a youth – a youth who inevitably resembles her brother – Viola travels to the Illyrian court, like many a hero of romance before her, to seek her fortune. It is as though she leaves the mourning, solitary sister behind: donning her costume, Viola propels herself into a comic world of mysterious disguises, capricious love and crazy topsy-turvydom.

Twelfth Night, as befits its place in Shakespeare's canon – written around the same time as *Hamlet* – bridges worlds that are comic and those that are tragic. Soon after Viola arrives we are shown the household of the Illyrian countess Olivia, likewise in mourning. Shakespeare means the parallels between the two heroines to be uncanny: just as Olivia's name is a near anagram of Viola's, she too is grief-stricken for a dead brother. Yet her long-absent fool Feste gently reminds his mistress that perhaps it is time to rejoin the living. "Good madonna," he asks, "why mournest thou?"

OLIVIA Good fool, for my brother's death.
FESTE I think his soul is in hell, madonna.
OLIVIA I know his soul is in heaven, fool.
FESTE The more fool, madonna, to mourn for your brother's soul, being in heaven.

[1.5.62–7]

Comedy has the potential to heal grave emotional wounds, and with the clown's reappearance in Illyria the cast of *Twelfth Night* discovers, with Olivia, that to find happiness you first have to make yourself happy. The irony is that, before the play is out, more will be exposed as "fools" than they think.

Excess of it

Not all the sadness at the opening of *Twelfth Night* strikes such grave notes. Elsewhere in Illyria Duke Orsino is mournful with love – worse, he is mournful with love for Olivia, who cannot bring herself to requite him. In fact the play begins with Orsino (though there is a long stage tradition of opening with the shipwreck), and with some of the most-quoted lines in Shakespeare. "If music be the food of love," he calls to his musicians,

> *An improbable world of hair's-breadth rescues at sea, romantic disguises,*
> *idealistic friendships and sudden, irrational loves. This is not quite the country*
> *behind the North Wind, but it approaches those latitudes.*
>
> Anne Barton, "*As You Like It* and *Twelfth Night*: Shakespeare's sense of an ending" (1972)

> Play on,
> Give me excess of it that, surfeiting,
> The appetite may sicken and so die.
> That strain again, it had a dying fall.
> O, it came over my ear like the sweet sound
> That breathes upon a bank of violets.
> Stealing and giving odour. Enough, no more,
> 'Tis not so sweet now as it was before.
>
> [1.1.1–8]

Orsino wants nothing less than too much: he demands "excess" in the hope that somehow it will cure his "appetite" for tears by killing it. Although he is in love, he begs to be out of it; though he listens to music, he wants it to stop. "So full of shapes is fancy," Orsino reflects to himself, "that it alone is high fantastical" (1.1.14–15). Orsino is in love with love itself – and with the power of his own "fantastical" imagination.

Before long both he and Olivia find themselves more authentically in love, but the consequences are unexpected. In one of Shakespeare's most inspired pieces of mischief, both fall for Viola – someone who is, in the strange logic of Shakespearian comedy, both "maid and man" (5.1.261). Before *Twelfth Night* gets there, however, other craziness ensues. Much of it centres on the aptly named Sir Toby Belch, Olivia's boozy cousin, and his companion Sir Andrew Aguecheek. Perpetually short of money because of his riotous lifestyle (in this he echoes Falstaff), Sir Toby cultivates the rich but dim Sir Andrew, persuading him to make yet another doomed attempt for Olivia's love. After all, as he patiently explains, there is a great deal of revelry to do:

> SIR TOBY Not to be abed after midnight is to be up betimes, and *diliculo*
> *surgere*, thou knowest.
> SIR ANDREW Nay, by my troth, I know not; but I know to be up late is to be
> up late.
> SIR TOBY A false conclusion. I hate it as an unfilled can. To be up after
> midnight and to go to bed then is early; so that to go to bed after midnight
> is to go to bed betimes.
>
> [2.3.1–9]

"Twelfth Night" was the closing feast of the Christmas season and its crazed climax. Historically, it was a medieval celebration that survived until the eighteenth century, an occasion upon which "misrule" (the inversion of social hierarchies) and carnivalesque licence were allowed full voice. Turning night into day with drinking and dancing, Sir Toby embodies the antic spirit of the play's title, doing his utmost to turn *Twelfth Night* the drama into Twelfth Night the festival.

That is and is not

Not everyone here is willing to let that happen. When Sir Toby's midnight revelry threatens to spin out of control, Olivia's puritanical retainer Malvolio bursts in and furiously demands that they call a halt. Sir Toby is appalled that a jumped-up "steward" should presume to say anything of the kind, but it is Malvolio's fellow servant Maria – egged on by Sir Toby – who hatches a satisfyingly cruel revenge: she will write a letter to Malvolio, purportedly from Olivia, hinting that she wishes to be more intimate with him. The plot catches fire immediately, and the letter itself is a comic masterstroke. Casually coming across it while out taking the air, Malvolio thinks that his chance for glory has finally come. "By my life, this is my lady's hand," he exclaims – then begins to puzzle away at the cryptic message it expresses:

> 'I may command where I adore.' Why, she may command me. I serve her, she is my lady. Why, this is evident to any formal capacity. There is no obstruction in this … I do not now fool myself, to let imagination jade me; for every reason excites to this, that my lady loves me.
>
> [2.5.113–60]

Malvolio does indeed "fool" himself, and furthermore makes a fool *of* himself by being convinced so easily – and on such implausible grounds – that Olivia loves him. Like Orsino, he has fallen in love with a reflection of his own figure: as Olivia astutely realized, he is "sick of self-love" (1.5.86).

The joke had real attractions for Shakespeare's contemporaries, themselves keenly aware of how "serving" in someone's household could, and sometimes did, encompass a suggestive range of possibilities. The error Malvolio makes is to mix up his mistress (his boss) with his mistress (his lover), and it is one that a seventeenth-century spectator of *Twelfth Night*, a lawyer named John Manningham, who saw one of its earliest performances, was particularly impressed by. Noting that "a good practice in it [was] to make the steward believe his lady widow was in love with him", Manningham relates in his account of the play that Malvolio's embarrassment does not stop at this. Instructed by the letter to don ridiculous yellow stockings in order to signal to Olivia that he has understood her message, Malvolio does so – and is promptly locked up because everyone "took him to be mad". The incarcerated Malvolio attempts to right the situation by insisting on his sanity, but the omnipresent Feste (Olivia's "allowed", or professional, fool) neatly turns it back on him:

> MALVOLIO Fool, there was never man so notoriously abused. I am as well in my wits, fool, as thou art.
> FESTE But as well? Then you are mad indeed, if you be no better in your wits than a fool.
>
> [4.2.89–92]

Boy meets girl

While the public theatre of other European countries allowed women to act, in Renaissance England they did not. No one is quite sure why: Spain, France and Italy had similar medieval, male traditions of academic and guild-sponsored theatre, but from around the middle of the sixteenth century women began to perform in public there. In England, however, boys and men continued to be employed in transvestite roles until 1642 and the closure of the theatres. The term "actress" did not become current until after the Restoration.

Most writers who attacked the theatre singled out the "wanton" practice of stage transvestism for especial vitriol, arguing that theatre – already dangerously sexual – encouraged its audiences to indulge in homoerotic fantasies. **Philip Stubbes**, one of the most prolific and compulsive pamphleteers during the period, screeched in his *Anatomy of Abuses* (1585) that people who had been to see plays were tempted to "play the sodomites or worse", while his fellow Puritan **John Rainoldes** reminded readers that Scripture outlawed precisely this kind of "beastly filthiness".

Yet wider society had ambivalent feelings about male homosexuality (the word itself is a nineteenth-century invention). Sodomy was a crime technically punishable by death, but on the other hand passionate friendships between young men seem to have been relatively commonplace. The position of the boy players themselves (and "boys" might be as old as 17; adolescence seems to have occurred later in the sixteenth century) was correspondingly ambiguous: apprenticed to adult players, they were thought by some to be exploitable youths working in an exploitative industry. And yet the idea of males pretending to be females on stage seems not to have bothered too many theatregoers – pretending to be a member of the opposite sex just took skill in acting, like anything else. The late Elizabethan fashion for women with small breasts and narrow hips can only have helped.

It is with these multiple ambiguities that Shakespeare's comedies teasingly flirt. Most often the device of swapping gender accomplishes a fixed purpose – allowing female characters to roam at large without attracting what *The Two Gentlemen*'s Julia calls "the loose encounters of lascivious men" (2.7.41). But in later plays the capacity for cross-dressed double entrendres becomes wickedly playful. *Twelfth Night*'s Viola finds her "masculine usurped attire" presents only problems: falling for her master Orsino, she realizes that the countess Olivia has also fallen for her disguise. *As You Like It*'s Rosalind, by contrast, employs her new identity more mischievously, renaming herself "Ganymede" – recalling not just Jove's cup-bearer in Roman mythology, but also Elizabethan slang for a homosexual youth. And she uses that sexual camouflage to winning advantage: first escaping to Ardenne, then teasing herself (and us) by pretending to be Rosalind so that Orlando can polish his wooing technique – the most dizzying Shakespearian transformation of all, in which a boy actor pretending to be a girl pretends to be a boy pretending to be a girl.

Malvolio hotly retorts that "I am as well in my wits as any man in Illyria" (4.2.109–10), but by the time he says it the claim is beginning to look double-edged. He is not the only character exhibiting signs of insanity. Having turned down Orsino, Olivia finds that she has become attracted to Cesario, his page (in other words, the disguised Viola), while Viola herself – resisting Olivia's impassioned advances – is sick for the sight of Orsino. "How will this fadge [turn out]?" Viola wonders at one point:

> My master loves her dearly,
> And I, poor monster, fond as much on him,
> And she, mistaken, seems to dote on me.
> What will become of this? As I am man,
> My state is desperate for my master's love.
> As I am woman, now, alas the day,
> What thriftless sighs shall poor Olivia breathe!
> O time, thou must untangle this, not I.

> [2.2.33–40]

Time will indeed unscramble things, though Malvolio's treatment is hard to forgive (he leaves the play vowing to be "revenged on the whole pack of you" (5.1.374)) and, in the shorter term, it will make Viola's life considerably more complicated. By this stage of *Twelfth Night* we know that her grief at the beginning of the play has been too hasty: though Sebastian has been separated by the shipwreck, he has in fact survived and is at this moment also wandering around Illyria. In a throwback to the perplexities of *The Comedy of Errors*, it is only inevitable that confusion between them will result – first when Sebastian's companion and rescuer Antonio mistakes Viola for her twin, again when Sir Andrew, emboldened by love for Olivia (and plenty of prompting by Sir Toby), attacks Sebastian in the belief that he is Cesario/Viola. In the play's most startling moment, however, it is Olivia's inability to tell the twins apart that has the most far-reaching consequences. Protecting Sebastian from his assailants, she begs, "Go with me to my house":

> Do not deny. Beshrew his soul for me,
> He started one poor heart of mine in thee.
> SEBASTIAN
> What relish is in this? How runs the stream?
> Or I am mad, or else this is a dream ...

> [4.1.53–60]

Neither is quite true, though madness is certainly in the air when the love-struck Sebastian agrees to be "ruled by" (and very rapidly married to) Olivia. Despite her best efforts – and the convolutions of Shakespeare's gender-bending plot – she has succeeded in getting wed to a man.

Although in *Twelfth Night* it frequently seems as if everyone has fallen in love with everyone else (even Sir Toby ends up hitched to Maria), the play allows these tangles to be untied, as so often, in a climactic final scene. It begins darkly: captured by Orsino's men, Antonio is stunned that the "ingrateful boy" Cesario (whom he thinks is Sebastian) should now pretend not to know him. "His life I gave him," he bitterly reflects,

> and did thereto add
> My love without retention or restraint,
> All his in dedication.

> [5.1.76–8]

Again the languages of service and of love entwine – so closely that modern directors have sometimes played the relationship between Antonio and Sebastian as a homosexual one. Shakespeare is more ambiguous as well as more subtle: Antonio has given his all for Sebastian, a "love" that is among the play's truest. It is the kind of devoted service also expected by Orsino, the reason he is so appalled when Olivia arrives and announces that she has married Cesario (a marriage that, in a teasing Shakespearian joke, has seemingly not involved any exchange of names). Despite Viola's genuine protestations of innocence, for a few tense moments it looks as though her duplicity throughout risks turning into something much more serious. But then Sebastian appears, and the play's most complicated moment – the presence on stage of identical twins of different sexes – dazzlingly resolves into its simplest. The recognition between the twins is winningly easy, not so much a genuine surprise as a rehearsal of facts the audience already knows to be true:

VIOLA
    My father had a mole upon his brow.
SEBASTIAN And so had mine.
VIOLA
    And died that day when Viola from her birth
    Had numbered thirteen years.
SEBASTIAN
    O, that record is lively in my soul.

                      [5.1.240–4]

From death Shakespeare conjures "lively" life: Sebastian's "sister … whom the blind waves and surges have devoured" (5.1.226–7) is standing here in front of him. Though the pair have, as Orsino murmurs, "one face, one voice, one habit," they are also "two persons, / A natural perspective, that is and is not" (5.2.213–4). In this way Shakespeare adds a new dimension to his assertion in the Sonnets – many of which may have been written by the time *Twelfth Night* debuted – that "love is not love / Which alters when it alteration finds" (116, 2–3). What the play's characters discover is that love can "alter" and yet find truth: that Olivia can fall in love with a girl and yet marry a boy; that Orsino, deceived, can find himself "betrothed to both a maid and man" (5.1.261); and that twins can be the same as well as different, and different as well as the same.

Stage history and adaptations

Unusually, we know a handful of facts about *Twelfth Night*'s early stage history: a 1602 performance at the legal hall **Middle Temple** was recorded by a contemporary diarist (see p.470), and some have speculated that it might also have been the unnamed play acted at **court** the year before. It seems likely that Feste was written for the chief clown in Shakespeare's company, **Robert Armin** – noted for his thoughtful approach to comedic roles (see p.36).

The comedy remained popular up to the closure of the theatres in 1642, and after the Restoration it was revived in an adaptation by **William Davenant**. Pepys saw this version twice and pronounced it "silly", however, and within a few decades it had been supplanted by modernized reworkings. **William Wycherly**'s *The Plain-Dealer* held the stage from 1674, and **William Burnaby**'s *Love Betrayed* first appeared in 1703, its published text proudly insisting that while it used much of Shakespeare's plot, nearly all his lines were cut. But Burnaby's version only had a couple of performances, and afterwards *Twelfth Night* disappeared from theatres entirely.

Its fortunes would be reversed by **Charles Macklin**, who acted the comedy at Drury Lane in 1741 and made it one of Shakespeare's most popular. Macklin founded a theatrical tradition by seizing on the role of Malvolio, which he performed to **Hannah Pritchard**'s Viola and **Kitty Clive**'s Olivia. *Twelfth Night* was played in countless London revivals over the next half-century, and appeared in New York in 1804. In 1820, **Frederick Reynolds** and **Henry Bishop** tried to get a musical version boasting songs "selected *entirely* from … Shakespeare" off the ground and saw some success, but, as usual with Reynolds's productions, few of those came from the play in question. **Samuel Phelps** was more faithful to the text at Sadler's Wells in 1848, playing a frosty Malvolio, while two years later **Charles Kean** chose to open his series of spectacular Shakespearian revivals at the Princess's Theatre with the comedy.

Other producers found success with the play – among them the **Duke of Saxe-Meinigen**'s company, who toured to Britain in 1881 with *Twelfth Night*, *The Winter's Tale* and *Julius Caesar* – and it remained an integral part of the Victorian repertoire. **Henry Irving**'s Lyceum performances were lavishly staged and well cast (Irving played an emotive Malvolio to **Ellen Terry**'s Viola), but struggled to attract audiences – a problem not experienced by **Herbert Beerbohm Tree** in 1901, whose production was seen by many thousands of people over the years. Tree starred as Malvolio, but it was the impressiveness of his staging that struck audiences with wonder: the Italianate garden of **Maud Jefferies**'s Olivia was painstakingly copied from illustrations in *Country Life*, and took so long to set that the scenes there had to be run consecutively. Nearly as invasive were **Augustin Daly**'s various New York-based productions from 1894, with **Ada Rehan** a buoyant Viola, which again rearranged the play's running order.

The backlash was soon under way. **William Poel** staged *Twelfth Night* several times, first in 1895 with an amateur cast and Elizabethan music, and again in 1905. Many were unimpressed by Poel's attempts at historically informed staging, yet they laid the ground for **Harley Granville-Barker**'s ground-breaking production at the Savoy in 1912, often called the first truly "modern" version. **Norman Wilkinson**'s elegant black-and-silver design dominated and the staging was rapid and fluid, but it was Granville-Barker's cast that put *Twelfth Night* in a fresh light: **Lillah McCarthy**'s Viola was passionate and **Henry Ainley**'s Malvolio a "dry puritan", but eyewitnesses were especially struck by **Hayden Coffin**'s lugubrious Feste. The Paris-based production by **Jacques Copeau** two years later gained nearly as many fans (Granville-Barker was one), though the temptation to tinker got the better of **William Bridges-Adams** at Stratford in 1932 – he softened the play's conclusion by axeing the prison scene.

"Smilest thou?" Mark Rylance's Olivia is nonplussed by Stephen Fry as a leering, yellow-stockinged Malvolio. Tim Carroll's all-male Globe production opened at Lincoln's Inn in 2002, four hundred years after the play first appeared there, and was revived in 2012.

The difficulty of how best to reconcile *Twelfth Night*'s comic and tragic elements also caused problems for **John Gielgud**, directing at Stratford in 1955, though admittedly he wasn't helped by **Laurence Olivier**'s hysterically camp and hammy Malvolio (Olivier insisted on falling backwards off a bench in the garden scene, though Gielgud begged him not to). Three years later **Peter Hall** produced a version at the same venue still often cited as a cornerstone: it put **Dorothy Tutin**'s Viola into service at **Lila de Nobili**'s gorgeously designed Cavalier court, described by one critic as a "rich symphony in russet". Reviewers were ambivalent about **Geraldine McEwan**'s unusually youthful Olivia (one called her a "kittenish typist"), but **Max Adrian**'s melancholy Feste was warmly received. The production was revived in 1960 with a slightly reworked cast – among them **Ian Richardson** as Sir Andrew and **Eric Porter**'s Malvolio – and continued to attract plaudits.

Also much revived was **John Barton**'s 1969 version, with an impressive line-up including **Judi Dench**'s powerful but level-headed Viola and **Donald Sinden**'s richly characterized Malvolio. Barton's reading of the play was Chekhovian – one witness commented that he couldn't recall a production "that held all the comedy's elements in such harmony" – and many audiences remembered its elegant staging, surrounded on three sides by a gauze box. **Peter Gill**'s 1974 version, again at the RSC, took a less romantic view of the play (Gill's theory that it was all about narcissism was represented by an image of Narcissus himself above the stage), and also emphasized its homosexual entanglements. **Terry Hands** took a literal-minded view of the play's post-Christmas setting, but as his 1979 production wore on green shoots sprung up beneath the snow; it wasn't an approach that convinced everyone, but **Cherie Lunghi**'s expressive Viola apparently did.

The RSC revival by **John Caird** from 1983 returned to the familiar theme of self-love (**Zoë Wanamaker** was distinctly unsettled by Orsino's advances), but a year previously **Ariane Mnouchkine** struck out in bold new directions with her Théâtre du Soleil production, which drew influences from Japan and India in order to construct a self-consciously exotic Illyria. Back at Stratford, **Bill Alexander**'s 1987 staging was dominated by **Antony Sher**'s striking Malvolio, who was driven literally mad after being chained to a stake. Elsewhere in the cast **Harriet Walter**'s Viola was acclaimed, as was **David Bradley**'s maudlin Sir Andrew. **Declan Donnellan**'s production with Cheek by Jowl the same year was utterly different, stressing instead the wild sexualities of the play along with its comic conclusion – Malvolio was brought back into the fold, and even Antonio and Feste paired off at the end.

It's difficult to generalize about a play which has had so rich a stage history as *Twelfth Night*, and recent approaches testify to the apparently endless ways of performing it. **Peter Hall**'s return to the comedy in 1991 at the Playhouse Theatre, 36 years after first doing it, impressed many critics with its straight-down-the-line approach, but in general directors have searched for new angles – something Hall was reacting against. **Adrian Noble**'s 1997 RSC production was a case in point: creating a fantasy world of primary colours (reminiscent of Komisarjevsky's famous 1938 *Comedy of Errors*), Noble played it for laughs at the expense of the play's melancholy dimension – thus delighting audiences but upsetting the critics.

Of the 100-plus productions over the last twenty years, in the UK and US alone, it is impossible to mention more than a handful, especially given that the American festival circuit averages roughly five per year. Elizabethan approaches to the text have been attempted by **Ian Judge** at the RSC (1994) and **Tim Carroll** at Shakespeare's Globe (2002), though Carroll's all-male production gained stronger reviews; **Mark Rylance**'s Olivia was particularly excellent, bringing touching comic pathos to the character, and the production was restaged at the Globe in 2012, with **Stephen Fry** stepping into Malvolio's yellow stockings, before transferring to Broadway the following year. **Edward Hall**'s production, which opened at the Old Vic in 2007, was also all-male, with the cast emerging from dust-sheeted wardrobes to re-enact the storm. Acclaimed for its attention to the text, Hall's production boasted fine performances from **Dugald Bruce-Lockardt** as a powerful Olivia and **Tony Bell** as a lugubrious Feste.

Sam Mendes chose the play for his final season at London's Donmar in 2002, pairing it with Chekhov's *Uncle Vanya*, and his cast (which included Simon Russell Beale as an especially fastidious Malvolio and Helen McCrory as a sexy and wilful Olivia) captured the melancholic essence of the play as well as its riotous comedy. Also autumnal was was Declan Donnellan's Russian-language version, which began a worldwide tour in 2003. This achieved its impact through the slenderest of means, balancing the play's contrasting moods with pinpoint precision and suggesting that the urge to dress up was as much psychological refuge as theatrical play-acting.

Twelfth Night's return to the West End in 2008, in a slightly old-fashioned Donmar production directed by Michael Grandage, was centred on Derek Jacobi's majestically prissy turn as Malvolio – comic catnip to some, allergy-provoking to others. Gregory Doran's Mediterranean-style revival at the RSC the following year boasted the attractive pairing of Nancy Carroll as Viola and Alexandra Gilbreath as Olivia, but was similarly accused of over-egging the humour in the strutting shape of Richard Wilson's Malvolio. Across at Stratford, Ontario in 2011, Des McAnuff took his cue from Orsino, filling (or perhaps overfilling) the play with music and offering costumes that reminded some of *Sgt. Pepper's Lonely Hearts Club Band*; "give me excess of it ... and so die", declared the *Globe and Mail*'s critic, somewhat wearily. Altogether different was the version offered by the young New York troupe Bedlam in 2015 in a tiny room in the Garment district off-Broadway – minimally designed, with a small cast and one scene that took place entirely in the dark. A delighted *New York Times* critic declared that witnessing it was evidence that "acting might just be the most satisfying profession on the planet".

Twelfth Night has long been a favourite far beyond British and North American shores: an extremely conservative recent estimate numbers well over 100 productions in the last half-century, many of them not in English – all the way from Yakov Fried's Russian-language *Dvenadtsataia Noch* of 1955 to Martin van Zundert's Flemish adaptation *Driekoningenavond* of 1972, not to mention any number of *Was Ihr Wollts* (in German the comedy goes under its alternative title, "What You Will"). Like many of the comedies, it was adapted in India early and multiple times, including a musical version created by the New Alfred Dramatic Company in Mumbai in 1905, in which the Viola and Sebastian characters are caught in a train crash rather than a shipwreck. Repaying the compliment in London in 2004, British director Stephen Beresford updated the play to contemporary India, with Paul Bhattacharjee's officious government-nabob Malvolio and Kulvinder Ghir's Bollywood-wannabe Feste both being singled out for special praise. At the World Shakespeare Festival in 2012, it was staged – perhaps fittingly – twice, once by the RSC in a dark-hued performance by David Farr, part of a "shipwreck" trilogy; and again in a gleefully impious version translated into Hindi by Atul Kumar's Company Theatre from Mumbai.

On screen, *Twelfth Night* has cropped up in various places. In addition to a number of BBC productions – the latest being the Time-Life collaboration starring Felicity Kendal's Viola alongside Alec McCowen's Malvolio (1980) – it has also appeared on commercial TV, most recently at the behest of Britain's Channel 4 with a production by Tim Supple that offered the play as a parable about multicultural society (2004). On the big screen, Yan Fried's Russian film (1955) has been joined by Trevor Nunn's

1995 English-language version, set in Victorian Cornwall and starring **Imogen Stubbs** (Viola) and **Nigel Hawthorne** (Malvolio), in addition to recent cinema broadcasts of live theatre versions.

SCREEN

Twelfth Night
F. Turner, C. Kent, J.S. Gordon; Charles Kent (dir.) USA, 1910 > on Silent Shakespeare (BFI) DVD

Its redaction of the plot may well have left early audiences puzzled, but this Vitagraph *Twelfth Night*, like their *Dream* (see p.316) has oodles of charm. Like productions before and after it, this version begins in the sea – and with what appears to be a real shipwreck sticking out of the lapping waves, richly contrasted with the fussiness of Orsino's court. Florence Turner's expressive (and unbelievably tiny) Viola comes close to stealing the show, at first touchingly melancholy but responding quizzically to Olivia's advances. Director Charles Kent's lofty Malvolio provides stiff competiton, though, as does Turner's double for Sebastian – the scene where they appear together really does seem convincing on century-old film.

Twelfth Night
I. Stubbs, H. Bonham-Carter, N. Hawthorne; Trevor Nunn (dir.) UK, 1995 > EIV / Warner DVD

Filmed a couple of years after Branagh's *Much Ado*, Nunn's rendering of *Twelfth Night* employs a similar formula: well-known names, picturesque locations, mellow interpretation. Nunn is a subtler director of actors, however, and his choice of period setting – stately-home Victorian, with the gloriously unlikely edifice of St Michael's Mount as Orsino's pleasure-dome – sets up some interesting collisions between gothicky fantasy and social reality, given further urgency by a played-up conflict between Illyria and Messaline. The film could perhaps be pacier, but a few performances really shine, notably Nigel Hawthorne's tight-lipped Malvolio and Imogen Stubbs's Viola (Stubbs carries a moustache surprisingly well), while Helena Bonham-Carter gets the little-girl lunacy of Olivia almost exactly right. Ben Kingsley's folkish, semi-Celtic Feste, however, may well make you want to wrap his accordion around his neck.

Twelfth Night
M. Rylance, S. Fry, S. Barnett; Tim Carroll (dir.) UK, 2012 > Shakespeare's Globe DVD

Deservedly a hit when it opened at the Globe in 2002, Tim Carroll's all-male *Twelfth Night* with Mark Rylance as Olivia was even bigger news when it returned a decade later, with many of the original cast in place. It opens with a teasing backstage tableau in which we see the cast dressing and putting on their make-up, and play-acting of all kinds is very much the theme, with Rylance's oboe-voiced Olivia, by turns imperious and genuinely vulnerable, leading the way. Johnny Flynn's Viola is a tad more blokeish than Michael Brown in the original production, but the rest of the cast are very fine, and – with the exception of Stephen Fry's somewhat over-ripe cameo as Malvolio – they get the play's balance between midsummer madness and wintry chill exactly right. Even the reunion between the twins, plastered in white make-up and wearing costumes that make them resemble figures of frosted icing, is both visually and emotionally convincing.

AUDIO

Twelfth Night
S. Gonet, G. Murphy, L. Whybrow; David Timson (dir.) UK, 1999 > Naxos ◉ ⬇

There is much to recommend this Naxos *Twelfth Night*, certainly when compared with the somewhat leaden BBC offering that is its main rival. The cast are consistently excellent: high praise goes to Stella Gonet's mature (and appealingly world-weary) Viola, Jonathan Keeble's strongly spoken Orsino and Gerard Murphy's fruity Sir Toby, although the fussy Feste offered by David Timson – also the director – takes much of the danger out of the role. Olivia receives a persuasively humane performance from Lucy Whybrow, nicely set off by Christopher Godwin's petty tyrant Malvolio. Most importantly, however, this recording has that spirit of mystery without which no performance of the play would be complete.

EDITIONS

Arden Shakespeare (third edition)
Keir Elam (ed.); 2008 > Bloomsbury

This edition is a superb achievement and a clear first choice. Keir Elam is known for his detailed work on the seductive, slippery sides of Shakespeare's language, work that's much in evidence in his introduction, but he is also brilliantly alive to the theatrical nature of *Twelfth Night*, particularly the ways it corralls (sometimes coerces) us to make of it what we will. The performance history is extensive and wide-ranging, featuring plenty about the play's life on screen as well as the way individual characters have been interpreted through the ages, and the text itself is helpfully glossed.

SOME CRITICISM

Twelfth Night and Shakespearian Comedy
Clifford Leech; 1965 > Toronto UP [o/p]

Leech's slim book collects a series of three lectures given at Dalhousie University during the tercentenary of Shakespeare's birth. It's an elegant and urbane study that starts from the very beginnings of comedy before moving to more immediate sixteenth-century influences and an illuminating attempt to place *Twelfth Night* in the context of Shakespeare's development as a dramatist. Leech's subtle reading of the play is well-attuned to its discordances and careful intermingling of opposing forces, and in his second lecture he argues that its conclusion "gives over the comic idea", decisively returning us to the wind and rain of Feste's parting song – and eventually to the problem comedies themselves.

William Shakespeare
Terry Eagleton; 1986 > Blackwell

Terry Eagleton is excessively proud of the fact that Prince Charles once described him as "dreadful", and during a long career as Britain's most loved/reviled/industrious Marxist literary critic he has turned controversy-making into high art. This polemical little book on Shakespeare is maddening and brilliant by turns, it being entirely in character for Eagleton to insist, with as much seriousness as whimsy, that "it is difficult to read Shakespeare without feeling that he was almost certainly familiar with the writings of Hegel, Marx, Nietzsche, Freud, Wittgenstein and Derrida". His article on *Dream* and *Twelfth Night* appeared in a very early form back in 1968, and is in some ways the best in the book – the play perhaps being more suited to his Theory-led approach than others. You sense that he's particularly at home writing about Feste, a character with all the wily linguistic tactics of an Oxford professor of English.

The Two Gentlemen of Verona

T hough it is probably Shakespeare's earliest surviving piece for the stage, *The Two Gentlemen of Verona* sets out ideas that would interest and engage the playwright until the dying days of his career. The problem explored in this comedy – a comedy that often risks becoming far more serious – is what happens when male friends fall in love with the same woman, and how they reconcile that love with their friendship for each other: an almost identical storyline to his final work, *The Two Noble Kinsmen*. Like that play and many in between, Shakespeare's *The Two Gentlemen* is very much about growing up, a test that the selfish and self-serving male leads come agonizingly close to failing. But it is also about far more than the "gentlemen" of the title. Although the drama takes its cue from courtly Elizabethan comedies about the value of male friendship, at its emotional heart are a pair of assertive, intelligent female leads whose devotion to their menfolk is difficult to understand – something that becomes glaringly apparent in a troubling and bitter conclusion. But perhaps the play's most winning achievements are those it offers in light relief: it contains some fine comic moments, not to mention the most coveted non-speaking role in the canon – that for a dog.

DATE > In all likelihood the first of Shakespeare's plays to be penned, *The Two Gentlemen* was described in 1598 as encapsulating his talent for "Comedy". It was probably composed some time earlier, perhaps 1589–90.

SOURCES > A version of Montemayor's pastoral romance, *Diana* (1559), describing the tale of "Felix and Felismena", provided the outline of the Proteus–Julia story. Thomas Elyot's 1531 version of the tale of "Titus and Gisippus" from Boccaccio's *Decameron* also had some influence, as did Ovid's *Metamorphoses* and Arthur Brooke's 1562 *Romeus and Juliet*.

TEXTS > The 1623 Folio – a relatively clean job – is the only extant text.

Interpreting the play

When the Elizabethan schoolmaster and writer Francis Meres drew up a record of Shakespeare's plays (the earliest of its kind, and a unique testimony to the young poet's career), a play called "his *Gentlemen of Verona*" appears at the top of the list. For all that Meres might have been impressed by this particular comedy, his write-up is usually taken as evidence that *The Two Gentlemen* is Shakespeare's first surviving play. Many agree that it seems to be the work of a talented but relatively inexperienced

MAJOR CHARACTERS & SYNOPSIS

Proteus, a gentleman from Verona

Valentine, another gentleman from Verona, Proteus's close friend

Lance, Proteus's clownish servant (accompanied by his dog **Crab**)

Julia, Proteus's beloved (later disguised as "Sebastian")

Lucetta, Julia's waiting-woman

Speed, Valentine's page

Duke of Milan

Silvia, the Duke's daughter

Thurio, Silvia's rich suitor

Antonio, Proteus's father

Panthino, Antonio's servant

Host who lodges Julia

Eglamour, a Milanese courtier and Silvia's friend

A band of **Outlaws** living in the forest outside Milan

ACT 1 Valentine and Proteus are best friends, albeit with contrasting views of the world – Valentine is anxious to leave Verona, while Proteus is content to remain at home with his beloved Julia (much to Valentine's disgust). Though Proteus loves Julia, she, so far, has shown little interest in him, and when her maid-servant Lucetta gives her a letter from him, she flies into a rage and tears it up. Just as things start to go right for Proteus – he has finally received a response from Julia – his father Antonio decides to send him to join Valentine at the Milanese court.

ACT 2 In Milan, meanwhile, Valentine has fallen for Silvia – much to his servant Speed's amusement – despite the fact that her father, the Duke, favours the dim-witted but rich Thurio. Silvia, in turn, loves Valentine, but will not say so; instead she persuades him to write a love letter supposedly for another suitor but actually intended for himself. Back in Verona, Julia and Proteus vow eternal fidelity and exchange rings, while Proteus's servant Lance parts sadly from his family. Arriving in Milan, Proteus is reunited with Valentine and meets Silvia; Valentine then discloses how he plans to elope with her and enlists Proteus's help. But Proteus is so struck by Silvia that he resolves to woo her himself. Meanwhile Julia is missing her lover and decides to follow him disguised as a page – despite Lucetta's misgivings.

ACT 3 Proteus reveals his friend's plan to the Duke, who banishes Valentine upon pain of death. The Duke then asks Proteus to help Thurio find favour in Silvia's eyes by slandering Valentine and praising Thurio. Proteus eagerly agrees, hoping to win Silvia's affections for himself. Lance, meanwhile, has fallen for a milkmaid and recounts to a bemused Speed her various attractions.

ACT 4 Valentine and Speed are heading back to Verona through the forest when they are ambushed by outlaws. Impressed by Valentine's bearing, they ask him to lead them. Back at court, Proteus is troubled by his conscience but continues to woo Silvia, who is shocked at his betrayal of Valentine and Julia. When the disguised Julia arrives she immediately discovers what is going on, but bides her time. Silvia, on the other hand, has decided to act: she plans to escape her impending marriage to Thurio and, with the help of her friend Sir Eglamour, join Valentine in Mantua. In the meantime, Proteus has recruited Julia (renamed Sebastian) to deliver a letter and a ring to Silvia – the very ring that Julia had given him. But Silvia, out of sympathy for Julia, again rejects Proteus's advances. Lance, all this time, has been sorting out the problems caused by his troublesome dog, Crab.

ACT 5 News has reached the Duke about his daughter's flight, and when Proteus, Thurio and Julia hear of it, they each determine to find her. Proteus succeeds first, rescuing Silvia from the outlaws who have captured her. When, however, she continues to reject him, he resolves to take her by force – unaware that Valentine is watching. Valentine intervenes, rescues Silvia and denounces the treachery of his friend. But when Proteus begs forgiveness, Valentine not only immediately consents but also declares that Proteus can have Silvia after all. At this, Julia/Sebastian, who has been present the whole time, faints – whereupon her real identity is uncovered and she is reunited with a penitent Proteus. The Outlaws enter with the captured Duke and Thurio, who initially claims Silvia but gives her up when threatened by Valentine. The Duke then consents to the marriage of Silvia and Valentine, and pardons all the Outlaws.

dramatist, one who was still learning his craft. The comedy borrows from writers such as John Lyly – whose *Euphues*, a prose tale about two young gentlemen, was published in 1580 – as well as experimenting in a limited way with the resources of the stage. It employs a tiny cast, the playwright's smallest, often using just two or three actors at a time, and the script is bedevilled by narrative inconsistencies, among them a muddle between the various Italian locations it describes (though for Shakespeare, for whom geography is a fluid and imaginative concept at the best of times, this last is entirely in character).

Crucially, like *Romeo and Juliet* a few years later, *The Two Gentlemen* is also about what it feels like to be young. The "gentlemen" of the title, Valentine and Proteus, are youthful best friends at an emotional crossroads. Proteus is passionately in love, while Valentine longs to get out of Verona and see what he calls "the wonders of the world" (1.1.6). The play opens at a parting of the ways that would seem familiar to the wealthiest among Shakespeare's audience: while Proteus stays "sluggardized at home" (1.1.7), Valentine is off to exciting new places, the kind of destinations regarded by rich Elizabethans as sources of gentlemanliness. Some of their contemporaries, says Panthino, are sent "to seek preferment out,"

> Some to the wars, to try their fortune there,
> Some to discover islands far away,
> Some to the studious universities.

> [1.3.7–10]

Antonio, Proteus's father, agrees with this analysis. "Experience is by industry achieved," he observes, "and perfected by the swift course of time" (1.3.22–3). If Proteus is to achieve anything in life, he needs to get out there and see it. For a dramatist who had recently left Stratford behind, along with his wife and three children, the plot line must surely have had resonance.

In love

But Proteus, unlike a playwright in his mid-20s, is portrayed as a teenager, and like any teenager is not exactly desperate to take his father's advice. Leaving Verona means abandoning his beloved Julia, and for the young lovers that means being separated from their very selves. It is a strong irony, then, that the absent Valentine – sent away to become the perfect gentleman – learns some unexpected lessons in Milan. He, too, falls in love, as his page Speed sarcastically explains:

VALENTINE Why, how know you that I am in love?

SPEED Marry, by these special marks: first, you have learned, like Sir
Proteus, to wreath your arms like a malcontent; to relish a love-song,
like a robin redbreast; to walk along like one that had the pestilence;
to sigh, like a schoolboy that had lost his ABC; to weep, like a young
wench that had buried her grandmam; to fast, like one that takes diet;
to watch, like one that fears robbing; to speak puling [whining], like a
beggar at Hallowmas … [Y]ou are metamorphosed with a mistress, that
when I look on you I can hardly think you my master.

[2.1.16–30]

Valentine cannot find a way of expressing love which is anything other than ridiculous. Love – or at least his idea of it – has made him, as it also makes Proteus, into
something less than a man.

This version of love, which receives unsparing scrutiny in *The Two Gentlemen* (as in
many of Shakespeare's subsequent comedies), has a lot to do with words and not very
much to do with reality. At first struck dumb by their mistresses, both Proteus and
Valentine then talk themselves into mournful passion. In truth they have little excuse:
unlike their counterparts in later plays, the two young men experience few problems
having their feelings reciprocated. Julia, though at first she tries to hide it, finds herself
falling for Proteus – as is obvious when, in a glorious piece of stage business, she rips
up a letter from him in order to demonstrate that she couldn't care less, then spends the
next few minutes trying desperately to reassemble the pieces. For his part, Valentine
is so self-obsessed that he fails to realize his mistress Silvia feels the same way he does.
Instructing Valentine to write a letter (the play is full of them) to a "secret, nameless
friend", she then orders her baffled would-be lover to present it to himself:

SILVIA
A pretty period. Well, I guess the sequel.
And yet I will not name it. And yet I care not.
And yet, take this again.
         She offers him the letter
         And yet I thank you,
Meaning henceforth to trouble you no more.
SPEED (*aside*)
And yet you will, and yet another yet.
VALENTINE
What means your ladyship? Do you not like it?
SILVIA
Yes, yes. The lines are very quaintly writ,
But since unwillingly, take them again.

[2.1.109–16]

Silvia's "jest", wittily imitating the fickle mistress of Valentine's imagination, gently
satirizes his self-absorption while also signalling that she is in fact interested – a

message that Speed, unlike his obtuse master, quickly decodes. Silvia needs to operate in secret because her father wants to marry her to someone else, though it will be the end of the scene before Valentine finally catches up.

This kind of high-bred game-playing is thrown nicely into relief by Proteus's servant Lance, whose opinions on marriage are distinctly less elevated. Having met a likely match, a milkmaid, he first compiles a "catalogue of her conditions" (3.1.271) describing the things that are best – and worst – about her. Unlike the fantastical (though admittedly beautiful) song, "Who is Silvia? What is she?", written by Proteus on behalf of Thurio later in the play, Lance's list lives solidly in the real world. Among the "virtues" he mentions are the fact that his milkmaid can fetch and carry, milk, brew ale, sew, knit, wash and scour; among her "vices" are bad breath, talking in her sleep, having no teeth and being "slow in words". It's not exactly romantic, but then in reality Lance only has eyes for his dog Crab, as we later learn. He reveals the truth in a garrulous – and slightly bizarre – tale which is also one of Shakespeare's funniest comic speeches. "You shall judge," he declares of his beloved pet's behaviour:

> He thrusts me himself into the company of three or four gentleman-like dogs under the Duke's table. He had not been there—bless the mark—a pissing-while but all the chamber smelled him. 'Out with the dog,' says one. 'What cur is that?' says another. 'Whip him out,' says the third. 'Hang him up,' says the Duke. I, having been acquainted with the smell before, knew it was Crab, and goes to the fellow that whips the dogs. 'Friend,' quoth I, 'you mean to whip the dog.' 'Ay, marry do I,' quoth he. 'You do him the more wrong,' quoth I, ''twas I did the thing you wot of.' He makes me no more ado, but whips me out of the chamber.
>
> [4.4.13–28]

"How many masters would do this for his servant?" he concludes, and it's surely true that the number would not be high. Lance's love for Crab inverts the relationship between dog and man, but also plays off the notion of male lovers (like Valentine and Proteus) blindly serving their mistresses. Those mistresses are eternally scornful, just as Crab is "cruel-hearted" (2.3.9) in his reluctance to be properly doggish and worship Lance, instead of the other way round.

Metamorphosed with a mistress

Every bit as devoted, it seems, is Julia, who decides with the kind of pragmatism also exhibited by Silvia that she cannot bear to stay in Verona while Proteus is gone. The first in a long line of strong Shakespearian women, all markedly more in control of the situation than their menfolk, she takes the route chosen by heroines like Rosalind and Viola and dons male disguise in order to travel to Milan. What she discovers when she arrives is a shock: her beloved Proteus, "his heart as far from fraud as heaven from earth", is in fact mooning over someone else (2.6.78). And not just anyone else: Proteus's new object of desire is Silvia. The parallels between Julia and Lance – slavish devotion to worthless dogs – are disturbingly strong, but the comedy steadily becomes bleached out. In one of the play's few soliloquies Proteus reflects grimly on where it leaves him. "Even as one heat another heat expels, / Or as one nail by strength drives out another," he begins,

> So the remembrance of my former love
> Is by a newer object quite forgotten.
> Is it mine eye, or Valentine's praise,
> Her true perfection, or my false transgression
> That makes me, reasonless, to reason thus?
> She is fair, and so is Julia that I love—
> That I did love, for now my love is thawed,
> Which like a waxen image 'gainst a fire
> Bears no impression of the thing it was.
>
> [2.4.190–200]

That sickening change of tense – "I love" to "I did love" – shows Proteus shifting shape like the Greek god for whom he is named. Characteristically, he is unsure whether it is Silvia's apparent "perfection" or Valentine's description that has excited his lust: this is all about male competition, and dispensing with his "former love" is apparently done as easily as saying the words.

This is a dark, and until now unexplored, side of love. It puts under considerable pressure Proteus's insistence near the opening of the play that his feelings for Julia have "metamorphosed" him (and equally Speed's obervation that Valentine, too, has been "metamorphosed with a mistress"): here Proteus is solely responsible for the swiftness of his alteration. Having resolved to forget Julia and pursue Silvia instead, he quickly realizes that Valentine – whose own name signposts him as the ideal lover – needs to be dispatched if he is to stand a chance. Exposing to Silvia's father the couple's plan to elope, Proteus ensures that Valentine is banished from Milan – for, as he coldly ruminates, "I cannot now prove constant to myself / Without some treachery used to Valentine" (2.6.32–3).

Fortunately Silvia is not so fickle, stoutly refusing the advances of this "subtle, perjured, false, disloyal man", as she boldly calls him to his face (4.2.92). And Julia is tragic in her constancy: shadowing Proteus disguised as a young man called Sebastian, she even agrees to deliver his messages of love to Silvia in order to get close to him. Although Proteus's actions do their utmost to make the women enemies, in fact Julia and Silvia end up reinforcing one another. When Silvia hears Sebastian/Julia recount the story of Proteus's "poor mistress", the affinity between them is touching. "Alas, poor lady, desolate and left," Silvia reflects,

> I weep myself to think upon thy words.
> Here, youth. This is my purse. I give thee this
> For thy sweet mistress' sake, because thou lov'st her.
>
> [4.4.171–4]

The final and most difficult test explored by *The Two Gentlemen* is whether the warring men can ever be reconciled. As the plot builds to its climax, it looks as if they cannot: Valentine, forced into banishment, has become an outlaw in the woods while Proteus continues to chase after Silvia. When she escapes Milan, he follows her into the forest; and when she refuses him for the last time, he bursts into terrifying violence:

PROTEUS
    Nay, if the gentle spirit of moving words
    Can no way change you to a milder form
    I'll woo you like a soldier, at arm's end,
    And love you 'gainst the nature of love: force ye.
SILVIA
    O heaven!
PROTEUS (*assailing her*) I'll force thee yield to my desire.

                                   [5.4.55–9]

The attempted rape gets, mercifully, no further; the nearby Valentine has heard the commotion and bursts in.

While in Shakespeare's source for the play, a novella by the Portuguese writer Jorge de Montemayor, Silvia's equivalent dies so that the two men can be reconciled, in *The Two Gentlemen* the resolution – though it avoids death – is somehow even more grisly. Accepting Proteus's apology on the spot, Valentine gladly announces, "Then I am paid,"

    And once again I do receive thee honest.
    Who by repentance is not satisfied
    Is nor of heaven nor earth. For these are pleased;
    By penitence th' Eternal wrath's appeased.
    And that my love may appear plain and free,
    All that was mine in Silvia I give thee.

                                   [5.4.77–83]

Rereading this scene while she waited anxiously for her lover George Henry Lewes to finalize his divorce, Marian Evans (better known as George Eliot) confessed herself "disgusted" by it, and even without external pressures like those, it is impossible not to agree. Before even accepting Proteus's skimpy apology Valentine does not so much as bother to check how Silvia is, then promptly tries to hand her over. They exchange not another word for the rest of the play.

It's hard to understand what Shakespeare means us to think here, and some have suggested that Valentine's bizarre and apparently indefensible move is simply the result of shallow dramatization. But perhaps we shouldn't rush to condemn the playwright's handiwork. Some of his contemporaries argued that male friendship was the summit of perfection, the kind of perfection described in Lyly's play *Endymion* (1588) as "the image of eternity in which there is nothing moveable, nothing mischievous", and which would always outweigh relationships between a man and a woman. In creating such a painful dramatic twist, Shakespeare asks his audiences bold and urgent questions: can any of us ever believe that? Would we want to? They are issues to which he would return in *Love's Labour's Lost*, where male comradeship is likewise disastrously ill-equipped to deal with reality.

In this scene Valentine commits the same crass blunder that he and Proteus are guilty of all along: for all their talk of love, they are simply not mature enough for it. Valentine means his gesture to be a noble sacrifice, but in order to achieve this ideal he proves himself, like Proteus, capable of astonishing changes of face. As Julia says moments later, "it is the lesser blot, modesty finds, / Women to change their shapes than men change their minds" (5.4.107–8). While stereotype accuses women of changefulness, in this play at least it is the men who prove themselves muddled and inconstant.

Typically, perhaps, the men do little to help the play find a more satisfactory resolution: it is only when Julia faints and her disguise is removed that Proteus is forced to rethink what has happened. "'Tis true," he admits after Julia's damning words.

> O heaven, were man
> But constant, he were perfect. That one error
> Fills him with faults, makes him run through all th' sins;
> Inconstancy falls off ere it begins.

> [5.4.109–12]

The Two Gentlemen seems to ask, at the very least, whether ideals purchased at this kind of price are worth their cost. Is Valentine's ideal of friendship worth abandoning the woman he is engaged to marry? Can Proteus ever be trusted again? Ultimately the play stops short of demanding answers from its characters: Julia is dramatically unmasked and reunited with a penitent Proteus, Silvia and Valentine stay together, and two marriages result. But we in the audience might wonder what happens after the curtain has come down.

Stage history and adaptations

The stage history of *The Two Gentlemen* makes for rapid reading. If Francis Meres's note has been interpreted correctly and it is Shakespeare's first surviving play (c. 1589–90), we know nothing of its early years – aside from the fact that it may have still been among the King's Men's repertoire as late as 1606. The comic role of Lance was almost certainly written for the clown **William Kempe**, though the identity of his sidekick, the dog Crab, has unfortunately passed into obscurity.

The Two Gentlemen doesn't appear to have been revived at the Restoration, and it wasn't until 1762 that we can be sure a performance actually took place (only *Love's Labour's Lost* stayed out of the repertoire longer). This was in fact a free adaptation by **Benjamin Victor,** which softened the conclusion and beefed up the comic elements to showcase **Richard Yates**, the most famous comedian of his day. But even though the renowned singer **Joseph Vernon** also starred as Thurio, the production flopped.

It wouldn't reappear until 1784, this time at Covent Garden, in a production cheekily advertised as "SHAXESPEARE's, with alterations" (and including scenes from other plays). **John Quick** played Lance, but this time the play sank after only one performance. Six years later **John Philip Kemble**'s Drury Lane adaptation did a little better, but it still followed Victor's lead by moralizing plot and characters alike: Valentine, played by Kemble himself in an 1808 revival over at Covent Garden, was a model of gentlemanliness.

Adaptations continued in 1821 with what proved to be *The Two Gentlemen*'s most popular nineteenth-century production: an "operatic" version by **George Reynolds** that employed Kemble's text alongside some awe-inspiring scenery. The following year **William Charles Macready** attempted a return to Shakespeare's script in Bristol, but it wasn't until 1841 that he staged a production in London. Although it was well received (again, mainly for its impressive sets), this version foundered – as did **Charles Kean**'s attempt to export it to New York in 1846. Kean tried again in London two years later, and did somewhat better; among his cast were **Ellen Tree** as Silvia and **Rob Keeley**'s Lance. But *The Two Gentlemen* was still a long way from being a favourite: when London's Olympic Theatre chose the comedy for its debut production in 1849, the *Examiner* actually praised the audience for sitting patiently through until the final curtain. **Samuel Phelps**'s 1857 version at Sadler's Wells also stumbled, as did **Osmond Teale**'s at Stratford in 1890, although in New York the great American actress **Ada Rehan** gained plaudits as Julia in 1895, directed by **Augustin Daly**.

By the dawn of the twentieth century *The Two Gentlemen* was ripe for rediscovery. Two pioneers, **William Poel** and his disciple **Harley Granville-Barker**, both attempted it within a few years, but amid their experiments the play itself rarely attracted comment – reviewers were more struck by Poel's alterations to His Majesty's Theatre in 1910, which included covering the stalls with an apron stage and destroying most of the sightlines. **Frank Benson** put it on at Stratford that same year as his "revival play", casting his wife **Constance**, then in middle age, as Julia to **Norah Lancaster**'s Silvia; and the comedy appeared once again in Shakespeare's home town in 1916, this time directed by **Ben Greet** and with **Sybil Thorndike** as Julia.

During the interwar years several productions appeared in both Stratford and London, but the play's nickname of "The Walking Gentlemen" (theatrical slang for a walk-on role) defeated its proponents. **Ben Iden Payne**'s colourful Stratford version from 1938, which name-checked Giotto and Palladio among its design influences, was reviewed more positively, if criticized for making the play too polite – a problem that didn't afflict **Hans Rothe**'s hugely popular German translation from five years previously, which eventually fell foul of Goebbels. In Britain, *The Two Gentlemen*'s turnaround came after World War II, with **Denis Carey**'s 1952 staging at the Bristol Old Vic. Carey employed a young cast (among them **John Neville**) and interpolated plenty of music, and found he had a surprise hit on his hands. **Michael Langham**'s 1957 production at the London Old Vic also gained plaudits, but this time for its Regency staging; among Langham's cast were **Barbara Jefford** and **Ingrid Hafner**, while **Keith Michell**'s Byronesque Proteus turned heads.

Peter Hall's 1960 version just predated the arrival of the RSC and state subsidy, and its autumnal setting failed to win hearts or profits. More divisive was **Robin Phillips**'s staging at the same venue ten years later, which transplanted the play to modern dress and camped it up, with **Peter Egan**'s Valentine and **Ian Richardson**'s Proteus spending

"This cruel-hearted cur": Crab (Woolly) looks the other way while his master, Lance (Richard Moore), pours out his heart to the audience. From David Thacker's RSC *Two Gentlemen* (1992).

much of their time playing beach-ball while **Patrick Stewart** stole the show as a sober, dignified Lance. **John Guare** and **Mel Shapiro**'s musical adaptation, which debuted on Broadway in 1971, was loved by audiences and critics alike and transferred to the West End, before being revived again in New York in 2005. That North American audiences seem to have warmed to the play is attested to by the fact that it also received successful productions at the **Oregon Shakespeare Festival** (1966, 1981), the **Colorado Shakespeare Festival** (1966) and **Stratford, Ontario** (1975). It was also turned into a TV movie by **Hans Dieter Schwarze** in Germany in 1963, which was surprisingly well received. The same could not be said of **John Barton**'s 1981 double bill of *Titus* and *The Two Gentlemen* at Stratford-upon-Avon, which opened to terrible reviews and quickly disappeared.

There are signs that *Two Gentlemen* is less unpopular than it was. Stratford, Ontario has mounted it no fewer than four times since the 1980s, most recently in 2010 in a cut-down vaudeville-style production by **Dean Gabourie**. **David Thacker**'s 1992 RSC production was set a little later, in the 1930s, and had Cole Porter lyrics to prove it; while on Bankside in 1996 the comedy formed part of the Shakespeare's Globe "prologue" season in an enthusiastically received production by **Jack Shepherd**. **Edward Hall** also chose the play for a debut – this time his own first appearance at Stratford in 1998, 41 years after his father Peter made his own entrance. Hall's lively and youthful production was quickly headlined "cappuccino Shakespeare" for its sharply tailored

Italian setting, and saw excellent performances from **Tom Goodman-Hill**'s sober Valentine and **Poppy Miller**'s Silvia in particular. Following David Thacker twelve years before, **Fiona Buffini**'s 2004 touring RSC version was staged during the interwar period, but went one further in suggesting a Brideshead-style ambiguity in relations between Proteus and Valentine; "when [they] part," wrote Michael Billington in the *Guardian*, "you half expect them to indulge in a farewell kiss". Caught between the two was **Rachel Pickup**'s vulnerable Silvia.

German audiences, like American ones, have had several recent opportunities to see the play, notably at the replica Globe in **Neuss** in 2006 and a student performance offered under the aegis of the prestigious **Berliner Ensemble** in 2014. In Britain, it remains neglected, though it featured in the RSC's Complete Works season (2006–07) in a production by Portuguese drama school **Nos do Morro**, and also as part of the World Shakespeare Festival in 2012, where a Shona-language production turned it literally into a two-hander, with actors **Denton Chikura** and **Tonderai Munyebvu** making the attempt in a witty and fleet-footed adaptation by **Arne Pohlmeier**. Across at the RSC, **Simon Godwin**'s Italian-style production was the first time the play had appeared on the company's main stage in nearly 50 years, and was widely acclaimed: "a production that brings out the identity-transforming nature of love," according to the *Guardian*.

On screen *The Two Gentlemen* has yet to make much of a splash – a fleeting appearance in **Tom Stoppard** and **Marc Norman**'s 1998 *Shakespeare in Love* notwithstanding (see p.398). The BBC/Time-Life version (1983) was directed by **Don Taylor**, featuring **Tessa Peake-Jones**'s Julia and **Joanne Pearce**'s Silvia opposite the Valentine and Proteus of **John Hudson** and **Tyler Butterworth**. A recording of Godwin's live RSC version from 2014 is also available

SCREEN

The Two Gentlemen of Verona
T. Butterworth, J. Hudson, T. Peake-Jones; Don Taylor (dir.) UK, 1983 ❯ BBC **DVD**

Don Taylor's *The Two Gentlemen* is bathed in what is presumably intended to be lustrous Mediterranean light – and, compared to the crepuscular interiors of other BBC Shakespeares, the effect is not unbecoming. Realism is a dangerous game in a TV studio, however, and elsewhere (for instance in hiring two cherubs, painting them gold and having them cavort between the lovers) Taylor attempts a more riskily stylized approach to the comedy. It's difficult to feel that either aspect of this production solidly works, though, and ultimately what makes it more than just watchable is its youthful and energetic cast – top marks go to the women in particular, Tessa Peake-Jones's touching Julia and Joanne Pearce's vivacious Silvia. All too often, however, over-coiffed hair creates its own problems of credibility.

The Two Gentlemen of Verona
M. Arends, M. Marcus, P. Chanda; Simon Godwin (dir.) UK, 2014 ❯ RSC/Opus Arte **DVD**

Simon Godwin's unfussily contemporary *Two Gentlemen* was the director's RSC debut, and this recording, filmed in front of a live audience inside the Royal Shakespeare Theatre, sparkles with youthful brio (it features a bunga-bunga-ing club scene that may remind some of the shenanigans of ex-Italian prime minister Silvio Berlusconi). Michael Marcus's Valentine and Mark Arends's Proteus rival each other for offhand callowness as well as Silvia's affections, but the focus is solidly on Pearl Chanda's earnest, somewhat rueful Julia as she embarks on her troubling journey of discovery; when the men forgive each other and embrace it's a genuinely painful moment. As the play concludes, to the plangent cry of a solo clarinet, you can't help feeling that the relationship between Roger Morlidge's long-suffering Lance and a preternaturally patient wolfhound is the only one it's possible to believe in.

AUDIO

The Two Gentlemen of Verona
M. Maloney, D. Lewis, S. Wickham; Clive Brill (dir.)
UK, 1998 > Arkangel ⊙ ☁

The relationship between Valentine and Proteus is crucial to any performance of the play – it's definitely rivalrous here, with plenty of aggression beneath the surface (sometimes not too deep) – but what listening to this recording makes you realize is that pace is all-important. *The Two Gentlemen*'s frequent wordplay needs to be fleet-footed if it isn't to stagnate, and fortunately old hand Clive Brill works his cast hard and edits rapidly. That said, speed (or Speed) isn't the only impression: John Woodvine's Lance is delightfully lugubrious, and more than takes his time, Lucy Robinson is a moving Julia, while Saskia Wickham provides a pert and persuasive Silvia.

EDITIONS

Arden Shakespeare (third edition)
William C. Carroll (ed.); 2004 > Bloomsbury

Carroll's Arden 3 is a clear front-runner, significantly fuller than its rivals and mercifully free of hand-wringing about the quality of the play. Instead of seeing *Two Gentlemen* as a piece of flawed juvenilia, Carroll sites it in a long Renaissance tradition analysing male friendship, from Cicero to Lyly, suggesting that it both expands and subverts convention. His on-page glosses are enlivened by a keen ear for language, and the performance history is nicely covered. Crab the dog (who, after all, usually steals the show) even gets an introductory chapterlet to himself.

SOME CRITICISM

Two Gentlemen of Verona: Critical Essays
June Schlueter (ed.); 1996 > Routledge

This *Critical Essays* volume is as useful as others in the series and particularly valuable for this often marginalized play. It unites classic essays, among them Harold Brooks's well-known "Two Clowns in a Comedy (To Say Nothing of the Dog)" from 1963, with some more recent fare, and closes with a helpful selection of theatre reviews from 1821 to 1991.

Shakespeare and Comedy
R.W. Maslen; 2005 > Bloomsbury

Arden's growing list of critical companions comes highly recommended, small but packed with flavour. R.W. Maslen's *Shakespeare and Comedy* is typically fine, racing very readably through no fewer than ten comedies in just over 250 pages. His starting point, too, is what was most likely Shakespeare's, *Two Gentlemen*, offering the play as a kind of "comic manifesto" for worlds that would be fleshed out later, particularly their balance of pure laughter with something much bleaker. There's fine coverage of many of the biggest issues in Shakespearian comedy and the context it springs from, and, using the example of *Measure for Measure*, an afterword probes how Shakespeare's writing darkened as the Jacobean period dawned.

The Two Noble Kinsmen

After the high-stakes political intrigues of *Henry VIII*, the play that followed it onto the stage could barely be more different. *The Two Noble Kinsmen* brought the curtain down on Shakespeare's professional theatrical career, and although it was also co-written with John Fletcher, their collaboration seems to have been markedly less intimate than before. And despite being elegant and courtly – its source is Chaucer's "Knight's Tale", its dramatic language heavily influenced by elaborate Jacobean masques – the tone of *Kinsmen* is mixed, and often difficult to gauge. While the story of two men who fall in love with the same woman points back to Shakespeare's earliest comedies, most obviously *The Two Gentlemen of Verona*, in this play resolution proves strikingly difficult to achieve. The "kinsmen", Palamon and Arcite, claim to be closer to each other than anyone alive, but their journey from extravagant devotion to bitter hatred undermines the chivalric ideals both claim to serve – and in the handful of professional performances the play has received they have often been quite outshone by another character, the nameless Jailer's Daughter, who falls hopelessly and tragically in love with Palamon. Dominated by loss and compromise – never more so than in its gruesome, troubling conclusion – *Kinsmen* feels a world away not just from *Henry VIII*, but from the renunciations and reconciliations offered by *The Tempest*, often assumed to be Shakespeare's cordial farewell to his art.

DATE > Featuring Shakespeare's last writing for the professional stage, *The Two Noble Kinsmen* was first performed in 1613–14, possibly at the indoor Blackfriars theatre.
SOURCES > Chaucer's "Knight's Tale" is the play's key source, as for *A Midsummer Night's Dream* – itself another influence. The masque in Act Three is lifted from Francis Beaumont's *Masque of the Inner Temple* (1613).

TEXTS > One of several Shakespeare plays not to make it into the First Folio (1623), *Kinsmen* was printed in a 1634 quarto edition proclaiming that it was co-written with John Fletcher – a plausible excuse for its earlier exclusion. Though regularly published in editions of Fletcher, it was not generally believed to be Shakespeare's work until the nineteenth century.

Interpreting the play

The Two Noble Kinsmen is, it's been suggested, a kind of *Midsummer Night's Dream* part two: both plays draw upon Chaucer's "Knight's Tale", the graceful and courtly

MAJOR CHARACTERS & SYNOPSIS

Prologue and **Epilogue**
Palamon and **Arcite**, cousins (the two "noble kinsmen"), both nephews of King Creon
Theseus, Duke of Athens
Hippolyta, Queen of the Amazons, later Theseus's wife
Emilia, Hippolyta's sister
A **Woman,** Emilia's attendant
Pirithous, Theseus's close friend
Artesius, an Athenian soldier
Three Queens, widows to kings killed at the siege of Thebes
Hymen, god of marriage
Valerius, a Theban
Six **Knights**, attending Arcite and Palamon
A **Jailer** at Theseus's prison
The **Jailer's Daughter** and her **Wooer**
A **Doctor**
Six **Countrymen**, led by the schoolmaster **Gerald**

ACT 1 In Athens, preparations for the marriage of King Theseus and Hippolyta are disrupted by the sudden appearance of three queens, whose husbands have died fighting the evil King Creon of Thebes. Denied the right to bury their husbands – whose bodies still lie on the battlefield – the women demand that Theseus take up their cause and attack Thebes. At that moment, Palamon and Arcite (Creon's nephews) are debating whether to escape the corruption of Thebes when a messenger arrives with news that Theseus is threatening the city. Despite their disgust with their uncle, the two kinsmen decide to remain and fight. Theseus triumphs, however, and the wounded Palamon and Arcite are captured and imprisoned.

ACT 2 In jail in Athens, Palamon and Arcite are consoling themselves with their friendship when Palamon spots the beautiful Emilia (Hippolyta's sister) gathering flowers outside. Both men fall instantly in love, but Palamon claims precedence for having seen her first, and the cousins immediately begin to argue. Their quarrel is broken off only when Arcite is suddenly released. Though banished from Athens, Arcite takes the opportunity to appear in disguise at Theseus's games, where he impresses all with his wrestling skills and noble bearing. His reward, fittingly, is to be bestowed on Emilia as a servant. Meanwhile, the

Jailer's Daughter has arranged Palamon's escape in the vain hope of winning his love.

ACT 3 Separated from the royal party while out celebrating May Day, Arcite is suddenly confronted by Palamon. The two men argue over Emilia once more, before agreeing to fight a duel for her. At the same time, the Jailer's Daughter is desperately searching the woods for Palamon when she stumbles across a group of countrymen rehearsing an entertainment. Realizing that she has lost her mind, the performers include her in their masque, which they then present to Theseus and his companions. In another part of the wood, Arcite brings his cousin armour but no sooner do the two begin to fight than they are interrupted by Theseus and his party. When the Duke condemns them to death, Emilia pleads for the sentence to be commuted to banishment, but the kinsmen refuse this offer (both preferring to die rather than never see her again). Theseus then demands that Emilia choose between them, but when she is unable to do so he agrees to supervise a final contest for her hand.

ACT 4 The Jailer's Daughter, now completely mad, is reunited with her father. Observing her behaviour, the Doctor advises that the only possible remedy is that a former suitor (the Wooer) should pretend that he is Palamon. Meantime, Emilia is still unable to choose between her suitors – the contest between the rivals must go ahead.

ACT 5 Palamon and Arcite, each accompanied by three knights, separately pray for success, while Emilia prays that whoever loves her best will be the victor. Back at the jail, the Doctor's treatment of the Jailer's Daughter seems to be working, and he encourages the Wooer to sleep with her. At court the contest begins, but Emilia refuses to attend and its progress is reported to her. Though at first it seems that Palamon will triumph, he is eventually defeated: Arcite wins Emilia's hand while Palamon and his knights are condemned to death. But just as Palamon is about to be executed, news arrives that Arcite has been fatally injured in a riding accident. As the cousins are briefly reunited, Arcite bestows Emilia on Palamon with his dying breath.

story told by the worthy, wise and "parfit gentil" Knight to the assembled gaggle of pilgrims as the first of *The Canterbury Tales*. But where the *Dream* merely takes up the Athenian setting of Chaucer's narrative and the wedding between the Duke Theseus and his bride Hippolyta, discarding the rest, *Kinsmen* is a full dramatization of the tale itself, that of two cousins, "yonge knyghtes" captured by Theseus as prisoners of war, who tragically fall for the same woman. That Shakespeare returned once more to a medieval author who had served him well before (most obviously in *Troilus and Cressida* as well as *Dream*) attests not only to Chaucer's continued popularity – an expanded edition of his works appeared a decade or so before *Kinsmen* reached the stage – but also to a Jacobean taste for medieval romance. The small, indoor Blackfriars became the King's Men's winter playhouse from around 1609, and the refined audiences who attended that theatre a few years later would surely have been flattered to hear that "Chaucer, of all admired" was providing their night's entertainment, as the Prologue announces. "If we let fall the nobleness of this," he goes on,

> And the first sound this child hear be a hiss,
> How it will shake the bones of that good man,
> And make him cry from under ground, 'O fan
> From me the witless chaff of such a writer,
> That blasts my bays and my famed works makes lighter
> Than Robin Hood'? This is the fear we bring,
> For to say truth, it were an endless thing
> And too ambitious to aspire to him,
> Weak as we are, and almost breathless swim
> In this deep water.

> [PROLOGUE, 13–25]

Begging its audience not to "hiss" – if only to preserve Chaucer's "sweet sleep" and keep him from spinning in his grave – the "child" play attempts a similar trick to the earlier *Pericles*, apologizing for, yet also showing off, its prestigious paternity. The authors keep their promise, too: while in previous scripts based on Chaucer Shakespeare reworks his material intensively (*Troilus and Cressida* is the most obvious example), in *Kinsmen* he and Fletcher are more restrained. This is to be a properly Chaucerian play.

Dearer in love

Even so – and though the work of writing *Kinsmen* was shared with Fletcher – it will also be a convincingly Shakespearian one. As well as taking its cue from Chaucer, the story of cousins Palamon and Arcite gestures back to early comedies such as *The Two Gentlemen of Verona* and *Love's Labour's Lost*, in which intimate male friendships occupy a central position in the drama. In *Kinsmen* nowhere is this clearer than after the battle between Theseus and Creon that occurs in the middle of Act One. Despite the fact that the kinsmen have been captured by Theseus following the Theban defeat and thrown into prison, their Athenian jailer and his daughter are amazed by the prisoners' buoyant spirits. "They eat well, look merrily, discourse of many things, but nothing of their own restraint and disasters," the Jailer's Daughter wonderingly observes (2.1.38–40), and it soon becomes clear that what sustains the two men, "dearer in love than blood", is their own friendship (1.2.1). Arcite describes it extravagantly. "Even from the bottom of these miseries, / From all that fortune can inflict upon us," he declares,

> I see two comforts rising—two mere blessings,
> If the gods please, to hold here a brave patience,
> And the enjoying of our griefs together.
> Whilst Palamon is with me, let me perish
> If I think this our prison.
>
> [2.2.56–62]

Their intimacy is such that it overcomes mere physical hardship, and Palamon echoes not only his friend's thoughts but his high-flown way of expressing it. "Let's think this prison holy sanctuary," he concurs,

> To keep us from corruption of worse men.
> We are young, and yet desire the ways of honour,
> That liberty and common conversation,
> The poison of pure spirits, might, like women,
> Woo us to wander from. What worthy blessing
> Can be but our imaginations
> May make it ours? And here being thus together,
> We are an endless mine to one another:
> We are one another's wife, ever begetting
> New births of love; we are father, friends, acquaintance;
> We are in one another, families …
>
> [2.2.71–82]

This doctrine of mutual self-sufficiency is incredible in every sense of the word. Rewriting their imprisonment as something they have chosen voluntarily, like life in a monastery, Palamon suggests that they provide the substance of each other's lives – friends, family, even spouse. Though it's undeniably more grandiose, this pact echoes the "deep oaths" signed at the outset of Love's Labour's Lost by the King of Navarre and his three lords, and like those ivory-tower fantasies it will prove unsustainable. Palamon and Arcite, though they persuade themselves otherwise, are only this close because circumstance has brought them together, and when circumstance changes so will everything else.

The transformation comes more immediately than anyone – even perhaps the audience – expects. Just a few moments later Palamon and Arcite are joined onstage by Emilia, Queen Hippolyta's sister, who appears outside the prison languorously picking flowers. "She is wondrous fair," says Arcite, and Palamon echoes him, sighing, "She is all the beauty extant" (2.2.148). So closely attuned to each other that they boast of being each other's "wife", the cousins, with the most ironic inevitability, fall for exactly the same woman. But it isn't long before the pair find themselves exchanging terms of high refinement for something less noble. "What think you of this beauty?" Palamon asks, suddenly suspicious:

> ARCITE   'Tis a rare one.
> PALAMON
>   Is't but a rare one?
> ARCITE   Yes, a matchless beauty.
> PALAMON
>   Might not a man well lose himself and love her?
> ARCITE
>   I cannot tell what you have done; I have,
>   Beshrew mine eyes for't! Now I feel my shackles.
> PALAMON
>   You love her, then?
> ARCITE Who would not?
> PALAMON And desire her?
> ARCITE Before my liberty.
> PALAMON
>   I saw her first.
>
>   [2.2.154–63]

Palamon's childish interjection is genuinely funny, but it also indicates how easy it has been for these two young men to renounce vows sworn so passionately just a few minutes earlier.

Palamon and Arcite are not alone in feeling the violent tremors created by love. When Arcite is suddenly banished from Greece, Palamon is left alone in prison – an arrangement that suits the Jailer's Daughter, who is earnestly trying to catch the stranger's eye. Acknowledging the social gulf between them, she admits that "to marry him is hopeless, / To be his whore is witless" (2.4.4–5) but can see no other way out. Then an idea strikes. "Say I ventured / To set him free?" she wonders,

>   What says the law then? Thus much
> For law or kindred! I will do it,
> And this night or tomorrow he shall love me.
>
>   [2.4.30–3]

The play does not make things that easy, however. Palamon remains aloof, seeming not to cotton on to the fact that she has wild ideas about marrying him.

Shakespeare and Fletcher took the story of the Jailer's Daughter (they give her no other name) from the tiniest of hints in the "Knight's Tale" – there it is merely a mysterious "freend" who helps Palamon escape – but what they make out of it becomes utterly crucial to the play. Against the narrative of the two kinsmen, which becomes more contorted than ever – Arcite manages to work his way into Theseus's court in

> *Palamon's unexpected salvation from execution is not the metaphorical resurrection of Shakespeare's other late plays, but just one more turning that will delay for a little his arrival in the marketplace of death.*
>
> Helen Cooper, "Jacobean Chaucer: *The Two Noble Kinsmen* and other Chaucerian plays" (1998)

disguise, while Palamon hides in the forest – the playwrights set four haunting scenes that trace her emotional collapse. "Let not my sense unsettle," she begs when she is unable to find her beloved (3.2.29), but a scene later these fears have been realized. As she addresses the audience in soliloquy (almost the only person in the play to do so), it becomes apparent that her sanity is gone. "I am very cold," she shivers,

> and all the stars are out too,
> The little stars and all, that look like aglets—
> The sun has seen my folly. Palamon!
> Alas, no; he's in heaven. Where am I now?
> Yonder's the sea and there's a ship—how't tumbles!
> And there's a rock lies watching under water—
> Now, now, it beats upon it—now, now, now,
> There's a leak sprung, a sound one—how they cry!
> Open her before the wind—you'll lose all else.
> Up with a course or two, and tack about, boys.
> Good night, good night, you're gone.
>
> [3.4.1–11]

Shakespeare is usually credited with Act One of *Kinsmen*, the first two scenes of Act Three and three scenes in Act Five, including the play's very last – but even if this soliloquy is Fletcher's handiwork it reads like an assemblage of Shakespearian motifs. Mumbling scraps of folk ballads, the Jailer's Daughter resembles *Hamlet*'s Ophelia, though her habit of repeating words resembles that of King Lear. More tragically even than these, she calls to mind the equally nameless maiden in *A Lover's Complaint*, a poem of Shakespeare's likewise given over to the story of a grief-stricken and abandoned young woman, perhaps written a few years before.

For what we lack

Yet the plight of the Jailer's Daughter, in loving someone socially beyond her reach, is unusual in Shakespeare (Helen in *All's Well* is her closest relative), unusual enough for the Restoration dramatist William Davenant to enhance her status in his adaptation so that she can marry Palamon after all (see p.500). *The Two Noble Kinsmen* itself does not permit itself such a tidy conclusion, and in this play the remainder of the Daughter's experience is wretched. A doctor persuades her father that the best cure for her illness is simply for the man who was wooing her previously (the script just calls him "Wooer") to seize advantage of her mental imbalance. "Take upon you, young sir," he tells the Wooer, the name of Palamon; say you come to eat with her, and to commune of love. This will catch her attention, for this her mind beats upon … Sing to her such green songs of love as she says Palamon hath sung in prison; come to her stuck in as sweet flowers as the season is mistress of, and thereto make an addition of some other compounded odours which are grateful to the sense. All this shall become Palamon, for Palamon can sing, and Palamon is sweet and ev'ry good thing.

[4.3.72–84]

"It is a falsehood she is in," the Doctor smartly concludes, "which is with falsehoods to be combated" (4.3.90–1), and many real-life Renaissance physicians would have agreed with his treatment. Even so the tone of the play is difficult here, balanced between comedy and something incalculably more perplexed – as it was a few scenes earlier, when the Daughter happened upon a group of country folk who took advantage of her insanity by getting her to join their chorus line and perform for Duke Theseus. While the rustic performance is of course another nod to *A Midsummer Night's Dream*, the suggestion in *Kinsmen* that it doesn't really matter whom the Daughter loves, Palamon or another man pretending to be him, also replays some of that comedy's concerns in a far doomier key, as well as gesturing towards later Jacobean plays such as Thomas Middleton's *The Changeling*, with its sexual game-playing and unsettling scenes in a madhouse (see p.638).

A little earlier the Jailer's Daughter is reported as having attempted to drown herself, and death is a nagging theme in *Kinsmen*. Having opened on a scene in which three widowed queens plead with Theseus for their slaughtered husbands to be given a decent burial, the play's finale resolves the conflict between Palamon and Arcite only in the messiest and most gruesome of ways. Finding the two kinsmen fighting in the woods, Theseus decides that unless Emilia can decide between them, they must face each other in combat one last time, with whoever loses facing execution. In what is probably a nod to the masques increasingly popular with the King's Men's royal employer, this climactic contest – like the queens' formal appeals to Theseus – will be performed with plenty of courtly, pseudo-medieval trappings. Each combatant is attended by three knights, and Theseus orders that whoever succeeds in touching a pyramid he sets up (an ancient symbol of success) will win the lady's hand. Yet at the heart of these intricate performances lies a stark emotional crisis. Emilia has no answer to the terrible quandary she faces, and in a later scene she is movingly depicted debating which of the two men is better (she cannot ultimately decide). Earlier Arcite had declared with characteristic fervour that to be removed from her sight would be "death / Beyond imagination" (2.3.4–5), but here the risk he and Palamon face is painfully real: Emilia's inability to choose between her suitors guarantees that one of them must die.

As the tournament nears, the two rivals ready themselves for combat. Once again gesturing towards the stylized devices of masque, the play has them perform elaborate and lengthy rituals of preparation (rituals that also guarantee some impressive special effects): Arcite prays to Mars to the sound of clanging armour, Palamon invokes Venus accompanied by strains of mystical music – and even Emilia calls upon

Diana for guidance, being rewarded with a blossoming rose tree that springs from the altar at which she kneels. Even when the competition finally arrives, though, the audience is kept guessing. The fight takes place offstage, with only background noise indicating what is going on. At first it seems that Palamon is winning, but then the cries for "Arcite" begin to filter through. When the news becomes more certain, the fretful Emilia greets the news with joy. "Half sights saw / That Arcite was no babe," she exclaims.

> God's lid, his richness
> And costliness of spirit looked through him—it could
> No more be hid in him than fire in flax,
> Than humble banks can go to law with waters
> That drift winds force to raging. I did think
> Good Palamon would miscarry, yet I knew not
> Why I did think so.

[5.5.95–102]

Geraldine Alexander as Emilia in Tim Carroll's 2000 folkloric production of *Kinsmen*, one of only a handful of times the play has been revived professionally in the last twenty years.

She accepts Arcite gladly, and Theseus concurs, announcing that "the gods by their divine arbitrariment / Have given you this knight" (5.5.107–8).

But in the play's lurching final move Shakespeare and Fletcher show that the gods' will is not always so easily interpreted. Palamon is about to be beheaded when a messenger bursts in, calling on the executioner to halt. Pirithous breathlessly follows, with news that it is Arcite who is on the point of death: the "hot horse, hot as fire" bestowed upon him by Emilia as a token of her love has bolted, and crushed the victorious knight. In a supreme but troubling sacrifice that directly recalls *The Two Gentlemen*, the dying Arcite insists that his kinsman should take his place: against all expectation it is Palamon, not his cousin, who is to marry Emilia. If the gods have declared their wish, as Theseus insisted before, their messages are achingly difficult to interpret. The Duke is permitted to address them one last time. "O you heavenly charmers," he calls,

> What things you make of us! For what we lack
> We laugh, for what we have, are sorry; still
> Are children in some kind. Let us be thankful
> For that which is, and with you leave dispute
> That are above our question.

> [5.6.131–6]

This scene is probably by Shakespeare, and as a conclusion to his career these halting words of Theseus are infinitely more painful than anything voiced by Prospero at the close of *The Tempest*. Everything is provisional, they imply – and the human condition is one in which comedy and tragedy are so closely entwined that we may never finally know which is which.

Stage history and adaptations

About the first years of *Kinsmen* there is much speculation and precious little evidence. Given that it debuted around 1613, soon after the destruction of the Globe – the Prologue mentions "our losses" in what may be a reference to the fire – it's likely to have first been performed at the intimate **Blackfriars** playhouse. About casting we can only guess: both of the King's Men's star actors, **Richard Burbage** and **John Lowin**, were probably too long in the tooth, though some critics think the play may not have been performed by Shakespeare and Fletcher's troupe at all but another company. At any rate, we know it was considered for performance at **court** in 1619–20, but probably never staged, and the text (omitted from the First Folio) wasn't printed until 1634.

Exactly thirty years later it reappeared in the Restoration theatre in adapted form, a version by **William Davenant** entitled *The Rivals*. As with Davenant's other reworkings, this cut many of the play's most unsettling aspects and made it into a straight comedy. Arcite is spared death while "Celania" (the Jailer's Daughter in the original play) is magically cured and married to "Philander", Davenant's Palamon, who was played by **Thomas Betterton** in the original production. **Moll Davies** took the part of Celania in a later revival, and caught the eye of Charles II – perhaps fittingly, she became one of his many mistresses soon afterwards.

In the eighteenth century, too, *Kinsmen* only reached the stage in heavily modified form. The playwright **Richard Cumberland** had limited success with his *Palamon and Arcite; or, The Noble Kinsmen* from 1779, which like Davenant's version sentimentalized the play but made it into a tragedy instead. In an altogether different vein was **Godolphin Waldron**'s *Love and Madness; or, The Two Noble Kinsmen*, which premiered in London in 1795. Unlike Cumberland's adaptation this ended happily, with Palamon cheerfully deciding to accept the advances of the mad "Hermia" on condition that his death will be stayed.

After these performances *Kinsmen* dropped out of the theatrical record entirely: its only verifiable stage history exists in the twentieth century. After over three centuries in abeyance, it was revived at the Old Vic in 1928 with **Eric Portman** as Arcite, **Ernest Milton** as Palamon and **Jean Forbes-Robertson** as the Jailer's Daughter. This staging played it safe by choosing a medieval setting ("an experiment in prettiness", according to one observer), although Milton found himself forced to play Palamon as a comic character after audiences tittered at his wig. The production sparked only mild curiosity, however, and for the next forty years *Kinsmen* became the preserve of academic and amateur productions. Many of these were impressive, however – an open-air staging by renowned Chaucerian and Shakespearian scholar **Neville Coghill** in the gardens of Merton College, Oxford in 1957 attracted attention – and bravely kept its spirit alive.

Its next foray into professional theatre came under **Richard Digby Day** at York's Theatre Royal in 1973. This presented a beautiful but skewed version of the play, cutting the rustics along with much of the comedy and concentrating instead on its timeless qualities. A French adaptation by **Véronique Réand** from 1979 offered a tragic view of its material, while an English-language Edinburgh Fringe production the same year by **Andrew Visnevski**'s Cherub Company stressed the intimate homosocial ties between the two kinsmen with an all-male cast. Despite heavy cutting and confrontational staging, many reviewers were struck by the emotional Jailer's Daughter of **Anthony Best**. Other performances followed, several in the US: **Walter Scholz**'s production at Los Angeles's Globe Playhouse was well reviewed with **Suzanna Peters**'s Jailer's Daughter a highlight.

The production with the greatest impact to date, however, appeared in 1986, and in fact opened the RSC's brand-new Swan Theatre, itself based on Jacobean models. **Barry Kyle** used Japanese-influenced staging and costumes to draw out the play's stylized qualities, but it was the calibre of his cast that really shone through. **Gerard Murphy**'s Palamon played opposite the Arcite of **Hugh Quarshie** (an early instance of colour-blind casting in Britain) while **Imogen Stubbs** very nearly stole the show as an uninhibited and hugely affecting Jailer's Daughter. Elements of Kyle's staging – notably the suspended cage in which the prison scene was played – irritated some, but his interpretation of *Kinsmen* has gone down in theatrical history as perhaps the finest yet.

Not that there has been much competition: fewer than a handful of professional productions have made it past the drawing board, and the play was regarded as sufficiently obscure that it only merited a rehearsed reading in the RSC's Complete Works festival of 2006–07 and was omitted from the World Shakespeare Festival of 2012 altogether. British audiences had a rare chance to catch *Kinsmen* courtesy of **Tim Carroll** at Shakespeare's Globe in London in summer 2000, but the cast – to its director's irritation – fell into the trap of performing the play for laughs. Despite powerful performances from **Will Keen** (Palamon), **Jasper Britton** (Arcite), **Geraldine Alexander** (Emilia) and **Kate Fleetwood** (Jailer's Daughter), it faced heavy fire from critics and has not been revived.

North American audiences have been luckier. **Darko Tresnjak**'s staging at New York's Public Theater (2003) received plaudits from reviewers impressed that so obscure a play had such power to move. Acting in Tresnjak's "crisp" production were **David Harbour** and **Graham Hamilton** as the Kinsmen, while **Doan Ly** attracted positive notices for a spirited Emilia. Indeed, North American audiences have been given a number of opportunities to judge the play's qualities for themselves. It was staged in the medieval style by **Nagle Jackson** at the Oregon Shakespeare Festival in 1994, and again at San Diego's Old Globe in 2004 (a pared-down production by Darko Tresnjak), then inside the replica Blackfriars Playhouse at **Staunton, Virginia** in 2013, in an acclaimed actor-led production – "better than it had a right to be," in the intriguing words of one local paper. The festival at Stratford, Ontario has even mounted the play twice, once in 1985, directed by **Charles MacFarland**, and again in 2002 when **David Latham** created a Japanese-inflected production with a team of young actors.

Not admitted into the BBC/Time-Life series owing to doubts about authorship (and, presumably, anxieties about budget), *Kinsmen* has yet to find a producer willing to capture it on film or TV.

AUDIO

The Two Noble Kinsmen
J. Firth, N. Cooke, H. Schlesinger; Clive Brill (dir.) UK, 1999 > Arkangel ◉

Employing Simon Russell Beale to speak the Prologue elevates expectations, and – even considering the lack of competition – this production of *Kinsmen* does not disappoint. The masques and songs come across surprisingly well, with Dominique Le Gendre's vibrant music evoking well the kinds of spectacle your mind's eye might supply. The interplay between Jonathan Firth's Palamon and Nigel Cooke's Arcite is effectively intimate, and while they don't always relish the more arcane corners of the play's verse, these Kinsmen never run the risk of blurring into each other – Firth seems youthful and open, Cooke more reserved and shadier. Sarah-Jane Holm makes a poignant Jailer's Daughter, while Helen Schlesinger's wistful Emilia also communicates the character's emotional resilience. Only the occasionally obtrusive sound effects (chain-rattling in the jail scenes) weaken this recording's appeal.

EDITIONS

Arden Shakespeare (third series)
Lois Potter (ed.); rev. 2015 > Bloomsbury

It's pleasing that Arden has expended effort in attempting to cover the lesser-known areas of the Shakespearian canon before going for the really major works, and Lois Potter's recently refreshed edition of *Kinsmen* demonstrates what a first-rate version can do for the play. Potter covers the question of authorship without getting in the least bogged down by it, and likewise her analysis of its tragicomic genre is sensitive and subtle. Glancing at this book, too, you'd have little sense that the play's stage history is sparse – Potter's detailed coverage fills more than thirty pages.

SOME CRITICISM

Shakespeare's Chaucer

Ann Thompson; 1978 > Liverpool UP / Rowman & Littlefield [o/p]

Thompson's was the earliest study to look in detail at what (surprisingly) had been a comparatively understudied area: the relation between Shakespeare and one of his most famous of literary antecedents. What emerges is evidence that Shakespeare not only knew his Chaucer well (the fact that he wrote two plays, *Troilus and Cressida* and *Kinsmen*, on Chaucerian models makes that clear) but that Chaucerian echoes permeate his work – all the way from half-remembered asides to large-scale liftings. *Shakespeare's Chaucer* devotes plenty of space to *Kinsmen*, travelling through the play scene by scene and comparing it with the "Knight's Tale"; and although some of Thompson's conclusions about the different intentions of Fletcher and Shakespeare might not suit everyone's taste (she argues that Fletcher was writing for the market, Shakespeare for all time), the book is thoughtful as well as helpful.

Shakespeare, Fletcher and The Two Noble Kinsmen

Charles H. Frey (ed.); 1989 > Missouri UP [o/p]

It testifies to the interest in *The Two Noble Kinsmen* following the RSC's production of 1986 that a few years later a Shakespeare Association of America conference devoted itself entirely to the subject of the play. The convenor of that seminar, Charles Frey, decided to bring together the papers given there and the result is this book. It's a valuable collection covering everything from textual compositors (prepare yourself for lots of tables and signature marks) to the role of sadness in the play (a slightly whimsical essay by Frey himself), plus a particularly intriguing article by Hugh Richmond on *Kinsmen*'s performance history. There's also a detailed bibliography, though obviously not up to date.

The Winter's Tale

To call something a "winter's tale" was Jacobean slang for something fanciful, unreal – a fireside story. The tale told by the play itself has sometimes been called that, too, but initially at least it promises little in the way of light-hearted entertainment. It relates the story of a king whose jealousy is so strong, yet so without ground, that it loses him not only his wife but his young son and his baby daughter. In this *The Winter's Tale* closely resembles an earlier play of jealousy, *Othello*, and for over half its length the drama seems to be an even bleaker remake – until, that is, the mystical appearance of Time (himself personified on stage) and the shift to a mysterious new location, one where a cure for the play's romantic ills gradually blossoms. Shakespeare's source, a novella by his long-dead theatrical rival Robert Greene entitled *Pandosto: or, The Triumph of Time*, suggests that time can heal even the most violent of fractures, and therefore that the tale doesn't have to end in disaster; and after an improbable sequence of events, the play delivers a powerful, almost mythical, resolution. Its final scene, which can still astonish unprepared audiences, is justifiably famous and marks a decisive transformation from tragic winter into reviving spring.

DATE > Difficult to pinpoint – a version of the play was performed on May 15, 1611, but much of it may have been written several years earlier.

SOURCES > Shakespeare reworked Robert Greene's popular tragic novella, *Pandosto* (pub. 1588), changing its characters' names and modifying its plot. Passing references to other sources have been identified, Puttenham's *Art of English Poesie* and Ovid's *Metamorphoses* among them.

TEXTS > The play seems to have been squeezed into the First Folio (1623) at the last minute by the scribe Ralph Crane, and his text forms the basis of all subsequent editions.

Interpreting the play

The title of *The Winter's Tale* seems to announce a return to the kind of throwaway, whimsical phrases that predominate in Shakespeare's middle comedies. Along with *Twelfth Night; or, What You Will* and *As You Like It*, it has a kind of take-it-or-leave-it quality – perhaps a kind of built-in defence against audiences taking anything too seriously. But the "tale" of this play's title is of more than symbolic importance: it appears within the action itself. Early in Act One, the heavily pregnant Queen Hermione and her attendants are idly amusing themselves at Leontes's court when Hermione hits upon an idea. "Pray you sit by us," she calls to her son Mamillius, "and tell's a tale":

MAJOR CHARACTERS & SYNOPSIS

Leontes, King of Sicily
Hermione, Leontes' wife
Mamillius, their son
Perdita, their daughter
Camillo, **Antigonus**, **Cleomenes** and **Dion**, lords at Leontes' court
Paulina, Antigonus's wife
Emilia, Hermione's attendant
Polixenes, King of Bohemia
Florizel (initially disguised as the countryman "Doricles"), Polixenes's son
Archidamus, a Bohemian lord
Autolycus, a con man
Old Shepherd, Perdita's foster father
Clown, the Shepherd's son
Mopsa and **Dorcas**, shepherdesses
The figure of **Time**, acting as a chorus

ACT 1 King Polixenes is staying at the court of his close childhood friend, Leontes, but after nine months away he has decided to return home to Bohemia. When Polixenes reluctantly refuses all entreaties to stay another week, Leontes asks his wife to intercede – but then interprets her success as evidence of an adulterous relationship between the two of them. Convinced that he is right, Leontes orders Camillo to poison Polixenes, but instead Camillo tips him off and both of them leave, in secret, for Bohemia.

ACT 2 Hermione is with her son Mamillius when Leontes rushes in, having heard of Polixenes's and Camillo's flight. Taking this as proof of his former friend's guilt, Leontes confronts Hermione and accuses her of adultery. Though she vehemently denies it, he has her imprisoned, ignoring the pleas of those who defend her. Leontes then announces that he has sent messengers to Apollo's oracle at Delphos, in the expectation that it will confirm her guilt. When Hermione gives birth to a daughter in prison, her friend Paulina takes the child to Leontes, hoping to persuade the King that the baby is his. He is outraged, however, and orders that Paulina and the baby be burnt to death. When his lords refuse, he relents and instructs Antigonus to abandon the child in a deserted place outside the kingdom. As news arrives that the messengers are returning from Delphos, Leontes orders Hermione to stand trial.

ACT 3 Leontes formally accuses Hermione of adultery and plotting to kill him, but she remains firm and declares that Apollo will be her judge. But when the oracle's words – which describe Hermione as utterly blameless – are read out, Leontes declares them to be false and orders the trial to continue. Everything is thrown into disarray, however, when news arrives of Mamillius's sudden death: Hermione collapses and is carried away, as Leontes begins to regret his terrible mistake. Paulina arrives and bitterly renounces Leontes before announcing that the Queen has died. Antigonus, meanwhile, has abandoned the baby (whom he calls Perdita) in Bohemia, where she is discovered by the Shepherd and his son, who take her home.

ACT 4 The figure of Time restarts the action some sixteen years later, during which time Perdita has grown up in Bohemia as the daughter of the Shepherd. More recently, she has been wooed by Florizel, Polixenes's son. Hearing of this, Polixenes and Camillo decide to attend the shepherd's shearing feast in disguise in order to spy on the couple. When Florizel (known to Perdita as Doricles) admits that he intends to marry her, his father angrily reveals himself, condemns the Shepherd to death, and threatens to disinherit his son. After he departs, Camillo hatches a scheme whereby the young couple will elope to Sicily and present themselves to Leontes. In the meantime, the Shepherd and his son are on the way to plead with Polixenes, when they are fleeced by Autolycus, the local con man.

ACT 5 In Sicily, Leontes, still in mourning for Hermione, vows not to marry again without Paulina's consent. When Florizel and Perdita arrive, Leontes is captivated by the young couple, but Polixenes has discovered their flight and has pursued them. The truth is revealed, however: the Shepherd relates his discovery of the infant Perdita, and father and daughter are happily reunited. All then go together to Paulina's house to view the statue of Hermione recently erected there. While the company marvels at its life-like qualities, Paulina commands the statue to descend. The living Hermione steps forward.

MAMILLIUS Merry or sad shall't be?
HERMIONE As merry as you will.
MAMILLIUS
    A sad tale's best for winter. I have one
    Of sprites and goblins.
HERMIONE   Let's have that, good sir.
    Come on, sit down, come on, and do your best
    To fright me with your sprites.

[2.1.23–30]

Though she calls for a childish ghost story to while away the time, there is in fact more than enough to "fright" Hermione – and the audience – in real life. Her husband, Leontes, is in the process of persuading himself that his wife has been unfaithful, and his instinct has hardened into deadly conviction. Leontes has invented his own "sprites and goblins", and though, like Mamillius's story, it is nothing but a "winter's tale" – a fairy story – its consequences will be horribly real. As she sits down to listen to her son's tale, Hermione has not an inkling of the danger she, or her unborn child, are in.

A spider steeped

The story of a king who becomes convinced that his wife has slept with his best friend, and is about to give birth to an illegitimate child, was an old one, and Shakespeare encountered it – if not at his mother's knee – in a wildly successful collection of tales by Robert Greene, an old playwriting rival (see p.142). In Greene's version, *Pandosto*, the king of that name is happily married to Bellaria (Hermione in the play) when his good friend Egistus (Polixenes) arrives to stay. After they have spent hour after hour in each other's company, enjoying what Greene calls their "secret uniting of affections", Pandosto begins to suspect that all is not as it should be. Wrestling with his conscience, he finally concludes that they have been unfaithful with each other, and is driven to seek revenge.

But in Shakespeare's play there is nothing whatsoever to back up Leontes's jealousy, so sudden and brutal in its onset that, when he demands that she hand over their son just a few lines later, Hermione at first thinks he is joking:

LEONTES   Give me the boy. I am glad you did not nurse him.
    Though he does bear some signs of me, yet you
    Have too much blood in him.
HERMIONE   What is this? Sport?
LEONTES   *(to a Lord)*
    Bear the boy hence. He shall not come about her.
    Away with him, and let her sport herself
    With that she's big with, *(to Hermione)* for 'tis Polixenes
    Has made thee swell thus.

[2.1.58–64]

Barely a scene after he first announced his suspicions, Leontes has become utterly possessed by the belief that he has been cuckolded – a change so abrupt that actors often struggle to present it convincingly, as if in having written about jealousy so often before Shakespeare felt at liberty to represent it here in brutal shorthand. Instead of being a joyful celebration of married love, Hermione's pregnancy, coming to term nine months after Polixenes's arrival in Sicily, becomes evidence of her adultery, even though – as becomes clear in the humiliating trial scene to which he subjects her later in the play – the King has not one scintilla of proof.

As numerous critics have argued, Leontes's jealousy is rooted in hatred – and fear – of women, apparently brought on by reminiscing about his childhood companionship with Polixenes, an era before the females that would separate those "two twinned lambs" were even dreamt of. "Temptations have since then been born to's," Polixenes laughingly tells Hermione when they are all together, "for / In those unfledged days was my wife a girl."

> Your precious self had then not crossed the eyes
> Of my young playfellow.
>
> [1.2.79–82]

Polixenes's tone is playful, but – as Hermione immediately picks up – this description of an Edenic boyhood existence, free from "tempting" females, casts the two queens as "devils", a pair of corrupting Eves to their husbands' sinless Adams. Yet Shakespeare, characteristically, shades things even more subtly. Hermione's position in this scene is complex: she clearly feels close to Polixenes, and in her passionate attempts to make him stay (prompted, of course, by Leontes) she uses all the resources she can. "Force me to keep you as a prisoner," she laughingly offers Polixenes, drifting dangerously close to the line (1.2.53). And we also find out that things have not always been easy between Hermione and Leontes; it took him "three crabbèd months", he claims, to convince her to love him (1.2.104), and the image of his wife speaking so intimately with his best friend – so warmly that Polixenes relents and agrees to stay in Sicily, though Leontes himself could not make him – clearly begins to eat away at the King's mind.

Leontes, like Shakespeare's other jealous males, is unable to shake off the idea that sexuality itself is a kind of loss of innocence. Though one might wish for blissful ignorance, Leontes muses ("Many thousand on's / Have the disease and feel't not" (1.2.207–8)), that sin only lies dormant, waiting to poison its victim. "How blest am I in my just censure, in my true opinion!" he congratulates himself, appallingly, hearing of Polixenes's terrified flight from Sicily:

> Alack, for lesser knowledge—how accursed
> In being so blessed! There may be in the cup
> A spider steeped, and one may drink, depart,
> And yet partake no venom, for his knowledge
> Is not infected; but if one present
> Th'abhorred ingredient to his eye, make known

How he hath drunk, he cracks his gorge, his sides,
With violent hefts. I have drunk and seen the spider.

[2.1.38–47]

Knowledge itself, Leontes reflects, is the danger: it is the real "venom". The irony here is that the King thinks that he is looking the truth squarely in the face, swallowing the terrible reality; but, of course, the "spider" he sees, like Macbeth's ethereal dagger, proceeds entirely from his own brain.

In one of the most famously difficult of his speeches in the play, jealousy has a kind of clotting effect on Leontes's tongue. Calling his little son to him, he stutters, "Affection, thy intention stabs the centre":

Thou dost make possible things not so held,
Communicat'st with dreams—how can this be?—
With what's unreal thou coactive art,
And fellow'st nothing. Then 'tis very credent
Thou mayst co-join with something, and thou dost—
And that beyond commission; and I find it—
And that to the infection of my brains
And hard'ning of my brows.

[1.2.140–48]

As broken thoughts race through his mind, Leontes is almost impossible to understand, and not just for the young son he addresses – Shakespeare's first audiences, too, would surely have struggled. If "affection" means sexual passion, he seems to be communicating the idea that if sex can "co-join" (or "breed", since breeding is on his mind) with "dreams", then it will certainly do so with realities. He could also mean that his own jealousy is eating away at his sense of what is real, or that his state of mind ("affection") is wildly out of control. But the central thought is that "nothing" is as dangerous as "something" – and so Hermione is guilty whether she has done anything or not, because Leontes suspects as much (his brows "harden" in the expectation that cuckold's horns will shoot out of his head, a fear that also afflicts Othello). Over all this, the unmistakable impression is of a man spewing diseased thoughts from a mind which is struggling to work out how realities can be made to fit fantasies.

Yet the problem is not so much that everyone believes Leontes's version of events, as in *Othello*: where in that earlier play the rest of the cast are taken in by Iago's brilliant improvisation, Leontes has to fight tooth and nail to assert his belief that Hermione is guilty. After threatening to dismiss his advisers if they so much as speak in her defence, Leontes answers Antigonus's scalding criticism that he has tried her "only in [his] silent judgement" (2.1.173) by publicly humiliating Hermione, who has just given birth to their daughter, under the pretence of testing her in court. As she lucidly announces at her trial, she is caught in a terrible catch-22: by testifying on her own behalf she only incriminates herself in Leontes's eyes. "My life," she tells him, "stands in the level of your dreams" (3.2.80): her husband and his brittle fantasies have absolute power.

A course more promising

But Leontes's "dreams", unlike Othello's, encounter resistance. The bustling energy of the girl's arrival (she is, says Emilia, "lusty, and like to live" (2.2.29)) seems to offer promise. When good news arrives from the Delphic oracle, which Leontes has consulted in the hope of silencing his critics, it seems as if everything, finally, will be resolved. "Hermione is chaste," it proclaims,

> Polixenes blameless, Camillo a true subject, Leontes a jealous tyrant, his innocent babe truly begotten, and the King shall live without an heir if that which is lost be not found.
>
> [3.2.132–5]

In language of crystalline clarity (Shakespeare copies it almost verbatim from his source), the oracle dismisses the King's crabbed fantasies in an instant. Redemption beckons. But Leontes, crying out that it is "mere falsehood", will not accept a verdict which differs from his own, and by this time he has already ordered that the newborn child should be taken out of the kingdom and exposed to the elements, "where chance may nurse or end it" (2.3.183). Upon that "chance" – and with the oracle's challenge of dire consequences if "that which is lost be not found" – the rest of *The Winter's Tale* will hang.

The next shock is sudden: Mamillius is announced to have died. Hermione faints at the news, then it is declared that she, too, is dead. Paulina, her steadfast defender, is outspoken in grief. "I say she's dead," she screams at Leontes, "I'll swear it."

> If you can bring
> Tincture or lustre in her lip, her eye,
> Heat outwardly or breath within, I'll serve you
> As I would do the gods. But O thou tyrant,
> Do not repent these things, for they are heavier
> Than all thy woes can stir. Therefore betake thee
> To nothing but despair. A thousand knees,
> Ten thousand years together, naked, fasting,
> Upon a barren mountain, and still winter
> In storm perpetual, could not move the gods
> To look that way thou wert.
>
> [3.2.203–13]

The barriers to any kind of resolution seem as impenetrable as any futile penance Leontes could trouble himself with. The play seems frozen in tragedy.

Yet *The Winter's Tale* does not, like Mamillius's story (or even *Pandosto*), end sadly. Antigonus has abandoned the child in Bohemia – she is called Perdita, "lost" – whereupon, in the middle of a furious storm, she is discovered by a kindly shepherd. Like the fishermen in *Pericles* who haul the hero from the ocean and cheerfully promise to care for him, the Old Shepherd proves an unstoppably kindly force. "What have we here?" he exclaims:

Mercy on's, a bairn! A very pretty bairn. A boy or a child, I wonder? A pretty one, a very pretty one. Sure some scape. Though I am not bookish, yet I can read 'waiting-gentlewoman' in the scape. This has been some stair-work, some trunk-work, some behind-door-work. They were warmer that got this than the poor thing is here. I'll take it up for pity …

[3.3.68–74]

Assuming the child has been abandoned because it is illegitimate (conceived, he chuckles, on the stairs, perhaps, or in a trunk, behind a door), he converts at a stroke what has been Leontes's public nightmare into something entirely unexceptional. It doesn't matter if the baby is a bastard – but it does matter that it is looked after. Hearing of the terrible storm at sea, the Shepherd tells his son, "Thou metst with things dying, I with things new-born" (3.3.111).

Those "new-born" things turn the play around. Following the intercession of Time, a personification of whom appears on stage to advertise (and apologize for) a sixteen-year gap in the action, *The Winter's Tale* continues with a fully grown Perdita who, like Guiderius and Aviragus in *Cymbeline*, somehow manages to exude royal breeding despite her humble upbringing with the Shepherd. But then Bohemia, like Ardenne in *As You Like It*, is an exotic and pastoral location, complete with a real bear, which in an infamous stage direction chases away and kills Antigonus (in the original Globe production the creature possibly came from a nearby bear-baiting pit). It also has a con man, Autolycus, straight out of Jacobean city comedy; and a fictional sea-coast, all of which seem to announce that Shakespeare has no intention that his location be taken too literally. In Bohemia there are in fact hardly any mentions of the main plot: people apparently spend their time having fun, with Florizel casually wooing the strangely beautiful girl in his land without revealing his royal identity. Nothing, it seems, can dent their joy. When Perdita promises to "strew" her "sweet friend" with garlands, he is momentarily shaken:

FLORIZEL   What, like a corpse?
PERDITA
   No, like a bank, for love to lie and play on,
   Not like a corpse—or if, not to be buried,
   But quick and in my arms.

[4.4.129–32]

The wonderfully vibrant sexuality implicit in Perdita's words hints that death can be banished by love, and that the play's winter can be transformed into a flower-filled spring. Bohemia contains everything the play needs to become a comedy: Perdita herself, her sweetheart Florizel and the kindly Camillo. Even the tall tales of the con man Autolycus, who roams the Bohemian countryside relating fantastical stories to the country's open-mouthed inhabitants, have a certain bizarre charm. Though Florizel's father Polixenes is displeased that his son has fallen for (he thinks) a shepherdess, it is not long before Camillo persuades the lovers to elope. All they

> *The real world [at the end of The Winter's Tale] has none of the customary qualities of reality. It is the world symbolized by nature's power of renewal; it is the world we want; it is the world we hope our gods would want for us if they were worth worshipping.*
>
> Northrop Frye, *A Natural Perspective* (1965)

have to do, he explains, is trust in providence, follow "a course more promising / Than a wild dedication of yourselves / To unpathed waters, undreamed shores" (4.4.565–6).

Yet the couple's destination is not "undreamed" – it is Sicily, and the play is very nearly home. But though we are not shown on stage what seems to be the point of the action, the long-lost daughter's reunion with her father (as we are in *Pericles*), Shakespeare has a yet more impressive coup de théâtre up his sleeve. Grieving for his dead wife, Leontes has been promised a commemorative statue of her, commissioned by Paulina. The time for it to be unveiled drawing near, Perdita joins her father to witness her first-ever sight of her mother, but as the curtain is drawn it is Leontes who seems most moved by what he sees in front of him. Then something incredible happens. Paulina calls out to the statue, "'Tis time. Descend."

> Be stone no more. Approach.
> Strike all that look upon with marvel. Come,
> I'll fill your grave up. Stir. Nay, come away.
> Bequeath to death your numbness, for from him
> Dear life redeems you.
>
> [5.3.99–103]

The moment is near impossible to reproduce on the page, not least because Hermione's apparent reawakening from the dead is as much a shock for the offstage audience as it is for the dumbstruck Leontes. The last we heard, Hermione collapsed, apparently fatally – yet here she is, alive and (as Leontes breathlessly observes) "warm". "If this be magic," he exclaims, "let it be an art / Lawful as eating" (5.3.110–1). Paulina's earlier threat to the King, that only if he could give the dead Hermione "heat outwardly or breath within" would she serve him, has come mystically true. The moment is astonishing not merely because it is unlooked-for, but because it is undeserved: Leontes has no right to expect his wife to be restored, just as there is no reason Hermione should want to go back to the husband who destroyed everything they shared. But Shakespeare, preparing his audience for an improbable "winter's tale", lets us – if we want to – believe in something infinitely more wondrous. Paulina's words to Leontes address the audience too. "That she is living," she proclaims,

> Were it but told you, should be hooted at
> Like an old tale. But it appears she lives …
>
> [5.3.116–8]

Stage history and adaptations

The astrologer Simon Forman saw the first recorded performance of *The Winter's Tale* in May 1611 at the **Globe**, and the play was also popular at **court**: no fewer than six performances across two decades are in the records and when Charles II attended in 1634 it was apparently "liked" by spectators. For all that, it didn't survive past the Restoration and remained off the stage well into the next century. **Henry Giffard** staged a performance at Goodman's Fields in 1741, and later that same year it appeared at Covent Garden with **Samuel Stephens** as Leontes and **Christiana Horton** as Hermione. The production foundered, though – despite a rural "Grand Ballet" in the Bohemia scenes – and when the play next appeared it was in an adaptation by **Macnamara Morgan**. This was named *The Sheep-Shearing; or, Florizel and Perdita* (it cut the first half of Shakespeare's script entirely) and opened at Covent Garden in 1754 with the magnetic **Spranger Barry** as Florizel opposite **Isabella Nossiter**'s Perdita. Hot on Morgan's heels was **David Garrick**'s own adaptation, also called *Florizel and Perdita*, which appeared in direct competition later that year. Both versions excised nearly all the tragedy and concentrated instead on the play's magical reunion, acted movingly for Garrick by **Hannah Pritchard** as Hermione, though lighter fare was offered in the form of **Richard Yates**'s Autolycus (Yates apparently excelled in "characters of low and vulgar mould"). It was Morgan's adaptation that persisted, however, and as late as 1795 it was still being performed in preference to Shakespeare as far away as New York.

The man responsible for bringing *The Winter's Tale* back from the dead was **John Philip Kemble**, who produced it several times in the first years of the nineteenth century. These productions were grand affairs – the prison scene was designed after Piranesi – with Kemble playing a dignified Leontes to **Sarah Siddons**'s passionate Hermione (one critic gushed that Siddons "towered beyond all praise"). **William Charles Macready** took on the play in 1823 but tried to inject it with more life: his own Leontes expressed such passion in the recognition scene that **Helen Faucit**, playing Hermione, was nearly overcome. **Samuel Phelps**'s Leontes (from 1845) was more restrained as well as more prudish: he dropped some of the play's "indelicacies". Phelps's Sadler's Wells boasted impressive sets, but they were soon outdone by **Charles Kean**, who centred his 1856 production on spectacular designs by **William Grieve** – to the extent that the script was pruned to remove any references that contradicted the Grecian setting. Kean's success even sparked a burlesque by **William Brough** entitled *Perdita; or, The Royal Milkmaid* that poked fun at the producer's serious-minded staging; in it the bear was instructed to be "respectably dressed".

English audiences were won over by the arrival of the **Duke of Saxe-Meiningen**'s company with *The Winter's Tale* in 1881, which set standards for ensemble performance far exceeding those of home-grown troupes. The 1887 staging at the Lyceum was a case in point, being a vehicle for the American actress **Mary Anderson**, who not only directed and starred, but played both Hermione and Perdita to **Johnston Forbes-Robertson**'s Leontes. Many loved it, though, and the production saw over 160 performances, later transferring to New York. **Frank Benson** attempted to draw on insights learnt from the Saxe-Meiningen approach, but his 1903 Stratford staging was still dominated by his own Leontes. **Herbert Beerbohm Tree**, as so often, produced a version that took to an extreme the indulgences of Victorian actor-managers: his 1906 production reduced the play to three acts so as not to distract from the grandiloquent staging.

The turnaround for *The Winter's Tale* came in 1912, with **Harley Granville-Barker**'s avant-garde production at the Savoy. Granville-Barker restored a full text and played it at lightning speed (too fast for many critics to keep up). **Henry Ainley** brought new life to Leontes by playing him with frightening psychological realism, while the elegant and simple designs by the fashionable **Albert Rutherston** were strong on atmosphere rather than straightforwardly realistic. **Jacques Copeau** would go still further eight years later in Paris, setting the play on an entirely bare stage, but in England Granville-Barker's ideas were too radical for many: his production was a critical failure. **Michael McOwan**'s Old Vic staging (1936) went for a softer, Italianate style while **Anthony Quayle**'s postwar Stratford version (1948) harked back to the spectacular tastes of the nineteenth century. Nevertheless **Esmond Knight**'s raging Leontes impressed, as did **Claire Bloom**'s fragile Perdita.

Quayle's Hermione was the alluring **Diana Wynyard**, who returned to the role under **Peter Brook** in a famous Phoenix Theatre production of 1951. Opposite Wynyard's flaxen-haired Queen was **John Gielgud**'s Leontes, who brought a brooding intensity to the role that reached its climax in the recognition scene. Brook muted the play's laughter – his bear was tragic, not comic – and was rewarded with commercial success. In North America two productions from 1958 offered fresh insights as well as bringing the play to new audiences: the staging by **John Houseman** and **Jack Landau** at Stratford, Connecticut was modern (Time wore a business suit and carried an umbrella); while at Stratford, Ontario **Douglas Campbell** encouraged **Christopher Plummer** to play Leontes as victim rather than villain. Back in Stratford-upon-Avon in 1960, **Peter Wood**'s production was blessed with an enviable cast, among it **Eric Porter** (Leontes), **Elizabeth Sellars** (Hermione) and **Peggy Ashcroft** (Paulina), but it was Wood's attention to detail that most impressed audiences: the small scenes were carefully staged, while the dances in Bohemia were full-bloodedly rural.

By contrast **Trevor Nunn**'s production at the same venue in 1969 emphasized the otherworldly qualities of *The Winter's Tale*: set wholly in a white box, it used props prompted by the play's language and enacted Leontes's perverted fantasies in dumb-show. **Barry Ingham** played a cool King to **Judi Dench**'s Hermione and Perdita (shades of Mary Anderson), but **Alton Kumado** came close to stealing the show as Time and a rural Green Man – a doubling intended to cast doubt on the innocence of the play's Bohemia. Less obviously an example of director's theatre was Nunn's return to the play with **John Barton** in 1976, dominated by **Ian McKellen**'s dangerously unstable Leontes. It wasn't without meaningful design touches, though: the pastoral landscape of Act Four was overshadowed by a single bare tree. **Peter Hall** offered the play at the National Theatre in 1988 as part of his triple bill of romances in a staging that was shadowier than its predecessors, featuring **Tim Pigott-Smith** as a nervy Leontes to **Sally Dexter**'s Hermione and hinting that the reconciliation between the pair might be merely provisional. **Ingmar Bergman**'s lavish 1995 production at the Royal Dramatic Theatre in Stockholm relied on theatrical magic, offering the main action as a kind of nineteenth-century play-within-the-play that gradually came to

"This brat is none of mine" ... Alex Jennings is unmoved by the sight of his newborn daughter, Perdita, brought on stage by the faithful Paulina (Deborah Findlay) in Nicholas Hytner's National Theatre production from 2001.

life. Dominated by expressionist scenography – including a statue scene staged like a Renaissance *pietà* – the production was "imbued with the calm authority of genius," in the words of the *New Yorker*.

The small number of major productions have preferred to emphasize the play's unsettling qualities. **Annabel Arden**'s Complicite version (1992) concluded peacefully, but hinted that not all that much had changed between **Simon McBurney**'s Leontes and **Gabrielle Reidy**'s Hermione. That same year **Adrian Noble**'s RSC version, his second after a touring version in 1984, had a set dominated by a large gauze box in which characters came eerily into view, notably **Samantha Bond**'s Hermione (who was actually pregnant at the time). Even so, Noble's Bohemia was a resolutely English vision, complete with village band. **Gregory Doran**'s 1998 version pitched Sicily as stuffily Edwardian, but it was **Antony Sher**'s clinically psychologized Leontes, not the staging, that attracted the warmest reviews. A Russian-language collaboration between **Declan Donnellan** and St Petersburg's Maly Theatre debuted in 1997; making no concessions to redemption, it ended in what the *Guardian* called "as great a piece of theatre as you are ever likely to see", **Natalia Akimova**'s Hermione visibly broken by her long years in isolation.

The 2001 National Theatre production, directed by **Nicholas Hytner**, was praised for **Alex Jennings**'s finely nuanced portrayal of Leontes, in which the character's fluctuating mental states were communicated with extraordinary precision. Not every critic welcomed Hytner's decision to make the rustic Act Four a Glastonbury-type festival, but **Phil Daniels** proved convincing as a Cockney wide-boy Autolycus. **Dominic Cooke**'s 2006 production at the RSC paired *The Winter's Tale* with *Pericles* in a form of communal ritual, allowing the cast to mingle among the audience as well as cross over beteween the two plays. **Anton Lesser's** brittle, repressed Leontes proved a strong foil for **Kate Fleetwood's** wide-eyed Hermione, while the transformation from a chilly 1940s to a flower-power 60s was deftly managed: a radio simply switched from "Catch a Falling Star" to "California Dreaming". **David Farr** offered an expressive interpretation in 2009, again at Stratford, dominated by **Jon Bausor's** awe-inspiring design (which included a library that collapsed on stage) and a lean, pallid **Greg Hicks** as Leontes. At Shakespeare's Globe in London, the play formed part of **Mark Rylance's** farewell season alongside *Pericles* and *The Tempest* in 2005; **John Dove's** Jacobean-era production, with **Paul Jesson** and **Yolanda Vazquez**, was respectfully rather than enthusiastically received.

The play remains as popular as ever globally, not least in India, where it has been adapted multiple times, first in 1876 in Bengali, and also in Marathi (**Nevalkar**, 1894), Gujarati (**V.A. Oza**, 1894) and Urdu (**Munshi Hasan**, 1898), perhaps because the figure of Hermione has echoes with virtuous female figures in the Hindu epics. In 2013 it was staged in a mixture of English and Hindustani by Delhi's **Tadpole** company in a beautifully realized promenade setting outdoors, directed by **Anirudh Nair** and **Neel Chaudhuri**. Over in North America, the play is even more popular in the twenty-first century than during the nineteenth, with at least ten productions in major festival venues. At Oregon in 2006, director **Libby Appel** offered a Ruritanian fantasy world that budded into sping; in Stratford, Ontario in 2010, it was more soberly realized by **Marti Maraden**, with costumes a mixture of Renaissance and Victorian styles and a young cast. It reappeared in Britain as part of the World Shakespeare Festival in 2012, in a Nigerian production from **Renegade Theatre** that made extensive use of Yoruba folk tales and suggested that Hermione's rebirth was only temporary.

The Winter's Tale has fared relatively poorly on screen: it appeared in a 1910 silent adaptation by **Theodore Marston**, followed by a version in 1913 from Italy's **Milano** company. In 1968 **Frank Dunlop** filmed his Edinburgh Festival stage production of two years earlier, with **Laurence Harvey** as Leontes, **Moira Redmond** as Hermione and **Jim Dale** as Autolycus, but it has never been made available on video or DVD. Two British television productions exist: one in 1961, in which **Robert Shaw** and **Rosalie Crutchley** played the estranged couple, and another in 1981. The latter, directed by **Jane Howell** and featuring **Jeremy Kemp** (Leontes) alongside **Anna Calder-Marshall** (Hermione), was part of the BBC/Time-Life project. More recently, tapings of Gregory Doran's 1998 staging have become available.

SCREEN

The Winter's Tale

J. Kemp, A. Calder-Marshall, M. Kendall; Jane Howell (dir.) UK, 1981 ❯ BBC `DVD`

The most immediately striking thing about this *Winter's Tale* is probably its set, a stark space tinted a blinding white in Sicily, moody gray at the Bohemian coasts and a rich gold in Bohemia itself. More stylistically ambitious than elsewhere in the series, Howell's inventive production did much to rescue the BBC project from its reputation for turgidity, though whether her work has dated well is more open to question (watch out for the bear and you'll understand). At any rate Howell's aim was to focus attention on the cast, and here we are rewarded: Jeremy Kemp, an inky-coated King in a sea of white, responds well to the intimacy of the camera and produces a memorable first phase of the play with Anna Calder-Marshall's intense Hermione and Robert Stephens's somewhat louche Polixenes. Kemp is perhaps too cool in the finale and Howell's staging is less effective here than elsewhere, but Margaret Tyzack's Paulina is powerful and the ending works – just.

The Winter's Tale
A. Sher, A. Gilbreath, E. Kohler; Gregory Doran (dir.)
UK, 1998 > Heritage/RSC **DVD**

Though undeniably traditional, Greg Doran's 1998 *The Winter's Tale* for the RSC made persuasive sense of the text and was quietly intelligent throughout. That it works less well on film is largely due to Antony Sher – after quizzing psychologists about Leontes's behaviour, Sher became convinced that the character was suffering from a condition called "morbid jealousy" and on stage he produces a full menu of symptoms. This approach makes for a somewhat jagged interpretation, and some may feel (especially in close-up) that Sher doesn't succeed in joining all the dots. But he is ably supported by a poignant Hermione from Alexandra Gilbreath, Estelle Kohler's gim-let-eyed Paulina is close to perfect, and the rest of the cast is strong. Also available from Heritage is a fascinating "Casebook" version, which places excerpts from the production alongside interviews with its key personnel.

AUDIO

The Winter's Tale
C. Hinds, S. Cusack, J. Gielgud; Clive Brill (dir.) UK, 1998 > Arkangel ◉ ☁

John Gielgud contributed to this recording as one of his last acting projects before his death in 2000, and his near-operatic performance as the magical healer, Time, is fitting testament to a career lasting some sixty years. By the time he appears half the play is done, but fortunately there are plenty of other highlights along the way. Ciaran Hinds makes a high-quality Leontes, exploding with fearsome power in the jealousy scenes and audibly aged at the end, but he is more than equalled by Sinéad Cusack's passionate Hermione. Other parts are well filled: especially charming is Alison Reid's rustic and uninhibited Perdita, while Alex Jennings's Autolycus rightly dominates the Bohemian part of the play. The statue scene is almost unbearably moving here – on audio you realize how the final miracle moves the lead characters to dumbfounded silence, Paulina (wonderfully voiced by Eileen Atkins) incanting this spellbinding metamorphosis in a wonderful solo aria.

EDITIONS

New Cambridge Shakespeare
Susan Snyder and Deborah T. Curren-Aquino (eds); 2007 > Cambridge UP

Originally slated to be edited by Snyder alone until serious illness intervened, this edition was completed by colleague Deborah Curren-Aquino. It is a fine monument, with the text largely based on Snyder's scrupulous notes and Curren-Aquino providing the critical apparatus. She begins with novelist Jane Smiley's suggestive comment that *The Winter's Tale* is an answer to the desolation of *King Lear*, and has a watchful sense of the play's tragedy as well as its comedy, pointing out that, if the text is followed faithfully, Leontes is far less reformed at the end than many assume. Curren-Aquino weaves performance history into her analysis of the play and its themes, and this edition is generously illustrated with a large number of production stills, with a chronology at the back.

SOME CRITICISM

A Natural Perspective
Northrop Frye; 1965 > Columbia UP

Frye was one of the earliest to move the study of myth and its themes towards the centre of Shakespearian studies, and in *A Natural Perspective* he argues that the romances are, in some deep sense, the summation of Shakespeare's work – plays which return to ancient traditions of storytelling in order to repair the devastation of the major tragedies. Despite recent cynicism about Frye's work (it's easier to see the cracks in Shakespeare's miraculous conclusions than he allows), his argument that the world of the romances is "symbolized by nature's power of renewal; it is the world we want" is a compelling one. It seems particularly pertinent to a play such as *The Winter's Tale*, which ends as much in death-suspending fantasy as any kind of conventional reality. The 1995 edition is published with an insightful foreword by Stanley Cavell, a very fine critic in his own right.

Shakespeare: The Last Plays
Kiernan Ryan (ed.); 1999 > Routledge

Ryan's anthology of essays unites an all-star cast, who are as insightful on *The Winter's Tale* as on the rest of the late comedies. It kicks off with Anne Barton's justifiably classic "Leontes and the Spider", a bravura study of the play's tongue-twisting language; and Carol Thomas Neely offers a wise defence of Hermione and Shakespeare's own perspective on women, which sits neatly next to an impressive piece of Derridean deconstruction of the text by Howard Felperin. Also good are Stephen Greenblatt on power games in *The Tempest* and Leah Marcus on the complicated historical contexts that underpin *Cymbeline*.

SHAKE-SPEARES, SONNETS.

FRom faireſt creatures we deſire increaſe,
That thereby beauties *Roſe* might neuer die,
ut as the riper ſhould by time deceaſe,
is tender heire might beare his memory:

The poems

nd only herauld to the gaudy ſpring,
Vithin thine owne bud burieſt thy content,
nd tender chorle makſt waſt in niggarding:
Pitty the world, or elſe this glutton be,
To eate the worlds due, by the graue and thee.

2

VVHen fortie Winters ſhall beſeige thy brow,
And digge deep trenches in thy beauties field,
hy youthes proud liuery ſo gaz'd on now,
Vil be a totter'd weed of ſmal worth held:
hen being askt, where all thy beautie lies,
Vhere all the treaſure of thy luſty daies;
o ſay within thine owne deepe ſunken eyes,
Vere an all-eating ſhame, and thriftleſſe praiſe.
ow much more praiſe deſeru'd thy beauties vſe,
thou couldſt anſwere this faire child of mine
hall ſum my count, and make my old excuſe
roouing his beautie by ſucceſſion thine.

A   B   This

A Lover's Complaint

O riginally published as the final part of the volume entitled *Shakespeare's Sonnets*, *A Lover's Complaint*, a narrative poem some three hundred lines long, engages with many of the same themes as the sonnet sequence – love, lust, betrayal, sorrow. In a broader historical context, the poem is perhaps best understood as Shakespeare's idiosyncratic contribution to an English tradition of "complaint": the haunting and dark tale told by this poem is one of desolation in the ancient sense of that word – from the Latin *desolatus*, "left alone, forsaken", and it relates the enigmatic confession of a woman betrayed by her lover and discovered in grief-stricken solitude. Though it is one of Shakespeare's most poignant and beautiful poems, its critical history is almost as gloomy as the story it tells – neglected for centuries, only recently has it come to enjoy anything like the attention it deserves.

DATE > On the basis of parallels with *All's Well* and *Measure for Measure*, some commentators plump for a date of c. 1600, while stylometric tests (see p.678) suggest that the *Complaint* was completed up to a decade later. Others have it both ways, arguing that the poem was begun early, but revised prior to publication. Based upon similar tests, some have claimed that it was written by someone else entirely.

SOURCES > Though no sources as such exist, the poetic form of a "complaint" was well used – enough to seem somewhat old-fashioned by 1609. In the 1590s, poets Samuel Daniel, Thomas Lodge and Richard Barnfield all wrote sonnet sequences capped by "complaints".

TEXTS > First printed as part of the 1609 quarto *Shakespeare's Sonnets*, the *Complaint* was excluded from the 1623 Folio, which printed only play-texts.

Interpreting the poem

Commentators have given the impression of being puzzled – even embarrassed – by the 329-line poem *A Lover's Complaint*, which is written in a markedly different style from much of Shakespeare's other work. Many have doubted whether he had a hand in it at all – or if he did, why the poem reads quite like it does. Criticisms of its "pedantry", "artificiality" and "ill-digested" scholarship (in the words of early twentieth-century scholar J.W. Mackail) have been legion, and arguments about authorship continue. Some scholars have used computer-based analysis to suggest that Shakespeare never went near the poem, and it is by an otherwise obscure writer named John Davies. Others defend it as indissolubly Shakespearian, a natural companion to the anguished lyricism of the Sonnets. According to the chilly assessment offered by the critic Hallett Smith, writing in the popular one-volume *Riverside Shakespeare*, "if it is by Shakespeare, it neither detracts from his achievement nor adds anything to it."

While out in the countryside, the poet-narrator describes hearing the voice of a crying woman echoing from the hillside. Tracing the sound, he comes across a once beautiful "maid" seated by the edge of a river. Highly distraught and with her hair dishevelled, she is reading and tearing up letters, and throwing love tokens into the water. The poet then observes the approach of a "reverend man" who sits down near the woman and asks her the cause of her unhappiness.

She relates that she has been ruined after falling for a beautiful and brilliant youth, so handsome that both men and women find him utterly irresistible. At first she held out, but gradually her resistance was broken down by the power of his eloquence.

Despite his callous behaviour towards previous lovers and an appalling reputation, the young man flatters her that she is the only woman he really cares for – arguing that, though he has seduced others, they meant nothing to him. He even shows her the tokens they sent, boasting that a nun was once so desperate for his love that she promised to renounce her vows. Moved by his tearful entreaties, the maid confesses that, despite herself, she slept with him. She goes on to suggest that no one, least of all someone as inexperienced as her, could resist the sheer subtlety of his advances. And though she regrets it, she wonders whether she would be able to refuse him were he ever to try again.

We may never know for sure who wrote *A Lover's Complaint* – and perhaps it doesn't entirely matter. What is beyond doubt is that the poem itself does not make things easy for its readers. While the Sonnets are uniquely intense and demand a great deal, they allow glimpses of shared intimacy – of love, anger, paranoia, fear, delusion, ecstasy. By comparison, the *Complaint* is oblique, dense, even deliberately perplexing. "From off a hill," it begins,

> whose concave womb re-worded
> A plaintful story from a sist'ring vale,
> My spirits t'attend this double voice accorded,
> And down I laid to list the sad-tuned tale;
> Ere long espied a fickle maid full pale,
> Tearing of papers, breaking rings a-twain,
> Storming her world with sorrow's wind and rain.

[1–7]

This enigmatic opening prepares the reader for what is to follow. While out walking in the countryside, the poet hears a "double voice" resounding off a hill – "double" because it is an echo of the desperate cries of a young woman standing by a river, the "fickle maid", whose weeping catches the poet's ear and tempts him to sit down and eavesdrop on what she has to say. Her story turns out to be as distressing as her appearance: joined on the riverbank by another figure, a "reverend man" who acts as her confessor, the maid tearfully relates how a beautiful but treacherous youth used all his persuasiveness to woo her – and how, despite knowing of his reputation, she surrendered her virginity. Thus seduced, she was cruelly abandoned.

Despite the simplicity of the tale – it doesn't take long to describe the plot of *A Lover's Complaint* – this opening scene is weirdly theatrical: the "maid" seems to inhabit not a real-life landscape but a terrain of the mind, where hills "re-word" her sorrow and her own tears and sighs are every bit as destructive as storms and rain. To that extent she resembles King Lear, but she is even closer to the mad Ophelia in *Hamlet*, whose "untucked" hair and distracted manner she seems to emulate.

The poem is as structurally complex and multi-vocal as any drama. It is ostensibly voiced by an eavesdropping poet – apparently unseen by both maid and reverend man – but after setting up the framing narrative (a form borrowed from medieval pastoral verse), he falls out of view, saying nothing more and simply relaying the maid's confession as if from the margins. The reverend man, too, remains all but silent, becoming just another pair of ears; a few of his words are reported by the poet, but no other response is recorded. And although it is the maid's lament that dominates *A Lover's Complaint* and brings it to a close, much of her speech quotes the young man who has deserted her. The poem is an echo-chamber of different voices, all of them nameless and bewilderingly blurred together.

But critics who condemn the *Complaint* on the grounds that it is too unfathomable or esoteric to be worth bothering with are blind to the poem's troubling brilliance. Arguably, the old-fashioned language and archaic style of *A Lover's Complaint* are designed to make it look older than it is – a 45-year-old author's tribute to the kind of poetry he was reading in his twenties, or even (if he came across similar kinds of poems at school) much earlier. And the *Complaint* also looks back in the sense that it is Shakespeare's final narrative poem, published long after the pair that made his name as a poet, *Venus and Adonis* and *The Rape of Lucrece*. Though up to fifteen years and nearly twenty plays separate the *Complaint* from these early works, the poem returns to similar themes – and one theme in particular, that of frustrated desire. In *Venus and Adonis* Shakespeare plays the subject mainly for laughs: the poem tells the tale of Venus, the eternally desirable love goddess, who nevertheless fails to bed the beautiful mortal Adonis – despite her enthusiastic attempts at wooing (at one stage she simply grabs him and pulls him on top of her), he remains indifferent. In *Lucrece*, however, the theme becomes grimly tragic: when the eponymous Roman heroine resists the advances of one of her husband's military colleagues, he viciously rapes her, leaving her to commit suicide in despair at the loss of her honour and the shame to her family.

Gilded in his smiling

In *A Lover's Complaint*, it is as if Shakespeare attempted what seems like the impossible – to unite the contrasting experiences of his two early heroines. The "maid" who is his protagonist in this poem has, like Lucrece, been violated and bitterly regrets it; but, like Venus, she keenly wanted to be, seduced by the "youthful suit" of a divinely handsome young man. "His browny locks did hang in crookèd curls," she says,

> 'And every light occasion of the wind
> Upon his lips their silken parcels hurls.

What's sweet to do, to do will aptly find.
Each eye that saw him did enchant the mind,
For on his visage was in little drawn
What largeness thinks in paradise was sawn.'

[85–91]

This youthful, even androgynous, figure is a close relative of the boyish/girlish Adonis, but where Adonis was insistent that he was far too young to be tempted by Venus, *A Lover's Complaint* reverses those polarities: its nameless youth is only too eager to take advantage of the maid, and does everything he can to persuade her to sleep with him.

After spending several tantalizing stanzas describing his beauty, the maid reveals that she was far from the only person susceptible to his charms: "maidens' eyes stuck over all his face", she claims (81); and this paragon of loveliness was so perfect that "sexes both" fell under his spell (128). A major component in that shimmering attraction appears to have been the young man's eloquence, which reputedly wins over everyone who encounters him. Sensually linking his sexual appeal with his oratorical prowess, she declares that

'On the tip of his subduing tongue
All kinds of arguments and question deep,
All replication prompt, and reason strong,
For his advantage did wake and sleep.
To make the weeper laugh, the laugher weep,
He had the dialect and different skill,
Catching all passions in his craft of will …'

[120–6]

Someone who has mastered all these different "dialects" rather resembles the figures mentioned in one of Shakespeare's most intriguing but riddling sonnets, number 94, which describes a kind of ideal people "who have power to hurt and will do none … who moving others are themselves as stone" (94, 1–3). Such as these, the sonnet claims, "rightly do inherit heaven's graces" (5), but the youth of *A Lover's Complaint* makes that assertion sound jaggedly ironic: far from embodying Christian virtue, he is callously deceitful and shamelessly immoral. Worse, the maid knew all this even before she relented. "For further could I say this man's untrue," she goes on,

'And knew the patterns of his foul beguiling;
Heard where his plants in others' orchards grew,
Saw how deceits were gilded in his smiling,
Knew vows were brokers to defiling,
Thought characters and words merely but art,
And bastards of his foul adulterate heart.'

[169–75]

Lovers make moan

While our understanding of "**complaint**" is nowadays fairly impoverished – it carries connotations of criticizing, grumbling, moaning – for Shakespeare's first readers the word would have been richly resonant, and possessed of serious literary credentials. Writing in the late fourteenth century, Chaucer was one of the first English figures to use "complaint" to describe a kind of poetry that voiced mourning and lament: his *The Book of the Duchesse*, probably written at the prompting of John of Gaunt, Duke of Lancaster, to commemorate his wife's death in 1368, uses complaint as a touching way of dealing with the horrors of bereavement. Employing a familiar device in medieval poetry, Chaucer's poet describes a strange dream encounter in which he meets a knight clad "al in blake", "ful pitous pale and nothyng red", mourning the loss of his lady. "I stalked even unto hys bak", the poet says,

> And ther I stood as stille as ought,
> That, soth to saye, he saw me nought;
> For-why he heng hys had adoune
> And with a dedly sorwful soun
> He made of rym ten vers or twelve
> Of a compleynte to hymselve—
> The moste pitee, the moste rowthe
>   [sorrowful],
> That ever I herde; for, by my trowthe,
> Hit was gret wonder that Nature
> Myght suffre any creature
> To have such sorwe and be not ded.
>   [458–69]

The poet goes on to relate the knight's desperate "compleynte" in full, before awakening in his bed and discovering that the whole thing was a dream, but nevertheless promising to write it down as a poem – the poem being, of course, *The Book of the Duchesse* itself. Though this complainant is male, his resemblances to the pale and tearful "maid" in *A Lover's Complaint* are obvious enough, and this poet, like Shakespeare's, is (at least initially) invisible to the speaker.

For in Shakespeare's period, six or seven generations later, "complaints", more commonly listing the grievances of female speakers disappointed in love, had begun to shoot up in anthologies of poetry such as Richard Tottel's *Songs and Sonnets* (1557), George Gascoigne's *Hundredth Sundry Flowers* (1573) and John Flasket's collection *England's Helicon* (1600). Despite the sixteenth-century popularity of the genre, however, some critics have traced the roots of female-voiced complaint back even earlier, to Ovid (see p.309), whose *Heroides* is a collection of passionate imaginary letters written by the most famous women of classical mythology (Dido, Hero, Helen of Troy, Medea), many of which rebuke their lovers for abandoning them. Edmund Spenser, the most famous writer of the generation preceding Shakespeare's, certainly knew Ovid, and also translated a series of complaints by the French poet Du Bellay that lament the impermanence of civilization and the grinding erosions of time. Spenser's *Amoretti* (1595), a collection of love sonnets, closely influenced Shakespeare's own, as did several other sonnet sequences – two of which, Samuel Daniel's *Delia* (1592) and Thomas Lodge's *Phillis* (1593), were published with "complaints" which relate the sorrows of abandoned women closely resembling the "maid" in Shakespeare's poem.

The young man is entirely able to separate himself from the "true" meaning of "characters and words", as if they, too, were the illegitimate children that he has so callously sired and abandoned. This chilling coldness is most graphically illustrated by one of his seductive ploys, which is nothing less than to boast and exhibit how many "tributes" he has received from previous lovers. Among the "pallid pearls and rubies red as blood" (198), the locks of hair "with twisted mettle amorously impleached" (205), the

> *The young maiden's unrepentant, unfinished testimony reveals Shakespeare's interest in both the elusiveness of confession and the narrative instabilities involved in recording it.*
>
> Katherine Craik, "Shakespeare's *A Lover's Complaint* and Early Modern Criminal Confession" (2002)

"deep-brained sonnets" (209) that have been sent by lovelorn admirers, one love token even came from a "nun, / A sister sanctified of holiest note", lured into renouncing her religious vows and joining the young man's cult (233). It is only too clear that this devilish tempter exemplifies a particular kind of evil, one that does indeed, as Sonnet 94 has it, possess the "power to hurt". He would, Shakespeare insinuates, make a dangerously good actor – or indeed a poet.

For although the young man of the *Complaint* resembles the "lovely boy" of the first sequence of Sonnets (who has likewise apparently been unfaithful), he also calls to mind the alluring but duplicitous Bertram in *All's Well That Ends Well*, who refuses to consummate his marriage so that he can sow his wild oats elsewhere. In fact, though commentators have so often been reluctant to allow it into the canon, *A Lover's Complaint* seems compellingly Shakespearian in its concern with the sweet temptations and bitter realities of sexual passion, the kind of concerns that lie close to the surface of the poet's middle period (though published in 1609, the *Complaint* is sometimes argued to have been written earlier in the decade). Another play morbidly interested in these themes, *Measure for Measure*, also betrays intriguing similarities: it, too, contains a nun, Isabella, repeatedly pressured to leave her novitiate; it, too, features a mysterious "reverend man" well acquainted with the "ruffle ... Of court, of city" (56–9), the Duke of Vienna, who dons the disguise of a friar apparently in order to spy out his city's corruptions, but ends up fatefully implicated. Most strikingly, that play also offers a woman bitterly betrayed in love – Mariana, betrothed to the Duke's deputy but abandoned by him when she lost her fortune. He "left her in her tears," the Duke claims, "and dried not one of them with his comfort" (3.1.227).

But where Mariana wins back the man she loves (her unstinting devotion is one of the play's many puzzles), no such consolation is offered to the nameless maid of the *Complaint*. Her predicament is precisely that she is no longer a "maid" in the sense of "virgin", and although she spends more time describing the young man's beauty than listing her sorrows – it is perhaps impossible to separate them – it seems clear that the experience has left a physical as well as emotional mark. Her admission that she gave up her virginity is not only poetically gorgeous; it implies that she has, like those "other" lovers, become pregnant as a consequence:

> 'There my white stole of chastity I daffed,
> Shook off my sober guards and civil fears;
> Appear to him as he to me appears,
> All melting, though our drops this diff'rence bore:
> His poisoned me, and mine did him restore.'

[297–301]

This is the obverse to the urging that fills the early Sonnets, which is that the young man they address should seize the day and have children, thus leaving behind an image of his beauty. Responding to that suggestion, the *Complaint* points out that, from the perspective of a "poisoned" maid ruined in order to "restore" her vampiric lover, doing so can be cruelly destructive. It is clear that the maid, movingly described earlier as "the carcass of a beauty spent and done" (11), has sacrificed her own youth and beauty in order to preserve the young man's. Love can imprison as much as emancipate.

That is perhaps the *Complaint*'s final and most disturbing paradox, and the reason why its difficulties as a text are closely bound up with its strange brilliance. The poem's religious confessor does not absolve or counsel the maid, still less the long-departed youth; despite being a complaint, the poem's female complainant can find no way out of a brittle obsession with her former lover. In her closing words the maid tries to claim that she is desperate to be rid of him, but what at first seems like it will be a curse against his memory becomes something far more compromised. "O that infected moisture of his eye," she sighs,

'O that false fire which in his cheek so glowed,
O that forced thunder from his heart did fly,
O that sad breath his spongy lungs bestowed,
O all that borrowed motion seeming owed
Would yet again betray the fore-betrayed,
And new pervert a reconcilèd maid.'

[323–9]

Instead of condemning the youth's attractiveness, inseparable from his falsity, the maid persuades herself that, given the opportunity, she would fall for him all over again. There will be no cure; the poem ends where it began.

EDITIONS

Oxford Shakespeare
Colin Burrow (ed.); 2002 ❯ Oxford UP

The Oxford *Complete Sonnets and Poems* contains the entirety of Shakespeare's poetic work, and in the case of the little-studied *A Lover's Complaint*, this broad context is especially valuable. Burrow's seven-page essay on the *Complaint* seems slender in a volume this thick – a wrist-snapping 750 pages – but it's lucid and sympathetic nonetheless, drawing attention to the *Complaint*'s links with the other narrative works and emphasizing its echoes of Spenser's earlier Elizabethan work.

SOME CRITICISM

Motives of Woe
John Kerrigan (ed.); 1991 ❯ Oxford UP

Bookstore shelves are hardly groaning with criticism on the *Complaint*, and this title will almost certainly be hard to come by (not least because, frustratingly, it has never made paperback). That said, this really is worth the effort, and not just for the light it casts on Shakespeare. Though the book began life as an essay on the *Complaint*, it quickly expanded into an historical anthology of poems in the same mode. Kerrigan's selection is excellent, ranging from haunting medieval lyrics such as "Als i me rode" (c. 1300) to gems such as Mary Sidney's wonderful sixteenth-century rendering of Psalm 137. In this setting, the *Complaint* begins to look less like a baffling oddity and more like the masterful expression of the genre that it is.

The Rape of Lucrece

Almost certainly the "graver labour" promised to his patron in the dedication to *Venus and Adonis*, Shakespeare's *The Rape of Lucrece* is a polished and ambitious follow-up, in every sense the more serious work of the two. Published just a year after that earlier narrative poem, *Lucrece* retells the anguished story of the Roman wife Lucretia, who is brutally raped by Sextus Tarquinius, son of her king, and who commits suicide soon afterwards, blaming herself for the attack. From the bare bones of this tale – which Shakespeare could have read in Latin versions by Ovid and the Roman historian Livy, as well as by medieval English poets Chaucer and Gower – he creates a lengthy and brooding composition that does justice to the gravity of its theme. And while its dense and rhetorically sophisticated style can be difficult to adjust to, *Lucrece* is much more than a display piece: in its fraught depiction of the heroine's trauma and self-loathing, the poem offers uncomfortable insights into the effects of sexual violence that still ring true. Though written for print publiction rather than live performance, it is in many respects the most dramatic work of Shakespeare's early career.

DATE > Printed by summer 1594 (see below), *Lucrece* was most likely written soon beforehand, presumably after *Venus and Adonis*, published the previous year.

SOURCES > Ovid's *Fasti* ("Chronicles") is the main source for the story of Lucrece's plight, but Shakespeare also turned to Livy's account in the *Historia* (probably in a 1566 translation by William Painter) as well as Chaucer's version in *The Legend of Good Women* (c. 1384).

TEXTS > Like *Venus and Adonis*, *Lucrece* was immaculately printed by his fellow Warwickshireman Richard Field. The quarto text (Q1) was much reprinted subsequently and remains the basis for modern editions.

Interpreting the poem

Fresh from the success of *Venus and Adonis* and still unable to work in the London theatres – which remained closed by plague for nearly two years – Shakespeare decided during late 1593 or early 1594 to write another narrative poem, which made it into print around the same time his first was being republished. This was "The Ravishment of Lucrece", as it was registered to be printed, simply *Lucrece* on its first title-page. Though there is some debate over precisely what the poem should properly be called (its traditional name, *The Rape of Lucrece*, might have been withdrawn and replaced with the less explicit *Lucrece* after the text was printed), there is no doubt that Shakespeare had the project in mind for some time. In the dedication to the light-hearted *Venus and Adonis* he promised his patron, the Earl of Southampton, that he

SYNOPSIS

An abbreviated synopsis of Lucrece, perhaps by Shakespeare, is included in the "Argument" to the poem, following its dedication, but differs from the poem itself in a few details.

Sextus Tarquinius (Tarquin), son of the Roman king Tarquinius Superbus, is riding full-tilt to visit Lucretia (Lucrece), the virtuous wife of his friend Collatinus (Collatine). Tarquin does not have good intentions: having heard Lucrece's loveliness praised by Collatine, he is eager to experience her for himself in her husband's absence. Suspecting nothing, the beautiful and innocent Lucrece welcomes her royal guest before the two retire for the night.

Tormented by lust for Lucrece, however, Tarquin soon rises and debates in anguish what to do. Though acknowledging the terrible nature of the crime, he resolves to ravish her and steals to her bedroom. Once inside, he gazes upon Lucrece's sleeping body but she awakes and pleads with him not to go through with the attack. Deaf to her appeals,

he gags and rapes her before escaping shamefully into the night.

Lucrece is devastated, at first hoping that morning will never come, then embarking on a lengthy sequence of laments. In despair she finally decides that suicide is the only way to safeguard her reputation and that of her husband, but resolves to tell Collatine what has happened beforehand. Dispatching a brief letter urging him to rush home, she burns with shame in front of her maid and the messenger, then sadly contemplates a painting of the fall of Troy, identifying herself with the grieving figure of Hecuba. As soon as Collatine arrives, in the company of her father Lucretius and other lords, she explains everything but holds back the rapist's name until the men have sworn to avenge the deed. Having secured their promises, to their shock she suddenly stabs herself. As she bleeds to death, Collatine's colleague Junius Brutus appeals to Collatine and the others to remember their vow. Lucrece's body is carried through Rome and – by popular consent – Tarquin and his family are banished.

---

had every intention of turning himself to "some graver labour" as soon as he could, and *Lucrece* undeniably fits that bill. Indeed, readers not forewarned might have got a shock if they were expecting a replay of the witty energy of *Venus and Adonis*: the tone of this poem, as befits its subject matter, is altogether different.

Opening the volume as it was published, purchasers were confronted by a grand-sounding "Argument" introducing *Lucrece*'s narrative and explaining its historical context. After relating the backstory of the kings of Rome, it describes how the son of the current incumbent, Sextus Tarquinius (Tarquin in the poem), was "enflamed with Lucrece' beauty" despite her "incomparable chastity" and marriage to Collatinus (Collatine). Abandoning his colleagues at their camp at Ardea, Tarquin heads surreptitiously for Lucrece's dwelling at Collatium, where she innocently welcomes him and encourages him to stay. She little suspects what will happen next:

> The same night he treacherously stealeth into her chamber, violently ravished her, and early in the morning speedeth away. Lucrece, in this lamentable plight, hastily dispatcheth messengers—one to Rome for her father, another to the camp for Collatine. They came, the one accompanied with Junius Brutus, the other with Publius Valerius, and, finding Lucrece attired in mourning habit, demanded the cause of her

sorrow. She, first taking an oath of them for her revenge, revealed the actor and whole manner of his dealing, and withal suddenly stabbed herself. Which done, with one consent they all vowed to root out the whole hated family of the Tarquins, and, bearing the dead body to Rome, Brutus acquainted the people with the doer and manner of the vile deed, with a bitter invective against the tyranny of the King ...

[ARGUMENT, 19–30]

Despite the appallingly personal nature of his crime, Tarquin's punishment proves political: his family is ejected from Rome and the city becomes a republic. It remained so until the series of events covered by Shakespeare in *Julius Caesar*, during which Caesar is offered the throne but murdered by conspirators led by another Brutus before he can accept it. The end of *Antony and Cleopatra* coincides with yet another turning point in Roman history: the accession of Augustus (Octavius Caesar), the first of the emperors.

Some have speculated that the poem's interest in republicanism might have well flattered the politics of Shakespeare's patron, and in other ways too *Lucrece* hints that it is addressed to a very specific audience. The poem's dedication resembles that printed in *Venus and Adonis*, but it is markedly warmer in tone, implying that the poet did indeed get some kind of reward from the Earl of Southampton – perhaps even the reward of his friendship. "The love I dedicate to your lordship is without end," the dedication begins, and continues more fervently,

What I have done is yours; what I have to do is yours, being part in all I have, devoted yours.

[DEDICATION, 1–7]

The poet hints at a special intimacy with this glamorous and well-known aristocrat, and many readers have seized upon this as evidence that Shakespeare was emotionally close to the 20-year-old Southampton – perhaps close enough for him to be the "lovely boy" addressed in the Sonnets and the mysterious "Mr. W. H." mentioned in that text (Southampton's initials were "H.W.", though he was certainly not a mere "Mr"; see p.543). Whether the story has any truth or not, it is likely to remain a mystery.

In time of sorrow

And all this is to ignore the biggest issue raised by *Lucrece* – a harrowing and horrifying act of rape. One of the most striking things about the poem is its sheer scale: stretching over 1,855 lines, longer than *The Comedy of Errors* and written in the doleful, slow-moving rhyme-royal form (see p.677), the action moves with painful deliberation as it follows Tarquin from his own bed to Lucrece's chamber in the dead of night. Shakespeare makes it agonizingly clear that Tarquin knows exactly what he is about to do, even as he battles with himself about whether he should go through with it; an "inward debate" that lasts a remarkable twenty-three stanzas. Once outside her room, time halts again as he pauses once more:

> The locks between her chamber and his will,
> Each one by him enforced, retires his ward;
> But as they open they all rate his ill,
> Which drives the creeping thief to some regard.
> The threshold grates the door to have him heard,
> > Night-wand'ring weasels shriek to see him there.
> > They fright him, yet he still pursues his fear.

> [302–8]

The task of opening Lucrece's door takes another age, and forty lines later Tarquin will still not be inside her chamber. Shakespeare would recall this eternal moment much later in his career, when he makes Macbeth think of "Tarquin's ravishing strides" while he too is stealing through the night, this time to King Duncan's bedroom (2.1.55). Here it is the poem's slow-motion movement that is terrible to observe, as well as its depiction of a world where everything – the locks, the creaking door, the weasels outside, even a needle stuck in one of Lucrece's gloves – attempts to resist the rape, yet has no effect. Before long Tarquin will violate Lucrece just as unstoppably as he, the "creeping thief", has broken into her room.

Where *Venus and Adonis* makes light of Venus's inability to seduce the man-child Adonis – it is funny as well as touching that the goddess of love finds herself desiring someone beyond her reach – in *Lucrece* we know only too well that physical force will count against the heroine. Tarquin is not only capable of forcing himself on his victim but he will, as the poem repeatedly puts it, have his "will". Standing over her bed, "rolling his greedy eye-balls in his head" (368), Tarquin takes in the view of the slumbering woman lying in front of him:

> Her lily hand her rosy cheek lies under,
> Coz'ning the pillow of a lawful kiss,
> Who therefore angry seems to part in sunder,
> Swelling on either side to want his bliss;
> Between whose hills her head entombèd is,
> > Where like a virtuous monument she lies
> > To be admired of lewd unhallowed eyes.

> [386–92]

Tarquin's gaze imposes on Lucrece an eroticism over which she has no control – to his mind the very pillows want to "kiss" her – yet in which she is fatefully implicated. This description implicates readers, too: our "unhallowed eyes" are also witnesses, forced to gaze on Lucrece just as Tarquin does. It is a grotesque, suffocating kind of intimacy. Forcing us to act as mute audience to the terrible events of the poem, Shakespeare hints that we, too, will be tainted by what is about to occur.

The same disgrace

Yet Lucrece herself proves stronger and more vocal than either we or Tarquin might expect. Waking to find a stranger in her innermost chamber, Shakespeare's heroine does not dumbly accept her fate, as in other versions of the poem she does, but speaks up against her attacker with fierce eloquence. After she appeals to Tarquin's relationship with Collatine and urges him to be careful of his reputation, he cuts in with an angry exclamation that "my uncontrollèd tide / Turns not" (645–6). But Lucrece remains rhetorically in control, passionately turning his argument back on him:

> 'Thou art,' quoth she, 'a sea, a sovereign king,
> And lo, there falls into thy boundless flood
> Black lust, dishonour, shame, misgoverning,
> Who seek to stain the ocean of thy blood.'

[652–8]

Lucrece appeals consistently to the good in her aggressor, to the sense that his innate nobility is being "stained" by forces from outside. Her words clearly touch a nerve, but

The frontispiece to John Quarles's 1655 edition of *The Rape of Lucrece*, engraved by William Faithorne. Quarles's own bombastic poem, *The Banishment of Tarquin*, appeared alongside Shakespeare's work as a sequel.

Tarquin's response is not to back down: a moment later he stamps out the light, gags Lucrece and attacks her. Like Lavinia in *Titus Andronicus*, whose tongue is cut out after she is raped (Shakespeare may have written play and poem around the same time), Lucrece's words are taken violently away.

One of the most distressing things about Lucrece's rape – Shakespeare does not describe it directly, but allows readers to imagine the worst – is that it taints everything. We know (and are repeatedly told by the ever-present narrator) that Tarquin is evil and Lucrece blameless, but in the wake of the attack Lucrece herself begins to doubt that she is free from guilt. While Tarquin wishes for dawn to arrive so that he can forget about everything, Lucrece is desperate for it to remain dark so that she will not have to confront what she awkwardly terms "night's scapes" (747). Describing her "true eyes", she weeps to herself,

'They think not but that every eye can see
The same disgrace which they themselves behold,
And therefore would they still in darkness be,
To have their unseen sin remain untold.
For they their guilt with weeping will unfold,
    And grave, like water that doth eat in steel,
    Upon my cheeks what helpless shame I feel.'

[750–6]

Lucrece's words are painfully moving, but most troubling of all is perhaps her sense that her "eyes" – and by extension herself – have some culpability in her "disgrace". In a harrowing image, the heroine imagines her tears – marks of her innocence and terrible sorrow – visibly eating into her face, just as Tarquin has polluted her body.

Lucrece's response to her violation is as comprehensible as it is psychologically realistic (many rape victims relate that they feel blame, no matter how unfounded), but in Shakespeare's poem the heroine's sense of guilt sets her on a path to self-destruction. Unlike Tarquin, who has little problem adjusting to the thought of a crime that is both "shameful" and "hateful" yet utterly doable (239–40), Lucrece cannot accommodate a world in which, as Hamlet will later put it, "one may smile and smile and be a villain" (*Hamlet*, 1.5.109). Gazing later on a painting of the fall of Troy that decorates her bedchamber – itself ominous enough – she peers at the portrait of the treacherous Sinon (a Greek who persuaded the Trojans to take the wooden horse into their city) in disbelief, unable to comprehend that someone who looks so honest can have done something so evil:

'It cannot be,' quoth she, 'that so much guile'—
She would have said 'can lurk in such a look',
But Tarquin's shape came in her mind the while,
And from her tongue 'can lurk' from 'cannot' took.
'It cannot be' she in that sense forsook,
    And turned it thus: 'It cannot be, I find,
    But such a face should bear a wicked mind.'

[1534–40]

Lucrece, still in shock, struggles to adjust to a world in which appearances do not map onto realities – and with the violent appearance of Tarquin's "shape" in her mind, it is as if her rape risks being committed all over again.

That is not the only way in which Lucrece fails to counter the chaotic complexity of her situation. She appears to be certain that she must be at fault – not least of having

[Lucrece's] despair after the rape is despair for an irredeemably lost simplicity, a simplicity inconsistent with the experience of injustice, conflict, and duplicity.

Katharine Eisaman Maus, "Taking Tropes Seriously: Language and Violence in Shakespeare's *Rape of Lucrece*" (1986)

Rhyming it royal

In two of his narrative poems, *The Rape of Lucrece* and *A Lover's Complaint*, Shakespeare employs an unusual poetic form, **rhyme royal**. Analytically speaking, this form is made up of seven-line, decasyllabic stanzas in the rhyme-scheme *ababbcc* – that is to say, each stanza contains seven lines, and each line has ten syllables. The blueprint connecting each is visible in stanza 18 of *Lucrece*, for instance, where the poet describes Tarquin on his way to bed:

> For then is Tarquin brought unto his bed,
> Intending weariness with heavy sprite;
> For after supper long he questionèd
> With modest Lucrece, and wore out the
>   night.
> Now leaden slumber with life's strength
>   doth fight,
>   And everyone to rest himself betakes,
>   Save thieves, and cares, and troubled
>   minds that wakes.
>
>   [120–6]

Here the lines rhyme first in pairs across one another ("bed"/"questionèd"; "sprite"/"night"), then conclude in a couplet ("betake"/"wake"). Between these, the fifth line brings the two kinds of rhymes together, introducing with "fight" another rhyme for "night" and making it, too, into a couplet – in other words, forcing line four in two directions at once and thus binding the whole stanza tightly together.

The effect of rhyme royal can be unsettling: it sets up a steady rhyming pulse for four lines which then falters in line five, anxiously treading water; and, though it does go on, the final couplet acts as a kind of conclusion (as in the Sonnets) which feels reluctant to travel anywhere further. Then the whole process begins again in the next stanza. Rhyme royal is a halting, limping

way to tell a story – particularly given that, as some critics have suggested, it is a hobbled version of the elegant and courtly Italian *ottava rima* (literally "eighth rhyme"), an eight-line stanza form rhyming *abababcc*, which was deployed in Renaissance classics such as **Boccaccio**'s *Filostrato* (c. 1335) and **Ariosto**'s *Orlando Furioso* (1516).

Furthermore, by the time Shakespeare turned to it, rhyme royal was sounding distinctly creaky. **Geoffrey Chaucer** pioneered its use in English, and it became so closely associated with his *Troilus and Criseyde* (early 1380s) that the form was initially known as the "*Troilus* stanza". Poets influenced by Chaucer frequently employed it in the years to come, notably **Hoccleve**, **Dunbar** and **Henryson** (who himself based his rhyme-royal *Testament of Cresseid* on Chaucer's poem). Its regal name seems to have appeared early in the next century, and by the time the poet, dramatist and sometime soldier **George Gascoigne** referred to it in 1575, the "royal" appellation had come to describe the way in which it was suited to grave, solemn subject matter.

But by the end of that century, the form was beginning to sound old-fashioned. While its use in *The Rape of Lucrece* presumably bears witness to Shakespeare's desire to provide a serious form for what he termed his "graver labour" after the erotic fripperies of *Venus and Adonis* (1593), by the time of the *Complaint*'s publication fifteen years later its antique patina would have been highly visible. Further into the seventeenth century, rhyme royal's days as a serious poetic option were numbered. Shakespeare's contemporary and fellow Warwickshireman **Michael Drayton** initially composed his historical poem *Mortimeriados* in the form, but, when revising it prior to 1619, decided to go for *ottava rima* instead.

betrayed her husband with "violated troth" (1059), a phrase that sounds as if it should come from someone guilty of adultery rather than a victim of violent assault. "Deep drenchèd in a sea of care" (1100), she becomes her own worst enemy in this latter section of the poem, railing helplessly against the various forces she sees as having conspired against her – night, time, even the "opportunity" that has allowed Tarquin to attack. These laments and complaints occupy a significant stretch of the action after the rape scene, and commentators have argued that they are not poetically successful, too artificial and empty to have much impact. But that is Lucrece's sense, too, and if anything the wide range of her appeals succeeds in charting her utter desperation. "In vain I rail at opportunity," she insists, acutely conscious of the futility of it all,

> 'At time, at Tarquin, and uncheerful night.
> In vain I cavil with mine infamy,
> In vain I spurn at my confirmed despite.
> This helpless smoke of words doth me no right;
>   The remedy indeed to do me good
>   Is to let forth my foul defilèd blood.'

>   [1023–9]

Blood-letting was a common treatment in the Renaissance (used, sometimes disastrously, for all manner of illnesses), but here Lucrece means nothing less than suicide. Her decision to go through with the deed is unhappily ironic: to medieval commentators influenced by St Augustine's views on the matter, it was Lucretia's decision to take her own life that proved her guilt and thus condemned her. Lucrece's position, Shakespeare makes clear, is a terrible catch-22: if she stays alive, she brings shame to her husband and risks giving birth to an illegitimate child (childbirth was itself a significant hazard in the Roman period as it was, too, during Shakespeare's time); if she commits suicide, she stands accused of complicity in the rape, even of arrogance in paying such heed to her reputation. Yet Lucrece herself is tragically unaware of these complications, insisting to herself that

> 'To clear this spot by death, at least I give
> A badge of fame to slander's livery,
> A dying life to living infamy.'

>   [1053–5]

Like many things in the poem, this pulls two ways: Lucrece's death, too, will bring her "infamy". History weighs heavily not only on the heroine, but also on Tarquin – who worries before the rape that going through with it will cause him "dishonour" (198), and later threatens Lucrece that if she resists he will simply ravish her anyway and leave her body lying with "some worthless slave" (515), thus poisoning not only her reputation but that of her husband. Shakespeare does not let his readers forget that posterity is a harsh judge.

And it is Lucrece's loss of control over her identity that is perhaps the most tragic thing of all: in killing herself she also loses the ability to speak for herself. Although she talks until the last possible moment, once the heroine is dead it is the responsibility of the men that surround her (no women are allowed into *Lucrece*'s conclusion) to interpret what has happened and act accordingly. Their solution, a "revenge" that turns out to be solely political, utterly fails to take into account the emotional impact of what has just happened, an impact of which we as readers are only too aware. Their treatment of her corpse, like that of Julius Caesar in Shakespeare's play, seems like the final insult. "They did conclude to bear dead Lucrece thence," the narrator sadly tells us,

> To show her bleeding body thorough Rome,
> And so to publish Tarquin's foul offence …

[1849–52]

This, of course, is not the only thing that is being "published". Even in death, Lucrece's public humiliation is not over.

AUDIO

The Rape of Lucrece
E. Best, O. Le Sueur, D. Burke; David Timson (dir.)
UK, 2006 ➤ Naxos ◉ ☁

While David Timson's Naxos recording of the major narrative poems struggles to find the right key for *Venus and Adonis* (see p.555), his version of *Lucrece*, which stretches over two CDs, is more successful. Partly that is to do with the poem itself, which has a more complex interplay of characters and thus translates effectively to full-scale drama. Partly, too, it relates to Eve Best's searing performance as Lucrece, touchingly aware of the heroine's moral torments. And Oliver Le Sueur's Tarquin, less out-and-out baddie than callow opportunist, refuses to play to stereotype. Narrator David Burke – who shoulders a large portion of the script – seems slightly colourless, but does well in the poem's more intimate sections.

The Rape of Lucrece
C. O'Sullivan, F. Murray; Elizabeth Freestone (dir.)
UK, 2014 ➤ RSC ◉

"Just to warn you, there may be some singing," declares Irish vocalist Camille O'Sullivan in the introduction to this live recording – and what singing it is. Somewhere between recitation, recital and seance, this adaptation was originally offered on stage in Edinburgh, London and Stratford-upon-Avon, and sets Shakespeare's text to new music by Fergal Murray, who also plays piano. But central in every sense is O'Sullivan, one of the most mesmerizing performers on the cabaret scene, who embodies Lucrece in wild and blisteringly powerful vocals – screaming, sobbing and stamping as she tries to find a voice for this most tragic of heroines. Often the results of this contemporary reworking are intense; sometimes they're almost too harrowing to listen to.

EDITIONS

Oxford Shakespeare
Colin Burrow (ed.); 2002 ➤ Oxford UP

As elsewhere with Shakespeare's poetry, the top recommendation for *Lucrece* comes in the bulky form of Colin Burrow's single-volume edition of the *Complete Sonnets and Poems*. Burrow is particularly sensitive in his handling of this poem and the notes are extremely observant, particularly when dealing with what the printed realities of the poems offered to their early readers (an interest also dealt with at length in the introduction). He also provides plenty of insight into the different versions of the Lucretia tale that Shakespeare drew upon, and discusses the impact of Shakespeare's humanistic education on this early work.

SOME CRITICISM

Captive Victors
Heather Dubrow; 1987 ➤ Cornell UP [o/p]

The title of Dubrow's book is a quotation from *Lucrece* and, though she also deals with *Venus and Adonis* and the Sonnets, it is Shakespeare's tragic poem that dominates her imagination. Dubrow has a sharp eye for slippery, twisting language and she proves an expert guide to (and robust defender of) the apparent rhetorical excesses of *Lucrece*, arguing that its range of linguistic techniques is an index of its psychological insight rather than its greatest flaw. *Captive Victors* is also an impassioned and convincing response to those critics who have suggested Lucrece's own culpability in what she suffers, though some readers might wish that the further reaches of Dubrow's arguments were more grounded in the text.

The Sonnets

Wordsworth thought them the key to Shakespeare's heart; Keats remarked that they were "full of fine things said unintentionally". Ralph Waldo Emerson asked whether they did not speak of "the confusion of sentiments in the most susceptible, and, at the same time, the most intellectual of men?". More recently Shakespeare has been outed as a gay icon, the man who wrote over a hundred poems to a mysterious male lover. Despite the difficulties of trying to read the Sonnets as autobiographical testament, the temptation never entirely passes, so utterly believable do these rich, intense and passionate poems seem. They are the only works of Shakespeare in which the poet seems to speak in his own voice: to wonder about who is writing them, and to whom, and why, is part of the intimate encounter. Yet "SHAKE-SPEARES SONNETS. Neuer before Imprinted", as they were first published, guard their secrets well. As well as being a monumental poetic achievement – they may have taken two decades to reach their published form – the Sonnets are also some of Shakespeare's most difficult works to interpret, quite literally so given their concentrated and sometimes dizzyingly complex language. Yet they reward patient and careful attention, and, despite the best attempts of love-poetry anthologists, it seems impossible to exhaust their brilliance.

DATE > The volume entitled *Shakespeare's Sonnets* was published in 1609, though the individual poems that make it up might have been composed nearly twenty years earlier. Stylometric analysis suggests that composition fell into four main groups between 1591 and 1604.

SOURCES > Numerous sonnet sequences were published during the 1590s, of which Philip Sidney's *Astrophil and Stella* (first printed in 1591), Samuel Daniel's *Delia* (1592) and Edmund Spenser's *Amoretti* (1595) are only the most famous.

TEXTS > Only one early edition, the 1609 *Shakespeare's Sonnets* (Q1), exists – poems were not printed in the plays-only First Folio (1623) – and is on the whole a good text with few errors. Unpopular compared with Shakespeare's narrative poems, it was not reprinted until a heavily revised version of 1640.

Interpreting the poems

Along with love poetry in general, sonnets do not get a great press in Shakespeare's plays. In *Love's Labour's Lost* the Lords try frantically to woo their respective Ladies with a succession of cringeworthy verses; in *Much Ado* the quick-witted Benedick is stumped by his inability to write anything but "halting sonnets" to his new-found mistress Beatrice. Even the endlessly eloquent Hamlet, when he attempts to distil his feelings for Ophelia into verse, churns out what can best be described as doggerel. Not

SYNOPSIS

There is no straightforward narrative connecting Shakespeare's 154 Sonnets, leading some scholars to conjecture that they were printed without the author's consent and not put into any kind of order. The last statement is not quite accurate, and in fact there are two major groupings: Sonnets 1–126 appear to be addressed to a beautiful and anonymous young man; while Sonnets 127–152 mostly describe, or are addressed to, a similarly anonymous black-haired woman (153 and 154 are poems on Cupid, the god of love).

The sequence addressed to the young man is the more carefully ordered, and contains several mini-sequences, albeit some little more than a collection of related ideas. Sonnets 1–17 urge the young man to find a partner and have children; 41 and 42 hint that the poet's mistress has seduced him during the poet's absence; 78–86 describe a rival author who has apparently tempted the young man away from the poet; 87–90 worry that the young man has forgotten the poet altogether; 91–96 suggest that the poet and young man have been reconciled; 100–103 describe the poet's struggles with his "truant muse"; 117–120 apparently apologize for the poet's own inconstancy to his subject; 126 brings an end to the "lovely boy" sequence.

127–152 are more loosely organized, though many are addressed to a mistress described as black-haired (130), "tyrannous" (131) and unfaithful (133–134). Sonnets 135, 136 and 143 pun on "Will" (Shakespeare's first name), while other sonnets in this section of the book dwell on the pain and humiliation of love.

---

that Shakespeare is always so ironic. In *Romeo and Juliet* he achieves a heart-stopping effect by having the lovers address each other for the first time:

ROMEO
    If I profane with my unworthiest hand
        This holy shrine, the gentler sin is this:
    My lips, two blushing pilgrims, ready stand
        To smooth that rough touch with a tender kiss.
JULIET
    Good pilgrim, you do wrong your hand too much,
        Which mannerly devotion shows in this.
    For saints have hands that pilgrims' hands do touch,
        And palm to palm is holy palmers' kiss.
ROMEO
    Have not saints lips, and holy palmers, too?
JULIET
    Ay, pilgrim, lips that they must use in prayer.
ROMEO
    O then, dear saint, let lips do what hands do:
        They pray; grant thou, lest faith turn to despair.
JULIET
    Saints do not move, though grant for prayers' sake.
ROMEO
    Then move not while my prayer's effect I take.
     He kisses her

[*ROMEO AND JULIET*, 1.5.92–105]

Laid out on the page – and possible to detect in performance through its rhyme-scheme – Shakespeare's lovers speak, in interweaving union and with apparent artlessness, a form known as a Shakespearian sonnet (see p.538). The fourteen-line pentameter pattern is elegant: the first twelve lines rhyme across each other ("hand/stand", "this/kiss") before concluding in a two-line couplet in which the rhymes are identical ("sake/take"). Despite these taut formal constraints the effect here is betwitchingly fresh, because Juliet and Romeo produce the words as it were without realizing it. But the moment has darker ramifications: though the sonnet is intense, it is also intensely short. These lovers will not be together for long.

The only begetter

Delicately beautiful though it is, the solitary sonnet in *Romeo and Juliet* is dwarfed by *Shakespeare's Sonnets*, a volume containing not just 154 sonnets, nearly all in the same "Shakespearian" form – outrunning even Sidney's 108 in *Astrophil and Stella* – but the 329-line narrative poem *A Lover's Complaint* (see p.519). Yet some have doubted that the author even intended the volume so loudly published in his name ever to reach print. There is a long-standing theory that Shakespeare's Sonnets were stolen from the poet by an unscrupulous printer (as Sidney's had been) and published behind his back. The infamous title-page to *Sonnets*, which addresses the book "TO . THE . ONLIE. BEGETTER . OF . / THESE . INSVING . SONNETS.", a mysterious man called only "MR. W . H .", does little to solve the puzzle: instead of being signed by Shakespeare, the initials of the printer, Thomas Thorpe, close this carefully typeset dedication. Some scholars have assumed as a consequence that Thorpe liberated these poems from Shakespeare's grasp and smuggled them into the printing house.

Setting aside the equally long-running dispute over who exactly "W. H." really is (if anyone at all; see p.543), readers have discovered other hints that Shakespeare never intended these poems to reach the reading public – something apparently believed by their earliest critic, the Elizabethan author Francis Meres, who commented that the poet's "sugared Sonnets" circulated only "among his private friends". As if to confirm that claim, Sonnet 145 is one of the most intimately clandestine poems in the collection. It plays tenderly with the name of the poet's wife, married nearly thirty years earlier and usually supposed to be living in Stratford while her husband's career was down in London. "Those lips that love's own hand did make," it begins,

> Breathed forth the sound that said 'I hate'
> To me that languished for her sake
> But when she saw my woeful state,
> Straight in her heart did mercy come,
> Chiding that tongue that ever sweet
> Was used in giving gentle doom,
> And taught it thus anew to greet:
> 'I hate' she altered with an end

> That followed it as gentle day
> Doth follow night who, like a fiend,
> From heaven to hell is flown away.
>
> [145, 1–12]

Adding "hate" to "away", as the sonnet suggests, makes something passably close to Anne Shakespeare's maiden name, Hathaway; without that knowledge, the poem makes little sense. Its audience might, rather wonderfully, be a private audience of one.

Just as this poem appears to glance at a real-life love affair (it is sometimes argued to be Shakespeare's first sonnet), readers of the Sonnets have long attempted to find similar biographical keys to the rest of the poems, which constantly open the way to a complex series of private narratives but teasingly refuse to go any further. Sometimes those readers have been baffled, even disgusted by what they have found: one

KEY SOURCE > Petrarch and Renaissance sonneteers

One of the most portable of poetic forms, the **sonnet** has been in Europe from the beginning of the Renaissance. Its name and origins are thought to be Italian: *sonetto* means "a small sound or song", and poems we think of as sonnets first started to appear in Italy as long ago as the thirteenth century. Though a variant on the form was used by Dante, the name of **Francesco Petrarca** (1304–74), Petrarch in English, always surfaces in connection with the sonnet. Petrarch formalized its delicate and intricate architecture (its metre and pattern of rhyme) and, building on medieval traditions of lyric, made the poem an expression of beautifully crafted but eternally unrequited love. Petrarch's sonnets are addressed to a mysterious figure named "Laura", who the poet claimed was a lady he met while living in Avignon but who suddenly died, perhaps killed by plague, leaving him grief-stricken and desperate for creative solace. It is not known whether Laura ever existed, but for the poems inspired by her it doesn't entirely matter. Petrarch uses the certainty of his mistress's absence – even the sense that she might be entirely imaginary – to construct an image of womanhood that rarely touches reality. His Laura is impossibly beautiful, unequalled in virtuousness, always just out of reach. She is an idea.

Writers influenced by Petrarch carried the form through the high Renaissance and into other countries: in France and Spain poets readily joined the cult, and by the first decades of the sixteenth century their counterparts in England had done so too. Two of the first home-grown exponents of the sonnet, **Sir Thomas Wyatt** (?1503–42) and **Henry Howard, Earl of Surrey** (?1517–47), travelled on the continent under Henry VIII, and were soon translating fashionable work by Petrarch and his successors. By the 1590s, when Shakespeare was making his name as a dramatist, poets such as **Sir Philip Sidney**, **Samuel Daniel** and **Edmund Spenser** had all seen sonnets published under their names (in Sidney's case a printer was responsible for publication, the poet himself being dead) and the concept of a "sonnet sequence" – a linked collection of sonnets, sometimes numbering fifty or more – had become entrenched. The sophisticated titles of these respective collections, *Astrophil and Stella* (first printed 1592), *Delia* (1592) and *Amoretti* (1595), reveal that, though the poems themselves are in English, being seen as continental was very much the thing. But the vogue for Elizabethan sonnets, brilliantly intense though it was, soon passed: no major sequences were published after 1600, and when the Jacobean poet **John Donne** revisited the form in his *Holy Sonnets*, what emerged – erotic verse linked with fervent Christianity – was shockingly iconoclastic.

nameless seventeenth-century commentator was sufficiently moved to scrawl "what a heap of wretched Infidel stuff" in his copy of the book, while the eighteenth-century editor George Steevens refused to include them in his 1793 edition of Shakespeare's works on the basis that "the strongest act of Parliament that could be framed, would fail to compel readers into their service".

One basis for such heated vituperation may be the boldest and most intriguing fact about the Sonnets: most of them appear to be written to a man. More than that, they are often surprisingly frank about the appeals – and difficulties – of what we now call homosexuality (the word itself, a Victorian invention, was not known by Shakespeare or his contemporaries, though sodomy was technically illegal). Sonnet 20, for instance, toys with some gender-bending questions:

> A woman's face with nature's own hand painted
> Hast thou, the master-mistress of my passion;
> A woman's gentle heart, but not acquainted
> With shifting change as is false women's fashion …

[20, 1–4]

The attractions of women, the poet continues, pale beside those of the young man to whom this sonnet is addressed, along with perhaps a hundred others. Lest we should miss the point, he declares, "But since she pricked thee out for women's pleasure, / Mine be thy love and thy love's use their treasure" (13–14), punning rather heavily on the still-current slang for penis. The poem perhaps calls to mind the intimate male friendships described in plays including *The Two Gentlemen of Verona* (from one end of Shakespeare's career) and *The Two Noble Kinsmen* (from the other): Palamon and Arcite, the paired "kinsmen" of the last play, declare that they may as well be "one another's wife", so close are they to each other (2.2.80). But this sonnet, mischievously, goes far further – flirtatiously insinuating that the poet and his addressee have shared, or desire to share, a good deal more than platonic companionship.

Not that all the Sonnets speak to a man. After Sonnet 126, which addresses "thou my lovely boy" for what appears to be the last time (the poem lacks two lines, as if the sonnet itself had exhausted its formal possibilities), there begins a second internal sequence apparently written to, and sometimes about, a female subject. Tradition calls this woman Shakespeare's "Dark Lady", but in the poems themselves the narrator is a good deal less refined. "Th'expense of spirit in a waste of shame / Is lust in action," Sonnet 129 begins, ferociously, and does not stop for another eleven lines,

> and till action, lust
> Is perjured, murd'rous, bloody, full of blame,
> Savage, extreme, rude, cruel, not to trust,
> Enjoyed no sooner but despisèd straight,
> Past reason hunted, and so sooner had
> Past reason hated as a swallowed bait
> On purpose laid to make the taker mad;
> Mad in pursuit and in possession so,

Had, having, and in quest to have, extreme;
A bliss in proof and proved, a very woe;
Before, a joy proposed; behind, a dream.

[129, 1–12]

"All this the world well knows, yet none knows well / To shun the heaven that leads men to this hell," the narrator finishes in a poisonous concluding couplet. Though many of the Sonnets are hard, this poem is more difficult to untangle than most – yet its denunciation of "lust" takes on a clearer, and nastier, resonance if you listen to some of its puns: "spirit" can mean semen; "hell" was Elizabethan slang for vagina. What Sonnet 129 stops just short of declaring is that male "lust" for sex, a desire "enjoyed no sooner but despisèd straight", should be blamed solely on women. Though the Sonnets are sometimes thought of as the greatest love poems of all time, their dark and sometimes astringent tone seems to belie, or complicate, that reputation – and suggest they are impossible to pigeonhole.

Outright misogyny is rarely far away in the Sonnets, as indeed the dynamic of the Petrarchan tradition – all cruel mistresses and wounded males – somewhat encourages. In the poems addressed by Shakespeare's narrator to the young man, women are repeatedly cast as inferior, limited, changeable; in those to the female mistress, she is accused of adultery, tyranny, deceit, perhaps even of having contracted venereal disease. Her very appearance comes in for harsh criticism: "My mistress' eyes are nothing like the sun", declares Sonnet 130, famously drawing attention to her "dun"-coloured chest and wiry black hair. And yet this poem, like others in the final sequence of the Sonnets, also has more interesting and engaging things to offer. Part of Sonnet 130's argument is that verse extolling the beauty of matchless mistresses rarely has much time for imperfect human realities. "I love to hear her speak," the poet says,

TO . THE . ONLIE . BEGETTER . OF .
THESE . INSVING . SONNETS .
Mr. W. H. ALL . HAPPINESSE .
AND . THAT . ETERNITIE .
PROMISED .

BY .

OVR . EVER-LIVING . POET .

WISHETH .

THE . WELL-WISHING .
ADVENTVRER . IN .
SETTING .
FORTH .

T. T.

Behind the bald, formulaic title page of Shakespeare's Sonnets "never before Imprinted" lie any number of literary enigmas.

> yet well I know
> That music hath a far more pleasing sound.
> I grant I never saw a goddess go:
> My mistress when she walks treads on the ground.
>   And yet, by heaven, I think my love as rare
>   As any she belied with false compare.

[130, 9–14]

The poet's mistress is not just "any she": her imperfections, what Sonnet 141 more brutally calls her "thousand errors" (141, 2), make her who she is, just as the narrator's own flaws (catalogued in Sonnet 138) do the same for him. Read in this company, Sonnet 116's famous declaration that "love is not love / Which alters when it alteration finds," sounds more tentative than seems to be the case first time around. "O no, it is an ever fixèd mark / That looks on tempests and is never shaken," the narrator cries,

> It is the star to every wand'ring barque,
> Whose worth's unknown although his height be taken.
> Love's not time's fool, though rosy lips and cheeks
> Within his bending sickle's compass come;
> Love alters not with his brief hours and weeks,
> But bears it out even to the edge of doom.

[116, 2–12]

The poem is often interpreted as celebrating the eternal constancy of love, and it may indeed be so. Set alongside others in the sequence, though, the message is more disconcerting, and perhaps more insightful. The narrator speaks of noble ideals, but the poet of the sonnets to the dark-eyed mistress knows – as perhaps we all do – that ideals can go only so far. The Sonnets continually remind us that love is not fixed, or beyond time: it is something more mutable and human, and that is also what makes it so potent.

So long lives this

Attempting to read *Shakespeare's Sonnets* as a narrative about Shakespeare's own life is an engaging but ultimately frustrating occupation, and, whether or not the poet was gay or straight in any modern sense of those words, we should be wary of drawing any stable conclusions. For one thing, male sexuality in the Renaissance was an ambiguous and sometimes flexible reality, not easy to map onto modern-day values and beliefs. For another, these poems, no matter the strength of their emotional feeling, continually remind us of their intense, often intricate, intellect. They are reluctant to take anything at face value – sometimes literally. "My glass shall not persuade me I am old," begins Sonnet 22,

> So long as youth and thou are of one date,
> But when in thee time's furrows I behold,

Then look I death my days should expiate.
For all that beauty that doth cover thee
Is but the seemly raiment of my heart,
Which in thy breast doth live, as thine in me;
How can I then be elder than thou art?

[22, 1–8]

The poem (and the poet) play a complex philosophical and linguistic game with their young and beautiful subject, suggesting that because the poet's "heart" beats within the youth's breast, and vice versa, they are in fact the same age. Despite outward appearances – the older poet ruefully declares elsewhere that he is "beated and chapped with tanned antiquity" (62, 10) – love draws them together and makes them live as one.

Sonnet 22 develops into new territory the argument put forward in this first group of sonnets, that the nameless young man they address should get on and procreate lest his beauty be lost to the world – something also urged by the heroine of *Venus and Adonis*, who is eager to taste the joys of the young Adonis for herself. The Sonnets are rarely that explicit, though as the sequence builds the poet often returns to the promise that it is his words alone that can make the young man live for eternity. While held together by their address to the youth, Sonnets 1–126 range through an amazing variety of topics – from nobility of birth to the role of art, from the nature of inspiration to simple envy – and call upon a restless array of poetic locations. Sonnet 30 imagines love operating in a kind of "sessions", or law court; Sonnet 73 places the poet in a late autumnal world where "yellow leaves, or none, or few, do hang" (73, 2); Sonnet 23 sets its speaker in a position that must have been familiar to the poem's author, that of "an unperfect actor on the stage / Who with his fear is put besides his part" (23, 1–2). In a different world entirely, Sonnet 107 begins by gesturing towards recent historical events (many think it refers to the death of Elizabeth I in 1603 and the arrival of her successor James) but concludes with the resonant declaration that, because of this poem, the youth will outlast mere monarchs. Leaving "death" to "insult o'er dull and speechless tribes", the poet proclaims,

thou in this shalt find thy monument
When tyrants' crests and tombs of brass are spent.

[107, 13–14]

The idea that poetry conferred eternity on its subjects was not new, but Shakespeare makes the thought seem fresh-minted, a gift of transcendent certainty in a world all too eager to forget. Much the same argument is put forward by the most famous sonnet of all, number 18, which begins by asking "Shall I compare thee to a summer's day?" and concludes that it is only the poet's "eternal lines" that can make the young man known to posterity. "So long as men can breathe or eyes can see," the narrator exults,

So long lives this, and this gives life to thee.

[18, 13–14]

Mr Who He?

Even before the poems start, the Sonnets play with its readers. The volume is dedicated to "THE . ONLIE . BEGETTER . OF . THESE . INSVING . SONNETS", a man called "MR. W . H .". To get inside the poems, this note implies, you have to figure out who is behind those two initials; that revelation, it hints, awaits those in the know.

The temptation to crack the code seems to have passed Shakespeare's early readers by – but interest awoke in the late eighteenth century. Edmund Malone's 1780 edition of the poems arrived at just the right time for the first Romantic critics to discover the Sonnets and wonder at what they revealed of Shakespeare's life and passions. Speculation over the identity of "W. H." – taken to be the "lovely boy" addressed in Sonnets 1–126 – followed close behind. Two aristocratic candidates, both connected to Shakespeare's published work, jostled for pre-eminence. The first, proposed in 1817, was **Henry Wriothesley**, Earl of Southampton, the man to whom *Venus and Adonis* and *Lucrece* were addressed. The second was another Earl, this time of Pembroke: **William Herbert**, co-dedicatee of the First Folio and nephew of Sir Philip Sidney, who was proposed in 1823.

For much of the nineteenth century, arguments over the relative merits of these pair bounced back and forth. Both are plausible, though Pembroke perhaps has the edge: in addition to his initials being the right way round, his life story has been taken to support the genesis of the Sonnets. After refusing several times to marry women selected for him, the 20-year-old Pembroke succeeded in getting Mary Fitton, a maid of honour to Queen Elizabeth, pregnant – but refused to wed her, too, and was briefly imprisoned. The theory goes that Shakespeare was called in by Pembroke's exasperated parents and commanded to write a set of poems telling him to get on and marry before it was too late. Tempting as this connection seems, there is no other evidence of it and Pembroke, and his status-conscious peers, would surely have taken it as a gross insult to be addressed as a mere "Mr".

The search for alternative "W. H."s raged on. Some suggested **William Harvey**, Southampton's stepfather; others **William Hathaway**, Shakespeare's brother-in-law; others even diagnosed a case of poetic narcissism, either on the basis of a misprint ("W. H." for "W. Sh.") or a cunning insertion ("W[illiam] H[imself]"). The most creative theory was dreamt up by **Oscar Wilde**, whose *The Portrait of Mr W.H.* (1889) spins the elegant story of a man claiming to own a portrait of the youth adored by Shakespeare, a boy actor called **Willie Hughes** for whom the playwright's greatest female roles were written. The echoes with Wilde's doomed love for Lord Alfred Douglas were acknowledged by Wilde and played a fateful part in his downfall: a letter to Douglas, described by Wilde as "like a little sonnet of Shakespeare", was produced at his trial in 1895 and helped to secure his conviction on counts of gross indecency.

Speculation as to the identity of Shakespeare's so-called "**Dark Lady**" has, if anything, been even more fevered – probably because many nineteenth-century scholars were unhappy confronting the notion that their idol might actually have loved a man. Lacking the evidence of even a pair of initials, theories have been remarkably ingenious. Mary Fitton, who carried Pembroke's child before being abandoned by him, has the attraction of fitting the most unimaginative biographical theory, that the Sonnets relate the story of their relationship with each other and Shakespeare. Fitton was fair (not "black"), however, and more exotic candidates have been lined up to compete – among them **Emilia Lanier**, herself well-known as a poet, who came from a family of Venetian musicians and has been linked with Sonnet 128 ("How oft, when thou, my music, music play'st"). Other rivals include the black-eyed **Lady Rich**, loved by Philip Sidney and ostensibly the "Stella" of his sonnets; **Jane Davenant**, mother of playwright William, who liked to claim he was Shakespeare's love child; and even a nameless black prostitute who caught the poet's eye.

> *I have long felt convinced, after repeated perusals of the Sonnets, that the greater number of them was composed in an assumed character, on different subjects, and at different times, for the amusement, and probably at the suggestion, of the author's intimate associates.*
>
> Alexander Dyce, in his edition of the *Poems* (1832)

This sense that it is through poetry that the poet can himself triumph over what Sonnet 19 calls "devouring time" is one of the most magnificent aspects of the book published as *Shakespeare's Sonnets*, and probably its most consistent single philosophy.

That need not surprise us: some evidence suggests that the poems printed in the volume were written over as much as a twenty-year period, so in that sense alone the work is a fitting testament to Shakespeare's career as a poet, a career that he appears to have continued even while his hands were more than full with writing plays. Revelling in its own power, Sonnet 55 offers a brave challenge to the erosions of "sluttish time":

> Not marble nor the gilded monuments
> Of princes shall outlive this powerful rhyme,
> But you shall shine more bright in these contents
> Than unswept stone besmeared with sluttish time.
> When wasteful war shall statues overturn,
> And broils root out the work of masonry,
> Nor Mars his sword nor war's quick fire shall burn
> The living record of your memory.
> 'Gainst death and all oblivious enmity
> Shall you pace forth; your praise shall still find room
> Even in the eyes of all posterity
> That wear this world out to the ending doom.
>> So, till the judgement that yourself arise,
>> You live in this, and dwell in lovers' eyes.

[55, 1–14]

And as long as they go on being kept alive by readers, that pledge will seem true enough.

AUDIO

The Sonnets

John Gielgud, UK, 1963 › HarperCollins
(Caedmon) ⬇

John Gielgud was widely acclaimed as having one of the most beautiful theatrical voices of his generation, perhaps even of the century. Even if the rest of his work perished, these 1963 tapings of the Sonnets would testify to his powers, for in them Gielgud is on transcendent form. What can in some other contexts seem like reserve or aloofness is here transformed into vivid urgency: when the speaker claims in Sonnet 147 that he is "past cure ... past care", here you utterly believe him. These are gloriously full-bodied readings that express their emotions – and Gielgud's understanding of the poems' turbulent moods – intimately. The text followed is that of the 1609 first quarto.

The Sonnets
Alex Jennings, UK, 1997 > Naxos ◉ ⬤

Listening to an audio performance of the Sonnets can be an odd experience: poems that you're used to imagining one way are suddenly taken out of your control and made someone else's. It's as if Jennings addressed himself to this conundrum when recording these sessions, always striving for a crisp, quiet approach that doesn't indulge itself in extremes. Less ostentatious than Gielgud, he's also more interested in driving a narrative through the different poems. If at times you wish that Jennings gave more of himself, his downbeat style is subtly shaded and grows in appeal with repeated listening.

The Sonnets
Kim Cattrall, Simon Russell Beale, Ruth Negga, David Tennant, Dominic West and others; John Wyver (dir.) UK, 2012 > Illuminations **DVD** ⬤

One way of dealing with the Sonnets' dazzling multiplicity is to have a whole cast of people read them; and production company Illuminations have secured an impressive range of talent – leading-name actors of all ages and backgrounds alongside academics (James Shapiro, Katherine Duncan-Jones), poets (Andrew Motion, Don Paterson), even the odd celebrity (Stephen Fry). There are some masterful interpretations here, notably a cool Simon Russell Beale in Sonnet 20 ("A woman's face ...") and Kate Fleetwood's arched, ironic interpretation of numbers 31, 46, 47 and 122, and many others are very good indeed. The performers' ability to be intimate with the camera varies, and you can't help feeling that some poems would work better as audio-only, but you can always switch the screen off – or download the MP3s.

EDITIONS

Oxford Shakespeare
Colin Burrow (ed.); 2002 > Oxford UP

Colin Burrow's *Complete Sonnets and Poems*, 750 pages long, includes not only *A Lover's Complaint* and the two major narrative poems but *The Passionate Pilgrim*, "The Phoenix and the Turtle" (though the editor doesn't call it that) and several poems that Shakespeare's contemporaries thought might be his – a condition that gets Burrow off the hook of including the woefully bad "A Funeral Elegy" (see p.618). This collective context gives Burrow plenty of reason to reposition Shakespeare as a major poet in his own right rather than someone who tossed off the odd sonnet in his spare time. His treatment of the Sonnets is typically excellent, with insightful but sensible notes and an extended introductory essay that provides detail on biographical puzzles while refusing to get lost in them.

New Penguin Shakespeare
John Kerrigan (ed.); 1986 > Penguin

Despite Colin Burrow's attempts to corner the market, other editions of the Sonnets (there are many available) have plenty to offer. Kerrigan's version is particularly recommended. There are no on-page notes and glosses, for one thing, but this apparent hindrance allows Kerrigan to exercise his intellect in an extended sequence of detailed mini-essays masquerading as notes. These take up nearly two-thirds of the book, but you have the option to ignore the lot and scan a clean text – as the first readers of *Shakespeare's Sonnets* did – instead. And Penguin have even reprinted this edition of the Sonnets in a slimline pocket format without notes, perfect whether you're reading them on the bus or slipping them under a lover's door. The narrative poem *A Lover's Complaint*, published after the Sonnets in the 1609 text, is also included.

SOME CRITICISM

The Art of Shakespeare's Sonnets
Helen Vendler; 1997 > Harvard UP

Whatever else this book is – and it offers much – *The Art of Shakespeare's Sonnets* is beautiful to use, in its hardback edition especially. Attractively designed and wonderfully printed, its format is also ingenious: each sonnet is printed both in original facsimile and a modernized text, with a long interpretative essay on the facing page. Vendler is one of the most perspicacious critics around, equally well known for her writing on contemporary poetry as for historical work, and here she's in her element, teasing out the most intricate of meanings then zooming out for the long shot. Ultra-close readings of these poems have much to offer, and even if you quibble with the details you will still find yourself in Vendler's debt.

Shakespeare's Sonnets: Critical Essays
James Schiffer (ed.); 1999 > Routledge

While single-author interpretations of the Sonnets have their merits – Stephen Booth's *Essay on Shakespeare's Sonnets* (1969) and Joel Fineman's *Shakespeare's Perjured Eye* (1986) are just two brilliant examples – in order to taste a fuller range of commentary on these poems it's worth digging out an anthology. The Garland one is typically excellent, though unlike some others in the series it includes historical criticism in overview rather than directly. Nevertheless Schiffer has some provocative contributions – notably from Margreta de Grazia and Peter Stallybrass – among fifteen specially commissioned essays. If you're interested in browsing older work, it's worth tracking down Peter Jones's fine (if long out-of-print) *Shakespeare's Sonnets: A Casebook* (1977).

Venus and Adonis

Exuberant, sexy, funny, yet also tenderly sad, *Venus and Adonis* was Shakespeare's first work to be printed under his name – and it was a rapid and roaring success. Published in spring 1593, four or five years after the author first arrived in London, the book was reprinted six times in the next seven years, making it by some margin Shakespeare's most popular and well-known work during his lifetime. The great scholar Muriel Bradbrook once suggested that the poet wrote this to thumb his nose at his competitor Robert Greene (see p.176), and even if the story has no basis in fact, it might as well be true. Shakespeare lifted the story of the goddess Venus and her frustrated love affair with Adonis from Ovid's *Metamorphoses*, but gave it a glorious new twist: in this poem Adonis simply will not be seduced, and Venus is driven to ever more ridiculous lengths to persuade him into it. Despite the tongue-in-cheek comedy that ensues, however, *Venus and Adonis* ends in tragedy, with a touching finale demonstrating a subtle and impressive shift in dramatic mood. Described by the poet in his dedication as "the first heir of my invention", *Venus and Adonis* is where Shakespeare's career – and not just as a poet – really began to take flight.

DATE > On bookstands by summer 1593, *Venus and Adonis* was perhaps written shortly beforehand, during a period of unemployment following the plague closures (see below).

SOURCES > Ovid's retelling of the Venus and Adonis story in *Metamorphoses* was Shakespeare's main source, but other details creep into it from elsewhere in Ovid and perhaps even Christopher Marlowe's *Hero and Leander*, written around the same time.

TEXTS > The poem was printed by Richard Field (also from Stratford-upon-Avon and possibly Shakespeare's schoolfellow) in a quarto text noted for its careful typesetting. It was immediately popular, with no fewer than sixteen editions appearing over the next half-century.

Interpreting the poem

Most likely penned during 1592 or early the following year, *Venus and Adonis* arrived during a difficult time for its author. After plague struck London during the summer and the death toll soared, the authorities quickly ordered that the playhouses be closed down. Ostensibly they posed a risk to public health, but there may also have been other motives at work. In the years to come Shakespeare and his colleagues found themselves locked in a bitter vendetta with the City fathers, who were continually trying to put the playhouses out of business. The spiritual as well as physical health of the population was at stake: only a few years previously

SYNOPSIS

As dawn breaks, the beautiful youth Adonis heads out hunting, little suspecting that the goddess Venus has him in her sights. Adonis is not remotely interested in love, however, as Venus discovers when she drags him from his horse and attempts to pin him to the forest floor with kisses. Although he manages to resist her – despite her many entreaties and her insistence that it's his duty to procreate – it is midday before he manages to spring free from her clutches. But just as he is about to get away, an in-heat mare gallops into view, prompting Adonis's steed to romp after her into the woods, leaving his master with no means of transport.

As Adonis sits down on the forest floor in a sulk, Venus again attempts to seduce him, but with the same lack of success. Appalled by his indifference, she faints, whereupon the shocked Adonis – thinking she might be dead – attempts to bring her round by kissing her. After Venus regains consciousness, Adonis agrees to a final kiss if they can then say goodnight, but the excited Venus sees this as an opportunity to get as much of him as she can. Eventually separating, Venus attempts to make a date with Adonis for the following day, but he informs her that he plans to go boar-hunting with his friends. Alarmed at the idea, Venus grabs him and pulls him down so that he's sitting on top of her, but, to her frustration, still nothing much happens. Finally, she attempts to convince him of the terrible dangers of hunting, but he refuses to be moved, and – angrily accusing her of lust rather than love – heads off home, leaving Venus to weep the night away.

As dawn arrives once more, Venus hears the sound of the hunt and, rushing towards it, comes across a blood-stained boar. Wavering between fear and hope, her worst misgivings are realized when she discovers Adonis's mangled body lying in the woods. Initially stunned into silence, she pays a moving tribute to his beauty and predicts that love itself will be diminished by his loss. But as she watches over him, Adonis's body disappears and a purple and white flower springs up in its place.

---

a London preacher had insisted in a sermon that "the cause of plagues is sin … and the cause of sin are plays", and many men in power agreed. The plague killed over ten thousand citizens in 1593, and it also caused devastation in the theatre industry: venues stood idle, actors died, companies were forced out on tour and fell apart. During these nervous years it must have been clearer than ever, even for a man as gifted as Shakespeare, that writing and acting in plays was not a stable profession.

It was only to be expected that he would explore other artistic avenues. *Venus and Adonis*, the first of Shakespeare's clutch of "narrative" poems (poems, that is, which tell a story), is sometimes written off as a juvenile irrelevance in a career otherwise spent in playhouses. But in the early 1590s most of Shakespeare's dramatic work still lay in front of him and, like many of his colleagues, he was not solely a man of the theatre. There was sound practical as well as artisic sense in trying a different path – composing a poetic work in a style then becoming fashionable, and dedicating it to an aristocratic patron in the hope of artistic and financial reward.

The dedicatee for *Venus and Adonis* was a typically canny choice: the young and glamorous Earl of Southampton, known for his excellent prospects, fine literary taste and encouragement of artists (he was famously painted by Nicholas Hilliard

547

at around this time). The poem's dedication addresses the Earl directly in an unashamed attempt to curry favour. "Right Honourable," the poet begins,

> I know not how I shall offend in dedicating my unpolished lines to your Lordship, nor how the world will censure me for choosing so strong a prop to support so weak a burden. Only, if your honour seem but pleased, I account myself highly praised, and vow to take advantage of all idle hours till I have honoured you with some graver labour. But if the first heir of my invention prove deformed, I shall be sorry it had so noble a godfather, and never after ear so barren a land for fear it yield me still so bad a harvest.
>
> [DEDICATION, 5–12]

"Your honour's in all duty," the newly published poet signs off with a flourish, "William Shakespeare".

Whether poet and Earl ever met is not known – Shakespeare's tone, confident but properly deferential, gives little away – and largely beside the point. The dedication to *Venus and Adonis*, the first ever appearance of Shakespeare's name in print, stakes his claim. Those "idle hours" may have been forced on him, but there is more here than a bitter joke at the theatre's expense. Shakespeare declares himself a man who is seizing control of his time and using it to his own professional advantage.

Shakespeare targeted his poem with some cunning. Southampton had an interest in fashionable Ovidian verse, but he was not by any means alone. Indeed, we don't know whether or not Shakespeare garnered any kind of financial reward from Southampton for his "labour" – the Earl ran into money worries soon after the publication of *The Rape of Lucrece* and Shakespeare apparently never went near him again – but we do know that *Venus and Adonis* found a ready market at the booksellers. It raced through at least sixteen editions in the next half-century, many of which have simply not survived due to readers' enthusiastic thumbing.

It's little surprise that this unabashedly erotic poem appears to have been popular with hormonal young men, particularly those studying at the universities or in London. Ironically enough, it was via some of those readers that Shakespeare's first full-time poetic venture even found its way onto the stage: it makes a fleeting appearance in a play put on at Cambridge around 1598, in which one of the characters promises to "worship sweet Mr. Shakspeare," and to "lay his *Venus and Adonis* under my pillow". Shakespeare's contemporaries were, in fact, to make more references to this work than any other he wrote.

If our poet had any moral design in view, he has been unfortunate in his conduct of it. The shield which he lifts in defence of chastity is wrought with such meretricious imagery, as cannot fail to counterpose a moral purpose.

George Steevens, note from *The Plays and Poems of William Shakespeare*, ed. Edmond Malone (1821)

By law of nature

And if *Venus and Adonis* was written in anything approaching desperate circumstances (Shakespeare's income is likely to have collapsed with the closure of the theatres), this joyous and often very funny poem gives little hint of it. It gives little hint, too, of being written in a city – so convincingly rural that many commentators have assumed Shakespeare arrived from Stratford with a finished draft in his pocket, or else wrote it far removed from the clamour and squalor of London. Over two-thirds of the way into the poem the narrator describes in gorgeously vivid language the goddess Venus scampering through the forest in search of Adonis, the youthful object of her desire:

> And as she runs, the bushes in the way
> Some catch her by the neck, some kiss her face,
> Some twine about her thigh to make her stay.
> She wildly breaketh from their strict embrace,
>   Like a milch doe whose swelling dugs do ache,
>   Hasting to feed her fawn hid in some brake.

[871–6]

Here Venus is compared, half-humorously, to a "milch doe", or female deer who feeds her young, and elsewhere the poem teems with all the bustle of the natural world. *Venus and Adonis* is noisy with nature: larks trill, hares scurry, waterbirds dip and dart, hunting dogs bray – the narrator even spends eleven stanzas describing Adonis's "strong-necked" horse, who catches sight of a "jennet" (female horse) who takes his fancy and promptly races after her. This is of course the central joke of the poem, and one reason it presents its bucolic setting with such helter-skelter glee: all around in the forest, fecund nature is doing what it does best, renewing and reproducing itself, while at the centre of the action stand the lovers, one of whom refuses to do anything of the kind.

Shakespeare borrowed the story of the goddess Venus and her encounter with the youthful mortal Adonis from Ovid's compendium of tales and legends, *Metamorphoses*, but he made one crucial change. In Ovid Venus falls helplessly for Adonis ("She loved Adonis more / Than heaven", Ovid's narrator exclaims in the translation Shakespeare used), and her love is reciprocated. The two head off hunting together. Shakespeare, however, turns the story around: his Adonis is a moody but perhaps surprisingly frigid teen whose beauty is matched only by his conspicuous lack of interest in Venus's advances. Fertility goddess she may be – and lusted after by gods and mortals alike – but this poem presents Venus as a woman whose unembarrassed sexuality is something to run away from rather than succumb to. Attempting to seduce the youth as she reclines fetchingly on a bank of primroses, she tries to convince Adonis that "by law of nature thou art bound to breed," (171), and that, really, love is just a matter of doing as the plants do. "Things growing to themselves are growth's abuse," she urges him,

> Seeds spring from seeds, and beauty breedeth beauty:
> Thou wast begot; to get it is thy duty.

[166–8]

Anticipating many of the arguments put forward in the first sequence of the Sonnets (which urge the young man to whom they are addressed "to breed another thee", as Sonnet 6 has it), Venus tries to caress her lover and make him stay. "I'll be a park," she eagerly cries, "and thou shalt be my deer" (231).

So bold with his name

By the late 1590s, Shakespeare had made his reputation as a published writer. His narrative poems *Venus and Adonis* and *Lucrece* were selling well, and 1598 saw the publication of editions of *Richard II* and *Love's Labour's Lost* with their author's name printed boldly on the title-page. That same year a self-appointed critic named **Francis Meres** published a survey of Shakespeare's work that acclaimed him as one of the brightest stars of the London stage. Meres also noted that Shakespeare was a poet, before adding enticingly that he was also the author of certain "sugared sonnets", which had never reached print and had only been seen by his "private friends".

Though Shakespeare must have been glad of the attention – yet another edition of *Venus and Adonis* followed soon afterwards – this threw up unforeseen problems. Before 1599 was out, a publisher named **William Jaggard** had put out a collection of poems entitled *The Passionate Pilgrim* and supposedly by "W. Shakespeare". Eager to cash in on that name, Jaggard declined to mention that most of the works in *The Passionate Pilgrim* were by other people, Shakespeare's contribution most likely limited to early versions of Sonnets 138 and 144 and some reheated excerpts from *Love's Labour's Lost*. Alongside work by Marlowe and Sir Walter Ralegh, the rest of the book was padded out with vaguely Shakespearian verse by other writers.

It's highly unlikely that Shakespeare sanctioned *The Passionate Pilgrim*, and hints of his feelings on the matter are communicated by colleague **Thomas Heywood**, who complained heatedly after the book was reprinted in 1612 that Shakespeare was "much offended with M. Jaggard" for presuming "to make so bold with his name" (nor was Heywood impressed that "lines" of his own had been included). Perhaps unwilling to make yet more enemies, Jaggard backed down soon afterwards: a second version of the title-page for the 1612 edition drops Shakespeare's name entirely. Perhaps forgiven, a decade later Jaggard was commissioned by Shakespeare's colleagues to print the First Folio.

Conspicuously more Shakespearian than *The Passionate Pilgrim* is the lyric poem "**The Phoenix and the Turtle**", published under his name in 1601 alongside poems by "the best and chiefest of our modern writers", including Ben Jonson, George Chapman and John Marston. All these poems take up the theme of a rambling work by a painfully obscure writer named Robert Chester, entitled *Love's Martyr*, which describes the tale of the legendary phoenix bird and her love for a turtle dove. Shakespeare's response concentrates on the final moments of the story, the lovers' decision to commit suicide by immolating themselves in flames, although his work is sufficiently mysterious in tone that many have suspected that the poem is an allegory for something else, as yet unknown.

Nor does "The Phoenix and the Turtle" bring an end to the speculation over Shakespeare's poetic career. Later in the seventeenth century many people ascribed poems to him, the most famous of which is probably a short work beginning "**Shall I die?**", copied down in two poetic miscellanies from the 1630s and included – to much scholarly horror and disbelief – in the 1986 Oxford *Complete Works*. Another poem, "A Funeral Elegy" (see p.618), has generated even more friction among critics, but wasn't connected with Shakespeare until 1989. The hunger for Shakespeare's name, it seems, has only intensified in the four centuries

Venus's somewhat frantic efforts to get the attention of a young man rather more eager to go hunting with his mates reveal the rich seam of comedy that runs through *Venus and Adonis*. One of the multiple jokes played out here is that Venus, goddess and irresistible embodiment of female love, finds herself stuck in a position conventionally assigned to men, that of the devoted but frustrated suitor held in thrall by a disdainful mistress. That dynamic (lovelorn man, cruel woman) animates much of the Italian courtly verse known by Shakespeare and his contemporaries, but here it is Adonis who refuses to become entangled in love, which is (as he anxiously observes) reputed to be "a life in death" (413).

Nor is that the only inversion set up by *Venus and Adonis*. As in *A Lover's Complaint*, the poem smudges the boundaries separating man and woman in its loving description of the "sweet" Adonis, so boyish that he's practically girlish, with his "maiden" cheeks, "soft bosom" and "coral mouth" (50, 81, 542). Adonis's plight – and it is touchingly rendered – is that he seems entirely unable to be interested in women, and is immaturely puzzled by what Venus so eagerly proposes. "'Fair queen,'" he begs with a virginal quiver,

> 'if any love you owe me,
> Measure my strangeness with my unripe years.
> Before I know myself, seek not to know me.'

> [523–5]

It's not that he is knowingly disdainful or coy, Adonis pleads, simply that it isn't yet time. This poem is all about different kinds of "love", but the platonic variety the youth prefers just doesn't provide the sexual pleasure Venus wants so keenly – and it is left to readers to imagine how they would respond if they found themselves, quite literally, in his position.

If Adonis, "frosty in desire" (36), most often seems divinely unattainable, the same cannot be said for Venus, who is painted by Shakespeare in vivid and realistic colours. Though a woman, she takes charge of the situation like a "bold-faced suitor" (4); though a goddess, she is depicted in ripe human detail. Early in the morning she is strong enough to pluck Adonis from his horse and fold him under her arm, and when midday arrives, it is she, not he, who begins to "sweat" in the heat (175). When Venus swoons a little later on, unable to cope with Adonis's harsh words, she simply flops onto the ground while he attempts some limp-wristed first aid. And when she is revived by his penitent kisses, she is eager not to let him go – and pulls him down on top. "Now quick desire hath caught the yielding prey," the narrator says, somewhat greedily,

> And glutton-like she feeds, yet never filleth.
> Her lips are conquerors, his lips obey,
> Paying what ransom the insulter willeth,
>   Whose vulture thought doth pitch the price so high
>   That she will draw his lips' rich treasure dry …

> [547–52]

A rare staging of *Venus and Adonis* came to the London Globe in 2012, part of the World Shakespeare Festival. South Africa's Isango Ensemble offered the poem in no fewer than six languages – English, isiZulu, isiXhosa, Sesotho, Setswana and Afrikaans.

Not for the first time, Venus's attempts at seduction are described in frankly predatory terms. Yet she is also wonderfully chimerical: forceful one moment, weak-kneed the next; tender and gentle yet gifted with an iron grip; a touch voluptuous, yet airy enough to lie on "forceless flowers" and be drawn through the clouds by "strengthless doves" (152–3). It's difficult to think that when he came to write the part of the Egyptian Queen in *Antony and Cleopatra* (herself associated with Venus by Antony's companion Enobarbus) Shakespeare didn't think back fifteen years earlier to his portrait of a goddess every bit as changeable.

Variable passions

Mutability is a key component of *Venus and Adonis*, as in all Shakespeare's works influenced by Ovid, and Adonis's stubborn refusal to submit himself to the changes wrought by love commits him – as Shakespeare's readers would have known from the outset – to a grisly end. The poem races through time (it is dawn at the opening, midday soon afterwards, dusk when Venus faints and "dark night" by the time she warns her lover about hunting the boar), yet also makes it strangely elastic, pausing to digress or dwell upon a picturesque detail but always heading relentlessly towards its conclusion. The poem's comic high-point – the moment when Adonis ends up on top of Venus, but "will not manage her", as the narrator cheekily puts it (598) – foreshadows its mournful finale, in which Adonis is gored by the boar he has set out to hunt.

Although she does not see the connection between her attempts to pursue Adonis and the boar's own actions, Venus does sense that something terrible lies just around the forest corner. It shows Shakespeare's sensitivity to his material, though, that he resists making her plight seem ridiculous. As night falls, the poem too makes a decisive shift into a darker mood as Venus is left alone for the first time. Gazing forlornly after Adonis, the narrator movingly describes her "eye",

> Which after him she darts, as one on shore
> Gazing upon a late-embarkèd friend
> Till the wild waves will have him seen no more,
> Whose ridges with the meeting clouds contend.
>   So did the merciless and pitchy night
>   Fold in the object that did feed her sight.

[817–22]

As time and experience move on, so too does the forest. Instead of forming a fertile counterpoint to her attempts to ensnare Adonis – as the woodland hums with life, it is almost as if it urges them both on – the "mistrustful wood" (826) now begins to compound Venus's misery, swallowing her lover, then making everything else disappear from sight. Like the "concave womb" of the hills at the outset of *A Lover's Complaint*, which echo the sound of the wailing female lover, in *Venus and Adonis* too the "neighbour caves" pick up the heroine's laments and amplify their grief:

'Ay me,' she cries, and twenty times 'Woe, woe!'
And twenty echoes twenty times cry so.

[833–4]

As night shifts to dawn (again the change is accomplished speedily), that sound will soon be joined by the hunting dogs, whose "dismal cry" resounding through the forest seems to insist that something has gone tragically wrong. When Venus stumbles across the boar, whose "frothy mouth" is grotesquely "bepainted all with red" (901), she is right to fear the worst.

By refusing to clarify precisely what has gone wrong for another twenty-odd stanzas, Shakespeare tightens the tension almost to breaking point. The precise moment of Adonis's death is left unclear, and the heroine is plunged into terrible uncertainty, at one moment positive that he is gone (and cursing Death as a "hard-favoured tyrant"), at another confident that he has survived (at which point she asks Death for pardon). Change is yet again near the surface of the poem. "Variable passions throng her constant woe," the narrator remarks, not unkindly, "As striving who should best become her grief" (967–8). Even so, the instant of discovery still shocks – and Shakespeare startles his readers by focusing not on what Venus discovers lying on the forest floor, but how she reacts. As she faints with shock, her eyelids clamp shut as if flinching from the sight:

>   her eyes, as murdered with the view,
> Like stars ashamed of day, themselves withdrew.
>
> Or as the snail, whose tender horns being hit
> Shrinks backward in his shelly cave with pain,
> And there, all smothered up in shade doth sit,
> Long after fearing to creep forth again;
>   So at his bloody view her eyes are fled
>   Into the deep dark cabins of her head ...

[1031–8]

What Venus cannot face is also withheld from us (Keats was so impressed by the effect that he copied it out in a letter to a friend). It is some lines before the narrator can bring himself to describe the gory sight of Adonis, lying blood-stained on the ground with a "wide wound" underneath his ribs. As Venus faints for the second time in the poem, it is as if time has repeated itself, and tragically: when she comes round it is to find her lover not alive in her arms but sprawled on the forest floor.

But this is not quite an end. *Venus and Adonis*'s final transformation is still to come. Returning to his Ovidian source, Shakespeare moves away from the earthy detail that characterized the opening phase and shifts into the supernatural. As Venus stands by, bitterly complaining her loss, something astonishing occurs:

> By this, the boy that by her side lay killed
> Was melted like a vapour from her sight,

And in his blood that on the ground lay spilled
A purple flower sprung up, chequered with white,
    Resembling well his pale cheeks, and the blood
    Which in round drops upon their whiteness stood.

[1165–70]

Shakespeare's contemporaries would have known that the flower associated with Adonis was the anemone, ravishingly described by the great English herbalist, John Parkinson, as "so full of variety and so dainty, so pleasant and so delightsome … that the sight of them doth enforce an earnest longing desire in the mind of anyone to be a possessor of some." But, intriguingly, Shakespeare engineers his own transformation here: the purple-and-white "chequered" species he describes is not an anemone at all but a Snake's Head Fritillary, a plant that flowers in early summer – around the same time that *Venus and Adonis* initially appeared in print. And if the poem's first readers paused to admire this beautiful and fragile plant, perhaps they, too, would have been tempted to imitate Venus in the last few lines of the poem. Plucking the flower from the blood-soaked ground, the unhappy heroine cradles it to her bosom, finally achieving the captive intimacy with Adonis that has eluded her all along:

'Here was thy father's bed, here in my breast.
Thou art the next of blood, and 'tis thy right.
Lo, in this hollow cradle take thy rest;
My throbbing heart shall rock thee day and night.
    There shall not be one minute in an hour
    Wherein I will not kiss my sweet love's flower.'

[1183–8]

AUDIO

Venus and Adonis
D. Burke, C. Corbett, B. Soames; David Timson (dir.)
UK, 2006 ❯ Naxos ◉ ⬇

Anyone seeking to turn *Venus and Adonis* into performance poetry has a tough call to make: whether to use a full cast, or – as did Gregory Doran with the RSC and the Little Angel Theatre in 2004 – allow one voice to read out the lot. David Timson opts to use three actors, and it's difficult not to feel that the poem's particular intimacy suffers as a result. This performance is rather stately, even sober, and little of Shakespeare's sly wit survives, most noticeably with David Burke's rather glum-sounding narrator. That said, Clare Corbett brings a charming earnestness to Venus and Benjamin Soames is nicely sulky as Adonis – and the poem's bittersweet conclusion is beautifully done.

EDITIONS

Oxford Shakespeare
Colin Burrow (ed.); 2002 ❯ Oxford UP

During its author's lifetime *Venus and Adonis* was his most printed work, so it's good to be reminded – as Colin Burrow frequently states – that Shakespeare's efforts as a poet are integral to a complete understanding of his career. Comprehensiveness is very much the point of this Oxford edition of the *Complete Sonnets and Poems*, which brings together all the poetic work Shakespeare is known to have penned and some he almost certainly didn't (it also includes some hopeful seventeenth-century attributions). *Venus* is sensitively treated, Burrow's introduction capturing very nicely its rhetorical and intellectual innovation without losing sight of its fun.

SOME CRITICISM

Elizabethan Erotic Narratives
William Keach; 1977 ➤ Harvester / Rutgers [o/p]

Part of the problem when studying *Venus and Adonis* and poems influenced by it (a kind of Jacobethan mini-genre) is what on earth to call them – hence the slightly catch-all title of this book, one of the first to consider them in relation to each other. Keach races neatly through poems such as Marlowe's *Hero and Leander*, Thomas Lodge's *Glaucus and Scilla*, Marston's *Metamorphosis of Pigmalion's Image* and others. He keeps in view the teasing ambiguities favoured by these works, a kind of generic playfulness that goes back to Ovid – the poet in whose shadow they were written – but which also (as Keach says) has more serious things to say about "the turbulence and contradiction in erotic experience". Lest all that sound too sober, it must be said that Keach's style is bright, interesting and readable.

Contexts

Shakespeare's life

I t's been said that all the facts we know about Shakespeare's biography fit onto a postcard (or, if you're feeling especially gloomy, a postage stamp). Not true. In fact, from contemporary records we have access to more information about Shakespeare than any of his playwright colleagues – except perhaps Ben Jonson, a man who did a great deal more to preserve his own reputation for posterity. The problem for Shakespeare is that, for all the extensive documentary evidence, little gives us access to the man himself. There is plenty on his extensive land holdings, property investments and involvement with the law; but almost nothing suggesting what kind of person he really was – no manuscripts, none of his books, no diaries. Most of the portraits we possess are of questionable authority; even his few surviving signatures don't entirely match up. Jonson's famous declaration that Shakespeare was "not of an age, but for all time" actually points up something rather discomfiting – that in writing about his life it can be difficult to pin him down.

A Midlands childhood [1564–70]

The story of William Shakespeare's life has its beginning and end in one place: the bustling town of **Stratford-upon-Avon**, in an area where the surname is still relatively commonplace. Nowadays Stratford is in the shadow of nearby **Birmingham**, the industrialized capital of the West Midlands and Britain's second-largest city, its sprawling suburban outskirts just twenty or so miles distant. Yet some two centuries before the Industrial Revolution, sixteenth-century Birmingham had a population of 1,500 and was merely "a good market town", as one contemporary historian described it. The most significant regional focus was **Warwick**, dominated by the medieval castle (seat of the Earls of Warwick, several of whom feature in Shakespeare's history plays), a trading centre for the area and the shire town that gives its name to the county. Stratford itself, eight miles to Warwick's southwest, began as a crossing point over the River Avon and became a planned settlement around 1200. By the mid-sixteenth century it was registered as a market town and became a thriving place to do business (it had three "very large streets" to Birmingham's pair), particularly for travellers on their way to the cathedral communities of **Coventry** and **Worcester** in the same area.

William Shakespeare was born directly into this mercantile Midlands environment. His father **John** (c. 1530–1601) was most likely the son of a local farmer – John's brother **Henry**, the playwright's uncle, was one as well – but like many of his generation moved from the countryside into town, in John's case to train as a glover, wool-dealer and whittawer (skilled tanner of leather). William, too, might have taken up the family trade for a few years, and indeed memories of it intermittently appear in his written work. For his own part John seems not to have been able to write – a pair of compasses, a symbol of his trade, is one of the marks he used in place of a signature – and the same is apparently true for his wife **Mary** (born Mary Arden; only her death date, 1608, is known), who likewise used a cross to sign her name. Many people in this period could read but not handle a pen, however – and in any case this limitation proved no barrier for John Shakespeare. In 1558, six years before the birth of his eldest son, he was sworn in as a town constable and rapidly ascended the corporate ladder, being made a burgess six years later and an alderman in 1567. The position of **chief alderman** (in effect mayor) followed a few years later.

By this time John and Mary had six of their eight children. The Shakespeares were typical in having a large family, and given that their first two daughters, **Joan** (b. 1558) and **Margaret** (b. 1562), both died in infancy, it is easy to comprehend why. **William** was their first son, followed by **Gilbert** (1566–1612), another **Joan** (1569–1646), **Anne** (1571–79), **Richard** (1574–1613) and **Edmund** (1580–1607). All except Anne made it into adulthood, but only Joan outlived her eldest brother – and then by thirty years.

All we know concerning William's arrival is that he was christened at Holy Trinity Church, Stratford, on 26 April, 1564. Patriotic tradition holds that he was born three days earlier, on St George's Day (also the date on which he died), but it might as easily have been the 21st or 22nd. The Shakespeares were then living in a large house in **Henley Street** – we know because John was fined in 1552 for having an illegal rubbish-tip outside – and as a consequence the building is now known, perhaps over-reverentially, as the "**Birthplace**". It's probable that John plied his trade at the same address, perhaps with his workshop downstairs, but soon after William's birth both work and family will have been overtaken by wider events. During the summer of 1564 **bubonic plague** hit Stratford, killing around two hundred people, perhaps a sixth of the town's population. As a member of the council, John was closely involved in dealing with the crisis, and is recorded as attending a meeting – held out of doors to avoid contagion – to arrange emergency financial assistance for those made destitute by the deadly outbreak.

At school [1571–81]

It is not an overstatement to say that his father's position and influence in Stratford made Shakespeare's subsequent career possible. Though the records have since perished, it is all but certain that William attended the town's **King's New School,** a grammar school foundation dating from the fifteenth century, for as the son of an alderman he would have been guaranteed a place. Boys usually began at grammar school at the age of 6 or 7, having attended a "petty school" for two or three years where they were taught how to read, write and count (only a handful of schools accepted girls in the sixteenth century, and then just for the junior years; private tuition was the only other option). Though with some forty pupils Stratford grammar school was small, it was run by a university-educated master – Oxford graduates **Thomas Jenkins** and **John Cottom** are likely to have taught Shakespeare – who had an assistant to help with the younger boys.

Unwillingly to school

The image evoked by As You Like It's Jaques of "the whining schoolboy with his satchel / And shining morning face, creeping like snail / Unwillingly to school" (2.7.145–7), has become a cliché almost as weary as Jaques himself, but it presents an experience common to many Elizabethans. Though the records have since perished, it's overwhelmingly likely that Shakespeare attended the **King's New School** at Stratford, and if he didn't "creep", others certainly did. Lessons typically began at 6 or 7am six days a week, there was three hours' work before breakfast arrived, and the afternoons were long – most schools finished at 6pm, though pupils did get two hours for lunch, the main meal of the day.

Yet Shakespeare was incalculably lucky to benefit – however unwillingly – from a recent explosion of interest in the design of children's learning. Humanist thinkers such as Erasmus and Colet argued that school, not university, should be the top priority for educationalists, and Elizabethan treatises such as the schoolmaster **William Kempe**'s Education of Children in Learning (1588) painstakingly laid out the curriculum. Between the ages of around 5 and 7 a child should attend a **petty school** for the rudiments of pronunciation and writing, practising with a "hornbook" that presented the alphabet, numbers and the Lord's Prayer. Then he – girls would usually stop here, unless they were lucky enough to have private tuition – would progress to one of the new **grammar schools** (nearly 150 were founded in Britain during the

sixteenth century) to acquire the basics of Latin, frequently administered through the standard textbook, **William Lily** and **John Colet**'s Grammar (1567), which argued that Latin grammar was the "foundation and ground work" of all thought. Once this was mastered, pupils developed skill in reading and translating, and in the upper forms used some of the great Roman authors – Cicero and Quintilian were favoured, as were the poets Virgil and Ovid (see p.309) – to present arguments and test ideas. The practice of imitatio (creative imitation), was crucial: students often used books containing extravagant lists of sententiae (memorable phrases) for them to learn and regurgitate. The value of speaking – performing – was hard-wired into the humanist curriculum, and the use of play-texts such as those by Plautus and Terence would have given the young Shakespeare an early taste for theatre.

Nevertheless, for all its benefits, what this added up to was up to ten years of extremely hard work, much of it based on learning by rote: an experience Shakespeare will hardly have recalled with unmixed pleasure. An entire scene in The Merry Wives of Windsor is devoted to the struggles of a small boy – knowingly named William – to master basic Latin (see p.616), while Henry VI Part II sees Jack Cade, leader of a Kentish rebellion, threaten to execute Lord Saye, one of the King's aristocratic supporters, because he has "most traitorously corrupted the youth of the realm in erecting a grammar school" (4.7.30–1).

The curriculum at Stratford grammar will have been difficult, and left an impressive mark. Ben Jonson's waspish jibe that his colleague possessed "small Latin and less Greek" came from a man who was fiercely proud of his learning, but in fact the 15-year-old Shakespeare will have known as much Latin as many classics graduates today (see box above). As with any child growing up in the Elizabethan era, **Protestant Christianity** will have also played a significant part in Shakespeare's boyhood. He will have attended church twice every Sunday for morning and evening services – attendance was compulsory by law – and taken Holy Communion several times a year. Shakespeare's formal education will also have covered religious matters (he will have learnt the catechism in Latin as well as English, and spent time translating the Geneva Bible into Latin), each school day opening and closing with formal devotions. Despite the possibility that John Shakespeare had sympathies with the old Catholic faith (see p.564), it is all but certain that his son's education will have been in orthodox Elizabethan Protestantism.

Aside from the teasing (and usually ironic) references to education in Shakespeare's plays, we don't know a great deal more about this period of his life. But in his last years at school his family circumstances were to change dramatically. During the mid-1570s the Midlands entered a prolonged **economic recession** that blighted Stratford especially hard: some records indicate that by the end of the century half of the town's population was living in poverty. John Shakespeare and his family were not remotely close to being among them, but evidence of their decline nevertheless accumulates in the records: John stopped attending council meetings in 1576, sold off part of his considerable land holdings in 1578 and began to owe money to a variety of creditors. An expensive and socially ambitious scheme to acquire a coat of arms, begun a few years earlier, was likewise dropped, and in 1586 his colleagues at the council voted to replace him as alderman.

One source suggests that as a result of his father's financial difficulties William was taken away from school, but by then he would anyway have been close to the leaving age. Unlike Christopher Marlowe (who came from a background humbler than Shakespeare's but won a scholarship to Cambridge), William never attended either of the **universities**. John Shakespeare's lack of funds might have stymied any ambitions his son had in that respect, but there is no reason to suppose that he wanted to attend. In the sixteenth century both Oxford and Cambridge were essentially prestigious theological colleges intended for well-connected young men, which also offered training in specialisms such as medicine and the law. University education might well have seemed a costly irrelevance; Ben Jonson, notably, did not go to college either.

Wife and children [1582–85]

And there were soon to be other ties holding Shakespeare to Stratford. The strongest is also the most striking: his marriage in November 1582 to **Anne Hathaway**. Shakespeare was just 18; Anne was 26 at the time of her wedding, and pregnant. By all accounts, it was a rushed process: the couple were forced to apply for a special licence because the date fell during the church season of Advent, when marriages were normally not performed, and had to travel to the bishop's court at Worcester in order to do so. The ceremony itself took place in late November, but we have no record as to where – one tempting suggestion is the village of **Temple Grafton**, where the priest had a lax reputation, but the neighbouring **Luddington** and **Bishopton** could equally have played host. There is another puzzle, too: in the records at Worcester Anne's surname is given as "Whateley", not Hathaway, and the pregnant bride is described as a "maiden" (virgin). Though this divergence has encouraged some to guess that the young Shakespeare had somehow got himself betrothed to two women simultaneously, the prosaic likelihood is that the clerks simply made a slip – another Whateley had appeared in court that day – and were not too curious about her condition.

The unprepossessing dwelling-cum-workshop where William Shakespeare was born in April 1564 is now a destination for pilgrims worldwide, and the cultic centre of Stratford-upon-Avon's tourist industry.

Infinitely more certain is that almost exactly six months later Anne gave birth to their first child. **Susanna** was christened, like her father, in Holy Trinity, Stratford on 26 May, 1583.

Shakespeare's wife is one of the most mysterious characters in his life story. The facts don't take us far: Anne was apparently the eldest daughter of a farmer – perhaps one of John Shakespeare's business contacts – from nearby Shottery, and from backdating her tombstone it is possible to work out that she was born in 1555 or thereabouts, making her seven or eight years older than her new husband. The sizeable farmhouse in which she grew up, now famously going by the name of **Anne Hathaway's Cottage**, stands around a mile away from the centre of Stratford and has since been swallowed by the growth of the town, but William would have passed through fields on the way to visit.

There are no records as to what Anne looked like – a pen-and-ink portrait, added in 1708 to a seventeenth-century edition of the works, is highly unlikely to be authentic – and the nature of her relationship with William has remained similarly shadowy. Some biographers have guessed that the marriage, which began in straitened circumstances, was unhappy, but the truth is that what little evidence we have points the other way – one of Shakespeare's Sonnets, number 145, plays tenderly with Anne's surname and might recall their courtship (see p.538). In marked contrast to William's parents, the couple had just two other children, the twins **Hamnet** and **Judith**, christened in February 1585, and when Hamnet died at the age of 11 just the daughters were left. At any rate the couple, who might well have moved in together with William's family in Henley Street, were not in the same place for long. Within seven years Shakespeare was in London, and making his name as a dramatist.

Years lost [1585–92]

We don't know how Shakespeare landed himself a job writing for the London theatre, and indeed the period between the twins' christening (1585) and the first surviving reference to his work as a playwright (1592) – the biggest surviving blank in the documentary record of his adult life – is conventionally known as "**the lost years**", and although a 1589 court case mentioning him has since surfaced it adds little detail to the record. In the absence of solid evidence, hearsay and tradition have come up with several options for Shakespeare's movements during this time. On the livelier end of the scale is the yarn that Shakespeare was punished for poaching the deer of **Sir Thomas Lucy**, master of nearby Charlecote (the playwright is meant to have got his own back by satirizing him in *The Merry Wives of Windsor*), but this story fails to deal with the fact that Lucy didn't keep deer until 1618, two years after the supposed poacher's death. More workmanlike is the suggestion that Shakespeare was employed as a **lawyer's clerk** in Stratford or elsewhere, but again it is unlikely that no written evidence would have survived. Another option is even simpler: that he worked with his father in the **gloving trade** for a few years – by marrying he had excluded himself from an official apprenticeship – and thereby supported his young family.

Altogether more mysterious is a theory first mooted by seventeenth-century biographer John Aubrey, which is that Shakespeare left Stratford in order to work as a "schoolmaster in the country" (and perhaps soon after leaving school himself). Investigation has uncovered mention of one "William Shakeshafte" among the household of **Alexander Hoghton** of Lea Hall near Preston in Lancashire, around a hundred miles from Stratford. Yet if Shakeshafte is our Shakespeare he will have been there several years beforehand, in 1581 – just a year before he married Stratford-based Anne Hathaway and presumably less time still before he got her pregnant.

Yet the connection remains intriguing, not least because the Hoghtons were **underground Catholics**, known as "recusants". According to a religious confession discovered by eighteenth-century workmen in the roof of the Henley Street house (but since lost), so was John Shakespeare, and it's not unlikely that the teenage William could have gained work in the Hoghton household through Catholic connections, perhaps involving his teacher at the King's New School, the Lancastrian John Cottom. Even more enticing is the possibility that William first gained experience of the theatre in Lancashire: the Hoghtons maintained players (the same will that mentions Shakeshaft describes musical instruments and "play-clothes"), and after Alexander's death his half-brother **Sir Thomas Hesketh** might have kept on the company – and was himself connected to **Ferdinando, Lord Strange**, patron of the London-based Strange's Men. If Shakespeare and his near-namesake are one and the same, this could have been a convenient route into a full-time theatrical career.

To London [late 1580s]

Though the Lancashire theory has numerous flaws, one advantage is that it appears to solve the central conundrum of the "lost years": how Shakespeare came to be working in London. His interest in the theatre might well have been kindled back at home, however, for the Midlands were hardly deprived of theatrical spectacles (see p.581).

Among the travelling troupes that visited Stratford during 1586–87 were the **Queen's Men**, a leading state-sponsored company led by the comedian **Richard Tarlton** and specializing in nationalistic English history plays. Before it reached Stratford one of the troupe's leading actors was killed by a fellow player in a brawl, and some have speculated that the 23-year-old Shakespeare was recruited to fill the gap – a seductive possibility, as yet unproven.

However he reached it, though, there is no doubt that **London** was Shakespeare's eventual destination. Easily the most important city in the realm, standing comparison with any in Europe, the capital had some 50,000 inhabitants by 1500 and four times that number just a century later. A bustling cosmopolitan metropolis, London grew to England's pre-eminent port through its position on the Thames and eventually stood at the hub of trade networks spanning the globe. Having left its medieval boundaries far behind, the city migrated restlessly westwards during the sixteenth and seventeenth centuries, eroding the traditional distinction between the court based at Westminster and the City of London to its east, though the City still remained London's financial and religious heart, dominated by the towering Gothic cathedral of St Paul's, the brand-new Royal Exchange and the great markets of Newgate, Cheap and Leadenhall. It astounded and appalled visitors and residents alike – who repeatedly commented on its ever-increasing size, its fine houses, its slums, its bountiful opportunities, its squalid poverty.

London was also a young city (sky-high mortality rates and a constant influx of population from the countryside guaranteed that), and one that took entertainment seriously. The first purpose-built, professional theatres had been erected north of the Thames in Shoreditch, but **Southwark**, across the river and outside restrictive City jurisdiction in the so-called "liberties" (see p.583), became the centre of London's burgeoning entertainment industry during the 1580s. It was around this time, presumably towards the decade's end, that Shakespeare first appeared in town. One tradition holds that he first got a job holding playgoers' horses before moving inside the theatre, perhaps to the position of **prompter's assistant**. But all that we can be sure of is that by 1592 he was not merely acting, but writing.

Young upstart [early 1590s]

We know this because someone tells us. It's somewhat ironic that the first recorded mention of Shakespeare as a playwright accuses him of plagiarism, but a vituperative attack published in the name of **Robert Greene**, referring knowingly to "an upstart crow" who "is in his own conceit the only Shake-scene in a country", parodies lines from *Henry VI Part III* to suggest that a non-university-educated writer who had begun as a mere player was stealing tricks from his more upmarket rivals. Greene died soon afterwards, but his colleague **Henry Chettle** (who transcribed and published the attack, and may even have authored it) soon published a retraction – indicating perhaps that Shakespeare, already well-known enough to be worth savaging in print, was also worth apologizing to.

If by that time *Henry VI Part III* had appeared – and done well enough to discomfit Greene and his fellow dramatists **Thomas Nashe** and **Christopher Marlowe**, two of

Who wrote Shakespeare?

A seemingly perverse question, but one that has been asked time and again. Unable – or unwilling – to square the facts of Shakespeare's life with the soaring genius of his art, some have dared to think the unthinkable: is William Shakespeare even the right man?

As Shakespearian traditions go, the notion that he isn't is relatively modern. A stout book by the American writer **Delia Bacon** entitled *The Philosophy of the Plays of Shakespeare Unfolded* (1857) was the first to broach for a wide readership what others had been gossiping about for a decade or so: the theory that William from Stratford (a "stupid, ignorant, third-rate play-actor") was not the author of the works usually attributed to him. So-called **"anti-Stratfordian"** arguments multiplied as the nineteenth century wore on, fed by Victorian suspicions about the vulgarity of the popular stage and disbelief that a mere middle-class actor could have been the greatest poet England had ever produced. Unhindered by conventional scholarship – or the fact that many of Shakespeare's colleagues and successors testified to his identity – speculation about conspiracy theories and cover-ups had snowballed by the century's end, reaching their apogee in a fad for "cryptographic" analyses, each purporting to show by numerological keys buried in Shakespeare's works that he was not responsible. While **Henry James** was merely unsettled by these theories (remarking in 1903 that "I am ... haunted by the conviction that the divine William is the biggest and most successful fraud ever practised on a patient world"), **Mark Twain** remains the movement's most famous literary convert. A century later, debates about authorship and conspiracy still have not died down; a conference on the subject was even staged at the London Globe during summer 2003, and four years later the actors **Mark Rylance** and **Sir Derek Jacobi** invited doubters to sign a "Declaration of Reasonable Doubt" – so far well over a thousand people have done so.

So if not Stratford Will, whom? Before losing her sanity and being confined to an asylum, Delia eventually settled on her namesake **Francis Bacon** as her chosen candidate, this connection later strengthened by apparent resemblances between Bacon's works and the plays of "Shakespeare". Others prefer the claims of **Christopher Marlowe** or **Edward de Vere**, the Earl of Oxford, but the earliest proponent for the latter, the resplendently named **Thomas J. Looney,** failed to overcome the inconvenient fact that Oxford died in 1604, six years before *The Tempest* – the easiest late play to date – was written. Still others argue that a shadowy consortium was behind the plays, and an extreme sect have even argued that **Elizabeth I** somehow found time to pen them.

Whoever the playwright may have collaborated with over his long career, no serious authorities believe that Shakespeare was, well, anyone else (evidence enough for a conspiracy, say some). Arguments otherwise are distinguished mainly by their disregard for plain evidence, their intellectual naivety and their rank snobbery. Shakespeare didn't attend university, but neither did he need to: his grammar-school education gave him an enviable advantage (see p.561). Nor did he need to be a lawyer like Bacon or a noble like Oxford to work out how to reproduce a court on stage, any more than he needed to be black or a woman to find words for an Othello or a Rosalind. As the critic David Bevington observes, the amazing thing is not that a middle-class man from Warwickshire wrote Shakespeare's works – it's that anyone could have written them at all.

These and other arguments are eloquently put by Jonathan Bate in *The Genius of Shakespeare* (1997), which argues convincingly that conspiracy theories about Shakespeare's identity are closely related to his promotion to Romantic "genius". And if you're interested in finding out more, check out our list of websites (p.665) devoted to the subject.

the so-called "university wits" – the rest of the Henry VI cycle may have already been written, or at least sketched out. This three-part historical extravaganza was a bold feat for a young dramatist (Shakespeare was just 28 in 1592), and outpaced anything that the Elizabethan stage had yet seen. Shakespeare had already tried his hand at comedy in the mode of **John Lyly**, another university wit, with *The Two Gentlemen of Verona* (c.1598–90); and *Titus Andronicus*, his first attempt at high-style Roman tragedy, followed in around 1594. The exact chronology of his first professional plays is diffi-cult to untangle, rarely more so than with *The Taming of the Shrew*: a stripped-down version of the script reached print in 1594, but was either a source for Shakespeare's comedy or an adaptation of it. *The Comedy of Errors*, an academic comedy to balance the learned tragedy of Titus, is also early, perhaps as early as 1591, though could date from a few years later.

During the first period of his professional writing life there is no evidence as to Shakespeare's ties with a specific theatrical company, and he may well have worked, like many of his colleagues, as a freelancer. A collaborative work, additions to a play entitled *Sir Thomas More* mainly written by Anthony Munday and Henry Chettle (see p.190), perhaps dates from this period, and given what we know about his later working practices it's likely that Shakespeare also found work tidying and polishing up old scripts, feeding the voracious hunger of competing London troupes.

His own plays were acted by a variety of different companies. Titus was performed by **Sussex's Men**, *The Comedy of Errors* and *Henry VI Part III* by **Pembroke's Men**; and his work appeared at different venues – the Inns of Court for *Errors*, *Titus* at the Rose playhouse on Bankside, and perhaps elsewhere for both. If Shakespeare hadn't joined the Queen's Men while they were on tour in 1586–87, he may well have been involved with them later on, given that a number of his plays – notably *Henry V*, *King John* and *King Lear* – draw upon scripts first performed by that company. It is hard to be sure: during the first years of the 1590s London theatres and companies were in a state of confusion and flux, not least because of the intermittent appearance of **plague**. In summer 1592 the Puritan city fathers seized the opportunity of a devastating out-break to close the theatres down, regarding them (inaccurately) as breeding grounds for pestilence as well as (perhaps more rightly) all manner of unwholesomeness. In the end they were closed for almost two years.

Poems and patrons [1593–94]

Shakespeare's response, just a few years after beginning to write for the professional stage, was to seek other employment. Despite a long-standing legend that he took the opportunity to travel in **Italy** (highly unlikely, even if he could afford it), it's almost certain that the playwright spent this period transforming himself into a poet. *Venus and Adonis*, the first of his narrative poems, was published in 1593 by his fellow Stratfordian (perhaps schoolfriend) **Richard Field** and dedicated to **Henry Wriothesley**, the influential and cultured Earl of Southampton. Wriothesley supported numerous poets as well as being an enthusiastic playgoer, and so made an attractive target for Shakespeare's attempt to secure patronage. The titillating *Venus and Adonis* flew off the booksellers' shelves and gave Shakespeare's reputation a boost, and was followed a year later by what he described as a "graver labour" – a longer tragic poem on the story of Lucrece, the celebrated Roman wife who is raped by a Roman prince, then commits suicide. *The Rape of Lucrece* was again dedicated to Wriothesley, but seemingly did less well in the shops.

Yet if Shakespeare had any intentions of making a career as a poet, they seem not to have lasted. In addition to the publication of *Lucrece*, 1594 brought events that would change the whole of his writing life. After plague had died down that autumn and the theatres reopened, Lord Hunsdon, Elizabeth's Lord Chamberlain, arranged for his troupe to be reformed as the **Chamberlain's Men**. Listed as among its members are Shakespeare, the great clown (and successor to Tarlton) **William Kempe** and **Richard Burbage**, who would become the company's star and take the lead in many of Shakespeare's subsequent plays. Also in the group were **George Bryan**, **John Heminges**, **Augustine Philips**, **Thomas Pope** and **William Sly**, all actor-sharers who had a stake in the company and supported it financially (see p.570). Other actors, notably **John Sincler**, were involved on a more informal basis.

The new Chamberlain's Men first played for the impresario and theatre-owner **Philip Henslowe** in June 1594, and then at court during the Christmas festivities, and seem to have been almost immediately successful despite the challenge offered by another company formed at the same time, the **Admiral's Men**. This was led by **Edward Alleyn**, famous for his leading roles in Marlowe's great tragedies *Tamburlaine* (1587), *Doctor Faustus* (c. 1588), *The Jew of Malta* (c. 1590) and *Edward II* (c. 1592). Between them the Lord Chamberlain's and Admiral's Men, based respectively at the Shoreditch **Theatre** and the Bankside **Rose**, were given a near duopoly over performances in London.

Now that Shakespeare's new company had a permanent home, it could get on with the serious business of theatre. Shakespeare's decision to join will have been a boost, for he seems to have brought his existing play-texts to the group, forming a core repertoire which expanded by two plays a year, on average, for the rest of his working life. This unusually stable arrangement – Shakespeare was his company's "ordinary poet", its playwright-in-residence – ensured a steady source of income for both writer and company, and gave Shakespeare the creative challenge of writing for an intimate and tight-knit company of fellow actors.

Lyrical love [1594–99]

Richard III, the sequel to the *Henry VI* trilogy, may have been performed as early as 1592–93, yet became wildly successful in London after the plague reopenings, reaching print in a text of 1597. The first years of Shakespeare's involvement with the Chamberlain's Men are often known as his "**lyrical period**", and represent the first flowering of his mature talent. Four works (***Love's Labour's Lost***, ***Romeo and Juliet***, ***A Midsummer Night's Dream*** and ***Richard II***) are usually assigned to this period, and their rich variety – two comedies, a love tragedy and a rhetorically sophisticated history – demonstrates that the playwright was expanding the bounds of theatre more fully than anyone of his generation. That at least was the view of **Francis Meres**, a schoolmaster and writer born a year after Shakespeare and the poet's first eulogist. Meres's

Palladis Tamadia (1598) includes a head-by-head comparison of celebrated Latin, Roman and Italian authors with their English equivalents, among which Shakespeare is hailed as the "best" for comedy (with *The Two Gentlemen of Verona*, *The Comedy of Errors*, *Love's Labour's Lost*, *Love's Labour's Won*, *The Merchant of Venice*) as well as tragedy (*Richard II*, *Richard III*, *Henry IV*, *King John*, *Titus Andronicus* and *Romeo and Juliet*). He also garners praise for being a "mellifluous and honey-tongued" poet, the author of numerous "sugared Sonnets" – seemingly the first mention of the works that would be printed as *Shakespeare's Sonnets* eleven years later.

Meres's list, invaluable to theatre historians, includes several plays Shakespeare wrote after he had finished the lyrical comedies – **King John** and **The Merchant of Venice** seemed to have followed very rapidly – but also a ghost, the mysterious **Love's Labour's Won**. Satisfactory identification has so far eluded critics, but this may well refer to a lost work, possibly one of several that have failed to survive (see p.242). But the greatest theatrical hit of 1598 was another history play, **Henry IV**, which traces the story of Richard II's deposer Henry Bolingbroke. It was soon followed by a pair of sequels, **Henry IV Part II** and **Henry V**, to form the second of Shakespeare's historical tetralogies (often known, half-seriously, as his "Henriad"). *Henry IV* also provided what may have been the playwright's first brush with trouble: the runaway popularity of its dissolute antihero, Sir John Oldcastle, aroused the ire of the powerful descendants of a Protestant martyr of the same name, and Shakespeare was forced to rechristen him "Falstaff" and insert a public retraction (see p.118). Falstaff's fame was such that he seems to have spawned a suburban comedy, **The Merry Wives of Windsor**, though sections of this play were possibly performed for **Elizabeth I** as early as April 1597 (one dubious story holds that they were commanded by her). *Henry V*'s connection with Elizabeth is far more solid and makes it much easier to date, in fact the easiest of all Shakespeare's plays – its description of "the General of our Gracious Empress", referring to the Earl of Essex, makes it almost certain to have been written while Essex was campaigning in Ireland, from March to September 1599, and before he returned in disgrace.

Around the Globe [1599–1602]

In the midst of a great run of triumphant productions, calamity struck the Chamberlain's Men. The lease to the Shoreditch Theatre had been due to expire in 1597, but when James Burbage (who had built the playhouse in the first place), his actor son and colleagues attempted to renew it, **Giles Allen**, the landlord, proved intractable – first insisting on nearly doubling the rent, then pulling out of negotiations the following year. After performing sporadically at the nearby **Curtain**, the players were on the verge of securing a fresh deal when Allen abruptly decided to repossess his land and demolish the Theatre. With the play-hating authorities hardly likely to give them support, the Chamberlain's Men decided on a novel solution – to engage the carpenter **Peter Street** and have him supervise the dismantling of the building and its transportation elsewhere. This was accomplished overnight in December 1598, with at least some of the timbers being moved to a new site across the river and rebuilt "in a new form" as the largest amphitheatre London had yet seen:

As well as being one of Europe's most populous cities, London also became renowned for its entertainment districts during Shakespeare's lifetime. Bankside, depicted in this detail from Visscher's massive panorama (c. 1625), tempted punters with bear-baiting, brothels and – of course – theatres.

the **Globe**. Though all this was legal – the wily James Burbage had insisted on a clause allowing it in the original contract – Allen was furious and three years later was still doing his best to sue (to no avail).

The sizeable cost of doing all this was met by a **syndicate** of various partners, among them original members of the Chamberlain's Men including Shakespeare, but also Richard and his brother Cuthbert Burbage. Shakespeare's shareholding began as a tenth and fluctuated as new partners entered and old ones left, yet testifies to his growing wealth and continued financial investment in the company. His artistic investment continued, too, though on Bankside the playwright turned his back on the English histories that had prospered at the Shoreditch Theatre and headed back to Italian comedy and Roman tragedy.

Much Ado About Nothing perhaps premiered in 1599, and *Julius Caesar* was seen by a Swiss tourist visiting the new Globe that same autumn. No such testimony describes early performances of the comedy *As You Like It*, which probably dates from that year or the next, but one theatrical tradition holds that Shakespeare himself took the role of Old Adam. Noting the small size of the part, some have assumed that the playwright was no great talent as an actor – a story apparently confirmed by his other starring role as the Ghost in *Hamlet*, a part he could well have performed silently with another actor's voice supplied from under the stage. (These stories may be unfair: Ben Jonson listed Shakespeare at the top of the list of "principal comedians" in his 1616 *Works*.)

Hamlet itself, Shakespeare's most adventurous work to date and for some audiences his finest of all, seems to have been written on the cusp of the new century; one version was onstage in London by 1600, though the revised script may not have appeared until the following year, and also seems to have been performed in Oxford and Cambridge among other places, indicating that some members of the Lord's Chamberlain's Men continued to tour when they found the opportunity (if Shakespeare joined them in Oxford he will have only been half a day's ride away from Stratford). *Twelfth Night*, which dates from around 1601, was also successful away from the Globe, being performed at the law college of Middle Temple in February 1602.

New places [1602–04]

And even at the apex of his London career, Shakespeare did not turn away from his family and Warwickshire. The years had witnessed changes there, too, notably the funeral of his only son Hamnet in August 1596 – an event that Shakespeare presumably attended, though no records survive. By this stage William's success seems to have had material benefits for the Shakespeare clan. John Shakespeare's application for a **coat of arms** was renewed later that year, probably at his son's behest, and was successful (in that respect at least John must have been content when he died five years later). In May 1597 William took an even larger social and financial step, buying one of Stratford's grandest premises, **New Place**. Though it has long since been demolished, this was a capacious five-gabled house of three storeys with at least ten rooms, reputedly the town's second-largest structure, and testifies to Shakespeare's eagerness to make an impact in his home town as well as in London (though it's possible at least some of the money came from John, whose finances had improved). New Place had gardens covering three-quarters of an acre with several outbuildings, and legend has it that Shakespeare himself planted a **mulberry tree** there. (The tree survived until 1758, when it was cut down by eager relic-hunters.)

It is not certain how often Shakespeare returned to Stratford to enjoy his new property, but it is usually thought that he made the journey at least once a year, perhaps more often if his schedule allowed. Back in London, unpaid tax records – not uncommon – reveal that he had been living in the upmarket area of **Bishopsgate** (the Shoreditch Theatre was just up the road), but he seems to have relocated to **Southwark** when the Chamberlain's Men moved south of the river in 1599. He moved back over the river a few years later, this time to the middle-class area of **Cripplegate** in the northwest corner of the city, lodging with the French Huguenot wig-maker **Christopher Mountjoy** and his wife **Mary**. Though undoubtedly wealthy enough to buy a London house, Shakespeare preferred to rent; Stratford, perhaps, was still his home. Subsequent references to property in the sources generally relate to investments – two Stratford land purchases in 1602, an outlay for Stratford tithes in 1605, the acquisition of a house in Blackfriars in 1614 – and point to the fact that Shakespeare's assets, and his willingness to invest, were steadily growing. He was also careful to hang on to what he had accumulated: when a Stratford neighbour, **Philip Rogers**, defaulted on a payment he owed the playwright in 1604, Shakespeare promptly sued. While Ben Jonson's recollection of his rival, recorded long after Shakespeare's death, as "honest, and of an open and free nature" may be accurate, it is clear that Shakespeare was not prepared to be taken for a ride financially.

Work continued, of course, with *Troilus and Cressida* (c.1601–02) and *All's Well That Ends Well* (1604–05), often grouped together as "**problem**" **plays** because of their uncertain and frequently bitter tone. The country's political mood was jittery around this time, too: the childless Queen was 69 and had yet to announce who would take the throne in her place. When Elizabeth became ill in late 1602, many sensed that it was the end, and just a few months after seeing the Chamberlain's Men act for the last time, commanding a full round of performances that winter, Elizabeth died on 24 March, 1603. Having waited until the last possible moment, the Queen had finally agreed that **James VI of Scotland** would be her successor, and he began the journey to London from Edinburgh soon afterwards.

Royal Shakespeare [1604–07]

The transition to a new regime must have been nerve-racking – Shakespeare and his colleagues had good cause to fear that James would be less sympathetic to theatre than his predecessor, or would favour one of their rivals. But news came quickly, and was good: James I, as he was crowned, munificently decreed that he would take the old chamberlain's company under his wing and rename them the **King's Men**. Whether *Measure for Measure*, performed for James at court in December 1604, was Shakespeare's way of repaying the compliment is a point as open to debate as the play itself (it does engage with the King's interest in justice and mercy), but in any case the company was now recognized as the country's finest, being guaranteed per-formances at court as well as at the Globe. Unfortunately, another outburst of **plague** closed the theatres once again soon afterwards and delayed the royal festivities, but the King's Men were there to parade in the postponed coronation procession in March 1604.

They also set about playing in earnest for their new patron. The court records indicate no fewer than eleven performances during the winter season of 1604–05, including seven plays by Shakespeare. Among them were old standards like *The Comedy of Errors*, *Love's Labour's Lost*, *Henry V* and *The Merry Wives of Windsor*, but the author had also penned a new tragedy, **Othello**, which was acted at Whitehall in November 1604. Another new play, **Macbeth**, seems to have been written around this time with the Scottish king expressly in mind (it unites the story of Banquo – believed to be an ancestor of the Stuarts – and James's interest in witchcraft), and was also performed at the Globe.

Revivals of Shakespeare's earlier work might have given him more time to spend on writing new material, so perhaps this explains why his great series of tragedies, beginning with *Othello* and *Macbeth* and continuing with **King Lear** (c. 1605) and **Antony and Cleopatra** (c.1606–07), appeared during this period. As well as featuring older parts for Shakespeare's familiar collaborator, Richard Burbage, all four contain a starring role, perhaps for the same leading boy actor. Despite the fact that he may have created the roles of Desdemona, Lady Macbeth, Cordelia and – most impressively – Cleopatra, we do not know his name.

Though Shakespeare felt freer to write what he wanted – an unbroken run of non-comic work might have been commercially risky earlier in his career – it appears that his work rate slowed slightly during this period. The bitterly pessimistic *Timon of Athens* is another product of this time, perhaps co-written with Thomas Middleton, sixteen years Shakespeare's junior. It's possible that the kind of plays he was writing took more time (*Lear* seems to have been revised soon afterwards, perhaps because the playwright was unhappy with it), but it is also conceivable that the 41-year-old was feeling his age.

Going private [1608–09]

Professionally, however, circumstances continued to improve. While Ben Jonson had managed to secure himself the lucrative position of chief poet and masque-deviser to King James, Shakespeare's company also found themselves gifted with an opportunity to go upmarket, albeit on a less extravagant scale. Years earlier, while the lease of the Shoreditch Theatre hung in the balance, James Burbage had bought a new property in **Blackfriars**, a well-to-do district on the north side of the Thames, just down from St Paul's. Intending to convert part of the former Dominican monastery there into an indoor playhouse, Burbage began work but was halted by a petition from local residents angered by the prospect of a common theatre in their midst. When Burbage died soon afterwards, the Chamberlain's Men opted for relocation instead, and the Blackfriars theatre was leased to a company of boy players run by **Henry Evans**.

But while the boys may have been upmarket enough for the good folk of Blackfriars, they specialized in satirical work and frequently aroused the indignation of powerful figures at court. When in 1608 Evans's company produced **George Chapman**'s incendiary *Conspiracy and Tragedy of Charles, Duke of Byron*, King James stepped in to disband them. As the Bankside playhouses were then closed due to plague, Richard Burbage swiftly moved to complete what his father had begun and set up another syndicate in order to regain control of the **Blackfriars playhouse**, clearly hoping that his position as a King's servant would overcome any objections. It did. The indoor theatre became the main winter home of King's Men's – catering for more select audiences than the great Elizabethan amphitheatres – though the company did by no means retire from large-scale public drama, keeping on the Bankside Globe for summer seasons until significantly later in the century.

Performances began at the Blackfriars in winter 1609, as soon as the plague (which had surfaced once again) abated, but as in the early 1590s Shakespeare had not been standing idle while his theatres were unavailable. Earlier that year a slender quarto entitled **Shakespeare's Sonnets** had emerged from the press of **Thomas Thorpe**, containing a sequence of 154 sonnets capped by a longish poem, the "Complaint" of a nameless "Lover" about her seduction and abandonment by a handsome young man. A similar youth stalks the pages of the first group of Sonnets, the object of the poet's adoration and frustration, but a second internal sequence is addressed to a mysterious dark-eyed woman who has apparently been unfaithful to the poet. This enigmatic set of characters, along with the sometimes haphazard printing, has led many to believe that Shakespeare was not involved in publication, and that these were private poems never intended to see print. Though not many credit that theory nowadays, debate still rages as to the identity of the various parties, particularly the "lovely boy" praised by the poet and (perhaps) addressed in a riddling dedication to "ᴍʳ. ᴡ. ʜ.", signed not by Shakespeare himself but by the printer. Could "W. H." be **William Herbert**, Earl of Pembroke and co-dedicatee of the 1623 First Folio? Or (with the initials reversed) Shakespeare's former patron Henry Wriothesley? Or even anyone at all? (See p.543 for more.)

Look here upon this picture

The most familiar image of the playwright is just that, a portrait that commemorates his work in the theatre. This is the so-called **Droeshout engraving**, done by a young artist of Flemish descent named Martin Droeshout and placed conspicuously on the title-page of the monumental *Mr William Shakespeare's Comedies, Histories, & Tragedies*, the First Folio of 1623 (see p.577). As with all copperplate engravings, Droeshout's technique will have been simple: he inscribed lines into a sheet of copper with a metal stylus, the plate then being covered with ink and pressed onto dampened paper. The artist probably didn't work from life: Droeshout was just 15 when his subject died, and even in 1623 the engraving, perhaps copied from a long-lost miniature of the playwright, must have been an early commission. That fact is sometimes taken to excuse some of its apparent failings: Shakespeare's forehead (memorably described by one commentator as "that horrible hydrocephalus development") is awkwardly modelled, the head itself sits precariously on an enormous ruff, while the body seems far too small. Generally, too, the Droeshout portrait looks stiff and uncomfortable; this is a middle-aged Shakespeare in his Sunday best. Late printings of the Folio are even more unflattering to their subject: as the plate wore down it gave the poet a coating of stubble and a blotchy complexion to boot.

Even so, the Droeshout engraving was accepted by Shakespeare's theatrical colleagues and cannot have been that far from the real thing. More authenticated still is the **Janssen bust**, part of the funeral monument to Shakespeare in Stratford parish church. This time the artist, Geerhardt Janssen, was Dutch, though he was based around the corner from the Globe in Southwark. Despite the likelihood that Janssen knew Shakespeare personally – and that the monument was approved by the playwright's relatives – the bust has come in for even more flak than the Droeshout engraving: it's been slated as "incompetent", portraying a man who looks like "a self-satisfied pork butcher" (in the words of one critic) and who might have already been a corpse when Janssen did his preliminary sketches.

The problem with both Droeshout and Janssen for most bardolaters is that they aren't nearly romantic enough – they don't depict a man who looks like he wrestled with *Hamlet*, still less poached deer or had a covert affair with a dark-eyed lady. These legends, which gathered impetus during the eighteenth and nineteenth centuries, fed the need to find a likeness communicating more of Shakespeare's spirit. Newly popular in this period was the **Chandos portrait** (c.1610), an oil on wood painting that may have been painted in the flesh, and which has the advantage of capturing a more rakish poet, complete with ear-ring and open collar. Though its authenticity and authorship have been much debated, Chandos was endlessly copied in the nineteenth century and remains a popular alternative, particularly for publishers eager

Romantic tales [1609–13]

Shakespeare, however, did not renounce the stage (as the disillusioned Jonson would eventually do). In fact the Blackfriars inspired a run of new work, much of it in a different key. **Coriolanus** (c.1608–09) is in some ways a transitory play: composed at around the same time as *Antony and Cleopatra* (and having a common source in Plutarch's *Lives*), it is far less expansive in scope, focusing on one man and his fiery path to self-destruction. It was followed by the late tragicomedies, now often referred to as the **romances** because of their thematic connections (see p.355). These plays are notable for their use of music and elaborate special effects, and are written on a more

"Supposedly we are to conceive of the poet as declaiming verses he has just composed," wrote one critic of Shakespeare's funeral monument, "but he appears for all the world to be struggling with indigestion." Even so, Janssen's bust is probably the most reliable representation we have.

to illustrate a fashionably unconformist Shakespeare.

Other portraits – and there are many – range from the mildly spurious to the gloriously unlikely. Many are copies, some are copies of copies, legacies of the burgeoning trade in Shakespeare's image. Into this category come the **Flower**, **Ely Palace** and **Ashbourne** portraits, touted as long-lost originals but all in fact derivatives of Droeshout. Easily the most artistically accomplished candidate is a gorgeous miniature of an unknown young man by **Nicholas Hilliard**. The connection with Shakespeare requires a lot of ingenious footwork – the scholar who suggested it, Leslie Hotson, devoted the whole of a somewhat bizarre book to it – and the obvious expense of the young man's garments (let alone the cost of employing Hilliard) pushes it further into the realms of implausibility. At this youthful age Shakespeare had a wife and children to worry about, and quite probably a very unstable income.

Somewhat more plausible, but not much more, is the **Sanders portrait**, discovered in 1908, rediscovered in 2001 and subject to a barrage of publicity. As a book on the subject, *Shakespeare's Face* (2003), argues at length, there is much to like about this portrait: its shyly smiling sitter has auburn hair, as Shakespeare is thought to have done (one minus point for Chandos, which has black), and does somewhat resemble the older man captured by Droeshout. Perhaps the best thing about Sanders is that it offers access to a Shakespeare well before the genteel and well-heeled retirement – a Shakespeare who looks like he is in the middle of work, perhaps eager to get back to it. Whether it *is* Shakespeare (the date of 1603, when Shakespeare was 39, counts against what appears to be a much younger man) remains pretty doubtful, however. Whether we like them or not, the handiwork of Droeshout and Janssen will be with us for a while yet.

intimate scale than earlier works, indicating that they were almost certainly composed with the small, candlelit Blackfriars theatre in mind. Even so, they were transportable: several were also performed at the Globe and for command performances inside the Banqueting House at Whitehall. In 1613 the King's Men were employed to help celebrate the **wedding** of James's daughter and offered no fewer than fourteen plays for watching courtiers, including *The Tempest* and *The Winter's Tale*.

The first play of Shakespeare's final phase was most likely *Pericles* (c. 1607), the most romance-like work of all with its tale of a wandering hero separated from and eventually reunited with his wife and daughter. Not included in the 1623 First Folio, *Pericles* is something of a mystery to scholars: perhaps written in collaboration with the minor writer **George Wilkins**, its text seems to be damaged or somehow incomplete. Few such puzzles surround *The Winter's Tale* (c.1610), though again its plot – climaxing in a theatrically astonishing recognition scene – challenges its audiences' capacity for wonder, and perhaps their credulity. More esoteric in terms of narrative is *Cymbeline* (c.1610), set in the distant British past and with a famously impressive conclusion in which apparent tragedy is repeatedly transformed into resolution. The most famous romance is undeniably *The Tempest* (c. 1610), quite possibly Shakespeare's final solo work and the one in which he is traditionally assumed to bid a graceful farewell to the stage, just as the magician Prospero swears to give up his "so potent art" at the drama's end.

Unfortunately for that theory, Shakespeare's art did not judder to a halt with *The Tempest*'s completion. He was to write two, perhaps three, more plays before retirement, but, now in his late forties, would not do so alone. His co-author was **John Fletcher** (1579–1625), an up-and-coming dramatist then being groomed to take over. It's not known whether the decision to work together was part of the handover process or emerged because Shakespeare was attempting to lighten his workload, but at any rate the first of their collaborations seems to have been the enigmatic *Cardenio* (?1612), a play based on Cervantes' *Don Quixote* that left only scattered traces in the records and has long since vanished (see p.242).

The second, *Henry VIII* (also known as *All Is True*), made a greater impression in every way – it was the cause of a **fire** which burnt down the Globe in June 1613. The blaze began when a piece of burning material from a stage cannon ignited the theatre's thatch roof, and although no one is known to have died, nothing was left of the building's fabric and the King's Men's investment. By the end of that year Shakespeare and Fletcher seem to have completed their final collaboration, *The Two Noble Kinsmen*, and as a consequence of the fire it probably opened at the Blackfriars. *Kinsmen* almost certainly contains Shakespeare's last writing for the stage, and it is tempting to feel that at least some of the tragicomedy's melancholy tone – a world away from the multiple miracles of the earlier romances – is the work of a man who felt death close at hand.

Back home [1614–15]

In April 1614 Shakespeare turned 50. His last few years in London had been difficult. The death of his brother Richard in February 1613 was the latest in a litany of funerals: Edmund (who became a player like his brother, but found little success) died at the age

MR. WILLIAM
SHAKESPEARES
COMEDIES,
HISTORIES, &
TRAGEDIES.

Published according to the True Originall Copies.

Martin Droeshout sculpsit London.

LONDON
Printed by Isaac Iaggard, and Ed. Blount. 1623.

"Published according to the True Originall Copies", Heminges and Condell's First Folio (1623), graced by Droeshout's engraving, rescued the scripts of eighteen plays from almost certain oblivion; pristine examples now fetch anything up to $4 million at auction.

of just 27 in 1607, Mary followed in 1608, Gilbert in 1612. In just six years William and Joan had lost their mother and three of their younger siblings. The Globe fire might well have been the end for the playwright. Though his colleagues swiftly regrouped – they built a **second Globe**, this time with a tile roof, which opened within a few years – Shakespeare took no part in the venture and appears to have sold his shares soon afterwards. He returned one last time to Stratford.

Though it took place a few years earlier, one of Shakespeare's final recorded engagements in London was to testify in court during the 1612 **Belott v. Mountjoy suit** involving his old landlord, Christopher Mountjoy, and Mountjoy's former apprentice Stephen Belott. The case was fractious: after marrying Mountjoy's daughter Mary, Belott had set up a rival business and Mountjoy had failed to provide the agreed dowry, upon which Belott sued. Shakespeare, as the man who had arranged the marriage and acted as a go-between, was a crucial witness. But in the event his memory appears to have failed him: he could not tell the court what had been originally agreed and the case ended inconclusively.

Back in Stratford, scandal would attach itself to Shakespeare's own family a few years later. In 1607 his eldest daughter Susanna had married the respectable and pious physician **John Hall** (Hall's medical practice would later become known throughout the Midlands), but six years later she was publicly accused by one John Lane of having cheated on Hall – and of having caught gonorrhoea as a result. There seem to have been no grounds to the charges: Susanna immediately sued for slander, Lane failed to turn up in court, and the case was closed. Hall stood by his wife.

Susanna's sister Judith was less fortunate, particularly in her marriage. At what was then the advanced age of 31 she wed a wine merchant named **Thomas Quiney** in February 1616, but the match was deemed illegal because it had taken place during Lent and the couple had failed to acquire a special licence (unlike Judith's father all those years before). The offence was not serious, but Quiney was nevertheless excommunicated for failing to attend the hearing. He was far more unreliable in other ways, too: seven or eight months earlier he had managed to get another woman pregnant, and both mother and infant died in childbirth just a month after Judith and Thomas wed. Thomas was once more called upon to attend a church court, this time to admit charges of fornication. In the event he got off with a fine, but in a close-knit community such as Stratford the scandal will surely have blighted his and Judith's nuptials.

Wills and monuments [1616]

Some have suggested that the shock of all this hastened their father's end. In March 1616 Shakespeare had just weeks to live, and may already have been ailing. Earlier that winter he had set about preparing a **will**: unlike his involvement with the Mountjoy suit, Shakespeare would not be forgetful of his own financial affairs. Though much of the will, which organizes the sharing-out of his considerable estate, is conventional enough, there are some enlivening details. Shakespeare clearly had second thoughts about what to leave Judith, and was careful to ensure that Quiney would not defraud her. More celebrated – in fact notorious – is Shakespeare's treatment of his wife, which if not actively shabby is certainly equivocal. He does not mention Anne by name, and famously bequeaths her his "**second-best bed**", a gift which most biographers have assumed to be insulting. This might not be so: some believe that this was the marriage bed, the best being kept for guests, but in reality – as so often with his plays – there is no way of knowing what Shakespeare intended. Though no other specific bequests to Anne are made, it is fairly safe to assume that she would be provided for, presumably by Susanna and Dr Hall, who were left New Place.

Shakespeare signed each page of the will and stated (in a formulaic legal phrase) that it had been drawn up "in perfect health and memory", but on the final sheet his signature begins to break down: he was not a well man. He lingered for a few more months, but on 23 April, 1616, during an unusually temperate spring, he died. Though there is a seventeenth-century legend that he contracted a "fever" while out drinking with old poet friends Ben Jonson and Michael Drayton, other diseases are more likely to have ended his life. **Typhoid**, virulent in warmer weather, is one possibility, but some have speculated that **syphilis** may have been a root cause. Again there is no evidence, and if Dr Hall treated his father-in-law (as surely he did) there is, unfortunately, no record.

Shakespeare was buried two days later, on 25 April, in the same place (and on nearly the same date) that he had been christened: Holy Trinity Church, Stratford. There is no surviving description of the funeral, but within a few years a sizeable **monument** was commissioned from **Geerhart Janssen**, an Anglo-Flemish sculptor based near the Globe in Southwark: the monument now stands in Stratford parish church (see p.574). Although biographers have questioned the bust's accuracy (it does not look like any other representation), it was presumably paid for and sanctioned by Shakespeare's family, and thus has good grounds to be called authentic. There is no other way of guessing what he looked like: an inscription upon Shakespeare's **gravestone** warns that anyone who "moves my bones" will be "cursed", a warning which to date has – despite a few close calls – been heeded.

But the poet's greatest monument was still to come. In his will Shakespeare bequeathed money to three of his closest theatrical friends, Richard Burbage, John Heminges and Henry Condell, and asked that they "remember" him. Heminges and Condell did so magnificently, collecting together nearly all of their dead colleague's plays and publishing them in impressive form. *Mr. William Shakespeare's Comedies, Histories & Tragedies*, the magisterial **First Folio**, appeared in print in the winter of 1623, just a few months after Anne's death, the most fitting tribute of all to a life devoted to drama.

Reading on

William Shakespeare: A compact documentary life
Samuel Schoenbaum; rev. 1987 > Oxford UP

Distilled from his earlier, sumptuously illustrated *Documentary Life* (1977), this is Schoenbaum's answer to the solid scholarship laid down by E.K. Chambers' fine but now outdated two-volume *William Shakespeare: A study of facts and problems* (1930). Determined to

"chasten speculative elaboration or romantic indulgence", Schoenbaum concentrates solely on what the records tell us about Shakespeare, and if you feel in need of hard facts, this is the place to come. Not that the author is dry: everything is written with the same flair and wry instinct for detail as Schoenbaum's monumental *Shakespeare's Lives* (see p.657). While other biographers can suffocate the reader under a weight of information, Schoenbaum never forgets to tell a story.

Shakespeare: A life
Park Honan; 1998 > Oxford UP

Though it's getting on for two decades old, this remains the most elegant, detailed and reliable life of Shakespeare. Many literary biographers have trouble aligning the life with the work, but Honan puts plenty of emphasis on Shakespeare's experience as a player and offers sophisticated critical judgement on his output. He also has a knack of making familiar details come up freshly scrubbed, suggesting supporting connections not specifically tied to Shakespeare but drawn from the wider social tapestry of his era. In attempting to put flesh on the bones of his hero, Honan undoubtedly engages in what Schoenbaum (see above) would term "speculative elaboration" – and some might find his conclusions too indulgent – but his approach delivers impressive insights nonetheless. Equally fine, and more perceptive than Honan on the works, is René Weis's *Shakespeare Revealed* (2007), published in the US as *Shakespeare Unbound*.

1599
James Shapiro; 2005 > Faber / HarperCollins

Subtitled "a year in the life of William Shakespeare", this engaging eyewitness-style narrative travels from the unlikely transportation across the Thames of the timbers that became the Globe (see p.569) to what Shapiro argues are the playwright's first thoughts on *Hamlet*. It's quite a journey, and the book excels at picking up long-familiar facts and scrubbing them clean – an approach that has much to offer Shakespeare studies, where it sometimes feels as if the life story has long been rinsed for all it's worth. Shapiro's larger argument, that 1599 was Shakespeare's breakthrough year, sometimes feels strained – but this is an illuminating read nonetheless, and wears its learning with disarming lightness. Its successor, *1606: The Year of Lear* (2015), is also highly recommended, arguing perceptively that Shakespeare evolved into a notably different playwright after the accession of James I.

The Lodger
Charles Nicholl; 2007 > Penguin

Already used to sleuthing around Elizabethan London for his excellent book *The Reckoning* (1992), which traced the final hours in Christopher Marlowe's life, Nicholl turns his attention to Marlowe's great contemporary and rival. Although the story of Shakespeare lodging with a Huguenot wig-maker and his wife in London's Bishopsgate is undeniably less thrilling than the tale of Marlowe's gory end, Nicholl nonetheless teases out some intriguing details from the historical case notes, notably the tale of the middle-aged playwright being cast in the unlikely role of go-between between two young lovers. Like James Shapiro's *1599* and *1606* (see above), this is keyhole biography at its best – vivid and evocative.

Shakespeare's Wife
Germaine Greer; 2007 > Bloomsbury

What's in a name? Sometimes a lot. For instance: strange how people always call Ann Shakespeare by her maiden title of Hathaway (usually they spell Ann with an "e", too, but Germaine Greer prefers the plainer version). You don't have to take such an approach to nomenclature as evidence of some vast phallocentric conspiracy, but Greer does have a point – and it is about time that someone paid some attention to the most important woman in Shakespeare's life. Despite some reflex lashing-out at male dons, there is valuable work in this biography, much of it based on unglamorous trawling through local records. The image of Ann that emerges – capable, organized, fiercely independent – feels idealized, to put it mildly, but is nonetheless an indication of what Jacobethan women were expected to live up to. A shame, then, that in praising Mrs Shakespeare Greer can't resist burying her husband: her claims that he was a syphilitic, abusive egomaniac would have anyone alive phoning up their lawyers.

Shakespeare's stages

Shakespeare wrote for the professional stage for twenty-five of the most eventful and exciting years English drama has ever seen. It's easy to forget that when he arrived in London, probably in the late 1580s, secular public theatre was still an astonishingly new medium – audiences nationwide had been living with it less than the time that we in the twenty-first century have had access to the world wide web. Renaissance drama melded together aristocratic entertainments, academic theatre and the carnival of the street; and in the bustling and often cut-throat world of Elizabethan London, popular plays became a remarkably versatile form. Moulded by talents such as John Lyly, Thomas Nashe, Thomas Kyd and Christopher Marlowe, then Shakespeare himself and his younger contemporary Ben Jonson, drama was not merely among the most successful entertainments of its time, but became one of the most revolutionary art forms in early modern Europe.

Miraculous shows

No one is quite certain when Shakespeare first attended theatrical performances, and unlike several of his famous contemporaries – his star actor Richard Burbage being the most obvious example – he was not born into a theatre family. But as a boy growing up in the prosperous and cultivated West Midlands he had plentiful opportunity to see the distinct varieties of theatre that Elizabethan England offered. At one end of the scale were the medieval **mystery** and **miracle plays**, performed at nearby Coventry during the festival of Corpus Christi (which generally falls in May or June) as late as 1579, when Shakespeare was 15 and may just have left Stratford grammar school. These epic religious narratives were usually put on by local craft guilds, who each took responsibility for one or more plays in the sequence – so in the York mystery cycles, for instance, the Shipwrights acted the story of Noah and the Ark, while at Coventry the Shearmen and Taylors took on the Annunciation, the birth of Christ and Herod's Massacre of the Innocents. During their medieval heyday these appeared every few years or so, but by the late 1570s Queen Elizabeth's Protestant authorities were suspicious of pageants preserved from Catholic days and they appear to have been suppressed, or replaced with more religiously appropriate spectacles.

Elizabeth will have been more sympathetic to the spectacular festivities put on in her honour during her 1575 "progress" (one of her numerous summer tours around the nation), during which she visited Warwickshire, Shakespeare's county. For the twelve days during which she stayed with her intimate friend – gossip held him to be more than that – Robert Dudley, Earl of Leicester at **Kenilworth**, the Queen was honoured with numerous pageants and parties, some of which admitted the public.

Dudley's impressive castle was just twelve miles from Stratford, and it seems more than possible that John Shakespeare took along his eldest son to be among the crowds. (*A Midsummer Night's Dream* contains teasing references to events strikingly like those at Kenilworth.)

Less rarefied theatrical occasions might also have been part of Shakespeare's youthful experience. Stratford itself frequently hosted travelling troupes of actors, never more frequently than during 1586–87, when no fewer than five companies performed in the town's Gild Hall as well as other venues. Among them were the state-sponsored **Queen's Men**, then the leading company of the day, who specialized in propagandistic, rambunctious English history plays. It has been suggested that Shakespeare may have joined the company at some point (several of his own plays bear marks of their influence), but no evidence survives. The life of **travelling players** was hard: despite good rewards income was sometimes fitful, towns en route could be less than welcoming, the travelling itself was arduous – a company would need to carry all its props and costumes. On the road tensions within companies sometimes boiled over: soon before the Queen's Men visited Stratford, they lost their star actor, killed in a brawl with a colleague. It was little wonder that many troupes wanted a home in London, the theatrical capital of the nation.

Outside the law

Theatre in London was well established, but so was the troublesome relationship between its practitioners and the rest of society. A government **Act** from 1572 announced that "Common Players in Interludes & Minstrels" who weren't affiliated to a patron (usually a nobleman) would be regarded as "Rogues, Vagabonds and Sturdy Beggars". Elizabeth's ministers were constantly trying to regulate theatre, demanding that companies be properly licensed and even attempting to control what kinds of plays they performed. A royal proclamation of 1559 required that they steer clear of subject matter covering "either matters of religion or of the governance of the estate of the common weal", in effect anything that could be taken as criticism of Elizabeth's reign. The Queen's **Master of the Revels** – her events manager – was given powers in 1581 to license "players of comedies, tragedies, interludes, or what other shows soever", which involved hearing or reading whatever plays were to be performed publicly and, if necessary, censoring them. That **Edmund Tilney** (who stayed in the job from 1579 to 1610, covering nearly all of Shakespeare's career) took these responsibilities seriously is not in doubt: the manuscript of *Sir Thomas More*, in which Shakespeare probably had a hand (see p.190), shows marks of his interventions to tone down the script.

Theatre companies were more carefully regulated than ever before. When Elizabeth's ministers formed the Queen's Men in 1583, cherry-picking the finest actors in London (among them Robert Wilson, John Laneham, Richard Tarlton, John Dutton, John Bentley and John Singer), the intention was to keep a close eye on their activities. As well as giving the company's members the duty of acting at court and the right to tour during the summer months, this move also granted them a near monopoly over performances in London. But this in itself guaranteed nothing: the City authorities took a consistently dim view of playing and players, and were always threatening to

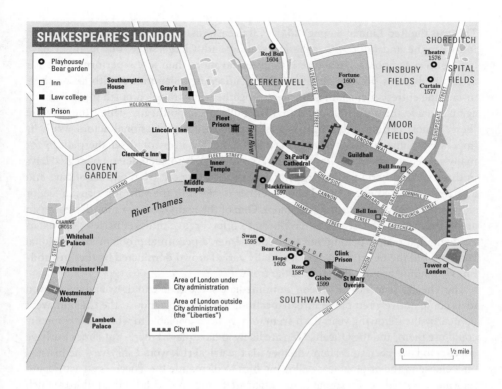

SHAKESPEARE'S LONDON

close them down by whatever means possible. A 1585 declaration announced that entertainments would be "tolerated", but on strict conditions: that they should not play at night, nor on the Sabbath; that the authorities shut theatres if bubonic plague threatened; and that only the Queen's Men were to be licensed. All other companies were effectively forbidden from playing in the City of London.

The first playhouses

So where did the Queen's Men play? **Inns** were most likely the first venues for acting companies, and during the 1580s the troupe is on record as having performed at City pubs the **Bell** and the **Bull**, where makeshift stages will have been constructed for their performances. But the City fathers never approved of this arrangement, and in 1595 succeeded in banning companies from performing at inns altogether. In order to escape restrictive jurisdiction, there was only one option: to make a dash for the suburbs, which meant travelling outside the City's medieval walls. These extended from the Fleet River to the west all the way to Aldgate and the Tower of London on the eastern side; to the north they reached as far as Moorgate and Bishopsgate, with the Thames forming the City's southern border. Outside these boundaries (and in isolated pockets within) the authorities had little power over what went on, and in these so-called "**liberties**" theatres began to spring up.

London's first purpose-built playhouse appeared in 1567 (three years after Shakespeare's birth, but twenty or so before he would make his way to the capital).

This was the **Red Lion** at Stepney to the City's east, financed by a businessman named **John Brayne** and built with galleried seating and a large stage, but it might have been only a temporary structure lasting for no more than a few performances. Far more durable was Brayne's next venture, organized in collaboration with his brother-in-law, the entrepreneur **James Burbage**. Together they travelled north to Shoreditch, again outside the City walls, and in 1576 built an amphitheatre called the **Theatre** there, almost certainly the capital's first playhouse for professional actors. With its impressive name (from the Latin *theatrum*), the Theatre would set the pattern for many subsequent houses – it was "round" (actually polygonal, made up of angled bays in three vertical tiers) with a large internal stage jutting out from one set of bays and an open yard. Audiences could choose either to stand in the yard for a cheap fee, or sit in one of the galleries for rather more. One of the main incentives for designing an amphitheatre like this seems to have been to offer a range of ticket prices – as well as ensuring that people paid before they could enter, a perennial problem in traditional venues – but the net effect was of a socially varied crowd dominated by the "**groundlings**" standing around the stage at the front.

The Theatre seems to have had an immediate success, able to draw audiences even to its comparatively remote suburban location, and a rival playhouse, the **Curtain**, went up nearby the following year. Both seem to have been available to whichever company could use them, and the Queen's Men are likely to have played there. But James Burbage appears to have been uncertain whether his theatrical risk would survive – he insisted on a clause in the original lease allowing him to dismantle the Theatre's structure and relocate it if need be. Presumably he anticipated problems with their landlord (which would indeed surface in 1597; see p.569), or perhaps he foresaw the **plague closures** that dogged the London theatres on and off for the next thirty years. As part of their 1585 settlement the London authorities retained the right to close down public venues in an attempt to restrict contagion – the disease was believed to be spread through human contact – and were particularly harsh on the theatres. As one recent biographer has pointed out, it is a small irony that the hazelnuts munched by many theatregoers (remnants of which have been found by archeologists) may, if anything, have kept away the fleas carrying the bubonic bacillus. Nonetheless those in power were unrelenting, and during closures many companies were forced back on to the road – assuming news of plague did not overtake them – to tour for their survival. Some stayed in England, but a hardy few went overseas, accompanying ambassadors on trips to destinations including the Netherlands and Denmark (a possible source for *Hamlet*; see p.95), or striking out on the trade routes that extended across northern Europe.

On Bankside

By the time that a plague outbreak initiated the first major theatrical shutdowns of Shakespeare's London career, in 1592 and 1593, the Curtain and the Theatre had been joined by other London playhouses. Instead of being located to the north of the city, however, **Bankside** to the south of the Thames had become the area of choice, encouraging Southwark's development into London's premier entertainment quarter. Here punters could be tempted by fishponds and bear-baiting, or prostitution, which

Elizabethan plays often ended with a "jig" performed by the company; at the Globe these were led by the clown William Kempe (right), who after leaving Shakespeare's troupe danced all the way from London to Norwich accompanied by his pipe and tabor player, Thomas Sly.

was rife (none other than the Bishop of Winchester was the area's largest brothel-owner). In 1603 the Privy Council was told that the area was teeming with "thieves, horse-stealers, whoremongers, cozeners, coney-catchers", and indeed most critics of the theatre seem to have regarded playgoing, too, as practically a criminal activity – partly because prostitutes tried to pick up trade outside the doors.

Right next to three of the largest brothels on Bankside, an impresario named **Philip Henslowe** built a playhouse he called the **Rose**, which opened for business in 1587. Although it followed the basic design of the Theatre and Curtain, the Rose seems to have been smaller than either, with a narrow, tapered stage. From archeological evidence we know that it was thatched, and Henslowe steadily built up its capabilities – extending the structure in order to squeeze in more spectators in 1592, and fitting a "throne in the heavens", presumably a device to fly an actor onto the stage, a few years later. That we know so much about the operation of the Rose is due to Henslowe's *Diary* (really an account-book of his expenses and business dealings, logging most of the transactions involving the theatre), and also to the discovery in 1989 of the playhouse's foundations.

Henslowe's theatre became crucial to the story of London theatre in 1594, when the Queen's Men – who had dominated throughout the 1580s – broke up. They had been ailing for years, having struggled to overcome the death of Richard Tarlton in 1588, and several other companies (with actors moving freely between them) had emerged to fill the gap – among them **Lord Strange's Men**, the **Admiral's Men**, the **Earl of**

Pembroke's Men and the **Earl of Sussex's Men**. But with the plague and through sheer competition it had been difficult for any of these to prosper, and after the theatre reopenings in 1594 just two new companies emerged from the wreckage. They were the renovated **Admiral's Men**, and a brand-new troupe called the **Lord Chamberlain's Men**, sponsored by Elizabeth's Chamberlain, Lord Hunsdon (see p.568). Both initially performed at Henslowe's Rose, but as part of the new deal agreed with the court they were given separate venues at different ends of London – the Admiral's staying with Henslowe on Bankside, the Lord Chamberlain's travelling to the Theatre at Shoreditch. Personal connections seem to have played a major role in this agreement: the Admiral's Men were led by **Edward Alleyn**, who had married Henslowe's stepdaughter and was the leading tragedian of his day, known for his "strutting" style, while their rivals were run by a consortium including James's son **Richard Burbage**, the famous clown **William Kempe** and **William Shakespeare** (Shakespeare's first appearance in the records as an actor). Other actors – some records suggest that as many as 200 were cast out of work at this point – took to the road in England and mainland Europe.

In rep

With their new duopoly in place the Chamberlain's and Admiral's Men were stable at last, and London theatregoers were rewarded with near unbroken seasons for the first time ever – during the 1594–95 season the Admiral's Men played for a non-stop 49 weeks, six days a week, breaking only for Lent and some much-needed renovations to the Rose. Both companies adopted a furious pace of repertory theatre, with constant changes in their fare: during that same season alone the Admiral's Men acted 38 plays (nearly Shakespeare's lifelong output), of which 21 were new. Only eight plays would make it through to the next year, and it's reasonable to suppose that the Chamberlain's Men consumed material at a similar rate. Actors would have just a few weeks to rehearse a new piece while still performing older plays in the evenings, so it seems likely that acting styles will have been standardized and formulaic, and also likely that playwrights – Shakespeare included – were put to work polishing old scripts so that the companies could revive them in new productions.

In order to limit piracy as best they could, companies frequently gave their actors not whole texts, but expurgated versions that contained just one part. Companies held copyright (such as it was) over an author's plays, and retained the right to **publish** them as they saw fit – as many did during the plague closures of 1592–93, when doing so created a much-needed stream of income. Playwrights themselves were initially used on a freelance basis, but over time might become contracted as an "**ordinary poet**", a writer-in-residence. These deals typically required the writer to produce a certain number of new works a year, in return for a steady salary as well as a fee each time a play was performed. Shakespeare seems to have begun as a freelance writer for a variety of companies (among them Sussex's and Pembroke's Men), but somehow managed to hang on to his early playscripts, perhaps offering them as collateral when he joined the Chamberlain's Men. After that date he seems to have become the new company's chief writer, producing an average of two plays a year during an exceptionally stable working relationship that lasted until the end of his career.

Team work

Most playwrights were not that lucky – or that consistent. What has come down to us today is undoubtedly the cream of Elizabethan drama, and it's likely that much of what appeared during these furiously busy years was hackwork (the average play took something like four to six weeks to write, usually involving a team of writers, and most new works failed to get a repeat performance). Yet there were many brilliant talents in London, partly an effect of the lack of jobs for grammar-school-educated men like Shakespeare. Probably the most notable writers of the 1570s and 80s were those known as the "**university wits**", a talented and correspondingly loud-mouthed group who are often credited with revolutionizing the early Tudor theatre pioneered by **John Heywood** and **Henry Medwall**, two of the earliest "playwrights" (though the word itself does not appear until the late seventeenth century). Among the wits' number were **Thomas Lodge, Thomas Nashe, George Peele, Robert Greene** and **John Lyly**. As was customary in the competitive (and underpaid) world of Elizabethan theatre, none focused exclusively on writing plays – Lodge, Greene and Nashe penned sensational romances, satires and pamphlets, while Peele was known for his poetry.

But their real superstar was the brilliant **Christopher Marlowe**, whose iconoclastic dramas (and dangerous private life) were the talk of the town when Shakespeare arrived in London. Born in the same year as Shakespeare, Marlowe made his name far more rapidly, writing an unprecedented string of successes – including the two-part *Tamburlaine* (1587–88), *Doctor Faustus* (c. 1588), *The Jew of Malta* (c. 1590) and *Edward II* (c. 1592) – that redefined the rules of English drama. Had he not been killed at the age of 30 in one of the most notorious murders of the Elizabethan period (see p.624), it seems possible that Marlowe would have matured into a greater writer even than Shakespeare himself. Almost as notorious as Marlowe was his former room-mate **Thomas Kyd**, who found himself caught up in the witch-hunt following his companion's death and was arrested soon afterwards. Kyd's most famous hit, *The Spanish Tragedy* (1592), became the must-see play of the early 1590s and launched a vogue for blood-soaked revenge drama that lasted well into the Jacobean period (see p.623).

At least in terms of intrigue, Marlowe's and Kyd's careers make Shakespeare's seem pedestrian by comparison, and his near-contemporary **Ben Jonson** (see p.534) also enjoyed a taste for danger. Jonson once killed a fellow-actor in a duel (he escaped punishment by pleading benefit of clergy) and, never a man to be cowed by authority, was imprisoned no less than twice for his involvement in writing plays that offended those in power, *The Isle of Dogs* (1597) and *Eastward Ho* (1605). Jonson had been forced to patch up his differences with **John Marston** (see p.630) in order to work on the later play, for a few years earlier both had been drawn into the "**Poets' War**", in which Jonson vied for ascendancy with challengers including fellow Londoners Marston and **Thomas Dekker** (see p.629), a writer noted for his romantic comedies. Jonson was initially involved with the Admiral's Men but flitted restlessly around, writing not only for the Chamberlain's but later for the all-boys' company run by Henry Evans that was based at the Blackfriars playhouse on the western tip of the City.

Also writing for the boys' company was **George Chapman**, slightly older than Shakespeare and nowadays better known as a translator of Homer. His translations

Period drama – and the rebirth of the Globe

From the little we know about costuming on the Elizabethan stage, Shakespeare's contemporaries had an eclectic and piecemeal view of history. The "Peacham drawing", supposedly by writer and artist Henry Peacham, appears to illustrate Shakespeare's early Roman tragedy, *Titus Andronicus*. Though Titus himself is shown in a toga in deference to the play's classical setting, the soldiers accompanying him wear Elizabethan armour and carry halberds. As with the play's language (which is defiantly Elizabethan), there is little attempt at consistency of staging, a practice that predominated in theatre until well into the nineteenth century. **David Garrick** performed in modern dress, and though his competitor **Charles Macklin** introduced "Highland" costume in his productions of *Macbeth*, it wasn't until the extravagant productions of **Charles Kean** in the 1830s and later that "historical" staging (whether painstakingly researched Roman for *Julius Caesar* or beautifully constructed Tudor for *Henry VIII*) became the norm.

The notion of returning to "Elizabethan" theatrical practice – dismissed as primitive by succeeding generations – would not properly surface until the entry of the innovative and eccentric actor named **William Poel** (1852–1934). Instead of employing the resources of Victorian theatre to create realistic period settings, Poel instead attempted to guess how Elizabethan companies had acted Shakespeare's plays. Later writing that "realism, so often thought healthy and natural, is with scarcely any exception only perverse sentimentality", he staged a watershed production of the so-called "bad" quarto of *Hamlet* at London's St George's Hall in April 1881. This employed a fit-up Elizabethan stage surrounded by curtains that blocked out the proscenium arch, while his cast wore scrupulously researched Elizabethan costume (his "Ofelia" even played the lute). Poel's passionately held views were controversial: his 1898 *Merchant* upended Victorian fashion by pitching Shylock as a snarling, fright-wigged villain, while an apron stage for his *Two Gentlemen* (1910) covered most of the stalls in an attempt to recreate an authentic space. Following his founding of the **Elizabethan Stage Society** in 1895, Poel directed numerous productions that cast fresh light not only on Shakespeare but

seem to have been read by Shakespeare, particularly during the composition of *Troilus and Cressida*, and there is another connection via the poetic collection *The Passionate Pilgrim*, where some of Chapman's verse appears alongside Shakespeare's (see p.550). Indebted to Shakespeare, by contrast, was the younger writer **Thomas Middleton** (see p.636), who appears to have revised parts of *Macbeth* for performance in the seventeenth century, and perhaps *Measure for Measure* too – testament to the continued taste for Shakespeare's work up to and immediately after his death. That taste was also fed by the work of John Webster (see p.632), whose most famous works, *The Duchess of Malfi* and *The White Devil*, adapt many of the motifs of Shakespearian tragedy to suit Jacobean audiences' curious obsession with Italianate courtly skulduggery. More directly associated with Shakespeare was **John Fletcher** (see p.634), who collaborated on three of his last plays but was also known for his close writing partnership with **Francis Beaumont** (see p.635).

For all these writers and others, conditions were far from perfect: cash was perennially short, work was piecemeal – **plague** or **rioting** could close the theatres at a stroke – and competition between rival companies was intense. London was the country's only real theatrical centre, and the dramatic community was fiercely close-knit (not least because many ostensible respectable citizens regarded players with disdain, for on many of his contemporaries too. Not that audiences always got the point: Max Beerbohm once wrote to an actress friend that "poor William Poel's honoured name is a guarantee of badness".

And although he revolutionized theatrical approaches – partly through disciples like **Harley Granville-Barker** and **Robert Atkins**, who argued for fluid staging and fuller texts – Poel never lived to see a full-scale reconstruction of an Elizabethan playhouse. And while "replica" Globes in various locations across North America sprang up in the 1930s, a major attraction at World's Fairs in Chicago, Cleveland and San Diego, they bore little architectural relation to Shakespeare's own theatre.

But a young actor performing at Cleveland in 1936 with an outfit called the New Globe Players had an idea: why not build a properly researched replica in London, as close to the site of the original Globe as possible? **Sam Wanamaker** became the moving force behind the rebuilding of "Shakespeare's Globe", as it became known. The project took nearly thirty years and was conducted in the teeth of aggrieved opposition from Southwark Council and a hostile press, who didn't take kindly to an American attempt-

ing to erect what they saw as a piece of Disneyfied "Merrie England" on Bankside. Wanamaker succumbed to cancer in 1993, before his new-old theatre could be officially opened, but its remarkable success in the years since, first under Mark Rylance (1995–2005) and then Dominic Dromgoole (2005–2015), stands as testament to his achievement. Despite initial scepticism that it would be little more than a tourist attraction, the Globe now welcomes over 350,000 ticket-buyers annually into its wooden "O" and has been a leading exponent of "original practices" performances.

In 2014 Shakespeare's Globe went one better, and opened a new indoor space it christened the **Sam Wanamaker Playhouse**. Not a reconstruction of the Blackfriars (a replica had already opened at the American Shakespeare Center in Staunton, Virginia, in 2001), the Wanamaker was constructed following detailed designs from later in the seventeenth century by **John Webb**, an assistant of the pioneering neoclassical architect Inigo Jones. A glistening jewel box of oak and gold leaf, candlelit and spine-tinglingly intimate, the Wanamaker is the best guess yet as to what Jacobean indoor theatre might have looked, felt and sounded like.

all that they visited the theatres in massive numbers). As well as drinking and living together, many playwrights collaborated, sometimes penning the odd scene or even just a handful of lines for a collaborative project that might have involved four or five writers. **Thomas Heywood** (see p.626), though now one of the least known of Elizabethan writers, once claimed to have had a hand (or, as he colourfully put it, "at least a main finger") in no fewer than 220 plays. Although few of his colleagues were quite so industrious, the claim is not wild. (For more detailed biographies of Shakespeare's key colleagues and rivals, and tasters of their work, see the chapter devoted to the subject on p.622.)

The great globe itself

The Blackfriars was leased to the boys by none other than the Chamberlain's Men, who had been looking to relocate as early as 1597, when the landlord of the Theatre, **Giles Allen**, began to create difficulties about renewing their lease. Negotiations eventually broke down, but James Burbage's plan to develop a base in the City came off the rails when the wealthy inhabitants of Blackfriars protested about having a theatre in their midst. Burbage died soon afterwards, leaving the Chamberlain's Men with just

The reconstructed Bankside Globe was modelled using contemporary sources and painstakingly rebuilt with "original" materials. Fire regulations limit audiences to 1,500, however, with 700 jostling on foot – half the house Shakespeare might have hoped for.

one other option: to exercise their right to dismantle the Theatre and move it. With the aid of master carpenter **Peter Street**, this they duly did (to Allen's lasting chagrin), and transported some of the timbers of the old building through the City and across the Thames to a new site. They, too, were to have a Southwark playhouse, while the Blackfriars could be rented to Evans's boys.

What resulted was the most famous theatre of the age, enshrined in Prospero's metatheatrical reference to "the great globe itself" and (so a slightly suspect legend has it) with Jaques's "all the world's a stage" as its motto. This was the **Globe**, probably opened during the 1599 season and the theatre for which, despite its ignominious origins, Shakespeare wrote his most famous plays. In reality there was little new about the Globe – unless its timbers were reshaped it will have been structurally similar to the old Theatre – and yet by the time it was built the resources of the Elizabethan playhouse had been honed by long experience and offered sophisticated dramatic possibilities. No expense seems to have been spared on the job of rebuilding (the considerable cost had to be borne by the Chamberlain's Men's "**sharers**", one of whom was Shakespeare; see p.570), and the theatre that emerged was probably larger than anything London had yet seen.

Its **dimensions** have been estimated at around 30 metres (100ft) in diameter at the outside walls, some 9 metres (30ft) larger than the Rose. Inside the walls, the yard must have been around 25 metres (80ft) wide, though some authorities have since scaled down all these estimates. No surviving evidence indicates the proportions of the Globe's stage, but scholars think that it might have been nearly square, perhaps with a width of around 12 metres (40ft). It will have been backed by a flat-faced *frons scenae* (stage wall), which probably had three doors – two smaller ones to the left and right, and a larger one in the centre opening into a **discovery space**. This was a room behind the stage and opening out onto it, suggesting an "interior" area into which a bed or other large prop could be inserted; Shakespeare calls for this kind of resource comparatively rarely, but the moment at which Ferdinand and Miranda are magically "discovered" playing chess near the conclusion of *The Tempest* shows him using it, as may Desdemona's bedroom scene in *Othello*.

Other kinds of transformations offered by the stage include **trapdoors**, one down into the space underneath (colloquially known as the "hell") and perhaps another in the "**heavens**" above, a canopy covering the stage, richly painted (perhaps with the astrological signs of the zodiac) and supported by two huge pillars. The heavens originally protected the cast and their expensive costumes from the rain, but came to offer theatrical possibilities in their own right – one of which was some kind of **winch mechanism** via which personnel could be flown in from above. Players could also appear in the "**aloft**" space directly above the central doors, shallow rooms with open windows looking out over the stage (the balcony scene in *Romeo and Juliet* is Shakespeare's most famous use of this resource) which, later on, might have been adapted and expanded to contain **musicians**. Behind the stage and under the aloft spaces lay the **tiring house**, a room or complex of rooms in which actors could change and put on make-up, and where their costumes and promptbooks were most likely stored.

Props and practice

Elizabethans talked of going to "hear" a play, not to see it, and they were far more used to using their ears – long weekly sermons guaranteed that – than most modern-day audiences. In a theatre so reliant on the transformative power of words, **scenery** at the Globe and other theatres like it was correspondingly sparse, with the possible exception of drapes and hangings. The great pillars of the heavens could be used (hidden behind or clambered up), as could the aloft areas and other spaces, but bulky props were probably avoided, particularly if a company was forced to take a play on the road. One exception would have been a chair of state upon which monarchs would sit, while beds and tents would also have been required. Judging by the inventory in Henslowe's *Diary*, small **props** – letters, books, candles and many more exotic things – seem to have been relatively commonplace. To make up for the lack of scenery, **costuming** at the Globe, as at other Elizabethan theatres, was magnificent – it's even been suggested that a ready source of ecclesiastical garb, repeatedly used in Shakespeare's history plays, would be real church robes flogged off at the Reformation. Much of a company's finance would be sunk into its costumes, though from surviving evidence the Elizabethan approach to representation was eclectic (see p.588).

Theatrical tricks such as blood, much in use during violent revenge plays like *The Spanish Tragedy*, will have probably used bladders filled with real pigs' or sheep's gore. **Swordplay** itself was likely to be impressive, especially because the young, male sections of the audience would have had a near-professional interest in the techniques of fighting, and the players themselves were likely to have plenty of physical skill (they also seem to have **danced** at the conclusion of each performance). **Sound effects** would include "thunder" – achieved, if the preface to Jonson's *Every Man In His Humour* is to be believed, by rolling a cannon ball around a drum or a tin trough – and extended to noises off representing anything from armies massing to the sound of birdsong. **Music** could vary from trumpet flourishes and drum rolls to full-scale incidental compositions (especially after Shakespeare's company moved to the Blackfriars; see p.597). Other "realistic" effects seem to have become more commonplace and refined during Shakespeare's late career: one of *The Tempest*'s first stage directions calls for the entrance of sailors soaked to the skin by the storm, though whether Antigonus's famous exit "pursued by a bear" in *The Winter's Tale* used a real animal from one of the baiting arenas nearby is still hotly debated.

In general plays were acted rapidly and with no breaks between scenes, one group of characters entering as another left. In *Romeo and Juliet*, the Chorus's description of the "two-hours' traffic of our stage" might seem optimistic – the length of Shakespeare's mature plays implies it was nearer three – but all the Globe's performances would have taken place in the afternoons and during **daylight**, night-time scenes being represented by actors dressing appropriately or carrying torches (or indeed discussing the prevailing conditions, as they do at the frosty opening of *Hamlet*). *Hamlet* is something of a mystery, in fact, as in its longest incarnation (see p.93), it would have been near impossible to perform before it became dark on all but a handful of days. This suggests that **cuts** to the script were probably a feature of theatrical life, though presumably the playwright would often have been involved with the process of trimming for performance.

Shakespeare may not have had the same luxury with **casting**, though in all likelihood as a resident poet he would have known exactly who would take the main roles in a new play, and adapted them accordingly – powerful leading parts for a star such as **Richard Burbage** alongside roles for character actors such as the skinny **John Sinklo** and the heavyset **John Lowin**. Comic characters, hugely important in the popular theatre of Shakespeare's day, were crucial, and that Shakespeare seems to have customized his writing for his colleagues is revealed by the quite different parts he wrote for **William Kempe** (big, physical roles such as Dogberry in *Much Ado* and Bottom in *A Midsummer Night's Dream*) and **Robert Armin**, whose more intellectual, quizzical style leaves its imprint on Touchstone in *As You Like It*, Feste in *Twelfth Night* and the Fool in *King Lear*.

The most obvious casting difference between Elizabethan practice and modern theatre was that companies were **all-male**; no women would act on the English public stage until after the Restoration in 1660, although they did so on the continent (see p.471). Boys took many of the female roles (there is some disagreement about what happened with older female characters), joining the companies young and staying with them until their voices broke – an event which often occurred later in the early modern period than it does now, perhaps as late as 16 or 17. Certain plays required

De Witt's drawing of the Swan, copied by a friend, is the only surviving image of an Elizabethan playhouse from an audience perspective – apparently sketched mid-performance, and with the theatre's features helpfully labelled.

Royal Shakespeare

The **Royal Shakespeare Company** can seem like a permanent feature of the British cultural landscape (too much so, say its detractors), but in its present form it's less than a half-century old. It was the brainchild of artistic director **Peter Hall**, who had been involved at Stratford's Shakespeare Memorial Theatre since 1957. Despite the theatre's many successes under its postwar artistic director, **Anthony Quayle**, Hall concluded that management needed a serious overhaul if it were to survive. Inspired by theatres in mainland Europe, particularly Germany, Hall proposed a permanent company of actors tied to three-year contracts, based in Stratford but with a regular London home at the Aldwych. Most impressively, Hall also secured dramatically increased state funding via the postwar Arts Council. In 1961 the RSC was born.

Its first years were every bit as radical and exciting as Hall had planned. In addition to committing his company to performing new work, Hall commissioned directors willing to take the RSC in bold directions.

Peter Brook's austere *King Lear* from 1962 immediately made waves (see p.234), and a year later *The Wars of the Roses*, a co-production of the English histories by Hall and **John Barton**, came close to defining a house style, hard-hitting Brechtian theatre that left Stratford audiences stunned in their seats. Hall's 1965 *Hamlet* (see p.108) located the zeitgeist even more precisely, presenting David Warner's Prince as an undergraduate too cynical about politics to care.

Following Hall's departure in 1968, **Trevor Nunn** steered the company into its next phase, which saw the opening of a studio space called **The Other Place** (originally little more than a shed down the road from the main house) that offered vivid, stripped-down productions under the stewardship of the ground-breaking **Buzz Goodbody**, the first female director ever to work in the company. After Goodbody's untimely suicide in 1975 at the age of just 29, Nunn took over TOP, as it became known, and directed there himself as well as in the main house. When **Terry Hands** became involved in running

Elisabeth Scott's Art Deco Stratford Memorial Theatre opened in 1932, but the "Jam Factory" was never much loved. A brand-new theatre complex boasting a thrust stage reopened inside the shell of the original building in 2010.

things in 1978, the company remained innovative, drawing in new directorial talent and continuing to expand its operations. In 1977 the RSC began touring to Newcastle; in 1982 it moved into a permanent London base at the **Barbican**; and four years later it opened yet another new Stratford theatre, a Jacobean-style playhouse called the **Swan**. But the going was not always smooth. The biggest test came in 2001, when then artistic director **Adrian Noble** announced that he would sever ties to the Barbican and abandon long-term actors' contracts, as well as declaring that the only way to solve long-standing problems with Elisabeth Scott's 1932 Art Deco Shakespeare Memorial Theatre (whose barn-like acoustics and appalling sightlines were criticized from its opening night) was to demolish it entirely. After months of wrangling Noble resigned, leaving the job to insider **Michael Boyd** in 2002, who rebuilt the company and kept the critics at bay. The **Complete Works season** of 2006–07, which showcased international companies alongside home-grown talent, was hailed as a masterstroke, and Boyd's eye for the grand gesture was enshrined in his histories season of 2006–08, in which a company of 34 actors tackled the two tetralogies on a temporary thrust stage, the **Courtyard**, built on The Other Place's foundations.

In November 2010 Boyd and his team delivered a long-awaited vision, a brand-new **Royal Shakespeare Theatre** inside the carcass of the gutted Memorial Theatre. With 1,040 seats and a thrust stage, the new space is essentially a larger version of the much-loved Swan, and has been warmly received – though it has created its own difficulties, the most obvious of which is that it is now a challenge to tour productions designed for the space. Travelling to New York in 2011, the company turned up with its own port-able theatre; and under incoming director Gregory Doran, another insider who took the job in 2012, it has announced a cautious return to the Barbican. Nonetheless the RSC still lacks a permanent London home, and although Doran has delivered his own grand gestures – notably a series of live cinema broadcasts and a project to perform the complete works over a six-year period – it is an open question what the future will hold. Still, the company looks in rude health. The RSC's current annual turnover runs at £60 million-plus, a quarter funded by the tax-payer, and it staged nearly 2,000 perform-ances of 22 productions in 2013–14, with 1.7m tickets sold in Stratford, London and on tour in Britain and North America. From being a modest troupe located in a small market town, it is now – like Shakespeare himself – a leading force in world drama.

plenty of extras, and as well as extensive use of **doubling**, in which actors played two or three separate roles in the course of a drama, there is some evidence that companies simply employed whichever people they could find in non-speaking roles, luring them off the street with the promise of free admission.

Plural playhouses

The Admiral's Men were seemingly irritated by the fact that their chief competitors had moved into the Globe next door, and soon after Burbage and his company arrived on Bankside they upped sticks and moved – to Shoreditch. Edward Alleyn came out of retirement to lead them once more, leasing a plot and employing Peter Street to build a new house called the **Fortune**. Street had been the specialist carpenter who had moved the Globe, so it's not surprising that Alleyn commissioned a theatre very similar to that of their rivals – with the key difference that it was square rather than polygonal. It was slightly smaller, too, but the stage and other fittings were copied from those in the Globe. As a consequence it took Street only six months to get it up and running, and Alleyn's company were performing there by autumn 1600. The Fortune would stay in use past Alleyn's second and final retirement, but in the end he outlived it – the house burnt down in December 1621.

The Admiral's Men's departure did not leave their rivals with a monopoly on Bankside, however. Four years before the Globe appeared there, a goldsmith and minor court official named **Francis Langley** had bought a plot to the west end of Bankside and erected a theatre there that he called the **Swan**. Langley's sole connection with Shakespeare was an attempt to sue him in 1596, and it appears that the Chamberlain's Men never played there. Instead companies including the Earl of Pembroke's Men appeared there – unluckily, as it turned out, because after their performance of Jonson and Nashe's scandalous *Isle of Dogs* in 1597 the theatre was shut down by the authorities. When it reopened, a hoaxer named **Richard Vennar** conned an audience into paying for a non-existent show (one featuring women, no less), and though he managed to flee, the disgruntled punters took out their frustration on the building and destroyed much of its fabric.

The Swan's chief interest for theatre historians is a sketch of the building made soon after it opened by a Dutch scholar named **Johannes de Witt**. The original drawing has since disappeared – a copy by his friend **Arend van Buchell** (see p.593) is all that survives – and, though it is the only contemporaneous illustration of an Elizabethan playhouse's interior, it remains contentious. While the basic details make sense, De Witt depicts a round building (the Globe and others like it were polygonal) and one in which the area under the stage seems open to the audience. There are only two stage doors, not three (no discovery space), and the "aloft" area, if it exists, appears not to be in use. Even more perplexing is De Witt's assertion in his notes that the Swan was built "out of a mass of flint stones", which seems highly unlikely.

Two other later playhouses deserve mention, one in Bankside, the other north of the river, though Shakespeare is not known to have had personal dealings with either. The first was the **Hope**, built by Edward Alleyn and Philip Henslowe near the Swan and replacing the old Paris Garden bear-baiting arena. Similar in design to the Fortune, it was completed in 1614. The other theatre, the **Red Bull**, had been converted from the remnants of a Clerkenwell inn ten years earlier. It lasted until the closure of the theatres in 1642, and even beyond, being employed by **Thomas Killigrew** for performances soon after the Restoration (although Pepys gave the house a damning review and Killigrew's company left for more commodious premises as soon as possible).

The private sector

During their years at the Globe the Chamberlain's Men played at a variety of other venues (among them law inns, as with *Twelfth Night* in 1602) and for other select gatherings. The "old" **Banqueting House** at Whitehall – "old" because after it burnt down in 1619 James I commissioned Inigo Jones to replace it with a sumptuous neoclassical edifice – was a familiar venue for Shakespeare's company, and after James's accession in 1603 they played there more frequently than ever before. Though they had not been allowed in, the **Blackfriars** playhouse, too, had not been gathering dust: Henry Evans's

In 2014 the team running the London Globe followed their predecessors in Shakespeare's company by unveiling an indoor space to match the amphitheatre outside. Candlelit and crafted from original-style materials, the Sam Wanamaker Playhouse is the best guess yet as to what it might have been like to step into a Jacobean private theatre.

children's troupe had been using it for their infamous – and increasingly scandalous – performances of satires. But when the boys acted **George Chapman**'s politically risqué *The Conspiracy and Tragedy of Charles, Duke of Byron* in March 1608, they went too far: James I took offence and shut them down.

The boys' downfall was a unique opportunity for Burbage, Shakespeare and their company. Recently adopted by James as the **King's Men**, they had acquired a powerful patron and at long last taking possession of the Blackfriars seemed possible. They moved in immediately, though because of more plague closures were unable to present their first plays there until the winter of 1609. But when they did, they acquired the holy grail of Jacobethan companies – an indoor winter venue. A Blackfriars address also offered enviable social cachet, and in this smaller, "private" theatre, with space for perhaps only 500 patrons, the company could charge higher ticket prices and attract a more exclusive clientele. Though they came nowhere near to abandoning the Globe, which remained in use during the summer months – indeed, when it burnt down during a performance of *Henry VIII* in 1613 (see p.185), they rebuilt it on a grander scale than before – the King's Men began to move upmarket.

Little evidence survives of the Blackfriars interior, which was converted from part of the old Dominican monastery that gave the site its name, as the complex was demolished in 1655, thirteen years after the theatres had been closed by the Republican government. Nevertheless it's possible to make some educated guesses, not least about

dimensions, which were considerably smaller than in the amphitheatres: around 20 metres (66ft) in length and 14m (46ft) wide, with the theatre itself rectangular rather than polygonal in shape. There will have been a **tiring house**, as before, though the **stage** was probably much smaller than at the Globe, edged with rails and cramped by audiences' boxes on both sides.

These restrictions will have had a huge impact on **staging**, presumably ruling out all but the most small-scale swordfights and shrinking the number of personnel that could appear at any one time. Shakespeare's late plays especially make much of this intimacy – the bedroom scene in *Cymbeline* is a classic example – though they did continue to be performed at the Globe too. *Cymbeline* might also have been the play in which Shakespeare first used one of the most controversial props of his time. This took the form of a table with two head-shaped holes cut in it and it called for two actors: one poked his head out, while the other's body lay on top with his head poking down and out of sight. The effect was of a decapitated body, though how convincing it was we can only guess.

In addition to seats in front of the stage (equivalent to modern-day "stalls") there were perhaps three audience **galleries** at the Blackfriars, though some spectators got intimate with the action by paying a premium to sit on the stage itself – presumably desiring to lord it over their social inferiors as much as watch the play. As in a modern theatre, audiences paid more the closer they sat, and starting prices were in any case up to six times higher than at the Globe. The resources of the stage itself – trap doors, aloft and discovery spaces – would presumably have resembled the open-air theatres, and it is almost certain that flights would have been possible here. **Music** was a notable feature of the Blackfriars: the theatre's instrumentalists were famous, often accompanying theatrical special effects such as the use of the flight machine, and in fact the theatre was refitted to include a purpose-built music space on a balcony above the stage.

The last great innovation was the use of **candlelight**, though many plays continued to be performed in the afternoons to make the most of natural light from the theatre's windows. As the candle wicks had to be trimmed regularly, plays began to have several **intervals** during which the musicians would perform. One upshot was that Shakespeare's late works began to use a five-act structure with breaks in between, his earlier plays being adapted to suit the new arrangements; the late plays in particular make expressive use of the contrast between dark and light.

This brief survey of the theatrical environment in which Shakespeare and his colleagues worked can do little more than outline some facts (and guesses) about the busiest and most exciting period the English stage has probably ever seen. Within three decades of Shakespeare's death, the Jacobethan public theatre would be gone, banned in 1642 by Parliament because it offered "spectacles of pleasure, too commonly expressing lascivious mirth and levity", unfitting for a country then tearing itself apart through war. When drama re-emerged following the Restoration of Charles II, Shakespeare and his contemporaries would have had difficulty recognizing it: women were on the stage, theatrical technology was astounding, courtly fashions held sway. The era of adaptation and innovation was about to commence.

Reading on

Shakespeare's Professional Career
Peter Thomson; 1992 > Canto

Instead of being a conventional biography or standard theatre history, *Shakespeare's Professional Career* takes the insights achieved by people like Andrew Gurr (see below) and puts them into practice. Practicality is in fact very much the focus of Peter Thomson's lively and compact book, which looks at how Shakespeare's job developed and altered over the two and a half decades during which he wrote for the London stage. It provides a vivid sense of the rewards (few) and difficulties (numerous) of a career in the early modern theatrical business – all the way from patrons and printing to plague, punishment and Puritans.

The Globe Restored
C. Walter Hodges; rev. 1968 > Oxford UP [o/p]

The Globe Restored united Walter Hodges's considerable scholarship with his skills as an artist (although many illustrations here are taken from a variety of historical sources too) to provide an enthusiastic introduction to the stages that Shakespeare wrote for – and even if some of his conclusions have been superseded by subsequent research, this book remains a fine survey. Other titles by Hodges are also worth seeking out: *Enter the Whole Army* (1999) brings together a range of his illustrations for the New Cambridge Shakespeare and looks pragmatically at how staging might have operated on a play-by-play basis.

Shakespeare's Globe: A theatrical experiment
Christie Carson & Farah Karim-Cooper (eds); 2008 > Cambridge UP

A sumptuously produced selection of essays from scholars, historians and (perhaps most importantly) practitioners, *Shakespeare's Globe: A theatrical experience* supplies an excellent account of the new Globe on Bankside, published 13 years after it first opened to the public and nearly 40 years after Sam Wanamaker first had the idea of reconstructing Shakespeare's most famous playhouse in London. Many of the contributions here are good, especially on such practical matters as stage make-up and music; especially insightful is a conversation with founding artistic director Mark Rylance on what the space has taught him as an actor.

The Shakespearean Stage: 1574–1642
Andrew Gurr; rev. 2009 > Cambridge UP

Andrew Gurr is the leading authority on the theatre of Shakespeare's time, and *The Shakespearean Stage* has remained the most useful textbook on the subject ever since it appeared in 1970. The book has now been revised no fewer than four times, a fact which is also its key attraction: Gurr is alert to the ephemerality of the Jacobethan theatrical enterprise as well as the ways in which scholarship has evolved in response to new research (such as the chance discovery of the Rose Theatre's foundations in 1989). The same author's *Playgoing in Shakespeare's London* (rev. 1996) is an offshoot from the final chapter of the earlier book, and remains an admirably full survey of social attitudes to playing and playgoing.

Actors and Acting in Shakespeare's Time
John H. Astington; 2010 > Cambridge UP

Subtitled "the art of stage playing", Astington's timely study turns the spotlight on the people very much at the centre of the plays – the actors they were written for. Scholars have only recently begun to understand how intimately Shakespeare worked with colleagues such as Richard Burbage and Robert Armin, tailoring and tuning his works to their particular talents. Spanning the period 1558–1660, Astington's survey covers the period between the birth of Elizabethan theatre and the seismic changes brought about by the Restoration, and includes a great deal, from training and rehearsal to costuming and acting styles. The working life of an actor in – and outside – Renaissance London makes for absorbing reading, and will make you wonder afresh at the creativity (and stamina) of these titans of the stage. It might usefully be combined with David Mann's fascinating *Shakespeare's Women* (2008), which looks in detail at the cross-dressing tradition and how the playwright conceptualized female roles.

Shakespeare's language

Y ou don't have to study Shakespeare's language to understand his plays: in the hands of good actors even the knottiest of lines make fine dramatic sense, and a decent edition of the text will solve problems with reading at a stroke. But Shakespeare's restless experiments with language make reading him uniquely thrilling, and if you're hoping to delve a little deeper into the texture of his writing, it is worth considering what transform-ations are happening beneath the surface. English in the Renaissance period was a language in volcanic flux, and Shakespeare himself did much to deepen and enrich its capabilities, playing familiar usages off against each other as well as adding new words to the dictionary. Similarly, it's worth knowing about the ways in which he and his contemporaries crafted straightforward words into theatrical rhetoric. And while in some aspects Early Modern English is strik-ingly like the English we speak now, in other ways it is immeasurably alien: four centuries is an aeon in the history of language.

On the move

The language spoken by Shakespeare and his contemporaries was a language experiencing dizzying change. When the sixteenth century began, England was still undeniably in the medieval period, and English still a largely medieval tongue – spoken day-to-day, written down as needs must, but regarded with suspicion by the educated elite. **Latin** was taught in schools (as was Greek) and was the default language for scholarly or ecclesiastical communication, while law courts used **French**, as did many wings of government. English, by contrast, was the language of lower-caste society. It was often described as rough or barbaric by contemporaries, attacked for being the mongrel offspring of Anglo-Saxon and Romance roots, and regarded as incapable of attaining the sophistication or polish of foreign languages. In one sense the difference was age-old, simply a distinction between oral and written culture: English was the language of the street, not that of literature.

Of course there were many exceptions to this – not least Chaucer's middle-English poetry, written over a century before (see p.459) – and, as the sixteenth century passed, several interlinked developments kick-started the development of English into a respectable linguistic force. One was the steady rise in **literacy rates**, which created a fresh class of people eager to read and, to a lesser extent, write. Another was the ever-increasing impact of **printing**, which transformed during the period from a coterie activity to a mass-media industry, making texts of many different kinds available to a wide audience more cheaply than ever before. Among the most enthusiastic adherents of printing were Protestant **religious reformers**, who spotted in the new technology a cost-effective way to get their message across. Although the English authorities refused to sanction a translation of the Bible into the vernacular for many years (the first appeared under Henry VIII in 1539), fearing what would happen if common readers got their hands on the word of God, Protestants in exile kept native believers supplied with a steady stream of samizdat Bibles and religious texts, many of them printed abroad. All contributed to the evolution of English.

As this woodcut illustrates, Renaissance printing was an unmechanized, laborious and dirty business. Even so, print shops became the intellectual powerhouses of Europe.

Rapid urbanization and steady **immigration** also played their part, particularly in London, the city in which Shakespeare made his career, where trade sucked in business people and tourists from all over the globe, and where political upheavals in continental Europe brought in waves of refugees. Domestic politics also had an influence: following Henry VIII's break with Rome, England attempted to make its own way as a Protestant country, a policy that encouraged a spirit of home-grown nationalism and ignited widespread interest in what made the country distinctive, most significantly its native history and language. Even so, English did not look inward in this period, in fact quite the opposite: according to one estimate, almost 30,000 words were incorporated into the language between 1500 and the 1650s, most of them from Latin.

We label the language that evolved through and out of all these changes, which occurred over a 200-odd-year period, as **Early Modern English**, thus marking it as the junction between **Old English/Anglo-Saxon** (c.500–1100) and **Medieval English** (c. 1100–1450) on one side, and **Modern English** (c. 1650–present) on the other. That codification is actually quite helpful, because it highlights the fact that Early Modern English is actually far closer to modern-day English than is sometimes realized. Although the language that Chaucer used seems to us about as straightforward as any in the medieval period – partly because the London-based dialect in which he wrote became the basis for modern English – it seems alien to us most obviously in its **lexis** (vocabulary), which features many words no longer in use. In Early Modern

English, by contrast, both **orthography** (spelling) and lexis are much closer to Modern English, such that it is possible to read or listen to entire passages by an Elizabethan or Jacobean writer without being puzzled by any of the words used. Some have become outmoded, or signify concepts that no longer exist, while others have subtly shifted their meanings in ways that can catch us out – but, overall, the language that Shakespeare and his audiences took for granted, perhaps as much as 90 per cent of it, is usually taken for granted by modern speakers of English too.

Up close

There are, of course, specific differences. **Pronouns** were evolving in this period, but the old distinction between the personal pronouns **thou/thee/thine** and **you/yours** was still in play. In Early Modern English, as in modern French (*tu*/*vous*) or German (*du*/*Sie*), the distinction was sometimes to do with number (thou singular, you plural) but also reflected hierarchy. *Thou* was used between friends, or when addressing someone of lower social status (or in an attempt at particular intimacy, as when addressing God). *You*, meanwhile, was used to address a social superior, and members of the upper classes preferred it among themselves. These social niceties would have had solid force in the Jacobethan period, a rigidly stratified society, and audiences would have been alert to the subtle changes in address Shakespeare employed – for instance in *King Lear*, where the King's collapse in status is charted in part by the increasing number of times he is addressed as "thou" rather than something more socially appropriate.

In terms of **grammar**, using *thou* also had an effect on verbs, activating the now-dead inflected ending -*st* ("thou thinkest", "thou wouldst"). Another old inflection, -*th* was sometimes also used in the third person, although not consistently ("he taketh", "she runneth") and increasingly passed out of fashion as the sixteenth century wore on. Even where there are no such grammatical challenges, word order can also be rather archaic, particularly when it unsettles the strong modern bonds between subject, verb and object: Richard II declares "of comfort no man speak" (*Richard II*, 3.2.140) instead of saying "no man speak of comfort", as we would nowadays.

But the greatest hurdle to a present-day reader attempting to read a Jacobethan text in its original, unmodernized form concerns **orthography**, where the spelling of words sometimes bears only the faintest resemblance to current practice. In an era before systematic English dictionaries, there were no hard-and-fast rules, so spelling was primarily a matter of personal preference rather than rigid custom, even when it came to people's names. Indeed, Shakespeare spelt his own surname in at least three different ways, "Shaksper", "Shakspere" and "Shakspeare", all of them utterly valid, while in several documents Christopher Marlowe appears as "Marley".

Spelling also reflected **pronunciation**, which, several centuries before the arrival of mass broadcasting, varied wildly across the many dialects of the British Isles. Many of these different sounds creep into Shakespeare's plays, particularly those featuring characters from countries such as Wales and Scotland or identifiable English regions, whether they are middle-class folk from Berkshire or the inhabitants of London's slums. Shakespeare's own accent, for all that he lived in the capital for thirty-odd years, must have retained strong touches of his Warwickshire upbringing, though working out what he might have sounded like is made almost impossible by the paucity of documents featuring his preferred spellings. In any case he and his contemporaries were in the midst of what linguists call the **Great Vowel Shift**, a subtle change in the pronunciation of long English vowels that took place from the late medieval period onwards, and which marked the evolution of the language to its modern form (some of the changes have been fossilized in the different pronunciations of words such as "crime" and "criminal" or "grateful" and "gratitude").

The modern eye notices other peculiar features on the Early Modern English page. While many **contractions** or abbreviations appear familiar, others seem strange: the commonest are *on't* for "on it", *is't* for "is it", *e'er* for "ever", *ne'er* for "never", *o'er* for "over" and *a* for "he". **Apostrophes** are rarely used, either for possessives (it was normal to write "Richards" rather than "Richard's") or to mark elision ("wont" rather than "won't"). Other letters have different functions altogether. The distinction between **u** and **v** had not yet solidified, although some printers attempted to be consistent by using *v* at the start of words ("vnlesse", "vpon") and *u* in the middle ("loue", "aliue"). The letters **i** and **j** were also often interchangeable, especially in handwritten documents, though printers attempted to regularize things by using *i* as an initial ("iust", "ielly") even if the sound j was represented. Another surprising feature to modern eyes is the **long "s"**, so called because it looks rather like a lower-case *f* on which the horizontal bar is either radically trimmed or missing entirely. It is usually found where the letter *s* began a word ("fince") or when doubled within it ("illneffe"). Many of these features can be seen in this passage from the 1623 First Folio, the very opening of *The Merchant of Venice*:

> *Anthonio.*
>
> N footh I know not why I am fo fad,
> It wearies me : you fay it wearies you ;
> But how I caught it, found it, or came by it,
> What ftuffe 'tis made of, whereof it is borne,
> I am to learne : and fuch a Want-wit fadneffe makes of
>   mee,
> That I haue much ado to know my felfe.

ANTONIO

> In sooth, I know not why I am so sad.
> It wearies me, you say it wearies you,
> But how I caught it, found it, or came by it,
> What stuff 'tis made of, whereof it is born,
> I am to learn;
> And such a want-wit sadness makes of me
> That I have much ado to know myself.

[*THE MERCHANT OF VENICE*, 1.1.1–7]

This speech, although short, is a compendium of common orthographical features: multiple long "s"s, a *u* used in place of *v* in "haue", a standard contraction ('*tis* for "it is") and a number of spellings that look peculiar to modern eyes. There are also small but crucial differences such as the use of capitals, punctuation and lineation, probably at the typesetter's behest rather than the author's. All are cleaned up and regularized by modern editors, but together they help to indicate how much English was changing during the sixteenth and seventeenth centuries, and how much the written language differs from ours.

Rhetoric: figuring it out

Like any newly self-confident language, Early Modern English was also painfully self-conscious, and during the Elizabethan period a small army of linguists and commentators produced various self-help guides aimed at users who wanted to refine their style. Many of these works focused on rhetoric, capaciously defined by one early theoretician as "an art to set forth, by utterance of words, matter at large" – a description that includes almost anything – but more specifically referring to the technical tricks students could employ to refine their spoken or written language. In accordance with the principles of **humanism**, the study of ancient Greek and Roman oratory formed a major part of the school curriculum in Tudor grammar schools (see p.561), and all Elizabethan schoolboys (girls were rarely educated to this level, unless they were lucky enough to be tutored privately) were put through their paces in rhetoric. This would involve examining famous texts from the past, particularly those of celebrated classical orators such as Cicero and Quintilian, then teasing apart the devices and effects employed, each of them painstakingly classified and named, and finally practising those effects to strengthen the pupil's own eloquence and ability to persuade.

Determined to prove that the English language was every bit as polished as its classical forbears, Elizabethan linguists – in some ways the first students of English literature – revived a dizzying array of classical **tropes** and **figures** to describe different rhetorical techniques. Handbooks on the subject covered everything from how to identify particular turns of phrase to sorting through the various ways of constructing a sentence, from suggesting strategies for winning over an audience to employing specific patterns of sounds. Almost all these technical terms have passed out of general use, but it is striking how many of the concepts remain current: what Renaissance theoreticians call *accismus* (from the Greek meaning "coyness") describes the rhetorical device of pretending to refuse something while in fact keenly wanting it, as in the phrase "I couldn't possibly". Likewise what was named *litotes*, the practice of deliberate understatement, often set up by denying the opposite of something you want to emphasize, lives on whenever someone says "no mean feat" or "not bad". Other rhetorical concepts – irony, oxymoron, paradox – have become familiar parts of modern discourse, and it is not just academic linguists who use them to describe the way we speak.

In Shakespeare's case, the detailed drilling in rhetoric he received at school stood him in good stead for a career as a poet and dramatist – a pleasing irony, given that many humanist teachers regarded the stage with horror, hoping that their charges would use their training in the law courts or as clergymen. While the young Shakespeare may have had his first taste of dramatic performances courtesy of travelling players,

KEY SOURCE > The Bible

It is difficult to overstate the importance of the **Bible** to a writer of Shakespeare's generation. The battle to translate it from Latin into English during the Reformation was arguably the single most important publishing event of the sixteenth century, while its morality, stories and language saturated society at every level.

Whatever a person's private religious convictions, Christian faith was a matter of social obligation in this period, upheld by legal requirements enforcing worship in a form laid down by Elizabeth I's Anglican Protestant government. Although it was technically possible to avoid attending church (many Catholics took the risk), doing so attracted unwelcome suspicion and meant paying heavy fines. **Recusants**, as they were known, also faced significant danger if the political situation took a turn for the worse, as they were usually the first to be persecuted in religious clampdowns.

Like anyone growing up in Elizabethan England, Shakespeare will have come into contact with the Bible early on, and it stayed with him throughout his life. Schoolchildren were required to learn the **Psalms** by rote, and everyone who attended church heard large sections from the scriptures on a weekly basis, not only in the official translation known as the **Bishops' Bible** (1568) but also via the **Book of Common Prayer**, the first incarnation of which was compiled in 1549 under Edward VI. Both texts drew on major English translations, notably by the great religious agitators **Miles Coverdale** (1488–1568), **Thomas Cranmer** (1489–1556) and **William Tyndale** (?1492–1536), the clarity and poetic grace of whose words still influence biblical scholarship. It is also clear that Shakespeare followed the reformers' injunction that the Bible should be read as well as listened to. From detailed references in his works, his preferred edition seems to have been the **Geneva Bible**, published in 1560, a translation whose forceful style and Calvinist tone made it popular among lay readers, although he also knew the slightly more straight-laced Bishops' version too.

References to both translations permeate the plays and poems so thoroughly that the two books must be considered Shakespeare's biggest sources, though primarily because they formed part of his imaginative universe rather than being texts he actively consulted. That said, he obviously lingered on the Old Testament books of **Ecclesiasticus** and **Job** (the latter's account of its hero's sufferings so influenced *King Lear* that one critic declared that the play was "a new Book of Job"). His eye was also caught by **St Paul**'s letters in the New Testament, notably those to the Corinthians and the Romans. The **gospel** accounts of Jesus's life, with their obvious dramatic content and scene-setting parables, surface at many points – rarely more so than in *Measure for Measure*, whose title is taken from the **Book of Matthew** and whose ambiguous hero, Duke Vincentio, has a taste for Christ-like intervention. King David, traditionally assumed to be author of the **Psalms**, is often touched on in *Henry V*, particularly with reference to his slaying of Goliath, while *The Tempest* draws on the **Book of Genesis** for its themes of creation and providence – though perhaps not as heavily as some scholars (eager to align Prospero, God and Shakespeare) have suggested. References to other biblical texts occur on almost every page of Shakespeare's works.

Some have suggested that Shakespeare had an even closer involvement with the Bible – that he was a nameless contributor to its most famous incarnation, the so-called **King James version** of 1611, which was compiled by a large committee appointed by James I to provide a newly "authorized" edition of the text. No evidence survives, however, and the connection some have drawn with the 1623 First Folio seems a little far-fetched – testament to the cultural influence of these two magnificent seventeenth-century books, perhaps, rather than because their authors were one and the same.

If you're interested in tracking Shakespeare's use of this most valuable of texts, Hannibal Hamlin's *The Bible in Shakespeare* (2014) is an excellent account.

it is all but certain that his first taste of acting will have happened in the schoolroom, where he was trained in disputation and argument along set themes, all part of the Renaissance educational toolkit.

Appropriately, nearly every rhetorical technique codified by his contemporaries appears somewhere in Shakespeare's output. Among hundreds of effects, he uses *chiasmus*, the balanced repetition of ideas in inverted order (as in Iago's "Who dotes yet doubts, suspects yet fondly loves"), to add a classical-sounding poise to phrases; elsewhere he uses *alliteration*, the repetition of consonants at the beginning of words (as in Marcus's "If I do dream, would all my wealth would wake me" from *Titus Andronicus*), to make them sound insistent. *Anacoluthon*, the device of springing surprise grammatical interruptions, is often used to express a character's tormented state of mind, particularly in the late plays and rarely more powerfully than in *The Winter's Tale*, when Leontes' language begins to clot as he watches his wife flirting (he thinks) with another man:

> But to be paddling palms and pinching fingers,
> As now they are, and making practised smiles
> As in a looking-glass; and then to sigh, as 'twere
> The mort o'th'deer—O, that is entertainment
> My bosom likes not, nor my brows ...
>
> [*THE WINTER'S TALE*, 1.2.117–21]

Hendiadys, the device of pairing near-identical nouns ("angels and ministers of grace defend us"), is an unmistakable hallmark of *Hamlet*, while Shakespeare uses *apostrophe*, the practice of changing which audience one is addressing (for instance appealing to a particular person in a crowd) as an insistent effect in *Julius Caesar*, a play in which characters vie with one another to control people through public speech. There are scores more. Of course it isn't necessary to know the technical terminology in order to appreciate the effects – and someone as talented as Shakespeare would undeniably have been able to employ these devices without having been taught them – but rhetoric was an essential part of the Elizabethan educational framework, and touched almost every aspect of its literature.

Shakespeare's command of **simile** and **metaphor**, the literary techniques for comparing things with each other or describing them in other terms, are perhaps the most striking examples of his use of rhetoric – more sophisticated, more thrilling and (sometimes) more bewildering than anything exhibited by any of his contemporaries. Almost any sentence contains one or the other, all the way from straightforward similes such as "as cold as any stone" (*Henry V*, 2.3.23) or "like as the waves do make towards the pebbled shore" (Sonnet 60, 1) or "his delights / Were dolphin-like" (*Antony and Cleopatra*, 5.2.87–8) to the most intricate of and memorable of metaphors:

> Now is the winter of our discontent
> Made glorious summer by this son of York ...
>
> [*RICHARD III*, 1.1.1–2]

When I do tell thee 'There my hopes lie drowned',
Reply not in how many fathoms deep
They lie endrenched.

[*TROILUS AND CRESSIDA*, 1.1.49–51]

It [love] is the star to every wand'ring barque,
Whose worth's unknown although his height be taken.

[SONNET 116, 7–8]

This music crept by me upon the waters,
Allaying both their fury and my passion
With its sweet air.

[*THE TEMPEST*, 1.2.394–6]

In all these examples and many more, what linguists call the **tenor** and the **vehicle**, the thing being described and the thing used to describe it, sizzle in new and unexpected ways: so Sonnet 116's description of love as "the star to every wand'ring barque" hints

Printed emblem collections distilled everyday metaphors and maxims into printed images, often with explanatory text attached. This example, published in 1635, reads *Nulla dies sine linea* – "don't let a day pass without writing a line".

not only at its fixity but at the feeling of being unmoored by passion, while Richard III's celebrated opening lines give a straightforward seasonal metaphor unexpected brilliance by punning on "son"/"sun".

Shakespeare is also supremely expert at what is sometimes called **extended metaphor**, the technique of pursuing a transformational image over several sentences, or even an entire poem or play, in order to draw out its many diverse shades of meaning. Sonnet 30 is a stunning example, though there are many hundreds on offer:

> When to the sessions of sweet silent thought
> I summon up remembrance of things past,
> I sigh the lack of many a thing I sought,
> And with old woes new wail my dear time's waste.
> Then can I drown an eye unused to flow
> For precious friends hid in death's dateless night,
> And weep afresh love's long-since-cancelled woe,
> And moan th'expense of many a vanished sight.
> Then can I grieve at grievances foregone,
> And heavily from woe to woe tell o'er
> The sad account of fore-bemoanèd moan,
> Which I new pay as if not paid before.
>   But if the while I think on thee, dear friend,
>   All losses are restored, and sorrows end.

[SONNET 30, 1–14]

The poem describes the process of retreating into memory and thought as entering a law court or "sessions", into which "things past" can be "summoned", a legalistic/ money-obsessed metaphor that intensifies through the poem to outline every aspect of his relationship with the absent lover. "Waste", "cancelled", "expense", "grievance", "account", "pay ... paid", "losses" – all these technical words construct the impression of a love affair called to account, viewed on a balance sheet, and add a bitter tang to the phrase "dear friend", which plays on the buried meaning of *dear* to mean "expensive".

From verse ...

The skills that rhetoric fostered in the young Shakespeare – acute awareness about the placement of words, an ear sensitive to patterns in language, a virtuosic control of linguistic effects – proved invaluable when it came to handling **metre**, the rhythmic patterns of syllables that make up poetic verse. Almost all modern-day plays, films or TV scripts are written in prose, a literary representation of "ordinary" or "natural" speech in which no attempt is made to impose any kind of rhythmic pattern. In the sixteenth century, however, the opposite was true. Nearly every play was written in verse, usually in what linguists call **blank verse**, in which the pattern of beats follows an unvarying rhythm but there is no requirement to rhyme the ends of lines with each other (hence "blank"). English writers borrowed blank verse from Italian early in the Renaissance and dramatists in particular clung to it, attracted by its balance and seriousness, its close affinity with the natural pulse of spoken English and because actors found it easy to project blank verse into large spaces – essential in an era when as many as 3,000 people were crammed into open-air theatres. Under Marlowe, Shakespeare and their contemporaries, blank verse became something like the staple metre of English drama, and remained so until well after Milton in the seventeenth century.

But what actually is blank verse? Its technical name is **iambic pentameter**, which simply means that each line is built up of five pairs of syllables (sometimes called metrical feet), with the stress or beat falling on the second syllable in each pair: de-*dum*, de-*dum*, de-*dum*, de-*dum*, de-*dum*, five iambs per line. The essential pattern can clearly be seen in this speech from the early play *Titus Andronicus*, in which the villain Aaron is advising two brothers to stop quarrelling with each other and work together instead:

> For **shame**, be **friends**, and **join** for **that** you **jar**.
> 'Tis **policy** and **stratagem** must **do**
> That **you** affect, and **so** must **you** re**solve**
> That **what** you **can**not **as** you **would** ach**ieve**,
> You **must** per**force** ac**comp**lish **as** you **may**.

[*TITUS ANDRONICUS*, 2.1.104–8]

With the stressed syllables marked in bold, the metrical pattern of blank verse can clearly be seen. It is a pattern Shakespeare uses more or less by default throughout his dramatic career.

That said, however, he experiments ceaselessly with the basic components of blank verse. Sometimes lines are **end-stopped** with rhymes, particularly at the end of scenes, to draw them to a symmetrical close. Sometimes Shakespeare adds in extra syllables or leaves lines short for effect, or allows different rhythms to play against each other within the line. This is particularly true in plays written after the turn of the seventeenth century, when Shakespeare was at the height of his powers – one of the earliest of which is *Hamlet*, a play which achieves a new kind of expressive freedom in verse. The kind of complicated metrical effects it contains can be witnessed in this fevered dialogue between Hamlet and his mother Gertrude, in which the Prince accuses her of sullying his father's memory by sleeping with his brother:

> QUEEN GERTRUDE   O Hamlet, speak no more!
>   Thou turn'st mine eyes into my very soul,
>   And there I see such black and grainèd spots
>   As will not leave their tinct.
> HAMLET   Nay, but to live
>   In the rank sweat of an enseamèd bed,
>   Stewed in corruption, honeying and making love
>   Over the nasty sty—
> QUEEN GERTRUDE   O, speak to me no more!
>   These words like daggers enter in mine ears,
>   No more, sweet Hamlet.

[*HAMLET*, 3.4.78–86]

To make the metrical patterns clear to actors, many editors mark up words requiring unusual pronunciation (here "grainèd" and "enseamèd", two and three syllables respectively). But although the Queen's speech begins metrically enough, Hamlet's sudden intervention unsettles the rhythm of the exchange. It is impossible to say the exceptionally vivid phrase "rank sweat" without stressing both words, while the line that follows gets off literally on the wrong foot, with a stress on another forceful word, "stewed", and ends up two syllables too long, drawing out Hamlet's intensely queasy image of his mother and uncle in bed together. When Gertrude interrupts in turn, the line they share ends up too long once again – adding metrical support for her desperate appeal that Hamlet should say "no more". Although the speed of the exchange makes it difficult to pick up such subtleties without studying them on the page, Elizabethan audiences, who were far more orally aware than ours, would have listened out for them.

... to prose

On the Elizabethan stage, verse was usually given to noble characters, whether in the sense that they were high-born or simply "good". So-called common people, however, were often assigned prose, usually because their speech was not intended to sound as high-flown or poetic, but natural and non-dramatic – echoing the rigid social divisions present in real life. In scripts, prose is represented by lines that travel all the way to the right-hand side of the column. Witness, for instance, these words spoken by Bottom in *A Midsummer Night's Dream*, uttered as he awakens from a fairy-induced trance:

> I have had a most rare vision. I have had a dream past the wit of man to say what dream it was. Man is but an ass if he go about t'expound this dream. Methought I was—there is no man can tell what. Methought I was, and methought I had—but man is but a patched fool if he will offer to say what methought I had.
>
> [*A MIDSUMMER NIGHT'S DREAM*, 4.1.202–8]

As Bottom flounders to put into words what exactly his "dream" entailed, his use of prose is undeniably prosaic. Full of pauses, false starts and repetitions, this is Shakespeare deploying human speech at its most unvarnished, a world away from the courtly, stylized verse used elsewhere in the play. Not that Bottom's use of prose implies that he is stupid (although Shakespeare often pokes gentle fun at him), nor is it the case that his commonness makes him somehow linguistically inadequate – Shakespeare's characterization and social awareness are too rounded for that. Bottom simply talks straight.

Later on, *A Midsummer Night's Dream* counterpoints verse and prose in subtle ways, weaving them delicately in and out of one another to alter the tempo of the action and create different effects. In the last main scene of the play the artisans, among them Bottom, put on an entertainment for their masters at court starring the lovers Pyramus and Thisbe, an entertainment whose dramatic limitations soon become woefully obvious not just to us but to members of the onstage audience. The courtiers keep heckling, in fact, even at the first climax of the action, where Bottom, acting Pyramus, attempts to spy Thisbe through a wall played by one of his colleagues:

> BOTTOM *(as Pyramus)*
>> Thanks, courteous wall. Jove shield thee well for this.
>>> But what see I? No Thisbe do I see.
>> O wicked wall, through whom I see no bliss,
>>> Cursed be thy stones for thus deceiving me.
> THESEUS The wall methinks, being sensible, should curse again.
> BOTTOM *(to Theseus)* No, in truth, sir, he should not. 'Deceiving me' is
>> Thisbe's cue. She is to enter now, and I am to spy her through the wall.
>> You shall see, it will fall pat as I told you.
>> *Enter Flute as Thisbe*
>> Yonder she comes.
>
> [5.1.176–85]

Shakespeare gains rich comedy here not simply in the set-up, ridiculous as is it is, but via clever use of verse and prose. Bottom's lines in the play, spoken in lumbering pentameter lines, rhymed in the manner of old-style drama, give way to Theseus's interruption – which, although the Duke elsewhere speaks verse (as befits his public status), is here in relaxed, chatty prose. Bottom's reply, forcing him to come out of character, is also in prose – so creating the gentle social joke that he has descended to the Duke's level. One of the scene's many subtleties is the gallant efforts of Bottom and his colleagues to maintain the integrity of their verse style, even under sustained (prose) attack from their so-called social betters.

Not that prose implies being tongue-tied. While Shakespeare's early plays explore the expressive possibilities of verse more fully than ever before, his great mid-period comedies *Much Ado About Nothing* and *The Merry Wives of Windsor* are composed overwhelmingly in prose: almost 90 per cent in the latter. The prose ratio of *Much Ado* is slightly lower, 70 per cent, but Shakespeare still reserves much of his most exquisitely turned dialogue for scenes in which characters address each other in prose:

> BEATRICE I wonder that you will still be talking, Signor Benedick. Nobody
>> marks you.
> BENEDICK What, my dear Lady Disdain! Are you yet living?
> BEATRICE Is it possible disdain should die while she hath such meet food
>> to feed it as Signor Benedick? Courtesy itself must convert to disdain
>> if you come in her presence.
> BENEDICK Then is courtesy a turncoat. But it is certain I am loved of all
>> ladies, only you excepted. And I would I could find in my heart that I
>> had not a hard heart, for truly I love none.
> BEATRICE A dear happiness to women.
>
> [*MUCH ADO ABOUT NOTHING*, 1.1.110–22]

The sardonic comedy that flickers through this exchange seems straightforward enough, but is in fact anything but, a complicated game whose rules have long since been laid down. When verse is used in this play, it is often at moments of tension or strain, as if its characters find such formality something of a straitjacket:

> BENEDICK
> Do you not love me?
> BEATRICE   Why no, no more than reason.
> BENEDICK
> Why then, your uncle and the Prince and Claudio
> Have been deceived. They swore you did.
> BEATRICE
> Do you not love me?
> BENEDICK   Troth no, no more than reason.
>
> [5.4.74–7]

When Beatrice and Benedick do finally admit to loving each other, a few lines later, they do so in the language that they have shared for almost the entire play: prose.

Elsewhere, the shift between verse and prose reflects a change in social setting, or the shift between public pronouncement and private speech. In *Henry IV Part I*, a play that brings a striking range of voices into intimate contact with each other, in which working horsemen rub shoulders with members of the royal family, the many complex social relationships it portrays are explored partly via metrical means. Take this exchange between Prince Hal and his lowlife companion Poins, in which the two of them are discussing a plot to humiliate Sir John Falstaff by ambushing him in disguise:

> POINS   The virtue of this jest will be the incomprehensible lies that this
>   same fat rogue will tell us when we meet at supper: how thirty at least
>   he fought with, what wards, what blows, what extremities he endured;
>   and in the reproof of this lives the jest.
> PRINCE HARRY   Well, I'll go with thee. Provide us all things necessary, and
>   meet me tomorrow night in Eastcheap; there I'll sup. Farewell.
> POINS   Farewell, my lord.
>   *Exit*
> PRINCE HARRY
>   I know you all, and will a while uphold
>   The unyoked humour of your idleness.
>   Yet herein will I imitate the sun,
>   Who doth permit the base contagious clouds
>   To smother up his beauty from the world …
>
> [*1 HENRY IV*, 1.2.193–7]

Despite the apparently genuine warmth between Poins and Hal, the switch in tone once Poins disappears offstage is striking, indeed chilling. Hal's change to formal verse underlines the fact that the plan to abandon his Eastcheap pals when he comes to power is coldly sincere, all the colder because it is uttered in soliloquy, when Hal is addressing no one but the audience. "The Prince studies his companions, / Like a strange tongue, wherein, to gain the language," claims the Earl of Warwick in *Henry IV Part II* (4.3.68–9), and at moments like this the claim seems utterly believable. Henry's skill at what linguists call code-switching – adapting his speech to prevailing social conditions – is impressive, and it will help him as a ruler too. In *Henry V*, called upon not simply to exhort his soldiers before battle but to talk with them honestly about their worries, he dons disguise and wanders among the rank and file:

> KING HARRY I myself heard the King say he would not be ransomed.
> WILLIAMS Ay, he said so, to make us fight cheerfully, but when our throats
>   are cut he may be ransomed, and we ne'er the wiser.
> KING HARRY If I live to see it, I will never trust his word after.
> WILLIAMS You pay him then!
>
> [*HENRY V*, 4.1.189–96]

Pointedly, this exchange rests on the value of Henry's "word", and although the King has a hard time persuading the cynical soldier Williams of the case for war, the believability of his prose is not in question. Language is just another useful disguise.

Words, words, words

People often get fixated on the idea of Shakespeare as a great inventor of words. Francis Meres, a self-appointed critic who spotted the playwright's talent early on, remarked in 1598 that Shakespeare and other poets including Marlowe, Spenser and Sidney "mightily enriched" the English language, filling it with "rare ornaments and splendid habiliments". Some modern observers, meanwhile, have credited Shakespeare with coining more new words than any other author. It is also sometimes said that Shakespeare's vocabulary was prodigiously large, unfathomably so by modern standards. Neither statement is quite accurate. Despite the eager efforts of one theorist, who suggested that Shakespeare minted over 10,000 words, the more realistic figure accepted by most scholars is that he came up with about **1,700 neologisms**, over 600 of them borrowed from Latin (far from all have stayed with us). And although Shakespeare knew significantly more words than most of his contemporaries – his total lexicon is estimated at between 17,000 and 20,000 English words, variously measured – the number is still less than most fluent English-speakers today.

This is not in any way to play down Shakespeare's linguistic achievement, merely to suggest that his skill lay as much in transforming and enriching the language that he learned as in coining thousands of new words. Expanding the possibilities of language, however it's done, is inevitably a complex process – some old words will readily take on new meanings, others won't. Some new words will take flight and become part of everyday usage, others stubbornly refuse to. Sometimes Shakespeare's very fluency leads him down bizarre linguistic alleyways; other times he is more interested in how

Words, words, words

Coinages that stuck ...	... and those that didn't
Assassination	Attask (verb) *to take to task*
Champion (verb)	Cadent (adjective) *falling*
Excitement	Congreet (verb) *to greet mutually*
Frugal	Crimeless (adjective) *faultless, innocent*
Gust	Dispunge (verb) *to discharge, as from*
Hurry (verb)	*a sponge*
Immediacy	Immoment (adjective) *trifling*
Lacklustre	Insisture (noun) *persistency*
Puking	Plantage (noun) *vegetation*
Savagery	Primy (adjective) *something in its prime*
Transcendence	Reprobance (noun) *being reprobate*
Unreal	Rigol (noun) *a ring or circle*
Watchdog	Unsisting (adjective) *unhelpful*

language fails us, or times when words simply will not work. Always Shakespeare is thinking about language as a working dramatist, one whose plays and poems are populated by talking people, and acted by living ones.

There is also the difficulty of quantifying the number of new words, and working out whether Shakespeare actually invented them or simply set them down in the earliest form that has been picked up. The most detailed wordbank of its kind, compiled and updated by the *Oxford English Dictionary*, notoriously relies far too much on Shakespeare's work because his texts were readily available when the groundwork for the dictionary was being done in the nineteenth century. Problems also appear because of spelling and hyphenation (problematic with a compound word such as "leapfrog", which appears as "Leape-frogge" in *Henry V* but is surely likely to have been in wide oral currency). And there is also the question of whether Shakespeare's addition of a brand-new sense to an existing word actually counts as a coinage. A noun such as "critic", for instance, circulated in various forms well before Shakespeare put it into the mouth of Biron in *Love's Labour's Lost* – an insult, as it happens, though far removed from the modern sense of a professional paid to produce opinions.

All that said, however, Shakespeare's use of words is of course amazingly varied as well as endlessly inventive. Often it is his broadening of a word's existing senses that is most dazzling to watch. If we observe the changes explored in the word "sense" itself, to pick one tiny but famous example, we can get some indication of it. Here are its appearances in *Measure for Measure*:

> One who never feels
> The wanton stings and motions of the **sense** ...
> **[*MEASURE FOR MEASURE*, 1.4.57–8]**

[He] hath picked out an act

Under whose heavy **sense** your brother's life
Falls into forfeit ...

[1.4.63–5]

Your bum is the greatest thing about you; so that, in the beastliest **sense**,
you are Pompey the Great ...

[2.1.208–10]

[Isabella] speaks, and 'tis such **sense**
That my **sense** breeds with it ...

[2.2.144–5]

Can it be
That modesty may more betray our **sense**
Than woman's lightness?

[2.2.173–5]

Nay, but hear me.
Your **sense** pursues not mine.

[2.4.73–4]

The **sense** of death is most in apprehension ...

[3.1.76]

He should have lived
Save that his riotous youth, with dangerous **sense**,
Might in the times to come have ta'en revenge ...

[4.4.27–9]

Poor soul,
She speaks this in th'infirmity of **sense**.

[5.1.46–7]

Her madness hath the oddest frame of **sense** ...

[5.1.61]

As there is **sense** in truth, and truth in virtue,
I am affianced this man's wife ...

[5.1.224–5]

Against all **sense** you do importune her.

[5.1.430]

The word is used by a small cast of characters and appears only thirteen times in
the play, but, as the critic William Empson once observed, "almost all of them carry

forward a puzzle which is essential to its thought". Shakespeare encourages *sense* to mean – and encourages us to observe it meaning – everything from solid good sense ("against all sense") to riotous abandon ("dangerous sense"), from playful linguistic analysis ("the beastliest sense") to basic comprehension ("your sense pursues not mine"), from general awareness of things ("our sense") to incredibly particularized sensuality ("my sense"). Among the ten closely packed columns devoted to the word's history in the *Oxford English Dictionary*, it is difficult to find a shade of meaning that Shakespeare doesn't hint at in *Measure for Measure*: and, moreover, all of them collide and commingle. When the corrupt ruler Angelo says to Isabella "your sense pursues not mine", outwardly implying that he doesn't catch her gist, it is impossible not to think back to his (private) admission earlier on that he finds her way of speaking a turn-on, her "sense" breeding with his. Alert audiences will also be reminded of the claim, early on in the play, that Angelo is a cold fish sexually, doesn't feel "the wanton stings and motions of the sense".

As becomes apparent in this surprisingly telling example, Shakespeare's mind was particularly alive to the possibilities of the pun, the word that can mean many things at once (also, as it happens, another way in which he deployed metaphor). Very often Shakespeare's wordplay tends towards the bawdy end of the spectrum, something that horrified many nineteenth-century commentators; but, in our less censorious age, his unbridled enthusiasm for sexualized language seems merely part of his abundant interest in humanity. Sometimes Shakespeare's puns are consciously set up, sometimes they are meant to seem artless. Sometimes they are both at once, as in this thumbnail sketch of a language lesson in *The Merry Wives of Windsor*:

EVANS What is your genitive case plural, William?
WILLIAM Genitive case?
EVANS Ay.
WILLIAM *Genitivo: 'horum, harum, horum'.*
MISTRESS QUICKLY Vengeance of Jenny's case. Fie on her! Never name
    her, child, if she be a whore.
EVANS For shame, 'oman!

[*THE MERRY WIVES OF WINDSOR*, 4.1.52–58]

As the child – slyly named William – declines a noun in front of his teacher, several schoolboy-level puns leap out, playing on the obvious similarity between "genitive" and "genital", then "horum" and "whore". Lest we miss the point, the always linguistically challenged Mistress Quickly, who happens to be watching the lesson, leaps ham-fistedly in – apparently not understanding what is going on, and introducing another Elizabethan dirty joke ("case" was slang for "vagina") en route. The moment may not make audiences laugh as hard as it once did, but Shakespeare's willingness to indulge in a spot of simple kidult humour alongside the most elevated rhetoric is hard not to admire.

Although pretty much everyone in the Elizabethan audience would have got the gag here, it has sometimes been suggested that Shakespeare's biggest battle, especially late in his career, was with **comprehension** – particularly after the turn of the seventeenth century, when his willingness to make audiences work harder than ever before seems to reach a new level. Some have even speculated that one reason the younger playwright John Fletcher was brought in to work alongside him was to help Shakespeare unknot the dense language employed in his late solo plays, among them *Cymbeline* and *The Winter's Tale*, and return them to a form readily understood by audiences. In truth, it is difficult to avoid the sense that Shakespeare was always pushing and prodding at the boundaries of language, whether to explore the extremities of experience via copious words, or the opposite, to find a place in consciousness where language no longer acts as it should. His plays and poems are as full of characters who never really grasp the full extent of their words as of those who stand in total control of what they say, as dominated by the failures and fissures of language as by the dazzling power of eloquence. This restless attitude to language, to the problems it creates as well as those it solves, is perhaps his greatest achievement of all.

Reading on

Shakespeare's Language
Frank Kermode; 2000 > Penguin

David Garrick famously introduced his 1748 adaptation of *Romeo and Juliet* with the claim that he had attempted to "clear the original as much as possible from the jingle and quibble which were always thought the great objections to reviving it". Frank Kermode had some sympathy with this view, as did his (and Garrick's) mentor Samuel Johnson, who also complained that Shakespeare's pen ran away with him rather too often. Kermode likes clarity – he attacks the playwright for unnecessarily "terse" moments in *All's Well*, criticizes *Cymbeline* for being "over-worked" – and is thus sometimes unwilling to hear that peculiarly Shakespearian trick of using words to frustrate as well as communicate, even for characters (like *Macbeth*) speaking to no one but themselves. But Kermode is genuinely enthusiastic about language, as well as perceptive about it, and if nothing else this book will make you listen and read more attentively.

Shakespeare and the Arts of Language
Russ McDonald; 2001 > Oxford UP

Recent years have been a boom time for Shakespearian reference works, spearheaded by OUP, whose selection of pocket-sized "Shakespeare Topics" books includes some real gems. One such is Russ McDonald's slim but informative *Shakespeare and the Arts of Language*, which takes a less tendentious – if less complete – approach than Kermode's *Shakespeare's Language* and comes up with some real insights about the playwright (there's not much on the poems) and his linguistic toolkits. Very informative and a delight to read. For further reading on Shakespeare's language, see p.648.

Shakespeare's canon

For a collection of plays sometimes imagined to have been inscribed on tablets of stone, Shakespeare's canon has proved remarkably unstable in the years since his death. Though John Heminges and Henry Condell, actor-editors of the all-important **First Folio** (1623), have earned the gratitude of countless Shakespearians for reproducing eighteen texts – among them *As You Like It, Julius Caesar, Twelfth Night, Macbeth, Twelfth Night* and *The Tempest* – which would otherwise have disappeared, their decision to include just 36 plays (and no poems) has since proved hugely controversial. Put simply, no one is entirely sure how much Shakespeare actually wrote – still less when he wrote it.

Labour's lost?

In addition to Heminges and Condell's 36, two plays from other sources, **Pericles** and **The Two Noble Kinsmen**, are usually regarded as canonical, alongside the three major narrative poems and the Sonnets. Added to these are a pair of missing plays, **Cardenio** and **Love's Labour's Won** (see p.242), and the collaborative drama **Sir Thomas More**, to which Shakespeare probably contributed (see p.190). But a number of other works published during this time boast that they too were authored by Shakespeare. In addition to several minor poems, no fewer than six Jacobethan plays made this claim – *Locrine* (1595), *Thomas Lord Cromwell* (1602), *The London Prodigal* (first attributed in 1605), *The Puritan* (1607), *A Yorkshire Tragedy* (1608) and *Sir John Oldcastle* (1619) – and others followed before the century was out. Though their Shakespearian connections are vigorously defended in some quarters, most authorities believe the playwright never went near them, and they are most often grouped together as "**apocrypha**".

Opinions change, however. A few years ago, the press was abuzz with news of a work entitled "**A Funeral Elegy**", printed in February 1612 in order to rescue the reputation of a Devon man named William Peter, who had been stabbed in the back of the head a few weeks earlier during a drunken brawl. Computer-aided statistical analysis supposedly confirmed that the title-page's enigmatic "W. S." was in fact Shakespeare, and some scholars staked reputations on the attribution – despite the fact that the poem lamented a man with no evident connection to the playwright, and appeared during weeks when Shakespeare was far more likely to have been attending to another funeral, that of his brother Gilbert. Most readers find the "Elegy" cringingly bad, too, and all but impossible to imagine as the product of Shakespeare's maturity. Sceptics have recently been gaining the upper hand: scholar Brian Vickers suggests that a more plausible author might be **John Ford**, whose later works include *'Tis Pity She's a Whore* (c.1628), and who sometimes imitated Shakespeare's style. More recently, Vickers has also used stylometric analysis to call the authorship of *A Lover's Complaint* once more into question, suggesting it to be the work of an otherwise obscure poet named John Davies of Hereford (see p.519). Some scholars have been persuaded, while others refute his findings; it's hard not to feel that maybe we should simply enjoy the poem on its undoubted merits, irrespective of authorship.

Another contender, the history play *Edward III*, has had a comparably tough time of it. Retelling the exploits – both martial and marital – of the illustrious King and his son the Black Prince (respectively Richard II's grandfather and father), the play was thought of as apocryphal until relatively recently. All the same, it has steadily made inroads on the canon: in 1997 it was included in the revised *Riverside Shakespeare* – albeit with the cagey statement that "if Shakespeare had not written at least some of [it] … he certainly should have" – and a year later was published as a single-volume edition in the New Cambridge series, edited by Giorgio Melchiori. *Edward III* was performed by the RSC as a "new play by Shakespeare" in 2003, and in 2005 the editors of the *Oxford Shakespeare* finally relented, electing to include the text in their new *Complete Works* alongside the full script of *Sir Thomas More*. Following that edition, this book has done the same; you can read all about the play, and about the controversy surrounding its authorship, on p.84.

Minding your Fs and Qs

If you do even a little exploration in the texts of Shakespeare, sooner or later you'll have to confront the jargon – the F1s and Q4s, the ominous-sounding "foul papers" and "bad quartos". Although these terms sound cryptic and puzzling, they're relatively easy to decode.

A logical place to start is **F**, bibliographical shorthand for **Folio**. Folios (from the Latin *folium*, "leaf") are books made up of paper folded in half, creating two leaves or four pages. In the early modern publishing trade large folio volumes were grand and prestigious products, typically reserved for serious works of history, theology and philosophy such as the multimillion-word *Chronicles* (1587) edited by Raphael Holinshed, and Sir Walter Ralegh's *History of the World* (1614). Folios were not, in other words, for ephemera like playscripts – mere "tinsel", as one printer memorably described them.

Never a man to be cowed by convention, **Ben Jonson** bucked the trend in 1616 by publishing what he entitled (with typical audacity) his *Works*, the first time that plays had been printed in folio. And when the actors **John Heminges** and **Henry Condell** came to collect Shakespeare's plays after his death the same year, they decided on the same red-carpet treatment for their friend and colleague. What they produced in 1623 – a handsome volume entitled *Mr. William Shakespeares Comedies, Histories, & Tragedies* – has become known as the **First Folio**, or **F1** for short, and it's the earliest and most important collected edition of his work. The book was so popular that a corrected version was printed nine years later (**F2**), another appeared in 1663 (**F3**), one more in 1685 (**F4**), and a last edition (**F5**) made it in around 1700. Shakespeare used the word "folio" only once, in the mouth of Don Armado, *Love's Labour's Lost*'s preening show-off, so he might have been bemused by – or quietly amused at – such unremitting demand for his printed words.

Quartos (Q) were cheaper and smaller. Their name refers to the paper being folded in half twice to make four leaves (eight pages), which then had to be cut along one edge. Individual plays were printed in quarto, and around half of Shakespeare's appeared in this way while he was alive, with the narrative poems being printed in the even smaller **octavo** (O) format (in which the pages are folded three times). On the whole, however, printers preferred not to publish plays, which – then as now – didn't sell particularly well: gossipy broadsheets, almanacs, Bibles and sermons generally did a much better trade.

Each play was owned by the company that commissioned and performed it, or the publisher that arranged for it to be printed: writers exercised no legal rights over their text, and what we now call "intellectual copyright" did not emerge until nearly a century after Shakespeare's death. Partly as a consequence, in the publishing industry of the time there appears to have been a trade in **pirated copy**, where play-texts were stolen and printed illicitly. So while some of Shakespeare's plays were printed from his **foul papers** (working manuscripts) or **fair copies** (transcripts), sometimes referred to as "**good quartos**", others were not authorized and are frequently inaccurate – those so-called "**bad quartos**". In recent years, however, many scholars have argued that such value-obsessed labels miss the point, and that many apparently "bad" (or "short") texts reveal things that more polished or approved versions do not.

About time

Dating Shakespeare's output is still difficult and involves interpreting a complex set of data – records of performance, early texts, availability of sources, allusions by other writers, linguistic evidence and much more. The picture is further complicated by the likelihood that playscripts were performed or published in multiple versions and a variety of places; and even the Sonnets may have been written over a fourteen-year period. If one thing is clear, it's that Shakespeare didn't have the luxury of dividing his time neatly – he was most likely juggling several projects at once, writing and revising almost continually for 25 industrious years.

The table opposite follows the order suggested by Stanley Wells and Gary Taylor in *William Shakespeare: A Textual Companion* (1987), with the addition of *King Edward III*, which was excluded from the first edition of the *Oxford Shakespeare* but included in the second (see p.619).

Late 1580s–early 1590s

The Two Gentlemen of Verona [1589–90]

The Taming of the Shrew [c.1590]

Henry VI Part II [1590–91]

Henry VI Part III [c.1591]

Henry VI Part I [1592]

Titus Andronicus [1593]

Edward III [1592–93]

Richard III [1592–93]

Venus and Adonis [1593]

Mid-1590s

The Rape of Lucrece [1594]

The Comedy of Errors [?1594]

Love's Labour's Lost [1594–95]

Richard II [1594–95]

Romeo and Juliet [1595–96]

A Midsummer Night's Dream [1595–96]

King John [1595–97]

Late 1590s

The Merchant of Venice [1596–97]

Henry IV Part I [1596]

The Merry Wives of Windsor [1597–98]

Henry IV Part II [1598]

Much Ado About Nothing [1598–99]

Henry V [1599]

Julius Caesar [1599]

Early 1600s

As You Like It [1600]

Hamlet [c.1600]

Twelfth Night [1601–02]

Troilus and Cressida [1601–02]

Sonnets and A Lover's Complaint [1591–1604]

Sir Thomas More [?never performed]

Measure for Measure [1603–04]

Mid-1600s

Othello [?1603–04]

All's Well That Ends Well [1604–05]

Timon of Athens [1605–08]

King Lear [1605]

Macbeth [1606]

Antony and Cleopatra [1606–07]

Late 1600s

Pericles [1607–08]

Coriolanus [1608–09]

The Winter's Tale [1609–11]

Early 1610s

Cymbeline [1610–11]

The Tempest [1610–11]

Henry VIII [1613]

Cardenio [c.1613, lost play]

The Two Noble Kinsmen [1613–14]

Colleagues and rivals

S hakespeare was far from the only show in Jacobethan London. The city was hungry for entertainment, and playgoing was a genuinely popular pastime: up to 25,000 Londoners visited the theatre each week during the Elizabethan period, and jobs in the sector were comparatively plentiful – especially for educated, ambitious men with nowhere else to go. Never before (and perhaps not since) had such a constellation of theatrical talent been concentrated in a few square miles. And although rivalry between playwrights was intense, especially with theatre companies competing for the best writing and acting talent, theatreland was a close-knit, incestuous environment in which everyone rubbed shoulders. Of the nine playwrights included in this chapter, all knew Shakespeare: some simply acted or drank with him, others knew him simply as a hugely successful rival, still others supplied him with ideas, rewrote his work or collaborated with him (see p.84). And although their plays are not so widely performed as Shakespeare's, they are well worth exploring, not simply because they help widen our appreciation of Renaissance drama but because so many of them are brilliant in their own right.

Thomas Kyd (1558–94)

Born in 1558 to a well-to-do London scrivener (a skilled clerical copyist, responsible for drawing up neat versions of documents), Thomas Kyd studied, like Shakespeare, at grammar school – in his case at the newly founded Merchant Taylors' in London. Like Shakespeare he didn't go to university, and seems to have worked in the family business for a while. Clerical experience may well have been his passport into theatreland, where copyists could make themselves extremely useful, but all we know for sure is that by 1592 he was well-known enough to be noticed by critic Francis Meres, who named him alongside Shakespeare and Marlowe as one of the new generation of playwrights then revolutionizing English drama.

As with Marlowe, when it comes to the end of Kyd's life the facts come in a rush – partly, indeed, because the two were closely involved. Following the so-called "Dutch libel", a crude note found pinned to the wall of a London church threatening violence against immigrant merchants in May 1593, the authorities were tipped off that Kyd was most likely its author, and he was hauled in. Under arrest, and possibly tortured, he tried to

> *Oh eyes, no eyes but fountains fraught with tears,*
> *Oh life, no life; but lively form of death:*
> *Oh world, no world but mass of public wrongs,*
> *Confused and filled with murder and misdeeds.*
>
> Hieronimo, in *The Spanish Tragedy* (3.2.1–4)

pass off incriminating atheistic papers found in his room as Marlowe's, left behind when they shared rooms together a few years earlier, and made a point of distancing himself from the younger man's "monstrous opinions". Although he was later released, Kyd died, his career ruined, in August 1594.

Dekker would praise him ten years later as "industrious Kyd", but little of that industry survives. Three plays are usually associated with him. The first is *The Spanish Tragedy*, which premiered around 1587 and caught the public imagination for at least the next half-century. It was the first work to bring the bloodthirsty world of Senecan revenge tragedy (see p.444) to mass audiences, and they seem to have loved it: along with Marlowe's *Jew of Malta* and another work since lost, *The Spanish Tragedy* was one of the most attended plays of the mid-1590s. The second play associated with Kyd, *Cornelia*, a neoclassical tragedy, may have been his last work.

The third is far more shadowy: the so-called ur-*Hamlet*, a supposed source for Shakespeare's play (*ur* is German for "original") often ascribed to Kyd. Just a few scattered references to the play survive, among them a jibing reference by Thomas Nashe to playwrights who steal from Seneca "whole Hamlets – I should say handfuls – of tragical speeches" and another by Thomas Lodge, which refers to "the ghost which cried so miserably at the theatre, like an oyster-wife, 'Hamlet, revenge' ". Both of these references appear too early to refer to Shakespeare's *Hamlet*, and another clue in Nashe's account points the finger at Kyd – raising the possibility that the play-wright behind *The Spanish Tragedy* might also have laid the ground for that later, and infinitely greater, play.

The Spanish Tragedy

Five Revenge Tragedies, Emma Smith (ed.);
2012 ❯ Penguin

A sensational hit that ignited the Jacobethan craze for plays about revenge – a ghost and the spirit of Revenge act as the chorus – *The Spanish Tragedy* influenced dramatists right up to Cromwell's closure of the theatres. Set in the Spanish court, its complex plot revolves around the figure of Hieronimo, an elderly knight out to avenge the murder of his son Horatio at the hands of two young noblemen who were seemingly his friends. Although often creaky, the play is powerfully affecting – not least during Hieronimo's grief-provoked bouts of insanity.

Christopher Marlowe (1564–93)

The facts of Marlowe's life, and the manner of his death, alone make him one of the most compelling figures of his generation. But the market in mass-produced intrigue has a habit of crowding out the one undeniably astonishing thing about the man: his writing. Despite his hectic and unstable life Marlowe wrote a series of plays that changed the course of literary history, doing more than any previous poet to wrench English theatre out of its post-medieval corsetry and into a living, breathing drama. If he hadn't died before reaching 30, it's possible he could have been an even greater writer than Shakespeare himself.

The biographical similarities between the pair are striking: born in the same year as Shakespeare, 1564, Marlowe came from similarly obscure origins, the son of a Canterbury shoemaker. Like Shakespeare, he was rescued from comparative oblivion by receiving a top-notch grammar school education, in Marlowe's case at the King's School in Canterbury, and went at the age of sixteen to Bene't College, Cambridge (now Corpus Christi) on a scholarship. Marlowe's unexplained absences while he was supposed to be studying – and a government note excusing him because of services "in matters touching the benefit of his country" – have been taken to imply that he was recruited into the Elizabethan government's army of spies while at university, but there is no direct evidence (hardly surprising). What is definite is that Marlowe began writing at Cambridge, translating Ovid and experimenting with various literary forms.

In 1587 he burst onto the public stage with the impressive, ambitious *Tamburlaine the Great*, which offered a glorious part for another man marked as a rising star, the young Edward Alleyn (see p.568). It became an overnight sensation, and Marlowe followed it with a sequel, performed in 1590. Over the next three years he dominated London theatres with a string of successes including *Doctor Faustus*, *The Jew of Malta*, *Edward II* and *The Massacre at Paris*, a body of work whose range and ambition undoubtedly overshadows that of his contemporaries, all the more remarkable for being written in just three years.

Whether Marlowe's surveillance work continued alongside his success as a dramatist isn't clear, but in any case he appears to have been closely knit into the shady and semi-criminal networks that made up the Elizabethan secret service. In 1589 he was imprisoned after being involved in a brawl in which a man was stabbed to death, and was sent home from army service in the Netherlands during 1592 for counterfeiting money. Marlowe also courted a more respectable form of rebellion by joining the group of free-thinkers that surrounded Sir Walter Ralegh, but his controversial reputation got him into severe trouble in 1593 when a personal attack by a former room-mate and probable fellow spy, Richard Baines, reached the attention of the Privy Council. Baines alleged, colourfully, that Marlowe entertained any number of dubious religious opinions, openly suggested "all they that love not tobacco and boys were fools" and – most gravely – poured scorn on the existence of God. When others (including Thomas Kyd; see p.622) corroborated Baines's testimony, Marlowe was arrested on charges of heresy and bailed. But he was never to make it to trial: after spending most of 30 May, 1593 in a pub at Deptford, south London, a tussle broke out in which he was killed. He was 29.

Speculation about Marlowe's killing has run rife, with two main conspiracy theories in circulation – one that his murder was ordered by the authorities, the other questioning whether he actually died at all. With respect to the first, historians point out that if Marlowe's death was a targeted hit it seems to have been bungled, to put it mildly: Marlowe was stabbed in the face, and according to a detailed coroner's report the fight started after a dispute about the "reckoning", or bill. All the evidence points to the obvious conclusion, that a brawl between men who had spent all day drinking got badly out of control. With respect to the second theory, many of whose adherents cling to the hope that Marlowe faked his own death, again the evidence doesn't stack up. We actually know more about Marlowe's last hours alive than almost anything else about him, and are as certain as we can be that he did indeed die that day.

> BARNADINE *Thou hast committed—*
> BARABAS *Fornication? But that was in another country; and besides, the wench is dead.*
>
> The Jew of Malta (4.1.41–3)

The curious theory that he stayed alive and went on to write the plays of Shakespeare in disguise is little more than wishful thinking (see p.566).

Yet, from a literary point of view, the relationship between Shakespeare and Marlowe remains an intriguing one. Many of their plays share similarities, and Shakespeare, forced into a late start by very different life circumstances, only seems to have found his feet as a dramatist after Marlowe's death. It is one of the strange might-have-beens of literary history that, if one man had never got into a fight in Deptford, the other might never have blossomed into the greatest dramatist in the English language. Shakespeare's innermost feelings about Marlowe will never be known, but there may be a buried clue in one of his plays – a comment by Touchstone in *As You Like It*, who remarks in passing that "when a man's verses cannot be understood … it strikes a man more dead than a great reckoning in a little room" (3.3.9–12). The reference to Marlowe's murder is subtle, even muffled, but seems too deliberate to be coincidental. Years after the death of his greatest rival, it appears that Shakespeare was unable to get the memory out of his head.

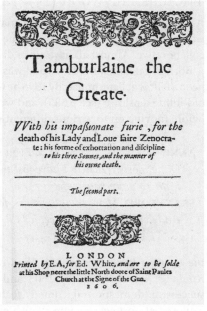

Tamburlaine, the first of Marlowe's many power-crazed antiheroes, left an obvious impression on Shakespeare.

Doctor Faustus and Other Plays

Doctor Faustus and Other Plays, David Bevington & Eric Rasmussen (eds); 1995 > Oxford UP

Doctor Faustus Overweening (anti) heroes are a Marlovian speciality, and this twist on the folk tale of a man who trades his soul with the Devil for unearthly rewards is, outwardly at least, a straightforward morality tale. What makes it more exciting than that is Marlowe's dramatic intelligence, and his gorgeous, searching verse: the appearance onstage of Helen of Troy sparks one of the most famous rhetorical questions in drama, "Was this the face that launched a thousand ships ...?" It's arguably his finest work – a mature play from a poet who died far too young.

Edward II Its frank depiction of love between men may have secured Marlowe's status as a gay icon, but from a literary point of view the relationship worth investigating is with Shakespeare, whose *Richard II* was written at very nearly the same time, indicating that the two writers had intimate knowledge of each others' work. In any case, draped in the rainbow flag this play is not: by falling for Gaveston, his beautiful but duplicitous favourite, Edward exhibits his weakness as a ruler and comes to a notoriously painful end – in full view of the audience.

The Jew of Malta Whereas Shakespeare treats the story of a Jew adrift in Christian society as a tragedy of sorts, Marlowe – whose play precedes *The Merchant of Venice* by four or five years – has no such qualms. His Jewish moneylender, Barabas, is an out-and-out villain, rapacious and greedy, who poisons an entire nunnery (not to mention his own daughter) when cornered by Malta's Christians. Unsubtle it may be, but the play's satire on religion, which insinuates that all faiths are as bad as each other, is thrillingly heterodox, and the script sparkles with energy.

Tamburlaine the Great, Parts I and II What Jonson called Marlowe's "mighty line" is glitteringly on show in *Tamburlaine*, a double-decker drama he wrote soon after leaving university. Muscular, action-packed and bursting with grandiloquent language, this tale of a shepherd from Scythia who tries to take over the world (the real-life Timur) is an appropriately pushy subject for Marlowe's London debut, and it bristles with youthful confidence. (Shakespeare's cheeky response was to parody Tamburlaine as the bombastic character Pistol in *2 Henry IV*.)

Thomas Heywood (1573/4–1641)

Although the least known of the major Jacobethan dramatists, Thomas Heywood was easily the most prolific: he claimed to have penned 200-plus plays, most of them collaborative. Almost all have since disappeared.

Born in Lincolnshire, Heywood was probably educated at Cambridge and may have been a fellow at Peterhouse. By 1596 he was writing for the Admiral's Men under the aegis of Philip Henslowe (see p.585), and went on to become a shareholder in the company before moving on to various different groups. His first work may have been *The Four Prentices of London*, a story of four young Englishmen who set off for the crusades – the kind of chivalric tall tale sent up by Beaumont and Fletcher's *Knight of the Burning Pestle* (see p.635). Heywood's most revived play, *A Woman Killed with Kindness*, was on stage by 1603 and represents the mode in which he was most successful: domestic tragicomedy featuring vividly drawn characters. But Heywood explored almost every genre available to him, including contemporary history plays, classical saga (including a version of *The Rape of Lucrece*), farce and comedy. His magnum opus, little known now, was a five-part series of *Ages* narrating the mythological history of mankind. Its third instalment, *The Iron Age*, covers the Trojan War and shows the influence of Shakespeare's *Troilus and Cressida*. The preface to his late drama *The English Traveller*, printed in 1633, contains Heywood's claim that it was merely one of "among two hundred and twenty, in which I have had either an entire hand, or at the least a main finger".

> ANNE   *To call you husband!*
> *O me most wretched, I have lost that name;*
> *I am no more your wife.*
> FRANKFORD   *Spare thou thy tears, for I will weep for thee;*
> *And keep thy countenance, for I'll blush for thee.*
>
> A Woman Killed with Kindness (Sc. 13, 82–6)

Heywood also maintained an industrious career as a poet and writer of prose. His *Apology for Actors*, of 1612, is one of the most interesting surviving pieces of Jacobean theatrical criticism, offering the author's views on the acting trade alongside plenty of colourful anecdotes. In its preface Heywood complains noisily that some of his own poems were printed in *The Passionate Pilgrim* under Shakespeare's name (see p.550).

A Woman Killed with Kindness

A Woman Killed with Kindness, Brian Scobie (ed.); 1985 ➤ New Mermaids

A world away from the Italianate intrigues that obsessed his contemporaries, *A Woman Killed with Kindness* is an intimate portrait of a middle-class marriage that goes disastrously wrong, set in the homely environment of rural England. The "woman" of the title is the newly married Anne Frankford, caught in an unfortunate clinch with a houseguest. She is punished by her husband not by violence or murder, but with something far crueller – the "kindness" of being estranged from her family forever.

Ben Jonson (1572–1637)

Even 370 years after his death, it feels easier to get a hold on Ben Jonson than any of his contemporaries (Shakespeare included). In part that's because he made things easy for biographers, leaving an extensive paper trail documenting many facets of his physical and creative life. But it's also because Jonson, possessed of one of the largest egos in the Renaissance theatreworld, wove his personality into almost everything he wrote. Determined that plays should be thought of as literature rather than entertainment, he did much to forge the idea of the author – the notion that a writer was a fully fledged artist, not merely a jobbing craftsman.

Jonson's prickliness on this subject (and many others) may relate to his background. His father, a Protestant minister, died before his birth, and his mother remarried a London bricklayer. With the help of a shadowy patron, Jonson attended Westminster School and he remained obsessed by academic study for the rest of his life. After leaving Westminster at 16, he became apprenticed to his stepfather – reluctantly, it seems, because he soon left to fight in the Netherlands, where, so he later boasted, he killed a man in single combat. He married in 1594 and had a son, also christened Ben, who died at the age of seven – an event Jonson mourned in one of his most touching poems, which begins "Farewell, thou child of my right hand, and joy". He had three more children, but all died young.

Jonson apparently left the family home early in order to become an actor, and seems to have begun writing soon afterwards. As was usual, his early plays were produced in collaboration with others – among them a satire (now lost) called *The Isle of Dogs*, written with Thomas Nashe, which appeared in 1597 and immediately resulted in a clampdown by the authorities. Jonson was thrown in prison, and soon after being released found himself in trouble yet again, this time for killing another actor in Hoxton, north London. He escaped the death penalty because of

> *Yet, I glory*
> *More in the cunning purchase of my wealth*
> *Than in the glad possession; since I gain*
> *No common way: I use no trade, no venture;*
> *I wound no earth with ploughshares; fat no beasts*
> *To feed the shambles ...*
>
> Volpone, in *Volpone* (1.1.30–35)

a medieval legal loophole favouring anyone who could read, and converted to Catholicism while awaiting trial, but was imprisoned again a few years later for his part in another court satire, *Eastward Ho* (1605). In the meantime Jonson's playwriting career had taken off. *Every Man in His Humour* (1597) was one of the biggest successes to be seen at the Curtain theatre, while his great middle-period plays – the Roman tragedy *Sejanus, His Fall* (1603), and the brilliant comedies *Volpone* (1607), *The Alchemist* (1612), *Bartholomew Fair* (1614) and *The Devil is an Ass* (1616) – made him into a superstar on a par with Shakespeare. Yet he was not above wrangling with rivals: during the so-called "war of the theatres" (see p.631) he caricatured Marston and Dekker.

In truth Jonson had a troubled relationship with what he once called the "loathed stage" itself, continually ranting at what he saw as dumbing-down in the public theatres. Following James I's accession Jonson put an increasing amount of energy into courtly drama, pioneering with architect Inigo Jones a new species of spectacular royal entertainment known as the masque (see p.629). Success won Jonson friends in high places, and his reputation was sealed when in 1616, the year of Shakespeare's death, he published a folio volume called *Works*, a breathtaking act of self-promotion crowned when the playwright was granted a royal pension (becoming, in effect, England's first poet laureate). Yet after Charles I came to the throne in 1625 Jonson's star began to wane, and following a stroke, then a spectacular falling-out with Jones, he retreated from court life. A final spurt of plays in the late 1620s and early 1630s followed, but they did not halt the decline. A heavy drinker and eater throughout his life, Jonson died rather like Shakespeare's Falstaff – overweight, underfunded and tended by his devoted serving woman.

Jonson's relationship with Shakespeare was even touchier than those with his other colleagues; encouraged, perhaps, by their contrasting personalities and competing talents. For all that they may have been close professionally (Shakespeare acted in at least one of Jonson's plays), Jonson several times sounded off about Shakespeare's apparent failings as a writer: his lack of "art", his factual slips, his use of unfashionable dramatic techniques. Jonson's tribute in the 1623 Folio is typically double-edged. Though he famously praises Shakespeare as "not of an age, but for all time", almost the greatest compliment anyone could pay him, Jonson couldn't resist mocking the older poet's shoddy language skills – claiming that despite ranking with the great classical tragedians Aeschylus, Euripides and Sophocles, Shakespeare had "poor Latin and less Greek".

The Alchemist

The Alchemist, Elizabeth Cook (ed.);
2004 > New Mermaids

Set in a London besieged by plague and wormy with moral decay, *The Alchemist* is a sour take on urban life, populated by villains, whores, gamblers and their gullible victims. With his master away, the enterprising Face joins forces with prostitute Doll Common and Subtle, the con-alchemist of the title, to separate as many people from their money as possible. With its multiple plots, the play is not an easy read, but it sparkles on stage, animated by earthy language, a plentiful supply of outlandish characters and a stream of fine gags.

Bartholomew Fair

Bartholomew Fair, Suzanne Gossett (ed.);
2000 > Revels

The last of Jonson's big comedies turns an unflattering mirror on London in holiday mood. A rogue's gallery of citizens is out and about at the fair, among them the hypocritical puritan Busy and justice of the peace Adam Overdo. When the two collide at a puppet-drama send-up of Marlowe's *Hero and Leander*, Jonson has fun with both dramatic conventions and social stereotypes: the performance is interrupted first by Busy, who objects to its cross-dressing (as did many real-life puritans); then the disguised Overdo unmasks himself and puts all to rights (a nod to *Measure for Measure*'s fictional Duke Vincentio).

Eastward Ho

Eastward Ho, C.G. Petter (ed.);
1973 > New Mermaids

Written with George Chapman and John Marston, *Eastward Ho!* caused a sensation when it was premiered, landing Jonson and Chapman in prison for sneering at the Scots (James VI of Scotland had recently become the first Stuart king of England). The plot follows the fortunes of a goldsmith, his apprentices and daughters, one of whom marries an insolvent adventurer who absconds to Virginia at the first opportunity. The fact that he gets no further than the Isle of Dogs turns the joke not merely on London itself but on the city's imperial ambitions.

Volpone

Volpone, Robert N. Watson (ed.);
2003 > New Mermaids

Prefaced by an extended advertisement to the author's talent, *Volpone* is a slick comedy, skilfully delivered, which follows the intrigues of a wealthy Venetian who fakes his own death in order to defraud his friends. Eventually the plot is unmasked, but not before it has sucked in any number of moneygrubbers, each doing their utmost to con the others – one even prepared to pimp his wife in order to gain an advantage. The central characters are named in Italian for the creatures they embody – the fox, the fly, the vulture, the raven – revealing the play's origins in animal fable.

Behind the masque

Shakespeare and his colleagues had numerous brushes with royalty. Elizabeth I's staff ordered several of their plays to be performed before the Queen, among them *Love's Labour's Lost* and *The Merry Wives of Windsor*, while James I took the company under his wing, rechristening them the King's Men and making them official court servants. It would have been unthinkable for either monarch to have visited the London playhouses in person; one of the many perks of Renaissance royalty was that theatre came to you, not the other way around.

As well as sampling fine public drama, both Elizabeth and James I encouraged another form of theatre, the **masque** – dramatic entertainments involving costume, dance and music, loosely based on Italian forms but mingled with the dumbshows and so-called "guisings" of the Tudor court. In Elizabeth's reign these were straightforward if lavish affairs, often created to honour her arrival in some far-flung corner of the kingdom – the young Shakespeare may have witnessed one when she visited Warwickshire in 1575 (see p.582).

When James came to the throne, however, he and his courtiers put enormous amounts of energy into Whitehall entertainment, massively increasing expenditure on masques and commissioning some of the leading artists of the day. Masque culture reached its apex with the partnership of **Ben Jonson** and the architect-cum-designer **Inigo Jones**, who collaborated on a number of one-off pieces commemorating major events during James's rule, beginning in 1605 and continuing for a quarter-century. The masques they created were elaborate and eye-wateringly expensive, often invested with complex allegorical or political messages, and – Jonson's innovation – sometimes preceded by so-called **antic-** or **antimasques**, in which scenes of evil or low comedy provided a foil to the main event, the entry of the courtiers themselves and the emblematic restoration of peace and harmony. Given that the casts were composed of aristocratic amateurs (sometimes a little tipsy), it is unlikely that Jonson's ultra-sophisticated texts were done justice, but Jones's sets and costumes – not to mention the music – must have made for a remarkable spectacle.

Masques survived well into the reign of Charles I (arguably the greatest example is Milton's *Comus*, written in 1634 and set to music by Henry Lawes), but the partnership between Jones and Jonson did not. The pair fell out in 1631, bitterly feuding about who had ultimate creative control. Shakespeare, notably, refrained from getting involved – though the masque-like scenes in his late plays, notably *Cymbeline* and *The Tempest*, suggest that he must have witnessed their handiwork.

Court masques, David Lindley (ed.); 1995 > Oxford UP

Scripts of long-gone royal entertainments aren't the easiest to read, but it's worth persevering. Of the eighteen masques in this collection, ten are by Jonson; of these *The Masque of Blackness* (1605), *Masque of Queens* (1609) and *Christmas His Masque* (1616) are the most approachable, and an eye-opening introduction to this unique form of drama.

Thomas Dekker (c. 1572–1632)

London-born and -bred, Thomas Dekker retained an intense affection for his city, an affection that makes itself felt in nearly everything he wrote. Characterful and vivid, his work captures what life must have been like in the early modern metropolis.

Dekker's date of birth relies on guesswork from a much later reference to his age, and had he not extolled London as "mother of my life, nurse of my being" in one of his plague pamphlets, we would have no firm evidence where he was brought up. From

> SIMON EYRE *Peace, you bombast-cotton-candle-quean—away, Queen of Clubs,*
> *quarrel not with me and my men, with me and my fine Firk. I'll firk you if you do.*
> MARGERY *Yea, yea, man, you may use me as you please …*
>
> The Shoemaker's Holiday (Sc.7, 38–43)

the level of education revealed in his writings, it is usually assumed that he went to grammar school, though it isn't known which one. In fact almost the first real proof of Dekker's existence relates to his imprisonment in 1598 for debt, in his mid-20s; he was imprisoned again in 1612 for similar reasons and spent nearly seven years inside.

Evidence relating to his playwriting career surfaces around the same time, chiefly courtesy of theatre impresario Philip Henslowe, who kept detailed (if sometimes haphazard) records of what appeared at his theatre, the Rose. Henslowe gave Dekker work as one of his regular playwrights, often writing for the Lord Admiral's Men and usually collaborating with Jonson, Webster and Michael Drayton – we know that Dekker, apparently kept busy by shortage of cash, was involved in over 40 plays, but nearly all are lost. *The Shoemaker's Holiday*, a rare solo piece and in every way his biggest success, appeared in 1598–99 and was performed in front of the Queen. Another comedy, *Old Fortunatus*, was published alongside it and also seems to have been given a royal performance. The majority of Dekker's theatre career was a succession of collaborations, initially in the so-called "war of the theatres" (see p.631), and later with playwrights including Middleton, Henry Chettle, William Rowley, Massinger and John Ford. There is barely a writer of the period with whom Dekker didn't have dealings – he even crossed paths with Shakespeare when both were involved in *Sir Thomas More* (see p.190).

Dekker also kept himself busy with prose, churning out numerous pamphlets, diaries and tracts. Some of these dwelt on his experiences in prison, for instance the prose narrative *Lantern and Candlelight* (revised 1616); others paint a vibrant picture of city life. *The Wonderful Year* is one of his finest non-dramatic works, describing with a journalist's eye the ghastly events of 1603, in which London was decimated by the plague (quite literally: 10 percent of its population died in just two months).

The Shoemaker's Holiday

The Shoemaker's Holiday, Anthony Parr (ed.);
1990 ❯ New Mermaids

Bustling, characterful and bursting with comic energy, *The Shoemaker's Holiday* focuses on the real-life story of a humble cobbler, Simon Eyre, and his rise to become Lord Mayor of London. Dekker offsets this slightly humdrum plot with a double romance that binds together the city's warring classes, one involving a young aristocrat, Rowland Lacy, who disguises himself as a Dutch shoemaker in order to woo the homely Rose Oatley. The play abounds with the earthy vernacular of the streets, most memorably in Eyre's sharp-tongued wife Margery and his foul-mouthed journeyman Firk.

John Marston (c.1575–1634)

Son of a well-known London lawyer who married the daughter of an Italian doctor, Marston studied at Oxford then went to Middle Temple in the mid-1590s to take up the family trade. Despite his father's dying wish that he would concentrate on the law,

At war

In a theatrical environment as hectic and rivalrous as Elizabethan London, professional tensions were par for the course: different companies competed not only for audiences but also for actors and writers, disputes were commonplace, and sometimes rivalries even erupted into violence.

Yet one of the strangest disputes in the history of Renaissance drama has to be the so-called **war of the theatres**, a long-running battle of words between several of the city's leading playwrights at the turn of the seventeenth century. The story goes that the first salvo was fired by **John Marston**, who seems to have taken against **Ben Jonson** – just why isn't known, though Jonson fell out with most people at one time or another – and ridiculed him as a boastful bore in his play *Histriomastix* (1599). Jonson promptly responded with an attack on Marston's apparently prolix style in *Every Man Out of His Humour*, whereupon Marston hit back with *Jack Drum's Entertainment*, which features a self-satisfied, malicious critic ostensibly modelled on Jonson. Jonson replied by sending up both Marston and **Thomas Dekker** in *Cynthia's Revels*, and the feud continued through several more plays. Jonson's final potshot, in *The Poetaster*, portrayed himself as the poet Horace forcing the satirist Crispinus/Marston to vomit up his words. Marston's riposte in *Satiromastix* (1601) is arguably funnier: the play contains a scene in which the poet Horace is depicted struggling to compose a brown-nosing commendatory ode – a literary form that Jonson very much made his own.

Given that satire in these plays has long since passed its sell-by date, no one is entirely sure what really lay behind this curious confrontation, genuine enmity or cunningly choreographed self-promotion (given that Jonson and Marston worked together on *Eastward Ho* just a few years later, the bitterness can't have run that deep). But even Shakespeare managed to get involved. In addition to a fleeting reference to the poets' war in a version of *Hamlet*, it has been suggested by some scholars that the doltish portrait of Ajax in *Troilus and Cressida* (1601–02) was in fact a dig at Jonson.

Marston spent more and more time writing, publishing satires at first anonymously, then under his own name. His first professional dramatic work seems to have been for the children's company based at the indoor Blackfriars theatre (which Shakespeare's company would later occupy; see p.589). Like many of his contemporaries, Marston soon found himself working for Philip Henslowe, who records paying him 40 shillings in May 1599 as an advance for a play.

Marston's growing success seems to have brought him into conflict with Jonson, a rivalry which lasted several years and may have been the basis for the "war of the theatres" (see above). Jonson caricatured his rival as insufferably pretentious in his play *The Poetaster* (1601) and even claimed to have beaten him up and stolen his pistol. Marston, together with Dekker, responded by producing *Satiromastix*, a thinly veiled attack on Jonson that sent up his delusions of poetic grandeur. Whether this dispute was the genuine article or a convoluted publicity stunt is difficult to fathom (see above), but in any case a few years later Jonson and Marston seem to have buried the hatchet. They worked together on *Eastward Ho*, which landed Jonson and their co-author George Chapman in prison because of its ill-timed jokes against James I, but Marston appears to have fled and escaped arrest.

> MENDOZA *To accomplish this now, thus now: the Duke is in the forest next*
> *the sea; single him, kill him, hurl him i' the main, and proclaim thou*
> *sawest wolves eat him.*
> MALEVOLE *Um, not so good.*
>
> The Malcontent (3.3.100–3)

Like Marston's early satires, *The Malcontent* (1604), written initially for the boys at Blackfriars, was successful enough to be adapted by Webster for the King's Men ten years later. Another satirical play, *The Dutch Courtesan*, appeared in 1605, the same year that Marston married Mary Wilkes, daughter of one of James I's chaplains (Jonson once quipped that Marston wrote his father-in-law's sermons while Wilkes was responsible for the comedies). His light-hearted experiment into different approaches to playwriting entitled *What You Will*, printed in 1607 but perhaps performed six years earlier, appears to borrow Shakespeare's subtitle for *Twelfth Night* (unless, of course, Marston got there first).

Whether or not his marriage into a church family was responsible, in 1609 Marston abandoned the stage to train as a clergyman – much to the astonishment of his theatrical colleagues. His plays carried on being performed and printed, but when his works were brought together for publication in 1633 he seems not to have been involved.

The Malcontent

The Malcontent, W. David Kay (ed.); 1998 ❯ New Mermaids

With a plot concerning the deposed Duke of Genoa, who disguises himself to spy on his court – and thus uncovers infidelity and intrigue aplenty – *The Malcontent* reads like a rerun of *Measure for Measure* that is both funnier and nastier than the original. Its hero, Malevole, is gifted with a satirical bent and the sharpest of tongues, while the play's metatheatrical induction, written by John Webster for performance at the Globe, pokes fun at Shakespeare's actor colleagues Burbage, Lowin and Condell.

John Webster (c. 1579–c.1634)

Strikingly little is known about the life of John Webster. His date of birth isn't clear, we have no idea what he looked like, and the only reference to his death is a passing comment by an ex-colleague. Even so, he was responsible for two of the greatest masterpieces of the Jacobean theatre, *The Duchess of Malfi* and *The White Devil*: searing, intense tragedies that absorbed the influence of Shakespeare and brought it to a new generation of theatregoers.

Son of a prosperous London coachmaker who was a member of the Merchant Taylors' Company, Webster is likely to have been educated at the guild's own school – the same one attended by Kyd, twenty-odd years before. From legal references in his writing, it is possible that he trained as a lawyer, and

> *I know death hath ten thousand several doors*
> *For men to take their exits; and 'tis found*
> *They go on such strange geometrical hinges,*
> *You may open them both ways …*
>
> The Duchess, in *The Duchess of Malfi* (4.2.209–12)

The Duchess of Malfi was the opening show at the Sam Wanamaker Playhouse in 2014 – a fittingly dark debut for this candlelit space. Gemma Arterton played a morally unimpeachable Duchess to David Dawson's scheming Ferdinand.

a "John Webster" who attended the law college Middle Temple in 1598 might well be him. He married in 1605, by which time he had been working for several years in Philip Henslowe's writing team at the Rose theatre, along with Anthony Munday and Michael Drayton as well as Middleton, Heywood and Jonson. He added new material to Marston's *The Malcontent* for the King's Men in 1604 (which may well have put him in contact with Shakespeare) and had a hand in two city comedies, *Westward Ho!* and *Northward Ho!*, written with Dekker, as well as assorted group projects.

Webster's first known solo work dates from five or six years later, and it isn't clear what he did in the interim. One clue may lie in the printed preface to *The White Devil*, published in 1612, in which the author defends himself against accusations that he was a slow writer. (The preface is also touchy about the poor reception that greeted the play, blaming it on the weather, the venue and ultimately the audience.) Even so, this impressive tragedy was a leap forward for Webster, and seems to have sparked a new enthusiasm for playwriting. *The Duchess of Malfi*, probably his masterpiece, followed a year later, and he contributed to a collection of character sketches by fellow lawyer Thomas Overbury in 1615.

Webster's last extant solo play, *The Devil's Law Case*, a tragicomedy stuffed with bizarre plot-points, dates from around 1619, although a lost work entitled *Guise* may have followed it. He continued to collaborate with other playwrights through the 1620s, and perhaps died later that decade or early in the next.

The Duchess of Malfi

The Duchess of Malfi, Brian Gibbons (ed.); 1993 > New Mermaids

Its plot is as hair-raising as any in Jacobean drama: a widowed duchess remarries beneath her to the disgust of her brothers, who plot her murder with the help of their agent, the malcontent Bosola. Death, madness and a blood-spattered finale ensue, but the play is saved from mere sensationalism by sinewy writing and a sophisticated portrait of its imperious heroine. T.S. Eliot's claim that Webster "saw the skull beneath the skin" seems particularly apt during the thrillingly spooky scene in which the Duchess prepares for death by discussing it at length with her murderer.

The White Devil

The White Devil, Christina Luckyj (ed.); 1996 > New Mermaids

An Italian revenge tragedy loosely based on actual events, *The White Devil* is filled with murderous intrigue and double-crossing aplenty. When Duke Brachiano develops a passion for Vittoria Corombona, her brother Flamineo arranges the murder of their respective spouses – with predictably gruesome consequences. In Vittoria, the "devil" of the title, Webster creates another great female role, though she's rivalled by her mother Cornelia, who in her late, great mourning scene resembles a cross between Ophelia and Lady Macbeth.

John Fletcher (1579–1625)

Most writers in this period collaborated with others, either through circumstance or for reasons of money, but the Jacobean playwright John Fletcher seems to have particularly relished writing as part of a team. Nearly fifty dramas have been attached to his name, many of them written with colleagues.

Almost nothing is known of Fletcher's first years. He was born at Rye in Sussex in 1579, the son of a clergyman who rose to become Bishop of London but died heavily in debt. By that time John had entered Bene't College, Cambridge – now Corpus Christi, also Christopher Marlowe's old college – but little evidence survives of his time at the university and he next crops up a decade later in London, among the dramatists, poets and actors who drank at the Mermaid Tavern in London's Bread Street. Ben Jonson was a regular, and tradition holds that Shakespeare also socialized there (in truth there's little evidence).

It may well have been at the Mermaid that Fletcher met his greatest collaborator and closest companion, Francis Beaumont (1584–1616). Despite their differing backgrounds – Beaumont was from a wealthy family and had trained as a lawyer – the two men began to write with each other, and seventeenth-century diarist John Aubrey reports (with a characteristic eye for gossip) that they became so close that they moved in together, dressed alike and "had one wench in the house between them". Fletcher never married, and whatever the precise details of his relationship with Beaumont, their professional partnership prospered. In the years before Beaumont's untimely death, the pair had written around six plays, although at least fifty would be ascribed to them in subsequent years. Among their joint creations is most likely *The Knight of the Burning Pestle*.

Fletcher also worked with another man who died in 1616, William Shakespeare. Shakespeare was fifteen years Fletcher's senior, and in the last few years of his career it seems that Fletcher was groomed by Shakespeare's

> PETRUCCIO *Why, this is a riddle*
>   *I love you, and I love you not.*
> MARIA *It is so.*
>   *And till your own experience do untie it,*
>   *This distance I must keep.*
> PETRUCCIO *If you talk more, I am angry, very angry.*
> MARIA *I am glad on't, and I will talk.*
>
> The Tamer Tamed (1.3.568–74)

company as his successor. They first came together for *Cardenio*, but that play has been lost (see p.242), making their earliest extant collaboration *Henry VIII*, written around 1613. Their only other work together was Shakespeare's last: *The Two Noble Kinsmen*, which dates from slightly later. It isn't clear how Fletcher and Shakespeare divided the writing of these plays, and attempts to separate their work on internal evidence haven't produced solid results – hardly surprising, given that Fletcher in particular was used to writing in a variety of styles. The task of working out who wrote what is further complicated by the likelihood that each revised the other's material.

The Knight of the Burning Pestle

The Knight of the Burning Pestle, Michael Hattaway (ed.); 2002 ➤ New Mermaids

It may be thoroughly Jacobean, but this benevolent comedy scrubs up surprisingly well. Written with Fletcher's regular collaborator Francis Beaumont (some critics regard it as entirely Beaumont's work), the metatheatrical plot is almost too silly to relate. A London grocer, his wife and a pair of apprentices interrupt a play and demand something more to their taste, whereupon one of the apprentices leaps on stage to become a knight errant journeying through the enchanted forests of suburbia. The play scores some subtle hits, both against audiences and dramatic contemporaries, including Shakespeare.

The Tamer Tamed

The Tamer Tamed, Celia R. Daileader & Gary Taylor (eds); 2006 ➤ Revels

The Tamer Tamed continues where Shakespeare's *Taming of the Shrew* leaves off, disposing of Katherine and supplying Petruccio with a new wife, Maria, whose task it is to administer some long-overdue humiliation. She organizes a female rebellion, whereby wives will withhold sex until their husbands are more respectful (an idea borrowed from Aristophanes' *Lysistrata*). The play's date is not known, making it unclear whether *The Tamer Tamed* was the work that brought Fletcher to Shakespeare's attention, or was written after his demise – or even whether Shakespeare gave it his blessing as a sequel.

Thomas Middleton (1580–1627)

Sixteen years younger than Shakespeare and one of his apprentices in the King's Men, Thomas Middleton learnt much from his older colleague and almost certainly collaborated with him – facts which have seen him dismissed as a mere copycat whose best writing was created in the shadow of others. In recent years, however, Middleton's work has been increasingly highly valued, and he has come to be seen as one of the few Renaissance writers whose talent genuinely rivalled Shakespeare's.

Son of a well-to-do London bricklayer who died when Thomas was five, Middleton had a difficult relationship with his impecunious stepfather, who tried to snatch the young boy's inheritance. Middleton studied at Oxford, though left without taking a degree, and began writing young: he was just 17 when his name first appeared in print, on the title-page of a group of satirical poems; and by 19 he wrote a poem in the style of Shakespeare's *Lucrece*. Soon afterwards Middleton was working in the theatre, perhaps as an actor but soon as a writer, initially patching up old plays in Philip Henslowe's stable of playwrights based at the Rose. The closure of the theatres by plague in 1603 forced Middleton to turn his hand to pamphlet-writing (he also married that year), but he returned energetically to drama as soon as he could. His first solo projects were undertaken for a boys' company who specialized in risqué London comedies, usually able to get away with their mature subject matter because the actors were so young. Among them were *The Phoenix* (1603), *Michaelmas Term* (1604), *A Trick to Catch the Old One* and *A Mad World, My Masters* (both 1605), and *The Puritan Widow* (1606), all of which appear to have been roaring successes.

Soon afterwards Middleton found himself writing for the King's Men during the same period as Shakespeare, at first on the heavily *Hamlet*-influenced *The Revenger's Tragedy* (1606), then apparently on *A Yorkshire Tragedy*, a short work based on a real-life family murder. Although its title-page claims that the play is Shakespeare's (see p.618), most scholars suspect that Middleton was in fact the author. The pair appear more likely to have collaborated on *Timon of Athens*, which also appeared in 1605–06, with Middleton writing most of the central act. Whether they were so closely involved over a rewrite of *Macbeth* in which Middleton appears to have added several sections from his own play *The Witch* (1616) is less certain; it's possible that he simply adapted the text after Shakespeare's death. Something similar may have happened with *Measure for Measure*.

Of the twenty-odd plays that follow – not to mention numerous pageants – the majority are collaborations with other authors, some of them piecework written when Middleton was short of money (he was arrested for debt in 1608). But others are among his finest dramas, including *The Roaring Girl*, shared with Dekker (1611), and *The Changeling*, written with the actor William Rowley (1622). Yet Middleton, one of the most flexible writers of his generation, also worked brilliantly on his own, as evidenced by the comedy *A Chaste Maid in Cheapside* (1613), the tragedy *Women Beware*

> *Does every proud and self-affecting dame*
> *Camphor her face for this, and grieve her maker*
> *In sinful baths of milk, when many an infant starves*
> *For her superfluous outside—all for this?*
>
> Vindice, in *The Revenger's Tragedy* (3.5.83–6)

Women (1621) and *A Game at Chess* (1624), a scintillatingly original take on contemporary politics in which all the major players become chess figures.

A Game at Chess caused a major diplomatic incident, and it may well have finished Middleton's career – after running for nine performances (an unheard-of number), and having been seen by perhaps 30,000 people, over a tenth of London's population, it was pulled and Middleton went into hiding. It was the last work he wrote, and he died at home in Newington Butts, just around the corner from the theatres that had hosted his greatest successes.

The Collected Works

Gary Taylor & John Lavagnino (eds);
2007 ➤ Oxford UP

The Changeling Often revived, and with good reason, *The Changeling* is a thrillingly tense essay in love, madness and death. Somewhat in the manner of Webster, it boasts a powerful central female role in the ostensibly virtuous heroine Beatrice-Joanna, who is in love with one man but betrothed to another. But it is her relationship with her obsessed servant, the disfigured De Flores, that strays into the darkest psychosexual territory and becomes one of the most compellingly kinky in all Jacobean drama. Middleton's collaborator, William Rowley, was probably responsible for the brilliantly off-kilter asylum scenes.

A Chaste Maid in Cheapside Best-known for his tragedies, Middleton was equally adept at generating laughter, especially via so-called "city" or "citizen" comedies, which sent up contemporary London life and the moneygrubbing middle classes. One of his best is *A Chaste Maid*, the scabrous saga of a dissolute knight, Sir Walter Whorehound, and his attempts to get his mistress (the tongue-in-cheek "maid" of the title) married off to the son of a rich goldsmith. Balancing this acrid satire is a sweet tale of young love between the goldsmith's daughter, Moll, and her admirer Touchwood; a plot device that somewhat calls to mind Shakespeare's *Merry Wives*, though Middleton's world view is less forgiving.

The Revenger's Tragedy Although its authorship is still disputed (for a long time it was attributed to the otherwise little-known Cyril Tourneur), the format of *The Revenger's Tragedy* is not: it packs all the usual revenge formulas into a furiously complicated plot and stars a hero, Vindice, whose name literally means "revenge". Set in yet another depraved Italian court, the target of Vindice's wrath is the Duke, who poisoned Vindice's betrothed when she refused him. Vindice must also protect the honour of his sister Castiza, one of the few incorruptible women in a Middleton tragedy. The play crackles with satirical wit, some of it at *Hamlet*'s expense, and is an unusually lively read.

Women Beware Women Every bit as good as *The Changeling*, though not so widely known, *Women Beware Women* is set among the Medici of Renaissance Florence. It's as cynical about sex as you'd expect from Middleton: the young nobleman Hippolito deceives his own niece into sleeping with him, the Duke of Florence seduces a newly-wed Bianca – both intrigues helped along by a widow named Livia, who in turn has her eye on Bianca's husband. The climactic wedding masque ends in wholesale massacre, some of it via the appropriately Catholic medium of poisoned incense.

Reading on

Shakespeare, Co-author
Brian Vickers; 2002 ➤ Oxford UP

The fullest recent account of collaboration in English Renaissance drama, Vickers' typically pugnacious study focuses on the four men who, he argues, worked most closely with Shakespeare: George Peele, Thomas Middleton, George Wilkins and John Fletcher. Undeniably in-depth (tables of stylometric analysis abound), *Shakespeare, Co-Author* is essentially a detailed analysis of the processes by which scholars decide who wrote what, but also offers plenty of information about what writers wrote, and how.

Shakespeare & Co
Stanley Wells; 2006 ➤ Penguin

Wells's sprightly, novel-sized paperback is perhaps the best place to start, full of detail on the theatrical ecology of Shakespeare and his contemporaries and packed with colourful anecdotes. Marlowe, Dekker, Jonson, Middleton, Fletcher and Webster get a chapter each, but plenty of lesser names feature alongside. A further bonus is Wells's insightful and subtle chapter on Shakespeare's relationship with his actor colleagues, a useful corrective to author-centred theatre history.

Shakespeare for kids

P resented imaginatively and enthusiastically, Shakespeare's plays can prove life-changing whatever your age. But it's easy for children to be put off by a heavy-handed approach, especially when accompanied by the idea that Shakespeare is somehow good for them. There are many ways of giving young people a taste of the action – from watching a DVD to performing a play for themselves, from reading a text-based adaptation in print or ebook to trying out a graphic-novel version. What works for one child won't work for another, and what follows are simply a handful of suggestions on how to kindle a passion for Shakespeare's work. We haven't separated out recommendations by age, but we have given a rough indication of which group particular adaptations are aimed at. It's also worth making the obvious point that, in terms of their content, certain plays might be more suitable than others. Above all, share your enthusiasm without forcing it down a child's throat. It's not compulsory to enjoy Shakespeare.

Screen

An imaginative film version can be an ideal way of getting inside plays that would otherwise be difficult for young audiences to enjoy. Camerawork, whether it's point-of-view shots or illusionistic trickery, can bring aspects of a text alive in startlingly vivid ways. And it's worth remembering that an approach that seems unsophisticated to a seasoned Shakespearian might well appeal to someone experiencing a play for the first time. Reviews of film versions of specific plays can be found at the end of each chapter earlier in this book, though we've also included a few general recommendations here.

Shakespeare: The Animated Tales
Various animators, directors and actors;
UK, 1992–94 > Metrodome **DVD**

This series of twelve half-hour animated Shakespeare films, produced by BBC Wales and Russia's Soyuzmultfilm, has rightly achieved classic status. Cleverly abridged by Leon Garfield, the plays retain Shakespeare's language (with occasional sections of added narration), with some fine British stage actors – Anthony Sher as Richard III, Timothy West as Prospero – supplying the voices. The decision to use different artists and directors for each film means that the mood of each play can be reinforced by the visual style – a dark and painterly approach for *Hamlet*, but brighter and more conventionally cartoonish for *Romeo and Juliet*.

● AGE: 11–15 (AND YOUNGER)

Shakespeare in Love
J. Fiennes, G. Paltrow, G. Rush; John Madden (dir.)
US, 1998 > Universal **DVD**

Struggling to complete a play for cash-strapped theatre manager Philip Henslowe (Geoffrey Rush), the young Shakespeare (Joseph Fiennes) finds himself strangely drawn to the boy who auditions for a role in his yet-to-be-finished play. In fact the "boy" turns out to be the aristocratic Viola de Lesseps (Gwyneth Paltrow), with whom he embarks on a passionate secret affair. Essentially an Elizabethan rom-com, *Shakespeare in Love* is redeemed by a gloriously witty script by Tom Stoppard and Marc Norman. It also has a great deal of fun playing off Shakespearian myths and realities – the rivalry with Marlowe, the pressures of showbiz – in ways that are insightful and enjoyable for viewers of any age. Also highly plausible as a version of *Romeo and Juliet*.

● AGE: 11–15

Books

Shakespeare's inventive use of language is one of the most thrilling aspects of his work (see p.600), but a good deal of it is challenging for any reader – young or old – to grapple with. By contrast, many of the stories behind the plays are compellingly clear, not least because they are often based on folk tales or older sources, and from the nineteenth century onwards have been retold for young readers in a variety of forms. In recent years, too, a spate of graphic novels have come into their own – some more successful than others. A no less enjoyable route into Shakespeare's world can be through narratives set in the theatre of his time, several of which are recommended below. We've put the recommendations in approximate age order.

Henry V: The Graphic Novel

John McDonald and others;
2007 > Classical Comics

Many of Shakespeare's plays now exist in graphic novel or comic-book form (with *Macbeth* and *Dream* proving the most popular). Classical Comics have produced two of the best, not least because they have found a good solution to the language's difficulty by producing each play in three versions: a full original script, a plain-English version and a quick-text adaptation. The graphics, done by a team of artists, are lively and colourful, if a little unsophisticated.

● AGE: 8–12

Macbeth: The Graphic Novel

John McDonald and others;
2007 > Classical Comics

The artwork for this *Macbeth* is mostly the responsibility of a single artist, Jon Haward, and although it is in a similarly traditional comic-book style it's a little more polished and dynamic than Classical Comics' *Henry V*. Excitingly cinematic viewpoints enhance the drama and Macbeth is very much a muscle-bound, Hollywood action hero – albeit one dominated by his button-nosed yet fearsome wife. At the back of both books the publishers provide historical background about Shakespeare and the play.

● AGE: 8–12

The Orchard Book of Classic Shakespeare Stories

Andrew Matthews; 2014 > Orchard Books

These retellings adopt the most modern and prosaic approach, using hardly any of Shakespeare's text. Nevertheless, the stories are imaginatively told (*Hamlet* is written in the first person) and Angela Barrett's colour illustrations have a startling, jewel-like intensity. Eight of the best-known plays are covered, including *A Midsummer Night's Dream*, *Romeo and Juliet* and *Macbeth*.

● AGE: 8–12

Shakespeare's Romeo and Juliet

Michael Rosen & Jane Ray; 2004 > Walker

This version is "presented" by its writer and illustrator, a verb that does full justice to a gorgeously produced volume. It's not quite accurate to call this a retelling of *Romeo and Juliet*, more a guided tour, offering speeches from the play (difficult words are explained in the margins) alongside Rosen's atmospheric commentary and Ray's expressive watercolours – an approach that seamlessly blends verse and prose, drama and narrative, image and story. Best of all, it preserves the thrill of the original while combining it with a vivid sense of what the play is like to experience in the theatre.

● AGE: 8–12

Tales from Shakespeare

Charles & Mary Lamb; 1807 > Penguin

Written by a brother and sister team, *Tales from Shakespeare* is the classic retelling of Shakespeare for children, beautifully fresh despite being two centuries old. The Lambs cover twenty plays in all (not all of them obvious choices), and tell their stories without too much elaboration, using a fair amount of Shakespeare's own words. There are numerous editions available in print and eBook; as well as the Penguin edition (which has an introduction by Marina Warner), there's a beautifully produced selection of six of the tales published by Abrams, with bold illustrations by Joëlle Jolivet.

● AGE: 8–12

Bearkeeper

Josh Lacey; 2007 > Marion Lloyd

Twelve-year-old Pip is living with his mother and sisters in Mildmay, just outside London, when some heavies show up demanding the repayment of mysterious debts. Driven by thoughts of revenge, Pip heads to London and an eye-opening discovery in the Bear gardens and theatres of Southwark. *Bearkeeper* is a rip-roaring adventure, packed with the sights and smells of Elizabethan England, which interweaves the author's own explorations of the same territory with delightful cameos of Shakespeare and his contemporaries.

● AGE: 10+

King of Shadows
Susan Cooper; 1999 ❯ Red Fox

Nat Field is a member of a modern-day, boys-only theatre company, which travels from the US to London in order to perform at the newly rebuilt Globe. While rehearsing *A Midsummer Night's Dream* Nat falls sick and finds himself transported back in time to 1599, this time to the original Globe, where he is to play Puck opposite no less a figure than Shakespeare himself. A brilliantly sustained novel, it convincingly evokes the Elizabethan theatre while wearing its historical knowledge lightly.

● AGE: 10–12

Kill Shakespeare
Anthony Del Col, Conor McCreery and others; 2011–14 ❯ IDW

More *Lord of the Rings*-ish than the *Manga Shakespeare* below, *Kill Shakespeare* is a twelve-part comic book series, a free-form montage of Shakespearian themes that brings many of the playwright's most celebrated creations – Hamlet, Juliet and Romeo, Feste, Falstaff and many others – back to life and installs them in an epic adventure story, vigorously illustrated, that's as addictive as a video game. It's been so successful that it's spawned two follow-up series, *The Tide of Blood* and *The Mask of the Night*, with more expected.

● AGE: 12+

King Lear
Ian Pollock; 1984 ❯ Can of Worms Press

This comic-book *Lear* operates in a very different artistic and psychological universe from that of Classical Comics (above). Ian Pollock's expressive drawings provide a disturbingly absurdist vision of the play, with the minimal settings placing the spotlight firmly on the characters. At the centre of the action is Lear himself, pop-eyed, whiskery and irascible, whose descent into madness and despair is movingly portrayed but also illuminated with sharp wit.

● AGE: 12+

Manga Shakespeare: Hamlet
Emma Vieceli; 2007 ❯ SelfMadeHero

Edgy and bold, the style of this series will jump out to anyone familiar with the Japanese comic books read by millions of people worldwide every year. As well as being hugely popular throughout Asia, *Manga* Shakespeare has also made its presence felt in the west courtesy of publisher SelfMadeHero, who have produced a series of plays with different illustrators. *Hamlet* is slightly mixed – older readers may find Emma Vieceli's black-and-white drawings a touch too cute, and its futuristic setting now seems dated. But the pages fly by, and this adaptation is great at getting right where it matters: inside its teenage hero's head. Paul Duffield's *Manga Tempest*, slightly more subtly illustrated, also comes highly recommended.

● AGE: 12+

Stratford Boys
Jan Mark; 2003 ❯ Hodder

This light-hearted look at Will Shakespeare, teenager, finds him taking time out from his father's glove shop in order to write and mount a play for Stratford's Whitsun celebrations. With the help of his good friend Adrian, an oddball company of friends and neighbours is assembled and – after several mishaps – *Fortune My Foe* receives its premiere. Mixing period detail with modern language, this is a genuinely witty imagining of how Shakespeare might have got started.

● AGE: 12+

The Shakespeare Secret
Jennifer Lee Carrell; 2008 ❯ Sphere / Plume

Technically aimed at adults (and published in the US as *Interred with Their Bones*), Carrell's thriller might appeal to Young Adult readers for whom the other recommendations here are a bit soft-edged. It cleverly entwines a modern-day murder mystery set in the replica Globe (which promptly burns down) with elements of Shakespearian history and more than a hint of the *Da Vinci Code*. Carrell certainly knows her stuff and the pages fly by as we follow theatre director Kate Stanley as she attempts to track down the key to an ancient curse. *Haunt Me Still*, a *Macbeth*-themed sequel, appeared in 2010.

● AGE: 14+

Audio

Audio versions, whether as CDs or downloads, offer a useful way of getting to know the plays and plenty of opportunity for imagination to fill in the gaps. As with films, every play in this book has at least one audio version recommended at the end of each chapter, but for most younger listeners a full performance would be a daunting prospect, probably even harder to understand without the action. With that in mind,

The education team at Shakespeare's Globe in London run a series of workshops and performances tailored for young people; this 2014 *Merchant of Venice* was played for an audience composed of schoolchildren from across London.

the following are recommended primarily as helpful listening experiences in advance of seeing things on stage or screen, though they might be an excellent option for car journeys too.

Lamb's Tales from Shakespeare
M. Jarvis, R. Ayres; UK, 2004 ❯ CSA Word ◉ ⬇

Originally published in 1807, the series of short, narrative adaptations by brother and sister Charles and Mary Lamb – initially only Charles was credited – became one of the most popular children's books of all time, translated into countless languages. Reading aloud helps to make the slightly old-fashioned language seem rather less so and Martin Jarvis is a master; sharing honours with his wife Rosalind Ayres, he brings an engaging authority to the stories without ever sounding patronizing. Eleven of the best-known tales have been recorded, and each unabridged retelling lasts approximately 30 minutes.

● AGE: 8–12

Stories from Shakespeare
J. Stevenson, M. Sheen; David Timson (dir.) UK, 2005–08 ❯ Naxos ◉ ⬇

David Timson, the producer of several Naxos audio recordings of Shakespeare, has abridged 26 of the plays somewhat in the manner of Leon Garfield's scripts for *The Animated Tales*, reducing them to around half an hour but retaining much of the dialogue while introducing a narrator to link the scenes. Ten of the plays use extracts from Naxos's own recordings, while the others have had them specially recorded. The results are a little more immediate and exciting than the Lamb recording.

● AGE: 10+

From school to stage

A final question might be the most obvious: why not just take kids to a "proper" performance? Shakespeare's works were written primarily to be performed rather than read, and there can be few things more thrilling than live theatre for audiences of any age. But given that uncut versions of the plays are consistently over two hours long and employ challenging language, a full-length staging might not be the best starting point, especially if a child is under the age of 12. That said, of course both children and productions vary, and many companies now specialize in family-friendly versions of Shakespeare, whether as part of their education programme or in the main repertoire. While certain plays are more suitable than others, less obvious or more difficult works can also inspire if you're lucky enough to catch a great performance. Conversely, there's nothing like flat-footed or over-complicated staging to put anyone off. The best advice is probably to trust your instincts, but also do a bit of homework: read up on reviews, look out for recommendations online and consider – especially with younger children – talking about the story of a play in advance.

Kids are almost certain to come across Shakespeare in school, of course, particularly in the UK, where studying one of his works is a compulsory part of the curriculum. Although reading out a play with students trapped behind desks is less common than it used to be, unimaginative lessons can put students off for life, and constant pressure to prepare for exams often does little to enhance enjoyment. It may be worth finding out whether your child's school has a drama club, or links with a theatre, to shake things up a bit. Many theatres, particularly large ones, have excellent education departments and offer discounted tickets. Educational progammes often involve close contact with actors, as well as customized workshops in directing and performance, emphasizing that Shakespeare's plays were written to be acted, and come to life in collaboration and performance. Try some of their websites for details (see p.662), and cross-check the recommended books for teachers and school students on p.644.

In 2008 the RSC launched an educational manifesto, *Stand up for Shakespeare*, whose excellent suggestions echo those of other education departments and are well worth repeating here – not least because they offer a challenge to parents and relatives as well as teachers. Children should be encouraged to get inside the plays by acting them out, the manifesto argues, responding orally and physically to the characters and stories through theatre-based learning. They should be encouraged to grapple with the language, perhaps using an edited text to aid understanding. It's also important that kids get the opportunity to experience live performance, whether by professional companies or amateur groups. And it's crucial that they gain access to Shakespeare early, ideally while still in primary or junior school – far younger than most syllabuses require. Not only can these approaches help young people get to know and appreciate Shakespeare, they give a good chance of igniting a passion for theatre in all its forms. You can find out more at: rsc.org.uk/sufs

Books

S omeone once estimated that a new book on Shakespeare is published every single day. The following clutch of titles isn't intended as a shopping list, still less is it complete (there are entire tomes dedicated to Shakespeare bibliography). It's merely meant to illuminate some pathways. Critical recommendations on specific works and themes are covered in the first portions of this book; this fills some remaining gaps with what is hopefully a lively mix of standard reference works and other reading. Classifying books on the Bard is a complex exercise, so it's worth skimming through the lot to find titles that interest you.

Complete editions

Though the individual editions recommended under each work are the most relevant if you're interested in, or studying, a particular play/poem in any depth, you'll soon want a *Complete Works*. Each is designed to provide an internally consistent approach to editing the text, which is why critical studies covering more than one work are frequently keyed to one of the standard editions (as this book is to the Oxford *Complete Works*). But each has its quirks, and none is ideal.

Mr William Shakespeares Comedies, Histories, and Tragedies
Charlton Hinman (ed.); rev. 1996 ❯ Norton

A pristine copy of the 1623 First Folio fetched $6.1 million at auction not so long ago, such is the fetish for a book produced seven years after Shakespeare's death and in which he had no involvement whatsoever. *The Norton Facsimile* enables you to own a copy without mortgaging your grandparents, and to inspect the famous Droeshout portrait at close quarters. Other facsimiles are available, but this contains the standardized "Through Line Numbers" (line numbers without the act/scene divisions imposed by later editors) and uses several versions of the Folio to achieve a "perfect" copy. Understanding how a seventeenth-century book works is, as it happens, an education in itself.

The Norton Shakespeare
Stephen Greenblatt et al (eds); rev. 2015 ❯ Norton

Recognizing that the *Oxford Shakespeare* (see below) lacked the reader-friendly equipment of other major editions and unwilling to invest in a revision, OUP gave permission to a team led by Stephen Greenblatt to use that text and construct a "full" edition around it. The result is extremely hefty (3,536 bible-thin pages), complete with one-word glosses; fuller notes at the bottom of each page; critical intros; and numerous appendices. The whole enterprise is heavily influenced by the new historicism movement – there's much on "Otherness" and censorship, for instance – and the hyper-student-friendly editorial matter may jar for some. But *Norton* offers many of the positive aspects of *Oxford*, while taking a less take-it-or-leave-it approach: so you'll find a *Hamlet* which unites (by clever use of typography) the two main texts without conflating them; and no fewer than three *Lears*. Recently republished with an enhanced ebook.

The Oxford Shakespeare
Stanley Wells & Gary Taylor (eds);
rev. 2005 ❯ Oxford UP

The Oxford Shakespeare ignited a furore when it first appeared in 1986, turning its back on a tradition of editing that strived to recreate "original" texts as Shakespeare "intended" them to exist (a task which resulted in a good deal of cobbling together). Pointing out that Shakespeare worked as an actor and director, the Oxford editors argue that each text has its own local value, as well as its own relationship with forces other than that of the playwright. Thus they generally print the "theatrical" versions of texts, producing two versions of *King Lear*, a play which seems to have been revised post-performance; *2 Henry VI* and others are known by their original titles; and they suggest that Shakespeare worked with collaborators as a matter of course. The second edition takes that work to its logical conclusion, including *Edward III* for the first time and printing a full version of *Sir Thomas More*. Two caveats: the editors are more creative than some would prefer; and even though the introductory matter has been beefed up somewhat, the editorial matter remains scanty (no on-page notes, for instance).

The Riverside Shakespeare (second edition)
G. Blakemore Evans et al (eds);
rev. 1997 ❯ Houghton Mifflin

Though not as textually avant-garde as *Oxford* and *Norton*, and utilizing traditions of scholarship that now seem a little old-fashioned, *Riverside* may nonetheless be more useful for many readers (and is the basis for Spevack's *Concordance*; see p.649). For a start it has explanatory

notes and glosses, and each work is preceded by a sizeable critical essay – Anne Barton's introductions to the comedies and Frank Kermode's to the major tragedies are particularly recommended. Then there is the rest: lavish colour sections; essays on critical trends and stage history; documents relating to Shakespeare; texts for the possibly apocryphal *Edward III* and "A Funeral Elegy".

The RSC Shakespeare
Jonathan Bate & Eric Rasmussen (eds);
2007 ❯ Macmillan

Another Complete Works? This one is different: the first modern edition of the 1623 First Folio, and very nicely produced (and priced) it is too. As such it's testament to a trend in Shakespeare editing, away from seeing Shakespeare as a soloistic genius whose first thoughts were never bettered, and towards an image of him as a team player who happily accommodated the views of colleagues and collaborators. Bate and co.'s ruling to follow the Folio script wherever possible – it was edited by two of those colleagues – has the faint hint of fundamentalism about it, relegating apparently sensible corrections to the dustbin, but has the merit of consistency. It's only a shame that *A Lover's Complaint* doesn't make the cut of the print edition.

General reference and companions

With Shakespeare making his presence felt on school and university curriculums across the globe, it's little surprise that publishers have fought hard to get a foothold in the student market. The three books recommended below offer different ways in, and should also interest readers simply wanting to get hold of more information.

The New Cambridge Companion to Shakespeare
Margreta de Grazia & Stanley Wells (eds);
2010 ❯ Cambridge UP

If you're looking for a companion on your journey through Shakespeare, Oxford and Cambridge have the market sewn up – and veteran scholar Stanley Wells plays for both sides. Actually, the books are quite different: whereas *Oxford* (see below) is a large A–Z, the recently updated *Cambridge Companion* is a collection of undergraduate-level essays (20 in total) by academic contributors on various themes. It's an all-star international team: Stephen Greenblatt on the playwright's life; Tiffany Stern on the theatrical environment; Ton Hoenselaars on the history plays; Stephen Orgel on sex and gender; and Paul Prescott on Shakespeare and popular culture. They're level-headed and spryly written, and the book contains a useful section on further reading. There are also useful Cambridge Companions to individual Shakespearian

subjects – comedies, tragedies, the last plays, and more – available separately.

A Companion to Shakespeare
David Scott Kastan; 1997 ❯ Blackwell / Wiley

David Scott Kastan, general editor of the Arden Shakespeare, brings together an excellent collection of new essays in this chunky Blackwell *Companion*, all distinguished by their original approach. At opposite ends of the volume David Bevington explores what Shakespeare might have been like as a man and Michael Bristol launches a hard-nosed (but not unsympathetic) examination of "Shakespeare: The Myth". In between lie pieces grouped under "Living" (social and geographical history), "Reading" (education and detail on sources), "Writing" (contexts for Shakespeare's output), "Playing" (the Jacobethan theatre industry) and "Printing" (the realities of publication). All are readable, many excellent, some unique.

The Oxford Companion to Shakespeare
Michael Dobson & Stanley Wells (eds);
rev. 2015 ❯ Oxford UP

It is difficult to believe that a book like this didn't exist until relatively recently, so handy has this large and generously illustrated encyclopedia proved. Intelligent short articles from a wide range of contributors are punctuated by longer pieces on individual works, providing brief accounts of texts, sources, performance and critical history, and a scene-by-scene synopsis for each. It is a bold venture – and despite being on one level a supreme example of bardolatry, the *Companion* never takes itself too seriously.

Shakespeare on stage

Shakespeare was an actor as well as a playwright for most of his working life, and remains perhaps the world's most performed stage writer. Even so, looking at the performance histories of individual works – such as those provided earlier in this book – can provide a slightly fragmented impression of overall historical trends. Several books specifically to do with Shakespeare and his contemporaneous theatrical environment are recommended in the "Shakespeare's Stages" section on p.599. If you want to find out more about individual actors and directors, the *Oxford Companion* (above) has many brief articles and suggestions for further reading; and if you're keen to keep pace with contemporary approaches worldwide, it's best to use a website such as the University of Victoria's Internet Shakespeare Editions, which aims to keep abreast of major productions as they happen (see p.659).

Colorblind Shakespeare
Ayanna Thompson (ed.); 2006 ❯ Routledge

The practice of "colour-blind" casting – in which actors of all heritages are encouraged to perform alongside each other, irrespective of ethnicity – has gone from being a far-out experiment at places such as the New York Public Theater in the 1950s to an accepted part of the mainstream. Thompson's collection is the first to examine the topic from an academic perspective, bringing together eleven original essays from multinational contributors including Ania Loomba, Angela C. Pao and Lisa M. Anderson. Many key productions are covered, from the Shakespeare productions mounted by New York's African American African Theatre in the 1820s onwards, and Thompson does not duck the difficult debates that surround the changing face(s) of stage representation.

The Oxford Illustrated History of Shakespeare on Stage
Jonathan Bate & Russell Jackson (eds);
rev. 2001 ❯ Oxford UP [o/p]

This book could do with an update, but is still hugely useful – a pleasure to browse because of its copious illustrations, and its contributors' consistently pithy and humane comments. It also contains a detailed list of further reading on specific theatrical periods. *The Cambridge Companion to Shakespeare on Stage* (2002) also packs much of international interest into an essay-based format (though, again, is ripe for revision).

Great Shakespeare Actors
Stanley Wells; 2015 ❯ Oxford UP

After decades of auteur theory, in which scholars concentrated on the intentions of playwright and/or director to the exclusion of all else, there has been a recent surge of interest in the role(s) played by Shakespeare's own actors and their successors. Stanley Wells's guide is excellent, thoroughly researched but written with spirit and verve, and tries to reconstruct the performances of 39 different leading men and women from Richard Burbage to Kenneth Branagh, with fascinating side essays on topics such as "Who was the first Shakespearian actress?". If you're interested in following the thread, Michael Dobson's *Performing Shakespeare's Tragedies Today* (2006) contains interviews with leading British thesps, including Imogen Stubbs, Antony Sher and Samuel West.

Shakespeare from Betterton to Irving
George C. Odell; 1920 ❯ Forgotten Books

Odell's goliath two-volume study takes on over two centuries of staging, offering a compendious history of the changes and chances in Shakespearian theatre from the Restoration stage of Thomas Betterton to that of his Victorian successor Henry Irving. It's an elderly book and the style can veer towards the orotund, yet there's so much here – all the way from lighting and physical staging to commentary on individual acting styles, with plentiful eyewitness detail. Recently available as a reprint.

Shakespeare in Performance
Keith Parsons & Pamela Mason (eds); 1995 >
Random House/Salamander [o/p]

Shakespeare in Performance is a glossy collection of nearly four hundred images of influential productions, with a slant towards twentieth-century British stagings. It's a visual banquet, and the text, which provides potted stage histories linked thematically to the plays, is also good. The RSC is over-represented, and it's obviously not remotely up to date, but that's a minor quibble when what's here is so good – it's revelatory to see images of historic productions you've only ever read about.

Shakespeare in Performance: Contemporary Critical Essays
Robert Shaughnessy (ed.); 2000 > Macmillan

Not to be confused with the coffee-table-style book immediately above, Robert Shaughnessy's valuable anthology marshals spiky and combative essays on feminist, Marxist, new-historicist, cultural-materialist, postcolonial and psychoanalytical topics, focusing on the fissures and complications that underpin contemporary performances of Shakespeare, particularly those that claim to be "authentic". Kathleen McLuskie examines the paradoxes of Elizabethan gender-bending, Robert Weimann investigates the politics of authority and Alan Sinfield examines the changing ideology of the Royal Shakespeare Company. W.B. Worthen's essay even casts doubt on the trustworthiness of performance criticism itself.

Shakespeare in Production
Various editors > Cambridge UP

Not one book, but an expanding series. CUP is picking up where earlier publishers left off, producing a hugely useful collection of individual plays with on-page notes, using nuggets from promptbooks and reviews to piece together a strong sense of how different productions have handled the text. Each also provides a detailed narrative stage history and illustrations, as well as tables saying who did what when. Titles now available include

Antony and Cleopatra, Hamlet, Henry V, The Merchant of Venice, Twelfth Night and *The Tempest*; see the website at www.cambridge.org for more.

Shakespeare in the Theatre
Stanley Wells (ed.); rev. 2000 > Oxford UP

An anthology of valuable snippets and reviews from such varied commentators as William Hazlitt, George Bernard Shaw and Virginia Woolf, which is as much a study of changing ways of reviewing performances as anything else. For all that, it provides a heady whiff of the greasepaint and a sense of what it might have been like to bitch with Evelyn Waugh over an interval drink.

Shakespeare on the Stage
Robert Speaight; 1973 > Collins / Little, Brown [o/p]

Long out of print but well worth finding, Speaight's "illustrated history" follows the story of performance from one Shakespearian titan (Richard Burbage) to another (Laurence Olivier), spending a refreshing amount of time out of Britain along the way. Speaight was a fine actor himself, and he handles his subject adroitly, giving a real sense of evolving trends in performance while providing plenty of colour on specific theatrical productions and their designs.

Talking to the Audience
Bridget Escolme; 2005 > Routledge

Escolme's fascinating study starts from a simple question – what happens when a Shakespearian actor addresses the audience? From there it flits through a fascinating number of performative issues, investigating the monologue, the soliloquy, and arguing that the notion of subjectivity is strongest in the direct encounter between performer and spectator. Escolme grounds her argument in theories drawn from Stanislavski and Brecht, but it bursts to life in her accounts of productions she has seen, ranging from Mark Rylance's Hamlet at Shakespeare's Globe in 2000 to fascinating stagings of *Julius Caesar* and *Hamlet* by the Italian experimental troupe Socìetas Raffaello Sanzio.

Shakespeare on film

Shakespearian movies date to the dawn of the silent era, not just in England and the United States (where directors seized on the plays to prove how highbrow their new medium could be) but in India, where theatre companies based in what became Bollywood were among the very first to record their versions of Shakespeare for posterity. Western academics are still struggling to catch up with the global reach of Shakespearian cinema, which extends across every continent on earth, but there are still some useful primers, which could be combined with a website such as IMDb.

100 Shakespeare Films
Daniel Rosenthal; 2007 **>** BFI

This BFI guide covers everything from the earliest silents (James Keane's 1912 *Richard III*) to modern multiplex fodder (Branagh's recent *As You Like It*), from the straightest of the straight (Heston's *Antony and Cleopatra*) to the eccentric fringes (Kaurismäki's *Hamlet Goes Business*). Rosenthal's write-ups are democratic and free of fuss, and even if one sometimes yearns for sharper prose there's no denying the range of his expertise: where else could you find *Scotland, PA* rubbing shoulders with Kurosawa's *Throne of Blood*? (Answer: the *Macbeth* section.) Also well worth checking out is Rosenthal's lushly illustrated, coffee-table-scale *Shakespeare on Screen* (2000), now out of print but well worth tracking down.

The Cambridge Companion to Shakespeare on Film
Russell Jackson (ed.); rev. 2007 **>** Cambridge UP

Jackson's selection is an adroit and concise collection of essays, if occasionally a little too prone to film-studies jargon. It's well positioned to discuss the second renaissance in Shakespeare film-making in addition to previous trends. The *Companion* is divided into four sections: "Adaptation and its Contexts"; a group of essays on genres and specific plays; pieces on specific directors (Olivier, Welles, Kozintsev, Zeffirelli and Branagh); and finally what the book calls "critical issues", including those involving Shakespeare's women on film and "filming the supernatural".

New Wave Shakespeare on Screen
Thomas Cartelli and Katherine Rowe (eds); 2007 **>** Polity

More playful and skittish than the *Cambridge Companion* and Rosenthal's *100 Shakespeare Films*, Cartelli and Rowe's collection addresses what it terms the "new wave" – the surge of experimentation in Shakespearian film-making (Taymor, Almereyda, Luhrmann) that swept to prominence at the end of the twentieth century. It's theory-heavy and occasionally over-hip, but there are real insights to be gleaned, particularly the essay on "adaptation as cultural process".

Shakespeare and World Cinema
Mark Thornton Burnett; 2013 **>** Cambridge UP

There has long been a hole at the centre of Shakespearian film studies – the world outside the Anglo-American canon, whether it's Bollywood movies (hundreds of adaptations from the silent period on), Latin American cinema or the rich corpus of East Asian film. Burnett's book is a long-overdue attempt to make up the debt – far from comprehensive, but a great start. He's a savvy critic, and intelligently weaves together many different movies from locations as far-flung as Malaysia, Venezuela and the Arctic, with a major focus on Indian auteurs Vishal Bhardwaj and Jayraaj Rajasekharan Nair. An excellent introduction to the field.

Shakespeare on Screen: An international filmography
Kenneth Rothwell & Annabel Henkin Meltzer; 1990 **>** Continuum

The book is sorely in need of an update – or some kind of digital rebirth tied to IMDb – but Rothwell and Meltzer remains the standard reference work, a goldmine of information on hundreds of Shakespearian movies, all the way from the major movies by Kurosawa, Kozintsev, Olivier and Branagh to spin-offs such as the 1937 American short *Hamlet and Eggs* to the brief scene referencing "To be, or not to be" in Katharine Hepburn and Douglas Fairbanks's classic comedy *Morning Glory* (1933). There are citations to articles, with information on distribution, medium and duration. Although it calls itself "international", the book's coverage outside the English language is pretty thin, however (there's very little on Asia or Africa, for instance).

Shakespeare on Silent Film
Judith Buchanan; 2009 **>** Cambridge UP

Critics get so obsessed with Shakespeare's language that it's easy to forget there was an entire pre-history to Shakespeare on film – the silent period, which lasted from 1899 (the year Beerbohm Tree's minute-and-a-half-long *King John* was screened) to the dawn of the talkie era in the late 1920s, and involved in excess of 300 films in all. Buchanan is an alert and engaging guide to the period, and draws out many fascinating strands, particularly strong on the numerous silent versions of *Hamlet*, including the celebrated 1920 version with Asta Nielsen as a gamine female hero(ine). As elsewhere, the book's only limitation is its near-non-existent coverage of Indian silent films – an extensive and fascinating world. Also worth referring to is Robert Hamilton Ball's classic account *Shakespeare on Silent Film: A Strange Eventful History* (1968).

Shakespeare's life and context

The paucity of hard evidence about Shakespeare's cultural milieu can make it rewarding to do some wider background reading, in addition to the conventional biographies recommended on p.579. Generalized historical and cultural studies have not been thick on the ground in recent years, perhaps because historians, more interested in particularities than ever, have fought shy of attempting to summarize entire swaths of Jacobethan life. The books recommended below deal – highly selectively – with aspects of this topic.

A Companion to English Renaissance Literature and Culture
Michael Hattaway (ed.); 2000 ❯ Blackwell / Wiley

There are no fewer than sixty essays here from a large team of writers – many of them acknowledged leaders in their field – covering what seems to be everything from the Reformation (Patrick Collinson), travel writing (Peter Womack) and education (Jean R. Brink) to sexuality (James Knowles) and rhetoric (Marion Trousdale). The vast span of topics sometimes threatens to overwhelm the essay-based format, although Diana E. Henderson, to cite one example, does rather well to introduce "love poetry" in just thirteen pages. On the whole, though, this is a usefully provocative volume that never threatens to become worthy.

The Elizabethan World Picture
E.M.W. Tillyard; 1943 ❯ Pimlico / Vintage

Though regarded with a mixture of scorn and horror by some, this remains an intriguing (and attractively slender) introduction to the period. Outlining a thesis grounded a few years later in *Shakespeare's History Plays* (see p.162), Tillyard suggests that the static elements in Elizabethan thought, which he terms the "chain of being" – order and degree, focused on God and mirrored by the four elements and the celestial spheres – ultimately governed Elizabethan society. At best this argument is selective, at worst it's hokum, but there is still much to learn.

Religion and the Decline of Magic
Keith Thomas; 1971 ❯ Penguin / Macmillan

Thomas's study remains one of the finest and most suggestive introductions to a period that was less modern in many respects than we sometimes think. Thomas accomplishes the impressive feat of providing a lucid and illuminating guide to a dimly lit, sometimes little-documented world: one in which astrology, witchcraft, ghosts and fairies still loomed large in everyday life. It's fascinating both in terms of social history and anthropology, and has a very pragmatic resonance for students of Shakespeare, in whose work ghosts and the supernatural are frequently present.

Shakespeare: The poet and his plays
Stanley Wells; rev. 2001 ❯ Methuen

Originally published as *Shakespeare: A dramatic life*, this is now in its second incarnation. It's not a biography as such, but rather a critical introduction of each group of works in the order in which they were probably written. The enviable breadth of Wells's experience makes this a pleasant (if slightly indulgent) read, spiced with detail from the countless productions he's witnessed and including an eloquent chapter on why Shakespeare should be seen as well as read.

This Stage-Play World
Julia Briggs; rev. 1997 ❯ Oxford UP

Briggs wrote *This Stage-Play World* for English students interested in knowing more about the historical period as well as historians wanting access to literary texts. In truth anyone can learn something from this sophisticated and readable study of what is sometimes called the "high renaissance", the period from the second decade of Elizabeth I's reign to the last years of her successor James. Shakespeare's working life is neatly bounded by those dates, but there's also plenty on Bacon, Spenser, Marlowe, Dekker, Sidney and many others, making this the best introduction to Shakespeare's contemporaries as well as the cultural environment that nourished them all.

Language and concordances

As the chapter on the topic suggests (see p.600), Shakespeare has no peer as a craftsman of the English language – which is why it's worth exploring a little further into the words he used and had access to, and why he selected the ones he did. Words he didn't have access to were no barrier: he came up with over six hundred coinages in all, many of them drawn from Latin. The recommendations below cover both reference companions and discursive introductions, and there are more suggestions on p.617.

A Glossary of Shakespeare's Sexual Language
Gordon Williams; 1997 > Continuum

Contrary to what self-appointed guardians of public morality would have you believe, sex really does permeate the work of England's National Poet, and nowhere is that more evident than in his willingness to pun on sexual slang. Eric Partridge's *Shakespeare's Bawdy* (1955) was for generations the standard work in the area and still remains an engaging read, though Gordon Williams's more upfront and complete work provides a fine replacement. Also worth dipping into is the hugely fun *Shakespeare's Insults* (1991), edited by Wayne F. Hill and Cynthia J. Öttchen, which offers advice on Shakespeare-style abuse as well as a play-by-play compendium of insults.

The Harvard Concordance to Shakespeare
Marvin Spevack (ed.); 1973 > Harvard UP [o/p]

The single-volume *Harvard Concordance* is actually a redaction of Spevack's nine-part monster (1968–80), which contains all sorts of fascinatingly geeky extras. The slimmer version is certainly more useable, though, and will accommodate all but the most esoteric needs. It includes every single one of the 30,000-odd words Shakespeare used (with obvious functional exceptions) and the phrases in which they appear, with full references to locations in *The Riverside Shakespeare* (see p.644). Spevack also includes data on each word's absolute frequency, its relative frequency, and how often it appears in verse and prose. Digital tools (see p.659) will soon offer much more,

but you can pick up this handsome hardback for a song secondhand.

A Shakespeare Glossary
C.T. Onions, rev. Robert D. Eagleson; 1986 > Oxford UP

Although to an extent superseded by the Crystals' more recent (and larger) *Shakespeare's Words* (see below), it would be churlish not to mention this long-standing favourite. Onions was one of the original editors of the *Oxford English Dictionary* and took it upon himself to produce a small guide to elucidate problematic and arcane words in Shakespeare, which first appeared in 1911 and was immediately popular because of the clarity of its explanations and range of reference. If you're interested in how the words fit together, Onions can be supported with another trusty Victorian reference, E.A. Abbot's *Shakespearian Grammar* (1869).

Shakespeare's Words
David & Ben Crystal; 2002 > Penguin

Shakespeare's Words is primarily a Shakespearian glossary, referring to the works and cross-checked with the *Oxford English Dictionary* (see above). As such its usefulness extends beyond being a replacement for C.T. Onions' standard *Shakespeare Glossary*: it can be employed as a stop-gap concordance, and in addition contains lists of names, synopses and engaging boxes on such topics as "Exclamations" and "Sounds". The only disappointment in this admirably clear book is that the Crystals didn't key everything to a standard *Complete Works*, such as Oxford or Riverside, but instead used Penguin's patchy New Shakespeare editions.

Sources and influences

It can be a surprise to learn how much Shakespeare depended on sources and analogues for his plays and poems – all the way from sensationalist romances to serious tomes such as Holinshed's *Chronicles* and Plutarch's *Lives*. In addition to listing the key work in the field, Bullough's *Narrative and Dramatic Sources of Shakespeare*, we also review several other studies and modern editions containing some of Shakespeare's favourite reading. Single editions of the plays and poems often contain excerpts from key sources; see the individual reviews earlier in this book for details.

Narrative and Dramatic Sources of Shakespeare
G. Bullough (ed.); 1957–75 > Columbia UP

Over a period of nearly thirty years, Geoffrey Bullough scoured libraries and archives for everything Shakespeare had access to when writing his plays and poems – and came up with some items he possibly didn't, classified

here as "analogues". The result is the most complete collection of sources available, usually printed in generous excerpts with plentiful commentary. The series as a whole takes up eight volumes covering various groups of work (Roman plays, major tragedies and so on), and though out of print, it is possible to buy individual copies secondhand for around £20/$30 each. Bullough's tomes are supplemented by G. Harold Metz's *Sources of Four Plays Ascribed to Shakespeare* (1989), which covers *Edward III*,

Sir Thomas More, Cardenio and *The Two Noble Kinsmen.* Some volumes of Bullough are available for free online in PDF form, so it's worth doing a search to see what comes up.

The Geneva Bible (1560 edition)
Lloyd E. Berry (ed.); 1981 ❯ Hendrickson

So-called because of its translation into English by Protestant exiles based at the Academy there, the "Geneva" Bible, first published in 1560, was the version most Elizabethans grew up with. Shakespeare refers to it in the most varied (and oddest) of places, making it one of the major sources for his work (though his plays show that he was familiar with the 1568 Bishops' Bible too). Various facsimile editions of this hefty tome are available – none of them cheap – but an infinitely easier option is to get hold of the more familiar King James version, published a few years before Shakespeare's death, whose resonant, lapidary style owes much to Geneva. If you're looking for more detail on what Shakespeare actually did with this text, Hannibal Hamlin's *The Bible in Shakespeare* (2013) is an excellent starting point.

Ovid's Metamorphoses [trans. Golding]
Madeleine Forey (ed.); 2002 ❯ Penguin

Madeleine Forey's edition of Arthur Golding's Elizabethan classic is elegant, up to date and well presented, with endnotes and a handy glossary (Golding has a habit of relishing, sometimes inventing, colourful but obscure language). Golding himself is an engaging and never less than personable translator – it's Ovid, but he takes the task of "Englishing" his Latin very seriously. If what sometimes emerges struggles to sound as suave as you might expect, that's all part of the fun (and Shakespeare enjoyed it, too, as his version of "Pyramus and Thisbe" in *A Midsummer Night's Dream* shows; see p.305).

The Riverside Chaucer
Larry D. Benson et al (eds); rev. 2000 ❯ Oxford UP

Although only the long and tragic poem *Troilus and Criseyde* and the "Knight's Tale" from *The Canterbury Tales* form large-scale sources (in *Troilus and Cressida*, *A Midsummer Night's Dream* and *The Two Noble Kinsmen* respectively), we know that Shakespeare often turned to his copy of Chaucer, probably in Francis Thynne's sixteenth-century edition. While the relevant excerpts from these and other Chaucerian classics are readily available in Bullough, it's worth reading Chaucer in a deluxe (but not expensive) edition such as this one, with a full range of notes and appendices.

Shakespeare's English Kings
Peter Saccio; rev. 2000 ❯ Oxford UP

It's been said that the English learn their theology from Milton and their history from Shakespeare. The perils of doing the latter are suggested by *Shakespeare's English Kings*, which provides plenty of facts to counterbalance Shakespeare's numerous excursions from historical truth. A manageable and useful book that offers abundant detail from the chronicle sources, while also providing a convincing survey of each Shakespearian royal; only its slightly juiceless prose lets it down.

Shakespeare's Plutarch
T.J.B. Spencer (ed.); 1964 ❯ Penguin [o/p]

Spencer's anthology of Plutarch's *Parallel Lives*, which excerpts parts of Sir Thomas North's 1579 translation, is the most helpful book of its kind, containing the big four lives – Julius Caesar, Brutus, Antony and Coriolanus – that Shakespeare used intensively for his Roman dramas. Spencer helpfully prints snippets from the plays alongside relevant passages. Long out of print, but it's relatively easy to find a decent copy of this paperback secondhand. If you can't, Cambridge publish a useful selection edited by P. Giles (2014), again using North's translation.

Shakespeare's Reading
Robert S. Miola; 2000 ❯ Oxford UP

If you're looking for a quick, no-nonsense guide to Shakespeare's sources and how he used them, this slim paperback is almost certainly the best place to start. Miola sketches out the Elizabethan intellectual climate with admirable brevity and skill, before going on to look at groups of sources in turn – for the poems, the histories, the comedies, the tragedies, before concluding with some suggestive thoughts on how Shakespeare was a "competitive" reader, determined to hoover up all the material he could before overmastering it.

Shakespere's Smalle Latin and Lesse Greeke
T.W. Baldwin; 1947 ❯ Illinois UP [o/p]

Not for novices and only available second-hand, Baldwin's monumental work is nevertheless the most complete survey of Shakespeare's education. It takes at face value Ben Jonson's snooty observation that Shakespeare had only "small Latin and less Greek" and demonstrates that, in fact, he had more than many modern-day classicists. Fascinating if somewhat forbidding. Colin Burrow's excellent *Shakespeare and Classical Antiquity* (2013) is a more approachable alternative, thoughtful on who and what Shakespeare read, and richly suggestive on what the classical world might have meant to him.

Shakespeare's work and texts

In the sections on Shakespeare's life and stages (see p.559 and p.581) we've already recommended studies that deal with the main fabric of Shakespeare's biography and work. But in recent years, encouraged by new scholarly interest in the materiality of texts and publishing practice, attention has focused on the environment in which he and his contemporaries actually wrote. Below you'll find reviews of some engaging academic studies that approach the issue from different perspectives – rehearsal, publication and revision.

Rehearsal from Shakespeare to Sheridan
Tiffany Stern; 2000 > Oxford UP

Interpreting the term "rehearsal" broadly, Stern's enlightening study investigates how rehearsals were handled over two centuries of theatrical history – not just as preparations for performance, but try-outs of new work and even actors' private study. Stern's most contentious point is that players during this period were working exclusively from "parts" containing only their lines and had no idea about the rest of the play until it was performed. As shown by the experimental work of Stern's uncle Patrick Tucker – who presents plays with Elizabethan-style rehearsal schedules – if this lack of preparation is true, Burbage and his ilk must have been finer actors than we can imagine.

Shakespeare and the New Bibliography
F.P. Wilson, rev. Helen Gardner; 1970 > Oxford UP [o/p]

In a general sense, the so-called "new bibliography" of the mid-twentieth century steered a path through the chaotic conditions of early English publishing by attempting to reconstruct single, "ideal" texts as the author might have intended them to see print – a formidable task, particularly for Shakespeare (see p.618). Nowadays editors tend to scorn such ambitions, but even so *Shakespeare and the New Bibliography* is a lucid exposition of the subject, and an excellent introduction to the study of printed texts in the Renaissance.

Shakespeare as Literary Dramatist
Lukas Erne; rev. 2013 > Cambridge UP

Two interlocking theories about Shakespeare – that he was careless about publication during his lifetime and (narrative poems aside) wrote for the theatre rather than print – have been received wisdom for decades. Lukas Erne's provocative book attempts to overturn convention by showing not merely that play-texts had a higher status in the booksellers' market than has often been supposed, but that Shakespeare managed his published image with some care. His further thesis, that the long and "literary" Folio texts represent scripts consciously worked up for publication, has caused controversy, but nevertheless makes for interesting reading.

Shakespeare at Work
John Jones; 1995 > Oxford UP

Jones's account is a fascinating and lively study of what you might call Shakespeare the tinkerer – a playwright who can never resist playing around with his text, the kind of man we glimpse in the one surviving manuscript in his own hand, *The Book of Sir Thomas More* (see p.190), only too ready to cross things out and try another option. *Sir Thomas More* forms Jones's first chapter, and other plays – *Hamlet*, *Lear* and *Othello* – are a major part of the book, which tries to suggest that variant texts as they survive contain clues to Shakespeare's habits of revision and reworking. Some of this rests on shaky ground, but *Shakespeare at Work* is nonetheless absorbing.

Unediting the Renaissance
Leah S. Marcus; 1996 > Routledge

The thrust of *Unediting the Renaissance* is that the kind of text you're reading matters a great deal: even supposedly minor issues can completely alter the way that people perform and write about Shakespeare. Marcus's initial illustration of this is Sycorax, the witch in *The Tempest* who is "blew ey'd" in the Folio text; despite the obvious enough meaning (that her eyes are blue), Marcus reveals how generations of editors have tried to claim almost everything else – that her eyelids are blue as a sign of pregnancy, that she has blackened eyes, that "blew" isn't really blue – in an attempt to water down Shakespeare's striking but shocking image of an Algerian witch with glittering cobalt eyes. A tiny instance, but suggestive and provocative – as indeed is the rest of the book.

Shakespeare in music, art and literature

Shakespeare's influence on visual and musical art has been every bit as profound as on the written word. As well as the many songs in his plays, set to music by succeeding generations of composers, many of the plays themselves have been turned into operas – the most notable being the three by Verdi. Painters have been no less fired up by his writings, whether as recorders of the great performances of their age – as in the work of Zoffany – or as inspired interpreters in their own right, as in the case of Blake, Fuseli, Delacroix and Millais. And of course there can be few writers who would claim not to have been influenced by this most august of literary forbears.

After Shakespeare: An anthology
John Gross (ed.); 2002 > Oxford UP [o/p]

Set out to read literature inspired by Shakespeare and you'd never reach the end. John Gross's marvellous anthology allows you to dip into a decent spread of homages, misquotations and half-heard echoes without signing away the rest of your life. There are excerpts here from a wonderful range of writers, all the way from wittily precise Cole Porter lyrics to a typically windy offering from Walt Whitman, from juicy quotes lifted out of Pepys's diary to a rather good Max Beerbohm Pepys parody. Bardolaters should keep it constantly within arm's reach.

Searching for Shakespeare
Tarnya Cooper (ed.); 2006 > National Portrait Gallery

Produced as a companion to the National Portrait Gallery's 2006 exhibition, this volume purports to take you on a hunt through the ages for Shakespeare's shifting shape. In truth the whole exercise was a faintly suspicious attempt to lend credence to the NPG's founding acquisition, the (almost certainly doubtful) Chandos portrait (see p.574). Even so, the range of treasures the curators brought to one place was truly mind-boggling: nearly every major Shakespearian document, plus plenty more, featured in the show, and all are lovingly catalogued here. Ignore the mugshots and go straight to the beautifully photographed documents and *objets d'art*.

Shakespeare and the Artist
W. Moelwyn Merchant; 1959 > Oxford UP [o/p]

Shakespeare's theatre employed a cornucopia of visual symbols, all the way from lavish costumes to the richly decorated stage canopy (and even the printed borders of texts). Merchant insightfully weaves together what evidence exists for the relationship between the visual arts and the Elizabethan theatre, and moves forward into an energetic history of the artist-as-designer, from Inigo Jones to John Piper. The second part of the book concentrates on specific examples – a post-Poussin illustration of *Coriolanus* by Kirkall (1709), John

Runciman's *King Lear in the Storm* (1767) and the designs for Charles Kean's *Winter's Tale* (1856) among them.

Shakespeare and the Dance
Alan Brissenden; rev. 2014 > Dance Books / Pre Textos

Alan Brissenden's *Shakespeare and the Dance* suggests among much else that dance was utterly central to the social fabric of Shakespeare's era. Building on an elegant chapter covering "Dance and the Elizabethans", which adopts some similar positions on harmony and order to E.M.W. Tillyard (see p.648), Brissenden then goes on to suggest ways in which dance in Shakespeare's plays offers an image of lively movement within overall cohesion: initially in the marriages of the early and middle-period comedies, then in the masques and pageants of his late work. The author even finds time for the (ostensibly dance-free) histories, presenting a subtle analysis of their imagistic concern with dance-like movement.

Shakespeare and Music
David Lindley; 2005 > Bloomsbury

Part of the new Arden critical companions series, Lindley's slim, affordable and elegantly informative study tells you everything you need to know about music as Shakespeare and his contemporaries understood it. A third of the book focuses on Renaissance musical theory; the rest is devoted to practice, both inside Shakespeare's plays and elsewhere. Everything is coloured by Lindley's sense that Jacobean society loved the rituals of performance, from gloriously stylized ceremonials at court to the simplest tavern song.

Shakespeare in Art
Jane Martineau (ed.); 2003 > Merrell [o/p]

Built around the excellent Dulwich Picture Gallery/ Ferrara Arte Spa exhibition, this catalogue is gorgeously produced. It discusses the whole range of visual representations of Shakespeare's work in the eighteenth and nineteenth centuries, including performer portraits, the eighteenth-century print market, the influence of Boydell's Shakespeare Gallery, and the set designs of the nineteenth-century Grieve family. Plus, of course, the many pictures painted for exhibition, all lovingly presented and extensively contextualized.

Shakespeare in Music
Phyllis Hartnoll (ed.); 1964 ➤ Macmillan [o/p]

Still the most helpful single collection despite its date, *Shakespeare in Music* offers contributions from such specialists in the field as John Stevens (who provides a brilliant introductory essay reconstructing Shakespeare's musical environment), Charles Cudworth (writing on settings of the songs, 1660–1960) and Roger Fiske ("Shakespeare in the concert hall", a lively if somewhat tendentious essay that gets as far as Prokofiev). The book closes with a useful – if obviously not up-to-date – catalogue of musical works.

A Shakespeare Music Catalogue
Bryan N.S. Gooch & David Thatcher (eds); 1991 ➤ Oxford UP

This monumental five-volume resource attempts the ambitious task of listing every single musical composition related to or inspired by Shakespeare. The focus is on art music – operas, ballets, orchestral works and so on – but even so the editors find space to cram in details of incidental music and songs. Volume 5 may be of most interest to non-specialist readers who can afford it (at about two-thirds the price of the others, it's still around £60/$100 new): it contains useful articles on topics including Shakespeare's knowledge of music and his choice of titles.

Shakespeare: The life, the works, the treasures
Catherine M.S. Alexander (ed.); 2006 ➤ André Deutsch

Open the pages, and all manner of historical documents – wills, legal documents, letters – tumble out. This curious volume, published in large format in association with the RSC, gives a decisively hands-on approach to the documentary record, mixing facsimiles of original manuscripts with bite-size chunks of history to tell the story of Shakespeare's life and posthumous reputation. Perhaps a bit too lift-the-flaps for most adults, but it will no doubt entrance the Bardolater who has everything.

Shakespeare's Songbook
Ross W. Duffin; 2004 ➤ Norton

Compiled using the enviable resources of the Folger Shakespeare Library in Washington DC, this beautifully produced volume aims to corral together every single song quoted or referred to in Shakespeare's plays, provide some explanatory context, and reprint the music. Duffin does a fine job and there's even an audio CD containing decent (if slightly earnest) performances of the songs. Peter J. Seng's *The Vocal Songs in the Plays of Shakespeare* (1967) is the standard reference work and admirably complete, but is only available secondhand.

Global Shakespeares

Translated into a tumult of different languages and performed in a riot of different performance styles – from Chicago hip-hop to Indian Kathak – the plays have touched the culture of almost every nation on the face of the planet over the last four centuries, making Shakespeare almost certainly the most read and translated secular author in history. This book tries to be as global as possible in its coverage of performance history and film adaptations, but if you're interested in this fascinating and fast-expanding field here are some suggestions to help map out a journey.

Chinese Shakespeares
Alexander C. Y. Huang; 2009 ➤ Columbia UP

It's a tad theory-heavy and not for the faint-hearted, but Huang's introduction to the world of Chinese Shakespeare (subtitled "Two centuries of cultural exchange") is sharp and alert, full of insights and ranging across a great deal of territory. It tells the story from the arrival of the Lambs' *Tales from Shakespeare* in the early twentieth century, covers the rebirth of Chinese drama they provoked, and offers numerous sidelights at Shakespeare in Mandarin film, traditional opera and many other forms besides, with a particularly sharp eye on "intercultural" remakes.

Also well worth consulting is Li Ruru's more pragmatic *Shashibiya: Staging Shakespeare in China* (2003), which focuses tightly on performance history.

The Critical Reception of Shakespeare in Germany
Roger Paulin; 2003 ➤ Olms

Revered by Goethe and Schiller and crucial to the rebirth of German literature in the *Sturm und Drang*, Shakespeare is felt by many Germans to be very much a native – and there are reckoned to be more performances of the plays here each year than in the UK. Hugely detailed and far from the easiest to read, Paulin's study nevertheless does exactly what it says on the tin, tracking the playwright's extensive influence on German life and literature from the late seventeenth century to the outbreak of World War I. If you're looking for performance history, the paired *Shakespeare on Stage* volumes by Simon Williams (1990, covering 1586–1914) and Wilhelm Hortmann (1998, on the twentieth century) are the best places to go; both are published by Cambridge.

German Shakespeare Studies at the Turn of the Twenty- First Century
Christa Jansohn (ed.); 2006 > Delaware UP

Christa Jansohn's study offers a snapshot of new-ish German scholarly approaches, from Horst Meller on *The Merchant of Venice* in postwar Germany to Ulrich Broich on Botho Strauss's 1983 adaptation of the *Dream*. The book's final section dwells on the fascinating – and sometimes troubling – history of the German Shakespeare Society, the world's oldest, which came fully under Nazi influence during World War II.

India's Shakespeare
Poonam Trivedi and Dennis Bartholomeusz (eds); 2005 > Pearson

An anthology featuring many leading names in Indian Shakespeare scholarship, *India's Shakespeare* threw long-overdue light on the vibrant life of Shakespeare on the subcontinent, which began when British colonizers introduced the plays in the eighteenth century yet soon expanded to fill almost every nook and cranny in Indian culture. There's a huge amount here, from essays on mind-bending Parsi adaptations in the late 1800s, folk theatre and Bollywood movies, to histories of the Bard in literary Bengal and a piece on Shakespeare's own view of the "Indies".

Re-playing Shakespeare in Asia
Poonam Trivedi and Minami Ryuta (eds); 2010 > Routledge

Chiefly a survey of different performance approaches, Trivedi and Ryuta's collection is valuable for the wide net it throws across many different kinds of Asian Shakespeare. Indian adaptations of the comedies and versions of the tragedies in Japan are well covered, but so too are stagings in the Philippines, Taiwan, Bali, Korea and mainland China, with a welcome emphasis on marginal or "minor" productions far outside the ambit of conventional Anglo-American Shakespeare studies. Hugely useful, especially given the increasing importance of Asian culture globally.

Shakespeare in America
Vaughan, Alden T. and Virginia Mason Vaughan; 2012 > Oxford UP

Slim but full of information, the Vaughans' *Shakespeare in America* – one of the Oxford Shakespeare Topics series – is the best place to start if you're interested in pursuing the Bard as he travelled out from the libraries of the Founding Fathers (Jefferson and John Adams were particular fans), through the fast-expanding United States in the nineteenth century, to become a powerful part of American cultural superpower. Their focus on multicultural Shakespeare is particularly welcome, as is coverage of popular American Shakespeares, from early Hollywood silents to the brief fad for Shakespearian musicals in the 1930s – a tradition energetically continued on social media. If you want pictures to go along with the words, the Vaughans' *Shakespeare in American Life*, the catalogue for a 2007 Folger exhibition, is lavishly illustrated.

Shakespeare in China
Murray J. Levith; 2004 > Continuum

More journalistic than either Huang or Li's accounts (see above), this is a good place to begin if you're encountering Chinese Shakespeares for the first time. Levith tells the story historically, focusing on nuts, bolts, names and dates, from a fleeting mention of the playwright in an 1856 encyclopedia to the period beyond the Cultural Revolution, during which Shakespeare (along with so much else) was banned. His chapter on Shakespeare and Confucianism is particularly fascinating.

Shakespeare in Eastern Europe
Stříbrný, Zdeněk; 2000 > Oxford UP

Courtesy of travelling English actors who toured bare-as-bones adaptations in the late sixteenth and seventeenth centuries, Eastern Europe was perhaps the first place outside England to encounter Shakespeare's work, and the tradition remains strong in present-day Poland and Russia, to name just two countries. Stříbrný is a welcoming and insightful guide to the territory, and particularly excellent on Shakespeare under communism, both during and after the Russian Revolution, when the plays became a means of smuggling protest into ostensibly state-sanctioned settings.

Shakespeare International Yearbook
Tom Bishop and Alexander C. Y. Huang (eds); 2000–present > Ashgate

Technically a journal, to date the *SIY* has published fifteen elegant issues, bringing together essays by many leading scholars from across the globe. Generally they focus on an individual geographical areas: vols 8

(Europe), 9 (South Africa) and 12 (India) are particularly valuable, but there are also volumes devoted to issues of place in Early Modern Europe (vol 11) and digital Shakespeares (14).

Shakespeare and Renaissance Europe
Andrew Hadfield and Paul Hammond (eds); 2005 ➤ Bloomsbury

Shakespeare started to go global even within his own lifetime, as the numerous worlds he put on stage amply demonstrate. Hadfield and Hammond's short essay collection is an excellent place to begin mapping the varied cultures of Renaissance Europe that trickled into the plays, from English tourists sending back travellers' tales to the changing geopolitical environment of the playwright's own lifetime. The Italian context for the comedies is well covered, as is the Moroccan backdrop to *Othello* – poised between Europe and North Africa – and there's a fine essay on "Shakespeare's imaginary geography" by Francis Laroque.

Shakespeare on the American Stage
Charles H. Shattuck; 1976 ➤ Folger [o/p]

An elegantly produced volume published by Washington DC's renowned Folger Shakespeare Library, it's well worth getting hold of this book secondhand if you're interested in how Shakespeare has appeared in American theatres from the eighteenth century onwards. Shattuck knows every nook and cranny of US performance history, and is an engaging and often very droll guide – his coverage of barnstorming nineteenth-century stars such as Edwin Forrest and Charlotte Cushman is superlative.

South Africa, Shakespeare, and Post-Colonial Culture
Natasha Distiller; 2004 ➤ Edwin Mellen

Few countries have experienced the colonial tensions and agonies of twentieth-century South Africa – one reason among many why the teaching and performance of a white European writer is still hugely controversial, over 20 years after the end of apartheid. Distiller doesn't duck the issues, examining the relationship between Shakespeare studies and South African culture from many different angles, and covering a panoply of responses to the plays in fiction, theatre, autobiography, journalism and other forms. Also well worth consulting is Distiller's slim essay collection, *Shakespeare and the Coconuts*, which examines the plays in light of intercultural controversies in Africa more broadly (a "coconut" being in this instance a derogatory term for someone black accused of wanting to be "white").

Romeo and Juliet in Palestine
Tom Sperlinger; 2014 ➤ Zero Books

Quite different to the academic studies and surveys elsewhere in this section, *Romeo and Juliet in Palestine: Teaching Under Occupation* is a personal account from a British academic of what it was like to work on Shakespeare – and Kafka, and Malcom X – with university students in the West Bank for five months at the beginning of 2013. The story is told with a cool eye for detail, and is often quietly moving as Sperlinger and his students battle with the realities of what the author calls "this mad reality" in the Occupied Territories.

World-wide Shakespeares
Sonia Massai (ed.); 2005 ➤ Routledge

Sonia Massai's excellent anthology focuses on film and stage performance, and thus might be a useful extension to the books recommended in the Shakespeare on Stage/Film sections above. In keeping with its title, Massai's contributors put a girdle round about the earth, all the way from Derek Walcott (Tobias Döring), Canadian auteur Robert Lepage (Margaret Jane Kidnie) to the tangled history of *The Merchant of Venice* in postwar Germany (Sabine Schülting). There's a huge amount that's fascinating, from all corners of the globe.

Worlds Elsewhere
Andrew Dickson; 2015 ➤ Bodley Head / Henry Holt

A literary travelogue rather than a straightforward academic study, *Worlds Elsewhere* narrates journeys through six countries where Shakespeare's work has made a home for itself – Poland, Germany, the US, India, South Africa and China, ranging from the late sixteenth century to the present day. Touching on such topics as Joseph Goebbels's adoration for the English Bard, the history of Shakespeare in apartheid South Africa and the surprising popularity of the plays in the Wild West, it blends historical material with eyewitness accounts of performances and films. If you're interested in the expanding topic of global Shakespeare, it's a good place to start. (Yes, the author also wrote the *Globe Guide*, so perhaps we're biased.)

A few critical trends

Individual works of criticism from many periods and walks of life are recommended earlier in the book with reference to specific plays and poems (though most will have links to other works). But if you'd like to find out about some overall trends, ranging from Romanticism to post-colonialism, the works listed below offer some pointers; most are anthologies.

A Feminist Companion to Shakespeare
Dympna Callaghan (ed.); 2000 > Blackwell

Including work by a number of well-known contributors – among them Juliet Dusinberre, one of the first critics to apply the "f"-word to Shakespeare with any seriousness – this collection of essays argues that we need feminist criticism now more than ever. The book helpfully covers the history of the movement before moving off in more esoteric directions; not every essay is of equal quality, but all show that feminism continues to innovate and agitate within academia, as outside it.

Johnson on Shakespeare
Bertrand H. Bronson & Jean O'Meara (eds); 1986 > Yale UP [o/p]

Among eighteenth-century critics Samuel Johnson was the most brilliant, able to distil views shared by his age and society yet make them his own. His largest contribution to Shakespeare scholarship was the monumental 1765 edition of the plays, the *Preface* to which remains perhaps the most lucid statement of its kind ever written. In it, Johnson's famous insistence that it is nonsense to claim (as Voltaire and other critics did) that Shakespeare's plays were jumbled and chaotic, rings true even now. Despite his distaste for Shakespeare's less moralistic moments and over-ingenious wordplay, Johnson is always an astute critic, and this valuable collection brings together the *Preface* and the earlier *Proposals for Printing ... the Dramatic Works of William Shakespeare* (1756) with the editor's numerous comments on specific scenes in the plays, both textual and dramatic.

Post-colonial Shakespeares
Ania Loomba & Martin Orkin (eds); 1998 > Routledge

It's the emphasis on variety and contingency that makes this anthology so worth reading, and which enables it to escape beyond well-worn commentary on *Othello* and *The Tempest*. Kim F. Hall's "Literary whiteness in Shakespeare's Sonnets" is involving and surprising, and Michael Neill's "Post-colonial Shakespeare? Writing away from the centre" raises a sardonic eyebrow in the direction of the whole enterprise – while also suggesting some convincing ways in which it has meaning.

Reinventing Shakespeare
Gary Taylor; 1989 > Oxford UP [o/p]

Gary Taylor knows plenty about reworking the Bard, having ruffled many feathers with his involvement

with the *Oxford Shakespeare* (see p.643), an edition that restored to the canon the poem "Shall I die?", an attribution still resisted by many. This book is subtitled a "cultural history from the Restoration to the present day" and takes a view of Shakespeare's engagement with varied historical periods which is as combative (and occasionally facetious) as much of Taylor's other writing. Terrific fun to read, and enlivening in its focus on the plurality of Shakespeare's reputation.

The Romantics on Shakespeare
Jonathan Bate; 1992 > Penguin [o/p]

Bate's anthology covers a solid chunk of one of the most exciting periods in Shakespeare appreciation. In this hefty paperback (571 pages) you'll find sizeable gobbets from contributors including Goethe, Schlegel, Hugo, Coleridge and Hazlitt – showing, as much as anything else, that by the late eighteenth and early nineteenth centuries Shakespeare had become a pan-European intellectual figure. If you feel like reading more from Coleridge, particularly his engaging marginalia, try R.A. Foakes's *Coleridge's Criticism of Shakespeare* (1989), which includes nearly everything of interest.

Shakespeare and the Question of Theory
Patricia Parker & Geoffrey Hartman (eds); 1985 > Routledge

In the heady mid-1980s, essay collections appeared bearing fierce titles like *Political Shakespeare* and *Alternative Shakespeares*, committed to annihilating dead-white-male readings of the Bard with brave new methods and theories (some Marxist, many imported from France and the US). *Shakespeare and the Question of Theory* is probably the scariest of the lot, but contains much work of interest and value, grouping separate essays under headings including "Language, rhetoric, deconstruction" and "Politics, economy, history". The book concludes with three essays on *Hamlet*, the most questioning play of all.

Shakespeare Criticism in the Twentieth Century
Michael Taylor; 2001 > Oxford UP

Taylor's admirably slim book skilfully digests some stodgy fare: he races through all the major critical debates over the past century, detailing their key exponents and signature works, quoting extensively, and highlighting the insights and limitations opened up by each. Probably the best introduction for beginners – or indeed anyone wanting to see wood rather than trees.

Shakespeare, Trauma and Contemporary Performance

Catherine Silverstone; 2011 > Routledge

Taking its cue from recent stage and movie productions in South Africa (*Titus Andronicus*, 2005), New Zealand (*The Maori Merchant of Venice*, 2002) and Nicholas Hytner's Iraq-war-influenced *Henry V* (2003), Silverstone's short monograph attempts to unite Shakespearian performance studies with contemporary theories about trauma. It's controversial stuff, but there's fascinating thinking here, as she attempts to piece together how the traumas in Shakespeare's dramas can mirror – and sometimes help heal – the after-effects of war, colonialism, homophobia and racism in the twenty-first century.

Shakespeare's Festive Comedy

C.L. Barber; rev. 2011 > Princeton UP

Barber's landmark study asserts on its opening page that "much comedy is festive – all comedy, if the word festive is pressed far enough". It goes on to demonstrate that the word is indeed suficiently flexible to describe not only Shakespear's comedies, but other Renaissance entertainments and pageants too. Though Barber's approach seems innocent, even conformist, today, his readings remain influential and critically as well as historically interesting. François Laroque's excellent *Shakespeare's Festive World* (1991) takes up many of Barber's insights and updates them in light of subsequent work by the practitioner of all things carnivalesque, Mikhail Bakhtin.

Shakespeare's Lives

Samuel Schoenbaum; rev. 1991 > Oxford UP [o/p]

The great insight offered by *Shakespeare's Lives* is that what people have written about the poet's life forms an uncanny shadow image of what they think about his work. Shakespeare was applauded for his untutored wisdom by Johnson, lauded as a solitary hero by Coleridge and subject to endless conspiracy theories in the more suspicious reaches of the nineteenth century. Schoenbaum lollops freely across the lot, drawing together a lively narrative of Shakespearian life-writing from the moment the man was buried until the late twentieth century. The author's superlative scorn for scholarship he doesn't like is one of the book's most winning features.

William Shakespeare: The critical heritage

Brian Vickers (ed.); 6 vols, 1974–81
> Routledge [o/p]

If you fancy getting more of a hold on the topic than a small study like Michael Taylor's allows, Vickers's six-volume beast will certainly show you the way. It contains lashings of criticism from all corners of the Shakespearian galaxy, all the way from (Margaret) Cavendish to Coleridge. Each volume covers a span of almost a half-century, reaching from 1623 to 1801, and is able because of its size to quote at length.

Teaching and learning Shakespeare

Throughout the *Globe Guide* we've tried to recommend books that are useful to everyone, whether you're an enthusiastic beginner or a postgraduate student; here are recommendations aimed specifically at teachers and school students. Dozens of books are available, but these are a handful of the best. It might be worth cross-referring with the books listed in the "Shakespeare for kids" chapter on p.638.

Creative Shakespeare

Fiona Banks; 2013 > Bloomsbury

Banks, a former teacher, now helps run the education programme at the Globe in London, and this slim but extremely useful book is full of practical ideas on how to make Shakespeare enjoyable to teach as well as learn. It marshals advice from a number of contributors, including text expert Giles Block and RSC voice coach Cicely Berry, and includes plentiful lesson tips, with an emphasis on making the texts active and collaborative.

Globe Education Shakespeare

Fiona Banks, Paul Shuter & Patrick Spottiswoode (eds); 2011– > Hodder

A series of individual play texts designed for British GCSE students, but which might also be useful for anyone trying to get to grips with a particular play. A full text is included with helpful glosses on difficult words, and there's good focus on how the plays work on stage, with small sections focusing on key exam topics – mood, humour, relationships and the like. So far *Romeo and Juliet, Macbeth, A Midsummer Night's Dream* and *Much Ado* are featured. Also available in iBook formats, with plenty of audio and video and other bells and whistles. Also highly recommended are texts in the Cambridge School Shakespeare series, recently and attractively republished, which now covers 14 major plays; and the Folger Library's *Shakespeare Set Free* series, which has a more American focus.

and writing assignments. Mary Elen Dakin's *Reading Shakespeare with Young Adults* (2009), also published by the NCTE, is likewise useful.

Performance Approaches to Teaching Shakespeare
Edward L. Rocklin; 2005 **>** National Council of Teachers

Over 400 pages long, Rocklin's resource is impressively detailed and contains a ton of ideas aimed specifically at American high-school educators and learners. As well as offering general tips for textual analysis, casting and rehearsal, the book focuses on *The Taming of the Shrew*, *Richard III* and *Hamlet*, suggesting lesson plans

Teaching Shakespeare
Rex Gibson; 1998 **>** Cambridge UP

Rex Gibson was for many years the *éminence grise* of Shakespearian education, the founding general editor of the Cambridge School Shakespeare series. This handbook is now regarded as a classic, and many of its principles – keep learning active, focus on performance – have become standard practice in classrooms across the globe. Gibson's *Stepping into Shakespeare* (2000) is aimed specifically at younger learners.

Shakespeare periodicals and journals

Reviews of major works on Shakespeare often make the mainstream press, and scholarly titles are frequently reviewed in the *Times Literary Supplement* and, less regularly, the *New York Review of Books* and the *London Review of Books*. But the journals listed below make a policy of catching pretty much everything Shakespearian in addition to carrying scholarly articles from the vanguard of research, so they're a good place to go if you want to find out what academics are debating at the moment. All maintain digital presences, with single articles or issues downloadable in PDF format. And if you're looking for still more routes into the ever-expanding Shakespearian universe, the best and most up-to-date option is to check an online bibliography such as the World Shakespeare Bibliography or websites recommended in the next chapter.

Shakespeare Quarterly
1950–present > Johns Hopkins UP

Shakespeare Quarterly has expanded immensely in the last few decades to cover not just standard fodder like special articles and book reviews, but scholarly exchanges and appraisals of Shakespearian performances across the globe. Like the Washington-based Folger Library, which publishes the journal, it's an entirely admirable, somewhat plush and enviably well-resourced American institution, and attracts high-calibre contributors. The *Quarterly* also publishes the annual *World Shakespeare Bibliography*, which attempts the remorseless task of tracking what's been published in the area that year (see p.669).

Shakespeare Studies
1965–present > Farleigh Dickinson UP

Shakespeare Studies has become an engaging and interesting annual forum for Shakespearian debate, one able to offer distinctive contributions (predominantly US-based) to the scholarly field. A few years ago this saw the editors introduce "review articles", which identify

and discuss current critical trends and build round-table debate around it – so, for instance, a recent edition saw pieces focusing on theatre in the 1580s, while a later volume concentrated on "material culture" in the Renaissance (from texts to textiles).

Shakespeare Survey
1948–present > Cambridge UP

The brainchild of great Shakespearian scholar Allardyce Nicoll and currently in the hands of Peter Holland, *Shakespeare Survey* was set up as a British-based journal that would cover not only academic and critical work but pay close heed to Shakespeare in performance, something confirmed by its ties with what was then the Shakespeare Memorial Theatre (now the Royal Shakespeare Theatre and Company). The format has remained consistent over the years: each annual volume has a specified topic (among them "Shakespeare in his Own Age", "Shakespeare and Sexuality" and "Shakespeare as Cultural Catalyst") with various essays tied to it, some one-off pieces, and reviews of productions in the UK and occasionally elsewhere.

Websites and apps

Welcome to one of the busiest – and most useful – areas for Shakespeare studies. The web has revolutionized the process of finding out about Shakespeare: nowadays you can watch video footage of influential interpretations, try out your theories on a discussion group or social media, download academic articles or ebooks, or just simply download a movie to watch at your leisure. Alongside these, there's also a growing selection of Shakespeare apps for mobile devices, which can do ever more sophisticated things. This directory picks the best of what's currently available.

Shakespeare gateways

A great way to get started, these are websites about websites – lists of links put together and recommended by human beings rather than search engines.

Global Shakespeares
globalshakespeares.mit.edu

Although mainly a scholarly resource, Global Shakespeares is hugely valuable nonetheless, centred around a unique collection of film and video recordings of plays from across the world – an Arabic *Taming of the Shrew* from 1962 to a new Brazilian *Timon of Athens*. The coverage of Asian performance is particularly valuable.

Internet Shakespeare Editions
ise.uvic.ca

Supported by Canada's University of Victoria, ISE's aim is to create reliable and scholarly texts native to the web. Recently revamped and almost certainly the best place to start, it now features in-depth sections on each of the plays and poems that link to reliable editions, facsimiles of a range of early texts, an evolving database of productions worldwide, information on Shakespeare's life and context and – particularly useful – links to relevant source materials. The list of Shakespeare sites in the so-called "Annex" is reason enough for visiting.

Literature Network
online-literature.com/shakespeare

The Literature Network's real attraction is its forum, which has over 70,000 members and buzzes with conversation on a bewildering variety of topics. Shakespeare is just one of over a hundred authors represented, and for a small

subscription fee you can get access to teacher-specific resources.

Play Shakespeare
playshakespeare.com

Play Shakespeare is an excellent jumping-off point, with a busy forum, a good news section, a range of dedicated apps and plentiful reviews of new productions in the US. You have to register to access the library, but there's plenty available – translations, edited versions of early texts, facsimiles and much more.

Shakespeare Online
shakespeare-online.com

Run by freelance writer and Bardic enthusiast Amanda Mabillard, Shakespeare Online has few frills (the design looks distinctly mid-2000s) but is a goldmine of useful information, especially if you're a student – full texts with notes, helpful articles and resources, biographies and excerpts from key critics, detail on theatres of Shakespeare's time and much more.

Shakespeare Resource Center
bardweb.net

A bit thinner than the other big gateways, the SRC nonetheless contains some useful things – useful essays on language and studying Shakespeare by Illinois-based editor J.M. Pressley (who has run the site since 1997), a news section with lots of links out, and thoughtful articles on subjects as varied as rival contenders to the authorship debate and life in Elizabethan England.

Sh:in:E – Shakespeare in Europe
shine.unibas.ch

A straightforward, no-frills metasite, Shakespeare in Europe springs from an educational philosophy that promotes cultural cross-pollination – the Bard being selected because of his unique international appeal. There are plenty of good sites recommended on these pages, and Sh:in:E's affiliation with the University of Basel links it to diverse academic content too.

Touchstone
touchstone.bham.ac.uk

It's now looking a bit old-fashioned, but Touchstone is valuable nonetheless, bringing together such things as a centralized catalogue for Shakespearian library resources, databases of British Shakespeare performances (including Traffic of the Stage, which lists productions from 1997 to 2003), links to global Shakespeare organizations and listings of scholarly and educational events. It even hosts an enquiry service, promising to answer any Shakespearian question you care to ask, or at least point you in the right direction.

Online video and audio

Since online video became globally popular with the advent of YouTube in 2005, it's become ever-easier to access video and audio content online, either via download services such as Audible and iTunes or streaming facilities such as Netflix and Lovefilm (and increasingly the boundaries are blurred, as the companies launch their own apps and bespoke digital content). Many Shakespeare films won't be available this way, particularly older or more obscure titles, but it's worth trying nonetheless.

Amazon/Lovefilm [UK]
amazon.co.uk/lovefilm

Now swallowed into Amazon's mighty maw, this UK company offers a DVD and Blu-ray mail rental service that is still popular among those who haven't made the leap to streaming or downloads. There's an excellent and surprisingly deep catalogue, including a number of Shakespearian movies.

Audible.com
audible.com [US]   audible.co.uk [UK]

Another Amazon purchase, Audible.com were one of the first companies to get into the downloadable audio market, and they deserve credit for rejuvenating the dusty world of audiobooks. Their range now covers some 180,000 titles (a quick search reveals six separate versions of Antony and Cleopatra, for instance).

Digital Theatre
digitaltheatre.com

Set up in 2009, DT pioneered high-definition filming of live theatre performances from a number of UK theatres, offering the videos on demand for streaming or download. The quality is high, shooting and editing both excellent, and the back catalogue is valuable, offering a number of fine Shakespeare productions alongside much newer work. Some British theatres have since launched their own video services in cinema or on the web, notably the National Theatre and Shakespeare's Globe (see p.662–3).

iTunes
apple.com/itunes [US]
apple.com/uk/itunes [UK]

iTunes also offers an ever-expanding selection of movies and TV shows, including many Shakespeare adaptations, and in 2015 started a streaming service, Apple Music, that offers an as-yet small selection of spoken-word albums.

Netflix
netflix.com

Netflix has become a leading streaming service for online video, and an increasingly powerful producer of bespoke content such as the popular House of Cards series (based, as it happens, on Richard III). Subscribers have access to a vast back catalogue, including many Shakespeare titles.

Spotify
spotify.com

Spotify has plenty of Shakespearian nuggets buried in its darker recesses – Edith Evans reading the Sonnets, playlists for tragedies and comedies, as well as every musical adaptation you can mention, including Kiss Me Kate and Laura Marling's folky music for a recent RSC As You Like It. It's haphazardly organized, but there's a heap of stuff here if you have the time to investigate.

YouTube
youtube.com

Alongside all the cat videos and webcam comedy sketches, YouTube is the strangest performance history database ever created, full of priceless oddities and rarities. Search for "Shakespeare", and before long you'll turn up Richard Burton plugging the Electronivision

version of his 1964 *Hamlet*, clips from John Barton's revelatory *Playing Shakespeare* TV series from 1984, the Beatles doing a full scene from *Dream* (John Lennon is Thisbe), and any number of Bollywood and other movie adaptations. Many of these clips are of dubious legality, meaning that they could disappear at any time, and quality is wildly variable, but rummage around for long enough and you're bound to dig up some gems.

Texts, concordances, dictionaries

Free online texts are an excellent quick fix: supremely handy for looking up quotations. Despite the convenience, any results should always be double-checked with a printed text if you're at all concerned about accuracy.

British Library
bl.uk

The reason for Bardolaters to visit the BL on the web is its excellent Shakespeare in Quarto microsite, which offers digital scans of 93 early printed copies of the plays, plus scholarly background, all accessible via a brilliantly idiot-proof interface (you can even compare separate editions side by side). The BL's vast master catalogue is a click away, and there are also plenty of online learning resources in a range of subjects.

The Furness Collection
sceti.library.upenn.edu/sceti/furness

With every major research library in the world rushing to digitize its collections and showcasing them online, there's never been a better time to get close to the holiest of holies, the 1623 First Folio. The University of Pennsylvania offers the swishest version: an extensive collection of electronic editions residing in the Furness Library, not just Shakespeare texts but plenty of other early printed books too. Undeniably the best introduction to the area currently on the web.

Hamlet Works
hamletworks.org

It's long been said that the internet – fundamentally decentralized, always evolving, able to present almost infinite amounts of information in new and radically different forms – offers the way forward for editing. The problem, as always, is money: few publishers or universities have committed serious resources to digital texts. All praise, then, to Hamlet Works for trying to do exactly that: this is a serious attempt to provide a "variorium" edition of the play (one that lists every variant of every separate version) that is far more complete than anything achievable in print. It's experimental, and not terribly pretty, but it offers as good a sense as any of what the future might hold.

LEME
leme.library.utoronto.ca

Geekily specialist, but amazingly useful, LEME – the acronym stands for Lexicons of Early Modern English – is a massive database of early dictionaries and lexicons containing contents of over 160 reference books printed between 1480 and 1702. Want to find out what Shakespeare's contemporaries understood by the word "dictionary", for instance, and you get lengthy quotations from sources including John Florio's *New World of Words* (1611) and Thomas Wilson's *Christian Dictionary* (1612). The database is free for everyone to use, but paying subscribers get access to more sophisticated search options and fuller results. A valuable complement to the *OED* (see p.669).

Open Source Shakespeare
opensourceshakespeare.com

OSS is one of the best free concordances we've come across – swift and seemingly accurate, and it contains the Sonnets and narrative poems too. The brainchild of US newspaperman Eric Johnson, the site is free from clunks and easy to use, the advanced search being particularly powerful. Texts are generally from that venerable Internet standard, the Moby Shakespeare, though a few are sourced from Project Gutenberg (still no *Two Noble Kinsmen*, however). Even better for those of a techie disposition, its software runs on democratic open-source principles and can even be built into other websites. It's also worth trying the Internet Shakespeare Editions (see above, p.659).

Oxford Shakespeare
bartleby.com/70

In case you're wondering, not the textually avant-garde *Oxford Shakespeare* of 2005, but the more elderly incarnation of 1914 – so again no *Noble Kinsmen*. Haphazard search results might require some trawling, though the friendly interface makes it a doddle to use as an online text if that's what you're after. All of Bartleby's other reference tools – from *Gray's Anatomy* to the works of Walt Whitman – are just a click away, and fully searchable.

Project Gutenberg
www.gutenberg.net

The granddaddy of them all, Project Gutenberg has been putting copyright-free texts on the web since ancient history – in fact since 1971, when its founder sent a computerized US Declaration of Independence to some pals. Now Gutenberg has more than 100,000 ebooks

online, in a variety of formats – from Kindle and epub to low-tech, plain-text format. The editing is often unreliable, but you have to applaud the democratic principles.

Shakespeare Apocrypha
www.republicofheaven.org.uk/ sh_apocrypha.htm

Does exactly what it claims to: brings together a list of all the plays that have ever been suggested as Shakespearian (all the way from *Noble Kinsmen* and *Pericles* to the wackier reaches of *George A Greene* and *Edmund Ironside*) and provides links to online texts, usually from Project Gutenberg. Unfussy and very helpful.

Shakespeare theatres, companies and festivals

While Shakespeare can be – and, thankfully, is – performed anywhere from scout halls to factory floors, there are a number of theatres worldwide devoted to performing his plays, and several Shakespeare festivals of international standing. If you're simply interested in tracking what's on at the theatre centres of London's West End or Broadway, Official London Theatre (officiallondontheatre.co.uk) and Playbill (playbill.com) should do the trick. In the US, try the Folger Shakespeare in American Life site (shakespeareinamericanlife. org), which features an interactive map of companies and performances, perhaps cross-checked with the list at Electronic Shakespeare (wfu.edu/~tedforrl/shakespeare).

American Shakespeare Center
americanshakespearecenter.com

Based in the pretty Virginia town of Staunton, a few hours down the freeway from Washington DC, the ASC is home to the Blackfriars, the first (and still the only) replica of Shakespeare's indoor playhouse to be built anywhere in the world. If you're anywhere nearby it's well worth dropping in to experience the space and the ASC's dauntingly active programme, which includes fully staged performances of Shakespeare and much else, excellent educational activities and the famous "Ren seasons", an annual attempt to replicate Renaissance staging practice by giving professional actors no director and minimal rehearsal time (more revealing than it sounds – it's an amazing feat).

National Theatre, London
nationaltheatre.org.uk

Though its four theatres stage a wide range of plays, there have been many fine Shakespeare productions since the National Theatre first opened with *Hamlet* starring Peter O'Toole in 1963 (the website lists all subsequent Shakespeare stagings). Artistic director Rufus Norris has maintained the tradition, but given it a sharper edge, mixing classics with some offbeat conceptual pieces. Recent highlights include Nicholas Hytner's *Timon of*

Athens, and a well-regarded *As You Like It* by young director Polly Findlay. Many are now broadcast globally in cinemas via National Theatre Live.

New York Shakespeare Festival
publictheater.org

Justly famous for its unique "Shakespeare in the Park" series, which runs every summer and attracts many thousands of spectators, Joe Papp's Public Theater began life in the 1950s as a workshop devoted to the Bard and has kept alive a strong Shakespearian tradition since. Many stars have graced its stage – James Earl Jones, Kevin Kline, Meryl Streep and Christopher Walken, among others – and the folk at the Public Theater downtown continue to develop bright and interesting work.

Oregon Shakespeare Festival
osfashland.org

In operation nearly nine months of the year (and it's been going since 1935), the OSF is the largest not-for-profit theatre organization in the US, with over 450 professional actors performing in its three houses at Ashland, Oregon. Repertoire is anchored in Shakespeare, naturally, but there's plenty else besides, both classic and contemporary – their 2015 season saw *Much Ado About Nothing* and

Pericles rubbing shoulders with *Guys and Dolls* and *Long Day's Journey into Night*.

Royal Shakespeare Company
rsc.org.uk

One of the world's most famous classical companies has an excellent site, allowing you to do all sorts of things: see what's on at Stratford, London or one of their UK/ international venues, buy tickets to shows or cinema screenings, look up the RSC's learning zone, or browse their extensive online archives, including photos from hundreds of historical productions. If you're planning a trip to the town, Stratford's web presence (**stratford-upon-avon.co.uk**) should provide pointers.

Shakespeare Festival of Canada
www.stratford-festival.on.ca

Based at the "other" Stratford – in fact Stratford, Ontario is just one of several in North America – the Stratford Shakespeare Festival has always been one of the most well-respected and artistically engaging set-ups of its kind in the world. Founded in the 1950s by a local journalist who decided that a gala devoted to Shakespeare was the best way for the town to stave off economic depression, the festival has attracted a wealth of talent both international and home-grown, all eager to perform on Tanya Moiseiwitsch's famous open stage, plus three other theatres. Nowadays there's even a fringe.

Shakespeare's Globe
shakespearesglobe.com

Written off by some as little more than a heritage tourist attraction when it opened in 1995, the London Globe (built just a few feet away from the site of the original) has proved to be very much more than that. At their best, productions here provide unique insights into Shakespearian performance practice, and involve the audience in a far more direct way than happens in more conventional spaces. Their website has improved in recent years – it now includes a "Globe Player" offering downloads or video streams of productions for around £3 a pop – but to get the authentic experience you'll have to arrange a visit. The Globe Education department also offers a range of courses and performance workshops, both in school and at the theatre itself.

Shakespeare Theater, Washington DC
shakespearedc.org

Headed these days by internationally recognized artistic director Michael Kahn, the Shakespeare Theater in the nation's capital was originally part of the Folger Library (see p.666), but split away in 1992 when it left to occupy the Lansburgh Theater in downtown DC. Generally regarded as one of the finest companies of its kind in the United States, the Shakespeare Theater has produced drama of international standing. The company website is well maintained and contains plenty of detail on all their activities.

Study guides & educational sites

There is a lot of lowest-common-denominator Shakespearian content online, much of it catering for the market in homework hints and cheats. But if you know where to look there are some outstanding educational information out there, often served up attractively and with an eye to making learning as fun as possible. Several respected institutions now run so-called video-based MOOCs (massive open online courses), which can lead to qualifications. If none of the sites recommended below offers quite what you want, try combing reviews and recommendations at one of the big Shakespeare gateways (see p.659). As is the case for almost every subject under the sun, trusting the infamously patchy Wikipedia is risky if you want your work to have more than basic academic credibility.

About Shakespeare
shakespeare.about.com

It's a sign that your subject has arrived when knowledge giants About.com begin to cover it. In these pages, authored by Lee Jamieson, Shakespeare gets a typically thorough working-over, with plenty of original, convincing articles, some fun quizzes, videos and links to useful sites elsewhere.

Britannica
britannica.com/biography/ William-Shakespeare

A decent offering from info titans Britannica, this website is well worth exploring: reliable biographies of Shakespeare and his contemporaries, information on the plays, snippets of audio and video, images, even the odd quiz.

Futurelearn
futurelearn.com

Distance learning has been in existence for over a century, but MOOCs have been a big story in recent years – attempts by major educational institutions to increase their outreach by offering open-access courses exclusively online, using a mixture of video lectures, collaborative teaching materials and online assessment, often free or for little cost. Shakespeare has been relatively underserved until now, but the University of Warwick and the Shakespeare Birthplace Trust have recently launched a free introduction to "Shakespeare and his World", and at the time of writing the University of Birmingham are about to run courses on *Hamlet* and *Much Ado*. Other institutions are sure to dip a toe into these waters soon. Futurelearn is the best place to go for UK-based courses; Coursera (coursera.org) is the most useful US equivalent.

Guardian Teacher Network
theguardian.com/teacher-network

Though it's run and edited by a team of journalists, who provide conventional content such as news stories, online debates, advice columns and review articles, all the best stuff at the Guardian's Teacher Network is provided by teachers themselves – lesson plans and suggestions on everything from how to interest kids in Mars to tips on how to teach migration. There's a lot of Shakespeare and other Eng Lit-related material on offer, much of it in PDF, from the role of music in *A Midsummer Night's Dream* to recommendations of the best movies for GCSE students.

OUP Shakespeare Centre
ukcatalogue.oup.com/category/academic/shakespeare.do

Oxford University Press have become the foremost publisher of Shakespeare titles, and their various publications on the subject are brought together in this useful site. Though it's basically promotional material, there are original articles here and much else of interest.

RSC Shakespeare
www.palgrave.com/page/rsc-shakespeare/

The online home of Macmillan's gargantuan RSC Complete Works, a modernized version of the First Folio released in 2007 (see p.644), this site offers some decent goodies, including synopses and RSC-centred stage histories with cast lists for each and every play.

Shake Sphere
shakespearestudyguide.com

A US site aimed at schools and maintained by Michael J. Cummings "as a public service", Shake Sphere brings nearly everything you want onto its extensive – and slightly daunting – front page. There are essays on a wide range of topics, plot summaries and lists of characters for no fewer than 41 plays (*Edward III*, *Sir Thomas More* and *Cardenio* featuring too), study guides, glossaries of literary terms, biographies, texts – you name it. Reliable and intelligent, which is the best thing of all.

Shakespeare's Globe Playground
shakespearesglobe.com/playground

Intended for 6 to 10-year-olds, the Globe's Playground is stuffed with fun ways in to Shakespeare, as far removed from dry and dusty schoolwork as possible. You can watch cartoons of the Globe's resident "company" of wild animals performing minute-long adaptations, take part in quizzes and games, download recipes and colouring-in sheets, all backed up by reliable educational material including PDF factsheets and more. Older students might get something out of Staging It, a companion project that allows you to "direct" a scene by assembling video footage recorded on the Globe stage (shakespearesglobe.com/education).

SparkNotes
sparknotes.com/shakespeare

A hipper alternative to the venerable Cliff's Notes and a firm favourite of American high-schoolers looking to save their grades, SparkNotes study guides aren't sophisticated (and tend to be frowned on by teachers who see gobbets cut and pasted with wearisome regularity), but they are free and have their uses. Probably the best bit of the site is No-Fear Shakespeare, full texts of the plays with facing translations into modern English, backed up by detailed and very readable plot summaries. There are also plenty of tie-ins, including a publishing franchise, and now an app.

Discussion groups

Feel the need to vent your opinions? Test-drive an extravagant new theory? Or simply to find out something from the experts? Then you might well be interested in that venerable internet concept, the online discussion group. Whether it's an old-style list, where subscribers communicate via email, or employing social media such as Facebook, Shakespearian news and views bounce around the world with increasing speed. Here are a couple of the best; many of the big gateway sites host their own discussion groups, and you can follow others on Twitter, too.

Google Groups
groups.google.com/forum/#!forum/ humanities.lit.authors.shakespeare

As the web address indicates, they are defiantly old-school – but Google Groups are still going strong, nearly 20 years after they first appeared, and the Shakespeare forum is intimidatingly active. There's plenty of lunatic stuff here (conversations about the authorship "debate" are tedious and frequent), but some good threads too, and it's easy to ask a question and get a swift reply.

SHAKSPER
shaksper.net

The doyen of Shakespeare discussion groups, SHAKSPER is subscribed to by a large swathe of academics, experts and Bard enthusiasts – but even if you aren't admitted to join the party (applications are vetted) every single thread is searchable on the web, enabling you to comb the crop for whatever interests you most. The standard of conversation is high and some genuinely interesting things get hammered out.

The authorship debate

Like other conspiracy theories, the internet has provided a cosy roost for devotees of the so-called "authorship debate" (see p.566). Despite the tangible air of derangement that attends most things in this area – and that goes for all sides of the argument – it can be intriguing to explore the options, and even to ask whether it really matters whether some of the greatest plays ever written were composed by a middle-class man from Stratford, or someone socially better connected.

Shakespeare Oxford Fellowship
shakespeareoxfordfellowship.org

Although better laid out than its Baconian adversary, the website of the Shakespeare Oxford Fellowship – who suggest that Edward de Vere, Seventeenth Earl of Oxford, handed scripts to an actor called Shakespeare in order to preserve his courtly reputation – has significant mountains to climb. One is Oxford's surviving poems, which rarely rise above doggerel; another is the fact that he died in 1604, well before about a third of the plays were written (including *The Tempest*, which is securely dated around 1610). Despite the yawning gaps in their case, though, the Oxonians scramble some precarious peaks with energy and occasional panache.

Sir Francis Bacon's New Advancement of Learning
sirbacon.org

Behind the lurid exterior lies one of the largest anti-Stratfordian sites on the web, arguing that polymath Francis Bacon – a man whom everyone agrees to have been one of the great geniuses of his age (conspicuously unlike the Earl of Oxford) was behind Shakespeare. There's lots here, and it's not the easiest to browse through, but nevertheless it offers the sum total of Baconian arguments: if you're not persuaded by this, you won't be convinced by anything else.

Shakespeare Authorship
shakespeareauthorship.com

A site "dedicated to the proposition that Shakespeare wrote Shakespeare": well-tempered and on the whole good-humoured, but nonetheless intent on its task. David Kathman marshals the standard arguments effectively, producing a range of bite-sized ripostes to every anti-Stratfordian suggestion under the sun, including a nicely witty review of Roland Emmerich's inadvertently hilarious film *Anonymous* (2011). Even super-sceptics might pause for thought.

Libraries, organizations and other institutions

Many of the world's leading libraries contain work by Shakespeare, and a few were even built to honour his work. Some of these institutions have been at the forefront of web presentation, offering access to their enviable collections – particularly in the last few years, when new technology has made it easier than ever before to see digital texts and online exhibitions.

British Shakespeare Association
britishshakespeare.ws

Formed in 2003, BSA is essentially a scholarly organization connecting academics in the field, but also maintains strong links with performers and is open to members of the public. It arranges conferences, debates and events and keeps a blog that also acts as an informal noticeboard for British Bardophiles.

Canadian Adaptations of Shakespeare
canadianshakespeares.ca

CASP tracks how Shakespeare has been accommodated into Canadian culture but has interest far beyond that – its tale of how an Englishman became an honorary Canadian has been replicated in countless countries worldwide. Proudly decorated with the Sanders portrait (rediscovered in Ottawa; see p.575), the site was originally built for students looking for unusual ways into Shakespeare but has since developed into a terrific storehouse of information on Canadian Shakespeariana – describing plays, songs, TV shows and films, much of it supported by multimedia backup.

Deutsche Shakespeare-Gesellschaft
shakespeare-gesellschaft.de/english

The German Shakespeare Society goes all the way back to 1864, laying claim to be the oldest scholarly society of its kind in the world – fitting testament to the special relationship between Shakespeare and Germany. The Society does all sorts of things, including running a well-regarded journal (*Shakespeare Jahrbuch*, which has contributions in English as well as German), supporting translation and editing activities, and holding international conferences. This bilingual site is sometimes haphazard, but contains among much else a worldwide diary for Shakespeare events, reviews of productions and links to relevant German-language resources and institutions.

Folger Shakespeare Library
folger.edu

The Folger is perhaps the world's most important Shakespearian archive (it's located, fittingly enough, on Capitol Hill in Washington DC). On its shelves are over 250,000 volumes, including a remarkable selection of early printed books and early modern manuscripts. An increasing amount is digitized, and there is plenty of information on the Folger's many events and real-life exhibitions, plus some useful learning materials.

Huntington Library
huntington.org

The Huntington has something of holy-grail status among research libraries – as well as containing all manner of wonderful books (among them copious Shakespeariana), the complex houses a recently restored art gallery and is surrounded by 150 acres of gardens. With the California beach only a few miles away, it's a wonder visiting scholars actually get any work done. The website contains plenty of interest, though.

Shakespeare Birthplace Trust
www.shakespeare.org.uk

The SBT guards the flame of Shakespeare in Stratford, maintaining the five properties associated with him as well as supporting an excellent library (which boasts the RSC's archives, including an online database of productions, and local records going all the way back to 1879). Unsurprisingly the site is mainly aimed at those intending pilgrimage, but there's also some useful background and educational information, and the SBT now runs some well-regarded online courses in collaboration with Warwick University. The Trust also has an excellent specialist bookshop, which offers to mail titles worldwide, with all profits ploughed back into the SBT.

Shakespeare Institute
shakespeare.bham.ac.uk

Affiliated to Birmingham University's English Department, the Shakespeare Institute was founded in the early 1950s by Renaissance scholar Allardyce Nicoll (also the first editor of the journal *Shakespeare Survey*; see p.658) and now houses a fine library as well as running postgrad courses in Shakespeare studies. There's plenty going on both academically and with public events, so it's worth checking the site if you're planning to be in the area.

Shakespeare's World
shakespeare.emory.edu

Based at Georgia's Emory University, this boutique site is run by Harry Rusche, a member of the English department there. It's in two main sections, both of them fascinating: "Shakespeare and the Players", an online exhibition of images commemorating American and British actors from the nineteenth and early twentieth centuries, many of them in postcard form; and a work in progress entitled "Shakespeare Illustrated", a compendium of nineteenth-century paintings and criticism. Both are great resources, intelligently and straightforwardly presented.

Journals and criticism

Scholarly debate and discussion have prospered online. All the major journals now have web presences, and there are even a few that run solely in digital space.

Early Modern Literary Studies
shu.ac.uk/emls

EMLS is how an online journal should be done: it's a no-frills site, a little dated in its appearance, but offers an impressive range of content. Everything is peer-refereed, and there's also an active readers' forum enabling people to respond to anything that appears. Specialization is in sixteenth- and seventeenth-century literature, but there's lots of online scholarship too, and plentiful reviews.

London Review of Books
lrb.co.uk

The biweekly *LRB* is politically combative and painfully hip – in a tweedy sort of way. It offers more considered but esoteric reviews than are published elsewhere, many of them to do with literature. The website is geared up for print subscribers, who have access to an archive dating back to 1998, but also offers a free taster of what's available. There's also an excellent blog.

New York Review of Books
nybooks.com

The *NYRB* is a slightly-less-than-biweekly literary/political magazine with an all-star selection of contributors and a markedly liberal bent. If you're not a subscriber to the print magazine, you can pay a one-off fee of $3 to download single articles.

Shakespeare and His Critics
shakespearean.org.uk

Maintained by Shakespeare student and enthusiast Thomas Larque, Shakespeare and His Critics offers a fine collection of critical work in the area, much of it nineteenth-century or earlier in origin. There's stuff here by usual suspects Coleridge and Samuel Johnson, but also some more unusual pieces – including an article by actress Helen Faucit on Ophelia and an electronic edition of Samuel Daniel's *Delia* (a sonnet sequence read by Shakespeare and probably a model for his own).

Shakespeare Quarterly
muse.jhu.edu/journals/shakespeare_quarterly

Unless you're able to access it through an institutional subscription, SQ's homepage offers little more than a list of what's currently in this well-respected journal (see p.658) and in previous editions, but it can be worth dropping by just to see what's going on.

Shakespeare Survey
cambridge.org

As with *Shakespeare Quarterly*, the website for the British *Shakespeare Survey* (see p.658), navigable via the main CUP homepage, won't tell you much more than what's in the current edition, but makes a handy reference nonetheless: unlike many other journals it's easy to purchase single copies rather than having to subscribe. They're about £35 per paperback.

Times Literary Supplement
the-tls.co.uk

The *TLS* is the UK humanities community's journal of record, reviewing nearly every significant scholarly title published on these shores and keeping an eagle eye on plenty else besides. You have to pay to access the archive.

Renaissance gateways and tools

While Shakespeare may have the lion's share of online coverage, there are huge amounts of other stuff out there, and if you want to broaden your knowledge of the Renaissance, the web offers plenty of routes to enlightenment (and ultimately to the Enlightenment). Here are some of the best.

CERES
www.english.cam.ac.uk/ceres

Ceres is a classical nature goddess associated with fecundity and fertility; "CERES" stands for the Cambridge English Renaissance Electronic Service. Go figure. Despite an over-fondness for Latinate acronyms, this website, run by academics in the university's English department, is a fantastic resource, offering pointers to Renaissance material on the web. The links page alone is worth a visit, and there are sections specializing in Spenser and Sidney.

English Short-Title Catalogue
estc.bl.uk

This one really is for experts: a full-spec electronic database of every English book that appeared in print between 1475 and 1801, plus serials, newspapers and plenty more. Distilled from the hard-copy *Short-Title Catalogue* edited by Pollard, Redgrave and Wing, ESTC is uniquely useful if you're digging around in bibliographical history. After years of subscriber-only access, it's now free to use via the British Library – hurrah.

Perseus Digital Library
perseus.tufts.edu

Not a portal as such, but then it's pretty hard to say exactly what Perseus is – apart from original and supremely handy. At base it's a collection of electronic texts (a corpus that is geographically ever-expanding, as its innovative map on the homepage shows) but has a series of invaluable research tools, among them online versions of Latin and Greek dictionaries, as well as an area devoted especially to the English Renaissance. Holinshed is here, as are Marlowe, Peacham and even James I.

REED
eir.library.utoronto.ca/reed

For thirty-odd years, the Records of Early English Drama team has been trawling dramatic texts and records referring to performances, aiming to construct a picture of what local drama was like in England between the middle ages and the closure of the theatres in 1642. As well as publishing their findings in scholarly editions, they also run this site, which enables you to search for specific events, performers and works or browse interactive geographical maps. Everything you need, in other words, to work out what your ancestors were booking for, 400 years before the advent of *Les Mis*.

Voice of the Shuttle
vos.ucsb.edu

An old favourite, Voice of the Shuttle (the term comes from Aristotle's *Poetics*) is a vast gateway for humanities research worldwide, with particular expertise in the opportunities offered by new media. Everything is searchable, but you can also drill down through specialist directories to find what you want.

Subscription-only sites

It's an unpalatable truth that few of the serious literary research tools – the reliable texts, the facsimiles, the dictionaries – are free to access online: they're costly to create and maintain, and inevitably that gets passed on to consumers (or, more usually, institutions who can afford to pay the subscription rates). Even so, we've listed the most impressive ones here in case you're lucky enough to have access, and in the hope that they become more democratically available in years to come.

Early English Books Online
eebo.chadwyck.com

Another Chadwyck-Healey venture (see Literature Online below), EEBO is how all online databases should operate: it's unfussily designed, a breeze to use and contains most of what you want. In this case the contents are electronic versions of the microfilm scans most research libraries undertook years ago to record and preserve their collections. What that boils down to is facsimile versions of 100,000 or so early English printed books in the Adobe Acrobat (PDF) file format, all a few clicks away and downloadable to your computer – so within seconds you can be scanning the Bodleian's copy of *Venus and Adonis* annotated by Edmund Malone (or indeed browsing for some naughty sixteenth-century woodcuts). Even more exciting is the ongoing project to make each file text-searchable, so that you can find individual words and phrases.

Encyclopædia Britannica
britannica.com

Not quite fair to call this subscription-only: although for most of the deep content you'll have to fork out, information lying closer to the surface is yours for free. If you do want to subscribe, you'll find rates aren't horrendous (about £50/$70 per annum), or your library may have have a subscription. Information is generally much more reliable than Wikipedia.

JSTOR Archive
jstor.org

JSTOR collects 700-plus academic journals and publishes images of every page in every edition. Unwieldy at times (these can be quite large files), but this system enables you to read – or print off – text just as it originally appeared in the printed format, with footnotes, typos and all. Main attractions for Shakespearians are current and back issues of renowned journal *Shakespeare Quarterly* (see p.658), though other literary titles in the Renaissance area include *Representations*, *ELH* and *Studies in English Literature*. Subscription fees vary; contact JSTOR for details.

Literature Online
lion.chadwyck.com

An enviable (and relatively non-specialist) resource for those fortunate enough to have access is Chadwyck-Healey's Literature Online, which boasts over 350,000 full-text English works in poetry, drama and prose, plus 190-odd journals, reference works, biographies, video clips ... What this means is that you can search and browse literary works from Anglo-Saxon verse all the way up to contemporary fiction, for individual keywords if required, and find out copious detail on everything contained within. It's designed for institutional use, however, and individual subscribers are rarely granted access.

Oxford English Dictionary
oed.com

Incredible to consider the energy, organization and resources that went into assembling the first versions of the *OED* all those years ago – slips of paper instead of computers for a start, although the *Dictionary* is nowadays updated digitally and a new print edition seems unlikely (the last in 1989 spanned 20 volumes). Especially because the advantages of the digital interface are considerable: as well as searching very precisely, you can sift through results in all sorts of creative ways and do a bazillion funky things besides. The downside, as ever, is the cost: around £215/$300 per annum for individuals at the time of writing, though many public libraries have access.

World Shakespeare Bibliography
worldshakesbib.org

Though it may seem that there can be no method of keeping track of the rampant Shakespeare publishing industry, there is, and this is it: a regularly updated bibliography of every book, article and review from 1966 to the present, with plentiful other Shakespeariana besides. Even more astounding is the fact that the World Shakespeare Bibliography is truly global in reach, covering some 98 languages: altogether there are over 116,000 entries. At the time of writing, individual subscriptions were $90 per annum.

Apps

A good percentage of the books recommended in this guide are available as ebooks, but purpose-designed apps can be infinitely richer: introductory guides, educational tools, video clips and more, even the odd game.

Shakespeare
iOS/Android

All Bardolaters should have this as standard. A reliable, nicely designed version of the complete works (poems and some apocrypha included), fully searchable and bookmarkable, plus an integrated glossary, all for free. A "pro", paid-for option has extra bells and whistles.

Shakespeare at Play
iOS

An innovative attempt to combine text with live video, this lets you watch stagings of scenes from *Romeo and Juliet*, *Macbeth*, *A Midsummer Night's Dream* and *Hamlet* while a script scrolls past beneath. It's nicely produced and very elegantly designed, and if you don't understand a word you can tap it and a definition will pop up.

Shakespeare Dictionary
iOS

Over 4,500 Shakespearian and early modern words are included in this fully searchable dictionary from study guide publishers BookCaps, with sensible and detailed explanations. This is the one to tap if you can't tell your "zephyr" from your "zenith".

Shakespeare's Globe 360
iOS

If you can't make it to Southwark, this 3D model is the next best thing. Stroll around a virtual digital model and explore the building's story and architectural features.

Shakespeare in Bits
iOS

Part of the best-designed educational app series on the market, Shakespeare in Bits offers a full text with a video animation that plays alongside, with top-quality actors such as Fiona Shaw and Stephen Dillane saying the words. It also provides character guides, a glossary feature, plot summaries and more. Not cheap (£10/$15), but if you're studying or teaching one play it could help bring the text alive. So far *Julius Caesar*, *Romeo and Juliet*, *Hamlet*, *Macbeth* and *Dream* are available.

Shakespeare's London
iOS

Pacing out the city that Shakespeare inhabited for most of his working life is – surprisingly – still very much possible, given how much of the street plan has survived. This geolocation app points you in the right direction, and contains plenty of useful explanatory nuggets about what you'll find. An audio tour is included.

Shakespeare or Die
iOS/Android

Put scrambled Shakespearian quotations in the right order and save the damsel in distress! Not the slickest product out there, but surprisingly addictive.

Shakespeare Translator
iOS

Just as it says, the Translator lets you enter whatever text you wish and have it rendered into cod-Elizabethan, whether it's Coldplay lyrics ("Coil that can be not y-cleped / Tigers waiting to be tamed ...") or common phrases. Fun for kids of every age.

Starting Shakespeare
iOS

Designed primary for primary-school students and their teachers, the app uses *A Midsummer Night's Dream* and *Macbeth* as introductions to Shakespeare's work, with video snippets, games, teaching tips and more.

SwipeSpeare
iOS/Android

Move smoothly from an edited text to a modern English translation with a simple swipe across the screen. Also contains a dictionary.

Glossary of useful terms

Although this book tries to keep jargon to a minimum, on occasion we've used specialist technical terms, many of them drawn from Renaissance printing and theatre practice. This glossary lists and defines the most useful, supplemented by some relevant literary terminology. (If the word you're hunting for doesn't feature below, see our recommendations for further reading on p.679.) Cross-references appear in **colour**.

Alliteration > The technique of repeating sounds that occur at the beginning of words, nearly always consonants. Shakespeare's Sonnet 12, which begins "When I do count the clock that tells the time", has two stressed alliterative patterns, one on *c* and the other on *t* (with three unstressed *th*s as well).

Aside > Words spoken by a character when there are other people on stage but not meant to be heard by them – and thus addressed to the audience instead. Compare **soliloquy**.

Autograph > When referring to text, "autograph" copy is a manuscript in the author's own hand – something that, with the exception of the collaborative play *Sir Thomas More* (see p.190), we don't possess for Shakespeare's work. Sometimes also known as "holograph".

"Bad" quarto > A **quarto** with serious problems of some kind: from erroneous printing and poor layout to major omissions of the script, or obviously nonsensical text. "Bad" versions sometimes result when copy is stolen or

pirated, or when text has been memorially reconstructed (see **pirate(d copy)** and **memorial reconstruction**), for instance in the 1603 quarto of *Hamlet*. Some argue against using such value-laden terminology, and that supposedly "bad" texts provide information that more polished ones don't.

Blank verse > The overwhelming majority of Shakespeare's verse is in so-called blank verse or "iambic pentameter". In this metrical scheme, each line breaks down into five pairs of syllables, with the stress on the second (de-*dum*, de-*dum*, de-*dum*, de-*dum*, de-*dum*); the "blank" refers to the fact that lines are not rhymed. This basic pattern is clear enough in a line such as Romeo's "The precious treasure of his eyesight lost" (1.1.230). See p.608 for more.

Chorus > In Shakespearian plays, an individual who speaks before and sometimes during the performance, presenting and commenting on its action, and often describing events not shown on stage. Shakespeare's include the Chorus in *Henry V*, a character called "Rumour" in *2 Henry IV*, and the medieval poet John Gower in *Pericles*. See also **Prologue** and **Epilogue**.

Clown > See **Fool**.

Comedy > As with **tragedy**, understanding what Shakespeare thought of as "comic" can be a full-time occupation. Laughs come into it, but so too does the expectation of social harmony, usually achieved through marriage between major characters. See p.355 for more.

Commonplace book > Many educated people in the Renaissance – Hamlet is one – kept a notebook (sometimes called "tables") in which they jotted down aphorisms or useful quotes as practice for their own writing or speaking. This practice was encouraged by humanist educators, who argued that rhetorical skill was the foundation of civil society.

Compositor > In a printshop, the person responsible for setting type within the grid laid out for each page in preparation for printing. Usually several compositors worked on a book at the same time; up to nine might have collaborated on the 1623 First Folio.

Deus ex machina > Literally "the god from a machine", a theatrical device derived from ancient Greek drama, in which a god intervenes in the human action. Usually the deity is flown (lowered) on stage via some kind of mechanical device, and resolves the complications of the plot at a stroke. Shakespearian examples include the appearance of the marriage god Hymen in *As You Like It*, and of Jupiter, king of the gods, in *Cymbeline*.

Discovery space > In sixteenth- and seventeenth-century theatres, an open room just behind the main stage and fronting onto it. Doors or a curtain usually hid the space from view, but could be opened to "discover" whatever lay within – sometimes a bed or other large prop, or even (in the case of *The Tempest*) two lovers silently playing chess.

Doubling > The practice whereby one actor plays multiple parts. It's especially prevalent in Shakespeare's histories, where the list of characters often far exceeds the number of personnel that would have been available to him.

Dramatis personae > List of characters in a play (from the Latin).

Epilogue > A short speech concluding a play, usually spoken after its action has finished. Sometimes Shakespeare's heroes and heroines step outside the play to act as epilogues; Rosalind in *As You Like It* and Prospero in *The Tempest* are two celebrated examples.

Fair copy > Before a text was published it had ideally to be copied out in neat, so that the printers could follow it accurately. This work might be done by a playwright, or (more likely) by a professional scribe.

Farce > Since the eighteenth century farce has been categorized as a form (usually dramatic) designed to move the spectator to unreflective, simple laughter – as distinct from **comedy**, which also encourages thought. Samuel Taylor Coleridge claimed that "a proper farce is mainly distinguished from comedy by the licence allowed, and even required, in the fable, in order to produce strange and laughable situations. The story need not be probable; it is enough that it is possible."

Feminist criticism > Since the 1970s, supported by the growing political movement for women's rights, much academic criticism has focused on the place of women in literary culture – both within texts and as producers of them. Though much of this work has been banded together as "feminist", exploration of issues relating to gender and sexuality has taken a variety of forms and directions, especially in recent years.

Folio > A large-format book, usually prestigious and expensive, for which each sheet of printer's paper was folded in half to make two leaves (*folium* is Latin for "leaf"), or four pages. See p.619 for more.

Fool > In the Elizabethan and Jacobean theatre professional comedians were great stars, playwrights often tailoring roles specially for them. Fools (also known as "clowns") usually wore distinctive costumes, specializing in singing, dancing and witty wordplay as well as physical comedy – some powerful families even employed a jester for their own private entertainment. Shakespeare's fools (he writes parts for at least thirteen) are often given license to say things that other characters cannot, offering a sardonic perspective on the events of the play. See p.36 for more.

Formalism > An academic movement that reached its apogee in the mid-twentieth century, which stressed the (internal) literary or aesthetic

qualities of writing as opposed to their (external) placement in a historical or cultural setting. In Shakespeare studies, the term most often refers to "New" critics such as Cleanth Brooks (see p.267), who stressed the importance of looking past an author's "intentions" to what the text actually achieved.

Foul papers > A playwright's rough manuscript(s), containing – as the name implies – redrafted and revised work rather than a finished or "fair" copy.

Frons scenae > The wall forming the back of the stage in Jacobethan theatres, also the outside wall of the **tiring house** and into which stage doors were set. The *frons scenae* was often elaborately painted, and could have been decorated, for example with tapestries, for individual performances where required.

Groundlings > Members of the audience who stood in the **yard**, closest to the stage in Jacobethan outdoor theatres. Because they had no seats, groundlings paid the lowest rate (usually a penny) to see plays.

Heavens > The multi-functional canopy surmounting sixteenth- and seventeenth-century stages. It kept rain from spoiling expensive costumes and props, but also (in later, more sophisticated theatres especially) provided a room aloft from which actors or props could be "flown" in – descending, as if literally, from the sky. Like the **frons scenae**, it was often colourfully painted, perhaps with the signs of the zodiac.

Holograph > See **autograph**.

Humanism > There are many ways of understanding humanism, but in the

Renaissance it is most closely identified with an educational movement, centred in northern Europe, that stressed the value of classical Greek and Roman culture and texts (see p.604). Many reforming humanists set up schools – called "grammar" schools because of their emphasis on classical linguistic training – among them the King's New School in Stratford, which Shakespeare probably attended (see p.560).

Iambic pentameter > See blank verse.

Jig > A sprightly dance with folk roots. According to eyewitness testimony, Elizabethan actors danced and sang jigs at the end of a play, perhaps in order to show off the talents of their master dancer (the clown William Kempe took the lead in Shakespeare's company from 1594 to 1599; see p.568). Many surviving jig texts are bawdy, often involving adultery – so perhaps the romantic climaxes of Shakespearian comedy weren't originally as innocent as they now appear.

Masque > A form of courtly entertainment that reached its extravagant height in the reigns of Elizabeth I, James I and his son Charles I. The Jacobean indoor masque combined music, dancing and poetry with lavish costumes and impressive stage effects, performed for (and by) courtiers, often in homage to the King. Masques usually included mythological or allegorical references, designed to flatter the learning and breeding of everyone involved. See p.629 for more.

Memorial reconstruction > Some plays appear to have been pirated and sold to printers by people claiming to have memorized the text – perhaps noted it down at a performance, or reconstructed it for themselves through their own involvement in the play (as with *Hamlet*; see p.93). Full scripts will not have been widely available to actors, perhaps in an attempt to forestall this practice; see p.568. Many of these texts were printed, producing what are sometimes called "bad" quartos.

Metaphor > Literally "transference" in Greek, a metaphor is a figure of speech in which one thing is described in terms of another, usually by way of a comparison. The claim in Sonnet 116 that love is "the star to every wand'ring barque [boat]" (7) is a resonant example of metaphor (see p.606). Compare simile.

Miracle play > See mystery play.

Morality play > A variety of religious drama that was especially popular in Europe in the late medieval period. Morality plays had a simple Christian message, often dramatizing the experience of man through temptation and sin (frequently personified by characters called, for example, "Vice" and "Pride") towards salvation. Shakespeare's Falstaff and Iago are descended from morality archetypes, both versions of the "Vice" character.

Mystery play > Mystery plays were a familiar part of English popular culture for over three hundred years until the late sixteenth century. They were usually dramatizations of biblical scenes, sometimes part of extended "cycles" performed in large towns to celebrate major religious festivals. The cycles of York, Wakefield and Chester are perhaps the most famous, though only two plays from the Coventry cycle (which Shakespeare could have seen; see p.582) have survived. "Miracle" plays drew upon the lives of saints rather than directly biblical sources.

Neoclassicism > Although significant swathes of Renaissance culture could be characterized as "neoclassical" in the sense that they gave new life to ideas derived from ancient Greece and Rome, here the term is commonly used to describe Restoration and early eighteenth-century approaches to Shakespeare. Influenced by continental models, neoclassical critics were united in distaste for Shakespeare's formal deficiencies (chiefly his reluctance to conform to Aristotle's **Unities**), lack of morality and "barbarous" phrases, and often resorted to adaptation in order to make him fit their "enlightened" age (see p.230).

New Criticism > A kind of criticism emphasizing the aesthetic importance of the text rather than its historical or cultural setting. See **Formalism**.

New historicism > A critical movement spearheaded primarily by American academics, which seeks to distinguish itself from the "old" historicism practised by critics such as E.M.W. Tillyard and Lily B. Campbell (see p.154). New historicism often attempts to throw light on canonical literary texts by reading them alongside more unconventional ones, arguing that historical culture is itself formed by texts of all varieties, from travel reports and works of history to marginal jottings and books of accounts.

Octavo > A small-format book, exactly half the size of a **quarto**, in which the pages are folded three times to make eight leaves – hence the name – or sixteen pages. See p.620 for more.

Part > For the theatres in which Shakespeare worked and wrote, an actor's role (sometimes several if he was "**doubling**" another part) was copied out individually, there being just one copy of the full-text **promptbook**. Parts would contain all a character's speeches as well as cues so that he knew when to appear and/or speak.

Patron > In sixteenth- and seventeenth-century England (and indeed much later), patrons were an essential part of the cultural and economic environment. Poets would often look for patronage to support their work, and theatre companies were required by law to have an aristocratic patron who would subsidize and protect the players in exchange for whatever kudos they might gain by involvement.

Pirate(d copy) > The concept of intellectual copyright largely being non-existent for authors in Jacobethan England (though Shakespeare was accused of plagiarism; see p.565), there was little to stop publishers from stealing text from writers and printing it without their permission. Sir Philip Sidney's sonnet sequence *Astrophil and Stella* reached print in a pirated edition of 1591 – Sidney himself was long dead – though debate rages as to whether Shakespeare's own Sonnets were lifted from their author and printed behind his back.

Pit > The area directly in front of the stage in "private" theatres such as the Blackfriars (see p.597), which inverted the hierarchies of the Elizabethan outdoor theatres by containing the most expensive seats.

Playbook > See **promptbook**.

Printers (and publishers) > In Renaissance England printers owned type and a press on which to set it, while publishers acquired the rights to a text, registered it to be printed and arranged for distribution. Most title-pages from the period provide information about who was responsible: the first quarto of *Richard III* (1597) states that it was "printed by Valentine Sims [printer], for Andrew Wise [publisher]", though Shakespeare's own name does not get a mention.

Problem play > Originally applied to the kind of drama pioneered by Ibsen and Shaw in the late nineteenth century, the term "problem play" was first used to describe Shakespeare in the 1890s. Its alternative, "problem comedy", points to a group of plays written in the first years of the seventeenth century – usually *Measure for Measure*, *All's Well That Ends Well* and *Troilus and Cressida*, though other works have been admitted too. These have in common an interest in sexual and social issues, but also a nagging sense that Shakespearian comic form – with its emphasis on social and sexual resolution in the finale – might be rendered problematic by the events of the plot.

Prologue > A short speech introducing a play, usually spoken before its action begins. See also **Chorus** and **Epilogue**.

Promptbook > Also known as a "playbook", this would have been in all probability the only full text of a play in the Jacobethan theatre – a valuable commodity, and usually kept in the playhouse itself. Actors' parts would be copied from it, although prompting in the modern sense (reminding actors of their lines during a performance) seems to have been uncommon.

Publisher > See **printers (and publishers)**.

Pun > A literary trick in which a word is mistaken for another that sounds similar, so bringing into play their various meanings. As with Panthino's pun in *The Two Gentleman of Verona*, which exchanges "tail" for "tale" (2.3.45), the aim is usually to get laughs, and the pun often has bawdy undertones (see p.616).

Quarto > A medium-sized book format, half the size of a **folio**, in which each sheet of paper was folded twice to make four leaves (hence the name) or eight pages. When Shakespeare's works were printed during his lifetime, the portable quarto format was nearly always the one chosen. See p.620 for more.

Rhetoric > Following the prompting of **humanist** educators, the study of oratory – chiefly as it was practised in ancient Greece and Rome – became an integral part of the curriculums of Renaissance grammar schools and universities. Rhetoric, the command of the spoken (and then written) word, was both prized and systematized, with students taught to use complex classical systems of schemes and devices in order to achieve eloquent and persuasive speech. As his works repeatedly show,

Shakespeare put his schoolboy experience of rhetoric to good use – as a writer of plays and poems he employed it on a daily basis. For more see p.604.

Rhyme royal > A seven-line poetic form used by Shakespeare in his poems *Lucrece* and *A Lover's Complaint*; see p.532 for more.

Romance > Although not to be confused with **Romanticism**, the term first appears in relation to Shakespeare in the nineteenth century. Generally it refers to his final comedies *Pericles*, *Cymbeline*, *The Winter's Tale* and *The Tempest*, which deploy motifs reminiscent of romance tales both ancient and medieval – they feature great journeys, wandering heroes, tempests and shipwrecks, separation and magical reunion – but add something particularly Shakespearian. Father-daughter reunions loom large in these plays, and spectacular staging is a highly visible part of their dramatic language (see p.355).

Romanticism > A cultural, philosophical and political movement that eventually touched every corner of the creative arts, from painting and music to theatre and architecture, Romanticism is often traced to the late eighteenth and early nineteenth centuries, when artists and writers rebelled against what they saw as the rationalism and formality of the **neoclassical** period. In Britain Shakespeare was pressed into service by first-generation Romantics including Coleridge and Hazlitt, who alike stressed the importance of unfettered imagination and saw in Shakespeare's art a triumph of protean genius. Both were impressed by the acting of

Edmund Kean, whose passionate and improvisatory performances as Richard III, Shylock and Othello became hallmarks of the Romantic style.

Scribal copy > In dramatic work the phrase describes text – usually "fair" or neat – copied out by a professional scribe or "scrivener", perhaps for the purposes of printing. Much literature circulated in manuscript, however, and scribes were often employed to copy out these texts too; some of Shakespeare's Sonnets might well have been read in this form before they reached print in 1609 (see p.535).

Signature > In Renaissance printing, the method of marking up groups of pages with alphabetical or numerical signs in the order that they were to appear in the book, designed to assist those responsible for assembling it to get everything in the right place (page numbers did not regularly appear until later in the period).

Simile > While resembling **metaphor** in its transfer of the meanings of one word to another, simile keeps the distinction between them at greater distance, often with the formula "like" or "as", which can then be followed by "so". Sonnet 60, a poem which describes the inexorable passage of time, begins, "Like as the waves make towards the pebbled shore / So do our minutes hasten to their end." In *Romeo and Juliet*, Capulet reacts to the sight of the apparently dead Juliet by saying: "Death lies on her like an untimely frost / Upon the sweetest flower of all the field." (4.4.55–6). For more see p.606.

Soliloquy > In plays, a solo speech, usually spoken by a character alone on stage. By convention, a soliloquy is addressed by the character to him-/herself, as if thinking out loud. This makes it an important way of revealing a character's thoughts and feelings, and providing clues as to his/her motivation. However, a soliloquy can also be addressed directly to the audience, as in the opening speech of Richard III (see p.374). Shakespeare's master soliloquist is Hamlet, also the playwright's largest role. Compare **aside**.

Sonnet > A fourteen-line lyric form popular in several European languages throughout the Renaissance, often associated with love poetry. Several versions exist, employing different patterns of rhyme, but in the kind of sonnet preferred by Shakespeare the lines are ten syllables long and rhyme in the pattern *ababcdcdefef*, before closing with a final couplet *gg*. See p.538 for more.

Speech prefix > A cue in a dramatic script identifying who is speaking, an often haphazard system in early printed texts – in fact some of Shakespeare's plays were printed with the name of the actor appearing by mistake.

Stage direction > As with **speech prefixes**, a sometimes chaotic system for cueing players to perform actions outside the spoken text, or informing readers that a particular device was used in performance. Many printed versions of Shakespeare's earlier plays have few stage directions (modern editors often opt to insert them), although others – particularly his last plays – have very detailed cues describing how particular moments should be staged.

Stationers' Register > The detailed accounts of the Stationers' Company, which licensed printers and (theoretically) ensured who had rights to publish a particular text. Everything printed was meant to be recorded in the Register, making it a valuable resource for modern scholars.

Staying order > An entry in the **Stationers' Register** designed to assert ownership of a particular text, and thus prevent it from being published illegally by others. Although an entry theoretically declared an intention to print, publishers did not always go ahead and do so.

Stylometrics > An analytical technique that tries to identify which stylistic forms (such as vocabulary, syntax, metre) are characteristically employed by a particular author, usually in an attempt to work out precisely what s/he wrote. Since the nineteenth century many different stylometric tests have been applied to Shakespeare, recently with the aid of sophisticated computer-aided statistics, but it is notoriously hard to prove anything beyond doubt without drawing on other evidence.

Tiring house > The "attiring" or dressing-room space of the Jacobethan theatre, traditionally located directly behind the stage and leading onto it via several doors.

Tragedy > Understanding (and defining) the concept of tragedy has been an obsession in Western culture at least since Aristotle, and Renaissance theorists had many views – chief among them that a tragic play should end sadly, usually with the death of a princely protagonist. See p.355 for more.

Trap > The door in the floor of many Renaissance stages, colloquially known as the "hell". Actors could climb out of the trap, bodies could be buried in it and sound effects could be supplied by someone standing underneath the stage.

Unities, the > The theory that for drama to be convincing it should be "unified" in place, action and time – that a play should take place in one location, have one plot and possess a time-frame corresponding to the literal time of performance. The idea was developed by **neoclassical** critics from Aristotle's fragmentary treatise on *Poetics*. Shakespeare had no such concerns, as he repeatedly demonstrates (only *The Tempest* fits this description, and even then has subplots), and his plays were frequently adapted to make them more neoclassical from the Restoration onwards.

Yard > In Jacobethan outdoor theatres, the space surrounding the stage in which **groundlings** were allowed to stand for the cheapest entrance fee. Its origins lay in the inn-yards where temporary stages were erected, an arrangement that continued with touring companies well into the seventeenth century.

Reading on

This glossary cannot hope to cover everything, and it may prompt more questions than it answers. The chapter on Shakespeare's language should provide some tips (see p.600), but more detailed discussions of literary terms can be found in Chris Baldick's *Oxford Concise Dictionary of Literary Terms* (2001) – helpfully available as web-linked ebook – but perhaps the ultimate resource in this field is *The Princeton Encyclopedia of Poetry and Poetics* (rev. 2012), which contains extensive and often hugely insightful essays on technical topics and literary genres.

Questions on matters of Renaissance staging might be answered by *The Oxford Companion to Shakespeare* (see p.645), perhaps in collaboration with a general drama encyclopedia such as *The Oxford Companion to Theatre and Performance* (2010), edited by Dennis Kennedy.

If you want to find out more about rhetoric, the system of codifying and shaping speech that Shakespeare will have learnt at school, head online, where an excellent website called The Forest of Rhetoric at humanities.byu.edu/rhetoric/silva.htm should answer your queries and direct you to further resources. See p.659 for an extensive directory of Shakespeare-related websites.

Photo credits

Index

For ease of reference, Shakespeare's major works are listed individually as part of the alphabetical sequence; the main account for each is highlighted in colour. Entries highlighted in **bold** indicate that the subject is covered in a feature box or extended article; numbers in *italics* reference an illustration or caption.

H